THE PASSION
OF
AYN RAND

THE PASSION
OF
AYN RAND

Barbara Branden

ANCHOR BOOKS
DOUBLEDAY
NEW YORK LONDON TORONTO SYDNEY AUCKLAND

AN ANCHOR BOOK
PUBLISHED BY DOUBLEDAY
a division of Bantam Doubleday Dell Publishing Group, Inc.
1540 Broadway, New York, New York 10036

ANCHOR BOOKS, DOUBLEDAY, and the portrayal
of an anchor are trademarks of Doubleday, a division of
Bantam Doubleday Dell Publishing Group, Inc.

The Passion of Ayn Rand was originally published
in hardcover by Doubleday in 1986.
The Anchor Books edition is published
by arrangement with Doubleday.

Library of Congress Cataloging-in-Publication Data
Branden, Barbara.
   The passion of Ayn Rand.
   Includes index.
   1. Rand, Ayn—Biography. 2. Novelists, American—
20th century—Biography. I. Title.
PS3535.A547Z57   1986   813'.52[B]   85-20704
ISBN 0-385-24388-X (pbk.)

9

Acknowledgments

I extend my grateful thanks to the many people—the list exceeds two hundred—who freely gave me hours, even days, of their time, to speak of their memories of Ayn Rand. Much of whatever merit this book may be found to have is a direct result of their kindness. I cannot list all of the people I interviewed; some of them, for various reasons of their own, prefer not to be named. But I thank each one of them: Dean Ahmed, Thadeus Ashby, Neera Badhwar, Fred Beck, Gladys Beck, Petr Beckmann, Michael Berger, Robert Berole, Laurie Biedemier, Shirley Maxwell Black, James Blanchard III, Robert Bleiberg, Winfred Blevius, Allan Blumenthal, Joan Mitchell Blumenthal, David Boaz, Nathaniel Branden, Marc Brewer, Fern Brown, Harry Browne, William F. Buckley, Jr., Roger Callahan, Mae Beth Carpenter, Stephen Carr, Thomas Carr, Douglas Casey, Graham Chalmers, John Chamberlain, Roy A. Childs, Jr., Ed Clark, Catherine Collins, Lilyan Courtois, Myrna Culbreath, Rex Dante, Lillian Davison, Richard DeMille, Jeanne Drew, E. Drobishcheva, Murray Dworetzky, Edith Efron, Jean Elliott, Albert Ellis, Don Ernsberger, Bruce Evoy, Bee Fetcher, Rosina Florio, Nancy Fooshee, Arly Fritts, Michael Gara, Tony Giannone, Mirra Ginsberg, Lillian Gish, Mimi Reisel Gladstein, Larry Gneiting, Minna Goldberg, Bettina Bien Greaves, Daniel Green, Alan Greenspan, Wallis Grover, Walter Grover, Muriel Hall, Marjorie Hansen, Henry Hazlitt, David R. Henderson, Susan Herald, Jack High, Ruth Beebe Hill, Jonathan Hirschfeld, Rick Holden, Cranston Holman, Erika Holzer, Henry Mark Holzer, Sidney Hook, John Hospers, Lester Hunt, Marc Jaffe, Elayne Kalberman, Harry Kalberman, Joe Kalt, Daryn Kent-Duncan, Robert Kephart, Manny Klausner, Richard Kleinow, Donald Klopfer, Bertha Krantz, Moshe Kroy, Roger Lee, Robert LeFevre, Candace Leigh, Leon Louw, Tibor Machan, Eric Mack, Ruth Inglis Matthews, Gerard McCauley, Scott McDonald, Wendy McElroy, Mike Mentzer, Cindie Messenger, Douglas Messenger, Margit von Mises, Charles Murray, Dmitri Nabokov, Tonie Nathan, O. T. Nelson, Edwin Newman, Alan Nitikman, David Nolan, Robert Nozick, Edward Opitz, Kerry O'Quinn, Millicent Paton, Jeffrey Paul, Ron Paul, Durk Pearson, Lee Plunkett, Paul Poirot, Robert W. Poole, Jack Portnoy, Robert Prechter, John Pugsley, Gerald Rafferty, Dick Randolph, Douglas B. Rasmussen, Jacquelyn Reinach, Andrea Millen Rich, Sheldon Richman, Jeff Riggenbach, Jennifer Roback, Ralph Roseman, Murray Rothbard, J. Neil Schulman, Wilfred Schwartz, Lawrence A. Scott, Sandy Shaw, Marge Shilcoat,

Devon Showley, Julius Shulman, Joyce Shulman, Lee Shulman, Stirling Silliphant, Sid Simms, George Smith, Kay Nolte Smith, Phillip Smith, Mimi Sutton, Truman Talley, Chris Tame, Joan Kennedy Taylor, Don Ventura, Mike Wallace, Beatrice Waller, Dave Walters, Jim Weidman, Miriam Weidman, Sidney Weidman, Jack Wheeler, Meta Carpenter Wilde, Walter Williams, Marie Windsor, Walter Wingo, Anne Wortham, Virginia Sale Wren, Clara Mae Wright, Evan T. Wright.

Apart from the people interviewed, there were others who helped in a variety of ways—by supplying information and leads, by locating library and other materials, by translating Russian and other documents, by looking up old records, by sending me their reminiscences, their letters, their journals, their photographs. I extend my thanks to the following: Forry Ackerman, Katherine Allen, Mary Barkhouse, Inez Barras, Don Cormier, Richard Cornuelle, Bruce Dovner, Paul Genteman, Marc Greenberg, Marie Greenberg, Ken Gregg, Edward M. Hall, John Hall, Vernon Harbin, David Hayes, Bruce Henstel, Anthony Hiss, Wayne Locke, Linda Mehr, Cynthia Nelson, Sarah Paris, John J. Pierce, Monica Pignotti, Ron Poulen, Dignora Rodriguez, Valerie Roop, Kelly Ross, Eric Schultz, Collette Shulman, Mary Simkins, Ethel Sanford-Smith, David Solan, Chris Tame, Bruce Torrance, Mike Wanamaker, Sam Wells, Jr., James J. Wheaton II, Marjorie Wheaton.

Staff librarians at a number of libraries and institutions provided invaluable information and guidance, finding the unfindable and locating the unlocatable. Foremost among them is the Community Access Library Line; its staff—Marilee Marrero, Marie Kaneko, Sheri Ryewuski, Chris Yuek, Helen Tsai, and Machiko Morita—cheerfully and doggedly answered hundreds of requests for information, performing miracles to supply me with the facts I needed. Other research librarians who were especially helpful were those at UCLA; USC; California State University, Northridge; California State University, Long Beach; the American Film Institute; The Academy of Motion Pictures Arts and Sciences; the University of Oregon; Denison University; the University of Wisconsin Center for Theater Research; Columbia University; the public libraries in New York, Boston, and Los Angeles; the Los Angeles County Museum of Art; and the Mormon Genealogical Library.

I am especially grateful to Susan Grode, my attorney, who believed in this project from the beginning—perhaps before I did—who pushed and prodded and worked for it through the five years of its conception and development, and who continues to do so.

I often used to think wistfully of the brilliant and caring editors of the early years of this century, and wonder why such editors no longer seemed to exist. Through working with my own editor, I have learned that at least one of their caliber does exist. Thank you, Loretta Barrett.

Contents

Introduction

The life of Ayn Rand was the material of fiction. But if one attempted to write it as a novel, the result would be preposterously unbelievable. Everything about her life and her person was of an epic scale. Her seventy-seven years encompassed the outer limits of triumph and defeat, of exaltation and tragedy, of passionate love and intransigent hatred, of dedicated effort and despairing passivity. Her person encompassed the grandeur of the heroes of her novels, their iron determination, their vast powers of intellect and imagination, their impassioned pursuit of their goals, their worship of achievement, their courage, their pride, and their love of life—as well as the terrors, the self-doubts, the lack of emotional balance, the private agonies that are so alien to an Ayn Rand hero. Her virtues were larger than life—and so were her shortcomings.

Few figures in this century have been so admired and so savagely attacked. She is viewed as goddess and as malefactor, as a seminal genius and an ominously dangerous corrupter of the young, as the mightiest of voices for reason and the destroyer of traditional values, as the espouser of joy and the exponent of mindless greed, as the great defender of freedom and the introducer of malevolent values into the mainstream of American thought. It is all but impossible to find a neutral voice among the millions who have read her works; each reader takes an unequivocal stand for or against that which she represents. When her name is mentioned in any gathering, it is met with explosions of grateful, loving admiration or enraged disapproval. In the course of conducting more than two hundred interviews with people whose lives were touched by her or by her work, I have yet to encounter a single person who spoke of her with indifference.

Yet despite the furor her ideas have generated—despite the fact that they fill the pages of thirteen books, which, as of this writing, have sold more than twenty million copies—despite the fact that her philosophy has had a powerful and still-accelerating influence on the culture in which we live—little is known about the human being who was Ayn Rand. Still less is known about the woman who was Ayn Rand. Her public and professional activities took place on a lighted stage; her private life was lived backstage, curtained from view.

I first met Ayn Rand in 1950. At the age of forty-five, she had already achieved a singular renown as the author of *The Fountainhead,* and was writing her magnum opus, *Atlas Shrugged*—the work that was to skyrocket her to international fame and place her in the center of a hurricane of controversy. I was attending UCLA with my friend and later my husband, Nathaniel Branden. I was majoring in philosophy, he in psychology. We had both read *The Fountainhead*—and then *We the Living* and *Anthem,* Ayn Rand's two earlier novels—and we deeply admired and were influenced by her work. Learning that she was living in Southern California, Nathaniel wrote her a letter, asking philosophical questions about *The Fountainhead* and *We the Living.* Impressed with his questions, she arranged to meet with him; a week later, I joined them for a second meeting.

It was the beginning of an intimate friendship with Ayn and her husband, Frank O'Connor, lasting across nineteen years, during which we met with Ayn or spoke with her by telephone almost every day; for a number of years, we lived in the same New York apartment building. I was engaged in the passions and pains of Ayn's life, first as her student and later as teacher of her philosophy. We became privy to each other's personal and professional lives, to each other's joys and sorrows, triumphs and defeats. It was the beginning of the endless captivation of observing at close hand the unfolding of a great and growing literary and philosophical talent, of a mind of towering intellectual power, of a tormented, passionate, searching spirit. It was the beginning of years filled with wonder, with excitement, with exaltation—and with suffering and tragedy and heartbreak.

I shall not forget my first sight of Ayn Rand. When the door to her home opened that spring evening in 1950, I found myself facing the most astonishing human being I had ever encountered. It was the eyes. The eyes were dark, too large for the face, fringed with dark lashes, alive with an intensity of intelligence I had never imagined human eyes could hold. They seemed the eyes of a human being who was composed of the power of sight.

As the years passed, I was to observe all the many changes of expression of those incredible eyes. I saw them ferocious with concentration on a new idea or question that had not occurred to her before, on a difficult passage in *Atlas Shrugged,* with a single-minded intensity that seemed as if it might set fire to the person or page she was addressing. I saw them cold, so icily, inhumanly cold that they froze one's heart and mind. I saw them radiant with the uninhibited delight of a child—I saw them menacing with anger at any hint of what she considered the irrational in human action—I saw them helpless and womanly when she gazed at her husband—I saw them bitter, resentful, and full of pain—I saw them glow with the special, earnest charm that was uniquely hers, and that no one who met her was immune to—I saw them pulled tight with loathing, wild with uncontrollable rage—I saw them kind, touchingly kind, tender with the desire to help and to protect—I saw the merciless, accusing eyes of the moralist, judging, condemning, unforgiving, the power of her reason becoming a whip to scourge the heretic—I saw them shyly solemn like a young girl when a boy, my husband, took her hand. But I never saw those eyes without the light of a vast, consuming intelligence, the light of a ruthless intellect that was at once cold and passionate; this was the core of her life, the motor of her soul.

There was something I never saw in Ayn Rand's eyes. They never held an inward look—a look of turning inside to learn one's own spirit and consciousness. They gazed only and always outward. It was many years before I was to understand the absence of that inward look, and what it revealed. It was to require all the knowledge of all the years to understand it.

To this day, when I think of Ayn Rand, I see her eyes. They haunted me through nineteen years. Perhaps they haunt me still.

Nathaniel and I were twenty-five years younger than Ayn. But it was not unusual for her, then or later, to seek friends among men and women considerably younger than herself. It was in young people that she found the eager, actively questioning minds that she deeply cherished, minds like her own, which constantly sought new perspectives, new ideas, new ways of dealing with the world. Her contemporaries, she said, were too often closed to ideas they had not heard before, they did not care to be shaken from whatever uneasy mix of concepts had come to form their philosophy of life. And young people, still in the process of being formed and of selecting the values and concepts that would guide their lives, offered her something more, which she did not name and probably did not recognize. Ayn Rand was a woman with a powerful need for control—control of her own life, of her own destiny, and of the belief system of those she chose as her friends. The passionate admiration she elicited from the young, their vulnerability and need for intellectual guidance, made possible an intellectual and moral dominance less likely to occur with accomplished men and women of her own age.

As I look back on my friendship with Ayn Rand, it seems almost as if the whole of that period were my preparation for the writing of this biography. From the beginning of our relationship, I was fascinated by her personality; my fascination led me to study her, to struggle to understand her character and motivation, in precisely the form in which a biographer studies and struggles to understand his or her subject. The years of my association with Ayn Rand, the years of her work on *Atlas Shrugged* and of the dramatic consequences of its publication, were filled for her with titanic effort, with explosive conflict, with the growth of her moral and philosophical influence which can today be found in the highest reaches of academia, in the halls of government, in the conference rooms of giant corporations, in popular television series, and in quiet living rooms all over the world. They were the years in which her personal life was filled with a similarly explosive conflict, a conflict which led, ultimately, to haunting and destructive tragedy.

In the early sixties, I was given an opportunity to learn still more about her, to examine and study her life with a depth and scope that few biographers are fortunate enough to attain.

Not long after the publication of *Atlas Shrugged* in 1957, Nathaniel and I decided to write a book entitled *Who Is Ayn Rand?* It consisted of four essays; in three of them, Nathaniel analyzed the moral theories presented in *Atlas Shrugged*, the view of human psychology it embodied, and Ayn's literary method; my own contribution was a short biographical sketch of Ayn. *Who Is Ayn Rand?* was published by Random House in 1962.

In preparation for the biographical sketch, Ayn agreed that I might interview her and tape our conversations. We met nineteen times, on each occasion for a minimum of two hours, while she spoke of her past life—her childhood and early womanhood in Russia, the nightmare of the Communist revolution and its consequences, her early years in America, her passionate professional struggle to succeed in a new world and with a new language, her meeting with Frank O'Connor and their courtship and marriage, her friends, her loves, her enemies, her disappointments, and her successes. She spoke not only of the events of her life, but also of the personal meaning of those events, how she felt and judged and what she learned and failed to learn from the days of her life. And when I had turned off the tape recorder and our formal interview was at an end, we often spent many hours in informal, less structured conversations about the material on the tapes.[1] Had she had in mind only the sketch which I wrote for *Who Is Ayn Rand?*, the interviews would have been much fewer in number and shorter in length. But, as Ayn made clear on one or two of the tapes, she thought that I might one day wish to write a full biography, and she spoke with a view to that possibility.

It was an intriguing and exciting experience—particularly so because Ayn rarely reminisced; she was always more interested in the future than in the past. And still more rarely, if she did speak of past events, would she speak of her emotional reaction to those events. Most especially, she did not speak of her years in Russia. In all my interviews with those who had known her, some intimately, I found not a single person with whom she had spoken at any length about the days of her childhood and young womanhood in Russia. Her memories of that period were associated in her mind with an excruciating and, to her, a humiliating pain; for Ayn Rand, pain *was* humiliation, it was not something to be discussed in casual conversation; the meaning of a human life was the joy one achieved, and suffering was only an irrelevant accident. There was a second, equally important cause of her silence about her early years: her commitment to the idea that human beings are in no sense inevitably the creatures of their environments; we do not *have* to be influenced or formed by the people and events around us, she believed; we are free to make choices, to evaluate, to come to our own conclusions. "Man," she wrote, "is a being of self-made soul." It would have seemed to her pointless to talk about her childhood with the implication that its events had something to do with the woman she became; parents,

---

[1] In the chapters that follow, quotations from Ayn Rand's works, speeches, and articles are specified as such, as are the reports from other people of statements she made to them. Where a source is not specified, the quotation is from my interview tapes, or from my own conversations with Ayn, or from her conversations with others at which I was present; I have edited such comments only for clarity.

friends, the experiences of youth, all were irrelevant to the being whose spirit and values she had molded.

After 1968, when our relationship ended, I saw Ayn only once more before her death. But a number of close friends of mine remained her intimate friends, and, along with more casual acquaintances of Ayn, they were of invaluable assistance in filling in the gaps in my knowledge of those years, in giving me the sense that I was present even then, that I was continuing to observe the unfolding of her life as I had observed it for so long.

Over the years, many people have suggested that it was time for me to write Ayn Rand's biography. But I had come to believe that I would never do so, that I could not again immerse myself in those days of wonder and pain and again struggle to emerge from them whole. For some time after the ending of our relationship, I doubted that I had achieved the necessary objectivity to write about a woman and a life that had so powerfully affected and altered my own life.

But by 1981, I knew that I had made my peace with Ayn Rand and our years together. The pain had lost its keenness; the wonder had endured. And I was left with the awareness that a life and a work as remarkable as hers should be committed to paper, that whatever understanding of her I had gained should not end with me. Her story should be told; it, and the woman who lived it, was unique and important.

The writing of Ayn Rand's biography has been a matchless experience; it has been a four-year-long journey into the life and spirit of one of the most remarkable and complex individuals of our time. And because she affected me so deeply, because, for so long, my life was tied to hers, it has been, as well, a journey in self-discovery. Both journeys have enriched my life. For this, as for so many other things, I am grateful to Ayn Rand.

Those who worship Ayn Rand and those who damn her do her the same disservice: they make her unreal and they deny her humanity. I hope to show in her story that she was something infinitely more fascinating and infinitely more valuable than either goddess or sinner. She was a human being. She lived, she loved, she fought her battles, and she knew triumph and defeat. The scale was epic; the principle is inherent in human existence.

PART I

PROLOGUE

Chapter One

Alice Rosenbaum was born in one of the most beautiful and cultured cities on earth—in the wake of one terrible carnage and amid the ominous warnings of a vaster and more savage carnage to come. It was a sophisticated, glittering world —that was slowly descending into hell.

On February 2, 1905, the day of Alice's birth, St. Petersburg sparkled in the rare winter sunshine. The city's broad, gracious avenues, its golden spires, onion-shaped church domes, and colored cupolas drank in the light. Elegant ladies, wrapped in sables and chattering to each other in French, returned from tea in horse-drawn troikas, and prepared to don formal gowns and their finest jewels for an evening at the Maryinsky Ballet. Along the Nevsky Prospect, in the city's restaurants, diners looked out over the wintry metallic gray of the Neva River to the Peter and Paul Fortress on the northern bank, where the bodies of former Czars lay in state; they talked of the works of Tolstoy and Maxim Gorki, of Pushkin and Turgenev and Dostoievsky, of the exhibit at the Hermitage where the paintings of Matisse, Cézanne, Gauguin, and Monet were hung, and of the city's smart new western nightclubs. Their glances slid past the troops of booted Cossacks thundering along the Nevsky on horseback, rifles on their backs and whips in their hands, seeking suspected revolutionaries. Revolution was sweeping the impoverished countryside as enraged and starving peasants, in the wake of the massacre of "Bloody Sunday," set fire to manor houses and crops.

By 1906, when Alice celebrated her first birthday, the revolution had been put down. Czar Nicholas had sold to the peasants, at low prices, more than four million acres of land, creating a new class in Russia: a class of peasant small landowners. He had transformed Russia from an autocracy to a semiconstitutional monarchy with an elected parliament, the Duma; although the Duma had minimal power, the principle of constitutional monarchy was established. But the hatred engendered by the revolution continued to fester, as if awaiting its time to erupt in an explosion of devastating violence.

The Rosenbaum family lived in a large, comfortable apartment overlooking one of the great squares of St. Petersburg. Beneath the apartment, on the ground floor, was the chemist shop owned by Alice's father. Fronz Rosenbaum was of slightly more than medium height, stocky and dark-haired, a silent, grim-faced man of severe integrity. His greatest pride lay in the fact that he was a rarity in Russia: a self-made man. His family had been poor, he had struggled to support himself through university, and, when he began to achieve success as a chemist, he had supported six sisters and a brother when their time came to enter the university. He had not wanted to become a chemist, but there were few universities that Jews could attend, and even those had strict quotas; when there was an opening for a Jew in the department of chemistry, he had snatched at the opportunity to enter a profession. He was a serious man whom Alice never knew to have a close personal friend; in his leisure time, he enjoyed reading the works of social criticism which were becoming popular in Russia, works by writers who defended European civilization and the British political system as against the mysticism and political absolutism of Russia. Weekends, when relatives visited, he spent hours in solemn games of whist.

"He had firm convictions," Alice later was to say, "but you'd never know it, because he was mostly silent, and argued very little. Mother argued politics, but Father never did. He seemed uninterested in intellectual issues, but I sensed even as a child that he took ideas much more seriously than Mother. He once told me that what he would have wanted was to be a writer; he considered ideas and the spread of ideas the most important thing of all. It was only after the Communist revolution that he began to discuss political ideas with Mother and other adults, and it was then that I could form some idea of his moral code and convictions about life in general. His strongest issue was individualism; he was committed to reason, but unfortunately not by stated conviction; he was nonreligious, although he never objected to Mother's religious ideas—he expressed the idea: 'Well, one never can tell.'

"I felt a friendly respect for him in childhood, not a strong affection, a dutiful 'official' affection—although probably even then I loved him more than I loved Mother. I liked him as a person, but in childhood I had very little to do with him. Children's education was totally in the hands of the mother in those days. Father never interfered, so he exercised no influence. It was when he and I began discussing ideas when I was fourteen, when we became political allies, that I felt a real love, a love that meant something."

Alice's mother was the opposite of her father. A graceful, pretty woman with sparkling, intense eyes, Anna Rosenbaum seemed always to be rushing about the apartment, giving orders to cook, maid, nurse, and governess; organizing the formal banquets she loved to give; arranging for a pianist to entertain; reveling in the role of intellectual hostess among the lawyers, doctors, and other professional people who attended her lively parties. When she was not entertaining, she read the French literary magazines that were scattered about the apartment, or rushed off to lectures, to the theater, to the ballet.

All during Alice's childhood, her relationship with her mother had the quality of a pitched battle. "I disliked her quite a lot. We really didn't get along. She was my exact opposite, and I thought so in childhood, and now," said Alice years later. "She was by principle and basic style, by sense of life, extremely social. She was not really interested in ideas, she was much more interested in the social aspect. Our clashes in childhood were that I was antisocial, I was insufficiently interested in other children, I didn't play with them, I didn't have girlfriends; this was a nagging refrain always. She disapproved of me in every respect except one: she was proud of my intelligence and proud to show me off to the rest of the family."

Her father's seeming indifference to her and her mother's disapproval had to be sources of anguish to the child. Yet as an adult she always spoke as if they were simple facts of reality, of no emotional significance to her then or later. One can only conclude that a process of self-protective emotional repression—which was so clearly to characterize her adult years—was becoming deeply rooted even in early childhood.

In Alice's later writings, her contempt for the "social" was to be a constantly recurring theme. Lillian Rearden, the major woman villain in *Atlas Shrugged,* is characterized as someone whose emptiness of spirit is exemplified by her passion for social interaction, for parties, for being the center of a crowd of people. As she characterized Anna Rosenbaum in her discussions, so Ayn Rand characterized Lillian Rearden: the "intellectual hostess" fundamentally indifferent to the world of ideas. To the end of her life, for Alice to say of someone that he or she had a deep need for the company of other people was to dismiss that person as essentially without value.

An equal source of conflict with her mother was Alice's loathing of physical activity. Anna Rosenbaum believed that it was necessary, for health reasons, that children have fresh air every day, whatever the weather. St. Petersburg's winters were freezing; darkness fell early in the afternoon and lasted until the middle of the following morning, with icy winds and whirling snowstorms and a Neva hard as steel. Alice detested the long walks she was forced to take in the snow and sleet. When expensive gymnastic equipment was purchased for her, she refused to go near it. "Make movements, Alice," was her mother's constant angry refrain. The child—and the woman she was to become—*never* willingly "made movements"; she was sedentary to the point of endangering her health. Even in the final years of her life, when a minimum of physical activity was recommended to her for medical reasons, she angrily refused any form of exercise—as if still defying the mother who demanded that she engage in activities that bored her.

The Rosenbaum household was a chaotic one, alive with Anna's comings and goings, with visiting friends, with relatives. An uncle and aunt of Alice's lived in the same apartment building, and Alice's first companion was little Nina, her cousin, a year and a half older than she. Alice's uncles appear to have been responsible for the family's partial protection from the anti-Semitism of Czarist Russia; one or more of them, an American cousin of Anna Rosenbaum's recalled, carried on the family tradition of being bootmaker to the army.

In the Rosenbaum home, religion had little meaning or place. Although Anna was religious—in what Alice was to term an "emotional-traditional way, not out of conviction, more out of devotion to the religion of her own mother"—she gave her children no religious training. The family perfunctorily observed one or two holy days a year—lighting candles and serving specified foods—then gradually gave up any formal observance. Alice had not enjoyed the observances, and did not miss them. Nor did she appear to recall ever hearing the problems of anti-Semitism, raging throughout Russia, discussed in her home—although her parents must have been painfully aware of pogroms and the frighteningly ubiquitous hatred of Jews. Alice was never to deny that she was Jewish; in later years, as a committed atheist, she would say "I was *born* Jewish"; but it had no significance to her, she had no emotional tie or sense of identification with Jews or things Jewish.[1]

One of Alice's earliest memories was of her fascination with the great city in which she lived. Still a toddler, she sat on the windowsill of her apartment, her father beside her, looking out into the winter street at one of the first streetcars to appear in St. Petersburg. It was evening, and she gazed in wonderment at the blinking yellow and red lights of the streetcar, as her father explained their purpose. Perhaps this was the beginning of the love of technology, of what she later was to call the physical manifestations of the power of man's mind, that she would carry with her as a banner—as a proud crusade—throughout all the years of her life.

Her second memory was of fear. Walking with her nurse one day, she happened to notice a sheet of glass in a wooden crate, propped along a wall. Curious, Alice approached and touched the edge of the glass. The frightened nurse pulled her away; she mustn't touch it, glass was sharp, it could cut her, it was dangerous. For days afterward, the child worried that invisible particles of glass somehow had gotten into her skin and would seriously hurt her. She felt a sense of danger hanging somewhere over her head. This, too, as a number of her friends would observe, was a reaction she was to carry with her all of her life, unadmitted and unrecognized but with a singular motivational effect: the feeling that the physical world held neither safety nor ease for her. As the years passed, her sense of a fundamental alienation from the material existence she would exalt in her writings was to take on a quality of obsession.

---

[1] In all of my conversations with Ayn Rand about her years in Russia, she never once mentioned to me—nor, to the best of my knowledge, to anyone else—any encounter she might have had with anti-Semitism. It is all but impossible that there were not such encounters. One can only assume that, as with the pain caused by the indifference of her parents, the pain and terror of anti-Semitism was ultimately blocked from her memory—in both cases, perhaps, because the memory would have carried with it an unacceptable feeling of humiliation.

By the time Alice was five, the family had grown to include two younger sisters, Natasha and Elena, called Nora. Alice's intellectual precocity, recognized by those around her even in earliest childhood, had turned her focus to the fascinating job of asking endless questions, of struggling to understand the objects and events around her; when she felt she understood the phenomenon of "babies," her sisters had nothing more to offer her. She much preferred the company of adults. She was often included in adult activities; Anna liked to have her precocious daughter present to be admired. At parties in her home, Alice was brought from the nursery to be hugged by her doting grandmother, Anna's mother, a dour martinet except with Alice, whom she adored as the first child of her best-loved daughter, and to be praised by the other adults for her large dark eyes that gazed with grave, questioning solemnity at the world around her.

Implicit in Alice's reminiscences about her childhood is the fact that, from her parents and from the other adults she encountered, love and admiration were purchased by the qualities of her mind. When her mother paraded her before the relatives, it was because Alice's bright lucidity inspired their admiration; when her father smiled at her during his visits to the nursery at the end of the day, it was because she had told him of some activity—a game she had invented, a picture in a children's book she had built a story around—that demonstrated the quickness of her mind. Alice learned well the lesson contained in the reactions she received. As a child, and as an adult, the first question she asked about anyone she met was: Is he intelligent? It was the first question—and, in a deeply personal way, the last. Intelligence was the quality she most admired, that she responded to with the greatest pleasure and respect. Her own remarkable intelligence created that reaction in part; a mind needs the stimulation of its equals. But she placed on intelligence what can only be termed a *moral* value; intelligence and virtue were to become inextricably linked in her mind and her emotions; where she saw no unusual intelligence—nor the capacity for dedicated productive work that she believed to be its consequence—she saw no value that meant anything to her in personal terms. One never heard her say of anyone, as a *significant* compliment: "He's generous," or "He's kind," or "He's thoughtful"; none of our common coinage of admiration—particularly the admiration we pay to qualities of character involving the treatment of other people— reached the place in her where Alice Rosenbaum's deepest values lived.

On a bright summer day, Alice discovered a passion that *did* reach into her most private spirit. Each summer, the Rosenbaums traveled to the Crimea for two months, renting a summer house and spending long lazy hours on the white beaches, wandering through the green, lush countryside and through a sunlit park. At a bandstand in the park, beneath a line of white birch trees, a military band played through the warm afternoons. One day, Alice pulled away from her governess to stop before the bandstand. The musicians were playing the first military marches she had ever heard. Then the little Russian girl listened, astonished and transfixed, to the sounds of "Yippy Yi Yippy Yi Yay"—then "It's a Long Way to Tipperary"—then the gay lilt of American and German light classics. Her small body began to move in time to the music. Thereafter, she demanded to be taken every afternoon to the bandstand in the park. In the terms of a six-year-old child, she appeared to sense that here, for the first time, was music that contained no pain, no tragedy, none of the gloom she associated with the Russian music she had heard in her home; it was music that bore no awareness that pain *ever* could exist. In later years, in America, she scoured record shops until she had collected most of the music she first had heard in a park in the Crimea, and begged Americans traveling to Europe to scour the record shops there. She called it her "tiddlywink" music.

Over the years, other pieces she heard and loved were added to her list, oddly disparate pieces such as "My Irish Molly," Chopin's "Minute Waltz," "C'mon Get Happy," Prokofiev's "March" from *Love for Three Oranges,* selections from the operettas of Léhar and Kálmán. In the happiest moments of her life, her thoughts would go to that music, she would listen to it, her body would sway to its beat. It was *her* music, she felt. It was untouched by the world, untouched by alien values. It was a pure, unsullied hymn to joy.

As the child worshipped joy, so did the adult she would become. Forever after, she believed that pain and frustration and suffering were meaningless aberrations, never a normal part of life, never to be accepted as the inevitable nature of human existence—and never to be considered important. This would be a theme in her writings, and despite the pain and bitterness that her life would contain, it remained a theme she struggled to keep alive in her psychology—where it was often muted, sometimes almost indiscernible, sometimes battered into silence, but always present. In *Atlas Shrugged,* the first words Dagny Taggart, the novel's heroine, speaks to John Galt—the man she has waited all her life to meet—are: "We never had to take any of it seriously, did we?" And Galt answers: "No, we never had to."

For a long time, Alice considered most classical music to be "sheer boredom." But when she heard the Overture and the Drinking Song from *La Traviata* and a few Chopin pieces, she understood that she could love—though never as much as her tiddlywink music—the works of serious composers. It was not until she lived in America that Alice first heard the music of Rachmaninoff; his Second Piano Concerto became her great love, and her standard of great music ever after.

When Alice spoke of the wonders of her tiddlywink music to her mother and other adult relatives, they were appalled that such a bright child—"Why?" and "Please explain" always on her lips—should have what they considered such uncultured tastes. It was the beginning of a series of value clashes with the people around her that was to mark the whole of her life. Years later, she remembered feeling—and still projected—an angry defiance in the face of their rejection of her musical choices. It was a defiance that was to characterize her attitude toward all of her values. "*I* know, but they don't. This is *mine.* It's not theirs."

"You're too violent, Alice," her mother constantly told the child. "Either you're tongue-tied, and won't talk to people at all, or—if they don't like something you like—you get angry and rude."

She claimed not to feel the same anger at *personal* rejection. One day, Anna Rosenbaum shouted at her daughters, "I never wanted children at all! I look after you because it's my duty to do so." Alice listened quietly, thinking: Why does she blame us for being born? We didn't ask for it. Even at this early age, Alice had learned not to expect appreciation except for her intellectual abilities; she had learned it so thoroughly that she appears not to have consciously experienced lack of appreciation as painful (although at a deeper level she must have suffered at a mother's rejection). Throughout Alice's life, she would expect, even demand, that her intellectual qualities be perceived and admired; she would react with pleasure, but with an authentic air of bewilderment, if any other aspect of her character or personality were understood or loved.

It was the following summer that Alice discovered a second passion—like her tiddlywink music, it remained in her mind as a discovery of major importance in her development—about which she felt, "This is *mine*. This is what *I* like." But this time, she did not discuss her newfound love with anyone; it seems clear that she was learning, painfully, to keep her deepest emotional reactions locked up inside herself, to view them as too personal, too private to be shared or made vulnerable to the rejection of others. This, too, was a trend that was to progressively characterize her life: as an adult, she spoke easily and in strongly emotional terms of whatever elicited her disapproval, her contempt, her anger; she spoke much more rarely—and then usually in objectively impersonal terms—of that which she most profoundly loved.

In the Crimean resort where the Rosenbaums vacationed, a smart, expensive hotel had recently been built, patronized mainly by foreign visitors. Occasionally, Anna took Alice to the hotel for lunch; from the dining room, they could see the tennis court—itself an unusual phenomenon in Russia. One day, gazing out at the court, Alice's attention was caught by a slender, graceful young girl racing effortlessly after a ball and decisively smashing it across the net. She was a twelve-year-old English visitor, Alice was told, named Daisy Gerhardi. Alice stared, fascinated, at this "sophisticated, foreign" figure—doing something no Russian girl was allowed to do, and doing it with consummate grace. When she was fifty-five years old, Alice glowed as she talked of Daisy. "It amazed me," she said. "It was a creature out of a different world, my idea of what a woman should be. She was a symbol of the independent woman from abroad. I felt what today I'd feel for Dagny Taggart. I only saw her that one summer, but the symbol was magnificent—I can still see her today, a very active, tall, long-legged girl in motion; I don't remember the face, only the long-legged agility, and black stockings worn with white tennis shoes. For years, her outfit seemed the most attractive I had ever seen. . . . I didn't long to approach her or to get acquainted, I was content to admire her from afar."[2]

[2] In his autobiography, *Memoirs of a Polyglot,* published in 1931, the eminent British novelist William Gerhardi wrote about his family and about Daisy. Alice never learned that the girl she admired was

Daisy served for Alice as a focus, a projection, an image that she was to use in her fiction—most particularly, she later said, in the creation of the heroine of *Atlas Shrugged,* Dagny Taggart, the beautiful woman who ran a great railroad. It was an image which she "held defiantly against everyone else. I didn't want others to share this value. I felt: This is *my* value, and anyone who shares it has to be extraordinary. I was extremely jealous—it was literal jealousy—of anyone who would pretend to like something I liked, if I didn't like that person. I had an almost anxious feeling about it, that it wasn't right. They have no right to admire it, they're unworthy of it."

The passionate concern with spiritual consistency—with a single-tracked purity of value-choices—was a significant element in alienating the small child from the people and the world around her. She felt, always, as she later said, a painful kind of anger—of contempt—for anyone who seemed to love what she loved, but also responded to what she considered boring and stupid; it was as if, through such a response, her love was desecrated. One may not light a candle before a god—and also before the figure of a clown.

The intelligence that boiled inside the child, that already had made her the center of attention in the adult world—"They all seemed to see something unusual in me," she reported—was creating its pressure to be fed. A year before she was to enter school, Alice had taught herself to read and write. By watching her parents and other adults reading, she grasped what the phenomenon consisted of; she asked them to show her how to write her name in block letters, then to show her other words, so she could learn more letters. By that method, she quickly learned the alphabet, and soon was reading and writing with ease. She was allowed to take a special examination to determine whether she was ready for school; she won acceptance with ease.

Alice was delighted at the prospect of entering school; it would be something *interesting,* she felt, and she would learn new things that she wanted to know. But by the end of the first year, she was bored with all of her classes except arithmetic. Arithmetic was pure deduction, which all her life was to be a source of joy to her.

"The teacher would lecture straight from the textbook, and explain what was in it—which I already understood; she would not expand or elaborate; and I was at least three lessons ahead. I felt I could learn better and faster at home. I felt that the slow girls needed this, but I didn't." Her boredom soon became torture, and she longed to catch cold, longed for the school to close, for her teacher to be sick. She was happy when she contracted measles and was quarantined at her

---

her neighbor in St. Petersburg; the Gerhardis owned the largest cotton mill in Russia, situated on the Nevsky Prospect; the family had migrated to St. Petersburg from England two generations earlier. William Gerhardi, like his youngest sister Marguerite, called Daisy, was Russian-born. Daisy, "a courageous little girl," was William's favorite of his five siblings, and his playmate. One summer, he wrote, "we all went tennis mad," and the family spent the summer playing their favorite game at a seaside resort. Daisy suffered from a lung disease, and later was sent to school in Switzerland; when the family lost its mill and its wealth after the Bolshevik revolution, they left Russia. Daisy ultimately settled in Paris, where she married a Frenchman.

grandmother's; there, she could do what she pleased, without rules, without assignments except of her own choosing.

Alice had been at school only a few days when a little girl approached her and said "Let's be girlfriends." The two children talked occasionally over the next few days, but within a week, her "friend" stopped approaching her. Alice felt regretful—she would have liked to have a friend—and "I felt I had failed her in something she wanted, I had no idea what." She never forgot her sudden awareness that she was different from the other girls, that she was too serious, too intense—and, at the same time, too shy—her realization that the other children got along with each other with an ease and understanding that she did not possess; she did not know why. Her continuing inability to form relationships with other children remained in her mind throughout childhood as a troubling question.

Anna Rosenbaum, recognizing that Alice's lessons at school and at home— her Belgian governess was teaching her French and German—were not enough to occupy her, and that she had made no friends among her schoolmates, began subscribing to French children's magazines in the hope that they would interest the child. At first, Alice was bored with the stories, and the magazines accumulated unread. Alice later said, "My contempt for those stories was exactly the same, only more primitive, as what I would feel today about stories of the folks next door or naturalism."

Then a serial that fascinated her appeared in one of the magazines. It was about a heroic French detective in pursuit of a dangerous jewel thief. The detective overcame all obstacles in pursuit of his goal, and, in the end, was triumphant. This is interesting, Alice thought, because he's doing something important. It's more interesting than what's going on around me. *His story is of a battle between good and evil.* The battle between good and evil was to engage her ever after. It was to be the major element she sought in literature, it was to be the perspective from which she viewed the world. It would later draw her to such disparate literary figures as Victor Hugo and Mickey Spillane; it would cause her to see the world as a giant battlefield in which her personal god and devil were locked in endless conflict. There was good in the world, and there was evil; one had to choose sides in the battle, one had—as writer and as human being—to enlist one's energies and one's life on the side of the good. As Alice matured, the detective and the jewel thief became opposing philosophical ideas, but the principle remained the same.

The idea of writing stories began to intrigue Alice; if others could do it, she could do it. The invention of stories soon became more absorbing than anything around her. She would sit in school, barricaded behind a book, scribbling furiously at her latest adventure, wanting only to be left alone, to write, to devise dangerous exploits for her characters.

Inventing stories and writing came to her with great ease: it was not work, it was a pure, ecstatic pleasure. She later said, in a tone of wistfulness, "The ease with which I wrote has remained to this day as a kind of Atlantis behind me, a lost Garden of Eden." Alice's style was precise and dry, she wrote with the naïve directness of a child, in synopsislike narrative. As it was to remain throughout her lifetime, her primary concern was with clarity, with expressing precisely what she wanted to say. Her greatest pleasure was inventing plots. And when the plot had been put into words, she discovered the heady feeling of living in the world of her own creation. She experienced the joy of creating a world more interesting than the world around her, of creating purposes more important than the purposes around her, of creating characters more admirable and heroic than the people around her. She was discovering, without yet the words to name it, the Aristotelian principle that the fiction writer creates the world "as it might be and ought to be."

It was during the summer of 1914 that she read a story which she recognized, then and later, as marking a crucial turning point in her life.

One quiet afternoon, Alice turned, as she often did, to her stacks of French magazines. Leafing through a boys' magazine of adventure stories, she stopped at one entitled "The Mysterious Valley," and began to read. Time stood still. Her life stood still, as if waiting for its purpose. Many years later, she talked about the story and her feeling for it.

"It was a love affair for me from the first installment. It was about English officers in India, kidnapped by an evil rajah, a monstrous old villain who is plotting to overthrow British rule. Two officers set out to avenge their friends, who they think are dead; then there follow a number of exciting adventures, until the men find the mysterious valley where the hero and the other men are imprisoned in a cage in a temple; the rajah is going to kill them. But the hero, Cyrus—the kind of feeling I had for him, it still exists, it's in essence everything that I've ever felt for Roark, Galt, Nathan, Frank, or all my values. There's nothing that I can add in quality to any important love later on that wasn't contained in that. Except that being the first, the intensity was almost unbearable. I was a woman in love in a serious sense. The whole reality around me lost all meaning. If, before, I felt that I was imprisoned among dull people, now it was: They don't know, but *I* do—*this* is what's possible.

"One illustration that particularly impressed me was a picture of Cyrus standing with a sword. He was a perfect drawing of my present hero: tall, long-legged, with leggings but no jacket, just an open collar, his shirt torn in front, open very low, sleeves rolled to the elbows, and hair falling down over one eye. The appearance of my heroes, and what is *my* type of man, was completely taken from that illustration."

As Ayn Rand, in middle age, talked about Cyrus, the excitement of youth was in her voice and face, like a woman remembering her first love, never to be challenged, never again to be matched.

"Cyrus was a man of enormous audaciousness, defiant independence. All the other officers in the prison were afraid of the rajah and broken in spirit—except Cyrus. He stood holding on to the bars of the cage, hurling insults at the rajah.

He was threatened with torture, with whipping, but he was completely defiant—he laughed!

"One of the rescuers climbed on the shoulders of an enormous idol in the temple, put two flashlights into the eyes of the idol and flashed their beams over the assemblage. The Indians were terror-stricken by the lights, and fled, abandoning the cages. Then began the difficulty of escaping the valley—all kinds of adventures, with secret corridors and a pool filled with crocodiles. At the last moment, they found that the rajah was holding a beautiful blond English girl prisoner; they rescued her, and escaped with her.

"In the last installment, they are climbing a steep ladder of metal rungs up the side of a cliff. Cyrus is carrying the girl on his shoulders. They had planted dynamite to go off just as the Indians were pursuing them—a dam broke, water covered the valley, and all the villains perished—and the hero married the girl."

During the years of my friendship with Ayn Rand, I was always impressed with the range and exactitude of her memory; I was never so much impressed as when, in 1982, I was able to locate "The Mysterious Valley." It was written by Maurice Champagne and published in France in 1914 after magazine serialization. I discovered that Ayn, who had recounted the story at considerable length, had recalled almost every detail, major and minor, of a work she had not read since she was nine years old.

"Cyrus was a *personal* inspiration," she explained, "a concrete of what one should be like, and what a man should be like. He was a man of action who was totally self-confident, and no one could stand in his way. No matter what the circumstances, he'd always find a solution. He helped me to concretize what I called 'my kind of man'—that expression, which I carried thereafter, began with that story. Intelligence, independence, courage. The heroic man."

In the child who was Alice Rosenbaum, Ayn Rand was being born. One can observe in her novels that the spirit of Cyrus became the spirit of all the fictional heroes she would create. Howard Roark in *The Fountainhead* was Cyrus, John Galt and Hank Rearden and Francisco d'Anconia in *Atlas Shrugged* were Cyrus. The name "Kira," which she chose for the heroine of *We the Living*, is the Russian feminine version of "Cyrus." As an adult, she would translate Cyrus's courage and daring into intellectual terms; but the basic nature of "the heroic man" was never to alter. Alice Rosenbaum, age nine, was on fire with the human possibility she had seen; Ayn Rand was to hold that fire throughout her life, as the source of a literary career that burned into the consciousness of generations of men and women. It was not the stories in her novels, it was not the literary style, it was not the events that most accounted for the fame she was to achieve; it was the portrayal of the human potential: it was Cyrus.

Talking about her childhood discovery, Alice said: "Thereafter, for the next three years, Cyrus was my exclusive love. I felt totally out of the concerns or reality of anybody. What they were interested in didn't matter at all to me, because I knew something much higher. The story made the reality around me more bearable, because it made concrete the reality of what I valued. My feeling was 'This is what *I* want out of life.' "

It made the reality around her more bearable, but it increased her estrangement from other people, both adults and children. *She* saw what was possible, they did not; *she* cared with desperate passion about her new love, they neither grasped nor cared about it; it was *hers,* it was not theirs. "I was shocked to hear that one girl in my class was receiving the same magazine, a girl I never particularly liked. I felt real jealousy. I felt violently: she has no right to it."

That same summer of 1914, Alice spent what she always recalled as an idyllic period. With her family, she traveled abroad, first for a week in Vienna, then for six weeks in Switzerland. She later spoke of that period in Switzerland as the springboard for the description in *Atlas Shrugged* of the childhood of Francisco d'Anconia and Dagny Taggart. Their childhood is spent in the country; it is a period of inventive, purposeful, adventurous activity, in a world that seems always to be lit by a brilliant sun, a joyful childhood devoted to learning the skills that will make them creative adults. Alice's own summer in Switzerland was spent climbing through the mountains—the first physical activity she had ever enjoyed—her skirt torn and her legs scratched, scaling difficult heights and searching for wild strawberries. Her companion was a young boy whom she met at a Swiss hotel. She chose him because he was intelligent and physically daring. "When we parted, I firmly intended to meet him again when I grew up. . . . Sometimes, to this day, I wonder what happened to him."

That summer, with its pure, ecstatic sense of adventure, ended in terror. As the family was traveling from Switzerland to Paris, World War I began. The family hurried to London to find a ship which would take them across the North Sea, the only route to Russia left open. They returned to Russia across a sea treacherous with German mines; the ship that had left just before theirs hit a mine and exploded, as did the one that followed them. It was a journey filled with fear and the imminence of death. "The war marked the end of the world," she later remarked.

If one world ended for Alice, another had just begun. Walking along a London street with her governess, while the family awaited the ship that would take them home, Alice stopped before a theater featuring a musical revue; she stared in fascination at a poster that showed attractive, blond young women with page-boy haircuts. When she returned to her hotel room, she began inventing stories about the girls in the poster, telling their adventures to her spellbound sisters, who always demanded to hear her latest story. As she talked and happily invented, it suddenly occurred to her for the first time: "This is what people *do*— people become writers, and they spend their *lives* writing stories." She stopped to examine the thought, as a wondrous possibility. Writing was not merely the most interesting activity of all—it could be a way of life. Her next thought was: This is what *I'm* going to do. I'm going to be a writer. The nine-year-old girl felt very solemn. Now I have a purpose, she told herself. I'm going to be a writer.

Arriving home in St. Petersburg, Alice turned to her new purpose with a blinding absorption. She wrote at home, in school, at night, whenever she was free of the demands of childhood and family and school, demands which she resented and despised more bitterly than ever. "The Mysterious Valley" was the symbol of what she wanted, the standard toward which she intended to grow. When she heard that two other girls wanted to be writers, she felt both a professional solidarity and a sense of rivalry. She was eager to learn what kind of stories they were writing, like—she later said—a businessman wanting to know what the competition is doing.

She was fully aware, she would always insist, that the motor moving her in devising her stories was, above all, the vision of the heroic she had found in Cyrus. She wanted to see heroes, so she invented characters who were daring, independent, courageous. She wanted life to be interesting, so she invented characters pursuing demanding goals and overcoming obstacles. She had been bored by the plotless mood stories she had read, so she struggled to invent dramatic events that led to unexpected climaxes. She disliked the sentimental tragedy of Russian children's stories, and her own stories had a sunlit, benevolent quality and culminated in the success of her heroes.

Convinced she could not find in the life around her the heroism, the drama, the benevolence that she had found in Cyrus—it stood in her mind as "My kind of people don't exist around me, but they exist somewhere, and when I grow up and am on my own, I'll find them"—she turned increasingly to books for the emotional nourishment she required.

One of the stories she found remained in her memory because it seemed to sum up her attitude toward her present and her future. It was a child's biography of Catherine the Great, the little German princess who became an empress. Catherine was presented as an intelligent child, more active than the other children of her background. But she was seen by her parents and others around her "as something between a misfit and an ugly duckling, because she didn't behave like a conventional little princess." At a royal party given for children of the German nobility, a fortune-teller was summoned to tell them what their futures would be. The reigning favorite among the children was a very beautiful little princess, so beautiful that everyone was sure she would marry a great king and have a glorious life. No one had great expectations for Catherine; her parents were of the second rank, and she was not beautiful. The children stood around the fortune-teller. "Do you see a crown on her brow?" asked one of the adults, pointing to the beautiful little princess. "No," answered the fortune-teller—then suddenly she turned to Catherine and cried, "But here is a girl on whose forehead I see the mark of *two* crowns."

"This was my feeling as a child," said Alice many years later. "I thought that I was exactly like Catherine. I didn't fit into their schemes, and they didn't know that there was a mark on my forehead—and how much I wished that somebody would see it." Then Ayn Rand, aged fifty-five, remarked sadly, "You know something—I'm still waiting, to this day. . . ."

Chapter Two

The destiny that young Alice awaited seemed to recede farther into the future when the family returned to St. Petersburg in the late summer of 1914. A tragically unprepared Russia was at war with Germany and Austria. The front was eight hundred miles away, weapons were outdated and inadequate, the army command was disorganized and incompetent. By the end of the year, Russian losses were staggering, averaging more than three hundred thousand men a month. Their weapons nearly exhausted, soldiers were fighting with clubs, searching for rifles among the bodies of enemy soldiers; around their feet, instead of the shoes which had long ago disintegrated, they wrapped shreds of newspaper.

By the following summer, 1,400,000 men had been killed or wounded in the terrible cold and icy storms of the front, almost a million more were prisoners of war. St. Petersburg—now Petrograd, its Germanic name changed by the Czar to the more Slavic Petrograd—stirred uneasily and prayed for an ever-receding victory.

The events seething in the world outside her barely penetrated Alice's consciousness in the years from 1914 to 1916. Children should not know about the terrible carnage in the world, her protective parents believed, and the war rarely was discussed in the presence of the Rosenbaum children; nor were they permitted to read newspapers. But perhaps more relevantly, her major focus continued to be on her writing. "I was writing in every spare moment. I felt I was preparing for the future, for the world I would enter when I grew up." Nothing could be allowed to distract her from the dedicated singleness of purpose that was to guide her life for the next forty years.

In school, Alice's class was beginning to read Russian classics. It was "torture" for Alice, it was "sheer official boredom." The sole pleasure of her class assignments was that, in presenting her own views, she felt like a crusader. In her middle years, she smiled with affection as she spoke of the child who had felt, as she gravely presented her views: " 'Thus spake little Alice'. . . . I felt that I was now naming the truth, and I was proud that I was able to do it."

She came to believe that one of the reasons adults were so impressed with the young girl—and perhaps one of the reasons other children kept a careful distance—was the precocity of her articulateness. She could never recall a time when she had had difficulty expressing what she thought or, when necessary, defending it. None of her acquaintances of later years, who unanimously spoke with deep respect of the quality of her mind and her astonishing ability to present complex intellectual issues in terms intelligible to the least knowledgeable of her listeners, ever doubted the validity of her memory.

She was no more than ten years old, she would recall, when she concluded, in conscious terms, not only that the realm of ideas was important, but that it was *her* realm to deal with. One day, her mother showed her an article in a Petrograd newspaper—it did not involve politics and so was not forbidden—that Anna thought would be instructive for the young girl. It was an interview with a woman who was a specialist in education; she declared that the purpose of education was to provide children with their ideals. "If a child does not acquire ideals from school, he will never acquire them," the woman wrote. Alice felt a "violent, outraged anger," an anger so intense that she never forgot the episode. "At that age," she later said, "I had a value-world of my own, it mainly took the form of the stories I was writing, I felt that what *I* valued or wanted was superior to what others valued or wanted, and school bored me, especially in the value realm. I did not share their values. I did not learn my values from school. I thought 'Wait until I grow up and I'll show those people, and I'll denounce this particular woman. If I don't agree, it's my job to fight it.' " Ideas were important, fighting for the "right ideas" was important, and so was denouncing the "wrong ideas."

Mystified, Alice observed that the other girls in her class found it difficult to form opinions of what they were reading and observing and to articulate whatever opinions they did form. Several of them came to her to ask how she could do it so easily. Alice wondered, "with an edge of contempt," why anyone would find it difficult. One read, one observed, one thought, one arrived at conclusions, and one expressed them.

"Contempt" is a curiously adult reaction to find in a child. But when Ayn Rand spoke of her childhood, it is a term that she used again and again to describe her feelings toward most of the people around her. It is a term that— accompanied by a dismissive wave of her hand and a grimace of distaste—dotted her conversations throughout her adult years.

In childhood, and all of her life, it appears that her most intense scorn was reserved for women. That scorn was evident in her recollections of childhood, and, equally, it is the impression of many of the people who knew her in later years. Even before adolescence, she was what she later called "an anti-feminist. I regarded man as a superior value." In her writing during that period, what interested her was to create a conflict for a hero, a conflict aimed at the achievement of some serious purpose; in her stories, it was the man, not the woman, who represented the qualities of struggle and purpose. "I would not have said that it was improper for a woman, I would have been extremely indignant at any touch of the idea that woman's place is in the home or 'young ladies should be young ladies'. . . . I was always in favor of tomboys, and of intellectual equality, but women as such didn't interest me."

The human qualities she cared about were, she believed, specifically masculine attributes; above all, purposefulness and strength. She would later insist that she had never regretted being a woman, but "it was hero worship from the first." And she would later *define* femininity as "hero worship." Man, she would say, is defined by his relationship to reality; woman—by her relationship to man. Far into old age, she would comment about herself proudly, "I'm a hero worshipper."

It was in the winter of 1916 that Alice's absorption in her inner life was interrupted. The world was beginning to knock loudly at her door, and she turned from reading and writing to admit it. For the first time, a keen interest in politics, which she was never to lose, began to take shape.

Petrograd was disintegrating. Almost a million troops had deserted the front; despairing, angry, and hungry, they headed for home, looting and destroying everything in their path and clogging the starving, inflation-ravaged cities, vainly looking for work. In towns, countrysides, and cities, the muttering against the Czar's conduct of the war grew loud. Petrograd's bread lines lengthened as the bitterly cold winter passed. Mass strikes, accompanied by outbreaks of violence, became daily occurrences. Crime became a plague, and no one was secure in his home. There was little heat in the city, and in their kitchens, people were burning furniture for fuel. The great city was dying, with only its terrible flailing agony as a sign of life. Throughout Petrograd—throughout Russia—the muttering began to grow to a furious bellow.

On the day of Alice's twelfth birthday, in February of 1917, the temperature stood at 35 degrees below zero. Demonstrators clogged the broad avenues of the city, shouting "Down with the monarchy!" Speakers stood at every street corner, handing out pamphlets and cursing the war. In the capital of a country that had a centuries-long heritage of revolution, an enraged population once more was moving to reclaim that heritage.

But this time, the revolution was virtually bloodless. Alice witnessed its beginning. She stood on the balcony of her apartment as a huge crowd gathered on the square below, shouting anti-Czarist slogans. A unit of the National Guard appeared and ordered the crowd to disperse. The crowd screamed its defiance—the soldiers raised their rifles—and Alice heard the first shots of the Russian Revolution. Unwillingly, the crowd scattered. But the next day, they returned in still-greater numbers: the soldiers who had fired upon them had now joined the revolution. Throughout the city, exultant crowds took over the public buildings and the courts. Fires blazed in the streets like beacons of hope.

By the end of February, political power had passed to the Duma in a revolution created by Russian citizens—by workers, by students, by the middle class, and by sympathetic soldiers. The Czar abdicated; the immeasurable power of the Romanovs was no more. Alexander Kerensky, a young lawyer with bristling hair, a powerful voice, and a gift for bold and effective oratory, became Prime Minister.

There were wild celebrations in Petrograd. But amid the cheers and the celebrations, an ominous note was sounding. Bolshevik revolutionaries were returning to Petrograd from exile. Molotov returned, and Trotsky, and a young party member named Stalin. At the railroad station, Lenin was welcomed by cheering Bolshevik crowds; his return was made possible by Germany, eager to see a Bolshevik government that would sue for a separate peace. In *The World Crisis,* Winston Churchill was to write: "The German leaders turned upon Russia the most grisly of all weapons. They transported Lenin in a sealed truck like a plague bacillus from Switzerland into Russia."

It is rare that history is so obliging as to present us with a morality play in the form of events that scream out their meaning—scream out the moral significance of the philosophical premises and world views responsible for those events. But for Alice Rosenbaum, the terrible years that lay ahead sometimes seemed precisely such a morality play.

"My concept of good and evil," she would later comment, "already in the process of being formed, saw its vindication everywhere"—as if reality had become the sort of fiction she later would create: a conflict, written larger than life, between two opposing views of man, two opposing views of human society, two opposing views of morality.

In the beginning, it seemed to Alice "that everybody of any political denomination was in favor of the February revolution. And everybody was against the Czar. What fascinated me was that it fit in with my own stage of development— it was the only time I was synchronized with history. It was almost like fiction taking place in reality. That was why I became so interested. I know that I romanticized it a great deal. It seemed the fight for freedom; since that's what they were talking about, I took it literally—by which *I* meant individualism: it's *man* who must be free."

Even at so early an age, Alice had concluded that she was opposed to "the government or society or any authorities imposing anything on anyone." With the February revolution, "I began to understand that politics was a *moral* issue." It was a perception she never was to lose or waver from: Is man free to choose his own purposes and set his own goals—or is he forced to accept and live by the goals and purposes of others? Freedom was the issue; in the realm of politics, it was the *only* issue, it was the heart and soul of political philosophy.

Alexander Kerensky, thought Alice—hearing the adults discuss his ringing speeches in defense of liberty—was a man who stood for freedom and the individual. Kerensky became important to her as the first man outside of books and her own imagination whom she could admire. She listened eagerly to everything the adults said about him, and surreptitiously scanned the forbidden newspapers for further stories. She reported, "I could never be allowed to go to a political meeting where he spoke, so my great dream was to catch a glimpse of him somewhere. I never did." But Alice collected his photographs, and despite her mother's annoyance, she plastered her bedroom walls with them, as American girls thousands of miles and a generation away would plaster their walls with pictures of matinee idols.

"My infatuation with Kerensky had a very important influence on me in one respect," Alice later said. "I decided that I could never be in love with an ordinary man. I said to Mother, 'I'm in love with Kerensky.' The adults said it was an infatuation, not love—so I stopped telling them. I concluded that I *am* in love, it's not just infatuation. And since he was married, I would never marry—because I could never be in love with anyone but a hero. In my last years in high school, when girls began to go out on dates, I remember feeling a very superior contempt: How can they be interested in just ordinary boys? *I* have to have a hero. By then, I had given up the idea that I'd never marry, but one thing did remain, and remains to this day: I can never be in love with anybody but a hero."

Alice's first real-life hero was engaged in a desperate struggle to save his beleaguered land from its terrible economic crisis, and to keep the army fighting. But the task was impossible. The railroads were falling apart, supplies could not move to the front, the streets of the cities were filled with vagabonds and deserters, the factories were closing. By summer, society was on the verge of dissolution.

The Bolsheviks saw their opportunity. On October 10, Bolshevik troops swarmed across the Neva into Petrograd. Within a handful of blood-soaked days, the helpless city was theirs. The desperate government called a meeting in the Winter Palace. But as the ministers conferred—to the sound of shrapnel shells bursting in the air over the Peter and Paul Fortress—armored Bolshevik tanks were bursting onto the grounds of the Winter Palace. Troops swarmed into the meeting room, and Kerensky's ministers were led out under arrest. Ten days after the Bolshevik revolution had begun, the hope of democracy was no more. The streets of Petrograd grew quiet, as the citizens huddled inside their homes in terror of what was to come.

Kerensky escaped the fate of his fellow ministers; during the siege of the Winter Palace, he was able to flee abroad. From then on, he roamed the world, writing, speaking, passionately recounting the story of the stillbirth of freedom in Russia. In one of the dramatic coincidences so typical of her life, Alice did, many years later, realize her childhood dream of "catching a glimpse" of Kerensky. In 1945, he attended a party in New York, given by political conservatives of her acquaintance—and Alice Rosenbaum was introduced to Alexander Kerensky. "But by then," Ayn Rand reported sadly, "I had no illusions about him. And he was worse that I would have expected. He was a real mediocrity."

As Alice had witnessed the first shots of the Kerensky revolution from her balcony, so she witnessed its last rites: the funeral procession of the delegates to the Constitutional Assembly who had been shot down by the Bolsheviks. It was an event that, even thirty-five years later, she spoke of with a shudder of horror. On the day of the funeral, in a gesture of defiance against the new regime, shops and schools closed; all of Petrograd swarmed into the streets to salute the fallen delegates. As the open coffins moved slowly beneath her window, to the sound of drum rolls and the thunder of cannons, the twelve-year-old girl looked down at the body of a beautiful young woman whose white face and black hair were vivid against a scarlet pillow.

In the city streets, as the weeks passed, the funeral was replaced by its cause: soldiers with bayonets and a hooligan manner—and by its effect: one's sense of being helplessly in the power of something brutal, savage, and mindless. The terror had begun.

"It will be the bloodiest revolution in history," Fronz Rosenbaum prophesied. During the revolution's first days, his frightened wife had begged him to consider fleeing the country. He had refused. He couldn't leave his business, he explained. Soon, there was no business to save.

On an afternoon that she remembered vividly all of her life, Alice stood in her father's chemist shop, watching in bewilderment as Fronz Rosenbaum gathered together the few personal possessions he kept in the shop, and hurried to hide them in the apartment. As he was returning, armed soldiers burst into the shop, and stamped a red seal on the door. The shop was nationalized in the name of the people. Anna Rosenbaum rushed Alice back to the apartment—but not before she had seen the look on her father's face. "I felt the way he looked. His look was one of helpless, murderous frustration and indignation—but he could do absolutely nothing. . . . It was a horrible silent spectacle of brutality and injustice. I thought: *that's* the principle of communism."

Along with all other private property, the banks were nationalized, and all safety deposit boxes were confiscated. An aunt of Alice's, who had kept her jewelry in a safety deposit box, wept bitterly over its loss. But Fronz Rosenbaum had uneasily foreseen what was to come, and had removed his funds and his wife's jewelry from the bank. After the seizure of his shop, the family eked out a bare, miserable survival on his savings.

The savings began to wither away; the state did not.

"Even at that age," Alice later said, "I could see what was wrong with communism. It meant living for the State. I realized they were saying that the illiterate and the poor had to be the rulers of the earth, *because* they were illiterate and poor." She was startled by the fact that while everyone complained bitterly about the physical hardships created by the Communists, no one seemed equally indignant about their ideology. When she first heard the Communist slogan—shrilled in the Bolsheviks' every speech and article and plastered on walls throughout the city—that man must live for the State, she knew that this was the horror at the root of all the other horrors taking place around her. This was the source of the bloodshed, the confiscations, the arrests in the night, the fear gripping the city she loved—of the beautiful young woman's dead face against a scarlet pillow. "I felt incredulous that such a statement could be uttered, and I felt a cold loathing for anyone who would accept it. I saw in that slogan the vision of Cyrus on a sacrificial altar, crucified in the name of mediocrity." She heard in it the statement that the purpose of *her* life was not her own to choose, that her life and her work must be given in selfless servitude to others —she saw the life of the men of intelligence, of ambition, of independence, the life of the men whose proud worshipper she had chosen to be, claimed as the property of the mob. "It was the demand for the sacrifice of the best among men, and for the enshrinement of the commonplace, that I saw as the unspeakable evil of communism."

Her answer to that slogan, in the form of a conscious conviction and of a passionate dedication—an answer that would become a major theme of all her future work—was that *nothing* could be higher or more important than an individual's right to his own life, that that was a right beyond the claim of any other individual or group or collective or state or the whole population of the globe.

The course of her life—which before had been moved forward by her vision of a god, the god that was Cyrus and what he represented—now was moved forward as well by a devil: the philosophy of sacrifice. Again, in the complex soul that was Alice Rosenbaum, Ayn Rand was being born.

Despite the accelerating terror and misery of the Bolshevik regime, Alice was not wholly absorbed with politics. In 1917 and 1918, two events occurred which she felt even then were as important for her future as the political nightmare around her.

The first event was a change in her method of thinking. She called her new method "thinking in principles." "I began to formulate reasons *consciously,*" she later said. "I began to ask myself the *why* of the ideas I believed, and to integrate them. Before, I had very strong value-judgments, but they were not very connected." She saw her new method as a major step toward the adulthood for which she longed. It was adults who formulated their ideas in conscious, conceptual terms, who constructed logical chains of *why's,* who identified the deepest reasons of their convictions, who asked themselves what they believed, and why they believed it. Now, she was learning to do it too. Alice was following a path not unusual in highly intelligent children entering adolescence; but in a manner that always was to be an essential element in her psychology and method of intellectual functioning—a method that perhaps in part explains the range and controlled power of her mind—she stopped to try to name her path, to grasp it, to conceptualize it, and, most important, to put it under her conscious control. She began to keep a diary in which she wrote down not the events of her life, not the terror and suffering of the political upheaval, but the ideas she was thinking about and the stories she was planning to write. It was, she reported, a period of "wonderfully intense intellectual excitement."

The changes in her method of thinking affected her writing in a manner that was, at first, frightening to her. "Before, I don't remember the genesis of any of my stories—they would come to me as a whole, I would have the idea 'wouldn't it be interesting if . . . ?'—and I would have the whole story. I had no critical faculty, I would write whatever my subconscious had connected. But now, I began to project an idea in *abstract* terms. I began to be self-critical, and I gave myself the assignment of what *sort* of story I wanted it to be. I would have the abstract intention, and the characters, but no specific plot. No concrete climax. And when I tried to fill it in, I couldn't. I could not find the concretes. Suddenly, for the first time in my life, I couldn't invent a story. It was a terrifying experience. My 'block' trouble started then, at the age of twelve. Thereafter, until I left Russia, I was writing themes down, I had lots of ideas either for plays or novels, I always got an idea that was part theme and part situations that would be clear, and never filled out the rest. Some were more filled out than others, some I left for future reference. I began to list themes and situations to write when I grew up. I knew I didn't yet have the knowledge to carry them out."

With the Bolshevik revolution, Alice's story themes became political. All of them concerned individualistic heroes, fighting against the Communists or against a king. "They were usually laid abroad, I never intended to write stories laid in Russia. Russia was too flat, too commonplace . . . it's stupid, backward, mystical, and sentimental. But abroad, or in historical dramas—*that* is civilization, *that* is intellectual, rational people."

All of her life, Alice—despite her love for the gracious city of her birth—was to speak of Russia with loathing, a loathing, she reported, that she felt even before the Communist revolution. She saw Russia as a nation that glorified the tragic and the malevolent, glorified the very qualities that were the antithesis of what she wanted in her own life and what she wanted to create in her stories. "It was the antithesis of my tiddlywink music," she later recalled thinking. It was the antithesis of the joy that she held as her birthright and her goal. And as, over the years, she became more consciously and passionately anti-mystical and pro-reason, championing man's reasoning faculty as the source of any value life might hold and denouncing faith as anti-man and anti-life, what she would call "Russian mysticism" became the synonym for all that was dark and evil and dedicated to the destruction of human life. It was the West—England in her early years, when she knew little of America—that was her ideal. When, in college in Petrograd, she began to see American movies, her allegiance was transferred to all things she saw as "typically American." All her life, she was to respond to men and women who had an appearance and manner she believed to be "the best of the American type": the tall, blond, long-legged, emotionally reserved men and women who would typify the heroes of her novels. When the movie of *The Fountainhead* was made in 1948, she hoped, although she had no power of decision, that Gary Cooper would be chosen for the part of Howard Roark; his appearance was what she had visualized for her character; and she was delighted when he was chosen. In the 1970s, Farrah Fawcett—so archetypical an American girl, an American version of Daisy—became a favorite of hers, and her choice for the part of Dagny Taggart had *Atlas Shrugged* been filmed. Many people, even among her close friends, were incredulous that so intellectual a woman as Ayn Rand was fascinated by such nonintellectual types as Gary Cooper and Farrah Fawcett: they did not know Alice Rosenbaum, the little girl in love with the gaiety, the benevolence, the clean-limbed agility, the "non-Russian soul" of Americans. Frank O'Connor, the man she married and loved for more than fifty years, might, in appearance, have been a brother of Gary Cooper.

The second great event in Alice's life during the immediate post-revolutionary period was the discovery of a writer whose work profoundly influenced her future literary development: Victor Hugo. She was later to say that he was the *single* influence on her in all literature.

In her classes in school, Alice had been exposed to the great classics of Russian literature—which, predominantly, she hated. She later said, "In Russian literature, there was nothing that would answer to my particular taste. There are either the great naturalists like Turgenev and Chekhov and Tolstoy, or the romantics like Pushkin or some others, usually poets, who are always Byronic and malevolent. I *loathed* stories of tragic, hopeless romance, I was extremely contemptuous of love stories. I *despised* the idea of love as the main concern, even at twelve, and from then on more so."

While the Bolshevik revolution raged on the streets of Petrograd, Anna Rosenbaum, determined that Alice further improve her French, gave her Hugo's *The Man Who Laughs*. It was a thunderclap of light exploding in the dull grayness of her life. After reading it, she turned to *Les Misérables*, then to all the rest of Hugo's novels. "I was fascinated by Hugo's sense of life," she said many years later, still glowing from the radiance of the memory. "It was someone writing about something *important.* I felt that this is the kind of writer I would like to be, but I didn't know how long it would take. I knew I could not now dream of touching the way he wrote. I was aware of to what extent he was a giant literarily. I knew that *The Man Who Laughs* was not my kind of heroic story in adult terms that 'The Mysterious Valley' was for me as a child. 'The Mysterious Valley' was nearer to my sense of life than Hugo." But she had discovered, she felt, a world of unprecedented scope and grandeur, of magnificently ingenious plots, of inexhaustible imaginativeness, of an exalted sense of life—of man seen as a hero.

"*Les Misérables* was *the* big experience. Everything about it became important to me, holy; everything that reminded me of it was a souvenir of my love. It was my first view of how one should see life, wider than any concretes of the story. I didn't approve of the ideas about the poor and the disinherited, except that Hugo set them up in a way that I could sympathize with; they were the victims of government, of the aristocracy, or established authority. The personal inspiration for me was that I wanted to match the grandeur, the heroic scale, the plot inventiveness, and those eloquent dramatic touches."

In recounting her reaction to Hugo, Alice was defining what was to be her own literary approach: the heroic, larger-than-life scale of men and events; the invention of complex, ingenious plots; the drama and inner consistency of the stories; the creation of events that are at once startlingly unexpected and logically inevitable. She always insisted that she did not learn her literary approach from Hugo—an approach she was later to term "Romantic Realism"—that it already had been contained, in embryo, in her stories—but that she found it eloquently realized and at its most heroic scale in Hugo. She found it in the form in which her mind, in childhood and always, required it: graspable, definable, able to be formulated and thereafter to be in her *conscious* control. Particularly in *We the Living,* her first novel, one can see the concrete, specific influence of Victor Hugo; as she continued to write and to grow, she found her own unique voice, but in the beginning she was a writer still reeling from the blinding vision of everything she wanted to achieve.

"I began to be conscious of style for the first time," she added. "I began to be aware that Hugo has a way of using language that *makes* the drama of the incidents; a synopsis of the same events wouldn't be as good. I saw the importance of style as a means to an end. . . . I was not then, or now, in love with the mere beauty of writing; I judge it by its purpose. But before that, I thought it didn't matter how you wrote, it's what you say. I began to realize that what you say depends on *how* you say it. And I was aware of his integration of themes, ideas, and action. I was struggling to find actions for all my many themes, and could not, and he was doing it expertly. He served as an ideal inspiration—it can be done. I had no idea of *how* I could do it, just a patient determination—I have to discover it."

Among Hugo's characters, she found her favorite in *Les Misérables.* It was not Jean Valjean, the leading character, nor Marius, the younger hero. It was Enjolras, the young leader of the insurrectionists, who dies fighting on the barricades in one of the most exalted and powerful scenes in all of Hugo's novels. "All of the other characters, like Jean Valjean and Marius, were presented as average men, however grandly presented. I fell in love with Enjolras. Enjolras is the man of exclusive, dedicated purpose, a man heroically dedicated to a one-track-mind purpose." In Enjolras, the austere, implacable rebel—whom Hugo described as "the marble lover of liberty," who "had but one passion, the right; but one thought, to remove all obstacles"—she saw the dedicated purposefulness and the love of rectitude that were to form her own concept of human greatness. Howard Roark, Henry Rearden, Francisco d'Anconia, John Galt—they too are austere, implacable rebels, who have "but one passion, the right; but one thought, to remove all obstacles."

This, thought Alice Rosenbaum, is what matters—Hugo's novels and the figure of Enjolras. Not the dismal, tortured existence to which she and all those around her were condemned. This, she felt, is what one lives for—this sense of life and this view of man. *This,* she thought, is what *I* shall live for.

Nothing could have been more typical of Alice—and of Ayn Rand—than her passionate enthusiasm for the values she had found in Hugo. It was to be rare in her life that she would discover objects of her admiration; but when she did find them, she became their ardent, dedicated spokesman, both privately and publically, happy to talk glowingly for hours about the priceless qualities she saw in a man, an event, a work of art, an idea, an achievement. They became her spiritual fuel, moving her forward, as Hugo was her fuel in childhood.

Ecstatic from the intellectual fervor of her new interests, Alice, for the first time, longed to find someone with whom she could share her thoughts. "But there was no one. I was desperately alone." Aware that she was unable to approach people or to deal with them in terms they could accept—increasingly uncomfortable with the mixture of painful shyness and emotional violence that characterized her—Alice began to carefully observe one of the girls in her class. It was a girl whom she liked very much, one of the best students in the class, attractive, independent, self-confident, very popular with the other young girls without appearing to court popularity. "I felt that she had somewhat my attitude toward life," Alice later recalled, "but she handled people quite differently, in what way I could not define. I wanted to know what was the difference between us, and what the similarity." One day at school, Alice walked over to the girl and said—without context or explanation: "Would you tell me what is the most important thing in life to you?" The girl looked startled, but she thought for a moment and then answered quietly: "My mother."

"That killed this ideal for me thoroughly," Alice was to say indignantly. "It was the first most important event in my life socially which made me see that it's not significant why some people, who seem to be individualistic, get along with the crowd, and I don't. My emotional reaction was like an elevator crashing—enormous disappointment and contempt. I had thought that she was a serious girl and that she was after serious things, but she was just conventional and ordinary, a mediocrity, she didn't mean anything as a person. It was really like a fallen idol. I felt the kind of contempt that made it unnecessary for me to continue. All I said to her was: Oh, I see."

Nothing could have been more typical of Alice—and of Ayn Rand—than the response revealed in this proudly and sadly told story: the instantaneous judgment, the sweeping contempt for values that were not hers, for a love that was not hers, as well as the unquestioning assumption that she understood, at once, everything that needed to be understood about the meaning of the young girl's answer to her, the failure to ask any other questions, to consider the possibility of a legitimate context not known to her. It *was,* as she later said, an important event in her life socially. Perhaps it was a decisive event in shaping the direction of her human encounters. A process of alienation appears to have been sweeping through her life with ever-increasing force, to wreak its ever-increasing havoc on her future.

Alice's precocious, intensely theoretical intelligence would serve her superbly throughout her long life; it would lead her, in the area of philosophy, to ask the incisive and seminal questions about the nature of man, about morality, about metaphysics and epistemology, that others did not think to ask, and never to accept the vague and the approximate as an answer; in the realm of philosophical investigation, her patient devotion to finding the truth, however complex and however difficult, was the heart and core of her methodology. But her psychological nature—arrogant, demanding, dogmatically wedded to its first passionate perceptions—would make her, in the realm of human relationships, *impatient* with methodology, with the calm and painstaking pursuit of hidden truth. In the realm of philosophy, she would be aware of subtleties, of context, of meanings not apparent at first glance; in the realm of social dealings, there would be for her no subtleties, no context, no hidden meanings; there was only: this is *mine*— or this is mediocre, evil, contemptible; there was only: This is *like me*—or this is valueless; there was only: I *value*—or I *despise*.

Since she was bored by the children she met, by her lessons, without friends except for her cousin Nina, indifferent to most of the activities and duties of childhood, it seems evident that it was only the richness and color of Alice's inner life, her writing, her reading, her newborn thoughts about the world, that absorbed and delighted the young girl. Her life *was* an inner life, as it would remain.

Alice did make one girlfriend, also a classmate, shortly after the February revolution. The girl was a sister of Vladimir Nabokov; her father was a cabinet minister in the Kerensky government. "She was very interested in politics, as was I, and this brought us together. It was a friendship based on conscious common interest. Earlier, when there were no specified common values, I was never able to be interested in anyone or to interest anyone. I was incapable of a personal, non-ideological friendship. As you know," she said smilingly in middle age, "I still am." The two girls discussed their ideas on the revolution—the Nabokov girl defended constitutional monarchy, but Alice believed in a republic, in the rule of law. They exchanged political pamphlets which were sold on the streets of Petrograd but which were forbidden by their parents; they read the pamphlets secretly, and discussed them. The friendship lasted only a short time. The girl's father, realizing that conditions were getting worse and that it was dangerous to remain, left Russia with his family at the end of the year. Alice never saw her friend again.[1]

By the fall of 1918, the position of the Rosenbaum family, as ex-bourgeoisie, was becoming increasingly precarious. Their savings were running out, and there was little food or fuel in the city. No one could be sure whether or not he would eat the next day. A citizen accused of hoarding sour cream was lynched by his hungry fellow citizens. During a single month, there were more than fifteen thousand reported burglaries in Petrograd, more than nine thousand holdups of shops, and a hundred and fifty murders. Rumors were spreading through the appalled city about the brutal slaying of the Romanovs. The Czar,

[1] I corresponded with Dmitri Nabokov, the son of Vladimir, in an effort to locate and talk to his aunt. I learned from him that his father had had two sisters, one of whom had died; the other one, whom he was kind enough to question for me, had no memory of Alice Rosenbaum; Alice's young friend must have been the deceased sister.

the Czarina, and all of their children had been shot by order of the Bolsheviks—then their dead bodies had been dismembered, then burned, then dissolved in sulfuric acid.

In the South and in the Ukraine, newly mobilized White armies were locked in civil war with the Communist Red armies; parts of the country, including sections of the Crimea, were in the hands of the Whites. Desperately seeking refuge from the growing Communist tyranny, Anna Rosenbaum decided that the family must leave Petrograd and journey to the Crimea. Travel permits were difficult to obtain, but with the appropriate bribery and with a doctor's certificate saying that the health of Nora, Alice's youngest sister—who twice had had pneumonia—required that she go south, the family obtained the documents permitting them to leave the shattered city they once had loved.

Chapter Three

In the fall of 1918, Alice and her family set out for what they hoped would be a haven in the Crimea.

As they rode to the train station, Alice could not avoid seeing the political posters that papered the city's buildings and back fences. The posters, crudely and roughly drawn, contained virulent characterizations of the regime's class enemies and expressions of class hatred—linked with exhortations for the people to brush their teeth and with denunciations of illiteracy. As an adult, recalling those posters, Alice shuddered with the same revulsion she had felt then as she spoke of the artists who had created the posters. With few exceptions, Russia's artists had flocked to join the Communist revolution; trains and riverboats over much of the country were splashed with their posters and their slogans, and in Petrograd an orchestra, its instruments consisting of factory steam whistles, played symphonies to the glory of the revolution. "It seemed to me a desecration that anyone sane could sanction communism, but it was almost physically sickening that artists—who are supposed to know and to express the highest possibilities of human existence—could give their talents to an ideology dedicated to the destruction of the best in man."

Because of the difficulty of travel in a country whose railroads were falling apart or were seized by deserting soldiers, and where roving bandits threatened the safety of passengers, the Rosenbaum family spent the winter months in the Ukraine. It was a tense, unhappy period, made bearable only by the news of White Army victories in the Crimea. In early spring, they headed south. When they reached the Crimean peninsula, they boarded a train which was to take them to their destination in a small, remote town.

On the evening of the second day, the train jerked to an unscheduled halt. The track ahead had been blown up, perhaps by Reds, perhaps by Whites, perhaps by bandits; no one knew. They knew only that they were stranded in the dark midst of an empty countryside, miles from Odessa, the nearest city, and that no one could guess when the train might again be able to move. Some of the passengers chose to remain in a nearby village; others, Alice's family among them, hired local peasants with horse-drawn carts to take them to Odessa. Alice threw her suitcase into an open cart and climbed behind the peasant driver to sit on the thin straw covering the wooden floor. The carts proceeded slowly, moving fearfully through uninhabited plains, bumping jerkily over the frozen ground. Suddenly, by the head of the horse drawing Alice's cart, a shot rang through the night—and an angry voice ordered: "Halt!" A group of armed, ragged men, wearing the uniforms of ex-soldiers, emerged from the darkness and commanded the terrified passengers to step down and hand over their money. If anyone tried to hide his money, the gang leader warned, he would be shot instantly. The passengers handed over their money, as the bandits quickly searched the wagons. Fronz gave his wallet to one of the bandits; it contained eight rubles; he had hidden several thousand rubles in the straw of his cart. The passengers were ordered to stand with their backs to the bandits. An elderly woman screamed out that they all would be shot, she wept and made the sign of the cross.

The possibility of death had never before been real to Alice; it was real now. Standing with the other passengers, her back to the bandits' guns, her body trembling under her rough sweater and old black skirt, the night stretching bleakly around her, she wondered if she would die. If it *is* the end—she thought —still, I have had something great in my life. I have had the image of Enjolras. If I'm going to be shot, I'll think of him at the last, I'll think of how *he* faced death. I want to die as well as he did. I want to be worthy of him. I want to die in my kind of world.

After what seemed an eternity of time, the passengers were ordered back into their carts, and allowed to continue their journey. It was early morning when they saw the buildings of Odessa in the distance.

When the family had settled in the Crimean town—in the tiny, damp house, with inadequate heating and tattered old furniture, which was all they could find in an area bursting with refugees from communism, and all they could afford— Fronz Rosenbaum opened a still tinier chemist shop. For a time, he eked out a meager living, and the family began to think that the future once again might hold some measure of hope. In the building that housed the precarious government, the Russian Imperial flag flew proudly, and the peeling walls held pictures of the dead Czar Nicholas.

Their hopes soon were dashed. During the next three years, the Crimea changed hands four times. "It was like living on a battlefield," Alice later recalled. "Finally, we began to starve. Food was unobtainable. At last, we ate only millet. Except that Mother insisted on obtaining raw onions, which she fried in linseed oil; scurvy had become a terrible problem and Mother had read that onions prevented it." It was in this period that Anna Rosenbaum's jewelry, carefully hoarded against disaster, began to trickle away, replaced by almost useless rubles. The jewelry was not missed; there were no ballets at which to wear it, no elegant gowns, no gay, carefree parties; there was only drudgery, and fear, and worn, patched garments growing shabbier month by month.

In the misery of the Crimean years, an event of a personal nature occurred which was a significant source of happiness to Alice: her stern, remote father became her "intellectual ally." One day, under the White regime, it was announced that a political lecture was to be held; the lecturer was a well-known anti-Communist. Despite their straitened financial circumstances, Fronz Rosenbaum decided to allow himself the rare luxury of attending the lecture. When Alice announced that she wanted to go with him, he was so amazed by an interest he did not know she possessed, that, despite his conviction that children should take no interest in politics, he allowed her to join him. Alice later recalled that the lecture was interesting—but the conversation with her father afterwards was fascinating. Alice learned, for the first time, the extent of the intellectual sympathy between them in the realm of politics; she had known that he was opposed to communism; she had not known that he shared her belief in individualism. She had known that he was a thoughtful man; she had not known that he took ideas with a profound, respectful seriousness. And, for the first time, he was speaking to her as an adult; *her* ideas were to be taken seriously.

Years later, when Alice described her new relationship with her father, there was a soft smile on her face and a faint tremor in her voice. It was evident that at last, to her great happiness, she was receiving the sanction, the approval, of the man who had given her so little throughout her childhood. It was evident that she loved him—and that it was the first time in the fifteen years of her life that she had loved, and been loved in return. And it was evident that the terms of that love were the only ones she knew, the only ones she respected and could understand: a philosophical mutuality.

It was during the Crimean years that Alice's relationship with her two sisters became closer. "My sisters were growing up and beginning to have personalities of their own, and the age distance lessened. . . . I really loved my youngest sister." In Alice's view, she and Nora shared important values: "We liked the same books, she was developing exactly in my direction, and she wanted to be an artist, a painter. Our personalities were the same, and she was very intelligent." In *We the Living,* Alice would create—in Irina, a minor character—one of the most sympathetic women in all of her writings, an aspiring artist of great charm and courage whom she acknowledged was inspired by her memory of her little sister Nora. It is not surprising that in the description of Irina's drawings, one finds the gay, impudent spirit of Alice's tiddlywink music.

Alice felt that she had nothing in common with Natasha, her middle sister. "I would not have picked her as a friend, it was only a family affection. She was my exact opposite: she was not intellectual, and she was very 'feminine'—when the family was in rags, she was interested in her personal appearance; she was more interested in young men than I was, she had girlfriends in school, which neither I nor my little sister ever had, she was much more conventional. But she was enormously efficient; for instance, she wanted to be a pianist, and she practiced eight to ten hours a day—driving everybody and herself crazy. She had a marvelous technique but very little expression; she was strictly a *virtuoso* pianist. You can see in what way that would be different from me."

Alice entered high school in the Crimea. In these early years of communism, the school was not yet ideologically controlled, even under the Red regimes. The teachers were old-fashioned, pro-Czarist ladies, who endured the rise of communism with grim resignation. For the first time, Alice became a class leader intellectually. Because she came from the sophisticated North, "I was forgiven for my intelligence." In Petrograd, the grim, desperately earnest little girl had been an outcast at school, by mutual, silent consent. She had shared no extracurricular activities with her schoolmates, and had made no friends among them. But in the Crimea "there was a tacit recognition of my superiority. I made no personal friends, I had no girlfriends, but I was recognized as the 'brain of the class,' which surprised me." On the first day of high school, a classmate approached Alice to ask for her help with her algebra homework. Alice explained the assignment, and what had to be done. The girl said that she had been given a different answer by a classmate. Alice replied, "Well, she's wrong. *This* is the right answer." "But the girl who gave me a different answer is our best student," Alice's classmate answered. Alice replied, "How do you know that *I* won't be?" The story spread instantly through the school that Alice had announced she would be the best student in the school—which she became. "And my answer to the assignment was the right one."

Alice's method of learning, a method that had seemed to her self-evident, but which she was now grasping was not self-evident to others, was to *understand.* Despite her remarkable memory, memory never was the tool she employed for learning. Her method was deduction: to grasp the stated or unstated axioms underlying a conclusion, to grasp the steps of moving from axiom to conclusion, to grasp the logical implications of the conclusion.

One incident at school, she later said, "influenced my thinking for life. One girl, a very nice, conscientious dummy, came to me because she could not understand her lesson, it dealt with a complex geometric problem. I explained it very thoroughly, I showed her all the connections. I realized she could not fill in the connections herself—I had to show her every step. The girl said, astonished, 'Why don't the teachers explain this the way you do?' I concluded that you can reach people's intelligence if you know how to present things clearly. I knew better than the teacher how to present things, and it was only an issue of logical progression and clarity. It gave me an enormous confidence in the common man, in the power of intelligence—some people were not as fast as I was, they could not connect by themselves, but people can be taught if it's explained properly. I still have that premise."

Alice never rejected "that premise." Throughout her life, she often said that the simplest of men, the least educated, had the power to grasp complex ideas if they were led through the necessary logical steps. It was a view that gave her infinite patience with minds slower and less competent than hers, so long as she believed that the mind was honest and seeking. Some of her friends of later years have commented that they observed her discussing politics, art, even metaphysics, for hours on end, with people she considered "the common man"—with a fifteen-year-old high school student, with her housekeeper, with her gardener— speaking in simple but philosophically accurate terms until her position was fully understood. She believed that such people had a capacity for logic, for understanding, an intellectual integrity uncorrupted by what she contemptuously called "modern education"; her patience and respect for the uncorrupted "common man" made her superbly able, in her personal dealings and through her writings, to reach him.

An element of the powerful charisma of her personality in her adult years was precisely her remarkable gifts as a teacher, her talent for breaking down the most complex ideas into their easily graspable parts—as well as her obvious pleasure in the process of teaching. In speaking to people who knew her, one hears, again and again, "She explained ideas with a clarity and power that was overwhelming"—or, "I had never dreamed that abstract philosophical issues could be made so fascinating, so easy to grasp"—or, "I'd been indifferent to philosophy until she began discussing it with me, and then I saw how important it is, and how enormously interesting"—or, "She had a way of raising precisely the concepts that were most relevant to me, and of demonstrating the crucial role of philosophy in the living of one's life."

Throughout her high school days, Alice continued to be very vocal about ideas that were important to her. "I argued at the slightest provocation, whether people did or did not want to hear. I criticized myself for this. I was very aware they didn't really want to talk, and I was forcing the conversation. I knew it was wrong." Her passion for ideas, her conviction that they were of paramount importance, led Alice, all her life, to "force conversations." One might make the mildest of off-hand comments—and suddenly find oneself engaged in an all-night philosophical conversation about the wider meaning and implications of one's comment.

Now an adolescent, Alice decided that it was time to learn about sex. The other girls were beginning to talk about boys and some of them were going out on dates; Alice was not invited on dates. She overheard girls whispering about sex, but she was not sufficiently friendly with any of her classmates to question them; and a Russian girl from a respectable family did not consult her parents about such issues. She had already decided that she would never have children. "It was for the same reason as today," she later explained. "I would not have time for it. I wanted to be a writer, that was the only thing I was interested in, and I knew that's a full-time job; children would require primary attention, they could not be neglected, and I would not want to have that responsibility—it would interfere with my career. A career has to take your full time." She began doggedly looking up words pertaining to sex in dictionaries in the school library, until she arrived at "an approximate understanding of the nature of sex."

One day, she overheard a girl explaining to an eager group that sexual desire is very different from spiritual love—that it is a desire unrelated to one's spiritual choices. In describing the event many years later, Alice said: "I was as violently opposed to that idea then as I am today. I felt that if it is true that sex is only physical, then no proper man could experience it. There could be no such thing as a desire or an action which had nothing to do with your mind, and with what you value. I told the girl indignantly, 'If this is true, it's wrong and I'm against it.' The girl answered—as if talking about men were somehow sinful— that I didn't understand men or sex. I said, 'I don't know what kind of men you know. *My* kind of man would be a hero, and he would have no such emotions.' I would project kissing or embracing or romance, and by introspection I knew it would be impossible for me to feel any such desire, to consider anything romantic, if it had nothing to do with the man's character. It couldn't be just good looks without mind. I knew I couldn't possibly experience it, yet I took life and values more seriously than anybody else, and a heroic man would be the same: he would take life and values as seriously as I. No intelligent man could tolerate a desire which had nothing to do with his understanding, and which is stronger than his mind. The theme in a lot of Russian novels of the chambermaid sort was about an irresistible passion that sweeps you off your feet against your judgment, particularly when it is a man or woman one despises. That, to me, was talking about another species. Not only would I not understand emotionally what it is like, but contempt would prevent me from even inquiring psychologically. It was a passion which is against your values that I despised. By fifteen, my sex theory was already formed."

The years of Alice's childhood continued to be unhappy for the most part. Childhood was an overture, she concluded, a preparation for the future, with no significance in itself. "Nothing existential gave me any great pleasure. And progressively, as my ideas developed, I had more and more a sense of loneliness. I felt a driving ambition, and in that sense it was pleasant, but I was enormously unhappy with my position at home; I did not like being a child, I did not like being attached to a family. I resented enormously the implication that anything to do with the family was binding on me—or anything to do with anybody—I had no obligation to unchosen values. Boredom was a cardinal emotion in relation to the events available to me. I didn't care about any of the immediate reality, there was nothing in it for me. *My* world was the future. Today, I would know that the difference between me and others was my romantic sense of life, my more heroic sense of life. My whole development was desiring and looking for things which are interesting, versus the boredom of the routine or the conventional, looking for the unusual or purposeful. The heroic concept of man: that's what interested me."

Until now, when she had projected her longed-for future, Alice had assumed that she would write in the Russian language, but would live abroad most of the time. Her real home, she believed, was the European culture. She had not thought of living in the United States; it had seemed as distant and unreal as

Mars. But in her last two years in the Crimea, she took classes in American history, and learned about the Declaration of Independence and the American system of government. "To me it was incredible. I saw America as the country of individualism, of strong men, of freedom and important purposes. I thought: 'This is the kind of government I approve of.' " The germ of a possibility was planted: perhaps she would visit the United States one day; perhaps it would become her home.

The subject she most enjoyed during her high school years, the one subject of which she never tired, was mathematics. "My mathematics teacher was delighted with me. When I graduated, he said, 'It will be a crime if you don't go into mathematics.' I said only, 'That's not enough of a career.' I felt that it was too abstract, it had nothing to do with actual life. I loved it, but I didn't intend to be an engineer or to go into any applied profession, and to study mathematics as such seemed too ivory tower, too purposeless—and I would say so today." Mathematics, she thought, was a *method*. Like logic, it was an invaluable tool, but it was a means to an end, not an end in itself. She wanted an activity that, while drawing on her theoretical capacity, would unite theory and its practical application. That desire was an essential element in the continuing appeal that fiction held for her: fiction made possible the integration of wide abstract principles and their direct expression in and application to man's life. She wanted to define a moral ideal, to present her kind of man—and to project, through fiction, the living reality of that ideal. She wanted to project it, using as her tool the precise, unsentimental mind of a mathematician.

The course that Alice found most fascinating, next to mathematics, was logic. "The first syllogism made an enormous impression on me. It was like a light bulb going off in my mind. The syllogism was 'All cats have tails, this is a cat, therefore it has a tail.' My first reaction was: That's wrong; when people say, for instance, that all Frenchmen are no good, they don't really mean every one of them, it's just an expression. Then I grasped, as a revelation, that when you say 'all,' you must really *mean* 'all.' I was converted to consistency from then on. It made me conscious of the importance of precision, and to what extent you have to use words exactly. I felt an enormous admiration for the discipline of logic, and a faint guilt: They were right, this is how one should handle words and thoughts, and I was wrong. I told myself that I must never forget this." Consistency became a passion for Alice, and remained so throughout her life. Her proudest boast about the philosophical system she would later devise was that if one accepted any part of it, consistency required that one accept the total of it.

Alice continued to keep a diary of her ideas. One entry read, "Today, I decided to be an atheist." She later explained, "I had decided that the concept of God is degrading to men. Since they say God is perfect, and man can never be that perfect, then man is low and imperfect and there is something above him—which is wrong." Her second reason was that "no proof of the existence of God exists; the concept is an untenable invention." It was all decided in one day, she said. "Since the concept of God is rationally untenable and degrading to man,

I'm against it. It was as simple as that. The essence of my present belief is there. It focused the issue of reason versus mysticism. I had the feeling that atheism was an integration of something that had been growing in me for a long time, not a sudden new thought. When I focused on the subject for the first time, the convictions were already there."

Alice never turned back from these convictions; she remained a lifelong atheist. She was not, she would often say, "a militant atheist"; the belief in God seemed to her so patently irrational that it did not deserve to be fought. It was not the concept of God that she would battle throughout her life; it was what she saw as its source, its wider meaning: the rejection of reason. It was to the battle for reason—the tool and the glory of the heroic man—that she would dedicate her life.

Although Alice would argue heatedly about any other issue, she stubbornly refused to engage in any argument about the validity of reason. It was not debatable. She would say only, "You're talking about faith. I haven't any—and it doesn't make sense to me." Man's mind—his reasoning faculty, his power to grasp logical connections—is his basic tool of survival, she would contend throughout her life; and mysticism, the anti-rational, the anti-logical, is the instrument of death.

As reason was an absolute not open to question, so was the value of intelligence. People who did not value intelligence as she did, she wrote in her diary, were "totally negligible. They were not anything human." She felt neither hatred nor anger in the presence of such people. She felt nothing.

Before this period, she had reacted *as if* those who did not hold her values were wrong. Now it became a conscious conviction; her values were objective "because I could prove my case. Reason is on my side. I felt they were either stupid or dishonest if they disagreed with me. If they were my own age, they were stupid. I knew that many philosophers and writers had a view of life which was wrong, and I considered them vicious and dishonest." This is an estimate of those who disagreed with her ideas which remained a part of Alice's character to the end of her life; she would "allow" disagreement until a philosophical opponent had heard her case; after that, if agreement were not forthcoming, she was faced with "vicious dishonesty."

Classics of foreign literature were not taught in Crimean schools. But Alice liked *only* foreign works, so she haunted the town's small library for French books. She read Rostand's *Cyrano de Bergerac*. "I cried my eyes out," she reported. In her adult years in America, she often recommended it as one of the world's greatest literary works.

The only novel, apart from the works of Victor Hugo, to which she strongly responded was *Quo Vadis?* Petronius, the worldly "arbiter of elegance," was her favorite character; years later, writing about Gail Wynand in *The Fountainhead*, she would describe him as "a modern Petronius."

She read—and intensely disliked—George Sand. "It was feminine, sentimental, romantic in a wishy-washy way; it was all love stories, studies of the relationship between men and women, which I considered totally unimportant subjects. I had felt almost rivalistic in advance, because I thought she was the most famous woman writer in the world; but I felt nothing but contempt for her feminine preoccupation with romantic passions. Great romance is important, and all of my projected novels had great romances—but it is not the main concern. Love has to be part of a great cause, never the main focus for the man or for the woman."

The outside world continued to intrude harshly on Alice's world of school and reading and writing and the fascination of her own developing thoughts. Most of the time, she and her family were hungry, ragged, cold, and frightened of the regime that ruled them, whether it was Red or White. The news of Petrograd and of the countryside was increasingly bleak, as if to match the physical bleakness of their life. The workers were struggling to run the nationalized factories, mines, banks—and were failing. People were fleeing the unrest of the cities; Petrograd alone lost almost two-thirds of its population. The Whites, still fighting their doomed battle, were beginning to lose the civil war. And the peasants, maddened by hunger and the fear of an unknowable future, were slaughtering landowners, pillaging and burning. By 1920, a package of cigarettes cost a million rubles. In the frozen winter of that year, the water supply failed, and fuel for heating was almost nonexistent. Cholera raged through the nation; everywhere one saw people with shaved heads, in an attempt to defeat the germ-carrying lice. It was a year of civil war, of famine, of disease, of political repression.

Early in 1921, the Red government of the Crimea declared a "week of poverty." Soldiers went to every home in the town, and if anyone owned "too much," the excess was taken from him to be given to the town's poorer population. Some people were left with only the clothes on their backs. When the soldiers burst into the Rosenbaum home, they took the family's one priceless luxury, saved from Fronz Rosenbaum's chemist shop: a few bars of soap. During that week, the father of a girl in Alice's class—a former industrialist who had owned a small industry under the White regime—was arrested and shot; his body was found on the seashore. From the loot the soldiers had taken, each school class was sent a single used dress; the girls were to draw lots to determine which one of them would receive the tattered dress. "I can't tell you the horror I felt," Alice later said, "when my class received a dress that had belonged to the daughter of the murdered man. That poor girl just sat numbly at her desk, watching silently as her dress was presented to the group. None of the girls wanted it; they refused to draw lots. But one 'socially minded girl' declared that she wanted it, she had a right to it, she was poor and her clothes were ragged—and she took it."

It was in the spring of this apocalyptic year that Alice graduated from high school. By the summer, with the family more desperate for food than ever before, Anna Rosenbaum was able to obtain work for Alice and herself, as teachers. Alice's job was to teach a class of illiterate Red Army soldiers to read and write. She went to her class, the first day, seething with rage and terror. But to her astonishment, she found the work interesting. She was delighted by the eagerness and earnestness with which these rude men struggled to learn. "They treated me, as a teacher, with awed respect, and I felt safe among them." One of the men, a peasant, made constant lists, in the block letters which were the only writing he had painfully learned, of the name of each science he heard mentioned; then he would ask Alice to explain what the science consisted of. A greater delight for Alice than teaching was that she was able to take home the first money she had ever earned.

That spring and summer, the Crimea was again under the occupation of the Red Army. But this time the Whites had been driven back permanently. The civil war was over. Russia lay crushed under the Bolshevik heel, helpless, angry, and hopeless. Wearily, Fronz Rosenbaum decided that the family should return to Petrograd. Before the final Red occupation of the Crimea, many people had escaped Russia; Anna Rosenbaum had begged her husband to allow the family to follow the exiles across the Black Sea. "Father's greatest mistake was that he didn't want to go," Alice later said. "He still hoped that communism would not last. He thought that Europe and the world at large would not allow it to last, and he would get his property—his business and his building—back."

The family had gone South to wait for a change in the government. Now, there was nothing left to wait for. The final blow in a three-year-period that had consisted of nothing but blows was that White Army rubles—which were all that the Rosenbaums' possessed—were declared invalid. They had become pieces of paper to be disposed of.

The Rosenbaums set out on the return journey to Petrograd. Before they left, Alice carefully burned the diary containing her philosophical ideas and plans for stories; she knew that it could mean imprisonment at best if such heretical views were discovered in Communist Petrograd.

The sixteen-year-old girl who boarded the train for the journey was not yet an adult, but she was no longer a child. In the midst of the terrors of civil war, she had thought about the supreme importance of the human mind; waiting wearily in ever-growing queues for ever-diminishing rations of food, she had struggled to grasp the meaning of good and evil; trudging to school through mud puddles against a piercing Crimean wind, wearing thin, patched shoes and her mother's cut-down summer coat, she had formulated her concept of individualism. The essence of her value-system and her character were formed. She felt that she was now an adult. That she was to be a writer was no longer a decision for an indefinite future; it had become real as an immediate, practical issue.

During the journey, the family had to change trains in Moscow, and wait there for a few hours. It was Alice's first sight of Moscow, the first time she had seen a large city since leaving Petrograd when she was thirteen years old. She stood on a square by the railroad station, gazing at the vast city. "It suddenly struck me how enormous it is, and how many people, and it's just one city. I had a concrete sense of how large the world is, there were so many large cities, and I had to address all of them, all those numbers had to hear of me and of what I was going to say. It was a case of suddenly the nature of my ambition being fully concrete and specific—and universal. The feeling was marvelously solemn. It was a moment of dedication, of doors opening."

Chapter Four

The first doors that opened for Alice were the doors of Petrograd. After a train journey that should have taken three days but had required rocking across Russia's devastated plains for three weeks, the exhausted Rosenbaum family alighted at the Petrograd station. "The first thing we saw," Alice would recall, "were huge red signs on the station's bare plaster walls. They said, LONG LIVE THE DICTATORSHIP OF THE PROLETARIAT! Other signs said, BEWARE OF CHOLERA! DO NOT DRINK RAW WATER! A gold hammer and sickle hung over the station door, beside a picture of a giant red louse bearing the words: LICE SPREAD DISEASE! The station reeked of carbolic acid; diseases were pouring into the city on every train, and buildings had to be disinfected against them."

When they left the station, Alice saw familiar streets with unfamiliar rows of abandoned shops, their glass panes shattered by the revolution's bullets. In front of a shop bearing the sign PROVISION CENTER, a line of ragged, emaciated people stretched around the block. An old woman stood on a street corner, holding a tray of saccharine and timidly offering it for sale to the passersby; she wore a tattered coat that once had been expensive, but now hung limply over her gaunt, stooped frame. Along Nevsky Prospect emblazoned with red banners were a few tiny private shops, opened as a result of the New Economic Policy; their signs were made of strips of cotton, which waved hopefully in the wind.

By part miracle, part bribery, the family was able to obtain an apartment—in the building Fronz Rosenbaum had once owned. To reach the apartment, they walked up four flights of stone stairs to three tiny rooms and a minuscule kitchen. Grim, silent days were spent hunting for furniture they could afford; when they had found it, the apartment was complete: it contained a few chairs with missing legs, a rusty samovar, two beds, heavy tin cutlery, and the scarred old grand piano that Anna Rosenbaum had managed to procure from the people who lived in their former home and who had no use for so frivolous a luxury.

The apartment had neither water nor electricity; they carried water up the four flights of stairs in iron pails. To light the dark evenings, a wick floated in a saucer of linseed oil; it cast its flickering shadow against an uncurtained window.

They soon joined the long lines at the government stores, where they roasted in summer and froze in winter. One purchased whatever was offered: dry herring, or lentils, or millet. Anna Rosenbaum chopped acorns for coffee, and cooked their food in lard. Breakfast was millet, lunch was millet, dinner was lentils and dried fish—when they were fortunate enough to get dried fish.

At night, few people dared to leave their homes; crime was rampant and no one was safe in the streets. They were no safer in their homes: the GPU made constant night arrests of "anti-Soviet conspirators," and Petrograd joked bitterly that soon there would be no one left to conspire. Private enterprises, opened under the NEP, kept failing; only a few well-dressed men and women were ever seen to enter them; their goods were priced at more than ten times that of the government cooperatives. But in the poverty and suffering of the city, some men were successful; Alice saw them emerging from limousines, wearing fur coats, escorting their jeweled wives. They sat in the front rows of theaters, they went to the new confectioners to buy cakes, they hired taxis. They were the speculators, who smuggled in food from the countryside, to be sold at huge prices. Disdainfully, Petrogradians called the speculators "Nep Men"—and stared at them with a mixture of envy and rage.

In the fall of the year, Alice entered the University of Petrograd, which was free to all students. (When Lenin died in 1924, its name was changed to the University of Leningrad, as the city's name was changed to Leningrad.) She had decided to major in history. Her writing was to deal with broad social issues, and history would give her the background she needed. A major in literature held no appeal to her. "I didn't want to study, as examples, writers who bored me and whom I despised." Nor did philosophy interest her as a primary focus; she felt that it was removed from life, and "I was convinced a lot of it would be mystical chaos."

Fronz Rosenbaum, who rarely interfered with decisions his wife had sanctioned, raised strong objections to Alice's choice of a major. She must not study something as theoretical as history, he told her. She must have a profession, such as medicine or engineering. "The most important thing in life," he said, "is financial independence. Especially in Russia today." In the face of her father's intense disapproval, Alice hesitated. How can I *know* that I have a talent for writing? she asked herself. How do I *know* I will succeed? She decided to reread the chapters of a novel she had begun in the Crimea. If she saw in those chapters a significant talent, she would study history. If not, she would consider, not medicine, which she loathed, but engineering. Typically, it did not enter her mind to submit her work to any recognized literary authority; she trusted her own objectivity; *she* was the only authority on her own work, then or in the future. It was a policy which, whatever its drawbacks, would keep her moving through years of literary rejection.

She reread the chapters. She told her father she was going to the university to study history. Fronz Rosenbaum—who knew the strength of his eldest daughter's will when she had made a decision—sighed in resignation and said nothing more.

No streetcars were running in the city. Each day, Alice walked three miles to school and three miles back, wearing old, torn summer shoes. When the teeth-chattering snows began, she put on a thin winter coat. At school, she sat with the other students in drafty, unheated auditoriums, her mittened hands clasped around her body. She came home to eat a skimpy dinner and to study by the shimmering light of the wick that was the apartment's only illumination.

Although the Soviet Government had not yet established total ideological control over Russia's universities, certain "Soviet subjects" were required of all students. One of them was historical materialism. Students were required to learn, from an official textbook presented with the reverence that religion gives its Bible, the history of the Communist philosophy. The study began with Plato, whom the regime claimed as the forerunner of historical materialism, then went to Hegel, then to Marx. For the rest of her life, Alice knew that she understood the theory of dialectical materialism—and had on her body and spirit the scars of its practice—as few Americans ever would; she did not bear with equanimity the remarks of anyone who ventured to tell her "what communism really was all about."

Despite her doubts about the value of formal philosophy, she chose as an elective a course on the history of ancient philosophy. The course was taught by Professor N. O. Losky, a distinguished international authority on Plato. To her surprise, the course turned out to be her favorite. She was profoundly impressed by Aristotle's definition of the laws of logic, and rejected completely "the mysticism, and collectivism" of Plato. In subsequent years in America, she would delve deeply into the works of Aristotle; her own philosophical system was to be powerfully influenced by him; he was the only figure in the history of philosophy to whom she acknowledged a significant intellectual debt.

Professor Losky was a stern, exacting man, contemptuous of all students, particularly of women. It was said that he failed most students the first time they took his examination, and that he was especially hard on women. In the spring, his students went to his home for their oral examination; a long line of them stood outside his study, nervously awaiting their turn. Alice hoped that she would be questioned on Aristotle. But when she entered his study, he questioned her only about Plato. She had studied carefully, and she answered easily and precisely. After a while, although she had not stated any estimate, Professor Losky said sardonically: "You don't agree with Plato, do you?" "No, I don't," she answered. "Tell me why," he demanded. She replied, "My philosophical views are not part of the history of philosophy yet. But they will be." "Give me your examination book," he ordered. He wrote in the book and handed it back to her. "Next student," he said. He had written: Perfect.

In 1921, it still was possible for university students vocally to oppose communism. The students at the University of Petrograd were divided into two camps: the larger faction was the anti-Communists, who defiantly wore the green student caps of the old days; the Communists wore red kerchiefs and military leather jackets. At a meeting to elect the student council, representatives of each side were passionately outspoken. The young Communists talked of service to the proletariat, and of sacrificing one's selfish interests to the good of the state. Alice listened eagerly—as a freshman, she had no right to speak—when the students in green caps spoke about political repression, and hunger, and tyranny. In *We the Living*, Alice would write sadly about the anti-Communist students: "They were raising their voices for the first time, while the country around them had long since spoken its last." One young man particularly impressed Alice, because he made a violently anti-Soviet speech. The students elected a council composed overwhelmingly of anti-Communists.

Because of the young orator's arrogant outspokenness, Alice felt "the first stirrings of a romantic interest." She did not speak to him, she felt she was too young to interest him, but she stared at him in fascination whenever she saw him in the halls of the university.

By the end of that school year, there were no more anti-Communist speeches on campus, and there were no more anti-Communists on the student council. The purge of students had begun. Alice never forgot the shock of the day she arrived at school to discover that the arrogant young man had been arrested in the night, and was to be sent to the slow, terrible death of Siberia. She never saw or heard of him again. That night, she lay awake, slow, heavy tears coursing down her cheeks. And she lay awake with terror pounding in her chest, expecting at any moment to hear soldiers' fists pounding on the door: in a rage of revulsion, she had shouted at a Communist student that he and his comrades ultimately would hang from the lamp posts of the city.

Because of the dire shortage of medicine among the population—people were collapsing on the streets from malnutrition and disease—the government grudgingly allowed a few private chemist shops to open and to do what the government shops could not. Former owners of chemist shops banded together, since no one was permitted to own a shop individually. With five other men, Fronz Rosenbaum opened a small shop, and was able to run it for almost a year. This was the only period during which the family had some relief from their grinding poverty; for a while, there was food on the table, and a few necessary articles of clothing were bought. But as soon as the new shops began doing well, the government abruptly nationalized them; that had been the purpose of the New Economic Policy: to allow former bourgeoisie to work long enough to present the regime with businesses worth looting. Fronz Rosenbaum, again without work and with no source of income, grimly refused to seek a job as a Soviet employee. "I won't work for them," he told the family in a rare burst of fury. "Not now and not ever. Not if we all starve." The family listened in silence. Alice knew—as they all knew—that they *might* starve; but she would later speak of the sudden stab of admiration she had felt, the fresh love for her tormented father.

With Fronz not working, growing more silent, more gaunt, more withdrawn as each day passed, Anna Rosenbaum became the main support of the family. Against her husband's passionate disapproval, and with her customary resilience, she found work teaching languages in a high school. They were going to eat, she told her family, if she had to work for the devil himself; besides, weren't the Communists bringing about interesting innovations in the schools? Perhaps it wouldn't be so bad, after all. Anna's salary, for long, wearying hours of work, was tiny, and Alice was able to contribute only the few ration cards she received as a university student, cards that did not allow enough food even for one person.

"That was the real time of starvation, those years," Alice later grimly recalled. One evening, after a dinner consisting of a handful of dried peas, she felt her legs sagging under her. She sank to the floor, too weakened by hunger and fright to stand. A small portion of peas was being saved for Fronz's arrival home. "May I have . . . just one of Father's peas?" Alice asked. Her mother handed her a single pea, on her face the most terrible anguish Alice had ever seen in a human face.

As Alice spoke of those years, it was clear that the worst of her suffering was not the hunger. It was the terrible sordidness of life—the colorlessness of a world where men dreamed only of obtaining half a pound of butter through a doctor's prescription—where they talked only of what government cooperative had stocked millet that was not rancid—where men's souls grew shabbier and pettier with each dreary year, as if to match their material existence. She could bear the hunger, Alice sometimes thought, a scream rising inside her; she could bear the rags and the cold and the threats of violence; but she did not know if she could bear the ugliness, the sense of hopelessness that was everywhere around her. As if to impose a final unendurable burden, epidemics of typhus swept the exhausted city. The lice which transmitted the disease became as terrifying as the Communists. Most people who caught typhus died, some of them falling to the streets, their bodies ignored by their fellow citizens who, in order to live, were becoming inured to the unspeakable suffering that surrounded them. The young girl who believed that joy is the meaning and purpose of human existence, rubbed carnation oil and kerosene into her hair as the only available protection against typhus. Streetcars were running again, but to take a streetcar was to risk one's life. Alice tried not to see the lice on the people she tried not to squeeze against. To the panic of hunger and the horror of disease, a persistent, gnawing fear of arrest was added; the Communist stranglehold continued to tighten, and no former bourgeois could be certain of living beyond the immediate moment.

Throughout Alice's university years, her reading of fiction continued. She read all of Schiller's plays, in French, and was passionately enthusiastic about them. "He is the only classical dramatist in whom I sensed an enormous hero worship," she later said.

As a student, Alice was required to read the complete works of Shakespeare, which she intensely disliked. "I was indignant at the tragedy and malevolence, but the malevolence was secondary. I disliked most precisely what his virtues are supposed to be: that he is a detached Olympian, who takes no sides. When we were taught in classes that Shakespeare holds up a mirror to human nature, that set me even more against him. He is a determinist, a nonvaluer, and I had no admiration for any of his characters. Caesar and Mark Antony are stock, cardboard characters, they are official bromides, they are what you are historically supposed to admire, but they are not alive; there is nothing individual about them. I refused to believe that Lear and Macbeth represent what man really is."

That same year, Alice discovered the novels of Dostoevsky. She admired his work, but for more narrowly literary and technical reasons than she had liked Schiller; her feeling was not a personal passion. "For a long time, I studied his plots carefully, to see how he integrated his plots to his ideas. I identified, in his work, what kind of events express what kind of theme, and why. He was very valuable for my subconscious integration concerning plot and theme."

The great philosophical discovery of those years was the works of Friedrich Nietzsche. Alice learned about him when an older cousin said to her, grinning with a touch of malice, "Here is someone you should read, because he beat you to all your ideas." Curious, Alice began reading *Thus Spake Zarathustra*. It was, for her, an exciting, unexpected discovery of a spiritual ally, the first she had ever found on an adult level. Here was a writer "who felt as I did about man, who saw and wanted the heroic in man; here was a writer who believed that a man should have a great purpose, a purpose which is for his own sake, for his own happiness and his own selfish motives. Here was a writer who revered the heroic in man, who defended individualism and despised altruism."

Nietzsche's defense of psychological determinism troubled her. "By introspection, I was convinced that free will was a reality, that men were free to make choices." But so great was her joy at finding ideas with which she could agree, that she focused predominantly on those, and often reread *Thus Spake Zara-thustra*. "The first book I bought myself in America was an English version of *Thus Spake Zarathustra*, and I underscored all my favorite sections."

Even in her first readings of *Thus Spake Zarathustra*, Alice was aware that Nietzsche was "equivocal about the issue of power. I assumed he really meant spiritual power, the conquest of nature, not power over others. He is very much like the Bible, he writes poetically, and you can take it as a metaphor or not; I took it metaphorically. I believed that the superior man could not be bothered enslaving others, that slavery is immoral, that to enslave his inferiors is an unworthy occupation for the heroic man." When she read further in Nietzsche, and discovered, in *The Birth of Tragedy*, that he was "statedly anti-reason," her early enthusiasm began to abate. "He said that reason is an inferior faculty, that drunken-orgy emotions were superior. That finished him as a spiritual ally."

It was toward the end of Alice's first year of college that she made a discovery that swept away her intellectual discoveries, her literary discoveries, even the sordid horror of life under communism—swept it away for enchanted hours at a time and gave her the living reality of the world she had to reach. There were two Soviet theaters in Petrograd—formerly Imperial theaters; one presented grand opera and ballet; the other, light operas and classical operettas. It was the light operas and operettas that drew Alice—like a giant magnet pulling her to an existence where the purpose of life was enjoyment. "The theater had four balconies, and the fourth was very cheap, and very hard to get. The box office opened for the week on Saturday at 10 A.M. I got up every Saturday at 5 A.M. to be there by 6, and I waited outside for three hours even in the Russian winters; at 9, they opened the lobby, and I could wait inside for the next hour. By 10, there were lines around the block for the cheap seats. For two years, I was there Saturday every time, and I would be either first or second in line. When streetcars were reestablished, my parents had given me money for tickets to go to the university; I walked, so I could save the fare; it was the only way I could afford the cheap theater seats. The first operas I saw were Verdi—the whole spectacle was of a sort of glamorous medieval existence, the productions were of pre-revolutionary days, marvelous sets and costumes. To see that after coming in from the Soviet reality was worth anything. I began going at least three times a week.

"Then I discovered operettas—and they saved my life. They were the most marvelous benevolent-universe shot in the arm—the one positive fuel I could have. They kept my sense of life going. My favorites—I saw one eleven times, another eight times—were Millocher's *The Beggar Student,* Offenbach's *Grand Duchess,* Kalman's *The Bayadere,* and Lehar's *The Song of the Lark. The Song of the Lark* was presented in modern costume; the actors wore fashionable clothes in the latest foreign style; the men wore top hats; I remember one scene of a ball, and a huge window showing a lighted street of a foreign city. That was more important to me than Nietzsche and the whole university. You know my love for city lights, city streets, skyscrapers—it was all that category of value. That's what I expected from abroad.

"They were the symbol of living for your own pleasure and for enjoyment—not for duty or service or misery. They were everything that was non-Soviet. Yet I was very uninterested in things like the new nightclubs that had opened up—my cousin Nina would occasionally be taken by her boyfriends to a nightclub, and I didn't want to go. None of the physical or obvious trimmings of the operetta style interested me. Nina—she was on the surface the operetta type, but really very malevolent inside, and I was very solemn, grim, aggressive on the outside, always engaging people in serious philosophical discussions—once said to me: 'I feel inside the way you act—and you feel inside the way *I* act.' It was true. Inside I was enormously cheerful and happy. I was very contemptuous of any book or theory that would preach that life was only suffering." Suffering was the accidental, the unimportant; it was never to be taken seriously, never to blur one's vision of joy, never to become *metaphysical.*

Alice's conviction of the unimportance of suffering was to be put to still another test.

Occasionally, she attended a party given by one of her cousins or their girl-friends. Parties were rare in Soviet Russia. For small or large gatherings, guests were asked to bring whatever they could—a few slices of black bread, a log or two of wood. "One issue that was very painful to me, in the feminine, personal sense, was that I was in rags; most of my wardrobe was Mother's old dresses, remodeled for me. For parties, I had only one dress, made from an old embroidered summer coat of Mother's; I wore it for several years, until it was so shiny that the only thing to do was to turn it inside out and use the other side. The idea of having clothes belonged to abroad—or to another planet. It was a handicap because my idea on clothes was just like today—either I would be perfectly groomed or not at all, and the result was not at all. And it's not at all to this day. The girls were spending an enormous lot of time on very intelligent makeshifts, but I didn't like the in-between. To be semi-decently dressed took enormous time. Most parties were costume parties, because you could make funny costumes out of anything—we'd ransack old trunks of someone's mother and grandmother for remnants of material, and put together pieces of inappropriate materials that would last one evening. At the parties, someone would play the piano, and one could dance. People really tried to be gay, tried to have intelligent light conversation. I really loved the parties. My feeling for them was the same as for the foreign operettas: they were non-Soviet, they were for a selfish, private pleasure only."

It was a cold night in 1922. A group of young people sat huddled around a fireplace, struggling to keep warm and struggling still harder, in their makeshift finery, to be cheerful. Alice glanced up as a young man strode into the room. "I couldn't quite believe it. He didn't look real—he was so perfectly good-looking. It was *my* type of face, except that his hair was dark; he was very tall and thin, with light gray eyes and sharp features. It was a very intelligent face, very determined, clear-cut, aristocratic, self-confident. What I liked most was the arrogance and the haughty smile—the smile that said: 'Well, world, you have to admire me.' " Alice was introduced to the young man and learned that his name was Leo—an Americanized version of the Russian "Lev"—that he was a student of engineering, that he was three or four years older than she. "But nothing unusual happened, except that I couldn't stop staring at him."

It was not until several months later that they met again at another party. That evening, Leo paid particular attention to her, and spent most of his time talking with her. "I was astonished," she reported, as she always would be astonished by male attention. He asked if he might accompany her home. "I don't remember the conversation on the way home, we just talked, nothing romantic. But he had a manner of projecting that he's a man and you're a woman and he's aware of it. By the time I arrived home, I was madly and desperately in love."

From that evening on, Alice's life and her thoughts revolved obsessively around Leo, around the sound of his voice, the way his hair fell over his forehead, his long, slender body, his aristocratic, arrogant smile. He began to take her out, and the sordid world around her seemed to be dancing to her operetta melodies—until she learned that he was also seeing several other girls. "I think he had to conquer almost any girl he met. It wasn't sexual conquest—that wasn't really possible then with young girls—but he had to be sure she was interested in him, and then he was not particularly interested any longer. I didn't especially like that in him, but I thought it was simply a man who desperately wanted to live an interesting life."

They went together, for a few months, to gatherings of friends and to the theater. Alice knew that she was openly showing her violent, almost painful passion for him. The young girl who had always been—and remained—so witheringly contemptuous of "emotions that swept you off your feet," who had not known her own desperate vulnerability, was swept helplessly away by her first love. "I knew he didn't like it, I knew it was wrong. I reproached myself, and there was no way for me not to do it. I didn't make verbal declarations, but my manner and the way I looked at him showed how I felt. . . . Perhaps if I had been more restrained, it would have lasted longer. Because as I showed more intensity, he began to draw away. . . . Of all the young people, he was the only one who seemed to value himself, who projected authentic self-esteem; he projected that he was something enormously important. That was a top value for me."

One particular action that she learned about seemed to bear out her most benevolent evaluation of the man she never ceased to love. Leo, whose parents were dead, lived alone with an elder sister. One day, a friend approached him about two young members of the underground who had to go into hiding while they waited to be smuggled abroad. Leo—whose sister was out of town and therefore would not be endangered—agreed to take the boys into his home; he agreed calmly, without a second thought, risking his future and his life during the anxious weeks before they could be sent to freedom.

"When it was over," Alice recalled, "when he stopped asking to see me, that was the most prolonged period of pain in my life. You see—perhaps it's not easy to understand when one has known only the freedom of America—Leo was, to me, life in the present, and the only life I had there. The only human being who mattered to me in a personal way. Before Leo, I had regarded everything as something to get over with; life begins in the future, and all that matters is what I'm thinking and what books I will write; concrete reality doesn't matter. Now, it mattered. He was my entry into life." And he was gone.

From then on, Alice and Leo encountered each other only at parties, where Leo paid scant attention to her. For months, she questioned everyone who knew him about his activities; for months, she went to gatherings of young people only in the hope of seeing him; for months, she allowed her pain and loneliness to wash over her life and drain it of everything but her longing to be with him. It was as if all the desperate intensity devoted before to books, to writing, to ideas, had found a new focus: the face and figure of the man she loved.

And then, one day, she stopped. Slowly, painfully, step by small step, her contempt for suffering began to restore her to life. She would not allow her love for Leo to be a tragedy, and to become a scar on her soul, she told herself angrily. She would not let pain win its one permanent victory: to make her forget her conviction that joy is the meaning of human existence. "Life is ahead," she told herself ferociously. She stopped questioning his friends about him, she stopped seeking him out—she tried to stop thinking about him. But in 1961, in her middle years, at the height of her powers and strength, when it seemed as if the whole world were spread out before her, offering her everything she had ever dreamed of, she said, with an almost childlike wistfulness, "I am not indifferent to Leo, to this day." Then she added softly, "But you see, it was fortunate that he didn't ask me to marry him. I would have said yes, I would have stayed in Russia—and I would have died there."

She was to keep the memory of Leo alive throughout her life and her literary career. She named the hero of *We the Living* Leo; his description matches that of the young man she had loved. And she would acknowledge that Francisco, one of the heroes of *Atlas Shrugged,* also was, in appearance and in manner, inspired by her first love. She did not love easily or often; but when she did, it was with a consuming and lasting passion.

Alice turned again to reading, to thinking, to planning the books she would create. The young girl who had been future-oriented from earliest childhood, whose suffering in Soviet Russia had inevitably increased her sense that the expectation of happiness must be relegated to tomorrow—turned again from the present, which she had so briefly and hopefully visited, to her interior life and to her dreams of the future. Tomorrow existed for her with a blazing, compelling reality, beckoning her onward, enlisting her most passionate determination; she believed in happiness, she *would* be happy, she believed in life, she *would* live it . . . only not today.

Her rejection by Leo clearly had increased her already strong sense of alienation from the world around her; it seemed still further evidence that it could offer her nothing of significant personal meaning. Only the future offered it. The future was to be her home, with a few rare exceptions, for the rest of her life: she would live in the richness and complexity of her thoughts, her plans for the books she would write, her single-minded pursuit of her goals. Tragically, when she reached a point in her life when the world around her at last offered its rewards—rewards of fame, of love, of respect, of appreciation, of material wealth—it was too late; perhaps it was too late from the last day she saw Leo. She could no longer live in the present, no longer stop to notice it, no longer remove her mental focus from tomorrow. Several of the people who knew her most intimately in later years, commented that they never once saw her fully enjoy an event or activity that was here and now. The ability to take pleasure in the shining moment, fragile from the beginning of her life, received its final and mortal blow with the loss of Leo, never to be regained.

Near the end of Alice's second year at the University of Petrograd, there appeared on the bulletin board—and in all institutions of higher education throughout Russia—a large notice with huge letters in red pencil: THE PURGE. The schools were to be cleansed of all socially undesirable persons. Those found socially undesirable were to be expelled, never to be admitted to any college again. Newspapers roared over the country like trumpets: "We shall not educate our class enemies!" All students were required to fill out questionnaires about their parents and their grandparents; if any close relatives had owned a business before the revolution, the student was not to be educated. As Alice slowly filled out her questionnaire and more slowly signed her name to it, she felt that she was signing the death warrant of her future. No one dared to think what awaited those who were to be expelled. In the corridors of the university, troubled students whispered that if you were of "bourgeois descent" you were a "class enemy," even though you were starving. They joked bitterly that you must try, if you could, at the price of your immortal soul, if you had one, to prove your origin from the workbench or the plow. Alice knew she could not prove it. She tried to think about what she would do when she was dismissed from the university, but for the first time in her life she could not think. Her mind closed on the horror of what lurked ahead of her.

A few days before the purge was to take effect, a convention of prominent British scientists journeyed to Petrograd, to witness the "noble experiment" taking place there. Alice was to describe, through Kira in *We the Living,* what she acknowledged were her own feelings when she saw the delegates at a compulsory demonstration staged by the Soviet Government to honor them. As she marched by in the long snake of citizens, "Kira's eyes saw but one person: the woman delegate of the British Trade Unions. She was tall, thin, not young, with the worried face of a school teacher. But she wore a tan sports coat and that coat yelled louder than the hurrahs of the crowd, louder than the 'Internationale,' that it was *foreign.* With firm, pressed folds of rich material, trim, well-fitted, serene, that coat did not moan, like all those others around Kira, of the misery of the muscles underneath. The British comrade wore silk stockings; a rich, brownish sheen, tight on feet in trim, new, well-polished brown shoes.

"And suddenly Kira wanted to scream and to hurl herself at the stand, and to grab those thin, glittering legs and hang on with her teeth as to an anchor, and be carried away with them into their world which was possible somewhere, which was now here, close, within hearing of a cry for help."

After the parade, the members of the delegation learned, through a chance remark, about the proposed purge of schools. They were indignant about it. Eager to impress visitors who could tell the world about the glories of the Soviet state, the government—only hours before the list of those purged was to be posted—decided to cancel it for some of the students. Those students who were to be seniors the next year would be allowed to finish their education; all others on the list were expelled. Alice was taking a three-year course; she was to become a senior in the fall. The possibility that she might have a future was created by a freak occurrence that was never to occur in Soviet Russia. Shaking with relief, Alice waited for the next disaster.

Chapter Five

The future was moving closer. At the age of eighteen, Alice felt that she was nearly an adult, ready to begin creating stories that would contain the qualities she identified with professional literature of "her kind": stories of heroic men and women involved in suspenseful, demanding events; stories which would be the vehicle for the ideas that had been forming in her mind for years and now were approaching their final form. As she spoke, years later, of how she had visualized "her kind" of stories, it was clear that her concept of her work would bring her to the day when she would be seen, by readers and critics, not simply as a novelist, but in the terms that would please her most; as novelist-*philosopher*. The tie between writing stories and presenting philosophical ideas was becoming firm in her mind.

While most eighteen-year-olds were groping helplessly in the world of ideas, seeking the intellectual moorings it might take them years to find, the small, ferociously intense young Alice Rosenbaum was engaged in a determined effort to name, to prove, to systematize and integrate the separate philosophical ideas she had been grappling with since the beginning of adolescence. When formed, those ideas were never to alter in any of their essentials; they would be honed and clarified and expanded; but what she believed at eighteen, she believed undeviatingly, without a backward glance or hesitation or doubt, for the rest of her life. In later years, she would say: "I have held the same philosophy I now hold, for as far back as I can remember. I have learned a great deal through the years and expanded my knowledge of details, of specific issues, of definitions, of applications—and I intend to continue expanding it—but I have never had to change any of my fundamentals. My philosophy, in essence, is the concept of man as a heroic being, with his own happiness as the moral purpose of his life, with productive achievement as his noblest activity, and reason as his only absolute."

She had begun to work on a detailed outline for a novel that she later smilingly referred to as "the grandfather of *Atlas Shrugged.*" *Atlas Shrugged,* which was to be written in the nineteen forties and fifties, is the story of "the mind on strike": the creators and originators in every field of endeavor withdraw from society, refusing to offer benefits—to offer the fruits of their reasoning minds—to a world that penalizes them for their ability; when they have gone, the world collapses into chaos and anarchy. *Atlas Shrugged* would be the richly complex, brilliantly plotted achievement of Alice's full maturity, containing the essence of the system of philosophy she was to name Objectivism. And its immensely sophisticated theme was foreshadowed by an eighteen-year-old girl's halting, angular jottings on a cheap school tablet.

As Alice later described the story (she was hesitant to describe it at all: "It's so primitive," she said, laughing) of the "grandfather of *Atlas Shrugged,*" the leader of the strike was a woman of so astonishing a beauty that any man who saw her had to follow her, and join her for the rest of his life. "It is not just physical beauty," Alice would explain, "but also its spiritual meaning. Her beauty is symbolic; lesser men would be perfectly indifferent to her, but if a man were an unusual soul, he would not be able to resist her." The story opens as men of achievement from all over Europe—statesmen, inventors, scientists, artists—begin to vanish, and friends can gather only that the night before each disappearance, the man was seen with an exquisitely beautiful woman. One by one, Europe's men of ability are disappearing. The reader learns that the heroine has not told the men the nature of her goal, she has asked only that they follow her. When she has drawn out the leading brains of Europe, she explains her purpose to them: to take them to the United States, to break all ties with an increasingly collectivist Europe, and to allow Europe to collapse.

Before they can leave, however, one new figure arises. He is the hero, a great French inventor named Francis;[1] he is the last genius left and Europe's one remaining intellectual weapon. He resents the woman, whom he has never seen, because he thinks she is attempting to rule the world. He gives a public test of an airplane he has invented that flies faster than any plane yet devised. When he lands, the heroine sees him—and *she* falls in love.

"That night, in his laboratory," Alice would recount, "Francis gets a private wireless message from her. She wires: 'I need your services. I will buy you. I offer one million dollars.' He wires back his answer: 'I don't need your services. I will buy *you.* I offer two million dollars.' A few moments later, he sits in his laboratory shaken, emotionally reached for the first time in his life, because the answer has come back: 'I accept.' He replies that he will expect her in his laboratory on this exact day and time next year.

"A year has passed. He is in his laboratory again. At the exact hour and minute of the woman's original message, there is a knock on his door. She

[1] One of the major characters in *Atlas Shrugged* was to be Francisco, and Frank O'Connor's name was Francis.

enters, wearing a black cape and veiled. He puts two million dollars on the table between them. She takes off her veil and cape; she is naked.

"The next morning, the newspaper headlines announce that the inventor has disappeared. He becomes the leader of America; she has merely been the spirit of the strike. They declare war on Europe, which they conquer easily because all the machinery, the inventions and the brains are on their side. The book ends on a free world and on their triumph."

It is interesting to note that this story marks the first foreshadowing of a psychological pattern Alice was to follow all her life. She was not a beautiful girl, though her appearance was arresting and unusual; she was small, she struggled with her weight; her movements had a jaggedness, a lack of rhythm, an indifferent carelessness out of keeping with the superbly functioning mechanism of her intelligence. She never liked her physical appearance; she would often say regretfully that she felt as if her body were an annoying burden which she had to drag behind her. But in her novels, she created exquisite heroines with streamlined, gracefully slender bodies and light hair and eyes. It is most unusual for a woman writer not to create, as heroines, idealized versions of her own physical type. But Alice was to write only about her exact physical opposite. In life, she was unhappy with her appearance; in fiction, it was transformed into irresistible beauty.

In life, Alice was not sought out by young men, and was rejected by the first man she loved. In fiction, she created heroines so remarkable that "any man who sees her has to follow her, and join her for the rest of his life . . . if a man were an unusual soul, he would not be able to resist her."

Through her fiction, Alice had found the philosopher's stone. She took the base metals of her own life, its mud and dross and suffering—and transformed it into the gold of her work.

Alice continued to work on other stories as well, some of which illustrated her interest—an interest that was to remain central to her literary imagination—in works set in the future. The events of *Atlas Shrugged* occur in an unspecified future, as do the events of a novelette entitled *Anthem* that she wrote years later but had planned in Russia.

In the spring of 1924, Alice graduated from the university with the highest honors. Her degree was a useless piece of paper; she had mastered the subjects she had wanted to master, but the degree was a key to a door leading to a blank wall in a society where workers and peasants were extolled as the highest types of humanity, and intellectuals, unless they employed their intelligence in selfless service to the state, were denounced as parasitical. Alice's life, like her country's, was controlled by the ever more repressive Communist regime; she, too, was hungry and ragged. But she was not despairing, she would later recall. When her mind was not preoccupied with her developing stories, when her emotions gave her a few hours' freedom from her longing for Leo, she was engaged in a ferocious intellectual struggle to find some way to build for herself, even in Soviet

Russia if she could find no way to leave, the kind of future she had to have, whose beckoning brightness she could not turn away from.

But first, it was necessary to find employment. Fronz Rosenbaum, now the shattered, weary shadow of the man Alice had known, was no longer "on strike"; he had found a job as a clerk in a drugstore far at the end of the city— far from the shop he once had proudly owned. But his income was tiny, and Anna Rosenbaum, continuing her work as a teacher of languages in several high schools, remained the family's main support. Alice's sisters, Nora and Natasha, were at school; when Alice graduated, Natasha, who had finished high school, went to a conservatory of music to study the piano, preparing diligently for the career she was never to have.

Through Anna Rosenbaum's connections, Alice was hired as a tour guide at the Peter and Paul Fortress. She lectured one day a week on the fortress's history to excursion groups—to silent rows of peasants and workers who were as bored and indifferent as she was to the information she imparted and to the exhibits they dully and dutifully studied. It was a job she loathed, that had no tie to the work she wanted to do, that had no future, no meaning; but it supplied food, and clothes, and physical survival.

It was at the beginning of 1925 that the unimaginable happened. A letter from the United States arrived at the Rosenbaum home—a letter on clean white paper, shining like the silk stockings of the woman union delegate whom Kira wanted to scream to, with sharp black marks that jerked open the doors to life, to hope, to tomorrow.

In 1889, a strong, gentle man named Harry Portnoy had left Russia and emigrated to the United States, taking his small family to the promised land. Like hundreds of thousands of Russian Jews, he had set off to escape the anti-Semitism of Russia, the hopelessness of life there for a Jew, and the prospect of his sons facing years of forced service in the Army. With Eva, his wife, and with their four small children, Isaac, Jacob, Gertie, and Anna, Harry Portnoy embarked on the long, difficult journey. Settling at last in Chicago, he became a tailor, working the diligent, uncomplaining eighteen-hour days of the immigrant. Shortly after the family's arrival, Sarah was born in their small rented home at 213 West Twelfth Street, then Mandel, then Lilly, then Minna. When Harry had decided to leave Russia, he had not been able to afford the full cost of the steerage passage; the rest of the money was supplied by the family of his wife's niece, Anna Rosenbaum. The two families had remained in contact by mail until World War I, when mail delivery to Russia was interrupted. The Portnoy family had worried and wondered about the fate of their Russian relatives; now, in 1925, they had at last located them.

The letter around which the Rosenbaum family huddled breathlessly was from little Sarah Portnoy, now Sarah Lipski, a grown woman with children of her own. Was the family well? she inquired. In the United States, one heard frightening stories about the fate of the bourgeoisie under communism. What had happened to them during the long years of silence?

The Rosenbaums read the letter again and again, talking excitedly about the account of their relatives' golden life in Chicago. Uncharacteristically, Alice did not join the conversation. She would always recall those moments when she sat silently, a slow, deep chill shuddering through her body, as an almost terrifying thought fought its way into her consciousness. America . . . the future . . . freedom. . . . Hadn't she heard people speak of Russian citizens who had been allowed to visit foreign countries because they had relatives abroad who sent the necessary papers? Could the Portnoy family arrange it? Could *she* be allowed to visit? Visit—and never return? Could she escape this hell to which someone had condemned her for a crime she had never commited? Then another thought—a name—slashed through her body like a knife. *Leo.* . . . Never to return. . . . For an instant, his face seemed to form in the space before her, smiling at her arrogantly. It lingered, stopping her breath with its beauty. Until, with a hot spurt of anger, she brushed it sharply away, as she would brush away a cobweb blurring her vision.

When the rest of the family had dispersed to their different activities, Alice turned to her mother. The words tumbled out. "Write them, Mother. Write and tell them. *I have to go to America.* Ask them to help. Do it today. Do it now. *I have to go to America.*" On her mother's face was a look Alice had seen there only once before: the time when, half starved, she had begged for one extra dried pea from her father's plate; she was half starved now, but not for physical food, and she saw the knowledge in her mother's eyes, and the same look of anguish on her mother's face. "I'll write them, Alice," Anna Rosenbaum answered quietly. "I'll ask them."

The correspondence began. Mail was slow and uncertain, and weeks passed before each arrival of a white envelope with its foreign stamp. An investigation had to be made before the Portnoy family's help could be requested; Anna Rosenbaum had to discover, slowly and carefully, without arousing questions or suspicions, what were the rules of the moment governing Russians who wished to visit the United States. After many guarded inquiries, she learned that, with the proper affidavits from America, the proper promises of financial support, the proper guarantees that the visitor would return to Russia—it was sometimes allowed, and sometimes not. The reasons were not known by anyone.

Anna Rosenbaum wrote often to her Chicago relatives, responding to as many of their questions as she safely could—all mail was censored, and no bourgeois dared write of the persecution of the bourgeoisie—and telling them of her delight at their good fortune. There was a source of sadness in the correspondence; Eva Portnoy, Anna's aunt, had died a few years earlier. When the correspondence was established, Anna asked the Portnoy family if they would be willing to have her oldest daughter come to the United States to visit them for a few months. Anna knew, as did Fronz—who shook his head at the thought of his child traveling alone halfway across the world, and protested, as he had done for eight years, that communism could not last, that life in Russia would one day again be civilized—that there was to be no visit. Alice was determined that if she went to the United States, she would never return; but the request had to be worded carefully, the pretense kept up. It might take months before they could know if Alice would be allowed to leave, weeks before they would learn if the Portnoys could help, Anna warned her daughter. It might never happen at all. Alice must be prepared for failure. She must be prepared to stay in Russia. Alice nodded dutifully, wondering how one prepared for blank nothingness. She began to live two lives, she would later recall. In one, she went through the motions of guiding her tours, instructing visitors on the horrors of slavery and imprisonment and tyranny under the Czar, she went through the motions of reading, of walking to the streetcar, of eating and sleeping and smiling and frowning and talking. In the other—the only one that was real—she prepared for America.

Her first step was to enroll in a school that had recently opened in Petrograd, a school for young men and women interested in a career in the developing Russian movie industry. Until her last year at the university, the few movie theaters that existed in Petrograd had been prohibitively expensive, and although Alice had yearned to see foreign movies, it would have been "like owning a yacht, totally out of reach. And since I didn't go out with young men, there was no one to take me." But when Russia again became interested in trade with Europe and the United States, more and cheaper movie theaters began opening, and Alice was able to attend third- and fourth-run theaters. Foreign movies came to serve, for her, the same function, providing the same emotional fuel, that operettas had done. "I was fascinated, because they were a much more specific, rather than simply symbolic, view of life than operettas." It was the great romantic period of the German silent movies—the period of Fritz Lang and Ernst Lubitsch, of Conrad Veidt and Mia May and Hans Albers, of *Siegfried* and *The Indian Tomb* and *The Oyster Princess.* These were her favorites, and they seemed to glow from the screens of the theater like the glow of the first sunrise over a darkened earth. "I began to go to movies every night. They were my private avenue to the world outside."

When American movies at last appeared in Petrograd, Alice felt that she was seeing the universe she had glimpsed, years ago, in its abstract essence in "The Mysterious Valley"—a world of free, joyously purposeful, active men. Once in a while, she would see a long shot of New York City—of slender buildings shimmering with light, streaking upward into the sky; she would sit through two shows for the sake of a single brief glimpse, before returning to the darkened streets of Petrograd. As she spoke, years later, of the movies she had loved, she laughed, throwing back her head in a rare gesture of uninhibited pleasure. "I can't tell you how *glamorous* it was," she said. "It still is. I have no other perspective, not really. My real enthusiasm for America, apart from its political principles, was formed then. I saw the essence of what Americans could be and ought to be. My favorite American movies were in the Milton Sills tradition— action, enormous benevolent freedom; they were not philosophical, but that's what I liked, it was as if Atlantis had already arrived, the ideal was right here on earth, and one did not have to be philosophical, certainly not political, all those

problems were already solved, and it was the perfect free existence for purposeful men."

The idea that she would write movies was born. Typically, when she became
aware of something important to her, her first thought was how to incorporate it
into her own life and purposes. If she went to the United States—*when she went
to the United States*—she would write movie scenarios; that way, she might
quickly make her name and her fortune, and then be free to write her novels.

The movie school was a disappointment. She had hoped to learn the craft of
scenario writing, but she found that the first period of study was devoted to
acting, and it was only in subsequent years that writing and production would be
taught. She continued to attend, in order to pick up whatever scraps of useful
information might be available.

With her mother's help, she found a teacher of English, an Englishwoman
married to a Russian citizen—and began the process of learning the language
that she was ultimately, as a writer, to master superbly, learning its subtlest
nuances and connotations to an extent rare among foreign-born writers. But she
never lost her heavy, guttural Russian accent, which, in later years, especially
after hearing her own voice on tape, she intensely disliked. She had battled with
her English teacher because she refused to imitate an English accent; the process
of mimicking was not something she could accept.

She knew she must continue to think—must *force* herself to think—about
what she would do it she could not go to the United States. She knew she could
not openly write her kind of stories in Russia, not if she wished to survive. But
what if she wrote scenarios for the Russian film industry in which the apparent
villain was really the hero, the alleged hero really the villain? What if she could
appear to be pro-Communist, while smuggling in her own message and her own
values?—smuggling in veiled political messages which the audience would understand, but the Communists would not. At the movie school, she met a young
Communist—"He was very enthusiastic about the screen and very impressed
with me." She decided to test one of her veiled story ideas by telling it to him.
Watching the young Communist's face closely as she recounted her story—her
own face blank and innocent—Alice could see that even he, who was not very
intelligent, knew that something was wrong; on the surface, everything was in
order, there was nothing he could object to—but he knew. And Alice knew that
she had no hope of smuggling her values into the Soviet film industry.

Sometimes, she would think of trying to escape abroad illegally, of heading for
a frontier and trying to make her way across it, unseen. "But I would probably
not have tried it. I was much too helpless to know how to go about it."

A letter arrived from Sarah Lipski. It contained an affidavit, satisfactory to
the American authorities, stating that the Portnoy family had invited Alice to
visit them, and that they would be financially responsible for her during her stay;
it also contained a promise from Anna Portnoy, now Anna Stone, to pay for
Alice's passage.

The first step had been taken. Her heart pounding, Alice filled out her application for a Russian passport. Then she waited, and tried to survive the waiting. The months crawled by, while someone—she could not know who or why or by what standard—decided her fate.

That summer, because Anna, Fronz, and Alice were working, was the first summer since the revolution that the Rosenbaum family could afford to rent a summer house in the country—a poor, shabby house by comparison with their pre-revolutionary standards, but a way to spend the summer by the seashore. Among trees and flowers and the burgeoning life around her, Alice waited to learn if her own life was to begin.

It was then that she did "something very inexcusable, though not malicious," as she later described it. She and her sister Natasha met a young man by the seashore, and "We made a bet, cold-bloodedly, about who would win him. Natasha was somewhat seriously taken with him, but he was not my type, although I did like him. He was rather intelligent, and very conscientious, but he was a typical Russian young man, not particularly distinguished. I went after him to prove to myself that I could win a man; and it would be something glamorous to counteract the enormous burden of tragedy I felt over Leo, the constant inner pain. And I did it. I astonished myself. It was a deliberate campaign; I worked to be charming and interesting. He fell desperately in love with me, and proposed. I said neither yes nor no. I never told him I loved him, but I acted as if I were in love. I felt quite guilty about it. . . . I feel guilty as I tell the story. I felt that what I was doing *in fact* wasn't right, but my inner motivation *was* right: I wanted glamour."

In the fall of 1925, a heavy envelope, thick with official seals, arrived from Moscow at the Rosenbaum home. Alice's hands shook as she opened it—and then shook still more: it was a Russian passport, permitting her to visit the United States for six months. She was free to go. She was free to live. *She was free.*

Anna Rosenbaum wrote to the French steamship line in Moscow that handled the passage of Russians to the United States and arranged for train transportation across Europe. Shortly after Alice's passport arrived, another envelope reached the Rosenbaum home: a packet of travel folders from the French Line. Friends and relatives came to leaf through the brightly printed colored pictures of the world outside of Russia, "so cheerful and so non-Soviet that we all were somewhat stunned." Alice moved through the next few months of arrangements and planning and farewells like a sleepwalker, feeling as if she could not quite see or understand the people and events around her, as if her eyes and mind were blinded by the afterimage of the gaily colored pictures in the travel folders.

There was one final, terrifying hurdle to be crossed before she could know if the gates of the United States would open for her. Affidavits from the United States and a Russian passport were not enough. Alice would have to travel to Riga, in neighboring Latvia, then an independent country, for final approval of her departure by the American consul who was based there; the United States had not officially recognized the Soviet Union, and there were no American officials within Russia. Through one of her uncles, Alice corresponded with a Latvian couple; they warned her that she had only one chance in a hundred of receiving a visitor's visa from the American consulate. Hundreds of people had been refused, the consul was very severe, White Russians from all over the world were desperately trying to get to the United States, swearing that they would return although they had no intention of doing so. Alice would receive her final visa only if she could convince the consul that she did not plan to remain in the United States; if he had the slightest doubt of her intentions, he was free to refuse her. Grimly, despite her sense of helplessness in the physical world, Alice resolved that if she were refused, she would vanish into the anonymity of Latvia and find a way to flee to Europe.

In January 1926, on the evening before Alice's departure, Anna and Fronz gave a farewell party for her. Leo was invited. Alice arranged that, at dinner, he would be her partner. "I thought I could permit myself that last touch." During dinner—abruptly and without context—Leo smiled at her radiantly and said, "You know, we should meet again when you're about thirty years old. You'll be at your best then." Years later, Alice said, her voice soft, "I'll always see him as he was then. I can't imagine him as an older man. I've tried, and I can't."

During the evening, one of the guests, a man whom Alice knew only slightly, whispered to her, with the sudden, harsh earnestness of desperation, "If they ask you, in America—tell them that Russia is a huge cemetery, and that we are all dying slowly." "I'll tell them," she promised.

The next morning, Alice stood on the platform at the train station, the suitcase her grandmother had given her at her feet, an old Remington-Rand typewriter clutched tightly in her arms, three hundred dollars—the result of Anna Rosenbaum's sale of the last of her jewelry—her passport and affidavits and tickets in her battered black purse, saying what she did not know were her final good-byes to her family and a few friends, and to Leo. Her mother wept, and hugged her tightly; her father's face was expressionless as he patted her shoulder silently, again and again; her two sisters gazed at her in awe, as they might have gazed at an astronaut about to leave for the moon. She would see them again, soon, Alice told her stricken family; either the Soviets would collapse, or she would make enough money in America to bring them out, to bring them to freedom with her.

Before she boarded the train, Leo bent to kiss her hand, his dark hair falling over his forehead. "It was the most personal thing that ever happened between us. I had never even kissed him."

The train seemed to hurtle over the icy plains between Petrograd and Latvia, pushed by the energy of her heartbeats. Then the border was in sight, almost close enough to touch. Then it was behind her. The years of dismal grayness dropped away. Russia was the past. It was prologue. An unobstructed world lay ahead.

At the train station in Riga, Alice was met by her uncle's friends—and by armed Latvian guards. With the other Russians on the train—even those merely traveling to Europe, or visiting Latvia on business—she was taken to a camp on the outskirts of the city, surrounded by barbed wire. The small, threatened state did not intend to be overrun by a neighbor enraged that its citizens made their escape through Latvia; it would finally be overrun with less reason or cause. When Alice wished to leave the camp, she was given a large brass ticket to attach to her coat, indicating that she had been released on official business and was to return. After a few frightening days, her uncle's friends were able to arrange for her to stay at their home while she waited for her appointment at the American consulate. She learned that if her visa were refused, it would be almost impossible to vanish; she would be arrested immediately and shipped back to Russia. She did not dare even to contemplate what would happen if she were refused; vaguely, she thought that she would go to every consulate, begging for admission to any country but Russia; but she knew the hopelessness of such an attempt: penniless Russian refugees were not welcome anywhere. She waited and tried to plan; but each plan seemed to lead to another dead end. Then the day and time of her appointment arrived.

When she entered the office of the consul—"a young man, a good American type, very severe"—she thought that she must tell him every reason she could invent to convince him that she wished to return to Russia. There was one reason she did not think of, at first.

As the American consul questioned her—and as she desperately explained that her family was in Russia, and her friends, and her work, and her life—she noticed a card lying on the desk across from her; from time to time, the man glanced down at it; she could not see the name on it, but it had to be her dossier. As she strained to read it, one phrase leaped out at her: "Engaged to an American citizen." "It's not true!" she protested, pointing to the card and remembering the boy who had proposed marriage. "It's a mistake! I'm not engaged to an American. There's a young man in Russia whom I intend to marry when I return. He's asked me to marry him. We're engaged." The consulate looked at the card, and shook his head. "Somebody did make a mistake," he said. "The card has your name on it, but it's information about someone else. It's fortunate that you noticed it. I was about to refuse you a visa. Now it's all right. I'll okay it."

It was a bitterly cold January day. The cobblestones of the street were covered with a solid sheet of ice. "I had the oddest feeling as I left the consulate. As if my feet weren't touching the ground. I was walking drunkenly, dimly knowing that the ice was dangerous, but I felt as if nothing bad could ever happen to me again; I was walking without even looking at the traffic—and it was like flying. There haven't been many wonderful concrete moments in my life. But that was one of them."

There was last-minute packing to be done again, and a final few arrangements to be made, and farewells to be said, and another train to be boarded—and Alice moved through all of it in a drunken excitement. Her first major stop was Berlin, where she was met by her cousin Vera, who had left Russia a few months earlier to study medicine in Berlin. It was her first sight of a major European city. "I think it was beautiful—I don't really know. Someone took me to a big revue, with half-naked girls and Gershwin music. I bought a collection of photographs of my favorite movie stars; I still have the one of Conrad Veidt." She celebrated her twenty-first birthday, on February 2, in Berlin. But it's not my twenty-first birthday, she thought; this is the first day of my life.

"When I reached Paris, I was met at the station by a funny woman somebody knew who was a Russian widow with two children, 'living by her wits,' I think; she helped me select the stores I shopped in." Alice bought her first foreign dresses, a lipstick, and silk stockings. She walked through the Louvre, and the streets of the city. "I was fascinated by Berlin and Paris, but I couldn't quite focus on them; I felt as if I were just in flight, or like looking out of a speeding train window. I can remember only broken highlights, with nothing in between. It was one streak of exhilaration—and the feeling: This isn't it yet, but I'm out, and everything begins overseas."

She boarded the boat train to Le Havre. For the first time, she felt a pang of homesickness. She wired Anna Rosenbaum from Le Havre, to say that she was about to board the *De Grasse* and would wire again from New York. "As I stood in the post office, composing the wire, I felt the sadness of parting for the first time; it was more real than at the station in Petrograd. It was my last message from Europe."

On the afternoon of February 10, Alice walked up the gangplank of the *De Grasse*. She went to her cabin quickly, to leave her luggage, and returned to the deck. In the early evening, the ship shuddered faintly—and she watched the coastline begin to recede; it was dark, she could see only a dim line of hills, and a few dots of lights. She stayed on deck until only the lights were left, flickering in the distance. "This is my last salute to Europe," she thought. From now on, it was to be *her* world.

In her cabin, she unpacked her new French dresses, marveling at the fine materials, the warm, soft colors, the expert workmanship. She applied her new lipstick, and stared at herself in the mirror. The face that gazed back at her— that still gazes back from her passport picture—did not belong with glamorous clothes and bright lipstick. Framed by its short, straight hair, its squarish shape stressed by a firmly set jaw, its sensual wide mouth held in tight restraint, its huge dark eyes black with intensity, it seemed the face of a martyr or an inquisitor . . . or a saint. The eyes burned with a passion that was at once emotional and intellectual—as if they would sear the onlooker and leave their dark light as a flame on his body.

But she was twenty-one years old. Tossing sleeplessly on her bed that night as the ship rolled gently beneath her, she wondered which of her new dresses she would wear tomorrow. The woman who had guided her through Paris had firmly informed her that on ships to America there were many millionaires, there was dancing and gaiety and delicious food, and she must see to it that she met wonderful company. Alice smiled happily, anticipating the glamorous evening she would have—then dropped suddenly off to sleep like an exhausted child.

When she woke in the morning, she jumped quickly out of bed, looked through the porthole at the roughened sea and the thick fog—and the cabin began to spin around her. Gingerly, she lowered herself back to bed, where she remained for the rest of the voyage, unable to eat or move or care about new dresses and gay parties and exotic food. The voyage was expected to take seven days; because of the rolling seas and thick fog of February, it lasted eight days.

On the last evening, when the ship was motionless not far from New York Harbor, waiting to enter when the fog lifted, Alice's seasickness abated. She put on a French dress, lipstick, and her new silk stockings. "I was able to have dinner in the dining room; I didn't meet anyone, because I felt very bashful and uncertain, I didn't know how one behaves in a restaurant outside of Russia. I enjoyed watching the dancing, it was exciting and beautiful, but I desperately looked for a system in the new dancing. I didn't understand then that there was no system, that one just moved around.

"My great disappointment was that I didn't see the skyline of New York or the Statue of Liberty. As we approached Quarantine Island in the late afternoon —it was still very foggy—all I could see was a barrackslike building. A small boat approached our liner, and immigration officials boarded. All the passengers coming to America for the first time had to wait in a salon for their papers to be examined. An official asked me how much money I had, and when I told him fifty dollars, he looked amused and said: 'What do you expect to do with *that?*' I was astonished, because it seemed a fortune to me. After the questioning, I went back to my cabin; waiting there was a little dark woman, holding a picture of me that had been sent to my Chicago relatives; they had asked for the picture so that they could have someone meet and identify me when the ship docked. I didn't realize we had arrived, I thought she'd somehow come from midocean. 'Who are you?' I asked. 'And how do you have my picture?' She explained that she was from a Travelers Aid Society and had come to meet me. 'Where are we?' I asked. 'We're in New York.' I was terribly disappointed. I had missed something that would never happen again."

A few minutes later, all disappointment forgotten, she stood on a pier at the Hudson River. She had disembarked with a new name: *Ayn* Rosenbaum—Ayn was the name of a Finnish writer whose work she had not read, but whose name she liked and adopted as her own; everything had to be shining and new in her shining new world. And she had embarked with a sword: the fifty dollars in her purse, the typewriter held in her arms, the stories outlined in her mind, and the sense of life as exaltation.

Ayn stood on the pier at the Hudson River. It was 7 P.M. It was snowing faintly. Through the snow, she could see the lighted skyscrapers of New York. On her stern young face she felt the marks of tears and snowflakes.

PART II

WE THE LIVING

Chapter Six

It was the best of times. The young immigrant from Soviet Russia had left behind her the stranglehold of a blood-soaked dictatorship, the soul-shriveling terror of a life without hope or a future, and had marched with resolute steps and tear-filled eyes from a snowy pier on the Hudson River into a New York City—into a United States—boiling with energy and limitless ambition, in love with the new, drunk on the idea of endless progress, prosperous beyond the dreams of earlier generations. It was the twenties, and the streets were paved with gold. It was the zany, optimistic, shockingly violent and heartbreakingly youthful decade where poverty and suffering seemed only momentary obstacles to be vaulted over, where horizons had no limit and man could remake the earth in the image of his heart's desire. The worst of times would never come. Here and there might be crazed pockets of wild-eyed advocates of communism and dictatorship, but America was the land of the free, of Thomas Jefferson and the Constitution and the beckoning arms of the Statue of Liberty, where the might and majesty of the free-enterprise system had been amply demonstrated. There could be struggle ahead, and setbacks, and backbreaking work to be done; there could never, in this golden United States, be ultimate defeat.

The immigrant girl who landed in New York never ceased to love her new country, with the passionate, near painful devotion that perhaps only the foreign-born fully understand, and never ceased to be aware that America had given her life, and hope, and freedom, and the possibility of achieving everything denied to her in Soviet Russia. To the end of her life, she would say: "America is the greatest country on earth. No—it's the *only* country."

Ayn Rosenbaum spent her first days in her new world at the home of friends of her American relatives, so that she might see the city she had dreamed of for so long. "I saw Broadway at night, and when I wrote Mother about all the lights, she said she wished my letter could be published in a magazine. I remember especially the Maxwell House Coffee animated sign, with the words 'good to the last drop,' and the falling drop of coffee. I'll never forget it—it seemed so incredibly cheerful and frivolous, so non-Soviet! I saw my first movie in America, in a huge Broadway theater—which was very thrilling; it was *The Sea Beast,* with John Barrymore."

As she spoke, thirty-five years later, of her first days in New York, her face was illuminated by a smile that must have been very like the smile she wore then: the gravity of years was swept away, replaced by a childlike, infinitely touching gaiety. A friend of hers once said—echoing the many friends who made similar comments—"I thought I understood her reasonably well, that her personality was basically sober and serious—and then I brought her a little gift, it was an inexpensive necklace that looked as if it were made of gold mail—and her eyes lit up and she suddenly looked about ten years old—except that I've never seen a ten-year-old having such a good time—and then I knew I'd have to start trying to understand her all over again." Whatever the mud and dross of the years, that capacity for enjoyment—particularly enchanting and unexpected in a woman who so rarely lived in the present—never wholly left her. Seeing it, one felt: This is what she was intended to be, this is how she started. . . .

Most of all, to Ayn New York was its buildings. They were to her, then and always, the symbols and the tangible reality of the achievement possible to free men. And she remembered that in Petrograd, waiting through two showings of a movie for a breathless glimpse of New York's skyline, she had vowed one day to write a novel that would capture the meaning of those skyscrapers and of the human spirit that had made them possible. As she walked, enraptured, through the canyons of the city that was to remain her abiding love, she silently repeated her vow.

Within a week, Ayn was once more en route, this time to her mother's family in Chicago. As the train rushed through the wintry cities and the countryside, she was again oblivious to the sights and sounds around her: her thoughts were on the future. The future was writing—writing and life in America. Both seemed precarious, and both were absolutes in her mind. Despite the lessons she had had in Russia, her English was halting and uncertain; she knew she could not expect to write competently in English for many months, perhaps not for a few years. And her visa was valid for only six months; it could be renewed, but only for a limited period. The pressure of time, which was to haunt her all her life, was driving her faster than the engine of the train.

That she must find a way to remain in the United States had been settled in Ayn's mind long before. It had been settled when the first letter arrived in Russia from her American relatives. She would never go back to Russia. "I would no more have thought of returning than of jumping off a building." If necessary, when she could get no further extensions of her visa, she would go to Canada or to Mexico and wait until she could be readmitted on the Russian quota. The quota was filled for seven years. She would wait. She would wait wherever she had to wait, doing whatever she could find to do. There was nothing to think about, only a gnawing, lonely fear to suppress inside her chest. In New York, the people she had stayed with had told her that many refugees were coming into the United States from Canada without visas, and that no one cared or checked. She had answered: "I don't want to stay here illegally. Someday I will be famous, and it would be discovered."

As she rocked gently to the motion of the train—her typewriter jammed, for safety, between her leg and the side of the passenger car, her old black coat wrapped tightly around her against the chill of the air—her plans, dimly formulated before, began to take definite shape. When she reached Chicago, she would begin writing screen originals. Since movies were silent, she could be successful without writing finished screenplays, which her halting English would not permit her to do. She would create the outlines of film stories, the basic plot ideas, and other scenarists could devise the titles. She would stay in Chicago only long enough to write several originals, then she would go to Hollywood and attempt to sell her story outlines.

The fear began to lift from her chest. It would not be too difficult. She knew the value of her work.

From her earliest childhood stories, Ayn seems never to have doubted the value of her work. Now, a timid young immigrant unable to speak or write the language of her new country, she retained that confidence—a deep, calm, unwavering faith in herself and her talents—as she would retain it for the rest of her life. Its source was within herself: she was to feel pain at the harshness of many of the criticisms she would receive, but not self-doubt; she was to feel pleasure at the praise and adulation she would receive, but not a greater self-value. She knew what she had the capacity to do.

The greeting that awaited her in Chicago dispelled, for a time, the last faint edges of her fear. The smiling faces of her aunts greeted her at the train station— little red-haired, vibrant Minna; the motherly Anna; Sarah, delighted that her letter writing and planning had brought a new niece to the family; serene, cheerful Gertrude—and Ayn was wrapped in the warmth of embraces that welcomed her as a long-anticipated member of the family; she was one of them, their greeting projected; she belonged to them. She had not expected it, and she could not understand it, as she was never able to understand an unconditional personal acceptance; but she basked in its warmth, and her grave young face brightened.

Within days, she was hard at work on her film ideas, noticing Chicago only when her aunts and uncles insisted that she come sight-seeing with them, visiting other relatives only when firmly pressed to do so, talking to her young cousins only when politeness required. "I disliked Chicago enormously," she said years later. "I felt I was not yet in an American city. And after New York, I felt I had no right to anything—now it's life or death, I've got to sell something, I've got to establish myself."

In the early evenings, whenever possible, she went to a movie, watching intently with a professional interest in the art of film writing and in order to improve her English; she knew, as many foreign-born people have discovered, that by seeing dialogue with the action that matched it, she could learn the language more quickly than by reading or listening to people speak. Sarah and her husband owned a small neighborhood theater, where Sarah played the piano and sang each evening, and Ayn could go there to a double feature when the films changed every few nights.

It had been the family's intention that Ayn live with Anna Stone and her family as long as she remained in Chicago, but, as her aunt Minna Goldberg explained many years later, "Ayn didn't get along in a daily routine, she had very strange habits, and finally Anna couldn't take it, and sent her to me. After a couple of months, I'd send her back to Anna, who would keep her as long as she could, then I'd get her back." The warm, close family was fond of Ayn, and happy to welcome her, but they found her dedicated self-absorption difficult. "We didn't have much money in those days," Minna said, "and my husband and I lived in a small apartment, with the children and my father, Harry Portnoy. My eight-year-old daughter, Fern, slept in a cot in the dining room; but when Ayn came, Fern moved to the living room couch, and Ayn took her cot. Ayn kept her typewriter on the dining room table, and that was where she worked. But she liked to work at night, until very late, and none of us could get to sleep when she was typing. My husband was in the grocery business, and he had to get up at 5 A.M.—and her typing didn't begin until midnight. . . ."

What Minna was too generous to say was that Ayn, who spoke often of her debt to her relatives, who said that they had saved her life, seemed astonishingly indifferent to their context and needs. She was consumed by her need to write. That powerful, undeviating drive, so central to her character and to her later success, was often to make her oblivious to the people around her.

"Her way of life was so different than ours," Minna added. "When she'd want to go to a movie, my father would give her the money, but she wouldn't go to any movie we wanted to see, she'd pick exactly what she wanted, and that's what we all had to see. She wasn't mean or anything, just thoughtless; she was very ambitious; she made up her mind, and she did what she set out to do.

"The worst of all was that late at night she'd want to have a bath, and she'd run the water first for hours, because she had the phobia that water was clean only if you let it run for a long time. The sound of the water running would keep us all awake if the typewriter didn't."

Minna appears to have been correct in calling Ayn's attitude toward germs phobic. She had learned her terror early, from her mother. Anna Rosenbaum held very firm ideas about the omnipresent danger of disease. When Ayn and her sisters were small, no guests were allowed into the nursery without first removing their outdoor clothing, which might be contaminated, and without carefully scrubbing their hands; every toy brought into the nursery was first disinfected in carbolic acid. After the Communist revolution, Anna Rosenbaum's fears had seemed justified; the sole means of protection against the terrifying cholera was a Spartan, dedicated cleanliness. But her mother's attitude, even before the revolution, had appeared reasonable to her eldest daughter. For years in the United

States, Ayn would scald dishes in boiling water if she had entertained dinner guests, she would keep an anxious space between herself and anyone who had even a cold, she would worry if a friend went outdoors in cold weather without appropriately warm clothing. What she—who desperately needed the sense that she was in full control of her life and her fate—found unbearable was the idea that she might inadvertently fail to take precautions against an external danger that could be averted; then the fault would be hers, she would often say, the responsibility hers, the disaster of her own making. With regard to illness and disease, as in so many other ways, she perceived the world outside her own being as a threat to be kept at bay.

During her stay in Chicago, she never talked to her relatives about Russia or her family there. To their bewilderment, she would briefly answer whatever questions her relatives asked, and drop the subject at once, as if it were of no importance. "She only talked about what she was going to be and what she was going to do," Minna said. "She never mentioned her mother or her father. She just wanted to put everything about Russia out of her mind, because she hated it there." Russia was the past, she projected, and only the future mattered; she had so little time to ensure her professional success and her safety in the United States; despite her pangs of homesickness, it was only her writing that was of importance; the pangs were merely emotions.

Her relatives recalled that Ayn seemed happy. Minna explained: "She sang a lot around the house. She'd sing 'I'm Sitting on Top of the World.' That was her song, and she'd dance around the room to it. She loved it." Ayn *was* happy; something inside her was blazing with a fierce, exultant joy; she was *free,* and the concept rang inside her like a great bell, like a call to live and work and achieve and then to achieve more and still more. The road was clear, and nothing could stop her.

Minna's daughter Fern—today Fern Brown, a well-known writer of books for children—later recalled how Ayn came to choose the name "Rand" for herself. "She had an old typewriter that she had come with," Fern said. "One day, she was sitting at the typewriter and she called me over. She said, 'I'm going to be called Ayn.' 'That's pretty,' I said. 'It's different. How do you spell it?' And she wrote it in her slanty foreign handwriting: A Y N.[1] 'But I need a last name,' she said. 'I want it to begin with an R, because that's my real initial.' She was writing down different possible names, and then she looked at the typewriter—it was a Remington-Rand—and she said, 'Ayn Remington . . . No, that's wrong. . . . I know!—Ayn Rand!' That's how she got her name."

Ayn never told her family in Russia the new name she had chosen. She had no doubt that she would one day be famous, and she feared that if it were known in Russia that she was Alice Rosenbaum, daughter of Fronz and Anna, her family's safety, even their lives, would be endangered by their relationship to a vocal anti-Communist. Through all the years that she corresponded with her

---

[1] Pronounced to rhyme with "mine."

family, until, just before World War II, Russia refused entry to mail from the United States and she lost track of them—they never knew that she had become "Ayn Rand." In her early years in the United States, her original name was known by a number of people, and appeared on all official documents; but after her marriage, when her name legally become O'Connor, she refused to tell anyone what it had been.[2]

During her stay in Chicago, Ayn often expressed her deep gratitude to her American family; she would not have survived in Russia if they had not gotten her out, she said; she would never forget what they had done for her. "When I make a lot of money," she told her aunt Minna, "I'm going to get you a Rolls-Royce." Sadly, in the years that followed, they felt that she *had* forgotten. "I didn't want the Rolls-Royce," Minna explained. "It wasn't money. It was to be remembered." For several years after her departure, Ayn corresponded with them and sent autographed copies of her books, but the intervals between letters gradually grew longer, until finally the letters stopped. When Fern Brown's first book was published, she wrote to tell Ayn about it, and to say that she was following in Ayn's footsteps by becoming a writer. "I thought she'd be thrilled that I had written a book," Fern said. "But she never answered my letter. So I knew she wasn't interested in us. However, a few years later, when she gave a lecture in Chicago, she sent us tickets, and of course we went, and she seemed glad to see us."

In fact, Ayn never did forget what her relatives had done for her. Over the years, she would sometimes say, "They saved my life." And when members of the family visited Los Angeles or New York, she was always cordial, inviting them to lunch or dinner. She was cordial, she was polite—but they sensed that her interest extended no farther than that. Two issues were involved in the gradual separation. There was little in common between Ayn and her Chicago family; it was a family such as she had never encountered—warm, loving, deeply concerned with each other's lives and welfare. And they were deeply concerned with living as Jews; the synagogue they attended and their Jewish heritage were profoundly meaningful to them. Ayn did not understand their values, they were not hers—they were not, as she understood it, "intellectual values." In this circumstance, she found it difficult to remain close to them. But equally important was Ayn's attitude toward the phenomenon of "family." It was a phenomenon to which she seemed monumentally indifferent. "It's not *chosen* values," she would often say when the issue arose in conversation. "One is simply born into a family. Therefore it's of no real significance." She did not appear to share nor really understand the sense others had of a bond to parents or siblings, even to more distant relatives, that arises out of the family relationship itself. This lack of understanding and sympathy for such bonds made her unintentionally cruel; she would occasionally talk to a friend about that friend's mother, or sister, or other relative, in the most scathingly negative terms, oblivious to the fact that

[2] I discovered it only in 1983, when I obtained copies of her birth certificate and her marriage license.

she was causing pain to her listener, oblivious to the fact that there could be a love not tied to intellectual values.

There was one exception to her indifference to her Chicago relatives. Her young cousin Burton Stone, Anna Stone's son, admired her intensely; he often said that she was the most brilliant person he had ever met. Over many years, Ayn and Burton remained in touch, and would see each other when Burton visited Los Angeles or, later, New York. This was a relationship that Ayn understood: they talked ideas far into the night, and Burton was eager to hear about her philosophy. Although she did not attend Harry Portnoy's funeral, or other painful or happy events in the family, she did travel to Chicago for Burton's funeral. It was a rare exception for her, since she hated traveling and never felt she had the right to take time away from her work.

In midsummer of her first year in the United States, Ayn decided that it was time to leave Chicago and set out for the world of motion pictures. Her visitor's visa had expired, but her relatives had taken the necessary steps to have it renewed; they bought her a train ticket, and they gave her one hundred dollars, which they could not easily spare, with which to begin her new life. Her aunt Sarah, who was friendly with a Chicago movie distributor, obtained from him a letter of introduction for Ayn to a woman who worked in the publicity department of the Cecil B. DeMille Studio. DeMille had always been Ayn's favorite American director—"He did plot pictures, and most of them were glamorous and romantic. His religious pictures were not shown in Russia, so I didn't know about them; but he was famous in Russia for society glamour, sex, and adventure. He was my particular ideal of the American screen. My relatives could have given me a letter to any of the studios, but I chose DeMille."

Ayn had completed four screen originals. "I could barely write English," she later recalled, "I could read it, and I could speak it, although I constantly had to ask people to speak slowly, but my grammar was atrocious. A young cousin of mine put my writing into proper English. The originals were very flamboyant; one had a 'skyscraper hero'—he was a noble crook who went around jumping from skyscraper to skyscraper by means of a parachute—so you can imagine what the rest of them were like! I knew even at the time that they were too wild and too exaggerated; I had no real material yet, no real knowledge. But they were the best I could do."

Chapter Seven

It was a warm summer day in 1926 when the girl who had been Alice Rosenbaum said her good-byes to her Chicago family and to the last remnant of her past life, and boarded the train for Los Angeles. In later years, she recalled very little of the train ride—only that she sat uncomfortably in a day coach for two days and two nights, and that a fellow passenger, who alighted before Los Angeles, gave her the pillow which the passenger had rented for twenty-five cents; Ayn had not rented a pillow, it was too expensive, and she remembered thinking that her seatmate must be wealthy indeed to afford such a luxury.

She did not remember the train ride, but she remembered, with the clarity of a vivid series of pictures unwinding before the screen of her consciousness, the days immediately following her arrival in Los Angeles.

When she reached the sunlit, sprawling city, Ayn headed for the YWCA in downtown Los Angeles; her relatives had suggested it as the cheapest and best place for her to stay. As she registered at the reception desk, chilled by the building's seediness, she mentioned that she was interested in working in pictures. "Go to the Hollywood Studio Club," the desk clerk urged her. "That's the place for you." It *was* the place for her.

In earlier years, girls on a limited budget who poured into Los Angeles to seek work in the movie industry could find only cheap rooming houses and cheaper hotels in which to live. In 1916, a group of Hollywood businessmen decided to rent a small, cramped old house on Carlos Place in Hollywood in which some of these girls could live inexpensively. Then Mrs. Cecil B. DeMille and Mary Pickford became interested in the young women's plight, and enlisted the help of the motion picture industry. They solicited contributions from studios and individuals, and an architect—Julia Morgan, who designed the Hearst mansion in San Simeon—was hired to design a larger and more comfortable house. The new Studio Club, on Lodi Place, a few blocks from Sunset and Vine, opened in May of 1926 under the directorship of the YWCA, housing eighty-eight girls in all branches of film—actresses, dancers, writers, costume designers, cutters, studio clerks and secretaries.

The three-story Mediterranean-style building, with its crisp white wicker furniture, its central courtyard with a fountain beneath which goldfish swam, its roof sundeck, its rehearsal hall, and its cheerful dining room, became a haven for young aspirants come to conquer Hollywood. Some of them did conquer it; at different periods over the years, until the club closed its doors for lack of money in the seventies, Janet Blair lived there, as did Barbara Britton, Linda Darnell, Barbara Hale, Evelyn Keyes, Dorothy Malone, Maureen O'Sullivan, Donna Reed, Marie Windsor, Rita Moreno, and Kim Novak; the biggest star arrived in 1948, registering as Norma Jean Baker; her name was later changed to Marilyn Monroe. But many of the girls found the pressures and struggle of Hollywood, the constant money problems, the part-time jobs they had to take as secretaries and waitresses when they weren't studying or auditioning, the endless rejections and disappointments, too difficult; a few attempted suicide, and others went home, in despair or resignation, to their cities and towns scattered across the United States.

When Ayn Rand timidly registered at the Studio Club, her dark hair straight, her square, solemn face innocent of makeup, her dark plain Russian clothes too warm for the California climate, and announced in her heavy accent that she intended to be a screenwriter—she must have seemed an odd apparition to the pretty, fresh, cheerful young American women who felt at home in their world —and in their skin—in a way that Ayn was never to feel. But Ayn was warmly welcomed. The girls knew that life was difficult in Hollywood, and whatever they could do for each other, they did; they helped each other with makeup and hairdos, they traded clothes for special occasions, they advised each other about the latest fashions and the latest studio call, they comforted each other when one of them failed to get an especially attractive role or lost a boyfriend. The Studio Club was not a rooming house; it was a home for these homeless young women, full of life and energy and good-fellowship. And it was a place to work; they were allowed to practice their art in the rehearsal hall, to play their songs on its grand piano, to test their work on one another; they staged showcases, with borrowed costumes, and the studios regularly sent scouts to see them.

Ayn paid her first week's rent—ten dollars for a room and two meals a day— to Marjorie Williams, the club's much-loved director. The club's two ironclad rules were explained to her: young men were welcome to attend the weekly parties and dinners, but were never allowed upstairs to the girls' rooms; and the rent must be paid on time. As Ayn's money ran short, she was to discover that although the first rule was stringently enforced, the second was not; like many of the girls, she was often behind in her rent, and Marjorie Williams waited with patient understanding until payments could be made. "During the two years I lived at the Studio Club," Ayn later said, "I had only the two meals a day— breakfast and dinner—that the Club provided. I could never afford lunch; I had to be very economical. And I was always hungry, no matter how much I ate; I could never seem to get enough. In Chicago, I had eaten constantly. It was because of the starvation in Russia; it took several years for the constant hunger to disappear."

Ten years later, Ayn Rand would write to Marjorie Williams: "The Studio Club is the only organization I know of personally that carries on, quietly and modestly, this great work which is needed so badly—help for young talent. It not only provides human, decent living accommodations, which a poor beginner could not afford anywhere else, but it provides that other great necessity of life: understanding. It makes a beginner feel that he is not, after all, an intruder with all the world laughing at him and rejecting him at every step, but that there are people who consider it worthwhile to dedicate their work to helping and encouraging him." After *We the Living* was published, she sent an autographed copy to Marjorie Williams; the inscription read: "From the little Russian girl in Room 318."

The day after the arrival of "the little Russian girl" in Hollywood and her establishment in Room 318 of the Hollywood Studio Club—it was a foggy, chill morning—Ayn took her letter of introduction and her screen stories and headed for the DeMille Studio in Culver City. Again one of the fortuitous happenings that marked her life occurred. She had been told to wait on a certain street corner for a bus with an orange roof. When she reached the corner, she saw buses going in both directions; when one arrived, she boarded it—only to discover, too late, that it was heading west instead of east and that its destination was Universal Studios, at the opposite end of the line. At Universal, she found the streetcar she needed; but she had lost more than an hour. Had she not made that mistake, two meetings, one that day and the other the following week—meetings which dramatically affected the rest of her life—would not have occurred.

When she at last reached the Colonial mansion that was the studio's main building, she found her way to the publicity department and presented her letter of introduction to "a very nice young woman." She soon realized that the interview was only a formality, that the publicity department had no power to arrange a screenwriting job for her.

Disheartened, with no idea of what her next step ought to be, Ayn headed down the studio driveway toward the exit gate.

As she walked, she happened to notice an open roadster—an unfamiliar, glamorous sight—parked against a curb; the driver was deep in conversation with a man who stood at the curb and whose face she never saw—because she stopped short, stunned, as she recognized the man at the wheel. It was Cecil B. DeMille. She had seen photographs of him in Russia, and she had never forgotten the distinctive face and manner. For long moments, she stood still, staring at him; then, aware that she must not be rude, she forced herself to continue walking. But when she reached the gate, she could not resist stopping again to catch one last glimpse of him before he drove by and out of her life.

The roadster pulled up to the gate—and stopped beside her. Smiling pleasantly, DeMille asked, "Why were you staring at me?" "I . . . I just arrived from Russia," she replied, stumbling over her words, miserably aware that her accent was heavier than usual, "and I'm very happy to see you." "Get in," DeMille said, opening the car door. Not knowing why, nor where they were going, and not caring, Ayn obeyed. As they drove, she told him that she wanted to be a screenwriter, and that he was her favorite director; he listened attentively, interested and amused. "He had a sense of drama," Ayn later said. "I think that's why it all happened." Much later, when Ayn was famous, DeMille released the story of their meeting, a story presumably written by a press agent: it said that Ayn had been starving, that DeMille had taken her to his home, and that Mrs. DeMille had placed her in the Studio Club.

They drove into the hills, where *The King of Kings* was shooting on location; they suddenly seemed to be driving on a Jerusalem street; it did not astonish her, because nothing could astonish her in her state of dreamlike unreality; anything was possible, and normal. "I was so breathlessly numb," Ayn always recalled, "that to this day I can remember the feeling. I probably showed it, but I controlled myself fairly well, I didn't get too emotional, but I was tense and bewildered, like being in an adventure that hadn't yet sunk in." As they left the car and walked onto the set, DeMille explained that if she wanted to work in pictures, she should begin by seeing how pictures were made. It was Ayn's first view of the shooting of a motion picture—and her first full day in Hollywood.

DeMille introduced her to a few people on the set—"and they acted as if I were visiting royalty. I learned later that there was a whole court around him, and anyone to whom he showed favoritism was carefully watched; it was a real Louis XIV setup." Entranced, she watched the shooting until the end of the day. Then DeMille approached her to ask, "Do you want to come tomorrow?" He gave her a personally signed pass—"And I went home dazed."

For the next four days, Ayn returned to the studio each morning to watch the shooting of a major movie. Each day, DeMille was on the set; each day, he gave her another pass. Shyly, not wanting to intrude, she never approached him; but at least once during the day he would come to talk to her about how pictures were produced and how screenwriters worked.

Lunch was served daily for the mobs of extras, but "I felt I wasn't entitled to eat; I was only a visitor. When I was asked if I wanted lunch, I said I wasn't hungry. The girls at the Studio Club told me that nobody would mind if I had lunch, but I never did—but I envied the marvelous cafeteria food, served at long wooden tables under a big tent."

At the end of the week, DeMille asked her, "Are you all right financially? What are you doing?" "I'm all right," she answered quickly, appalled that he might think she wanted money from him, "I have enough. But I want to work." "You can have a job as an extra if you want it," he said.

Ayn was hired as an extra, working with three hundred other extras on the huge mob scenes, at a salary of $7.50 a day. It seemed a fortune. "I worked for so long that I could live on my earnings for the next year; I worked daily for several months. The number of extras needed varied at times, but DeMille kept me on every day that extras were required at all. He probably liked me, in a sort of indifferent manner, and he liked the unusual circumstances. And he was interested in discovering talent."

On her first day as an extra, she was sent to the wardrobe department to receive a costume. "The costumes were thrown out at random from big baskets, they didn't even look at you, and I got something that was horrible, like sackcloth, and I had to put on dirty body makeup and a black wig. I didn't like it, and I complained that it was dirty, so they sent me to a young assistant designer; he gave me special scarves and neckpieces, and fixed me up beautifully, he made me a patrician lady instead of a street beggar." The young assistant was Adrian, later to be one of Hollywood's most distinguished designers and, with his wife, Janet Gaynor, Ayn's neighbor and friend.

"I met Joseph Schildkraut on the set. He played Judas in the movie, and he was a big star. He took me to lunch one day, and he somewhat flirted, and gave me an autographed picture. He was enormously good-looking and he was marvelous in his costume. I'd seen him once in Russia, in an earlier DeMille picture."

Ayn plucked up the courage to tell DeMille about the screen originals she had written, and at his request, she gave them to him. "He didn't read them himself, he gave them to the head of the scenario department, an old-maidish woman who disliked me on sight and I disliked her; she gave the originals a very bad report: she said that they were improbable and farfetched, not human enough. Even then, with all the faults those stories had, I knew this was the enemy; I sensed something anti-romantic in her. I still hate her to this day. . . . No, I don't hate her, but I dislike her intensely."

This episode marked the beginning of a criticism of Ayn's writing that she was to hear throughout her life: that her characters and events were too romanticized and extravagant, that "real people don't behave that way," that she must write about people as they are, about human frailty and failure. She was to hear the criticism throughout her life—and she was to react to it exactly as she reacted the first time: with contempt and revulsion. Untouched within her was her conviction that the purpose of art was to show the heroic potential of man; that was what she wanted, what she loved, and what she would do with her days on earth.

Each morning, Ayn left the Studio Club in the dimness of predawn; she was required to be at the studio at 6 A.M. to report for makeup and dress. No buses ran that early, and she had to take two streetcars to reach Culver City; the ride took more than two hours. She didn't mind the long ride. "It was necessary, and I felt very businesslike."

It was a morning during Ayn's second week in Hollywood. She sat on the streetcar, gazing abstractedly out of the window. "I didn't see him enter, but then I noticed him some benches away. I suddenly caught sight of his face—and that was it."

He was tall and slender; a strand of fair hair fell over his forehead; he wore an open shirt, and slacks over long legs. The skin of his face was taut against high cheekbones. His mouth was long and thin. His eyes were a cold, clear blue. He was half dozing, his body relaxed with the boneless elegance of a cat.

Ayn felt a shock of astonishment—a sense almost of recognition—and an emotion of such intensity that she could not know if it was pleasure or pain. She would recall thinking that if she were a painter and were asked to put on canvas her own private vision of the perfect human face and figure, it would be this face and this figure that she would struggle to create. She felt as if she were chained to her seat—or chained to him—unable to move.

"Don't let them tell me about love at first sight," she said in future years. "It *was* love at first sight. I was always on the lookout for *my* kind of face, I often saw faces that seemed interesting, but here was my *ideal* face. I have never seen a face that would fit my view of the ideal man quite as well." Here was Cyrus, here was Enjolras, here was everything she loved and everything she wanted.

Then she felt the jolt of a sudden terror: he would get off the streetcar and she would never see him again. Desperately, she tried to think of a way to speak to him, of some excuse, any excuse, but her shyness and her sense that it would be improper held her paralyzed. How could she approach a total stranger? He was not a stranger to her; he was someone she had known all her life, and loved all her life, but she was a stranger to him. There was nothing she could do. She sat very still, huddled into herself, her mind racing helplessly and hopelessly, feeling as if the world had simultaneously begun—and ended.

Chapter Eight

Ayn held her breath as the streetcar made its periodic stops and the man did not rise to his feet. Then the streetcar—and her heart—stopped at Culver City. She *had* to get up, she *had* to leave, she could not be late for her job. Slowly, painfully, she stood up—and saw that he was rising too, and hurrying to the exit door. She watched for a moment in dazed disbelief as he got off the streetcar and headed toward the studio gate; then she quickly followed him as if a magnet were pulling her in his wake.

Ayn dashed to the dressing rooms to change into her costume, and rushed to the set. He was the first person she saw.

"He was *magnificent,*" she would recall, describing his appearance decades later as if her wondering eyes were still seeing him. "He was wearing a short tunic, and a big toga over it with an embroidered collar, and sandals laced to the knees. There was a Roman-looking scarf around his head, with the ends streaming down. The costume was enormously becoming. He was an actor, playing a bit part in the movie. Later, from memory, I drew a picture of him in that costume. I couldn't forget his profile, and how he looked with that headdress.

"I spent the next three days just staring at him on the huge, crowded set, watching his every move, and trying to figure out how to meet him. I watched to see if anyone spoke to him whom I knew, but he was enormously anti-social— and of course I liked that. His manner suggested an aloof, confident self-suffi- ciency. I never caught him speaking to anyone, he always sat alone, his every position graceful. . . . I was following him like a camera. One day, when he was sitting on a flight of steps, I sat beside him, staring at him, but he didn't turn; and I didn't have the courage to talk to him.

"By the fourth day, I had decided what to do. They were filming a big street scene in Jerusalem, Christ was carrying the cross to the Crucifixion, surrounded by a mob; the extras were to mill about chaotically, some shaking their fists and yelling insults at Christ, others weeping and pleading with the Roman officials. The scene was done over many times. Each time, I watched very carefully to see where he went; he had a special routine to follow and a specific pattern of action, since he was a bit player. After I had my plan all calculated, they began shooting the scene again. I walked toward him, stepped directly into the path I knew he had to follow—and stuck my foot out. He stumbled and almost fell. He apologized, and we began talking. I don't know to this day what we said; all I really heard was that his name was Frank O'Connor.

"At the end of the day, I ran to the cashier for my pay; I knew he would have to come there too, so I stood aside until I saw him approaching; as if by accident, I got in the line next to him, and we talked again. He was just asking me how I got home—much later, I learned that he had intended to take me home—when someone he knew came up and offered him a lift, and he took it. I blame him for his indecisiveness—he told me later he regretted accepting the lift, so why did he? His brothers told me that when he got home that day, he said 'I met a very interesting and funny Russian girl on the set. I couldn't understand a word she said.'

"The sad and very painful part was that he had finished work that day, which I didn't know. When I got to the set next day, I waited to see him, but he didn't come; I waited for days before I learned that he wasn't coming back. I didn't know his address, or how to find him, he wasn't in the phone book, and I didn't know anyone who might know him. I finally went to the casting office, and told them I had a book of his which I wanted to return, and I needed his address; but they said they didn't have it. He had vanished, and there was no way for me to find him.

"For the next nine months, I drove one girlfriend of mine at the Studio Club —she was kind of my confidante—almost crazy: I could talk about nothing but Frank. I called him only 'the DeMille extra'—because I didn't want to give anyone his name. I was seriously in love. It was an absolute that this was the man I wanted. In those days, I fully believed that appearance showed character, that my type of face necessarily showed a good character, my kind of man. I was not fully wrong, I couldn't yet really distinguish which part is physical and which spiritual, as I could today; and in Frank's case I was right. It was a combination of how he looked and how he acted on the set, the style of the personality. I loved the aloof, aristocratic look, the look of something strong and independent, something cold and graceful. Even Frank's touch of repression goes with my type. I was desperately afraid that I would never see him again . . . but yet, deeper than the terror, I would often feel that I *would* see him again, that it would happen because it *had* to happen."

The entire event—from Ayn's first sight of Frank O'Connor on the streetcar to the edge of calm certainty that she would somehow find him again—has so much the stamp of Ayn Rand's personality and character that if it had not occurred, one could invent it and know that it might have happened. Her instant and never-to-be-altered decision that here was *her* type of face and therefore *her* type of man—her timidity about approaching him, despite the depth of her feeling—her carefully thought out and executed plan to meet him—her positive reaction to his "anti-social aloofness"—her childlike helplessness in the face of the practical problem of finding him again—her refusal to tell her friend his name, because it was too private, too personal, too precious to be shared—the desperation of her longing and loneliness for a man with whom she had exchanged only a few words—the deep, oddly serene conviction that they would meet again because it was *right* that they should meet again—all contain the unique, intriguing mixture of elements that formed the soul and view of the world that was hers in childhood and was hers in old age. And all are permeated with the fantasy elements—the fictionlike re-creation of a man whom she found physically beautiful into the heroic being of her own need—that was to become so marked in Ayn's relationships with people.

Among Ayn's acquaintances at the Studio Club was Virginia Sale, who was to become a well-known screen and vaudeville comedienne, and who, many years later, clearly recalled Ayn Rand. She spoke of Ayn's reaction to the disappearance of Frank. "Ayn used to weep in her room," Virginia said. "We'd all hear her crying and crying. We'd go to her door, and we'd say 'Can we do anything for you, Ayn?' And she would say, in her Russian accent, 'Go back! Go back!' She wouldn't talk to us about what was wrong, she wouldn't let us help. One weekend, we were terribly worried about her; she didn't return to the Studio Club after work, and we didn't know where she was. We were afraid she had committed suicide. But she returned after the weekend. She seemed all right, though very sad, and she wouldn't say where she had been. We never found out."

It was a situation for which nothing in Ayn's psychology had prepared her: she had learned to deal with disappointment, she had learned to deal with frustration, she had learned to deal with pain—so long as action and control were still open to her. But helplessness in the face of something she passionately wanted—and the lack of control over her destiny which that represented—was and remained the unbearable, the unacceptable. All avenues seemed closed, and she gritted her teeth against the agony; she could do nothing but hope, without the possibility of action.

Her sole emotional salvation was in her work, where she *could* take action. Not with regard to writing, but at least in her job as movie extra; that was the means for which writing was the end, and she would do it as well as it could be done.

Within a few weeks, *The King of Kings* was almost completed. DeMille approached Ayn on the set one day, and offered a job as a junior writer to the young woman he affectionately called "Caviar." She would be employed to do detailed synopses of properties he owned, and to outline her suggestions for adapting them to the screen; if her ideas were useful, other writers would complete the adaptations. She would be paid twenty-five dollars a week.

She was not yet rich and famous; but she was in Hollywood, she was a professional screenwriter—and twenty-five dollars a week seemed not far from riches.

To her deep disappointment, she found the work painful, boring, and frustrating. "The stories they gave me were impossible, and I didn't do well. I had terrible 'squirms,' I felt blocked, and couldn't come up with ideas I really liked. The first story they gave me was entitled 'My Dog,' " she was to recall with a shudder, "so you can just imagine how I felt." Although her adaptation suggestions were never used in full, she was pleased, when she attended films made from scripts she had struggled with, to see that at least some of her ideas were used—a small dramatic touch or a stylized line of dialogue here and there.

In the summer of 1927, DeMille gave her a story entitled *The Skyscraper,* a screen original about the rivalry of two construction workers in love with the same girl. Ayn made an appointment with the construction superintendent of a new building going up on Hollywood Boulevard, in order to interview him and to watch the men working; she knew she had to learn about construction in order to adapt the story properly.[1] When she arrived at the building, a message awaited her: the superintendent had been detained, and would not be able to see her for an hour. Ayn walked aimlessly along Hollywood Boulevard, then decided to go to a nearby library and read until it was time for her appointment. She entered the library—and saw Frank.

The event which "had to happen," happened.

Frank, who was also waiting for a delayed appointment, was reading a book. When Ayn saw him—and stopped still as if paralyzed—he looked up from his book, and smiled at her. He had not forgotten her. He rose to his feet, took her arm, and said "Let's go out."

"We walked for blocks, just talking," she would later say. "We talked about movies, and the movie originals that he wanted to write, all outrageous comedies. He talked very eagerly—which is unusual for him to this day." Unusual for Ayn, she talked very little, ecstatic to be beside Frank and to hear the sound of his voice. But she quickly asked him where he lived; she was not going to lose him again. He lived with his two elder brothers: Nick, a reporter on the Los Angeles *Evening Herald,* and Joe, an actor; the three brothers had taken rooms in downtown Los Angeles, at the home of an Army friend of Nick's; that was why she had not been able to find Frank in the telephone book: it was the friend who was listed, not the O'Connors. She had not needed to ask: as they walked, Frank invited her to his home for dinner that evening. The relationship that was to last more than fifty years had begun.

Throughout those fifty years, people who knew them slightly, and even people who knew them well, confessed to one another their inability to understand the bond that had drawn Ayn and Frank together and held them together. They seemed so oddly mismatched a couple—the handsome, elegant gentleman, quiet,

---

[1] DeMille finally produced the story in its original version. *The Skyscraper,* starring William Boyd and Alan Hale, was released in 1928.

unintellectual and passive, and the small, aggressive, ferociously intellectual woman. And yet, if one examines their lives before their first encounter, one feels that their meeting and their enduring relationship had a quality of the inevitable; that had they not found each other, they would have found startlingly similar loves, similar mates, similar life partners.

Charles Francis O'Connor was born September 22, 1897, in the small steel town of Lorain, Ohio, to Dennis and Mary Agnes O'Connor. The O'Connor family consisted of seven children, Nick, Joe, Frank, Agnes, Margaret, Bill, and Elizabeth; three other children had been born, but two died at birth and the third of scarlet fever at the age of six. Mary Agnes—her name had been "Minerva," but when she married Dennis she had converted to Catholicism and abandoned her pagan name—considered herself a cut above her husband; her father had been a violin maker and music teacher; Mary Agnes had been brought up in a cultured background and with expectations for her future that were dashed when she fell in love with the handsome young Irishman with his twinkling blue eyes and reddish-blond hair and tall, muscular frame. Dennis was a steel worker who had little education and no ambition except to do well at his work; it was not work that his wife respected. Dennis, too, thought that the aristocratic Mary Agnes was a cut above him; his respect and admiration for her intimidated him, silencing him when she used the term "steel worker" to his sons as an epithet.

His sons learned very young that their proud, strong mother had one overriding ambition: to bring them up to have a different, better life than their father; they were not to remain in provincial Lorain; they were to be educated; they were to understand art and music—and, above all, they were not to be physical laborers. Despite her dark-haired, blue-eyed fragility, Mary Agnes was a stern disciplinarian: the children's table manners had to be exemplary, their clothes spotless, their carriage erect. When Frank was not yet ten years old, his mother spent long, exhausting hours washing and ironing for the nuns at the parochial school the children attended so that the nuns would give Frank singing lessons; each Sunday, he obediently took the streetcar to nearby Cleveland to sing in the cathedral choir. She purchased a piano at a crushing cost, and Nick took piano lessons. Mary Agnes's sons were to have the life she had missed, she told them. She did not tell them that they must despise their father, but the message was clear and her power over the boys was complete; they loved their gentle, hard-drinking father, but they did not respect the life he had chosen.

It would have been difficult not to love Dennis. He was a warm, kindly man, and his children knew that he would never physically punish them. If they had misbehaved, Dennis would arrive home from work to find them on their knees, praying ardently; he would wait patiently to scold them until they had finished their prayers—but they were careful not to finish until, tired of waiting and unwilling to interrupt so devout an activity, he sighed resignedly and left the room.

Mrs. David (Mimi) Sutton, the daughter of Frank's sister Agnes, remembered her grandfather with great affection, and remembered especially the color and gentleness of his personality. She recalled enchanted afternoons spent with Dennis in his den, curled up in a deep leather chair in front of the potbellied stove and reading, knowing that all was well with the world because her grandfather was there. She recalled his old seaman friend with the glass eye, who needed a place to stay for a few days; Dennis gave him an extra room—and Tom stayed for ten years, doing chores to pay for his keep; Dennis never suggested to him that it might be time to leave. "I can picture him so clearly," Mimi said many years after Dennis's death. "First thing every morning, he would go down to the kitchen and pour himself a glass of beer. Then he'd break a raw egg into it, and pour in a shot of whiskey—the whiskey was home brew and he made it himself. I can still see the prettiness of the sun shining through the kitchen window into the glass, and the egg making a lump in his throat as he drank it down—and then he'd say a great, satisfied 'Ah!' When he was dying—he was in his late seventies—and in the hospital, almost too weak to speak, with his children around him, he asked for a drink. The nun who was nursing him indignantly refused, but Nick insisted that it no longer mattered, and poured him a shot of whiskey. Dennis took the glass, drank it down in one motion, said a great, satisfied 'Ah!'—and died."

The boys worshipped their domineering mother, Frank's sister Agnes would recall. And Mary Agnes was proud of her three eldest sons. Besides being obedient and gentlemanly, they were remarkably attractive, tall, long-legged, with finely drawn aristocratic features—Joe with his mop of shining blond hair and mysteriously aloof manner; Nick with bright blue, penetrating eyes, and a wickedly dry humor; and Frank with soft, light-brown hair, eyes of a slatey blue, and an endearing gentleness of spirit.

The O'Connor children led the cheerfully active lives of young people growing up in a small town. Frank loved anything that was small and helpless; when a neighbor's chickens were sick, he would sneak into the hen roost and steal them, carrying them home to nurse them gently back to health and to apply tiny splints to broken wings. His neighbors learned where to look for their missing animals, but if they had not healed, Frank would stoutly deny the theft, sneaking them back to their owners only when they were fully recovered.

The one sour note in their childhood was that the O'Connor children hated the parochial school they attended and the martinet nuns who taught them. With the exception of Elizabeth, none of the children were religious in later life. Frank once said that when he was only six, he had, as usual, been taken to church one Sunday morning; but this particular week the priest was explaining that all babies are born in sin, and must be cleansed of their evil. The child was shocked at the idea; he knew that sin meant lying and stealing; how could an infant lie and steal? If that was what religion taught, he decided, then it didn't make sense; there was something wrong with it, something *bad*.

When the first primitive two-reel moving pictures came to Lorain, Frank was immediately fascinated by the medium. At his instigation, the O'Connor children began putting on plays, in barns and attics and basements, for their neighbors and friends. If they did not find a play they wanted to do, Nick would write one; they borrowed makeshift costumes where they could, slathered on makeup, built primitive sets out of whatever materials they could scrounge, robbed a nearby graveyard for flowers when they needed them—giving their sisters hair ribbons pulled off the bunches of flowers—and sold tickets for which they charged one pin.

In her early forties, Mary Agnes developed breast cancer, and underwent a radical mastectomy, an operation rarely performed in those days. When she recovered, she found it painful to move her right arm, and Joe, Nick, and Frank learned to shop for groceries, to cook, to set the table and to serve, eager to spare their mother. A few years later, the cancer recurred and could not be halted; when their mother died at the age of forty-five, the children were emotionally devastated. So terrible was the blow to seventeen-year-old Nick that he attempted suicide, and fifteen-year-old Frank's behavior, for many months, was uncharacteristically brusque and insensitive.

Shortly after Mary Agnes's death, Frank, Joe, and Nick decided to go to New York, where the major movie studios were located. All three were interested in working in films, although Nick was later to become a newspaper reporter. They left Lorain a year later, and gradually worked their way from city to city toward their destination, picking up whatever jobs they could find. It was almost three years before they reached New York.

Thomas (Tommy) Carr, who had been an actor since childhood and later directed both movies and television, knew the three O'Connors in their days in New York, and later knew Ayn as well. "It was tough for young actors in New York at that time," he said many years later. "And Frank was not a very dedicated actor. He tried to make a living, like we all did, but he didn't go all out for it. He was very quiet and soft-spoken, a thoughtful and considerate person. I never heard anyone say a negative word about him, not then and not even after Ayn became famous; everyone liked him."

In his years in New York before meeting Ayn, Frank struggled hard enough to ensure at least a precarious living; he made the rounds of the studios regularly and found occasional bit parts and work as an extra. Despite his startling good looks, parts were difficult to obtain for a young man without professional experience or contacts. During World War I, Joe and Nick left to join the Army. They were sent to France; it was an experience from which they would come home, two years later, physically shattered. Both had been gassed in the fighting. Both were frail and often ill for the rest of their lives, and worked only occasionally, subsisting on government disability pensions.

One July day in Central Park, Frank helped a truck driver to change a flat tire. What could he do in return? the driver asked. "Take me *there*," Frank said, pointing to the name printed on the side of the truck: D. W. GRIFFITH STUDIO. By the end of the day, he was helping an assistant director to repair a boat at the Griffith studio in Mamaroneck; by the end of the week, he was an extra on the set of *Orphans of the Storm.* During the filming of the picture, he worked in almost every department of the studio: he worked in the wardrobe, he designed costumes, he painted sets, he assisted the director, he was an extra in mob scenes, he had a bit part in the movie's opening scene.

When Griffith left to make a movie in Europe, Frank remained in Mamaroneck, working for a department store, delivering furniture and decorating windows until Griffith returned and the studio reopened. This was the pattern of the next several years: while a movie was in production, Frank worked at the studio; in the intervals between productions, he took whatever jobs he could find.

In 1925, Griffith left permanently for Hollywood, where the studios were moving. Frank decided to follow the studios, and to join his two brothers, who were now living in Hollywood. Once again, he worked his way to his destination, as steward on a freighter going through the Panama Canal. His first movie job in Hollywood was as a bit player in *The King of Kings.* The first person he spoke with on the set was a "very interesting and funny Russian girl" named Ayn Rand.

Many years after their meeting, Frank reminisced about what had drawn him to Ayn in the early months of their relationship. "One of the most striking things about her was her complete openness—the absence of any trace of deviousness. The total honesty. You knew that it would be inconceivable for her ever to act against her own principles. Other people professed so many things that had no connection to what they actually did. But you knew that anything Ayn said, she *meant.* . . . She had a tremendous capacity for enjoyment. Whether it was a piece of music she liked or a story or some present I bought her that cost a dollar —she was so expressively and radiantly delighted. . . . She constantly passed value judgments. If she liked something, she liked it violently. If she didn't like something, she would communicate *that* violently, too. . . . When we were with other people, she was reserved, even shy—until they began discussing ideas. Then all the shyness vanished. She was as confident then, in her early twenties, as she is now. . . . The people we knew all talked about the things they were going to do in the future, *if* they got 'the breaks.' Ayn never spoke that way. She never thought about 'breaks.' She was convinced that it was up to her—and she was absolutely determined that she would get where she wanted to go. It didn't matter how difficult it was, or what hell she had to go through. She never wondered if she was going to succeed. The only question was how long it would take."

It was evident to everyone who knew them, then and through the years, that Frank deeply respected Ayn and was proud of her achievements. But he rarely spoke of such feelings. Ayn often spoke about what Frank meant to her. His physical appearance was never irrelevant to her love for him; she once told a friend—more seriously than not—"I married him because he is so beautiful." But most of all, she would say, her appreciation was based on what she defined as their deep and enduring value-affinity. She spoke of him as a man who shared her most intimate view of life, who understood her and her work, her loves and her hates, her joys and her suffering and her passionate aspirations, and who stood by her unflinchingly, as no one else ever had or would; she spoke of him as a man who, in his deepest being, held the same sense of life she did, worshipped the same values, was dedicated to the same concept of rationality. It was clear that he was the only human being she ever accepted fully into *"her* universe." She knew that Frank did not have the words for the convictions they shared. Although he would listen quietly to her discussion of philosophical concepts, he could bring little to the conversation. But that always appeared to be unimportant to Ayn; with Frank, she could accept and cherish an emotional understanding that he could not make explicit. Despite the disasters that were to occur in their life together, despite the bottomless agony she was to cause him, he was the love of her life. Always, there was Frank—and there was the rest of the world. She had no other loves before him.

Yet the friends who knew them most intimately were to agree that the man Ayn spoke of in such extravagant terms had little to do with the real human being who was Frank. As they listened to her praise his intelligence, his insights, his philosophical and psychological perceptiveness, they were often embarrassed —as Frank, too, appeared to be—by the nature of her compliments. It seemed that she could not allow Frank merely to be consort to a queen; she needed to announce to the world—and to herself—the validity of her choice of a husband. They felt—and they wondered if Frank, too, felt it—that his actual character and virtues were not visible to or appreciated by Ayn, that she responded, instead, to the heroic virtues he did not possess. Frank was a gentle, kind, sensitive man; he was not a giant of the intellect, he was not a world-mover. But for Ayn, he *had* to be a hero. "I could only love a hero," she had said. "Femininity *is* hero-worship," she had said. If she were to find herself the worshipper of a deeply flawed man, what would that mean about *her* soul and *her* femininity?

The words Ayn and Frank spoke about each other, and even the view between the lines in their attitudes toward each other, seem only a part of the picture, only a part of the intense bond that linked them. The picture has another component, crucial to its meaning and composition and to the sometimes dark and brooding, sometimes sunlit colors that formed its background: that component arose from the markedly similar patterns in their experiences long before they met.

Patterns. Each human life has its own unique recurring patterns, its own unique repetitions, from childhood to old age—patterns of action and emotion and choice that form a central part of it. And perhaps it is our experience of the relationship between our parents, in childhood—our observations of the two people most important to us, for good or for ill—that first tells us what *love* is to be for us, tells us what it *means* when a man and woman choose to spend their lives together, tells us what is the appropriate way for a couple to function and interrelate. This unnamed and unidentified conclusion profoundly influences our later emotional responses, influences whom we choose, whom we love, and how we behave in our most passionate human dealings; it forms the patterns that our loving relationships are to follow. Some people, as the years pass, question their early conclusions, alter them, and go on to make choices widely at variance with their youthful patterns. Most do not. Some change the patterns of their romantic choices. Ayn and Frank did not.

Frank, as a child, saw a vivid and unmistakable pattern in the relationship of his parents—even in the relationships of his grandparents and other relatives. Dennis O'Connor's mother, Bridget, was a strong, tyrannical woman, who ruled her home and her passive husband with an iron determination. Bridget's sister, Ellen, was cast from the same mold; she was a woman of great fire and unswervable will; at the age of eighty-two, contemptuously refusing any offers of help, she could be seen laying cement for her sidewalk. Mary Agnes, Frank's proudly domineering mother, made all the important decisions in her home and about the raising of "her" children; she strode through her short life with a band of steel hardening her spine, her eyes fixed steadfastly on her goal of improving the lot of her sons.

Without any significant exception, the men who surrounded Frank in his childhood—including his beloved elder brothers—although they were distinctively different personalities in many ways, shared common characteristics: they were kindly, passive personalities, emotionally repressed, hiding their resentments and their pains behind a wall of silence, controlled by the powerful women in their lives. Without any important exception—including his own sisters—the women who surrounded Frank were the exact opposite: dominant, aggressive, ambitious, ruling their husbands by means of the husbands' admiration for them and by the single-tracked intensity of their purposes.

For the young boy—and for the man he became—this must have seemed to be the way life was, the nature of men and women, and the inevitable nature of the relationships among them. It is not surprising that this view became embedded in his subconscious mind, to function as a powerful motivating force. It is not surprising that he chose Ayn Rand.

If one examines the photograph, taken in St. Petersburg about 1908, of the toddler Alice Rosenbaum and her family, it is with a sense of *déjà vu—déjà vu* after having investigated the men and women in Frank's family. In the center of the photograph, surrounded by her children, their mates, and her grandchildren, Ayn's maternal grandmother sits solidly, her heavy body erect and confident, her square, expressionless face under tightly pulled-back hair rigid and severe, her mouth held inflexibly taut—clearly the feared matriarch and the soul of her family. Beside her sits her husband, his shoulders somewhat slumped, his eyes soft and sad and without intensity. To the grandmother's right are Fronz and Anna Rosenbaum, Alice's parents. Anna is leaning forward, as if ready to leap into motion; her large dark eyes are wide and intense, flashing even in a still picture; one sees the energy in her posture and her face—but her mouth, like her mother's, is held tight and tense with resolve; her posture, like her mother's, is confident and precise. Beside her is Fronz. Fronz and Anna lean in opposite directions, as if avoiding each other. Like his father-in-law, Fronz's shoulders sag faintly; the fingers of his fleshy hands are parted and lax; his body seems to be moving backward, as if away from the watching camera. His heavy-lidded eyes are not fully open, as if he does not care intently to perceive the world; his eyes hold a look of quietly uncontested sadness.

The message of the photograph is confirmed by the facts of the life of Ayn's parents. It was Anna who was the dominant figure in the Rosenbaum household, as Ayn, despite her lack of warm feeling for Anna, always acknowledged. Fronz was a quiet, retiring man, content to leave decisions in the capable hands of his wife. He had his work—the exception to his passivity, for in that area he performed with considerable success—and he had his weekend games of whist; he seemed to require nothing more. It was Anna's firm convictions that were expressed and Fronz who listened silently, even when her convictions were not his. It was Anna who decided what the children should be taught and how they should be raised. It was Anna who determined the direction her family's lives should take. It was Anna who decided, after the Communist revolution, that the family must seek safety in the Crimea; it was Anna who found the way to get them there. It was Anna who supported the family when they returned to Petrograd, despite Fronz's disapproval of her working for the Communists. It was Anna who decided that Ayn should be allowed to emigrate to America, despite Fronz's fears for her safety. It was Anna who took responsibility for handling the complicated process of securing Ayn's passport and making the necessary arrangements. In the life of his family, Fronz was a dim, passive figure; Anna was the power.

It was also clear that Ayn saw nothing remarkable in the relationship between her parents. Even this woman of so uniquely a firsthand vision, carried the emotional baggage born of the characters of Fronz and Anna Rosenbaum. Her mother's dominance appeared to her both normal and appropriate. When she spoke of her early years, Ayn would say, again and again, "Mother decided"— always without comment or question. Like Frank, she had accepted as valid the pattern of the marriage she was born into. For the young girl—and for the woman she became—this seemed to be the way life was, this seemed to be the nature of men and women, and the inevitable nature of the relationships among them. It is not surprising that her view became embedded in her subconscious mind, to function as a powerful motivating force. It is not surprising that she chose Frank O'Connor.

The period following Ayn's rediscovery of Frank was one of the happiest of her life. They began to see each other regularly, to go walking, to movies, to dinner, to visit Frank's brothers and his friends. She remembered always the moment when he came to the Studio Club for the first time, and she saw the beauty of his tall figure moving across the room toward her. She remembered the day he brought her an impossibly extravagant bunch of golden chrysanthemums, the first flowers she had ever received, which she kept in their vase long after they had died. And she remembered the first time he kissed her: they were in the rumble seat of a friend's car, passing the dim shapes of orange groves; she remembered the sweet smell of the oranges, the clear, starlit summer sky of California, the touch of his narrow mouth on hers, spreading its heat through her body. At the Studio Club, she was never far from the telephone, waiting eagerly for the sound of Frank's voice. "Sometimes, he didn't call when he said he would, and two days passed. When there was no call, I would sometimes call him—at a desperate cost emotionally. I believed that a girl shouldn't do that, but I had to, I couldn't stand it, it wasn't by decision, it was by breakdown. Years later, he told me that he didn't call when he wasn't working and had no money to take me out."

But this period—in a different respect—was one of the hardest of Ayn's life. DeMille closed his studio, moving to Metro-Goldwyn-Mayer as an independent producer—and she was out of a job. For the next year and a half, she had to take whatever jobs she could find. She found employment as a waitress, but "I was fired after the first day. I didn't even properly know the names of the food, so I didn't know what to carry to what customers, and I didn't fake too well." At her next waitressing job, at a roadside diner, "I lasted a whole week. I was beginning to be good, but they let me go because there was not much business." Calls would come to the Studio Club with offers of temporary jobs; Ayn drearily stuffed envelopes for a few endless weeks. She tried to sell newspaper subscriptions to the *Hollywood Citizen:* "I sold *one.* That would be the last thing in the world I would know how to do."

There was one month, after she had moved out of the Studio Club, when she lived on thirty cents a day. In the morning, she ate a chocolate bar in her room, with hot water from the bathroom; during the day, she ate a can of cold spaghetti or beans. By the end of the month, enduring painful stomach cramps, she went to a restaurant and ordered a bowl of soup. "I held my poverty against myself," she would later say. "I had expected to be famous in a year at most, but I had learned that that was too fast to expect. I didn't blame anyone for my poverty. I knew I had no profession, I was not trained for anything but unskilled labor, and I had no time to train."

When she worked as a waitress, she took jobs in outlying districts of Los Angeles, in the slum areas, more than an hour's streetcar ride from Hollywood. Her reason, she would proudly recall when she spoke of those days, was to be certain Frank would not see her there. He never knew of her financial hardships, nor the sort of work she was doing. She was not ashamed of her work, but he, too, was struggling on an irregular income, and she did not want him to think that she needed help. It was typical of her psychology that she refused to share her pain with him. A passage she would later write for *Atlas Shrugged,* describing Hank Rearden's thoughts as he faces Dagny Taggart, equally, she once said, described Ayn's attitude of that time: "He grasped a feeling that he had always experienced, but never identified because it had always been absolute and immediate: a feeling that forbade him ever to face her in pain. It was much more than the pride of wishing to conceal his suffering: it was the feeling that suffering must not be granted recognition in her presence, that no form of claim between them should ever be motivated by pain and aimed at pity. It was not pity that he brought here or came here to find."

Despite her financial worries, despite the fact that she could not do the only work she cared to do, it was in her first years with Frank that the warmth, the charm and the quality of youth in Ayn's personality blossomed as never before. The girls at the Studio Club had found her grim and remote; she had not joined in their activities or discussions; she had no part, and clearly no interest, in their social life. Each month, a dancing party was held at the club; Ayn never attended. The girls traded clothes and silk stockings and gossip; Ayn, focused as always on the future, haunted by the pressure of time, severely went her own way. But now, in her happiness, they saw a new, a kinder and gentler, part of her.

Virginia Sale would later speak of an event that typified what the girls saw as "the new Ayn." Virginia was working on a one-woman comedy show, and discovered, to her astonishment, that Ayn laughed uproariously at her jokes. The night she first showed her act to girls at the club, Ayn stood behind a drape, enthusiastically banging pots and pans to create the required sound effects. She told Virginia that her show was wonderful and could not help but succeed, and Virginia, who had been considering taking it on the vaudeville circuit, and heartened by Ayn's enthusiasm, decided to do so—with great success.

The cost of board and room at the club had gone from ten to eleven dollars shortly after Ayn began seeing Frank, and she was often late in her payments. Marjorie Williams, the club's director, took an interest in all the girls, and was troubled by Ayn's struggles and her poverty and the shabby clothes she wore. One day, a woman in the motion picture industry, a patron of the club, offered to give a needy girl a gift of fifty dollars. She asked Marjorie Williams to recommend a deserving recipient, and Miss Williams suggested Ayn. A few days after receiving the money, a beaming Ayn walked into the director's office, carrying a large box. "Would you like to see what I got with the money?" she asked. She opened the box—to proudly display her new black lingerie. It is a story which is still told in Hollywood.

A year after encountering Frank in the library, Ayn moved out of the Studio Club. She wanted a place where she could spend time alone with Frank, and she took a minuscule furnished room, struggling with more determination than ever to meet the small rental payments. Ayn's sexual relationship with Frank, the first for both of them, began. When, many years later, she admitted that she and Frank had made love prior to their marriage, it was in a manner of shy pride: shyness at revealing so intimate a secret, and pride in what she saw as her daring flouting of convention. Sex was always very important in her life, and central to her relationship with Frank; physically, he was *her* type of man, and as such, powerfully sexually attractive to her; the intensity that was her trademark dominated every aspect of her relationship with Frank.

"I don't remember how the question of marriage came up," she was to say. "There was no 'official' proposal. It came about by unspoken understanding."

Several of the young people who were friendly with Ayn and Frank during those days have since said, separately, that "everyone knew" the reason for the marriage was the imminent expiration of Ayn's visa; she had had several extensions, but no more were possible. Tommy Carr said, "Frank and Ayn got married so that she could stay in this country. Her time was running out, and she had to do something about it, and that was the way she solved it. No one thought Frank was in love with her; he did it for *her,* basically; he was that kind of a guy, very easygoing, very kind. It wasn't a question of love, but of convenience. That was common knowledge. All my family and our friends thought it was a very nice thing for him to do." And Millicent Paton, who was friendly with Nick O'Connor and through him with Ayn and Frank, echoed the same belief, adding, "Frank didn't seem to be in love. He was fond of her, he respected her, but one didn't have the feeling of love. Nick told me he married her because of the visa issue."

And Ayn once said, many years after her marriage, recalling with amusement that Frank and Nick had joked about which one of them should save her from deportation by marrying her, "Ours was a shotgun wedding—with Uncle Sam holding the shotgun." All of their friends knew that Ayn adored Frank; it was clear in her words, in her manner, in the way she looked at him, in her reliance on him, on her need to have him always with her. But one never fully knew what Frank felt. It was apparent that he felt respect and admiration, and a deep attachment; but their friends never sensed in him the presence of passionate romantic love. It seems that, in their decision to marry—as well as in their future lives together—it was Ayn who was the motive power.

Ayn and Frank were married on April 15, 1929. (On the marriage certificate, her occupation is listed as "Waiter.") "It was a 'proper' nonreligious ceremony in a judge's chambers in the Los Angeles Hall of Justice," she later said. "It was a very unromantic marriage in one sense, because there was no real celebration; we didn't know many people, and the people we did know were all broke." Ayn wore her old black coat for the ceremony; it was the best garment she owned. On it, she pinned a corsage of flowers, tiny white roses that were a gift from Nick. A sculptor friend gave her two embroidered handkerchiefs, which she kept long after they were shabby and worn. After the wedding, there was a quiet dinner in the home Frank had lived in with his brothers. "I almost didn't want anyone there. I felt very private about the ceremony. I wanted total privacy or an enormous formal wedding with a white veil and ballroom dresses—that had always been my idea of how it should be." But when Frank stood beside her as her husband, and when she signed her name "Mrs. Frank O'Connor," her wedding day became a dream of romance.

The young couple moved into a furnished room, and began their life together. As if to complete her happiness, Ayn found work in the wardrobe department of RKO. She began as a filing clerk, at twenty dollars a week; but she learned rapidly and worked hard, and within six months her salary was raised by five dollars. Within a year, she was head of the department—at a salary of forty-five dollars a week. "I loathed and hated it," she would recall. "The work was filing and purchase supervising, keeping track of the costumes and accessories and seeing that the actors got the right costumes. I loathed it, but it was a godsend. I was always grateful to have it, especially when the Depression began and everybody was out of work."

The RKO job solved their financial problems. Ayn was able to form contacts in the Central Casting office, and Frank was kept working steadily, for several days each week. They moved from the furnished room, and rented an apartment near RKO. "Frank decorated the apartment beautifully, out of nothing. It was the first time I saw his artistic ability. He built shelves, and framed inexpensive prints, and hunted for the little secondhand-shop ornaments that he was always finding. We bought our first car, on time, a secondhand Nash convertible—and it was wonderful. Frank designed a desk for me, and had it made to order; it's the desk I still use. We even got a radio."

In late June, two months after their marriage, Ayn and Frank drove to Mexico, so that she could reenter the United States as the wife of a citizen. When they returned, she applied for American citizenship. For the first time, she felt politically—and emotionally—secure.

Chapter Nine

It was the worst of times. It was the decade of the thirties, and the crash of the stock market had brought its thunderous repercussions into the lives of all Americans. Never again would they feel quite safe, their world unassailable. Never again would life have the innocence it once had had.

By 1933, fifteen million people were out of work, and Roosevelt had inaugurated his National Recovery Administration—an action undreamed of by any former American President—by which the nation's industry, agriculture, and manufacturing became subject to centralized economic planning; the break with the laissez-faire free market was gathering momentum. The ambition, the energy, the sense of unlimited horizons that were the hallmark of the twenties, were fading into the memory of a golden age; the streets paved with gold had tarnished.

Soon, the rush to collectivism, which would earn the thirties the title of "the Red Decade," would begin. Writers and artists and professors and theologians and publishers and scientists and social workers and journalists and labor leaders and wealthy dilettantes would flock to embrace the doctrines of totalitarian communism. Soon, Granville Hicks, "the literary terrorist of the left," would write in the prestigious *New Masses:* "To be a good writer, a man must first become a proper communist"—and Stuart Chase would ask: "Why should the Russians have all the fun of remaking a world?" and Dorothy Parker would announce: "There is no longer 'I,' there is 'WE'! The day of the individual is dead."

But in the early years of the 1930s, the signs of what was to come were not yet clear, even to so prophetic an intelligence as Ayn's. "I had no idea, then," she later explained, "of the degree of leftist penetration in America. I knew few people in Hollywood, but those were certainly not left. Russia was not yet recognized, and I simply thought that although people were not sufficiently aware of the menace and evil of communism, they were decidedly not in sympathy with it. And I took it for granted that no one could advocate altruism except the worst kind of hypocrites—that most Americans, explicitly or not, lived in effect by *my* code. I did not see the enormity of what had to be fought."

And Ayn was involved in a project that required her whole mind, her whole attention; it blotted out everything in the world around her. In 1930, she had begun outlining her first novel. Its working title was *Air Tight*. She was to change it to *We the Living*.

Her initial thought had been to develop one of the story outlines she had devised while still in Russia, but all of them involved heroes and heroines older than herself, whom she did not yet feel comfortable working with. "I wanted to do something of which I felt certain," she later recalled. "I did not really want to do a major novel—that is, a novel that would have *my* kind of hero and *my* philosophy; I felt more sure of myself writing about characters in their early twenties, about a major character who was a woman, and about a theme that was political rather than more widely philosophical."

Frank and his brother Nick—who, with Joe O'Connor, was now her neighbor and close friend—argued that she should tell the world the nature of her Russian nightmare; people must know what was happening in Russia, and why it was happening, and no one was telling them. As they spoke, she thought of the farewell party her mother had given for her shortly before her departure for America; she thought of the guest who had approached her and said, "If they ask you in America—tell them that Russia is a huge cemetery and that we are all dying slowly." "I'll tell them," she had promised. She decided to write *We the Living*.

"*We the Living* was to be a protest," she later said, "and an introduction to my philosophy." She wanted to show that communism destroys not only the average man but most particularly the best among men—the brightest and the most creative, those with the greatest gifts to offer the world.

She began preparing her outline in the manner that was to characterize all of her future writing: in exhaustive, painstaking detail. Before a word was committed to paper in her angular, stark handwriting, each scene, each development and each character was fully spelled out, fully in her conscious control. She knew that writing required complex subconscious integrations, but she attempted to leave as little to her subconscious as possible. To work primarily by "feel," by inspiration, was abhorrent to her; as in every area of her life, she had to *know* what she intended, she had to remain in conscious control, the work had to be an *intellectual,* not an emotional process.

The outline was completed in several months.

Set in the years immediately following the Communist revolution, *We the Living* is the story of Kira Argounova, a girl of fierce independence, and—in the mold of future Ayn Rand heroines—dedicated to two purposes: the work she has chosen to do, and the man she loves. Kira plans to be an engineer, a builder of bridges, of mighty spans of steel and aluminum crossing wide blue rivers. But she is the daughter of the bourgeoisie; as a "class enemy," she is expelled from the university—in the student purge that Alice Rosenbaum had so narrowly escaped—and prevented from pursuing her education. She knows that she cannot leave this brave new world of Soviet communism—not merely because the state forbids it, but because there is no power on earth that can tear her away from Leo Kovalensky, the tall, slender aristocrat with the severe, contemptuous mouth and "a face that was like a drug to her, inexplicable, unconditional, consummate like music."

And then a power arises which threatens to rob her of her love, threatens to smash Leo's life and her own: he develops incipient tuberculosis, the disease of poverty and dirt, the rampaging physical disease brought to epidemic proportions by the intellectual plague of totalitarianism. Leo's only salvation lies in admission to a sanatorium in the South. The son of aristocrats and the daughter of the middle class cannot hope for the largesse of the state; Kira's desperate efforts to secure the necessary permissions are in vain; the doors of the sanatoriums are locked air tight to Leo, as air tight as the suffering spirits of the regime's victims.

There is one way . . . a way unbearable to contemplate . . . until Kira listens in anguish, night after night, to the accelerating, racking cough of her young god, and sees his sunken cheekbones, and knows that he will die. The way is Andrei Taganov, the Communist who loves her.

Andrei is Ayn's idealized version of a young Communist. In *We the Living,* the preponderance of Communists are villains—malicious, cynical, using the tenets of their faith for their own aggrandizement, in the mold of the altruists and statists who would appear in her future novels. But through the character of Andrei, she wished to show the Communist at his best potential, a potential possible only in the early days of the revolution, before the malice and cynicism and lust for self-aggrandizement of the regime itself became too overwhelmingly apparent for many of its most devoted adherents to stomach. When Andrei confesses his love to Kira, she shrinks from him as a lover, despite her affection for him as a friend—and then she thinks of red bubbles on dying lips, and she answers, "I love you."

Kira becomes Andrei's secret mistress. He does not know that his gifts of money are sent to a private sanatorium in the South, where they purchase Leo's life.

The dramatic climax of *We the Living* comes when Andrei, searching Leo's apartment for evidence of black market activities, finds in a closet the evidence of a second crime, in the form of a woman's clothes—a black velvet dress, a coat with a fur collar, a white blouse—that he recognizes. "Whose are these?" he asks, his voice empty. "My mistress's," answers Leo. "Citizen Kovalensky, you're under arrest."

Kira goes to Andrei to scream to him that his love and his body meant to her only a pack of ten-ruble bills with a sickle and hammer printed in the corner, which have bought back the life of the man she loved long before she met Andrei. Andrei learns at last what communism has done to—has made of—the woman who is "his highest reverence," and he understands the irreplaceable value of that thing in his spirit which is able to revere. The Party is dead for him, and communism—along with his desire to live and act. His last act before his suicide is to free Leo.

But he has sent back to Kira only the shadowy remnant of a man. Believing that Kira has betrayed him with Andrei, seeing no future and no hope for a human life in Russia, his spirit and his will eroded by years of dismal days, Leo announces to Kira that he is leaving her for a middle-aged, wealthy woman who wants him.

Now she will go. She will try to escape abroad. There is nothing left to hold her, neither work nor love. Kira makes her way across the Latvian border alone, on foot. Wearing white clothes to hide her in the snow, she begins her long crawl toward freedom in the bitter cold of the winter darkness.

Hours later, a Russian border guard sees something moving in the snow, far away. He raises his rifle to his shoulder and fires. "Just a rabbit, most likely," he mutters.

She can still walk, despite the little hole in her jacket and something warm and sticky slithering down her skin. She goes on, trembling and swaying and calling Leo's name as a plea for help from across the border. At dawn, she falls on the edge of a slope and knows that she cannot rise again. There is a smile on her face, the last shape of her hymn to the life she has never betrayed.

Ayn would later say that *We the Living* was not an autobiography in the literal, but only in the intellectual sense—that Kira's convictions and values were hers, and the background was real, but the plot and the events of Kira's life were fictional creations.

The background *is* real: the setting is the Russia in which Ayn had lived and suffered—the grayness, the terror, the ignominy of life under the Soviets. But the novel as a whole is nearer to autobiography than its author chose to say publically. Many of the characters—most especially the major male character, Leo—appear to be closely modeled after people she had known; the choice of the name "Leo" for the hero was not accidental; and Leo's inner conflict—that he teeters on the edge of a cynical, self-destructive despair, from which Kira cannot save him—is Ayn's interpretation of the mystery of her first love. The passionate, exalted worship that Kira feels for Leo is, most signally, the passion of Ayn Rand.

The character of Kira's Uncle Vassily—who refuses to work for the Soviets and stubbornly retains the conviction that communism cannot last, that his suffering country will be saved—was, Ayn would privately admit, "copied, both in appearance and in essential characteristics, from Father. Not in literal detail —he is slightly exaggerated for fiction. But the unbending character, the repressed integrity, that is Father." And the character of Galina Petrovna, Kira's mother, was borrowed from Ayn's own mother—"her politically liberal attitude, her tolerance for the Revolution, her social snobbery about the Revolution." The young couple, Irina and Sasha, who are sentenced to Siberia because of Sasha's underground activities, are taken from a boy and girl Ayn had known in Petrograd, who had suffered the same fate for the same reason. And Irina's work as an artist is modeled after that of Ayn's favorite sister, Nora.

When the outline was completed, Ayn began the writing, working in longhand as she was always to do. It proceeded with agonizing slowness. Her hours at RKO were long, there was often overtime and weekend work which she could not refuse at a time when more and more people were losing their jobs to the Depression. Her job increasingly came to feel like a jail sentence, despite its financial value. She would arrive home in the evenings exhausted, she would cook dinner for Frank and talk to him for a while, then find herself staring at a blank page of paper that demanded to be filled, her body aching and her mind a weary blank. After weeks of struggling to write at night, she knew that, at least in the early stages of the book, it was impossible for her, and that she could continue only on Sundays and on her yearly vacation. It meant that the novel would take years to complete. That was all right, she told herself grimly; she was moving, and that was all she could demand. She would reach her goals more slowly than she had expected. But she would reach them.

During the evenings, she and Frank often visited with Frank's brother Nick— he had changed his name to Nick Carter—to whom Ayn grew increasingly close, finding in him an intellectual stimulation that she did not find in her adored husband. Throughout her life, she was to draw to her intellectual young men with whom she could share the philosophical interests she could not share with Frank. As the months and years passed, Ayn and Frank seemed to talk less and less with each other, Frank seemed progressively to fade still farther into Ayn's background, and Ayn turned to others for the conceptual understanding and the passionate concern with ideas that she needed.

Ayn was, and remained, helpless and contemptuous in the realm of what she called "small talk." Parties held no interest for her, and she avoided them whenever possible. Her manner at purely social gatherings was one of shy, aloof boredom, that she neither knew how to conceal nor cared to. Millicent Paton, who occasionally saw Ayn and Frank when they moved to New York a few years later, was to recall: "We had a summer place in Darien, Connecticut, and I invited Ayn and Frank for the weekend. I gathered a group I thought would be compatible, or at least understanding of her; I wanted a light sort of thing, and to have these friends get to know her somewhat; but she just sat very grimly without making any attempt at conversation. I said to her: 'Ayn, you're so quiet tonight.' She answered: 'I cannot make small talk.' I said: 'Oh dear, isn't that a shame, because it would be so dull if we all just made profound remarks.' She didn't answer, she just looked at me as if I were the stupidest person on earth. Frank, on the other hand, was extremely pleasant; and when he had a chance, he could be very amusing, telling funny little anecdotes. But she didn't like to have too much of that 'silly talk,' as she called it. . . . Nick and Frank were quite close, as close as one could be with Ayn in the picture. Frank was all hers, and she made that clear. . . . Frank was not an aggressive man. If Ayn had wanted it, she could have really pushed his career . . . but I think she preferred to have him right by her side. Things had to be her way, no doubt about that; she was so positive, so brilliant. Nick once said to me: 'You don't ever try to change Ayn. If you have different views, keep them to yourself.' "

In one sense, Ayn was a surprisingly social being. When she and Frank visited with their few friends—a Russian actor who had helped Ayn get her job at RKO, a young ballerina who lived at the Studio Club, the family of Tommy Carr, a sculptor—Ayn was fascinated if the evenings consisted of intense philosophical and political discussions. She enjoyed nothing more than surrounding herself with people with whom she could discuss metaphysics or morality or politics or art, and she hungered, above all, for people who shared her own vision of life and man. When she found such people, she was happy to see them night after night and month after month. Her friends would observe that she seemed rarely to spend an evening alone or with Frank when philosophical discussion was possible instead.

It is interesting to note that during this period, when Ayn was only in her middle twenties, the people she met, whether friends or merely acquaintances— from the head of her department at RKO to Virginia Sale to the family of Tommy Carr to Frank's brothers to the struggling young artists she and Frank associated with—all seemed aware of her remarkable intelligence, of the breadth and scope of her mind, of her drive and ambition. She talked often of the novels she would write—as most of the young people in Hollywood spoke of the great things they would one day accomplish; but the people who knew Ayn *believed* her; they expected that she *would* accomplish what she said she would accomplish, that her name and her talents would eventually be widely known and recognized, that her work would be insightful and controversial. Even though she was so young, awed by her new country, struggling with a new language, socially awkward, working at an undistinguished job, her blazing conviction of her own abilities was infectious, her charismatic certainty was convincing. Nick, with whom Ayn and Frank spent most of their free time, was especially enchanted by Ayn. It was evident to those who knew Nick that he, vastly more sophisticated and worldly than Frank, regarded her with a deep, affectionate esteem; he and Frank were united in their conviction that if Ayn believed she would startle the world as novelist and as philosopher, then she would do precisely that; they were united in feeling that they were watching the first steps of a major talent, a major and provocative intellect.

Nick was an interesting and complex man, warm, outgoing, highly intelligent, with gaiety and style and great charm. "He made everything exciting and exotic," his niece Mimi Sutton once said. "He brought gaiety to everything and everyone he touched. He'd tell thrilling stories, and one knew they weren't quite true, but it didn't matter; it was his way of making life interesting.

"But in a terrible way, his whole life was a disaster. Because he had been gassed in the war—over the years, he was hospitalized with lung trouble a number of times—he received a lifelong pension, just enough to scrape by on. So he never *had* to work seriously. He'd talk about being a novelist, and he did do some writing; once, he sold a couple of short stories; and he'd work off and on for newspapers. But none of it ever came to much. . . . For a while, he lived with a young man, who I suppose was his lover. In those days, it was not something one could talk about; Ayn suspected that he was homosexual, and Frank did too, but it was never discussed. Nick would talk as if he were a ladies' man, and one sensed the pain he felt at having to pretend."

Ayn spent many long evenings talking to Nick about her ideas for *We the Living* and about her developing philosophical concepts. But always—as remained true throughout their lives—she wanted Frank to be with her; she appeared to need him at her side, to see him, to touch him, to experience the sense of visibility that he gave her. Sometimes, Frank would doze off during an all-night conversation, wanting nothing more than to go to bed; but Ayn would insist that he stay, as if his mere physical presence were a source of spiritual fuel. "Just a few more minutes," she would say as the hours passed, oblivious to his boredom and his need for sleep.

Frank read very little, but with Nick, Ayn could discuss the books she was reading, which she obtained from a rental library in her neighborhood. She was never a voracious reader, and as the years passed she read less and less, despairing of finding material that would suit her particular tastes and uninterested in anything else; although she could intellectually appreciate technical ability or sensitivity of characterization or narrative power, she responded in a personal, emotional manner only to novels that presented man at his highest potential through the medium of a skillfully devised plot; where she did not find these values, no "lesser" values had the power to move her. But she wanted to have some familiarity with current and representative American and British literature, and to continue improving her English. She discovered little that she liked.

One of her few favorites was O. Henry, whom she admired for the gaiety and imaginativeness of his stories. She was to say that, more than any other writer, O. Henry represented the spirit of youth—"the expectation of finding something wonderfully unexpected around all of life's corners." She read the novels of Sinclair Lewis, and appreciated "his characterization and an intelligent mind writing purposefully, though journalistically; but he's not my sense of life." She read Hemingway's *A Farewell to Arms*, "which I hated; it's mushy, morbid malevolence; the heroine, in the end, dies in childbirth, and that's the finish of the passionate romance, it's a totally gratuitous and accidental tragedy."

She began Thomas Mann's *The Magic Mountain*, but gave it up after three hundred pages—"It's a pretentious piece of nothing at all; I remember only dry, cataloguelike descriptions of precisely how tuberculosis patients were put to bed on the veranda, and pointless conversations about the meaning of life." It was after attempting to read Mann that she asked the librarian, an elderly, kindly woman, "Do you have anything that is a good plot story but has some serious ideas?" The woman answered sadly, "I know exactly what you mean. They don't write them anymore." And Ayn thought: Well, I will.

She did, however, find the book that became her "favorite novel." It was entitled *Calumet "K"*, written by Merwin and Webster and originally published in *The Saturday Evening Post* in 1901. It was given to her by Cecil B. DeMille, who admired it as work projecting the drama and heroism of a construction job. *Calumet "K"* is a work of light fiction, dealing with the struggle of its hero, against great odds, to construct a grain elevator. Its style, Ayn would acknowledge, although straightforward and competent, is undistinguished, and it lacks what was, for her, the most important ingredient of good fiction, a plot structure. But she loved the book, then and always, because "it has one element that I have never found in any other novel: the portrait of a strong, confident, cheerfully *efficacious* man—in a universe where victory and fulfillment are possible."

Calumet "K" was, to Ayn, who reread it every few years for the rest of her life, the quintessentially *American* novel. To the American reader, it is a startlingly light, nonphilosophical story to be beloved by so philosophical a woman. Yet between 1926 and 1930, she had written several short stories which seem similarly startling from the pen of Ayn Rand: in marked contrast to her future work, they are without explicit philosophical content; they are charming, almost magazinelike fiction, adventurous and cheerful and lighthearted.[1] In a deeper sense, neither those stories nor her love for *Calumet "K"* are startling at all: they represented to the young Russian émigré—as did her tiddlywink music and the American movies she had seen while still under the nightmare of communism—a world where one did not *have* to be philosophical; all philosophical problems were solved, and one was free simply to act and to achieve. In her response to *Calumet "K"* and in these early stories, one sees a manifestation of the youthful, life-intoxicated joy that still danced somewhere within the increasingly severe and serious woman.

Until almost the end of her life, Ayn spoke of wanting to write a novel in the manner of those early stories: a novel of action and high adventure that would make the point, but only by implication, that evil is the exception in life and that one lives for the achievement of happiness; she would write of a world in which "Atlantis had already arrived, the ideal was right here on earth, and it was the perfect free existence for purposeful men." She chose the name of the hero of the novel: he was to be Faustin Donnegal—a name that made her smile whenever she said it, and represented the extravagantly lighthearted approach she wished to achieve. But as the years passed, she knew that there was too much pain in her: she could no longer write that kind of story. She always hoped that the day would come when she *could* write her novel of pure, unsullied joy. The day did not come.

It was during this period of the early 1930s that Ayn received news of Leo from Russia. Her cousin Nina, with whom she occasionally corresponded, wrote that Leo had married a girl who was "neither intelligent nor attractive, a real

---

[1] Published posthumously in *The Early Ayn Rand,* they illustrate her rapidly growing mastery of her new language.

homebody." Nina had visited Leo and his wife, and said that theirs was "a typical lower-middle-class bourgeois household—the kind of home where the wife puts little lace doilies on the arms of the armchairs, and was just the little woman. Leo seemed embarrassed and enormously unhappy." The news shocked and pained Ayn; it was, she said many years later, "a horrible mystery. I still feel that Leo is an unfinished mystery story in my mind, I didn't really understand him, I knew only what I saw in him. But I can never feel that he's a total mediocrity and that I just invented him. I think that he *was* like Leo in *We the Living,* that his marriage was a deliberate act of self-destruction, that he consigned himself to mediocrity because higher values were not possible to him."

Oddly, nothing Ayn ever said about Leo seemed to warrant her ascription of such noble motivation to him; apart from what his appearance suggested, and his admirable act of courage in hiding members of the underground, there was nothing to indicate that he was the self-doomed hero of *We the Living.* Perhaps it is the case that what she did with Frank, she also did with Leo: they *had* to be heroes, to justify her love. They had to be transformed into the stuff of fiction—the fiction of Ayn Rand.

Even before learning the story of his marriage, Ayn had said her final farewell to Leo. Not in Russia, when he had bowed to kiss her hand at the train station, but in America. She had done it in the form of a short story which she wrote in her early months in America. The story, entitled "The Husband I Bought,"[2] is written awkwardly, sometimes ungrammatically, and clearly is a first attempt to write in a language still foreign to her. But it trembles with the doomed passion of its female narrator for the man she adores, and it leaves the reader feeling an exalted, exquisite agony. It is astonishing that a newcomer to the English language could capture, with such precision and power—the precision and power that were to become Ayn's literary trademark—the wrenching, bottomless pain of unrequited love.

Ayn never attempted to publish the story, nor did she wish to do so; she was too aware of its flaws. She did not even sign it with her own name, but with an invented name, "Allan Raynor." (As she once said, writers and criminals keep their initials when they change their names.) It was written as a literary exercise, as practice in writing in English—and as her final exorcism of Leo. She never forgot him, she often thought of him, she wrote of him in *We the Living,* but her thoughts were no longer blurred and heavy with pain. She had taken her love and her hero-worship—sensitively capturing her feeling for her "ideal man," her feeling for Leo, for Cyrus, for Enjolras, and for the men she was yet to create, Roark and Galt, in its purest essence—and had put those feelings on paper, where her life was most truly to be lived.

As the world plunged deeper into the chaos of the thirties, the writing of *We the Living* continued to proceed with agonizing slowness; Ayn could not begin to foresee its completion. Writing a novel in English was a painful process; some-

[2] It appears in *The Early Ayn Rand.*

times, she thought in English, sometimes in Russian—even, occasionally, in French. Sometimes, American idioms and ways of phrasing came to her mind automatically; sometimes, a style that was typically Russian was, to her disgust, evident on the pages before her. Clarity and precision were the highest of her literary values; she shuddered at an inexact phrase, an approximate metaphor, an irrelevant sentence, an awkwardly expressed thought. Often, she would spend an entire day struggling with a single short paragraph that dissatisfied her.

She had little difficulty with the plot ideas; the central concept of the story had come to her relatively easily, complete in its initial form. "I seldom remember getting the idea for a story or for any particular situation," she later said. "When I'm working, it's as if it is a living entity; getting the ideas is a constant process which you don't remember until it's set, and then, when it is set, it feels as if it was always that way. But I do recall the day I thought of the central situation of *We the Living*—that is, the idea of the Communist who has to arrest the other man, and he discovers the truth during the search: the twist on the old bromide of the woman giving herself to someone to save the man she loves, the twist being that the villain is really morally superior to the hero, that the tragedy is greater for him than for the woman. I don't mean that Andrei is *essentially* a better man than Leo, but in the setup, in the stage where they are at the climax, Andrei is more idealistic than Leo, and the worst blow is to him, not to Kira or to Leo. That idea of the search was the center from which all the rest of the story developed."

Nor did she have difficulty with characterization. "Characterization was always what I have given least thought to. I'm always very clear on the *concept* of the character, but not in the technical sense of *how* to project the kind of character I have in mind. I'd have to be very clear on what are the major and minor premises and motivation of each character, on what makes him tick, what he is after—and I could state it in words. But I would not project in advance *how* to show, for instance, that Andrei is brave. I had almost a block against characterization, I was contemptuous of the issue because of the irrational importance given to it by the kind of stories and schools of literature that say characterization is a primary, and there's detailed character delineations of people who do nothing at all. Throughout the writing, I was astonished that I was keeping to a very great consistency of characterization; apparently, my subconscious premises were set."

With *We the Living*, stylistic issues presented the greatest difficulties—both because she was writing in a new language, and because "I felt throughout that I was expressing only approximately what I wanted, not fully; I was fully satisfied with the presentation of the ideas and the theme, but not with my way of saying things, with the narrative, linguistic aspects. For instance, many of the early passages pertaining to Kira's reactions to Leo are not quite right, they are too brief, too understated. Particularly in emotional scenes, I felt that there was so much I wanted to project that I did not know how to capture it all; I was not yet at home with writing in essentials about emotions and moods; one has to do that by practice, one can't do it theoretically. I worked very hard, everything was rewritten many times, particularly the first chapter. But I was not yet at home with my own particular style. Style pertains to *what* you choose to say, and *how* you say it; my particular style consists of writing in *essentials* about emotions or mood. I could not yet express everything I wanted to express: that did not happen until *The Fountainhead*. In *We the Living*, everything was difficult."

In writing *We the Living*, Ayn was aware of the influence on her of Victor Hugo, which she struggled to avoid. "His influence shows itself in a certain kind of overassertive, overeditorial, and slightly overdramatic turn of sentences. My mind worked in those literary forms that had most impressed me, because I could not yet have any of my own, not on a first novel. My mind seemed to act in Hugo's kind of pattern, but I was learning in the process how to form my own method of expression. When you first begin, you will be influenced by those values that impressed you most; that is the way you'd think of expressing yourself, the most forceful way you have ever seen."

Late in 1931, unendurably frustrated by the slowness of her work on the novel —she had done only the outline and two chapters—Ayn decided to interrupt her work to write a screen original. If she could sell it, she would have the money to quit RKO and spend full time on the novel. The original she wrote was entitled *Red Pawn*.[3]

Red Pawn is a flamboyantly dramatic story—more typical of the later Ayn Rand than anything she had so far written—about a beautiful woman who becomes the adored mistress of the commandant of a Soviet prison for men convicted of political crimes; she becomes his mistress in order to free her husband who, unknown to the commandant, is one of his prisoners. It contains, in sharp, abbreviated focus, the dramatic twists, the plot inventiveness combined with keen philosophical insight, that were to reach their climax in *Atlas Shrugged*.

While *Red Pawn* was making the rounds of the studios—Ayn was able to secure the services of an agent through her contacts at RKO—she showed the synopsis to an acquaintance who was an executive assistant at the studio. "It will *never* sell," the woman told her. "The story is too improbable."

The story editor of a major studio, who had given a newspaper interview saying that he was interested in discovering fresh new talent and original ideas, read the synopsis and called Ayn in for an interview. He wouldn't buy the story, he explained, but he wanted to give her some advice. "We're interested in realistic stories about average people," he said. "That's what you should write about. Write about the people you know."

The theme that Ayn was to hear all her professional life, that was to haunt her in book reviews of her work, in articles, in interviews, in discussions of Ayn Rand, was sounding. Choose more realistic themes, write about more realistic

[3] It consisted of an eight-page synopsis, which she later expanded into short-story length and which appears in *The Early Ayn Rand*.

problems; your stories are too romantic, your plots are implausible, your characters larger than life. Write about life as it *is*. She rarely attempted to explain that she wrote in order to create the kind of people she would *like* to know, and to project what life *should* be like. She did not want to create Babbitt, but Enjolras; not Main Street, but a golden Atlantis.

Early in 1932, Universal Studios made an offer for *Red Pawn*. "When my agent called to say they wanted to buy it," Ayn later laughed delightedly, "I had to go to a *hospital* to talk to Universal's business manager; we settled the deal right there, in his hospital room where he was recovering from surgery. I was to be paid seven hundred dollars for the story, and another eight hundred for doing a treatment and the screenplay—a total of fifteen hundred dollars! I was enormously thrilled and proud."

From the hospital room, Ayn took her last bus ride to RKO—and quit her job.

A three-year jail sentence had come to an end.

Chapter Ten

Ayn wrote one of her aunts in Chicago and told her, with happy excitement, of the events surrounding the sale of *Red Pawn*. Universal had bought the story for their rising young star, Tala Birell, who was being groomed as the new Dietrich; Ayn had been given a two-month contract to write the script. She reported that Universal was very pleased with her script, and that she expected it to go into production soon. If the movie were successful, she could get a long-term screen-writing contract with Universal and still have time to work on *We the Living*. The most difficult part of her struggle, she said, seemed now to be at an end.

The struggle was not at an end. A film that had been intended to establish Tala Birell's career was a financial and critical disaster, and the studio released her. *Red Pawn* was put on a shelf.

But shortly thereafter, Universal traded *Red Pawn* to Paramount Pictures for an E. Phillips Oppenheim story for which Paramount had paid twenty thousand dollars. Ayn told her friends that she felt no resentment that a story which had earned her fifteen hundred dollars was sold for twenty thousand; despite her desperate need for money, she was thrilled by the compliment to her work.

Paramount decided to produce *Red Pawn* with Marlene Dietrich, and with Josef von Sternberg directing. It was Dietrich whom Ayn had envisioned when she wrote the story. Ayn was called in to do final work on the screenplay. "I sat in the studio at one hundred dollars a week for four weeks, doing nothing," Ayn later said. "Von Sternberg had the okay on the choice of stories for Dietrich, and I could not start work until they had sold him on making my story. Paramount had my preliminary screenplay from Universal, and I was to work with Von Sternberg on the final script. But Von Sternberg turned it down. He had just done *The Scarlet Empress* with Dietrich, a bad picture about Catherine the Great, and he didn't want to do another Russian story. Instead, he chose a ghastly, plotless story, it was a terrible flop, and Paramount let him go. He never made a comeback, and I always thought that that served him right. It was as contemptible a thing as anybody has ever done to me artistically—the kind of thing he preferred to my work."

Red Pawn was removed to another shelf, where it still remains, unproduced.

In the letter to her aunt, Ayn had reported that she and Frank were as happy as ever, "even happier, if such a thing is possible. Frank is simply wonderful." The family had never met Frank, and Ayn suggested that if they were curious, they could see him in a picture entitled *Three on a Match,* produced by Warner Brothers and starring Bette Davis; near the beginning, there was "a good, long closeup of him."

While Ayn's star was beginning to rise and she was embarking on her first major work and selling her first professional screen play, Frank's career, never successful, was moving steadily toward oblivion. He continued to work as an extra or bit player when he could, appearing in such unmemorable movies as *Smashing the Rackets* and *Hold 'em Up.* In *Cimarron* (the movie from the novel by Edna Ferber, starring Richard Dix and Irene Dunne) he was given a scene in the opening sequence, as the young fiancé of the heroine, whom she leaves for the hero; it was his first part with dialogue.[1]

Frank's important "break" came in a comedy entitled *As Husbands Go.* He was hired for the Los Angeles road company production of the Rachel Crothers stage play. But he played—as Ayn later termed it, while Frank nodded his head in agreement—"a tall, ungainly young professor having a romance with a young girl; they were the comedy relief. The part was totally wrong for Frank. Then Fox bought the movie rights and Frank did the same role on the screen. After the first day of shooting, he was told not to wear makeup, because he was too good-looking! It was heartbreaking for me to see him trying to be as ungainly as he could and to clown as much as he could."

Frank was bitterly unhappy with the progress of his career, and he was losing interest in acting. He continued working at it because it was what he knew, and he and Ayn needed the money. As time passed, he had less and less hope of achieving the kind of success he had wanted. As Ayn grew more fired with ambition and purpose, Frank was sinking deeper into passivity and a quiet, unacknowledged defeat. "That particular break in *As Husbands Go* really finished him," Ayn said. "And even if he had gotten big parts, Hollywood would have done to him what they did to Gary Cooper. I don't know if Frank would have stood for it, or if he would have fallen to pieces."

Acting was the only work that Frank had ever timidly wanted; it was crumbling to dust with each day's new defeat, and his gentle spirit, his capacity to want *anything,* seemed slowly to be crumbling with it. Progressively, his friends and colleagues observed, he was becoming *only* Ayn's consort, his own identity

---

[1] When the movie recently appeared, uncut, on cable television, no such scene appeared; presumably it had been removed from the film years earlier. All that remained was a dinner party during which one saw Frank in two or three brief glimpses.

dimming and fading beside the power and demands of a personality obsessed with its own purposes and needs.

Ayn had begun full-time work on *We the Living*. Although the writing still was difficult, the manuscript pages on her desk kept growing. But by 1933, money was again running short; Frank's employment was precarious, and little remained of the money from *Red Pawn*.

On an evening which Ayn would always remember as a turning point in her life, she and Frank went to see a play, a melodrama comedy set in a courtroom, entitled *The Trial of Mary Dugan*. (It had been produced earlier on Broadway by Al Woods, then made into an MGM movie.) "I didn't especially like it, but I thought the form was dramatic. I thought: Wouldn't it be interesting if someone wrote a courtroom drama with an indeterminate ending, one in which the jury would be drawn from the audience and would decide whether the accused is guilty or not guilty. My next thought was: Why don't *I* write it?"

"Wouldn't it be interesting if? . . ." is a crucial key to Ayn's literary approach. In 1940, she would write a short story entitled "The Simplest Thing in the World." The "simplest thing," writer Henry Dorn tells himself, would be to turn out hack work, "to be stupid on order," to toss off some popular nonsense that would sell—unlike the novel he had spent five years working on, "writing as carefully, as scrupulously, as delicately as he knew how," and which had not sold. I'll write a good commercial story, he decides, and make a lot of money. But whatever "stupid, human, bromidic" idea he gets, soon leads to the thought: Wouldn't it be interesting if? . . . and he finds himself creating, in his mind, *his* sort of story, romantic, intellectual, controversial, important. In the end, knowing what he cannot do, he reaches for the *Times* Help Wanted ads.

Ayn did not try to do "the simplest thing in the world." She understood, as Henry Dorn did not, that an artist's sense of life, his values, his philosophy, direct the creative process, that he cannot alter his basic identity, he cannot leap out of his own soul. But Dorn's method of working was Ayn's method: to project, in imagination, the most interesting, colorful characters and the most dramatic and important events she could devise—then to build on that, to make her story and her people still more interesting and more colorful—to build drama on drama and abstraction on abstraction until she had created the world that was the motive power of her writing.

After seeing *The Trial of Mary Dugan* and considering the possibility of writing a courtroom drama—she had always wanted to write a play; even in Russia many of her story ideas were for plays—Ayn remembered an event that had blazed across the headlines of the world's newspapers: the suicide of the Swedish "Match King," Ivar Kreuger, after the crash of his vast financial empire, and the subsequent shocking revelations that his empire was a gigantic fraud. Ayn had felt sympathetic toward Kreuger; she believed that it was not essentially his methods, his ruthlessness and dishonesty, that accounted for the storm of denunciations that followed the financial revelations; it was his ambition. She was to say: "It was a spree of gloating malice. Its leitmotif was not: 'How did he fall?' but: 'How did he dare to rise?' "

From *The Trial of Mary Dugan,* from the story of Ivar Kreuger—and from "Wouldn't it be interesting if . . ." the idea for *Penthouse Legend* was born.

Once again, interested in the project and hoping to make money from it, Ayn took off a few months from her work on *We the Living* and turned to her new project. *Penthouse Legend* is the story of Bjorn Faulkner, an arrogant, ruthless industrialist, and Karen Andre, the powerful, beautiful woman who loved him, worked with him, obeyed his every wish—and is on trial for his murder. As in "The Husband I Bought" and in *We the Living,* the major male character is not yet Ayn's "ideal man"; rather, Ayn was concerned to show a woman's *feeling* for her ideal man.

Her intention was that the factual evidence of the heroine's guilt or innocence be evenly balanced, so that the verdict must be determined by the moral philosophy of the jurors. Jurors would be selected each night from the audience; they would witness the play and decide on their verdict at the end of the last act, judging, by the standard of their own values, the diametrically opposite characters of the woman on trial and the major witness against her, characters which represent two different types of humanity. "The events," Ayn wrote, "feature the confrontation of two extremes, two opposite ways of facing existence: passionate self-assertiveness, self-confidence, ambition, audacity, independence—versus conventionality, servility, envy, hatred, power-lust." Thus, it is not only Karen Andre, but the jurors, who are on trial. As the defense attorney tells the jury, "It is your own souls that will be brought to light when your decision is rendered."

Commenting on the fact that Faulkner, like Kreuger, was a swindler, Ayn explained many years later: "It's not to be taken literally. Fraud and crookedness are not and were not my idea of individualism; but the issue that interested me was the man who stood alone versus conventional society; that's the way a young person, which I was, sees the issue of individualism. At the time I wrote it, I was not as conscious as I would be today that the concretes were symbolic, I was not as clear that Faulkner's morality, if taken literally, is the opposite of mine."

Ayn was very pleased with the play. "I was more in control of technique than with *We the Living,* because it was simpler and involved no narration, only plot and dialogue. It was with narrative that I was not yet fully in control." The major difficulty was the legal research: she had never been inside a courtroom and knew nothing about the law. Through DeMille, whom she still occasionally visited in his office and who always seemed happy to see her and interested in the progress of her career, she was able to get a pass to a famous murder trial; she attended for one day only, in order to see a courtroom. She obtained a transcript of part of the trial, and studied it carefully to learn general courtroom procedure and principles. A lawyer later checked the play, and Ayn was delighted that he had few objections to make.

Although *Penthouse Legend* was written as a stage play, MGM learned about it, became interested, and took an option on it. An MGM producer, Lucien Hubbard, wanted it as a vehicle for Loretta Young, who was under contract to MGM and was in the process of departing from her usual role of innocent, sweet maidenhood. Ayn went to MGM to write a screen adaptation, without, of course, the device of the jury chosen from the audience. "I had a very miserable time with it," she would later recall. "Hubbard kept insisting that I 'humanize' it. He had a reputation for never leaving anything in the original. Some MGM writers told me—they swore it was true—that he had bought a Broadway play by a well-known writer, then changed it so completely that nothing of the original was left in the movie version; the writer then bought his play back and said he would write his own screen adaptation and submit it to another studio; Hubbard said to him, 'If you get an offer for the screenplay, give me first option.'

"Every so often Hubbard would say that we needed to insert a comedy scene. I struggled to be funny—how is one funny to order?—I had the naïve idea that it was a flaw in me that I couldn't write comedy; whenever I tried, what came out was enormously phony. Fortunately, Hubbard would read it and say: 'Well, let's forget it.' When the script was finished—without being humanized—he didn't like it and MGM didn't pick up the option. But at least this gave us more money."

While her agent was submitting the play to theatrical producers, Ayn returned to *We the Living.* As it approached its final chapters, rejections for *Penthouse Legend* began coming in. Most of the producers rejected it because of the jury device, feeling that it would destroy the theatrical illusion; Ayn was convinced that the device was the play's particular strength. She was deeply disappointed, but *We the Living* was approaching completion, and that mattered to her more than a hundred plays and a hundred producers.

She was working on the climactic scene of *We the Living*—the scene in which the three leading characters face each other in Leo's apartment and Andrei learns that Kira is Leo's mistress—when an incident occurred which Ayn always recalled with great amusement. Frank had a bit part in a movie that day, but Ayn expected him home for dinner. When he did not arrive, she called the studio and was told that the shooting was running overtime. She returned to work. It had been an inspired day; she was writing her favorite scene, and she knew it was right, exactly as she had wanted it to be. About ten-thirty, the telephone rang, and a gruff masculine voice said "Mrs. O'Connor? This is the Lincoln Heights jail. We're holding a Mr. Frank O'Connor here." Ayn had immediate visions of horror: with her Russian background, to be held by faceless authorities was the ultimate in peril. When she finally stammered: "What for?" she was told, "For speeding. His sentence is to spend the night in jail." Ayn called Nick immediately: they *had* to raise the money to get Frank out at once. But Nick told her, "Don't interfere. Let him do what he wants to do." Frank had been fined for speeding, had insisted that he was "framed," had argued indignantly with the judge, refused to pay the fine, and chose to go to jail. Miserably, fearfully, Ayn accepted Nick's insistence that Frank be allowed his own choice. "I was terribly upset at the thought of *Frank* in jail; I stayed up all night waiting for him, I couldn't think of sleeping. I continued writing—and to my astonishment I did very good work, my mind was very clear. At six in the morning, a sheepish Frank came home, looking like a guilty jailbird. I made him take off all his clothes in the foyer, and shower, it must be terribly unhygienic in jail—I was very angry, but he just kept laughing. . . . I've always remembered that the best sequence in *We the Living* was written while Frank was in jail."

Toward the end of 1933, Ayn completed *We the Living*. It had taken her four years.

The moment of completing it remained with her forever. Beaming, she handed the thick manuscript to Frank, and her own eyes suddenly grew wet as she saw the tears in his eyes. Perhaps it had not taken four years, but twenty-eight. The days of her life, the ambition, the capacity for concentrated work, the indifference to obstacles, the values and the philosophy that were uniquely hers, had finally brought her to this day. She had transformed the base metal of her wretched years in Russia into the shining gold of a novel. She had done what she set out to do.

Chapter Eleven

"While writing *We the Living,* I was literally living in that world," Ayn said.

Now it was time to emerge from the crystalline, luminous world of her imagination and to cope with the world of other people, other values, other attitudes, a world from which she always had felt remote and alienated. What was to come was itself like fiction: the events of the next years seemed devised by some demonic fiction writer first to raise her hopes for professional success by presenting her with opportunities she had only dreamed of—and then to send them crashing and crushed, as if determined to increase her remoteness, her alienation, her anger and frustration.

But at the time she completed *We the Living,* her hopes were high. And the work, Nick confided to Frank, seemed to have smoothed some of the rougher edges of her personality. It had an important personal-psychological, as separate from professional, value for Ayn. Her experiences in Russia had remained a painful issue, driving her on relentlessly to tell their meaning to the world, and haunting her with memories of fear and suffering that had often jerked her, sobbing, from sleep. *"We the Living* got Russia out of my system," she said. "By the time the book was finished, the issue of Russia was also finished for me."

Though *We the Living* did not satisfy her completely, because of her language difficulties and problems with style, certain aspects of it were a deep and lasting source of pride. She later explained, "What I liked most, literarily, was the plot structure; it was a single-tracked series of events leading to a dramatic climax, a highly personal novel set against a social background. With the plot, I succeeded completely in what I had wanted." And she added, "Ideologically, I had said exactly what I wanted, and I had had no difficulty in expressing my ideas. I had wanted to write a novel about Man against the State. I had wanted to show, as the basic theme, the sanctity—the supreme value—of human life, and the immorality of treating men as sacrificial animals and ruling them by physical force. I did so."

The stylistic problems, however, continued to disturb her. "The events leading to Andrei's suicide and the suicide itself were among the very few places where I was able to achieve the deliberate understatement and indirection and implication that is crucial to me literarily; those scenes were conscious *underwriting*. It wasn't until later novels that I *fully* succeeded in the art of implication—that is, building a strong emotional situation, then not naming it for the reader but writing around it. That makes the emotional impact stronger."

Interestingly, this aspect of *We the Living* which Ayn considered a defect was precisely the aspect that would cause many of its readers to prefer it to her later novels. *We the Living* is a passionate work. Although Kira dies in the end, the overall emotional tone of the book is not tragic, but life-affirming: the State has the power to end Kira's life, it does not have the power to destroy her spiritually; she remains as she had begun, loyal to her knowledge of what life could be and should be. Throughout most of the novel, the emotion is *in* the lines, most particularly in Kira's words and reactions and manner. The writing is lush and romantic. True to Ayn's purpose, the emotion in the novels that would follow *We the Living* became predominantly *between* the lines: it became implicit rather than explicit, understated, and projected by action alone, as she mastered "the art of implication"—and as she began subordinating emotion to the intellectual message she wished to impart. Her style—culminating in *Atlas Shrugged*—became increasingly cerebral.

The progression of Ayn's work, inevitably, closely followed what was to be the progression of her life. During the struggle and disappointments of the years following the completion of *We the Living,* her own emotions began to sink below the surface of her life, replaced by intense rational cerebration. In her later novels, the passionate intensity results from the cumulative power of the events, but one does not *see* it—as one was ceasing to see it in Ayn Rand.

There was another element in *We the Living* that Ayn evidently considered a defect, although she never spoke of it, because many years later she was to remove it from a new edition. That element represented the influence of Nietzsche on her early thinking. In the original version of the book, Kira tells Andrei, "I loathe your ideals, I admire your methods. If one believes one's right, one shouldn't wait to convince millions of fools, one might just as well force them. Except that I don't know, however, whether I'd include blood in my methods." In the Foreword to the 1959 edition—from which that statement was removed— she would write: "I have not added or eliminated to or from the content of the novel. I have cut some sentences and a few paragraphs that were repetitious or so confusing in their implications that to clarify them would have necessitated lengthy additions. In brief, all the changes are merely editorial line-changes."

Some of her readers were disturbed when they discovered this and similar changes. It is unfortunate that Ayn did not choose to explain it, rather than to ignore it. It appears likely that even at the time of writing *We the Living,* had she been asked if she intended *literally* that one should force "fools" at gun point—she would have said that she did not intend it; it appears likely because, in all of her later writing, she was to stress, consistently and constantly, that "Whatever may be open to disagreement, there is one act of evil that may not, the act that no man may commit against others and no man may sanction or forgive. So long as men desire to live together, no man may *initiate* . . . no man may *start*—the use of force against others." This conviction was the core of her rejection of socialism, of communism, of fascism, of any "ism" that presumed to allow some men to force others to act against their will and convictions; it was the basic premise of her own political philosophy. Force might, and should, be answered by force; under no circumstance, for no reason, for no holy cause or purpose or goal, might it be *initiated.* Like Nietzsche, Ayn worshipped "the superior man" —by which she meant "the man of the mind," the rational, purposeful, independent, courageous hero who lives by his own effort and for his own happiness; unlike Nietzsche, she rejected as unforgivably immoral any suggestion that the superior man had the right to employ physical force as a means to his end.

During the writing of *We the Living,* Frank, and Nick, whose intelligence and literary sensitivity she found invaluable, had read the manuscript as it progressed—or rather, she had read it *to* Frank, as she was always to do. With the completion of the manuscript, she asked Gouverneur Morris, the well-known fiction writer whom she had met while working on the scenario of *Red Pawn* and with whom she had become friendly—he had autographed one of his stories to her with the words: "To the only genius I've ever met"—if he would read *We the Living.* Morris read the novel and thought it a remarkable and important work. He immediately recommended it to his New York agent, Jean Weick. Ayn, not knowing how she would otherwise have enlisted the services of a New York agent, was delighted to send the manuscript to her.

The story of Gouverneur Morris was typical of the course of Ayn's career: one man or woman discovering her work, responding to it enthusiastically, believing that she had a great and rare talent, and taking action to help her professionally despite her status as an unknown writer in the early years of her career, and, later, despite her status as a writer whose works were considered dangerously controversial. Her personal, charismatic intellectual powers had the same consequences; always, there were people around her who spoke of her in their own circles of friends and associates as a woman of so astonishing an intellect that she yet might change the world.

Jean Weick began submitting *We the Living* to publishers. The first response was a rejection. Then another, and another, and another, until Ayn lost count. "It was a terribly painful period," she was to remember. "I went to the mailbox twice a day—and all I got were more rejections. I was very shocked. I thought, It's wrong, injustice, and I have to find my kind of editors. Jean Weick—who was primarily a magazine agent, and whom I later discovered didn't take my book very seriously—didn't give me any *reasons,* I didn't *know* why it was being refused. I finally learned that she had been hearing from editors that I was too concerned with *ideas,* that the book was too intellectual. I knew that was the enemy attitude."

During the agony of waiting, Ayn recalled something she had been told several years earlier. She had been borrowing books from a lending library owned by a White Russian woman. One day, as the two women were talking, Ayn had said that she was writing a novel about Soviet Russia. The woman had answered: "You'll have a hard time and a lot of opposition; the Communists have tremendous influence on American intellectuals." Ayn had been indignant and had not believed it. "I thought it was typical Russian panic-mongering. I told her it was possible there would be some opposition, but not the majority of American opinion."

But she later heard from Weick that a number of publishing houses had not troubled to disguise the fact that the cause of their rejection was not literary, but political: they saw no possibility of making a profit on a book that denounced Soviet Russia.

The O'Connors' main income now was from Frank's sporadic acting work. The last of Ayn's money was gone, and she was close to desperation professionally and economically—when an offer came for *Penthouse Legend.*

The offer came from Al Woods, the famous New York theatrical producer. It seemed to Ayn almost miraculous that a man who was a legend in the theatrical world, who was inundated with the work of known and unknown playwrights, should wish to produce the first play she had written; it seemed to her almost miraculous—and utterly appropriate. A contract with Woods would mean a Broadway production, and all that that entailed professionally and financially; it was a once-in-a-lifetime opportunity to break forever out of anonymity and to begin her playwriting career at the top. Again, one man had seen, by his own judgment, the value of her work, and had responded by taking action.

Ayn rejected the offer.

Woods had insisted that he be granted the right to make changes in the script. She would not grant it. Her reason was not that she considered her play to be flawless; it was that she knew, then and always, that her survival as a writer required fidelity to her own firsthand vision; she could not allow her work to be given into the hands of someone else—*anyone* else—to be altered by the dictates of a vision that was not her own.

Ayn was beginning to be known and talked about in Hollywood through her sale of *Red Pawn,* through Gouverneur Morris' enthusiasm for her work, and, she suspected, through the audacity of her refusal of Al Woods's offer. It was not long before another offer came for *Penthouse Legend,* this one from screen actor E. E. Clive, whose first love was the theater and who produced occasional plays on a modest budget at the Hollywood Playhouse, a small local theater. In terms of professional advancement and monetary reward, there was no comparison and no contest between his offer and Woods's.

It was with E. E. Clive that Ayn signed a contract.

The rehearsals of the play were not happy occasions for her. "Instead of being glamorous, it was nerve-wracking day after day to hear people reading my lines and not really knowing what they were saying, and very few did it properly. Clive was a good director, and really respected the play and my kind of writing. But there was not much he could do with those actors. A special kind of conscious focus is required for my sort of lines."

The play opened at the Hollywood Playhouse in October 1934, under the title: *Woman on Trial.* Ayn had made the title change at Clive's request; he felt that the original title suggested a fantasy. Arriving at the theater on opening night, standing on the pavement before the brilliantly illuminated entrance, Ayn looked up at her name and the title of her play sparkling on the marquee. *"That* gave me a real thrill, because I had read about it in Russia, in American film magazines. But the play was spoiled for me because of the acting, and because my own lines had become a bromide to me through repetition during the rehearsals. To this day," she would say almost thirty years later, "I can still hear all the different voices of that company and subsequent companies. So opening night meant nothing to me, because it was not the way I wanted the lines to be given."

Because of Clive's reputation as a producer, a number of Hollywood celebrities attended the opening, including Marlene Dietrich—who was, second only to Greta Garbo, Ayn's favorite actress. An actor friend gave a festive party after the show. Ayn, as was usual at social occasions, felt uncomfortable at the party: "I felt that none of these people spoke my language. It was only a social strain, the necessity of being introduced, smiling, saying 'Thank you very much.'"

Tragically for the woman who wrote so convincingly of the joy possible in human life, it was indicative of the manner in which Ayn was developing psychologically that she took little pleasure in the rehearsals or in the presentation of her play. Where she saw, in her view, both good and bad, she was tending increasingly to react emotionally to the bad, to focus on it, to discuss it, and to remember it. Except for those times when she listened to the music she loved— her tiddlywink music, Rachmaninoff's Second Piano Concerto, some Chopin pieces, and a few others—she could rarely abandon herself nonjudgmentally and benevolently to the living moment. The stern, unforgiving judge in Ayn, present since childhood but now in the ascendancy, was beginning to stand as an impassible wall between her spirit and the happiness that life offered her.

"The big shock to me were the reviews of *Woman on Trial,"* Ayn would recall. "I never really recovered from it."

The reviews, predominantly, were highly complimentary. But the play was praised for aspects which she considered of secondary importance; that which she considered most original and ingenious was ignored or mentioned only in passing. She had the sense that her play had not been *seen.* "My attitude always toward reviews and compliments, since my high school days, was that I expect superlatives or nothing, and I wanted raves that raved about the right things. The reviews were not intelligent, there was no mention that is was a play of ideas; the stress was on the melodrama and suspense. There were three or four reviews in all, and they hardly mentioned the gimmick of choosing the jury from the audience. . . . The one really bad review was in the Los Angeles *Times,* by a man named Paul Jordan Smith; it was a hooligan misrepresentation. He wrote as if it were trite and violent, and never mentioned the ideas, as if it didn't have any. The irony is that he later gave a favorable review to *Atlas Shrugged.* I've never been able to explain it. . . . I suppose it's just the usual irrationality of people."

Woman on Trial ran to less than full houses, but did sufficiently well to justify its short run.

When the closing was announced, Al Woods renewed his offer. Ayn learned that he had been stunned by her earlier refusal; unknown playwrights did not turn down offers from Broadway producers. After long, nerve-wracking negotiations, Woods finally agreed to make minor alterations in the clause pertaining to his right to make changes in the script, although, Ayn said, "it was very dubiously worded. I was wary of it, but I thought that the Hollywood production would give me a certain bargaining power with Woods. I decided to take a chance on it, a calculated risk."

Ayn signed the contract with Al Woods for a Broadway production of *Penthouse Legend.* Woods planned immediate production, and asked Ayn to come to New York at once.

In the late fall of 1934, Ayn and Frank, in their battered secondhand convertible—"We couldn't even think of affording a train"—set out for New York. They had little more than one hundred dollars between them: the money from Woods for the first month of his option on the play.

Ayn carried with her a new novelette, *Ideal,* which she had written during her last six months in Hollywood.[1] Although it was written after *We the Living,* it showed more clearly than the novel her struggle with her new language. "It sounded as if the writer were thinking in a foreign language," she later said. "Perhaps the problem was that it was laid in America."

Ideal is a strange and bitter and very beautiful work, in the emotionally explicit tradition of "The Husband I Bought" and *We the Living.* The idea of the novelette came to her in the following way. A middle-aged woman of her acquaintance, pleasant but undistinguished and conventional—"a kind of *Mrs. Babbitt*"—spoke one day of Greta Garbo and of her intense admiration of Garbo. "If only I could meet her!" she gushed. "I'd give my life for it!" Would you? Ayn wondered. What do your values actually mean to you? Wouldn't it be interesting if . . . ?

Ideal is the story of a movie actress whose appearance and personality suggest so exquisite a beauty of spirit that her audiences see in her the embodiment of their own deepest values and ideals. Desperately needing to know that there are others who share her exalted sense of life, she attempts to discover whether those

---

[1] It was never published until it appeared, posthumously, in the play form to which she had later adapted it, in *The Early Ayn Rand.*

who claim to worship her do want, in actual reality, that which she represents—
or whether they want it to remain only a distant, unrealizable dream. As the
story progresses, all of them betray her, in different ways and for different reasons, just as they betray their own ideals—all but one: a young man who gives
his life for her when he believes that her life is threatened; in so doing, he shows
her that there exist on earth a few rare men who are not content merely to
dream, who will live—or die if they must—for their values.

Ideal is both angry and exaltedly idealistic, a tortured hymn to integrity. In it
one sees the union of attitudes so marked in Ayn: the union of passionate idealism with a profound scorn for those who are *only* idealists, who renounce the
responsibility of translating their ideals into action and reality. And in it one sees
Ayn's desperate loneliness for people who saw the world as she did. She felt that
in all her twenty-nine years she had found only one man who shared her exalted
vision of life, the man she had married. She had discovered other values in other
people, but never that most basic value of all. Where were the people she was
seeking? She could not doubt that they existed somewhere. Would she find them
in New York?

As Ayn and Frank began their long drive, they talked excitedly of what
awaited them in New York, of the new world that seemed to be opening its arms
to take them in its embrace. But their excitement was soon marred. "We were
barely out of Hollywood," Ayn later recalled with a shudder, "when the brake
lining burned out, then the battery went—which meant more expenses. When
we got to Virginia, a stretch of road was being repaired; suddenly there was a dip
in the road where the pavement became a dirt road, the car went out of control,
we slid onto an embankment over a sharp drop, we started turning over—but at
the last moment the car stopped on its side. A small rock was holding one of the
back wheels. It was a miracle we weren't killed. We had to be towed to town.
The damage was too expensive to repair, so we sold the car, for very little, to the
repair man, and we went on by bus. It was not a very happy procedure."

But New York was where Ayn had wanted to live since her first sight of it as
she stood, a timid twenty-one-year-old immigrant, on a pier on the Hudson
River. When she again saw its gleaming skyscrapers, she felt that she was home
at last. To the end of her life, she would leave New York only when absolutely
necessary for professional reasons, or for her very rare vacations. She seldom
took advantage of the cultural offerings that New York uniquely possessed—art
galleries, theater, ballet—but to know that the great city was there, just outside
her window, seemed to give fuel to her spirit. New York was, to her, the symbol
of human achievement, the living, breathing reality of the accomplishments
possible to the mind of man. With her writing, and with Frank, it was her life's
great love.

The O'Connors had arrived with almost no money. Nick had moved to New
York several months earlier, and was working as a reporter; they were able to
borrow some money from him—a limited amount, since he had little to spare.
Ayn turned to Millicent Paton, their friend from Hollywood. "Ayn called me

and said, 'I'm here, and we don't have one penny,' " Millicent would recall. "She said, 'I'm putting my play on. You must lend me some money.' She was very direct and frank, no subterfuge. We were happy to lend it. And she paid it back—every penny—when she could."

Another disaster struck shortly after their arrival. Al Woods explained that he had not been able to arrange financial backing for the immediate production he had planned. Ayn would continue to receive one hundred dollars a month until the play was produced—but Woods could not say when that would be.

The Depression was at its height, and unemployment was rampant. Frank spent his days desperately searching for work, any kind of work, but no jobs were to be found. Ann Watkins, Ayn's new agent, began seeking work as a script reader for Ayn.

As the writer of a play soon to be on Broadway, it was no longer difficult for Ayn to interest an important agent in her work, and she had been dissatisfied with Jean Weick. A friend arranged an introduction to the much respected Ann Watkins. "I liked Ann Watkins very much at our first meeting," Ayn would recall. "We got along well, and she took *We the Living*. I showed her *Ideal,* which she liked, although she recognized that the style was shaky. She submitted it to a few magazines, but there were no buyers; most magazines then were publishing detective and action stories, and *Ideal* was an episodic story."

Ann Watkins found a job for Ayn as a free-lance reader, first at RKO and later at MGM. Her work consisted of reading books and manuscripts submitted to the studio, synopsizing them and evaluating their screen potentiality. RKO paid two dollars for a brief synopsis, and five dollars for a long one—"Few were long, because the material was awful. My advantage was that I could read French, Russian, and enough German to manage, so I got the foreign stuff, even Soviet plays."

That money, with the option payments from Woods, was what Ayn and Frank lived on for almost a year. Ayn was a promising playwright with a play about to go into production—and she was struggling to buy enough food to survive. At RKO, she earned about eleven dollars a week, at MGM about twenty dollars a week. Rent was forty dollars a month; her payments were often late. "I'd buy one lamb chop for dinner for Frank," Ayn would recall. "I had to diet anyway, so I would do without. One day, we had fifty cents between us, and our only food was the remains of a box of oatmeal. It was slightly Russian. . . . You see why I'm not very glamour-conscious and don't like to live glamorously. I gave up the idea long before then, but that helped. There was no time to think of it. . . . The tension was enormous because of our financial situation. I was planning *The Fountainhead* at that time, but I had no peace of mind to really work, I could neither work nor not work—I was running a race with an undefined bank account." And month by month, Ayn waited for word that Al Woods had obtained his backing.

The O'Connors made an arrangement with Nick that was financially helpful to all of them: Nick came to their small furnished room on East Sixty-fifth Street for dinner each night, helping with the shopping and cooking, and paying his share of the expenses.

Another intellectual young man came into Ayn's life that year. They became close friends, in a relationship that lasted for many years. Albert Mannheimer was a budding and talented writer—and a convinced Marxist. Ayn had violent political arguments with him, but she liked "Fuzzy"—his nickname due to the unmanageable frizz of his brown hair—for his lively intelligence and his eager curiosity about ideas diametrically opposed to his own. "You're an honest man," Ayn told him. "I'll convert you to capitalism in a year." He laughed at such a preposterous idea. It took less than a year. Albert became one of the first "students" of her philosophy and she spent long evenings and nights—while Frank listened quietly and served drinks and coffee—presenting her ideas to him. Twenty years later, Albert was still telling the story of their friendship, saying that he had been fascinated, "almost hypnotized" by her intellectual brilliance and by the power of her personality.

Rehearsals for *Penthouse Legend* finally began in the summer of 1935; Woods had obtained the financial backing he needed. At his insistence, Ayn grudgingly agreed to change the title to *Night of January 16th;* the alternative he offered her was *The Black Sedan.* It was to open on Broadway, at the Ambassador Theater, on September 16.

During the period of the rehearsals, lonely except for Nick and Albert; and beginning to relax after a year of unrelieved tension, Ayn and Frank began to meet people in New York—a young director, Bob Grey, actors Ivan Lebedeff and Robert Shayne, writer Jeanne Temple—and once more to spend evenings devoted to discussing the subjects Ayn loved best. She had not yet entered the world of New York political conservatives; she had not yet developed the passionate interest in American politics that was later to characterize her. But people were seeking her out, drawn as if to a magnet, as word of her talents and her ever-increasing intellectual powers began to spread.

But the demonic fiction writer was still at work, and Ayn emerged from the rehearsals and production of *Night of January 16th* with the sense of having escaped a medieval torture chamber. In an interview with Rex Reed in 1973, she would say: "The entire history of the play has been the worst hell I ever lived through. It was produced in 1935 by Al Woods, a famous producer of melodramas, who . . . turned it into a junk heap of clichés that clashed with the style and confused the audience. . . . He was a faithful adherent to the school of thought that believes if a literary work is serious, it must bore people to death; if it's entertaining, it must not communicate anything of importance."

"Al Woods," Ayn would say bitterly when recalling the production of the play, "was really an old scoundrel, uneducated, and a pathological liar. He tried to get anything dishonestly, even if he could get it honestly. His one redeeming value was that he had a marvelous dramatic sense—his taste was vulgar, but he loved whodunit action. I later discovered why he bought the play: he had learned about the jury gag, and when the more intellectual producers were saying it would destroy the theatrical illusion, he thought it was a marvelous idea. But it was mutual hatred between us from beginning to end. He was impatient of what he called my 'highfalutin speeches, sweetheart,' and he cut them all to the bone, so they were meaningless. . . .

"Casting on Broadway was supposed to be by mutual okay of the producer and the writer. I suggested Walter Pidgeon for the part of Guts Regan [the criminal who is in love with Karen Andre]. At that time he was out of the movies, he didn't catch on in talkies, and Woods said he was a has-been. But I had seen him at the Hollywood Playhouse in *Androcles and the Lion,* and he was very good. Woods finally gave him the part—and as a result Pidgeon got an MGM contract, which started him on his big career. I was later told that he said publically that my play was responsible for his contract. And he did Guts Regan very well, he was the best in the cast.

"Karen Andre was played by an unknown whom Woods had discovered: Doris Nolan. She was the right physical type, very attractive, but not a sensational actress. The rest of the cast was okay.

"The director, John Hayden, was a very ratty Broadway hanger-on.[2] I didn't get along with him at all. Anything good in the direction was supplied by Woods —he knew how to make things move." By the terms of his contract with Ayn, Woods was permitted to hire a collaborator; he chose John Hayden, paying him one percent of Ayn's royalties.

"I sat through rehearsals every day for three weeks, I began to dislike the actors very much; they kept wanting to change words or lines, they'd say 'I can't *feel* it the way it is'—they were the kind who suddenly find difficulty in saying 'The cat is on the mat.' You know how I write, the extent to which every statement is weighed, even for rhythm. It was plain torture. . . .

"What I most objected to was not the cuts, but the additions: Woods insisted that there be a gun in the play, so I had to write it in—and it had nothing to do with the story. He'd weigh down the action with stuff like that, and then cut out the speeches. I could only argue. The contract was really in his favor. . . . He kept saying 'This is your first play, and I've had forty years in the theater. Don't you respect my judgment?' And I kept explaining that if the elevator boy suggested something, and had a reason, I'd accept it—or if the greatest authority in the world suggested something without reasons, I wouldn't accept it. . . .

"The worst of all was that he decided to put an extra character in the last act, Roberta Van Rensselaer. Her part was written by the director. She didn't belong at all, and it held up the action—but Woods liked the idea of a chorus girl with furs. The girl who played it was said to be the mistress of Lee Shubert, who owned the theater and who was Woods's main financial angel."

In an article that appeared in the New York *Herald Tribune* on November 17, 1935, John Hayden wrote about his preproduction concern for the play. He and

---

[2] Ayn's evaluation of Hayden seems illustrative of her growing inability to acknowledge any worth in someone in whom she found significant flaws; Hayden had had a long career as a Broadway director; only a year earlier he had directed his own revised version of *Lost Horizon.*

Woods were told by a prominent manager that it was ridiculous to believe that members of the audience would leave their seats and pass three entire acts on the stage. People come to the theater to be entertained, not to be made a part of the show; they would be embarrassed if asked to go on the stage. "After listening to these and many more reasons why the idea was all wrong we felt a little ashamed at having started it and a whole lot concerned about the expense that had been incurred in ripping out the orchestra pit, installing a new platform, steps and so forth. . . .

"With all this to worry about it was a perturbed production staff that settled down in Philadelphia to see if it would work. When the first juror's name was called he answered it promptly and alertly stepped right up on the stage. I then went out and had my first drink. Continued elimination of obstacles provided me with enough excuses to arrive at a very mellow stage by the time the play was over. Our week out of town proved the prophecies wrong. Not only would the public serve on the jury gladly, but it was pulling wires to get the chance."

Although the reviews were reasonably good and the reactions of the audiences enthusiastic, the Philadelphia tryouts were a special agony for Ayn. Woods insisted that she make script changes before almost every performance; she worked day and night to create material she believed served only to damage her play.

"One day in Philadelphia," Ayn later recalled, "I was walking along the street with Frank and Nick, who had come with us, and I started to cry. I tried to walk behind them so they wouldn't see me. I felt that the whole thing was blind experimentation, like a child and the surgeon is trying to decide which organs he can cut out."

As if to make a miserable situation still worse, Woods horrified her by bringing in a play doctor, Louis Weitzenkorn. Ayn considered him "a terrible sort of creature. He described himself as a Marxist, and we had violent political arguments." Ayn was not told that Woods planned to pay Weitzenkorn one percent of her royalties. When she later learned it, she insisted that the matter go before the American Arbitration Association. "I was not going to pay him out of my own money for nonsense."[3] Weitzenkorn's contribution to her play, Ayn told the arbiters, was to have the district attorney say to Guts Regan, "You bastard!" He wanted that line inserted, she explained, because the tag line of *The Front Page,* a major Broadway hit a few years earlier, had been a character saying "the son-of-a-bitch stole my watch!"—and he decided the scene was funny because of the word. Woods had tried it, the audience did not respond, and Woods took it out. "When I told this to the board, Mrs. Vincent Astor, a member of the board, leaned forward and said 'That was *all* he did?' You should have seen the look on her face!" The board decided for Ayn.

[3] Ayn was represented at the arbitration by Pincus ("Pinky") Berner, a renowned theatrical attorney, who was to become a friend and to remain her attorney until his death in 1961; after he died, Ayn stayed with his firm; in her will she appointed among the executors of her estate Paul Gitlin and Eugene Winick of the firm Berner had headed.

Opening night on Broadway, Ayn sat in the back row of the theater—and yawned. It was not out of nervous tension—she was neither excited nor fearful —but out of acute boredom. The play was dead for her. It was no longer a play about ideas.

To create excitement in the audience, Woods had arranged for boxing champion Jack Dempsey to be among the jurors on opening night. The verdict was Not Guilty.

Next morning, in The New York *Times*, Brooks Atkinson wrote: "It is routine theater with the usual brew of hokum. . . . It involves gangsters, millions, airplanes, grave-robbing and several noble flourishes to a man's devotion to the woman of his dreams, with perhaps a little suggestion of abnormality thrown in to spice the dish."

Other reviews, including that of Walter Winchell, praised the play, but their praise was embarrassing to Ayn. "They praised it as a plain good melodrama. The whole thing was such a messy compromise, I wanted to run. I felt that making my name with that kind of a play was a handicap, it was the wrong kind of name."

The Atkinson review and other negative reviews damaged the play, but did not destroy it. Despite Ayn's unhappiness with it, it continued to run to slightly less than capacity audiences. It was considered successful, although not a smash hit. One performance was given for an audience of the blind, with Helen Keller serving as foreman of the jury and newscaster Graham McNamee describing the scenes. The verdict that night was Guilty. Helen Keller herself, whom Ayn admired and later wrote about with great respect, voted Not Guilty.[4]

Through the gloom of this period, one event had burst through like an explosion of sunlight in an underground cavern. During the Philadelphia tryouts, a telegram from Ann Watkins had been delivered to Ayn's hotel room. The Macmillan Company had made an offer for *We the Living*.

Ayn signed a contract with Macmillan. Her advance was two hundred and fifty dollars.

Ann Watkins told her how the offer had come about. The Macmillan editors had been deeply divided on the manuscript; some wanted to publish it, some did

---

[4] In the years following the Broadway production, the play has been astoundingly successful, up to and including the present time. Two road companies went on highly successful tours. It was produced in Britain and other foreign countries. It has been played endlessly in summer stock; it is still, more than fifty years after its first production, a classic of the summer stock repertoire. It has been presented on radio and on television. To Ayn's great delight, it was staged, in 1936, by a summer theater in Stony Creek, Connecticut, with Frank playing the part of Guts Regan. In 1937, in a presentation in Suffern, New York, José Ferrer appeared in the cast. After World War II, it was performed by the USO for the American troops occupying Berlin. Amateur groups continue to perform it regularly, in a bowdlerized version not written by Ayn, directed to the amateur market. In 1941, Paramount released a movie version of the play with Ellen Drew and Robert Preston; it could not, of course, contain the play's most original feature, the choosing of the jurors from the audience. Rex Reed quoted Ayn as saying: "I had nothing to do with the screen adaptation. There is nothing of mine in that movie except the names of some of the characters and one line of dialogue, 'The court will now adjourn until ten o'clock tomorrow morning.' " The movie, she said, was "cheap, trashy, and vulgar."

not. Stanley Young, an editor who was also a poet and playwright, had fought for it stubbornly. The man who was most violently and intransigently against it was Granville Hicks—a member of the Communist Party and editor of *The New Masses,* who had written that "to be a good writer, a man must first become a proper communist." The final argument was given by George P. Brett, Sr., former president of Macmillan and still involved in its operations, who said: "I don't know if we'll make money on it or not, but it's a novel that should be published."

Substantial royalties for *Night of January 16th* began coming in. On good weeks at the box office, Ayn received as much as twelve hundred dollars. For the first time since the Communist revolution she was not on the edge of financial panic. She and Frank moved into a sunny, comfortable apartment at 66 Park Avenue. Frank was intensely proud of his young wife and her accomplishments; cheerfully, he told a newspaper interviewer, "I've been called 'Mr. Rand' so much that I'm going to have my name changed legally to that of my wife." Ayn, still not quite certain that their new comfort was real, began shopping, a little tentatively, for the clothes she could never before afford; the days of her dark Russian garb were over, and she wore casual American clothes, simply cut, straight-lined, and belted.

Because she now had the financial means to arrange it, Ayn made her first attempt to keep her promise to her family: to bring them to the United States. The matter had to be handled with great care, so that her anti-communism would not be known to the Soviet authorities. As Ayn had waited in 1925, so the Rosenbaums now waited to learn if they would be granted permission to leave Russia. Permission was not granted. When war began in 1939, Ayn lost all contact with her family, as completely as if they had died. Many years later she learned that Fronz and Anna *had* died in the German siege of Leningrad; the Soviets' refusal to allow them to emigrate had cost them their lives.

In March of 1936, a month after *Night of January 16th* had ended its run of 283 performances, *We the Living* was published.

Ayn sent a copy of her book to Frank's father, Dennis—whom she had not met—inscribed: "To my American father, from his Russian daughter." She sent a copy to Cecil B. DeMille inscribed: "From a little Russian immigrant to whom he gave her first chance at writing." She sent copies to her Chicago relatives, and wrote them: "I am glad to think that you believe the book justifies all the trouble you've had in bringing me to this country and in keeping me here. . . . From now on, I think, it will be easier and you won't have to wait for years to hear of my success."

But the demonic fiction writer was waiting in the wings. *We the Living* was born and it died within a scant few months.

"The way *We the Living* was published was enormously painful to me—really enormously," Ayn later said. "Apparently it was way down on Macmillan's list of important books, and they concentrated any publicity only on their two or three leaders. I got only a couple of ads in conjunction with other books, and that was all. *Nothing* was done for it. That terrified me.

"Then the reviews started appearing—*not* appearing, really. There were no daily reviews in New York at all, only a couple in the weekend magazine sections. The New York *Times* review was ghastly; the reviewer panned it unmercifully, and said it was 'slavishly warped to the dictates of propaganda.' There were a few complimentary out-of-town reviews, but they didn't praise it in the right way or understand the ideas. I blamed the reviewers totally, not myself. If they had given me justice for what was good, and said the style was rough or uneven, then okay, I would have taken the blame. But they wrote things like 'God is too frequently on the side of the non-Soviets,' and 'the author pours out her hatred for a collectivist world,' and 'the tale is good reading, but bad pleading; it is not a valuable document concerning the Russian experiment.' I always knew I would be controversial, but I was concerned only with reaching my kind of readers." There was no means for *We the Living* to reach Ayn's kind of readers: without advertising or publicity, with only a few, mostly negative reviews, published at the height of Americans' excitement about "the noble experiment" occurring in Russia, her potential public did not learn that the book existed.

Like Henry Dorn in her short story "The Simplest Thing in the World," what made the reactions to *We the Living* harder to bear was that she knew the value of her work. As Henry Dorn had written his novel, so she had written *We the Living* "as carefully, as scrupulously, as delicately as [she] knew how." Like Henry Dorn, "[she] read [her] book over again, very carefully, and [she] was happy when [she] found a bad sentence in it, or a muddled paragraph, or a thought that did not seem clear; [she] said, they're right, it isn't there, it isn't clear at all, it was perfectly fair of them to miss it and the world is a human place to live in. But after [she] had read all of [her] book, to the end, [she] knew that it was there, that it was clear and beautiful and very important, that [she] could not have done it any better—and that [she'll] never understand the answer. That [she] had better not try to understand it, if [she] wished to remain alive."

The review that most angered Ayn appeared in the *Saturday Review of Literature*. "It was the most disgusting," she said, "because it gave a synopsis only, expressing absolutely no opinion." The review was written by Irina Skariatina, a former Russian countess who had fled to America in 1922, married an American, and returned with him ten years later to visit her homeland. In 1933, her book, entitled *First to Go Back,* was published by Bobbs-Merrill. Written during the period of some of the worst Communist atrocities against the Russian people, it glows with accounts of the "new Russia" in such statements as, "Truly the worker is sitting on top of his world with everything conceivable being tried that would be of benefit to him."

Ayn met Irina Skariatina at a party a few years later. "She approached me and gushed about what a wonderful book I'd written. I said, violently and coldly, 'Why didn't you say this in print?' She giggled with embarrassment, shrugged, and changed the subject."

After publication of *We the Living,* Ann Watkins was working to get Ayn a screenwriter's job in Hollywood. Ayn knew that her income from the play would not last indefinitely, and publication of *We the Living* was evidently not to add to her income. A screenwriter's job seemed the solution; it would provide money to live on, and give her free time to work on her next novel. Ayn had burst out of obscurity—she had a successful play on Broadway, a published novel, she had begun giving occasional anti-Communist talks to club and luncheon meetings, articles were appearing about her in the newspapers—and Watkins expected no difficulties. But no job was to be found. "We can't get a job for Ayn Rand," a Hollywood associate reported to Ann Watkins, "because she talks too much about Soviet Russia." "It really was the red decade," Ayn later said. "I was blacklisted."

A year after publication, sales of *We the Living* suddenly started to climb. Recommendations of people who had discovered it on their own were beginning to break through the barriers of opposition and indifference; the novel was becoming talked about and known. This was to be the pattern of all Ayn's future books. In an industry in which a novel usually has its highest sales in the first few months after publication, then begins diminishing, Ayn's work reversed the pattern; sales were not immediately large but kept growing through word-of-mouth recommendations, and in the second year they increased rather than diminished. But it was too late for *We the Living.* After issuing a first edition of three thousand copies, Macmillan, convinced that the book would not sell, had destroyed the type. Apart from her small advance, Ayn earned in royalties on the American sales of *We the Living,* a total of one hundred dollars.[5]

[5] In 1937, *We the Living* was published by Cassell in London, and began appearing in other foreign editions. In 1959, it was reissued by Random House. In 1960, New American Library published a paperback edition, and printed more than 400,000 copies within one year, twenty-four years after the novel's original publication. By 1984, American editions of the book that was "too intellectual" and "too anti-Soviet" to have a market, had sold more than two million copies. First editions are now selling on the private market for more than one thousand dollars—and the price is rising.

PART III

THE FOUNTAINHEAD

Chapter Twelve

It was time. The concept of "the ideal man," its seeds planted early in Ayn's childhood, developed and refined over the years, had grown to fruition in her mind as *she* developed through her twenties. It was, as it always had been, as it always would be, the focus of her literary and philosophical interests; it was the radiant center of her soul.

Now, she was ready. Now, that radiant center demanded expression, demanded an entrance into life, like a child struggling to be born. Ayn endured its birth pangs, severe and passionate as a martyr to a noble cause.

The man-child struggling to be born was Howard Roark. His universe was *The Fountainhead.*

And it *was* a universe that she would create. If one examines the history of art, one will conclude that the writers whose works have lived across time—like the composers and painters and sculptors—share an essential characteristic. Their unique and personal stamp, their unique and personal *spirit,* emanates from every page of their writing, and one knows that it could have been created by no other sense of life, no other consciousness, no other intellect. The literary universe of Dostoievsky, its tone, its emotional quality, the conflicts that rend it—its metaphysics, so to speak—can never be confused with that of Henry James or Victor Hugo or Oscar Wilde or Thomas Wolfe—just as the musical universe of Chopin can never be confused with that of Handel or Wagner or Prokofiev. Dostoievsky's world of aspiration and betrayal and martyrdom is *his* world, the manifestation of the internal spiritual universe in which he alone lived. In the presence of such an artistic creation, one has the sense of being led through a self-consistent new planet, born of an inimitable perspective. And so it is with the work of Ayn Rand. One turns the pages of *The Fountainhead* or *Atlas Shrugged,* and one has entered *her* spot in the literary galaxy, formed out of chaos in the image of the world view and the values that were hers alone.

During the years of writing *We the Living,* she had known she was not ready, in philosophical knowledge or literary experience, to attempt a full portrait of her concept of the ideal man. The ideal is only suggested in what Kira sees in Leo, that potential he might have realized had he lived in a free country. *"We the Living,"* she once said, "was only an exercise, it was not fully *my* novel yet. My first *serious* novel had to present my type of man." When *We the Living* was completed, she knew she now could write her "serious" novel, a novel that would present her philosophy and would be written fully in the literary style that had been struggling slowly and painfully into life. She had learned enough about her new country confidently to place the novel's action in America. She was, at the age of thirty, fully an adult, prepared to handle adult characters.

She knew what the theme of her new novel was to be; while still writing *We the Living,* she had worked on it in what she called "small glances"—that is, it was not a systematic activity, but something her mind went to whenever she was momentarily free of other responsibilities.

The theme of *The Fountainhead*—which she identified as "individualism versus collectivism, not in politics, but in man's soul"—had been born on the day that Ayn grasped the distinction between two basic types of human motivation. It had been a day while she still was living in Hollywood, before the sale of *Night of January 16th* to Al Woods had brought her to New York. A young woman who lived in the same apartment house as Ayn and Frank had an important position as an executive assistant at RKO, where Ayn was working in the wardrobe department. Ayn watched the woman's professional struggle with fascination. She was battling, Ayn felt, with a desperate, amoral ferocity, scheming, manipulating and conniving, to advance her career. Ayn would later say "I liked the fact that she took her career very seriously—yet I disliked everything about her and her outlook on her career as against mine." The woman was passionately ambitious; so was Ayn. The woman was enormously hardworking; so was Ayn. Yet Ayn sensed a basic difference in the nature of their ambition—a difference of profound moral and psychological importance.

Seeking a clue to the principle involved, she asked the young woman one day, "What is your goal in life? What is it that you want to achieve?" The young woman answered immediately, as if the answer had long been clear in her mind: "I'll tell you what I want. If nobody had an automobile, then *I* would want to have *one* automobile. If some people have *one,* then *I* want to have *two.*"

Ayn was never to forget her feeling of incredulity, indignation, contempt. Her mind raced with the implications she saw in the young woman's statement; she knew that in a few brief sentences, she had been given the key to answer the question she had wondered about for years, the question about people whose values and actions seemed incomprehensibly irrational: *But how* can *they?* In future years she would say wonderingly, "It was like a light bulb going on. Without that statement, I don't think I could have ever arrived at the explanation. I owe *The Fountainhead* to that." It was typical of Ayn's method of thinking that she searched for a fundamental principle that would make the woman's attitude intelligible, rather than leaving the matter at: "All she cares about is material possessions," or "She wants to feel superior," or "She's a social climber." It was typical of her method of considering intellectual issues that from a brief verbal exchange, she would work her way to a dissection of human motivation.

The woman, Ayn thought, would conventionally be called "selfish." But wasn't a *self*—that which thinks, judges, values, and chooses—precisely what she lacked? *I* want to achieve things that are important—important objectively, in reality, in fact—thought Ayn; *she* wants only to make an impression on others. I choose my own goals, I decided *that* I wanted to write, and *what* I wanted to write; she struggles to imitate the goals chosen by others. I set my own standards; her desires are dictated by the standards of others. *Why?* What is the concept that will name the essence of the difference involved . . . ?

She was led to define two different ways of facing life—two antagonists—two types of man. The man of self-sufficient ego, of firsthand, independent judgment —and the spiritual parasite, the dependent who rejects the responsibility of judging. The man whose convictions, values, and purposes are the product of his own mind—and the parasite who is molded and directed by other men. The man who lives for his own sake—and the collectivist of the spirit, who places others above self. The prime mover, whose source of movement is within his own spirit —and the soulless being who is movement without an internal mover. The creater—and the secondhander. Howard Roark—and Peter Keating.

Her earliest notes for *The Fountainhead* began with the statement: "The first purpose of this book is *a defense of egoism in its real meaning.*"

She was always to say that she had grasped the political implications of her purpose immediately. "The question of what makes a person an individualist or a collectivist *politically,* what is the principle, had interested me. The conversation with that girl gave me not just the key to personal motivation, but to political motivation as well."[1]

In Ayn's notes, one finds an interesting insight into her first thoughts about Roark's characterization: "How he feels is entirely a matter of his own, which cannot be influenced by anything or anyone on the outside. His feeling is a steady, unruffled flame . . . a profound joy of living and of knowing his power, a joy that is not even conscious of being joy, because it is so steady, natural and unchangeable. If outside life brings him disappointment—well, it is merely a detail of the battle. He will have to struggle harder—that's all. . . . He is in conflict with the world in every possible way—and at complete peace with himself."

[1] By chance, Ayn met the woman who had given her the key to *The Fountainhead* after the book was published. She had married, and had given up her career. She had read *The Fountainhead,* and she spoke of how proud she was of Ayn's success. "She was basking in my reflected glory," Ayn said, "and talking of how we had lived in the same apartment house and been struggling young girls together. I was dying to tell her how much she contributed to the book—that she was *Miss* Peter Keating. But I couldn't do it. It would have been pointless cruelty." I agree with Ayn, and that is why the woman's name is not included in this description.

She knew that her hero must represent the creative principle in man, and she chose architecture as Roark's profession. It gave her the opportunity she had always wanted: to glorify the American skyscraper as a symbol of achievement and of life on earth. And because the profession of architecture involves art, science, and business, she could illustrate the creative principle in man's three major types of productive careers.

She had arrived at the concept of Dominique Francon, the heroine, shortly after the conversation with the young woman who was to be Peter Keating in *The Fountainhead*. As she and Frank were driving through Virginia on their way to New York for the production of *Night of January 16th,* she had happened to notice a chain gang of convicts working on a road under construction. A little later, she noticed an old and very beautiful Southern mansion, with graceful white columns and weathered, dark red brick walls, which had the air of a feudal castle. The two images suddenly united in her mind, and she had the essence of the quarry scene in *The Fountainhead:* Dominique, fragile, delicately austere, aristocratic, the chatelaine of the surrounding countryside, walks from her estate to the granite quarry owned by her father—to see Howard Roark, a nameless worker drilling granite under the broiling sun, his face streaked with stone dust, his shirt clinging to his gaunt body, looking up at her with a glance that is an act of ownership. That scene led Ayn to the famous "rape scene," in which Roark, his identity still unknown to Dominique, takes her sexually despite her violent, terrified struggle—a struggle which she wants only to lose.[2]

"Until then," Ayn later said, "I knew about the heroine only that she and Roark were to have a romance, and since this was to be *my* kind of novel and the events were to represent 'what could be and ought to be,' the ideal romance had to start with violent antagonism. It was seeing the convicts and the mansion that gave me the idea for what would be the most romantic first encounter possible in my kind of style. . . . So while we were being towed through Virginia in a broken-down car, my whole mind was on that scene.

"After getting the quarry scene I was stopped for a while by what would be the exact nature of Dominique's conflict with Roark. The problem was that I could not give her a *moral* conflict, but there had to be a conflict that would make her oppose Roark."

Ayn arrived at the essence of the inner conflict that would set Dominique in opposition to Roark, by introspection. "Dominique," she later remarked, "is myself in a bad mood." She projected what she herself felt in moments of disgust or depression, during the worst of her indignation against injustice, her contempt for depravity, her passionate rebellion against the rule of mediocrity—and asked herself: "What if I really believed that that is all there is in life, that values and heroes have no chance in the world?" What if she believed that the "journalistic" facts around her were *metaphysical*—necessary and unalterable by the

---

[2] Many years later, when Ayn was asked during a radio interview why Dominique was raped, she replied, "If it's rape—it's rape by engraved invitation."

nature of reality? Thus she projected the psychology of a woman who is motivated by the bitter conviction that values and greatness have no chance among men and are doomed to destruction—a woman who is stopped and paralyzed by contempt—a woman who withdraws from the world because of the intensity of her idealism—a woman who fights against the man she loves in order to make him renounce his career before his inevitable destruction.

In all of her writing, Ayn was to argue that evil, by its nature, is impotent, that only the good—the rational—can ultimately triumph; in *Atlas Shrugged,* "the impotence of evil" is a significant theme. Evil can destroy, it cannot build, it cannot create. Yet she knew too well the inner state of a Dominique, the revulsion and disgust from which such an attitude stems.

Ayn told close friends—although she never stated it publically—"The other source of Dominique was Frank. I knew that here was someone stopped by enormous contempt for the world and indignation at the world—what I later would have called 'he's on strike.' I felt that that would be Dominique's premise —a withdrawal from the world not out of bad motives or cowardice but out of an unbearable idealism which does not know how to function in journalistic reality as it is. The key to Dominique is that she is myself in a bad mood—and Frank if he were a woman."

Whenever Ayn told this story, her friends wondered, dumbfounded, at her lack of objectivity; some of them felt that she had invented two characters: Dominique—and Frank. Frank was not the spiritual giant that Ayn spoke of; and his motivation was not Dominique's. Frank could become angry—especially when he felt that Ayn had been treated unjustly—he was a very protective man; he could become disgusted with behavior he called "nonsense" and Ayn called "immoral and irrational"; but no one who knew him ever saw moral indignation or contempt in Frank's attitude. When Ayn was furious at a friend or acquaintance, it was Frank who tried to make excuses for actions that Ayn would not excuse, it was Frank who tried to calm Ayn and be the peacemaker, it was Frank who would comfort the often bewildered, emotionally shattered victim. One saw his warmth—the frustrated warmth of a lonely man—especially in his dealings with the animals he loved; he treated the least stray animal with the exquisite gentleness of a parent; a part of Frank always remained the boy who had stolen sick chickens from his neighbors in order to heal them. Bitterness? Contempt? Passion? These were not attributes that had relevance to Frank.

Like Dominique, he had withdrawn from the world; unlike Dominique, he had withdrawn into silence and passivity. Throughout the years he and Ayn spent in New York, from the mid-thirties to the early forties, he rarely worked at a job or in the theater which he loved. Jobs were difficult to obtain during the decade of the Depression, and Frank was not a man who knew how to obtain whatever work was available; he was profoundly helpless in the practical world. But his withdrawal, his noncommunicativeness, his lack of deep attachment to any long-range goal was not the result of frustrated, embittered idealism. The reasons appear to have arisen out of his own character as it formed through a childhood dominated by powerful women—and out of his marriage. His respect and admiration for Ayn were deep and enduring; he knew that he had married an extraordinary woman; he was disarmed by his admiration. And Ayn required, psychologically, that she and her work and her interests be the center of the world for both of them; he did not have the strength to resist the force of her will, he did not resist—and sadly, he *was* becoming, as he had jokingly predicted, "*Mr.* Ayn Rand."

It was Ayn's genius—and in one sense her curse—that she could envision men of the stature of her heroes. In her intellectual and spiritual loneliness, she longed, throughout her life, for such a man: a man who would be her equal, who would see the world as she saw it, and who would represent the challenge she had never found. She told herself—and the world—that Frank was that man. But it seems more than possible that *had* Ayn married a man who in fact *was* like her heroes, the marriage would have shattered to rubble in terrible bursts of rage. Two people equally obsessed by their careers, equally singled-tracked, equally convinced of the validity of their ideas and the rectitude of their positions, equally dominating, could not have lived together with any serenity. One of the tragedies of Ayn's life was her painful, lifelong yearning for what she could never have endured.

The twin sources of Dominique's characterization may well be the reason why, even in the view of many readers who greatly admire Ayn's work, she was to be the most unsatisfactory figure in the novel. Dominique, who loves Roark, was to spend years attempting to destroy his career; it could have been no more intense and carefully structured a vendetta had she hated him. And she was to spend years trying to destroy herself and her own vision of life, that sense of what the world ought to be that was the cause of her torture at what is; she was to do it by leaving Roark and marrying two men she despised: first Peter Keating, then Gail Wynand. She was to be one of the most intriguing and complex of Ayn's characters, but ultimately she lacked the reality of the other characters. Ayn would ask for too great a "willing suspension of disbelief." By forming Dominique from herself "in a bad mood" and from an unrealistic vision of Frank, Ayn was dealing with a level of abstraction different from the level that was the source of her other characters. Roark, Keating, Wynand, and Toohey, the major male protagonists, *are* symbols; they represent four distinct psychologies and ways of dealing with good and evil; but they may also be taken as realistically possible individuals engaged in realistically possible courses of action. Only Dominique stands solely as a symbol—the symbol of idealism frozen by contempt. If one were to meet Dominique in life, one would be appalled by her marriages and by her treatment of the man she adores; one would find it impossible to accept her motivation.

It was late in 1935 when Ayn felt she could begin spending all of her time systematically planning *The Fountainhead*. *Night of January 16th* was running successfully on Broadway, royalties were coming in, and for the first time it seemed possible that she could complete a project of her own choosing without the strain of financial worries and without the need to interrupt her work to earn a living. She and Frank were ensconced in a new apartment, where their continuing arrangement to share household tasks with Nick eased Ayn's responsibilities for marketing and cooking. To Frank's great pleasure, he and Ayn had once more begun attending occasional movies and theatrical performances, rare events in their lives because of their straitened financial circumstances and because of Ayn's work; during the evenings in which she was not working on a project, she preferred to discuss philosophy with friends or to sit quietly listening to her favorite music and thinking about her writing. Still tentatively, still not quite certain that their new means were real, Ayn had begun shopping for furniture—a modern bedroom set in pale wood, a comfortable, overstuffed couch and chairs for the living room—and for the clothes she could never before afford. It was Nick who was Ayn's worldly Petronius. It was from Nick that both Ayn and Frank, oblivious to social conventions, learned how to entertain their guests, what food to serve, what wine or liquor was appropriate. It was Nick who urged Ayn not to wear the too feminine, fluffy clothes she occasionally bought. Mimi Sutton, Frank and Nick's niece, would later recall that on one of her visits to New York, "Ayn proudly purchased a small white 'Dutch' hat with a starched peak and a blue netty veil—it was awful! Frank very gently said that it wasn't right—but Nick said 'Take it off at once. It's ridiculous!' Ayn was a little hurt, she thought it was pretty—but she never wore it again." She began to wear the dramatic flowing capes that became her trademark; for a few years she jauntily carried a slim black cane with a silver head. It was Nick who made her aware that she had pretty legs; with her indifference to her physical person, Ayn had not been aware of it, but she was delighted to be convinced.

One of Ayn's most charming qualities was her attitude toward beautiful women. That *she* was not beautiful, nor even the physical type she admired, was a fact she appeared to accept with characteristic realism; nonetheless it was evidently a painful fact—perhaps more painful than she permitted herself to know. One might speculate that had she looked like Dominique or Dagny—tall and slender and fair—her life would have been vastly different and her relationships with men vastly more satisfying; nor would she have found it necessary to insist—implicitly at first and finally, years later, by explicit statement—that she, as the greatest of hero worshippers, was the standard of feminine worth, and that by their response to her all men were to be judged. Yet despite her dislike of her appearance, she took great pleasure in the beauty of other women; it was an aesthetic delight in which there appeared to be no tinge of envy. When she met an attractive woman, she was disposed in advance to like her—taking the physical beauty as the sign of an inner spiritual loveliness. None of her friends ever reported seeing envy in Ayn toward anyone; she *wanted* to see success and happiness and beauty in others; it buttressed her conviction that it was a "benevolent universe," where joy and accomplishment were possible.

With her decision to devote her time to planning The Fountainhead, Ayn turned from her brief sally into the world of "glamour," of entertaining and of buying clothes—"with an immense feeling of relief," she would later laughingly admit—and lost herself once more in the world where she felt most at home. Because of the considerable success of her play, she had become talked about and known in the literary and theatrical world; there were opportunities for her to meet people who might have helped her career, there were invitations to speak and to appear on radio; she was not interested. The book came first, as her writing was always to come first in her life. Any other value, apart from Frank, was essentially a distraction, emotionally trivial in comparison to her passionate need to work.

The characters of Roark, Keating, and Dominique were clearly set in her mind. Now, she began to devise two other central characters: Gail Wynand, the brilliant newspaper publisher, a man of great stature who makes the destructive error of seeking power over other men, and who tries to attain it by publishing whatever his readers want to hear; and Ellsworth Toohey, architectural critic of the Wynand newspapers and the archvillain of the story, who preaches the nobility of self-sacrifice in order to rob men of their self-esteem, their courage, their virtue, and their honor and to turn them into willing sacrificial victims.

"I thought of the four men this way," Ayn was to say. "If I took the ideal man as the center, in relationship to him I would show three other types. Every character was devised in relation to the main theme. Roark is the man who could be the ideal man—and was; Wynand is a man who could have been—but wasn't; Keating, who wasn't—and didn't know it; Toohey, who wasn't—and knew it. These were not fundamental definitions, but they were the ones most helpful to me; they were the definitions I used for myself as to why I take these as the key figures. I asked myself what would happen to Roark if he surrendered to others—he would be the man of good premises who had given in—and that's how I arrived at Wynand. Then I asked who would be the archopposite and enemy of Roark and Wynand—and I arrived at Toohey. The average man who rides on evil without fully knowing it was Keating; from the beginning he was my idea of the girl in Hollywood."

There was to be considerable speculation over the years that Wynand was modeled after William Randolph Hearst. "Yes and no," Ayn said privately. "One could equally say he was Hearst or Henry Luce or Pulitzer. The common abstraction was: in order to rise from scratch and establish a great newspaper chain or magazine, you have to have some firsthand premises and ability and independence; how can that man dedicate his career to giving the public what it wants to hear? Some people thought Wynand was Hearst because—and I only learned this long after Wynand was clear in my mind—there were particular things about Wynand that resembled Hearst." In *The Fountainhead*, Wynand was to own an important art collection, one of the few things on earth he loved; before meeting Dominique, he had added to his collection an ecstatic nude statue of her. "How did you know about Hearst's statue?" Ayn was asked by a man who was acquainted with Hearst. "What statue?" Ayn replied. She was told that Hearst had a statue of a nude woman which was one of his prized art treasures.

"One thing *was* influential to me about Hearst," Ayn explained. "He was enormously ambitious politically; at the height of his success, he had tried to run for office and had been badly beaten. What impressed me was that when he tried to use all that influence for an ideological issue and to have people follow his ideas, he couldn't do it. That was a lead to Wynand's character: if a man goes after power by appealing to mob taste, he has the least power of anyone."

There were more direct sources for Ayn's characterization of Ellsworth Toohey. One day, Ayn's attorney and friend Pincus Berner and his wife invited the O'Connors to attend a lecture at The New School for Social Research. The speaker was to be Harold Laski, the British Socialist who was influential in the development of the British Labour Party. Ayn had only a vague knowledge of who Laski was. "Isn't he a socialist?" she asked. Yes, the Berners replied, but he was charming and witty, a wonderful speaker, and to hear him would be a cultural treat. Ayn was and continued to be emphatic in her disapproval of giving any form of sanction to "evil"—she maintained in later years that one should not attend such events as the Bolshoi Ballet, that to do so was to morally sanction and financially contribute to the Soviet Union; she felt "somewhat guilty" about going to Laski's lecture; but since the Berners had already purchased the tickets, she told herself "It's on their conscience," and agreed to join them. Several months later, when Laski returned for another lecture, Ayn and Frank eagerly purchased tickets; in this instance, she felt fully justified: Laski and his intellectual brothers would be infinitely more damaged by her use of them in *The Fountainhead* than they would be helped by a two-dollar admission payment.

"When I saw Laski, I knew I was seeing the soul of Ellsworth Toohey in the flesh," she was to recall. "Thereafter, I just had to remember how Laski lectured —his mannerisms, the pseudo-intellectual snideness, the whole manner of speaking on important subjects with inappropriate sarcasm as his only weapon, acting as though he were a charming scholar in a drawing room, but you could sense the bared teeth behind the smile, you could feel something evil—and I would know how Toohey would act in any circumstance; it gave me the complete sense of life of that type. Toohey is larger scale than Laski, who was a cheap little snide collectivist, but Laski projected Toohey's essential characteristics. Even his appearance was ideal. I drew a sketch during the lecture, with the narrow cadaverous face and glasses and big ears, and I gave all of it to Toohey."

There were other spiritual sources for Toohey. One was Heywood Broun, who wrote a column entitled "It Seems to Me" for several New York newspapers. "He would lecture the world on everything, always collectivist. He made one especially horrifying statement: that a man cannot form his own philosophy of life, but has to, in effect, find it ready made. He was a busybody, like Toohey, butting into every possible intellectual issue." Another was Lewis Mumford, architectural critic for *The New Republic.* "He was the only writer on architec-

ture who went into social-political issues, as Toohey did, and he was a collectivist of a medieval kind, he defended medieval cities and the medieval way of life
against the modern machine age." The final source was Clifton Fadiman, book
editor of *The New Yorker*. "He was the archliterateur of the left, an elegant
literary type, very intellectual, who made constant references in his articles to
the history of literature of the seventeenth century, and general name-dropping
literary phoniness. That intellectual superciliousness combined with leftism was
just right for Toohey." (Many years later, after *Atlas Shrugged* was published,
Ayn met Clifton Fadiman—and discovered that she rather liked him, and that
he appeared to admire *Atlas Shrugged*. "I lifted him a few rungs in hell," she
said.)

"I had had Toohey in mind before," Ayn said, "but it was like an abstract
drawing, and these four helped me to fill in the details."

With the four major protagonists now devised, her next step was to do the
necessary architectural research. She had never been interested in architecture,
and knew nothing about it except that she liked modern and Gothic buildings,
and disliked classical and eclectic architecture. She went to the New York Public
Library and asked for a reading list of books that would acquaint her with the
history, the aesthetics, and the profession of architecture. Within a few days, she
was given an excellent list, and began her reading. "One of the first thrilling
things was that Frank bought me a very expensive book—it was on sale but it
was still a luxury—it was a good history of modern architecture and its problems, with illustrations." She also read a number of architectural magazines, to
get the sense of how professionals discussed their problems, and what were the
specific, immediate problems that arose for them.

A biography of Frank Lloyd Wright, about whom she knew only that he was
famous in the field, was among the recommended books. After publication,
many of her readers would assume that Roark was patterned after Wright. She
would respond: "The only resemblance between Howard Roark and Frank
Lloyd Wright is in their basic architectural principles and in the fact that Wright
was an innovator fighting for modern architecture against tradition. There is no
similarity in their respective characters, nor in their philosophical convictions,
nor in the events of their lives."

While working on the architectural research for *The Fountainhead*, Ayn was
simultaneously struggling with the plot. Devising the concrete events of the
story, presenting the theme in terms of action, "was the hardest assignment I
have ever had," she later said. The difficulty was inherent in the assignment: she
had to devise a tightly integrated, unified progression of events that would cover
Roark's entire career. In her early notes, she described her assignment as follows: "The story is the story of Howard Roark's triumph. . . . It has to show
every conceivable hardship and obstacle on his way—and how he triumphs over
them, why he *has to* triumph. These obstacles, of course, can come from only
one source: other men. It is *Society*, with all its boggled chaos of selflessness,
compromise, servility, and lies, that stands in the way of Howard Roark. As he

goes on, it is every conceivable form of 'second-hand living' that comes to fight him, that tries to crush him in every possible manner . . . and fails in the attempt. To every second-hand creature he stands as a contrast, a reproach and a lesson."

Ayn had set herself a unique literary and philosophical goal. Historically, the originators of moral philosophies presented their theories in the form of treatises, as non-fiction. The writers of fiction who *dramatized* moral concepts were not philosophical originators; writers of the Romantic school, such as Hugo, Schiller, Dostoievsky, Rostand, took as their base the moral code of the culture of their time, which the majority of their readers accepted. But as Ayn was to say throughout her life, she was interested in philosophical principles only as they affected the actual existence of men; and in men only as they reflected philosophical principles. "An abstract theory that has no relation to reality is worse than nonsense; and men who act without relation to principles are less than animals. Those who say that theory and practice are two unrelated realms are fools in one and scoundrels in the other. I wanted to present my abstract theory where it belongs—in concrete reality—in the actions of men." Like the philosophers, Ayn intended to present a *new* moral theory. Like the fiction writers, she intended to *dramatize* it in a novel. She had rejected the common context, the conventional view of morality, in favor of an unprecedented concept of good and evil, a new definition of egoism, a radical view of man—and intended to present it not in the form of a treatise, but concretized and illustrated in human action, in the character of Howard Roark, in the events of a story. It was an assignment of stunning intellectual audacity.

She once said, "If all philosophers were required to present their ideas in novels, to dramatize the exact meaning and consequences of their philosophies in human life, there would be far fewer philosophers—and far better ones."

Working out the plot of *The Fountainhead* involved a long process of experimentation, of trying and dropping various possibilities. She reread *Les Miserables,* and wrote an outline of its structure in order to understand how Hugo had created a unified story that spanned the lifetime of his major character. "That helped bring some sort of order into what was an immense vacuum; but I still had no specific event or conflict to hang the story on, only the abstract conflict of the characters and their professions. . . . I devised certain events very slowly, by pure conscious calculation: what would be the key points of Roark's career, how would he start, what would be the early difficulties, how would he become famous. I wanted to show how, even when he succeeded to some extent, the combined evil of the villains could throw him down. . . . I had a lot of trouble with Dominique: in one version, she was to be Wynand's wife from the beginning, and Roark wouldn't meet her until Part IV; Vesta Dunning was to be the romantic interest in the first part of the story."

The character of Vesta Dunning, included in Ayn's early thinking about the novel—it was to appear in the first typed version—was removed before publication. Vesta was to be a young and idealistic actress who falls in love with Roark;

they have a love affair, although he knows she is not his final or lasting romantic choice. The reader was to see her gradual spiritual decay as she began to debase her great talent in order to win public acceptance. Years after the end of their relationship, she would meet Roark again; she had become a world-famous actress—and a mediocrity.[3]

Ayn's major plot difficulty was that she could not, for a long period of time, devise the book's climax, and any other events she projected could only be tentative until she had done so. "That was the real mind-breaker. I wanted an event for the climax connected with architecture, that would put Roark in great danger and antagonize the whole of society, and that would involve all the major characters. It was such a torturous process, I couldn't know when I could even start writing. I felt almost like a fake talking about my novel, since nothing was set and I didn't even know the central part of it. . . . I was really against the idea of a novel that takes eighteen years of time, but the theme required it."

By the summer of 1937—a year and a half after making her first notes on *The Fountainhead*—Ayn still had no idea for the central integrating climax. Frank was working in summer stock in Stony Creek, Connecticut, playing Guts Regan in *Night of January 16th* and doing small parts in other productions, and Ayn joined him for the summer. "I spent the whole time walking around in the country working on the plot, and going crazy. I would sit on a raft on Long Island Sound and think about it, then I'd walk through the woods, tearing my hair in despair—but every day I started again. By late in the summer, I still had no ending."

Exhausted from her fruitless struggle to devise the novel's climax, and desperately needing to write rather than to spend all of her time vainly *planning* to write, Ayn took off the last weeks of the summer to write *Anthem,* a novelette she had conceived while still in Russia. "I wrote it as a rest from plotting," she was to say.

Anthem (originally entitled *Ego*) is the most lyrical of any of her work, the most abstract and stylized in its literary method. It has the beauty and cadence of a prose poem—and, as always in Ayn's writing, the action is integrated with the philosophical theme. The story is laid in a world of the future, a totally collectivized world in which even the word "I" has long been forgotten; an individual refers to himself as "we," and to another individual as "they." The achievements of the past—industrial, artistic, and scientific—have vanished from men's world and from their memories. Until one man arises with the passionate, single-minded determination to pursue knowledge. Working alone, at night, in secret, he rediscovers the electric light—and is forced to flee when the

---

[3] Some excerpts from the Vesta Dunning story were published in *The Early Ayn Rand.* They show an aspect of Roark which does not appear in the published novel: a steely indifference to a woman with whom he is sexually involved, an unjust intolerance of her failure fully to see the world as he does, a bewildering severity in his treatment of her. Presumably, these sections would have been substantially edited before publication; but as they stand, Ayn did the book, and the character of Roark, a service by removing them.

rulers order the destruction of his light. In an uncharted forest, with the woman who loves him and follows him into the wilderness, he discovers the word—and the meaning of—"I," and plans to establish a new society. "I shall call to me all the men and the women whose spirit has not been killed within them and who suffer under the yoke of their brothers. . . . And here, in this uncharted wilderness, I and they, my chosen friends, my fellow-builders, shall write the first chapter in the new history of man."

Anthem is illustrative of an important distinction between Ayn and other writers who have described collectivist societies laid in the future. The idea of projecting such a society was not new: it was part of the literary intellectual ferment of the twenties in Russia. Yevgeny Zamyatin wrote his novel *We* in 1920–21; it could not be published in Soviet Russia but was read to writers' groups and widely discussed throughout Petrograd. In *We*, as in the world of *Anthem*, men's names have been replaced by numbers in a totalitarian world where the human spirit is crushed. But unlike the world of *Anthem*, the enemy of freedom in *We* is the rule of reason, which flourishes in the form of superb technological achievements. Like the anti-utopian novels to follow—most notably George Orwell's *1984*—Zamyatin projected his society as brilliantly mechanized and industrialized, on the implicit premise that slaves will continue to think, to work, to achieve.

Ayn believed that slavery is *not* practical. In her society of brute force the achievements possible only to free minds have ceased to exist. This was an issue that was to form the theme of *Atlas Shrugged*, where she would show the inevitable destruction of industrial civilization in a world where human intelligence no longer functions.

Ann Watkins, Ayn's agent, could find no buyer for *Anthem* in the American magazine market, where Ayn wanted to publish it, or in the book publishing market. "The author does not understand socialism," was one editor's comment. A year later, it was sold to the English publisher of *We the Living*, Cassell, but continued to be rejected by American publishers.[4]

When Ayn and Frank returned to New York from Stony Creek, Ayn decided to spend a few months working in an architect's office, without pay, in order to become familiar with the day-by-day activities of the profession. Through a friend, she met the famous New York architect Ely Jacques Kahn and he agreed to her plan. Ayn's friends were aware that her social shyness had made it difficult for her to approach a stranger and request a favor; but they also knew that when her work was involved, she allowed nothing to interfere. Ayn spent six months working in Kahn's office as a filing clerk, typist, and general assistant.

[4] In 1946, Pamphleteers, Inc., a small politically conservative house, put out an edition of five thousand paperback copies. Caxton Press took it over from Pamphleteers, and in 1961 New American Library issued a paperback edition, which has had a continuing sale to the present. Like all of Ayn's fiction, *Anthem* has become a classic, rediscovered by each new generation, not through major advertising campaigns but through readers who discover it, love it, and recommend it.

He was the only one in the office who knew that her real purpose was research for a novel, and he seemed charmed by the adventure of having her there.

After leaving his employ, Ayn did not see Kahn again until *The Fountainhead* was in galleys, when she asked him to check it for any architectural inaccuracies. "He found none, except that I used the term 'silver granite' in the quarry scene and he said it should be 'gray granite'—and another of that kind. I was tremendously pleased—I was really delighted. Kahn was very complimentary about the book, and pleased by its glorification of his profession, but I could sense that the philosophy frightened him to pieces. I asked if he wanted an acknowledgment for his assistance, and he said no, it was not professionally appropriate, but that he would like me to give a general acknowledgment to the profession because they get so little recognition. And that's why I put the note in the front of the book, I felt I had to." The note reads: "I offer my profound gratitude to the great profession of architecture and its heroes who have given us some of the highest expressions of man's genius, yet have remained unknown, undiscovered by the majority of men." In post-publication interviews about *The Fountainhead,* Ayn, at Kahn's request, kept his name confidential. "I knew he was afraid of the book and thought it might be embarrassing. By the time it was a bestseller and the movie rights were sold, he kept announcing that I had worked there, and when I saw him again he said it was fine to mention his name. He was so open about it that I couldn't resent it."

It was while working for Kahn that Ayn solved the problem of devising a climax for her novel. One day, she asked Kahn "What is the biggest technical problem in architecture at the moment?" He told her it was in the field of housing projects, and that the difficulty lay in finding a means of building modern structures at the lowest possible cost. Many architects had tried to solve the problem but had done badly: in one project, he said, the architects had left off the closet doors for the sake of economy. "When he said 'housing,'" Ayn would later say, "something clicked for me. I thought that this was both a political issue and an architectural issue, and that it fitted my purposes. I knew that it was a good lead . . . but I didn't yet know what to do with it."

Ayn went to lunch at a nearby Schrafft's that day. She sat with an uneaten sandwich, thinking of the problem of housing. "Suddenly—like Newton's apple—the total of the climax fell into place. I saw how it would unite Roark, Keating, Wynand, Toohey, and Dominique, and how it would fit my theme. I saw how it would involve all the chief characters in an action way, and bring all the chief conflicts and problems into focus. From then on, it was easy."

Ayn's idea for the climax of *The Fountainhead* was that Howard Roark would dynamite Cortlandt Homes, the housing project he had created.

Excited by the possibilities, she immediately began to work out the details, partly in her racing mind and partly on paper. Peter Keating would see an opportunity to rise from the debris of his failing career by designing Cortlandt Homes, a gigantic government housing project to be built on the shore of the East River and to serve as a model for the whole world. But he knows he cannot design it. He asks Roark to do it for him, and to allow him to present it as his own work.

Roark agrees. He has spent years working on the problem of low-cost housing, he has solved its problems—and he knows he will never be given a chance to build it: he will never be hired by any group, board, council, or committee, public or private.

Roark attaches one condition to his agreement. Cortlandt is to be built exactly as Roark designs it; that is his purpose, his goal and his reward: his own work, done his own way.

Keating agrees. Roark designs Cortlandt. The building of Cortlandt begins—and Keating fights, the first fight of his life, to save it "from so many people involved, each with authority, each wanting to exercise it in some way or another." He fails to save it. Roark's structural and engineering plans, without which the project would not have been possible, are retained, but the finished building has only "the skeleton of what Roark had designed, with the remnants of ten different breeds piled on the lovely symmetry of the bones." With a charge of dynamite, Roark destroys the butchered body of his creation.

The climax of *The Fountainhead,* worked out over a sandwich in Schrafft's, is an archetypical illustration of Ayn's powers as a plot writer. It involves each of the novel's leading characters intimately and brings each of them to his final victory or defeat. Simultaneously, it dramatizes Ayn's philosophical theme: the rights of the individual versus the claims of the collective. It dramatizes the crucial role of the creator, the thinker, the initiator in making human survival possible, and the manner in which the morality of altruism victimizes him.

Through the working out of the climax, Peter Keating would be brought to professional disaster and to the realization of his self-created mediocrity. Gail Wynand would attempt to use his newspapers to defend Roark, to fight for the first time for a cause in which he believed—then see the public rising against him and learn that it was not he who had directed public opinion, but public opinion that had controlled and directed him. With the closing of Wynand's newspaper, the channel for his destructive philosophy, Toohey would discover that he must begin his struggle for power all over again; his years of scheming and plotting had led him only to defeat. And Dominique would witness what she had most feared: the man she loved in the greatest danger he had ever faced; but this time, she would not be afraid for him; this time, she would know that he was right, that he would not be destroyed by a malevolent world—and she finds her way back to him after painful years of separation.

Almost from the moment that Ayn conceived the climax, she decided that a trial had to follow the dynamiting: the trial would be the occasion for a statement to the jury by Roark that would summarize the philosophy which the events of the novel—and of Roark's life—had illustrated: that progress and achievement come only from the independent mind; that altruism is the second-handers' weapon for enslaving the creator; that man is not a sacrificial animal, but has the right to exist for his own sake. It did not require a separate act of thought for her to conclude that Roark would be acquitted: his acquittal would serve as the final confirmation of her conviction that the moral is the practical.

In 1938, almost four years after Ayn had conceived the original idea for *The Fountainhead,* she completed the plot structure and began the writing of the novel.

With the words that open the story: "Howard Roark laughed"—the ideal man was born.

Chapter Thirteen

As she began writing *The Fountainhead,* Ayn hoped—and expected—that the work would move quickly. It did not. It moved with painful slowness. The plot was clear in her mind, and the specific events, and the characters, and the philosophical ideas; but as before with *We the Living,* Ayn's literary difficulties were stylistic. Now it was the cadence and the beat, the expression of emotions and the narrative, that forced her to keep rewriting again and again. Frank often heard her reading paragraphs aloud to herself, time after time, to ensure that the rhythm was precisely as she wanted it. She would spend hours and days on a single paragraph, struggling to capture exactly the emotional quality she intended. She went over each page of her work as if with a powerful microscope, never abandoning a word or a sentence at the approximate, working far into many nights until she was fully satisfied. In *Atlas Shrugged,* when Richard Halley, the composer, denounces those who claim that art represents the spontaneous outpouring of the artist's blind feelings, and tells Dagny Taggart: "I, who know what discipline, what effort, what tension of mind, what unrelenting strain upon one's power of clarity are needed to produce a work of art—I, who know that it requires a labor which makes a chain gang look like rest and a severity no army-drilling sadist could impose . . ." he speaks for the author of *The Fountainhead.*

Ayn had thought that her carefully hoarded royalties from *Night of January 16th* would guarantee that she would be able to write her novel without interruption and without financial worries. But as the weeks and then the months went by and she was still struggling with the first chapters, rewriting them constantly, she began once more to feel driven by the sense of a race against time and a dwindling bank account that had haunted her for so long. Frank was not working, and the occasional screenwriting job Ayn had tried to obtain was closed to

her "because she talks too much about Soviet Russia." She wondered anxiously
if her money would last long enough and what she would do if it did not last.

Despite the passionate romanticism of Ayn's nature, there was a firm and
unyielding realism in her; she had always uncomplainingly believed that her life
and her future were in her own hands, that there was no one who could or
should remove that responsibility from her. In her later comments on this period, she neither expressed nor projected any resentment at Frank's failure to
contribute to their expenses, although it is difficult to imagine that she did not
feel it, at least at times. She communicated implicitly that she saw their financial
support as wholly her responsibility, and she appeared never to question it. But
perhaps, somewhere inside her, she did question it, for as the years were passing
her love for Frank seemed to remain as powerful as ever but their unspoken
emotional rapport, their friends observed, was diminishing. For the first time,
there were occasional flashes of temper between them, and progressively, in the
rare social time she allowed herself, Ayn chose to be in the company of friends
rather than alone with Frank. Mimi Sutton, who spent her summer vacations
with the O'Connors in New York and observed them with an intimacy not
available to their other friends during this period, thought at times that the glue
holding their marriage together was Nick. Nick's gaiety and spirited conversation livened the silent hours Ayn and Frank would have spent together, as they
had less and less to say to each other; when they quarreled, Nick made peace
between them; when Ayn seemed lonely, he was her companion, as he was
Frank's companion in *his* loneliness.

It was at this time, when her nerves were on edge from the slowness of her
work and the beginning of new worries about money, that Ayn began contemplating the first of the series of interruptions that were to plague the writing of
The Fountainhead. Ann Watkins approached her to suggest that, since no publisher had been found for *Ideal* in its novelette form, Ayn ought to rewrite it as a
play. The timing was appropriate: Ayn had earned a reputation as the writer of a
successful and controversial Broadway play—a play becoming equally successful
on its road company tours—and it seemed likely that a new play would be
eagerly sought after in the theatrical world.

Ayn did not want to do it. She dreaded taking time away from *The Fountainhead,* but a new play, if successful, would bring new royalties, enabling her to
finish the novel even at its present slow pace, and would establish her reputation
more securely.

Ayn had never been fully satisfied with *Ideal* as a novelette; however, she told
her agent, she was not convinced that it was appropriate play material because
of its episodic structure. But Ann Watkins continued to urge her, and finally,
unhappily but believing it was a reasonable and practical step to take, Ayn tore
herself from her work on *The Fountainhead* and began to turn *Ideal* into a play.

This was an ability she had always had, and would retain: the ability to cope
with more than one writing project at a time. It was painful to do, and it
remained painful, but she had schooled herself to switch literary assignments

when she was a junior screenwriter for DeMille and wrote short stories in her free time; and she had rigorously schooled herself never to hope that financial problems would somehow dissolve unaided.

She was delighted to discover that the adaptation of *Ideal* proceeded rapidly, and was soon completed. Ann Watkins began submitting *Ideal* to theatrical producers; she reported that there was active interest. But the interest soon began to fade and rejections began coming in—until the prestigious Theater Guild told Ann Watkins that they were considering making an offer. The Guild held the play for several months, while Ayn nervously waited and wondered. At last, Ann Watkins called to say that Theresa Helburn of the Guild wanted to talk to Ayn. During their interview, Theresa Helburn praised the play—"She seemed to like it a great deal, and to understand it," Ayn would later say. She said she wanted to do it but was concerned that it was highly experimental and that its episodic nature, requiring many sets and many actors, made it very expensive to produce. After still more weeks of consideration and conversation, the Guild regretfully decided against production. Ann Watkins could find no other producer.[1]

Ayn was "almost relieved" that *Ideal* was not produced; once more she was free to devote herself to *The Fountainhead*. But as she turned back to the novel, it was with an intensified concern about money. It had been a year since she had begun writing, and she was still struggling with the early chapters. Unable to work with a clear mind, knowing that now there was little likelihood that her bank account would last to the end, she soon again painfully faced the need to interupt the novel and attempt to earn money.

She had had an idea for a play, "a philosophical murder mystery," which she believed had much greater commercial possibilities than *Ideal.* She began to write *Think Twice*. "I did it strictly for commercial purposes," she was to say, "and it was one of the most pleasurable writing jobs I ever did. I had thought out the plot between other activities, and I wrote it in three weeks. It's a much better play than *January 16th. . . .* We had a gray Persian cat named Turtle Cat, whose food was very expensive; she'd eat only raw hamburger. I would economize on my food and Frank's, but not on hers. I told Frank that the play would be dedicated to Turtle Cat, 'who costs fifteen cents a day and sometimes a quarter.' "

Think Twice is an ingenious thriller, in the tradition of *Night of January 16th* and *Atlas Shrugged* rather than *Ideal* or *Anthem*—that is, the stress is on intricate and complex action and the emotional power is between the lines, the cumulative effect of the action. It is a union of mystery and philosophy, and thus a precursor of *Atlas Shrugged,* where the reader's attention is held by a series of

---

[1] When Ayn later returned to Hollywood and became established in the film industry, studio representatives approached her from time to time, asking to see the play for possible movie adaptation; every few years, Ayn rewrote it, making improvements in a work that never fully pleased her. In the end, *Ideal* remained unproduced and unpublished until 1984, when the play version appeared posthumously in *The Early Ayn Rand.*

grippingly unexplained events at the same time that he is learning a radical new philosophy. In *Think Twice,* in the simplified form of a play, one sees in clear relief Ayn's greatest literary strength: the ability to make exciting events carry a profound philosophical message, to tie plot and abstract ideas into a single integrated unit.

Like *Night of January 16th,* with its device of choosing the jury from the audience, *Think Twice* has what Ayn loved to call "a gimmick." Its hero, young scientist Steve Ingalls, commits a morally justified murder—commits it stupidly, clumsily, leaving behind a trail of clues which unequivocally point to his guilt. The district attorney, knowing the quality of Steve's mind, concludes that Steve is being deliberately framed—just as Steve had wanted him to conclude. In a dramatic flashback, we observe Steve talking to his intended victim just before the murder. "I will have no alibi of any kind," he says. "It will be the sloppiest and most obvious murder ever committed. And that is why it will be the perfect crime."

To Ayn's great disappointment, *Think Twice* could not be sold.[2] She had taken more time from *The Fountainhead,* and now she had less money than before.

It was then that she received an excited telephone call from Ann Watkins. Eugenie Leontovich had read *We the Living,* had heard there was an unproduced play version of it, and wanted to do the role of Kira. Ayn *had* written a play version, entitled *The Unconquered,* shortly after publication of the novel when Broadway producer Jerome Mayer had expressed interest in it; Mayer had been unable to arrange a production, and Ayn had not attempted to do anything further with the play. As a result of Leontovich's interest, Ann Watkins told Ayn, the famous producer George Abbott was now interested in producing it. Ayn had serious misgivings about the project because of Leontovich's age—she was in her forties and would be playing a young girl—and because Abbott's reputation had been made predominantly in the field of comedy. But she knew she had no choice but to agree.

"And it was a disaster," she said many years later. "Abbott was pleasant, honorable, a well-educated gentleman, but intellectually he was a farce man, capable of nothing more. He had an inferiority complex about the intellect which he had given up but could have had. He often spoke wistfully of Maxwell Anderson, with whom he went to college, and he would say 'Somehow he became a serious playwright, and that's what I always wanted to be.' And you know what a phony Maxwell Anderson is! . . . William Saroyan's first play had opened, and Abbott said 'I couldn't understand it, that's why I knew it was deep.' I used that line for a villain in *The Fountainhead.*

"Abbott was totally inept about drama. He was a realist, unstylized, and he wanted 'the folks next door.' He disliked the directness and brevity of my dialogue, and if a line was simple, he wanted me to complicate it and use ten words instead of three. He'd say 'All right, if you want it to be arty'—when the 'arti-

---

[2] Like *Ideal, Think Twice* was published posthumously in *The Early Ayn Rand.*

ness' consisted of simplicity, economy, and purposefulness. He wanted it to be the sloppy way people really talk."

Learning from her bitter experience with *Night of January 16th,* Ayn had refused to sell *The Unconquered* unless she were given script control. "I like to permit changes if they're not too awful, I didn't want to be arbitrary—especially since he had to direct it—but this was a succession of flat no's, one after another. It was terrible to deal with, particularly on *We the Living,* which was more important and which I took much more seriously than *January 16th.*

"There were endless rewrites, Abbott sacrificed everything for comedy, and the direction was miserable. Eugenie Leontovich was terrible, no one could do anything with her; she played in the old Moscow Art Theater hammy way and wouldn't take direction. The road reviews were miserable, and Abbott told me that if we went to New York, we had to get rid of Leontovich; I agreed fully. He asked if I would tell her, and say the decision was mine, since they were old friends; and besides, I had the okay on cast. It was cowardice on his part, but I agreed to do it—and it was done."

The play was recast for the New York opening. Abbott chose for the part of Kira a young actress named Helen Craig, whom Ayn considered "not the type, but a rather good actress." At Ayn's insistence, Dean Jagger played Andrei; "his performance was the best in New York," Ayn said. John Emory played Leo. Ayn liked Emory personally, and they soon became friends. Frank had a small part as a GPU man, and understudied Emory. "Frank was much better than Emory, who was sort of a ham, but we had to have names."

The young actor John Davis Lodge was hired for the part of Andrei in New York. "He was a terrible actor," Ayn recalled; "he couldn't deliver Andrei's speech. Abbott labored with him but could do nothing. We knew we had to let him go. But this time, Abbott fired him. When I got home from rehearsal the day Lodge was fired, Frank and Nick were there, and Mrs. Francesca Lodge, whom I had never met. She was furious and practically hysterical, demanding to know why I had fired her husband—if it were on the stage, I'd be sure she'd pull a gun. She asked if I was against her husband, and I said, yes, I was, I didn't hide behind Abbott, and I very calmly explained what he did wrong and why he couldn't do the part. She finally left, not happy but no longer angry, just resigned. Nick complimented me enormously on how I handled it, but all I did was be rational. . . . When John Lodge became governor of Connecticut, I thought I'd better not go there."

Ayn's experience with *The Unconquered* was a nightmarish repeat of *Night of January 16th.* "Even the script was bad," she felt. "It was a compromise between ten different versions. The sets were expensive but totally wrong for the play. Abbott had really done his best, which made it even worse; I could not accuse him like Woods." Ayn did not drink—she disliked both the taste and the effect—and was in later years to be vehement in her disapproval of the drug culture. How could anyone be irrational enough to tamper with his *mind?*—she would demand. The vigorous clarity and precision of her mind was the most precious of her possessions; to interfere with its functioning would have been to her a mortal sin. But Ayn got drunk, for the first and last time in her life, just before the dress rehearsal of *The Unconquered.* "I knew it was going to be a disaster, and I could not stand the idea of seeing it one more time. Frank was at the theater, and I was with Nick at home. I took a glass and a half of straight gin—it tasted horrible—but I gulped it down. When we arrived at the theater, I was marching down the aisle weaving from side to side and trying to control it—but it worked, it cut off any emotional reaction, and I could watch the rehearsal feeling nothing." After the rehearsal, Frank, seeing the state she was in, was furious with Nick for allowing Ayn to drink. Upset by the ordeal of the play, and even more upset by Frank's anger, Ayn burst into tears.

Mimi Sutton was again visiting Ayn and Frank in New York during this hectic summer, and the twenty-year-old girl felt as if she had been dropped into the center of a hurricane of emotion. She loved her aunt and uncle, and was painfully moved by Ayn's misery. Mimi had first met Ayn several years earlier, an experience she never forgot and still talked of almost forty years later. The thirteen-year-old girl had dutifully kissed her new aunt on the cheek. "Ayn was polite," Mimi recalled, "and inquired about me, but she was a little remote. After a few minutes, she said, 'Tell me, Mimi, are you afraid of me?' I *was* a little in awe, but I said, rather defiantly, 'Why should I be?' That got us off on the right foot."

It is true that the small, dark woman with the huge dark eyes, who was stiffly polite and shy at a first meeting, always seemed to inspire immediate awe, and not merely in children. It is also true that Mimi's answer *would* have "got us off on the right foot." All her life, Ayn sensed that people were intimidated by her; she would at rare intervals refer to it as a source of considerable pain, further alienating her from those around her. To say "how do you do?"—and to see a flicker of fear in the eyes of the person one is greeting—fear that appeared not to be predominantly the result of Ayn's professional or personal reputation, nor even of her "thus spake Ayn Rand" manner, but of her directness, her intensity, and her perceptiveness—was a singularly unhappy relationship to have with other people. That a little blond, blue-eyed child stood up to her bravely, would indeed have been a rare source of pleasure for Ayn. It was soon after that meeting that Ayn and Frank invited Mimi to spend her summer vacations with them. They treated Mimi with warmth and affection throughout their lives.

There had been another meeting with Ayn that Mimi was never to forget. She was sixteen when Dennis, Frank's father, had died and Ayn and Frank had traveled to Lorain for the funeral. Ayn was there, she told Mimi, because she wanted to see where Frank had been born and brought up—and because she was curious to view the body, to see if Frank resembled his father. "We escaped the wake," Mimi would recall, "and went back to her hotel room. I was telling her about my latest crush, on a boy named Peter, and she said that that was the name of a terrible person in the novel she was writing. We took off our shoes and lay on twin beds, and she told me the entire story of *The Fountainhead;* it wasn't written, but it was all planned. She made me feel as if the people were real, and the story was real, and I was living through it all. She wanted to get a kid's reaction. I was *fascinated.* She even told me about the rape scene!"

It was at the funeral, Mimi recalled, that most of the O'Connor family met Ayn for the first time. They found her aloof and difficult. They felt that Frank had abandoned the family after his marriage, rarely contacting them or showing concern for them, and they blamed Ayn for the loss of the brother to whom they had once been close.

Ayn was *not* interested in Frank's family, a fact which she did not hide from Frank. It is unlikely that she questioned him about *his* feelings for them; through all their lives together, she seemed always to take it as self-evident that her feelings must also be his. But had Frank spoken of his love for his family, it is equally likely that, out of her love for him, Ayn would have agreed to see them and would have been cordial and friendly; no one who knew Ayn and Frank ever saw her refuse him a firmly expressed wish. But the time had long passed when Frank spoke openly about his feelings or desires; as the world outside came to hold less and less for him, his retreat into isolation and passivity was beginning to accelerate.

During what Mimi often referred to as "that incredible summer of *The Unconquered,*" it was evident that this entire period—the worries about money, the constant interruptions of *The Fountainhead,* the failure to sell *Ideal* and *Think Twice,* the knowledge that *The Unconquered* was heading for disaster—was agony for Ayn. The one thing she wanted was to work on the novel she had been waiting all her life to write, and it was the one thing she could not do.

And it was agony for Frank. Not only because of his concern for Ayn, but because he was unable to help, as he was to admit in later years; he was unable to find work that would support himself, much less his wife. And because, as some of their friends observed, Ayn, in her pain, resorted to the only means she knew to deal with it emotionally: sudden rages over trifles—sometimes bewilderingly directed at Frank—to which he listened silently and helplessly; frightening periods of paralyzed, mute depression; all of which must have profoundly increased Frank's already intense sense of failure as a husband and removed from him his sole armor against an unintelligible world: the strength and certainty of Ayn Rand.

"Frank and I would go places together and talk that summer," Mimi recalled. "He seemed to talk more freely when Ayn wasn't with us. . . . He'd often say how proud he was of Ayn. Once, he told me that he'd like to have had a child, but it wouldn't have fitted into Ayn's life. He sometimes seemed upset over Ayn's breaks with people."

In this last statement, Mimi was noting a phenomenon that no one who knew Ayn well failed to observe: a series of angry ruptures with people who had been her friends, accompanied by condemnations of them for irrationality or moral treason. Ayn often was warm and generous with her friends, generous with her concern, her time and her attention. But when, in her view, a line had been crossed, when she saw an action as unjust to her, or as intellectually dishonest, or as morally wrong, she became an avenging angel and the relationship ended in a burst of rage. It was a pattern of behavior that was to escalate disastrously through the years that followed. "She was close for a while with Eugenie Leontovich," Mimi recalled, "and I used to hear Ayn's long telephone conversations with her, half in English and half in Russian. Then Ayn got furious with her one day; God help you if you were on the other end of that conversation! They never saw each other again. . . . There were other good friends, and then something happened, and they'd just disappear. Frank would try to say: 'Well, we differed on some things and we don't see them anymore'; he'd try to smooth things over."

Fascinated and thrilled, Mimi attended some of the rehearsals for *The Unconquered*. "I got to meet the cast, and George Abbott, and S. N. Behrman, who wrote *No Time for Comedy*—he'd been called in as play doctor because things were going badly." At the rehearsals, Mimi observed a characteristic in Ayn which other friends would later comment upon. Dean Jagger, an attractive and gallant man, was warmly attentive to Ayn during the rehearsals. Ayn was unused to masculine attention that was not of an exclusively intellectual nature; men were intimidated by her, and she knew—this woman who wrote with such passion about exalted romantic and sexual relationships, who would have flourished under masculine attention, who would have loved to flirt and tease like a romantic young girl—that she was only an incarnate intelligence to most of the men she met, not, in their eyes, a woman. Mimi saw a glow in Ayn's eyes when she spoke to Jagger: "I could see that she had a sort of crush on him." With the boldness of youth, Mimi said to Ayn one day, "You'd really like to investigate this further, wouldn't you?" "Yes," Ayn replied, smiling. "You're entranced with him, I bet you'd like to have an affair with him, but you'd be afraid to take a chance, because you'd be afraid of losing Frank," Mimi went on. "You're absolutely right," said Ayn calmly.

The Unconquered opened February 14, 1940—twelve days after Ayn's thirty-fifth birthday—at the Biltmore Theatre. "The crowd was good, and a lot of celebrities were there," Mimi remembered. "I saw Mary Pickford, wearing a chinchilla coat. Ayn had loaned me a beautiful dress, with a black velvet bodice and a black and white taffeta skirt. But we all knew the play was a disaster. We went to a party at Dean Jagger's house to wait for the reviews—he had a Japanese barman and maids serving the hors d'oeuvres—but when the papers came, it was *awful*. We went home. Ayn stayed in bed all the next day, crying, and no one could talk to her; Frank and Nick tried, but it was hopeless."

The reviews of *The Unconquered were* awful. "One of the season's mishaps," wrote Richard Watts in the New York *Herald Tribune*. "Sentimental melodrama," said the *Times*. In the *Daily News:* "The interest is held but the imagination is not fired nor the emotions noticeably stirred." In the *World-Telegram:* "If it is intended as anti-Bolshevik propaganda, it is neither impressive enough in its doctrine nor brilliant enough in its satire to arouse anything beyond the mildest interest in the subject."

The play closed after a five-day run. Ayn never again wrote for the theater.[3]

Her emotional salvation lay, as always, in her work. She returned to the writing of *The Fountainhead.*

The writing continued to go slowly.

There seemed one last chance to raise enough money to finish the book. As Ayn worked, negotiations were in progress for publication of *The Fountainhead.* Despite the commercial failure of *We the Living,* James Putnam, Ayn's editor at Macmillan, had inquired about her new novel. She explained the theme to him, and something of the story. He made an offer to publish *The Fountainhead*—on the same terms as *We the Living* had been published: the company would pay an advance of two hundred and fifty dollars. Ayn was willing to accept the small advance, but she insisted that, this time, she be given a guarantee that Macmillan would spend a minimum of twelve hundred dollars on publicity and advertising; she was not willing to have *The Fountainhead* vanish into the oblivion of *We the Living.* Macmillan refused to give the guarantee, and Ayn's association with her publisher was at an end.

When the first three chapters were completed, Ayn showed them to Ann Watkins. The agent was complimentary and enthusiastic. You can stop worrying about money, she told Ayn; if your money runs too low, I can get you an advance very easily, there will be no difficulties. "She had no business to say that," Ayn later said angrily. "She should have known that no matter how good the book is, one can guarantee nothing, particularly when the ideas are so controversial. I knew it would not be easy to get a contract."

Ayn agreed that Ann Watkins should begin submitting the early chapters. At first, it seemed that the agent had been correct; Ayn was immediately offered a contract by Knopf. She signed with them for an advance of one thousand dollars, which was not to be paid until the completed manuscript was delivered. They agreed to a small publicity guarantee, and gave Ayn one year to complete the manuscript.

There was no way for Ayn to speed up the writing process, not if she were to adhere to the literary standards she had set herself; and she never conceived of the possibility of accepting lesser standards. She worked for crushingly long hours and at a frantic pace to meet her deadline, seeing no one, rarely leaving her desk. As time began to run out, she had completed only one third of the manuscript. Desperate, she had Ann Watkins ask Knopf if they would extend the deadline, and pay her some part of the advance. Knopf read the completed section of the book, agreed to extend the deadline—but refused to pay any part of the advance. On the date of the deadline, the contract was dropped by mutual agreement.

"Now," Ayn later said, her face taut as if still enduring the strain of that

[3] *The Unconquered* is available now only in typescript at the New York Public Library.

period, "I didn't know if I'd be able to finish the book. We had no money at all. And I didn't even have a publisher. This was when the real horror began." Ann Watkins continued circulating the completed chapters, and rejections began coming in—eight rejections in all.

Ayn was upset when Ann Watkins, against her stated order that that "red house" was not for her, submitted the manuscript to Simon & Schuster. It was rejected. A friend of Ayn, who knew Henry Simon, insisted that the decision must have been made by the editors without Simon's knowledge, and that Simon was not politically to the left. He wanted Ayn to talk with Simon, and dubiously she agreed. "Simon was a tall, gawky type," she was to comment. "He was so intellectually out of focus that he could not be leftist or anything else. He said the house was not leftist, but that their editors hadn't liked the book, they'd thought it was badly written and that the hero was unsympathetic. Then he said, 'We're not Communists, we're really conservatives—we're so conservative we even published Trotsky!' I had to make an effort not to burst out laughing. It was so ludicrous I couldn't even be upset too much. It was like being turned down by the *Daily Worker* plus Mortimer Snerd."

It was after the eight rejections, Ayn always felt, that her agent's opinion of the book began to change. "She couldn't sell it, so she had to blame me. One day she said 'The real trouble is that you have an unsympathetic central character, and you can't have that in a book.' I said 'I don't see why you can't. Look at William Faulkner, his leading characters are always unsympathetic.' She said 'Mmm, yes'—and the way she said it was so eloquent. The look on her face was as if I had cut the ground from under her feet. I had refused to sanction what she was saying; she knew that *I* considered Roark sympathetic, and I was telling her I don't give a damn what you think, if you want to call him evil, fine. . . .

"Our relationship began to get very tense. One day she was talking about something being wrong with *The Fountainhead,* and I kept asking her what it was. She finally said, 'I don't know, I just *feel* it, I can't always give reasons.' I was still naïve enough so that that was a traumatic shock to me. I didn't expect anyone to say that seriously. I went home and wrote her a long letter, saying why one must always go by reason, and that this has to be a break with her. That's how I left her. I had no choice. She was to continue handling my past work, but now I no longer had an agent."

By then, the book had been rejected by twelve publishers. The intellectual world was dominated by collectivisim in politics and by naturalism in literature. Ayn had no doubt that the rejections were based on one or the other—or both— of these two allegiances. The reports declared that the novel was too controversial—that it went against the prevailing political climate of opinion—that it was too intellectual for a novel—that the story was improbable—that the hero was unsympathetic—that no one could identify himself with Roark. The verdict: *The Fountainhead* had no commercial possibilities.

Ayn continued to work steadily, burdened by the knowledge that her savings were dwindling with each page of manuscript. By the fall of 1940, she had only seven hundred dollars left.

It was under these circumstances that she took three months off from writing, using the last of her savings, to work for a political cause.

Chapter Fourteen

Ayn had been in the United States for several years before she began to take an interest in the American political scene. In her first years in her new country, there had been no time for political studies. Besides, she would say, "when a play or a movie preached some sort of drippy altruism, I took it to be just conventional hypocrisy which was of no cultural significance. The political institutions of America, the Declaration of Independence, were so individualistic, so much on *my* premises, that I thought altruism and statism were a dead issue."

The 1932 campaign of Franklin Delano Roosevelt had been the first presidential campaign to interest Ayn. She was by then, proudly, a citizen; her first vote was cast for Roosevelt. Her reason was his promise to fight for the repeal of Prohibition. "Prohibition was the political issue that aroused me," Ayn would recall. "I knew that this was a complete breach of individual rights, a collectivist-mystical issue serving the interest of the worst kind of pressure groups, created by a small religious and Bible Belt minority. . . . What shocked me was the hypocrisy with which the issue was handled by the Republicans. The Democrats came out with an uncompromising, absolute stand against Prohibition; the Republicans temporized—you know, the attitude of 'something can be said for both sides.'

"Besides, FDR seemed to have the more libertarian platform; he criticized Hoover for too much bureaucracy, that taxes were too high, that the national budget was too high. . . . I must confess that I did not follow all of Roosevelt's speeches, I was not yet a very careful political observer, I read only the highlights of an issue. Much later, I saw quotations from some of his speeches during that campaign that made me feel a little guilty—he said that this economy had reached its climax as far as production was concerned, that now it's an issue of distribution."

As she began to observe the American political scene more closely in the midthirties, it was with a growing sense of uneasiness. "It had become really apparent that Roosevelt was a collectivist, that he was moving toward a socialist program," she concluded. "Some of his Brain Trust were making speeches that were out-and-out Communist. I was violently indignant." She began to read in increasing numbers of newspapers and periodicals that the nightmare from which she had escaped was a "noble experiment." She began to hear intellectuals denouncing individualism, industry, and the profit motive in a manner she had not expected to hear outside of Russia; collectivism was being advocated more and more openly. She watched in stunned disbelief—and then in growing horror —as the country's intellectuals began their rush to the embrace of Stalinism. It had happened in Germany with Hitler, it had happened in Russia with the Communist revolution—she had seen it happen, she had lived with it: that the intellectuals—the men who ultimately determined a country's philosophy—were the first to ringingly endorse totalitarianism. "You can't make an omelet without breaking eggs," they proclaimed, indifferent to the fact that it was human bodies that were being broken and that the dish they were preparing was dictatorship.

She had never forgotten—she never would forget—the vision of America she had held while still in Russia, the golden, free America she had loved. She loved it still, it lived within her still—as she could not doubt that it lived within most Americans, struggling against the dead weight of altruism and collectivism that was beginning to choke its life. She watched her new country's steady march toward collectivism and began to grasp that she had walked down the gangplank of the De Grasse into an America that lived and worked by one moral code, but in its churches, its schools, its art, its literature, its departments of philosophy, it championed and preached and taught its young the exact opposite of that moral code, the exact opposite of the code that had made possible its unprecedented achievement and grandeur. She had come to an America that was vastly productive, whose industrialists and businessmen were raising the standard of living of the country to heights no gem-encrusted rajah had ever conceived, where scientists and inventors were lifting the centuries-old, backbreaking work of manual labor which had always been the life of most of mankind, where architects were building edifices that soared arrogantly to the sky as if to match the aspirations of the people who occupied them, where government was limited predominantly to the protection of human rights and had no mandate to be the big brother of its citizens or to distribute the wealth and achievement of some men for the unearned benefit of other men, where men were free to live for their own happiness and pursue their own goals and, in so doing, to create the most productive country that had ever existed. But she had come to an America that had been hurtling toward disaster and had not known it: an America where men were taught that humility was a high virtue, that self-sacrifice was a moral imperative, that poverty was noble, that material wealth was the sign of spiritual depravity.

She had come to an America that was cut in two. It lived by the moral code she had been struggling to formulate since the first days of the Communist revolution, since her first horrified sight of the posters informing her that man must exist for his brother men, for the state, for the collective; but it upheld, philosophically and morally, the sentiments of those scrawled red posters. She had come to an America that had never named or sanctioned its *own* unique code, the principles by which it lived and prospered and had become the last great hope of mankind.

Despite the professional activities in which she was engaged throughout the thirties, despite her work on *We the Living* and *Ideal* and *Anthem* and *Think Twice* and *The Unconquered* and *The Fountainhead,* she had begun to spend most of her spare moments—and to take more moments than she could spare— systematically studying economic theory and practice, reading every new book by conservative thinkers, following newspaper and magazine accounts of the political situation.

By 1940, she felt that "through the reading and thinking I had done, I was a real political expert. I was convinced that if Dewey or Taft were nominated, it would be complete disaster for the Republican Party and for the nation if one of them were elected—both were uninspiring compromisers without any righteous or moral stand, they were Republicans in the present-day sense. It was only Willkie who was—in the beginning—an outspoken and courageous defender of free enterprise."

Wendell Willkie was nominated to run against Roosevelt. Ayn believed that this was a crucial election, that if Roosevelt were reelected the country would accelerate its perilous roll toward political disaster, and that "this time *one has to do something.*" It was self-evident to Ayn that if she believed something should be done, she did not wait for others to do it; it was her job to leap into the fray. After long discussions, Ayn and Frank agreed that Ayn would temporarily stop work on *The Fountainhead,* they would live on the last seven hundred dollars of her savings, and they would join the Willkie campaign to fight for the preservation of the American political system.

It was a difficult and painful decision, made at a wrenching emotional cost. But when Ayn was asked if it were a "sacrifice" to abandon her novel and spend the last of her money, she denied it vehemently, saying that it was an act of pure selfishness to fight for her ideas and for a world in which she would be free to write.

Ayn knew no one in the political world, no one who might see to it that her name and her talents were properly utilized in the campaign. It was consistent with the modesty that coexisted with her certainty of her abilities that, with Frank, Ayn went to the headquarters of the Willkie Clubs, introduced herself as "Mrs. Frank O'Connor," and volunteered her services in any capacity required.

Frank's job—a job totally out of character for this reserved, retiring man— was to ring doorbells, hand out literature, and urge people to register and to vote for Willkie. Ayn became a typist. They both worked full time, and without pay. Within a week, Ayn suggested the formation of an "intellectual ammunition bureau"—a bureau that would analyze Roosevelt's speeches and prepare answers for Republican speakers across the country, that would unearth and disseminate facts and statistics damaging to the Democrats. Her suggestion was accepted, and she was put in charge of a group of hardworking, dedicated volunteer researchers.

"There was a real crusading spirit at first," she recalled. "I've never seen it in any election since. People were bristling with Willkie buttons. I wore five of them."

It was still early in the campaign when Ayn "began to see the disasters. Willkie began uttering such a mishmash of compromises that his popularity—he had had the enthusiastic support of millions in the beginning—began to fall and he never recovered. The torture for me was that each of Willkie's major speeches would defeat whatever good the other campaigners were doing; each was a worse disappointment than the preceding. The issue was capitalism versus the New Deal—and by abandoning his moral stand for capitalism, Willkie was the guiltiest man of any for destroying America, more guilty than Roosevelt, who was only the creature of his time, riding the current; but Willkie had had a chance single-handedly to stop or at least delay the disaster. It was horrible."

Ayn was passionately opposed to any American involvement in the war in Europe. And she was horrified that Willkie did not speak out unequivocally against such involvement. "It was Roosevelt," she said, "who was uncompromisingly anti-war. He swore he would never send American boys to fight on foreign soil."

As Ayn watched the campaign collapsing into ruins, she was given a new assignment by the Willkie Clubs—added to her "intellectual ammunition" work —which was an enormous source of pleasure to her. She had never enjoyed— and never would enjoy—formal public speaking; the few talks she had given following the publication of *We the Living* were done as a dutiful, nervous chore. But now she began enthusiastically addressing assorted, often vocally hostile, groups on street corners, in cafes, in parks, wherever she could find people who wanted to listen and question. Once, a heckler demanded: "Who the hell are you to talk about America? You're a foreigner!" Calmly, she answered: "That's right. I *chose* to be an American. What did *you* do, besides having been born?" The crowd laughed and applauded—and the heckler was silent.

The Gloria Swanson Theater on Fourteenth Street, near Union Square, a strongly pro-Roosevelt district, was showing Willkie campaign movies and had requested speakers to answer the audiences' questions. Seven times a day for two weeks, Ayn's shyness vanishing as it always did in the presence of eager, questioning minds, she happily answered questions from the stage of the theater. The experience further confirmed her in her respect for the American public, in her conviction that the so-called "common man" is singularly *un*common. The most intelligent and rational questions she heard anywhere were asked by the audiences from the working-class area of the theater.

She was delighted, too, by her newly discovered ability to make complex political issues instantly clear and to establish communication even with antagonistic audiences—and she found that she loved being in the thick of an intellectual battle. A friend from the Willkie Clubs sat in the audience to see the severe, cerebral Ayn Rand sparkling on that Fourteenth Street stage as the power of her words and the power of her personality held her audience entranced. Her ability to make complex issues effortlessly intelligible, to open wide the gates to the realm of ideas for even the most modest of intelligences, was newly discovered by Ayn, but had always been clearly perceived by those who knew her. It was a talent that was an essential part of the spell she was progressively to weave as the years passed, bringing even the most antagonistic audiences to their feet in thunderous applause for a woman—and a philosophy—they had been prepared to dislike. It was a talent that was to reach a towering height—a talent for finding the most devastating arguments for her case, for presenting her arguments with stunning clarity and precision—a charismatic power to convince.

The 1940 election was a landslide for Roosevelt. Ayn was bitterly disappointed, but she felt that Willkie had not deserved to win, that he had sabotaged his own campaign. A few weeks after the election, Ayn met Willkie at a party given by some of her new conservative acquaintances. "I approached him very timidly," she would recall. "I didn't quite know how to speak to people like that nor what was understood between us—and I asked naïvely, 'Can you tell me why, prior to the campaign, you were writing about individualism constantly, but you never mentioned it during the campaign?' He looked at me in a completely unfocused manner, I could tell that the eyes were not seeing me, and said 'Individualism? Well, I'm for it'—and walked off. This was a memorable moment for me. It was a horrible shock of disgust."

It was through her work in the campaign that Ayn began to meet prominent conservatives, to see them socially at her modest Manhattan apartment or in their homes, and to begin working with them on free-enterprise causes. The man she liked best was the distinguished novelist and playwright Channing Pollock. She was concerned that he was religious; the link between reason and freedom had always been firm in her mind; but, she was to say, "he was violently pro free enterprise, and he didn't mix religion with it, he was very sincere and militant." Although she disapproved philosophically of religious beliefs, she felt that they were an individual's private business—until and unless he attempted to justify his political philosophy on religious grounds, on faith rather than reason. That, she maintained, was the death knell of freedom. After the election, Ayn suggested to Pollock that what was now required was a union of intellectuals to take a philosophical and moral stand for capitalism; since Pollock had more of a public name than she, she suggested that he be the official organizer of such a group. Pollock was skeptical about the possibility of recruiting such a movement, but he agreed to test the idea during one of his lecture tours; he would announce that he was contemplating the formation of a pro-free-enterprise group, and request that people write him if they were interested. In the spring of the year, he returned from his lecture tour with eight thousand letters.

Pollock introduced Ayn to a number of important conservative thinkers and writers, feeling that her unique powers of persuasion would interest them in the group. "That's how I met the most extreme advocates of capitalism of the day," she later recalled. Among them were Ruth Alexander, prominent economist, writer, and lecturer; Albert J. Nock, one of this century's most significant influences on libertarian thought; Rose Wilder Lane, the brilliant political writer and theorist; and Isabel Paterson, a conservative theorist of fiery and outstanding intellectual range and power.

Many of the people Ayn spoke to were interested in helping with the group's formation, and several meetings were held to formulate plans. Ayn wrote an article for them entitled "The Only Path to Tomorrow," in which she stated her definitions of individualism: "Man is an independent entity with an inalienable right to the pursuit of his own happiness in a society where men deal with one another as equals in voluntary, unregulated exchange"—and collectivism: "the subjugation of the individual to a group—whether to a race, class or state does not matter."[1]

Ayn intended the paper as a draft of what the organization would stand for. Several meetings were held, but, Ayn soon concluded, "It was complete disaster. I had written my paper as a bromide, assuming all of them would be in favor of it; that it was a revelation to many of them was a shock to me. What disillusioned me was the realization that they were really nonphilosophical, and that education would have to begin with *them*." She had read and admired Nock's work, but she felt, meeting him, that his attitude was cynical and weary; he once told her that freedom was doomed, that it was a rare accidental exception in history, and there would always be majorities demanding handouts—and he wished the group well but refused to join it. "At one meeting," Ayn recalled, "Pollock brought in several professional 'gravy boys,' concerned only with how we would raise money rather than with what we would do. . . . It all fell apart, and I lost interest." Ayn continued to respect a number of the conservatives she had met, but she was becoming convinced that the "devotion" to free enterprise of many among them consisted of compromise, timidity, fence-sitting and an aggressive nonintellectuality.

"I didn't conclude then that conservatives were actually hopeless traitors," she later explained. "Just that a lot of them were weak and cowardly; I still thought that it's an issue of ignorance. It took years for me to gradually discover that it was an amoral, *anti*-moral attitude. This wasn't true of all of them, but most. The other killer was cynicism; they didn't believe capitalism could be saved." Characteristically, when Ayn made her final negative judgment on conservatives, it was in terms of immoral motivation; the possibility of an honest error involving such crucial issues seemed not to be in her lexicon.

[1] In January of 1944, the article was published in the *Reader's Digest.*

Ayn was to maintain her contacts with many of the conservatives she met, and over the next years she was to become acquainted with many more; she found Rose Wilder Lane particularly interesting. But it was her meeting with Isabel Paterson that marked the beginning of one of the most important friendships of her life.

Isabel Paterson—called "Pat"—was a widely respected conservative thinker and writer, a remarkable woman with a still more remarkable intelligence. Small, dark, and plain, Pat was the blazing firebrand of the conservative movement, ferociously dedicated to her principles and ferociously contemptuous of anyone who disagreed with her. "Stupid," "blockhead," "traitor," and "fool" were among the more kindly of her descriptions not just of her political opponents, but of any of her allies whom she found guilty of even the most minor intellectual heresy—descriptions she never hesitated to announce to them, waving her arms and shouting, both publically and privately. She wrote several novels which achieved a moderate success; one of them, *Never Ask the End,* was a Literary Guild Selection; she told her friend Muriel Hall[2] that she wrote them because it was relaxing, "like doing needlework."

When Ayn meet her, Pat was a columnist for the New York *Herald Tribune Books,* where she wrote a witty and brilliant Sunday column called "Turns With a Bookworm." Her column, intended to be about books, was as often about politics. At the same time, she was working on a major nonfiction book, *The God of the Machine,* which was to be a profoundly valuable addition to the library of free enterprise thought.[3]

"She was very pleasant to me when I met her," Ayn recalled. "We discussed politics, which I enjoyed—but I disliked her enormously as a person. The malice was so blatant. Later, I reproached myself for trusting a first impression. She contacted me to say that she liked my attitude toward politics and wanted to see me. That's how our friendship began."

Within a few weeks of their acquaintance, Pat invited Ayn to spend the weekend at her country home. It was one of the very few times that Ayn left the city for a weekend without Frank. She and Pat talked until sunrise, discussing philosophy and politics. The acquaintance soon became a warm friendship between these two women of great and passionately held principle. It was the first—and the last—important friendship with a contemporary that Ayn ever had. They saw each other constantly, and talked endlessly. Each Monday evening, when the *Herald Tribune* Sunday Book Section was going to press, Pat was in her office to check the final copy. It had become a tradition that a few conservative friends joined her for intellectual conversation, which continued until the small

---

[2] Muriel Hall, although much younger than Pat, was an admiring and loving friend, and finally the executor of Pat's estate. She is now Senior Staff Editor at the *Reader's Digest.*

[3] In 1982, conservative writer and critic John Chamberlain was to write: "It was Isabel Paterson's *The God of the Machine,* Rose Lane's *The Discovery of Freedom,* and Ayn Rand's *The Fountainhead* and (later) *Atlas Shrugged* . . . that made it plain that if life was to be something more than a naked scramble for government favors, a new attitude toward the producer must be created."

hours of the morning. Ayn soon became a member of the group, which included the writer and literary critic Will Cuppy and journalist Sam Wells, and looked forward eagerly to the Monday meetings.

Despite their closeness, Ayn had important philosophical disagreements with Isabel Paterson. "Pat could be totally rational," Ayn was to say when she later spoke of their friendship. "She once broke with a conservative friend because the friend had said she didn't always form her goals by reason, but by feelings or hunches; Pat had screamed at her: how *dare* she go by feelings when human lives and freedom were involved! But you never knew when, during the same week or even the same evening, she'd be at her best: a marvelous, enormously rational, abstract mind, who could talk fascinatingly and made the best philosophical identifications and connections—or at her worst, when she'd turn mystic. She told me that she believed in God, and when I said that was incompatible with rationality, she replied that she was absolutely for reason, but that reason itself can tell you what issues reason cannot handle. I insisted that she explain what on earth she was talking about, I'd bring up the issue from time to time, and she always maintained that she could explain it—if she hadn't, that would have been the end between us—but she never did. She even told me once that she believed in reincarnation, and that she'd been a German countess during the Renaissance. I listened as politely as I could, then said: I do not take cognizance of anything I cannot check. Whenever she'd start on mysticism, I'd cut her off so short that after a while she stopped talking about it."

The absolutism of reason with its corollary, the rejection of faith, was, and remained, the philosophical issue most important to Ayn. As early as adolescence, she had grasped that man's reasoning mind is his tool of survival; as early as 1934, she had written in her private notes, "Religion . . . is the first enemy of the ability to think. That ability is not used by men to one-tenth of its possibility, yet before they learn to think they are discouraged by being ordered to *take things on faith. Faith is the worst curse of mankind,* as the exact antithesis and enemy of *thought.*" Never would she see as less than evil, as less than anti-life, any explicit or implicit rejection of reason.

"Pat often told me," Muriel Hall later recalled, "that she thought Ayn was a genius—and 'genius' was a word she very rarely used. She was always very complimentary about Ayn's courage and integrity and intellect. . . . She loved some of Ayn's difficulties with the English language. Her favorite was Ayn saying once, 'It's an ungulfable bridge.'[4] . . . My brother, who used to attend the Monday discussions, told me that Ayn used to sit at Pat's feet—he saw it time after time. They would take an issue such as, for instance, the Supreme Court, and discuss it until Ayn had a full understanding." Pat had read widely and thoughtfully in American history, world history, economics, political philosophy, literature, and science, and while Ayn had a firm concept of freedom

[4] I, too, have memories of Ayn's occasional language problems, which lingered in her conversation long after they had been eliminated from her writing. Talking about the actor Louis Calhern, she said: "Frank looks like him—but not as ugly."

and free enterprise, she had little knowledge of American history or the Constitution or the history of American industry.

Mimi Sutton met Pat during one of Mimi's New York summers with Ayn and Frank. "Isabel Paterson was a dowdy woman, with no charm whatever," Mimi remembered. "But Ayn was entranced with her. They'd sit up until four or five in the morning—and Ayn would be sitting at the master's feet. One night, when they were talking, I went to bed, but I could hear the conversation, and it was as if Pat were the guru and teacher—and Ayn *didn't do that.* Ayn would be asking questions, and Pat would be answering. It was very strange."

It seems clear that Ayn's early relationship with Pat did have a strong element of student to teacher—not in the realm of philosophy, where Ayn held positive and rigorously thought-out convictions, but in areas of the history and interpretation of American politics and institutions. One of the rare and cherished pleasures of Ayn's life was precisely the opportunity to learn from others; she delighted in the occasions when she did not have to be the teacher, when she could "sit at someone's feet" and listen to ideas and theories that were new and valuable, and ask questions, and listen again. It gave her, if only for a few brief hours, the sense that she was not, after all, utterly alone in the world, that she was not alone to see, to understand, to grasp, to know. It made her a member of the human race, rather than some odd creature whose mind danced among the stars while others struggled in the mire below.

Years later, Ayn would write a scene in *Atlas Shrugged* in which Dagny Taggart shows the brilliant scientist Dr. Robert Stadler the remnants of a motor that represents a great new scientific breakthrough. " 'It's so wonderful,' said Dr. Stadler, his voice low. 'It's so wonderful to see a great, new, crucial idea which is not mine! . . . Those touchy mediocrities who sit trembling lest someone's work prove greater than their own—they have no inkling of the loneliness that comes when you reach the top. The loneliness for an equal—for a mind to respect and an achievement to admire. They bare their teeth at you from out of their rat holes, thinking that you take pleasure in letting your brilliance dim theirs—when you would give a year of your life to see a flicker of talent anywhere among them. They envy achievement, and their dream of greatness is a world where all men have become their acknowledged inferiors. They don't know that that dream is the infallible proof of mediocrity, because that sort of world is what the man of achievement would not be able to bear. They have no way of knowing what he feels when surrounded by inferiors—hatred? no, not hatred, but boredom—the terrible, hopeless, draining, paralyzing boredom. Of what account are praise and adulation from men whom you don't respect? Have you ever felt the longing for someone you could admire? For something, not to look down at, but up to?' "

The words are Robert Stadler's. The voice is Ayn Rand's.

The deep contradiction in Ayn's nature was that she so rarely allowed herself this pleasure, even when it was possible to her. Her own deeply rooted need to be teacher and guru, to dominate intellectually, was too powerful to permit her, with very rare exceptions, the relationship or any part of the relationship that she had with Pat.

It was that relationship that was the sole important value she found during the months she took from *The Fountainhead* to work for a doomed political campaign.

Chapter Fifteen

The summer and winter following the Willkie campaign were among the most difficult periods of Ayn's life. Three months and seven hundred dollars had been lost. She was financially unable to return to the writing of *The Fountainhead* and she had no way of knowing when it would be possible. She had no choice but to find a job—any job.

Richard Mealand, story editor of Paramount Pictures in New York, had seen the first part of *The Fountainhead* when Ann Watkins was submitting it and had arranged to meet Ayn. It was a great novel, he had told her. He had tried, without success, to convince Paramount to buy it. When Ayn told him that she was broke and wanted work as a reader, he shook his head sadly and hired her at once. Her wages were six dollars for a short synopsis and ten dollars for a long one. "The money seemed a gift from heaven," she said.

She had hoped to be able to snatch some time for writing, perhaps a few hours a week; but even that was not possible. She was a painfully slow reader; to keep up with her assignments and earn the money she needed, she worked twelve or more hours a day, seven days a week. *The Fountainhead* was relegated to "small glances."

"It was not a *fully* wasted period," Ayn later said. "My subconscious was working, which helped later to make the writing go very fast." But she longed for her work as one longs for a lost lover; it was a sensation of physical pain, somewhere in her chest, that never left her.

Frances Hazlitt—the wife of Henry Hazlitt, the conservative economist who was to have a long-running column in *Newsweek* and to publish a number of important books on economics—later herself a writer, was Mealand's assistant at Paramount, in charge of readers. She and Ayn became friendly. It was a relationship of mutual respect and affection that was to last for many years. Frances once told Ayn that she had been upset when she learned that Ayn Rand was to be their new reader: she had expected an arrogant, difficult woman who felt above her job. She was pleasantly surprised to find that she liked Ayn immediately and that Ayn was the most conscientious and hardworking of any of her readers. "I was terribly impressed with her resolution," she told William Buckley many years later. "Despite the kind of work she had to do, she kept talking about the great book she was writing." And she was pleased to observe that Ayn and Frank, despite their difficult financial circumstances, loaned small sums of money to out-of-work writers who were having an even more difficult time than they. Frances Hazlitt gave Ayn the pick of books for outside readers, and kept her busy even during slow periods.

Time dragged by as if some malevolent force were stretching out each hour. Sometimes, Ayn felt as if she were back at the beginning, back in the days of her arrival in America, when her work had been only a dream of the future.

She had been at Paramount for almost six months when Richard Mealand learned that she had left Ann Watkins and that *The Fountainhead* was no longer being submitted to publishing houses. Appalled, he offered to personally recommend it to any house of her choice. She had not thought to ask Mealand for help; she rarely asked anyone for help. It was characteristic of her that even when a friend would have been delighted to offer assistance, but did not know it was needed, her fierce independence prevented her from asking. If ever help were forthcoming unasked, she reacted with astonished pleasure; she never took it for granted—so much so that people who knew her were often startled by the extent of her gratitude when they did her the smallest of services, offering the kind of assistance one automatically offers a friend. Her gratitude was indicative of two facts: the extent of her passion for self-responsibility—and how rare it had been in her life that a hand was held out to her in simple human kindness. Perhaps the second is in part the sad result of the first: an independent spirit is expected to take care of herself, to give help, not receive it; those strong enough to bear burdens are given still heavier burdens to carry. And the Atlas who was Ayn Rand never shrugged. But it appears that the cause can also be found in her alienation from people, which led to a formality and aloofness of manner that intimidated those who might have wished to offer help; her manner made them feel that she might interpret good will as a pitying insult.

Ayn told Mealand that she would like her novel to be submitted to Little, Brown, which had a reputation for good salesmanship of serious novels. Mealand introduced her to the editor, Angus Cameron. Six weeks later, Cameron called to say they were rejecting the book. When she came to pick up her manuscript, against normal publishing procedure he showed her the report written by a member of the firm's editorial board. To the end of her life, Ayn remembered the wording of that report: "This is a work of almost-genius—'genius' in the power of its expression—'almost' in the sense of its enormous bitterness. I wish there were an audience for a book of this kind. But there isn't. It won't sell." This was typical, Cameron told her, of the other reports he had received. All had praised the novel—all had predicted commercial failure.

"Of the whole history of *The Fountainhead,*" Ayn said in later years, "this was the most depressing. I told Frank when I got home that if they had told me it's a bad novel, then okay, that's their bad standards. But to have it rejected because of its *greatness*—because it's *too good*—that's really a feeling of horror."

Mealand offered to submit it to another house, and asked Ayn to select a publisher. Once more, she felt uncomfortable about imposing, but when he insisted that he wanted to help, she agreed. Bobbs-Merrill had recently published Eugene Lyons's *The Red Decade,* so she knew they were not influenced by communism. She asked Mealand to submit *The Fountainhead* to Bobbs-Merrill. Mealand arranged a meeting with the new young editor, Archibald G. Ogden.

"When I walked into the Bobbs-Merrill office with the manuscript and saw Archie," Ayn recalled, "I thought 'This is no place for me'—because he acted like a complete Peter Keating—bright, smiling, almost too palsy and effervescent; he was friendly, but unserious and superficial. I thought there was no possible chance that this man would like my book."

Knowing that publishers usually required a month or more before reaching a decision on a manuscript, she was startled to receive a telephone call from Archie Ogden less than a week after she had submitted the book. He had called, he said, to tell her that *The Fountainhead* was magnificent. Still glowing with pleasure when she discussed their conversation many years later, Ayn said, "He proceeded to pay me the greatest compliments I ever had—he said it was great writing, that I was enormously talented, that I was writing in the tradition of *real* literature. He wasn't gushing, he was very solemn, and he told me specifically what he liked—he thought it was a great theme, marvelous characterization of Roark, that it was inspirational and uplifting. It was incredible."

Ayn had asked for an advance payment on royalties of twelve hundred dollars and for a year's time to finish the book. Archie explained that if she hadn't required what was a large sum for Bobbs-Merrill, he would be authorized to sign a contract immediately, but because of the advance, he had to send the manuscript to the company's head office in Indianapolis for a decision. He was sending it with a strong recommendation.

While she waited for word from Indianapolis, Ayn continued reading for Paramount—reading one undistinguished book after another and thinking of the book that had found no publisher. "You're casting pearls," Frank told her one day, "without getting even a pork chop in return." His remark found its way into *The Fountainhead,* where it is spoken by Dominique about Howard Roark's struggle.

Six weeks passed. Early one morning, as Ayn was wearily completing a rush assignment on which she had worked through the night, the telephone rang. It was Archie Ogden. He was ready to draw up a contract for the publication of *The Fountainhead.*

She soon learned the story behind the acceptance. On the strength of two reports on the novel from Indianapolis editors—one that called it a great book but said it would not sell, a second that said it was a bad book but *would* sell—

D. L. Chambers, the head of Bobbs-Merrill, had returned the manuscript to Archie, telling him to reject it. Archie was a young editor in an important position which he had held for only a few months. He staked his job on *The Fountainhead.* He wired Chambers: IF THIS IS NOT THE BOOK FOR YOU, THEN I AM NOT THE EDITOR FOR YOU. The return wire said: FAR BE IT FROM ME TO DAMPEN SUCH ENTHUSIASM. SIGN THE CONTRACT. BUT THE BOOK BETTER BE GOOD.

It is an interesting postscript that the man who fought for *The Fountainhead* was the man who rejected Dale Carnegie's *How to Win Friends and Influence People.* He often told the story cheerfully, saying that he never regretted either decision.

Radiant with exhilaration, Ayn took her completed synopsis to Paramount, and told Frances Hazlitt and Richard Mealand that she was to be published. However, she needed to continue working weekends; Archie had been able to get her an advance of only one thousand dollars, which would not last for a year. Mealand and Frances Hazlitt guaranteed that she would have as much work as she wanted—and the entire department joined in a celebration of her success.

The contract was signed in December 1941. Ayn had a year in which to complete the manuscript. Her deadline was January 1, 1943.

Before the contract could be signed, Pearl Harbor was bombed and America was at war. Archie told Ayn that had their oral agreement been made a week later, in wartime, he could not have put the contract through: the book would be long and expensive to produce, and publishers were already concerned about a new market situation and a possible shortage of paper. One week had saved her from another rejection.

Almost two thirds of the novel remained to be written. She began working day and night, with intense concentration and unlimited mental energy, seeing no one and going nowhere—in a state of happily agonized tension. And now, at last, she was writing rapidly, her mind freed from the chains that had inhibited the creative process. As the days and nights went by, Ayn measured time by the distance from January 1, and by the mounting stack of manuscript pages on the desk Frank had given her.

Mimi Sutton stayed with Ayn and Frank that summer. "I slept on the couch in the living room," she said, "and Ayn would be working in the dining area long after Frank and I were asleep. I remember waking at four in the morning, and she was still writing."

Once, when Ayn was depressed because of minor interruptions that had prevented her from working, Frank told her, jokingly, "It's nothing that a little writing won't cure." He repeated it often during the years to come. They both knew that it was true—that no negative emotion could long withstand the sense of achievement that writing gave her.

Isabel Paterson was also deep in her work, completing *The God of the Machine;* she and Ayn were running a friendly race to see who would finish first. Ayn had spent many evenings explaining her moral philosophy to Pat, clarifying and specifying the rationale behind it, and how it applied to human action; during their early discussions, Pat had argued against a morality of self-interest, but after months of often angry discussions, had finally been convinced. Now, she asked Ayn if she might include in her own book a defense of Ayn's moral theory as opposed to humanitarianism. Ayn agreed immediately. She later explained, "I felt pleased and flattered that Pat wanted to use my ideas. She told me that for certain reasons—she hated a lot of footnotes—she would rather not mention my name in her book. My consideration was only that the more the ideas are spread, the better, and that it would be wonderful to have them presented in a nonfiction book. I was totally idea-centered. So I told her, 'By all means, I don't want any credit.' "

Ayn's two mainstays during that hectic year were Frank and Nick—Frank, because of her sense that on an emotional level he comprehended her work and took a quiet joy in it—Nick, because she could discuss the book with him, know she was understood, and receive an intelligent feedback. The two brothers did whatever could be done to make that difficult year easier for her. Ayn had customarily helped with the marketing and cooking; now, they insisted that they would do all of it, and they bickered cheerfully about their division of household responsibilities. As always, Ayn first read her longhand drafts aloud to Frank. But as she wrote each sequence or chapter, then edited and typed it, it was Nick to whom she showed it for his criticism or approval.

"I'd be dozing on and off, late at night," Mimi recalled, "and Nick would come in. She'd read to him, and they would talk for hours. . . . Nick could be angry and annoyed with her, he could be terrified of her and intimidated—but he came as close to loving her as he could with any woman. He was proud of her —and proud that she valued his opinion." Both Nick—whom some of his friends called "a small-town Oscar Wilde"—and Frank, whose wit was wonderfully dry and unexpected, were especially helpful to Ayn with regard to the rare touches of humor in her work. A number of Frank's offhand comments—such as "throwing pearls and not getting even a pork chop in return"—were included in her books. Several of Ayn's friends had the impression that whatever occasional humor appeared in *The Fountainhead* was Frank's or Nick's.

Ayn had very little humor in her psychological makeup, and was suspicious of humor on principle. She roundly criticized the view that a sense of humor is an important human trait, and projected an especially withering contempt at the suggestion that one should be able to laugh at oneself. "That's the man who wants a blank check on flaws," she would say. Frank Lloyd Wright, whom she met a few years after completing *The Fountainhead,* once told her that he regretted Roark's lack of humor, particularly his lack of ability to laugh at himself; Roark would never say, for example, "What a damn fool I was!" Ayn replied stiffly: "Roark would admit errors, but he'd certainly never say a thing like that; he'd never think of himself as a fool; he would never take himself or his work lightly."

In *The Act of Creation,* Arthur Koestler—in a fascinating analysis of the nature and function of humor—wrote that the humor of a joke consists of being led to follow along a certain conceptual track, which, by the punch line, is abruptly switched—so that the punch line is both totally unexpected and perfectly logical in its own terms. The pattern is *"the sudden shift of ideas to a different type of logic or a new rule of the game."* The inclusion of the totally unexpected and perfectly logical was central to Ayn's purposes and method as a fiction writer. Yet those who knew her often had the chastening experience of telling her a joke which they thought was hilarious—then being greeted by a blank look of bewilderment—then having to give a lengthy explanation of what was the presumed humor. Having to explain *anything* to Ayn Rand was an unusual experience; having to explain one's humor made one less than eager to repeat the next hilarious story one heard.

It appeared as if, despite the brilliance and intricacy of her mind, she somehow failed even to *grasp* humor that was subtle or sophisticated; her tastes ran rather to the broad and obvious. Perhaps the cause was that her entire self-training was to rigorously follow a straight and undeviating line from a concept to its implications, to hold one single perspective from premises to conclusion; it was precisely *not* to shift perspective in midstream or ever to employ a "different kind of logic."

During this happiest and most hectic year of her life, the months—which previously had dragged by—now seemed to fly past Ayn at the same breakneck speed as the manuscript pages handed to Nick for proofreading. The only shadow on her pleasure was her weekend work for Paramount; she did the work efficiently and well, but never afterward remembered a single script she had read; the scripts existed in some dim unreality cut off from her emotional life.

Always, Ayn's mental energy was limitless; she was never too tired to continue a philosophical conversation, even after an eighteen-hour work day, even when those many years younger than she were collapsing with exhaustion. But always, she struggled with the problem of low physical energy, which she tried to alleviate with the dark Russian breads and rich cheeses and chocolates she loved, often adding too many pounds to her small frame. She had never been ill except for the normal diseases of childhood, never been in a hospital; at most, she caught a rare cold; but she would rise from long hours at her desk with severe pains in her shoulders and back, her body too weary to move or eat or even fall limply into bed.[1]

[1] It was during this period of nonstop work on *The Fountainhead* that Ayn went to see a doctor. She had heard there was a harmless pill one could take to increase one's energy and lessen one's appetite. The doctor, telling her there would be no negative consequences, prescribed a low dosage of a small green tablet which doctors had begun prescribing rather routinely. Its trade name was Dexamyl. Ayn took two of these pills each day for more than thirty years. They appeared to work: she felt that her physical energy had increased, although it was never high, and her weight stayed under reasonable control. In fact, medical opinion today suggests that they soon ceased to be a source of physical energy; their effect shortly became that of a placebo.

Dexamyl consists of two chemicals: an amphetamine and a barbiturate. It was not until the sixties that researchers investigated the effects of large doses of these chemicals. They found that extremely *high* doses were harmful, sometimes even resulting in paranoid symptoms; but to this day, there is

Early in December of 1942, as *The Fountainhead* neared completion, Ayn worked through a single unbroken stretch of thirty hours. For two nights and a day, she wrote steadily, without sleep, stopping only to eat, as one refuels a motor, so that she could continue to write. She felt exultantly clear-headed, as if she could continue indefinitely without tiring.

When she had time to notice, she knew that *The Fountainhead* was *right*. She had always resented the idea that a writer must inevitably feel some sense of dissatisfaction with his work, that he can never perfectly express what he wishes to say. While writing *We the Living,* she had still been in the process of mastering her technique and of developing her own unique style, and she had had the added difficulty of writing in a language which was not yet fully natural to her. But with *The Fountainhead*—which was far more complex in theme, plot, and characterization—she felt fully in control and fully satisfied with her means of expression: the means were perfectly matched to her end; she was achieving exactly what she wanted, in precisely the form she had intended.

She began the final typing of the manuscript, working around the clock, sleeping only for a few hours at long intervals—while Frank and Nick worked in twelve-hour shifts, proofreading the manuscript and collating pages.

In *The Fountainhead,* Gail Wynand asks Roark: "Howard, when you look back, does it seem to you as if all your days had rolled forward evenly, like a sort of typing exercise, all alike? Or were there stops—points reached—and then the typing rolled on again?" "There were stops," answers Roark. "Did you know them at the time—did you know that that's what they were?" asks Wynand. "Yes," says Roark.

As she walked toward the Bobbs-Merrill office in the brilliant crispness of a winter morning, Ayn knew that *this* was a stop for her—a point reached. It was December 31. She was carrying the completed manuscript.

A few hours earlier, she had typed the final sentence of *The Fountainhead:* "Then there was only the ocean and the sky and the figure of Howard Roark."

---

only the most fragmentary and contradictory scientific evidence to suggest that low doses such as Ayn took could be harmful. As one pharmacological specialist has said: "Perhaps they hurt her, and perhaps they didn't."

In the early seventies, when for the first time she became seriously ill, her doctor took her medical history, and, quite innocently, she told him about the Dexamyl. Disapproving, he ordered her to cease taking them at once. She never took another.

I include this discussion only because I have learned that a number of people, aware that she took this medication, have drawn ominous conclusions about Ayn's mental health; there is no scientific basis for their conclusions.

Chapter Sixteen

In the period before publication of *The Fountainhead,* Bobbs-Merrill, because of the imminent paper shortage, was concerned about the length of the manuscript. Ayn shortened the first part of the manuscript by approximately one third; the major cut was the elimination of Vesta Dunning. She was not unwilling to do it, she had felt some dissatisfaction herself, but, she later said, "Because of the cut, I've always thought Part I was a little slow. There's no major romantic relationship. If I had not planned Vesta Dunning from the beginning, I would have introduced Dominique earlier—not that she would have met Roark, but she would have been there as a presence, so that the main concern would not have been exclusively professional. But there was no time to readjust."

From the inception of the theme in her mind, she had called the novel *Second-hand Lives;* that had remained its working title until the end. But when Archie Ogden pointed out that it stressed the negative, that it made it appear the novel was essentially focused on Peter Keating, Ayn agreed at once and chose *The Fountainhead* instead.

Ayn was immensely gratified that she had no editorial difficulties with Bobbs-Merrill. She often complimented Archie as one of the rare editors who had a sensitive understanding of the intention of his writers, and never attempted to interfere with that intention. "We discussed the book only in *my* terms," she said. "He never interfered with the creative part or suggested *how* I should change it. We got along wonderfully. Editorial suggestions from Indianapolis were sent through Archie. He told me only one: that Chambers objected to the length of Roark's [courtroom] speech, particularly the fact that it was unbroken; he wanted it to be interrupted for descriptions of the characters and so on. I said no—it was absolutely wrong—and that was that."

Ayn did the final editing in galleys. Archie would come to her apartment in the evening after his office day to work with her; they would both remember as happily creative times those evenings over manuscript and coffee and the sweet rolls Ayn never could resist. Ayn remained staunchly loyal to Archie, continuing to see him at regular intervals until he moved to England in the early sixties. It was an unusual friendship for her: Archie was not the sort of man she normally liked. He was a man of charm and wit, but without the philosophical bent or the intensity that were important to her. But she never forgot that he had risked his job for her work, and would discuss what she saw as his shortcomings only with her most intimate friends.

Despite her pleasure in the completion of the novel and in her hopes for its success, Ayn, like the rest of the country, was living with the anguish of a nation fighting for its life. The early years of the forties were desperate years, as newspapers and radios trumpeted the news of Hitler's steady march through Europe, of the blinding speed of the fall of France, of Japanese successes in the Pacific, of young Americans bleeding and dying on foreign shores. Her own especial anguish was the news of the German siege of Leningrad, where her family—with her youngest and beloved sister, Nora, whom she thought of often and missed painfully—still lived. Since the beginning of the war, she had had no word of her family, no way to reach them. With the nine hundred days of the siege, she had no way to know if they were alive. In the terrible months from October of 1941 through April of 1942, almost half of Leningrad's three million people died in a city without heat, light, transport, food, or water; as the temperature fell to thirty degrees below zero; as bombs and shells rained down on the living and the dead; as men, women, and children with pencil-thin limbs and swollen bellies fell in the streets as often from starvation as from the effects of the bombings; as looting and stealing were replaced by cannibalism in a city with nothing left to steal but human bodies. The noble and gracious city, celebrated by its poets, had become a charnel house.[1]

Ayn returned to full-time work at Paramount. The advance payment of royalties had provided only enough money to enable her, with her weekend work, to finish the book. Now, the advance was gone. She did not mind returning to Paramount. Her main assignment was completed.

Over the last years, Frank had found, at best, occasional bit parts in the theater and roles in summer stock. Ayn often said that he willingly abandoned acting when they left Hollywood. That appears not to be so; in New York, the work he looked for was in the theater. It appears that he had left Hollywood because Ayn had to leave Hollywood; he had followed her unquestioningly, his life revolving around her as it had and always would. It appears that Ayn believed that if *she* felt his acting career had become futile, then *he* must feel it; if

---

[1] It was only many years later than Ayn learned that her parents had died in that charnel house. In the decades following the war, rumors of her sisters would reach her from time to time—from an American tourist with an unconfirmable report of having met Natasha, from a Russian refugee who *might* have talked with Nora. But the rumors never jelled into knowledge, and Ayn was afraid to enlist the help of the State Department; if her sisters were alive, official inquiries from the United States might destroy them. As year after year went by, even the faintest grounds for hope dissolved, and Ayn painfully accepted the fact that she had no family left to seek.

she wanted him to leave Hollywood and its last faint hope of a career in movies, then *he* must want it. Authentic emotional communication between them had ended long ago; Frank did not tell Ayn—or anyone else—what he really felt, what he really wanted, what brought him suffering or happiness. These two people, so different in most respects, were alike in the extent of their alienation from their own emotional lives, and now talked primarily of their day-to-day activities and of Ayn's career and work.

In order to help them over the period before publication, Frank began to seek work more actively; he found a job in a cigar store in Brooklyn. It was the uncontested end of his desire for a career of his own; he never looked for acting work again.

Shortly before publication, Ayn was delighted to be approached by Alan Collins, president of Curtis Brown, Ltd., one of the largest and most respected of literary agencies, asking to represent her. It was a remarkable tribute to her; she was the author of a successful play, *Night of January 16th,* but that had been followed by the failures of *We the Living* and *The Unconquered.* Alan Collins told her that he had seen galleys of *The Fountainhead* and was convinced that she had a great literary talent. "I always gave Alan credit for approaching me," Ayn later said. "No one could know how the book would sell." She no longer required an agent for the book rights, but they agreed that he would handle her future work and the movie rights to *The Fountainhead.* It was the beginning of a long and mutually respectful relationship; Alan Collins, a wise and gracious man of great integrity, remained Ayn's agent and friend until his death in 1968; after his death, Ayn remained with the firm.

When she received early copies of the novel, Ayn gave one of them to Isabel Paterson. She inscribed it with Roark's words to Gail Wynand: "To Pat—You have been the one encounter in my life that can never be repeated—Ayn—April 25, 1943."[2]

Discussing the novel with Pat one day, Ayn said: "If *The Fountainhead* does not make me famous, I'll continue to write, but I will not expect any recognition in my lifetime. I know the nature of this novel. I do not care to become famous for any other." "What sale would you consider a success?" Pat asked. "One hundred thousand copies," Ayn said. Pat gasped: "How can you set your desires in the stratosphere? Do you realize how few books *ever* sell that many copies?" "That's what I want," said Ayn. "If it sells a hundred thousand copies, then it will have reached my kind of readers, the right minds, wherever they are."

Publication day was approaching. From her experience with *We the Living,*

[2] When I interviewed Muriel Hall, she showed me the first-edition copy of *The Fountainhead* that was part of Pat's estate. I burst into somewhat appalled laughter when I began to thumb through the book. At some point, probably in later years, Pat had decided to edit Ayn; the first few pages of the novel show Pat's cuts of what she considered extraneous material. Among other things, she had eliminated *The Fountainhead*'s first sentence—and most famous line: "Howard Roark laughed." Muriel Hall asked me if I thought Pat had ever shown her editing to Ayn. "No," I answered, "I *know* she didn't." "How can you know it?" Muriel asked. I replied, "Because Pat lived to show you the book."

Ayn knew she could not count on reviews to accurately inform the public about her book. She could count only on Bobbs-Merrill, on an advertising campaign that would stress the revolutionary nature of *The Fountainhead*'s theme. Archie reported that the book was already causing a stir: he was receiving enthusiastic telephone calls from booksellers and editors of publications to whom advance copies had been sent; all the signs were good, he said exultantly.

On the day before publication, Frank told her, with happy confidence: "We've made it, this time."

The Fountainhead was published in May 1943.

The week of publication, Bobbs-Merrill sent Ayn an advance proof of the advertisement scheduled for the Sunday newspapers. It was a half-page advertisement, which described *The Fountainhead* as an interesting new book that would do for architecture what *Arrowsmith* did for medicine.

"I stood still in the middle of the living room holding the page," Ayn would later recall with a shudder, "and literally wished I could die on that spot. I've never experienced anything like that before or since. It was the most ghastly shock of anger and futility, and the feeling that there's absolutely nothing I can do about this and I don't want any part of a world in which this is done."

It was too late to change the first advertisement; the ones that followed continued to be, for the most part, Ayn said, "vague, noncommittal, and meaningless." There was no way for anyone to distinguish *The Fountainhead* from all the other allegedly "big" and "challenging" books offered to them daily by means of the same routine bromides.

One of the first reviews called it an interesting book about architecture, and said its message was that we ought to do something about the people in the slums. Another announced that the ideas it presented were selfish and reactionary. Another described Roark as a selfless architect. A socialist reviewer attacked it ferociously. There were many attacks, most of which ignored the ideological content and damned it as dull, badly written, with implausible characters; "Miss Rand has much to learn before she can write," said one. Another said, "Miss Rand can only create gargoyles, not characters." None of the major magazines, with the exception of *The Saturday Review*, even mentioned its existence. None of the reviewers, including those who praised it, stated the theme of the novel. The one fact—more than any other—that Ayn had wanted the public to know, was that this was a book about *individualism*. For all practical purposes, it was as if the press were under censorship; "individualism" seemed to be the forbidden, the terrifying word.

There was a storm of objections to the climax of *The Fountainhead*. In articles, reviews, and discussions, the assumption was often that Roark dynamited Cortlandt Homes "because somebody changed the look of his building, and he didn't like it, so he blew up the home of the poor." These critics had not read the fine—or the large—print. Ayn had made it clear that the issue involved was breach of contract. The contract for the building guaranteed that it would be erected as it was designed. It was a government project; the government could not be sued or forced to honor its contract without its consent. Roark had no legal recourse by which to undo the butchering of his work.

"I agreed to design Cortlandt," he told the jury at his trial, "for the purpose of seeing it erected as I designed it and for no other reason. That was the price I set for my work. I was not paid. . . . the owners of Cortlandt got what they needed from me. They wanted a scheme devised to build a structure as cheaply as possible. They found no one else who could do it to their satisfaction. I could and did. They took the benefit of my work and made me contribute it as a gift. But I am not an altruist. I do not contribute gifts of this nature.

"It is said that I have destroyed the home of the destitute. It is forgotten that but for me the destitute could not have had this particular home. Those who were concerned with the poor had to come to me, who have never been concerned, in order to help the poor. It is believed that the poverty of the future tenants gave them a right to my work. That their need constituted a claim in my life. That it was my duty to contribute anything demanded of me. This is the second-hander's creed now swallowing the world.

"I came here to say that I do not recognize anyone's right to one minute of my life. Nor to any part of my energy. Nor to any achievement of mine. No matter who makes the claim, how large their number or how great their need.

"I wished to come here and say that I am a man who does not exist for others.

"It had to be said. The world is perishing from an orgy of self-sacrifice."

There was an exception to the generality of the reviews. On a week day shortly after publication, Archie telephoned to say he wanted to read Ayn an advance copy of a review by Lorine Pruette which was to appear in the Sunday New York *Times Book Review.* "I don't want to hear it," Ayn said wearily. "I've had enough." "You'll want to hear this one," Archie told her.

Lorine Pruette wrote: "Ayn Rand is a writer of great power. She has a subtle and ingenious mind and the capacity of writing brilliantly, beautifully, bitterly." The review made explicitly clear that the theme of the book was individualism versus collectivism. "Good novels of ideas," Pruette stated, "are rare at any time. This is the only novel of ideas written by an American woman that I can recall. . . . You will not be able to read this masterful work without thinking through some of the basic concepts of our times."

"It saved my whole sense of the world at that time," Ayn was to say. "It's the only intelligent major review of a novel I have had in my whole career."

Later reviews, several of which Ayn considered intelligent and perceptive, came in from other cities. But professionally only New York reviews counted, she believed.

The first printing of *The Fountainhead* was 7,500 copies. Bobbs-Merrill's intention had been to print only 5,000, but they had raised it when advance sales seemed promising. After publication, sales were ominously slow. The book would appear at the bottom of one or another bestseller list, then vanish, then appear and vanish again. "All that summer," Ayn recalled, "I watched its progress. It looked as if it had been completely killed by a campaign of silence about its content. I fought with Bobbs-Merrill constantly about their ads, although I had no contractual right of control. They would advertise it once in a while, but the wording was terrible—to this day I can't think about it calmly. In one they had a drawing of a woman with an enormous bosom, and the copy said 'the amazing story of a ruthless woman.' They told me that would sell books. I kept telling them that people who would buy the book from such ads would *hate* it—and my real audience would be stopped from buying. . . . That whole summer I was thinking about how to plan the rest of my life. I'd need a job, and could continue to write only at night, and I'd have to get used to that sort of life."

Toward fall, Bobbs-Merrill scheduled a second printing of 2,500 copies. Archie demanded that they raise it at least to 5,000. The business manager refused: "This book will never sell more than a total of ten thousand copies," he said. Archie made a bet with him, for one dollar: If you don't increase this printing, you'll have to reprint by Thanksgiving. In November, the business manager walked into Archie's office and silently placed a dollar bill on his desk: sales had reached 18,000 copies.

In his posthumously published autobiography, Hiram Haydn, later to be Ayn's Random House editor for *Atlas Shrugged,* wrote: "A . . . startling example of Mr. Chambers' [the head of Bobbs-Merrill] penuriousness and stubbornness involved another novel Bobbs published that year: Ayn Rand's *The Fountainhead.* Despite an unmistakeable groundswell of excitement over this book, DLC, as we all knew him, gave it only the most perfunctory support."

Sales slowly began to accelerate, and the book appeared steadily on bestseller lists. But the paper shortage had become severe, and paper rationing began; quotas were set according to the amount of paper a publisher had used during an arbitrary base year. Bobbs-Merrill kept issuing small editions—then going out of print.[3]

It seemed as if *The Fountainhead* would follow *We the Living* into oblivion. Ayn was still working full time as a Paramount reader, Frank was working in a cigar store, and sales of the novel continued to limp along. Ayn had never felt closer to despair, nor had the future ever seemed more bleak.

In that painful year of publication, Ayn could not know that in 1945 alone— two years after publication—*The Fountainhead* would sell 100,000 copies. She could not know that the odyssey of *The Fountainhead,* unique in publishing history, was beginning.

It is an odyssey without an end. By 1948, sales would exceed 400,000 copies. In 1952, the New American Library would publish it in paperback. By 1962, it would have sold over 500,000 copies in hardcover editions and over a million

---

[3] It was not until 1944 that Bobbs-Merrill entered into an arrangement with Blakiston, a small publisher who, in the base year, had had a huge sale of a manual, and whose paper quota was now very large. The arrangement was that Blakiston would take over publication of *The Fountainhead* until the shortage ended, as it had taken over bestsellers from a number of major publishers. Blakiston issued very large editions, and in their ads, for the first time, the theme of the book was stated; they called it "the story of a rebellious, individualistic man."

copies in paperback. Today, the "noncommercial" book for which there was no audience has sold more than four million copies. The book that was "too intellectual" is read by truck drivers and farmers. The book that was "too controversial" is studied in university classrooms. *The Fountainhead* has achieved the status of a modern classic.

Ayn could not know what was to happen—but beneath her pain and despair still existed the bright core of conviction she had carried with her throughout her thirty-eight years: that human beings will ultimately respond to values. It might happen more slowly than she had expected, it might take longer; but *The Fountainhead* was an important book, and one day it would find its audience. Frances Hazlitt was never to forget Ayn telling her, even before the novel was accepted by Bobbs-Merrill, that her novel would become a bestseller, would have great impact, would change people's lives—that a movie would be made of it, and that she would demand a say in picking the actors; she would choose Gary Cooper as the male star.[4]

From the beginning, Ayn was deluged by mail from her readers. Publishers later said that they know of no other writer who inspired an equivalent response. The letters began to come—and would continue to come until Ayn's death—from professors and unskilled workers, from students and soldiers, from housewives and scientists and businessmen and artists. They wrote that they had found in Roark's moral intransigence a personal ideal—that the image of Roark had given them a greater courage to stand by their own convictions and to fight for their own achievements—that *The Fountainhead* had liberated them from the guilt they had experienced for their failure to live by the altruist ethics—that it had taught them to feel proud of their work—that after reading it, they gave up meaningless jobs which they had accepted as second best, and returned to the careers for which they had longed—that it had given them the sense of what is possible in life, what is possible to man, what is possible to *them.*

Many of the letters that Ayn most appreciated were from men in the armed services overseas. One letter from a group of air-force men said: "After every mission, we gather around a candle and read passages from *The Fountainhead* aloud." Another said: "I'd feel much better about the war if I thought it was being fought for the ideals of *The Fountainhead.*"[5]

Isabel Paterson's *The God of the Machine* had been published the same month

[4] Henry Hazlitt was later to say, "To our enormous surprise, but not Ayn's, it all came true."
[5] Finally unable to deal with the thousands of letters, Ayn would later have a "Letter from Ayn Rand" printed, in which she answered the questions most often asked. In it she wrote:
"The success of *The Fountainhead* has demonstrated its own thesis. It was rejected by twelve publishers who declared that it had no commercial possibilities, it would not sell, it was 'too intellectual,' it was 'too unconventional,' it went against every alleged popular trend. Yet the success of *The Fountainhead* was made by the public. Not by the public as an organized *collective*—but by single, individual readers who discovered it of their own choice, who read it on their own initiative and recommended it on their own judgment.
"I did not know that I was predicting my own future when I described the process of Roark's success: 'It was as if an underground stream flowed through the country and broke out in sudden springs that shot to the surface at random, in unpredictable places.' "

as *The Fountainhead.* In it was a chapter dealing with Ayn's theory of morality entitled "The Humanitarian with the Guillotine"—which contains a paraphrasing of Ayn's ideas. Today a reader of Ayn Rand would recognize the source of certain of the ideas in that chapter; but then, with *The Fountainhead* newly published, readers could legitimately assume that Isabel Paterson was the source of these radical new moral concepts. "It was only after the book came out," Ayn later said, "that I realized Pat had done something enormously improper. And she had a name, I did not; had she mentioned me, it could have helped me professionally." One can only take as an indication of Ayn's deep attachment to her friend, that this was not the occasion of a permanent rift.[6]

On an afternoon in the fall, Alan Collins telephoned Ayn with the news that Warner Brothers was interested in the movie rights to *The Fountainhead* and wanted to know her price. "I want fifty thousand dollars," Ayn calmly replied. Collins objected: that was a fantastic amount to ask, there had been no cross-bidding on the movie rights, and to demand so large a sum would probably cost her the deal. "Ask for twenty-five thousand," he said, "and settle for twenty." Ayn replied, "This book is going to be worth much more than fifty thousand dollars. But for now, that's a good price, and the money is important to me. If I take less, I'll regret it; if I get fifty thousand, I won't. I know the value of the book. I'll take the chance of losing the deal."

Ten days passed. Ayn, by now well-known in the conservative world, had maintained the contacts made during the Willkie campaign, and was attempting to interest conservative businessmen in contributing money for advertisements for her novel, advertisements that would stress its pro-individualist, pro-capitalist nature. She was turned down everywhere, by men who she concluded were unable to see that she was fighting for a cause that was theirs as well. "Of what importance are books in politics?" one of them demanded. "Of what importance was *Das Kapital?*" she asked. "I was ruthless with myself in those days," she later recalled. "I *hated* to work for a campaign for my own book, but I did it."

Still anxiously waiting to hear from Alan Collins, Ayn lunched with a businessman who had expressed interest in her campaign. "He was the usual type of conservative, not intellectual, he gave me the usual line about philosophical education being long-term, and our time being too short for that. I knew it was hopeless."

Arriving home from lunch, feeling weary and discouraged, she opened the apartment door to see Frank standing in the living room, an odd look on his face.

"Well, darling," he said, "while you were at lunch you earned fifty thousand dollars."

[6] When Nathaniel and I met Ayn and expressed an interest in economics, *The God of the Machine* was one of the handful of books she recommended to us. In 1964, when it was reissued after having been out of print for many years, she wrote an admiring review of it, terming it "an invaluable arsenal of intellectual ammunition for any advocate of capitalism. It is a sparkling book, with little gems of polemical fire scattered through almost every page, ranging from bright wit to the hard glitter of logic to the quiet radiance of a profound understanding."

Chapter Seventeen

The day she earned fifty thousand dollars, Ayn and Frank went for dinner, as they often did, to a neighborhood cafeteria on Lexington Avenue; they lived nearby, in the small, somewhat seedy apartment they had moved to when every penny was required for the writing of *The Fountainhead*. All afternoon, their moods had shifted between excited happiness and dazed disbelief. Whatever they needed to do of a physical nature, from dressing to feeding their cat to locking the apartment door behind them, they seemed able to do only with the automatic parts of their minds.

The cafeteria offered two types of meals: one cost forty-five cents, the other sixty-five cents. They had always ordered the former. They glanced at the menu, ignoring as usual the more expensive dishes, then stopped short, looked at each other—and burst out laughing. *Today* they could afford a sixty-five-cent dinner.

Ayn could not sleep that night. She sat at her desk "just gloating." When she heard Frank, who had gone to bed, still tossing and turning hours later, she asked, "Are you gloating too?" "Yes," he answered. "I'm afflicted." They stayed up all night, talking and smiling and hugging each other.

The day the contract with Warner Brothers was signed, Ayn and Frank went to the Roosevelt Hotel for champagne cocktails. "Although I don't like to drink," Ayn later said, "we had to celebrate. We were both walking on air. It was the most unreal period in my whole life. If I had become rich and successful by degrees, it would never have had such drama—it was the sudden switch from the bottom economically to fifty thousand dollars and a Hollywood contract. It was worth the whole struggle."

Ayn was wearing an old cloth coat, inexpensive when it was new and now, Frank told her, "a disgrace." He and Isabel Paterson insisted that she buy a mink coat. Ayn was horrified at the suggestion; she wanted to save her new riches so that she would never again lack time to write. She would buy a new coat, she agreed, but it would be cloth. Frank responded: "You can buy any kind of coat you want—provided it's fur; and any kind of fur you want—provided it's mink." It *was* mink.

The price of the coat was twenty-four hundred dollars. Little more than a year before, the fate of *The Fountainhead* had depended on getting an advance of twelve hundred dollars—which she didn't get. When she told Alan Collins of her new purchase, he laughed delightedly. "I've never yet had a woman client," he said, "who, if she sells the movie rights to her novel, doesn't buy a mink coat."

The contract with Warner Brothers required that Ayn come to Hollywood to write the preliminary script for the movie. She had accepted eagerly: she wanted to be the scriptwriter for *The Fountainhead*, and if Warner Brothers liked her preliminary work, they might hire her to do the final version. She knew that writing the script would not give her control over its fate, that the studio had the legal right to change it in any manner they chose, at any moment, for any reason. She knew she had taken a terrible risk by selling the movie rights; her sole weapon in fighting to protect the integrity of her work would be her power of persuasion.

If she could not save it, still, her freedom to write her next novel was financially assured. And the movie, if it merely followed the plot line of *The Fountainhead*, would communicate the essence of her ideas; and it would help the still-sagging sales of the novel. "I would never allow a cut version of the book to be published," she explained. "That's destroying the work itself, that's Roark's Cortlandt. But a film, however bad, leaves the book intact."

In December, Ayn and Frank left by train for Hollywood. On Ayn's first trip to Hollywood, seventeen years before, she had traveled by day coach; Frank had worked his way as steward on a freighter. Now, they took the luxurious Twentieth Century to Chicago, then a stateroom on the Chief, happily and incredulously reveling in a luxury that had never before been possible to them. "The transition to this way of life was incredible," she would always recall. "We both remember that trip as an enormous highlight in our lives. We went to the diner on the Twentieth Century, and Frank ordered steak—the feeling that we *could* do this, and that we had *earned* it, was marvelous. The only advantage to poverty is that if you can get out of it, the contrast is wonderful."

The first person Ayn met when she arrived in Hollywood was Henry Blanke, who was to produce *The Fountainhead*. "He was a charming, nice man," Ayn said, "but not strong." She was pleased that he was to be the producer, because he had done serious movies such as *The Story of Louis Pasteur*, and had worked with Ernst Lubitsch and Fritz Lang, both of whom Ayn admired—"although he did inexcusably awful B movies too." He was enthusiastic about the project. His first words were, "It's a great book. It's *magnificent.*" He said that he wanted her screenplay to be as faithful to the book as possible.

Blanke was later quoted as saying, "She told us that she would blow up the

Warner Brothers lot if we changed one word [of her script], and we believed her. Even Jack Warner believed her."

Ayn was disappointed to learn that, as a result of the wartime shortage of materials for the many sets the film would require, production had to be indefinitely delayed. In the end, she waited five years, through delay after delay—never knowing if she would be asked to do the final script—until production was finally scheduled.

Ayn and Frank moved into a furnished apartment in Hollywood until they could decide where they wanted to live—smuggling in Turtle Cat, who had traveled with them, against the rules of the building. The only pets they did not have to hide were Oscar and Oswald, the small stuffed lion cubs that Frank had given Ayn soon after their marriage. The cubs went with Ayn wherever she lived for the rest of her life, sitting sedately in the room where she wrote "as a symbol of the benevolent universe." Each Christmas—a holiday Ayn loved to celebrate, maintaining that in America it was essentially a pagan event, an excuse to give parties and exchange gifts with friends—the two cubs were brought out from her study, dressed in cheerful Christmas hats, and ensconced, slightly bedraggled with age, in the living room, where they were surrounded by colorfully wrapped gifts. The cubs fulfilled the same need as her tiddlywink music—and as the private affectionate names that new friends were always astonished to discover Ayn and Frank used for each other: he was "Cubby-hole" and she was "Fluff."

This severely austere intellectual took enormous pleasure in being called "Fluff." The woman who most of her life felt as if she were a brain encased in flesh, seemed never to feel more womanly than when Frank addressed her by her pet name. The woman who took no help, who fought her own battles and made her own decisions, reveled in the feeling of being fragile and delicate and protected.

Despite the delay in production of the movie, Warner Brothers wanted Ayn to write a preliminary script immediately. Blanke's instructions were that she was to make it as long as she wished and to include as much of the story as possible. Ayn completed it in six weeks; it was three hundred pages long; the final working script was under a hundred and fifty pages.

"I had no difficulties with the dramatic form as such," Ayn later said. "The difficulty was that I was not interested personally as a writer, I was very uninspired—I had worked for seven years to achieve the structure, and to tear it down was horrible; the better the integration, the harder it is to change it. I would have fought to the death to do the adaptation, but as a job it was very boring and painful; I had told the story in the proper form in the book. And I was certain that it couldn't be made into a *really* good movie: the length of time involved in the story, eighteen years, is too long to be ideal movie material, and too much of the action is psychological rather than physical. But Blanke liked the preliminary script very much."

It was Barbara Stanwyck, Ayn learned, who had interested Warner Brothers, to whom she was under contract, in *The Fountainhead*. Stanwyck had read it, admired it, and wanted the role of Dominique. She and Ayn lunched several times together to discuss the role, and although Ayn's first choice for Dominique was Greta Garbo—whom she knew would probably not be obtainable—she fought unsuccessfully to have the part given to Stanwyck. Stanwyck was not the physical type Ayn had envisioned, but Ayn admired her work, liked her personally, and was grateful for her help.

During the years before the movie went into production, it seemed as if every major star in Hollywood, male and female, wanted the role of Roark or Dominique. For a while, Humphrey Bogart was seriously considered, but to Ayn's great relief—her choice was Gary Cooper, and Bogart could not have been more opposite a type—he turned it down. A story about Clark Gable appeared in the newspapers, which he later verified to Ayn. Gable had been on leave from the Army and was traveling from New York to Hollywood; a friend gave him several books to read on the train, including *The Fountainhead*. In Chicago, Gable got off the train and telephoned MGM, to whom he was under contract, demanding that they buy the book for him immediately. He was furious when he learned it had already been purchased by Warner Brothers, and "he raised hell that while he was away fighting, his studio was not protecting his interests." MGM offered Warner Brothers four hundred and fifty thousand dollars for the property; the offer, which would have given the studio a four-hundred-thousand-dollar profit, was refused—and Gable demanded to be let out of his contract with MGM. Ayn had not been wrong in predicting that her book would one day be worth much more than fifty thousand dollars.

Joan Crawford gave a dinner party for Ayn—"It was very funny, she appeared dressed as Dominique, in a white Adrian dinner gown and loaded with aquamarines. She was a good actress, but she could never play an intellectual woman or a lady. . . . The funniest of all was Veronica Lake, who said the role was perfect for her because of her haircut—you know, she wore her blond hair over one eye—which Dominique didn't."

Ayn and Frank began to discuss the possibility of buying a house, in order to invest the money from the movie sale. Frank scoured the area until he found a small ranch at 10,000 Tampa Avenue in the San Fernando Valley—thirteen acres of land and a modern house of steel and glass designed by Richard Neutra. Ayn liked the design of the house—it is considered to be the most dramatic of Neutra's houses—but was hesitant about purchasing it, concerned by its twenty-mile distance from Hollywood and by what seemed so enormous an investment. Josef von Sternberg, the original owner, had paid less than fifteen thousand dollars for it; the present owner was asking twenty-four thousand. But Frank insisted that it would be a good investment, certain to increase in value.[1]

It was then that Ayn and Frank's landlady discovered their smuggled cat. "Get rid of the cat," she said, "or leave the apartment." "All right," Ayn told

---

[1] Frank was correct; in 1963, Ayn and Frank sold it for one hundred and seventy-five thousand dollars.

Frank, "we buy the house." Soon, she was working in a sunlit study facing the austere blue shapes of hills in the distance, with Oscar and Oswald on a couch near her desk.

Whenever Frank talked about his life on the ranch in later years, his friends observed, his face seemed to come alive with a smile that made him look younger than his age. The next few years appear to have been the happiest of Frank's life. He managed the ranch, reconditioned the land, landscaped the grounds, and grew acres of flowers and citrus trees for commercial sale. Soon, one could see among the flowers exquisite miniature gladiolas that he had developed himself. On one section of the land were cages of peacocks—cages that Frank, who could not bear to see any living thing imprisoned, had built without tops, so that the peacocks were free to fly. He often worked eighteen hours a day; he would enter the house in the evening exhausted, but uncharacteristically eager to talk of the things he had done that day. To work with beautiful things— his flowers and his peacocks—and to work with his hands, to make things grow —and to be engaged in activities that were *his*, not Ayn's, was a way of life that gave him deep contentment.

Thrown into the midst of unaccustomed luxury after years of struggle, Ayn often found herself thinking of a line quoted in Victor Hugo's *The Man Who Laughs:* "No man can pass abruptly from Siberia to Senegal without fainting." But much as Frank loved living on the ranch, Ayn came to dislike it. As she had feared, the distance to Hollywood became a severe problem. Frank had promised to teach her to drive their new Cadillac convertible, so that she would not be dependent on him. He gave her several driving lessons, then they both gave up the attempt in mutually enraged despair. Frank was a very bad driver—some of the most terrifying hours in the lives of his friends were spent in cars with Frank at the wheel—and Ayn, who found mechanical objects impossible to master, was unable to learn. Whenever she had to go to the city, Frank had to take her. The isolation began to trouble her: she felt cut off and trapped, unable to do what she wanted when she wanted. After her years in New York, she disliked California, which she called "the provinces"; she missed the activity and excitement of New York. She made an uncomfortable, complaining peace with her new way of life and was never happy with it.

Ayn and Frank soon began to enjoy inviting guests to their new home— always alive with Frank's flowers—as Ayn met political conservatives in California. Leonard Read, head of the Los Angeles Chamber of Commerce who was to become widely known and influential as the founder of The Foundation for Economic Education, was an occasional visitor. One evening, Read and another friend were at Ayn's home and began discussing the need for a book about a society of complete collectivism, showing the ultimate consequences of collectivist doctrine applied to the actual existence of man. "I have written just such a book," Ayn said. "It's a story called *Anthem.*" Leonard Read later wrote, "I borrowed her only copy and read it on the eastbound Stratoliner. My secretary, to whom I gave the book to be returned, read it during her lunch hour and said:

'This is a great book. Isn't it too bad that others can't read it?' Precisely what I had been thinking."

Through Pamphleteers, a small publishing house whose purpose was to further the cause of freedom and individualism, Read arranged for the publication of five thousand copies. *Anthem,* written in 1937 and published only in England, received its first American publication.

Other visitors to the ranch were people in the movie industry, such as Morrie Ryskind, writer of the sensationally successful *Of Thee I Sing,* and his wife, Mary. Janet Gaynor and her designer husband, Adrian, were Ayn and Frank's "neighbors"—which meant that they lived only a few miles away—and the two couples developed a warm relationship. A younger friend was Herbert Corneulle, later to move to Hawaii to head Dole Pineapple. Ayn's favorite of the political conservatives she met was William Mullendore, president of Consolidated Edison of California and an outspoken defender of free enterprise. He was a charming, attractive, courageous man, who spoke his mind with great dignity and effectiveness, and deeply admired Ayn's work. "He was the star of my Hollywood conservatives," Ayn would often say. "He went all over the country speaking for free enterprise; he was the only uncompromising businessman I've ever known."

Ayn had met Henry Hazlitt earlier in New York, through her friendship with Frances; she began to know him better during this period, on her rare visits to New York and his more frequent trips to California. "Frances was always very complimentary and enthusiastic about my work," Ayn was to say, "and Henry seemed to echo her, although I wasn't sure of his exact views, I didn't really know his reasons. But he projected respect for me and interest in my ideas, and that I was an important intellectual ally." And Henry Hazlitt was to say, "Frances and I both liked Ayn personally very much, considered her our friend—and did not get particularly upset by her occasional scoldings of us. I differed strongly with her on ethical problems, but sensed that any discussion of them would simply lead to a useless quarrel. I don't try to change someone's mind if I think it's a basic and set thing."

Through the Hazlitts, Ayn met the brilliant theoretical economist Ludwig von Mises, one of the founders of the "Austrian School" of free-market economics and later to become a seminal influence on twentieth-century economic thought. His major work, *Human Action,* deals with the nature, scope, and methodology of economics, and presents a comprehensive defense of the free market and free exchange. One of his students was Nobel Prize winner Friedrich von Hayek.[2]

Ayn was charmed by Von Mises. Along with a vast and searching intellect, he

[2] As late as the fifties, Von Mises was relatively unknown in the United States—his books were not published here before 1944—until, beginning in the late fifties and continuing for more than ten years, Ayn began a concerted campaign to have his work read and appreciated: she published reviews, she cited him in articles and in public speeches, she attended some of his seminars at New York University, she recommended him to admirers of her philosophy. A number of economists have said that it was largely as a result of Ayn's efforts that the work of Von Mises began to reach its potential audience.

had a gentleness, a warmth, and communicated a respect for whomever he talked with, that made him beloved by his friends and his students. "He seemed very impressed," Ayn recalled, "that a woman had read his books and was seriously interested in economics. He had read *The Fountainhead,* and he seemed to think highly of it. I didn't like his separation of morality and economics, but I assumed that it simply meant that morality was not his specialty and that he could not devise one of his own. At that time, I thought—about both Henry and Von Mises—that since they were fully committed to laissez-faire capitalism, the rest of their philosophy had contradictions only because they did not yet know how to integrate a full philosophy to capitalism. It didn't bother me; I knew *I* would present the full case."

Henry Hazlitt said to Ayn one day: "I just talked with Lu Mises a few days ago. He called you 'the most courageous man in America.' " "Did he say *man?*" asked Ayn. "Yes," he replied. Ayn was delighted.

While still in New York working on *The Fountainhead,* Ayn had hoped to meet Frank Lloyd Wright and to interview him about architecture. Through Ely Jacques Kahn, she had attended a banquet at which he spoke. "I spent three hundred and fifty dollars out of my savings to buy a black velvet dress and shoes and a cape, everything to match, at Bonwit Teller's, which I had never entered before," she would recall. "I felt this would be an unrepeatable occasion, because I was to meet a man who was really great." After the banquet, Kahn introduced her to Wright. When she told him she was writing a novel on architecture and wanted to interview him, he seemed disinterested and vague about his plans. She realized that she would have to show him her work; then he would be interested, she thought.

When three chapters were completed, she had sent them to Wright with a copy of *We the Living,* and again asked for an interview. She had received in return a brief, antagonistic note, saying, without explanation, that he liked nothing about the chapters. Ayn was deeply wounded. "I never could forgive him," she once said, "because he hurt me through his virtues; he could hurt me only because I admired him."

Now, in California, Ayn met Wright again at the home of his son, Lloyd Wright. This time, he was pleasant and cordial. He said he had not yet read *The Fountainhead,* but planned to do so. Ayn liked him, and believed that he liked her. "He talked as if he and I understood each other spiritually," she would explain, "as artists against the world. We had an interesting conversation about individualism. He was an extremely intelligent man. . . . He said one very funny thing. You know, he's very short, though he carries himself beautifully and with dignity. He said that from the early chapters I'd sent him, he hadn't liked the fact that Roark was so tall, and that he should not have red hair but a

---

Ayn also widely recommended and discussed Henry Hazlitt's brilliant presentation of basic economic issues for the laymen, *Economics in One Lesson.* But Hazlitt and his work were already known, and his book a bestseller.

mane of white hair. Lloyd said, 'Oh, Father, Miss Rand wasn't writing your biography!' He chuckled and said, 'That's true. . . .'

"He said to me at one point, 'I don't think you can write about integrity. You're too young to have suffered.' I answered, 'Oh yes, I have suffered. Do you want to know what was the worst of it? It was your letter.' He shook his head sadly. He seemed to recall the letter only vaguely. He'd thought I just wanted to use him for publicity, as so many people had tried to do. . . . As we were leaving that evening, he sat at the piano and began to play violently dramatic, exultant music. It was so false and phony. I felt sad and embarrassed that such a man had to express himself in that way. Because under the falseness was something very authentic—a heroic and romantic sense of life that he could express only in architecture."

When Wright read *The Fountainhead,* he wrote Ayn: "I've read every word of *The Fountainhead.* Your thesis is *the* great one. Especially at this time. . . . Your grasp of the architectural ins and outs of a degenerate profession astonishes me. . . . Your novel is Novel. Unusual material in unusual hands and, I hope, to an unusual end." Ayn was thrilled with the letter, but disappointed that he did not volunteer to be quoted. She learned later that he kept the book on his night table in Taliesin, and that, at his suggestion, almost every student in his architectural school had read it. But he made no public statement.

Wright invited Ayn and Frank to visit him, and they spent a weekend at Taliesin East. It was a shocking experience for Ayn. "It was like a feudal establishment," she was to say, recalling the weekend. "The buildings were magnificent, and thrilling to see after having seen pictures of them. They were connected by courts and galleries, built on sloping hills, and adapted perfectly to their site. But they were terribly neglected; there were broken window panes, doors that didn't fit, the floors creaked—he had a theoretical mind with no concern for how one would actually live, the practical side didn't interest him."

As Ayn described the scene, it was clear to her listeners that, unknowingly, she was describing her own attitude and her own way of life; Frank had always furnished their apartments attractively, as he did the house on the ranch, with the clean, modern lines that Ayn loved—but the furniture was soon ripped by the claws of their cats, the carpets were stained, the bathroom was rarely cleaned. Ayn "had a theoretical mind with no concern for how one would actually live."

At Taliesin, Ayn was startled to learn that Wright's students, who lived there, were required to pay for tuition and also to take care of the house, the grounds, and the farm, to cook and clean, to wait on tables, and to do the complex drafting of his buildings. She knew that his lectures and his criticisms of their work were invaluable, but felt that it was not right that he make them servants. She later commented disapprovingly, "They were like medieval serfs. The most horrible thing was that the menu for his table, where his guests also ate, was different than the menu for his students. We sat on a raised platform, high above the others, we ate fancy delicacies and they got fried eggs; it was a real caste system. The idea for all of it was his wife's. He was the deity of the place, its spirit, and she was the practical manager.

"Almost all his students seemed like emotional, out-of-focus hero-worshippers. Anything he said was right, there was an atmosphere of worshipful, awed obedience. When he and I began to argue about something, the students were against me instantly; they bared their teeth that I was disagreeing with the master. They showed me some of their work, which was badly imitative of Wright. What was tragic was that he did not want any of that; he was trying to get intellectual independence from them during the general discussions, but he didn't get anything except 'Yes, sir' or 'No, sir' and recitals of formulas from his writing. He wanted what I want: independent understanding; but he didn't know how to stimulate it. I felt sorry for him in that atmosphere. Although he was approaching eighty, by comparison with that retinue he was the youngest person there."

As Ayn described the Wrights' attitude, it was clear to her listeners that she was describing, unknowingly, conflicting aspects of her own attitude: the emotional need and demand for total agreement always at war with the equal, simultaneous longing for an independent response.

It was that weekend that Ayn commissioned Wright to design a home for her, to be built in the future. The sketches show a beautiful, complex structure of three stories, with her study at the top. Ayn would later tell a friend, Lawrence A. Scott, the final installment of the story of Ayn Rand and Frank Lloyd Wright. When Wright showed her the sketches of the house, she asked the price—and was stunned by the amount he named. It was well beyond her financial capabilities, she told him. "My dear lady," he replied. "That's no problem at all. Go out and make more money."

After her return to California from Taliesin, Ayn soon had less time for the political and philosophical discussions that she enjoyed. While completing the preliminary movie script of *The Fountainhead,* she had met Hal Wallis, producer of *Jezebel, Dark Victory* and *Casablanca,* who was working on the Warners lot. Soon after their meeting, Wallis quarreled with Jack Warner and walked off the lot to form his own production company. He offered Ayn a long-term screenwriting contract. Blanke had made her the same offer. Ayn told Wallis what she had told Blanke: she was ready to begin a new novel, and would sign a contract only with the provision that she work no more than six months each year. Blanke had refused; it was against studio policy and unprecedented in Hollywood. Wallis agreed. Ayn signed a five-year contract guaranteeing her six months work a year and six free months. "To this day, I like Wallis very much," Ayn said many years later. "He was a talented, sensitive, very intelligent man, though not intellectual; and he had a good dramatic sense. It was a pleasure working for him because he would always accept a rational argument—reason was an absolute to him." And Hal Wallis was to say, "Ayn was a brilliant writer, and totally an individualist in her person, her writing, and her ideas."

She began working harder than ever, under the pressure of Wallis's constant deadlines; often, she and Frank had no time to see each other except at the dinner table. But she did take time to go to Beverly Hills to make two purchases: the complete works of Aristotle and three suits by Adrian.

Ayn's first assignment for Hal Wallis was an adaptation of the novel *Love Letters,* written by Chris Massie. "I chose it out of sheer desperation from among the batch of plotless novels about someone's emotions that he showed me," she said. "He didn't see how I could make it dramatic—the book was junk. But I saw at least the possibility of a dramatic situation in it." Dubiously, Wallis agreed to let her try it.

The movie of *Love Letters,* a love story with a strong mystery element, starred Jennifer Jones and Joseph Cotten. It was a huge commercial success. To this day it can regularly be seen on late-night television. One finds the touch of Ayn Rand everywhere in the movie, in the considerable reworking of the original story and in the beauty and romanticism of the dialogue between the two lovers.

Her next assignment was *You Came Along,* the story of a dying airman and the woman who loves him. It was an original screenplay, which she felt was badly written. However, she liked the story, and agreed to redo it. "I kept whatever was good in the original script," she said, "and wrote the rest; I got second credit, which was fine even though I'd saved it." The movie, starring Robert Cummings and Lizabeth Scott, was also an unusual commercial success; it, too, can still be seen on late-night television.

Hal Wallis suggested to Ayn that she write a movie original: the story of the development of the atom bomb. The idea interested her, and she agreed to do it —on one condition: that she be allowed to write the story as she understood it, as a triumph of the human mind in a free society. Little information about the work done on the bomb in Germany was yet available—although the newspapers said that America and Germany had been in a frantic race to unlock its secret—but Ayn was convinced on principle that Hitler's Germany could not have developed it, that great achievements could not emerge from slaves in a slave state. Wallis accepted her condition. Ayn interviewed a number of physicists, among them General Leslie Groves, military head of the Manhattan Project, and J. Robert Oppenheimer, known as "the man who built the atom bomb." Ayn, who had never studied physics, had laboriously struggled through only the very technical Smythe Report on the bomb, when one of the physicists she interviewed said to her admiringly, "You must have a very extensive background in physics."

"When Wallis and I met with Oppenheimer," Ayn would recall, "he greeted us very suspiciously; he didn't like the idea of a Hollywood movie on the bomb; there was a lot of resentment of scientists for creating it, and he was afraid a movie might add to that. I told him what I wanted to do—to show the bomb as a great achievement of the human mind that could be done only by free minds in a free country—and he was my friend from that moment on. He told me everything I wanted to know, he kept us past the allotted time, he walked us to the car and invited us to come back again. We did return for a second interview.

"He told me that I was right about the impossibility of the bomb being created by Nazi Germany, that all through their work the scientists in America had known they were *not* in a race—and he projected an *Atlas Shrugged*-like satire on the constant interference of German bureaucrats with their scientists. German scientists had to flee to America to be effective. 'There was never a single bureaucratic order given to any scientist at Los Alamos,' he said."

It was Oppenheimer who would be the inspiration for physicist Dr. Robert Stadler in *Atlas Shrugged*. "I copied his appearance and manner, and what he suggested," Ayn said when discussing Oppenheimer. "An enormous intelligence, somewhat bitter, very much a gentleman, slightly otherworldly, with an almost ostentatious simplicity. I even copied his office for Stadler. He was a fascinating man."

Ayn had completed one third of the script when, without warning to her, Hal Wallis sold his rights to the movie, and Ayn's script, to MGM. Furious, Ayn asked to be released from her contract. Wallis compromised by extending her next free six months to a year.

It was in the mid-forties that Nick became seriously ill. He had been hospitalized a number of times with lung trouble, which had become more severe over the years since he was gassed in World War I. Ayn and Frank invited him to come to California and live with them until he was well. He did so, and for several months Frank cared tenderly for his beloved brother. But shortly after his return to New York, Nick entered the Veterans Hospital in Saranac, where he died. It was a painful loss to both Ayn and Frank. Neither of them talked about it, but one could see the suffering in Frank's eyes when his brother's name was mentioned.

Albert Mannheimer, Ayn's young friend from New York, had moved to Hollywood to write for the screen. Among other assignments, he collaborated with Garson Kanin on the screenplay of *Born Yesterday*. He came to the ranch regularly to visit Ayn and to discuss her philosophy, to which he was now dedicated. Albert was struggling to deal with a problem not uncommon to idealistic young men working in Hollywood: the clash between his moral values and what he believed to be the requirements of his job. The sense that he was not living up to his potential, that he was compromising the values he had learned from Ayn in order to achieve success in his career, led to attacks of anxiety. His anxiety was severely heightened when, after an unhappy love affair, the girl he had broken off with stole into his apartment and—in what appeared to be an act of vengeance—committed suicide there. Ayn tried to help Albert: to convince him he had no cause to feel guilt, that only the young woman bore the responsibility for her actions; and to help him learn how he might remain a Hollywood writer while maintaining his integrity. Despite the pressure of her own work, she took whatever time he required, whenever he required it, to talk with and advise him.

It was her first experience of systematically helping someone psychologically. Psychology was a field she had never studied, and had taken little interest in; she believed that people could make their decisions and lead their lives as she insisted that she did: by rational calculation; if they had emotional-psychological problems, they were functioning irrationally, and could choose not to do so. Now, through her conversations with Albert, she was learning that human motivation was more complex than she had known, and she began evolving theories in the field.

Essentially, her theories were elaborations of the views she already held: that a man *chooses* to be rational or irrational, and that if he is in psychological pain, the solution can be found by discovering the irrational, contradictory convictions that he consciously or subconsciously holds, identifying them, and changing them to rational convictions.

She was armed with two basic concepts of the nature of man. One was that man has free will, to which she gave a radically new and important definition. "Man," she would write in *Atlas Shrugged,* "must obtain his knowledge and choose his actions by a process of thinking, which nature will not force him to perform. . . . 'free will' is your mind's freedom to think or not, the only will you have, your only freedom, the choice that controls all the choices you make and determines your life and your character. Thinking is man's only basic virtue, from which all the others proceed. And his basic vice, the source of all his evils, is that nameless act which all of you practice, but struggle never to admit: the act of blanking out, the willful suspension of one's consciousness, the refusal to think—not blindness, but the refusal to see; not ignorance, but the refusal to know. It is the act of unfocusing your mind and inducing an inner fog to escape the responsibility of judgment. . . ."

The second concept, which she derived from the first, was that a human being's *emotions* are the result of the thinking he has done or has refused to do. If his emotions are consistent with his rational judgment, their source will be found in his constant choice to use the best of his mind and his intelligence, and in the conclusions he has reached thereby. To the extent that he has contradictory emotions, emotions that conflict with his rational judgment, *their* source will be found in intellectual error or in acts of "blanking out."

She would often give an interesting example as evidence of her theory that emotions are the result of cognition. "If a small baby sees someone pointing a gun at him," she would say, "he will not react with fear; he may smile, thinking he is being given a new toy. If an adult sees someone pointing a gun at him—he *will* feel fear: *he* knows the gun is dangerous and may kill him."

When Ayn announced proudly, as she often did, "I can account for every emotion I have"—she meant, astonishingly, that the total contents of her subconscious were instantly available to her conscious mind, that all of her emotions had resulted from deliberate acts of rational thought, and that she could name the thinking that had led her to each feeling. And she maintained that every human being is able, if he chooses to work at the job of identifying the source of his emotions, ultimately to arrive at the same clarity and control.

Both of these concepts—that emotions result from the thinking one has done or has failed to do, and that free will consists of the choice to think or not to think—have great importance philosophically and as guides to human psychology—and both, even in the opinion of many philosophers and psychologists who admire Ayn's work, are highly oversimplified. Because of their oversimplification, they can be explosively dangerous guides to the human psyche. It is precisely our *deepest* values, our most intimate feelings, our most cherished loves and passions—those emotions that we experience as forming our very souls and as having *always* formed our very souls—those emotions that Ayn called our "sense of life"—that are not amenable to easy, or even to difficult, reduction to a set of intellectual conclusions that we may then accept or reject according to their rationality or irrationality. And although we are sometimes able to say: I *should* have thought about this issue or that one, and I dimly recognized it at the time but I evaded—more often we can only say: I don't *know* if I failed to think through an issue because I evaded it, or simply because I wasn't aware that it was necessary to do so—I don't *know* if I blanked out or was merely lacking in knowledge. We are not omniscient, not about the world outside us, and not about the vast complexity of our own mental content and processes.

These two concepts—for which her arguments were powerfully convincing—formed the heart of Ayn's approach to psychology, to her method of attempting to help Albert—and, in later years, to help those of her young friends who were struggling with what they thought to be psychological problems. The result was that her psychological work consisted to a great extent of what can only be called "moral lectures"—that is, stern advice to find the failures, the irrationalities, the "blank-outs" that had led to the problems, to rethink the original errors, to form correct conclusions, and thereby to find one's way to health. If one did not finally succeed, one clearly was continuing to evade. One felt under a constant pressure to discover the irrationality buried in one's subconscious that had led to the confusions or self-doubts or self-damaging actions that were defined as "psychological problems."

The danger of Ayn's oversimplification became compounded by an aspect of her own psychology. She stated, and wrote, that one *could* make simple, non-willful errors in thinking and evaluating, which she termed "errors of knowledge" as opposed to "breaches of morality." But she very often behaved and responded as if *only* willful errors, *only* evasion, existed in the realm of contradictory emotions and irrational value choices. Her anger, her accusations, her indignation at the perception of any value differences between herself and others, could be understood only on the assumption that she felt herself to be dealing with deliberate irrationality.

Despite her best efforts, it was Ayn's impression that Albert "got a little better" over the long period of their psychological discussions, "but not much."

During their years on the ranch, Ayn and Frank became friendly with Ruth and Dr. Borroughs Hill. Ruth Beebe Hill was then researching the book that would become a bestseller many years later: *Hanta Yo*. Borroughs, known as "Buzzy," was a researcher in cancer at UCLA Medical Center. Ruth had read *The Fountainhead* shortly after it was published, and had fallen in love with it.

"Howard Roark," she said, "is what I'd want to be if I were a man. . . . I wanted everyone to love *The Fountainhead* as I did, and I think I became quite obnoxious. Buzzy once said to me, 'Do you realize that for the last three years you have spent *every* social evening talking about *The Fountainhead?*' "

Knowing what *The Fountainhead* meant to Ruth, Jean Elliott, a friend, telephoned one day to say, "I'm going to tell you something you won't believe. I'm going to be Ayn Rand's secretary! I'll be typing for her one day a week, on the recommendation of a neighbor of hers whom I know." Ruth replied, "No, I don't believe it. And I give you exactly ten days to arrange for me to meet her."

Ten days later, the Hills met the O'Connors. Ayn soon attended, at the American Association of University Women, one of the dramatic readings of *The Fountainhead* that Ruth had been presenting. Her comments on the presentation, Ruth recalled, "influenced me more as a writer than a year's course in writing. I learned from her the importance of constructing a story as an architect constructs a building—that the structure must be strong and enduring and logical."

At Ruth's urging, Ayn gave her first talk in Hollywood at a Books and Authors group—at which the attendance established a record for the organization. The fame of *The Fountainhead* was growing. She spoke for a few minutes, then asked for questions. At the first question, Ruth cringed with embarrassment. "Miss Rand," a woman said, "the sex scenes between Roark and Dominique are so wonderful! Do they come from your own experience? What is their source?" Ayn brought down the house when she replied in two words: "Wishful thinking."

Ayn gave another talk during this period. While she was still living in New York, Ely Jacques Kahn had arranged for her to address a luncheon of the American Association of Architects. Now, she was approached to speak at a meeting of the Los Angeles branch of the organization. During the question period, a man said, "You present Howard Roark as unconventional—but he wasn't really—he was, after all, faithful to one woman all his life!" Ayn replied, "Do you call *that* conventional?"—and the audience burst into laughter and applause.

Like many of the people who knew Ayn, Ruth Hill loved her deeply. And she felt a special tenderness for Frank. She often commented on the intensity of Ayn's love for him. Ayn once said, Ruth recalled, "Frank is the power behind the throne." To which Frank responded, "Sometimes I think I *am* the throne, the way I get sat on." In the same man-worshiping vein, Ayn told Ruth, "It's Buzzy I admire most. And if you're half the woman I think you are, you'll like that."

One day, talking to Ruth while dipping the heads of white chrysanthemums into pans of coloring, Frank grinned and said, "Not the sort of thing Howard Roark would do, is it?" Ruth would learn that, probably for the first time since his marriage, Frank had formed a friendship of his own, not of Ayn's choosing. His friend was an older woman, Aretha Fisher, who sold flowers in a nearby area. On many afternoons, Frank would visit her at her home, sometimes to talk, sometimes to join her for lunch, sometimes to relax in his favorite chair. Nothing was required of him by this kindly woman; with her, he was not "Mr. Ayn Rand," he was Frank, who grew beautiful flowers on his ranch and of whom she was fond. Ayn knew they were acquainted, but Frank never told her of the depth of their friendship nor of their constant meetings; like his work on the ranch, this friendship was *his.*

One day during this period, Ayn received a letter, signed "Thadeus Ashby"—a name she did not know—informing her that "Warner Brothers can't produce *The Fountainhead.* I can. I must talk to you about it." Amused when she learned that he was only twenty-one, and touched that he had read *The Fountainhead* while in the Air Force and was so eager to meet Ayn that he hitchhiked from New York to Hollywood to do so, Ayn agreed to meet him. The meeting went well. Ayn would later say, "He talked philosophy, he was very perceptive about *The Fountainhead*—he even understood that Wynand dramatized the Nietzschean philosophy—he was *very* intelligent. Frank is usually more severe on first impressions and I'm more mushy, but both of us liked him."

Ayn and Frank learned that Thadeus was working on a novel and a play—but he had no money and no job. Ayn soon invited him to live with them on the ranch so that he could work there without having to hold a job. She wanted to spare a young writer a painful struggle. While Ayn never believed that charity was a moral virtue or requirement, and did not give money to organized charities, she occasionally was financially helpful to people in whom she saw ability. In later years, she gave gifts of money, informal scholarships, to young people who could not otherwise complete their educations and in whom she saw intelligence and promise.

In the months he lived with Ayn and Frank, Thadeus was to recall, he was struck with their devotion to each other. "She was deeply in love with him," he said, "and he was always tender and affectionate with her. Their relationship seemed perfect to me; it served as a model. . . . From what I could observe, she always initiated sex between them, and though he was a passive man, he was always available; I'd often see them go upstairs to the bedroom, their arms around each other. . . . She used to say that Frank was on strike, that's why he had no career. I once asked him if that were true, and he answered, 'That's how Ayn interprets it.' "

Ayn appeared to accept Thadeus to an extent rare in her relationships. She inscribed his copy of *The Fountainhead:* "To that spirit which is yours and mine." But it was not long before she began to grow disillusioned. After almost six months, he had written only approximately twenty pages of his novel, and Ayn considered those pages to be "a terrible imitation of *The Fountainhead.*" She seemed not to understand that the imitativeness was almost inevitable. She had known why her own first writing was overly influenced by Victor Hugo: "My mind worked in those literary forms that had most impressed me." And she believed that her own literary approach, which she called "Romantic Realism," was the rational approach; it is not unlikely that she would have been equally indignant had Thadeus's writing been of a different school and a different style.

Ayn and Frank were planning a trip to New York; she asked Albert—the two young men had become friendly—to move in with Thadeus while they were away. Albert and Thadeus promised that the house would never be left empty, that one of them would be there at all times. Albert kept his word, Thadeus did not. When Ayn and Frank returned, Ayn was furiously angry that he had broken his promise, and soon after she asked him to move out. It was that disappointment, she would later say, that made her extremely reluctant to meet other fans in the future.

One of the sources of Ayn's frequent disappointments with people is evident in her relationship with Thadeus. Painfully hungry for intellectual companionship, judging people exclusively by their intellectual interests, their stated philosophy and their intelligence, she tended to move too fast, to accept someone as a friend on the basis of an apparent intellectual rapport without knowing anything about the person's character or background or life. As she saw more of her new friend, she often discovered that they had little in common, and that she disapproved of qualities and actions she had had no way of discerning from conversations about philosophy.

Almost forty years after their friendship ended, Thadeus was to say: "Ayn was a genius, the most brilliant person I have ever known. I really loved her—and I still do. . . . Although I have moved in different philosophical directions, I'm still an individualist; I learned individualism from her, and that remains. . . . But my separation from her was ultimately liberating. For a number of years, I didn't grow as a person, I was almost slavishly repeating her ideas. The break finally allowed me to grow philosophically."

He added that there had been a sexual element in his relationship with Ayn, despite her indisputable love for Frank; there had been a flirtatiousness, a sexual awareness of each other that cut across the nineteen-year difference in their ages. It was never acted upon, but their mutual attraction existed as a constant presence, and they openly named and discussed it on several occasions. "We debated whether or not to discuss our relationship with Frank," Thadeus said. "But we decided not to."

There seems reason to believe that something was coming to life in Ayn, that her dissatisfaction with her life with her husband was seeking expression—and that it could, one day, explode into action.

Chapter Eighteen

Because of *The Fountainhead*—by 1946, three years after its publication, a much-discussed bestseller—because of her friendships with political conservatives who were universally admiring of the brilliance and depth of her social-political reasoning, and because of her eagerness to talk about her political philosophy with anyone she met, Ayn had herself become much discussed in Hollywood as an active and vocal opponent of collectivism. And she had become progressively more concerned with the infiltration of Communist propaganda into American movies.

She wrote a pamphlet entitled "Screen Guide for Americans" for the Motion Picture Alliance for the Preservation of American Ideals, an anti-Communist organization with which she was for a time associated. Among its members over the years were John Wayne, Robert Taylor, Gary Cooper, Adolphe Menjou, Sam Woods, and Walt Disney; Ayn was unanimously elected to the board shortly after attending her first meeting. In the pamphlet, she wrote: "The purpose of the Communists in Hollywood is *not* the production of political movies openly advocating Communism. Their purpose is *to corrupt our moral premises by corrupting non-political movies*—by introducing small, casual bits of propaganda into innocent stories—thus making people absorb the basic principles of Collectivism *by indirection and implication.*" She made it clear that she was unalterably opposed to any form of legal restriction on the movie industry; she was offering suggestions for voluntary action. Don't smear the free enterprise system, she recommended to writers and producers; don't smear industrialists, don't glorify failure, don't glorify the collective, don't smear the independent man, don't smear American political institutions. And when you make pictures with political themes and implications—don't hire Communists to write, direct, or produce them. "The principle of free speech requires that we do not use police force to forbid the Communists the expression of their ideas—which means that we do not pass laws forbidding them to speak. But the principle of free speech does not require that we furnish the Communists with the means to preach their ideas, and does not imply that we owe them jobs and support to advocate our own destruction at our own expense."

Early in 1947, representatives from the House Un-American Activities Committee, preparing for hearings that would investigate Communist infiltration into the movie industry, arrived in Hollywood. They contacted Ayn and requested that she testify before the Committee in Washington. It was the beginning of a flood of angry controversy throughout the nation that set politician against politician and friend against friend—and that has not ended to this day.

The purpose of HUAC's October 1947 hearings, under the chairmanship of Representative J. Parnell Thomas of New Jersey, was to investigate Communist Party penetration of Hollywood: "to discover the truth and report it as it is . . . with such recommendations, if any, as to legislation on those subjects as the situation may require and as the duty of Congress to the American people may demand." HUAC subpoenaed a group of "unfriendly witnesses"—among them Ring Lardner, Jr., Dalton Trumbo, John Howard Lawson, and Edward Dmytryk. Among the "friendly witnesses" were Ayn Rand, Adolphe Menjou, Ronald Reagan, Robert Taylor, and Gary Cooper. A group of Hollywood personalities —Lauren Bacall, Jane Wyatt, Humphrey Bogart, Paul Henried—flew to Washington in a well-publicized campaign to register their opposition to the committee's work.

Ayn agreed to appear before the committee on one condition: that she be allowed to testify as she wished, without dictation from HUAC, and that she be allowed to speak on *ideological* issues. Two movies were run for her in Hollywood: *The Best Years of Our Lives,* an enormously popular 1946 release starring Fredric March, Myrna Loy, Teresa Wright, and Dana Andrews, and *The Song of Russia,* released in 1943 and starring Robert Taylor and Susan Peters. Ayn felt that *The Song of Russia*—the story of an American musician who tours Russia in 1941 and falls in love with an idealistic peasant girl—was so blatant in its pro-Soviet orientation that it "was totally meaningless; no one could really be taken in by it." Robert Taylor had been quoted by the newspapers as saying that he hadn't wanted to do the movie, but before he left for the Navy he had received word from Washington that if he did not accept the role, he would not get his commission.

The Best Years of Our Lives was a recent success, and a movie Ayn wanted to denounce ideologically. "Everyone was praising it," she would recall, "as a humanitarian achievement—you know, Fredric March played 'the banker with a heart,' who, in his big speech, decides that loans should be given without collateral. I agreed to go to Washington on condition that I could present a full case: I would start my testimony by reading from my 'Screen Guide for Americans' in order to establish my foundation, and then take up the two movies."

Considerable pressure was brought to bear on the anti-Communist witnesses to prevent them from testifying. Many of them were told, tacitly or openly, that cooperation with the committee would be professionally damaging to them. When an acquaintance of Ayn congratulated her on her courage in agreeing to testify, she replied, "I'm not brave enough to be a coward. I see the consequences too clearly."

The day Ayn arrived in Washington, Louis B. Mayer, a friendly witness, was testifying. Then the committee called her to the stand—to testify *only* about *The Song of Russia.* At the end of the day, Ayn recalled, "I threw a fit; I told the committee members that if I only spoke about an unimportant movie that was several years old, it would seem that that was the worst Hollywood had done— and it amounted almost to a whitewash. It was much more important to show the really serious propaganda going on right now, and about America." She was speaking to two members of the Committee, Parnell Thomas and a young congressman named Richard Nixon. She had become convinced that most of the committee members were "intellectually out of their depth, and motivated by a desire for headlines," but she was impressed with Nixon; he seemed intellectual and he seemed to understand the issue she was naming. But Thomas told her that the press coverage of the hearings had been so damning, that if a widely praised and popular movie like *The Best Years of Our Lives* were denounced, there would be a furor. Finally, in the face of Ayn's arguments, he capitulated; he promised that she would be called in a day or two to give the testimony she had come to give. Ayn stayed throughout the hearings—and was not called again.

"The hearings were a disgusting spectacle," Ayn was to say with contempt when she spoke of them in later years; she rarely spoke of them; it was a painfully unpleasant memory. "Each one of the unfriendly witnesses would make long denunciatory speeches to the committee—and when the chairman tried to stop him and get the answer to a question like 'Are you a writer?'—he'd say 'I'm answering in my own way'—and continue the denunciation. After putting up with this for hours at a time with each one of them, and getting no answers to his questions, Thomas finally held them in contempt of Congress. They were *not* jailed for being Communist Party members; they were jailed for contempt.

"Before each of them left the stand, *his Communist Party card* was produced. That was the dramatic part. It shocked the audience and the newspapers and all the liberals, who had been screaming that these men were being persecuted. But to this day, when people denounce the hearings, they don't even *know*—they are not told—that these people *were Communists.*

"The unfriendly witnesses' attitude was that if their unpopular political viewpoint became known, then people wouldn't attend their movies—so they had the right to put over a fraud. I kept yelling at the conservatives about the difference between the right to freedom of speech—which means the *government* cannot interfere—and the private right of people who don't want to deal with Communists, to boycott; and the private right of employers not to hire men whom they consider to be enemies of this country." Ayn's viewpoint was also unpopular, among both liberals and conservatives; it remains unpopular to this day. That was not a fact that troubled her then or at any time in her life. She was later to term herself a "radical for capitalism"; she knew very well the price to be paid for radical and innovative ideas, and she was calmly prepared to pay it.

When the hearings ended, furious that she had not been recalled, she held another angry session with Thomas. Apparently he was impressed with both her fire and her arguments; he said that he wanted to hold another set of hearings dealing specifically with ideology; he asked Ayn to be the chief investigator. Ayn refused. He said that he would allow her to testify exactly as she wished—and would pay her throughout the period before the hearings were held. Ayn refused.

It is well known and well documented that a number of the unfriendly witnesses were blacklisted by Hollywood after the hearings—although several of them continued working under false names and others worked in Europe. What is less well known—except to those involved and to those who have since researched the issue—was the silent, unpublicized persecution of friendly witnesses. "Everyone who had testified *for* the committee—not the big stars, but the lesser-known actors and writers who were considered dispensable, and those who were free-lancing and were not under contract to a major studio—lost their jobs," Ayn would recall bitterly. "Morrie Ryskind had had more work than he could handle; he never again worked in Hollywood. Adolphe Menjou, who was also free-lancing, got fewer and fewer jobs; after about a year, he could find no work at all. I was not victimized, because of *The Fountainhead* and because I had a contract with Hal Wallis."

Friends were later to observe that Ayn appeared to have uncomfortably mixed feelings about both the committee's validity and her own appearance before it. When she was questioned, her attitude ranged from calm, reasoned explanations to outraged defensiveness at any suggestion of disapproval of her actions. She often said that she and the other friendly witnesses had been so maligned by the press and public, that any of her doubts about the committee's legitimacy were irrelevant in the face of such injustice. But she granted that "It was a very dubious undertaking. I think that legally and constitutionally they had the right only to ask factual questions, such as party membership and Communist penetration of organizations. If their focus was to expose communism, it had to be done ideologically—but it's improper for a government agency to do it."

She had agreed to testify, she would explain, because she wanted the extent of Communist propaganda in movies to become publically known, and the committee was the only existing forum by which to accomplish it. "My real purpose was to get that information into the press; all the articles that had appeared about Communists in Hollywood were not about ideological penetration or propaganda on the screen, only that there were a few Communists around; they never discussed the content of the movies. I didn't think the hearings were immoral or improper under the circumstances, since congressional investigating committees had existed long before that; it was not an evil institution, but futile. And it did not interfere with anyone's freedom of speech." But when asked how she thought such a problem should be handled by government in the kind of society she advocated, she responded, "There would be no hearings."

Despite her misgivings, Ayn was convinced that something of value had arisen from the hearings: that Communist propaganda on the screen vanished after that, at least in the blatant form it had taken. "My 'Screen Guide for Americans' did that," she would say proudly. "It was reproduced on the front page of the Drama Section of the New York *Times,* and several other papers ran it. All the points I had made, particularly about the attacks on businessmen as villains, disappeared from the screen. I take credit for that."

But whenever the subject of the hearings arose in future years, Ayn would say, "The whole thing is a very unpleasant, ugly memory for me. I disliked being there, I disliked the attitude of most of the committee, I disliked the futility of the conservatives—they had no idea of how to fight an *intellectual* battle—and I was furious that I couldn't do what I went there to do."

Ayn returned to California weary, frustrated, and depressed. She had maintained her contact with Isabel Paterson, seeing her whenever she and Frank visited New York and engaging in long philosophical discussions with her by mail and telephone. It had been agreed that because Ayn was in a better financial position than Pat, she would one day give Pat the present of a trip to California. Now, thinking that a visit from her friend would lift her spirits, Ayn called Pat to invite her to spend a week. *The Freeman,* a new conservative magazine, was in the process of being formed; Pat was helping to raise money for it, and could combine her trip with meetings with Hollywood conservatives, to whom Ayn would introduce her.

When Pat arrived, Ayn was delighted to see her. But knowing her friend's hair-trigger temper, Ayn warned her firmly that the conservatives in Hollywood meant well, but they were not philosophical. She demanded, and received, Pat's promise not to insult any of them. She then began introducing Pat to all of her "best conservatives, a couple at a time, inviting them to my house." The first people to meet Pat were Janet Gaynor and Adrian, who had read *The God of the Machine* on Ayn's recommendation. To Ayn's relief, Pat was cordial and polite with them.

Ayn then invited Morrie Ryskind and his wife Mary. The evening went well, but when they left, Pat said, "I don't like Jewish intellectuals." Angrily, Ayn replied, "Then you don't like me." Pat laughed, insisting that she had not meant it "that way." Ayn's response was typical of her. She would not grant what she termed "the sanction of the victim." If Pat was implicitly insulting her by her remark about Morrie Ryskind, Ayn would not spare Pat's feelings by pretending she didn't know it. What others, out of pity or conventional good manners or fear preferred not to name, Ayn named.

"I had a constant stream of people in and out of the house," Ayn would recall, "and Pat kept her promise pretty well—until Janet and Adrian invited us to their home for dinner with a group of conservatives. Pat was horrible all through dinner. Adrian had begun painting, and when he showed us his work, she just looked away without saying a word. She kept telling people they knew nothing about politics, and everyone was humbly polite toward the great conservative."

Ayn was angry, and grew angrier still when Pat inadvertently revealed something that Ayn had long suspected but had been unable fully to believe. Just before publication of *The Fountainhead,* Pat had told Ayn that Irita van Doren, head of the *Herald Tribune* Book Section, had offered the book for review to a conservative woman—who had refused the assignment. "That's a moral crime," Ayn had said, wondering why Pat seemed oddly upset. Now, Pat revealed that *she* was the one who had been offered the review and had turned it down. Ayn was stunned. When she asked Pat her reasons, Pat said only that she did not agree with certain aspects of the book and had not wanted to attack it. "I was so sickened that I couldn't even question her much," Ayn was to say about the incident. "I felt I should throw her out, but even that didn't matter. Today, I suspect that she did like certain aspects of *The Fountainhead*—but really hated it because of its romanticism and anti-religion."[1]

Despite her anger, Ayn kept her promise to continue introducing Pat to conservatives. Her next guest was William Mullendore. She had explained to Pat that he was "my best friend in California politically, that I really liked him, and that she was to treat him accordingly." When Mullendore arrived, he began to tell Pat his reasons for agreeing that an intellectual magazine such as *The Freeman* would be important. "He was using all the arguments Pat had been using with other people," Ayn recalled. "I thought she'd be delighted. But she began to argue a bit, slightly switching her viewpoint. Then Janet and Adrian came in. Adrian suggested that the organizers of the magazine should make up a dummy, with one or two articles, perhaps written by Pat if she wanted, to show potential backers what the magazine would be. It was a perfectly good idea.

"Pat exploded. She began yelling that none of them appreciated her, didn't she work hard enough, why did she have to work more, the backers should take her word. She made it a totally personal issue. Then she whirled on Mullendore and said 'It's all the fault of businessmen, because they don't care about free enterprise and they do nothing about it—*none of them!*' Mullendore waited for her tirade to end, then got up, and with his usual dignity he said goodnight. I apologized to him at the door; he said he understood, he had heard of her reputation. But the whole thing was horrible.

"When Janet and Adrian left, I told Pat I wanted to know what on earth! I

---

[1] Ayn was correct in believing that Pat had mixed feelings about her work. Years later, when William Buckley's conservative *National Review* published the most violently antagonistic of any review of *Atlas Shrugged,* Pat denounced Buckley for "his treatment of a woman of Ayn's genius and courage and honor"—and broke with him. She was, her friend Muriel Hall said, "thrilled with Ayn's ability to take an intellectual concept and translate it into fiction; 'I couldn't do that,' she said." But she disagreed with much of Ayn's philosophy—she believed that "Ayn was limiting her talents and taking herself out of the mainstream by that Objectivism philosophy"—and she disliked Ayn's literary style.

told her this was a moral issue, that her actions had been immoral, and I told her why. She answered that she hadn't been insulting, and she had nothing more to say. I kept pressing. Finally she said, 'If that's the way you feel, I'll leave tomorrow.' I said, 'Fine. Until you agree to discuss this, we can have no other discussion.' "

The end had been coming, for Ayn, before this disastrous visit. The tension between the two women had been growing, predominantly because of their philosophical disagreements on issues of reason and faith. "Pat once said," Ayn would recall, "that her real self is nothing that can be materially perceived, it's not her actions or words or body or thoughts or books. I took that verbatim for James Taggart [one of the arch-villains of *Atlas Shrugged*]. And she was very helpful, in reverse, one time when she was arguing that logic can deal only with measurement, and therefore it can apply only to material, not spiritual, reality. I knew she was wrong, but I went home to think about it. That's when I arrived at my definition of logic as 'the art of noncontradictory identification.' " Ayn's definition of logic, with its application both to matter and to spirit, was to form a continuing theme in *Atlas Shrugged* and to serve as the base of her later writings on epistemology. But Ayn had long since stopped being the eager student to her older friend—their roles had been reversing themselves as Ayn had grown in intellectual power and breadth of thought; it was a reversal that Pat apparently could not accept.

Pat left the next day. At the airport, she told Ayn sadly that she would always wish her success and luck. Ayn replied, "I hope you'll be happier than you are." There was nothing more to say. The friendship was at an end. Ayn returned home feeling a mixture of depression, outrage, and loss.

For many years after their break, Ayn would occasionally mention Isabel Paterson in an offhand and disapproving manner, never indicating that the association had once been important to her; her conversation focused almost exclusively on the intellectual differences between them that had led to their rift. Her friends could not and did not suspect—and were startled to discover—that the two women had once been warmly friendly.

Ayn's manner of discussing Pat was illustrative of a growing trend in her psychology—a trend that consisted of "rewriting" the history of a relationship if that relationship ended, of retroactively demoting a former friend in stature and importance so that her past view would appear to conform to her present view. With Pat, and with other former friends, she would cease to see as significant, even as worthy of mention, aspects of their mind and character that once had aroused her enthusiastic approval; what she had once described as values were given a new and malevolent interpretation. Perhaps it was not done consciously; it appeared, rather, as though her new view of the person became so total an absolute, her damnation so thoroughgoing, that no former interpretation could be allowed reality; as though the vividness and conviction of her present estimate had to wipe out even the shameful memory that she once had had a different perspective. If she now viewed Isabel Paterson, or another former friend, as an individual she could not deeply care for—then she *had* never deeply cared. If she saw her as immoral and spiritually corrupt—then that had always, at bottom, been her estimate.

The source of this psychological mechanism is not difficult to find. Ayn—who proudly said: "I can explain the reason of any emotion I feel"—clearly was growing more alienated from her own emotions with each year that passed. Her thoughts, like her perceptive eyes, looked only and always outward. If she felt anger, she did not introspect to find the cause: the cause, self-evidently, was the "evil" of the person who had angered her; if she felt love, the cause was the heroic qualities in the person she loved; if she felt alienated from the world, the cause was the failures and irrationalities of the inhabitants of that world. More and more, as time passed, the actual nature of her emotions was retreating into some hidden, never-to-be-examined part of her, to work unseen and unacknowledged.

Nevertheless, Ayn's spirits were at a low ebb when Pat boarded the plane for New York. But then, as if timed to lift her depression, she received exciting news: the movie of *The Fountainhead* was shortly to go into production, and Ayn was to write the final script.

She did not know that she was about to wage a war to protect the integrity of her work, a war from which she would emerge battered, bleeding, and without illusions. She did not know that on the sets and in the boardrooms and offices of a movie studio, she was about to fight the most courageous battle of her life— that she would become once more the young woman on the stage of the Gloria Swanson Theater, in the thick of an intellectual battle which charged her with limitless energy and resolve, utilizing the whole of her charismatic power to convince.

In the beginning, she was primarily focused on her pleasure and relief that she had been assigned to do the final script. And then an event occurred that thrilled her. From the time she had begun writing *The Fountainhead,* when she had first considered the possibility that it might one day be made into a movie, Gary Cooper was the one actor she wanted for the role of Howard Roark. His physical appearance strongly suggested Roark to her; she saw him as the archetype of the American hero. "He looks like Frank," she often said. She had discussed her reasons for wanting him with everyone involved in the movie, but she could only suggest and advise, she had no power of decision. She was ecstatic when Gary Cooper was signed for the role.

Ayn was told that Cooper had read her preliminary script, and although he was not under contract to Warner Brothers, he had signed a two-picture-a-year deal with them on the condition that he be given the part of Howard Roark. A slightly different version of his desire to do the picture is presented by Larry Swindell in his book *Trouble in Paradise.* ". . . in Brentwood, Rocky Cooper [Gary Cooper's wife] was reading *The Fountainhead* and being enthralled by it. She was a reader, Gary wasn't, and she kept him informed of what was going on in the world of books although she made it a point never to advise him on matters of his career. . . . she broke her rule, and advised him to go after *The Fountainhead.*"

The first sign of trouble to come occurred when King Vidor, famous for such films as *The Big Parade, The Crowd,* and *The Champ,* was chosen to direct the movie. Ayn recognized the importance of having a director with a distinguished reputation, but she felt that he was "the worst man they could find for *The Fountainhead.* He was a naturalist, so he had no mind or imagination for the book; he seemed anxious to do right by it, but he was afraid of it."[2]

Ayn began working on the final script with Vidor. "He wanted a lot of things I didn't like artistically," she would later say, "but I was willing to give in on some of those. I kept my thunder for the intellectual issues. My real power— through all the arguing and fighting—was that nobody in the studio knew what to make of the book. They knew it was different than other books, but they didn't understand what would or would not ruin it, what would antagonize my readers. That was my protection and my weapon."

Warner Brothers continued with the casting as the scriptwriting progressed. "I asked Vidor about Garbo, whom he knew," Ayn recalled. "He thought she would be wonderful as Dominique, but he said the studios were afraid of her: she had so often agreed to do a picture, then changed her mind at the last minute; but he said he'd try to arouse her interest. Later, he told me he had sent her the script, and that she had called him enthusiastically and wanted to do it— but the next day, she changed her mind; she said she couldn't play love scenes with Cooper. . . . The story might or might not be true. I suspect that Vidor was dishonest, but it seemed true."

Apparently, Vidor's story to Ayn was true only in part. In *Trouble in Paradise,* Swindell wrote: "Vidor, an old friend, sent the script to Garbo. She came to his house to return it in person. 'Do you really think I should come back with this part?' she asked. Vidor knew there wasn't a chance she would do it, and he tended to feel it wasn't right for her, no matter how commercial her return to the screen would be. 'As a friend, I don't think you should,' he told her."

It seemed as if Warner Brothers were considering every major actress in Hollywood for the role of Dominique—Bette Davis, Ida Lupino, Barbara Stanwyck, Jennifer Jones, and Gene Tierney. Ayn was so violently opposed to Bette Davis, who she thought was too old for the part and impossibly difficult to work with, that she threatened to walk out and to remove her name from the screen play if Davis were chosen. Then Warner Brothers decided to test the beautiful young actress Patricia Neal, who had received rave reviews for her Broadway perfomance in Lillian Hellman's *Another Part of the Forest* and whom they were

---

[2] Critics do not agree that Vidor was a naturalist. In *Coop,* a biography of Gary Cooper, Stuart Kaminsky wrote: "The Vidor film [of *The Fountainhead*] is one of the most noteworthy of American films. It is one of the most antinaturalist films imaginable. . . . There is almost no attempt in the film to make the dialogue or scenes conform to the prevailing American goal of 'realism.' . . . Symbolism is overt with no apologies. . . . The very decision to ignore so-called realism makes the film a strange and courageous effort, rather like a building by Howard Roark."

grooming for stardom. "Her test was horrible," Ayn remembered. "Her appearance was really good, but she had a terrible voice and she couldn't read lines. Cooper happened to come to the set during the test. He turned to me and said 'What's *that?*' When I explained, he said he would stop this."

Cooper did not "stop this." Instead, during the course of the filming, he fell in love with his leading lady, and she with him, in one of Hollywood's most famous romances. "Patricia Neal worked very hard on her role," Ayn later said, "and she did improve." It was said in the studio that the improvement in her performance, especially in the love scenes, came from the inspiration of her love affair with Cooper. "I remember the day we drove up to Fresno to do our location shooting for *The Fountainhead,*" King Vidor reminisced to Stuart Kaminsky. "We met Patricia Neal there that night. It was the first time they had met. They went for each other right away. After dinner we never saw the two of them again except when we were shooting."

Both Henry Blanke and Ayn wanted Clifton Webb to play Toohey, but the studio refused; he had been hugely successful in several comedies, and Warner Brothers felt that his public would not want to see him as a villain. It was Robert Douglas who finally was selected. "He was too forceful for Toohey," Ayn felt, "and too strong for the rest of the cast. He should have been slippery and snide, not so openly villainous. But he delivered his lines with enormous intelligence."

In later years, Ayn laughed delightedly when she described a discussion she had had with Melvyn Douglas's agent, who wanted Douglas to be signed for the role of Gail Wynand. "I was totally against it," she said. "He would have been an awful type for Wynand. I told his agent I objected—and he said I didn't want him because of his political reputation. 'Has he a political reputation?' I asked innocently. 'I didn't know that. No, I object to him because he has a moustache.' " Ayn had an oddly intense dislike of facial hair. "A man wears a moustache or a beard," she would say, "because he wants to hide behind it; there's something he wants to conceal, not just a physical defect, but a spiritual defect; I would never trust such a man."[3]

Ayn was relieved when Raymond Massey, whom she considered a fine actor, was cast as Wynand. But when the shooting started, she began to feel that "Massey was overacting and he didn't fully understand the requirements of the role." Kent Smith was cast for the role of Peter Keating; although Ayn was not familiar with his work, she felt that, as physical type, he was right for the part.

Henry Blanke was determined to hire Frank Lloyd Wright to do the architectural drawings that would illustrate Roark's work on the screen. Ayn agreed enthusiastically; only an architect of Wright's caliber would be convincing as designer for Roark, and would immeasurably help to publicize the picture. She had written, as visual instructions at the beginning of her screenplay, "Among

---

[3] Many years later, a friend of mine who was a screenwriter arranged a meeting with Ayn to discuss his proposed screenplay of *Atlas Shrugged*. Before their meeting, I warned him—embarrassed but knowing it was necessary—that if he didn't shave his beard, he had no chance of getting the assignment.

present day architects, it is the style of Frank Lloyd Wright—and *only* of Frank Lloyd Wright—that must be taken as a model for Roark's buildings. Wright holds a unique position with the general public—even the people who cling to traditional architecture and hate modernism of the concrete-and-steel-pipe school. This is extremely important to us, since we must make the audience admire Roark's buildings." But Wright demanded two hundred and fifty thousand dollars as a fee, and the right to approve or reject the sets and the script. Unwilling to meet his terms—the right to the final say on sets and script would have made Wright, in effect, the film's director—Warner Brothers looked for another designer. "They gave Roark's buildings to a studio set designer [art director Edward Carrere], who had been trained as an architect but had never built anything," Ayn would recall with a shudder. "He and Vidor got pictures of *horrible* modernistic buildings and copied them. Architects criticized them enormously, with justice; they were embarrassingly bad." The *Hollywood Citizen* reported that Wright commented: "Warners sent an art director to ask me to design the sets. I said I would, for my regular fee of ten percent. He asked if I meant ten percent of the $400,000 budget for the sets. I said no, ten percent of the cost of the movie. . . . That amounted to a refusal. I think the art director was glad. . . . He wanted to design the sets himself."[4]

As the shooting progressed, Ayn became still more convinced that Vidor was not the director for *The Fountainhead*. She argued with him constantly, aware that he saw her as a meddler, but she cared only about the purity of the ideology for which she had fought all her life. There seems little doubt that she was often overprotective of her ideas; she was lonely and frightened in a hostile environment, an environment that intellectually was part of the mainstream of American thought, the very mainstream that her script opposed. Blanke stood by her sympathetically, for which she was grateful, but intellectually she had to fight alone. It appears that Vidor was, at worst, intimidated, or, at best, captivated by the blazing firebrand that was Ayn Rand and by the forceful logic of her arguments; he made concessions to her that were astonishing in Hollywood. "When he was ready to film the scene in which Dominique goes to Roark's apartment after she learns who he is," Ayn reported, "he told me he wasn't sure he could explain Dominique's psychology to Patricia Neal, and would I write it out for him. I did, and I also wrote out Roark's psychology for the scene. I think it's the best scene in the picture."

And when Roark's climactic courtroom speech was being shot, Vidor asked Ayn to work with Cooper. Cooper's attitude, too, was astonishing for an actor of his position and stature; he agreed, in effect, to be directed privately by Ayn. "I spent an entire day coaching him," Ayn would recall. "He was very good about it. I'd always liked him as a screen personality, and I liked him as a man. But I couldn't do much with him, he didn't quite get it."

[4] The Louisville, Kentucky, *Courier-Journal* reported that an indignant Frank Lloyd Wright said, after the movie was released: "Any move I make against such grossly abusive caricatures of my work by this film crew would only serve their purpose."

Ayn would never forget what was for her, emotionally, the worst moment of the shooting. She came to the set to watch the courtroom scene—and discovered that Vidor was shooting a cut version. Their unwritten agreement had been—after endless battles—that once the script was approved—and it had been approved—no changes were to be made on the set. "I rushed to Blanke's office, screaming at the top of my voice; I said I'd not only take my name off the movie, I would also see to it that my audience didn't come to it, I'd take ads denouncing it. Blanke went to see Jack Warner, and came back with an unprecedented ruling: no changes are to be made in the script."

Nevertheless, "the whole thing was an enormously miserable experience. I was anxious through it all; I never knew who or what would ruin it. I decided then that I'd never again sell a novel without getting script control, unless it were absolutely financially necessary."

Throughout the months of conferences and scriptwriting and casting and filming, Frank had to leave the ranch daily to drive Ayn to and from the studio. The ranch began to fall into disrepair. Once more, Frank's life revolved around Ayn; the peace he had found was replaced by exhausting evenings of listening to Ayn planning her next day's battle, marshaling the arguments she would need—sometimes pounding the arm of her chair in frustration, her pain and fear transformed, as always, into anger. He did not argue with her—as he never argued with her—but this period, some of their friends recognized, marked the beginning of something in Frank that was to grow and intensify as time passed: an impatience with Ayn, totally at variance with his usual personality, split-second bursts of furious, seemingly motiveless anger at her that were gone almost before they could be noticed. He did not shout at her because his gentle spirit cringed at her anger, he did not shout at her because *her* needs were taking from him the few moments of contentment he had found—he shouted at her because she was late in dressing for an appointment, or had forgotten her keys, or wore stockings with runs in them, or nagged him to wear a warm sweater on a balmy day. He had repressed too much of his emotional life over too many years: it could not forever remain underground. Now his inevitable resentment of Ayn—perhaps his resentment of his own failed life—burst out at unpredictable times and for unpredictable reasons. Ayn was bewildered by it. Her fantasy view of herself, of Frank, and of their relationship, did not permit her to understand the motivation she might have understood in someone else. Through the rest of their life together, as his outbursts of anger grew more frequent and more intense, it remained unintelligible to her.

Nor did she have time to think about it. From all sides, pressures to make ideological changes in her script began descending on her. Her response was to dig in her heels, straighten her spine, and defy the whole of the Hollywood establishment. Her battle was not unlike the battle she had waged with Al Woods for *Night of January 16th*—a constant struggle to preserve her script, to salvage the integrity of her work. It was a battle not unlike Howard Roark's battle to preserve Cortlandt Homes, when everyone seemed to have a say, every-

Alice Rosenbaum with her family in St. Petersburg. 1909. Center row, from left (identified with reasonable certainty): Fronz and Anna Rosenbaum; Alice's maternal grandmother; Alice's cousin Nina; Alice's maternal grandfather; on his knee, four-year-old Alice. (Picture courtesy of Mrs. Minna Goldberg)

The Portnoy family, Ayn's Chicago relatives who, in 1926, made it possible for her to leave Soviet Russia. 1916. Middle row, beginning second from left: Ayn's aunt Sarah; Eva and Harry Portnoy; Ayn's aunt Gertrude; Ayn's aunt Minna; back row, fourth from right, Ayn's aunt Anna; first row, far left, Ayn's cousin Burton Stone. (Picture courtesy of Mrs. Beatrice Waller)

Frank O'Connor.
About 1920.

Frank O'Connor as a bit player—back row, second from right—in D. W. Griffith's *Orphans of the Storm.* 1921.

Nick Carter, Frank's brother and Ayn's good friend during her first decades in the United States. Mid-1930s.

Isabel Paterson in her office at the *Herald Tribune*. (Picture courtesy of Muriel Hall)

The O'Connor home in Chatsworth, California, designed originally by Richard J. Neutra for Josef von Sternberg. 1947. (Photo by Julius Shulman)

Interior of O'Connor ranch home in California. 1947. (Photo by Julius Shulman)

Ayn and Frank in patio of ranch home with Richard Neutra. 1947. (Photo by Julius Shulman)

Ayn and Frank with friend and neighbor Janet Gaynor. 1947. (Photo by Julius Shulman)

Ayn working on *Atlas Shrugged* at the desk Frank designed for her, in study of ranch home. 1947. (Photo by Julius Shulman)

Ayn and Frank walking through the grounds of their ranch. The birch trees were a gift to Josef von Sternberg from Marlene Dietrich. 1947. (Photo by Julius Shulman)

Ayn testifying as a "friendly witness" before the HUAC hearings on communism in Hollywood. 1947. (Photo by Leonard McCombe, *Life* magazine © 1967 Time Inc.)

Ayn with Gary Cooper and Patricia Neal, the stars of Warner Brothers' movie of *The Fountainhead.* 1948. (From the Warner Bros. release *The Fountainhead* © 1949 Warner Bros. Pictures, Inc. Renewed 1976 United Artists Television, Inc.)

Ayn at Warner Brothers during the filming of *The Fountainhead.* 1948. (From the Warner Bros. release *The Fountainhead* © 1949 Warner Bros. Pictures, Inc. Renewed 1976 United Artists Television, Inc.)

Ayn on the movie set of *The Fountainhead*, with, left, director King Vidor and producer Henry Blanke. (From the Warner Bros. release *The Fountainhead* © 1949 Warner Bros. Pictures, Inc. Renewed 1976 United Artists Television, Inc.)

one had a vote, everyone had the right to mutilate the work Roark's life had gone into creating. She was under constant pressure to disguise, dilute, or tone down the philosophical theme of her novel, to turn her ideas into meaningless generalities that would shock no one, to destroy the forceful clarity and originality of her work by means of ideological bromides. In the most timid of all mediums, in an industry whose guiding principle was a quest to amuse the lowest common denominator, an industry convinced that the public was not interested in ideas and was specifically not ready for *Ayn's* ideas, she was fighting to present on the screen a moral code that defied the moral tradition of two and a half thousand years.

A major source of pressure was the Johnson Office, Hollywood's self-censoring agency. Oddly, they did not object to the "rape scene"—but to Roark's courtroom speech. "Two men came to see me," Ayn would recall, "one of whom was a Catholic scholar. He said they objected to the speech because it was 'materialistic.' I explained and explained—and he kept retreating, he knew he was on shaky ground because the Johnson Office was not supposed to discuss the philosophical content of a movie. Finally, I said 'Are you censoring me on the grounds of what does and does not accord with Catholic doctrine?' He backed up immediately—and I had no more trouble. That's how one should treat any underground pressure that doesn't dare come out into the open: make it open, name what they are implying."

Another source of pressure was the studio's business manager, who "wanted me to soften certain points about altruism, about man not being a sacrificial animal. 'So you think man *is* a sacrificial animal?' I asked. I argued in very clear and simple terms, and he, too, backed up."

Ayn's final ideological battle was with Gary Cooper's attorney. "He said that Cooper's audience was not intellectual, and if they heard him say such selfish things, they'd hold it against him, it might damage his reputation and his career. I bent over so far backward in defense of selfishness that I must have sounded like a monster—on the ground 'If this be treason, make the most of it.' He finally gave up."

With quietly intense pride, Ayn was to say, "My script was shot exactly as I wrote it." In 1926, she had come to Hollywood to conquer it. Now, twenty-one years later, she *had* conquered it. It was a victory unheard of in Hollywood. But in the end it was a hollow victory. When the shooting was completed, Ayn saw the first rough cut. "I knew it was no good," she said wearily. "And I never changed my mind. The people involved were not worthy of the assignment. I didn't even like the script; they wanted the movie to be under two hours, so the script was too short, it wasn't right. I was through with Hollywood. There's nothing there for me." Ayn turned her back on Hollywood forever, on the shining possibilities she had seen as a young girl in Russia, gazing, rapt and enchanted, at American movies glowing on the screen. She never wrote for films again.

Two previews of the movie were scheduled, one in Beverly Hills, the other in

Hollywood Park, a working-class district. Henry Blanke hoped the studio would give the first preview in Beverly Hills. Ayn told him she wanted it to be in Hollywood Park, because that was where her *real* audience would be.[5] It *was* in Hollywood Park. "I never saw so responsive an audience," she recalled. "They understood it all, and they applauded Roark's speech. After the previews, the top brass were gloating and delighted, they were sure it would be a big hit, and we had an enormous celebration. The Beverly Hills audience was not quite as responsive or perceptive, although they liked it. That's why I like the common man."

After the preview of the movie, in a strikingly modest gesture, Gary Cooper told Blanke, Jack Warner, and Ayn that only now did he really understand Roark's courtroom speech and how he should have done it. He felt that his performance had not been forceful enough. Silently, admiring the integrity of his gesture, Ayn agreed with him; she thought his performance was wooden, that he was unconvincing as an architect of genius, that "there were places where he was almost coy, and he was often embarrassing when he was supposed to show emotion."

The movie premiered at Warner's Theater in Hollywood in July of 1949. Ayn was able to forget her disappointment in the final product long enough to enjoy the extravagant glamour surrounding the premiere—stars in festive evening clothes, lines of eager theatergoers cheering their favorite stars, interviewers thrusting microphones at anyone of importance who would say a few words, brilliant searchlights sweeping in giant arcs across the night sky. "Frank and I talked about how we'd risen from the bottom of the ladder to this," she would recall with a smile. Her smile faded as she added, "And I told the interviewers how proud I was that my script had not been altered or cut."

Ayn and Frank entered the theater and took their seats. The movie began. Ayn watched uncomfortably, thinking that at least her script and her lines had been preserved. The final courtroom scene began—and suddenly, like a knife cutting through her body, she saw that Roark's most important line, the line that named the theme of the book and the total of its meaning—the line "I wished to come here and say that I am a man who does not exist for others"—had been cut.

All the work and struggle of months, all the arguing and persuading, all the dealings with irrationality and mediocrity—she felt in that moment—had been for nothing. She had lost her battle.[6]

Within a few days, she was able to remind herself that she had not lost, that the rest of her script and her ideas were untouched, that the novel's theme and meaning had been preserved. But whatever personal value there had been for her

[5] In 1950, *Variety* reported: "Politically intriguing is the word from London that 'The Fountainhead,' which preaches rugged individualism, is mopping up in the United Kingdom's industrial areas, where the government is nationalizing the steel industry."

[6] When Ayn learned from Henry Blanke that the cut had been made at the order of the front office, it was the end of her relationship with Warner Brothers. Furious, she called Alan Collins to say that when *Atlas Shrugged* was completed, it was never to be submitted to Warner Brothers.

in the movie was destroyed. Its sole remaining importance for her was that it did achieve her primary purpose: it brought large numbers of new readers, fascinated by the movie and by its stunning new ideas, to *The Fountainhead.* An unprecedented six years after publication, it put the book back on the bestseller lists. In the years that followed, hundreds of thousands of viewers did not agree with Ayn's negative judgment on the movie; it continues to bring the novel an ever wider readership to this day.

Warner Brothers' publicity campaign for the movie, though enthusiastic and extensive, virtually ignored its ideological content. The advertisements show Patricia Neal struggling to free herself from Cooper's embrace or huddled on the floor as Cooper gazes down at her with a look both sexual and menacing; the captions read: "No man takes what's mine!" The reviews were mixed; in many of the smaller newspapers, they were respectful and admiring; the major New York reviewers were appalled and angry. Several said, echoing the Vancouver *Sun:* "The Fountainhead is the story of an architect who coldly blows up a badly needed housing project rather than permit the slightest alteration in his designs." Another announced: "The novel's religious aspects have been removed from the screen version." Ayn, who never defended herself against printed attacks, knowing that to do so would give added publicity to the attacks, did—despite her anger at the studio—respond to Bosley Crowther's attack on Warner Brothers in the New York *Times.* She wrote a statement that was printed in the Letters column: "Mr. Crowther missed the fact that Warner Brothers have given a great demonstration of courage and consistency: they have produced the most faithful adaptation of a novel ever to appear on the screen."

Ten years after the movie was released, when it was making its still-frequent appearances in neighborhood theaters and on television, Ayn saw Patricia Neal at a party in New York. "Have you seen *The Fountainhead* on television?" Ayn asked. "It's a strange thing," Neal replied. "All my fans seem to have seen it on television—and they like it now better than they liked it originally." "That's because it's better on a small screen than a large one," Ayn said. "The intimacy of television is much better suited to the presentation of ideas. And because the ideas are working; what seemed outrageous in 1949, seems less so now. The book —and reality—are working."

The culture *has* changed since the forties, in significant part as a result of the works of Ayn Rand. Her ideas have spread, they have been heard, they have made a difference. The book—and reality—*are* working.

PART IV

ATLAS SHRUGGED

Chapter Nineteen

Ever since leaving New York to do the preliminary movie script for *The Fountainhead,* Ayn had spent every spare moment on the new novel that had come to absorb her wholly. She had returned to it the instant the script was completed, she had worked on it between assignments for Hal Wallis, she had devoted many evenings to it despite the turmoil of the shooting of the movie; gradually, she had begun to see fewer people, begrudging the time spent on social activities. Now, with the release of the movie, she was due to return to Wallis for another six months. Longing only to work in peace on her novel, she asked him to release her from her contract. Hollywood had been hit by a depression, fewer movies were being made, and to her great relief Wallis agreed to her request. She had worked for him three years of the projected five; her insistence on canceling the contract cost her more than seventy thousand dollars.

"A plot," Ayn would write, "is a purposeful progression of events. A plot-structure is a series of integrated, logically connected events, moved by a central purpose, leading to the resolution of a climax." Her novels have been criticized as romanticized and unrealistic; it has been said that the progression of a human life consists of a random series of disconnected, unchosen events, untied by any common theme or purpose, and leading, in the end, to the grave.

But the life of Ayn Rand—like her art—*was* a plot.

Her professional life was increasingly ravaged by conflicts, her emotional life was buried ever deeper in the underground of her spirit, her life as a woman was painfully unfulfilled—but she held fast to whatever was golden in her soul, carrying it untouched and unaltered through the years. Until, in the purposeful progression of her days, that store of gold led her to the moment that united and integrated all the separate threads of all the separate purposes of her life.

That moment was the first inception of the idea for *Atlas Shrugged.*

It was on an evening five years earlier, shortly after the publication of *The*

Fountainhead; the book was selling slowly and no one could predict its future spectacular success. During a telephone conversation with Isabel Paterson, Ayn was discussing her crushing disappointment with the sales of the novel. "People can't accept your moral philosophy in fiction form," Pat said. "You should write it as a nonfiction treatise." "No," Ayn replied emphatically. "I've presented my case in *The Fountainhead.* It's clear to any rational mind. If they don't respond, why should I wish to enlighten or help them further? I'm not an altruist." Pat continued to press her, arguing that if she wished her ideas to be known, she had a *duty* to write nonfiction; people *needed* it. "Oh, they do?" answered Ayn. "What if I went on strike? What if *all* the creative minds of the world went on strike?" She added, in passing, "That would make a good novel"—and they went on to discuss other matters. When she hung up the telephone, Frank, who had been in the room, remarked: "It *would* make a good novel."

Ayn turned to stare at him, her eyes widening—then narrowing as her mind retraced the words she had spoken to Pat, then flew back in time to her childhood story of the beautiful woman who withdrew the men of intelligence from a collectivist Europe. She talked excitedly all night, her mind racing with possibilities that were shaping themselves into a form more real to her than anything in the world around her: the form of a novel. By morning, she had decided that "the mind on strike" was to be the theme of her next novel. Its title was to be *Atlas Shrugged.*

From that night in 1943 through the success of *The Fountainhead,* through the emotionally barren periods of writing screenplays for Hal Wallis, through the frustration of the Hollywood hearings, through the fierce battle to preserve her movie script of *The Fountainhead,* through the accelerating decay of a marriage without intimacy or reality—*Atlas Shrugged* was the center of her life and thoughts, alive within her as her battle cry, her armor and her holy grail, as the invincible world in which her real life was lived.

As an early step in the project that was to absorb and obsess her for fourteen years, Ayn began to study the problems and the history of heavy industry, of railroads, steel, oil, copper. "I had to do less specific research than for *The Fountainhead,*" she would recall, "because I did not have to know any profession as thoroughly as I'd had to know architecture." She collected a small library of books and began reading them in the evenings. As she projected particular sequences in the novel which would demand highly specialized knowledge, she did more detailed research: in order to describe the breakout of a blast furnace at a steel mill, she struggled through the complex instructions contained in a technical manual for furnace foremen. She began a series of interviews of railroad and steel executives, and she and Frank drove between both coasts to visit steel plants and railroad yards.

Again Frank was pulled away from his beloved ranch. But he seemed to enjoy their trips as much as Ayn did, although the source of his pleasure was different from hers. Ayn was willing to travel only when she had a specific, preferably professional, purpose; Frank enjoyed, as an end in itself, the sight of mountains and streams and cities and hidden towns he had not seen before. They now had the money for pleasure travel had they wished it; Frank told a friend that he longed to see Europe. "But Ayn wouldn't go there," he said wistfully. It seemed not to be a possibility, as they understood their lives together, that Frank might travel alone.

Ayn had chosen railroads as the main background for her novel because they deal with all the other major industries, thus functioning as the blood system of the economy. On one of their trips to New York, she interviewed the vice president in charge of operations of the New York Central Railroad, a dignified, white-haired gentleman; she wondered what his reaction would be if he had known he was to become Dagny Taggart, a beautiful young woman of thirty-four.

She was planning a climactic scene in which Dagny and Rearden would ride in the engine of the train on the first run of the John Galt Line. She wanted to know firsthand what such an experience would be—and she was able to obtain the railroad's permission to ride in the engine of the Twentieth Century Limited. She would later say that, "It was one of the few existential experiences in my life that I really enjoyed every moment of." In a letter written to Isabel Paterson before their break, she described her adventure: "The most thrilling moment was when the engine started moving, and the ride through the underground tunnel out of Grand Central. Everything I thought of as heroic about man's technological achievements, was there concretely for me to feel for the first time in my life. . . . I was not afraid at all. It was the feeling of being in front and of knowing where I was going, instead of being dependent on some unknown power. . . . All I felt was a wonderful sense of excitement and complete security. . . . At Harmon they changed the engine, and I got into my first Diesel . . . the engine rides as if it were floating. It actually seems to glide; you don't feel the wheels under you at all. . . . The next morning, I had to get up at six o'clock, and got into the engine again at Elkhart, Indiana. During the night they had their first snowstorm. It was still dark when we started riding through the snow. . . . They put me into the engineer's seat and let me drive the engine myself. . . . *I have now driven the Twentieth Century Limited.* They let me start the engine from a small station, and of course, there were three men standing behind me watching, but still nobody touched a lever except me, and I started the train and accelerated it to eighty miles per hour . . . the signal lights seemed to be coming along every few seconds. . . . An old railroad man was riding on the cowcatcher of a switch engine on a siding; when he looked up, as our train came along with me in the engineer's seat, the look on his face was something I have never seen on any human face before. It was like an exaggerated close-up in a movie farce. *There* was a man who was staring, stunned and stupefied. . . . I am completely ruined now as a train passenger. I was bored all the way out of Chicago, riding in a compartment. That's much too tame. I would love to travel across the whole continent in the engine." The scene which was to result from this ride is one of the most movingly beautiful in any of Ayn's writing.

That same summer, returning to Los Angeles, she and Frank drove along the exact run of the John Galt Line: diagonally across Colorado from Cheyenne, Wyoming through Denver, then on southwest. For the location of *Atlas Shrugged*'s Atlantis, the hidden valley where the men who have gone on strike spend a month together each summer—they call it "Galt's Gulch"—Ayn had studied a Union Pacific Railroad map until she found an isolated valley high in the most uninhabited section of the Rockies. She and Frank drove to the location of the valley in Colorado—and found, to their astonishment, that there was a beautiful little town there, the town of Urey. "It was an old mining settlement," she would recall, "circled by mountains; at the time, it had just one street of very old houses and a tiny motel. It was cut off from everything, very difficult of access in the winter. I'll never forget how beautiful it was. Some day, I'd like to go back there."

Ayn's work on the plot of *Atlas Shrugged* was not beset with the years of difficulties she had encountered with *The Fountainhead*. Her talents as a plot-writer, always the core of her approach to fiction, had been honed during her struggles with *We the Living* and *The Fountainhead*. Within five months after she began outlining *Atlas,* the essential plot outline was completed. "I would walk around the garden and on the road near the alfalfa field," she was to say, "because there were no interruptions and no sounds of cars; that's where most of the plotting was done. At the end of five months, I knew the key events and developments, and in what order they would occur. Some of my notes are very generalized; I'd know *what* was to happen, but I didn't know *how* it would happen until I came to the chapter in the writing. Other events were fully worked out in the outline. I had first thought that the strike would have to begin three generations before the strike's present leader. But I soon grasped that a certain amount of foreshortening was permissible, and by that means I could show it occurring in one generation. My main worry was how I would show the economic disintegration of the country throughout the novel, concretely and plausibly, while enormously foreshortening it. A lot of the specifics in my mind had to be kept fluid, so that I could use whatever of them could be tied to all the developments and advance all the steps of the disintegration."

As she first conceived of the novel, Ayn had thought that her theme, "the mind on strike," would not require the presentation of new philosophical ideas. It would demonstrate the application of the theme of *The Fountainhead,* individualism, to the political-economic arena. The action, with a minimum of comment, would carry the philosophical message, it would demonstrate that capitalism rests on the mind and the freedom of the mind. It was when she began to concretize more specifically what her theme required, to outline the means by which she would show the role and importance of the mind in human society, that she began to have the first glimmering of the philosophical dimensions of what she had undertaken. One day, while she was working on the final movie script for *The Fountainhead,* a young Associated Press reporter came to the studio to interview her. He asked her about the new novel she was planning. She told him, "it will combine metaphysics, morality, economics, politics, and sex—and it will show the tie between metaphysics and economics." Ayn beamed like a young girl when she later told the story, adding, "I'll never forget his look. He said helplessly, 'I can't see how you'll manage it . . . but I guess you know what you're doing.' And he released the story exactly as I'd stated it."

In order to achieve full conceptual clarity before beginning to write the novel, Ayn made extensive notes on the ideas that were explicitly or implicitly to be involved. In these early notes, one sees the scope of the novel begin to grow and broaden.

"My most important job," she wrote, "is the formulation of a rational morality of and for man, of and for his life, of and for this earth."

While projecting what would happen if the men of the mind went on strike, while defining how and why civilization would collapse, she was led to a crucial question. If it is the men of the mind who carry the world on their shoulders and make civilization possible—why have they never recognized their own power? Why have they never challenged their torturers and expropriators? When she grasped the answer, she knew it was to be one of the most important moral concepts in the novel: the concept of "the sanction of the victim." She saw that it is the *victims,* the men of virtue and ability, who make the triumph of evil possible by their willingness to let their virtues be used against them: their willingness to bear injustice, to sacrifice their own interests, *to concede moral validity to the claims of their own destroyers.*

Her identification of the disastrous consequences of the soul-body dichotomy was another contributing element to the growth of the novel's scale; it would become a central philosophical issue. In her notes, she described the way in which this dichotomy has served as sanction and excuse for the persecution of industrialists and for the scorn directed against those who create the physical means of man's survival. She wrote: "Show that the real sources, key spots, spark plugs of material production (the inventors and industrialists) are creators in the same way, in the same sense, with the same heroic virtues, of the same high *spiritual* order, as the men usually thought of as creators—the artists. Show that *any* original rational idea, in any sphere of man's activity, is an act of creation and creativeness. *Vindicate* the industrialist—the author of material production."

She added, "It would be interesting to show how the same principle operates in relation to sex." She believed that just as men do not understand that the source of the production of wealth is man's mind, so they do not understand that the source of a man's sexual desires and choices is his philosophical values: both production and sex are scorned for the same reason, as mindless, animalistic activities that have no relation to man's spirit. The meaning of the soul-body dichotomy as applied to sex became a crucial part of the story. The manner in which it is tied, through the character and life of Hank Rearden, to the same dichotomy in the realm of economics and politics, constitutes one of the most brilliant feats of integration in *Atlas Shrugged.*

Excerpts from her notes provide an interesting illustration of the process by which she proceeded from wide abstractions to the concrete events of a specific story. "The collectivists and the champions of the 'common man,'" she wrote, "have screamed for so long about strikes, about the dependence of the industrialist upon his workers, about the workers supporting him, creating his wealth, making his livelihood possible, and what would happen to him if they walked out. Very well. I will now show who depends on whom, who supports whom, who creates what, who makes whose livelihood possible, and what happens to whom when who walks out."

One of her notes states: "Reverse the process of expansion that goes on in a society of producers: Henry Ford's automobile opened the way for [the expansion of many] industries: oil, roads, glass, rubber, plastics, etc. Now, in a society of parasites, the opposite takes place: a shrinking of industries and productive activities. A James Taggart at the head of a big concern would have exactly the opposite effect from that of a Henry Ford."

In another note, she wrote: "Since the essence of the creator's power is the ability of independent rational judgment, and since this is precisely what the parasite is incapable of—the key to every disaster in the story, to the whole disintegration of the world is, in each case (big or small), a situation where independent rational judgment is needed and cannot be produced (cannot—in the case of the parasites involved; will not—in the case of the creators)."

In devising the plot structure, Ayn had had to call upon her full power of dramatic integration. Each key event had to carry and illustrate the philosophical theme, and—simultaneously—contribute to the economic disintegration of the country, advance the personal relationships among the characters, and heighten the element of mystery and suspense created by the disappearance of one man of ability after another.

The mystery element was a major one because, as Nathaniel Branden later wrote in Who Is Ayn Rand? "Atlas Shrugged is a mystery story, 'not about the murder of a man's body, but about the murder—and rebirth—of man's spirit.' The reader is presented with a series of events that, in the beginning, appear incomprehensible: the world seems to be moving toward destruction, in a manner no one can identify and for reasons no one can understand. A brilliant industrialist—Francisco d'Anconia—appears suddenly to have abandoned all purpose and to have become a worthless playboy. A great composer—Richard Halley—renounces his career, after years of struggle, on the night of his triumph. Businessmen who have been single-tracked in their devotion to their work—such as Midas Mulligan, Ellis Wyatt, and Ken Danagger—retire without explanation, and disappear. A pirate—Ragnar Danneskjold—is loose on the high seas, attacking and robbing government relief ships. The world's most distinguished philosopher—Hugh Akston—leaves his university position and chooses to work as a cook in a diner. The abandoned remnant of a new type of motor that could have revolutionized industry, is found on a scrap heap in the ruins of a factory. And in the growing darkness of a crumbling civilization, in moments of hopelessness, bewilderment and despair, people are crying: 'Who is John Galt?'—without knowing exactly what the question means or where it came from or why they cry it. . . .

"*Atlas Shrugged* . . . is an action story on a grand scale, but it is a consciously philosophical action story, just as its heroes are consciously philosophical men of action. . . . It moves effortlessly and ingeniously from economics to epistemology to morality to metaphysics to psychology to the theory of sex, on the one hand—and, on the other, it has a playboy crusader who blows up a multi-billion-dollar industry, a philosopher-turned-pirate who attacks government relief ships, and a climax that involves the rescue of the hero from a torture chamber. Notwithstanding the austere solemnity of its abstract theme, her novel —as a work of art—projects the laughing, extravagantly imaginative virtuosity of a mind who has never heard that 'one is not supposed' to combine such elements as these in a single book."

As Ayn worked on the progression of the story, she began to devise the kind of characters who would represent the theme and enact that kind of story. "It took quite a long time for me to decide who would be the characters," she would explain, "except for Galt and Dagny."

Just as the person of John Galt would dominate all the events of *Atlas Shrugged*, so his spirit and image dominated the conception and writing of the novel. He is the man who conceived the strike, who initiated it, who sought out the men of the mind who would join it, and who brought it to its final climax and triumph. He is the man who said he would stop the motor of the world— and did. He is the man who gave his strikers their banner, the solemn oath that bound them together, and their rallying cry, in the form of the statement: "I swear by my life and my love of it that I will never live for the sake of another man, nor ask another man to live for mine."

"Galt's character was almost simultaneous with the idea of the strike," Ayn was to say. "It feels as if . . . as if his character was always there."

The character of John Galt *was* always there; Galt was to be her full and final statement of "the ideal man," the statement toward which the whole of her life had been moving her. He was to be the apotheosis of the human potential—the man of theoretical genius, of practical efficacy, the man who lives joyously, productively, courageously, triumphantly—the man who belongs on earth. When Dagny first meets John Galt—after her plane crashes in Atlantis—Ayn would describe Dagny's reactions in one of the most exalted tributes to her ideal in all of her writing:

"When she opened her eyes, she saw sunlight, green leaves and a man's face. She thought: I know what this is. This was the world as she had expected to see it at sixteen—and now she had reached it—and it seemed so simple, so unastonishing, that the thing she felt was like a blessing pronounced upon the universe by means of three words: But of course.

"She was looking up at the face of a man who knelt by her side, and she knew that in all the years behind her, *this* was what she would have given her life to see: a face that bore no mark of pain or fear or guilt. The shape of his mouth was pride, and more: it was as if he took pride in being proud. The angular planes of his cheeks made her think of arrogance, of tension, of scorn—yet the face had none of those qualities, it had their final sum: a look of serene determination and of certainty, and the look of a ruthless innocence which would not seek forgiveness or grant it. It was a face that had nothing to hide or to escape, a face with no fear of being seen or of seeing, so that the first thing she grasped about him was the intense perceptiveness of his eyes—he looked as if his faculty of sight were his best-loved tool and its exercise were a limitless, joyous adventure, as if his eyes imparted a superlative value to himself and to the world—to himself for his ability to see, to the world for being a place so eagerly worth seeing. . . .

"This was her world, she thought, this was the way men were meant to be and to face their existence—and all the rest of it, all the years of ugliness and struggle were only someone's senseless joke. She smiled at him, as at a fellow conspirator, in relief, in deliverance, in radiant mockery of all the things she would never have to consider important again. He smiled in answer, it was the same smile as her own, as if he felt what she felt and knew what she meant.

" 'We never had to take any of it seriously, did we?' she whispered.

" 'No, we never had to.' "

In these paragraphs, two women are in love: Dagny Taggart and Ayn Rand— "and all the years of ugliness and struggle were only someone's senseless joke." Those years would come to an end for Dagny, through the living reality of John Galt. They were not to end for Ayn. She never found the man whose "eyes imparted a superlative value to himself and to the world." But she would do what, perhaps, mattered to her even more than finding John Galt in life: she would give him reality in a work of art, she would shape her hero with her own mind and her own hands; and when the shaping was completed, she would have found her life's great love. He would never disappoint her, as every other love had disappointed her, as every later love would disappoint her. He would never leave her, he would never betray her. But he could never return her impassioned worship; like all the men she loved who lived and breathed in the real world— like Fronz, like Leo, like Frank, like the man who was soon to enter her life—he sentenced her to a lifetime of unrequited love.

The attributes most sharply emphasized in Galt's portrait were to be rationality, realism, serenity, self-esteem. An essential characteristic of Galt illustrates Ayn's view of what she called "the impotence of evil," a concept of great importance in her philosophy and in the structure of all her novels. Galt has a profound contempt for evil, a contempt based on the conviction that evil is the irrational and, therefore, the blind, the aberrated, the impotent. Evil is to be fought, when necessary, but not to be taken seriously in one's own view of life, not to be granted metaphysical power or significance; evil is to be despised, not hated or feared. One may observe this premise in the plot-structure of *Atlas:* the central lines of dramatic conflict are not between the good and the evil, but between the good and the good—between Galt and Francisco, the strikers, on the one hand, and Dagny and Rearden, who will not join the strike, on the other. The errors that set Dagny and Rearden in conflict with Galt and Francisco are what Ayn defined as errors of knowledge, not breaches of morality. This same pattern is apparent in *The Fountainhead;* the central conflict is Roark versus Dominique and Wynand. In both novels, the villains merely cash in on the consequences of the heroes' conflicts, but are not the initiators, the sources or the motive power of the story's events. "In my novels, and in actual life," Ayn often said, "the alleged victories of evil are made possible only by the flaws or the errors of those who are essentially good. Evil, left to its own devices, is impotent and self-defeating. To make my central conflicts a struggle between heroes and villains, would be to grant to evil an honor it doesn't deserve."

When she had devised the character and role of John Galt, Ayn turned to her heroine, Dagny Taggart, the woman who was to be worthy of loving Galt and being loved by him. "I had always been somewhat frustrated by my presentation of women, and eager to present *my* kind of woman," Ayn said. Dagny is Ayn's first portrait of "the ideal woman." Kira was still a young girl at the end of *We the Living;* Dominique was paralyzed by a profound inner conflict. But Dagny was to be free of psychological conflict, serene in her basic relationship to existence, passionately ambitious and creative. Ayn wished to project her as the woman thought to be impossible by the conventional view of life—and of sex: the woman engineer, dealing with the material world of metal rails and freight cars and Diesel engines, who is, simultaneously, a consummately feminine hero-worshipper.

"Dagny is myself, with any possible flaws eliminated," Ayn once said. "She is myself without my tiredness, without my chronic slightly anti-material feeling, without that which I consider the ivory tower element in me, or the theoretician versus the man of action. . . . Dagny is myself without a moment of exhaustion."

The character of Hank Rearden, the leading industrialist and the chief victim of the novel—whom many of Ayn's readers would consider the most attractive and memorable of her characters—was arrived at with considerable difficulty and over a considerable period of time. "As I first conceived him," Ayn was to say, "Rearden was not to be a romantic character, but a much older man. He was to be a key means of dramatizing the martyrdom of the men of the mind; he was to be the martyred industrialist, the concrete Atlas who carries the world on his shoulders and receives only torture in return; that never changed; but as long as I saw him as an older man, I could get nowhere with him, and I couldn't get a central plot line. Everything had to be in flux until that central line was established. Then I had the sudden idea that Rearden should be younger, that he and Dagny should have a romance—and that their romance should be the central plot line. From that decision, everything else fell into place quite easily. I could begin to organize all the tentative events into an orderly progression, and decide which of the many possible events I had in mind should be used."

The characterization of Rearden was to be unique in Ayn's work; he *is* a hero, he is a man whom one admires intensely for his dedication, his uncomplaining struggle, his achievement, his austere honor, the magnanimity of his personality. But he is a man torn by conflict—not only the conflict with the outside world that characterizes Ayn's other heroes, but by inner conflict: the conflict between his sexual passion for Dagny and his view that sex is degradation; the conflict between his love for Francisco and his conviction that the face of the playboy which Francisco presents to the world is the proof of depravity; the conflict between his love for Dagny and his sense of duty toward the wife he despises. It is Rearden's battle with himself, and the unflinching honesty with which he fights it, that engages the reader. He is a man who, within the context of his understanding, will not deceive himself. After his first sexual encounter with Dagny, he would tell her: "I held it as my honor that I would never need anyone. I need you. It had been my pride that I had always acted on my convictions. I've given in to a desire which I despise. It is a desire that has reduced my mind, my will, my being, my power to exist into an abject dependence upon you—not even upon the Dagny Taggart whom I admired—but upon your body, your hands, your mouth and the few seconds of a convulsion of your muscles. . . . Whatever I wanted, I was free to proclaim it aloud and achieve it in the sight of the whole world. Now my only desire is one I loathe to name even to myself. . . . I want no pretense, no evasion, no silent indulgence, with the nature of our actions left unnamed. . . . It's depravity—and I accept it as such —and there is no height of virtue that I wouldn't give up for it." In the end, Rearden would come to understand the nature of his mistake, and of all the central mistakes of his life; and the reader would understand the means by which a man of spiritual nobility faces his internal conflicts.

Francisco d'Anconia—Galt's closest friend and the first man to join him in the strike—would become one of Ayn's most colorful and dramatic figures: the man of ruthless purposefulness who assumes the role of a playboy in order to destroy his fortune in plain sight of the whole world. Francisco's leitmotif is a lighthearted gaiety: he is the man with a superlative capacity for the enjoyment of life, who is an iron-disciplined worker of unsurpassed productive energy and achievement. It is Francisco who would explain the meaning of the novel's title, and its theme, to Rearden and to the reader:

" 'Mr. Rearden,' said Francisco, his voice solemnly calm, 'if you saw Atlas, the giant who holds the world on his shoulders, if you saw that he stood, blood running down his chest, his knees buckling, his arms trembling but still trying to hold the world aloft with the last of his strength, and the greater his effort the heavier the world bore down upon his shoulders—what would you tell him to do?'

" 'I . . . don't know. What . . . could he do? What would *you* tell him?'

" 'To shrug.' "

"Francisco," Ayn would say, "is the philosophical expression—the concretization in a human character—of what I heard in the operetta music I fell in love with in my childhood. . . . I don't remember how or when I got the specific

Nathaniel Branden, Pacific Palisades, California, one year after his meeting with Ayn Rand. 1951.

Ayn Rand. 1951. (From the Warner Bros. release *The Fountainhead* © 1949 Warner Bros. Pictures, Inc. Renewed 1976 United Artists Television, Inc.)

Ayn and Frank as matron of honor and best man at the wedding of Barbara
and Nathaniel Branden. 1953.

Ayn and Nathaniel. About 1956.

Ayn with manuscript of *Atlas Shrugged*, only moments after completing it. 1957.

Frank beside pastel portrait by an unknown artist; the portrait was used by Random House in advertisements of *Atlas Shrugged*. 1957.

"Maybe it's a publicity stunt for 'Atlas Shrugged.'"

Cartoon which appeared in the New York *Times Book Review* shortly after the publication of *Atlas Shrugged*. November 17, 1957. (Copyright © 1957 by The New York Times Company. Reprinted by permission)

Wedding of Joan Mitchell and Allan Blumenthal, with some of the members of "the collective." Standing, from left, Leonard Peikoff; Harry Kalberman; Elayne Kalberman; Sholey Fox; Allan; Reva Fox; Frank; Nathaniel; Alan Greenspan; seated, from left, Mary Ann Rukavina; Joan; Ayn; Barbara. 1957. (Picture courtesy of Joan and Allan Blumenthal)

Ayn and Frank in their New York apartment, holding a copy of *Atlas Shrugged*. 1959. (Picture courtesy of Joan Kennedy Taylor)

Ayn and Nathaniel during question period following lecture at Nathaniel Branden Institute. About 1960.

One of Frank's early paintings. 1963.
(From Barbara Branden's personal collection) (Photo by George Reis)

Ayn, with Frank, Nathaniel and Barbara, receiving honorary doctorate of humane letters at Lewis
and Clark College, Oregon. 1963.

NBI baseball team—named "The Huns" after a concept in Ayn's *For the New Intellectual*—in Central Park. Back row, from left: Allan Gotthelf; center row, from left, Dan Fauci, Barbara, George Broderick, Alan Margolin; front row, from left, Larry Abrams, Kathryn Eickhoff. 1964.

Some members of "the collective." Standing, from left: Leonard Peikoff, Nathaniel, Alan Greenspan; seated, from left: Barbara, Mary Ann (Rukavina) Sures. 1966.

Barbara Branden.
Late 1960s.

Mimi Sutton, Frank's niece and Ayn
and Frank's good friend. About 1970.

concept of the character. More than any other character, he was Minerva—he came ready-made into my mind. I don't even remember how I got his name. I probably heard it somewhere; to this day I'm slightly afraid to discover that his name is some forgotten association." Ayn *had* forgotten that the name she had given to the French hero of "the grandfather of *Atlas Shrugged*"—was "François"; and it is interesting to note that the world's largest producer of copper, like Francisco in the novel, is *Anaconda* Copper.

To Ayn, Francisco's name—Francisco Domingo Carlos Andres Sebastian d'Anconia—symbolized the whole character. "He is the other axis of my type of man," she once said. "You know, there are two types of man in my novels: Roark, Galt, and Rearden are one line; Wynand, Bjorn Faulkner, Leo, and Francisco are the other. The Francisco type are the men who symbolize the enjoyment of life on earth. In my early attempts in Russia, the Francisco type was very prominent—so in devising the character of Francisco, I was cashing in on an enormous store of ideas."[1]

If the leitmotif of Francisco was to be an indestructible gaiety, the leitmotif of Ragnar Danneskjold—the philosopher who becomes a pirate—was to be an implacable sense of justice. ". . . my only love," Ragnar would tell Rearden, "the only value I care to live for, is that which has never been loved by the world, has never won recognition or friends or defenders: human ability. That is the love I am serving—and if I should lose my life, to what better purpose could I give it?"

In her early notes, Ayn wrote that Ragnar was to be the symbol of the good man's helpless indignation against evil. "That was my lead to his character—the indignation that all of us feel, that any victim feels—against evil. That was the justification for a superior type of man choosing a career of violence. He was to be the avenging angel."[2]

Once the major protagonists were formed in Ayn's mind, she turned to the creation of secondary characters—of Dagny's brother, James Taggart, who "hides in mystical nonsense to avoid moral judgment"; of Lillian Rearden, Hank Rearden's wife, "the archetype of the humanitarian liberal pseudo-intellectual who despises and hates the industrialist"; of Cheryl, the young girl who marries

---

[1] I asked Ayn one day, "Which type was Cyrus?" She smiled. "It still seems odd to me when you mention his name, Barbara. He's always been like a private secret. . . . Cyrus was the Roark, Rearden, Galt type—the grim, domineering man of action. I still remember him, and I'm still in love with Cyrus."

[2] When I read *Atlas Shrugged* in manuscript as Ayn was writing it, I was fascinated with Ragnar from his first description: the smile that "was like seeing the first green of spring on the sculptured planes of an iceberg"—"the startling beauty of physical perfection—the hard, proud features, the scornful mouth of a Viking's statue"—the golden hair and the sky blue eyes. Ayn happened to mention a woman striker whom I would later meet in Galt's Gulch—"a tall, fragile woman with pale blond hair and a face of such beauty that it seemed veiled by distance, as if the artist had been merely able to suggest it, not to make it quite real. . . . she was Kay Ludlow, the movie star who, once seen, could never be forgotten." Almost involuntarily, I said, "How can you keep Ragnar and Kay Ludlow apart? Two people who look as they do, should be together." Ayn laughed, looked thoughtful for a moment—then said, "Okay. I'll do it for you." In the final version of the novel, Ragnar and Kay are married.

James Taggart believing his pretense of greatness, and is destroyed when she grasps the horror of the truth; of Robert Stadler, the great scientist destroyed by his own cynicism; of Ellis Wyatt and Ken Danagger, industrialists who abandon the work they love and join Galt's strike. In her outline, Ayn did not determine the relative importance of the secondary characters; she planned to use them as the plot required, when it required them.

"One character is an exception in my whole writing career," she would later say, shaking her head as if still startled by the exception and by how it came about. "He's a character who, without my intention, seemed to write himself— he came out of the material inspirationally, as I was writing. All I had intended was to describe in one brief mention a modern young college boy bureaucrat." The character was the young man nicknamed "The Wet Nurse," sent by Washington to direct the "fair" distribution of the new metal Rearden had created. He was to be a boy who "had no inkling of any concept of morality; it had been bred out of him by his college; this had left him with an odd frankness, naïve and cynical at once, like the innocence of a savage." The character began to interest Ayn, she explained. "I realized that through this type of innocent savage—not corrupt enough to know how corrupt his actions are, innocent enough to admire Rearden, a boy who really accepted what he'd been taught in college—I could show the tragic representative of the good average young people. He would be a boy brought up as amoral, then awakening to moral understanding. I was idly listening to music one day, and I thought that it could be a beautifully tragic scene if he died trying to save Rearden—and that that would be the specific event I had been trying to devise, the event which would finally make Rearden quit and go on strike."

The Wet Nurse was to become the most endearing and touching of all Ayn's characters. In his last scene, during a riot at Rearden Steel staged on order from Washington, he would be shot in a last desperate effort to save Rearden's mills. Rearden takes the dying boy in his arms, to carry him to safety. But it is too late. "The boy's features had no power to form a smile, but it was a smile that spoke in his glance, as he looked at Rearden's face—as he looked at that which he had not known he had been seeking through the brief span of his life, seeking as the image of that which he had not known to be his values."

Another minor character whom Ayn had planned in her notes, but later decided not to use, was a priest. "He was to be one of the philosophical variants illustrating the evil of the morality of forgiveness," she said. "If you always take the burden of sin upon yourself—as God does—it amounts to the sanction of evil. The power of religion consists of the power of morality—that's what holds people to religion—and I wanted to show that religion's monopoly on values does not belong to religion, but to philosophy. The priest was to be a glamorized Thomist philosopher who thought he could combine reason and religion, and finally realizes the mistake of his choice, and joins the strike. I wanted to give him the benefit of the doubt, and to show a man attracted to religion by morality. But the problem was that he was not to be taken literally; all the other strikers are members of valuable professions, and to include a minister would be to sanction religion."

One of the minor characters—a woman striker in the valley—had a particular personal meaning to Ayn: the woman Ayn called "the fishwife," because her work was to provide the fish for the grocery market. As Dagny and Galt drive through the valley, Dagny was to see "a young woman . . . stretched on the sun-flooded planks, watching a battery of fishing rods. She glanced up at the sound of the car, then leaped to her feet in a single swift movement, a shade too swift, and ran to the road. She wore slacks, rolled above the knees of her bare legs, she had dark, disheveled hair and large eyes. . . . Dagny . . . saw the glance with which the young woman stood looking after Galt . . . hopelessness, serenely accepted, was part of the worship in that glance." Galt said, "She's a writer. The kind of writer who wouldn't be published outside. She believes that when one deals with words, one deals with the mind." The fishwife is Ayn's Hitchcock-like appearance in *Atlas Shrugged.*

In her notes, the fishwife originally was intended to have a larger role: "She has written a very good book, which has been totally neglected and is being killed. One lonely, dark evening, she is standing in front of a book-store window, looking for her book. She hears a voice saying, 'You'll never find it there.' It's one of the strikers—and that's how she goes on strike." Commenting on the notes, Ayn was to say wistfully, "It was wishful thinking on my part—it's what I wished to God would happen to me. I still do, in a certain sense. The woman was projected from that sense. But there was no room to handle it properly, so I finally used her only for that one scene in the valley. It amused me to have her be like me, as a private joke. . . . There were other things on that order that gave me enormous pleasure—like the use of the dollar sign [cigarettes produced in the valley were marked with a gold dollar sign, 'the initials of the United States, the only country where money was the symbol of man's right to his own mind, to his work, to his life, to his happiness']—and the gimmick of 'Who is John Galt' [the slang expression used as the novel's opening sentence and throughout the story as an expression of despair and a cry for help]—and the theme of the strike itself. These fantastic gimmicks are the real source of pleasure in fiction for me, the greatest pleasure. They capture the whole spirit and style of the book."

Throughout the last year of the forties, Ayn was working full time on the writing of *Atlas Shrugged.* The philosophical work was done, the plotting was done—and, since the ending of her contract with Hal Wallis, her time was her own. Her tendency to reclusiveness continued to increase as the world that interested her narrowed to the dimensions of her novel and the study in which she worked. Often, in the evenings, she would put on her favorite music—her tiddlywink pieces, selections from Rachmaninoff and Chopin, operettas—and think about her next day's work. The music she loved always inspired her, it gave her the sense that she did not leave *her* world, the world of *Atlas Shrugged,* when she left her study; some of her best literary ideas were arrived at as she listened to it.

The political conservatives she had met since moving to California continued to be among her rare social contacts. But she was becoming progressively and painfully disillusioned with them, progressively convinced that they did not know how to fight an *intellectual* battle; their concern was with political and economic issues, despite Ayn's efforts to convince them that the political-economic case for freedom had long ago been presented, but no one was listening, the march toward collectivism had not halted, and that what was needed was a *moral* justification for freedom. So long as men were taught to feel guilty for their success and their wealth, so long as altruism was accepted as a morality for life, men might give lip-service to freedom, but they would turn their backs on it. The dominant ideas in the world were faith, self-sacrifice and collectivism. "Historical trends are the inescapable product of philosophy," Ayn often said. "It is philosophy that has brought men to this state, and it is only philosophy that can lead them out." She continued to watch America's political progress, to watch— and to work on the book which she would offer as the solution to the decay of freedom.

The young immigrant girl who landed in New York had never ceased to love her new country, with the passionate, near-painful devotion that perhaps only the foreign-born fully understand, and had never ceased to be aware that America had given her life, and hope, and freedom, and the possibility of achieving everything denied to her in Soviet Russia. But Ayn Rand was a trader. She would write that ". . . the moral symbol of respect for human beings, is *the trader*. We, who live by values, not by loot, are traders, both in matter and in spirit. A trader is a man who earns what he gets and does not give or take the undeserved." She was to repay her adopted country for the gifts it offered her. She was to repay it by giving America its voice.

In *Atlas Shrugged,* Dagny Taggart would ask John Galt what he had told the inventors, the artists, the industrialists, the scientists, the men of the mind in every field of activity who had joined his strike, leaving behind their work and their lives—what he told them to convince them to abandon everything and to join him. Galt answers, "I told them they were right. . . . I gave them the pride they did not know they had. I gave them the words to identify it. I gave them that priceless possession which they had missed, had longed for, yet had not known they needed: a moral sanction."

This was to be Ayn's gift to America. A moral sanction. The philosophical demonstration that to live for one's own rational self-interest, to pursue one's own selfish, personal goals, to use one's mind in the service of one's own life and happiness, is the noblest, the highest, *the most moral* of human activities. Speaking of his strikers, Galt would say: "I have given them the weapon they had lacked: the knowledge of their own moral value. They, the great victims who had produced all the wonders of humanity's brief summer . . . had not discovered the nature of their right. They had known that theirs was the power. I taught them that theirs was the glory." Speaking to the unnamed, unchampioned, beating heart of her new land, Ayn was to say: "Yours is the glory."

Chapter Twenty

It was during this period of intensive work on the writing of *Atlas Shrugged* that Ayn agreed to meet two young fans of *The Fountainhead*.

She had received a letter from Nathaniel Branden,[1] asking philosophical and literary questions about *The Fountainhead* and *We the Living*. Since beginning the writing of the novel, she rarely took time to answer her mail; her "Letter from Ayn Rand" had been printed, and it dealt with many of the questions that were addressed to her. But Nathaniel's letter posed questions about philosophical inconsistencies he believed he had found in *We the Living* that intrigued her with their perceptiveness; she felt he deserved a thoughtful reply. In her lengthy response, she added that she was working on a new novel, and could not continue to engage in correspondence; but since he was living in Los Angeles, he could send her his telephone number if he had more questions, and perhaps she might call to arrange an appointment.

Ayn did not know that Nathaniel's telephone number—dropped off as he was speeding to tell me that he had heard from Ayn Rand—was in the mail five minutes after her letter arrived at his home.

Nathaniel and I were students at UCLA, he in psychology, I in philosophy. We had both separately discovered *The Fountainhead* when we were fifteen years old and had devoured it nonstop in a few rapt days of emotional and intellectual absorption; it had had a powerful influence on the development of our thinking. A few years later, it was because of the novel that we met. I was living in Winnipeg, Canada, with my family; Nathaniel, whose home was in Toronto, was spending a year in Winnipeg after his graduation from high school. A friend said to me one day: "There's a boy you must meet. You'll find him fascinating. He's

---

[1] At that time, his name was Nathan Blumenthal; he was later to change it to Nathaniel Branden; many of his friends, including Ayn, continued to call him "Nathan." My name was Barbara Weidman.

the only person who talks about *The Fountainhead* the way you do." My friend was correct: I *was* fascinated by the brilliant, erratic, passionately intellectual young man. We began to see each other frequently, and our relationship continued when our education took us to Los Angeles, as we struggled together to find a consistent view of a complex world, to find the answers to questions to which *The Fountainhead* had given us a key, but had not yet opened the door.

She did not really want to meet this new young fan, Ayn told Frank when Nathaniel's telephone number arrived, despite his apparent intelligence. She had been disappointed too many times by admirers of her work to whom she had been friendly and helpful; too often, young fans had tried to use her for personal advice, for professional advancement, for the social prestige of knowing the writer of an international bestseller. She would later recall, "I paced up and down in my office one late winter night, talking to Frank, trying to decide if I should or should not meet Nathan. Today, it's almost frightening to think how much depended on that decision. I finally made up my mind on a theoretical moral principle: that it was wrong to pass collective judgments on the basis of a few bad experiences, and I shouldn't be stopped by the fear of disappointment." Ayn went to the telephone. It was a few steps and a brief conversation that were to radically alter her life.

Ayn met Nathaniel at her home on an evening in March 1950.

When he arrived at my apartment early next morning—collecting a speeding ticket on the way—it was clear from his face that something of extraordinary meaning had happened to him. They had talked long into the night, he said excitedly; her conversation was brilliant, powerful, overwhelming in its clarity and consistency. She had talked about reason, and why reason versus mysticism, man's mind versus faith, was the most fundamental of all philosophical issues, of which capitalism versus collectivism was merely a derivative. As she discussed the absolutism of reason, he had interrupted to say uneasily, "But there's a problem." Ayn was later to explain that the exchange that followed was, for her, the highlight of the evening, convincing her that Nathaniel was an unusually intelligent and promising young man. He had said, "Even if I were somehow rationally convinced that I should murder, say, my wife, I don't think I'd be able to do it. So doesn't reason have limits?" "Did you say *rationally* convinced?" Ayn had asked quietly. "Oh . . . ." he had answered. Then he had laughed. "Of course."

"She's fascinating," he told me. "She . . . she's *Mrs.* Logic. She's everything I could have expected from the writer of *The Fountainhead*—no, she's more." Then he grinned and said, "She told me I'd be welcome to visit again. I'll ask if I can bring you with me."

"Of course, bring him," Ayn responded when Nathaniel called to say he'd like a friend, who admired her work as he did, to join him on his next visit. "It's not a 'him,' " he said. She laughed. "Fine. Bring her along."

In 1950, no freeways had yet been built between Los Angeles and most of its outlying towns. Chatsworth was over an hour's drive along narrow roads to what seemed less like a suburb than a country village. As we drove in Nathaniel's ancient LaSalle, we passed long stretches of open country where only the first few homes were beginning to rise. Today, the busy freeway passes used-car lots and fast-food restaurants and housing developments and banks; but it does not reach the house at 10,000 Tampa Avenue where Ayn Rand once lived: that house has long since been razed.

When we reached Ayn's home, secluded on a tree-lined street, it was to see an austere modern house that looked as if it might have leaped from the pages of *The Fountainhead* over the signature of Howard Roark. It was made of glass and aluminum-covered steel, the aluminum burnished to a satiny glow; it was light, airy, formed of straight, rising lines and with, incredibly, a curving moat—devised by Richard Neutra to ensure an extra measure of privacy—around the front of the house and surrounding a circular steel patio. The geometric forms of the house were reflected among the water reeds of the moat. It was already dark, but the shapes of fields could be seen behind the house and, nearer, flowering shrubs and a stand of small lush trees.

I no longer recall what I said or what Ayn said when we were introduced and I first heard her husky, Russian-accented voice. The total of my concentration was on the visual reality of the woman who stood before me. At first, I saw only her eyes—and I had the sudden, odd feeling, a feeling gone before I could grasp it, that I was naked before those fiercely perceptive eyes, and alone—and safe. It was the beat of a long moment before I could wrench my glance away to capture the full figure.

Ayn was a small, stocky woman, dressed in a pale green blouse and gray skirt, with short, dark hair—the hair style of the twenties, straight and bobbed and severe—and a full, sensuous mouth set firmly in a squarish face. She was not a conventionally attractive woman, but compelling in the remarkable combination of perceptiveness and sensuality, of intelligence and passionate intensity, that she projected.

Beside her stood a tall, gaunt man with the appearance and manner of an aristocrat. There was no touch or hint of aristocracy in Frank's background, only a long line of manual workers. But his figure had an elegance that spoke of generations of breeding. He had light, straight hair thrown back from a high forehead, gray-blue eyes, and the large, slightly gnarled hands of a laborer. He seemed a man from a different century, perhaps a member of the Southern landed gentry living in the nineteenth century. There was an easy, slow grace about him, a warmth, a gentleness, the spiritual and physical elegance of a man who would have been content in beautiful old surroundings with beautiful old possessions and a way of life that required only his particular quiet charm.

The living room of the house seemed inevitable for that house and for Ayn Rand. The room, its walls painted peacock blue, was large, filled with comfortable overstuffed furniture covered in shades of beige, with coffee tables and a record cabinet in blond wood; scattered over the tables were brightly colored ashtrays in vivid blue-green, Ayn's favorite color, and bowls of fresh flowers.

And everywhere, larger than life size, were giant plants, their colors and shapes bringing sunshine and daylight into the night room. Above, extending around two sides of the living room, was a gallery that formed the hallway of the second floor; from the gallery's peacock blue railing the green of more plants spilled down like a cheerful frame for the second story. Through a window, one could see the burnished walls of gray slate, open to the sky, which formed the outdoor patio.

As we began to talk, Ayn pulled out a cigarette holder and lighted the first of the evening's many cigarettes. She was rarely without the holder; even when she was not smoking, she held it almost as a weapon, punctuating her words with sharp, jagged gestures. All her gestures were abrupt, straight-lined, and unblurred, like her thoughts and her conversation.

After not more than ten minutes of getting-acquainted social conversation—she asked how Nathaniel and I had met, and seemed delighted to learn that it was because of *The Fountainhead:* "It's a wonderful fiction event," she laughed —we plunged into a discussion of precisely the sorts of issues Nathaniel and I had been struggling with for the past two years. An important part of the powerful effect of Ayn's personality on everyone who met her was that she appeared to have an acute sensitivity to the particular concepts most relevant to whomever she was addressing, a special antenna that gave her a direct line to what would be especially meaningful; many of her acquaintances had commented on this phenomenon, as many more were to do throughout her life.

Evidently pleased by our interest in philosophical questions—an interest for which she had been starved in her dealings with conservative friends whose concerns were narrowly political—she spoke, that evening, of her concept of "the benevolent universe," her view that man's *natural* state is one of achievement, fulfillment, and joy; she spoke of free will as the choice, or the refusal, to use one's mind to the limit of one's ability; she spoke of emotions as the product of an intellectual estimate, made consciously or subconsciously. Ayn was, by basic mental set, a superb teacher, taking endless joy in the activity of breaking down complex issues into their easily graspable parts, in communicating her thoughts, in working out the implications of her ideas in conversation, in honing the concepts she was developing in *Atlas Shrugged.* Nathaniel and I listened, argued, and questioned with an almost painfully intense eagerness, feeling as if she were weaving a personal miracle for us.

It was clear why Nathaniel had described Ayn as "Mrs. Logic." One could not encounter a human being in whom the psychological attribute of rationality was more pronounced; one grasped it almost as a visible presence. It was conveyed by the openness of her manner—by the precision and clarity of her speech —by the directness of her conversation and the fact that she gave reasons for her every statement—by the intense perceptiveness of her glance—by the natural, effortless pleasure she projected in the act of intellectual analysis.

Throughout the evening, Frank said little. But his silence was not aloof; he seemed to be listening carefully, smiling or nodding at times, his eyes very kind, his long body relaxed and graceful as a cat. Ayn often turned to him as she spoke, as if gaining some special comfort from the fact of his presence. After a few hours, he disappeared into the kitchen, and emerged with mugs of coffee and mounds of sweet pastry and a plate of Ayn's beloved Swiss chocolates.

We talked—or, rather, predominantly it was Ayn and Nathaniel who talked, as I struggled with a shyness I had not yet overcome—until the sun came out and lighted the black marble floor of the outdoor patio. The conversation dealt with metaphysics, with politics, with religion, with the nature of knowledge, with aesthetics, with morality, with the absolutism of reason and the power of the human mind—while I listened with a feeling of intellectual excitement I had never before experienced. There was something Ayn conveyed, something more than her words and their meaning, something as tangible as the sound of her voice, that seemed to have its own especial purity and beauty. *Here,* with this woman, in this room, ideas *mattered*—they were of life-and-death importance, they were the means of commerce among human beings, the only values to be traded. Here was a world ruled by the rigorous, cool elegance of rationality. I listened to Ayn Rand with a sense of wonder, and with tears stinging at the back of my eyes.

When Nathaniel and I finally tore ourselves away and headed back to Los Angeles, we carried with us Ayn's invitation to return again in a week. I recall saying to Nathaniel as we drove, "I feel as if, intellectually, I've always stood on a leaking life raft in the ocean, and as I jump to cover one leak with my foot, another spurts forth—and I leap to cover it—and then there's another. . . . But now I have the sense that it might be possible to stand on solid ground, to *understand,* to *know* what sort of world I live in. It's as if . . . as if for the first time the earth is firm under my feet." I began to laugh. "But Nathan, I'm nowhere *near* the ground—I'm floating six feet above it—and I feel wonderful! Is all this really possible? I know it's happening, but is it really possible?"

It *was* possible. What began for us was an enchanted period of time. We went through our university days talking not of our classes or our daily lives, but of the things we were learning from Ayn, and the new questions rising in our minds. And each week seemed to crawl by until our Saturday meetings with Ayn Rand.

Ayn had told Nathaniel that he might telephone her when he had philosophical issues to discuss. "Do you mean tomorrow?" he had asked. He began to call as often as she would permit, which soon became daily. His sister, Elayne, with whom he was living, was furious when her April telephone bill arrived. Chatsworth was a toll call's distance from Los Angeles—a ten-cent toll call. That first month, the bill for calls to Chatsworth was forty-three dollars. Despite the pressures of her work, Ayn welcomed his calls, her mind teeming with the issues she wished to discuss.

During the first weeks, Nathaniel and I drove to Chatsworth on Saturday evenings. Soon, other evenings and an occasional afternoon were added. Within a few months, we had graduated from young fans to the status of personal friends. Since early childhood, Ayn had scornfully rejected any human relationship not based on a philosophical mutuality; she often said that she was "incapable of a nonideological friendship." She rarely used the word "friend," or showed more than the most perfunctory interest, for any man or woman with whom she did not share a common philosophical interest and dedication. As a result, she had few intimate friends. She was no longer in contact with Isabel Paterson, and Thadeus Ashby had been gone from her life for several years. She enjoyed occasional meetings with the few friends she did respect, with Adrian and Janet Gaynor, with Ruth and Buzzy Hill, with William Mullendore, with Herbert Corneulle, with Henry and Frances Hazlitt on their rare visits to California; she continued to see Albert Mannheimer, although at less frequent intervals than before. But she felt that most of the people she met did not offer her the intellectual challenge she sought.

When Nathaniel and I asked Ayn why she spent so much of her time with us, particularly in a period when she had cut herself off from almost all social contacts, she answered, "Don't you know that the pleasure of dealing with active minds outweighs any differences in age or knowledge?" Despite Ayn's growing reputation, which brought to her doorstep mature men and women of similar renown, she was indifferent to reputation and social standing—her own or that of others; she preferred to spend her time with those, wherever they might be found, who wanted to discuss the burning issues of philosophy. And in her attitude toward the power and importance of ideas, she seemed closer to us than to many of her contemporaries: she was like a youth who had started out on the same quest, the quest to acquire a set of principles to guide one's actions in practice, but had never given up and had reached her goal, and could now show us the steps of that long road. Often, when we arrived in the evening, she would come out of her study, having had no time for dinner; she would look one step away from collapsing—then Nathaniel or I would mention some philosophical issue and the lines of exhaustion would vanish from her expression, she would begin to ask questions and to talk, and we would see the face of a forty-five-year-old woman become the face of a twenty-year-old-girl within the space of ten minutes.

It was particularly with Nathaniel that she experienced the philosophical give-and-take that was so rare in her experience. With Nathaniel, she felt that she was teacher, but not *merely* teacher; she was adviser, but not *merely* adviser. She was astonished and delighted to discover a young man deeply committed to her philosophical ideas who was equipped and eager to challenge, to argue, to debate with her. She was further delighted that, in the area of his own field, psychology, he was able to expose her to issues and problems she had never considered, broadening her understanding of human motivation.

Sometimes, on a bright afternoon, Ayn and I would walk together along the paths of the ranch, past the cages of Frank's exquisite preening peacocks and along the alfalfa field, whiie she scanned the ground for the colorful rocks she loved to collect. As we walked, I would tell her about the problems on my mind

—problems in my university classes where I was becoming a pariah by arguing violently in defense of her philosophy, family problems, intellectual and emotional problems—all the difficulties of a young girl on the verge of adulthood. Where I saw no avenue to a solution, she would point out what I had overlooked, with a sensitive, nonjudgmental understanding of my context and needs. I have never forgotten those sunlit walks and those equally sunlit discussions; in my memory they are endlessly lit by a gentle golden glow. It was during those golden days that I first came to love Ayn.

One afternoon, I began to speak of the difficulties in my relationship with Nathaniel, of my sadness that I could not passionately love a man whom I admired in so many respects. The bond between us was strong: we were growing up together, we were trying to understand the world together, we were sharing our thoughts, we were sharing the experience of knowing Ayn Rand and the excitement of the world view we were learning from her. As we became still more deeply involved with Ayn's philosophy, the bond had grown stronger still: we were fellow-fighters in a crusade. But I knew I did not—could not—return the emotional and physical intensity of his feeling for me. Ayn was very kind and sympathetic; but it was clear that she did not understand how there could be a barrier to my loving Nathaniel; she seemed bewildered that a young woman would not be passionately drawn to him. I recognized that it was not a problem I could share with her; for a while, her attitude puzzled me, but I soon dismissed it from my mind.

It was not until several years later that Ayn spoke in detail of her first impressions of Nathaniel and me. "My impression of you, Barbara, the evening we met," she said, "was of delicacy and strength, of someone of the Dominique style. I couldn't definitely estimate the personality, because you were so quiet, but I was aware of very great intelligence. Your mind worked in principles, and very fast. . . . The week before that, when Nathan first arrived, I remember that I was as usual slightly late dressing. Frank had let Nathan in, they were in the living room. When I came downstairs, I saw Nathan standing in profile to me. I was enormously impressed with his face. It was completely the face of my kind of man. . . . I'll never forget that moment.

"I was completely fascinated by him during the whole evening, totally emotionally sold on him, and Frank was too. He was brilliantly intelligent, totally open and honest, he spoke to the point, he spoke in principles, he asked the right questions. . . . He talked that evening more than I did, but it was not that he was trying to *tell* me, he was presenting philosophical issues that interested him and he wanted to know my views. . . . I knew he was testing me, but so openly and rationally that I was very pleased. I felt, 'I would have done the same thing.' He was checking on the consistency of my views. He projected enormous respect and total independence. . . . I was sold on both of you from the first meeting; the rest was taking the time to be sure rationally. I was committed that this was an important discovery in my life, a real value, from the very beginning."

As the weeks and months passed, Nathaniel and I came to know Ayn not just as a thinker and philosopher but through all the daily, prosaic events of life. We saw her well and ill, we saw her irritable and cheerful, we saw her loving and rejecting, we saw her laughing and . . . no, we did not see Ayn crying. She was a woman who did not hide her pain; pain, whatever its cause—from a torn hem in her dress to a disappointing day's writing to a human encounter that disgusted her—was always discussed with us and with Frank. But pain in Ayn was instantaneously transmuted into anger, into allegedly rationally motivated indignation, in a subconscious means of avoiding suffering.

I recall vividly—it has the impact of a still, unchanging photograph of Ayn, a photograph of something beneath any anger and pain, more true to her most intimate vision of life than her normal grave severity—the first time Nathaniel and I saw passionate joy in her, the first time we saw her totally happy and openly showing her feelings. As we were parking the car, we heard the sound of Ayn's tiddlywink music coming from the house. When we entered the living room, it was to the sight of this serious, austere woman, interested only in the most crucial issues of human life and thought, dancing around the room, spinning in circles and laughing, her head thrown back in a gesture of cheerful defiance, waving a baton that Frank had bought for her—like a child to whom life was an endlessly joyous adventure.

It was that same day that Ayn made dinner for us and another, faintly jarring aspect of her personality became apparent. Usually, her servant did the cooking, but tonight, as a special treat, Ayn was to create the dish of which she was most proud, an authentic Russian beef Stroganoff. I stood with her in the kitchen—she didn't want me to help—and watched her at work. Although she was an excellent cook, she worked painfully slowly, her movements awkwardly overprecise, and she projected an excruciating physical and emotional tension. "It's because," she said, "my mind is never really on working in the kitchen. It's because I can't fully focus on most of the necessities of daily life. So I have to be extra conscientious." She made a list of the ingredients necessary for each dish—even though she had prepared it many times before; she made another list of the amount of time necessary for cooking each dish; and she carefully checked the lists at every step of the process. This same tension over practical affairs was present in many other aspects of her daily routine. When she left the house, she would lock the front door, step away, come back, check the lock, head for the car, come back, check the lock again—distrusting herself initially to have given it the attention it required. In part, her distrust clearly was due to her concentration on her work and on the philosophical issues that concerned her; her concentration was so absolute and all-absorbing that it left her no mental space for anything else. But it seemed to be, as well, an indication of her alienation from the physical world, her sense of helplessness, tinged with fear, in dealing with material reality.

The same alienation was evident in her attitude toward her physical body, the carelessness with which she treated the body she had not chosen and did not like. Her one source of pride in her physical person was her shapely legs, which she cheerfully flaunted in short skirts. But her stockings usually were snagged, her lipstick smearily applied, her skirts often stained. Occasionally, she would make an effort to look, as she termed it, "glamorous." For important occasions, she wore Adrian designs, enjoying their drama and simplicity. But to dress for such occasions, to see that her hair was properly combed, her makeup perfect, her gown pressed, was always a tension-filled, irksome chore. But when she was dressed and groomed, she delighted in the compliments she was paid; she would come into the living room, beaming, and twirl around to be admired.

The alienation so apparent in her dealings with the material world, extended beyond the physical to encompass her emotional sense of herself as a woman. Ayn expected, and demanded, that the people around her appreciate and understand her literary and intellectual achievements. She exploded in anger and contempt when she did not receive what she believed to be her right. But she never expected that her emotional life, her motivation, her existence as a human being and especially as a woman, would be intelligible or even of interest to other people. Yet when she felt visible as a person, rather than solely as a mind, she reacted with astonished pleasure, as if she had received a gift she had never allowed herself to know she wanted. If she received a moment's understanding of herself as a woman, the bitterness of years seemed to fall away, replaced by a touchingly innocent gratitude.

One evening, when we were talking about *We the Living*—she had not yet told us the story of Alice Rosenbaum and Leo—I said to her: "Ayn, you knew a 'Leo' in Russia, didn't you?" She looked startled and asked, "How in the world did you know *that?*" I explained that I had guessed it because her choice of the name "Leo" for a literary hero was an out-of-character choice for her; it was not the sort of name she had given to her other heroes, who were Howard and Gail and Andrei. I had concluded that she chose the name because a man named Leo once had been important to her. She seemed bewildered that I had guessed this about her. During all the subsequent years of our friendship, she would occasionally again compliment me on my sensitivity in having understood her.

It was evident, quite early in our relationship, that something was involved between Ayn and me that was more than the exchange of ideas, something that was never named or acknowledged but that was always present as an unspoken element in our friendship. From the beginning, I was aware of the woman, hidden behind a battery of defenses, who co-existed with the intellect that was all she was willing to show to the world; I did not see her as merely a brain encased in flesh. I knew—and I somehow communicated it to her—that somewhere inside her was a woman's longing, a woman's emotions, a woman's struggle for self-expression. Sometimes, in our private conversations, she would speak with uncharacteristic ease not of her thoughts, but of her *feelings* about "the ideal man," of the loneliness of her early years in America, of her social shyness, of her painful awareness that the men she met were intimidated by her and thus oblivious to her femininity. I believe it was her awareness of my understanding which, many years later—when the world of the woman who was Ayn Rand was crashing around her—caused her to turn to me for help, for protection, for the solace of someone who knew the agony she was enduring.

Both Nathaniel and I often were asked if, in those early years when we were not yet fully adults, Ayn's attitude toward us was maternal. It was not. When she introduced us to her friends, as she soon began to do, she spoke of us as "the children"; she was protective of us, eager to encourage us in the pursuit of the careers we planned, concerned that we might be hurt, perhaps professionally damaged, by our espousal of a philosophy as radical as hers—but there was nothing of the maternal in her manner or personality. The special softness, the need to touch and be touched, the concern with day-to-day activities, the nonjudgmental tenderness, the unconditional acceptance that one associates with motherhood, were alien to Ayn. We were, so to speak, the children of her brain, not of her body.

The concept of unconditional love was totally foreign to Ayn's thinking. It soon became evident, as those who knew her were uncomfortably aware, that however much she previously had projected love and affection, one was always potentially on trial with her. At any time, an action, an emotion, a conviction that she deemed irrational, could result in an explosion of anger. One had no hoard of deposited virtue in the bank; one was judged moment by moment, loved or rejected moment by moment. Often, when a friend said or did something of which she disapproved, she would react as if suddenly she knew nothing about the person except the single issue under discussion. One was forever on trial, forever required to re-prove one's virtue and rationality. Clearly, she hated what she perceived as the irrational; but on a more subtle level, her hatred seemed to be rooted in a deep, terrible fear—as if the outside world was not merely an arena where wrong ideas were held and wrong actions taken: it was an arena fraught with danger. She was struggling, as she had always done, to create a safe haven around her, a smaller world within the larger irrational world that would consist of people who were predictable, intelligible, in accord with her thinking, devoted to her, convinced that she was the spiritual and intellectual equal of her heroes—and who, therefore, posed no threat to her. Any sign of the "irrational" appeared to threaten her safety, her world, her life; it could not be permitted to enter her safe haven. When she attacked "irrational values"— particularly in the few people for whom she deeply cared, the people she had allowed entrance into the innermost reaches of her safe haven and who therefore had the power to endanger it—her manner projected something oddly personal, as if she desperately needed to annihilate forever whatever irrational love they clutched to them. She needed not only to be loved and admired, but to know there were no conflicting loves in the haven she had built.

During the happy excitement of our first months of seeing Ayn—months full of questions and answers and talking and learning—it was Ayn's fear of "the irrational" that planted the first small seed of the problem that finally was to engulf all our lives. One evening, I casually mentioned that I liked to look at mountains and the ocean, that the sight of them gave me a special feeling of peace. "Why?" she demanded, a slight edge in her voice. "Because they're beautiful, and, I suppose, because they never change, they're always just what they are." "And human beings?" she asked. I shrugged. "Human beings change constantly, they shift, they seem to dissolve from one identity to another." The edge in her voice was sharper as she said, "That's always why people prefer nature to man." And she began to speak of skyscrapers, of city pavements, of giant industries, of all the mighty creations of the human mind—almost as if I had been denouncing man's achievement. "It's a 'malevolent universe' emotion —it's the subconscious belief that man's life is inevitably tragic—that makes you prefer nature to the man-made," she told me, and I saw, bewildered, that she was deeply angry.

I listened uncomfortably as she continued speaking, wondering why a philosophical disagreement—if that was indeed what was involved—had become the occasion for an analysis of my psychology. But I had learned the quality of Ayn's intelligence: that behind every statement stood an enormous breadth and complexity of thought and integration; if I took it seriously when that intelligence was directed to philosophical issues, then I had to take it no less seriously when it was directed to what she saw as errors in my thinking and reactions. And I knew that some part of what she said was true. Her sensitivity to the slightest implication of a statement was honing in like a laser beam to something that was real. Some part of me was *not* convinced of what my mind had accepted: that reason and achievement were man's natural state. The issue remained unresolved in my mind, and left behind the first faint tinge of guilt.

On another evening, we were discussing the aesthetics of literature. I was telling Ayn that I deeply loved the novels of Thomas Wolfe, that I had discovered *Look Homeward, Angel* when I was twelve years old, then devoured all of his work. As I spoke, I dimly observed that Ayn's face was an expressionless mask, and that her eyes, usually so warm when she looked at me, were icy with disapproval. She interrupted only to ask me an occasional question. When I was silent, she reminded me of our former discussions of literature. "Plot, theme, characterization, style—those are the essential ingredients of fiction, are they not?" I nodded. Her voice had become driving and sharp as the ice of her eyes, her words followed each other with machine-gun-like rapidity. With devastating logic, the logic that had drawn and held me to her from the beginning, she demonstrated Wolfe's shortcomings with regard to precisely the elements of fiction I had agreed were essential. She spoke of his indifference to plot; she spoke of his thematic confusions; she spoke of the overwriting that was an omnipresent part of his style. I had no answer; it seemed irrelevant to explain what he meant to me emotionally—that the majestic songs he sang had reached into my deepest being, that I often felt they *were* me.

I sat with my friends in a quiet room, talking in a civilized manner—and feeling a small death occurring inside me. In the choice between my emotions and the commandments of reason, I *had* no choice. Then, and always, the greatest value Ayn offered me was the rationality of her arguments; then and always, that was her greatest intellectual and emotional hold on me. I had told her, at our first meeting, that reason was an absolute to me; that had not changed, it could not change. Whatever the emotional consequences, I would not turn my back on what I believed to be the truth.

In the weeks that followed—indeed, the years—I never learned to tear out of myself my passionate response to Thomas Wolfe's novels. Instead, I learned repression, as so many of her young friends were to learn it in later years. I learned not to recognize my authentic feelings—not to recognize them nor to experience them nor to know that they remained, never to acknowledge them to myself or others. The first step toward placing my emotions into a destructive vise had been taken. I was to continue along that path for many years.

Ayn had convinced me—as she was to convince me that the paintings of Vincent van Gogh were too undisciplined, too chaotic and wild to be considered great art—as she was to convince me that Somerset Maugham's *Of Human Bondage* propounded a deeply malevolent view of life—as she was to convince me that Wagner's *Tristan and Isolde* was profoundly tragic. She convinced me, as, over the years, I would see her convince so many others, of the invalidity of their artistic tastes—the tastes and the loves that so often, in fact, represented the best within them. It did not happen all at once. It could not have happened all at once. Such conversations occurred over a space of months and years— always interspersed with the great experience of dealing with a mind that presented the rich texture of a total world view and a systematic philosophical system of awesome logical consistency.

When I had met Nathaniel, the first book he gave me to read was Rolland's *Jean Christophe*. But Rolland was a socialist, Ayn pointed out, and the philosophical underpinnings of socialism had made him a realist, rather than a romantic, in literature. While I was dealing with my private aesthetic agony, Nathaniel was abandoning *Jean Christophe*. Over the years, we were to hear Ayn excoriate the "grim, unfocused malevolence" of Rembrandt—to a painter; Shakespeare's "abysmal failure" to present human beings with free will—to a writer; Beethoven's "tragic sense of doom"—to a musician. And we were to see the painters, the writers, the musicians, fail hopelessly to refute her arguments and unhappily grant the logic of her position. Some ran from her, unwilling to renounce their deepest aesthetic values. Most remained, and from then on their work reflected the air-tight underground into which they had placed their aesthetic emotions: in the name of reason, their work became thin, and tight, and without originality.

But in those early months, when the future storms were only the first faint wisps of clouds far off at the horizon, there seemed nothing that could for long blemish for Nathaniel and for me the joy of our new intellectual discoveries, and our conviction that we had found a woman as noble and admirable as her ideas. Ayn was first and foremost a rationalist and a moralist. These qualities brought her admiration and respect; they did not bring her love. But Ayn *was* loved, by Nathaniel, by me, by many others who had been and were to be her friends. The source of that love, for some of us, was that quality in her which I often felt was most profoundly, most nakedly, Ayn Rand: the quality of passionate idealism, the exalted vision of life's possibilities. In *The Fountainhead,* she had written that love was "a command to rise." In Ayn's presence, and in her work, one felt that command: a command to function at one's best, to be the most that one could be, to drive oneself constantly harder, never to disappoint one's own highest ideals.

Chapter Twenty-one

Ayn spoke to us often about the new novel she was writing—as deliberate "teasers" to arouse our interest and curiosity. Privately, she and Frank were discussing her desire to show us the manuscript. One evening, she brought out the first chapter, a wide smile of anticipation on her face.

We read Chapter One that evening. We were fascinated by the drama of the story's beginning, intrigued by the mystery, and delighted to be meeting a new Ayn Rand heroine. So enthusiastic was our reaction that Ayn agreed to show us further chapters. Soon we were reading regularly, until we had read everything that had been typed. Ayn wrote in longhand, editing as she proceeded; when she was satisfied with a section, she gave it to her secretary to be typed. From then on, at each visit, she would show us the work completed in longhand since our previous visit.

It was an unrepeatable intellectual and emotional experience. Reading a new section of the book each week, we felt as if we had gained private entry into the world that had been a dominant focus of our thought since our discovery of *The Fountainhead,* as if we had left everyday reality and had entered a new planet fashioned by Ayn Rand. We were meeting, not the Babbitts we had seen as representative of businessmen until then, but the giants of ability and achievement who peopled her world; we were following the complex strands of a mystery more involving than any thriller; we were encountering a style of luminous clarity and consistency. We were hearing, on each page, a command to rise to heights of a greater nobility than we had ever conceived. We felt that we were now citizens of the world of Ayn Rand—of a world in which man's mind was efficacious, where achievement and happiness were possible, where life was a great adventure and the human potential was unlimited. We were eager to understand that world in every detail, to live up to the high standards it demanded, to be worthy of the exaltation it promised.

The process of writing continued to be arduous for Ayn. She could not, she would not, abandon herself uncritically to the literary inspiration, the free, un-censored flow of thought and feeling that emotions provide a creative artist; the process of inspirational writing was aborted before it could fully begin. She was rarely solely creator; she was editor as well, during the very act of creation, often devising each paragraph, each sentence, each phrase, sometimes each word, by conscious rational calculation.

"Writing *Atlas* is the most difficult thing I've ever done," she said. "It takes the total of all my intellectual circuits, it requires my full capacity. I could not handle anything wider. It's been difficult from the beginning. You see, nonfiction writing feels to me like the ease I had in writing before I was twelve; it feels natural to me. But in fiction, I feel as if my mind has to work on two tracks, one natural, the other forced; it's the fiction element—except for the action se-quences—that feels forced. The need to communicate moods, emotions, sensory perceptions, feels like it's impeding what I really want to say. I project every-thing in my mind in nonfiction terms, then I must drop that and allow myself to feel, and then project what I want by means of a feeling—and the words don't come. The main appeal of fiction to me has always been the presentation of the ideal man and the ideal manner of existence. In that sense, fiction is a means to an end for me. But philosophy alone is not yet life, it's only a blueprint for the future. So I feel that one without the other is not enough; only together do they give me the career and activity I really want, being simultaneously both a novel-ist and a philosopher."

Sometimes, she would come out of her study at midnight after fifteen uninter-rupted hours of work, her body aching from strain, looking frighteningly ex-hausted—having written that whole day and evening perhaps a page, perhaps only a paragraph. The cost in mental torment and tension was beginning to take its toll in every aspect of her life, in the form of a growing impatience, an intolerance, sudden, accelerating bursts of temper, and moods of black depres-sion.

But Ayn's enthusiasm for conversation continued unabated. Nathaniel and I began to introduce to her a few of our friends who were also admirers of her work. Among them were Joan Mitchell, a talented painter and my dearest friend since our childhood in Winnipeg, and my seventeen-year-old cousin Leonard Peikoff; in later years, both of them were to become close friends of Ayn's. One evening, I brought one of my UCLA philosophy professors to meet her. He was *not* an admirer of her work; his views were diametrically opposed to hers; but he was a man widely respected in his field who had expressed great interest in meeting Ayn. It was a memorable evening. They talked and argued with mutu-ally enthusiastic pleasure; Ayn was at her most incisive and spirited, marshaling powerful arguments for her positions. They discussed metaphysics: he was a Platonist, Ayn an Aristotelian; they discussed morality: he was a utilitarian, she an advocate of self-interest; they discussed politics: he was a socialist, she an advocate of capitalism. At dawn, as the professor and I left, he said to me, clearly distressed: "She's found gaping holes in every philosophical position I've maintained for the whole of my life—positions I teach my students, positions on which I'm a recognized authority—and I can't answer her arguments! I don't know what to do!" He found a solution: he refused to see Ayn again, and he went on maintaining his former views.

Ayn continued to be deep in conversations about psychology with Nathaniel. He had begun applying to his own field the philosophical concepts he was learning from her. Over the next eighteen years, this was to be his major intellectual focus. His work during those years was to culminate in his book, *The Psychology of Self-Esteem*, published in 1969. Within the framework of the Objectivist metaphysics, epistemology, and ethics, the book contains major new work of his own, which he had been honing in discussions with Ayn, particularly on the psychological nature and meaning of self-esteem, on the nature of mental health and illness, on the source of pathological anxiety, and on what he termed "the principle of psychological visibility," an explanation of why man needs human companionship and is motivated to find human beings he can value and love. Ayn often said, "Everything I know about psychology, I learned from Nathan."

One does not perceive the impossible. Ayn's growing and unique closeness with Nathaniel was evident to everyone who saw them together. It was clear that they felt an increasing affection for each other—an affection which included occasional touching and hand-holding. Their feeling was fully intelligible to me, and a source of pleasure. I had no hint of what was to come, of what was beginning to develop, unnamed and unacknowledged, between them. Neither did Nathaniel. Neither did Ayn.

Perhaps it might have been predicted by someone who knew of a battle that was raging in Ayn—as it had always raged, but never so intensely as now, when she had reached her mid-forties. It was the battle to remain a woman. Throughout her life, she had fought against what she saw as her feminine attributes—fought against her softness, her tenderness, her desire to yield to a stronger force, her need to give and to receive love; these were the enemies that would make her vulnerable to a world and to men that threatened her. She needed to control, she needed to dominate, she needed to set the rules and establish the terms; only therein lay her safety. She had married a man whom she *could* control, who posed no threat to her dominance. She had often selected friends who were much younger than she, who revered and loved her, who were captivated by the new world she opened up to them, a world in which she *had* set the rules and established the terms; she was the teacher, the mentor, the guide. Now, in writing *Atlas Shrugged,* she called upon all that she felt to be most male in her; although she was creating an ideal man, she was *God* creating man out of chaos; she was forming his identity, shaping his world, directing his philosophy. It was her intellect—chaste and sexless and impersonal—that directed her through the pages of her novel.

The only hint that there might be hidden complexities and drives in Ayn, self-doubts and confusions at variance with the self-sufficient woman whose face she presented to the world, the confident woman, at peace with herself, in full and serene command of her purposes and her life—was the mystery of her relationship with Frank. The people who knew Ayn and Frank often puzzled over the question of what had drawn and held her to him. Frank projected a sympathy, a wordless understanding, a kindness that was as essential a part of him as the color of his eyes, which touched his friends deeply; but they could not understand why these qualities were of value to Ayn—whose stated values of intellectuality, of ambition, of energy, of commitment, were alien to the values Frank possessed. It was impossible to doubt the reality of her love. It was evident in her constant need for his presence, in the compliments she continually paid to his appearance and his character, in the softness in her eyes when she looked at him, in a kind of hovering concern for his physical well-being. "Frank is my rock," she would say. "He always knows my context. He reacts just as I do, to people and to events. He always knows what I'm feeling and what things mean to me. He's never once let me down."

Occasionally, she would grow irritated with him, and they appeared to have little to say to each other. But none of their friends suspected the extent to which the relationship was troubled. A number of years later, Ayn was to admit that during this period the friction between them and their lack of intellectual communication had come to so frustrate her that she had seriously considered divorce. She had decided to put the issue out of her mind until *Atlas Shrugged* was completed. By then, she had changed her mind. It seems unlikely that she would have divorced Frank under any circumstances, however hard and long she had considered it; her need of him was too great; the place he filled, the place of nonthreatening lover and companion, was too vital ever to be abandoned.

As Ayn and Frank's relationship was silently deteriorating, my relationship with Nathaniel appeared to be improving, as a direct result of Ayn and *Atlas Shrugged.* In the novel, Francisco presents Ayn's theory of sex, saying: "A man's sexual choice is the result and the sum of his fundamental convictions. Tell me what a man finds sexually attractive and I will tell you his entire philosophy of life. Show me the woman he sleeps with and I will tell you his valuation of himself. . . . He will always be attracted to the woman who reflects his deepest vision of himself, the woman whose surrender permits him to experience—or to fake—a sense of self-esteem. The man who is proudly certain of his own value, will want the highest type of woman he can find, the woman he admires, the strongest, the hardest to conquer—because only the possession of a heroine will give him the sense of an achievement, not the possession of a brainless slut. . . . There is no conflict between the standards of his mind and the desire of his body. . . . Love is our response to our highest value—and can be nothing else."

It is an intriguing theory—and a potentially dangerous one, which already had had explosive effects on Ayn's life. It had led her to wildly aggrandize the men who were *her* sexual choices—Leo and Frank—and it would continue to do so in the future; if the men to whom she was attracted were not heroes, then what would her choices say about *her?* And it had led her to denounce and intimidate those of her friends who were not able to demonstrate that *their* choices were similarly exalted.

In retrospect, it seems clear that while one may grant that a man sexually drawn only to sluts suffers a deficiency of self-esteem, and that a man drawn to women of character and intelligence possesses a greater sense of self-value, the possibilities between these two extremes are so vast that the infant science of psychology can say little about them. Few things in life are so complex and so little understood as that which motivates our passionate sexual response; to require, as proof of psychological health, that this motivation lead only to the choice of a "hero," is to inflict, on oneself and others, inestimable damage.

But at the time, through long discussions with Ayn and Nathaniel, I came to accept Ayn's theory of sex. And I made a decision. Nathaniel appeared to embody the values I cherished. The difficulty had to lie in *me*, in psychological problems I had not dealt with. I must continue growing, I must continue learning, I must work to resolve my unidentified problems, and the day would come when I would respond to Nathaniel as I should and wanted to respond. The road would be cleared and I would be free to live my life rationally. It was all perfectly simple—and perfectly impossible of achievement.

On a cloudless day in the early summer of 1951, Ayn and Frank said good-bye to Nathaniel and to me as we left Los Angeles to return to our respective homes in Toronto and Winnipeg. I had always wanted to live in New York; ironically, it was Thomas Wolfe who first inculcated that desire in me, through his moving descriptions of the great city he loved. I had received my Bachelor of Arts degree from UCLA; I had enrolled in the philosophy department of New York University for the fall semester. Nathaniel had decided to join me; he would continue his work in psychology at NYU.

As we stood in the driveway of her home for the last time, Ayn said that we would visit each other from time to time, we would speak on the telephone often, we would write letters—and when *Atlas Shrugged* was finished, she and Frank would leave the city she disliked with increasing fervor and would join us in New York. But it would be a long parting; the novel, she believed, would require at least another two years for completion. As her dislike of California intensified, she was feeling a growing homesickness for New York—the first homesickness she had ever experienced for a geographical locality—but she did not want to interrupt her work and to move until the novel was finished. It was a painful parting; we felt that we had become a family, and although I wanted to leave its bonds and to build a life of my own, we would sorely miss one another and the never-ending excitement of our conversations.

"When your car drove out of the driveway," Ayn later said, "I found that I could barely speak and that I was crying. I tried not to cry, but my eyes were full of tears. And the kind of emptiness you left behind—that's when I fully realized how enormously important the two of you had become. You know, when something is growing day by day, you don't quite notice it. I hadn't known it meant quite that much."

Shortly before this, Ayn had met Evan Wright, a young marine who was studying English at UCLA and writing pro-free-enterprise letters in the university newspaper. She now began to spend occasional evenings in philosophical conversation with him, and hired him to do proofreading of her manuscript. She was touched and amused when Evan, because of her, met the girl who soon became his wife. He had gone to the bank to deposit his pay check; Mickey, the pretty teller, recognized Ayn's signature, and excitedly asked if Evan knew her. Three days later, after consulting with Ayn, Evan returned to the bank. "Would you like to meet Ayn Rand?" he asked Mickey. Five weeks later, they were married. "It will be a good marriage," said Ayn at the wedding, "because you share the same ideas."

Years later, Evan would recall—in an echo of Thadeus Ashby, whom he had never met—that there was an unnamed sexual element, a sexual awareness, in his relationship with Ayn. It was never discussed, but he did not doubt that she recognized it too. "I remember especially," he said, "one day when I was working on her manuscript, and she came to stand beside me silently, we were almost touching—and there was a powerful magnetism there, we both knew what we were feeling. I didn't look up—I suppose I was too shy—I don't know quite what would have happened if I had looked up. . . . Yes, perhaps I do know. After a long time, she walked away. . . ."

Like so many of those who came to know Ayn, Evan never forgot the constant fascination of being with her. "She was by far the most brilliant human being I have ever met. She was remarkable in so many ways, not like anyone else," he was to say, adding—thirty-five years after their meeting—"I still think of her, and Mickey and I often talk of her. . . . When I met Ayn, college had confused me about a lot of issues; she gave me direction, and part of her thinking became a lasting part of my own life. I owe her a great debt of gratitude. Because of her, I learned to think better and more clearly, I developed a logical power and a rationality, and clarified my thought processes. . . . But then I found it was impossible to disagree with her, and I didn't want that; I couldn't remain tied to her apron strings."

Ayn's parting from Nathaniel and me was briefer than any of us had imagined. In the fall, she telephoned to announce happily that she and Frank would arrive in New York in three weeks. The day after she finished the chapter called "Atlantis," she had found she could not bear to remain in California any longer. That same day, she talked it over with Frank—it was the quickest decision they ever made—and by evening they were making arrangements to move back to New York.

She talked it over with Frank, she said. But there is little doubt that, as always when Ayn had come to a decision involving both of them but felt that Frank must be consulted, her conversation consisted of telling Frank that she *had* to return to New York, and that she knew he wanted it too. And there is no doubt that Frank did *not* want it, although he did not tell her so. He had found, on the ranch, his first contentment in many years, and a work that he loved. He enjoyed working outdoors, he had made friends of his own among the men he hired to assist him, he took great pleasure in the physical beauty of California. New York offered him nothing. It was far too late for him to again consider an acting career; that possibility had ended when he and Ayn first left California in 1934; now, he was once more being torn away from a world and from goals that he had carved out for himself—and that were his one source of serious pleasure in what must have been, for him, the arid wilderness of Ayn's world—and he did not know what would ever again replace it. Ayn's decision to leave California ended a way of life that was precious to Frank, a way of life he lacked the strength to fight for. It was a tragedy built into their relationship from the beginning that it would not occur to Ayn that Frank's nod of assent to her decision was less than a wholehearted agreement. Or perhaps it did occur to her, somewhere in a part of her awareness, because for many years afterward she would talk of her love of New York and her loathing of California and say: "You feel the same way, don't you, Frank? Don't you?" She said it too often. She said it too insistently.

As Ayn and Frank made their plans to leave California, they asked Ruth and Buzzy Hill if they would move into the house; Ayn did not want to leave it unattended, nor rent it to strangers. In exchange for a nominal rent, the Hills agreed to care for the ranch and the grounds. They were to remain in the home they came to love for almost twenty-five years.

Once again, Ayn and Frank drove across the country. This time, they shared the ride with a passenger: a six-week old gray-and-white kitten, which a neighbor's cat had given birth to in the back seat of their car; they named the kitten "Frisco," in honor of Francisco d'Anconia.

On their arrival, Ayn told us, "Frank said that he thinks I decided to come to New York because of you two. It was an enormous contributing factor. I followed you across a continent." We began to visit more frequently than had been possible in California, often four or five evenings a week. Ayn once asked: "Don't you ever want to go out in the evenings, rather than spending it talking to two old fogies?" She said that our look of astonishment "told me that you would never prefer any lighter or less intellectual pleasures."

Ayn and Frank moved into an apartment in the Murray Hill area of the city, at 36 East Thirty-sixth Street. An eight-by-twelve-foot office, jammed tight with file cabinets and her battered desk, with a view of a few apartment buildings, replaced Ayn's luxurious, sun-filled California study—much to her delight. If she stood very close to the room's single window and craned her neck, she could see a part of the Empire State Building; she often stood there, her body angled in order to gaze at the building that gave her the reality of what she loved about the city: the *man-made*.

Back in New York after almost eight years in California, Ayn knew she would never build the country home that Frank Lloyd Wright had designed for her, no matter how much money she earned. Never again would she choose to live away from the city.

Within a few weeks, the city became only a presence to be seen from the window of her study, as she resumed the task of writing. She drove herself on a ruthless schedule, often working seven days a week, for as many hours as she was mentally and physically able to continue. It was not unusual for her to eat dinner at midnight. She no longer kept servants except for a weekly cleaning woman, and, with her oddly old-fashioned view of a woman's appropriate behavior, insisted on preparing dinner for herself and Frank no matter how late she finished working or how exhausted she was. The results were not beneficent. Frank was too thin, and needed to eat on a regular schedule; he should not have waited until midnight for what was usually his only full meal of the day. But Ayn needed to feel that she was functioning as a woman, and Frank, as always, did not cross her.

During the next several years of concentrated work, Ayn went out only rarely. She grew progressively disillusioned with the political conservatives who had been her friends, progressively convinced that her philosophical differences with them were greater than she had known, and, as a result, progressively certain that she and they were not, as she once had thought, fellow fighters in the battle for political freedom. She continued to contend that the reason why a laissez-faire economy was being rejected had little or nothing to do with economics as such, that the proof of the *practicality* of economic freedom had long been available in an endless series of writings and in the reality of the astounding growth of the United States; that it had not convinced people, that America was moving with ever increasing speed toward an ever more stifling welfare state, was a matter of morality. "If men feel they are faced with a choice between the moral and the practical," she said, "then proving to them that capitalism is practical will never motivate them. Men have always been willing to fight, and to die if necessary, for *moral* principles; they will not fight and die for *economic* principles. They will choose morality over practicality, whatever the cost. In order to turn the country to capitalism, one must first demonstrate the *morality* of capitalism." This was the view which she tried, in vain, to communicate to conservatives of her acquaintance, whom, she felt, wrote endlessly on political and economic subjects to no avail, since they had accepted an anti-capitalist morality, a religious morality, an altruist morality. This was the view which led her, finally, to conclude that conservatives were in no serious sense her allies, and that "conservative" was a term she could no longer apply to herself; she was, she said, "a radical for capitalism."

Occasionally, Ayn spent an evening with Henry and Frances Hazlitt or attended a gathering at the home of a conservative acquaintance. Margit von Mises[1] was to recall an early meeting with Ayn, at which Nathaniel and I were present, at the Von Mises home. "She was very kind and very friendly, like every other guest. I wouldn't have said she was haughty or arrogant, and I liked her.

[1] Margit von Mises, today still beautiful and blazing with energy, has written a biography of her late husband and is chairman of the Ludwig von Mises Institute.

. . . But Frank was like a slave to her. He never said a word, he just watched her, and if she needed something he was there. When she wanted to smoke a cigarette, he was there with his lighter."

One evening, the Hazlitts invited Ayn and Frank to dinner, with Dr. and Mrs. von Mises. The evening was a disaster. It was the first time Ayn had discussed moral philosophy in depth with either of the two men. "My impression," she was to say, "was that Von Mises did not care to consider moral issues, and Henry was seriously committed to altruism. . . . We argued quite violently. At one point, Von Mises lost his patience and screamed at me. We did not part enemies—except for Von Mises at the moment; about a year later, he and I met at a conservative dinner, and his wife made peace between us; neither of us wanted a feud, and we resumed a cordial relationship. . . . I continued to see the Hazlitts, and I consider him a valuable writer on politics and economics, but my interest vanished when I realized that his philosophical base was thoroughly modern and pragmatic."

Ayn was to denounce conservatives—and liberals as well—several years later in an article on the evil of censorship. (She did not intend to include Ludwig von Mises or Henry Hazlitt as the type of conservative she was discussing, since both were opposed to censorship and any form of government control of ideas.) "Both camps," she wrote, "hold the same premise—the *mind-body dichotomy*—but choose opposite sides of this lethal fallacy. The conservatives want freedom to act in the material world; they tend to oppose government control of production, of industry, of trade, of business, of physical goods, of material wealth. But they advocate government control of man's spirit, i.e., man's consciousness; they advocate the State's right to impose censorship, to determine moral values, to create and enforce a governmental establishment of morality, to rule the intellect. The liberals want freedom to act in the spiritual realm; they oppose censorship, they oppose government control of ideas, of the arts, of the press, of education. . . . But they advocate government control of material production, of business, of employment, of wages, of profits, of all physical property—they advocate it all the way down to total expropriation. . . . *each camp wants to control the realm it regards as metaphysically important; each grants freedom only to the activities it despises.*" Her article caused considerable furor among conservatives, by whom it was widely discussed. It marked her final break with her former allies.

In January of 1953, Ayn and Frank were matron of honor and best man at Nathaniel's and my marriage at the home of my relatives in White Plains. Nathaniel and I had met because of *The Fountainhead;* it seemed beautifully appropriate that Ayn and her husband should assist at the culmination of that meeting. When we arrived home and Nathaniel carried me over the threshold of our one-room apartment on Thirty-fifth Street, furnished with the few pieces we could afford to buy and with some of Ayn and Frank's old tables and chairs—it was to enter a garden. Frank had spent the day transforming the room into a

bower of apple blossoms; blossoms swept across the ceiling and the walls, delicately scenting the room and creating an exquisite honeymoon cottage.

It was in part our enthusiasm over his floral arrangements that led Frank to
take a job with a New York florist, where he sold and arranged flowers. For a
while, he made the rounds of office buildings, suggesting that he be engaged to
do weekly arrangements for the buildings' lobbies; although he lacked the drive
to pursue the idea with the sustained effort it required, he was hired by a few
buildings at a monthly fee. It was work that was important to him; it gave him
some sense of self-esteem, some sense of carrying at least a part of his financial
weight in his marriage.

Nathaniel and I continued introducing to Ayn young people we knew who
shared our admiration for *The Fountainhead* and were eagerly interested in its
ideas. Over the next several years, they attended regular Saturday evening discussions of philosophy at Ayn's home, as they began to be intellectually and
emotionally absorbed in her world. She nicknamed the group "the class of '43"
—because 1943 was the year *The Fountainhead* was published. Privately, we
referred to ourselves as "the collective"—because the term was so absurdly the
opposite of what we represented. While Ayn usually led the conversation, the
collective was not a formal organization, nor a formal class; it was a group of
friends who met together because of a common interest in ideas. Eventually,
because of the group's questions about *Atlas Shrugged,* and because of its relevance to the issues being discussed, Ayn allowed them to read *Atlas* in manuscript.

The group represented diverse professions, and all were concerned with the
application of the ideas of *Atlas* to their respective professions or fields. Alan
Greenspan was an economic consultant. Leonard Peikoff was now a student of
philosophy at NYU. Joan Mitchell (who had briefly been married to Alan
Greenspan) was a graduate student at the Institute of Fine Arts of NYU, as was
Mary Ann Rukavina. Allan Blumenthal was a physician who for a few years
abandoned medicine to pursue the career of a concert pianist. Harry Kalberman
was an account executive at Merrill Lynch. Elayne Blumenthal, Nathaniel's
sister, was a nurse. During the next few years, there were changes in the professional and personal lives of members of the group: Joan Mitchell and Allan
Blumenthal were married, and Allan returned to the field of medicine to become
a successful psychiatrist; Elayne Blumenthal and Harry Kalberman married and
became the parents of a daughter named Kira after the heroine of *We the Living;*
Leonard Peikoff received his doctorate in philosophy and began teaching; Alan
Greenspan headed his own consultant firm and was establishing the reputation
that would later make him adviser to three presidents.

As always, Ayn enjoyed her role as teacher, and enjoyed the new experience of
being surrounded by a number of young people who shared her philosophy and
were eager to learn more about it. Despite the grueling pressures of her work,
she never canceled a Saturday night meeting. She later explained, "As you
know, I barely went out at all, I didn't leave the apartment for weeks at a time, I

couldn't leave my desk; I'd been on the book for so long, and I *had* to finish it; and the integrations required were so vast that I couldn't interrupt them. On the few occasions when there was someone I had to see, the emotional and intellectual switch would cost me two or three days' work, it took me that long to get back into my own universe. The collective was my only contact with intellectual activity in a form which made it possible for me to take my mind off the story, but which wasn't a break. We could talk all night, and I'd go back to my desk in the morning with an uninterrupted sense of life; our conversations belonged in the same world as the novel.

"The nights they all read the manuscript were an especially great pleasure, and it was a pleasure to be able to talk about the book on nonreading nights; the group were the ideal sort of readers. All of them had an undivided eagerness to understand. It was the only kind of social contact I could have had. They, in their separate ways, were the next generation, the dramatized, concrete reality of what the world would be like if people were beginning to accept my philosophy."

Ayn went on to say, "Of you, Barbara, and of Nathan, I expect world-shaking achievements. I do expect miracles. As far as you're concerned, Barbara, career-wise, the turning point was when I saw the first few pages of that short story which you started and didn't finish. It was those pages that convinced me that you're going to be a great writer, and you've been developing, since then, everything I saw in those pages. . . . As to Nathan, I thought he was a genius from the first evening. I've never pronounced that judgment that immediately and objectively. For 'genius,' what's necessary is creative, initiating intelligence, total independence, the firsthand look of a creative mind, a mind constantly active on its own power. Nathan is the man to whom I want to leave my intellectual inheritance, whom I want to be my intellectual heir."

I was then, and am now, grateful that such were Ayn's views. But there was in her a deep and unnamed need to see Nathaniel and me as she did: as astonishing, once-in-a-lifetime creatures. She had made us an integral part of her world; in the inner reaches of her safe haven only giants of the intellect, only giants of ability, could be admitted. Not even Ayn, with her perceptiveness and impressive powers of prediction, could see a "great writer" in the few pages of a short story I wrote; not even Ayn, with her special sensitivity to intellectual creativity, could see "genius" in a brilliant young man who as yet had not demonstrated his powers in action. Just as Ayn formed—as a novelist must—fantasy figures in her mind to whom she gave reality by means of fiction—just as she formed a fantasy replacement of her real self and demanded to be seen as the archetype of virtue and rationality—just as she formed a fantasy replacement of Frank in the image of her novelistic heroes—so she seemed to be forming fantasy figures of Nathaniel and of me and attempting to live within that artistic conversion.

In the fall of 1954, Ayn and Frank took their first trip out of the country since their marriage twenty-five years earlier. Nathaniel and I, with his sister Elayne, intended visiting his family in Toronto, and Ayn and Frank had agreed to join us

—although Ayn was always nervous about traveling and particularly nervous about leaving the boundaries of the United States. She insisted that we drive; she had never flown, and despite writing with assured conviction and dramatic power about Dagny Taggart at the controls of her own airplane, she was frightened of flying.

It was an especially happy few days for Ayn. Away from her work, she seemed more relaxed than she had been in many months.

We headed back to New York on a chilly, sunlit Canadian day, with Frank driving, Ayn and Nathaniel beside him and Elayne and I in the back seat of the car. As the hours passed, I grew increasingly uncomfortable. I had the sense that, for the first time, I was observing something between Ayn and Nathaniel that was more than their usual enjoyment of each other's company. His arm was around her shoulders, her hand was in his, their heads were close together, they were talking and laughing with an intimacy that seemed to exclude the rest of us. Ayn often paid Nathaniel compliments, just as she did Frank, but now she was speaking of his intellectual achievements more extravagantly than ever before. An occasional glance passed between them that was too personal and that lasted too long, as if they were gazing deeply into each other and could not bear to look away. One could almost touch the vibration of the emotion that seemed to lock their eyes together, as they lapsed into silences that spoke more intimately than their words.

I did not want to see it. I did not want to believe it. But by the evening of that endless, terrible day, I could no longer doubt the evidence of my senses.

We were to stay overnight at a motel along the highway. We pulled up to our rooms at dusk. The darkness obscured Ayn and Nathaniel's expressions as they looked into each other's eyes and spoke quietly. But it was no longer necessary to see their faces or hear their words.

As Nathaniel and I entered our motel room, the explosion that had been building in me throughout the day erupted. "She's in love with you!" I shouted. "And you're in love with her!"

Chapter Twenty-two

Nathaniel stared at me with a look of stunned disbelief, as if I had suddenly gone mad. "What in *hell* are you talking about?"

I told him what I was talking about—I stumbled out the words—I shouted and paced the room as tears of rage and pain streamed down my face—while Nathaniel listened and watched as if paralyzed with incredulity. "She's in love with you!" I said. "And you're in love with her! I *know* what I saw! I *know* what it means!"

"For God's sake, I love *you!*" he replied, as his own eyes grew wet. "She—she's twenty-five years older than I am!"

I stood my ground. I knew what I had seen. I knew what it meant. But Nathaniel's response was authentic: he had not yet grasped nor named nor understood the new and unexpected feelings that were growing within him. I have sometimes wondered, in the years since, what might have occurred—or not occurred—had I kept silent.

The anguished conversation continued until, both of us weary and heartsick, we agreed to try to sleep; we would talk when we reached home. All night, I lay sleepless beside Nathaniel, the scenes from the afternoon running ceaselessly through my mind as if all the cameras in the world had jammed and I was doomed forever to stare at the same insistent, tormenting repetitions.

The few remaining hours of the drive home were silent and strained. Ayn and Nathaniel barely looked at each other, barely spoke, as if they were reeling from the blow of an event they could not name to each other nor to themselves. It was impossible to know if Frank was aware of yesterday's events; there was nothing to be observed in his face. Elayne talked cheerfully, aware only of the unusual silence among people whose conversation was characteristically uninterrupted.

It was the next day that Ayn telephoned Nathaniel. She had to see him at once, she said. It was important that they talk.

The nightmare that was to last for fourteen years, and was finally to smash many hundreds of lives, had begun.

When he hurried to her apartment, Ayn asked at once, without context or preliminary, "Do you understand what happened to us two days ago?" Did he understand its meaning? Did he know its consequences? Her questions had the odd style of an interrogation, an interrogation that was pushing him too fast. He was only beginning to understand his feelings—and he was utterly unaware of their consequences. He knew only that this was the woman he had idolized since childhood, since he had first read *The Fountainhead*—this was the woman whose spirit was formed in the image of the noblest of his values—this was the woman who saw him as a man of genius, who had given him a new, heady sense of his destiny—this was the woman who had ended his own deep alienation and had thrown wide the doors to a world of purpose, achievement and joy—this was the woman who was the symbol and the embodiment of that world—this was the woman toward whom he was now feeling strange and troubling emotions and whose passionate dark eyes were speaking to him of love.

And he was the boy who, through all the years that he was growing up, had been rejected by the girls he approached: he was too intellectual, he wasn't interested in parties or athletics, he frightened them with his intensity, they were bored by his philosophical conversations—he was the boy who, finally, had felt rejected by the wife he loved. And now, in answer to those years of rejection, *Ayn Rand*—the consummate hero-worshipper—had fallen in love with him. Intoxicated with the miracle that was happening to him, he answered her questions with the words: "I love you."

Many years later, Nathaniel was to say, "I know, in retrospect, that if she had let the matter die after the drive from Toronto, I would have let the matter die. But once we had spoken, it was too late."

It was a few days later that Ayn asked to see me. Nathaniel had gone ahead. In the living room of her apartment, Ayn and Nathaniel sat together on the couch, their hands clasped, an ashen-faced Frank half hidden in an overstuffed chair. Ayn said simply, almost matter-of-factly, that she and Nathaniel had fallen in love: it was no longer the love of a teacher and her student, it was no longer the love of intellectual comrades, it was no longer the love of close friends. It was the romantic, sexual love of a man and a woman. Her voice seemed to go on endlessly as Frank and I listened, stricken, grasping only a random sentence, a disconnected thought here and there. "You know what *I* am, you know what Nathan is. . . . By the total logic of who we are—by the total logic of what love and sex mean—we *had* to love each other. . . . It's not a threat to you, Frank, or to you, Barbara. . . . It's something separate, apart from both of you and from our normal lives. . . . Nathan has always represented the future to me—but now it's a future that exists in the present. . . . Whatever the two of you may be feeling, I know your intelligence, I know you recognize the rationality of what we feel for each other, and that you hold no value higher than reason. . . . There's nothing in our feeling that can hurt or threaten either of you. . . . There's nothing that alters my love for my husband, or Nathan's love for his wife. . . ."

The room seemed to be spinning, and Ayn's insistent voice was coming from some vast, lonely distance. Frank's face had remained expressionless, but he was paler still. I was the first to speak. "No!" I said. "I understand what the two of you feel. I think I even understand why you *have* to feel it. But it will be without *me!* I won't be any part of this." For the first time, Frank spoke. He jerked upright in his chair, and his voice was ferocious as he said, "And *I* won't be part of it." Now it was Nathaniel's face that was ashen. He walked to me and took my hand, as Ayn sat motionless. "What Ayn told you is true," he said. "There's no threat to you. You know what you are to me, what you've always been to me. But I love Ayn, too. It's real. We have to work this out. We can't run from reality."

Ayn's husky voice—hadn't it always been the voice of logic, of reason, of morality?—continued as if no one had spoken, and her marvelous eyes seemed to probe into Frank's brain and mine. "We're not suggesting an affair. Both of you must understand that. . . . We want it, but too much is at stake, and it's not the only important thing. . . . Besides, the age difference is far too great. . . . We've decided that we need to spend time alone, one afternoon and one evening a week, we want time together, for ourselves. . . . That's all. . . ."

Frank turned to look at me, a faint touch of relief on his face. They weren't talking about a sexual affair . . . not yet. This was something we could live with, perhaps. We could try. There was a long, heavy silence. Then I nodded my head. "I'll agree to that." Ayn turned to her husband. "Frank?" "I agree," he answered.

For the next few weeks—while Ayn spent one afternoon and one evening each week alone with Nathaniel—Frank and I tried to prepare for what we knew was coming. And it came. And we were not prepared.

The four of us sat in Ayn and Frank's apartment, as she discussed all the reasons why she and Nathaniel could no longer keep their original agreement—and all the reasons why Frank and I should understand their desire for a sexual relationship, and accept it—and all the reasons why the four of us could and should remain loving friends—and all the reasons why Ayn and Frank and Nathaniel and I could and should remain, respectively, loving husband and wife. As we talked hour after hour, there were moments when it seemed as if all of us had stumbled into a home for the insane—and there were other moments when Frank and I remembered that this was *Ayn,* her magical eyes had not lost their tenderness, and this was *Nathaniel,* and we knew who and what they were, they were sane and reasonable and just, they were the people we loved, and this quiet living room in New York City, where Frank was serving coffee and Frisco was tumbling across the floor with his ball, was not a chamber of horrors.

The conversations and the variations on the themes already sounded went on, day after day and week after week. "This isn't intended to be forever," Ayn kept saying. "Perhaps a year or so, that's all. If Nathan and I were the same age, it would be different. But we aren't the same age. An affair between us can only be temporary. . . . This is something out of space and out of time. If the four of us were lesser people, it could never have happened and you could never accept it. But we're not lesser people. . . . It's right and rational that Nathan and I should feel as we do for each other. But it's right and rational that a sexual affair between us can last only a few years. I could never be an old woman pursuing a younger man. . . ."

Nothing was to happen without our knowledge and consent, Ayn and Nathaniel told us. Nothing was to be hidden, there were to be no lies. After each discussion, Ayn would continue talking alone with Frank, and Nathaniel and I would return home to lapse into the long, empty silences that were the first since we had met. In the void of those silences, I tried to make sense of the senseless, as Frank was trying to do. In retrospect, it remains astonishing that there was even a question in Frank's mind or mine about what action to take; in retrospect, it remains astonishing that even the power of Ayn's personality could cause us to consider agreeing to an affair; but it was as if she had cast her spell long ago, and now it was too late to flee from its web.

Ayn's motivation appeared to Frank and to me as crystalline in its purity and clarity as the functioning of her mind. She had named her motivation, and we accepted her explanation. We had no real understanding of the psychological complexities and the desperate needs that drew her to Nathaniel. The need to live as a woman—so unfulfilled in her marriage—had at last burst forth. She could no longer live only as "Mrs. Logic." In *Atlas Shrugged,* through the relationship of Dagny and Galt, she was creating the "ideal" romance. She could no longer bear to create it *only* in fiction. She had to have it in her life—she had to have it before it was too late—she had to have it *now,* that feeling she had longed for since she discovered Cyrus in *The Mysterious Valley,* that passionate feeling she had given to Kira, to Leo, to Andrei, to Dominique, to Roark, to Rearden, to Francisco, to Dagny, to Galt. She had to *live* it, if only once, if only for a year—if only for a day. And her time was running out. She was fifty years old. The passion, the capacity for joy, the hero-worship, the violent sexuality, the longing for submission to a stronger force, that had found its outlet only in her novels, was screaming to be lived before it was too late, and could no longer be denied.

She could not find what she needed with a man who was a contemporary and an equal. Such a man might challenge the whole structure of the fantasy in which she progressively had begun to live—the fantasy in which she was flawless, serene, morally and intellectually superior to those around her, the apotheosis of rationality, the woman without self-doubts or inner conflicts. And so she chose a boy—a brilliant, talented boy, but still a boy, who posed no threat, who revered her and would confirm the fantasy picture she could allow no one to threaten. She chose him as, twenty-five years before, she had chosen Frank.

But Nathaniel offered her something that Frank, now totally defeated by her strength, his identity submerged in hers, could no longer offer. Ayn's respect for

Nathaniel, despite his youth and inexperience, the respect which from the beginning of their friendship was not solely for his intellectual precocity but for an attractive, even irresistible *man*—his face "was completely the face of my type of man," she had often said—had created a new confidence in him. Of all the young men Ayn knew—and the men who were not young—he was the only one who treated her as a human being and a woman, who knew and expressed that at times she needed a shoulder to lean on, that she could be fragile and hurt and soft, that she needed emotional as well as intellectual understanding; he was the only one who challenged her intellectually and, in the realm of psychology, was her teacher. She had long ago ceased to expect it. She could not renounce it. "A soul cannot live without fuel," she had said. She would *live* the great romance she wrote about, she and Nathaniel would *be* Dagny Taggart and John Galt—but with a crucial difference that would serve as her safety net: Nathaniel would be the hero worshipper, and she the immaculate hero.

Nathaniel had no power to resist the force that was Ayn Rand. Her passion for him was a triumph beyond any he had ever dreamed. It was a triumph that ennobled him, it was the proof of his worth, of his virtue, of the greatness that was to be his future—and he knelt as if before a queen to receive the gift of knighthood. It was more than knighthood, it was a morganatic marriage, and he was raised high to sit on the throne beside her.

Throughout the nightmare of the years that were to follow, it sometimes appeared that Nathaniel, despite his protestations, did not return the intensity of Ayn's passionate sexual feeling for him, and that his love for me was more real than his romantic devotion to Ayn. Many years later, he said that it was true, and that he had fought against it throughout the course of their love affair. By the madness of a coincidence that was not a coincidence at all, he and I were in the identical position: I believed that I *should* love Nathaniel, that I *should* feel an overwhelming sexual response that I did not feel; he believed that he *should* love Ayn, that he *should* feel an overwhelming sexual response that he did not feel. He never named or hinted it to Ayn. Not until it was much too late.

Frank and I met together often during the long weeks of conversations with Ayn and Nathaniel. His silent, helpless suffering was terrible to see. We talked for hours—predominantly, I talked—while he listened as I tried to make the irrational turn rational for both of us. I knew, very early, that I would agree to the affair; I knew that Frank would also agree. I thought I could survive it—perhaps even find some peace of mind—and I wanted Frank to survive it, too. We went for long walks, while I echoed Ayn's words: it isn't a threat to us; it will only be temporary; it makes sense that they feel as they do and want what they want; if it were otherwise, they would not be the people they are; we had accepted the validity of Ayn's theory of romantic and sexual love—we could not turn against what we knew to be true.

Ayn had taught that one's own emotional context is irrelevant in the face of knowledge of the right; personal pain is not in itself an appropriate motive for action. In hindsight, looking back on those anguished days, it seems clear that

Frank and I were struggling, as we had learned from Ayn to do, to ignore our own personal contexts; we were struggling to be the objective observers of four lives, deciding what was right; that two of those lives were ours, that we were suffering, was irrelevant to the justice of the situation. One day, I said, "Frank, I've asked myself what I would do if I could simply push a button, and none of this would have happened—Nathan and Ayn would never have met, never have fallen in love. I wouldn't push it. I want to live in the kind of world where people like that exist, and find each other, and love each other. I hate what's happening, but I don't want the alternative." Frank listened, and sometimes he nodded— and sometimes he exploded with rage and swore he'd leave Ayn and never see her again—and sometimes his eyes filled with tears and he said only, "No. No. No . . ."—and sometimes we clutched each other's hands and walked silently through the winter streets.

Again in hindsight, it is apparent that both Frank and I were carrying within our psychologies a lethal combination that disarmed us and left us helpless to leave Ayn, to leave Nathaniel, to leave the whole destructive situation, or to fight it and refuse our agreement. That combination was idealism—and guilt.

Ayn had established herself among her young friends, through the rigor of her argumentation and the forcefulness of her personality, as the epitome and the standard of the human potential, of everything we were struggling to become and everything we loved. I felt that she had given me so much, she had pulled me out of the intellectual morass of adolescence and had helped me to make sense of a complex, confusing world, she had given me friendship, and knowledge, and love. She had opened wide the doors of her own shining world to admit me, she had consistently encouraged me to achieve my most treasured goals, in my work, in my person, in my life; she had healed my wounds and ended my lonely distance from the world around me; she had taught me to exchange the leaking life raft on which I'd floundered for a sturdy, high-speed cruiser; she had shown me the grandeur and the limitless possibilities of existence. It was unthinkable that I should interfere with her happiness or that I should run from the sight of it. She had given me the possibility of mine.

Even so many years later, I cannot judge the precise extent to which my sense of guilt toward Nathaniel aided in forming my decision, except to know that it was significant. Since our marriage, although I had fought to change whatever in my psychology was preventing me from giving him the response he had a right to expect, I had failed. Nathaniel was painfully unfulfilled. One day, I still believed, it would be different. But it was not different yet. If he could find, with Ayn, the romantic and sexual fulfillment he sought, then my sanction would be the form in which I *did* have the power to make his life happier. I did not know that I was torturing myself in the name of a concept of the source and meaning of sexual love that I would finally reject as false to the infinite complexities and needs of the human psyche.

Frank's motivation seemed to be almost identical with mine. He, too, revered Ayn; he, too, believed that the love between Ayn and Nathaniel was inevitable;

he, too—the man who rescued sick chickens and left his peacocks free to fly—
could not bring suffering to the woman he had married. And he, too, was
tormented by the guilt of failure, the guilt of not being the hero he believed Ayn
deserved—the man of productive achievement, of limitless ambition, of unique,
self-generated intellect—the hero who would match her heroism.

Frank was further disarmed by a factor he alluded to only much later.
Throughout their marriage, Ayn had been the center of his life and his motive
force and his purpose; his life *belonged* to her. He had few skills, no trade, no
profession, no money of his own. Twelve years later, after a violent quarrel with
Ayn, Frank angrily stamped out of the living room. I followed him to the bedroom and found him sitting quietly, a look of uncontested anguish on the still-
beautiful planes of his face. As I tried to comfort him, he grasped my arm so
tightly that I winced. "I want to leave her," he said, his voice a hiss of rage and
despair. "I want to leave her!" His hand fell from my arm, and I could barely
hear his words as his voice dropped and he turned his face away to look into a
void. "But where would I go? . . . What would I do? . . ."

Together, walking through the streets of New York, Frank and I named the
decision that I had known I would make and that he had made twenty-five years
ago, on the day that he and Ayn stood in a county courthouse and listened to the
words that pronounced them man and wife. We would agree to Ayn and Nathaniel having an affair.

And so it began, that afternoon and evening of sex and love that Ayn and
Nathaniel spent together each week. And so we all careened toward disaster.

As I look back on the beginnings, I think of a question I have asked myself
many times in the years since. How did Ayn, who had lived in sophisticated
cities all her life and mingled with worldly, sophisticated people, not know that
the course on which she was embarking could lead only to tragedy? Surely, by
the age of fifty, one has seen enough of life and its complexities to have some
intimation of what was to follow. Surely, she had lived long enough to know that
she was presiding at the death of two marriages and at the corruption of four
lives in an ugly tangle of deceit and emotional savaging and pain. But Ayn was a
strikingly unsophisticated woman. She had had little personal experience of the
world, except as it related to her career; with the exception of Frank, she had
had no personal experience in intimate relationships with men. She had fought
valiant battles, she had endured revolution and dictatorship and the death of her
family and loneliness and joy and defeat and triumph—yet she had lived an
oddly sheltered life, locked within the confines of her special view of reality. To
Ayn, other people were not fully real; they were moving and breathing abstractions, they were, for good or for ill, the embodiments of moral and psychological
principles. They were not formed of flesh and blood and bone and sinew; they
were formed of the ideas that moved them. It was how she saw herself; it was
how she saw everyone else.

And if she *should* have known what awaited Frank, and Nathaniel, and herself, and me, if she *could* have known, if some hidden part of her suspected it but kept silent—if she was the guiltiest of the four of us, in a situation where no one was blameless—then it was she, in the end, who would pay the highest price of all.

Chapter Twenty-three

The timing of the love affair between Ayn and Nathaniel could not have been more unfortunate. During this first extended period in her life when she had unlimited time to devote herself to her novel, without the interruption of other literary assignments or the need to earn money, Ayn was writing the major and climactic philosophical speech of *Atlas Shrugged*. As the world races toward economic collapse, John Galt gives a radio address in which he explains his strike and presents the synopsized total of the philosophy of Objectivism.

It was the earlier speeches in *Atlas*—by Rearden, by Francisco, by Dagny—that had always created the greatest literary difficulties for Ayn. The problem had not been conceptual; she knew what issues she wanted to present. The problem had been to make her points clearly but not to lead the reader, or the characters who had not yet joined the strike, too quickly to the solution of the mystery of a disintegrating world—not to let them discover too soon that they were witnessing the strike of the world's productive geniuses. Sometimes, she would have to rewrite a speech five or six times, carefully measuring what could and what could not yet be said, while at the same time properly covering an intellectual issue.

She had known, long before she approached Galt's speech, that it would be the hardest challenge of *Atlas Shrugged*. It was to sum up, in essentials, all of the issues of the novel. But as she approached it, it kept growing in scale in her mind until she recognized that she could not predict how difficult it would be or how long it would take. And until she had finished the speech, she could not guess how long she would need to finish the book. She refused to submit the manuscript to publishers before Galt's speech was written; only then, she knew, could she estimate the time the final chapters would require.

When she began writing Galt's speech, Ayn thought that the purely conceptual planning had been done, that she knew precisely the issues she would cover.

But she found that new thinking was required and new ideas had to be included. The most notable was her theory of the origin of values, to which she had given only cursory consideration before. The statement of that theory was one of Ayn's outstanding intellectual achievements; in a few paragraphs in a novel, she took a major step toward solving the problem that has haunted philosophers since the time of Aristotle and Plato: the relationship of "ought" and "is"—the question of in what manner moral values can be derived from facts.

"There is only one fundamental alternative in the universe: existence or non-existence—and it pertains to a single class of entities: to living organisms," she wrote. "The existence of inanimate matter is unconditional, the existence of life is not: it depends on a specific course of action. Matter is indestructible, it changes its forms, but it cannot cease to exist. It is only a living organism that faces a constant alternative: the issue of life or death. . . . It is only the concept of 'Life' that makes the concept of 'Value' possible. It is only to a living entity that things can be good or evil. . . . Man has no automatic course of survival. His particular distinction from all other living species is the necessity to act in the face of alternatives, by means of *volitional choice*. . . . Man has been called a rational being, but rationality is a matter of choice—and the alternative his nature offers him is: rational being or suicidal animal. . . . A code of values accepted by choice is a code of morality."

In writing the speech, Ayn was attempting to complete the task she had begun in *We the Living:* the destruction of the altruist morality and the demonstration of a morality of reason. "My morality," Galt says, "the morality of reason, is contained in a single axiom: existence exists—and in a single choice: to live. The rest proceeds from these. To live, man must hold three things as the supreme and ruling values of his life: Reason—Purpose—Self-esteem. Reason, as his only tool of knowledge—Purpose, as his choice of the happiness which that tool must proceed to achieve—Self-esteem, as his inviolate certainty that his mind is competent to think and his person is worthy of happiness, which means: is worthy of living."

Ayn had expected that it would require three or four months to write the speech. It required two full years.

"The organization was a major difficulty," she said. "And the difficulty of legalistic definition, of covering all the loopholes and all the possible objections, the arguing without sounding like it was arguing. Galt had to present his explanations as if they were assertions; he wouldn't be debating with his opponents. . . . I first started writing the theoretical part of the speech beginning with metaphysics, then epistemology, then morality; that was the easiest way to do it. But then I realized, after a lot of pages, that you can't do that in fiction, you have to start with the presentation of the morality, which is the real theme of the book. I had to change the whole order, then sometimes spend weeks getting the original mental set out of my mind, then start rewriting."

The work was nerve-racking. The most difficult part was the need to impose a fictional form on philosophy. "I had to keep remembering the emotional part of the presentation," Ayn explained, "and to make it a rousing speech, and that kept getting in the way of the theoretical presentation. My assignment was to present the whole of my philosophy briefly and logically; to have to worry about emotions was pure hell. When I'd arrive at especially good formulations, that was a pleasure, but it was only drops-of-water-in-a-desert kind of torture. Frank said it was the worst he ever saw me go through."

The sixty-page speech was the culmination of a lifetime of thinking, a lifetime of devotion to philosophic truth, a lifetime of flogging her mind, her spirit and her body to do more and still more, to delve deeper, to work harder, to push to the limit of her endurance and beyond. Ayn suffered both physical and mental agonies in her struggle. Sometimes Frank would find her slumped over her desk as if she were unable ever to rise again; she would emerge from her study with new deep lines on her brow and her body sagging with weariness. At other times, she projected an emotional tension that was painful to see; she could not eat, or sleep, or even talk. She was reaching the limit of her endurance.

The emotional effects on Ayn of these two years of "pure hell" were destructive. As her literary and philosophical talents reached their zenith, her personal attitudes were falling into disrepair. The long period of unremitting intellectual effort and its accompanying emotional and physical tensions profoundly exacerbated the conflicts and unidentified self-doubts, the lack of sensitivity to the contexts of others, the need for control, the fears, the alienation and suspiciousness, the judgmental explosiveness, the tendency to self-aggrandizement, that were a part of her character.

Adding to the exacerbation was the fact that she had spent her days, for many years, giving life to her ideal human beings and her ideal world, making real, for herself and her readers, her vision of the human potential. That potential no longer existed only in her mind, it flamed from the pages of manuscript growing on her desk—and it made the rest of reality unendurable. She left her study each night—she left Galt and Dagny and Rearden and Francisco—to glance through newspapers and magazines and listen to news reports that brought word of the country she loved continuing its headlong hurtle toward catastrophe, toward an ever-growing welfarism, and she wondered whether anything could now stop it. She left Atlantis each day to deal with her disappointment in Isabel Paterson, the one friend who had been important to her, in Albert Mannheimer, whom she had struggled for so long to help and who had not contacted her since her departure from California, in Thadeus Ashby, whom she learned had now joined the religious right, in the conservatives such as Henry Hazlitt and Ludwig von Mises, whom she felt were no longer allies she could count on except in the narrow realm of politics and economics, even in William Mullendore, her favorite of the California conservatives, who appeared to be toying with Eastern mysticism.

As the last of her powers of endurance were spent, as her nervous state grew more jagged and fragile, the bitterness and pain in her personality began to take the ascendency. As always, her pain was converted into anger, the only means

she knew by which to deal with it. The lighter, gayer aspects of her personality
—the element in Ayn that responded to her special music and danced to its
strains—began to be buried somewhere out of sight and out of reach.

It was only the collective whom, she felt, offered her the sight of her own
world. "Our conversations," she had said, "belong in the same realm as the
novel." As time went by, others were joining the group around her, as *The
Fountainhead* continued its astonishing odyssey and attracted still more young
people to Ayn. Some, who lived in other cities—my brother Sidney and his wife,
Miriam, and Nathaniel's two sisters and their husbands, Florence and Hans
Hirschfeld and Reva and Sholey Fox—were present only at irregular intervals.
And what Ayn called "the junior collective" began to form: younger people who
had contacted one or another of her friends to express their interest in learning
more about Ayn's ideas. Ayn and the various "collectives" were becoming a
small society. Her dependence on them for the spiritual fuel provided by her
sense that they were a part of *her* world, markedly increased as they became,
except for a few rare evenings that she spent with others, her only social contacts
in a life steadily growing more reclusive, a life lived within the boundaries of
Atlas Shrugged. Her dependence became dangerous, both for her and for them;
her need to know that they would never betray her, that they would remain
unfailingly and unswervingly the consistent denizens of *her* world, became a
demand impossible to meet. Despite Ayn's affection for her friends, her relationship with them had always been marked, and marred, by the absolutism of her
moral condemnations of any deviation from the principles of Objectivism. Now,
as if to clasp them still more tightly to the universe of *Atlas Shrugged,* she began
to demand fidelity even in those areas that she herself had defined as subjective.

She had said, and continued to say, that the validity of one's musical tastes
could not be philosophically demonstrated: not enough was understood about
the mechanism by which music was interpreted by the brain and translated into
emotional responses. Yet if one of her young friends responded as she did to
Rachmaninoff, or especially to her lighter musical loves, she attached deep significance to their affinity. On the other hand, if a friend did not respond as she
did, she left no doubt that she considered that person morally and psychologically reprehensible. One evening, a friend remarked that he enjoyed the music of
Richard Strauss. When he left at the end of the evening, Ayn said, in a reaction
becoming increasingly typical, "Now I understand why he and I can never be
real soul mates. The distance in our sense of life is too great." Often, she did not
wait until a friend had left to make such remarks. If she was now demanding
adherence even in areas of subjective preferences, her demands in realms she
deemed rationally demonstrable became obsessive.

Ayn's childhood division of the world into the white of good and the black of
evil, with no shades of gray between them, was not lessening in this difficult
period of her life, but increasing. Innumerable times, her shocked friends witnessed her verbal flaying of those whom she felt had failed her and failed her
standards—a painter in whose work she saw a "malevolence" he was not work-

ing to correct—a journalist who she believed had compromised his principles—a student of philosophy who had been pleasant to a socialist professor who could advance his career—an economist who had not defended her publicly when she was attacked. They saw her denouncing people as evil, rejecting them, breaking off relationships of many years' standing. She seemed able to end relationships without suffering pain; during the life of a friendship, she was predominantly focused on its cerebral content, not on its emotional meaning to her, and thus could sever it without full awareness of what she was abandoning.

It was her new theorizing in psychology that became the weapon that Ayn began to use as an inquisitor might use fire and the rack.

Nathaniel had been developing a concept of human motivation that Ayn considered a major step forward in her understanding of the mechanisms of the human psyche. He called it "social metaphysics." He was to write on the subject: "A man of self-esteem and sovereign consciousness deals with reality, with nature, with an objective universe of facts; he holds his mind as his tool of survival and develops his ability to think. But the man who has abandoned his mind lives, not in a universe of facts, but in a *universe of people;* people, not facts, are *his* reality; people, not reason, are *his* tool of survival. It is with *them* that he has to deal, it is on *them* that his consciousness must focus, it is they whom he must understand or please or placate or deceive or maneuver or manipulate or obey.

"It is his success at this task that becomes his gauge of his fitness to exist—of his competence to live. . . . To the man I am describing, reality is *people:* in his mind, in his thinking, in the automatic connections of his consciousness, *people* occupy the place which, to the mind of a rational man, is occupied by *reality. . . .*"

Nathaniel was giving a psychological interpretation to the Peter Keatings of the world, in conjunction with Ayn's philosophical interpretation. As with many of Ayn's own interpretations, it represents a valuable *description* of an aspect of inner behavior, but it is not a fundamental motivational principle; it names how some people behave, but it does not name the underlying sources and base of such behavior.

Nevertheless, the diagnosis of "social metaphysics" became in Ayn's hands, and in Nathaniel's, both a means of accounting for human "irrationality" and a means of exercising control. The world, before divided into the Roarks and the Keatings, now was divided into the rationalists and the social metaphysicians—with the rationalists forming a minuscule portion of that division. When applied to one or other of Ayn's friends or close acquaintances, the diagnosis of social metaphysician—announced with the gravity of a medical doctor pronouncing a verdict of cancer, to which was added a moral opprobrium appropriate to a volitionally chosen cancer of the spirit—became a nightmare to be avoided at all costs. And once that verdict was pronounced, the consequences were clear: hours and weeks, even years, of psychological consultation with Nathaniel in an effort to rid one's spirit of the demon into whose hands one had given it; hours and weeks, even years, of work and thought and struggle to perform the necessary act of exorcism.

But was Ayn not writing—as Galt describes the world he and his strikers will create—"Such is the future you are capable of winning. It requires a struggle, as does any human value. All life is a purposeful struggle, and your only choice is the choice of a goal. Do you wish to continue the battle of your present or do you wish to fight for my world? . . . do you wish to undertake a struggle that consists of rising from ledge to ledge in a steady ascent to the top, a struggle where the hardships are investments in your future, and the victories bring you irreversibly closer to the world of your moral ideal, and should you die without reaching full sunlight, you will die on a level touched by its rays? Such is the choice before you. Let your mind and your love of existence decide."

No one, however young and inexperienced, would have accepted so cavalier and damning an explanation of his psychological state as social metaphysics, had the source of the explanation not been Ayn Rand. In Ayn's own terms, in the terms of one of the most important concepts of *Atlas Shrugged,* it was "the sanction of the victim" that gave her the power to inflict such damage: only her virtues made it possible. It was the same intellect that was presenting a comprehensive world view that made sense of human existence, the same intellect that was defining a moral code that made achievement and joy possible, the same intellect that was creating the inspirational fictional characters they wished to emulate—the same mesmerizing power to convince that had told them that their desire to live for their own happiness was the highest of virtues, that their most exalted goals were possible on earth—the same overwhelming breadth of mind that never made a philosophical statement without the backing of an endless list of logical justifications—the same towering intelligence whose derivation of morality from metaphysics they were reading with a sense of ecstatic release from the amorality they had been taught in their classrooms—the same exquisite acuity that had lifted them up to the heights of an exalted understanding—that was now dashing them down to the depths of tortured self-doubt and defining them as "social metaphysicians." They felt themselves on a roller coaster of conflicting messages and contradictory emotions. But they could not reject such a denunciation out of hand. It had to be taken seriously. Particularly when it was echoed—more often initiated—by the psychologist whom Ayn called a genius and had named her "intellectual heir."

A highly intelligent young woman of twenty, a dancer and a member of the "junior collective," had personal problems in her romantic relationship with a friend of Ayn's. Ayn, Frank, her lover, and I were present when Nathaniel called her in for a discussion of her psychology. Such evenings were becoming a commonplace in Ayn's dealings. The evidence was presented, the diagnosis of social metaphysician was made. In a paper she later wrote in an attempt to organize her thoughts, the young woman said—in an echo of others who felt as she did— "I have not been this unhappy since I was a kid, when I used to look out the window and calm down by watching the stars. But then I had the promise of a brilliant, beautiful future. Now I have the echo of an empty, futile past. . . . Everything is gone. Everything. . . . I began to see the pattern as Nathan went through example after example of what I had done. It was when he said 'and your self-esteem is tied to what other people think of you,' that I knew beyond a shadow of a doubt what was being said to me—the worst degradation, the worst muck. I had betrayed everything that has ever meant anything to me. . . . He said I could work to correct it and become a proper human being, or be like the people I hate for the rest of my life. . . . I'm afraid to care about anything, because I'm afraid I'll get all mixed up again. I have to find out if it's safe to care about something again. I don't know any longer what I want in a career, in anything—it doesn't seem to matter, and I'm afraid of the day when it is going to matter. . . . Yet I will always remember the day I met Ayn as one of the happiest days of my life. . . ."

That evening, Ayn exhibited a lack of human empathy that was astonishing. As Nathaniel, who conducted the conversation—it had the aura of a trial, except that the accused had no defense attorney—was pointing out the young woman's psychological deficiencies, he occasionally made some especially compelling point, succinct and well-phrased. Each time, Ayn chuckled with appreciation—and clapped her hands in applause.

The girl, like others of Ayn's friends caught in similar situations, was to find a means of ridding herself of guilt. The means, as her paper indicates, was emotional repression. "I'm afraid to care about anything, because I'm afraid I'll get all mixed up again." She, like they, began the process of changing from an open, spontaneous, enthusiastic young woman into a rigid thinking machine. It was done as an act of self-preservation: one must not experience emotions that might brand one as immoral.

The distance between the self-created myth of Ayn Rand and the real woman who lived and acted outside the world of her study, was growing steadily greater. In retrospect, it is evident that none of Ayn's young friends, including Nathaniel and myself, were helping Ayn to deal with the tensions that drove her. No one achieves power who does not seek it; had she not insisted upon being viewed as a goddess, she would not have been so viewed. Nevertheless, the adulation she received was a great disservice to her. She needed to be challenged when she applauded a young woman's agony—or when she spoke of Aristotle as the only thinker in history from whom she had had anything to learn—or when she demanded, in her affair with Nathaniel, that a set of rules be held as applicable to her that were not applicable to others—or when she flew into a rage, as she did with her attorney, Pincus Berner, at his suggestion that *everyone,* including herself, had at some time done what they knew to be wrong—or when she made it implicitly clear that any criticism of her was an act of treason to reason and morality. But had the attitude of her friends been different, it is likely that she would have renounced them and surrounded herself with people who would give her what she needed. It was not chance that her chosen friends were so many years younger than she—as it was not chance that her lover was so many years younger than she.

The sexual affair between Ayn and Nathaniel had begun early in 1955. Years later, Nathaniel would acknowledge that their romance was not truly lived in reality. Rather, it was theater—no, not theater, it was a scene from a novel by Ayn Rand, full of sexual dominance and surrender and the uncontrollable passion of two noble souls. Ayn, so desperate to live in the real world, not merely in her novels and in a future that never came—could not, after all, be content with reality. Once more, she was struggling to turn base metals—the painful, unsatisfactory fact of a woman having an adulterous affair with the too young husband of her closest friend—into the gold of a great and exalted romance. She succeeded in her fiction. She did not succeed in her life.

The practical realities under which the affair was conducted seemed designed to destroy whatever authentic joy might have been possible between Ayn and Nathaniel. Despite his pleas, Ayn refused to allow him to take a small apartment where they could meet; she was terrified at the possibility of being recognized if she were seen entering a man's apartment. She said that she would not be ashamed—she would be proud—if their story were featured on the front pages of the world's newspapers; but everything that was conventional in her silently said the opposite. Frank, Nathaniel, and I were sworn to lifelong secrecy about the affair; it was too personal, too precious to be shared with an irrational world.

Her fear created a situation more terrible for Frank than the affair itself. Twice a week over a period of years, knowing that Nathaniel was soon to arrive, Frank left the apartment. Sometimes, he was a few minutes late in leaving, and he would usher Nathaniel in, chat with him while Ayn finished dressing, kiss Ayn good-bye and listen to her admonitions to "Be careful"—be careful crossing the street, be careful to keep his coat warmly buttoned, be careful to be home in time for dinner—and then depart, leaving his wife to spend a few hours of love in his bedroom.

Frank was always vague about what he did when Ayn and Nathaniel were together. "I went for a walk," he would say. Or, "I saw a movie." Or, "I dropped into the bar at the Mayfair Hotel for an hour or two; I know some of the men who go there, and we talked." It was not until years later that the truth about how Frank spent that afternoon and evening each week was revealed. He did go for a walk—just as far as the bar he frequented. He did visit with some of the men at the bar: they were his drinking partners. Frank had always enjoyed a drink or two in the evening—his powerful martinis were guaranteed to elicit gasps at the first sip by an unsuspecting guest—but now his drinking began to be a way of life, an escape from an intolerable reality.

A friend of Frank's—now a recovered alcoholic—who sometimes joined him for the drink or two which became three and four and five and more, was convinced that Frank was an alcoholic. None of the friends Frank shared with Ayn were aware, during these years, that he drank to excess. But much later, his drinking was to become a painful and explosive source of friction between Ayn and Frank.

Perhaps some part of Ayn's shocking insensitivity toward Frank in matters involving her relationship with Nathaniel was, subconsciously, a means of punishing the husband who had failed her expectations. And perhaps a part of it was the hope that he would, at last, assert himself—that he would say: Enough! and forbid her the relationship. Apart from the indignity visited upon Frank by the private meetings in his home, there was, when the four of us were together, an element of flaunting their sexual feeling in Ayn and Nathaniel's manner, an unnecessary touching and hand-holding and gazing into each other's eyes, as if they were throwing their passion into Frank's face and mine, as if they were saying: *You* would not give me what I wanted, but *now* I have it despite you.

Throughout her marriage, Ayn, in her search for her own femininity, had given the appearance of deferring to Frank's judgment and preferences, saying, "May I do this, Frank?"—or, "Frank won't permit me to do that"—or, "Do you agree, Frank?"—or "Frank insisted" or "Frank refused" or "Frank wants" or "Frank demanded." Now, this dependency, more apparent than real, was transferred to Nathaniel's shoulders: both privately and publicly, Ayn constantly solicited his agreement, his sanction, his opinion, as if leaning on his knowledge and support; she praised him for the least accomplishment in extravagant and loving terms; she continually announced and stressed what she had learned from him about psychology, calling him her intellectual heir, stating that he was the spiritual equal of her heroes. Remarkably, among her closest circle of friends, only one, Joan Mitchell Blumenthal, wondered about the real nature of the relationship between Ayn and Nathaniel. The answer may be that it was inconceivable to them that the relationship could be sexual—and so it was not conceived.

The circumstances surrounding the liaison inevitably had their effects on Nathaniel as well as on Frank. It was not possible for Nathaniel to enter Ayn and Frank's apartment, talk with Frank, say good-bye to him when he left, wonder where he would go and what he was feeling—then turn to Ayn to see her drawn and tense and weary—and then move with her to the bedroom to become an inspired young lover. There were, of course, exceptions, when their deep feeling for each other was a stronger, more compelling force than any obstacles to its expression, and they could be simply a man and woman in love. Frank had never been a man of intense sexuality, and in their marriage it was Ayn who was predominantly the sexual initiator. Now her lover was a man of youth and vigor —a man wise enough to give her the sense of herself as a woman for which she had always yearned: the sense of being helplessly in the control of a male force stronger than her will.

But Nathaniel was struggling to deal with a deeply ingrained emotional repression which always had interfered with the spontaneous expression of his feelings. And the last of Ayn's patience and capacity for dogged endurance had gone into the manuscript pages on her desk; it was unbearable to her that he, the best gift the world had offered her, should now refuse her what she so desperately needed. She began reproving him for what she termed his "emotional distance," for his lack of verbal, easy communication of his love, for his periods of coldness and emotional withdrawal which raised frightening doubts of the authenticity of his love. She never said that the doubts were *hers;* the problem was *his;* it was not the result of the numbing existential circumstances, of her husband roaming the streets, of his wife sitting miserably at home, of the secrecy of their meetings; nor was it the result of her own ambivalence toward emotional intimacy, her simultaneous longing for it and dread of the self-confrontation that it entailed. It was the result of Nathaniel's psychological problems. As her reproaches escalated, his emotional distance inevitably grew more marked; each week, he entered her apartment wondering how he would fail her this time.

Often, Nathaniel would arrive home from a meeting with Ayn looking grim and tormented. He would say that Ayn had been furious with him—that they had spent their hours together analyzing his psychological problems and the reasons for his failure of spontaneous emotional communication. Many times, still angry, she telephoned him when he reached home, scolding, accusing, denouncing. Immersed in the insoluble problems of our own disintegrating relationship, neither Nathaniel nor I heard Ayn's unspoken cry for what she had missed all her life, and now, struggling to create *Atlas Shrugged,* missed more painfully than ever, we did not see the years of rejection and of silent, unacknowledged suffering beneath her demands, we did not recognize that in a lifetime of too many battles and too many personal defeats, she needed to receive strength from outside herself. All four of us were suffering, each in his or her own way and for his or her own reasons; each of us was lost in his own pain; none of us could hear the others': "I want!"—"I need!"—"I must have!" As Nathaniel listened to Ayn's voice over the telephone, his dream of love was becoming a nightmare.

The quarrels and reproaches had their effect on Nathaniel's life. Just as Ayn's too demanding struggles as a writer did not create, but did exacerbate, preexisting emotional problems, so Nathaniel's difficulties in his relationship with Ayn did not create, but did exacerbate, his own pre-existing problems. He and Ayn were alike in their lack of empathy with the suffering of others, in the alacrity with which they passed moral and psychological judgments. Just as these qualities were accelerating in Ayn, so they were accelerating in Nathaniel. Sometimes in the past, he had attempted to stand between Ayn and young friends in whom she was disappointed, soothing her, reassuring her, reminding her of the values which still remained. But now it was Nathaniel who was often the first to find grave fault, to condemn, to savage victims disarmed by the credentials Ayn had given him. The devastation inherent in the events of that car ride from Toronto to New York, was spreading its corruption over his spirit.

Nathaniel's pain and confusion were worsened by mine. Within a few months of the beginning of the affair, I awoke one night with my heart pounding, my pulse racing, my body drenched with perspiration—and with a feeling of uncontrollable, sourceless terror. I was convinced that I was having a heart attack. Allan Blumenthal rushed over to examine me. It was not a heart attack. It was the classic onset of an anxiety attack.

It was to continue, almost unabated, for more than a year and a half. It never completely left me during that period, it rarely significantly lessened in severity. For endless days and endless nights I walked the streets of New York, trying to stamp my emotions into the pavements of the city, trying to rush past the terror that fed on itself and created a terror that I would feel still more terror. As is typical of such attacks, the "free-floating," apparently causeless anxiety became attached to one object after another: it was heights that frightened me, I concluded, or flying in an airplane, or riding in an elevator—or any of a long list of concrete sources. In a vain attempt to battle my fears, I would go to the Empire State Building and take an elevator to the top and look out over the city from the observation deck—feeling that my thudding heart would stop at any moment; when I traveled, I would fly to my destination—feeling that to crash could not be worse than the agony of my fear. I felt that I was fighting for my sanity and my life.

I saw neither a physician nor a psychiatrist. Was I not married to a great psychologist? Of what importance was it that other psychologists did not treat their wives? He was helping me, and Ayn Rand was helping me. And another theory was evolving, for which I was the laboratory experiment, to take its place beside the theory of social metaphysics and to explain the terror in which I was drowning. The theory which Ayn and Nathaniel arrived at was called "emotionalism."

Ayn wrote a paper on the nature of emotionalism; she wrote it, as she often did with new concepts, as a private technique to clarify her thinking; she made no attempt to publish her many papers. "The Emotionalist's premise," she said, "is as follows: 'Reality is objective, but let other people deal with it, *my* role is only to form values (desires) in spirit, *their* role is to serve me and to provide me with the material means and the opportunity to translate my values into physical form, *their* role is to make reality somehow subservient to my desires'. . . . The Emotionalist bases his self-esteem on his 'intentions' or 'aspirations'. . . . I think that there are two different types of Emotionalists: those who became Emotionalists in childhood, by evasion—and those who acquired it later, by an error of knowledge. These last would be the Emotionalists who have a tremendous passion for values and a total sense of 'the stylized universe,' like F and B [Frank and Barbara]. They, I think, had started out in life as Rationalists. . . . The Emotionalist who becomes such later, in adolescence or youth, starts out as a purposeful, independent child. . . . The error which later throws him off is *Emotional Repression*. When he encounters disappointments in his clashes with other people, he represses his pain, in the name of his values, in the mistaken belief that suffering is weakness or betrayal of values. Once the habit of emotional repression is established, it grows and it handicaps his perception of reality, his thinking, his mind. It blocks one area of reality after another and reduces his rational faculty to a state of passivity. . . . This type of 'later-day' Emotionalist, no matter what errors or evasions he may proceed to commit, can never lose his self-made soul. He will always remain an entity, *a person*—in a manner which the 'childhood' Emotionalist does not possess or achieve."

The concept of emotionalism—the theory that the emotionalist attempts to grasp the world not by reason but through the medium of his emotions, and views his emotions as tools of cognition, just as the social metaphysician attempts to grasp the world through the medium of the opinions and values of others, and attempts to use the minds of others as *his* tools of cognition—was utilized by Ayn and Nathaniel, as they utilized the concept of social metaphysics, to account for a certain psychological syndrome. But Ayn considered emotionalism to be, morally, a giant step above the cancer of social metaphysics. And it seems likely that her division of emotionalists into two categories—the relatively corrupt category of the "childhood Emotionalist" and the relatively innocent category of the "later-day Emotionalist"—functioned as Ayn's means of keeping pure the souls of her husband and Nathaniel's wife.

In the theory of emotionalism—even in its name—one can glimpse Ayn's ambivalent attitude toward emotions. Her conviction that happiness is the proper goal and purpose of human life lies at the very heart of her moral code. Yet throughout her novels one reads of her heroes ruthlessly ignoring their emotions, damning emotions in others, taking pleasure only in their work, leading lives of Spartan self-discipline. It was so in her novels, and it was so in her own person. And many of her admirers learned to make it so in *their* own persons—they learned to deny their emotions, to ignore the inner signals their feelings were giving them, to abandon the evidence that was telling them who they really were and what they really loved, to devote their lives to work and to self-improvement, to deal with each other by means of philosophical abstractions. They learned emotional repression and its inevitable concomitant: the alienation from self.

The theory of emotionalism was the tool by which Ayn and Nathaniel attempted to deal with the problem of my anxiety. The anxiety did not lessen. In fact, it increased, as all the work I did, all the thinking, all the conversations about my psychology seemed unable to lead to a solution.

It was Nathaniel who arrived, in the end, at a concept which names, in abstract terms, what appears to be a fundamental psychological source of anxiety. In *The Psychology of Self-Esteem,* he would write: "The experience of pathological anxiety always involves and reflects conflict . . . and the acute anxiety attack is occasioned by the ego's confrontation with that conflict. . . . The conflict is the collision of two absolutes. . . . It is the conflict between 'I must' —and 'I can't' . . . between 'I must not'—and 'I am.' . . . There is always a conflict between some value imperative that is tied, in a crucial and profound way, to the person's self-appraisal and inner equilibrium—and some failure or inadequacy or action or emotion or desire that the person regards as a breach of that imperative, a breach that the person believes expresses or reflects a basic and unalterable fact of his 'nature.' "

This, as in retrospect I understand what was happening to me, names it precisely: the conflict between "I must" and "I can't"—the collision of two absolutes. One absolute was that I *must* accept my husband's love affair with Ayn, that it was right, it was rational—the other was the absolute screaming silently within me that *"I can't."*[1]

During that year and a half before my anxiety disappeared as mysteriously as it had come, Nathaniel suffered over my suffering—although, incredibly, neither he nor Ayn saw its connection to the situation in which we were all involved. Their love affair, they believed, was the inevitable and rational consequence of their estimate of each other; they believed that I had accepted it as fully as they had. The source of my symptoms was emotionalism, for which I was now paying the price. Ayn shifted between two attitudes toward me. Often, she spent hours and days and nights struggling to help me, to release me from anxiety; she was tender, and kind, and loving, she was the beloved friend who could not bear to see me in pain. At other times, she was impatient, angry, morally disapproving. But she had only one attitude when Nathaniel, having left me in the throes of a panic attack, would arrive at her apartment troubled and worn and fearful of admitting that he had not wanted to leave me: her attitude was rage. "How dare you worry about Barbara when you're with me!" she demanded. At times, she hinted broadly that he should divorce me, that he had no right to live with a woman so patently unworthy.

There was one night I shall never forget—the worst of all those years and of the years to come. It was about eleven o'clock, I had been walking all evening; the anxiety was building to a pitch greater than any I had ever experienced. I began to grow frantic; I believed that my mind might collapse from the bombardment of so great a terror. I had never called Ayn's apartment when she and Nathaniel were together; but that night, I stopped at a pay phone and dialed Ayn's number. When she answered, I told her what was happening, and that I wanted to come over to talk. Her explosion made the telephone drop from my hand—and a moment later I felt her voice pursuing me as I hurried away from it as from the cold clasp of hatred. "How dare you! Do you think *only* of yourself? Am I *completely* invisible to you? *I* don't ask anyone for help! There's your whole problem in the fact that you called—if you *want* something, that's all you know or care about! Don't dare to dream of coming here!" And on and on and on, until I was beyond the range of that terrible loathing. I did not, could not hear Ayn's unspoken cry that she had waited and worked all of her life for an evening such as this, an evening of love and passion and exaltation with the man she adored—and I was demanding that she give it up.

---

[1] According to recent scientific findings, pathological anxiety is believed to be primarily the result of a chemical imbalance in the brain, whatever else may be involved of a psychological nature, and is treatable by appropriate medication.

It was later, during an informal course Ayn gave on fiction writing for several friends who were interested in the subject, that the climax of her negative attitude toward me was reached. The course was fascinating, as Ayn explained her own principles of writing and the reasons for those principles, and illustrated her points with excerpts from her work and the works of other writers. One evening, she decided to compare three writers stylistically: Ayn Rand, Thomas Wolfe, and Mickey Spillane. Spillane had become her favorite contemporary novelist, from the aspects of originality, imagination, sense of drama and, above all, plot-structure; she admired him as "a moral crusader," saying that he approached conflicts in uncompromising black-and-white terms and that his hero, Mike Hammer, was a moral avenger.[2]

For the purposes of comparison and contrast, Ayn chose a section from *Atlas Shrugged,* one from Spillane's *I, the Jury,* and another from Wolfe's *Of Time and the River.* She insisted that I be the one to read the selections aloud: I had a very attractive speaking voice, she said: she always loved to hear me reading her work. The selection she had chosen from Wolfe—as an example of bad writing— was a few paragraphs of a description of New York that I had shown her, when we first discussed Wolfe, as an example of what I most loved and cherished in his work.

After her analysis of the excerpts, Ayn announced that last on the evening's agenda would be Nathaniel's reading of a short story. Apparently it was his suggestion, to which Ayn acceded, that the class should not be told who had written it. The group listened intently as Nathaniel read a rather charming story; but it was awkward stylistically, it seemed blatantly imitative of Ayn, and was without real drama despite an original and professionally handled plot. When he had finished, I was the first to present my negative opinions. Then Nathaniel announced that the title of the story, written in 1927, was "Good Copy." Its author was Ayn Rand.[3]

Ayn's face was a thundercloud, her eyes flashing a dark and ominous lightning. In the silence that fell over the room, she began to shout in outrage. What was wrong with me psychologically that I could so totally fail to appreciate her story and her sense of life?—I knew nothing about literature, I knew nothing about writing, and most of all I knew nothing about *her!* I sat in a state of numbed shock as her anger intensified, and the others, aware that they should not be present at such a scene, quietly took their leave. Ayn's fury continued unabated; she accused me of every imaginable psychological evil. It was too much. I could accept no part of what she said, and I stood my ground like a bulldog while the thunder of her voice crashed around me. It was impossible to

[2] When Ayn later met Mickey Spillane, she discovered that the admiration between them was mutual: he had read and loved her novels. It was a strange sight to see these two together: Spillane, who physically suggested a prize fighter or a dock worker, was courteous and pleasant, but nonphilosophical in his approach to writing, and Ayn painstakingly tried to make him aware of the philosophical meaning and value of what he had accomplished.
[3] Published in *The Early Ayn Rand.*

speak at any length, when I interrupted her she shouted louder, all I could do was keep repeating: "It isn't true"—"You're wrong"—"You're wrong"—"You're wrong." By four o'clock in the morning, she was likening my psychology to that of the archvillain of *The Fountainhead,* Ellsworth Toohey. At that point, I gave a shout of laughter and said, "Ayn, stop it!" She stopped it. We began talking quietly and sanely, and by the time the sun rose, she had retracted her accusations, and we were friends again.

In retrospect, it appears that the rejection of her story in itself only partially accounts for the intensity and injustice of Ayn's anger that night. More relevant is the fact that it was I, whom she had chosen, along with Nathaniel, as her closest friend, whom she had likened to her heroines, whom she had praised as an example and exemplar of her philosophy, was now invading the safe haven of *her* world not merely with alien values, but, still worse, with a repudiation of her work. And perhaps it was, as well, the explosion of all the frustrations of her affair with Nathaniel, all the unrecognized pain and guilt it was causing her, all that I stood for in her mind as the wife her lover steadfastly refused to leave. And no one heard her silent cry that life was intended for happiness and fulfillment—and why was that joy denied to her?

It was in this tortured, explosive fusion of overheated emotions, of anguish and rage and frustrated longings and bitterness—and of love and sexual passion and ecstatic fulfillment—that Ayn at last completed the writing of John Galt's speech.

Chapter Twenty-four

With the ordeal of John Galt's speech behind her, Ayn's boundless intellectual energy and enthusiasm began to return with astonishing rapidity. As if a spiritual switch had been thrown, she soon was once again the woman Nathaniel and I had met in California. All the tensions seemed to drain from her almost overnight; her exhaustion and sudden angers and accusations seemed only the memory of a distant storm.

There was more to be done on the novel, there were three long chapters still to be written, completing the climax begun by the speech and bringing the story to its final resolution. The remaining chapters would be "the cashing-in"; they were chapters predominantly of action and drama and suspense, precisely the kind of material she most enjoyed writing, and she could revel in the luxury of working with a single concern: that of dramatist and plot-writer.

As if a pall had been lifted from our lives, it began to seem as if the four of us were the triumphant survivors of a natural disaster, and we could begin to pick up the smashed pieces of our lives and gradually to regain the former closeness and love that had so tightly knitted us together. It began to seem as if the affair between Ayn and Nathaniel would become a tranquilly accepted part of our lives instead of the divisive and painful trauma it had been.

One could see in Ayn, during this period, a quality not manifest since the time of her meeting with Frank and her marriage: something bleak and grim had gone from her personality, replaced by a sensual quality, a pleasure in her own physical person, a concern with grooming, with clothes, with looking attractive. Her affair with Nathaniel had passed through its traumatic, tortured beginnings, and one began to see the emergence of a provocative, sexual woman. There was a new glow about her like a young woman in love; her stern features took on a softness and a femininity, as if cold marble had been warmed by an inner fire. Timidly, by slow, careful steps, Ayn was again attempting to live in the present, and was finding, in her work and in her romantic attachment—perhaps to her astonishment—a fulfillment the present had never before afforded her.

As Ayn began to consider the submission of the completed sections of her manuscript to publishing houses, Nathaniel was continuing his schooling at New York University and was busy and active as a psychological consultant; I, the period of anxiety behind me, had earned a master's degree in philosophy and was working in the editorial department of St. Martin's Press. And Frank, to his great joy, had at last found the work he loved to do and to which he wished to devote the remainder of his life.

The turning point in Frank's life came one evening when the collective was discussing painting. They were questioning whether or not certain careers required abilities that were innate and could not be taught, or if all forms of ability could be developed over time and with the appropriate knowledge. I said—only partly jokingly—that I felt myself so hopelessly lacking in the approach and perceptions of a visual artist, that I could never be taught to draw. Joan disagreed; any intelligent person, she maintained, granted a reasonable amount of interest and effort, could learn to draw with some degree of competence. She offered to prove it by giving lessons to anyone in the group who would care to attempt the experiment. Several of us laughingly agreed to try—including Frank.

At the first session of the class, hearts sank as Joan placed a white egg on a piece of white paper, and said that the assignment was to draw it. With her instructions, the group fell to work with varying degrees of success. But within a few sessions, what happened to Frank—who had never given any thought to painting or expressed any interest in the subject—had the quality of an explosion.

It was as if a subterranean talent, lying dormant for years, suddenly found an outlet and burst into the open. It was obvious that he was in a category by himself: while the other members of the class struggled slowly, and eventually did vindicate Joan in her claim, Frank shot forward like a rocket. His early drawings exhibited a violent self-assertiveness one would never have expected from so reserved and retiring a man, and an astonishing sense of drama and compositon in spite of their technical flaws. Ever since childhood, as an integral part of his interest in the theater and the movies, he had been preoccupied with the visual: with composition, with spatial tensions and relationships, with esthetic form and design. Now it was the accumulated visual observations of years that his imagination was calling on and using, filling his brain with dramatic sensory images.

He began to draw and sketch constantly. His drawings were scattered all over the apartment—and often, when one spoke to him, one saw that he had not heard, he was frowning in concentration and staring critically at some sketch halfway across the room. Soon he began working in pastels. He worked ceaselessly; he would come out of his room when guests arrived in the evening, his clothes smeared with chalk, in a state of quiet, ferocious rapture; he would utter a brief "Hello" and go back to his easel. And he was planning future work, projecting paintings he would do far into the future; he often talked of a painting of Icarus flying triumphantly into—and through—the sun, emerging unscathed and more beautiful than before. Frank was fifty-eight years old; he did not know how long it would take him to master the technique of painting. But *this,* he knew, was the work he wanted.

It was another giant boost to Ayn's morale. Here, at last, was what she had always hoped to see in Frank: a man working to the top limit of his capacity, working productively and happily, working for both short-and-long-range goals that elicited her deep admiration. And she felt that his painting revealed a startling artistic affinity to her own novels in his extravagant imaginativeness, in his sense of visual drama, in the union of tension and serenity, of austerity and sensuousness.[1] His silent agony over her love affair with Nathaniel seemed a thing of the past: it was as if he barely had time to notice it. And when he did take time to be with Ayn, the resentments and anxieties and raw, chafed nerves between them seemed equally a problem of the past.

Recognizing his need for technical training—although always impatient with it, like a man who has too much to do and too little time in which to do it and wants to focus only on the broad sweep of his work and not its details—Frank enrolled in the Art Students League. Rosina Florio, executive director of the League, has described the world-famous League as a "clutch of ateliers"—no credits or grades or diplomas are given, the students come to work five days each week, and work predominantly on their own from models or still-life setups provided for them, with critiques two days a week by a staff of teachers who have achieved eminent positions in the art world. She spoke of Frank with warm affection. "He worked very hard," she said. "He came every day, and progressed well. . . . He was a very private man, very kind and gentle, and everyone liked him. . . ."

Joan Mitchell Blumenthal was also working at the League. She did not know that Frank had never mentioned to anyone that his wife was Ayn Rand; his status was Frank O'Connor, painter. One day, Joan was talking with a group of students; one of them asked: "Is Frank married?" She replied that he was, and the student inquired: "What is his wife like?" "Her name is Ayn Rand," Joan answered. When she mentioned the incident to Frank, and saw the look of resigned pain on his face, Joan realized her mistake: he did not want to bask in Ayn's reflected glory, he wanted to be his own man and to stand or fall by his own work and his own considerable capacity to draw people to him; he was very popular among the other students—especially the women—for his courtly manners, his kindness, his unfailing helpfulness. "I wish you hadn't said it," he told Joan. "This is the one place where I'm liked for myself." But Rosina Florio would later say, "No one really cared at all who his wife was, only what sort of

---

[1] The Twenty-Fifth Anniversary edition of *The Fountainhead,* issued in 1968, has on its jacket a reproduction of Frank's painting *Man Also Rises.*

person he was, and what sort of work he did. Besides, Ayn rarely came to the League and people didn't pay much attention when she did. . . . I remember a party we all went to, given by one of our teachers, and my husband saw Ayn sitting alone while all the artists and their wives were discussing art; he went over to talk to her—he didn't have any idea who she was—and he later said to me, 'She's a strange woman. She answered my questions in one-sentence staccato assertions.' She couldn't be part of a group. You couldn't have a real conversation with her, an exchange. She seemed unable to handle not being the center of attention. Understandably so. She was an important writer, internationally famous, and here we were, a group of artists talking art, very shy and conscious of not wanting to disturb her."

One of Frank's classes was conducted by the distinguished painter Robert Brackman, member of the National Academy of Design. When asked his opinion of Frank's work, he said, "It was obvious almost immediately that Frank was not a student when he came to my class. He was already an artist. He had an absolutely individual way of doing things, right from the beginning. I saw that all he needed from me was technical advice—I would point out the kind of errors it would take him a long time to discover on his own—but in every other respect, I knew that he should be left free to develop in his own way. . . . With most students, one can see a dozen different historical influences reflected in their early work. There were no historical influences at all in his work. . . . I was floored at how quickly he learned. I didn't think that anyone could grow that fast. . . . Whatever subject he's given to paint, his first idea is always: What is the most dramatic way of presenting it? So far, composition is his strongest point technically. . . . Some people work at painting all their lives and never find themselves, never really find what they want to say or how they want to say it. Frank had found himself from the start."

Joan, an accomplished artist and a teacher of drawing and painting, was later asked her opinion of Frank's work, and what she thought to be its shortcomings. "His overwhelming virtue was his artistic imagination," she said. "He was able, for instance, to transform even the most uninteresting of the League's models into fascinating characters on canvas—or take a couple of onions in a still-life setup and create a dramatic fantasy. His work looked only like *his* work; it was uninfluenced by anyone else. . . . His problem areas were technical, particularly with regard to perspective, which he never mastered, and anatomy, which was always very faulty. One was aware of a lack of consonance in the perspective, as well as disturbing anatomical distortions. He was not at all interested in technical issues, and did not appear to see his errors. . . . One could not really *teach* Frank, one could only turn him loose to work in his own way and to exercise his admirable imagination. That was why Ayn was totally unsuccessful in influencing him artistically. She continually made suggestions about his work, and had long talks with him about what he should and should not do—but he paid no more attention to her than to anyone else."

It was in this happier atmosphere of the end of her own long ordeal with

Galt's speech and Frank's newfound joy in his creative activities, that Ayn began discussing with her literary agent, Alan Collins, the submission of *Atlas Shrugged* to a publisher. She was eager to have the issue settled before she completed the book. She was not willing to submit Galt's speech ahead of acceptance of the novel; Alan was to send out the manuscript up to but not including the speech.

By the terms of her contract with Bobbs-Merrill for *The Fountainhead,* Bobbs had the right to the first submission of her new novel. Ayn was determined that they would not again be her publisher; she could not forgive them for their handling of *The Fountainhead;* she was prepared to insist on terms to which they would not accede. But her proposed demands were unnecessary.

A few weeks after receiving the manuscript, Ross Baker, the company's New York representative, called Ayn to suggest that she and Alan Collins join him for dinner. "What is it you want to discuss?" Ayn asked. Baker replied, "The book is *much* too long. The editors and I have made a long list of possible cuts." "You may make an offer or not," Ayn said angrily. "I will *not* come to dinner and I will *not* discuss changes. The book is to be published *exactly as it is.*" "There are too many long speeches," Baker complained to Alan in a hurried telephone call —naming as an example a speech given by Francisco about the nature and meaning of money. He was naming one of the most powerful and effective speeches in the novel, which was later to be reprinted in journals and magazines and for private distribution across the country; it is aimed at those who say that money is the root of all evil, and upholds Ayn's view that money, as a tool of exchange, is the noble symbol, not of force nor of fraud, but of voluntary trade among men who produce. Baker concluded, "In its present form, I regret to say that the book is unsalable and unpublishable."

Discussing this event long after publication, Ayn chuckled gleefully. "I hope he remembers what he said. It was the history of *The Fountainhead* repeating itself."

Word flew through the publishing industry that Ayn's new novel was approaching completion and that she was free of her contract with Bobbs-Merrill. The phenomenal success story of *The Fountainhead* had become a publishing legend, and her new work had been awaited with intense anticipation. She no longer had to struggle to interest publishers in her work; instead, they courted *her,* with lunches, with telephone calls, with expressions of enthusiasm for *The Fountainhead.* Almost every major publisher approached Alan Collins to express interest in *Atlas Shrugged.*

Ayn's main concern was to find a publisher from whom she could expect, not necessarily agreement with her ideas—she knew that an innovator cannot expect that—but intellectual understanding and the courage to face the kind of antagonism her book inevitably would arouse. She made up a list of questions to keep in mind when she spoke to the publishers she was considering: Are they aggressive? Will they stand by a controversial book? What is their enthusiasm for publishing? Do they have initiative or are they routine-bound?

From among the inquiries, Ayn and Alan Collins selected four possibilities. McGraw-Hill, because "they wrote a very enthusiastic letter to Alan about the scope of the publicity campaign they would undertake, and because they were a big business house." Knopf, because "Alan had a great deal of confidence in Pat Knopf, who was just taking over the business from his parents." But Alan warned her that the senior Knopfs had "retired" several times, but had always returned; if it happened again, it would be a problem for her; they were difficult to deal with and he felt that they would not respond to her book as she wished. Viking, because Archie Ogden, who was no longer staff editor at a publishing house, had arranged with Viking that if he brought them a novel they wanted, he would edit it and would get a percentage of the profits. Ayn had never forgotten that Archie had risked his job for *The Fountainhead;* although she would not otherwise have considered Viking, she was eager to help him if she could—but not at the expense of *Atlas.*

The fourth contender was Random House. Hiram Haydn, editor-in-chief at Random House, had been an editor for Bobbs-Merrill; in those years he had lunched with Ayn at intervals to ask how her new novel was progressing; Ayn had liked him and felt she could deal with him. Haydn would later say, speaking of their meetings and of the power of Ayn's intellect: "Because of Ayn Rand, I have a foolproof method of judging honesty. If I introduce a friend to her, and they meet for a discussion, and the friend then tells me that their differences ended in a draw—I know he's a liar. If he tells me that their differences ended in his demonstrating the truth of his views—I know he's a hopeless, permanent, irredeemable liar."

In his posthumously published autobiography, *Words and Faces,* Haydn wrote: "I shall never forget (those words again, but true) my first meeting with Ayn. A short, squarish woman, with black hair cut in bangs and a Dutch bob. . . . Her eyes were as black as her hair, and piercing. We sat down for lunch at One Park Avenue, a place to which we were to return again and again because their eggs Benedict were good, and that was her invariable meal. I made one or two conventional remarks: she fixed me with those eyes and said, 'What are your premises?'

"Again and again, during the next decade, I was to hear that question—with anticipation when it was addressed to someone else, with discomfiture when to myself. For Ayn had built up a comprehensive systematic philosophy, which she calls Objectivism, and which, once you accept its first premises, is the most closely reasoned, rigorously logical and consistently interlocking world view and explanation since the great synthesis of Thomas Aquinas."

Now that Ayn was free of Bobbs, Haydn again began taking her to lunch for the purpose of selling her on Random House. "It was a benevolent joke on me," Ayn was to say. "For years I had considered Random House, next to Simon and Schuster, the worst possible place for my work; until the forties, when they published Whittaker Chambers's *Witness,* they were the most left-wing of all publishers." Despite Haydn's assurances that this was no longer the case, Ayn was hesitant. He asked that she and Alan Collins at least meet with the owners, Bennett Cerf and Donald Klopfer, so that she could judge for herself. "It's a fair request," Ayn said. "We'll meet for lunch."

The morning of the luncheon, everything seemed to go wrong. Ayn had an emergency dentist appointment; when she left the dentist's office, her jaw aching, it began raining heavily, and no cabs were to be found. She arrived at the restaurant feeling dutiful about the meeting and expecting nothing.

"It was the best and most exciting publisher's meeting I have ever had in my career," she later said.

"I liked Bennett and Donald immediately, they had such an open, active, intellectual attitude. They spoke as I would want publishers to speak—they faced ideas openly, they heard what I said, they were enthusiastic about my work, they answered all my questions straight. I explained my problem to them, that other publishers wanted a chance at the book, and that I had not decided to which of four publishers I should first submit. Bennett came up with a brilliant idea—and what I liked about him was the fact that he focused enough and had enough initiative to think on the spot and propose something. He proposed, in effect, a philosophical contest, by a method that at that time was daringly unprecedented in the publishing world. He proposed that, with their knowledge and consent, I should submit to all four publishers simultaneously, not for the purpose of getting cross-bidding on terms, but in order to learn their reactions, how they felt about the book, and how they proposed to handle it. By their answers, I could choose whom I wanted to deal with. . . . That he suggested such an idea told me that Bennett understood and took seriously exactly what I wanted. Alan and I said we would consider it and let them know.

"Another highlight of the luncheon was a statement by Donald. I had indicated only the general ideology of *Atlas,* that it was an extreme, uncompromising, moral defense of capitalism and presented a new philosophy. Donald's acumen startled me when he said, 'If it is a *moral* defense of capitalism, wouldn't it have to clash with the entire tradition of Judaeo-Christian ethics?' I had never heard anyone else observe the clash between capitalism and religion, and I was enormously pleased that he was so philosophical." Ayn did not ask him whether he agreed or disagreed with her position; what impressed her was that he had understood an issue which professional defenders of capitalism seemed unable to understand.

After the Random House luncheon, Ayn came home to talk about it ecstatically for several days. She was unbending in her condemnation of the bad, but when she discovered people or events that could elicit her positive response, she was as openly and happily enthusiastic as a child who has never been hurt, never been disappointed, never had cause for bitterness or suspicion.

Ayn and Alan Collins, with Archie Ogden, next met with Harold K. Guinzburg, the owner of Viking Press. "The whole tone, style and universe was totally different than Random House," Ayn reported. "The Viking people were uncomfortable discussing controversial issues, and when I mentioned Bennett's idea,

Guinzburg was very much against it; he said he had no personal objection to entering such a contest, but 'what would you really learn?—publishers will necessarily lie to you—they'll want the book and will say what you want to hear.' I'll remain naïve until I'm ninety, I'm sure, because that shocked me. He was cynically admitting his own lack of integrity. Then he explained how their editorial board functioned: major books are submitted to all eight editors, all of them read it and make suggestions to the writer. He was even saying it as an advantage, because, he said, 'If one or two editors said something was wrong, you wouldn't have to accept it; but if all eight said it, wouldn't you want to consider it?' I answered quietly, 'No, I wouldn't.' *He was saying that to the writer of* The Fountainhead."

The next luncheon was with Edward C. Aswell of McGraw-Hill—who had been one of Thomas Wolfe's editors. "That was the worst of the three lunches," Ayn reported. "He was cynical, bored, malevolent, as if nothing on earth were of any value or interest to him. He said, in an exhausted manner, that he didn't like the idea of the contest, because he'd have to go to all the trouble of reading the manuscript—and he might not get it. I knew it would be hopeless to try to deal with him."

At the final luncheon, Ayn met Pat Knopf. "He was very active and intellectual, he told me very intelligently and enthusiastically why he liked *The Fountainhead,* and controversy didn't seem to bother him. But he didn't make anywhere near as good an impression as the Random House men. . . . Perhaps there was a bit too much youthful enthusiasm—and he wasn't that young. . . . He was willing to accept the contest, but he said that his father was still officially head of the company, and would refuse—Alfred Knopf would consider it an insult to the Knopf imprint."

Ayn and Alan Collins returned to Collins's office to make their decision. But Ayn said that Bennett Cerf's idea had already worked, and that no actual contest was necessary. On the basis of his idea, she felt that she had the best test of Random House possible. "My mind was really made up at the first luncheon," she said. "If this is the campaign they staged to get me, they will be just as clever and active in selling my book."

Random House had been calling Alan Collins to ask if Ayn would accept the idea of the contest. She decided to stage the kind of dramatic scene she loved, and Alan got into the spirit of it. He made an appointment with Bennett, merely saying that he wanted to talk about the book; he did not mention that Ayn would be joining him. "When we entered Bennett's office," Ayn would report happily, "I said to him: 'You have the first, exclusive submission. The book is yours.' Bennett simply inclined his head silently for what seemed a full minute."

When Bennett, Donald Klopfer, and Hiram Haydn had read the manuscript, Bennett opened his next meeting with Ayn with the words: "It's a great book. Name your own terms."

"The whole atmosphere was wonderful and enthusiastic," Ayn said. "And the deal was completed the way Alan Greenspan told me Wall Street tycoons used to do it in the old days: in about five minutes. Alan Collins said we wanted a fifty-thousand-dollar advance—they said okay; he said we wanted a straight fifteen percent royalty, they said okay; Alan asked for a guaranteed first-edition printing—they said they'd print seventy-five or a hundred thousand with a minimum guaranteed advertising budget of twenty-five thousand dollars. There was no bargaining or bickering, it was settled just like that—in the spirit of an enormous celebration."

When the business part of their meeting ended, Ayn was told, to her delight, that when Bennett had finished reading the scene of the train ride on the John Galt Line, he ran out of his office and down the hall, waving the manuscript and shouting: "It's magnificent!" Donald Klopfer said that he had recently been flying over Detroit—and he'd suddenly felt glad that smoke was coming out of the factory chimneys, that the factories were still functioning. "They didn't pretend to be converted," Ayn said, "but they knew these were important ideas and they were very affected by the book. And Bennett was chortling about how they'd antagonize their neighbors." The Random House offices occupied one wing of a wonderful old Stanford White brownstone palazzo, across from St. Patrick's Cathedral; it had been built in 1885 as a private mansion, consisting of five buildings joined by a common courtyard. The other buildings were owned by the Catholic Church.

As Ayn and Alan Collins were leaving Random House, Hiram Haydn ran down the stairs after them to kiss Ayn and to say how much her decision meant to him. She asked, "Don't you want to hear all the details of how I arrived at my decision?" He answered: "I don't *care*—just so you did it!"

Later, Ayn met with Donald Klopfer—who had said that *Atlas* had caused him to change his mind about several issues—to ask him what those issues were. Ayn would always remember that "he said above all, what impressed him was the demonstration that industrial and business success depended on intelligence and ability. Before, he had felt faintly guilty when he was reproached for his success. After reading *Atlas,* he attended a party where someone was criticizing a famous doctor for charging high prices and being very rich—and Donald thought of *Atlas Shrugged* and suddenly said: 'And what's wrong with being rich, if he has earned it by ability?' "

In his posthumously published *At Random,* Bennett Cerf wrote about his first meeting with Ayn and the several years of their friendship. "I had heard of her philosophy, which I found absolutely horrifying. *The Fountainhead* was an absorbing story, nonetheless. . . . She had lunch with Hiram, Donald and me at the Ambassador Hotel, now unfortunately torn down, and asked us a lot of questions. I found myself liking her though I had not expected to. . . . She has piercing eyes that seem to look right through you and a wonderful way of pinning you to the wall. You can't make any loose statements to Ayn Rand; she hops on you and says, 'Let us examine your premises.' I am likely to shoot off my mouth occasionally and make statements that I don't quite mean or can't quite prove, and Ayn, again and again, would nail me. . . . Later on, after she came to Random House, she showed me a chart she had kept. She had visited about fifteen [sic] publishers, and when she got home she rated them on all the things they had said. I didn't realize, of course, that I was being examined this way, but I came out very high because I had been absolutely honest with her. I had said, 'I find your political philosophy abhorrent.' Nobody else had dared tell her this. I said, 'If we publish you, Miss Rand, nobody is going to try to censor you. You write anything you please, in fiction at least, and we'll publish it, whether or not we approve. . . .'

"Ayn and I became good friends. What I loved to do was trot her out for people who sneered at us for publishing her. Ayn would invariably charm them. For instance, Clifton Fadiman, who had snorted at the idea of our publishing Ayn Rand, sat talking with her until about three in the morning. George Axelrod, author of *The Seven Year Itch,* toward the end of a long, long evening at Ayn's, disappeared with her into another room and we couldn't get him to go home. Later he said, 'She knows me better after five hours than my analyst does after five years.' . . .

"Ayn's a very simple and modest woman. We were on our way to lunch in Radio City once, and as we passed one of those junk shops with all kinds of statues and knickknacks, she saw a little blue bracelet in the window, and like a twelve-year-old girl, Ayn said, 'Isn't that a beautiful bracelet!' So I went in and bought it for her. It cost exactly one dollar, but she was as happy as a child.

"She's so brilliant at expounding her theories! . . . People react violently to her iconoclastic statements. She's entirely against any religion. She thinks that strong, selfish people should prevail, and that, in reality, two percent of the population is supporting the other ninety-eight percent. . . . There's a lot in what she says."

Donald Klopfer, too, vividly recalled the initial luncheon with Ayn. He was to say, "Ayn *never* was reluctant to talk. At our first meeting, she talked about her book and her whole philosophy. She was a very difficult, very strange woman, but I liked her; she was *extremely* bright and she was fun to spar with, and fun to publish even if you disagreed, as I did, with almost everything she said. . . . We got along just fine. I respected her stubbornness, and her integrity by her own standards. We were very glad to be her publisher. She was one of the most interesting authors I've met in a very long career in publishing. A fascinating, strange, very strong woman."

After the frustrations and disappointments of her former dealings, it seemed to Ayn little short of a miracle that she had found publishers who believed in her work and seemed prepared to stand by her. In a note entitled "About the Author," which appears as a postscript at the back of *Atlas Shrugged,* she would pay Bennett Cerf and Donald Klopfer the highest tribute she had the power to offer: "I trust that no one will tell me that men such as I write about don't exist. That this book has been written—and published—is my proof that they do."

About eleven years earlier, in the first chapter of *Atlas,* she had written a description of Richard Halley's music, with the knowledge that she would repeat it verbatim in the last chapter. That description is the philosophical leitmotif of the novel; she knew that it would sound different the second time—that the same words would carry a greater meaning, a more specific conviction, a fuller reality, a deeper emotional power—and that the difference would tell a perceptive reader what it was that he had learned from the chapters between. Now, at last, she reached the day when she wrote that passage for the second time, in the opening paragraph of the novel's final sequence:

"It was a symphony of triumph. The notes flowed up, they spoke of rising and they were the rising itself, they were the essence and the form of upward motion, they seemed to embody every human act and thought that had ascent as its motive. It was a sunburst of triumph, breaking out of hiding and spreading open. It had the freedom of release and the tension of purpose. It swept space clean and left nothing but the joy of an unobstructed effort. Only a faint echo within the sounds spoke of that from which the music had escaped, but spoke in laughing astonishment at the discovery that there was no ugliness or pain, and there never had had to be. It was the song of an immense deliverance."

She had come out of the most brutal dictatorship in history, she had risen past years of poverty, of struggle, of intellectual isolation, she had moved by the power of her knowledge of man and of life as they could be, by the image of John Galt and of his world—and now she had given to that world and to the sense of life from which it came the reality of a superlative artistic projection. And she had named the motive power of that world when she said: "My philosophy, in essence, is the concept of man as a heroic being, with his own happiness as the moral purpose of his life, with productive achievement as his noblest activity, and reason as his only absolute."

As she had written in the novel: "To hold an unchanging youth is to reach, at the end, the vision with which one started."

On an evening in March 1957, she wrote on the last page of her manuscript:

" 'The road is cleared,' said Galt. 'We are going back to the world.'

"He raised his hand and over the desolate earth he traced in space the sign of the dollar."

Later, she could remember nothing of that evening, except that she stood up from her desk, walked out of her study in a state of dazed numbness and exaltation, and handed Frank the last page of her manuscript to let him see the words: "The End."

Chapter Twenty-five

The end of *Atlas Shrugged* marked a new beginning for Ayn. The work of her lifetime was completed, and she could relax, ravenously gulp down the sleep she had been starved for, and spend her waking hours looking over the manuscript and "just gloating." She was peacefully happy with every aspect of the novel she had created. Even the title delighted her. Originally, she had tentatively named the book: *The Strike*. But she had soon realized that that title gave away the mystery; and when a friend pointed out that it might be interpreted as a book about labor unions, she had scrapped it instantly. Briefly, she had considered *The Prime Mover*, a concept taken from Aristotle, but had decided that that was too philosophical and nonliterary a title. "Atlas Shrugged" had initially been a chapter title, but Frank had suggested that she use it for the title of the book. She had agreed at once: it captured for her the spirit and the whole meaning of the novel.

One sentence of the final manuscript is in Frank's handwriting. Ayn had found herself unable to formulate Francisco's farewell message to the world after he blows up d'Anconia Copper and disappears. The message had to contain—in the briefest possible form and in a style characteristic of Francisco—the essence of the motive behind his action. After many unsuccessful attempts, she explained her problem to Frank. "You mean," he asked, "that it should be something like 'Brother, you asked for it?'" "Not *like* it!" she cried, delighted. "That's it!" She handed him her pen. "It's your sentence," she said. "You write it."

As Random House moved toward its publication date of October 1957, it was time for Ayn to plunge into the editing and copy editing of the manuscript. But there was to be no editing. Ayn would allow no changes. In *At Random*, Bennett Cerf wrote ". . . arguing with her was like running your head against a stone wall. I remember when *Atlas Shrugged* was being edited by Hiram Haydn. The hero, John Galt, makes a speech that lasts about thirty-eight pages [Bennett was mistaken; it lasts sixty pages.] . . . but Hiram couldn't get her to cut a word. I very angrily said to him, 'You're some editor. Send her in to me. I'll fix it in no time.' So when Ayn came in and sat down, looking at me with those piercing eyes, I said, 'Ayn, nobody's going to read that. You've said it all three or four times before, and it's thirty-odd pages long. You've got to cut it.' She looked at me calmly and said, 'Would you cut the Bible?' So I gave up." The report that circulated in the publishing industry was that Bennett had replied, "Well, it would make more money!"

Ayn has often been criticized for refusing to allow any of her work to be edited. But in fact, in her earlier work, she had been amenable to editing; George Abbott had suggested a number of changes in her play, *The Unconquered,* to which she had acceded; and she had found Archie Ogden's suggestions for cuts in *The Fountainhead* acceptable and helpful. It was only now, with *Atlas Shrugged,* convinced of her own literary professionalism and convinced that she had worked long enough and hard enough to be certain that the work matched her intention, that she would not entertain suggestions for changes.

In his *Words and Faces,* Hiram Haydn was to write that although his contract with Random House stipulated that he was to receive a commission on books he brought in, Bennett Cerf and Donald Klopfer asked him, with some hesitancy, if he would forgo his usual commission for *Atlas;* it would be a very long, high-priced novel and expensive to produce. "I agreed immediately. I had felt all along some uneasiness of conscience. Ayn's philosophy, replete with social and political consequences, troubled me. Left to myself, I would not have published that book. Yet I had owed it to the partners to steer Ayn to them if I could, for she was a publishing catch, with 'best seller' stamped all over her. . . . Moreover, I believed that a publisher should publish books with all sorts of political and social coloration. Only I didn't want personally to make money on one so contrary to my own convictions. Yet again, I was willing to act as her editor for Random House. So, in a muddled way, I split my allegiance.

"How she would have laughed had she known the welter of contradictory reactions I was experiencing! And how well indeed I illustrated her concept of the softheaded, ambivalent, tortured liberal!"

Ayn would not have laughed had she known that her editor, left to himself, would not have published her book. Nor would she have laughed at his statement that: "In her novels, she wedded her ideas to a first-rate narrative skill; the pace of the action was usually fast, and she was proficient at suspense and the melodramatic, spectacular scene. But her style was drab, and although I respected her philosophy as one kind of arid intellectual triumph, a tour de force that commanded admiration even though she based it on an utterly false (as I see it) central premise—although that was how I felt in measured moments, there were times when I conceded that the world I lived in was most probably right, and she really was a crackpot, though of a noble sort.

"Even now I can't write about Ayn Rand without feeling upset, unhappy with myself. I know of no other relation with an author in which I played such shamefaced ball, never being wholly for or against her, never saying right out all the things I believed about her book or her ideas or life in general."

Although Haydn did not tell her his actual views, Ayn was aware of the deep intellectual gulf between them, and indignant at the editorial changes he suggested. After many futile sessions, recognizing that *Atlas Shrugged* was not to be edited, Haydn turned the manuscript over to Bertha Krantz, then Random House's chief copy editor and assistant managing editor.

Bertha Krantz found that copy-editing *Atlas Shrugged* was the single most difficult, nerve-racking assignment of her professional life: "Ayn and I worked together daily for several months. We were dealing with a manuscript that was more than a thousand pages long—and there were discussions about every comma, every semicolon, every word I questioned. Everything had to be explained to her in painstaking detail and, according to her philosophy, had to be *rational.* But I must say that she always listened to me, and when she felt I was 'right,' she'd accept my explanations, complimenting me on my reasonableness. I think the worst thing I had to contend with was that there was never a light moment—laughter, doing or saying something just for fun seemed to have no place at all in her life. I found that very sad."

Nevertheless, the two became friendly enough to lunch together occasionally, and Ayn even invited Bertha to her home. Gradually, Bertha "began to see that there was no reason to be afraid of her—those piercing eyes and stern manner had really frightened me at first—and our relationship got to be fairly easy. She could be very kind: she was concerned that my apartment was in what she considered an unsafe area, and she really worried that I traveled on the subway, thought it was dangerous. . . .

"She was such a brilliant woman, and to listen to her, one could be convinced that she had no fears, no contradictions. But we live every day, we live with the little things of life; once when I was at her home, I noticed that she almost boiled the dishes when she washed them; and she admitted that she was deathly afraid of germs. And, of course, she scoffed at 'superstition,' but I remember that when I commented on a little gold watch she always wore, she said she had found it in Los Angeles years ago, and that it was her good-luck watch. And I saw that she did indeed have contradictions—Ayn Rand believing in a good-luck charm! But I admired and respected her, and I never for a moment doubted the sincerity of her convictions.

"I made it clear to her that I could never think her way, and she seemed to accept it. But there was still an element of her trying to convert me. It seemed not to be second nature with her; it was *first* nature.

"In the end, I began to feel somewhat sorry for her. As I said, laughter did not come easily to her, and she seemed to have no capacity for simple enjoyment. Everything had to be carefully considered, analyzed—again, had to be *rational.* And her view of things was so limited. We'd be walking along somewhere, and she never 'saw' the sky or the trees or even any of the people: her attention seemed to be given only to the stone and glass buildings. . . . I went with her to a lecture she delivered at Columbia University, and I was struck by the number of students who obviously worshipped her; it had to be terribly hard to be regarded as an idol and to have to sustain that image to the world.

"But what I say reflects only my reactions. Certainly Ayn Rand and her philosophy represented—still represents—something very important to a lot of people."

Ayn was very excited when Bennett Cerf took the unprecedented step of asking her to speak about her book at a conference of the Random House salesmen. The meeting delighted her: the atmosphere was relaxed and cheerful, and the salesmen were full of enthusiasm for *Atlas.* One of them, concerned about how he would communicate her philosophy to book sellers, asked her jokingly: "Miss Rand—could you give the essence of your philosophy while standing on one foot?" She did. She said: "Metaphysics—objective reality; Epistemology—reason; Ethics—self-interest; Politics—capitalism."

During the months of preparation for the publication of *Atlas Shrugged,* Ayn was well aware that she could not expect the rest of the world to react to the novel as her young friends reacted. "I know that I am challenging the cultural tradition of two and a half thousand years," she said. She was ruefully amused when Leonard Peikoff, the youngest of the collective, seemed to hope that within a few years of publication, America would return to complete political freedom and a laissez-faire economy. "That's not how things happen, or can possibly happen," she insisted. "I *will* have an influence—*Atlas* will have an influence—but it will be a very slow process. We won't begin to see its concrete results in action for many years. *I* may not fully see them at all."

On an evening a few days before publication, Ayn, Frank, Nathaniel, and I—remembering that Random House always placed featured new books in its small window on Madison Avenue—drove to Random House to see if *Atlas* was there. We got out of the car and hurried to the window. *Atlas was* there, it was the only book in the window. I grinned, and, quite involuntarily, pointed at the colorful jacket that had been designed by Frank, and said: "That's us!" It was one of the few times I ever saw Ayn roar with delighted laughter.

On the back of the jacket was a photograph of Ayn taken by Phyllis Cerf, Bennett's wife: Ayn sits in front of a window with a view of New York, her head slightly raised, her expression cheerful, serene, intent, her large eyes looking upward. On a copy of that picture which she gave to Nathaniel and me, the inscription reads—in a phrase from Galt's words to Rearden and Francisco, to which she added the words in parentheses:—"To Nathan and Barbara—my first friends, my fellow-fighters, my fellow-out-casts (and fellow winners), in whose name and honor I speak—Ayn."

In my copy of *Atlas Shrugged,* she wrote a still more personal message: "To Barbara—for that sense of life which is mine and yours—for starting with the same values and accepting nothing less—to carry on my battle, my universe and *all* my values—Ayn." The underscoring of "all" was not accidental; it referred to Nathaniel.

The dedication page of the novel read: "To Frank O'Connor and Nathaniel Branden."

Shortly before publication, the collective decided to give a celebration surprise party for Ayn. The Cerfs were invited, the Klopfers, the Haydns, the Ogdens, the Collinses—all the people who had a professional part in bringing out *Atlas*. A private room at the Plaza Hotel was engaged, which Frank agreed to decorate with his exquisite floral arrangements, invitations were sent out with the explanation that Ayn was to know nothing about it, and an elaborate banquet, consisting of Ayn's favorite dishes, was ordered. Frank was to tell Ayn that he wanted to take her to a special dinner, just for the two of them, and that she was to dress accordingly.

When Ayn and Frank arrived at the banquet room, the guests shouted "Surprise!" and hurried to greet and congratulate her. Her first words were an angry: "I do *not* approve of surprises." The friends crowding around her had been talking and laughing; but the laughter stopped; it was evident that her words were not a startled reaction of the moment, that she was truly indignant. She sat grimly all through dinner, through the strained efforts at conversation and the toasts to her, and through Bennett Cerf's redoubled efforts—with the warmth and charm that was so delightful a part of his personality—to melt her chilly disapproval. Bennett was partly successful; Ayn began to join in the conversation—although she continued to say that she disliked surprises and should have been informed of the party in advance.

One touch that almost—but not quite—saved the evening was that Alan Collins and Bennett Cerf distributed packages of cigarettes they had had made, with a bright gold dollar sign printed on each cigarette; on the front of the packages, in gold lettering over the Random House insignia, were the words: WHO IS JOHN GALT? THEY KNOW AT RANDOM HOUSE." In *Atlas,* these cigarettes are manufactured in Galt's Gulch, with the dollar sign as the symbol of the trader. Ayn smoked several of the cigarettes—she had always been a heavy smoker— and saved the rest. As she puffed away happily, one saw again the childlike charm in the woman who a moment ago had been so sternly disapproving; she could scarcely believe that Bennett and Alan had taken the trouble to arrange something for the sole purpose of giving her personal pleasure.

In retrospect, it might have been predicted that a surprise party would not please Ayn, that she could not cope with the unexpected. Her reaction that evening seemed relevant to her lack of humor: she could not, would not, move abruptly from one context to another. She had expected a dinner alone with Frank; when the nature of the evening suddenly switched, she could not flow with the change of plans—and, typically, she reacted with anger and a touch of fear. It was as if she felt a painful pressure to force her mind to abandon its straight-line, single-track functioning and to make a mental leap not only to another context, but worse, to a context imposed upon her by other people.

When the first Random House advertisements for *Atlas* began to appear, as part of one of the most major and aggressive advertising-promotion campaigns in the firm's history—Ayn felt that they were essentially meaningless, and had her first quarrel with Bennett. But she was pleased when he ran an advertisement that she and Nathaniel had worked out together; it consisted of a dramatic portrait of Frank, with the caption "This is John Galt—who said he would stop the motor of the world—*and did.* Meet him in *Atlas Shrugged.*"

Atlas Shrugged was published on October 10, 1957.

And then it was over—over forever in Ayn's life—that happy period of excitement, and hope, and expectation. And with it seemed to go almost the last of her fragile capacity to live in reality.

The reviews of *We the Living* had been bad. The reviews of *The Fountainhead* had been worse. The reviews of *Atlas Shrugged* were savage. Incredibly, once again Granville Hicks came into Ayn's life: it was to Hicks that the New York *Times* gave the job of reviewing *Atlas.* "This Gargantuan book comes among us as a demonstrative rather than as a literary work," he wrote. "It seems an expression of the author's determination to crush the enemies of truth—her truth, of course—as a battering ram demolishes the walls of a hostile city. . . . Not in any literary sense a serious novel. . . . Loudly as Miss Rand proclaims her love of life, it seems clear that the book is written out of hate. . . ."

Patricia Donegan wrote in *The Commonweal:* "*Atlas Shrugged* is a cumbersome, lumbering vehicle"—its heroes "all subscribe merrily to the theory that morality lies in taking what one is capable of getting. . . . Miss Rand is all for the survival of the fittest, dog-eat-dog, *sauve qui peut* and other such bracing philosophies. . . . The destruction of the weak to the advantage of the strong is applauded . . . an outpouring of hate."

In the Los Angeles *Times,* Robert R. Kirsch wrote: "It would be hard to find such a display of grotesque eccentricity outside an asylum. . . . The reader looks on with the amazement of one who has been given access to another's nightmare. . . . Galt is really arguing for a dictatorship."

"Ayn Rand's philosophy is nearly perfect in its immorality," wrote Gore Vidal. Other reviewers wrote that the philosophy of *Atlas* "makes well-poisoning seem like one of the kindlier arts"—that it is "crack-brained ratiocination"—that it is "a pitiful exercise in something akin to paranoia"—that as a novel it is "execrable claptrap"—that it is "longer than life and twice as preposterous." Although many critics denounced Ayn for specifically literary incompetence, the reader could not judge the authenticity of such accusations, since they so often were combined with outrage at her philosophy.

The worst review of all appeared in William Buckley's conservative *National Review.* It was written by Whittaker Chambers, former Communist spy who reembraced religion. It would be difficult to find a reviewer whose intellectual history was more representative of the villains of *Atlas Shrugged*—the villains of "faith and force"—and more certain to be antagonized by its philosophy. The review was headlined: BIG SISTER IS WATCHING YOU. "The Dollar Sign is not merely provocative," Chambers wrote, "more importantly, it is meant to seal the fact that mankind is ready to submit abjectly to an elite of technocrats, and their accessories, in a New Order. . . . It is a forthright philosophic materialism. Upperclassmen might incline to sniff and say that the author has, with vast effort, contrived a simple materialist system, one, intellectually, at about the stage of the oxcart, though without mastering the principle of the wheel. . . . Systems of philosophical materialism, so long as they merely circle outside this world's atmosphere, matter little to most of us. The trouble is that they keep coming down to earth. It is when a system of materialist ideas presumes to give positive answers to real problems of our real life that mischief starts . . . a temptation sets in to let some species of Big Brother solve and supervise them. . . . Miss Rand calls in a Big Brother of her own . . . she plumps for a technocratic elite. . . . And in reality, too, by contrast with fiction, this can only head into a dictatorship. . . . From almost any page of *Atlas Shrugged,* a voice can be heard, from painful necessity, commanding: 'To a gas chamber—go!' "

It is astonishing that some attackers of Ayn's philosophy accused her of materialism and continue to do so—she, who wrote of the glory and magnificent achievements of the human spirit—as if, without the hypothesis of a divine creator, there can be no spirit, no values, no morality; and that they accused of lusting for dictatorship a thinker who places, at the very heart of her moral and political philosophy, the total rejection of force. Galt states: "Whatever may be open to disagreement, there is one act of evil that may not, the act that no man may commit against others and no man may sanction or forgive. So long as men desire to live together, no man may *initiate*—do you hear me? no man may *start* —the use of physical force against others. . . . Do not open your mouth to tell me that your mind has convinced you of your right to force my mind. Force and mind are opposites; morality ends where a gun begins. . . . It is only in retaliation that force may be used and only against the man who starts its use."

Whittaker Chambers's review began the now famous vendetta against Ayn and *Atlas Shrugged* by *National Review*—most particularly on the grounds of her opposition to religious faith—that has lasted to this day. In the pages of his magazine, William Buckley has attacked the "desiccated philosophy" of *Atlas Shrugged* and has written, "All that needed to be said about it had already been said in the Sermon on the Mount." He attacked again in both of the two newspaper columns he wrote about Ayn and her ideas immediately following her death, denouncing "the essential aridity of Miss Rand's philosophy" and quoting Chambers's references to *Atlas Shrugged*'s "tone of over-riding arrogance . . . its shrillness . . . its dogmatism."

Many years after the Whittaker Chambers review appeared, William Buckley was asked why he chose Chambers to review *Atlas* for *National Review*. "He volunteered," Buckley insisted. "He had read the first one hundred pages and had said that it was off to a wonderful narrative start, and he exclaimed over how thoroughly she knew her material. . . . I was in Europe when the review came out, so I didn't see it before it was published."

Asked if the review was representative of his own opinion, Buckley said, *"I never read the book* [italics mine]. When I read the review of it and saw the length of the book, I never picked it up. I *think* I read all her other novels. I didn't read her philosophy books. . . . One of these days I'll probably get around to reading *Atlas Shrugged."*

Despite the furor of negative reviews, many reviews were highly, often ecstatically, favorable. Critic John Chamberlain wrote that *Atlas Shrugged* was "directed toward the creation of an entirely new mental and moral force in the world." Ruth Alexander, in the New York *Mirror,* wrote that "Ayn Rand is destined to rank in history as the outstanding novelist and profound philosopher of the twentieth century." Other critics praised her striking narrative power, her skill at the creation of a complex and intricate plot, the breathtaking suspense which carries the reader headlong through the book's eleven hundred and sixty-eight pages. But, as with her earlier work, most of the rave reviews were published in papers and magazines outside of New York City.

The sales began slowly—not as slowly as *The Fountainhead,* but not as Random House had expected. Bennett Cerf wrote in *At Random,* "By the time we published *[Atlas],* we had an enormous advance sale. It was her first novel since *The Fountainhead* and we printed a hundred thousand copies, knowing there would be tremendous interest in it. Then the reviews came out. The critics were hostile, as they always were to Ayn Rand, and the sale was badly crimped for a while. We thought it was going to be a failure."

In an effort to publicize the novel, Ayn agreed to an interview with Mike Wallace, on his New York television show, "Night Beat," the hard-driving program that began his rise to prominence. They liked each other immediately, and were to visit together on a number of occasions over the following years. "She was perfect grist for the mill of 'Night Beat,' " Mike later said. "She voiced provocative opinions, she was anti-establishment and utterly unexpected, with a kind of close reasoning and a clarity that one had to admire; it was a remarkable interview. And the calls and letters that poured in about it shook the rafters."

Mike smiled ruefully as he spoke of sending his young staff of three for pre-interview talks with Ayn. "They all fell in love with her!" he said. "And they made life pretty difficult on the show at times, demanding an adherence to Ayn's ideas that I couldn't possibly give. . . . I liked to look at Ayn, her hair in the same kind of Dutch cut that I had as a small boy. She had such sparkling eyes and an extraordinary texture to her accent; and when she talked to you, she *really* talked to you, she *cared* about talking to you. She was fascinating."

As always in Ayn's professional career, it was predominantly word of mouth that caused the sagging sales of her novel to pick up—then to soar—then to skyrocket through printing after printing and edition after edition and year after year. Speaking of the success of *Atlas,* Bennett Cerf later remarked, "In all my years of publishing, I've never seen anything like it. To break through against such enormous opposition!" Its history is still more phenomenal than that of *The Fountainhead;* it has repeated the saga of *The Fountainhead,* but on a wider scale and with a more profound impact. By 1984, it had sold more than five million copies, and had been printed in most of the major languages of the world. In 1963, New American Library brought out a paperback edition which made publishing history; because of its length, NAL took the risk of pricing it above the top mass-market paperback price of fifty cents; they priced it at ninety-five cents.[1] Paperback sales zoomed skyward at once. Today, more than twenty million copies of Ayn's books have been sold; without advertising, the novels continue to sell at the rate of over three hundred thousand copies a year —more than the equivalent of new bestsellers. Like *The Fountainhead, Atlas Shrugged* is now a modern classic.

Each reader of *Atlas Shrugged* finds for himself, according to his own standards and judgment, its virtues and its flaws. Many among even its most admiring readers have found a major shortcoming in the characterization of the novel's hero, John Galt: despite his epic grandeur of intellect and imagination, he is, in the end, a shadowy, unknowable abstraction, he is the wholly cerebral man, the man whose passions we deduce but never experience. Another shortcoming has been found in a similar deep emotional remoteness in *all* the major characters, whose conversations, even in their most intimate moments, are predominantly without authentic intimacy, are philosophical presentations and debates; their minds touch, their bodies embrace, but their souls remain aloof, hidden in some unseen spiritual haven. Another—in the often bewildering severity of the moral judgments pronounced by its heroes and heroine, their blistering contempt for the world, their withering dismissal of lesser minds and less exalted goals. Another—in the faint sado-masochistic overtones of its love scenes, the troubling violence of the sexual encounters. Another—in the novel's often pedantic quality, its overdetailed spelling out of each new idea and new concept, with the resultant loss, in such passages, of literary spontaneity.

Necessarily, the novel's shortcomings—and its virtues—reflect its author's personality and psychology.

Like her characters, Ayn, too, was damaged by her rejection of the emotional and intuitive aspects of her nature, by her indifference and obliviousness to her deepest emotional needs, as she, like Galt, became increasingly a rigidly cerebral being, cut off from and unable to utilize the deep wells of knowledge contained in the noncerebral levels of her mind. As the years were passing, it was particularly the "feminine" aspects of her nature that she turned her back on. Increasingly, the once rejected child—rejected by her beloved father, who responded only to her intellectual qualities, rejected by her mother as socially inadequate,

[1] Truman Talley, then at New American Library with publisher Victor Weybright, has said, "When Victor was negotiating for the paperback rights of *Atlas Shrugged,* he felt that the novel would have to be cut, because he couldn't price it for more than fifty cents. Ayn Rand refused to cut it, and negotiations ceased. A year later, Victor agreed to do it at ninety-five cents—and even then it had to be printed in '8-point eyestrain.' "

rejected by young men, who chose prettier girls as the objects of their romantic interest, rejected by Leo, who won her with a single arrogant smile and left her bleeding and bereft—the child who had suffered from the rejection more than she ever permitted herself to recognize—was struggling to disallow her need for intimacy, for love, for comfort, for solace, for authentic emotional closeness in her human relationships, for the joy of a man's strong, protective arms. She was struggling to do it despite—or, perhaps, because of—her marriage and her love affair.

Philosophically, Ayn defined a woman's love as surrender. But her inability to make peace with her feminine needs had led to a conflict in her romantic life that never left her: the conflict between, on the one hand, her terror of surrender, a surrender that could bring in its wake the agony and humiliation born of her love of her father and of Leo, her fear of recognizing a will and a strength greater than her own, her horror at the possibility of any loss of her independence—and, on the other hand, her need, both passionate and timid, to find in a man the courage, the will, and the strength that would bring her helplessly to her knees. In her novels, that conflict took the form of a romanticized sexual violence. She had said, discussing Roark and Dominique, that theirs was to be the ideal romance, "so of course it had to start with violent antagonism." That the "of course" seemed self-evident to her was not a matter of abstract philosophy or of psychological theorizing, but of the deep division within her: in order for *her* to surrender, she needed to feel, like Dominique, like Dagny, that she was helpless in the power of a hero of overwhelming dominance and will. Only thus could she avoid feeling self-contempt for her feminine instincts.

But *Atlas Shrugged* is a great work of art—not merely in the grandeur and sweep of its story, the extraordinary power and originality of its plot—not merely in the inspirational quality of its heroes and heroine, the "command to rise" which they embody—not merely in its integration of complex, ingenious events with still more complex and stunning philosophical ideas—but most of all in the breathtaking intellectual audacity of what it attempts and encompasses.

As in *The Fountainhead*, Ayn Rand was presenting new philosophical ideas and concretizing them in the lives and actions of men. But as she once said, *"The Fountainhead* was only a prologue to *Atlas Shrugged."* In *Atlas,* she was attempting what no other philosopher and no other novelist had dreamed of: to present the *total of a self-consistent philosophical system*—a system and a world view that embraced metaphysics, epistemology, morality, politics, economics, and aesthetics, that included such issues as the meaning of free will—the relationship between mind and body—the nature of universals—the law of identity as the bridge between metaphysics and epistemology—the derivation of "ought" from "is"—the distinction between errors of knowledge and breaches of morality—the psychology of sex—the nature of logic—the spiritual meaning of money —the relationship between happiness and moral values—the creative man's attitude toward pain—the psychology of the secondhanders and why they hate the creators—the meaning of charity—the social conditions necessary for material production—the industrialists as exponents of man's creative ability. And she was doing it by *dramatizing and demonstrating each complex concept as it related to and affected men's life on earth,* she was concretizing the meaning of each concept in human action, in reality, as it led men to joy or tragedy, to achievement or parasitism, to triumph or defeat. She was doing it not in the dry and scholarly form of a treatise, but by uniting the cool, mathematical methodology of the philosopher with the novelist's passionate, imaginative projections through theme, style, characterization, and plot.

As with *The Fountainhead,* mail from the readers of *Atlas* began to pour in like a torrent which has continued to the present day. Hundreds, then thousands, of letters were written to Ayn, expressing enthusiasm for her achievement and asking philosophical questions, as she began attracting an ever growing following.

Within little more than a year after publication, Ayn was on her way to world fame, she was becoming wealthy, she was passionately admired by many thousands of devoted readers. She had written the novel she had been moving toward all of her life. She had achieved all the dreams of her childhood—and all the dreams of her adult life.

It was then that Ayn began sinking into a profound, terrible depression. It was a depression that would last almost without abatement for more than two long years. Her mood returned to what it had been when she was working on Galt's speech: tense, irritable, demanding, with violent outbursts of rage and bitterness. During some part of nearly every day, she wept in pain and frustration. Her agonizing physical tension returned, and the severe, debilitating pains in her shoulders and back. Her energy dissipated; she seemed to drag herself from assignment to assignment without interest or motivation. She had always played solitaire as a means of occupying herself when she was blocked on the writing of a passage or a scene; now, she sat at her desk daily, playing game after game; she did not read, she did not write, she was scarcely willing to talk. The life seemed to be draining out of her body and spirit in slow, anguished drops. She was gradually running down, like a mighty engine losing the fuel that is its life's blood.

It was not the bad reviews, she said. "I had told Bennett not to expect a single good review. If there were any, fine, but we couldn't count on it—although I did think I'd get more intelligent smears, I didn't expect them to be such abysmal, stupid hooliganism, to contain such self-contradictions and such total distortions of what I'd said." It was not the outpouring of hatred directed against her, she said. It was not the initial slow sales of *Atlas.* It was that there was no one to object to the attacks, no one to oppose them, no one with a public name, a public reputation, a public voice, to speak for her in that world which was villifying her, to defend her, to fight for her, to name the nature and the stature of her accomplishment. Ayn had never doubted her own uniqueness as novelist and as thinker. Her unwavering belief in the value of her work had always before protected her in the face of disappointments and attacks; now, it became her enemy. Since her achievement was beyond question, what was wrong with a world in which there was no one of stature to announce it from the rooftops?

"The whole state of the culture suddenly appears much worse then I had ever imagined," she said. "I no longer know to whom I'm addressing myself when I write. I no longer know where are the intelligences to which I've *always* addressed myself. I feel paralyzed by disgust and contempt. You can fight evil, but contempt is the most terrible feeling . . . you feel you are fighting lice, in a vacuum. And if I feel contempt for the whole culture—if it feels like I'm living in the last days of the Roman Empire—then what sense does it make to continue writing?"

Unfortunately, in a respect quite apart from its philosophical or literary content, *Atlas* inevitably antagonized the very group among which Ayn had expected to find the voices to speak for her: the intellectuals. Throughout the novel, her worst denunciations and the worst villainy are reserved precisely for modern intellectuals. "The parasites of subsidized classrooms," Galt calls them, echoing themes dotted throughout the story—"hatred-eaten mystics"—"professional cannibals"—the men of "evasive eyes and snarling words." It was not an attitude likely to cause intellectuals to rise to her defense. And, as is evident in the reviews, despite the shocking injustice of the "big brother" accusations, many readers were grasping or at least sensing a discrepancy between Ayn's steadfast political convictions and the authoritarianism of personality, the dogmatic conviction that only she possessed the truth, that had been growing in her over the years and had become apparent in her work. Some of these readers, not recognizing that the authoritarianism was present in the writer rather than in the philosophy, hurled their accusations at the wrong target.

But more appeared to be involved in Ayn's state of mind than she understood. Quite simply, she was physically, emotionally, and intellectually exhausted from the savagely intensive effort which had lasted, from the first idea of the novel, through fourteen years. All her life, she had fed her immense energy into her work; she had no reserves left with which to fight another battle.

Still more relevant was the fact that she had completed her life's work. She had at last, to her full satisfaction, created the ideal man, the figure who had been the source of her decision to be a novelist. Her motivation to write fiction, which had always been central to her sense of identity and had carried her through every day of her fifty-three years—was gone. All at once, fiction ceased to interest or attract her. She had done what she had set out to do, and now there seemed nothing worth doing. She could not conceive of a hero greater than John Galt, and she had no wish merely to present variations on Galt. She had written *Atlas Shrugged* too young. The motor of her life was gone, and suddenly, shockingly, she felt herself drifting without rudder or direction or purpose.

Her emotional reaction to the completion of her goal was mixed: she was desperately unhappy at the prospect of a future without purpose—but she was simultaneously deeply fulfilled. "I had no more inspiration for fiction," she later said, commenting on the years of depression. "Fiction, to me, *is Atlas Shrugged.*

My mission was done. . . . Until *Atlas* was completed, I always felt an enormous tension, the drive of a central purpose. My loafing so much during the years after *Atlas* was malevolent in that I felt desperate about the state of the world, I could not decide what to do with my life nor how to bear going around despising everybody—yet often, alone in my study, it *was* Atlantis, I'd sit at my desk in happy contemplation, with the feeling of complete peace. While I was working on *Atlas,* I felt I didn't care if a bomb dropped, just so long as I could finish this book. But after *Atlas* I was no longer pressured, my lifelong assignment was over, and I felt as if my time from then on was a gift."

In the black agony of depression, Ayn turned to Nathaniel for help. Frank suffered with her and for her, but he could not deal with the issues that were tormenting her. He would listen to her for hours as she railed bitterly against the irrationality of the world, shake his head in sympathy—and then escape to his painting. Her anguish became an increasingly heavy burden for Nathaniel, as she began leaning on him even more than before. All at once, his teacher, his mentor, his lover, was in agony, and it was *his* job to find a solution for the woman who had always been the source of so much of his own understanding.

For more than two years, Nathaniel spent hours each day in telephone conversation with Ayn, and two or three evenings each week talking with her in an attempt to motivate her once again, struggling to be her psychologist and teacher. He did not see the world as the bleak, irrational place that Ayn now considered it to be, and he searched desperately for reasons to give her hope, reasons to make her feel she was not living in the last days of the Roman Empire, reasons to convince her that there was more in the world around her than blank and corrupt mindlessness. His task was an almost impossible one. Ayn's dark view of the world, although now sharply intensified, was not new in her psychology; it had been present through most of her life, lurking out of sight for years at a time, but still present underground as if it awaited the events that would evoke it.

One must wonder if Ayn's suffering was not in part the price she paid, granted other elements in her psyche, for her astonishing intellectual powers. Historically, it is a price that men and women of vast intelligence have often paid. Such men and women stand alone, cut off from the world by a sense of distance from other people that is not an illness and cannot be cured. With the firsthand, blinding vision of the creator, they endure the loneliness of seeing farther and more clearly than others see, of understanding what others do not understand, of achieving what others cannot achieve, of moving forward with a dedication and tenacity that others cannot grasp. They feel invisible to the world—and in many respects they *are* invisible, as is every creative genius. For Ayn, the use of her mind, the solving of the most complex of problems, was an effortless, joyous activity, it was the sole unchanging and permanent source of happiness in her life. To think, to see, to understand, to know, seemed to her as simple and uncomplicated as drawing breath; and the conclusions she reached seemed as clear and evident as the need to draw those breaths. Why, then, did others not grasp what was so easy to grasp? Why did they not perceive what was so patently apparent? Why did they not understand what was so simple to understand? Why did they not know what she knew with such blazing clarity?

Ayn's depression brought to an end, with only a few unplanned exceptions, her sexual relationship with Nathaniel. She did not intend the ending to be permanent, she told him. She would recover emotionally, she knew she would recover; but she could not say how long it would take. And while she felt as she did, while her capacity for emotion seemed dead inside her, she was not able to cope with a love affair, she had nothing to give or to want. Her love for Nathaniel had not died, but her whole life, she said, was "on hold," and their romance must also be on hold. Nathaniel agreed without argument—and with some measure of relief. Just as Ayn could not cope with a love affair in her present state, he could not simultaneously be psychologist, the strong shoulder on which she leaned, the man who listened, day after day and month after month, to the worst of her anguished denunciations of the world—and an ardent, romantic lover.

The strain of dealing with Ayn's depression took its toll on Nathaniel. He had always been arrogant and judgmental in his dealings with people. Now, attempting to live his own life while finding for Ayn a reason to live, constantly tense, pressured by the weight of responsibilities to Ayn, he was more coldly arrogant and demanding than ever before. Within Ayn's circle of friends, widened since the inception of the collective, denunciation followed denunciation and moral recrimination followed moral recrimination—always buttressed and validated by the sanction of Ayn Rand, and often occurring in her presence and at her insistence as she became once more the avenging angel she had been during the writing of Galt's speech. Ayn's young friends had been disarmed in advance: they had learned from Ayn that reason required that one not "withhold your contempt from men's vices"; they had learned from Ayn and Nathaniel that irrationality and evasion were often found in the most innocent-seeming errors; they had learned that emotions were not a valid guide of behavior, that one must live by reason, that however loudly their emotions were screaming against the demands and the criticisms, that was not a reason for action.

The ultimate responsibility for the suffering of Ayn's friends lay neither with Ayn nor with Nathaniel. Her friends—including myself—were free; no gun was held to our heads; we could have said: "Enough!" We could have left and found our separate ways to life. We did not say "Enough!" We did not leave. The deadly mixture of idealism and a vulnerability to guilt—with all its variations and permutations in each individual—had formed the stout chains of our own devising that bound us tightly and made us willing to endure more and still more, that made us willing to endure, as the years passed, the awareness that our enthusiasm and zest for life were seeping away, that our authentic benevolence was losing its bright coloration, that our hope was diminishing. We could not abandon reason, we could not abandon morality, no matter what the cost. And that meant we could not, would not, abandon Ayn Rand.

In myself, I felt an emotional deadness steadily growing and beginning to encase me in a sheet of ice. I became perceived as cool, aloof, distant. My remoteness was enhanced by the secret I could not tell: the secret of Ayn and Nathaniel's affair. Often, I felt a desperate need for the release of confiding in a friend; but I believed myself bound by a vow of silence. I could not tell my own secret without revealing secrets that were not mine to share. And so I kept silent —and found myself growing farther and farther away from the people I loved.

A philosophy that exalted individualism and joy was becoming, in practice, a set of dreary duties and a source of agonized emotional repression. A philosophy that was a mighty hymn to the possibilities of human life was becoming, in practice, a dirge. The bright promise was fading. The golden days of enchantment were gone.

Chapter Twenty-six

It was in January of 1958, a few months after the publication of *Atlas Shrugged*, that the movement which was to make Ayn known not merely as novelist but as philosopher, which was to focus and speed the dissemination, the understanding and the influence of her ideas from one end of the country to the other—and to other continents—had its modest beginning. Ayn *would* see concrete results of her philosophy in action.

Nathaniel had conceived the idea of organizing Nathaniel Branden Institute[1] soon known as NBI, as a response to the growing tide of requests Ayn was receiving for a detailed, systematic presentation of her philosophy. He prepared a course of twenty lectures entitled "Basic Principles of Objectivism." The course presented Ayn's philosophy, including aspects not yet covered in her written works, and developed some of its implications for psychology; it included such topics as "Objectivity versus subjectivity"—"What is reason?"—"The nature of emotions"—"Are the arguments for the existence of God logically defensible?"—"The nature and meaning of volition"—"Why self-esteem is man's deepest psychological need"—"Social metaphysics"—"Foundation of the Objectivist ethics"—"The importance of passing moral judgments"—"The ethics of altruism"—"The principles of a proper political system: Freedom versus compulsion"—"The economics of a free society"—"The psychology of sex"—"The nature and purpose of art."

Ayn was dubious about the presentation of such a course. "When Nathan first had the idea for the lectures," she later explained, "I didn't expect very much to come of them, and I was concerned for him: I thought there was a good chance his project would fail, since the culture in general seemed totally indifferent to our ideas and to ideas in general." But when Nathaniel insisted that he knew the risks involved and believed the lectures had a reasonable chance of success, Ayn

[1] Its original name was Nathaniel Branden Lectures, which was later changed with incorporation.

agreed that he should attempt it. And she agreed to join him during the question period following each lecture, so that students might direct questions to her.

The lectures had Ayn's intellectual approval, but as a business venture, they were Nathaniel's independent undertaking. Nathaniel and I opened an "office" —which consisted of the combination desk–dining table in our apartment—and sent announcements to people in the New York area who had written especially interesting and intelligent letters to Ayn. We had no experience in the lecture field; we did not know that at that time it was unprecedented to offer lectures on philosophy privately, without a university affiliation. A few years later, the president of a large lecture agency commented, "I'll admit quite candidly that if you had come to me for advice then—I would have told you that what's happened is impossible. Lectures on *philosophy?*" He shook his head.

The course was presented for the first time to twenty-eight students in a small hotel room. When it was given again in the fall, there were forty-five students; the following February, the enrollment rose to sixty-five. The Institute began placing small advertisements in New York newspapers, and enrollment began to double with each course. The intellectual level of the students was impressive; then, and later, they predominantly consisted of remarkably intelligent men and women. The average age of the students was in the early thirties; in one series, the youngest student was a sixteen-year-old high school girl, the oldest a sixty-year-old professor of physics. The professional range was varied: there were college students, secretaries, businessmen, housewives, writers, economists, artists, teachers, lawyers, engineers, psychiatrists.

Students began asking for courses on other aspects of Objectivism, and NBI arranged for members of the collective to join the Institute as associate lecturers. Alan Greenspan began presenting a course on "The Economics of a Free Society"—Leonard Peikoff offered "A Critical History of Philosophy"—Mary Ann Rukavina gave a series on "The Esthetics of the Visual Arts"—Nathaniel added new courses on "Basic Principles of Objectivist Psychology" and "A Critical Analysis of Contemporary Psychology"—and I developed a course entitled "Principles of Efficient Thinking."

It was soon necessary for NBI to move to larger quarters. Nathaniel cut back on his practice of psychotherapy and spent his time lecturing and writing, and I devoted full time to the Institute as its executive director.

Ayn's first serious interest in the activities of NBI was sparked when mail started pouring in from all over the country—later, from all over the world—as word of the availability of formal presentations of Objectivism began to spread. Many of the letters asked for courses to be made available in other cities. A young Los Angeles couple, Jan and Peter Crosby, asked if the lectures could be put on tape, so that they might hear them. It occurred to me that we could tape our courses, appoint representatives to handle them, to do mailings, to advertise, to arrange for accommodations—and thus be able to offer lectures nationwide. It seemed an unlikely idea. How could one induce people to sit around a tape recorder, staring at a blank wall, listening to a lecture on epistemology or ethics or aesthetics? But soon, to Ayn's continuing astonishment, NBI was successfully offering courses in more than thirty cities, from Los Angeles to Toronto to Clear, Alaska, and a stream of requests began arriving from Europe, Africa, Asia, and Australia.

Slowly, by infinitesimal steps, the growing success of NBI, in conjunction with her two years of conversations with Nathaniel, began to pull Ayn out of her depression. "The man who really saved my life during this period," she later said, "was Nathan. I was almost paralyzed, and it was his understanding of the culture which helped me clarify and identify what was really happening. It was only Nathan who kept a steady point in a Hegelian universe.

"I felt that people had given up even the search for rational ideas, and that there was nothing to be done. But as a cultural sign, it was NBI that really changed my mind. With the passage of time, I began to see how even the least promising of students were not the same after the course, they were infinitely better people and more rational. I saw that rational ideas do take, even if in a manner which I did not know before, that part of the process is conscious and part is osmosis, but it works. The enormous response to the lectures gave me a preview of what can be done with a culture, and that pleased me enormously. It was what I needed in order to go on."

For the first time in several years, Ayn began to move outside the narrow circle of her friends to spend time with other people. Through his daughter, Joan Kennedy Taylor, an admirer of Ayn's work and a student at NBI, Ayn had met the renowned composer and music critic Deems Taylor. She began to spend occasional evenings with him, discussing music and listening to recordings of his compositions.

One evening some time later, New York University held a banquet to honor Deems Taylor, which Ayn and Frank attended. At her request, she sat next to John O'Hara; she admired the psychological perceptiveness of his work. O'Hara's biographer, Finnis Farr, was to quote his reaction in *O'Hara:* "I sat next to a woman called Ayn Rand, the author, whom I had often heard described as a terror, but we got along fine. She is an oddball, born in Russia, but what a talker! Fun, actually. . . . She asked me what my philosophy was, and that, of course, got me going. Turned out that I am diametrically opposed to her philosophy, but I didn't know that till later. . . ."

One day, to her stunned surprise, Ayn answered her telephone to hear the voice of Isabel Paterson. After complimenting her on *Atlas Shrugged,* Pat explained that she had been unable to sell her own novel. Ayn had seen and liked the initial chapters years ago. Would she recommend it to Random House? Pat asked. Ayn felt that the request was inexcusable after their break and the years of silence, but, she later explained, "I felt such pity I simply said that I didn't know if I could recommend it, I would have to read it first; if she'd drop it off, we could talk about it after I'd read it—and that I'd like to see her."

In the years since their last meeting, Pat had often talked of Ayn, and of how much she missed her and regretted their break. She spoke, too, of Frank, to whom she had been devoted and who was perhaps the one person in her life whom she had never insulted. As Ayn's fortunes were rising, Pat's were falling. Her hair-trigger temper, her bitter intransigence, her infinite capacity to embarrass friends publicly, had finally alienated her from all of her allies. One by one, she broke with them—from Rose Wilder Lane, a friend and source of intellectual stimulation over decades, to John Chamberlain, an admiring and admired fellow fighter, to Will Cuppy, the literary critic and writer who was for many years among the closest and most faithful of her friends, to Ayn Rand. Each time—unlike Ayn, who spoke without a suggestion of regret about rejected friends—Pat openly admitted to feeling painful regret over the breaches and painful loneliness for the lost relationships, but the rifts went too deep to be healed.

When she was forced to retire from the *Herald Tribune* with a tiny pension, she refused, on principle, to collect Social Security benefits. In 1959, elderly, ill and poor, this fiercely independent woman moved in with Muriel Hall and her husband. "We loved it," Muriel said. "It was better than any college education."

Pat had spent the last years working on her novel (still unfinished at her death in 1961). She wanted to find a publisher, and tried to contact old friends in the publishing industry; but she had antagonized all of them, and the novel was rejected. One day she told Muriel, "I think I'll ask Ayn to read it." Muriel's impression was that her real interest was not in literary criticism but in seeing Ayn once more.

Their final visit was a desperately sad one for both women. Ayn had read the manuscript, and was disappointed. She had never particularly admired Pat's fiction, but felt that this one was considerably below Pat's former standards; it was hopeless as a commercial property. Ayn felt obliged to say that she didn't think the novel would sell, and why. "Pat kept asking if I liked such-and-such a passage," Ayn would recall, "and when I could say I did, she beamed. It was heartbreaking. We talked philosophy a bit, and it was the same old mysticism. Then she left."

"There is no possibility of a reconciliation," Pat told Muriel Hall. "There's still a barrier that is never going to disappear."

Pat was to make a very interesting remark about Ayn's work: that Ayn, as a fiction writer, was in one sense the Harriet Beecher Stowe of this century—that like *Uncle Tom's Cabin,* her fiction had the rare and compelling power to change people's ideas and their lives. And it is true that the single statement most consistently made about Ayn's work by her readers—by people who grasped little of her philosophical ideas and by people who had studied them deeply, by businessmen and philosophers and engineers and students and stock brokers and housewives and newspapermen, by rich and poor and middle class, by liberals and conservatives and libertarians, by Americans and foreigners, by blacks and whites and Jews and Methodists and Catholics—is: "Ayn Rand's books changed my life." Usually, they mean it as a compliment; rarely, they mean it as a criticism. But always, *they mean it.*

Ayn was soon to feel disappointed in still another friend. Ruth and Buzzy Hill had continued to rent Ayn's California house, although Ayn was shortly to ask them to arrange for its sale, knowing she would never again choose to live there. Nathaniel wrote to Ruth and asked if she would be willing to locate interested people and present his lectures in Ayn's home. Ruth agreed, but asked that she first be allowed to hear a sample lecture, so she could judge the quality of Nathaniel's voice and become familiar with what she would be selling. An indignant letter from Nathaniel arrived, stating that Ayn was offended by her request; since Ayn had recommended him as a lecturer on her philosophy, the meaning of asking him for a sample tape was to discover if she were a reliable judge in such matters. He did not audition, he said. The matter was closed.

A few months later, Ruth was startled to see Ayn, Frank, and Nathaniel coming up the driveway; she had not known they were in Los Angeles on NBI business. As Ruth ran down the driveway to greet Ayn and Frank, she stopped short when she saw Ayn's furious look. She listened, numbed, to an angry tirade: How dare she question Ayn's judgment? How dare she presume to demand an audition of someone Ayn had recommended? Despite her love and admiration for Ayn, Ruth stood her ground firmly. "It was from you," she said quietly, "that I learned the importance of thinking for myself and going only by my own judgment." To be quoted in this context served only to increase Ayn's anger. When she left, she pointedly invited only Buzzy Hill to visit her in New York— although Frank winked at Ruth, as if to say "Don't worry, it will be all right," as he waved good-bye.

It was during these years, from the publication of *Atlas Shrugged* throughout the sixties, that an influx of new people, drawn to Ayn by her novel and by NBI —people who predominantly were accomplished adults rather than youngsters beginning their careers—began to enter the circle of Ayn's friends. Among them were television producer Ted Yates, writers Ira Levin and Al Ramrus, economists Murray Rothbard and Martin Anderson, historian Robert Hessen, artists Daniel Green and Jose Capuletti, businessman Wilfred Schwartz, psychologists Lee and Joyce Shulman and Roger Callahan, journalist Edith Efron, neurophysiologist Robert Efron, attorneys Henry Mark Holzer and Erika Holzer, actress Kay Nolte Smith, and actor and drama coach Phillip Smith. (A second generation began forming in the late sixties: Nathaniel's nephews Jonathan and Leonard Hirschfeld became interested in Objectivism and moved to New York, and my nephew, Jim Weidman, began to spend summers with us.)

These new people were drawn to Ayn by her work and her reputation—and held by the quality of her intelligence and the power of her personality; none had ever encountered so intellectually fascinating and provocative a human being. Friends have commented that they would see Ayn talk to physicists—she had studied almost nothing in the field—who were astounded by her grasp of the essentials of the field and her ability to draw penetrating inferences on the basis of a handful of facts. They saw her talk to economists who were stunned by the breadth and innovative nature of the conclusions she had derived from reading a handful of books on economics. They saw professional philosophers listening thunderstruck as she led them to grasp invaluable principles of metaphysics and epistemology; had the philosophers been told that her reading in academic philosophy was limited to a few college courses, the study of Plato and Aristotle, excerpts from key figures in the history of philosophy, and conversations with those among her friends who were students of philosophy, they would not have believed it.

Ayn did not lecture to men and women working in areas where her own factual knowledge was inadequate; she tended to be well aware of her lack of concrete information. Her method was Socratic: she would, for instance, question a physicist about his field, a barrage of questions posed by a mind that homed in like a laser beam on essentials, which would lead him to identify and examine his own most basic scientific axioms—so basic that he had barely known they were the source from which his thinking and his work proceeded. And the physicist would leave Ayn feeling that he—and his field—had been understood and appreciated as never before. Even in the field of literature, her method tended to be Socratic: she would read a few paragraphs of a writer's work—and after instantly naming for him the most self-revelatory aspects and small touches that he had thought intimately personal and evident only to himself—she would lead him, through a series of probing questions, to grasp and to consider the basic literary premises that motivated him. And the writer would leave Ayn feeling that he—and his field—were understood and appreciated as never before. Her methodology was an epistemological tour de force.

Her new friends felt that they were receiving an inestimably important gift—a gift which made many of them willing to ignore the times when her lack of knowledge did *not* stop her from pronouncing sweeping judgments. She would dismiss composers such as Wagner and Beethoven as without important merit—because their work was "malevolent." She would dismiss artists such as Rembrandt for the same reason, and the entire Impressionist school as "murky and unfocused." She would dismiss most of the history of literature as anti-Romantic and unstylized, and the history of philosophy, with the sole significant exceptions of Aristotle and aspects of Thomas Aquinas, as mystical, dishonest, and irrational.

The insights that Ayn gave to her friends were not a gift. They carried a price tag. The price was the adulation one was expected to offer her. Increasingly, as the years were passing, Ayn required that, among those who admired her, no other admiration was to threaten her preeminent place. Increasingly, as the years passed, this woman of outstanding talent and originality required that she be seen as *the* great novelist and *the* great philosopher. And a second payment was exacted as well: the willingness to accept her moral condemnation of any attitude, any action, any thought or feeling that seemed to her irrational. Some of her new friends circled in her orbit for only a few weeks, some remained for months, some remained for years; but with very few exceptions, the relationships were ruptured in anger as Ayn felt her friends to have failed reason, morality, and herself.

Clearly, Ayn never lost her underlying disappointment with the culture around her or the bitterness that accompanied it. But she nevertheless continued to work her way back to a more serene view of the world. In conjunction with the Institute, she entered into a flurry of activities, all geared to promoting the spread of Objectivism. She rarely missed attending the question period of any lecture given at NBI in New York, and worked with its lecturers to improve and perfect their course material; she made herself available to discuss advertisements and publicity and promotion. The results streamed in during the decade of the sixties with a speed and momentum she had not dreamed possible.

It was in 1963 that Ayn traveled to California, where Nathaniel was to give "live" the first lecture of his series, to participate in the question period. In San Francisco, a lecture room was engaged to accommodate two hundred and fifty people; five hundred came. In Los Angeles, NBI's representative engaged a room to hold six hundred people; eleven hundred arrived; the overflow listened in another room, through loudspeakers. The caliber of the students continued to be exceptional; during a series held in Boston, the students helping NBI's representative to process admissions included a neurologist, an anesthesiologist, and a researcher in biochemistry and genetics; the man ushering students to their seats was a biophysicist.

The response to Objectivism throughout the country received little acknowledgment in the press. But a teacher of English wrote, in *New University Thought,* about the "danger" of Ayn Rand's influence on college students. "For the past two or three semesters," he wrote, "no other author . . . has threatened to upset Miss Rand's commanding popularity. . . . I have had an opportunity to talk with several other college teachers, from various parts of the nation, and many of them informed me that they too have been troubled by Miss Rand's appeal . . . it is dismaying to contemplate the possibility that Ayn Rand is the single writer who engages the loyalties of the students I am perhaps ineffectually attempting to reach. All of the students I talked with struck me as intelligent . . . and most were quite able to verbalize the reasons of their admiration for Miss Rand."

A professor of English at Yeshiva University reported that he had given his freshman English class the assignment of writing a paper on the book they had most enjoyed during the past year and which had most impressed and influenced them. Twenty-five percent of his students wrote on one or other of Ayn's novels.

In the *Wall Street Journal,* John Chamberlain wrote: "Seated about in booths in college-town snack shops, the young Randites talk about their intellectual leader as their fathers and mothers a generation ago talked about Karl Marx, or John Maynard Keynes, or Thorstein Veblen. . . . And it is normally a matter of two decades before the young take over the seats of power in the name of what they have learned to believe 20 years ago."

The mail that NBI received gave Ayn further insight into the steps of Objectivism's motion through the country. "I heard people arguing about *Atlas Shrugged* at a dinner party—the book sounded interesting—so I went out and bought it." "I read *Atlas Shrugged* because people told me it was an evil book that no one should read." "After fighting with my professor for a month, I finally obtained permission to do my term paper on Objectivism." "I discovered the works of Ayn Rand when they were recommended in a course on psychology." "Can you recommend additional readings to supplement discussions of Objectivism in an ethics seminar?" "My psychiatrist suggested that I read *Atlas Shrugged* as a helpful adjunct to psychotherapy." "I heard about Ayn Rand when Galt's speech was quoted in a political science class."

Ayn Rand clubs soon began springing up on campuses, organized by college students for the purpose of discussing and studying Ayn's philosophy. Increasing numbers of requests for material arrived from teachers and professors who wished to include a discussion of Objectivism in their classes. Leonard Peikoff gave a course on "Objectivism's Theory of Knowledge" in the Graduate College of the University of Denver. In 1962, Random House published *Who Is Ayn Rand?*, a book containing an analysis by Nathaniel of Ayn's novels and a biographical essay which I wrote.[2] By the fall of 1963, NBI courses were offered in fifty-four cities in the United States and Canada. During the next year, more than thirty-five hundred students attended, as well as several thousand visitors who audited individual lectures. The most startling location was somewhere under the Atlantic Ocean, on the tour of a Polaris submarine. By 1965, courses were given in eighty cities; arrangements were underway to offer them to American soldiers in Vietnam who had expressed interest, and representatives were organizing courses in Greenland and Pakistan.

NBI opened a publishing wing, NBI Press, and issued *Calumet "K"* and Hugo's *The Man Who Laughs,* both with introductions written by Ayn. It was followed by NBI Book Service, through which Ayn's books and other works of interest and value to NBI students on economics, politics and philosophy, were sold by mail order. NBI Art Reproductions was formed, through which prints of paintings by Frank, Joan Mitchell Blumenthal, and a portrait of Ayn by Ilona (Ilona Royce Smithkin), were sold.

These were exciting years for Ayn and for everyone involved with NBI. Working twelve-hour days, often seven days a week, both directors and staff felt themselves engaged in a task of supreme importance: helping to move the philosophical trend of a country from faith to reason, from altruism to self-interest, from collectivism to capitalism; perhaps, it sometimes seemed as NBI's progress became intoxicating, even helping to change the world. The staff of the Institute, from file clerk to head of the production department, consisted almost entirely of young people who had taken or were taking its lecture courses. In the first years, "the production department" consisted of Gerald Rafferty, who had said, "Had

---

[2] *Who Is Ayn Rand?* was moderately successful, and more successful when it appeared in paperback. It is a book that was written in good faith, but in a spirit of uncritical adulation which neither Nathaniel nor I would defend today.

I been alive when Aristotle was living, I would have worked for him; I want to work for Ayn Rand," and an aged addressing machine upon which he performed constant miracles of repair, located in the office's kitchen; the staff had to squeeze past both man and machine to reach the coffeepot. They were dedicated to the work they did and cheerfully put in long hours and weekends to advance the intellectual cause that was their own.

And these were more hopeful and optimistic years for Ayn. "I'm beginning to believe that even *I* will see substantial changes in my lifetime," she said. "Reality and time are on our side. Young people, who will one day have public voices, are reacting more than one could have predicted; they *are* looking for direction. I expect eventually to see an established movement."

Chapter Twenty-seven

Since the publication of *Atlas Shrugged,* Ayn had received countless invitations to speak at universities. In her despair over the intellectual state of the culture, and because of her dislike of formal speech-making, she had refused all of them. But as her spirits had begun to lift—and as Nathaniel and I urged her to accept such invitations, feeling that it would be important as a means of publicizing her work and important as a demonstration to her that there *were* responsive intelligences in the world outside her living room—she unwillingly began to accept. Her decision was to have unanticipated and beneficent consequences.

It was in 1960 that Ayn agreed to give her first university talk, in response to an invitation from Yale Law School. It seemed an unfortunate choice: the Law School, Ayn said, was a totally un-American hotbed of liberalism and socialism.

On a cold February day, Ayn and Frank, with a group of friends, drove to Yale. In a pattern that was to continue throughout her university appearances, Ayn completed the writing of her talk—she always wrote out her talks in full, and read from the manuscript—in the car, fighting against the car sickness that afflicted her when she tried to write in a moving vehicle.

Lawrence Scott, then a student at Yale, later vividly recalled Ayn's appearance. The only announcement of the talk had been a couple of notices, nestled among hundreds of other notices, on the Law School Bulletin board. "There was no rally, and there were no other mentions of her talk," he said. "On the surface it seemed a few admirers would gather in a small classroom and visit with this very controversial author for an hour or two. . . . On that Friday night, every seat in the Yale Law School auditorium was packed wall to wall. In fact, the overflow was so great that loudspeakers had to be installed in the corridors on two floors—and that still wasn't enough! Additional loudspeakers were placed at the entrance to the school, and crowds gathered there to listen to Ayn Rand in the bitter cold of that night. . . . For fifty minutes, she delivered a stirring and eloquent presentation of 'Faith and Force: The Destroyers of the Modern World.' Occasionally, the audience applauded, but there were hisses and groans, too. . . . When the question period began, the young socialist attackers were out in force. One called from the balcony: 'Under your system, who will take care of the janitors?' Without an instant of hesitation, Ayn Rand replied in a powerful voice, and without anger, 'Young man: the janitors!' A roar of applause and laughter filled the auditorium."

When the question period ended, crowds of eager students gathered around Ayn with further questions; those who could not reach her, turned to the friends who had joined her, who for more than an hour happily answered philosophical and political questions. It seemed that Yale was applying for admission to the Union.

After this triumphant first appearance, Ayn accepted invitations from Princeton, Columbia, Hunter College, Johns Hopkins, the University of Wisconsin, Harvard, Massachusetts Institute of Technology, Purdue, the University of Michigan, Sarah Lawrence, Brown, and many others. Invariably, in the pattern that had begun with her first work and was to continue for the rest of her life, it was lone individuals who fought against enormous opposition to arrange that she be invited to speak. And invariably, her appearances attracted record audiences. All followed the pattern of Yale: many students and faculty members came to jeer, and remained to question; they came to hiss, and remained to applaud—and always, her audiences overflowed whatever hall had been engaged. It became a joke among her friends that just before a speaking engagement, I would contact the university to ask what size hall they planned to use; whatever answer they gave me, I would explain that they would require a larger room; I would then be told that, by precedent, they knew approximately how many people to expect; when the evening of the talk arrived, there was always a last-minute hectic switch to a larger auditorium, and still students gathered in hallways, other rooms, and under the stars to hear her speak.

Ayn was a strangely powerful speaker: this small, unprepossessing woman, dressed in a flowing black cape, her dress ornamented with a gold dollar sign, reading with little inflection in her heavy Russian accent from a prepared text— had the charismatic power of certainty. Her thoughts were new and intriguing to her audiences, her logic impeccable—her passionate conviction overwhelming in its force. No other modern writer has displayed a comparable capacity to generate intellectual excitement.

Marc Jaffe, now editorial director of Villard Books, commissioned Ayn to write an introduction to Victor Hugo's *Ninety-three* for Bantam Classics. He later spoke glowingly of his meetings with her, in terms relevant to the success of her lecture appearances. With a cheerful grin, he said, "I've been telling my colleagues that I was the man who was in love with Ayn Rand . . . at least for ten minutes. What I most remember about our meetings was the almost magical impact she had on me. She was not a beautiful woman, but she had an inexpressible charm, that wonderful deep and resonant voice, the words poured out of her in a way that excited both my mind and my emotions. When we talked about her notions of the romantic novel, I was fascinated and educated; what she said was very important and convincing. I felt that she had such an extraordinary mind and presence. I had read *The Fountainhead* and *Atlas Shrugged,* and I liked them both very much; apart from their wealth of ideas and characters, both have a compelling force that came in good part from the incredible energy of her personality."

But apart from the question periods, lecturing never became an activity Ayn enjoyed. "I didn't, and don't, want to do it," she said. "It's a duty I perform to advance the spread of my ideas. I know why they need to see me in person, that seeing me gives them the reality of Objectivist ideas existing here and now, not merely in a book. If this helps to spread Objectivism, and helps the sale of my books, then it's publicity for which I'm being paid, and I'm willing to do it. I don't like the personal adulation or any of the 'fan' atmosphere. It's not on my terms. I appreciate the intention in an impersonal, professional way, but it means nothing to me personally. When anyone compliments me, my first question is: What's my estimate of the source of the compliments? Is it a mind I respect? When it's a mind that understands what I've done, then it's an enormous pleasure. Anything less than that—no. I don't really want anything but the response of top minds. . . . How I would love to meet a really first-class mind, a first-class person. . . ."

At some of her university appearances, Ayn abandoned her cape for a new mink coat. She called the coat "a gift from *We the Living.*" She had learned from the State Department that during World War II, the Italian Government, as part of its policy of expropriating the works of foreign authors, had allowed a pirated film to be made of *We the Living;* Italian officials expected it to be effective propaganda because of its anti-Communist stand. Alida Valli and Rossano Brazzi had played Kira and Leo. When the movie was released, it was an immediate success; the enthusiasm it generated was even greater than the government had hoped. Proudly, Italian officials sent a print to the Nazi government in Germany—and received a blisteringly angry order to remove it from distribution immediately. The German Government understood what the audiences had grasped, but the Italian Government had not: that every scene in the movie was as much an indictment of fascism and naziism as of communism; it was an indictment of *all* dictatorships. The Italian Government complied with the order, and the distribution of the picture was halted. Some years after the end of the war, the American State Department successfully sued the government of Italy for its theft of American literary properties. Ayn's payment was her coat, with several thousand dollars remaining which she was determined to spend only on the most frivolous luxuries she could imagine.

Not surprisingly, Ayn found few luxuries on which to spend her "gift from *We the Living.*" She continued to live modestly, as she had always done, despite the large amounts of money she was earning. She cared nothing for jewelry, except for the occasional inexpensive costume piece that delighted her; she cared nothing for travel or luxurious living; her small apartment continued to please her;

she took no vacations; she had no interest in being lavishly entertained or in entertaining; attending the dinner party often given for her after a lecture engagement was a chore she dutifully performed, but rarely took pleasure in. And she never fully trusted her financial ease; she often said that, as a writer, one lived with perpetual insecurity, never knowing how long royalties would continue to be generated. Whatever money she did not require for day-to-day expenses remained in her savings account—to be eroded, as the years passed, by the continuing gallop of inflation. It was only years later that she could be persuaded to risk even the most careful of investments.

As her fame continued to grow, Ayn began writing a weekly column of opinion in The Los Angeles *Times,* dealing with topical issues from the perspective of Objectivism. The column was tremendously successful. Nick Williams, editor of the newspaper, wrote that he was swamped with letters, and that "the count has been running solidly for Miss Rand." She wrote a warmly beautiful and much-discussed column about the suicide of Marilyn Monroe, defending her as "an image of pure, innocent, childlike joy in living . . . facing life with the joyous self-flaunting of a child or a kitten who is happy to display its own attractiveness as the best gift it can offer the world," and deploring the fact that she "found herself regarded and ballyhooed as a vulgar symbol of obscenity . . . found herself answered by concerted efforts to negate, to degrade, to ridicule, to insult, to destroy her achievement."

Ayn had never been a dedicated reader, but in order to write her column she had to keep up with the latest political events in newspapers and magazines. The problem that had tormented her as a writer affected her reading as well. She found herself compulsively arguing with each line of print, rewriting in her mind, analyzing, considering the implications and sources of the writer's position. Reading became a laborious and impossibly time-consuming activity. By the end of the year, she realized she could no longer do it; she was not able to keep up with the material she felt it necessary to read. Regretfully, she discontinued her column.

In 1963, Lewis and Clark College in Portland, Oregon, invited Ayn to receive an honorary degree of Doctor of Humane Letters. To accept the degree, Ayn took her first airplane flight. She had always refused to fly, insisting that she did not trust "the modern psycho-epistemology [the method of mental functioning] of the mechanics and the pilots." It appeared, rather, that her powerful need for control, her need to run her own life, her abhorrence of ever dropping the reins and putting herself in the hands of someone else, was at the root of her fear. When Nathaniel and I agreed to join her and Frank on the flight to Portland, she uneasily acceded. It was typical of Ayn that, once she made the commitment to fly, she was no longer nervous; the unknown frightened her; a fact of reality did not. All through the flight—which was, at times, unpleasantly bumpy—she thoroughly enjoyed herself. It is remarkable that, in *Atlas*—before she ever flew —she was able to write with total credibility and full sensory reality a scene in which Dagny Taggart flies her own plane and crashes in Galt's Gulch; she had read a few paragraphs in a book on flying and airplanes, and her power to form abstractions from a handful of concretes gave her the rest.

Ayn spent two full days at Lewis and Clark, where the entire college listened to her lectures and participated in lively discussions of Objectivism. In preparation for the occasion, all of the faculty and all of the student body had read *Atlas Shrugged*.

It was the president of the college, Dr. John R. Howard, who had originated the proposal to confer the degree on Ayn and who had arranged the study program on Objectivism. When asked how he first became interested in Ayn's ideas, he replied: "A few years ago, when I was president of a college in Illinois, there was a student with whom I was engaged in a rather protracted discussion, involving some disagreement between us. One day, the student walked into my office, put a book down on my desk, and said, 'President Howard, here is a book that you absolutely have to read.' The book was *Atlas Shrugged*."

During the sixties—as the sales of *Atlas* continued to skyrocket, as the sales of *The Fountainhead* ran a close second, as the success of Ayn's university appearances became a legend in campuses across the country, as NBI's advertisements for lectures kept her name in the newspapers nationwide, as more and more cities were added to the NBI list, as more and more study clubs were formed—a profusion of articles about Ayn began to appear in major magazines and newspapers, and requests that she write articles piled up on her desk. The majority of the articles were strongly negative, but through their indication—often distorted —of some aspect of her thinking, they brought her still more readers. An NBI student said: "I had read *The Fountainhead* in the early fifties, and when I saw Granville Hicks's horrible review of *Atlas,* all I cared about was that it told me Ayn Rand had written a new book; I left my desk at the office and ran to the nearest bookstore."

When one of Ayn's talks was entered into the *Congressional Record,* Bennett Cerf said, "Now that you have made the *Congressional Record,* there is only one peak left for you to climb. I refer, of course, to *Playboy* magazine!" It was a "peak" she did climb. In March of 1964, after lengthy talks between Ayn and Alvin Toffler—talks that he termed "intellectually electric"—his interview was published in *Playboy.*[1] In an introduction to the interview—which was later twice published in book form, along with other interviews of men and women whom *Playboy* considered "among the movers and shakers of our time"—the editor wrote: "Ayn Rand, an intense, angry young woman of 61, [sic] is among the most outspoken—and important—intellectual voices in America today. She is the author of what is perhaps the most fiercely damned and admired best seller of the decade: *Atlas Shrugged.* . . . Despite [her] success, the literary establishment considers her an outsider. Almost to a man, critics have either ignored or denounced the book. She is an exile among philosophers, too, al-

[1] At his invitation, Ayn met Hugh Hefner during a trip to Chicago. Hefner spoke glowingly of the intellectual and emotional impact of her work on him. "I liked him," Ayn was to say. "He's very intelligent."

though *Atlas* is as much a work of philosophy as it is a novel. Liberals glower at the very mention of her name; but conservatives, too, swallow hard when she begins to speak. For Ayn Rand, whether anyone likes it or not, is sui generis, indubitably, irrevocably, intransigently individual."

Ayn received an invitation from Boston's prestigious Ford Hall Forum, asking her to give a talk on any subject of her choosing. Her first inclination was to refuse, believing that the Forum predominantly invited speakers of liberal-to-socialist orientation; but once again, in order to spread her ideas, she agreed to appear.

Of all her appearances, Ford Hall Forum became the one she loved best. She soon spoke admiringly of the Forum for its commitment to intellectual excellence and its determination, contrary to her original opinion, to throw open its doors to the widest possible diversity of opinion. The enthusiasm that greeted her from the huge crowd in attendance shook the walls of the old building—and astounded the Forum's representatives. From then on, she was invited to return every year; until her death, she missed only one year, because of a serious illness; lesser illnesses never kept her from the single public event that had personal meaning for her. Her speeches became landmark occasions for the Forum and for admirers of her work: by early morning before each talk, lines began forming outside the building, as crowds waited in heat or cold or sunshine or rain or snow to be certain of getting the seats that those who arrived in the afternoon would not get; the afternoon crowds would be seated in a second large auditorium where they would listen to the talk over loudspeakers; the evening crowds might or might not be admitted as standees. Her appearances became jokingly known among her admirers as "the Objectivist Easter," an occasion for celebration, and people came to stand uncomplainingly in line from Boston, from New York, from California, from all the states in between, from Canada and Europe and Australia and India. Only a few years before Ayn's death, the Forum honored her at a special banquet attended by more than eleven hundred people; after her death, with the agreement of her estate, they auctioned off the manuscript of one of her talks for ten thousand dollars.

A letter reached Ayn's desk from L. Quincy Mumford, Librarian of Congress. He wrote: "Among the most widely discussed philosophies of our time is that associated with your writings. In your fiction and essays you have made the Objectivist philosophy an issue affecting many levels of public discourse. When the history of our time is written, your work will have a prominent place. In order to insure that your work will be the subject of informed study, I invite you to place your manuscripts and personal papers in the Library of Congress."

Ayn was honored by the request, and agreed to accept it. But the material has not yet been placed with the Library of Congress.

With the spread of her fame and the accelerating influence of her ideas, Ayn's interest in writing had slowly begun to reemerge—but now, it was directed toward the writing of nonfiction.

In 1961, Random House had published Ayn's *For the New Intellectual,* which contained the main philosophical passages from her four novels, with a new and lengthy introductory essay in which she offered "an analysis of the development of Western culture, the causes of its progress, its decline, its present crisis, and the road to an intellectual renaissance"; in 1963, New American Library issued a paperback edition, with a first printing of two hundred thousand copies.

Philosopher Sidney Hook wrote a criticism of the book in the New York Times, saying: "Despite the great play with the word 'reason,' one is struck by the absence of any serious argument in this unique combination of tautology and extravagant absurdity." In response—since the Times refused to publish letters to the editor in excess of three hundred words—NBI took out an advertisement in which Nathaniel responded to Professor Hook's review.[2]

For the New Intellectual was to be the last of Ayn's works published by Random House. After its success, Bennett Cerf expressed interest in bringing out a collection of Ayn's university talks and articles. The selection which she gave him included a speech she had delivered at Ford Hall Forum, entitled "The Fascist New Frontier"; it was an analysis of the similarities between the ideology of fascism and the ideology contained in addresses given by President John F. Kennedy; its central point was that contrary to popular belief, the Kennedy administration's ideology was not socialistic but fascistic—that it had been using, propagating, and stressing the principle that the individual should be sacrificed to the "public interest" as no American administration had ever done before. It was to be the lead essay and the title of the book.

In At Random, Bennett wrote, "I read the piece and absolutely hit the roof. I called her and said we were not going to publish any book that claimed Hitler and Jack Kennedy were alike. Ayn charged in and reminded me that I had said when she came to us that we would publish anything she wrote. I reminded her that I had said fiction. I said, 'You can say anything you want in a novel, but this is something I didn't foresee. All we ask is that you leave this one essay out.' Ayn was enraged. . . . Finally, she gave me her ultimatum, 'You're going to print every word I've written—or I won't let you publish the book.' I said, 'That's that. Get yourself another publisher.' When Kennedy was assassinated that fall, I wrote Ayn to ask if she didn't agree now that she was wrong. She didn't agree at all. She said the assassination had nothing to do with what she had to say. It didn't change her opinion one iota. . . . I liked her and still do. I miss her."

Ayn was deeply indignant at Bennett's attitude. She insisted that at their first luncheon, "Bennett assured me that Random House was nonpolitical in its publishing policies, whatever his own views and Donald's might be, and that I

---

[2] Ayn was very angry with the review—an anger which created a difficult situation for me. I was unable, as I was expected to do, to dismiss Sidney Hook as dishonest and corrupt. He had been my professor and faculty advisor when I was studying philosophy at NYU; he was—and is—a man for whom I have the greatest respect and affection, a man of honor, of courage, of outstanding integrity. To my great surprise, when I could not join Ayn in denouncing him, she said nothing, and seemed to accept that I had a personal attitude toward him that was separate from our philosophical differences.

would never encounter any political objections there. I included 'The Fascist New Frontier' in the collection because the bookstores had heard about the talk and were asking for it. I didn't try to sell Bennett on the project; he sold me on it; he said that the coming election would make the book controversial, sensational, and a big seller. He even enthusiastically exclaimed, 'The Fascist New Frontier—by Ayn Rand—what a title!' He said he'd publish the book on his spring list; it was a firm commitment. I even have a note from him in which he wrote, 'I am sending word around to everybody at Random House that we will have a new nonfiction book by you on the Spring 1964 list called The Fascist New Frontier. I think this book will cause a *tremendous* amount of excitement.' "

She added that about a month later, Bennett called and said his editorial staff was violently protesting publication of the book, which shocked and disturbed him because he had not expected to hear political objections from his editors. "Three weeks later, he was agreeing with his editors; he made the decision not to publish without even consulting me, without giving me a hearing."

It was a sad parting for both Ayn and Bennett. He wrote her a warm letter, saying "I am deeply, deeply sorry that you no longer wish Random House to be your publisher, but I want you to know that wherever you go, I wish you well. I think you are one of the most wonderful people I ever have met in my life, and this decision of yours will not change my feeling in that respect in the least degree. I acted in the way that my heart dictated and could not have done otherwise. You did the same. I hope I may continue to consider you my friend." In her reply, Ayn wished Bennett well, and said, "I shall always give you credit for the many good actions you have taken in regard to me." She always did.

From then on, Ayn's books were published by New American Library, her paperback publisher, which had opened a successful hardcover division. She was on friendly terms with Victor Weybright, NAL's president; she liked and respected him, and their association remained a mutually rewarding one.

It was in writing the introductory essay to For the New Intellectual that Ayn discovered a fact which she found startling: that "nonfiction is my natural way of functioning. I enjoy the actual writing itself. I have difficulties and organizational problems, but it's an enormous pleasure to me even when it's difficult." She began speaking of writing an ambitious, full-length book on epistemology, on the Objectivist theory of knowledge, presenting her view of the nature, source and validation of concepts, and she began making personal notes on what she envisioned as a project which would take several years. In her notes, she stated:

"Aristotle established the right metaphysics by establishing the law of identity —which was all that was necessary (plus the identification of the fact that only concretes exist). But he destroyed his metaphysics by his cosmology—by the whole nonsense of the 'moving spheres,' 'the immovable mover,' teleology, etc.

"The real crux of this issue is that *philosophy is primarily epistemology*—the science of the means, the rules, and the methods of human knowledge. It is the base of all other sciences and the one necessary for man because man is a being of volitional consciousness—a being who has to discover, not only the content of his knowledge, but also the means by which he is to acquire knowledge. . . . All the fantastic irrationalities of philosophical metaphysics have been the result of epistemological errors, fallacies, or corruptions."

While writing *Atlas Shrugged,* she had thought that the philosophical material contained in Galt's speech "was all a rational man needed to guide him." She had believed that another philosopher could one day write a fully detailed nonfiction presentation of Objectivism from that material. "The thought of doing it myself was paralyzing to me," she said. "I had no interest in writing for people of lesser intelligence, there would be nothing in it for me. But as I began watching the state of the culture and reading essays on modern philosophy, I began to see that what I took as almost self-evident was not that at all. I began to see that the kind of issues not explicitly covered in *Atlas,* such as my theory of universals, were much more enormous departures from today's thinking than I had imagined. The magnitude of what needs to be done has become real to me—and I've become interested in it. I've become an intellectual detective, cutting through the nonsense of modern philosophy to find the basic error. I've begun to see that in writing on epistemology, I will be engaged in a crusade for reason, my top value, and that *does* inspire me."

A contributing influence in Ayn's decision to write nonfiction, she said, was her discussions of philosophy with John Hospers, who is today a professor of philosophy at the University of Southern California in Los Angeles and the author of a number of distinguished books on aesthetics and philosophy, and was then a philosophy professor at Brooklyn College. He later spoke of his first meeting with Ayn when she addressed the student body at Brooklyn College. "I had not yet read *Atlas Shrugged,"* he said. "After the lecture—during which her challenging intellect impressed me very much—I asked her to lunch. We talked from noon until six in the evening; the intellectual excitement of that afternoon remains as a high spot in my life. I realized that this was both a tremendously powerful intellect and a powerful personality, a person completely different from anyone I'd ever met. Her ideas did not fit into any of the usual philosophical categories—so I had to discover more."

Ayn and John soon developed a friendly relationship, and over many months he visited her regularly for lengthy philosophical conversations. "Sometimes we'd still be talking at eight in the morning, and she'd make me breakfast, and then I'd go off to teach my classes in a state of intellectual ferment." He read *Atlas Shrugged,* which he considered an aesthetic triumph. "I was overwhelmed by Ayn's detailed sense of organization, by the structure and texture of the novel—its literary architecture—by her brilliant use of recurring themes, by the power of the passages which deal with intellectual, dramatic confrontations between characters. But most important, it is that rare thing in the modern novel: a book of *ideas,* developed with consummate skill." In the course of their conversations, and through the readings in economics and politics which she suggested to him, John became convinced of the validity of her moral and political views. Their major area of disagreement was on issues of epistemology. The disagreements were often heated, and Ayn easily grew angry. "Her sudden anger was bewildering," John said. "She was like a different person. But I was always totally fascinated. . . . those compelling eyes that you can't get away from and don't want to get away from—they could be completely benign and benevolent, and a moment later totally merciless. . . . She had a marvelous smile, which melted me many times. . . . I would see this towering intellect, and then, at times, a vulnerable little girl. . . . I loved her, very much. . . . Now, although more than twenty years have passed, it still seems like yesterday, and I can't imagine my life without that experience—it was an emotional and intellectual high which never abated. . . . She gave me a renewed faith in my own profession, when she made it clear that it's not military or political leaders who make history, it's the men of ideas. I missed her enormously . . . I still do."

As with so many of the people who were important in her life, Ayn broke with John Hospers. At his invitation, she gave a talk at a meeting of the American Society of Aesthetics at Harvard, for which he was Program Chairman; her subject was "Art as Sense of Life." John's assignment, as commentator on her speech, was to present a critical analysis. Ayn took violent exception to his criticisms—and he never saw her again.

The effect of Ayn's conversations with a professional philosopher remained with her, and made her eager to write a nonfiction work on epistemology. She began to feel enthusiastically impatient to begin work, a feeling she had not experienced since finishing *Atlas Shrugged.* "It's the feeling of entering on a big assignment," she exclaimed happily. "It's wonderful!"

As her initial venture into nonfiction writing apart from the introductory essay to *For the New Intellectual,* Ayn began writing articles for *The Objectivist Newsletter,* a four-page monthly consisting of articles analyzing current events from the perspective of Objectivism, and reviews of recommended books. Ayn and Nathaniel were the publishers and editors; I was the managing editor and Elayne Kalberman the circulation manager. The majority of the articles were written by Ayn and Nathaniel, with other writers, such as Alan Greenspan, Leonard Peikoff, and myself, making occasional contributions. Ayn's articles included her public speeches; a number of the articles Nathaniel wrote later appeared in his *The Psychology of Self-Esteem.*

In 1966, the newsletter became a small magazine, *The Objectivist,* a monthly journal that dealt with the theoretical aspects of Objectivism, with its application to modern problems, and with the evaluation of present cultural trends. It featured articles by Ayn, by Nathaniel, and other contributors, as well as reviews of recommended books, and reports on Objectivist activities. Within a year, *The Objectivist*'s subscription rate was fifteen thousand copies; within two years, it was more than twenty-one thousand copies, and was continuing to grow.

Ayn began publishing collections of her articles from *The Objectivist Newsletter* and *The Objectivist,* organized thematically, in book form. In the years from 1964 to 1971, her nonfiction books were *The Virtue of Selfishness,* a discussion of the ethics of Objectivism, which included five articles by Nathaniel on related psychological themes—*Capitalism: The Unknown Ideal,* essays on the moral aspects of capitalism, which included articles by Nathaniel, Alan Greenspan, and Robert Hessen—*Introduction to Objectivist Epistemology,* a preview of her intended future book on Objectivism, which many professional philosophers consider to be her most important philosophical work—*The Romantic Manifesto: A Philosophy of Literature*—and *The New Left: The Anti-Industrial Revolution.* All of these collections, which have regularly been reprinted and have continued selling in both hardcover and paperback, added substantially to the dissemination of her ideas and to her fame. One important consequence of Ayn's nonfiction writing was that, because purely philosophical presentations of her ideas were in print, more and more college and university theses began to be written on Objectivism, more and more college and university professors began to assign books on Objectivism as required reading in their courses.

The response to Ayn's ideas continued to be astonishing, even to those who were convinced of the validity of those ideas. She appeared on Johnny Carson's "Tonight Show" on three occasions in 1967 and 1968. Johnny Carson had intended to interview her briefly, but as their time ran out, he scrapped the other appearances scheduled so that Ayn might continue speaking. NBC told her that the mail response was the largest in the history of the show; well over three thousand letters were received—and only twelve of them were negative in tone and content.

By the late sixties, Objectivism had become a firmly established movement, a firmly established part of the American culture. And the movement, begun on a dining-room table, was becoming a society. In 1967, NBI and *The Objectivist* moved out of their crowded offices at 120 East Thirty-fourth Street—the apartment building where Ayn and Frank now lived, as did Nathaniel and I, and Leonard Peikoff—to the Empire State Building. NBI now had a large auditorium, where lectures were given, a full production department, and ample office space. The move had a symbolic meaning to all those involved in it: the Empire State Building was more than a giant edifice; it was all the skyscrapers of *The Fountainhead*—it was New York—its soaring height was its own command to rise.

Many close friendships—even a number of marriages—had formed among NBI students. It seemed time to offer the students what they appeared to want: a social life that was integrated to their philosophical interests. To celebrate the anniversary of NBI, a formal dinner and ball was held at a New York hotel for students and their guests; it was so successful that it was repeated two years later; a year after that, it was held in San Francisco. Ayn did not attend the balls: she was uncomfortable at parties, and did not know how to dance; but she reveled vicariously in the sight of her intensely serious-minded students floating happily around a dance floor in evening dress, enjoying themselves in a completely nonphilosophical manner.

NBI organized a tour of Europe during the summer of 1967, for those students particularly interested in art who wanted to visit famous European museums, under the guidance of art historian Mary Ann Sures, formerly Mary Ann Rukavina. The new auditorium made possible opportunities that had not existed before, and NBI began showing a series of movies, "The Romantic Screen," with films such as *Dark Victory, The Brothers Karamazov, Quo Vadis,* and *Shane.* Many of the students were accomplished in theater, dance, and music, and they began sharing their talents in performances in the auditorium; one evening, a fashion show was held in which, to the delight of the audience, Frank at his most dashing walked down the aisle in an elegant dinner suit. At the suggestion of one of the more athletic students, two baseball teams were formed—called "Attilas" and "The Witch Doctors" after the philosophical villains Ayn had described in *For the New Intellectual*—to fight enthusiastically inept battles in Central Park; after each encounter, the less athletic limped about groaning from the pain of formerly unused muscles; after one encounter, the athletic student who had suggested the teams sheepishly arrived at NBI's offices on crutches.

A monthly tradition of dancing evenings at NBI began. Before the formal start of each evening, Robert Berole, a teacher of ballroom dancing, gave group lessons for those unsure of themselves on a dance floor, and demonstrations of each dance in which I—discovering depths of exhibitionism I had not known I possessed, and after painstaking lessons from Robert—joined him. One great pleasure of those evenings was that they were the cause of Ayn's decision, at the age of sixty-two, that it was time she learned to dance. She asked Robert Berole to give lessons to Frank and her at their apartment.

Robert was to recall those lessons as fascinating occasions. "Ayn was amazing," he said. "She went about learning to dance just as she went about the most philosophical of activities: with absolute concentration and dedication. During every lesson, she would make elaborate notes on the steps of each dance, so she could work on them before the next lesson. Although she had never danced before, she learned with remarkable speed; I never had to tell her anything twice. . . . The problem was Frank. When they'd be dancing together, he seemed almost paralyzed, he couldn't be spontaneous with her; when he and I worked together, he was fine. . . . After the lesson, Ayn would make coffee, and we'd talk for a couple of hours. It was a privilege I never expected to have. I'll never forget those wonderful conversations, nor how charming and sensitive she was. . . . Ayn particularly wanted to learn the Viennese waltz, the most difficult of all dances; she said it had always been her favorite. We worked on that one most of all."

One evening, Ayn decided that she was ready to dance in public. Wearing a softly colored cocktail dress and impeccably groomed, she arrived at NBI's auditorium—and Ayn and Robert whirled around the dance floor perfectly executing the complex steps of a Viennese waltz. The expression on her face varied between intense concentration and delighted pride in her new accomplishment. It was a picture of Ayn that NBI's students would not forget; they had regarded her with awe as a giant existing somewhere in the stratosphere with the ghosts of

Aristotle and Victor Hugo, and now watched with pleasure and astonishment the enchanting child-woman who had replaced the symbol.

But the symbol was waiting in the wings. In step with the rapid progress of Objectivism through the culture, an event was occurring within the narrower confines of the movement itself that was perhaps inevitable, that was tragic, that was ominous in its implications.

NBI students were, in the main, a remarkable group of people of unusually high intelligence and ambition, educated, sensitive, idealistic, as has been noted by countless observers; the appeal of Ayn's philosophy was the appeal to intelligence. They were disenchanted with the answers to their questions offered to them by their religious and social traditions, by their teachers, by their thinkers and philosophers. They were seeking understanding; they were seeking knowledge and certainty and reason; they were seeking a serious and intelligible philosophical framework that would enable them to understand the world and rational values by which to guide their lives.

Reading Ayn's books and attending lectures, they felt themselves entering the world they had sought. They felt they were discovering a comprehensive, intelligible, integrated view of existence, a view of unwavering internal consistency, a methodology by which to deal effectively with existence, and a noble, life-celebrating vision of their own possibilities, of the efficacy of their minds, of the heights and the happiness possible to them. And they were discovering the person of Ayn Rand. When she lectured before them or spoke to them individually, she discussed the widest of philosophical issues—and demonstrated the application of those issues to the urgent requirements of their own lives; like John Galt in *Atlas,* who solved the most complex and abstract problems of theoretical physics in order to build a better motor to benefit human life, she had worked on the most complex problems of philosophy in order to improve man's life on earth; metaphysics and epistemology did not exist in some ivory tower of the intellect, they were the means of providing men with a motor by which to power the course of their lives. Through her person, they encountered the concrete reality of a great mind, a seductive, hypnotic mind able to dance lightly through the web of problems and unanswered questions that enmeshed their lives and provide solutions of seemingly irrefutable logic. They encountered her special charm, as seductive as her intelligence.

But they encountered, as well, the puzzling shifts of emotional attitude that often characterized Ayn—the dogmatism implicit in her later writings, her conviction that rational consistency required not only the acceptance of the fundamentals of Objectivism but the acceptance of her specific applications of those principles to any and every issue.[3] They encountered the near-deification of Ayn

---

[3] British writer Colin Wilson became a victim of this demand for total acceptance. He wrote Ayn an enthusiastic letter praising her work—and including his objections to certain concepts. The response was a harshly denunciatory letter from Nathaniel, who had taken on, at Ayn's request, the job of screening and answering mail which he considered offensive to her; in this category she included letters which disagreed or argued with her philosophical ideas. Wilson persevered, believing that if

Rand that had emerged from her own inner conflicts and from the attitude of many of her friends, together with her idealization of Nathaniel and others in the circle around her as models to be emulated. (Once, she was asked, "Can heroes such as you write about really exist?" Proudly, she pointed first at herself, then at Frank, then at Nathaniel, and then at me, and replied: "Here is my proof that they can and *do* exist!" On another occasion, she called out from the audience, when Nathaniel had said that he didn't know if he spoke for Ayn in a particular instance, "You have my blank check, which I've never given to anyone else. You may *always* speak for me.") They encountered her austere and self-denying preoccupation with the future at the expense of the present—her focus on long-range goals at the expense of short-range pleasures and emotional spontaneity, her conviction that in making decisions and in dealing with other people, emotions are irrelevant and only one's rational judgment may be considered. They encountered her conviction that love and affection, as rewards to be earned, could and should be withdrawn at the least infraction of morality or rationality, that reason demands constantly passing moral judgments on one's own character and that of others. They encountered her view that they, like all men, teetered constantly on the edge of moral depravity, and that to the extent to which they failed to achieve the stature of a Howard Roark or a John Galt, self-contempt and guilt were the appropriate reactions.

They encountered all of this while still reeling from the onslaught of an avalanche of new and exciting ideas which they were struggling to grasp and integrate. Some of them were able to thread carefully through the maze of ideas, implications, and attitudes being simultaneously presented to them. Others left to find their own paths. Many of them accepted the total, as one inseparable package. Those who accepted the package were on their way to becoming true believers, growing self-alienated and alienated from others, intellectually rigid, guilty over their failures, quick to judge and accuse others. It was the path that had been followed by those of us in the circle they were expected to emulate, as they moved from the ecstasy of learning their own powers and the power of reason—to the agony of grasping their supposed failures and flaws and psychological problems and inadequacies—and then back to the ecstasy—and then back again to the agony, in a never-ending cycle of pleasure and pain, until at the end of that path pain became the dominant emotion.

On many occasions, I would walk to the podium when I gave my own lectures, see the admiring glances with which I was greeted, know that I was perceived as supremely controlled, aloof, self-contained, invulnerable—and I would cringe, feeling I was hidden behind a mask I did not know how to remove, a mask that hid suffering and vulnerability and the longing to be recognized as I truly was. I did not yet grasp the nature and meaning of what I saw in myself, in Ayn, in Nathaniel, in many of our friends and many of our students; I

---

he could get past Nathaniel to Ayn, a mutually beneficial correspondence would be possible. But his letters continued to be answered by Nathaniel.

knew only that I experienced a growing uneasiness. Sometimes, I would think grimly—it was a thought without context or evaluation—"I'll try until I'm forty, I'll continue the struggle, I'll continue to learn, I'll continue to grow; but then, if I've still found no way to be happy in the life I'm leading—I'll get out. I'll go, I don't care where, but I'll go!" For the present, I was held tightly. Eric Hoffer wrote in *The True Believer,* " 'Things which are not' are indeed mightier than 'things that are.' In all ages men have fought most desperately for beautiful cities yet to be built and gardens yet to be planted." I was still fighting for my beautiful city and my unplanted garden.

In the first years of the lectures, Ayn's appearance at question periods was an event eagerly anticipated by the students. She was usually courteous, considerate, and painstaking in her response if a question seemed to her valid and intelligent; the students recognized the enormous compliment to them which her attitude projected, her assumption that they required and would respond to only a rational argument. But if she did not believe the question to be valid and intelligent, she was scathing in her denunciation; her anger, she would insist, was rationally justified moral indignation. A young man asked: "How can you expect everyone to be rational and to arrive at correct philosophical conclusions, if they have not been taught rationality and have not been exposed to a philosophy of reason?" Ayn exploded. "*I* did it myself!" she shouted. "No one taught *me* how to think! Anyone can, who chooses to." The student later said to his friends, "How can she have it both ways? How can she consider herself a great innovator, yet insist that everyone should arrive at the conclusions she did?"

It was the question period—the event she once had most enjoyed—that gradually became the arena in which Ayn was especially bewildering and damaging to her students, all at once becoming enraged by an innocent question and lashing out furiously at the hapless questioner. Margit von Mises was to say, "Lu and I attended one or two of the Nathaniel Branden Institute lectures, and I was shocked at Ayn Rand's behavior. She was on the podium, smoking one of her cigarettes in that long black holder. Someone asked her a question, and she answered in such a rude, disagreeable way that I couldn't understand how anyone could take it. She just killed the questioner with her reply. You can do indescribable harm to people that way. I couldn't understand how she could hurt people, and I disliked her terribly for that."

Ultimately, students either ceased asking her questions, or framed them with such care that they became meaningless. After several years, Nathaniel and I gradually lengthened the time between Ayn's appearances at question periods; since she had come to dislike them, it was not difficult to do.

And yet, when one looks at the life of Ayn Rand, one must wonder if the dogmatic absolutism of her certainty, the blinding conviction of her own rectitude and her special place in the world, the callousness of her intolerance for opinions that were not hers, the unwavering assurance that she was alone to know the truth and that others must seek it from her—the eyes that looked neither to the left nor to the right, but only at the path ahead—the savage innocence of her personality—was not the fuel required for the height of achievement she attained. Just as when one looks at history's great achievers one so often encounters the desperate loneliness and alienation which is perhaps the emotional price paid by men and women who see farther than their brothers, so one also encounters these qualities of Ayn Rand. And one must wonder if they are not precisely the qualities that make possible the courage and uncompromising dedication of those who forge new paths through the unknown, enduring and persevering, shouting defiance at the enormity of the opposition which follows them at every step of their lonely journey, and adding new glories to our world. Would a lesser conviction have made it possible? The unyielding intransigence distorts the life and corrupts the personality of the innovator. But is it a tragic flaw—or is it, in the end, when one pushes past the rubble and the pain, neither tragic nor a flaw?

As the sixties proceeded, Ayn was deeply immersed in work, in lecturing, in providing intellectual guidance for the growing number of NBI lecturers, in writing for *The Objectivist,* in organizing collections of her articles for book publication, in planning her book on epistemology. And for the first time since the publication of *Atlas Shrugged,* she began to talk of writing another novel. It was not to be a philosophical novel, it would not present new ideas; it would show in action the meaning of ideas already presented in *Atlas.* The theme would be "the benevolent universe." In an appalling irony not evident at the time, she decided that the plot would involve the novel's protagonist, a woman, coping with the problem of unrequited love.

Ayn had not worked out the details of the plot, except that the heroine would be a ballet dancer, passionately in love with a man who rejects her and who, by his rejection and by his actions throughout the story, brings her terrible anguish.

Ayn had decided on the novel's ending. The man whom the heroine loves, now deeply in love with her, bitterly regretting what he has done and what he has failed to understand, at last tells her of his love. He asks her forgiveness for the pain she has endured. The last line of the novel was to be: " 'What pain?' she asked."

Ayn did not write her book on epistemology. She did not write her novel about the unimportance of pain. Instead, what was to come was itself like fiction. What had happened in her professional life after she completed *We the Living,* was now beginning to happen in her personal life: the events of the last half of the sixties seemed devised by some demonic fiction writer precisely to increase, to harden into unyielding stone her alienation, her anger, her frustration, her sense that the world was savagely, mindlessly irrational.

In one sense, she *did* write her novel. She wrote it not with pen and paper but in the events of her own life—and with a different last line.

Chapter Twenty-eight

Ayn was not yet sixty when all the doors of the world began opening for her. Her books had achieved a readership beyond her most extravagant expectations; they were read and pondered and discussed in cities around the world; their influence was beginning to be felt in her adopted country. She was not enormously wealthy, but her time and her comfort were assured for life; she would never again have to work at a job she loathed. Despite the disappointments that had dogged her, she sometimes spoke as if she had gained all her desires and all her dreams. With one exception.

It was in 1964, her spirits and enthusiasm for life rising, that Ayn turned once more to her personal life and to Nathaniel.

Nathaniel, she had said, was her tie to the world outside her own consciousness. In a life too often barren of emotional rewards, he was her unexpected gift from the world, the one reward for which she had not had to battle, which had come to her freely. He was the man who had given her a sense of visibility—as a thinker, as an artist, as a person, as a woman—that no one else had given her. He understood her work, and understood *her;* and because of his understanding, he had fallen in love with her and had made possible a romantic happiness she had long ceased to expect.

She had often said that Nathaniel was her future as well. He was her "intellectual heir," her public spokesman, the man who would carry on her philosophy and her ideals and add to her work by his own intellectual achievements.

It was now six years since she had put their affair on hold; since then, their relationship had rarely been sexual; they were loving friends—who always knew there was more between them, not yet to be given reality. For too long, she had lost her emotional resiliency; for too many years, she had been absorbed in struggling to understand the nature of the culture in which she lived; for too long, the only personal contacts that had been meaningful to her, aside from her relationship with Frank, had been with the small circle of her intimate friends. Now, her need to live fully, to live in the world rather than in the confines of her own mind, to be a *woman* again, to live vibrantly and joyously, to experience the personal happiness of which she had so long deprived herself, burst free of the chains that bound it. She was ready to resume her sexual affair with Nathaniel.

She did not know that it was much too late. A year earlier, Nathaniel had met a young woman, an NBI student, and had fallen in love with her. Patrecia Gullison was a beautiful and charming girl who worked as a model; she was not intellectual in her interests or approach to life, but she had an unusual emotional spontaneity and openness and, at times, a startlingly acute sensitivity. In their first meetings, Nathaniel did not admit to himself his growing feelings for her, but he found in their occasional encounters a response he had never received before, and that he needed desperately. For the first time in his life, he felt himself to be receiving the priceless gift of a woman's total acceptance. Patrecia did not require him to change, to grow, to learn, to improve; she loved and admired him precisely as he was. Throughout our marriage, Nathaniel and I constantly had made every presumed failure in each other, every deficiency, every confusion, every attribute deemed unworthy, the subject of long analyses and discussion and solemn chastisement. In Ayn's relationship with Nathaniel, the problem was vastly multiplied: she saw shortcomings and criticized him from the perspective of a philosophical height I had not attained. He felt that he was loved only to the extent that he was brilliant, that he manifested the qualities of Ayn's heroes, that he was the master of reality, that he was without flaw or inner conflict. With Patrecia, Nathaniel could be young again, he could be carefree and open and unafraid; he need not guard every word and every thought; he could be *himself,* and know that who he was satisfied Patrecia utterly. Her love was unconditional. It contradicted everything he had learned about the nature of love, everything he had taught others; and he discovered that he needed it as a drowning man needs air and breath and solidity beneath his feet.

Before their relationship had fully developed, Patrecia, believing Nathaniel to be out of reach, married Lawrence Scott, who was also an NBI student. Nathaniel continued to see her; it seemed an innocent friendship. But as time went by, it began to seem less innocent; both Larry and I began to suspect that the friendship had become love. Patrecia denied it to Larry, and Nathaniel denied it to me; if I doubted his fidelity, Nathaniel often told me, it was a sign that I had unidentified psychological problems; they were friends, and important to each other, nothing more. We did not know that Nathaniel and Patrecia were already involved in a sexual affair.

As I look back on the events of those years, I realize that the truth was evident. I did not see it—I did not fully believe the evidence of my senses—because it appeared to me impossible that Nathaniel would lie to me. He had been completely honest about his affair with Ayn. Why would he not be honest now?—especially when our marriage was in tatters, and there was little left to preserve. And I, too, had become romantically interested in someone else. I had told Nathaniel how I felt, and that I would not deceive him; if there were to be an affair, it would only be with his knowledge and consent. For two years, Nathaniel, expressing what appeared to be a genuine anguish, had refused his consent. It was early in 1964 that he finally acceded—without telling me that for several months he had been involved in a sexual affair with Patrecia. My relationship did not last, as it could not. The man I loved and I were overwhelmed by what appeared to be Nathaniel's magnanimity and benevolence toward us; it was an attitude that was fatal to our relationship. One cannot emotionally carry the burden of intense gratitude to another man, and at the same time feel that he has a right to that man's wife.

Nathaniel did not tell Ayn of his affair. It seemed to him that he *could* not. He had accepted—he was even teaching, in classes all over the country, as he had taught his clients and friends in therapy—Ayn's theory that romantic love is one's response to one's highest, most exalted values, and that to choose a lesser value over a greater one is an act of spiritual and moral depravity. Now, he was in love, not with Ayn Rand, not with the woman whom he believed exemplified all that was best and noblest in the human spirit—but with a young girl who did not comprehend the great issues and purposes that he told himself were all that was important in life.

Now, like so many of his students, like so many of his friends, Nathaniel swung between suffering and joy. He moved from the joy of his meetings with Patrecia, from the knowledge that he loved passionately and was loved as passionately in return—to the guilt of living a lie with Ayn and with me, the guilt of feeling that his love could not be displayed to the world, that by its very nature, it must be hidden from the day, and the still worse guilt of believing that he had betrayed the best within himself by his romantic choice.

It was then that Ayn told him she was ready to resume their affair. He had known it was coming, he had tried to be prepared, he was not prepared. He leaped to the first semi-honest response he could find. His marriage was shattering, he said; he was upset and had no emotional capacity left for anything else. Shocked, Ayn offered to help solve his marital problems. Nathaniel assured her that once they were resolved, whatever the resolution, their own relationship would be repaired and resurrected. Once more, Ayn put her emotional life on hold.

For several months, Ayn met with Nathaniel and me to discuss the conflicts that divided us, exhibiting a kindness, a generosity, a tenderness that had long seemed absent from her personality. Despite her desire for Nathaniel, despite her hectic professional schedule of public appearances and writing, she devoted priceless hours to the effort to understand and resolve the problems destroying the marriage of the man she loved. She blamed neither of us; there was no hint of moralism in her attitude or conversation, only a deep, loving desire for our happiness. But by then, the marriage that should never have begun had reached its final dead end.

During these months, Ayn was dealing with another problem that was emotionally devastating to her. Frank was growing increasingly frail and thin, and had developed a contraction of the tendons of his hands which seriously interfered with his painting. When he went into the hospital for surgery, Ayn was terrified. She had never been ill; she had never been hospitalized; the world of doctors and hospitals and surgery was strange to her, and frightening. She rarely left Frank's side during his hospital stay, she rarely slept, her tension was palpable in the room in which she sat. But the operation was successful, and Frank was soon able to return to his work and to the Art Students League. He had been elected to the League's Board of Control, its policy-making organization, where he served ably and conscientiously for three years. He rented a small apartment in the building where he and Ayn lived and converted it into a studio. He needed his work and his separate world of the League and his studio more than he had ever needed them; for the next years, he was to be a silent observer of conversations and encounters that shattered him emotionally, that he should not have been present at, and that he had no way to cope with.

In the summer of 1965—exhausted from years of struggling to feel what I did not feel, angry at my growing sense that I was not being told the truth about Patrecia—I told Nathaniel that I wanted a divorce. I took an apartment in the same Thirty-fourth Street building where we had lived for several years, and where Ayn and Frank were also living. Nathaniel and I continued to work together and spend time together, even to travel together to NBI lectures and events; we still were comrades-in-arms, we still were fighting for the same ideals; that had been the strongest bond between us, and it remained.

Not long after our marital parting, Larry and Patrecia were separated. Patrecia was free to see Nathaniel more regularly. But she was not free of guilt; Nathaniel had told her of his past relationship with Ayn and the events now unfolding between them. Patrecia felt that she, as well as Nathaniel, owed Ayn a debt that could never be repaid; and now they were betraying her. And she was not free of suffering; she knew Nathaniel believed that in choosing her, he had chosen a lesser value over a higher one, that he did not view her as a full citizen of the world he inhabited, that, even when both their marriages had ended, he still felt it necessary to hide their relationship. She endured the guilt and the pain because she loved him, as she, too, struggled to accept the unacceptable.

A river of anguish and betrayal and deceit was moving to swamp everyone involved in a situation that should never have begun. With Frank well again, and Nathaniel's marriage at an end, Ayn wanted to resume her interrupted love affair. But she was puzzled and upset by Nathaniel's behavior. She felt that he was withdrawing from her, that he was continually busy with other activities and other people, that he had less time for her and less interest in her, that even when they were together his emotional remoteness was interfering with the former closeness of their relationship. He engaged only in abstract philosophical and psychological conversations with her in a manner appropriate to a colleague but not to a lover. And he talked obsessively about his friendship with Patrecia, a young woman whom Ayn liked but did not believe warranted the sacrifice of Nathaniel's time and interest. How did he have time or interest for a friendship in view of what was unresolved between them?

Nathaniel tried to allay Ayn's uneasiness by assurances of his love, assurances that he needed and wanted her, that she was the most important person in his life—and he struggled to believe that it was so. He spoke vaguely of problems troubling him, of physical and emotional exhaustion, of depression, of being overworked, as Ayn tried conscientiously to listen and to help. But as his retreat from her and the progressive deterioration of their relationship continued to escalate through the ensuing months, she began to question the reality of his love. Yet still—struggling vainly with guilt and a sense of failure, desperately telling himself his feeling for Patrecia would somehow miraculously vanish, that Ayn need never know of it, that it would equally miraculously be replaced by a passionate sexual response to Ayn—Nathaniel continued to assure her that the problems besetting their relationship had nothing to do with his love for her.

It was the "triangle," he explained—the triangle consisting of Ayn, Frank, and himself—that seemed to him an insuperable emotional barrier. He was naming something that, like his weariness and depression, was an authentic problem, but not the basic problem. He spoke of his pain during the early days of their affair, his constant awareness that he shared her with another man, that he had no rights in their relationship and could make no claims, that her first loyalty was and had to be to her husband. His emotional state, he said, was caused by the knowledge that if they resumed their affair, he would be sentenced to that pain again; it was the fear of it that was causing his retreat from Ayn.

Trying to ignore her feeling that she was hearing only part of the reasons for his estrangement, her bewilderment that the difficulties of the triangle could be more important to Nathaniel than the value she represented to him—Ayn plunged into a period of working to help Nathaniel with this new conflict. She wrote lengthy papers on her analysis of his psychology, on the meaning and solution to what appeared to be tormenting him, they discussed her papers and her theories for long and futile hours. But the result of her best efforts was not an improvement in their relationship; it became still more gray and strained and empty. The romance whose meaning to her had been the enjoyment of life on earth, was deteriorating into endless psychological sessions, endless excruciatingly difficult labor for her—and the tortured sense that everything she did and said was somehow beside the point, that she was losing him.

Sometimes, she would tell Nathaniel her doubts of his love. Was that the *real* problem? she demanded. Was he afraid to say he no longer loved her? Always, he denied it, reassured her, insisted that he would make their relationship what it should be once his personal problems were solved, that he was painfully aware he had drifted away, but he would change that—insisting it still more vehemently in the privacy of his own thoughts. I love Ayn, he seemed to be telling himself; Patrecia is only a temporary need in my life. I love Ayn, but I can't release the feeling; something is blocking it—that's the only problem.

Sometimes, Ayn asked him: Is it the age difference? Is that what has come between us? She was to tell me, later, at the worst of her suffering, "As Nathan and I were talking, I looked down at my arm, and I saw the loose skin of a woman in her sixties . . . and I felt old. . . ." No, he insisted, the age difference did not matter, as it had never mattered. Always he denied it, appalled at the thought of what it would do to her if he admitted the truth: that their twenty-five year age difference *was* an impediment to him. In 1966, Nathaniel was thirty-six and Ayn was sixty-one; that had become one more barrier he did not know how to cross.

It was toward the end of that year that Nathaniel first told me, truthfully, what was happening between Ayn and himself—and, untruthfully, that he was only now about to begin a sexual affair with Patrecia. I was horrified, and frightened for both Ayn and Nathaniel. I well understood Nathaniel's conviction that he *must* love Ayn; I had spent years dealing with the identical conflict in my marriage. But he *had to* tell her the truth, I insisted, or he would destroy them both. When he said he could not, not yet, not without one more effort to break out of his dilemma, I understood; I felt, in some undefined way, that if Ayn were to break with him now—the inevitable result of telling her the truth—her moral disapproval and contempt would shatter him in a manner beyond mending. I agreed to keep his secret, either until he had given up Patrecia and cheerfully returned to his prior relationship with Ayn—or until he had told her the truth. I did not know what my silence was to cost me—or what it was to cost Ayn.

During these increasingly tormented years, although she continued her work, Ayn's world was narrowing down to the dimensions of her relationship with Nathaniel. It was her constant mental focus, her constant emotional focus. She seemed barely to notice Frank's quiet presence, their discussions of his painting grew less frequent, the distance dividing them grew greater. She became more impatient and intolerant of NBI's students, more demanding of her friends, quicker to anger as her personal life fell into disarray. But always, students and friends were told that it was their own irrationality that was the cause of her anger and demands; they could not know that they were struggling in a web of deceit they had not spun.

Ayn's only hold on her belief in Nathaniel's love was brief periods which she later described as "honeymoon periods," when he inexplicably seemed warmer, closer, more loving, when he experienced the return of his early feelings for her, and she could begin to hope that their conflicts were over, that he was not abandoning her after all. But each honeymoon soon ended, as Nathaniel was flung back into guilt, into remorse, into further deceit.

Early in 1968—as Nathaniel was working, in a hideous irony, on a series of articles for *The Objectivist* entitled "Self-Esteem and Romantic Love"—Ayn took me into her confidence, describing her bewilderment with Nathaniel and the events that had occurred between them during the past few years. A new "honeymoon period" had just ended as the others had ended, and for the first time in a lifetime of battles she was faced with a battle she could not handle alone. She turned to me for help—for someone to talk to, for someone who would understand what she was enduring, for someone who might be able to explain Nathaniel's unintelligible behavior and might know a way to reach him —in a manner that was infinitely moving and painful. All her life, she had fed her enormous energy into her work and into other people; now, she needed a source of energy outside herself. During that strange and agonized year, our relationship underwent a shift. Ayn, who had always been the strong, unchanging rock in my life, the person I had turned to for advice and knowledge and certainty, could no longer maintain the ruthless repression of pain, the repression of any emotion she saw as weakness, that had ruled her for so many years. She allowed me—and herself—entry into all the hidden vulnerability of her life, and I saw and loved again, as I had so often seen and loved when she listened to her tiddlywink music, the heartbreakingly innocent young girl she once had been. But now, as the wall of repression first cracked and then shattered before my eyes, I was not seeing that young girl's joy and exaltation, but all the rejections of all the years and all the unacknowledged, helpless anguish it had caused her. She leaned on me now as if *I* were the strong older friend, and she the lost and suffering child.

"The more Nathaniel and I talk," she said, "the less I understand. And I have the feeling that nothing I say or discover will be heard, that I'm working harder on his psychology and I care more about it than he. Why is he able to think brilliantly about theoretical problems of psychology or morality, but not about personal problems? He'll seem to understand something one day—then it's gone the next day. He's warm and loving with me one day, he'll kiss me in a way that's sexual, he'll tell me he can't live without me, and I'll feel that something magnificent is possible between us—then that's gone the next day. Nothing is stable or predictable, I'm always waiting for the ax to fall. . . . He seems neither to want to break with me nor to continue. Perhaps it's good that even in his desperate unhappiness and helplessness, he doesn't want a break; perhaps it means he *does* love me. . . . I don't know. . . .

"I'm beginning to think that the problem of the triangle is some sort of rationalization. If he feels for me what he says he feels, and sees in me what he says he sees—he'd be willing to be part of a harem. Doesn't he know that the great proof of my love for him is that I chose him *despite* a happy marriage and the difference in our ages? Doesn't he know that an exclusive commitment for life is impossible? . . .

"I'm constantly hovering on the edge of breaking with him. I feel that I know nothing about him. . . . He seems dominated by fear—but of *what?* . . . I'm getting enormously exhausted. . . . I cannot stand the mystery of the issue of Patrecia. He swears he's not in love with her, and I believe it. He knows perfectly well that the only other woman I would accept in his life is you, Barbara; it would have to be a woman of your stature. And I can't believe he would ever want someone of lesser stature. But why does he talk about her so much? Why is she important to him? He explains and explains, and none of it makes any sense. . . .

"Theoretically, I believe that he loves me, but it has no emotional reality. Where are the concretes that manifest it? I cannot stand the fact that his feeling for me is totally alien and incomprehensible to me."

I struggled to help her in every way I could devise. She discussed her endless papers about Nathaniel's psychology; at her request, I talked with him about those papers and about Ayn's changing theories of his motivation. And often, I begged him to return to sanity and to Ayn or to tell her the truth before it was too late for all of us. And then I saw his anguish and an anxiety that was leaping out of control, and I knew that he could neither resume his affair with Ayn nor confess the truth to her; I felt, as he appeared to feel, that the day he broke with Ayn would be the final break in his sense of self-value—and that I was demanding the impossible of him. And so I would return to Ayn, and talk with her again, as she evolved theory after theory to explain Nathaniel.

And I lived in my own anguish with the knowledge that I was aiding Nathaniel in his deception, that Ayn trusted me and I was keeping the truth from her. Every direction seemed to lead only to disaster. Was I to destroy Nathaniel by speaking? Or was I to allow Ayn to go on in her suffering, and continue to hope that Nathaniel would be finished with his passion for Patrecia so that Ayn's pain could end? I swung between the two impossible choices, racing from my office to Ayn in the middle of the day, or from my apartment to Ayn in the middle of the night, when she called to say she had a new idea that might explain Nathaniel, or she had no idea at all and she could no longer endure the situation—and then I ran to Nathaniel, to hear him say, tears streaming down his face, "Barbara, please help me! I don't know what to do!" And I wondered what had happened to the two giants of the intellect I had known, now lost and helpless in the morass of their emotions.

Throughout this year of endless nightmare, Ayn talked compulsively to Frank about Nathaniel and her problems with him. Frank saw the wife who was *his* strong rock, *his* certainty, *his* source of knowledge in a world with which he had never learned to cope, tortured by her romantic problems with another man. He did not speak of his feelings, as he had never spoken of them; but once, in sudden, contextless anger, he said, "That man is no damn good! Why won't you see it?" He grew increasingly irritable with Ayn. As a result of years of living in her shadow, of wiping his own desires out of existence, of suffering at the sight of her pain and being helpless to alter it, he snapped at her for the least thing in an anger that added to her emotional upset. Frank was seventy-one; his health and his strength were failing; he had no money except what Ayn had earned. He had nowhere to go. And so he stayed, and endured.

Frank was growing more vague and forgetful. He seemed sometimes not fully to understand what was said to him. Often, in his explosions at Ayn, he seemed emotionally out of control. Allan Blumenthal, who was in private practice as a psychiatrist, told me he believed the change in Frank was probably due to organic processes, the beginning of what we understood as senility. Whatever the physical source, as Frank sat through months of Ayn's conversations it was evident that his wife's devotion to Nathaniel and the torment it caused her were increasingly unbearable to him; he bore it in the only way he knew how: by gradually, month by month, understanding less of what was happening and what was being said, by retreating still farther into silence and passivity, by being present at those conversations only in body, his mind absent and blank. And he bore it another way, which neither Ayn nor any of her friends suspected: he spent many hours each day in his studio, but seemed to be producing less and less; he was not painting, he was drinking, drowning his grief and his failed life in liquor.

By May, Ayn was listening again as Nathaniel spoke of another difficulty besetting him—again real, again beside the point. Ayn's constant anger with him during the early period of their romantic relationship, he said, her moral accusations and condemnation when he did not behave as she thought he should, had caused him to feel that he was trying to deal with the unpredictable; he had never known when or why her fury would descend on him. It had shaken him profoundly with regard to the possibilities of a happy relationship with her. It was the scars of those early troubles, he said, that accounted for his present behavior.

He did not say that a love affair with Ayn Rand would have been impossible for any twenty-four-year-old to cope with, and that, with more maturity, he would never have embarked upon it. It had been a mistake on both their parts, doomed by its very nature. Now the consequences of that mistake were being reaped—and Ayn and Nathaniel were caught in a trap with no exit.

Once again, Ayn tried to solve the problem, but this time she felt no sympathy for it. She was unable to recognize the havoc she had caused, to Nathaniel and to others, by her use of morality as a whip, a scourge, an instrument of damnation. Nor could she look for failure in herself, not even for the most innocent of errors. The fantasy self-image of perfection that she had spent a lifetime constructing was not to be toppled. The destruction of her relationship with Nathaniel could only be *his* fault, *his* evasions, *his* guilt.

"Yes, *I am a moralist,* first and foremost, before I'm anything else," she told me. "It's my greatest pride. . . . Whatever I project with him, happiness, passion, despair, anger, just creates more guilt in him—I'm in a straitjacket. He sees me as some kind of unpredictable terror. . . . I feel so terribly invisible. . . . He doesn't really love me, it's a duty, he'd really like to find an escape and he's looking for a rationalization. . . . Everything is switching and swimming. . . . My fear is that I'm too much for him, and he wants something else. Everything keeps adding up to this. It's all so crazy, I don't believe anything we've identified about his present state, something is still being hidden from me and from himself —there's something he hasn't faced and doesn't want to face. . . .

"The worst pain of all is my feeling that it was so right that he should fall in love with me . . . yet he's been trying to kill his feeling, and he's succeeding."

I went to Nathaniel to demand that he tell Ayn he was not in love with her, even if he could not bring himself to tell her about Patrecia. "Don't leave her in this hell!" I said. But when I saw the look on his face, I grew silent. Soon after, he called me late one night to say, "Please come. I need you." I spent the rest of the night holding him in my arms, trying somehow to reassure him, somehow to force energy and hope into him, as he said, "Don't you think I know that my behavior is inexcusable? I'm in a maze, where every avenue leads only to tragedy."

On a morning in early July, Nathaniel telephoned me at NBI and asked me to come to his apartment. Once again, I flew from my desk, ignoring the curious looks of the staff; they could not avoid knowing—observing my continual unexplained absences, the hours I spent on the telephone in hushed conversations with Ayn or Nathaniel, and observing the tension in Nathaniel that hung about him like a black cloud—that something was terribly wrong. Ayn's friends knew it, too, but did not suspect the nature or dimensions of the problem.

When I reached Nathaniel's, he said that Ayn was to visit him that evening at eight o'clock, and that he had decided to tell her a part of the truth; this time, it would be a part that mattered. He would explain that the difference in their ages had become an impassable barrier to his sexual feeling. He wrote out what he wanted to communicate, in order not to stumble inadvertently into formulations even more hurtful than the facts. When she arrived, he would give her the paper, she would read it, and then they would talk. His paper was as tactful as such a document could be—but I shuddered at the thought of what Ayn would feel when she read it. What kind of nightmare would it be for a woman to learn that the man she loves finds her too old to inspire romantic feelings? This would be the final, crushing blow for her, the worst of all the blows she had received.

It was not yet nine o'clock in the evening when my telephone rang. It was Ayn —in a fury. "Come down at once," she demanded, "and see what this monster has done!" I was there within moments. I entered to find Ayn raging at an ashen-faced Nathaniel. The insult to her dignity, too overwhelming to bear, had been hurled out of conscious awareness—it was evident that she was, in those moments, totally unaware of her wounds—and what replaced it was anger, and outrage, and condemnation. Their relationship—*any* relationship between them —was over, she cried; she would never see or deal with him again.

Later, I was to ask Nathaniel, "Why didn't you take advantage, over the years, of the 'outs' Ayn offered you about the issue of her age? Why didn't you tell her then?" "Because I never believed that she would accept it," he replied. "I believed she raised it so that I would deny it. I thought that if I admitted it, it would end as it did end, and I would be morally condemned in her eyes and my own."

The tortured situation, in which those involved were simultaneously victims and executioners, began its rapid roll to the disastrous end that had begun fourteen years ago on a sunny winter's day drive from Toronto.

Ayn would not discuss the terrible injury to her of Nathaniel's sexual rejection. A scoundrel had no power to damage her sense of her femininity, she insisted angrily; the man she had thought Nathaniel to be, could have hurt her and did; the man he had become, could not and did not. There was agony in her eyes, and a twisted look to her mouth, but the protective wall of emotional repression had slammed down again.

She spoke, instead, of fear and horror and rage and furious indignation—and she shifted back and forth between her initial decision to break totally with Nathaniel, and her wish to give him "one more chance" to solve his problems. Her greatest fear appeared to be that she had given Nathaniel her public sanction, she had said that he spoke for her—and now she believed him to be a man capable of any outrage. "I can't predict what he'll do," she said, "and I'm terrified of what may happen to my name and reputation. I've put them in his hands—*this* is what the struggle of my life has gone into!—I've turned everything over to him because he said he loved me and I believed him—and now I have to wait in terror to see when he will disgrace me professionally. He *must* save me from this horror, or disconnect himself from me and my name and close NBI. If he doesn't save my name, then I'll break with him publicly, I'll disgrace him, it doesn't matter what happens to him now, I've got to protect myself! . . .

"The worst of all is that he has destroyed my view of him. . . . To see as a scoundrel the man I thought closest to me philosophically, personally, romantically—the man to whom I dedicated *Atlas Shrugged,* and told the world he was my intellectual heir! He has no right to other people or concerns, he has no right to go on vacations and lie in the sun and run around with casual people—he must be with me every evening and try to think and work, he must have no other life or concerns—he can't just say: sorry, I have a problem, so good-bye, I'm leaving you with the problem and me with all the advantages. It's too late to break, after all this hell. He has no right to a private life which is paid for by my life, to his beautiful apartment, paid for by what I went through with *Night of January 16th*—I will not retire from the scene and let him profit. He can't have a private life and the adulation and wealth that I created, after he has ditched me and abandoned me to my suffering."

Her voice grew low and weary. "How can I believe I will ever be visible to anyone? The best mind I ever knew, the man closest to me in every way, rejected me as a person. Everyone else profits from my ideas, but I am punished for them, punished for the happiness I bring to others, for initiating and living up to those ideas." Her voice was almost too low to be heard as she said, "There is nothing for me to look forward to, nothing to hope for in reality. My life is over. He has forced me into a permanent ivory tower. He took away this earth."

Ayn demanded that Nathaniel immediately cancel his plans for the stage production of *The Fountainhead.* A year earlier, NBI Theater had been established for the purpose of producing off-Broadway plays. Its first production was to be a dramatization of *The Fountainhead,* which I had written, and which Ayn had enthusiastically approved. There had been considerable interest in the roles among actors: Robert Lansing had expressed the desire to play Roark, and Jessica Walter and Susan Crane were considering the part of Dominique.

Through the winter of 1967 and into the summer of 1968, plans for the play had proceeded. Ralph Roseman, a man of both managerial and aesthetic talent, with years of successful experience as a stage producer and manager both on and off Broadway and in touring companies, was engaged as General Manager. Phillip Smith, an NBI student experienced as a stage director and acting teacher, was to direct. The Jan Hus Playhouse on East Seventy-fourth Street was leased for the production, which was to open in October. Cast auditions were conducted in the NBI auditorium.

In accordance with Ayn's wish, all plans for the production were canceled.

As if out of an instinct that would not die, Ayn still met with Nathaniel, although with much less frequency than before. She said that her purpose was to save her reputation by helping him psychologically. It was evident that that was only part of her purpose. Somewhere inside her remained the last faint remnant of a hope that all the problems and pain would vanish, and Nathaniel would again be the dashing young lover she had known so long ago.

The blows had not stopped falling on Ayn. On an evening in mid-July, she spent more than a dozen hours with Nathaniel, talking and suggesting and advising. It was then that he admitted—saying it was a realization he had come to only now—that he cared for Patrecia more than he had said. He denied that they were having a sexual affair, but he acknowledged the strength of his feelings. When he said, "I know what this must mean to you, to be rejected for a lesser value"—Ayn was outraged. "How *dare* you speak to me of 'lesser values'?" she demanded. "It's not an issue of that! It's far worse—the girl is nothing! In fact, in reality, this situation is obscene!"

It was the final affront for Ayn. "I don't believe he has just realized that he loves Patrecia," she said. "I believe *nothing* he has said, now or ever!" With instructions that I was to repeat her words to Nathaniel, whom she categorically refused to see, she said she would wait two months, until just before the fall NBI courses were to begin in New York and across the country, to decide if he would "regain his mind," and learn to apply Objectivism to his behavior no matter what his emotions. "If the rational part of him can still be saved, he may stay at NBI, and he may work on his writing, but Objectivism must become his exclusive career. He may create no disgrace in his personal life that will reflect on me. And I want a statement from him, in writing, that it is his intellectual judgment that my position on Patrecia is understood by him and is objective. The alternative is that *I* will create a public scandal."

Nathaniel, appalled by Ayn's terms, nevertheless agreed to them. Ayn had no legal power over NBI, although without her sanction it would be impossible to continue. It was not predominantly the fear of public scandal or the possible loss of NBI that motivated his agreement; it was the charismatic force of Ayn Rand. She still remained a moral authority, the fountainhead of morality.

On an evening in August, Ayn told me that she was about to call her attorney and make an appointment to change her will. Should Frank predecease her, Nathaniel was the heir to her estate, with the understanding that Frank would make similar provisions should she die first. "I intend *you* to be my heir," she said. "I'm changing my will at once." Somehow, I stumbled out my gratitude, invented the excuse of a pressing business meeting, and ran to Nathaniel's apartment.

"I've reached the end," I said. "Ayn is about to make me her heir. It is not possible for me to live with that and continue to hide the truth from her. It's too late for you to tell her. *I* have to do it. There's no argument in the world, no problem in the world, that will prevent it."

Nathaniel agreed. He did not speak of arguments or problems. He seemed relieved that the truth would be known at last, that he would finally be free of the crushing burden of lies.

And Ayn sat alone at the desk at which she had written *Atlas Shrugged,* mourning the loss of the man who had offered her the possibility of living richly in the world and living ecstatically as a woman, feeling abandoned to an incomprehensible mystery. She did not know that she soon was to lose, as well, the intellectual crusade that had been at the heart of her new fame as a philosopher.

Chapter Twenty-nine

The snowball of events had kept rolling and growing, while the four of us had stood as if at the bottom of a cold steep cliff, paralyzed, watching helplessly as it began its furious rush down the mountain to bury us all in white horror. Now, the events had reached their climax. We were hurled into the snow's pounding maelstrom, and we flailed blindly, unable to see each other, to reach each other, to touch each other's hand one last time.

Early on the morning of August 23, I telephoned Allan Blumenthal. I shuddered at the thought of the effects on Ayn when she learned the full truth; she would need help and support, but she would refuse to accept them from me; she would refuse ever to see me again. As a psychiatrist and a friend, Allan was the logical person to have standing by. I asked him to come to my apartment on an urgent matter. When he arrived, Nathaniel was with me; he had suggested that he be present to verify what I intended to tell Allan.

Breaking my vow of secrecy for the first time, I told Allan the events of the past fourteen years—of Ayn and Nathaniel's affair, of Nathaniel's relationship with Patrecia, of the lies and deceit that had followed. Allan was stunned and indignant, but his negative reaction was predominantly directed toward Ayn. "How could she have begun this whole nightmare?" he demanded. "And with a twenty-four-year-old kid! How could she have done this to Frank and to you, Barbara? How could she have failed to know where it would lead?"

When Frank opened the door that evening, Allan and I entered to greet a tense and agitated Ayn. Something in my voice when I made the appointment had told her there was another blow to come.

For the first and only time, everything I had learned about emotional repression stood me in good stead. When I began to speak, my words were measured and precise and my voice steady. I said that I had something to tell her that would profoundly upset her and would end our friendship. I explained why I had asked Allan to be present, and that it had been necessary for me to tell him of her romance with Nathaniel, because that was what I intended to discuss. For a moment, she looked puzzled; then there was a flash of anger in her eyes. She nodded silently. "Nathaniel has been lying to you," I said. "I've been lying to you. For almost five years, he has been in love with Patrecia and has been having an affair with her. I've known part of the truth for more than a year."

Ayn's face was expressionless as I continued to speak. She interrupted occasionally only to ask a question of fact. I told her the progression of Nathaniel's relationship with Patrecia; I told her what element of truth there had been in Nathaniel's various "explanations" of his withdrawal from her, and what untruths. I explained the cause of the depression and anxiety and guilt he had complained of. I told her my part in the deceit.

There was an eternity of silence in the room. Ayn's eyes seemed to have grown smaller, they had narrowed into slits, her sensuous mouth was pale, it was two white lines slashed across her face. She spoke—and her voice was frightening, because it sounded natural, even, without feeling. "Get him down here."

She leaped to her feet in a motion so violent that it ripped at the air of the room. *"Get that bastard down here!"* Her voice did not tremble, it was a hiss, as if it were being forced upward by something not visible that was seething and boiling inside her.

"Ayn," Allan said, "it's too dangerous. He can't handle a confrontation now."

"Get him down here!" The hiss was louder, its boiling source beginning to rise to the surface.

"Ayn," I said, "there's nothing you can say to him, no condemnation that he hasn't already pronounced on himself."

"Get that bastard down here, or I'll drag him here myself!" The slash of her mouth twisted downward, her jaw seemed frozen—her eyes were terrifying.

Allan went to the telephone. "Nathan, Ayn wants you to come here at once." He turned to Ayn. "He said 'Okay.'" Ayn remained standing. Frank had sunk too deeply into his chair; his eyes were half closed, as if he were almost asleep.

When Nathaniel entered, it seemed for a wild moment that the wrong person had come through the door. Instead of the arrogant, confident man he had been, the man with straight shoulders and a look of fiery intensity, he was a man whose eyes under drooping lids were smudged by purple circles, his body was stooped as if he had no power to hold it erect, his hands were clenched into trembling fists at his sides.

"Sit *there*," Ayn said, pointing to a straight-backed chair near the door. "I don't want you in my living room." He sagged into the chair, she stood straight before him, her eyes fixed, her mouth loose and wide. And then it began.

The seething agony, the loss, the humiliation and rejection—all poured out of Ayn in a single convulsion. She stood erect, but her intransigent spirit was battered to its knees, as the judgment, the control, the farsighted wisdom that had belonged to Ayn Rand, slipped from her grasp. "You—to whom I offered the world!—to whom I gave my love and the name I'd earned through an unspeakable battle—*you* did this to me! May you be damned to the hell you put me through! Do you *begin* to know what you've done? Do you *begin* to know what you've thrown away? *Me!*—your highest value, you said, the woman you couldn't live without, the woman you had dreamed of but never hoped to find— you rotten hypocrite!"

Her voice went on and on, filling the room with its implacable agony. There is a point at which pain wrenches the human spirit into twisted, unrecognizable shapes. Ayn had reached that point, as the years of unmet needs seemed for the endless, tragic space of that evening to have shattered what she had been, shattered what she was. Her eyes were huge and blazing. "How did you dare aspire to *me!* If you ever, for even a moment, had been the man you pretended to be— you would value me romantically above any woman on earth if I were eighty and in a wheel chair! You'd be blind to all other women! But you've *never* been what I thought you were! It was an act from the beginning, a sick, ugly act!"

Frank's body was limply relaxed, his eyes were closed. There was no presence where he sat.

"It's finished, your whole act!" Ayn cried. "I'll tear down your façade as I built it up! I'll denounce you publicly, I'll destroy you as I created you! I don't even care what it does to *me*. You won't have the career I gave you, or the name, or the wealth, or the prestige. You'll have nothing—just as you started, just as you came to me, just as you would have remained without me. You would have accomplished nothing if I hadn't handed you my life. *I* did it all!"

Nathaniel had not moved, he had not spoken. He sat numbly as the flood of sounds washed over him.

"You *dared* to reject *me?*" She was no longer screaming, her voice was guttural, choked, and all at once her accent was startlingly heavy—and it seemed for a moment that she no longer knew it was Nathaniel she was denouncing, she was in Russia, she was a girl again, she was damning those who had inflicted upon her a lifetime of rejection—damning her mother who had required as the price of love that she be glamorous and social and pretty, damning her father who had never touched her hand in affection, damning her schoolmates who had profited by her intelligence and excluded her from their lives and activities, damning all the men through all the years who had feared the power of her brain and so had been blind to the woman's body it inhabited—and damning Leo most of all, damning the man to whom she had offered her heart and her soul and who had been indifferent to them. Leo had been born again, more than forty years later, when she had become everything she had wanted to become and achieved everything she had wanted to achieve—and once more he had done to her the unthinkable, the unendurable, once more he had tried to destroy her life, once more she had offered him her heart and her soul and he had thrown them in her face.

As Ayn's voice went relentlessly on, denouncing, threatening, despising, Nathaniel's body gradually began to straighten and his look of passive acceptance faded, replaced by something intent and thoughtful. It was too much; even in his pit of guilt, the things Ayn was saying were too far removed from reality. They were ceasing to reach him, ceasing to destroy him as she wished him to be destroyed.

The choked voice spat out its last terrible sounds. "If you have an ounce of morality left in you, an ounce of psychological health—you'll be impotent for the next twenty years! And if you achieve any potency, you'll know it's a sign of still worse moral degradation!" The voice stopped too abruptly, as if stunned by its own words. There was silence.

Suddenly, with a sound that rang through the room like a shot—a shot fired at Nathaniel's heart and her own—Ayn's open hand arced through space to slash across Nathaniel's upturned face. It retreated, arced again—slashed again. And then once more.

"Now get out!" ordered a stranger's voice.

Nathaniel rose to his feet. Three red welts scarred his face. He had not flinched. He had not uttered a word. His glance flicked, once, to me. Then he turned and left the room. And left Ayn's life forever.

Ayn slumped heavily onto the couch. There was neither sound nor movement from Frank. "I've got to plan," she murmured. "I've got to decide what to do. . . . But I can't plan now. I have to sleep. I have to sleep. . . ."

"Ayn," I began, not knowing what my sentence was to be, "I. . . ."

"Not now," she interrupted. "We'll talk later." She looked older than her years, she looked as if there were nothing left inside her but exhaustion.

"Do you need me?" asked Allan. "Shall I stay?"

"I don't need anyone. . . . Barbara, you did a terrible thing. I think I understand part of it. You were caught between two loyalties. You chose the man you had married. . . . I'm tired. . . . We'll discuss it after I decide what to do about Nathan. . . ."

I nodded, astonished. I had not imagined that the bond between us could withstand what she had learned this night. Something within me whispered: Do I want it? Do I want to continue?

Then Ayn was alone with the silent man half buried in an overstuffed chair.

By the next day, events began moving with breakneck speed.

Ayn told me her demands. Nathaniel was to terminate his role in NBI and its several affiliates, and turn over full ownership to me. He was to transfer his fifty percent share of *The Objectivist* to her; I would become the magazine's co-editor in his place. He was to inform Ayn's friends and the NBI staff that he was doing so, and that the cause was immoralities he had committed that had caused Ayn to break with him irrevocably. Ayn would write a brief statement in *The Objectivist*, a single paragraph stating that because of moral failures on Nathaniel's part she had terminated their personal and professional relationship, and that he no longer spoke for her or for Objectivism.

As I listened, I felt, as I had felt the evening before, a great dull void forming between us—and so I reached out to stroke her hair and say, "We'll work it out. I'll do what has to be done."

There seemed no reason why her decision had to entail the abandonment of the valuable work of NBI; it might be possible to continue running it without Nathaniel. I asked for a few days to think about and project a means of salvaging the lecture operation. Ayn, somewhat hesitantly, agreed.

Then we spoke of her relationship with me. In the end, she said there were mitigating circumstances in my complicity with Nathaniel, and that, despite her strong disapproval of my actions, she did not believe I had acted out of unworthy motives. Our personal and professional relationship need not end.

I took her demands to Nathaniel. He was sunk in a deep, empty passivity. The red welts had faded from his face, replaced by the color of ashes. He answered dully, "I'll do whatever she wants." He knew that when it was over he would have no money, no friends, no honor. But he would have his writing, his work on the book now nearing completion, and he would have Patrecia. The first faint flicker of life and hope was in his eyes. It was ending, the years of nightmare were ending, he would be free of it, free of the load of guilt and suffering and lies that had crushed him to his knees.

A long time later, Nathaniel would say with a bitter smile, "Someone asked me what I did in 1968. I answered: 'I survived.' " I do not know how Ayn or Nathaniel or Frank survived that year, which was yet to bring us its final desolation. I know how I survived it.

Early in 1968, I had begun to see Robert Berole, the NBI student who was teaching Ayn to dance; later in the year, he became manager of NBI Book Service. I felt that I was discovering a near-miracle in the form of a man who cheerfully, benevolently enjoyed life, who was warm and loving and openly emotional, whose high intelligence was singularly reality-bound. Often, when he saw me floating somewhere in space in a cloud of abstract concepts, he would yank me back to the earth where he was so firmly rooted and demand that I look *there,* at empirical, living reality, for the answers I sought.

One day, feeling obliged to tell him what I could of the events affecting my life —he saw my periods of despair, my endless rushing between Ayn and Nathaniel, the frantic telephone calls I received in the middle of the night—I had said to him: "I'm doing something that I'm not free to explain. It involves my deceit of Ayn. I see no alternative to my present actions, but the situation I'm in can't go on much longer, the truth will come out, and when it does, Ayn will break with me. And she will require that you choose between your loyalty to her and to me. I want you to know that if you choose Ayn, I'll understand it and I won't reproach you." I waited for his answer. He was silent for a moment, looking at me intently—and then he burst out laughing. *"Why* would I choose Ayn?" he said. "I love *you*—of course she means a great deal to me—but it's *you* who make me happy. Why in the world would I choose someone else?" In the most astonished moment of my life, I realized I had no answer to give him. The self-evident had ceased to be self-evident. And slowly, painstakingly, like a child taking its first awkward steps, I began to move down the long road that consisted of allowing my authentic emotions entry into life, learning to respect them, to take them seriously, to listen carefully to their messages. I was to spend seven years with Robert, in the most fulfilling and untroubled relationship I had ever known. When we parted, it was with the knowledge that we would remain loving friends throughout our lives.

Robert was beside me, bringing sanity and perspective with him, as I moved through the trauma of the next weeks.

Ayn began speaking to her friends to tell them that, because of Nathaniel's immoral actions, she had broken off her personal and professional relationship with him. She gave no hint, nor did she plan to, of the love affair whose consequences had led to the break. She spoke of evasion and dishonesty, of personal exploitation of her, of moral corruption and depravity. They saw her open fury and her hidden hurt, they could not doubt her word, they could only wonder what terrible thing Nathaniel had done. They asked no questions and they dealt as best they could with their own devastating shock. For years, Ayn and Nathaniel had been their teachers, their psychologists. Now, they had to redefine their loyalties. The redefinition was the work of a moment; Nathaniel had been the source of too much pain for too long; they rallied to Ayn's support; most of them refused to see or speak with Nathaniel again.

On the evening of August 25, two days after the final confrontation between Ayn and Nathaniel, I went to Nathaniel with Henry Mark Holzer, Ayn's friend and her attorney for matters pertaining to Objectivism. At Ayn's demand, we brought with us papers transferring Nathaniel's half interest in *The Objectivist,* without financial recompense, to her. Nathaniel raised his pen to sign—then stopped. The magazine held the copyright to all his articles, including the psychological articles which he had written for use in his book. He and Ayn had had an unwritten agreement that each would retain full rights to his or her articles. Before he signed the transfer agreement, he said, he wanted the copyrights to his work legally assigned to him. Hank telephoned Ayn; Nathaniel's articles would remain his property, she agreed. Still, he hesitated: there was nothing in writing to substantiate his claim. Then he picked up the pen and signed his gift to Ayn.

Three days later, I called a meeting of the NBI and *The Objectivist* staffs. They gathered tensely in the auditorium, wondering if they were at last to be given an explanation of the tensions and chaos of the last months. When Nathaniel entered the room, they whirled to look at him; he had not been in the office for more than a month. I mounted the podium and spoke in a trembling voice. I told them that Ayn had broken with Nathaniel, and that he had resigned from all NBI organizations. I stood at the podium weeping helplessly as Nathaniel rose to speak; his hands gripped the lectern so tightly it seemed that either the lectern or his hands would break. "I have taken an action I know to be wrong," he said. "I have failed to practice the principles I taught to all of you. Miss Rand gave me a blank check on the use of her name, and I defaulted on my responsibility. She is fully within her moral rights in severing our relationship." Within moments, the auditorium was filled with the sounds of shock, of disbelief, of disillusionment, it was filled with the sounds of sobbing and outrage and despair.

The sounds were to keep reverberating as word of Nathaniel's statement raced through the Objectivist movement. NBI's telephone never stopped ringing; students from one end of the country to the other made frantic calls, demanding or pleading to be told what had happened. Was Nathaniel taking drugs? Was *that* the problem? Was he a secret drinker? Was he a bigamist? Had some horror from his past suddenly revealed itself? What had he *done?* A flurry of rumors flew back and forth, impossible to cope with or to stop.

During the last days of August, Wilfred Schwartz, NBI and *The Objectivist*'s business adviser, and I, with Robert and a few members of the NBI staff, worked eighteen hours a day to project the financial possibilities of a more modest lecture organization that could function without Nathaniel. We arrived at a set of figures that proved this to be feasible. (Wilfred, who had the major role in preparing the new plan, would later found and head the Federated Group, a large public chain of consumer electronic stores in California and other western states.) We prepared a lengthy report outlining the plan, with a projection of revenue and expense arrived at by a methodology that had been employed by NBI for five years; in those years, estimates had been correct within a two- to three-percent variation. *The Objectivist* would continue to be a subtenant of NBI, so that the responsibility for the rental costs would remain where it had been, with NBI. We talked and planned and projected and wrote down figures—and the thought kept pounding in my head: I don't want it to work!—I don't want it to be possible!—I want the whole madness to end!—I want to be through with it all, and free.

On the evening of September 2, Ayn met with Wilfred, Robert, Henry Mark Holzer and myself at her apartment. A frighteningly withdrawn Frank was at her side. Hank had seen our report and our figures, and, as Ayn's attorney, had given it his endorsement; it will *work,* he had said happily; the lectures can continue profitably. Ayn glanced at our plan for only a moment. And then she exploded. "I don't want it! I won't hand my endorsement and my reputation to *anyone,* for *any* reason! I don't want to read this thing"—she shook the thick sheaf of the report—"I can't run a business, and I can't let anyone else run it when it carries my name!" The subject was at an end; she was too agitated to consider any arguments against her position. It was her right to refuse to sanction a newly constituted lecture organization, and I agreed to drop the plan and to proceed with the liquidation of NBI. The philosophical movement that had spanned ten years and several continents, was dead.

Since Ayn's final confrontation with Nathaniel, the violence of her attacks on him had not diminished, it had intensified—and she turned once more to the subject at the forefront of her consciousness. He would not destroy her and the work of her life, she cried, pounding the arm of her chair, her eyes dark points of laserlike light. She would *not* write merely a single paragraph of repudiation in

The Objectivist, the whole world must know what he was! She would unmask him, she would destroy him as he had tried to destroy her!

And then she said, "I'll see that his book is *never* published. I'll stop it. It's all plagiarism of me! There isn't a single original idea in it! I'll use my influence with New American Library to break his contract! He'll never be published!"

Next afternoon, I spoke with two friends of my growing concern at Ayn's reckless accusations and threats against Nathaniel—my concern at her state of mind, and at the possibility of his professional destruction. Later in the day, as I was preparing for an urgent business meeting I had scheduled with Ayn for the evening, I received a message from her, through Hank Holzer, that she had changed the nature and purpose of our meeting. She had asked several of the collective to be present; I was to appear to answer charges of having made false and immoral accusations against her that afternoon.

I called Ayn immediately, but she refused to reconsider her decision, despite the fact that certain business issues had to be decided by the following morning. "I assume you're coming to the meeting. That's the only thing I want to know," she said coldly. "I'm willing to discuss with *you* anything you care to discuss," I answered. "I'm not willing to appear before a jury of my peers to answer charges." "Are you coming or not?" was her only response. I hesitated for a long moment. I knew what hung in the balance. "No," I said. The telephone slammed down. It was over. It was the end of the passionate engagement of nineteen years of my life.

The work of dismantling NBI began. Ayn had *The Objectivist* transferred to new quarters. NBI's representatives in other cities were informed that no further lectures would be given. Office equipment, furniture, books and prints were sold. NBI's first addressing machine, once ensconced in my kitchen, was removed from the office—along with a newer addressing machine that an excited staff had triumphantly toasted in champagne the night the first issue of *The Objectivist* was mailed.

The scene in the offices was of total hysteria. Students kept arriving from New York and from cities dotted around the country, upset, depressed, angry, crying, confused, stunned by the news of Ayn's break with Nathaniel and me and by the closing of NBI. Some of the students had come to denounce me; I had become a pariah along with Nathaniel, as the rumors continued to spread. I moved from selling prints of Frank's paintings and the file cabinets from my private office to endless questions about "what had happened." They knew only that the intellectual movement so important to them had ended; they did not know the reason; and neither Nathaniel nor I felt free to tell them.

The hysteria never completely died away. Even today, almost eighteen years after "the break," as it became known among Objectivists, the pain of disillusionment and bewilderment and indignation still is present in some of NBI's former students. They have never been told the truth. It has not ceased to be a living issue to them.

Students poured into the office; our friends did not. With few exceptions, our friends refused to speak either to Nathaniel or to me, refused to hear our under-standing of what had occurred. I would walk from the office to my apartment and pass friends I had known for fifteen years and more—to be met by contemp-tuously averted faces. One day, most of the NBI staff was gone; they too walked past me with averted faces, refusing to work for me any longer. The doors of NBI closed.

From the time of her last confrontation with Nathaniel, Ayn had begun de-manding an unquestioning loyalty from both friends and students. As she con-tinued to insist that sides in the dispute no one understood had to be taken, friend turned against friend, families split into warring factions, husband raged at wife and young people at parents, accusations were hurled with promiscuous abandon. Those who attempted to question Ayn's demand for loyalty in the absence of knowledge, or who refused to take sides, were denounced. Those who attempted to defend Nathaniel or me, were ostracized at once. Those who aligned themselves with either of us, lost their friends, some lost lovers and jobs and families. To this day, my cousin and friend, Leonard Peikoff, has refused to deal with me or to discuss the events of 1968; by my understanding, he knows and cares only that Ayn was deeply hurt by my actions. And I began to see if *this* were what the movement had finally created—if it had created true believers devoted to Ayn as to a guru—then perhaps it should never have come into existence.[1]

Ayn's despair and grief continued to impel her along a self-destructive path. She took an action more tragically out of character than any of her actions of that year, an action that would never have been possible to her before. She went to Curtis Brown, her literary agents and Nathaniel's, to insist that they cease representing Nathaniel. Gerard McCauley, who represented Nathaniel, later said, "Nathaniel was an unknown at the time, and Ayn was one of our most valuable clients, whom we certainly did not want to lose. But I said that I would quit Curtis Brown if any outside pressures were allowed to determine the writers we represented. There was no problem; nobody at Curtis Brown even considered accepting Ayn's demand. The answer we gave her was an emphatic 'No.' "

[1] For a number of years after 1968, I was to speak of myself, Nathaniel, and our friends and students, as having been members of a cult. More recently, as a result of considerable personal investigation and reading in the subject of cults, I have come to believe that that was not a valid designation of the Objectivist movement. The Oxford English Dictionary defines "cult" as "a particular form or system of religious worship." Although the Objectivist movement clearly had many of the trappings of a cult—the aggrandizement of the person of Ayn Rand, the too ready acceptance of her personal opinions on a host of subjects, the incessant moralizing—it is nevertheless significant that the funda-mental attraction of Objectivism to both the majority of her students and to her friends was the precise opposite of religous worship. It was the attraction to *reason*—to the intelligible, the grasp-able, the definable. It was the attraction to *individualism,* the view that one's life and one's destiny is and properly should be one's own responsibility, not to be dictated by state or society or any other human being. It was the attraction, not to the vision of a divine creator, but to a heroic vision of man. And it has been interesting for me to observe that among the many hundreds of men and women I have known who were deeply intellectually influenced by Ayn, that fundamental attraction has held: only a handful were later drawn to religion or any other form of cultism. The vast majority have remained committed to rationality and individualism.

In October, Ayn published a six-page article in *The Objectivist* entitled "To Whom It May Concern."[2] It began with the statement:

"This is to inform my readers and all those interested in Objectivism that Nathaniel Branden and Barbara Branden are no longer associated with this magazine, with me or with my philosophy.

"I have permanently broken all personal, professional and business association with them, and have withdrawn from them the permission to use my name in connection with their commercial, professional, intellectual or other activities.

"I hereby withdraw my endorsement of them and of their future works and activities. I repudiate both of them, totally and permanently, as spokesmen for me or for Objectivism."

The article outlined what she termed the specifics of the reasons for her repudiation, including Nathaniel's "gradual departure from the principles of Objectivism, a tendency toward non-intellectual concerns"—a trend manifested by such issues as his venture into the theater to produce a stage adaptation of *The Fountainhead* and his delays in writing articles for the magazine. She wrote that "my personal relationship with Mr. Branden was deteriorating in a puzzling manner: it was turning into a series of his constant demands on my time, constant pleas for advice, for help with his writing, for long discussions of his personal, philosophical and psychological problems . . . a policy of intellectual and professional exploitation," and that this year she had discovered that "he did not practice what he preached, that he demanded of his students a standard of conduct he failed to demand of himself."

The article continued: "About two months ago . . . Mr. Branden presented me with a written statement which was so irrational and so offensive to me that I had to break my personal association with him." There was no hint of the contents of that written statement, nor of the fourteen years of which it was the culmination.

"About two months later," the article went on, ". . . Mrs. Branden suddenly confessed that Mr. Branden had been concealing from me certain ugly actions and irrational behavior in his private life, which was grossly contradictory to Objectivist morality and which she had known about for two years.

"I confronted Mr. Branden with her accusation and he admitted it. He admitted that his actions had involved the deliberate deception of several persons for a period of some four years. . . . I have never accepted, condoned or tolerated conscious breaches of morality. This was the last of the evidence which caused me to break all professional, as well as personal association with him."

Ayn then outlined what she named as Nathaniel's "attempts to exploit [her] financially"—she wrote of loans from *The Objectivist* to NBI, which had not been repaid until she had recently demanded it, of "other, less costly instances of the same questionable policy." She did not write that she had often told Nathan-

---

[2] The issue of *The Objectivist* in which the article appeared is dated May 1968, but was not issued until October.

iel she did not wish to be troubled with the magazine's financial affairs, that he was to handle them, and that when he had mentioned the loan she had told him to do what he thought best.

Then the article turned to me. "During the period of the growing breach between Mr. Branden and me, she volunteered to act as my ally. . . . it was she who exposed the secret of his private life. I gave her credit for her somewhat belated honesty. . . ." On September 2, Ayn wrote, I had submitted a plan to her for the reorganization of NBI, which "did not offer any relevant factual material, but a *projection* (by an unspecified method) of future profits to be earned by a lecture organization patterned after NBI . . . a business arrangement of so questionable a nature that I rejected it at once. . . . Next day, a sudden switch occurred in [her] attitude. . . . Mrs. Branden began to utter veiled threats and undefined accusations against me. . . . Since this change in [her] attitude occurred when [she] realized that my business association with her was finished and that the gold mine involved in [her] use of my name was shut down, draw your own conclusions about the cause and motive of [her] behavior.

"Such is the sordid story, as of this present date. . . . I offer my apology to the readers of this magazine and to the students of NBI, who trusted Mr. and Mrs. Branden on my recommendation."

Following Ayn's article was a statement from NBI's Associate Lecturers: "Because Nathaniel Branden and Barbara Branden, in a series of actions, have betrayed fundamental principles of Objectivism, we condemn and repudiate these two persons irrevocably, and have terminated all association with them and with Nathaniel Branden Institute."

In retrospect, it is evident why Ayn believed it legitimate to write the article she chose to write—to manufacture reasons for her actions and refuse to name their real source. For many years, she had made her position clear: honesty was a high and noble virtue, dishonesty was a moral vice—except when one was put in a position, not of one's own making but *through the immorality of another,* where truth would be inimical to one's best interests. We do not owe truth to a robber who demands to know where the jewelry is hidden, she often said; we may morally tell him there *is* no jewelry. That appeared to be how she had interpreted her situation with Nathaniel: that he, not she, had brought her to the point where the truth would expose her to public humiliation; he had made it necessary for her to fight by any means possible for her life, for her reputation, for her work. It was not she who should pay the price of his deceit. Ayn, finally enslaved by the self-image she had created, unable to storm its impregnable barriers, was never to ask herself if she had helped to create the trap with no exits in which she found herself.

When Nathaniel and I read Ayn's article, reeling from the shock of its misleading implications, its half-truths and its fabrications, we knew we had to make an effort to salvage what little remained of our professional and personal reputations. With a feeling of desperate sadness at the need to issue such a response, we wrote our separate statements, had them printed as one article under the title, "In Answer to Ayn Rand," and sent them to *The Objectivist* mailing list. We answered the specific unwarranted charges Ayn had made against us, while admitting that we had deceived her. We, like Ayn, continued the policy of keeping private the real truth: that the source of all the conflicts and all the dissension and all the actions and all the madness that had followed, was Ayn's and Nathaniel's romantic relationship. Except that, at the conclusion of his statement, quoting Ayn's words that he had given her a "written statement which was so irrational and so offensive to me that I had to break my personal association with him"—Nathaniel wrote: "In writing the above, Miss Rand has given me the right to name that which I infinitely would have preferred to leave unnamed, out of respect for her privacy. I am obliged to report what was in that written paper of mine, in the name of justice and of self-defense. . . . It was a tortured, awkward, excruciatingly embarrassed attempt to make clear to her why I felt that an age distance between us of twenty-five years constituted an insuperable barrier, for me, to a romantic relationship."

The postscript to my section of "In Answer to Ayn Rand" stated: "We have learned that Miss Rand has chosen to dispute Mr. Branden's right to the use of his articles published in *The Objectivist*. She has set, as the price of her coopera- tion in this matter, a number of conditions, chief among which are the following: We must guarantee not to initiate an action for libel against her, and we must further guarantee not to defend ourselves against the charges made in her arti- cle, that is, to make no statements or comments of any kind, oral or written, about the article. We have rejected Miss Rand's conditions." On the advice of his attorney, Nathaniel was to include the relevant articles in his book without Ayn's permission; he heard no further word about it.

Later that year, Nathaniel submitted the completed manuscript of *The Psy- chology of Self-Esteem* to his publisher, New American Library. His submission, by the terms of his contract, was, he has said, a month or two late. New Ameri- can Library rejected his book, on the grounds of its lateness.

The Psychology of Self-Esteem was published by Nash Publishing Company in 1969, and went into paperback a year later. As of this date, it has sold almost a million copies.

With the publication of the "To Whom It May Concern" and "In Answer to Ayn Rand," the mail began pouring in. The confusion and grief of NBI's stu- dents had not diminished, it had increased in the wake of charges and counter- charges whose truth they had no way to determine. Most of the letters Ayn received were supportive and sympathetic. The writers had not forgotten the enormity of their intellectual debt to her; it was clear that she was suffering at the betrayal of the man she had named her "intellectual heir," and they offered her their loyalty and their gratitude. The majority of the letters Nathaniel re- ceived, and those I received, were angry and denunciatory; one of them, in a penultimate madness, was a curt note from my broker, an Objectivist, saying that he would no longer handle my account.[3] But more than two hundred of them expressed shock at the absence of authentic explanation in Ayn's article—and their sense that something crucial had not been said that might make sense of the whole dispute; the phrase "a woman scorned" appeared in letter after letter.

It was to be said again. Nathaniel and I considered the possibility of suing Ayn for libel. Back issues of *The Objectivist* would continue to be sold into the indefinite future, and new subscribers would read Ayn's attack, but not our response. Nathaniel's greatest concern was Ayn's charges of financial malfeasance—about which the man who was NBI's accountant and *The Objectivist*'s had said: "Miss Rand certainly *is* a fiction writer, isn't she"—and a former friend, one of the few willing to speak to us, had said: "Ayn knows perfectly well that Nathan is not dishonest." We soon rejected the idea of suing, unwilling to subject ourselves to more years of dealing with an issue we wished only to leave behind us. But before rejecting it, we made an appointment with George Berger, an attorney in the Louis Nizer office. He knew nothing about us, nothing about our conflict with Ayn; he knew only that we wanted his legal advice regarding a possible libel suit. Before saying more, Nathaniel handed him Ayn's "To Whom It May Concern." He read two or three pages, looked up and asked, "How old is she?" We answered, puzzled by the question, that she was sixty-three; he continued reading. After a few more moments, he shook his head sadly and said, "Hell hath no fury. . . ."

The most painful moment of all the painful moments of that year was my chance meeting with Frank. He entered the elevator in our apartment building one day to find that I had preceded him. He smiled, as gently as always, with a glance that told me his eyes and mind were alive. As we rode up together, he reached out his arms and hugged me, saying in a tone of despair, "Barbara, it's like a nightmare, I don't understand *any* of it!"—and I answered, clutching him tightly, "Frank, my dearest Frank . . . I don't either." The car stopped at his floor, he got out, and just before the door closed he turned back to say, "I love you, Barbara." "I love you, Frank," I responded. Then I stared at the closed door, sobbing. I never saw him again.[4]

---

[3] The ultimate madness was revealed to us several months later, when Nathaniel and I learned that a half-demented former student of NBI had raised the question of whether or not it would be morally appropriate to assassinate Nathaniel because of the suffering he had caused Ayn; the man concluded that it should not be done on practical grounds, but would be morally legitimate. Fortunately, he was shouted down at once by a group of appalled students. Had Ayn known of the incident, she would have been no less appalled.

[4] Robert and I decided to leave New York and move to Los Angeles; Nathaniel and Patrecia made the same decision. When we arrived, it was to find that most of NBI's California students had little of the near-religious attitude toward Ayn that was so prevalent in New York, where the force of her personality had its greatest impact upon her admirers, many of whom had regular dealings with her. The California students did not attack Ayn; their respect and admiration for her achievements and for the inner qualities that had made them possible, remained unchallenged; but they refused to take sides in an issue they did not understand.

For almost two years, I spent much of my time thinking about Ayn and my relationship with her, in order to understand what had brought and held me to her, and the meaning of the events of all

Ayn continued indignantly to deny that Nathaniel had made any significant contribution to her life or her work. She spoke of NBI as "a homemade" business enterprise of which she had never approved, and which had been of little professional value to her. Nathaniel's work in psychology had been merely an offshoot of her intellectual position, without originality or importance. Leonard Peikoff and Mary Ann Sures began giving lectures on aspects of Objectivism; before a prospective student could attend, he was required to sign a paper guaranteeing that he would have no dealings with Nathaniel or Barbara Branden, and that he would not purchase any of their future work. Ayn arranged to have the dedication to Nathaniel removed from all future printings of *Atlas Shrugged*.

For a time, I was angry with Ayn, but I could not remain angry indefinitely. The tragedy of witnessing the personal deterioration of so great a mind, the deterioration of a personality so valiant and enduring, was vivid in my mind. And I had loved Ayn for too long, she had meant too much to me and had done too much for me—ever to be able, even had I wished to do so, to tear that love out of me. I had seen too often her unique, heart-wrenching charm, and the enchanting young girl who still dwelt somewhere within her, I had witnessed too often, with a sense of wonder, the power and the passion of her intelligence. I had seen the change in her over the years of our friendship, I had seen the disappointments and loneliness of her life intensify her bitterness, her harsh moralism, her anger, the unreality of her view of herself—and I had seen the intransigent battles she had fought, and lost, to remain unscarred. I remembered the early days of our friendship, the exhilaration of my discovery of a new world of ideas, I remembered the days and nights of reading *Atlas Shrugged* in manuscript and feeling that its pages—and its creator—were speeding me in the direction of everything I wanted. I remembered Ayn's smile whenever I entered her door, and the touch of her hand when something was troubling me, and the hours she spent giving me the best of her intellectual powers in order to remove the frown from my face. I remembered her blowing a kiss whenever we parted. For nineteen years, despite the pain and anguish, it had seemed as if a brilliant, glowing light shone on my life and the world, never to go out. It remained, and still remains. As my love for Ayn Rand remains.

Regrettably, Nathaniel's anger against Ayn and against his former friends who rejected him appears not to have diminished but rather to have escalated

---

those years. When it was over, I had begun to make peace with the past, and I returned to the writing I had always wanted to do.

Nathaniel opened a practice as a therapist, and has published a number of successful books on his psychological theories, many of which are major departures from the views he once held. He and Patrecia were married in 1969. In 1977, Patrecia died in a drowning accident. It was a tragedy for him that paled any other tragedy in his life. Although the pain of Patrecia's death remains, he has since happily remarried.

After moving to Los Angeles, Patrecia and I grew increasingly fond of each other, and I continued to see Nathaniel. After her death, however, the bond of comrades-in-arms between Nathaniel and me began to fray, and finally to split. We have not met in several years.

during the years since 1968; too often, he has characterized and described them in terms that can only be considered unjust.

During the next years, the influence of Ayn's ideas was to continue, finally reaching vast proportions. But the organized, official movement vanished with the closing of NBI's doors. As it should have vanished, for with it went much of the true believer mentality that had damaged it. Pockets of true believers still remain, but in insignificant numbers. Ayn's influence takes its appropriate form, as each new generation reads her works, profits from them, learns from them, and goes on to lead independent lives of their own choosing.

As 1968 groaned slowly to its end, Ayn began to pick up the pieces of her life, and go on. She had always been a valiant fighter. She would not be stopped now. Her intransigent spirit, battered to its knees, rose again. The future beckoned to her. Its voice was fainter, but still it called to her, and she reached out her arms to embrace it. There were new battles to fight and new ideas to discover and new work to do. She marched on, her eyes fixed on her goal, to the lilt of her tiddlywink music.

PART V

DENOUEMENT

Chapter Thirty

The first of Ayn's new battles was to understand Nathaniel and the nineteen years of their relationship. Throughout her life, *to understand* had been, and would remain, fundamental to her approach to any problem confronting her; what her mind could grasp—however personally painful or shocking it might be —she could deal with and endure. For more than two years following the end of 1968, she was obsessed over her concern to interpret Nathaniel's psychology and actions in a manner that would make sense of the tragedy of their last years together.

She did not know that she was herself placing insurmountable barriers in the path of understanding. A tendency, present in her psychology since childhood, had grown and hardened over the years into an unquestioned absolute: that in any conflict between herself and another, the guilt, the blame, the responsibility could lie only with the other. Through sixty-three harsh years, she had forged her own soul and her own psychology—"man is a being of self-made soul," she had written—and the moral rectitude and rationality of that soul was not to be negated. As she had done with other friends with whom she had broken, so she did with Nathaniel: if she was his victim, still writhing in pain and anguish and confusion, then it was axiomatic that he was a moral monster; the estimate of him she once had held could not be allowed reality. Blinded to her own motivations in their relationship, she had no means of understanding his. "I've never had an emotion I could not identify," she continued to say, "or an emotion that clashed with reason."

And so her tormented questions were only: Had Nathaniel always been morally corrupt, or had it been only a seed in the beginning, too small to be noticed, that had blossomed at last to engulf him? If the corruption had always been there, how had he hidden it from her and from the world? What was the specific nature of the corruption? What were the terrible psychological errors he had made that had ended by drowning his intelligence? How could he have been the brilliant, electric teacher of her philosophy, yet failed to practice it in his own life? Had he ever loved her, or had he deluded her from the beginning? The variations on the questions were endless, and again Ayn wrote paper after paper in an effort to open the door to the mystery that was Nathaniel, never utilizing the key contained in the unasked question: What did *I* do that might have contributed to my own anguish and Nathaniel's? What are the hidden areas in my own psychology, the unnamed needs and the secret drives, that played their part in the events that destroyed our love?

Without that key to that unopened door, the answers she reached were tentative, switching, and unsatisfying. What remained, in the end, was the helpless, bewildered sense that human beings were irredeemably corrupt and irrational, that there was nothing to seek from the world outside her own consciousness and nothing for which to hope ever again—the desolate sense that all her worst fears about the world in which she lived were true.

Her friends struggled vainly to help her. She spent days and evenings and weeks and months discussing Nathaniel with them, going over and over the questions haunting her and the answers she reached that seemed valid one day and invalid the next—but never told them of the love affair whose consequences she needed their help to understand. Whatever some of them might have suspected, they were not given the essential piece of evidence that most basically explained her unhappiness and her wrath. It was only with Allan Blumenthal that she discussed the romance—but always from the absolute that it was Nathaniel who was to blame for whatever was blameworthy and that she was closed to any challenge of that absolute.

For many years, she had forcefully demanded the acquiescence of her younger friends to the fantasy self-image she carried with her; if they doubted it, the doubt lay in their own failures and betrayals. And she had wrapped her mantle around Nathaniel and me, describing us as she described herself, bristling at the remotest suggestion that there could be justification for criticism of either of us; in later years, as her relationship with Nathaniel began to disintegrate, I was alone to carry the burden of perfection. But despite their acquiescence to this unholy deification, which had made clear perception toxic, they could not avoid sight—sight of Ayn and Nathaniel's continuous switching between gentleness and harshness, between sensitive understanding and insensitive moral bludgeoning, between acceptance and rejection, between justice and injustice; and sight of my own chilly remoteness, which seemed a chronic commentary on the unworthiness of others. They had been deeply hurt by their treatment, but many of them had found no one to blame but themselves.

Now, with what appeared to be the defection of Nathaniel, there was an explanation for the pain they had endured. Nathaniel, as their therapist and teacher, privy to their most private inner lives, had wounded them sorely by his harshness and arrogance; it was he who received the full impact of the accumulated anger, hurt, bitterness and resentment of all those years. It was Nathaniel who had been their executioner and through whose fall they could at last account for their long suffering.

The same implicit reasoning was at work in the wider circle of Objectivists around Ayn, the students and friends who were continuing to grieve over the inexplicable death of the movement to which they had given their support and their work and their passionate idealism. They too, had been required to view Ayn, Nathaniel, and me as gods; they too, had suffered at our hands, and had suffered at the guilt of their own perceptions. They too, now found a villain to crucify in the person of Nathaniel. They stoked the fire of Ayn's denunciations, bringing her story after story of injustices, of acts of cruelty, of arrogance, of callousness. Had she required vindication of her new view of Nathaniel, it was given to her in full measure.

Ayn would not consider the possibility of any of her friends attempting to establish a new version of NBI. She did not want it, she had never wanted it, she would not give her name and sanction to anyone for any purpose ever again, she insisted. Lectures on her philosophy were being given in New York, by Allan Blumenthal on music, by Henry Mark Holzer on law, by Mary Ann Rukavina Sures (now married to attorney Charles Sures and living in Maryland) on art, by Leonard Peikoff on metaphysics and epistemology, but no formal organization or fountainhead of a movement existed.

For a while, their dealings with Ayn became easier and more pleasant for her friends and associates. More alone than she had ever been—perhaps relieved that the crushing weight of tension and suffering had been removed from her shoulders—she was touchingly grateful for their support, and all that was gentlest and most generous in her nature asserted itself. The magic that was Ayn Rand began to awake from its long nightmarish sleep, and they saw again the electric charm of her intellectual passion, of the mind that had forged new paths where others dared not go, of the sensitivity that made one feel, in conversation with her, that she knew precisely what one was most hungry to learn and that nothing was of more urgent concern to her. It was the magic that had caught them in the early days of their acquaintance with Ayn. It had held them through all the difficult years. Now, it caught and held them once more.

David Dawson, a former NBI student married to Joan Kennedy Taylor, was able to persuade Ayn to attend a performance of *La Bohème* at the Metropolitan Opera House. Attending any event with Ayn was usually a traumatic experience: she rarely went to a movie, a play, a ballet, an opera, and when she did so she would announce her judgments in a clearly audible voice—and her judgments usually were negative. "They must understand what immoral trash they're seeing," she would insist when friends begged her not to disturb the audience. There was nothing her friends could do but wish they could hide under their seats until the ordeal was over. But during the performance of *La Bohème,* she was raptly silent. As she and Frank walked along Broadway afterward, David recalled, "she was as happy as a child. She was skipping along the street. She kept saying, 'I haven't seen it since *Russia*—and I've always loved it so. It's wonderful!' I'd never seen her like that. *She* was wonderful!"

Through the early years of the seventies, Ayn was hard at work on *The Objectivist.* She was determined to keep the magazine going without Nathaniel, but it was impossible for her to do all the writing for it. Again, her friends rallied to her support, working on articles, book reviews, movie reviews. Few of them were professional writers, they were involved in their own careers and had no real interest in writing—and Ayn's requirements for any article appearing in her magazine were stringent. She was an astonishing editor; when she worked on one's articles one learned principles and specifics of writing that could have filled a year of classes. But she was a strict and unforgiving editor, and upset that the burden of the magazine now rested totally on her shoulders. If an article were not up to her rigorous standards, the writer was subjected to hours of conversation about the flaws in his "psycho-epistemology," his method of thinking, that had led to his literary failures. In one case, a young woman, a budding and later quite successful novelist, abandoned writing for more than a year after an all-encompassing criticism of her work that led her to conclude she was hopelessly without talent. And Leonard Peikoff was to spend fourteen years writing his book, *The Ominous Parallels,* under Ayn's editorial guidance. A few articles by others did appear in *The Objectivist* from time to time, and excerpts from Leonard's book, but primarily the work was done by Ayn. It took most of her time and all of her mind, she often worked until the first light of morning fell across her desk, and she grew further embittered by the sense that only she was competent and that all burdens were hers to carry.

The period of enchantment was coming to an end. Ayn's friends began to wonder if the agony they had thought was over had really been the sole result of Nathaniel's actions and Ayn's innocent unawareness of those actions.

Ayn had turned once more to Frank, seeking the special comfort that he alone could give her. He was the one man who had never betrayed her, who had always stood by her, who was her ally and her support through all the triumphs and traumas of her life. It appears that now, at last, she began truly to love the man she had married—or, perhaps, to accept the fact that she always had loved him, loved him as he was and as he had been. She still referred to him as a hero from her novels—she subjected him to the indignity of signing his name to a review of Lillian Gish's *The Movies, Mr. Griffith, and Me* which *she* had written —but that part of her life not spent on writing for *The Objectivist* and struggling with the dilemma of understanding Nathaniel, now once more revolved around Frank. The old needs returned, the need for his presence, for his approval, for the solace of his arms around her, for the touch of his hand. Ayn's headlong passions had been evoked by Nathaniel; but only Frank could invoke the soft and womanly aspects of her nature. Without the words to name it, he had always accepted and revered her as no one else had ever done, and the personal rejections of a lifetime made his understanding and acceptance more valuable to her than they had ever been before. She clung to him, hating to have him out of her sight, uneasy when they were not together; he was a part of her inner being, without whom she was incomplete. Despite the lifelong passion of her search for "the ideal man," the man of reason and productive genius, it was the relationship that was the most purely emotional of her life which gave her, in the end, the most satisfaction.

Ayn worried over Frank's increasing fragility and vagueness, and the series of minor illnesses that began to afflict him. She knew nothing of medical science, and did not recognize the increasingly clear signs of senility in Frank; it had not yet swamped his personality, he had days and weeks of lucidity, but for frightening periods he could not be reached, lost in the darkening corners of his mind. Even in later years, when the evidence of his mental decay was inescapable, Ayn never used the word "senility" to describe it. She had often said that she had a horror of mental illness, that a person whose mind had eroded, whatever the cause, was no longer a rational being and therefore no longer human in her eyes. But "love is exception-making," she had written—and at the worst of Frank's deterioration, she made her great exception for him, as she had done in so many other ways: Frank remained "human" to her to the end, he remained the husband and comrade he had always been, the one love who had stood steadfastly at her side.

In her inability to recognize what was happening to Frank, she took on another burden: the burden of trying to restore his mind to health. His problems were psycho-epistemological, she concluded; if he was forgetful, vague, often irritable with her, it was because he had not mastered the principles of efficient thinking; he forgot because he had never properly learned and integrated; he was vague because he had never properly conceptualized. Each week, she spent many hours with him, teaching him principles of psycho-epistemology, exerting every effort and every brain cell to train a mind that could no longer be reached by principles or training—not understanding why those sessions were agony for him, why they changed nothing, why his irritation with her kept increasing. It was a futile, tragic effort, but she would not give up, she would not abandon his mind, and week after week and year after year she lectured and explained, as Frank looked at her with increasingly distant blue eyes and struggled to grasp what increasingly he could not grasp.

Joan Blumenthal would later recall that "When Ayn was working with Frank on his psycho-epistemology, often daily, trying to get him to think more clearly and conceptually—which he could not do—asking him to write papers on his mental processes—which he could not do, Allan tried to make her understand that the mental changes in him were due to an organic condition, probably arteriosclerosis. She'd listen, she didn't disagree—and then she'd go back to the lessons. She was torturing him by trying to help him. He'd fly into a rage when she began lecturing him, but it was years before she finally stopped. She kept saying, in utter bewilderment, 'How can he be hostile to *me*? To me, of all people!' "

By 1971, Frank had formally dropped from the rolls of the Art Students

League. Occasionally, he would go there to visit, but he could no longer cope with formal painting classes. His fellow students and teachers were shocked by his physical and mental deterioration. He retained his studio in the apartment building where he and Ayn lived, and continued to spend his days there. And each week, when Ayn's housekeeper went to the studio to clean it, she found no new paintings but, instead, rows of empty liquor bottles.

One evening, Frank collapsed and was rushed to the hospital. Ayn was terrified as she had never been before; the thought of losing Frank was beyond bearing. It was believed that he had had a minor heart attack, although the diagnosis could not conclusively be determined; what was determined was that he was suffering from severe arteriosclerosis, diminishing the flow of blood and oxygen to all his organs and most ominously to his heart and brain. Long after Frank returned home from the hospital, Ayn's terror remained; it was never to leave her while he lived.

Yet Ayn still struggled, as she had always struggled, to keep alive her sense of life's promise. At times, she played her tiddlywink music—and all at once she was a girl again, knowing that life was beautiful and rare, that it was a sacred treasure to be guarded with all of one's energy and power. At times, she sat in her study and read sections of *Atlas Shrugged,* and the flickering fire within her blazed fiercely once more. And then she returned to working with Frank's problems of memory and focus, to running back and forth to the doctor with him, to her anxieties over his health—she returned to her memories of Nathaniel's abandonment and the anger that still seethed within her—she returned to writing articles for *The Objectivist,* which interested her less and less each month, and to teaching her young writers how to meet her literary requirements—she returned to a world she believed held nothing but irrationality and to a life that gave her, not rapture and fulfillment, but only a dull, empty pain. The promise of life lived within her, but its voice grew fainter.

Then an event occurred that spoke directly to her belief in life's exalted possibilities—an event that was fuel to her dying hopes. At the invitation of NASA, she and Frank attended the launch to the moon of Apollo ii. The guests were government officials, foreign dignitaries, and a few intellectuals selected to represent the American people and culture. She wrote one of the most beautiful of all her nonfiction pieces about the occasion. After a movingly evocative description of the physical sight of the launching, she wrote:

"What we had seen, in naked essentials—but in reality, not in a work of art—was the concretized abstraction of man's greatness.

"The meaning of the sight lay in the fact that when those dark-red wings of fire flared open, one knew that one was not looking at a normal occurrence, but at a cataclysm which, if unleashed by nature, would have wiped man out of existence—and one knew also that this cataclysm was planned, unleashed and *controlled* by man, that this unimaginable power was ruled by *his* power and, obediently serving his purpose, was making way for a slender, rising craft. One knew that this spectacle was not the product of inanimate nature, like some aurora borealis, nor of chance, nor of luck, that it was unmistakably human—with 'human,' for once, meaning *grandeur*—that a purpose and a long, sustained, disciplined effort had gone to achieve this series of moments, and that man was succeeding, succeeding, succeeding! . . .

"No event in contemporary history was as thrilling, here on earth, as three moments of the mission's climax: the moment when . . . there flashed the words: 'Lunar module has landed'—the moment when the faint, gray shape of the actual module came shivering from the moon to the screen—and the moment when the shining white blob which was Neil Armstrong took his immortal first step . . . he spoke of man. 'That's one small step for a man, one giant leap for mankind.' So it was.

"As to my personal reaction to the entire mission of Apollo 11, I can express it best by paraphrasing a passage from *Atlas Shrugged* that kept coming back to my mind: 'Why did I feel that joyous sense of confidence while watching the mission? In all of its giant course, two aspects pertaining to the inhuman were radiantly absent: the causeless and the purposeless. Every part of the mission was an embodied answer to "Why?" and "What for?"—like the steps of a life-course chosen by the sort of mind I worship.' The mission was a moral code enacted in space."

A friend spoke of Ayn's reaction to Apollo 11. "She was wonderful when she came back from the moon shot," the friend said. "She was so excited, she had loved every moment of it, and her eyes glowed when she talked about it. It was thrilling to hear how she felt, she spoke of what was possible to man—she was more happily animated than I'd seen her in years."

Ayn decided that she could no longer continue publishing *The Objectivist*. The circulation of the magazine had been falling dangerously; since the end of 1968—as her articles had grown more bitter, consisting predominantly of denunciations of evils—it had lost six thousand subscribers. And the demands of producing so many articles left her without time for any other activity; she still spoke of writing a novel and nonfiction work on the epistemology of Objectivism, although she spoke of it less often than before and with less conviction. The magazine was changed to a smaller newsletter format, and renamed *The Ayn Rand Letter*. *The Objectivist*, started with such high hopes, toasted in champagne drunk from paper cups the night of its first mailing, when it seemed that the movement would remake the world—was no more.

Over the next years, with the exception of Ford Hall Forum, Ayn refused almost all of the speaking invitations that continued to pour in, and almost all television and radio appearances. Speaking engagements no longer interested her, she had little enthusiasm left for working for "the cause"; when she had appeared on television or radio, she had too often found herself engaged in a pitched battle with an antagonist; she was unwilling to submit herself to it again. "Anyone is free to criticize or attack me," she said. "But not with my help."

She did, however, appear on Edwin Newman's "Speaking Freely," an hour-long unedited interview on NBC. She agreed to appear because of her confidence in Edwin Newman, whom she often watched on television. In recent years, she had begun setting demands for interviews that were almost impossible to meet: she insisted that all questions be submitted to her in advance, that she have veto power over them, that no critics of her work be quoted, that her words not be edited, and that she appear alone, not in a debate. For "Speaking Freely," she submitted no demands; had she submitted them, Edwin Newman would not have accepted them. It was a remarkable interview, in which the vast wasteland of television was illuminated by Ayn's discussion and dissection of complex philosophical issues ranging from Immanuel Kant to her concept of selfishness.

"When she came in, she seemed suspicious and on guard. She probably expected a polemical discussion, but that wasn't the purpose of the program," Edwin Newman later said. "She never did relax, she remained wary, and sat straight up in her chair throughout the discussion, never once leaning back. But she was tremendously attentive. Once it got going, I enjoyed the interview. She was a remarkably well-organized thinker, who knew exactly what she believed; I got direct, specific answers, right to the point. She was so strong in what she thought, so vigorous in the way she set it out. Word had gotten around that she was to appear on the show, and a lot of people came to the building just to catch a glimpse of her. That was most unusual in my experience."

Joseph Michaels, the producer of "Speaking Freely," later explained why Ayn had been invited. By 1972, a rebirth of free enterprise thought was becoming evident throughout the nation, and articles about Ayn and her influence on that rebirth were appearing. At the same time, Alan Greenspan, known to be Ayn's friend and an admirer of her philosophy, was emerging into national prominence.

Alan Greenspan's success was one of Ayn's rare sources of pleasure during the decade of the seventies. An advocate of fiscal responsibility, a balanced budget, and reduced government spending, Alan was an economic adviser to Nixon, and entered government as Chairman of the Council of Economic Advisers under Ford; with Reagan's presidency, he headed the commission which brought about changes in the Social Security laws; he remains, today, an adviser on economics to President Reagan, and a member of the President's Economic Policy Advisory Board and Foreign Intelligence Advisory Board. Ayn was delighted with his accomplishments, and delighted that he spoke openly and proudly about his admiration for her, for her work, for her philosophy. In an interview with *Time* in 1974, Ayn commented on their first meeting in the early fifties: "He impressed me as very intelligent, brilliant and unhappy. He was groping for a frame of reference. He had no fundamental view of life." Soon convinced of the logic of Ayn's philosophy in general terms, he had read *Atlas* in manuscript and had found his frame of reference. By the sixties, he was lecturing on economics for NBI, and contributing articles to *The Objectivist* and to Ayn's book of essays, *Capitalism: The Unknown Ideal*, advocating the abolition of antitrust laws and a return to the gold standard. Ayn was quick to acknowledge that Alan neither sought nor required her advice on the economic issues with which he was dealing as presidential adviser. But she was proud that a man who spoke for her economic-political ideas had risen to the inner circles of the White House. When Alan was sworn in as a member of Ford's administration, she and Frank traveled to Washington to attend the ceremony and to meet President Ford.

She was to go to the White House again, this time to attend a state dinner in honor of Malcolm Fraser, the Prime Minister of Australia. It was generally known in Australia that Ayn was his favorite author; when he was asked whom he wished to have at the dinner, he had named Ayn. She was thrilled by the occasion. It had been a long, hard journey from starvation and terror in Soviet Russia to attendance at the White House as the welcome and respected guest of an American President and an Australian Prime Minister. It was a sanction that she needed, and had earned.

In 1972, Ayn had made an excited announcement in *The Ayn Rand Letter:*

"I am very happy to announce that the motion picture rights to *Atlas Shrugged* have been bought by Albert S. Ruddy. Mr. Ruddy is Hollywood's top producer, who—in the face of enormous opposition—made the sensationally successful film *The Godfather.*

"For almost fifteen years, I had refused to sell *Atlas Shrugged* except on condition that I would have the right of approval of the film script, a right which Hollywood does not grant to authors. Mr. Ruddy had the courage (and the respect for *Atlas Shrugged)* to break the precedent and agree to my condition. Work on the film will begin at once. If all those concerned do their best—as we intend to—the cultural consequences will be incalculable."

Ayn had always been uneasy at the idea of a movie sale of *Atlas.* She had survived what was done to the movie of *The Fountainhead;* she did not know how she would survive if the great work of her life were butchered. And she knew that *Atlas,* because of its complexity of plot and philosophy, would be much more difficult to film than her earlier novels. Since publication of *Atlas,* there had been many expressions of interest in the movie and television rights; in the end, Ayn had backed away from each one, increasing her demands for control until one producer after another found them impossible to meet. But Al Ruddy had convinced her of his respect for her work, of his determination to maintain its integrity—and had met her most stringent demands. Their agreement was only oral; no contract had yet been signed.

Al Ruddy held a gala luncheon and press conference at the "21" Club, to announce the forthcoming film production of *Atlas Shrugged.* The press turned out in full force, and for once Ayn, glowing with hope and triumph, was at ease with reporters. This was *her* moment, and no one could take it from her.

Shortly after the press conference, while negotiations with Ruddy were continuing and the contract still unsigned, Ayn was approached by Kay and Phillip Smith, both friends of Ayn and former NBI students, both active in theater, requesting her permission to stage an off-Broadway production of *Night of January 16th.* They had been involved in theater for a number of years, Phillip as director, and Kay, under the stage name of Kay Gillian, as actress. Ayn was happy to grant permission. She respected their work, and she knew that their admiration for her and desire to help spread her ideas would guarantee that there would be no repeat of the personal agony of its original Broadway production. At last, *Night of January 16th* would be produced as she had written it, as she wanted it—just as it appeared that *Atlas* would be filmed as she wanted it. A contract was signed, and plans for production were soon underway. The play was retitled by its original name, *Penthouse Legend,* with Kay as the heroine, with Phillip as director, with Kay and Phillip as co-producers.

It was then that the deal with Al Ruddy fell through. Ayn angrily contended that she had been promised control of the final cut of the movie—which meant that she would have the right, when the shooting was at an end, to veto the movie and order it scrapped; it was improbable that she would do so, but she had insisted that the clause appear in the contract. Al Ruddy contended that he had made no such promise, that he could not have done so, that no producer could do so. All that remained of Ayn's moment of triumph was the small kitten that Ruddy, knowing her love of cats, had given her.

The failure of the movie production of *Atlas* was a battle painfully lost, but there still were battles to be fought and won. Ayn threw off her bitter disappointment—a disappointment mixed with a faint feeling of relief that her work was not to be distorted—and got to work. She cut out of the playscript *Night of January 16th* everything relating to the Broadway production, including the gun moll and the detective-story props, and updated some of the lines; the play was restored to its original form, which had never been produced. After thirty-eight years, it was *her* play again.

When the requisite money had been raised, the McAlpin Rooftop Theater was engaged for the run of the play; it was to open in February of 1973. Candace Leigh, a young publicity agent, was hired to handle the publicity.

"Ayn Rand was delightful!" Candace would recall. "She couldn't have been more gracious; she looked right in your eyes when you spoke, in order to grasp your full meaning. She had almost a little-girl charm about her. She seemed very excited about the play, and very much a part of it. She was willing to do anything for it that made sense, but she insisted on very strict conditions for print interviews; interviewers had to sign a list of conditions: they could use only the photograph that she submitted—the one by Phyllis Cerf on the back of *Atlas Shrugged*—and they had to submit all quotes and their context for her approval. My heart sank when she told me her requirements; I didn't think anyone would agree. But they did!—some refused, but many of them signed her list without an argument.

"When I called Rex Reed and risked suggesting that he interview Ayn, he said, 'I'd love it! *The Fountainhead* is my favorite book. It influenced me all through my college years.'"

Rex Reed's interview with Ayn—entitled "Ayn Rand: A Bold Voice in a Mealy-Mouthed Age"—was one of the best and fairest ever published about the woman whom he described as "the lady whose theories are studied by legions of college students like passages from the Bible, and denounced by others as if she were planning to destroy the world next Thursday." He went on to say: "She sits on the edge of a blue-velvet sofa, bristling with energy. In person, she is less formidable than either her writing or her reputation suggests, with round, luminous eyes that don't miss a trick, a Russian lilt to the voice . . . a natural curiosity about everything, and an intriguing way of shaping words with her hands as though she were fondling rare jade. When she speaks, it is with passion and authority. . . ."

"He told me later," Candace recalled, "that he got more mail in response to the interview than he had ever before received—and more positive letters. He said it was the best interview he ever had."

Ayn warned the Smiths to expect attacks from the reviewers. They must not count on even a single good review, she insisted; that had been the history of her work. But she thought that, with the ready-made audience of Objectivists who would rush to see it, word-of-mouth would spread quickly enough to bypass the reviews and ensure a long run.

The amount of pre-opening publicity the play received was astonishing for a modest off-Broadway production of an old work. The local ABC television station filmed a rehearsal and ran the film on the evening news. Other journalists published interviews, and Ayn appeared on a number of shows. A few times, interviewers spoke of Objectivists as a "cult." "My following is not a cult," Ayn responded hotly. "I am not a cult figure." "Unfortunately," Candace would recall, "she was often her own worst enemy during interviews: she could be very grim and brusque and intimidating when she sensed resistance."

Ayn attended the casting calls and many of the rehearsals. "One day," Kay Smith was to say, "she told me that from now on she was sending Frank to be her emissary; he would attend the rehearsals and report his reactions to her. . . . It was terribly sad. The first day he was there alone, he just sat silently in a corner. He was beyond even *trying* to participate. Next morning, Ayn called me and said it had been too much for Frank, and from now on she would be coming." Throughout the rehearsal period, Frank responded vaguely if spoken to, but he could seldom initiate a conversation. But both actors and the staff observed that Ayn's expression was invariably warm and loving when she spoke to him or about him.

Previews began two weeks before the opening. The previews were completely sold out. "Ayn was very complimentary about my performance," Kay recalled, "and about the directing, about the production. But Phillip and I knew there were real problems: the actors were competent, but no more than that, and we were seriously undercapitalized. There were a number of things Phillip wanted to do that would have greatly improved the production, but financial constraints made it impossible. He called it 'a C-plus production.' "

After the opening-night performance—again sold out—the Smiths held a celebration party for Ayn and the cast and waited for the reviews. "When the party began," Kay said, "it was very festive and gay. But when the reviews began appearing, the celebration became a wake. The critics were ruthless, the reviews were dreadful. The worst of all was John Simon's television review: it was a massacre."

The play limped along to small houses for another three weeks. Then it closed. Ayn was disappointed, but not crushed. The reviews had not surprised her. But she never doubted the value of her play, as she had never doubted the value of any of her work. "The culture isn't ready for it," she said.

Unfortunately, the play is dated; it required considerably more modernizing than Ayn gave it. That, plus the quality of the production and the inadequacies of some members of the cast, might have doomed it even without the reviews—particularly among sophisticated New York audiences. Nevertheless, it has continued to play in summer stock and repertory theaters across the country. What Ayn loved to call its "gimmicks"—its dramatic flourishes—along with the drama of its central situation and philosophical concepts, its unexpected twists and turns, and the ingenious idea of the jury chosen from the audience, has guaranteed an eager reception wherever it appears.

It was during the year of the production of *Penthouse Legend* that Ayn's vast energies began to diminish. She felt an aching physical exhaustion, she felt unmotivated, lethargic, often depressed. She did not know why. She grew more suspicious, more guarded in her conversations at the rare social events she attended, as if uneasily backing away from responsibilities too demanding for her to handle. Even to prepare to go out, to dress, to cross the street, to find a taxi, seemed to fray nerves already stretched to their breaking point. Events that might once have pleased her—or infuriated her—now received only an indifferent, dismissive wave of her hand. She was financially secure, she was famous throughout most of the world, she was surrounded by loving, appreciative friends, her revolutionary ideas were continuing their steady march through the American culture—and it seemed as if nothing could rouse her, nothing excite her, nothing engage her depleted energies. Until the day in 1973 that she received a telephone call that promised to change her life.

Late in 1971, an article had appeared in the United States Information Agency's magazine, *America Illustrated*—a magazine not available in America but distributed within the Soviet Union as part of a cultural exchange agreement—entitled: "On Discord." It featured photographs and biographical profiles of a number of prominent Americans from every part of the political spectrum; among them were Benjamin Spock, Abbie Hoffman, Linus Pauling, Robert Welch, Madalyn Murray O'Hair—and Ayn Rand. In Leningrad, in a Russian translation, the magazine was made available at the "Research and Development, U.S.A." exhibit.

In 1972, a stocky, graying Russian woman in her sixties, wandering through the exhibit, was handed a copy of the magazine. She took it, flipped through the pages—and stopped short, fighting a feeling of faintness.

In March of 1973, a letter from Leningrad arrived at the Washington offices of

America Illustrated. It was referred to the attention of the editor's assistant, Lilyan Courtois. It read: "I am writing to ask you a favor. Early in 1926, my sister left for Hollywood, U.S.A. Our family corresponded with her until the late 30's, but then the correspondence stopped and I never heard of her again. Late in 1972, I visited the exhibit Research and Development, U.S.A., where, along with some brochures, I was given *America* magazine, #182 Dec. 1971. In this magazine I came across a picture of my sister and a short feature about her. She is a writer. Her name is Ayn Rand (Mrs. Frank O'Connor). I wrote her a letter, but since I do not know her address, the magazine says she lives in New York, I am asking you to find out her address and forward the attached letter to her."

Lilyan Courtois checked on Ayn's address immediately. About to mail the two letters to her, she thought: This is too important to wait for mail delivery; if this really is Ayn Rand's sister, and not a hoax, Miss Rand will want to know about it at once. She picked up the telephone and dialed Ayn's number.

"I'll never forget our phone conversation," she later said wonderingly. "By the end of it, we both were weeping. I told her about the letter, and as I spoke, she kept crying: 'She's alive! She's alive! Oh my God, I thought she was dead! All these years, I thought she was dead!' She was sobbing, and asking me questions, and sobbing again. It was unbearably moving. In spite of the tears, she sounded so happy and so terribly excited. She said she hadn't seen her sister for *forty-seven years.* She kept thanking me again and again for telephoning."

It was Nora who had reappeared, as if resurrected from the dead. It was Nora, Ayn's youngest and favorite sister.

Her sister's letters were dispatched to Ayn, and a carefully worded reply was sent to Leningrad by the magazine. The wording was intended to let Nora know that the magazine had done what she had requested, but to say nothing that might create trouble for her with the Russian authorities. It read, in part: "We are pleased to comply with your request. All of us on the editorial staff of *America* are delighted to know that the copy you received at the 'Research and Development' exhibit was of particular interest to you. Good luck and best wishes."

To Ayn, Lilyan Courtois's call seemed like a miracle. Nora was alive! The little sister who had been so much like Ayn, who had shared the same values and the same interests, who had drawn such wonderful, gay pictures—had survived! Ayn flung herself into action, but she moved carefully and warily, making certain at every step of the process that Nora's safety would not be endangered. Following the advice of the State Department in every detail, she began an exchange of letters with her little sister, and invited Nora and her husband, Victor, to "visit" her in America. It would be like her own "visit" so many years ago. Nora would never return to Russia. Ayn would have her beloved sister with her always. She would have a friend of her own generation, with her own background and her own memories; she would have a friend she could trust and rely on, with whom she could share her life and thoughts for as long as she lived. She would have a sister!

In Leningrad, Nora waited breathlessly, as Ayn once had waited, for the passport and visa that would bring her to America. At last, permission was granted, plane reservations were made, farewells were said, luggage was packed —and Nora and Victor boarded an Aeroflot plane to New York. As they skimmed high over the clouds, a Soviet official spoke to selected passengers to tell them that if they wished to remain in America, arrangements could be made for them. The passengers to whom he spoke included Nora and Victor, and others who, like them, were elderly, unproductive, and living on pensions; the Soviet state would be glad to be free of the need to support them.

Ayn had been making excited plans for their arrival. She intended to give a welcoming party in a few days, she told her friends, and they, happy for her happiness, planned festive parties of their own. If Nora and Victor wished, she would buy them a small house in New Jersey, in an area settled by Russian immigrants; they would have a garden—Nora had loved flowers—and neighbors who spoke their language. There were a few empty apartments in Ayn's building on Thirty-fourth Street; she rented a furnished suite for her sister and brother-in-law, had it scrubbed until it shone, stocked the refrigerator and the kitchen with necessities and with every luxury unobtainable in Russia that she could think of, installed two cheerfully bright telephones, added, as a final touch, the few small mementos she had brought with her from Russia—and tried not to explode from the joyful strain of waiting. Only one thing disturbed her: she still was not feeling well, her energy remained at a low ebb, everything was an effort, and even the excitement of Nora's impending arrival could not rid her of her physical lethargy.

At last, the day of arrival dawned, bright and clear and welcoming. Ayn and Frank hired a chauffeured limousine and set out for the airport. They rushed into Aeroflot, a few minutes late because of unexpected traffic, to find an elderly, shabbily dressed couple huddled nervously together on a bench—but the woman, heavier and more stocky than Ayn, had Ayn's own face—it was the same squarish shape, with the same huge eyes and firmly sensuous mouth. The two women fell into each other's arms and wept, and clutched each other tightly, and wept again.

The trouble began on the drive home from the airport. Ayn eagerly questioned her sister, asking her about her life, about Russia, about their lost family—they spoke in Russian because Victor did not speak or understand English, although Nora did—but Nora kept pointing fearfully at the chauffeur, whispering, "We must not speak in front of him. He's a spy, don't you understand?" Victor, a small, sharp-faced man, nodded in emphatic agreement. Ayn laughed at first, reassuring them, but Nora shook her head angrily and refused to believe that America was not a hotbed of suspicious ears and watching eyes. A faint edge of tension grew between the two women.

Ayn showed Nora and Victor the apartment she had taken for them. They were awe-struck by its luxury. "It's just like a Hollywood movie set," Nora exclaimed.

When they went to Ayn's apartment, Eloise Huggins, Ayn's devoted house-keeper of many years, was waiting to serve the special combination of Russian and American delicacies that Ayn had ordered. Nora was convinced that Eloise, too, was an agent of some American version of the GPU, and despite Ayn's careful explanations, she refused to speak openly. Leonard Peikoff came in to welcome Nora and Victor; although Ayn introduced him as a man who had been her friend for more than twenty years, Nora fenced with him warily, to Ayn's increasing annoyance, answering his questions with curt brevity, clearly suspicious of him.

Perhaps Nora's uneasiness with strangers was understandable, perhaps inevitable. She had spent a lifetime living with distrust and fear and suspicion. But it seemed to Ayn that Nora understood nothing of the difference between Russia and America. How did she not know what it meant to be in a free country? How did she not know that she was safe, that no dark dungeon awaited her?

It was only when Eloise and Leonard had left that Nora was willing to speak of what her life had been since their parting so long ago. She confirmed what Ayn had long believed: that Anna, Fronz and Natasha Rosenbaum had died in the early forties, in the blood-soaked siege of Leningrad. And Ayn learned, to her indignation, that while Nora and Victor were not Communists, they were "good Soviet citizens," devoted to their beautiful city and unwilling to unequivocally damn their form of government. They lived well by Soviet standards. Until their retirement, Nora had been a set designer and Victor an engineer; he had invented a piece of equipment that had won them a higher pension than their work categories would have warranted, a fifth-floor walkup apartment consisting of a single room, and other small benefits unavailable to most Soviet citizens. Nora and her friends, in private, hushed conversations, spoke often of their desire to be free, she admitted; they were fully aware and resentful of their lack of freedom. "But after all," she added, "what good would freedom *really* be to me? I'm not a political activist."

Appalled, Ayn began to explain—and explain—and explain—at first calmly and quietly, then more and more angrily as she was met with an intransigence and impatience like her own. Where was her little sister? she began to wonder. Where was the girl whose mind and values had been like her own? Who was this alien Russian woman?

By the time the date of the first planned party arrived, Ayn no longer cared to introduce Nora and Victor to her friends; the parties were canceled. The sisters were engaged in pitched battles about politics, about Russia, about America, about philosophy. And Ayn knew that her sister's values were *not* hers, that they were *not* alike, that she was not to have the trusted friend and companion for whom she had longed.

In her desperate disappointment—and in her continuing physical weakness—Ayn was harder on her sister than she might otherwise have been, indifferent to the fact that Nora had been exposed, since childhood, to Soviet values and the Soviet way of life. "That's precisely why she *should* know better," Ayn insisted.

"She's *lived* with that horror. She *knows* what it's like. How dare she talk like an apologist! How dare she criticize America!"

Nora soon was critical of everything American. Elayne Kalberman took the couple on tours of the city, which they were eager to see, and which Ayn had neither the energy nor the inclination to conduct. "I took them to Radio City Music Hall," Elayne was to remember, "through Rockefeller Center, up and down Park Avenue and Fifth Avenue, into the stores—Nora especially wanted to see Macy's—and she was clearly impressed, clearly happy to be in a world where no one was telling her what to do or think. But she complained constantly about how dirty New York is, about the noise and pollution and crowds. Leningrad wasn't like that, she kept saying proudly. It was exactly the sort of thing that would infuriate Ayn.

"One day—it was both pathetic and annoying—Nora went to the market to buy toothpaste. When she came back, she was terribly upset and indignant. 'I asked one of the staff for toothpaste,' she said, 'and all he would do was show me to a big rack filled with different kinds of toothpaste. He wouldn't tell me which one to buy! Why wouldn't he tell me?' The multitude of choices available in this strange new country frightened her; she couldn't handle it. And she was astounded when Ayn explained that you didn't really have to count your change at the checkout counter; she couldn't believe that the staff wouldn't try to cheat her."

On another occasion—no longer convinced that she and Victor would remain permanently in America—Nora said, "What would I do if I stayed here? In Leningrad, I spend most of my time hunting down the food and other things I want, and waiting in lines. But here, if I go to the grocery store, everything is right there, half the time you don't even need to cook it! I'd have nothing to do!" The impression among the friends of Ayn who heard this comment was that Nora was proud of her ability to maneuver for the things she wanted, proud of her ability to be devious and conniving. In America, where life was easier, there seemed no outlet for that ability.

Ayn was achingly wounded that Nora did not take the trouble to read her books, and expressed little interest in them. And she was outraged when Nora began instead to buy books banned in Russia that she wanted to read—and soon was raving about Solzhenitsyn's work. Ayn detested Solzhenitsyn for his theocratic view of government. The tension and arguments between the two sisters continued to escalate.

Within the first weeks of their arrival, Victor, who had a history of heart trouble, suffered a heart attack. Allan Blumenthal rushed him to Bellevue Hospital, which has one of the finest cardiac care units in the country. He remained hospitalized for many days, at considerable expense to Ayn. Nora was astonished at the high quality of the care he received and by the kindness and concern of the doctors. She explained to Elayne that "doctors in Leningrad won't even talk to relatives of someone who's sick—and you can't get the proper medicines except on the black market." "What would have happened if he'd been this ill in Russia?" Elayne asked. "He probably would have died," Nora answered.

Nevertheless, by the time Victor was released from the hospital and pronounced well again, he and Nora had decided to return to Russia. Ayn and Nora were barely speaking, and when they did speak it was to continue angry arguments. Before leaving, Nora wanted to tour America and to see California's Disneyland. Ayn explained that she could not go on such a trip; she was feeling ill and tired, and she had responsibilities to meet with *The Ayn Rand Letter.* "That's ridiculous!" Nora snapped. "You're rich and famous—you can do anything you want."

Six weeks after their arrival, Nora and Victor returned to the airport to huddle together nervously on an Aeroflot bench, awaiting the plane that would take them to Leningrad.

Sadly, it does not appear that Ayn's childhood affection for Nora had been returned—or at least, if Nora had once loved her, even the memory of that love was erased in the traumatic encounter between them. As part of the research for this biography, I was able to locate Nora in Leningrad in 1982, where she and her husband still lived. I spoke to her by telephone. It was a frustrating interview, and lasted only a few minutes. Nora would not answer any of my questions, although I was requesting information only about the young Ayn Rand, about her personality, her activities, the quality of her mind. At three separate times during the conversation, Nora said only—in explanation of her refusal to answer—"It is our custom to speak only good of the dead, or say nothing at all. Therefore, I cannot tell you anything."

Before telephoning, I had checked with American authorities on Russian affairs, to be certain I would say nothing that might endanger Nora with the Soviets. I was told, "There will be *three* of you on the telephone: the Russian woman, yourself—and the GPU." It seems likely, therefore, that Nora was inhibited, perhaps frightened, by the knowledge that she dare not speak freely. Nevertheless, one cannot ignore three repetitions of "It is our custom to speak only good of the dead, or say nothing at all; therefore, I cannot tell you anything." Other formulations were possible—even a simple "I don't want to discuss it." In addition, I had the unfortunate task of telling Nora that Ayn had died; when I did so, she showed no sign of emotion; her voice remained calm, cool, severe.

"They're nothing!" Ayn told her friends with disgust. As always, she spoke only of her anger, her disapproval, her moral judgments—but not of her pain and hurt. The pain and hurt were bitter. Once more she had dared to hope for a value from the world, for something that was *hers* in the sea of irrationality in which she felt herself drowning. Once more her hope had turned to anguish and disillusionment. She was tired, desperately weary; the years were passing and her youth and strength were gone. What more would she have to endure?

There was much more yet to be endured. But before her physical and mental resources faced their most severe test, one small bright flicker of light entered her life, in the form of an invitation to address the graduating class of the United States Military Academy at West Point. She had always admired the Point, and now, intrigued by the prospect of seeing it and addressing the class, she accepted the invitation. "It was a wonderful, exciting occasion," a friend who went with Ayn would report. "She was taken on a tour of the Academy, a special banquet was given for her, and wherever she went she was surrounded by generals and colonels and professors and cadets asking her philosophical questions and hanging on every word she said. Ayn really enjoyed it."

The speech Ayn gave at West Point in March of 1974, entitled "Philosophy: Who Needs It"—later published posthumously as the title essay in a collection of her articles—was a fascinating discussion of the practical importance of abstract philosophical concepts.

"As a human being, you have no choice about the fact that you need a philosophy," she told the rows of gray-uniformed cadets and West Point officials and professors who overflowed the auditorium. "Your only choice is whether you define your philosophy by a conscious, rational, disciplined process of thought and scrupulously logical deliberation—or let your subconscious accumulate a junk heap of unwarranted conclusions, false generalizations, undefined contradictions, undigested slogans, unidentified wishes, doubts and fears, thrown together by chance, but integrated by your subconscious into a kind of mongrel philosophy and fused into a single, solid weight: *self-doubt,* like a ball and chain in the place where your mind's wings should have grown."

Her speech concluded: "West Point has given America a long line of heroes, known and unknown. You, this year's graduates, have a glorious tradition to carry on—which I admire profoundly, not because it is a tradition, but because it *is* glorious.

"Since I came from a country guilty of the worst tyranny on earth, I am particularly able to appreciate the meaning, the greatness and the supreme value of that which you are defending. So, in my own name and in the name of many people who think as I do, I want to say, to all the men of West Point, past, present and future: Thank you."

Ayn raised her hand in a military salute. The audience leaped to its feet as one man, cheering and applauding.

When Ayn returned home, she received word of heated philosophical conversations occurring among the cadets and in the classrooms. West Point requested, and received, permission to reprint her speech in a forthcoming philosophy textbook. Ayn's lecture was to be the text's first article—to serve as future officers' introduction to the subject of philosophy.

Cheered by the response to her talk, Ayn nevertheless felt more exhausted than before. She had learned to be a stoic, and she drove herself ruthlessly, working long and punishing hours on her newsletter and caring for her ailing husband. But at last, her ability to push her flagging energies, taxed beyond their limit, failed her. She could no longer concentrate or work, and at last, capitulating to the urging of friends, she agreed to seek medical advice.

The verdict was lung cancer.

Chapter Thirty-one

They sat in the office of Dr. Murray Dworetzky, he would later recall, discussing, as they had done so often in the years that he had been her internist, Ayn's heavy smoking. Since her late twenties, she had smoked two packages of cigarettes a day. "You've *got* to stop it," Dr. Dworetzky said. "It's terribly bad for you. It's dangerous."

With a gesture of defiance, Ayn took a long, deep puff from the slim cigarette in its gold and black holder. "But *why?*" she demanded. "And don't tell me about statistics; I've explained why statistics aren't proof. You have to give me a *rational* explanation. *Why* should I stop smoking?"

There was a tap on the door, and a nurse entered. "Mrs. O'Connor's X rays, Doctor," she said, sliding one of them into the view box on the wall and switching on the fluorescent bulb that illuminated it. Dr. Dworetzky turned to the X ray. He froze for an instant, then bent to examine it closely. With a heavy sigh, he turned back to Ayn, his face grim.

"*That's* why," he said, one finger pointing at a large white shadow in the center of the chest area, where no shadow should have been.

Ayn's face paled. "What's wrong? What is it?"

"I'm . . . sorry. It looks like a malignancy in one lung." Ayn looked down at the cigarette in her hand. She reached out to the ashtray on the table beside her, snubbed out the cigarette with a firm, precise movement, removed it from its holder and began replacing the holder in her purse; then she stopped, shrugged, and dropped the holder on the table.

"Now tell me everything I need to know," she said, her voice controlled. "But first, will this"—she pointed at the dead cigarette—"will it help?"

"I don't know. . . . We'll do what we can. I'm going to refer you to a specialist. The man I have in mind is very good."

Dr. Dworetzky was to say that Ayn "was a very tough, courageous lady. She seemed to have no emotional reaction to the diagnosis. She just asked me questions, as if we were talking about someone else. She remained totally objective. . . . She used to bring Mr. O'Connor in when he needed to see me—he was having a number of medical problems, occasionally acute—and she was always very nervous about his condition, she was extraordinarily devoted to him; she seemed much more anxious when the problem was his than when it was hers."

Ayn *was* courageous. She might lose emotional control and perspective, she might storm and complain and be frightened—but only when faced with what seemed to her the unintelligible. Uncertainty was unbearable, never certainty, however terrible that certainty might be. For the brief time until her admission to New York Hospital for surgery, her manner was calm, almost serene. She knew that the odds were not in her favor, that she might not survive a malignancy of the lung that had progressed as far as hers had. That was a fact of reality. She knew that in the person of her thoracic surgeon, Dr. Cranston W. Holman, she was in the best possible hands; what could be done, would be done. That, too, was a fact of reality. She would live with the facts, unselfpityingly—or she would die with the facts. She would spend her time with Frank, she would play her beloved music, she would read her favorite passages from *Atlas Shrugged:* she would enter Atlantis for a while. Then she would pack her bag and check into the hospital.

She made arrangements for Frank's care for the period of her hospitalization. It was unsafe for him to be alone. There were times when he did not recognize the people he knew—times when he did not recognize Ayn. Whenever he left the building by himself, which he insisted on doing, Ayn was tortured with fear that he might get lost or that he might unwittingly walk out in the street in front of a car. Mary Ann Sures agreed to come in from Maryland to stay with him for a week or two, at which time Leonard Peikoff would take over.

The surgery was long and arduous. When Ayn was finally brought from intensive care to her hospital room, Joan and Allan Blumenthal, who had been anxiously waiting, barely recognized her. It was as if twenty years had been added to her face, and although she had gained a considerable amount of weight in the last few years, her body seemed frail and boneless as a child. Dr. Holman had removed one lobe of the left lung, with the adjacent lymph nodes, he had removed one rib and divided a second rib. There was no evidence that the malignancy had spread to the lymph nodes. The prognosis, although necessarily guarded, was hopeful.

Ayn's will to live was a powerful subconscious force. Despite the tragedies that had punctuated her days, she clung to life with ferocious determination. In many respects, life held little for her now: she was not writing except for the newsletter she cared nothing about; she had no real plans to write; she had broken with so many people for whom she cared; she had lost Nathaniel; she had lost Nora. But she had Frank. One cannot know the precise medical relevancy of the will to live, but it is difficult to doubt that on some level, whether conscious in Ayn's mind or not, Frank's own gentle hold on life was significant in Ayn's survival. She would not leave him for her own sake, for the sake of her love of him—and she would not leave him, for his sake, to the care of strangers.

Ayn awoke from surgery to excruciating pain, typical of this type of operation. Joan spent every day in the hospital with her, and Allan, stealing time from his psychiatric practice, came in once or twice daily. Ayn's absence from home was distressingly difficult for Frank. He could not remember where she was or why; he became extremely agitated that she was not with him, requiring constant reminders and reassurances. Leonard brought him to the hospital in the evenings, where he sat silently by Ayn's bed, looking at her blankly as she held his hand in hers.

Ayn spent more than three weeks in the hospital. They were hard weeks both physically and emotionally. As she slowly began to recover, she seemed to lose the realism and strength that had enabled her to cope so well with her illness before surgery. Her nerves raw from the ordeal she had gone through, devastated that she had lost the iron control of her life and her fate that had been her great pride, that she and her future were helplessly under the guidance of others —she complained of pain even when heavy medication had reduced it considerably. She complained about the staff doctors and nurses: either they were young, and therefore incompetent because of their "modern psycho-epistemology"—or they were past middle age, and therefore too old to be treating her. She was upset that "young hippies in miniskirts" had been assigned to look after her in intensive care.

Several days after surgery, her doctors told her she must begin to move around, she must do a few simple exercises and she must stand and walk as much as possible, in order to minimize the danger of pneumonia or embolism. It was one more problem to cope with, when she had endured all that she could endure, and she flatly refused. "I'm in physical agony," she said. "No one has the right to ask me to do anything when I'm in such pain." Nothing would induce her to change her mind, not medical warnings, not Allan's insistence, not Joan's pleas. She refused even to dangle her feet over the side of the bed. "It's irrational to demand it," she kept insisting angrily. Her outbursts of temper began to antagonize the medical staff; they were in awe of her reputation, and intimidated by her manner. They began using Allan as their middleman to Ayn, rather than approaching her themselves.

"Allan, Leonard, and I," Joan would later say, "discussed among ourselves how serious and dangerous her emotional state was. We felt that she should be told she might be suffering needlessly, both physically and emotionally, because she had repressed a good deal of recent pain—the pain of losing Nathan, then Nora. We felt that if she could acknowledge and release her bottled-up feelings, she might be more relaxed and less prone to outbursts of temper, which would help her recovery. Allan agreed to talk to her about it. She listened to him, and politely disagreed. Then, months later, she told him she'd been terribly upset and angered by what he'd said. She did *not* repress, she insisted. She had *never* repressed."

Joan was to have a similar experience. One day, after Ayn had received a heavy dose of pain medication, she said that she could see the branches of a tree waving across the window pane. How could it reach so high, wasn't she on the ninth floor?—she asked, disturbed by the mystery. Joan realized she was seeing a reflection of the pole holding her intravenous equipment. She explained it to Ayn, adding that it was not uncommon to have mild hallucinatory experiences under heavy medication. Ayn refused to believe it. She continued to insist that it was a tree, she *knew* it was a tree. . . . "A number of months later," Joan recalled, "she called me in to discuss what she said was a serious matter. When I arrived, she shouted at me over the issue of the tree. How could I have tried to make her doubt her mind?—she demanded. How could I have attempted to undermine her rationality? Clearly, the issue had been festering ever since it occurred. There was no arguing with her. Allan and I were both very hurt. We had done everything possible to help her, I'd been with her constantly when most of her other friends had stayed away because they couldn't cope with her— and none of that seemed to matter."

It was inconceivable to Ayn that anything—illness, medication, stress—could affect her mind. It was axiomatic that the functioning and rationality of her intellect was in her control, even when her body was not. Her free choices ran her mind, nothing else. From time to time in the next months, she would raise, disturbed, the question of how she could have contracted cancer; she tended to think that cancer, as well as many other illnesses, was the result of what she termed "bad premises"—that is, of philosophical-psychological errors and evasions carried to their final dead end in the form of physical destruction. How could she have had a malignancy, when she had no bad premises? She demanded that the nature of her illness be kept secret, she wanted no one to know of it—as if it were shameful.

Joan and Allan asked her to make public her decision to stop smoking. For many years, questions about the dangers of smoking had been raised by NBI students and at Ayn's own lecture appearances. Each time, she had lit a cigarette with a defiant flourish, then discussed the "unscientific and irrational nature of the statistical evidence." "Many people still smoke," Allan and Joan explained, "because they respect you and respect your assessment of the evidence. Since you no longer smoke, you ought to tell them, you needn't mention the lung cancer if you prefer not to, you can simply say you've reconsidered the evidence." Ayn refused. "It's no one's business," she said wearily.

When Ayn returned home, her recovery proceeded very slowly. She still refused to exercise or take the walks she had been told she must take. Only when Frank was ordered to do more walking did she agree to dress, put on high heels, and go out with him to walk miserably for perhaps a half block, clutching his arm for support. Long after she was pronounced able to return to normal living, she spent much of her time in bed, watching detective shows on television at night and game shows during the day; occasionally, she would read a mystery novel, and sometimes she would drag herself to her desk to play hours of solitaire. She was sinking into a deep, lethargic passivity—interrupted only by bursts of anger.

She had good cause for her growing depression. Her life with Frank was becoming a torment. He could no longer handle even the simplest of responsibilities, such as preparing his own breakfast, feeding the cats, paying the rent and utilities bills. On several occasions, Ayn paid the rent only after an eviction notice had been taped to her door. In the early mornings, before Ayn had risen, a member of the newsletter staff came to the apartment with mail or papers requiring her attention. Frank, weaving, incoherent, and smelling of alcohol, would answer the door; he had been drinking throughout the night while Ayn slept. And what had once been his irritability with Ayn, now was becoming a frightening hostility. One evening, in terror that he was about to harm her physically, she packed a suitcase and was prepared to leave the apartment, until at last he calmed down. And once, exploding in a rage, he did strike her, and she had to run, in heartbroken disbelief, to Frank's nurse for help.

Remembering those days with a shudder, a friend said, "All Frank's hostility seemed directed at Ayn, never at anyone else, and that hurt her terribly. When I came into the apartment, he was as sweet and kind as he had always been. Even at his worst, he would stand up when I entered, and hold the chair for me. Sometimes, he'd whisper in my ear, 'Don't eat anything. She's trying to poison me, and maybe she'll try to poison you, too.' I would say, 'Okay, Frank, I won't eat.' And I didn't.

"It may have been because she was always trying to force food on him that his reaction took this form. He was much too thin, but he *couldn't* eat, not when he was drinking all the time."

Ayn was unable fully to face Frank's terrible disintegration. Although he rarely left the building, she bought him a mink coat. He never wore it. She seemed to keep hoping that somehow he would recover. She would tell him, "Please, Frank, if you'll just try to concentrate, you'll remember"—at a time when he could not remember if he had eaten breakfast. As a friend explained, "She was so helplessly dependent on him. One year, when she went to Ford Hall Forum to give a talk, it was impossible for Frank to go with her. I went instead, with a couple of other people. Ayn was literally trembling all the time she was there, her hands were shaking. She said she would never travel without him again."

Ayn's inability to accept the facts of Frank's condition and of his inner life had always been an integral part of their relationship. "When he was hospitalized after his collapse," Joan recalled, "his mind was wandering, he was disoriented, and from time to time he'd say a few rambling words. Ayn couldn't hear him, and she asked me what he was saying. 'He's dreaming about the ranch in California. He thinks he's there again,' I explained. Ayn answered tensely: 'But he *hated* California. He loves New York.' "

Ayn never returned to full physical health and strength. For the rest of her life, she remained tired and lethargic; she would rarely stand rather than sit, sit rather than recline; often, she would spend two or three days in bed, unwilling to move even as far as her desk to play solitaire. And her emotional energy never fully returned; there were sparks of it, there were rare bright flashes of vibrancy and enthusiasm during a discussion of a philosophical subject that particularly intrigued her, but her predominant state was a growing depression. The trauma of lung cancer and the sorrows and disappointments of the last years pressed down on her with crushing force. Once more, she grew angry, impatient, bitter in her criticisms at the smallest suggestion of wrongdoing. She never lost—it seemed her last hold on life—her intense gratification in her work and in what she had achieved; but she found no gratification in the world around her.

She spoke continually of her disappointment in the culture; her focus was increasingly turned to the irrationality of the world and its failure to accept her philosophy. She spoke of it with weary revulsion, with volcanic anger, with distraught wretchedness. At intervals, she would rouse herself sufficiently to attend a small gathering at the home of a friend—only to spend the evening on the same topic, the one topic that had the power fully to engage her. Friends, increasingly concerned with her passivity—the *Ayn Rand Letter,* now issued monthly rather than twice monthly, and usually many months late, occupied her only a day or two a week—tried to motivate her to undertake some purposeful activity that would interest her. Wasn't it time she thought about another book? they suggested. She expected them to understand that there was no one to write for, she stormed, no audience that she respected. "Besides," she said, "my writing is already out there, and if anyone is interested, they can read it." She ceased discussing future writing projects; several years earlier, she had received a large advance from New American Library for her projected novel on unrequited love; she returned the advance.

The world, once so shining with hope and love and achievement, had turned bleak and cold. She had lost too much, she had suffered too much. She had earned international fame and fortune—but not on the terms she had desired and expected. She had lost Leo and Nathaniel—and now Frank was slipping away, receding from her farther with each day. She had lost too many close friends—Isabel Paterson, Albert Mannheimer, Nora, myself; she had drifted away from Frances and Henry Hazlitt and all her old friends among political conservatives; she had broken with Bennett Cerf; years earlier, she had broken with Edith Efron, a later member of the collective; in the early seventies, she broke with Erika and Henry Mark Holzer, and a few years later with Kay and Phillip Smith. Alan Collins had died, and Archie Ogden. Her ties to her past were gone, most of the people she had loved were gone, life's bright promise had turned to gray ashes. Her alienation and withdrawal from a world she never stopped struggling to understand, but could neither understand nor cope with, had reached its tragic climax, from which not even the greatness of her mind could save her.

Elayne Kalberman once asked her, "If you could do anything you wanted, or be anywhere you wanted, what would you choose?" "I'd choose to be on a cloud," Ayn answered wistfully, "just floating by myself, with nothing and no-body to bother me . . . drifting serenely above the whole world."

One misty winter day, she stood in front of her living room window, gazing silently at the city veiled in fog. Wearily, she said, "What was it all for?"

She asked a friend, "Do you know what it's like to have no one to look up to —always to look down? Can you understand what it means still to hope, always to hope, and never to find it?"

The next few years dragged slowly by. Ayn learned to play Scrabble; many of her evenings were spent bending attentively over a Scrabble board. She spent long hours working on her stamp collection, a hobby of many years. In 1971, she had written an article in the *Minkus Stamp Journal* entitled "Why I Like Stamp Collecting"—and stamps continued to pour in from admirers all over the world. Her interest in stamps was not as a financial investment, it was aesthetic; she was pleased when she received, or occasionally purchased, a stamp that she enjoyed looking at.

Late in 1975, she discontinued publication of *The Ayn Rand Letter,* explaining to her readers that it gave her no time to work on a book—that "I do not care to go on analyzing and denouncing the same indecencies of the same irrationalism" —and that "the state of today's culture is so low that I do not care to spend my time watching and discussing it."

The few serious friendships she still maintained were becoming precarious. With the closing of *The Ayn Rand Letter,* Elayne and Harry Kalberman— Elayne had been the newsletter's subscription manager—began to drift away, to see Ayn less often, unable to deal with her emotional state. Ayn had returned to her former "psychologizing"—the translation of ideas and attitudes she thought irrational into psychological and psycho-epistemological terms—and her friends had to endure constant discussions of their "failings" and "betrayals." Leonard Peikoff was lecturing in New York on various aspects of Objectivism, taping his lectures, and sending them to groups in other cities; but he was reeling from the onslaught of her literary criticisms and insistence on rewrites of his unfinished book, *The Ominous Parallels,* for which she was to write an introduction. Allan and Joan were constantly on call, dropping their own work in order to comfort Ayn, to listen to her tortured complaints, to listen to her speak of Nora and Nathaniel.

In 1978, Joan and Allan ended their relationship with Ayn. Over the preceding few years, they had had many intense and upsetting discussions with Ayn about painting and music, the two artistic areas which most interested them and about which they were professionally knowledgeable, Joan as a painter and Allan as a former concert pianist. Ayn admired Dali and Vermeer, and dismissed Rem-brandt and French Impressionism as essentially without value; she admired Rachmaninoff, Chopin, and operetta music, and dismissed Mozart, Beethoven, Bach, and Handel. The Blumenthals made clear their disagreement with her choices, but would have been content to let the matter drop; Ayn was not content. Again and again she returned to the subject, again and again she spoke of the psychological and psycho-epistemological errors in their tastes, again and again she argued and scolded and "proved" and "re-proved."

"Her discussions of our artistic and musical choices grew very difficult," Allan was to say, "and often heated and condemning. She was relentless in her pursuit of so-called psychological errors. If an issue were once raised, she would never drop it; after an evening's conversation, she'd telephone the next day to ask what we had concluded about it overnight; if we hadn't thought about it, that led to another conversation about why we hadn't. It was becoming a nightmare."

Joan added, "By then there was something almost reckless in Ayn's attitude toward us. Along with Leonard, she considered us her closest friends, but, often, she would seem deliberately to insult and antagonize us. When we indicated that we would not take it, she would change abruptly and would become kind and loving—she always called me 'darling' after such episodes—and would say that she hadn't meant us to take the criticism personally. There was no other way to take it! At the time, we felt it was self-destructive on Ayn's part; she seemed almost to invite a break, as though it would confirm her attitude toward the world. Then, too, she did not want us to have a private life apart from her. We had friends who were not *her* friends and that made her unhappy. When we learned not to discuss our other friends or activities with her, she accused us of being secretive. There were endless discussions about the meaning of our desire for privacy. . . . And I had another problem: I could see that Ayn's artistic tastes, and the impressive logic with which she backed them, were impeding the development of my students. It disturbed me very much to see young artists, some of whom were very talented, struggling to do 'benevolent' pictures in the style of Dali, not daring to develop their own way of expressing themselves for fear of being judged irrational. Ayn knew I was troubled; she called my concern for self-expression 'suspicious.' "

And Allan said: "Many of her psychological concepts were perceptive and original; there was a complex logic in her approach, an internal consistency. She would integrate seemingly disparate psychological manifestations into plausible syndromes. But, often, these syndromes were rationalistic constructs that sounded ingenious, but were not necessarily based on reality. They were carefully derived from her pre-existing theories of human nature: she tended to reduce human problems to simple, free-will choices—the choice to think or not, to be rational or not—without regard for actual psychological mechanisms. . . . I was appalled by her contempt for those with psychological problems. She would say: 'I don't know how you can work with such people, how you can deal with depravity all the time.' Of course, this attitude contradicted her stated position that psychological problems were morally neutral, that the only issue of moral relevance was an individual's willingness to deal with his problems. One could argue that even that is overly simplified.

"For many years, I had been aware of negative effects of the philosophy on my Objectivist patients. At first, I attributed them to individual misinterpretations.

But then I began to see that the problem was too widespread. Objectivism's insistent moralism had made many patients afraid to face their own conflicts and that was counterproductive in psychotherapy. They were afraid of the judgments that they and other Objectivists would have to pass. They experienced, to an unwarranted degree, feelings of inadequacy and guilt and, consequently, they repressed massively. This led to a tragic loss of personal values. Instead of living for their own happiness—one of the ideas that attracted them to Objectivism in the first place—they sought safety by living to be 'moral,' to be what they were 'supposed' to be and, worse, to feel 'appropriate' emotions. Because they had learned the philosophy predominantly from fiction, the students of Objectivism thought they had to be like Ayn Rand heroes: they were not to be confused, not to be unhappy, and not to lack confidence. And because they could not meet these self-expectations, they bore the added burden of moral failure. These were people who were particularly concerned with morality. For them, what was seen as a failure in the moral realm was devastating. In that atmosphere, it was difficult for us to deal with the real problems."

The final break came because of Ayn's continuing insistence that they throw open their personal lives to her and have no life apart from her. They had been unwilling to leave so long as they believed that Frank would be hurt by their absence. But by now, he recognized people only rarely; they knew it was unlikely that he would be aware of their absence.

"I telephoned Ayn and said that we no longer wished to see her," Allan said. "I refused to discuss it further—she knew the reasons, of course, and *I* knew that any discussion would lead only to more days and weeks and months of futile discussions and recriminations."

Ayn wavered between apathy, hurt, and bewilderment at Joan and Allan's defection. Once more, she changed her will. Allan and Leonard had been her joint heirs; she removed Allan and left Leonard as the heir to her estate. And once more, she considered issuing a public denunciation, on the grounds that patients consulted Allan as a result of her recommendation. A friend argued that she should not do so, and Ayn, suddenly too weary to care, agreed. Her exhaustion, which so exacerbated her hair-trigger temper, was growing more intense: she had recovered from lung surgery, there were no signs of a recurrence of the malignancy, but now her sturdy heart was beginning to fail. She was diagnosed as having arteriosclerosis, for which she required constant medication.

Soon after, her relationship with the Kalbermans came to an end. "Our final conversation was a shouting match," Elayne recalled, "because of the things she was saying about Allan and Joan. I was shocked, and I told her I was shocked; they had been so good to her, particularly when she had had surgery. How could she have forgotten that? She was very upset; she began saying that Joan had tried to undermine her rationality over the issue of the tree, and that Allan had accused her of repression. The conversation went from bad to worse—and that was the end."

Of the original collective, Ayn's closest, most loving friends for years, Nathaniel and I were gone, and Joan and Allan, and Harry and Elayne; Mary Ann was living in Maryland and came to New York only rarely; Alan Greenspan was too busy to see Ayn often. Only Leonard remained to carry the burden of Ayn's unhappiness and Frank's illness. Even Frisco, Ayn's most beloved cat, had died; she sat with him, holding one small gray paw and petting him, throughout the night of his death; she had other cats, but Frisco—Francisco Domingo Carlos Andres Sebastian d'Anconia—once the tiny kitten who had motored with her from California to New York and had stubbornly dozed on her manuscript pages during the years of writing *Atlas,* had always been her favorite.

The people who now flocked around Ayn, with whom she talked and with whom she played Scrabble, were for the most part still younger than her former friends and for the most part of an intellectual and spiritual caliber she could not have tolerated in earlier years. She was bitterly lonely, and bitterly afraid as she watched Frank's slow march toward death. Her only sense of the reality of her own universe was the hours she spent alone in her study; only there could she find the world of Howard Roark and John Galt; only there could she find peace.

In the late seventies, when her life was running steadily downhill, an event occurred that lifted her spirits higher than they had been in many years. Jaffe Productions expressed interest in producing a television miniseries of *Atlas Shrugged,* and, somewhat to Ayn's astonishment, agreed to her terms: she was to have total control of the script. Ayn had long thought that a miniseries was a more appropriate form for *Atlas* than a feature movie: on television, it could run across several evenings and therefore include much more material, and she had always liked the immediacy of the television form. With the feeling that there might once again be point and meaning and a promise to her life, she accepted the offer. Contracts were signed between Ayn, Jaffe Productions, and NBC.

Writer Stirling Silliphant would later recall, "My agent called one day to ask if I'd be interested in flying to New York to be interviewed by Ayn Rand as the possible writer of a ten-hour television adaptation of *Atlas Shrugged.* He explained that she had seen *In the Heat of the Night* a number of years ago, had thought my film script was brilliant, and believed that I would understand *her* material. I was overwhelmed and flattered. In my college days, *Atlas* and her other works had been bibles for students, and I respected her immensely. Her writing style was incredible; she was a lot better writer than she's ever been given credit for.

"I flew to New York to meet her in the offices of Curtis Brown, her agent. As I waited—I arrived early—a little bird-like lady in a long black coat walked in, reminding me of someone's Russian mother. I spent the next hour-and-a-half talking with this little woman—and it was the most fascinating time I've ever spent with another person." Ayn quizzed him mercilessly, requiring detailed answers to why he wanted to do the adaptation, what he liked about the novel, what he saw as the problems inherent in transferring it to the medium of television and how he proposed to solve them. At the end of the meeting she announced: "I want you to do this. No one else is going to do it but you."

They worked together over the next year. For the first time in all the years of suffering, Ayn's thoughts and her hours were filled with a project she loved. As he completed stages of the work, Stirling Silliphant, with his producer Michael Jaffe, flew into New York for week-long meetings with Ayn. "Very specific rules had been set down," he explained. "I could not change a single word of dialogue in *Atlas Shrugged*; I could omit and juxtapose, but I could not create new dialogue. That was a very big problem, because in a lot of areas her dialogue was dated. But no way could you best this woman in an argument! Nor could I invent new scenes. So it was a question of editing and rearranging rather than a lot of new creative work. . . . But because of this arrangement, the script became an extremely faithful and haunting film version of the book. It kept the original purity and spirit and mood that the author had brought to the work. It would have been an incredible piece of film."

When they began working on John Galt's climactic radio speech—it was to be a television speech—Silliphant insisted that Ayn should be the one to cut and rewrite it; no one else could do it properly. And he suggested that they do something that had never been done on television: the speech should run the entire length of a fifteen-minute act. Ayn agreed to both suggestions, excited and delighted.

Only once during their association did Ayn's wrath descend on Stirling Silliphant. He had added the word "perhaps" to a statement made by Dagny—and Ayn angrily shouted: "You've destroyed Dagny's character on this page! You've made her qualify her thinking! She *always* knows what she's doing—she doesn't use words like 'perhaps' or 'maybe.' " The offending word was removed.

"Working with her was a great education for me," recalled Silliphant. "I learned so much, she was a brilliant teacher, constantly talking about the use of language, sentence structure, and so on. She could not tolerate sloppiness in language. It was an experience I will value all my life, a felicitous, happy experience. It was my first and only encounter with a world-class literary talent.

"I cared for her, and valued her. But although she could be delightfully charming, I knew that had our relationship become friendly, rather than professional, I would have had problems with her. She did not reflect the kind of humanity or warmth I like in people. And I think that had I challenged her as a writer, rather than being her literary student, there would have been serious trouble. She was the kind of person who required you to play by *her* rules."

When the script was completed, Ayn, Silliphant, and Michael Jaffe, proud of the work they had done, toasted the script—and each other—with champagne. Then the script was turned in to NBC.

"It was almost that same week," Stirling Silliphant said, "that NBC changed its administrative-production staff. In came Fred Silverman. One of the first things he did was cancel the production of *Atlas Shrugged*—and it was dead. Michael and I were heartbroken, and Ayn Rand was devastated."

A friend of Ayn was later to say, "I never fully believed that anything would come of the Jaffe project, even though she seemed so excited and happy about it.

It was clear almost from the beginning that she didn't *really* want it to be done, not deep inside her. She was too afraid that it would be ruined."

Perhaps the clearest and saddest evidence of Ayn's underlying despair and pessimism can be found in her attitude toward young writers. She had been wary for many years of anyone who wished to write about her books or her philosophy, she had discouraged such attempts, but now her wariness became a crusade. Mimi Gladstein, professor of literature at the University of Texas at El Paso, wrote to say that she was planning a book, *The Ayn Rand Companion,* which would consist of a bibliography and an overview of Ayn's fiction and nonfiction. In response, Mimi received a letter threatening her with a lawsuit if she proceeded with the project. Douglas Rasmussen, professor of philosophy at St. John's University, wrote to say that he was planning a book, *The Philosophic Thought of Ayn Rand,* a compilation of essays by a number of distinguished philosophers. He, too, received a letter warning him not to write the book. Ayn's view was that the writers who approached her were attempting to cash in on her efforts and fame in order to receive a renown they could not otherwise earn. Both Mimi and Douglas wrote and successfully published their manuscripts; Ayn had no legal power, of course, to stop them. And both books are valuable additions to the literature on Ayn Rand.

For a great many years, Ayn had repeatedly spoken of her longing to discover novels she could enjoy and admire, novels of her school of fiction, romantic, benevolent, expertly plotted, dealing with serious issues. The longing was a deep, frustrated ache inside her. Yet in these tortured years of the seventies, when a few such novels appeared on her desk, she scarcely glanced at them. She no longer believed the world could have any values to offer her, it was futile even to investigate, she would only be disappointed again. Erika Holzer, Ayn's former friend and an aspiring novelist, had learned her literary principles from Ayn; her work on her novel, *Double Crossing*—a novel about human rights, laid in the Soviet Union—was directed by those principles. Erika sent a copy of the manuscript to her, at Ayn's suggestion. "All through the years of writing *Double Crossing,*" Erika would say, "I kept thinking that Ayn would be so proud of me when she read it. That was my fuel. I was applying everything I'd learned from her, and speaking out on a subject very close to her heart." Ayn never read the manuscript.

Kay Smith, as Kay Nolte Smith, wrote *The Watcher,* again in Ayn's general literary tradition. Kay did not send it to her, but Ayn, who had enthusiastically praised Kay's articles for *The Objectivist,* knew of its publication and did not seek to read it.

Ayn had continued to force herself to appear at Ford Hall Forum, but fewer speaking invitations were coming in after her years of constant refusals. Nor would she have accepted them had they arrived. In May of 1979, however, she agreed to appear on "The Phil Donahue Show." It was a disaster. A young woman in the audience asked Ayn a question which made it clear that she thought her former admiration for Ayn's work had been an aberration of youth

—and Ayn, offended and insulted, pounced angrily, shouting at the girl; a substantial part of the show was devoted to their exchange.

In July of that year, she appeared on Tom Snyder's late-night "Tomorrow," to talk about her new book, *Introduction to Objectivist Epistemology,* a collection of articles from *The Objectivist* published by New American Library. It was an astonishing appearance. These two confident, abrasive people, polar opposites in their convictions, warmed to each other instantly, and some measure of Ayn's charm and color, never far beneath the surface, still ready to respond to the smallest sign of a response from the outside world, leaped into life. No other interviewer had had the courage to treat Ayn as Tom Snyder did; there was something almost paternal, something affectionate and tender, in his manner toward her, and she blossomed during their hour together, feeling safe. At one point, he asked her, "Would you say 'Thank God' for this country?" Ayn replied, smiling broadly, "Yes. I like what that expression means: it means the highest possible." As the interview came to an end, Snyder said, "God bless you"—and Ayn responded, "Thank you. The same to you."

One of the few personal contacts Ayn maintained was with Mimi Sutton, Frank's niece. They had met only rarely in later years; Mimi was widowed, and could not often travel to New York from her home in Chicago. But they spoke regularly on the telephone, and Mimi never forgot Ayn's birthday or Frank's. She was painfully aware that with each birthday call, her beloved uncle grew more confused; she knew that Ayn sometimes had to explain who she was. When she called on September 22, 1979, to congratulate Frank on his eighty-second birthday, Ayn, terribly distraught, explained, "He can't speak to you today. When he is rational and can understand, I'll tell him you called. But *I'll* know you remembered him . . . and somehow, *he'll* know it, too."

During Tom Snyder's interview with Ayn, he had said, "Ayn Rand doesn't fear death, does she?" Ayn had replied, "No. Not my own. Only the death of someone I love."

As 1979 drew to a close, Ayn rarely left Frank's side except to eat a hurried, untasted meal and to try to get the few hours' sleep that eluded her. Frank's heart was failing, and only a few rare sparks of his mind still flickered. Ayn held the fragile hands of the man to whom she had been married for fifty years, and kissed his sunken cheeks, and stroked his hair, and wept.

On November 9, as gently and quietly as he had lived, Frank O'Connor slipped out of life.

Chapter Thirty-two

Ayn moved through the next days as if she were carved out of ice—with a glacial control through which one sensed something so fragile that it would shatter at the first touch of heat or light.

Frank was gone, and with him went the last of life. There was nothing to hold her now, only the need to do for Frank the few last tasks that had to be done. When I learned of his death, I thought, with a chill of fear for her, of the lines from an old poem: "He first deceased. She, for a little, tried to live without him, liked it not, and died."

She did what had to be done, rarely dropping her silent remoteness to weep choking, desolate sobs. As arrangements for Frank's funeral were being made, she told a friend, "I feel better today. I've learned that when a couple lives together as long as Frank and I did, the one who remains tends not to survive more than six months. I won't have to suffer long."

Frank's coffin lay in the funeral home, surrounded by flowers. Groups of friends and admirers of Ayn came to say their last farewell to the man whom no one had ever deeply known but who had warmed them with the tenderness of his spirit. Ayn sat quietly, accepting condolences as if she could not quite hear the words or know who was speaking them; she was listening to the sounds of the organist playing the light lilting music that once had delighted Frank. One of the pieces was an old ballad, "With a Song in My Heart"; Ayn and Frank had first heard it the year they were married, and for both of them it had come to symbolize their coming together so long ago.

The private burial took place on a snowy slope in the nonsectarian Kenisco Cemetery in Valhalla, New York. At Ayn's request, the only ceremony at the graveside was a reading of Frank's and her favorite poem, Rudyard Kipling's "If." Then the coffin was lowered into the cold earth.

Ayn endured. Not even her longing for death was stronger than the life force that still beat within her as it had beaten throughout her seventy-four years. She had never learned to succumb; she could not learn it now. Ill, tired, heartbroken, without purpose or hope, she could not abandon the words she had written decades before: "There's your life . . . something so precious and rare, so beautiful that it's like a sacred treasure." In the name of that sacred treasure, she endured.

She spoke often to Mimi Sutton. "Talk to me about Frank," she would say. "Tell me everything you can remember about when he was young. It doesn't matter how small or insignificant it may seem; I want to hear." Mimi would dredge through her memory, telling Ayn the stories she remembered and the stories her family had related—about the sick chickens Frank had nursed back to health in his boyhood—about the plays he and his brothers and sisters had written and performed for the admission price of one pin—about the Sundays when he had sung in the church choir—about the nickname an aunt had given him when he was seven, "my little brown-haired robin." She spoke of Frank's brothers and sisters, of his mother's dreams for her sons, of his hard-drinking father's passionate love of his children. And each time she stopped, Ayn said, "Go on. Please go on. I want to know more."

The empty days dragged by—the weeks, the months, the year of waking each morning and learning not to leap out of bed to go to Frank—the year of learning not to think about the food she would prepare for him, and how she might coax him to eat a few bites—the year of learning not to wake from harrowing nightmares in terror that he was dead—the year of remembering Frank striding in to smile at her after a day of working on the ranch in California, his face and arms bronzed from the sun, his blue-gray eyes startlingly vivid against his tan—the year of remembering the sexual passion of their first years together, the nights of lying in his arms and knowing that she wanted nothing more of life than this— the year of suddenly discovering, with a jolt of panic, that his face and body had blurred in her memory, and running to her study to gaze at photographs of the beautiful, strong young man she had married, and wondering where their days had gone and why, and touching the glass over the paper face with her fingers, then her lips, and sobbing until she was past exhaustion.

There were random activities to occupy her. There was her editorial work on Leonard's manuscript and the introduction for it that she had agreed to write; there was the small magazine *The Objectivist Forum,* for which she had agreed to act as philosophical consultant; there were the mountains of fan mail that never stopped arriving; there were business matters to be attended to and discussions with her publishers and agents and attorneys; there were her favorite television detective programs and reruns of "The Twilight Zone" and "The Avengers" and "Perry Mason" and "The Untouchables" and "Kojak"; there were Scrabble and stamp collecting and novels by Ian Fleming and Donald Hamilton and S. S. van Dine; and sometimes there were philosophical conversations long into the night. Her hands were occupied, and an infinitesimal portion of her mind. The power of her intelligence and the passionate emotion that had raged through her life, lay dormant.

Until . . . in a series of tiny, almost unnoticeable inner motions, like a giant eagle slowly stretching the great span of its wings, the unextinguishable life force within her began to stir from its long sleep and to fight for air and light. She seemed to see once more the radiance of the world. There was life outside the four walls of her room, there was work and warmth and achievement still possible on earth as long as life endured, there was the sacred treasure she had always loved—its riches were waiting for her, calling her name, life was demanding to be lived.

She had always hated suffering. She had suffered too much, for too many years. She had always worshipped joy. She had been joyless for too long. She would start to move, she would move without motivation, with too little breath to fill her damaged lungs and too much pain as blood and oxygen struggled to reach her damaged heart . . . she would move without Frank. Her first steps would be small and halting, but perhaps one day her swift, confident stance would return. She would hold tight to her sacred treasure, she would fight for achievement and joy for all the days that remained to her. There remained one fight more—the best and the last.

Her first halting step was to go through the piles of letters and urgent telephone messages from universities and from television and radio shows, inviting her to appear. The letters had gone unopened for months, the telephone messages had been left unanswered. She decided to venture out into the world again, to fight for her ideas and to work for their dissemination. She chose "The Phil Donahue Show" as her first public appearance since Frank's death. It was to be a test, a way of discovering the limits of her newborn strength.

The show was one of Ayn's most sparkling, enchanting appearances in many years. She seemed alive again, she was serious and intense, she was light and witty, she was passionate and luminously profound. Following the lead of Donahue's questions, she danced effortlessly from a discussion of the importance of taking pride in one's accomplishments to her reasons, as a Romantic writer, for liking "Charlie's Angels," to why she was an atheist, to the damage men do themselves by repressing their emotions, to a discussion of Aristotle as the defender of reason and the father of logic, to the proper function of government as the defender of individual rights, adding: "Whoever tells you that you should exist for the collective, for the State—is, or wants to be, the State." The studio audience laughed and cheered and applauded. A young woman rose to say: "I want to tell you that my husband and I met and married because of our mutual interest in your work. The initial appeal of your writing, for me, was the idea that I should be proud of who I am and what I am."

As the hour drew to an end, Donahue said, "You have recently been widowed. Does the emotional impact of this kind of pain alter your philosophy in any way?" "No," Ayn replied. "It has only altered my position in regard to the world. I lost my top value. I'm not too interested in anything else. But I'll survive it, because I do love the world, and I do love ideas, and I do love man." "Isn't it tempting," Donahue asked, "to hope for a reunion with the person you love?" Ayn responded, "I've asked myself just that—and then I thought that if I really believed it, I'd commit suicide immediately, to go to him. . . . I've asked myself how I'd feel if I thought he were on trial before God or St. Peter—and I'm not with him. My first desire would be to run to help him, to say how good he was."

The Donahue appearance was a beginning for Ayn, it was a first small step back to life. And then the eagle's wings spread wide.

She had abandoned all expectation of discovering a writer who could bring *Atlas Shrugged* to the screen in the manner she envisioned; she had abandoned all interest in entrusting it to hands and minds that would not understand and cherish it. All her life, she had known that what she wanted was *her* responsibility to achieve. Very well, she decided. I want *Atlas Shrugged* to be brought to television as a miniseries. *I* shall write it, and, if necessary, *I* shall produce it.

She set to work on a nine-hour adaptation. She had to re-conceive, to approach in a totally new manner, the novel that had taken fourteen years to write. It was as difficult as any task she had undertaken. But as she sat at her desk and the weeks passed and the stack of pages grew, she knew that she was alive again. She was writing fiction, and she wondered why she had ever stopped. She was living in *her* world again, and she wondered why she had ever left it.

Her work was interrupted by another bout of physical illness. She had been having painful gallbladder attacks; surgery was indicated, but was dangerous because of her weakened heart. Finally, as the attacks grew worse and came oftener, an operation was performed—from which she recovered rapidly and well.

In May of 1981, a friend sent an audiocassette of Ayn's appearance on "The Phil Donahue Show," which I had not seen, to my home in Los Angeles. As I sat listening to it, I was deeply moved by the enthusiasm in her voice and by the love and dignity with which she spoke of Frank, and I knew that I wanted to speak with her once more. It had been almost thirteen years since I had seen her. I had kept informed of her activities and her physical health, as, over the years, I reestablished friendly relationships with those of the former collective and former NBI students and staff who were important to me—Joan and Allan Blumenthal, Edith Efron, Elayne and Harry Kalberman, Alan Greenspan, Henry and Erika Holzer, Kay and Phillip Smith. But now, I felt a sudden longing for some part of my broken contact with Ayn. I went to the telephone, thinking it likely that she would refuse to talk to me, that she would slam the receiver at the sound of my voice. I dialed the telephone number I had not forgotten.

"It's Barbara, Ayn," I said when she answered the telephone. There was a brief, stunned silence. Then she said, a sound of pleasure in her tone, "Barbara! How are you?" I told her that I had been listening to her interview, and what I had felt, and why I was calling. She barely let me finish, she wanted to know where I was, what I was doing, what had happened in my life since I left New

York—and all at once, Ayn and I were old friends again, catching up on each other's lives after too long an absence. Perhaps it was her need for that unique emotional understanding of each other we once had shared, perhaps it was her loneliness, perhaps it was my obvious love of Frank, perhaps it was her memory of the good days I had been a part of, before the world had darkened and grown cold—perhaps it was a combination of all these things. We talked for half an hour, until it seemed to both of us that at any moment I might come down from my apartment on Thirty-fourth Street to knock on her door and we would talk philosophy through the night.

"I haven't had much energy since my illness," she said. "I rarely go out in the evening anymore. I've been trying to plan a long-range writing project, but I'm still torn between fiction and nonfiction. . . ."

She interrupted herself to say, "I feel much more benevolent toward you than I would have expected. I truly wish you well. I'm not angry with you, although I'm very angry with Nathan. You probably were his victim, too." Then she went on to speak of her last Ford Hall Forum talk: "There was a mob there, they had to turn people away," to mention her break with the Blumenthals, and to ask me more questions about myself.

I told her I planned to be in New York in a couple of months. Could I visit her? "I'll be glad to see you," she answered. "Let me know when your plans are definite. We'll make a date." As if to warn me that I would find her physically changed, she added, "I'm getting older, as you know if you've seen me on television."

Two months later, as I walked in the early afternoon sunshine from my New York hotel toward Ayn's apartment, I wondered how I would feel when I saw her again. I had missed her, I cared for her as I had always done, but I knew that I could not pick up the strings of our former relationship, should she wish it; I could not again accept a friendship that was not on my terms, that did not permit me to think my own thoughts and feel my own feelings. I was free of the old bonds.

I stood before the apartment door where I had stood so many times, feeling the same faint trembling in my knees I had felt the first night I met her. When the door swung open, a smiling Ayn reached out her hands to take mine—and for a moment we stood silently as the years rolled back—and then we both laughed because we did not know what to say. How does one greet a friend one has not seen for thirteen years, but whom one has seen only yesterday?

Ayn looked more vibrant than she had in many years. She had aged, as she had warned me, one could see her seventy-six years in her face, but there was nothing in her face or stance that suggested illness; her huge dark eyes were shining, she was slenderer than I had ever known her to be. She wore a bright dress in a print she had always loved, and under it her body seemed alive with energy. When I complimented her on her appearance, she twirled around to show me how slim she was—"I weigh exactly what I weighed the day I arrived here from Russia," she said proudly. The apartment, once full of dingy furniture torn by her cats, looked fresh and new, furnished with the glass and chrome and pale gray upholstery over straight-lined sofas and chairs that she preferred. Eloise, her housekeeper, served coffee and the small sweet pastries I remembered.

And then we began to talk. Suddenly, an icy coldness was in her tone as she said, "You don't think you can ignore the past and the break between us. You know we have to talk about it." I had known it could not be ignored, but I had been unable to arrive at a satisfactory policy for dealing with it. Despite her appearance, I knew she was ill, she had lost Frank, she was elderly and terribly tired; I had no wish to upset her with recriminations, nor could I accept unearned guilt. The problem dissolved as she spoke. To my bewilderment, she began making excuses for me that I would never have dreamed of making for myself—and the gist of those excuses was that I had treated her badly out of misguided loyalty to Nathaniel. It was not the truth, but she would not be interrupted, she spoke of both of us as Nathaniel's joint victims, victims of the perverse psychology of a man we had loved and whom neither of us had understood.

Then I remembered that she had written, "The essence of femininity is hero-worship—the desire to look up to a man." And I grasped the meaning of her defense of me. What a woman chooses to do for a man's sake—for the sake of a man she believes to be a hero—cannot profoundly be condemned. It was the hero-worshipper who was defending me.

There was the beginning of anger in her voice when she mentioned Nathaniel, an anger that had never died and that revealed itself once more when she said, "Did you know that I've met his wife?" I *did* know it, I had been told it two years earlier by Nathaniel and Devers; but Ayn did not wait for my response. She chuckled bitterly and said, "I was coming home one day, and I found a woman standing in front of my apartment door who said she was Nathan's wife. I let her in because she insisted; there were people in the hall, and I didn't want a public scene. Can you believe that she wanted me to see Nathan! She talked some nonsense about how we had once loved each other, and should now meet again to say a civilized good-bye. I told her to stop talking like a bad Hollywood script, and that I would never see him, under any circumstances or for any reason. She said that coming to me was *her* idea, and that Nathan knew nothing about it. She expected me to believe that! . . . But when she dropped the subject of Nathan, she was rather nice, and we talked for a while. After that, she'd telephone when she was in New York; I think she still hoped she'd win me over to Nathan. Finally, one day after she had called, a messenger came to my door with a beautiful, huge, excessively expensive bouquet of flowers; they were from Devers. I didn't want them"—the anger rose in her voice and paled her face—"I didn't want *anything* that had come from Nathan. That evening, I had visitors; when they left, I gave them the flowers to take home. Two days later, Devers phoned again, upset that I hadn't called to thank her for the flowers; she had made a point of telling me what hotel she was staying in. I told her"—the anger rose higher, clearly directed not at Devers but at Nathaniel—"that if the gift was a gesture of friendship, it was presumptuous; if it was a bribe, it wasn't nearly enough." She chuckled again, as if pleased by the final slap she had delivered to Nathaniel; she did not speak of him again, except to say tensely, "Do you still see him?"

"No," I answered, "we haven't been friends for some time."

"I'm glad," she said. "He was a bad influence on you."

Ayn's face and body relaxed. She smiled at me warmly as she said, "Now tell me about the last thirteen years." I began speaking about my life, and she told me of hers.

In the hours of that golden afternoon, as the light from the window softened the stern planes of her face, Ayn spoke of Frank with love and longing and despair. "After he died," she said, "I couldn't write at all, not for a long time, I wasn't motivated to do anything. . . . Then I realized that I needed to do something that would be only for my own personal pleasure, something purposeful that I would do only because I enjoyed it. So I've begun taking lessons in mathematics. I have a private tutor who comes once a week to teach me algebra. It's wonderful! He can't believe how quickly I'm learning—he said he's never seen anyone move so swiftly. And it leads me in fascinating philosophical directions—there are so many intriguing connections between algebra and philosophy."

I listened to her, astounded, as she had always had the power to astound me. At the age of seventy-six, her concept of personal pleasure, of an exciting new activity, was to study algebra and to define its relationship to metaphysics and epistemology.

She spoke of politics—she disapproved of Ronald Reagan, whom she considered a typical conservative in his attempt to link politics and religion; she had refused to vote for him. She spoke of the activities she was engaged in and the work she was doing. She told me whom she saw and whom she no longer saw, and we gossiped cheerfully about old friends. We talked politics and philosophy and aesthetics—and it was not 1981, it was 1950, we were young and the world was young, and the glow of ideas outshone the sun.

When I rose to leave long after dusk—we would see each other again, we agreed, on my next visit to New York—we were both solemn, wondering when our next meeting would be . . . or if it would be. At the door, she blew me a final kiss, as she used to do when we parted, and I blew her a kiss in return. It was the last time I ever saw Ayn Rand.

Walking back to my hotel, I thought of the people, through the years, who had said to me, "How could you have stayed with Ayn all those years? How could you have allowed yourself to be a party to her affair with Nathaniel? How could you have been willing to endure all the pain of so many years? *I* would never have done it." I understood their perspective, but each time I heard the comment, I had thought, No, you would not have done it. The moments of joy and the passionate engagement, the struggle for the highest possible, would not have been worth their cost in agony. But they were worth it to me.

It was a few months later that I wrote Ayn to tell her I was planning to write her biography. I wanted her to learn of it from me, and to understand my reasons. Knowing she always procrastinated about letter-writing, I was not surprised when weeks went by without a response. Finally, I telephoned—but she refused to speak to me. I was certain that her refusal must stem from anger at the prospect of my writing her biography. But many months later, I happened to be speaking to an acquaintance who had a business relationship with Ayn. "Ayn was in the office to talk about a business matter," he told me. "And she said, 'Barbara was in New York a while ago. We spent a day together. She's going to write my biography.' She said it perfectly calmly, there was no anger in her voice or manner—and then we went back to our discussion." I can only assume that if anger was her initial reaction, her attitude later changed.

In the summer of 1981, Ayn received an invitation that was to bring her, at last, a value from the outside world that was in *her* terms.

At the age of eighteen, James U. Blanchard—later founder and Chairman of the National Committee for Monetary Reform, an organization dedicated to the reestablishment of a gold standard and to educating the American public in the benefits of free market economics—was severely injured in an automobile accident. One afternoon, as he sat listlessly on the front porch of his home, a friend approached, tossed a book on his lap, and said, "You'll really like this." The book was *Anthem*.

"After I read it," Jim recalled, "I read all her other books nonstop. I got *The Objectivist Newsletter* and started reading everything it recommended. I became particularly interested in economics, especially the Austrian School, and from that came my interest in investments and later in monetary reform—and from that came financial success. . . . Her work gave me a context within which to structure my life and make decisions—it gave me the sense of a consistent foundation on which I could build. That little book that was thrown on my lap changed my whole life."

In November of 1981, NCMR was to hold its annual conference in New Orleans for businessmen, bankers, financial consultants, entrepreneurs, investors, industrialists, economists, mutual-fund managers, and others in the financial world. Among the speakers would be Louis Rukeyser, Paul Erdman, Adam Smith, Harry Browne, Douglas R. Casey, Harry Schultz, and Howard Ruff.

"I wanted Ayn Rand to be our featured speaker," Jim said. "But I had been asking her to appear for about four years, thinking that the romance of talking to all these millionaires would reach her; there was never an answer to my letters. I began thinking how I might really excite her and convince her to come. I knew that the offer of a considerable fee wouldn't do it. Then I remembered her interest in the railroad industry and in trains—and I wrote again, saying that I would arrange for her to travel to New Orleans in a private rail car, with a butler and a gourmet chef. She accepted. Leonard Peikoff and Cynthia, his wife-to-be, were to join her. And then I faced the problem of *finding* a private car! I called around desperately for days, until I located Ray Thorpe, president of the Private Rail Car Association. When I told him what I wanted he said, 'Fantastic! Ayn Rand changed my whole life, I love her books. I'll give her my own private car and my personal chef. Ask her for a list of her favorite foods, so the chef can prepare them.'

"It was a marvelous car," Jim continued. "It looked like it was built in the nineteenth century, very ornate, with two private bedrooms and a formal dining area. We stocked it with everything she liked best, and added champagne and caviar. I knew she hadn't been anywhere or done anything for a long time; I wanted her to have the fun of the train ride, and to be where she would be appreciated and would see how many people she had affected—I had a feeling she didn't realize the depth of her influence."

Ayn did *not* realize the depth of her influence. Her reclusive life and her disinterest in the world outside her doors had prevented her from learning that her ideas were fast becoming a respected and astonishingly potent part of the culture of which she had despaired—that Objectivism was taught in university classrooms across the country, that books and scholarly articles expounding aspects of her philosophy were pouring out of the presses in a growing stream, that men and woman influential in government, in the arts, in the sciences, in industry and finance were carrying her standard because it was their own. Tragically, when she was reaching the pinnacle of the success for which she had yearned, when the voices she had sought *were,* at last, speaking for her—she was no longer listening.

Ayn arrived in New Orleans after a two-and-a-half-day journey, to be met by Jim and the limousine that would take her to and from her hotel suite. Her eyes were glowing. The trip had been hard, the road-bed rocky, but she had loved the sense of living in the pages of *Atlas Shrugged,* of riding in the same kind of railroad car as Dagny Taggart and Hank Rearden had done.

Jim held a small party for Ayn the evening before her appearance. Among the guests was economic writer Douglas Casey. Doug was to say, "She was very charming and gracious—although it was obvious she would not brook contradiction. I had picked up *The Virtue of Selfishness* when I was about twenty-two; I read the first page—then I had to put it down: I could *not* believe it—it wasn't possible that someone was saying these things. Then I read all of her books. I couldn't accept everything, I had to find my own path, but I agree with all her basic values. She's one of the great geniuses of modern history."

More than four thousand people, representing every geographical area in the country and many overseas areas, attended Ayn's speech. "When she got up on the stage," Jim would recall, "she came alive, she was so vibrant even though she was in ill health. The audience got to its feet and gave her a standing ovation —and her speech was constantly interrupted by applause. They *loved* her."

Ayn's talk, entitled "The Sanction of the Victim," was a tour de force. Its theme was that the producers, who carry the world on their shoulders and keep it alive, are being destroyed by their acceptance of the morality of altruism. They accept all the insults and accusations of materialism hurled against them, instead of proudly asserting their moral right to the profits they earn. "The greatest thrill," Jim said, "was that she announced publically for the first time that she was writing a miniseries script for *Atlas*, and that there was a strong possibility that she would be looking for outside financing to produce it."

The speech ended with a quote from John Galt:

"The world you desired can be won, it exists, it is real, it is possible, it's yours.

"But to win it requires your total dedication and a total break with the world of your past, with the doctrine that man is a sacrificial animal who exists for the pleasure of others. Fight for the value of your person. Fight for the virtue of your pride. Fight for the essence of that which is man: for his sovereign rational mind. Fight with the radiant certainty and the absolute rectitude of knowing that yours is the Morality of Life and that yours is the battle for any achievement, any value, any grandeur, any goodness, any joy that has ever existed on this earth."

The applause was an unending outburst of gratitude and love from members of a group that had never before received a moral sanction. Ayn stood, thunderstruck, listening to the wild cheering as the audience leaped to its feet. She had not imagined the extent of her power nor expected the tide of passionate admiration that flowed to her from the audience.

"The question-and-answer period was thrilling," Jim said. "She was razor-sharp. When it was over, lines of people crowded around her, wanting to know where they could sign up to invest in the project. . . . Did you know that my wife, Jackie, and I named our son 'Anthem'? We told Ayn about it, and she autographed the copy of the book I had originally read, for my son. . . . I really loved her."

In his *Dow Theory Letters* of December 3, Richard Russell, who had attended the conference, wrote: "Had an interesting conversation with guest of honor, Ayn Rand. . . . We talked about age (she's in her 70's), and the necessity of having intense interests. She said she would love to see the year 2000. I replied that I had made a study of people who live to be over 100, and I was convinced that she'd make it. She seemed pleased at the prospect."

She was not to make it. By the time the train brought Ayn back to New York, not even her excitement over her triumph could continue to feed energy to her body. She was desperately ill. Her face was gashed with new lines, she moved with enormous effort, her voice was raspy, as if not enough breath were being fed to it.

It was soon evident that her path led downhill. From December through January of 1982, she grew weaker and more frail. In February, she was hospitalized with cardiopulmonary problems. Leonard was with her constantly, knowing she had only a short time to live.

Ayn faced death as she had faced life. Death was a fact of reality. Facts had never frightened her; they did not frighten her now. She was scheduled to give her annual Ford Hall Forum talk in April; when she realized it would be impossible, she asked Leonard to give the talk she had prepared. Her work on the teleplay of *Atlas* was only one-fourth completed; she told Leonard to do whatever was possible to have it finished and produced. She had been planning a new collection of essays, *Philosophy: Who Needs It;* she had not completed the choice of articles to be included; she asked Leonard to complete it. She specified the arrangements she wished made for her funeral.

She had often quoted the saying: "It is not I who will die, it is the world that will end." Her world was coming to its end.

Early in March, Ayn said, "I want to go home. I want to die at home." Nothing more could be done for her, and the doctors agreed. She returned, with her nurses, to the apartment where she had lived with Frank. She was not in pain, but she grew progressively weaker as her valiant heart began to fail.

On the evening of March 5, Mimi Sutton telephoned. "The doctor had told me how sick she was, and I wanted to speak to her once more. I don't know if she fully understood, but I said, 'Ayn, I love you.' "

The morning of March 6, the nurse telephoned Leonard to come at once. He arrived moments too late. Ayn Rand was dead.

The New York *Times* wrote: "Ayn Rand's body lay next to the symbol she had adopted as her own—a six-foot dollar sign. Outside the funeral home, her followers, some in jeans and some in furs, stood in the cold waiting to pay her tribute.

"From 7 to 9 o'clock Monday night, 800 admirers of the novelist and philosopher passed through the Frank E. Campbell Funeral Home at Madison Avenue and 81st Street. Some wept as they spoke of her in hushed tones, and some glowed as they described how she had changed their lives.

"Those who came to the funeral home to pay their respects reflected Miss Rand's influence in political, economic and intellectual spheres. They included Alan Greenspan, chairman of President Ford's Council of Economic Advisers; Robert M. Bleiberg, editorial director of *Barron's* magazine; many of the leaders of the Libertarian Party, and professors of philosophy, business management and psychology at schools from Vassar College to York University in Toronto."

Ayn's body lay in an open coffin. Her gold wedding ring was on her finger, where it had been since Frank had placed it there on an April day in 1929. On her breast was a photograph of Frank, to be buried with her. The sounds of music sang through the flower-filled room as the mourners filed by the coffin. It was not a heroic symphony but the music she loved much better. It was her tiddlywink music that was ushering her out of life, as it had ushered her into life from a park bandstand in the Crimea.

As word of Ayn's death spread, it was announced on the front pages of newspapers all over the world. In their reports, she was given at last the title she had most cherished: "Ayn Rand, novelist-philosopher." Throughout America and in cities dotted across the map from Canada to India to Israel, groups of her admirers held memorials on college campuses, in private homes, in parks and in rented halls. They spoke of their love for Ayn Rand, and their grief, they spoke of her achievements and of the inestimable gifts they had received from those achievements.

The private burial was held in Valhalla. Two hundred people stood on a rolling hill by the graveside as huge snowflakes drifted down to cover the earth and the coffin and the bare white branches of trees. Kipling's "If" was read, as it had been read for Frank. As the coffin was slowly lowered to take its place beside Frank's, each of the mourners dropped a flower on the casket.

I visited Ayn and Frank's graves a year later, on a brilliant summer day. I stood on the same rolling hill, now green and softly glowing. Two pale gray stones stood side by side, joined in the back by a narrower strip of stone, near a maple tree and the swaying leaves of a weeping willow. On one stone is engraved: FRANK O'CONNOR, 1897–1979; on the other: AYN RAND O'CONNOR, 1905–1982."

As I stood remembering, I thought that I had often grieved for Ayn's unhappiness in her last years. And yet, was grief appropriate? In the life of Ayn Rand, I had seen something I had never seen before nor ever heard or read of. Ayn had begun life with a single passionate goal—to create her ideal world and her ideal man. And at the end of her life—despite the odds against her, despite the pain and the losses, despite illness and anguish and death—it was done. Perhaps it is for the rest of mankind that one should grieve.

I stood by the weeping willow and I thought how fitting it would be if the legends of Valhalla were true. Ayn would travel to the paradise of the brave, the paradise assigned to heroes slain in battle. Eight guards would rise to salute her and to escort her on her new journey. But they would not be the guards of the legends. They would be Cyrus, and Enjolras, and Leo, and Frank, and Howard Roark and Hank Rearden and Francisco d'Anconia and John Galt. Ayn had fought for Valhalla—for Atlantis—all of her life, and now she would enter its gates.

Weeping, I remembered what she had said at the conclusion of the interviews I had done with her in 1961. "It's a benevolent universe, and I love it, and any struggle was worth it. Struggle or unhappiness are so enormously unimportant. I don't regret a minute of my life."

PART VI

EPILOGUE

Chapter Thirty-three

A young black girl, brought up in the American South, joined the Peace Corps in the sixties. Wandering through a rummage shop in Kampala, Uganda, she noticed an old battered copy of a novel entitled *Atlas Shrugged.* "By the time my Peace Corps tour ended," she later said, "I had undergone the loneliest, most inspiring, and heartrending psycho-intellectual transformation, and all my plans upon returning to the United States had changed." Anne Wortham is now Assistant Professor of Public Policy at Harvard's Kennedy School of Government. The most significant consequence of Ayn Rand's influence in terms of Anne's intellectual output is her book, *The Other Side of Racism*—a denunciation of coercive egalitarianism and a clarion call to individualism in race relations. In her introductory courses on sociology, *The Fountainhead* is a text, and has elicited, in enthusiastic student papers, such comments as, "I have already recommended this novel to others and I only hope that they benefit as I did from Rand's insight into man's potential"—and, "The exaltation of man's great ability to achieve and succeed gave me an impetus to improve myself, for myself"—and, "*The Fountainhead* is a monument to the splendor of the ability of men to reason, think, create, build, achieve, and succeed."

Through her teaching and her writings of books and articles in academic journals, Anne Wortham is presenting a new and individualistic view of sociology and a new and individualistic perspective on the black experience. The fountainhead is Ayn Rand.

An admirer of *The Fountainhead*, at the threshold of his career as a psychologist, met Ayn Rand in 1950. He began the concentrated study of her ideas and their application to his own field. Today, Nathaniel Branden is a pioneer in the field of self-esteem; among his books are *The Psychology of Self-Esteem, The Disowned Self, The Psychology of Romantic Love,* and *Honoring the Self.* As director of the Biocentric Institute in Los Angeles, he offers workshops in major

American cities in self-esteem enhancement, man/woman relationships, and personal transformation.

"Intellectually," Nathaniel said, "I learned more from Ayn Rand than I can possibly summarize. She used to love to say 'check your premises and watch your implications.' I really learned that from her, both with regard to my own thinking and statements and those of other people. In other words, I feel she sharpened enormously my ability to think philosophically. Notwithstanding important areas of disagreement between us, I am generally very much in accord with the broad fundamentals of her philosophical perspective, and naturally that influences my own work. I recall that a neurophysiologist once said of *Atlas Shrugged*, 'This book was written by a great biologist.' I definitely learned what I have come to call the biocentric approach, at a very deep philosophical level, from Ayn. . . . She was a genius. She had provocative and innovative ideas in virtually every sphere of philosophy, from epistemology to aesthetics. I think the creativity of her countless insights will go on being discovered and appreciated and new for a very long time." Readers of Nathaniel's books and participants in his workshops have been and continue to be introduced to the metaphysical, moral, and political ideas of Objectivism through his work. The fountainhead is Ayn Rand.

An Alaskan legislator switched his allegiance from Republican to Libertarian and was reelected in 1978. During his years in office, Dick Randolph, along with Libertarian legislator Kenneth Fanning, fought for the deregulation of transportation and the privatization of government land, and successfully initiated a program by which royalties from mineral rights are distributed to Alaskans in the amount of four hundred million dollars a year. In 1982, at the request of Dick Randolph and four other representatives, the Alaskan Legislature issued a Citation in memoriam to Ayn Rand: "Controversial, brilliant, and talented, Ayn Rand's impress upon the American literary and political scene was poignant and indelible. She was standard-bearer for those fortunate ones who already believed that all change, progress, innovation and creativity lie within the individual, and mentor and educator for those who only dimly suspected that collectivism was never the blueprint of nature. Only after she had dared to celebrate self-esteem and competition in *Atlas Shrugged* and *The Fountainhead* did lagging social engineers and experts on human nature begin to recognize the necessary art of 'selfishness' and redefine it as success. . . . America had no more forceful voice for freedom. . . ." The citation was signed by the Speaker of the House and the President of the Senate. "Without Ayn Rand's influence, I would not be in office," Dick Randolph said. The fountainhead is Ayn Rand.

A twenty-four-year-old woman, who termed herself "a traditional housewife," read *Atlas Shrugged* and enrolled in NBI's lectures in New York. Today, Jacquelyn Reinach is a writer, composer, and entrepreneur; she is the author of *Sweet Pickles,* a series of children's books which have sold more than sixty million copies. "Dagny Taggart was an inspiration to me; she is a great feminist role model," Jackie said. "Ayn Rand's works gave me the courage to be and to do what I had dreamed of."

In 1963, a Czechoslovakian professor of physics defected to the United States. It was a difficult, painful decision; he was tormented by guilt, believing that because his former government had "provided" him with an education, he had a moral duty to return the fruits of that gift—until he read the works of Ayn Rand and understood that there can be no unchosen obligations. Today, Petr Beckmann, Professor Emeritus of the University of Colorado, publishes *Access To Energy*, a newsletter devoted to a rational, fact-based energy policy, and is the author of *The Health Hazards of* not *Going Nuclear.*[1]

A Canadian premedical student met Ayn Rand and began reading her works. Leonard Peikoff switched his major from medicine to philosophy, moved to New York to study with Ayn Rand and Nathaniel Branden, earned his Ph.D in philosophy, and is today the heir to and an executor of Ayn's literary estate. In 1982, Stein and Day published his book, *The Ominous Parallels,* in which he maintains that the deepest roots of Nazism lie in three philosophic ideas: the worship of unreason, the demand for self-sacrifice, and the elevation of society above the individual. Most recently, he has organized The Ayn Rand Institute: The Center for the Advancement of Objectivism, whose purpose is to help the spread of Objectivism to schools and colleges, to businessmen and to the general public.

A businessman began reading *Atlas Shrugged,* and "Within a few hundred pages I sensed clearly that I had ventured upon a lifetime of meaning. The philosophy of Ayn Rand nurtured growth, stability and integrity in my life. Her ideas permeated every aspect of my business, family and creative life." In 1973, in order to translate for his two young children the sense of life presented by Ayn Rand, O. Terry Nelson wrote *The Girl Who Owned a City,* an exciting story of a group of youngsters suddenly forced to survive in a world without adults; they are led by a heroic thirteen-year-old girl who organizes a new society based on reason and individualism. The novel has sold more than one hundred thousand copies, and is assigned to students in a number of schools across the country. The fountainhead is Ayn Rand.

A recent law school graduate read *Atlas Shrugged* and soon afterward met Ayn Rand, becoming her attorney for matters pertaining to Objectivism. "Dealing with Ayn Rand," he has said, "was like taking a post-doctoral course in mental functioning. The universe she created in her work holds out hope, and appeals to the best in man. Her lucidity and brilliance was a light so strong I don't think anything will ever be able to put it out." Today, Henry Mark Holzer is a constitutional lawyer and professor of law at Brooklyn Law School. He is the author of *The Gold Clause; Government's Money Monopoly;* and the recent *Sweet Land of Liberty? The Supreme Court and Individual Rights,* an examina-

---

[1] Not all of the people discussed above, or in the pages that follow, are wholly committed to Objectivism; many have significant disagreements; but all have been powerfully affected by her work and acknowledge an intellectual debt to Ayn Rand.

tion of the Court's consistent violation of individual rights in both the economic and social spheres. He co-represented teenage Walter Polovchak, "the littlest defector," seeking to prevent his forcible return to the Soviet Union, and also the 1985 Ukrainian defector, seaman Minoslav Medvid. In 1968, he purchased the Italian film version of *We the Living*, which Ayn edited before her death, and a subtitled version will be released in 1986. The fountainhead is Ayn Rand.

A young economist met Ayn and became a member of her "class of '43." Today, Alan Greenspan is one of the country's most prominent economists, adviser to three presidential administrations, and a member of the board of directors of major American corporations. He said, "At the time I met Ayn Rand in my mid-twenties, I had already developed a strong admiration for the efficiency of free-market capitalist economics. She demonstrated to me, however, that not only was laissez-faire capitalism an efficient and productive system, but was also the only system consistent with political freedom. By confronting issues I had never previously encountered, a whole new view of society was opened to me. Ayn Rand was, therefore, instrumental in significantly broadening the scope of my thinking and was clearly a major contributor to my intellectual development, for which I remain profoundly grateful to this day."

It was in 1981 that the New York *Times* noted, "If there is a novelist with unusual appeal among the Reagan organization, it is Ayn Rand, proponent of enlightened self-interest. Some of Reagan's closest advisors, including his director of domestic policy, Martin Anderson, sat at her feet when they were fledgling disciples and a Reagan Presidency just a gleam in the eye of G.E. Theater's host." David R. Henderson, former senior economist on Reagan's Council of Economic Advisors, has said, "Ayn Rand got me thinking about what kind of political system is proper for an autonomous human being to live in, and my thinking about that led me to become an economist. She helped me, perhaps more than anyone else, to live my life." Another among the men and women influenced by Ayn Rand who serve in the Administration is Kathryn Eickhoff, a former student of Nathaniel Branden Institute and Associate Director of the Office of Management and Budget. The fountainhead is Ayn Rand.

A refugee from Budapest, Hungary, smuggled to freedom in 1953, ultimately made his way to the United States. He was introduced to Ayn Rand's work and later became a professor of philosophy at several American universities. Tibor Machan is one of the most dedicated of philosophical fighters for many of the ideas of Ayn Rand, most particularly in the areas of morality and political philosophy. He is senior editor of *Reason,* senior Fellow of the Reason Foundation, and has written for numerous philosophical journals, magazines and newspapers. He is the editor of *The Libertarian Alternative,* a book of essays by contemporary defenders of libertarianism containing a comprehensive overview of libertarian thought on freedom and justice; and is at present editing *The Main Debate: Capitalism versus Communism,* soon to be published by Random House. The fountainhead is Ayn Rand.

The publisher and editorial director of one of the nation's most respected and influential financial weeklies read *Atlas Shrugged* shortly after its publication. "I couldn't put it down," said Robert Bleiberg of *Barron's.* "It was filling in great gaps in my economic theories and presenting a totally new philosophy. I'm in very substantial agreement with Ayn Rand; all the years have done is to confirm the wisdom of her ideas." Robert Bleiberg became friendly with Ayn, and began the occasional publication of her articles in his magazine, as well as publication of articles and editorials by Alan Greenspan and many others who had been influenced by Objectivism, a practice which he continues to this day. In 1984, *Barron's* republished Ayn's article on "The Morality of Capitalism," which first appeared in *The Objectivist Newsletter* in 1965. "She has had an enormous influence on the country," Robert Bleiberg said. "She deserves a great deal of the credit for the fact that we are beginning to get out of the statist muddle of the last decades. The intellectual ferment among defenders of freedom and capitalism over the past ten years or so, the remarkable upsurge, in theory and in practice, of freedom-oriented ideas—the fact that we have a President who cares about the free market—are staggering, and much of it is owing to Ayn Rand. To have arrived at where we are today is an astonishing intellectual voyage—and we have not yet seen the end of it; her influence continues to grow."

On the bookshelves in Robert Bleiberg's office, beside bound volumes of *The Wall Street Journal,* stand bound volumes of *The Objectivist.* "To the extent that I have had an influence," he said, "then so has Ayn!" The fountainhead is Ayn Rand.

A homemaker, married and the mother of three children, read the works of Ayn Rand and decided to return to school and complete her education, despite the heavy responsibilities involved. "My own move toward independence and liberation," she wrote in the *Journal of College English,* in an article entitled "Ayn Rand and Feminism: An Unlikely Alliance," "had been inspired by a popular novel. Pre-Friedan and pre-Millet, nascent feminism had been nurtured by the reading of *Atlas Shrugged.* . . . The neurotic, manipulated, or exploited female continues to be the mainstay of American fiction. . . . [But Rand's] novel has a protagonist who is a good example of a woman who is active, assertive, successful, and still retains the love and sexual admiration of three heroic men." Today, Mimi Gladstein is a literature professor at the University of Texas at El Paso, and author of the recent *The Ayn Rand Companion.* She had an opportunity to witness the effects of the character of Dagny Taggart on the young women students in her course, "Women in Fiction." "The course was very well attended," Mimi said, "and very depressing. In the world's great literature, women are either virtuous—which means passive, uninteresting, and unmotivated—or they are immoral—which means active, colorful, passionate . . . and doomed to defeat. I saw that my students were becoming more and more upset by this view of women's two possibilities, an alternative that no modern young woman could find acceptable—but I had found no other to offer them. And then it occurred to me to assign and discuss the character of Dagny Taggart in *Atlas Shrugged.* My students were *ecstatic.* Here, at last, was a woman they could admire and emulate, a woman who was both immensely effective and successful in the world, and intensely feminine. They responded with an excitement and pleasure that was gratifying to see. I felt as if I'd given them a treasured gift."

Despite the fact that Ayn Rand has been roundly attacked in the pages of *Ms.*—and was herself opposed to the feminist movement, focusing on the collectivist orientation of much of that movement—many feminists have found a source of inspiration in her presentation of an heroic woman who renounces neither career nor love, and in her rejection of the view of women as properly being objects of sacrifice in the name of children, family, and society. In an interview in *Playboy,* tennis champion Billie Jean King discussed the effects on her of *Atlas Shrugged,* which she read in 1972: " 'The book really turned me around, because, at the time, I was going through a bad period in tennis and thinking about quitting. People were constantly calling me and making me feel rotten if I didn't play in their tournament or help them out. I realized then that people were beginning to use my strength as a weakness—that they were using me as a pawn to help their own ends and if I wasn't careful, I'd end up losing myself. So, like Dagny Taggart, I had to learn how to be selfish, although selfish has the wrong connotation. As I see it, being selfish is really doing your own thing. Now I know that if I can make myself happy, I can make other people happy—and if that's being selfish, so be it. That's what I am.' "

A young man appeared at the offices of Nathaniel Branden Institute one day to sign up for courses and to seek—and find—work on NBI's staff. Robert Hessen, today a historian and Senior Fellow at the Hoover Institution in Stanford, is the author of *Steel Titan: The Life of Charles Schwab; In Defense of the Corporation;* and most recently he has edited and written an introduction to *Berlin Alert: The Memoirs and Reports of Truman Smith,* which has attracted major news stories in the Washington *Post* and the New York *Times.* Robert Hessen has said, "There were lots of defenses of capitalism versus socialism when *Atlas Shrugged* came out in the 1950s, but they were mostly 'bathtub economics'—you know, capitalism is superior because it's more efficient, and it makes bigger and better bathtubs than the Soviet system. Ayn Rand provided a *moral* defense that had an electrifying effect on people who had never heard capitalism defended in other than technological terms. She made it clear that a free society is also a productive society, but what matters is individual freedom."

"After you read *Atlas Shrugged,* " a young woman concluded, "you don't look at the world with the same perspective." Jennifer Roback is today Assistant Professor of Economics at Yale, a radio commentator and contributor to *Fortune, The Wall Street Journal,* the scholarly *Regulation* and the *Chicago Law Review,* as well as columnist for *Business Times.* In her courses at Yale on "Economics and Individualism," she includes readings from Ayn Rand.

A politically liberal professor of philosophy listened to a speech given by Ayn Rand, spent the rest of the day talking with her, and began to visit her regularly to discuss political philosophy, morality, and epistemology. In 1971, when a small group of people, disillusioned with the Republican Party, met in Denver to form the Libertarian Party, John Hospers wrote the statement of principles which was adopted unanimously and to roars of approval—a statement of Ayn Rand's principles of man's *moral* right to freedom, to self-interest, to the unfettered pursuit of his goals, and rejection of the use of physical force except in retaliation against the initiation of force. In 1972, John Hospers became the first presidential candidate of the new party—a party that in a few years would appear on the ballot in fifty states, win more than a million votes, and become the third largest political party in the United States. In an extraordinary break with historical precedent, he, along with his running mate Tonie Nathan— whose interest in libertarianism was created by her reading of Ayn Rand— received a vote in the Electoral College; Tonie Nathan thus became the first woman ever to receive an Electoral College vote. It was cast by college member Roger McBride, then a Republican and later the second Libertarian presidential candidate.

Today, John Hospers is an internationally respected philosopher, professor at USC, author of a number of important books on philosophy and aesthetics and of the first major work on the Objectivist-oriented philosophy of freedom, *Libertarianism.* He is president of The American Society of Aesthetics, and editor of one of the oldest and most respected journals of philosophy, *The Monist;* in scholarly journals he has edited over the last twenty years, he has arranged for the publication of numerous articles on aspects of Ayn's philosophy, firmly entrenching her name and importance in the philosophical literature.

John Hospers has said, "Ayn Rand was one of the most original thinkers I have ever met. There is no escape from facing the issues she raised. . . . At a time in my life when I thought I had learned at least the essentials of most philosophical views, being confronted with her, and having the privilege of extended discussions with her over a period of several years, suddenly changed the entire direction of my intellectual life, and placed every other thinker in a new perspective. Whatever subject one discusses thenceforth, one always has to take account of Ayn Rand."

In the years since its inception, the Libertarian Party has been racked by internal conflict between the Objectivist-oriented defenders of limited government and a strong defense posture, and the "anarcho-capitalists" led by noted economist and writer Murray Rothbard, a former student of Ludwig von Mises and a student in the first courses offered by Nathaniel Branden Institute. Though disagreeing with Ayn Rand's key concept of limited government, Murray Rothbard has stated that he "is in agreement basically with all her philosophy," and that it was she who convinced him of the theory of natural rights which his books uphold. In the opinion of many people, the anarchist wing has deeply undermined the effectiveness of the Libertarian Party in recent years. That wing was the particular source of Ayn Rand's indignant repudiation of the party that had been formed in the image of her political philosophy. But her influence in the party still is strong. Ed Clark, 1980 Libertarian presidential candidate and deputy general counsel at Atlantic Richfield, has said "I became involved in libertarian activities as a result of reading Ayn Rand. She was a great novelist, who had a profound effect on me and on hundreds of thousands of Americans. Her ideas are one of the most important streams of thought slowing down the march of collectivism in the Western world."

More important and more influential than the party, which necessarily deals only with narrow and specific political issues, is the wider and rapidly growing worldwide libertarian movement, unaffiliated with the party and concerned with fundamental issues of political philosophy. In recent years, it has had a powerful effect on the nation's discussions of the rights and sanctity of the individual, on the manner in which businessmen and entrepreneurs are viewed, on the new acceptance of the profit motive as a beneficent economic force; it has popularized such issues as the concept of victimless crimes, of deregulation of industry, of restitution for victims of crimes. "Without Ayn Rand," said David Nolan, the original founder of the Libertarian Party, "the libertarian movement would not exist."

In recent years, a number of effective magazines and journals with a libertarian orientation have sprung up, spearheaded by *Reason,* the best-known, most intellectually consistent and most influential of the libertarian magazines.

Reason—its subtitle is *Free Minds and Free Markets*—has grown rapidly since its modest beginnings in 1968. Founded by commercial artist Lanny Friedlander, it was purchased in 1969 by attorney Manny Klausner, philosopher Tibor Machan, and engineer Robert W. Poole. Its subscriptions—four hundred in 1970 —now exceed forty thousand copies monthly, and it is beginning to appear on newsstands in major American cities. Among its contributors are Nobel Laureates Friedrich von Hayek and Milton Friedman, psychiatrist Thomas Szasz, free-market economist Thomas Sowell, financial writer Howard Ruff; among its regular contributing editors are a former Reagan speechwriter, a prominent financial analyst, a syndicated literary critic, nationally known economists and philosophers; foreign correspondents contribute from countries around the world. *Reason*'s cover story on military testing was presented on "60 Minutes," its article on private fire departments caught the attention of both *Newsweek* and the ABC nightly news; its discovery of the misuse of funds in Cesar Chavez's farmworkers' union was picked up by ABC's "20–20." Excerpts from its articles regularly appear in magazines and newspapers throughout the country.

Reason—as its title and subtitle indicate—was consciously founded on the principles of Objectivism. Robert Poole, its editor and publisher, has said, "By the way we select articles and deal with issues, we try to imply a rational, clear-thinking approach that is consistent with individual rights, private property, and free markets and so forth—the same political and social principles that Ayn Rand advocated. . . . My basic philosophical view of the world was shaped by Rand's thinking. From her I learned the passion for ideas, the appreciation of the power of ideas to change things. It helped give me the idea for what I'm doing now—running a publication and an organization that is trying to change the course of events."

A significant force in attempting to change the course of events is the Reason Foundation. On its advisory board are professors from UCLA, the University of Colorado, the University of Victoria, Pace University, Carnegie-Mellon University, the University of Rochester, Johns Hopkins University, USC, Tulane University, the University of Chicago, George Mason University, Princeton University—as well as representatives of the Hoover Institution, The Center for Political Economy, and the Heritage Foundation. One of its primary objectives is to encourage and to disseminate information about the privatization of public services and to provide documentation on the thousands of public services that have been privatized; the New York *Times* acknowledged the Reason Foundation as a "citadel" of information on this subject. "It is no longer possible," said Robert Poole, "to shoot down a privatization proposal by attacking it as an untried idea." Unique among free-market think tanks, the foundation continues to work on the theoretical underpinnings of a free society. In 1983, it initiated an Adjunct Fellows program, assisting promising young academics with their careers, and brought together scholars from diverse fields for a conference on the *moral* arguments against the welfare state.

The fountainhead is Ayn Rand.

Other free market foundations and organizations devoted to the principles of liberty have sprung up as a direct result of the ideas of Ayn Rand. One of the most influential is the Society for Individual Liberty, a nationwide educational and activist group founded in 1969. Its directors and co-founders, Don Ernsberger and Dave Walter, have said, "SIL is primarily based upon Objectivist principles, and the basic works of Rand continue to be the most powerful influence on our membership."

Another is South Africa's Free Market Foundation, headed by Leon Louw, formed in 1965 by six young libertarians. Its purpose is to provide the intellectual leadership that will challenge the many South African laws that restrict the freedom of both blacks and whites. Leon Louw reported, "Recently, the stature of the foundation was considerably enhanced when 30 prominent South Africans became patrons . . . drawn largely from the business world but also including trade union, consumer, and public service leaders. . . . Another example of the new free market trends in southern Africa is that autonomous and semi-autonomous pro-free market associations have been or are being formed by local enthusiasts. These include the Soweto Committee for Economic Freedom (largely black members), the Cape Flats Free Enterprise Association (colored people, i.e., mixed blood . . .)."

In many pro-freedom foundations and organizations that did *not* arise out of the ideas of Ayn Rand, one nevertheless finds individuals in policy-making positions who have been influenced by her philosophy. They include the Hoover Institution, the Manhattan Institute for Policy Research, Canada's Fraser Institute, Cato Institute, and the Institute for Humane Studies. "Miss Rand was widely credited with influencing most of the current leaders of the libertarian moment in the United States," wrote the New York *Times* in 1982.

In the past two decades, bookstores have opened up in the United States and other countries which specialize in pro-freedom literature and particularly feature the books of Ayn Rand. Among them are New York's Laissez-Faire Books, the world's largest seller of books on liberty, Palo Alto Books in California, Second Renaissance Books in Toronto, The Alternative Bookstore in London, Free Forum Books in San Francisco.

"Seated about in booths in college-town snacks shops," wrote John Chamberlain in *The Wall Street Journal* in 1961, "the young Randites talk about their intellectual leader as their fathers and mothers a generation ago talked about Karl Marx, or John Maynard Keynes, or Thorstein Veblen. . . . And it is normally a matter of two decades before the young take over the seats of power in the name of what they have learned to believe 20 years ago."

More than twenty years have passed. A new generation sits in college-town snack shops and talks excitedly of their discovery of Ayn Rand, whose books continue to sell half a million copies each year. And the generation that talked of Ayn Rand in 1961 now teaches in the universities, sits on boards of directors, writes speeches for Ronald Reagan, composes and plays the music to which we tap our feet, produces and acts in motion pictures and television, directs publishing houses, advises government officials, produces scholarly works on philosophy, on aesthetics, on morality, on psychology, runs giant corporations and small businesses, writes novels and paints pictures—influenced, in varying degrees and aspects by the ideas of a small Russian woman with a giant brain and a passionately intransigent will.

In the universities—in addition to the above-mentioned Anne Wortham of Harvard, John Hospers of USC, Jennifer Roback of Yale, Henry Mark Holzer of Brooklyn Law School, Tibor Machan of Auburn, and Mimi Gladstein of the University of Texas—their names are Lester Hunt, professor of philosophy at the University of Wisconsin in Madison; Dean Ahmed, professor of astrophysics at the University of Maryland; John V. Cody, professor of classics at Northwestern University; Graham Chalmers, mathematician at California State University in Long Beach; Allen Gotthelf, Aristotelian scholar; Jack High, professor of economics at George Mason University; Edwin Locke, professor of psychology at the University of Maryland; Eric Mack, professor of philosophy at Tulane University and former Visiting Professor of Political Philosophy at Harvard; Jeffrey Paul, professor of philosophy at Bowling Green State University and Associate Director of the Social Philosophy and Policy Center; Tom Nagel, professor of marketing at Boston University; John O. Nelson, professor of philosophy at the University of Colorado; John Ridpath, professor of economics and intellectual history at York University in Toronto; Roger Lee, philosopher in the Department of Education at California State University; Joe Kalt, professor of economics at Harvard University; Fred Miller, professor of philosophy at Bowling Green State University; Devon Showley, head of the physics department at Cypress College; Harry Watson, professor of public policy at the University of Chicago; George Walsh, professor of philosophy at Salisbury State College; and Bruce Dovner, professor of mathematics at California State University. Douglas Rasmussen, professor of philosophy of St. John's University and Douglas Den Uyl, philosopher at Bellarmine College, are the editors of the recent book *The Philosophic Thought of Ayn Rand,* published by the University of Illinois Press and containing articles on aspects of Ayn Rand's ideas by a number of eminent philosophers. Among academic economists, reports Jack High of George Mason University, "most of the young economists who are 'Austrians,' [in the tradition of Ludwig von Mises] have been influenced by Ayn Rand."

This listing is only a small indication of the distinguished men and women in the academic world who have read the works of Ayn Rand—many of them once attended lectures at Nathaniel Branden Institute—and who, today, are presenting aspects of those ideas to their students. (I must stress that although some of them consider themselves to be Objectivists, by no means all of them do so; but all have felt to varying extents and in various ways the impact of the ideas of Ayn Rand and, in their work, are carrying forth that impact.) It is unlikely that there is a campus in America without, on its teaching faculty, at least one man or woman whose view of life has been deeply touched by Ayn Rand.

Books continue to issue from academic and mass market publishing houses which deal directly with the ideas of Ayn Rand and/or with concepts derived from her theories. In the scholarly journals of various disciplines, scarcely a month goes by without the appearance of an article concerning theories first defined by Ayn Rand. In the libraries of colleges and universities throughout the country may be found master's and doctoral theses—in subjects from philosophy to art to physics—written about Objectivism by a new generation of readers. On the campuses, active Objectivist clubs are discussing the philosophy of Ayn Rand. Similar discussion groups have formed in cities across the world—in India and Pakistan and Australia and Holland and Canada and Brazil and Switzerland and Hong Kong, in Austria and Argentina and Poland, in Turkey and Denmark and France and Japan and West Germany and Belgium and Norway and South Africa, in Finland and Sweden and Scotland and Greece and England and Mexico and Israel.

Private schools have been formed which have, as one of their purposes, the educational implementation of the concept of reason and individualism promulgated by Ayn Rand. Among them are the Culbreath Schools, based in California and headed by Myrna Culbreath, which teach remedial reading to adults. "Ayn Rand gave me an intellectual framework," Myrna Culbreath said, "and a knowledge of the important philosophical questions to be asked; she particularly influenced me in the field of epistemology." Myrna is co-writer, with Sondra Marshak, of a series of successful books dealing with the "Star Trek" television series and movies; she reports that a large number of the letters she receives about her books refer to Ayn Rand. Another institution based on Objectivist principles is the Flint School, a shipboard traveling school. A third is the American Renaissance School in White Plains, New York, founded by eight college professors for high-achieving students, a "private, pro-reason, pro-capitalism, profit-making school."

A major source of Ayn Rand's conflict with society was her belief that she was being ignored by the academic world, as indeed she was during the fifties and sixties. But today, it is not only her advocates who recognize the importance of her ideas. The distinguished philosopher Robert Nozick, professor of philosophy at Harvard, defender of libertarian principles and author of the remarkable *Anarchy, State and Utopia,* wrote a sharply critical article entitled "On the Randian Argument" in *The Personalist* but said, "I have found her two major novels exciting, powerful, illuminating and thought provoking . . . combined with a 'sense of life' that is worthy of man. . . . Miss Rand is an interesting thinker, worthy of attention." Professor Nozick discusses Ayn's libertarian concepts in his courses on political philosophy. Charles Murray, writer of *Losing Ground,* the path-breaking and controversial analysis of the failure of two decades of profligate welfare spending, first read Ayn Rand's works in high school and remains powerfully impressed with her "heroic vision of man and her accuracy and prescience regarding social issues."

Books criticizing the philosophy of Objectivism continue to appear, such as philosopher William F. O'Neill's *With Charity Toward None: An Analysis of Ayn Rand's Philosophy*—in which, despite his disagreements with Objectivism, he concludes, "Whatever else Miss Rand may have achieved, she continues to serve as a useful intellectual catalyst in a society which frequently suffers from philosophical 'tired blood' "; and Christian scholar John W. Robbins's *Answer to Ayn Rand;* and psychologist Albert Ellis's *Is Objectivism a Religion?*

In books, magazines, and newsletters on economics, finance, and politics, the influence of Ayn Rand is particularly evident. Robert Ringer, bestselling author of such works as *Restoring the American Dream* and publisher of the newsletter *The Tortoise Report,* acknowledges his debt to Ayn in helping him to construct his basic philosophy, as does Douglas Casey, economist and author of the hugely successful *Crisis Investing* and *Strategic Investing,* and James Blanchard, founder of The National Committee for Monetary Reform and publisher of *Wealth* magazine and *Market Alert.* Others of a similar orientation are investment advisor Robert Prechter, publisher and editor of *The Elliott Wave Theorist;* investment writer Mark Tier; Daniel Rosenthal, editor of *The Silver and Gold Report,* who wrote, "Miss Rand is one of the people who most deserve credit for the revival of the hard-money movement. She was the philosopher who espoused personal success in an era of altruism; capitalism in an era of socialism; and gold in an era of paper"; Takashi Uratu, Japanese economist presently translating *Atlas Shrugged* into Japanese; Harry D. Shultz, publisher of *The International Harry Shultz Letter,* who recommends that his readers send copies of Ayn Rand's books, as part of the fight for freedom, to "press/pulpit/politicians/VIPs/ friends/teachers"; John Pugsley, investment writer and publisher; Michael Berger, publisher of *On Principle,* who created and met the requirements for a self-directed degree program in Objectivism at Antioch College, thus becoming the first person to earn a degree in Objectivism.

Ayn Rand's influence extends far beyond the walls of academia, far beyond the realm of politics and political philosophy, far beyond popular books on economics. It can be found in every aspect of American life. As one looks at the vast panorama of American life, one must marvel at Ayn Rand's ability to generate a series of philosophical definitions and identifications that appear to be altering the face of America. One cannot yet estimate the *precise* extent of her influence; to do so would require many years of research and study—resulting one day, perhaps, in a book entitled *The Biography of an Idea.* Nor can one know with certainty the final results of that influence. But in the course of rather intensive investigations, I have observed her impact on every aspect of the American scene to which I have turned.

In the area of industry, a few among the titans who acknowledge her influence are Gordon McLendon, one of the four hundred wealthiest men in America, according to *Forbes* magazine; John Diebold of The Diebold Group, who is acknowledged as "the father of automation"; Whitney Stevens, former NBI student and chairman of the board and chief executive officer of J. P. Stevens Company; Edward Snider, principal owner of the Philadelphia Flyers, head of Spectator Corporation, and the driving force behind the founding of The Ayn Rand Institute; Jay Snider, president of the Philadelphia Flyers.

Ayn's impact can be found in executives, entrepreneurs and businessmen throughout the country—in Lillian Davison, president of Resource Retrieval, a toxic waste disposal company in New Jersey; in Ray Thorpe, president of the Private Railroad Association; in Robert Kephart, president of Kephart Communications; in Hans Hirschfeld, president of the Horizon Company of Canada; in Mike Oliver, real estate developer; in Lawrence Scott, president of Liaison Ltd.; in Rex Dante, one of the world's foremost memory experts; in Leonard Hirschfeld, marketing consultant; in Milton Engel, gold dealer; in Robert Fritts, housing developer; in Kerry O'Quinn, head of the Star Log Group and publisher of *Star Log* magazines and *Star Log Video Tapes.*

It can be found in Mike Mentzer, former Mr. America and Mr. Universe, publisher and editor-in-chief of *Workout* magazine; in Calvin Nash, an engineer working on nuclear power equipment; in former congressman from Texas Ron Paul, chairman of the Ludwig von Mises Institute; in Neil Peart of the rock group Rush—one of whose songs is entitled "Anthem" and one of whose albums is dedicated to Ayn Rand—and Simon LeBon of Duran Duran; in painters Joan Mitchell Blumenthal and Daniel Green (whose early portrait of Ayn appears on the jacket of *For the New Intellectual)* and sculptors Jonathan Hirschfeld and Don Ventura; in actors Raquel Welch—whom Ayn was interested in for the role of Dagny Taggart—and Rock Hudson and Jill St. John and Eileen Fulton; in Gerald Rafferty, publisher of Info Books; in neurosurgeon Avner Feldman.

It can be found in professional adventurer, philosopher, and writer Jack

Wheeler, who, in 1985, under the auspices of Citizens for America, organized the world's first congress of anti-Soviet guerrilla leaders at Jamba, Angola—an event, according to *Newsweek,* that was organized without the knowledge or approval of the State Department but with "tacit" White House endorsement; in science fiction writer Robert Heinlein, who has likened his political views to those of Ayn Rand and introduced a character in one of his novels called "the John Galt of the revolution"; in science fiction writer J. Neil Schulman's *The Rainbow Cadenza;* in Western writer Winfred Blevins and Edgar Award recipient Kay Nolte Smith; in Edith Efron, author of *The News Twisters* and *The Apocalyptics;* in novelists Ruth Beebe Hill and Erika Holzer; in computer writer Adam Smith, who names Ayn's *Introduction to Objectivist Epistemology* as a book that inspired his work; in *Ergo,* a student newspaper at MIT; and in *Aristos,* a journal of aesthetics; in the philosophical magazine *The Objectivist Forum* and newsletter *The Intellectual Activist;* in composer-conductor George Broderick and musician Douglas Messenger; in screen and television writer Al Ramrus; in Fred Stitt, architect and writer who once worked his way across the country to New York to attend Nathaniel Branden Institute, who teaches at Berkeley's architectural school and whose recent McGraw-Hill book *Designing Buildings That Work* is dedicated "to my first architectural mentor, Howard Roark."

It can be found in young philosopher David Kelley, whose recent book *The Evidence of the Senses* is a striking and valuable addition to the field of epistemology; in prominent libertarian writer and lecturer Roy A. Childs, Jr., who has said, "For thousands of people, *Atlas Shrugged* became more than a novel; it became a way of viewing the world. It became a part of people's minds, and they saw the world through that book."

It can be found in Walter Wingo, U.S. Business Editor of *U.S. News and World Report;* in William Hernstadt, former state legislator in Nevada and television station owner; in Alan Nitikman of Citicorp's "think tank"; in Wendy McElroy, feminist writer and editor of *Freedom, Feminism and the State;* in George Smith, author of *Atheism: The Case Against God;* in Ralph Roseman, senior partner of New York's Theatre Now; in David Hayes, biographer of the Bowery Boys; in psychologists Lee Shulman and Joyce Shulman and Roger Callahan and Edith Packer and Larry Gneiting and psychiatrist Allan Blumenthal; in economist George Reisman, author of *Government Against the Economy;* in author Karl Hess, former speechwriter for Barry Goldwater and Presidents Nixon and Ford; in John Piper, minister and professor of theology; in Walter Block of the Fraser Institute, author of *Defending the Undefendable;* in Durk Pearson and Sandy Shaw, authors of the sensationally successful *Life Extension.*

It can be found in disparate groups of people whose names are not publically known and may never be known: in a man who works on a crew boat ferrying scientists to the South Pole, and who observed that many of the scientists he takes to their months of isolation bring with them copies of *Atlas Shrugged;* in a young woman from an orthodox Jewish family who, forbidden to study Ayn

Rand, stood at the window of her darkened bedroom at night to read *Atlas Shrugged* by the glow of a street lamp; in a professional gambler; in a young coed who said, "It was only a few weeks after I read *Atlas Shrugged* that I left the Church"; in a Manhattan retail executive; in a senior at Vassar writing her undergraduate thesis on Ayn Rand. It can be found in an attorney and a barmaid and a woman construction worker; in a car designer for Datsun and a political pollster and a janitor and a Lockheed designer; in a travel agent and a Jesuit priest and a ghost writer and a masseur and a teacher of dressage; in a warehouse worker and a rabbi; in actors and actresses; in athletes and a lazerist and a drama critic and a banker and a farmer and a pediatrician and a gemologist; in a film processor and a financial planner and a nuclear plant engineer and a karate instructor; in an advertising director and a child prodigy in chemistry and a photographer and a veterinarian and a telephone company supervisor. It can be found in a young man who was the source of a solemn and fruitless investigation by both the Naval Investigative Service and the FBI when there was discovered, scratched on the body of a Navy plane, the inscription, "Who is John Galt?"—and in a young teacher who said, his eyes damp, "Ayn Rand taught me that life could be a wonderful experience."

It can be found in the Literary Guild's listing of *The Fountainhead*, more than forty years after publication, under the title "Best Selling Library"; in a quotation from *The Fountainhead*, "Throughout the centuries, there were men who took first steps down new roads armed with nothing but their own vision;" in Disney World's Great American Experience exhibit; in the 1984 article in *Vanity Fair* entitled "The Fountainhead Syndrome," a discussion of the architects who are "the Roarks of the 1980s"; in the course on Objectivism given at The New School for Social Research; in the constant reruns of the movie of *The Fountainhead* on television and in art theaters; in a college course entitled "Heroic Humanism: A Study of the Major Novels of Ayn Rand"; in the character of Mr. Spock in the "Star Trek" television series and movies; in a television news commentator announcing with approval that "free-wheeling capitalism" is creating wealth in countries in the Far East; in the continuing interest of companies such as MGM and United Artists, of directors such as Michael Cimino, of actors such as Tom Selleck, in a movie version of *Atlas Shrugged* and/or a remake of *The Fountainhead*, and in the sale of the movie rights of *Anthem* to Star Log Group; in the forthcoming release of the movie of the fifty-year-old *We the Living*; in the high prices offered and paid for first editions of Ayn's books and letters; in the host of crossword puzzles that cannot be completed without the name of the writer of *The Fountainhead* and *Atlas Shrugged*; in the question "What Ayn Rand novel begins with 'Who is John Galt?' " in the game of Trivial Pursuit; in bumper stickers which read, "Who is John Galt?"; in desk calendars featuring famous quotations from writers; in the constant public mentions of Ayn in such unlikely places as the popular movie of a few years ago *Boys in the Band* and a Simon and Garfunkel recording and the film remake of *Heaven Can Wait* and the movies *King of Hearts* and *Lost in America*; in the recommendation of the fast food chain Burger King, that its executives read Ayn's books; in letters to the editors of newspapers and magazines throughout the country, still dotted with comments about Ayn Rand. Ayn often said, only partly joking, that she would know her ideas were having a crucial impact on the culture when they had worked their way down from the ivory towers of the universities through popular writings and finally to mass market comic books; then she could be certain that her philosophy had become a part of the conventional wisdom. She would have been amused to learn that she *has* won this victory—as witness Steve Ditko, creator of the cartoon "Spider Man."

In the late 1940s, describing the success of *The Fountainhead,* Ayn said: "I did not know that I was predicting my own future when I described the process of Roark's success: 'It was as if an underground stream flowed through the country and broke out in sudden springs that shot to the surface at random, in unpredictable places.' " The stream has become a tidal wave, shooting out in every direction and to every continent of the world. The story of the influence of a series of novels on philosophic thought is unprecedented in literary history; it is a saga worthy of an Ayn Rand novel. It is Ayn's best statement of the power of the lone individual.

As one observes the bright sparks of thought that emanated from one mind and one ferocious will continuing to send out their lengthening rays, perhaps one can also see a small, passionately stalwart figure marching steadfastly forward into history.

Books by Ayn Rand

Anthem. London: Cassell and Company, 1938; revised edition, Los Angeles: Pamphleteers, Inc., 1946; Caldwell, Idaho: Caxton Printers, 1953; paperback edition, New York: New American Library, 1946.

Atlas Shrugged. New York: Random House, 1957; paperback edition, New York: New American Library, 1959.

Capitalism: The Unknown Ideal. New York: New American Library, 1966; paperback edition, New York: New American Library, 1967.

The Early Ayn Rand: A Selection from Her Unpublished Fiction. New York: New American Library, 1984; paperback edition, New York: New American Library, 1985.

For the New Intellectual. New York: Random House, 1961; paperback edition, New York: New American Library, 1961.

The Fountainhead. New York, Bobbs-Merrill: 1943; paperback edition, New York: New American Library, 1952.

Introduction to Objectivist Epistemology. paperback edition, New York: New American Library, 1979.

Night of January 16th. New York: Longmans Green, 1936; paperback edition, New York: World Publishing Company, 1968; New York: New American Library, 1971.

The New Left: The Anti-Industrial Revolution. paperback edition, New York: New American Library, 1971.

Philosophy: Who Needs It. New York: Bobbs-Merrill, 1982.

The Romantic Manifesto. New York: World Publishing Company, 1969; paperback edition, New York: New American Library, 1971.

The Virtue of Selfishness. New York: New American Library, 1965; paperback edition, New York: New American Library, 1964.

We the Living. New York, Macmillan: 1936; London: Cassell and Company, 1937; New York: Random House, 1959; paperback edition, New York: New American Library, 1959.

Index

MARK HODDER

PRESENTS

BURTON & SWINBURNE

in EXPEDITION TO THE

MOUNTAINS OF THE MOON

an imprint of **Prometheus Books**
Amherst, NY

Published 2011 by Pyr®, an imprint of Prometheus Books

Cover illustration copyright © Jon Sullivan
Cover design by Nicole Sommer-Lecht

Inquiries should be addressed to
Pyr
59 John Glenn Drive
Amherst, New York 14228–2119
VOICE: 716–691–0133
FAX: 716–691–0137
WWW.PYRSF.COM

15 14 13 12   5 4 3 2

Library of Congress Cataloging-in-Publication Data

Hodder, Mark, 1962–
     Expedition to the mountains of the moon / by Mark Hodder.
         p. cm.
     ISBN 978–1–61614–535–4 (pbk.)
     ISBN 978–1–61614–536–1 (ebook)
     1. Burton, Richard Francis, Sir, 1821–1890—Fiction. 2. Swinburne, Algernon Charles, 1837–1909—Fiction. 3. Time travel—Fiction. 4. Africa, Central—Discovery and exploration—Fiction. 5. Great Britain—History—19th century—Fiction. 6. Steampunk fiction. I≥ Title. II. Title: Burton & Swinburne in expedition to the Mountains of the Moon. III. Title: Burton and Swinburne in expedition to the Mountains of the Moon.

PR6108.O28E94 2012
823'.92—dc23

                                                                      2011037544

Printed in the United States of America

Dedicated to

REBECA CAMARA

"Time discovers truth."
—SENECA

ACKNOWLEDGMENTS

W hen I began writing these tales of Burton & Swinburne, I couldn't help but worry that I might be insulting the memory of men and women who, by virtue of their hard work and astonishing talents, had made their mark on history.

My concerns were assuaged when enthusiastic readers told me that, while reading my novels, they repeatedly consulted *Wikipedia* and other sources to learn more about the real lives of the people I had "hijacked."

This delights me. It means, for example, that PC53 William Trounce might now be recognised by a few more as the hero who stepped up to the mark when John Francis tried to assassinate Queen Victoria in 1842 (and yes, I meddled with that historical fact). It means a greater awareness of Richard Spruce, who, despite being treated as a villain in these works, was in truth a quiet and unassuming man possessed of sheer genius in the subject of botany. It means more people turning to Swinburne's astonishing poetry, more people marvelling at Lord Palmerston's political astuteness, more people wondering whether Samuel Gooch really existed, then finding out that he did, and that he was amazing.

This, I hope, will be considered by any descendants of the characters herein who might feel offended by my treatment of them. Please note that these novels are *very obviously* flights of utter fancy and very definitely *not* biography. My alternative histories are places where individuals have encountered different challenges and opportunities to those met in real life, and have thus developed into very, very different people. They should not be in any way regarded as accurate depictions of those who actually lived.

In this volume, my account of Africa circa 1863 follows closely the descriptions left to us by Sir Richard Francis Burton himself. His *The Lake Regions of Central Africa* (1860) is, in my opinion, by far the most fascinating journal of any of the Victorian explorers. Burton tended to adopt his own

7

spelling for villages, towns, and regions, and throughout the African chapters I've retained his version of place-names.

Finally, my thanks and deepest appreciation to Lou Anders, Emma Barnes, and Jon Sullivan.

THE VOYAGE TO AFRICA

"One of the gladdest moments in human life, methinks, is the departure upon a distant journey to unknown lands. Shaking off with one mighty effort the fetters of Habit, the leaden weight of Routine, the cloak of many Cares and the Slavery of Home, man feels once more happy. The blood flows with the fast circulation of childhood... afresh dawns the morn of life...."
    —Sir Richard Francis Burton's journal,
    2nd December, 1856.

CHAPTER 1

MURDER AT FRYSTON

"The future influences the present just as much as the past."
—FRIEDRICH NIETZSCHE

Sir Richard Francis Burton wriggled beneath a bush at the edge of a thicket in the top western corner of Green Park, London, and cursed himself for a fool. He should have realised that he'd lose consciousness. He should have arrived earlier to compensate. Now the whole mission was in jeopardy.

He lay flat for a moment, until the pain in his side abated, then hefted his rifle and propped himself up on his elbows, aiming the weapon at the crowd below. He glanced at the inscription on its stock. It read: *Lee–Enfield Mk III. Manufactured in Tabora, Africa, 1918.*

Squinting through the telescopic sight, he examined the faces of the people gathering around the path at the bottom of the slope.

Where was his target?

His eyes blurred. He shook his head slightly, trying to dispel an odd sense of dislocation, the horrible feeling that he was divided into two separate identities. He'd first experienced this illusion during fevered bouts of malaria in Africa back in '57, then again four years later, when he was made the king's agent. He thought he'd conquered it. Perhaps he had. After all, this time there really were two of him.

It was the afternoon of the 10th of June, 1840, and a much younger Richard Burton was currently travelling from Italy through Europe, on his way to enrol at Trinity College, Oxford.

Recalling that wayward, opinionated, and ill-disciplined youngster, he whispered, "Time changed me, thank goodness. The question is, can I return the favour?"

He aimed from face to face, seeking the man he'd come to shoot.

It was a mild day. The gentlemen sported light coats and top hats, and carried canes. The ladies were adorned in bonnets and dainty gloves and held parasols. They were all waiting to see Queen Victoria ride past in her carriage.

He levelled the crosshairs at one person after another. Young Edward Oxford was somewhere among the crowd, an insane eighteen-year-old with two flintlock pistols under his frock coat and murder on his mind. But Burton was not here to gun down the queen's would-be assassin.

"Damnation!" His hands were shaking. Lying stretched out like this would have been uncomfortable for any man his age—he was forty-seven years old—but it was made far worse by the two ribs the prime minister's man, Gregory Hare, had broken. They felt like a knife in his side.

He shifted cautiously, trying not to disturb the bush. It was vital that he remain concealed.

A face caught his attention. It was round, decorated with a large moustache, and possessed a palpable air of arrogance. Burton had never seen the individual before—at least not with this appearance—but he knew him: Henry de La Poer Beresford, 3rd Marquess of Waterford, called by many the "Mad Marquess." The man was the founder of the Libertines, a politically influential movement that preached freedom from social shackles and which passionately opposed technological progress. Three years from now, Beresford was going to lead a breakaway group of radicals, the Rakes, whose anarchic philosophy would challenge social propriety. The marquess believed that the human species was restricting its own evolution; that each individual had the potential to become a *trans-natural man*, a being entirely free of restraint, with no conscience or self-doubt, a thing that did whatever it wanted, whenever it wanted. It was a dangerous idea—the Great War had proved that to Burton—but not one that concerned him at this particular moment.

"I'll be dealing with you twenty-one years from now," he murmured.

A distant cheer echoed across the park. The gates of Buckingham Palace had opened and the royal carriage was steering out onto the path.

"Come on!" Burton whispered. "Where are you?"

Where was the man he'd come to kill?

Where was Spring Heeled Jack?

He peered through the 'scope. The scene he saw through its lens was incomprehensible. Shapes, movement, shadows, deep colours; they refused to coalesce into anything of substance. The world had shattered, and he was splintered and scattered among its debris.

Dead. Obviously, he was dead.

No. Stop it. This won't do. Don't submit to it. Not again.

He closed his eyes, dug his fingernails into his palms, and pulled his lips back over his teeth. By sheer force of will, he located the disparate pieces of himself and drew them together, until:

Frank Baker. My name is Frank Baker.

Good. That felt familiar.

He smelled cordite. Noise assaulted his ears. The air was hot.

Frank Baker. Yes. The name had slipped from his mouth in response to a medic's query.

"And what are you, Mr. Baker?"

A strange question.

"An observer."

An equally strange answer. Like the name, it had come out of nowhere, but the overworked medics were perfectly satisfied with it.

Spells of nothingness had followed. Fevers. Hallucinations. Then recovery. They'd assumed he was with the civilian Observer Corps, and placed him under the charge of the short squeaky-voiced individual currently standing at his side.

What else? What else? What were those things I was looking at?

He opened his eyes. There wasn't much light.

He became aware of something crushed in his fist, opened his hand, looked down at it, and found that he was holding a red poppy. It felt important. He didn't know why. He slipped it into his pocket.

Pushing the brim of his tin helmet back, he wiped sweat from his forehead, then lifted the top of his periscope over the lip of the trench and peered through its viewfinder again. To his left, the crest of a bloated sun was melting into a horizon that quivered in the heat, and ahead, in the gathering gloom, seven towering, long-legged arachnids were picking their way through the red weed that clogged no-man's-land. Steam was billowing from their exhaust funnels, pluming stark white against the darkening purple sky.

Harvestmen, he thought. *Those things are harvestmen spiders bred to a phenomenal size by the Technologists' Eugenicist faction. No, wait, not Eugenicists—they're the enemy—our lot are called Geneticists. The arachnids are grown and killed and gutted and engineers fit out their carapaces with steam-driven machinery.*

He examined the contraptions more closely and noted details that struck him as different—but different from what? There were, for instance, Gatling guns slung beneath their small bodies, where Baker expected to see cargo nets. They swivelled and glinted and flashed as they sent a hail of bullets into the German trenches, and their metallic clattering almost drowned out the chug of the vehicles' engines. The harvestmen were armour-plated, too, and each driver, rather than sitting on a seat fitted inside the hollowed-out body, was mounted on a sort of saddle on top of it, which suggested that the space inside the carapace was filled with bigger, more powerful machinery than—than—

What am I comparing them with?

"Quite a sight, isn't it?" came a high-pitched voice.

Baker cleared his throat. He wasn't ready to communicate, despite a vague suspicion that he'd already done so—that he and the small man beside him had made small talk not too many minutes ago.

He opened his mouth to speak, but his companion went on: "If I were a poet, I might do it justice, but it's too much of a challenge for a mere journalist. How the devil am I to describe such an unearthly scene? Anyone who hasn't actually witnessed it would think I'm writing a scientific romance. Perhaps they'll call me the new Jules Verne."

Think! Come on! String together the man's words. Break the back of the language. Glean meaning from it.

He sucked in a breath as a memory flowered. He was on a bed in the field hospital. There was a newspaper in his hands. He was reading a report, and it had been written by this short, plump little fellow.

Yes, that's it. Now speak, Baker. Open your mouth and speak!

"You'll manage," he said. "I read one of your articles the other day. You have a rare talent. Who's Jules Verne?"

He saw the little man narrow his eyes and examine him through the twilight, trying to make out his features.

"A French novelist. He was killed during the fall of Paris. You haven't heard of him?"

"I may have," Baker answered, "but I must confess, I remember so little about anything that I'm barely functional."

"Ah, of course. It's not an uncommon symptom of shell shock, or of fever, for that matter, and you suffered both severely by all accounts. Do you know why you were in the Lake Regions?"

The Lake Regions? They are in—they are in Africa! This is Africa!

"I haven't the foggiest notion. My first recollection is of being borne along on a litter. The next thing I knew, I was here, being poked at by the medical staff."

The journalist grunted and said, "I did some asking around. The men from the Survey Corps found you near the western shore of the Ukerewe Lake, on the outskirts of the Blood Jungle. A dangerous place to be—always swarming with Germans. You were unarmed, that odd glittering hieroglyph appeared to have been freshly tattooed into your head, and you were ranting like a madman."

Hieroglyph?

Baker reached up, pushed his hand beneath his helmet, and ran his fingers through his short hair. There were hard ridges in his scalp.

"I don't remember any of that."

I don't remember. I don't remember. I don't remember.

"The surveyors wanted to take you to Tabora but the route south was crawling with lurchers, so they legged it east until they hooked up with the battalions gathering here. You were in and out of consciousness throughout the hike but never lucid enough to explain yourself."

The correspondent was suddenly interrupted by the loud "Ulla! Ulla!" of a siren. It was a harvestman spider signalling its distress. He turned his attention back to his periscope and Baker followed suit.

One of the gigantic vehicles had become entangled. Scarlet tendrils were coiling around its stilt-like legs, snaking up toward the driver perched high above the ground. The man was desperately yanking at the control levers in an attempt to shake the writhing plant from his machine. He failed. The harvestman leaned farther and farther to its left, then toppled over, dragged down by the carnivorous weed. The siren gurgled and died. The driver rolled from his saddle, tried to stand, fell, and started to thrash about. He screeched as plant pods burst beneath his weight and sprayed him with acidic sap. His uniform erupted into flames and the flesh bubbled and fizzled from his bones. It took less than a minute for the weed to reduce him to a naked skeleton.

"Poor sod," the little man muttered. He lowered his surveillance instrument and shook dust from his right hand. "Did you see the weed arrive yesterday? I missed it. I was sleeping."

"No."

"Apparently a thin ribbon of cloud, like a snake, blew in from the sea and rained the seeds. The plant sprouted overnight and it's been growing ever since. It appears quite impassable. I tell you, Baker, those blasted Hun sorcerers know their stuff when it comes to weather and plants. It's how they still drum hundreds of thousands more Africans into the military than we do. The tribes are so superstitious, they'll do anything you say if they believe you can summon or prevent rain and grow them a good crop. Colonel Crowley is having a tough time opposing them—the sorcerers, I mean."

Baker struggled to process all this. Sorcerers? Plants? Weather control?

"Crowley?" he asked.

The shorter man raised his eyebrows. "Good lord! Your brain really is shot through! Colonel Aleister Crowley. Our chief medium. The wizard of wizards!"

Baker said nothing.

The correspondent shrugged in bafflement, pressed up against the side of the trench as a line of troops pushed past, chuckled as a sergeant said, with a grin and a wink, "Keep your heads down, gents, I don't want holes in those expensive helmets," then turned back to his 'scope. Baker watched this and struggled to overcome his sense of detachment.

I don't belong here. I don't understand any of it.

He wiped his sleeve across his mouth—the atmosphere was thick with humidity and he was sweating profusely—then put his eye to his periscope's lens.

Two more of the harvestmen were being pulled down into the wriggling flora. He said, "How many men must die before someone orders the blasted vehicles to pull back?"

"We won't retreat," came the answer. "This is our last chance. If we can capture German resources in Africa, we might be able to launch some sort of counterattack in Europe. If not, we're done for. So we'll do whatever it takes, even if it means pursuing forlorn hopes. Look! Another one has gone down!"

The three remaining harvestmen set their sirens screaming: "Ulla! Ulla! Ulla! Ulla!"

The journalist continued, "Terrible racket. One could almost believe the damned spiders are alive and terrified."

Baker shook his head slightly. "Strictly speaking, they're not spiders. Spiders are of the order *Aranaea*, whereas harvestmen are *Opiliones*."

How do I know that?

The war correspondent snorted. "They're not of any order now—not since our Technologists scraped 'em out!"

All along the British trenches, men started to blow on whistles.

"Damn! Here comes our daily dose of spores. Get your mask on."

Baker moved without thinking about it. His hands went to his belt, opened a canvas container, pulled out a thick rubber mask, and slid it over his face. He and his companion looked at each other through circular glass eyepieces.

"I hate the smell of these things," the smaller man said, his voice muffled. "And they make me claustrophobic. Far too stifling an item to wear in this infernal climate. What say we go back to the dugout for a brew? It's getting too dark for us to see much more here anyway. Time for a cuppa! Come on!"

Baker took a last glance through his periscope. His mask's eyepieces blurred the scene, and Africa's fast-descending night obscured it even further, but he could just make out that on the far side of the weed a thick yellow cloud was advancing, appearing luminescent against the inky sky. He shivered, turned, and followed the other along the front-line trench, into a communications ditch, and back to one of the dugouts. They passed masked soldiers—mostly Askari, African recruits, many of them barely out of childhood—who sat despondently, waiting to go over the top.

The two men arrived at a doorway, pushed a heavy curtain aside, and entered. They removed their helmets and face gear.

"Make sure the curtain is hooked back into place, it'll keep the spores out. I'll get us some light," the journalist said.

Moments later, a hurricane lamp illuminated the small underground bunker. It was sparsely furnished with two wooden beds, two tables, three chairs, and a couple of storage chests.

"Ugh!" Baker grunted. "Rats!"

"Nothing we can do about 'em. The little blighters are everywhere. They're the least of your problems. In a couple of days, that nice clean uniform of yours will be infested with lice and you'll feel like you're being eaten alive. Where's the bloody kettle? Ah, here!"

The little man got to work with a portable stove. In the light, his eyes were revealed to be a startling blue.

Baker stepped to the smaller of the two tables, which stood against the wall. There was a washbasin on it and a square mirror hanging on a nail just above. He sought his reflection but for some reason couldn't focus on it. Either his eyes wouldn't let him see himself, or he wasn't really there.

He moved to the other table, in the middle of the dugout, and sat down.

"The spores," he said. "What are they? Where do they come from?"

"They're more properly called A-Spores. The Hun propagate giant mushrooms, a eugenically altered version of the variety commonly known as the Destroying Angel, or *Amanita bisporigera*, if you prefer your botany, like your entomology, in Latin. It's deadly, and so are its spores. Breathe them in and within seconds you'll experience vomiting, cramps, delirium, convulsions, and diarrhoea. You'll be dead in less than ten minutes."

"Botanical weapons? The weed and now the mushroom spores. How horribly ingenious!"

The other man looked back at Baker with an expression of puzzlement. "It's common knowledge that the Germans use mostly plant-based armaments, surely? And occasional animal adaptations."

"Is it? I'm sorry. As I said, my amnesia is near total. You mentioned something called *lurchers?*"

"Ah. Hum. Yes. Carnivorous plants. They were one of the first weapons the Germans developed. Originally they were battle vehicles, used throughout Africa. Then one day they spontaneously mutated and consumed their drivers, which somehow resulted in them gaining a rudimentary intelligence. After that they spread rapidly and are now a danger to both sides. If you see one, and there isn't a flamethrower handy, run for your life. They're particularly prevalent in the Lake Regions, where you were found." The journalist paused, then added, "I didn't realise your memory was quite so defective. What about physically? How are you feeling?"

"Weak, but improving, and the ophthalmia has cleared up. I was half-blind when I regained consciousness in the hospital. That confounded ailment has plagued me on and off ever since India."

"You were in India?"

Baker frowned and rubbed his chin. "I don't know. That just popped into my head. Yes, I feel I may have been."

"India, by crikey! You should have stayed there. It might turn out to be the last bastion of civilisation on the whole bloody planet! Is that where you joined the Corps?"

"I suppose so."

There came a distant boom, then another, and another. The ground shook. The journalist glanced at the ceiling.

"Artillery. Peashooters. Firing from the outskirts of Dar es Salaam."

Baker muttered to himself, "Derived from *bandar es-salaam*, I should think. Ironic. It means *harbour of peace*." Aloud, he said: "The landscape and climate feel familiar to me. Are we south of Zanzibar? Is there a village in the area called Mzizima?"

"Hah! Mzizima and Dar es Salaam are one and the same, Baker! Incredible, isn't it, that the death of the British Empire had its origins in such an insignificant little place, and now we're back here."

"What do you mean?"

"It's generally believed that this is where the Great War began. Have you forgotten even that?"

"Yes, I fear I have. It began in Mzizima? How is that possible? As you say, it's an insignificant little place!"

"So you recall what Dar es Salaam used to be, at least?"

"I remember that it was once nothing more than a huddle of beehive huts."

"Quite so. But that huddle was visited by a group of German surveyors a little over fifty years ago. No one knows why they came, or what occurred, but for some reason, fighting broke out between them and Al-Manat."

"The pre-Islamic goddess of fate?"

"Is she, by gum! Not the same one, old chap. Al-Manat was the leader of a band of female guerrilla fighters. It's rumoured she was British but her true identity is shrouded in mystery. She's one of history's great enigmas. Anyway, the fighting escalated, Britain and Germany both sent more troops here, and Mzizima became the German East Africa Company's stronghold. The *Schutztruppe*—the Protection Force—formed there some forty years ago and rapidly expanded the settlement. It was renamed Dar es Salaam and the place has been thriving ever since. A situation our lads will reverse this weekend."

"What do you mean?"

"I mean, my friend, that on Saturday, HMA *Pegasus* and HMA *Astraea* are going to bomb the city to smithereens."

More explosions thumped outside. They were increasing in frequency. Everything shook. Baker glanced around nervously.

"Green peas," his companion noted.

"You can tell just from the noise?"

"Yes. Straightforward impact strikes, like big cannonballs. The yellow variety explode when they hit and send poisonous shrapnel flying everywhere. They annihilated millions of our lads in Europe, but, fortunately, the plants don't thrive in Africa."

Baker's fingers were gripping the edge of the table. The other man noticed, and reassured him: "We'll be all right. They take an age to get the range. Plus, of course, we're noncombatants, which means we're permitted to shelter in here, unlike the enlisted men. We'll be safe unless one of the blighters lands right on top of us, and the chances of that happening are very slim indeed."

He got the kettle going and they sat wordlessly, listening to the barrage until the water boiled, then he spooned tea leaves into a metal pot and grumbled, "Rations are low."

Baker noticed that his companion kept glancing back at him. He felt an inexplicable urge to duck out of the light, but there was no refuge from it. He looked on helplessly as the other man's face suddenly displayed a range of emotions in sequence: curiosity, perplexity, realisation, incredulity, shock.

The smaller man remained silent until the tea had brewed, then filled two tin mugs, added milk and sugar, handed one to Baker, sat down, blew the steam from his drink, and, raising his voice above the sound of pounding shells, asked: "I say, old chap, when did you last shave?"

Baker sighed. He murmured, "I wish I had a cigar," put a hand into his pocket, and pulled out the poppy. He stared at it and said, absently, "What?"

"Your most recent shave. When was it?"

"I don't know. Maybe three days ago? Why do you ask?"

"Because, my dear fellow, that stubble entirely ruins your disguise. Once bearded or moustachioed, your features become instantly recognisable. They are every bit as forceful as reported, every bit as ruthless and masterful! By golly, those sullen eyes! That iron jaw! The savage scar on your cheek!"

Baker snapped, "What the devil are you blathering about?"

"I'm talking of the completely impossible and utterly incredible—but also of the perfectly obvious and indisputable!" The journalist grinned. He had to shout now—the barrage was battering violently at their ears. "Come come! I'll brook no denial, sir! I'm no fool. It's out of the question that you could be anyone else, even though it makes no sense at all that you are who you are."

Baker glowered at him.

The other shouted, "Perhaps you'd care to explain? I assure you, I'm unusually open-minded, and I can keep a secret, if you want to impose that as a condition. My editor would never believe me anyway."

There was a detonation just outside. The room jerked. The tea slopped. Baker started, recovered himself, and said loudly, "I really don't know what you're talking about."

"Then allow me to make it clear. Frank Baker is most assuredly not your name."

"Isn't it?"

"Ha-ha! So you admit that you may not be who you say you are?"

"The name occurred to me when I was asked, but I'm by no means certain that it's correct."

Baker flinched as another impact rocked the room.

"Fair enough," the journalist shouted. "Well then, let us make proper introductions. I was presented to you as Mr. Wells. Drop it. No need for such formality. My name is Herbert. Herbert George. War Correspondent for the *Tabora Times*. Most people call me Bertie, so please feel free to do the same. And, believe me, I am both astonished and very happy to meet you." He held out his hand and it was duly clasped and shaken. "Really, don't worry about the shelling, we are much safer in here than it feels. The Hun artillery is trying for the support trenches rather than the front line. They'll gain more by destroying our supplies than by knocking off a few of the Askaris."

Baker gave a curt nod. His mouth worked silently for a moment. He kept glancing at the poppy in his hand, then he cleared his throat and said, "You know me, then? My actual name?"

"Yes, I know you," Wells replied. "I've read the biographies. I've seen the photographs. I know all about you. You are Sir Richard Francis Burton, the famous explorer and scholar. I cannot be mistaken." He took a sip of his tea. "It makes no sense, though."

"Why not?"

"Because, my dear fellow, you appear to be in your mid-forties, this is 1914, and I happen to know that you died of old age in 1890!"

Baker—Burton—shook his head. "Then I can't be who you think I am," he said, "for I'm neither old nor dead."

At which point, with a terrible blast, the world came to an end.

The world came to an end for Thomas Bendyshe on New Year's Day, 1863. He was dressed as the Grim Reaper when he died. A committed and outspoken atheist, his final words were: "Oh God! Oh, sweet Jesus! Please, Mary mother of God, save me!"

His fellow members of the Cannibal Club later blamed this uncharacteristic outburst on the fact that strychnine poisoning is an extremely painful way to go.

They were gathered at Fryston—Richard Monckton Milnes's Yorkshire manor house—for a combined New Year and farewell fancy dress party. The farewell wasn't intended for Bendyshe—his demise was utterly unforeseen—but for Sir Richard Francis Burton and his expedition, which was leaving en route for Africa later in the week.

Fryston, which dated from the Elizabethan Age, lacked a ballroom but behind its stone-mullioned windows there were many spacious oak-panelled chambers, warmed by inglenook fireplaces, and these were filled with costumed guests. They included the Pre-Raphaelite artists, leading Technologists, authors and poets and actors, government ministers, Scotland Yard officials, and members of the Royal Geographical Society. A number of high-ranking officers from His Majesty's Airship *Orpheus* were in attendance, and among the female notables were Miss Isabella Mayson, Sister Sadhvi Raghavendra, Mrs. Iris Angell, and the famous Eugenicist—now Geneticist—Nurse Florence Nightingale, making for a very well-attended soiree, such as Monckton Milnes was famous for.

In the smoking room, Bendyshe, in a black hooded cloak and a skull mask, spent the minutes leading up to his death happily pranking the Greek god Apollo. The diminutive flame-haired Olympian, actually the poet Algernon Charles Swinburne, dressed in a toga, with a laurel wreath upon his head and the gold-tipped arrow of Eros pushed through his waistband, was standing near a bay window with the Persian King Shahryār, Oliver Cromwell, Harlequin, and a cavalier; otherwise Sir Richard Francis Burton, the Secretary for War Sir George Cornewall Lewis, Monckton Milnes, and the Technologist captain of the *Orpheus*, Nathaniel Lawless.

Swinburne had just received a full glass of brandy from a passing waiter, who, like all the staff, was dressed in a Venetian *Medico Della Peste* costume, complete with its long-beaked bird mask. The poet took a gulp, placed the glass on an occasional table at his side, and turned back to Captain Lawless, saying: "But isn't it rather a large crew? I was under the impression that rotorships are flown by seven or eight, not—how many?"

"Counting myself," the captain replied, "there are twenty-six, and that's not even a full complement."

"My hat! How on earth do you keep yourselves occupied?"

Lawless laughed, his pale-grey eyes twinkling, his straight teeth whiter even than his snowy, tightly clipped beard. "I don't think you've quite grasped the size of the *Orpheus*," he said. "She's Mr. Brunel's biggest flying machine. A veritable titan. When you see her tomorrow, I'll wager she'll take your breath away."

The Technologist Daniel Gooch joined the group. As always, he was wearing a harness from which two extra mechanical arms extended. Swinburne had already expressed the opinion that the engineer should have outfitted himself as a giant insect. As a matter of fact, though, Gooch was dressed as a Russian Cossack. He said, "She's magnificent, Mr. Swinburne. Luxurious, too. Designed for passenger cruises. She'll carry the expedition, the supplies, and both your vehicles, with plenty of room to spare."

Bendyshe, standing just behind the poet, with his back to him and conversing with Charles Bradlaugh—who was done up as Dick Turpin—surreptitiously took the brandy glass from the table. He slipped it beneath his mask, drained it in a single gulp, put it back, and winked at Bradlaugh through his mask's right eye socket.

"Are all the crew positions filled, Captain?" Burton asked. "I hear you had some problems."

Lawless nodded. "The two funnel scrubbers supplied to us by the League of Chimney Sweeps proved rather too young and undisciplined for the job. They were playing silly beggars in the ventilation pipes and caused some considerable damage. I dismissed them at once." He addressed Gooch, who was serving as chief engineer aboard the vessel: "I understand the replacements will join us at Battersea?"

"Yes, sir, and they'll bring with them a new length of pipe from the League." One of his mechanical hands dipped into his jacket pocket and withdrew a notebook. He consulted it and said, "Their names are William Cornish and Tobias Threadneedle."

"Nippers?"

"Cornish is a youngster, sir. Apparently Mr. Threadneedle is considerably older, though I expect he'll prove childishly small in stature, like all his kind."

Unable to stop himself, Gooch glanced down at Swinburne, who poked out his tongue in response.

"A master sweep, no doubt," Burton offered. "I believe the Beetle is attempting to incorporate their Brotherhood into the League." He paused, then said, "Where have I heard the name William Cornish before?"

"From me," Swinburne answered, in his high, piping voice. "I know him. And a fine young scamp he is, too, though rather too eager to spend his evenings setting traps in graveyards in the hope of catching a resurrectionist or two!" He reached for his glass, raised it to his lips, started, looked at it ruefully, and muttered, "Blast!" He signalled to a waiter.

"Resurrectionists? The Beetle? Pipes? What in heaven's name are we talking about?" Cornewall Lewis exclaimed.

Burton answered, "The Beetle is the rather mysterious head of the sweeps' organisation. A boy. Very intelligent and well read. He lives in a factory chimney."

"Good Lord!"

Swinburne took another glass of brandy from the waiter, sipped it, and placed it on the table.

"I never met the Beetle," he said, "but I worked with Willy Cornish when I served under a master sweep named Vincent Sneed during Richard's investigation of the Spring Heeled Jack affair. Sneed was a vicious big-nosed lout whom I had the misfortune to bump into again during last summer's riots. I knocked the wind out of the swine."

"You fell on top of him," Burton corrected.

Unseen, Bendyshe took the poet's glass, swallowed almost all of its contents, and slid it back into position.

Bradlaugh whispered to him, "Are you sure that's wise, old man? You'll end up sloshed if you're not careful!"

"Nonshence," Bendyshe slurred. "I'm jober as a sudge."

Monckton Milnes turned to Lawless. "What exactly does a funnel scrubber do?"

"Normally, he'll be based at a landing field," the aeronaut answered, "and is responsible for keeping a ship's smoke and steam outlets clean and free of obstruction. However, in the bigger vessels, which fly at a higher altitude, extensive internal pipe systems circulate warm air to ensure that a comfortable temperature is maintained in every cabin. The pipes are wide enough for a nipper to crawl through, and it's a funnel scrubber's job to do just that, cleaning out the dust and moisture that accrues."

"That sounds like dashed hot and uncomfortable work!"

"Indeed. But not compared to cleaning chimneys." Lawless addressed Swinburne: "As you obviously know from personal experience, sweeps lead a dreadful existence. Those that get work as funnel scrubbers are considered the fortunate few."

"I hardly think that such a promotion completely justifies the word 'fortunate,'" put in Burton. "Funnel scrubbers are still emotionally and physically scarred by their years of poverty and brutality. The Beetle does what he can to protect his lads but he can't change the social order. To improve the lives of sweeps, we'd need to instigate a fundamental shift in the way wealth is distributed. We'd have to raise the masses out of the sucking quagmire of poverty into which the Empire's foundations are sunk."

He looked at Cornewall Lewis, who shrugged and stated, "I'm the secretary for war, Sir Richard. My job is to protect the Empire, not right its wrongs."

"Protect it, or expand it, along with its iniquities, sir?"

Monckton Milnes cleared his throat. "Now, now, Richard," he said, softly. "This isn't really the occasion, is it?"

Burton bit his lip and nodded. "My apologies, Sir George—I spoke out of turn. I've been rather sensitive to such matters since the Tichborne riots."

Cornewall Lewis opened his mouth to speak but was interrupted by Swinburne, who suddenly screeched: "What? What? Has the world gone giddy? How can I possibly be guzzling my drinks at this rate? I swear I've barely tasted a drop!"

Burton frowned down at his assistant. "Algy, please remember that you are Apollo, not Dionysus," he advised. "Try to regulate your imbibing."

"Regulate? Regulate? What in blue blazes are you jabbering about, Richard? Nobody drinks more regularly than me!"

The poet gazed at his empty glass with an expression of bemusement, then signalled to another waiter. Behind him, Bendyshe and Bradlaugh smothered their chuckles.

"Anyway," said Gooch, "when the nippers arrive, the crew will be complete." He produced a slip of paper from between the pages of his notebook. "I have the complete roster here, sir."

Lawless took the note, read it through, and nodded his approval.

"May I see that, Captain?" Burton asked.

"Certainly."

The king's agent took the list and scrutinised it. He read:

Commanding Officer: Captain Nathaniel Lawless
First Officer: William Samuel Henson
Second Officer: Wordsworth Pryce
Helmsman: Francis H. Wenham
Assistant Helmsman: Walter D'Aubigny
Navigator: Cedric Playfair
Meteorologist: Arthur Bingham
Chief Engineer: Daniel Gooch
Engineer: Harold Bloodmann
Engineer: Charles Henderson
Engineer: Cyril Goodenough

Engineer: James Bolling
Chief Rigger: Gordon Champion
Rigger: Alexander Priestley
Rigger: Winford Doe
Fireman: Walter Gerrard
Fireman: Peter Etheridge
Stoker: Thomas Beadle
Stoker: Gwyn Reece-Jones
Funnel Scrubber: ~~Ronald Welbergen~~ William Cornish
Funnel Scrubber: ~~Michael Drake~~ Tobias Threadneedle
Steward/Surgeon: Doctor Barnaby Quaint
Assistant Steward/Surgeon: Sister Sadhvi Raghavendra
Quartermaster: Frederick Butler
Assistant Quartermaster: Isabella Mayson
Cabin Boy: Oscar Wilde

"I trust Quips is living up to my recommendation?" Burton asked the captain.

"Quips?"

"Young Master Wilde."

"Ah. An appropriate nickname—he's a very witty young man. How old is he? Twelve-ish?"

"He celebrated his ninth birthday a couple of months ago."

"Good Lord! That young? And an orphan?"

"Yes. He lost his entire family to the Irish famine. He stowed away aboard a ship to Liverpool, made his way to London, and has been working there as a paperboy ever since."

"Well, I must say, I'm impressed by his industry. There's an unpleasant amount of bureaucracy associated with the captaincy of a rotorship and the youngster picked up the paperwork in a flash and keeps it better organised and up to date than I could ever hope to. Furthermore, I find that whenever I say 'hop to it,' he's already hopped. I wouldn't be at all surprised if Oscar Wilde captains his own ship one day." Lawless ran his fingers over his beard. "Sir Richard, what about these young ladies? Having women serving as crew isn't entirely without precedent, but are you sure it's wise to take the Sister with you on your expedition? Africa is harsh enough on a man, isn't it? And what about all that dashed cannibalism? Won't she be considered too dainty a morsel to resist?"

"It is indeed a cruel environment, as I know to my cost," Burton answered. "However, Sister Raghavendra is from India and possesses a natural immunity to many of the ills that assail a European in Africa. Furthermore, her medical skills are exceptional. I wish she'd been with me on my previous excursions. I assure you she'll be well looked after all the way to Kazeh, where she'll remain with our Arabian hosts while the rest of us hike north to the supposed position of the Mountains of the Moon."

"And the cannibals?"

The corners of Burton's mouth twitched slightly. "Those few tribes that feast on human flesh do so in a ritualistic fashion to mark their victory in battle. It's not as common a phenomenon as the storybooks would have you believe. For a daily meal of arm or leg, you'll have to go to the other side of the world, to Koluwai, a small island to the southeast of Papua New Guinea. There they will very happily have European visitors for dinner—and I don't mean as guests. Apparently, we taste like pork."

"Oof! I'm rather more in favour of lamb chops!" Lawless responded.

Cornewall Lewis interrupted: "You'll leave her with Arabians? Can they be trusted with the fair sex?"

Burton clicked his tongue impatiently. "Sir, if you choose to believe the lies propagated by your own government, that is up to you, but despite the calumnies that are circulated in the corridors of parliament, I have never found the Arabian race to be anything less than extraordinarily benevolent, courteous, and entirely honourable."

"I meant only to suggest that there might be a risk in leaving a woman of the Empire in non-Christian hands, Sir Richard."

"Christian? Do you then stand in opposition to Darwin's findings? Do you also believe that your God favours some races over others?"

"I use the word merely out of habit, as a synonym for civilised," Cornewall Lewis protested.

"Then I'm to take it you don't consider the Arabians civilised, despite that they invented modern mathematics, surgical instruments, soap and perfume, the windmill, the crankshaft, and a great many other things; despite that they realised the Earth is a sphere that circles the sun five hundred years before Galileo was tortured by your Christian church for supporting the same notion?"

The secretary for war pursed his lips uneasily.

"That reminds me," said Monckton Milnes. "Richard, I have the manuscript we discussed—the Persian treatise."

"The what?"

"The translation you were looking for." He stepped forward and hooked his arm through Burton's. "It's in the library. Come, I'll show you. Excuse us please, gentlemen, we shan't be long."

Before Burton could object he was pulled from the group and propelled through the guests toward the door.

"What blessed treatise?" he spluttered.

"A necessary fiction to remove you from the battlefield," Monckton Milnes hissed. "What the blazes has got into you? Why are you snapping like a rabid dog at Cornewall Lewis?"

They left the room, steered across a parlour, past a small gathering in the reception hall, entered a corridor, and stopped at a carved oak door. Monckton Milnes drew a key from a pocket in his costume, turned it in the lock, and, after they had entered into the room beyond, secured the door behind them.

They were in his famous and somewhat notorious library.

He pointed to big studded leather armchairs near the fireplace and snapped: "Go. Sit."

Burton obeyed.

Monckton Milnes went to a cabinet, retrieved a bottle and glasses from it, and poured two drinks. He joined Burton and handed one to him.

"Vintage *Touriga Nacional*, 1822, one of the finest ports ever produced," he murmured. "It cost me a bloody fortune. Don't gulp it down. Savour it."

Burton put the glass to his nose and inhaled the aroma. He took a taste, smacked his lips, then leaned back in his chair and considered his friend.

"My apologies, dear fellow."

"Spare me. I don't want 'em. I want an explanation. By God, Richard, I've seen you angry, I've seen you defeated, I've seen you wild with enthusiasm, and I've seen you drunk as a fiddler's bitch, but I've never before seen you jittery. What's the matter?"

Burton gazed into his drink and remained silent for a moment, then looked up and met his friend's eyes.

"They are making a puppet of me."

"Who are? How?"

"The bloody politicians. Sending me to Africa."

Monckton Milnes's face registered his surprise. "But it's what you've wanted!"

"Not under these circumstances."

"What circumstances? Stone me, man, if you haven't been handed a rare opportunity! The Royal Geographical Society was dead set against you going, but Palmerston—the prime minister himself!—forced their hand. You have another chance at the Nile, and no expedition has ever been so well funded and supported, not even Henry Stanley's! Why do you grumble so and flash those moody eyes of yours? Explain!"

Burton looked away, glanced around at the book-lined walls, and at the erotic statuettes that stood on plinths in various niches, pulled at his jacket and brushed lint from his sleeve, took another sip from his glass, and, reluctantly, returned his attention to Monckton Milnes.

"It's true, I have long wanted to return to Africa to finish what I began back in fifty-seven," he said. "To locate, once and for all, the source of the River Nile. Instead, I'm being dispatched to find and bring back a damned weapon!"

"A weapon?"

"A black diamond. An Eye of Nāga."

"What is that? How is a diamond a weapon? I don't understand."

Burton suddenly leaned forward and gripped his friend's wrist. A flame ignited in his dark eyes.

"You and I have known each other for a long time," he said, a slight hoarseness creeping into his voice. "I can trust you to keep a confidence, yes?"

"Of course you can. You have my word."

Burton sat back. "Do you remember once recommending to me the cheiromantist Countess Sabina?"

Monckton Milnes grunted an affirmation.

"These past weeks, she's been employing her talent as a seer for Palmerston. Her abilities are prodigious. She's able to catch astoundingly clear glimpses of the future—but not our future."

His friend frowned, took a swallow from his glass then laid it aside and rubbed a hand across his cheek, accidentally smudging the red harlequin makeup that surrounded his left eye.

"Whose, then?"

"No, you misunderstand. I mean, not the future you and I and everyone else in the world will experience."

"What other future is there?" Monckton Milnes asked in bewilderment.

Burton held his gaze, then said quietly, "This world, this time we live in, it is not as it should be."

"Not as—You're speaking in blessed riddles, Richard!"

"Do you recall all the hysteria eighteen months or so ago when people started to see Spring Heeled Jack left, right, and centre?"

"Yes, of course."

"It wasn't newspaper sensationalism. He was real."

"A prankster?"

"Far from it. He was a man from the future. He travelled back from the year 2202 to 1840 to prevent his ancestor, with whom he shared the name of Edward Oxford, from shooting at Queen Victoria. His mission went terribly wrong. What should have been a botched assassination attempt succeeded thanks to his interference. It altered everything his history had recorded and, what's more, it wiped him out of his own time."

Monckton Milnes sat motionless, his eyes widening.

"While he was trying to escape from the scene of the assassination," Burton continued, "Oxford's strange costume, which contained the machinery that enabled him to move through time, was damaged by a young constable with whom we are both acquainted. In fact, he's here tonight."

"Wh—who?"

"William Trounce. He was just eighteen years old. His intervention caused Oxford to be thrown back to the year 1837, where he was taken in and looked after by Henry de La Poer Beresford."

"The Mad Marquess?"

"Yes. While in his care, Oxford dropped vague hints about the shape and nature of the future. Those hints led directly to the establishment of the Technologist and Libertine castes and their offshoots, and sent us down a road entirely divorced from that which we were meant to tread. History altered dramatically, and so did people, for they were now offered opportunities and challenges they would not have otherwise encountered."

Monckton Milnes shook his head wonderingly. "Are—are—are you spinning one of your Arabian Night yarns?" he asked. "You're not in earnest, surely?"

"Entirely. I'm telling you the absolute truth."

"Very well. I shall—I shall attempt to suspend my incredulity and hear you out. Pray continue."

"Trapped in what, for him, was the distant past, Oxford began to lose his mind. He and the marquess, who himself was a near lunatic, cooked up a scheme by which Oxford might be able to reestablish his future existence by restoring his family lineage. This involved making short hops into the future to locate one of his ancestors, which he managed to do despite that his suit's mechanism was rapidly failing. One of those hops brought him to 1861. Beresford had, by this time, formed an alliance with Charles Darwin and Francis Galton. They intended to trap Oxford, steal his suit, and use it to create separate histories, moulding each one as they saw fit, manipulating us all. I had to kill them, and Oxford, to protect the world from their insane plans."

Monckton Milnes stared at Burton in shock. His mouth worked silently, then he managed to splutter: "This—this is beyond the realms of fantasy, Richard. Everyone knows that Darwin was murdered by religious extremists!"

"False information issued by the government. You'd better take another swallow of this fine port. There's a great deal more to the tale."

Monckton Milnes, forgetting his earlier directive to Burton, downed his drink in a single swig. He looked at the empty glass, stood up, paced over to the cabinet, and returned with the bottle.

"Go on," he said, pouring refills.

"Countess Sabina can see far more clearly into the other history—the original one—than she can into ours, perhaps because none of the decisions we make here can have an effect there. The histories are quite different, but there is one thing common to both. There is a war coming. A terrible war that will encompass the world and decimate an entire generation of men. That is why the prime minister wants the African diamond."

"War? My God. So what is it, this diamond? Why is it so important? What's it got to do with Spring Heeled Jack?"

"Are you familiar with the fabled Nāga?" Burton asked.

Monckton Milnes furrowed his brow. "I—yes—I believe—I believe I've come across references to them in various occult texts. Weren't they some sort of pre-human race?"

"Yes. There are carvings of them at Angkor Wat. They are portrayed as seven- or five-headed reptiles."

"So?"

"When this planet was young, an aerolite—a huge black diamond—broke into three pieces in its atmosphere. One piece fell to Earth in what became South America, another in Africa, and the last in the Far East. The Nāga built civilisations around the impact sites. They discovered that the diamonds possessed a very special property: they could store and maintain even the most subtle of electrical fields, such as those generated by a living brain. The Nāga used them to fuse their minds, to form a sort of unified intelligence."

"If any of that is true, how can you possibly know it?"

"That will become apparent," Burton responded. He went on speaking in a low and urgent tone: "The human race waged war on the Nāga, and the reptiles became extinct. The diamonds were lost until, in 1796, Sir Henry Tichborne discovered one—the South American stone."

"Tichborne!"

"Indeed. He brought it home and hid it beneath his estate. In the history that was meant to be, it remained there until just prior to the future Edward Oxford's time, when it was discovered after Tichborne House was demolished. Oxford cut small shards from it and used them in the machinery of his time suit. When he arrived in the past, those shards suddenly existed in two places at once. They were in his suit and they were also still a part of the diamond under the estate. This paradox caused a strange resonance between them, which extended even to the two as yet undiscovered Nāga diamonds. It caused them all to emit a low, almost inaudible musical drone. This led to the recovery of the Far Eastern stone, in Cambodia, which had been shattered into seven pieces when the humans conquered the Nāga many millennia ago."

"My head is spinning," Monckton Milnes murmured.

"Not just yours," Burton said. "The resonance also awoke a hitherto dormant part of the human mind. It made mediumistic abilities possible. Thus Countess Sabina, and thus a Russian named Helena Blavatsky."

"The woman they say destroyed the Rakes last year?"

"Quite so. She stole two of the Cambodian stones and used them to peer into the future."

"Which future—ours or the other one?"

"Ours. And in that future, in the year 1914, another Russian, a clairvoyant named Grigori Rasputin, was gazing back at us."

"Why?"

"Because he foresaw that the Great War, which was in his time raging, would lead to his assassination and the decimation of his beloved Russia. He came looking for the events that sparked off the conflict, and he found them here, in the 1860s."

Monckton Milnes regarded his friend through slitted eyes. "Are you referring to our role in the American hostilities?"

"No. The world war will pitch us against united German states, so I'm of the opinion that the recent Eugenicist exodus to Prussia, which was led by the botanist Richard Spruce and my former partner John Speke, might be the spark that lights the flame."

"So this Rasputin fellow observed the defectors at work? To what end?"

"He did much more than that. He possessed Blavatsky and used her to steal the rest of the Cambodian stones and recover the South American diamond from the Tichborne estate, thus changing history again. He then employed them to magnify and transmit his mesmeric influence, causing the working classes to riot. He intended nothing less than the wholesale destruction of the British Empire, so that United Germany might win the war against us without Russian assistance. Once that heinous outcome was achieved, Russia would swoop upon a weakened Germany and defeat her."

"Bloody hell!"

"Blavatsky didn't survive and the plot failed," Burton said. "I caused Rasputin to die in 1914, two years before his assassination, meaning that history has diverged yet again, although that particular bifurcation won't occur for another fifty-one years."

Monckton Milnes flexed his jaw. He clenched his fists. He blew out a breath, reached for his glass, emptied it, and refilled it again. He was trembling. "By thunder!" he muttered. "I actually believe all this! Where are the Cambodian and South American diamonds now?"

"The South American stone was broken into seven fragments when I defeated Rasputin. They are in Palmerston's possession. The Cambodian stones are embedded in a babbage probability calculator."

"They are? For what purpose?"

"During the Tichborne riots I was assisted by a philosopher named Herbert Spencer. He died with the stones in his pocket and his mind was imprinted onto them. Charles Babbage had designed a device to process just such an imprint. We fitted the diamonds into it and placed the mechanism in my clockwork valet. Herbert Spencer thus lives on, albeit in the form of a mechanical contraption. That is how I know the history of the Nāga, for the reptile intelligence remains in the stones, and Herbert can sense it. Actually, so can I, in a vague way. The Nāga came to me in a dream and left me with the phrase 'Only equivalence can lead to destruction or a final transcendence.' It was that which guided me in the final ruination of Rasputin."

Monckton Milnes again rubbed his face and again smudged his Harlequin makeup.

"So only the African diamond remains undiscovered and Palmerston is sending you to find it?"

"Precisely. As the last remaining unbroken stone, it will be more powerful than its splintered counterparts. He means to use the Eyes to wage a clandestine war on Prussia through clairvoyance, prophecy, and mediumistic assassinations. He intends that Bismarck will never unite the Germanic states. Do you see now why I'm wishing this expedition had never been commissioned?"

He received a weak nod of understanding. "Yes," came the whispered response. "You can't possibly allow Palmerston that kind of power. By God, he could manipulate the whole world!"

"Just as Darwin and Galton and their cronies would have done."

Monckton Milnes gazed at his friend a moment. "By James, I wouldn't be in your shoes for anything, Richard. What are you going to do?"

Burton shrugged. "I have to retrieve the stone if only to prevent it from falling into Prussian hands. I feel certain that my erstwhile partner is going after it, with Bismarck's sponsorship. As to what I'll do with it once I have it—I don't know. There's a further complication: it was the African Eye that Rasputin employed in 1914 to probe into the past. So I already know I'm fated to find it, and, after I do, it will somehow, eventually, be transported to Russia."

They sat in silence for a few minutes, then Burton muttered, "I feel like a bloody pawn in a game of chess."

Monckton Milnes roused himself from the reverie he'd fallen into. "I have every faith in you, Richard," he said. "Go to Africa. Do whatever you must. You'll find an answer, of that I'm certain."

Burton sighed and gave a slight jerk of his head. He became conscious of the buzz of conversation and merriment that filled Fryston. He looked down at himself, then at his friend, and suddenly chuckled. "Bismillah! King Shahryār of *A Thousand Nights and a Night* discussing fantastic notions with Harlequin! What a confounded joke!"

Monckton Milnes smiled. "Go back to the party. Relax. Enjoy yourself. I'll join you in a few minutes. I want to sit here a little longer."

Burton rose and crossed to the door. He looked back and said, "If Palmerston learns that we had this conversation, I'll be thrown into the Tower."

"Bedlam, more like," Monckton Milnes murmured.

"No. The government keeps secret rooms, including prison cells, beneath the Tower of London."

His friend held up his hands as if to ward off the king's agent. "Have mercy! No more, I beg of you!" he cried. "My capacity for revelations is all used up!"

Burton unlocked the door and left the room. He made his way back across the entrance hall, through the parlour, and into the smoking room.

"I say, Captain," Humpty Dumpty called as he entered. "Where's that wonderful housekeeper of yours?"

Burton turned to the rotund fairy-tale figure. "Is that you in there, Trounce?"

"Yes, and I feel an absolute ass, but it was Mrs. Trounce's idea and I thought it wise not to kick up a fuss, seeing as I'm abandoning her for the next few months. It's blasted awkward, I can tell you. I'm having dashed difficulty in steering food and wine lipwards, so to speak."

"I shouldn't complain. It looks like you could stand to lose a pound or two."

"That's quite enough of that, if you don't mind! You know full well that my current circumference is all padding!"

"If you say so. Who has the esteemed Mrs. Trounce come as?"

"Old Mother Hubbard, which, admittedly, didn't require much by way of dressing up. She's eager for a gossip with Mrs. Angell but what with all these fancy getups she can't locate the dear lady. So where is she and who, or what, has she come as?"

"She's a rather too matronly Queen Boadicea, and is off doing your wife's job, I think."

"What do you mean?"

"She's gone to give a dog a bone."

"Eh?"

"She's down in the kitchen procuring a morsel for Fidget, though I suspect she's actually seeking refuge from all these lords and ladies. She feels a little out of place, but I insisted upon her attendance. She deserves a taste of the high life after all I've put her through recently."

"You brought your confounded basset hound as well?"

"She made him a part of her costume—harnessed him to a toy war chariot and had him trotting along beside her. He was most indignant about it."

A loud high-pitched howl rose above the general hubbub.

"Would you excuse me?" Burton said. "It sounds like Algy needs to be reined in."

He moved back toward the bay window. As he reached the group gathered there, a waiter pushed a glass of port into his hand. Absently, Burton placed it on the table, his attention on Swinburne, who was hopping up and down, waving his arms like a madman.

"I'm not in the slightest bit tipsy!" the poet was protesting vociferously. "What an utter disaster! I've become immune to alcohol!"

"Through overfamiliarity, perhaps?" Cornewall Lewis offered.

"Nonsense! We meet frequently, I'll admit, but we're naught but nodding acquaintances!"

Doctor James Hunt, a Cannibal Club member, joined the group just in time to hear this. He roared with laughter and declared: "Hah! I rather think there's a great deal more intimacy than that, Algy! You and alcohol are practically wedded!"

"Tosh and piffle!" Swinburne objected. "Claptrap, balderdash, cobblers, and bunkum!"

Someone spoke quietly at Burton's side: "I should have you arrested."

The explorer turned and found himself facing Sir Richard Mayne, the lean-faced chief commissioner of Scotland Yard.

"Something to do with me whisking four of your men off to Africa?" he asked, with a raised eyebrow.

"Yes," Mayne answered, glancing disapprovingly at Swinburne's histrionics. "Trounce and Honesty are among my best detectives, Krishnamurthy commands my Flying Squad, and Constable Bhatti is in line for promotion. I can hardly afford to have them all gallivanting around the Dark Continent for a year. I can only conclude that you're in league with London's criminal underclasses. Am I right, Sir Richard? Are you getting my men out of the way prior to some villainous coup? Perhaps plotting to have them consumed by lions and tigers so you can break into the Tower of London and steal the Crown jewels?"

Burton smiled. "Funny, I was just talking about the Tower. But no, and there are no tigers in Africa, sir. Did Lord Palmerston explain the situation?"

"He delivered to me some vague waffle about it being a matter of national security."

"It is."

"And he ordered me in no uncertain terms to provide you with whatever you want. I shall do so, of course."

"Thank you. I ask only that the men receive extended leave and that their families are looked after."

"Have no worries on that account." The commissioner took a sip of his wine. He sighed. "Keep them safe, won't you?"

"I'll do my best."

They shook hands. Mayne wandered away. Burton reached for his drink and was surprised to find that his glass had mysteriously emptied itself. He pursed his lips and looked at his assistant, who was still stamping his feet and protesting his sobriety. He concluded that Swinburne was either in the midst of one of his infamous drinking sprees or he was the victim of mischief. Then he noticed the Grim Reaper hovering behind the little poet and, though he quickly recognised Thomas Bendyshe—which explained everything, for the anthropologist and atheist was Swinburne's most dedicated tormenter—he nevertheless felt a momentary chill needling at his spine.

"Richard!" Swinburne screeched. "You've seen me in my cups more than most. Do I seem inebriated to you?"

"Of all people, Algy, you are the one in whom it's hardest to tell the difference," Burton answered.

The poet gave a shriek of despair. He yelled for a waiter.

Time passed, the party continued, and the king's agent moved from group to group, chatting with some, debating with others, joking with a few.

At a quarter-past eleven, Monckton Milnes reappeared, with makeup restored, and herded his guests into the music room, where Florence Nightingale surprised Burton by demonstrating an unexpected proficiency on the piano as she accompanied Sister Raghavendra, whose singing voice proved equally impressive. They entertained the gathering until close on midnight, at which point everyone fell silent and listened to the chimes of the grandfather clock. As the final note clanged, they hooked their arms, Nightingale started playing, and the Sister sang:

> "Should old acquaintance be forgot,
> and never brought to mind?
> Should old acquaintance be forgot,
> and old lang syne?"

The guests happily launched into the chorus:

> "For auld lang syne, my dear,
> for auld lang syne,
> we'll take a cup of kindness yet,
> for auld lang syne!"

"And surely you'll buy your pint cup," the young singer trilled. "And surely I'll buy mine—"

"Oh God!" someone yelled.

"And we'll take a cup o' kindness yet, for auld lang syne."

"Oh, sweet Jesus!" came the agonised voice.

Burton peered around the room as the crowd launched into the chorus again.

> "For auld lang syne, my dear,
> for auld lang syne,
> we'll take a cup of—"

The song tailed off and the music stopped as someone screamed: "Please, Mary mother of God, save me!"

The explorer unhooked his arms from his neighbours, pushed people aside, and hurried toward a commotion near the fireplace. Men were kneeling beside a prone figure. It was Bendyshe. His skull mask had been removed and his face was contorted into a ghastly expression, eyes wide and glassy, mouth stretched into a hideous rictus grin. His whole body was convulsing with such ferocity that it required four men to hold him down. He writhed and jerked, his backbone arching, his heels drumming on the floor.

Detective Inspector Honesty—a slight, wiry man with a flamboyantly wide moustache that curled upward at the ends, who normally sported lacquered-flat hair, parted in the middle, and displayed a fussy dress sense, but who was currently outfitted as one of the Three Musketeers—appeared at Burton's side and muttered, "Fit. Overdoing it. Excessive indulgence."

"No," Burton said. "This is something else." He pushed forward until he reached Monckton Milnes's side and hissed, "Get the crowd out of here."

The host of the party looked at him and said, "Gad, what am I thinking? Of course."

Monckton Milnes turned and, in a loud voice, announced: "Ladies and gentlemen, unfortunately one of our fellows has been taken ill. Would you mind moving into the other rooms, please? We should give the poor chap space to breathe."

With utterances of sympathy, people started to wander away.

A hand gripped Burton by the elbow. It belonged to Doctor James Hunt.

"Come here," he whispered, and dragged the king's agent over to the window, away from everyone else.

"What is it, Jim? Is Bendyshe going to be all right?"

"No. Quite the opposite." Hunt caught his lower lip between his teeth. There was a sheen of sweat on his brow. "I'd recognise the symptoms any-where," he hissed. "Bloody strychnine. The poor devil's been poisoned!"

Burton momentarily fought for balance as his knees buckled. "*What?*"

"Poisoned. Purposely. A man doesn't get strychnine in his system by accident."

"Can you save him?"

"Not a chance. He'll be dead within the hour."

"No! Please, Jim, work with Nurse Nightingale and Sister Raghavendra. Do whatever you can for him."

Hunt gave Burton's arm a squeeze and returned to the dying man. The king's agent saw Trounce standing by the doorway and moved over to him.

"Get out of that ridiculous costume. There's trouble."

"What's happened?"

"Murder, Trounce. Someone has poisoned Tom Bendyshe."

"Great heavens! I—um—I'll round up the troops at once. Damn this bloody padding! Help me out of it, would you?"

Some minutes later, Trounce, Sir Richard Mayne, and Detective Inspector Honesty ushered the guests and staff upstairs, while Commander Krishnamurthy and Constable Bhatti guarded Fryston's front and back doors to ensure no one slipped out.

Bendyshe was now frothing at the mouth and thrashing even more wildly.

Charles Bradlaugh, sitting on his friend's legs and being bucked about as they spasmed beneath him, looked at Burton as the explorer squatted beside the dying man. "I can't believe it," he croaked, his eyes filling with tears. "Hunt says it's poison. Who would do this to poor Tom? He never hurt a soul!"

"I don't know, Charles. What was he up to before he was taken ill?"

"Singing along with the rest of us. He was rather sloshed—he's been stealing Algy's drinks all night."

Burton turned to James Hunt. "Could strychnine have been in one of the glasses?"

"Yes." The doctor nodded. "It's an incredibly bitter poison but if he was blotto enough he might have swallowed it without noticing the taste."

"He was half-cut, to be sure," Bradlaugh put in.

Burton reached past Nurse Nightingale, who was mopping Bendyshe's brow, and placed a hand on the man's chest. He could feel the muscles jumping beneath his palm.

"Tom," he whispered.

He cleared his throat, stood, and gestured for Hunt to follow him. The two men left the music room and went into the smoking room, crossing to the table near the bay window.

"The poison was probably in one of these glasses," Burton said, indicating the various empty vessels.

"If so, it won't be difficult to find out which one," the doctor answered. He picked up a glass, sniffed it, muttered, "Brandy," then dipped his index finger into the dregs at the bottom. He touched the finger to his tongue. "Not that one."

"You won't poison yourself?"

"Strychnine is occasionally used in small amounts as medical treatment. The merest dab won't harm me."

Hunt tested another glass, then a third and fourth. The fifth made him screw up his face.

"Bitter. The port would have gone some way to disguising it, but the taste is strong, nevertheless."

"The drink is port?"

"Yes."

Burton went through the other glasses one by one. As their shapes suggested, they had all contained either brandy or wine.

"Damnation," he muttered. "Get back to Tom. I'll talk to you later."

He strode off and made his way to the entrance hall where he found Richard Monckton Milnes, Algernon Swinburne, and Chief Commissioner Mayne in quiet conversation at the bottom of the staircase.

Mayne's expression was grim. "Are you certain it's attempted murder?" he said as Burton joined them.

"Not attempted. Successful. There's no antidote."

"But why kill Tom?" Swinburne asked, miserably.

"It was a mistake," Burton answered. "He wasn't the intended victim. I was."

CHAPTER 2

UNDERWORLD AND
THE *ORPHEUS*

GOVERNMENT NOTICE

IT IS ILLEGAL TO INTERFERE WITH STREET CRABS!

Those who seek to block a Street Crab's path,
entangle its legs, extinguish its furnace,
divert it into harm's way with a purposely laid trail of litter,
or in any other manner prevent it from fulfilling
its function, will be fined a minimum of £25.

STREET CRABS KEEP *YOUR* STREETS CLEAN!

"Y ou?"

Richard Monckton Milnes, Algernon Swinburne, and Sir Richard Mayne had all spoken at once.

Burton nodded. "The poison was in a glass of port. It was pushed into my hand by one of the waiters. Tom drank it by mistake." He addressed Monckton Milnes. "Would you order your waiting staff and household manager into the parlour, please? We'll question them there."

This was duly done, and it was quickly made apparent by Mr. Applebaum, the manager, that a man was missing.

"Two of the waiters are permanent here at Fryston," he told Burton. "The other four we hired from an agency, just for this party. These are the temporaries—" he indicated three of the men, "—and their colleague, sir, is the one that's made off."

"Where is the agency?" Burton asked.

"In Thorpe Willoughby, a village about four miles east of here. Howell's by name. It has offices over the high street bakery."

Burton turned to one of the hired hands, a small man whose fingers moved nervously. "What's your name?"

"Colin Parkes, sir."

"And the missing man?"

"Peter Pimlico, but he ain't one of us. It was meant to be Gordon Bailey workin' tonight, but he was taken poorly, like, with a bad tummy, so he sent this Pimlico fellow, what is a friend of his, along in his stead. Leastways, that's how Pimlico explained it."

"Do you know where he lives?"

"Pimlico? He said in Leeds, sir. He came with us in a carriage from Thorpe Willoughby. He's been renting a room there for the past few days. There are only two hostels and one inn in the village, so I reckon he's in one of them."

"What does he look like?"

"Blond. Big side whiskers. Blue eyes. A bit soft around the middle. I should say he eats more'n he serves."

"Thank you, Mr. Parkes."

Sir Richard Mayne sent the staff back upstairs and said, "I'm going to order my men to search the house."

Forty minutes later, the police commissioner reported back to Burton. "Commander Krishnamurthy found the missing man's fancy-dress costume dumped in a back room near the kitchen. The window was open. Doubtless that was his means of escape. I'll send Bhatti to the local railway station."

"Pointless," Burton said curtly. "There's no service at this time of night."

"Then where do you think he—?"

The commissioner was interrupted by Swinburne and Hunt, who joined them, their faces drawn.

"Tom Bendyshe is dead," the doctor said tonelessly. "Mercifully quick for strychnine. His heart gave out."

Burton turned back to Mayne. "I'd like to borrow Detective Inspector Trounce. I have my basset hound here—he's an excellent tracking dog. We'll give him a sniff of that *Medico Della Peste* outfit and see where he leads us."

"Very well."

Burton—after quickly changing into rather more suitable evening attire—found Fidget happily gnawing on a bone in the kitchen downstairs.

"Sorry, old thing," he said, lifting the dog's lead from a hook behind the door. "You're going to have to save that for later."

Fidget growled and complained as the explorer removed the bone and clipped the leash onto his collar. He whined and dragged at the tether until Burton got him out of the kitchen, then settled down and padded along beside his master, up the stairs and out of the back door.

A cold breeze was blowing outside. Burton's breath clouded and streamed away. Stars shone in a clear night sky and a three-quarters moon cast its silver light over Fryston's grounds.

Swinburne—now in his normal day clothes but with the laurel wreath still entwined in his hair—and Trounce were waiting by an open window. The Scotland Yard man was squatting on his haunches, holding a lantern over the ground. "Footprints in the flower bed," he said as the king's agent joined them.

Swinburne stepped back. Fidget had an unfortunate fondness for his ankles and had nipped at them throughout the train journey from London to Yorkshire. The poet held out a bundle of clothing and said, "Here's the waiter's costume, Richard."

Burton took the clothes and applied them to Fidget's nose.

"Seek, boy!" he urged. "Seek!"

The basset hound lowered his head to the ground and began to snuffle about, zigzagging back and forth. He quickly caught the trail and dragged Burton away from the window and across the lawn. Swinburne and Trounce followed. The frozen grass crunched beneath their feet.

"Pimlico must be almost two hours ahead of us by now," Trounce panted as he hurried along.

"We're heading east," Burton noted. "I suspect he's gone back to Thorpe Willoughby. If he had a vehicle waiting there, he'll have made off and we'll lose the trail, but if he intends to travel back to Leeds by railway, he has no choice but to wait until the morning, and we'll nab him."

Fidget pulled them to the edge of the estate, along the bordering wall, and over a stile. They proceeded down a country lane edged by hedgerows until they reached a junction. The basset hound veered right onto a better-travelled road, and, as they followed, the men saw a sign that read: *Thorpe Willoughby 3½ Miles.*

"Confound it!" Swinburne muttered as they pushed on. "Tom was one of my best friends, even if he was a giant pain in the rear end. Why did this Pimlico chap try to kill you, Richard? I don't recall his name. He's not someone we've had dealings with, is he?"

"What? You?" Trounce exclaimed, not having been privy to the revelation earlier.

"I was meant to be the victim," Burton confirmed, "but I've no idea why. As far as I know, Pimlico has no connection with any of our past cases. His motivation remains a mystery."

The road led them to the brow of a hill and down the other side. They saw the outlying houses of the village some little distance ahead, lying beyond patchwork fields and dark clumps of forest. From the centre of the settlement, an irregular line of steam curved up into the night air, slowly dissipating in the breeze. It was instantly recognisable as the trail of a rotorchair.

"Hell's bells!" Trounce growled. "It looks like our bird has flown!"

Fidget, making little *yip-yip* noises as he followed the scent, led them into the village.

The exertion kept the men warm despite the low temperature, and by the time they reached the houses, Trounce was puffing and had to wipe at his brow with a handkerchief.

They passed cottages and small terraced houses, kept going straight past the inn, and eventually arrived outside a square and rather dilapidated-looking residence. The ribbon of steam was slowly drifting away above it. A notice in one of the lower windows read: *Robin Hood's Rest. Bed & Breakfast. No Foreigners.* Fidget stopped at its front door and pawed at it, whining with frustration.

Trounce reached out, grasped the knocker, and hammered.

They waited.

He hammered again.

A muffled voice came from within: "Keep yer bleedin' hair on!"

The portal opened and a fat man in an off-grey dressing gown blinked at them.

"What the bloomin' 'eck are you wantin' at this time o' night?" he demanded, his jowls wobbling indignantly.

"Police," Trounce snapped. "Do you have a Peter Pimlico here?"

"More bloody visitors? I told him, none after ten o'clock, them's the rules o' the house, and what 'appens? I get nothin' but bleedin' visitors! You ain't foreigners, too, are yer?"

"We're English. Answer the question, man! Is Pimlico here?"

"Yus. He's in his room. I suppose you'll be wantin' to go up? You're police, you say? In trouble, is he?"

"It's distinctly possible," Trounce answered, pushing his way past the man and into the narrow hallway beyond. "Which room?"

"Up the stairs an' first on yer left."

Trounce started for the stairs but stopped when Burton asked the landlord, "You say there was a previous visitor for Mr. Pimlico? A foreigner?"

"Yus. A fat bloke with a big walrus moustache."

"Nationality?"

"How the bleedin' 'eck should I know? They're all the same to me!"

"And when was he here?"

"'Bout 'alf an hour ago. Woke me up landing his bloody contraption right outside, then thumped on the door. Pimlico came down the stairs like a bloomin' avalanche to answer it, they both stamped up to his room, then a little bit later the foreigner came clod-hopping back down an' slammed the door behind him afore setting the windows a-rattling again with his blasted flying machine. I tell yer, it's been like trying to sleep in the middle of a bleedin' earthquake, and you ain't helpin'. Am I to get any kip at all tonight?"

"We'll not disturb you for long, Mr.—?"

"Emery. Norman Emery."

"Mr. Emery. Remain here, please."

Burton tied Fidget's leash to the bottom of the banister, muttered: "Stay, boy," then, with Swinburne, followed Trounce up the stairs. The policeman knocked on the first door on the left. It swung open slightly under his knuckles. He looked at Burton and raised his eyebrows.

"Mr. Pimlico?" he called.

There was no reply.

The Yard man pushed the door open and peered into the room. He let out a grunt and turned to Swinburne. "Get Emery up here, would you?"

The poet, noting a grim aspect to the detective's face, obeyed without question.

"Look at this," Trounce said as he entered the room.

Burton stepped in after him and saw a man stretched out on the floor. His face was a blotchy purple, his tongue was sticking out between his teeth, and his eyes were bulging and glazed.

"Strangled to death," Trounce observed. "By Jove, look at the state of his neck! Whoever did this must be strong as an ox!"

"And a practised hand," Burton added, bending over the corpse. "See the bruising? Our murderer knew exactly where to place his fingers and thumbs to kill in the quickest and most efficient manner. Hmm, look at these perforations in the skin. It's almost as if the killer possessed claws instead of fingernails!"

Trounce began to search through the dead man's pockets.

Swinburne reappeared with the landlord, who, upon looking through the doorway and seeing the body, cried out, "Cripes! And he ain't even paid his rent!"

"Is this Peter Pimlico?" Burton asked.

"Yus."

Trounce uttered an exclamation and held up a small phial.

Burton took it, opened it, sniffed it, then tipped it until a drop of liquid spilled onto his finger. He put it to his tongue and screwed up his nose.

"Strychnine. No doubt about it."

"It was in his pocket," Trounce said. He addressed the landlord: "Does the village have a constable?"

"Yes, sir," Emery replied. "Timothy Flanagan. He lives at number twelve."

"Go and get him."

"He'll be asleep."

"Of course he'll be asleep! Bang on his door! Throw stones at his window! I don't care what you do—just wake him up and get him here, on the double!"

Emery nodded and disappeared down the stairs.

The detective turned back to the corpse, running his eyes over it, taking in every detail. He suddenly uttered an exclamation and bent close to Pimlico's swollen face.

"What is it?" Burton asked.

Trounce didn't answer. Instead, he pushed his fingers between the dead man's lips, groped to one side of the tongue, and pulled something out.

It was a small withered leaf, a dry brown colour with spitefully thorny edges, and it was attached to a tendril that, though Trounce gently tugged at it, refused to come out of Pimlico's mouth.

"Captain," he said. "Would you prise the jaw open, please?"

Burton squatted, placed his hands around the lower half of the corpse's face, and pulled the mouth wide while Trounce pushed his fingers deeper inside.

"What in the blazes . . . ?" the Yard man hissed as he drew out a second leaf and the vine to which it was attached tightened. "Look at this!"

He leaned back so Burton could peer into the mouth. The king's agent emitted a gasp of surprise, for the little plant was growing straight out of Pimlico's upper palate.

"I've never seen anything like it!" Trounce said. "How can it be possible?"

Burton shrugged distractedly and started to examine the dead man's head in minute detail. He quickly discovered other oddities. There were tiny green shoots in the hair, growing from the scalp, and a tangle of withered white roots issuing from the flesh behind both ears.

"I don't know what to make of it," he said, rising to his feet, "but whatever this plant growing out of him is, it's as dead as Pimlico. What else did he have in his pockets?"

Trounce went through the items. "Keys, a few shillings, a box of lucifers, a pipe and pouch of shag tobacco, a pencil, and a 'bus ticket."

"From where?"

"Leeds. Let's search the room."

Swinburne looked on from the landing as the two men went over the chamber inch by inch. They discovered a small suitcase under the bed but it contained only clothes. No other possessions were found.

"Nothing to tell us who the foreigner might be," Trounce ruminated. "And no clue as to where Pimlico lived in Leeds."

"There's this," Burton said. He held out the tobacco pouch—the brand was Ogden's Flake—with the flap open. On the inside, an address was printed in blue ink: *Tattleworth Tobacconist, 26 Meanwood Road, Leeds.*

"If this is his local supplier, perhaps the proprietor will know him."

"Humph!" Trounce grunted. "Well, that's something, anyway. Let's wait for the constable, then we'll leg it back to Fryston. There are plenty of rotor-chairs there—I'll commandeer one. It'll be close on dawn by the time I get to Leeds. No sleep for me tonight!"

"Nor for me," Burton said. "I'm coming with you."

"And so am I," Swinburne added.

Some minutes later, footsteps sounded on the stairs and a young policeman appeared, looking somewhat dishevelled and unshaven. Mr. Emery lurked behind him.

"There hasn't really been murder done, has there?" the constable blurted. He saw Pimlico's body. "Blimey! In Thorpe Willoughby! And who are you gentlemen, if you'll pardon my asking?"

"I'm Detective Inspector Trounce of Scotland Yard. This is His Majesty's agent, Sir Richard Francis Burton, and his assistant, Mr. Algernon Swinburne. To whom do you report, lad?"

"To Commissioner Sheridan in Leeds."

Trounce spoke rapidly: "Very well. I want you to wake up your local postmaster and get a message to the commissioner. Inform him that this chap—his name was Peter Pimlico—was strangled to death by an as yet unidentified foreigner. Then get the county coroner to call first at Fryston, then here to take care of business. I'll report to Commissioner Sheridan myself, later this morning."

"Yes, sir. Fryston, sir? Why so?"

"Because this scoundrel—" Trounce gave Pimlico's corpse a disdainful glance, "—poisoned to death a guest there."

Constable Flanagan gaped, swallowed, then saluted.

"What about me?" Emery grumbled. "Can I get back to me bleedin' bed?"

Trounce snorted. "If you think you can sleep with a corpse in the house, by all means. First, though, tell me—when did Pimlico start renting this room?"

"Five days ago."

"Did he receive any visitors before tonight?"

"Nope."

"What did he do while he was here?"

"Got drunk in the local boozer, mostly."

"Did he cause you any trouble?"

"Not so much as he's bleedin' well caused since he kicked the bucket! He just thumped up an' down the stairs when he was comin' an' goin', that's all."

"Were there any letters delivered for him?"

"Nope."

"Do you know anything about him?"

"Nope, 'cept he said he was here to get work with Howell's agency."

"Nothing else?"

"Nothin'."

A few minutes later, Trounce, Burton, Swinburne, and Fidget were retracing their steps to Monckton Milnes's place. Glancing back at Thorpe Willoughby, Swinburne noted that the trail of steam had almost vanished.

"Which direction to Leeds?" he asked.

"West," Trounce answered.

"Our strangler flew south. I wonder why he killed Pimlico?"

"Perhaps to stop him talking," Burton said. "I'm certain I've never encountered him before, so I doubt he had any personal motive for doing away with me. I rather think he was hired to do it by our mysterious foreigner. He probably expected to be paid and assisted in escaping from the area tonight. Instead, he was killed."

"Ruthless," Swinburne muttered, "although I can't say he didn't deserve his fate, the bounder! But what of the strange growth?"

"That," Burton said, "is a much bigger mystery. It seems unlikely that it was in his mouth earlier this evening, while he was playing waiter at Fryston. Such a rapidly growing monstrosity smells to me of the Eugenicists and the botanist Richard Spruce."

They reached Fryston and found that a great many of the guests had already departed, despite the hour.

"I've sealed off the music room," Monckton Milnes reported. "Poor Bendyshe will have to stay there until someone comes for him."

"The coroner is on his way," Burton reported. "May I ask a couple of favours of you?"

"Of course, anything I can do."

"We need to borrow three rotorchairs. We have to fly to Leeds immediately."

"Take mine, Jim Hunt's, and Charlie Bradlaugh's. They're on the front lawn. I'll walk you to them."

"Thank you. I presume Mrs. Angell has gone to bed?"

"Yes. I gave her one of my best guest rooms."

"Would you ask Captain Lawless to accompany her and Fidget to the airfield in the morning? Trounce, Algy, and I will have to fly there directly from Leeds. We'll see to it that the rotorchairs are delivered back to you later in the day."

"I'll take her myself, Richard. I want to see you off."

Monckton Milnes escorted his friends out of the house and to a group of flying machines parked in the grounds. As they walked, he pulled Burton back a little from Swinburne and Trounce and whispered, "Has this any connection with your mission to Africa?"

Burton shrugged. "I don't know. It's certainly possible, maybe even probable."

They reached the rotorchairs and Monckton Milnes watched as the three men placed their hats in the storage boxes, put goggles over their eyes, and buckled themselves into the big leather seats.

"See you later, chaps," he said. "And best of luck!"

They started their engines, which belched out clouds of steam. Above their heads, blade-like wings unfolded from vertical shafts and began to spin, rotating faster and faster until they became invisible to the eye.

Burton gave his friend a wave, then pulled back on a lever. The runners of his machine lifted from the grass and it rose rapidly on a cone of vapour. Swinburne and Trounce followed, and the three rotorchairs arced away and vanished into the night sky, leaving silvery white trails behind them.

An orange glow lit the eastern sky as three flying machines descended onto the cobbles of Black Brewery Road. Two of them touched the ground gently; the third hit it with a thump and skewed sideways for five feet amid a shower of sparks before coming to rest.

"Ridiculous bloody contraptions!" Trounce cursed. He turned off the engine, waited for the wings to fold, then disembarked and joined Burton and Swinburne.

It was their third landing in Leeds. The first had been to ask a constable on his night beat for directions. The second had been outside the Tattleworth Tobacconist on Meanwood Road.

Mr. Tattleworth, swearing volubly at his rude awakening, had eventually confirmed that he knew Peter Pimlico.

"A bloody thief," he'd said. "What you might call a denizen of the underworld. But a regular customer. Lives a couple o' streets away. Number seventeen Black Brewery Road."

They could have walked, but, preferring to keep their vehicles in sight, they took off and almost immediately landed again.

"It's this one," Swinburne said, pointing at a terrace. "Let's see how many profanities our next customer can spit at us!" He reached for the door knocker and banged it with gusto.

After a couple of minutes and a second attack on the door, a gruff and muffled voice came from behind it.

"Oo's thah?"

"Police," Trounce barked.

"Prove 'tis!"

"I have credentials," Trounce said impatiently. "Open up and I'll show you."

"Ah durn't believe thee. 'Tis a trick. Thou b'ain't no trapper. A tallyman, more like!"

Swinburne squealed. "Ha-ha! Tallyman Trounce!"

"Oo were thah?" came the voice.

"Algernon Swinburne!" Swinburne called. "The poet!"

There was a moment of silence, then the voice said, "Ah durn't need owt pottery fro' thee! Be off an' durn't come bah!"

"Sir!" Trounce bellowed. "Open the blasted door this very moment or I'll kick the damned thing in!"

The rattle of a chain sounded and a key turned in the lock. The door opened a crack and a rheumy eye peered out.

"Wah durst thou want? Ah aren't dressed. Am havin' us mornin' pipe."

"Does Peter Pimlico live here?" Trounce demanded.

"Aye. In t' flat upstairs. Ee durn't be in. Not fur'n week."

"I know. He's dead."

"Huh?"

"He was murdered earlier tonight."

"Good. Ee were a dirty oik an nowt else. So?"

"So we're here to search his rooms. Let us in."

The eye took in Trounce from his bowler hat to his police-issue boots, then flicked to Burton and examined his swarthy and scarred face and broad shoulders, then down to Swinburne, who stood with laurel leaves tangled in his long bright-red hair, which was sticking out wildly after the flight from Fryston.

"A poet wit' trappers?"

"Police pottery," Swinburne said. "Ceramics Squad. Stand aside, please!"

Trounce put his shoulder to the door and pushed, sending the man behind it reeling backward. "What's your name?" he demanded, stepping into the house.

The man, who would have been tall were it not for his rickets-twisted legs, stood shivering in his striped nightshirt. He was wearing a nightcap over his straggly brown hair and bed socks on his large feet. There was a hole in the left one and his big toe was poking out. A smoking corncob pipe was clutched in his gnarled hand.

"Ah be Matthew Keller. Thou can't barge int' us 'ouse like this!"

"Yes, I can. It's your premises? You're the owner?"

"Aye. Get thee out o' it!"

"Not yet. So you rent the upstairs to Pimlico, is that right?"

"Uh-huh, an' ah be glad t' be rid o' 'im, t' good-fer-nowt bastard."

"Trouble, was he?"

"Aye! Alweez drunk n' thievin'."

"Any visits from foreign gentlemen?"

"T'week past. Fat, ee were."

"Name?"

"Durn't knah."

"Nationality?"

"Durn't knah."

"Walrus moustache?"

"Aye. Now then, ah 'ave t' get dressed fr' work."

"You'll do nothing without my leave. We're going up to Pimlico's rooms."

"They be locked."

"Do you have a master key?"

"Aye."

"So get it!"

Keller sighed impatiently.

"Jump to it, man!" Trounce exploded.

The householder flinched, then moved to the rear of the small hallway, opened a door beneath the staircase, and took a key from a hook. He returned and passed it to the detective.

Trounce started up the stairs and Swinburne followed. As he passed Burton, who stepped up after him, the king's agent noticed that his assistant's grin had quickly faded.

By nature, Swinburne's emotions were as fiery and wild as his hair, always changing rapidly, never consistent, and often entirely inappropriate. The poet was subject to a physiological condition that caused him to feel pain as pleasure, and, it seemed to Burton, this might be the origin of his quirky, unpredictable character. Emotional hurt, such as that caused by Bendyshe's demise, became internalised and concealed behind wayward behaviour, which, unfortunately, frequently involved the consumption of copious amounts of alcohol. Swinburne's inability to judge what might harm him made him one of the bravest men Burton had ever met, but also one of the most dangerously self-destructive.

"Follow us, Mr. Keller," Trounce called. "I want to keep my eye on you."

Keller protested, "Us an't gon' t' do nowt," but mounted the stairs behind his unwelcome visitors and struggled up, groaning at the effort. "Legs," he complained. "Bad all us life."

Pimlico's flat consisted of a bed-sitting room and a kitchen. It stank of rancid lard and bacon and hadn't been cleaned in a long time. Threadbare clothes were scattered over the floor. A porcelain washbasin, containing dirty water and with a thick line of grime around its inner edge, stood on a dressing table in front of a cracked mirror. There was a cutthroat razor and a soiled bar of soap beside it. The sagging bed was unmade, a chair was piled with betting slips from the local dog track, and issues of the *Leeds Enquirer* were stacked beneath the window.

Swinburne and Keller hung back while Burton and Trounce went over the rooms.

"Notebook!" the Scotland Yard man exclaimed, lifting a small bound volume from the bed. He flicked through it, page by page. "Nothing but odds on dogs. He was a gambler, this Pimlico fellow."

"Ee were a loser," Keller said. "Lost every bleedin' penny ee earned. Nearly alweez late wit' rent."

"How was he employed?" Burton asked.

"At t' Pride-Manushi factory, packagin' velocipede parts what they send to salesrooms o'er in Coventry. But ee was laid off a fortnight since, after ee got nabbed fr' thievin'."

Burton's eyebrows arched. "What happened?"

"Ee climbed through t' window at Cat n' Fiddle, skanked a couple o' bottles o' whisky, an' jumped straight out int' arms o' trappers. Spent a night in clink."

Trounce frowned. "Just one night? After breaking into a public house?"

"Aye."

"Where was he held?"

"Farrow Lane Police Station."

Some minutes later, the detective inspector called to Burton, who was searching the kitchen: "Captain, your opinion, please."

Trounce pointed down at the bare floorboards near the window. Burton stepped over, looked, and saw a small glob of something blackish and fibrous. He squatted, took a pencil from his pocket, scraped its end in the dried-up substance, then raised it to his nose.

He winced in disgust. "Stinks of tooth decay—and something else. Mr. Keller, did Pimlico use chewing tobacco?"

"Nah. Ee smurked Ogden's Flake, same as what ah does."

Burton stood and addressed Trounce. "I've made a study of tobacco odours. I'm certain this is Kautabak, a Prussian brand. Not widely available in England."

"And you think it was left by the foreigner? Our murderer is Germanic?"

"I suspect exactly that, yes."

They spent another twenty minutes searching but found nothing of any further use.

"Well then," Trounce said, "we'll take our leave of you, Mr. Keller."

"Aye, an' ah'll not be sad t' see thee go," the householder muttered.

As they descended the stairs, he added, "Ee were expectin' t' come int' brass, ee were."

Trounce stopped. "What?"

"Pimlico. Ee were expectin' brass—were goin' t' pay me what ee owed in rent, or so ee said."

"Money? From where?"

"Durn't knah."

Outside the house, the Yard man looked up at the sky, which was now a pale overcast grey.

"As from today I'm officially on extended leave," he said, "but I'll be damned if I'll leave this alone." He turned to Burton and Swinburne. "Next stop, Farrow Lane. I want to know why Pimlico was released."

They climbed back into their vehicles and took to the air. Once again, they had to search for a constable to give them directions. Fifteen minutes later, they landed outside the police station and Burton and Swinburne waited in their vehicles while Trounce entered to make his enquiries. He was gone for twenty minutes, during which time the poet discussed his latest project, *Atlanta in Calydon*, with his friend.

"I'm moved to heighten the atheist sentiment by way of a tribute to old Bendyshe," he said. "He was determined to drive the last nails into the coffin that Darwin built for God."

"Tom would have appreciated that," Burton responded. "For all his larking around, he never had anything but praise for you, Algy, and he adored your poetry. He was one of your most dedicated advocates."

An uncharacteristic hardness came to the poet's eyes. "Do you remember me once telling you about how, in my youth, I wanted to be a cavalry officer?"

"Yes. Your father wouldn't allow it, so you climbed Culver Cliff on the Isle of Wight to prove to yourself that you possess courage."

"That's right, Richard. And at one point, I hung from that rock face by my fingertips, and I wasn't afraid. Since that occasion, I have never once shirked a challenge, no matter how dangerous. I don't baulk at the idea of warfare; of engaging with the enemy; of fighting for a principle. As a poet, my roots are deeply embedded in conflict."

"What's your point, Algy?"

"My point is this: as of now, I'm on a mission of vengeance."

The Royal Naval Air Service Station was situated some twenty miles east of Fryston. It had originally been established for the building of dirigibles, an endeavour the Technologists had abandoned after a sequence of disastrous crashes and explosions. Those failures had led to the development of rotating-wing flight mechanics, and a breathtaking example of that particular form of engineering ingenuity currently dominated the largest of the station's landing fields.

HMA *Orpheus* was the most colossal rotorship Sir Richard Francis Burton had ever seen. Side-on, she appeared long and flat, two decks high, with a humped cargo hold slightly to the rear of centre, a conning tower at the front, and a glass-enclosed observation deck occupying her pointed prow. Eight flight pylons extended from either side of her—a total of sixteen, which made her the most powerful rotorship ever constructed.

Most of the crew and passengers were already aboard, ready for the short trip to London. Burton, Swinburne—sans laurel wreath—Captain Lawless, and Detective Inspector Trounce stood at the base of the boarding ramp, bidding farewell to Monckton Milnes and Sir Richard Mayne. The latter, nervous of flying, had opted to ride the atmospheric railway to the capital later in the week.

"So the fat Prussian bailed Pimlico out," Trounce told the police commissioner. "He gave his name as Otto Steinrück, and an Essex address."

Swinburne added, "Probably false."

"No," Trounce said. "The address had to be verified before his bail could be accepted. It exists and it's registered in his name."

"You're off duty now, Detective Inspector," Mayne said, "but if you want to pursue this in an official capacity during what little time you have left before your departure, then you have my permission."

"I would, and thank you, sir."

Mayne nodded, then looked up at the ship. "What a monster!" he exclaimed.

"The first of a new breed," Lawless told him. "Mr. Brunel surpassed himself with this one!"

"And she'll take you all the way along the Nile?"

"Unfortunately, no."

Burton said, "Mechanical devices refuse to function in the Lake Regions, Chief Commissioner. Some sort of emanation prevents it. Henry Morton Stanley's rotorchairs were found there, and their engines were as dead as a doornail. We fear that if the *Orpheus* flew too close she'd drop like a stone, and since we have no clear idea of where the zone begins, we have little choice but to go in on foot."

"Besides which," Lawless added, "this ship sacrifices economy for speed, so she'll need to stop for fuel, which can't be done in Central Africa."

"So what's your route?" Monckton Milnes asked.

"Our first leg is London to Cairo," Lawless replied, "the second Cairo to Aden, then we'll fly to our final stop, Zanzibar, where the collier ship *Blackburn* awaits us with a hold full of coal. The expedition will disembark, we'll refuel, offload the vehicles and supplies on the mainland, and head home."

Burton added, "A hundred and fifty Wanyamwezi porters have been hired in Zanzibar and are already making their way inland with supplies purchased on the island. They'll deliver the goods to a village in the Dut'humi Hills and will await our arrival. When we get there, they'll be paid and fresh porters from the nearby Mgota tribes will be hired. We'll then push on and, hopefully, will reach Kazeh before we have to abandon the vehicles. From there, we'll hike north to the Lake Regions and the Mountains of the Moon."

Lawless said, "Well, chaps, we'll never achieve any of that if we don't get under way, so I'd better check that my ship is flight ready. We'll be off in ten minutes. I'll leave you to say your goodbyes." He gave a nod to Mayne and Monckton Milnes, touched a finger to the peak of his cap, and walked up the ramp and into the *Orpheus*.

Sir Richard Mayne drew Trounce aside and engaged him in a quiet conversation.

Monckton Milnes grasped Swinburne's hand and gave it a hearty shake. "Good luck, young 'un," he said. "You stay safe, do you hear me?"

"Perfectly well, old horse," Swinburne replied. "Don't you fret about me. I'll be fine. I'm too slight a morsel for a lion or crocodile to bother with, and I plan to keep myself soaked in gin to fend off the mosquitoes."

"Good lad! I look forward to some inspired poetry upon your return."

Swinburne caught Mayne's eye, gave him a salute, and boarded the ship.

"Are you sure he's up to it, Richard?" Monckton Milnes asked Burton. "As much as I admire him, he's the very last person I'd expect to be trekking through Africa."

Burton gave a wry smile. "You know as well as I do that he's far from the delicate flower he appears. He's a tough little blighter and I need his insight into the Nāga business. Anyway, he'd never forgive me if I left him behind."

"And you? What of your health? Last time you tried for the Nile you were blinded and crippled for months on end."

"True, but mostly because John Speke was pouring huge doses of Saltzmann's Tincture into me. But that aside, we have Sister Raghavendra with us. That should make a considerable difference to our well-being."

Monckton Milnes nodded thoughtfully. "The Sisterhood of Noble Benevolence is a confoundedly strange organisation. I've never understood how they move around the East End without coming to harm. You know there's a rumour they possess some sort of supernatural grace that protects them?"

"I've heard as much, yes. It may be that their ability to heal and soothe is, indeed, supernatural. Perhaps it's another effect of the resonance from the Nāga diamonds. Whatever the explanation, I'm sure she'll prove a most valuable member of the expedition." Burton looked up at the grey sky. "Africa again," he muttered. "Maybe this time—"

"You aren't obliged to put yourself through it, Richard," Monckton Milnes interrupted. "Palmerston can find other pawns for his chess game."

"For certain. But it's not just the diamond business. I want the Nile. Every day, I ask myself, 'Why?' and the only echo is, 'Damned fool! The devil drives!' That bloody continent has been shaping my life for nigh on a decade and I feel, instinctively, that it hasn't finished with me yet."

"Then go," said Monckton Milnes. "But Richard—"

"Yes?"

"Come back."

"I'll do my level best. Listen, old chap, on the subject of Palmerston, there's something you might do for me while I'm away."

"Anything."

"I'd like you to keep an eye on him. Follow, especially, his foreign policies with regard to Prussia, the other Germanic states, and Africa. You are one of the most politically astute men I know, and you have a plethora of friends in high places. Use them. When I return, I'll need you to give me an idea of which way the wind is blowing where our international relations are concerned."

"You think he's up to something?"

"Always."

Monckton Milnes promised to do everything he could.

They shook hands and bade each other farewell.

Detective Inspector Trounce returned and joined Burton on the gangplank.

With a final wave to their colleagues, the two men entered the rotorship.

The great swathe of the world's territory that Britain had once controlled was still referred to, in its final days, as the Empire, even though there'd been no British monarch since the death of Albert in 1900. "The King's African Rifles" was a misnomer for the same reason. Traditions die hard for the British, especially in the Army.

Two thousand of the KAR, led by sixty-two English officers, had set up camp at Ponde, a village about six miles to the south of Dar es Salaam and four miles behind the trenches that stretched around the city from the coast in the northwest to the coast in the southeast. Ponde's original beehive huts were buried somewhere deep in a sea of khaki tents, and their Uzaramo inhabitants—there were fewer than a hundred and fifty of them—had been recruited against their will as servants and porters. Mostly, they dealt with the ignominy by staying as drunk as possible, by running away when they could, or, in a few cases, by committing suicide.

Perhaps the only, if not happy, then at least satisfied villager was the man who brewed *pombe*—African beer—who'd set up a shack beneath a thicket of mangrove trees from which to sell the warm but surprisingly pleasant beverage. The shady area had been furnished with tables and chairs, and thus was born a mosquito-infested tavern of sorts. *No Askaris permitted! Officers and civilians only!*

It was eleven in the morning, and the individual who now thought of himself as Sir Richard Francis Burton was sitting at one of the tables. It was an oppressively humid day and the temperature was rising. The sky was a tear-inducing white. The air was thick with flies.

He'd refused *pombe*—it was far too early—and had been provided with a mug of tea instead, which sat steaming in front of him. His left forearm was bandaged. Beneath the dressing there was a deep laceration, held together by seven stitches. His face, now more fully bearded, was cut and bruised. A deep gash, scabbed and puckered, split his right eyebrow.

He dropped four cubes of sugar into his drink and stirred it, gazing fixedly at the swirling liquid.

His hands were shaking.

"There you are!" came a high-pitched exclamation. "Drink up. We have to get going."

He raised his eyes and found Bertie Wells standing beside him. The war correspondent, who looked much shorter and stouter in broad daylight, was leaning on crutches and his right calf was encased in a splint.

"Hello, old thing," Burton said. "Take the weight off. How is it?"

Wells remained standing. "As broken as it was yesterday and the day before. Do you know, I snapped the same bally leg when I was seven years old? You were still alive back then."

"I'm still alive now. Get going to where?"

"Up onto the ridge so we can watch the bombing. The ships should be here within the hour."

"Can you manage it? The walk?"

Wells flicked a mosquito from his neck. "I'm becoming a proficient hobbler. Would you do me a favour, Sir Richard? Next time I pontificate about the unlikelihood of a direct hit, will you strike me violently about the head and drag me clear of the area?"

"I'll be more than happy to. Even retrospectively."

"I must say, though, I thoroughly enjoyed the irony of it."

"Irony?"

"Yes. You affirm that you are quite impossibly in the land of the living, and seconds later, you almost aren't!"

"Ah, yes. Henceforth, I shall choose my words with a little more care. I did not at all enjoy being bombed and buried alive. And please drop the 'Sir.' Plain old 'Richard' is sufficient." He took a gulp of tea and stood up. "Shall we go and watch the fireworks, then?"

They left the makeshift tavern and began to move slowly through the tents, passing empty-eyed and slack-faced soldiers, and heading toward the northern border of the encampment.

The air smelled of sweat—and worse.

"Look at them," Wells said. "Have you ever seen such a heterogeneous throng of fighting men? They've been recruited from what's left of the British South Africans, from Australia and India, from the ragtag remains of our European forces, and from all the diverse tribes of East and Central Africa."

"They don't look at all happy about it."

"This isn't an easy country, as you know better than most. Dysentery, malaria, tsetse flies, mosquitoes, jigger fleas—the majority of the white men are as sick as dogs. As for the Africans, they're all serial deserters. There should be double the number of soldiers you see here."

They passed alongside a pen of oxen. One of the animals was lying dead, its carcass stinking and beginning to swell.

"Do you have a thing about poppies?" Wells asked. "You pulled one from your pocket just before we got bombed, and now I see you have a fresh one pinned to your lapel."

"I think—I have a feeling—that is to say—the flower seems as if it should mean something."

"I believe it symbolises sleep—or death," Wells responded.

"No, not that," Burton said. "Something else, but I can't put my finger on it."

"So you're still having trouble with your memory, then? I was hoping it'd returned. As you might imagine, I've been beside myself with curiosity these past few days. I have so many questions to ask."

"Odd scraps of it are back," Burton replied. "It's a peculiar sensation. I feel thoroughly disassembled. I'll submit to your interrogation, but if you manage to get anything out of me, you must keep it to yourself."

"I have little choice. If I publicised the fact that you're alive, my editor would laugh me right out of the news office and straight into the European Resistance, from which I'd never be seen again." Wells jerked his head, coughed, and spat. "These bloody flies! They're all over me! The moment I open my mouth, there's always one eager to buzz into it!" He saluted a passing officer, then said, "So what happened? Did some quirk of nature render you immortal, Richard? Did you fake your own death in 1890?"

"No. I have the impression that I came here directly from the year 1863."

"What? You stepped straight from three years before I was born into the here and now? By what means?"

"I don't know."

"Then why?"

"I don't know that, either. I'm not even sure which future this is."

"Which future? What on earth does that mean?"

"Again, I don't know—but I feel sure there are alternatives."

Wells shook his head. "My goodness. The impossibilities are accumulating. Yet here you are."

"Here I am," Burton agreed.

"An anachronic man," Wells muttered. He stopped to adjust his crutches.

Moans emerged from a nearby tent, its inhabitant obviously wracked by fever. The sound of his misery was drowned out as a group of Askaris filed past, singing a mournful song. Burton listened, fascinated by their deep voices, and was able to identify the language as Kichagga, a dialect of

Kiswahili, which suggested the men were from the Chagga tribes that originated in the north, from the lands below the Kilima Njaro mountain.

They were far from home.

So was he.

"I once discussed the possibility of journeying through time with young Huxley," Wells said, as the two of them got moving again. "It was his assertion that no method would ever be invented, for, if it were, then surely we'd have been overrun by visitors from the future. It didn't occur to either of us that they'd actually come from the past. You say you don't know how it was achieved? But was it through mechanical means or a—I don't know—a mental technique?"

"I have no idea. Who's Huxley?"

"A boy I was acquainted with. He had a prodigious intellect, though he was almost entirely blind and hardly out of short trousers. He was killed when the Hun destroyed London. I don't understand, Richard—how could movement through time have been possible in the 1860s yet remain a secret today?"

"My guess is that—that—that—wait—who is—was—is Palmerston?"

"Pah! That villain! In your day, he was prime minister."

"Yes!" Burton cried. "Yes! I remember now! He had a face like a waxwork!"

"What about him?"

"I think he might have suppressed the fact that the boundaries of time can be breached."

"The devil you say! I should have known! That wily old goat! Does he know you're here?"

"Not to my knowledge."

"Maybe my editor would help you to contact him."

"I have no means of sending a communiqué into the past."

"I mean now, here in 1914."

Burton exclaimed, "Surely you don't mean to suggest that he's still alive?"

"Ah. You didn't know. Yes, he's with us. Famously so. Or perhaps 'notoriously so' would be a more accurate assessment. He's a hundred and thirty years old!"

"Bismillah!" Burton gasped. "Palmerston! Alive! Is he still prime minister?"

"No, of course not. There's been no such thing since the Germans overran Europe. And let me tell you: few men who ever lived have had as much blood on their hands as Palmerston. He called us to war. We were making the future, he said, and hardly any of us troubled to think what future we were making." Wells waved his hand at the tents that surrounded them. "Behold!"

Burton looked puzzled. "But there's more than this, surely? What of the Empire?"

Wells stopped in his tracks. "Richard," he said quietly. "You have to understand. This is it."

"It?"

"All that remains. The men commanding these two battalions of Askaris, plus perhaps three thousand in the British Indian Expeditionary Force, scattered groups of soldiers around the Lake Regions, maybe twenty thousand civilians and Technologists in our stronghold at Tabora, and whatever's left of the British European Resistance—there's nothing else."

Burton looked shocked. "This is the Empire? What in heaven's name happened?"

"As I told you before, it all began here. By the 1870s, despite the efforts of Al-Manat, the German presence in Africa was growing. Palmerston was convinced that Bismarck intended a full-scale invasion. He believed that Germany was seeking to establish an empire as big as ours, so he posted a couple of battalions over here to prevent that from happening. The Hun responded by arming the natives, setting them against us. The conflict escalated. Palmerston sent more and more soldiers. Then, in 1900, Germany suddenly mobilised all its forces, including its Eugenicist weapons—but not here. It turns out that Bismarck never wanted Africa. He wanted Europe. France fell, then Belgium, then Denmark, then Austria–Hungary, then Serbia. The devastation was horrific. Britain fought wildly for five years, but our Army was divided. Almost a third of it was here, and when they tried to get home, Germany blockaded all the African ports. My God, what a consummate tactician Bismarck was! We didn't stand a chance. Then he gained Russia as an ally, and we were conquered. India, Australia, South Africa, and the West Indies all quickly declared their independence, British North America fell to a native and slave uprising, and the Empire disintegrated."

Burton sent a breath whistling through his teeth. "And Palmerston was to blame?"

"Completely. His foreign policy was misjudged in the extreme. No one really understands why he was so obsessed with Africa. A great many Britishers have called for him to be tried and executed. After all, it's not reasonable that those who gamble with men's lives should not pay with their own, and he was the greatest gambler of them all. But Crowley insists that he should be kept alive—that, somehow, the survival of Tabora, the last British city, depends on him."

They reached an area where the tents thinned out and row after row of Mark II Scorpion Tanks were parked, hunkered down on their legs, claws tucked in, tails curled up.

Burton noted that, though the war machines' design was new to him, the technology appeared to have advanced little since his own age.

"Let's rest again for a moment," Wells said. "This bloody leg is giving me gyp."

"All right."

Burton leaned against one of the arachnids and batted a fly from his face.

Memories were stirring. He was trying to recall the last time he'd met Lord Palmerston.

Shut the hell up, Burton! Am I to endure your insolence every time we meet? I'll not tolerate it! You have your orders! Do your bloody job, Captain!

The prime minister's voice echoed in a remote chamber of his mind but he was unable to associate it with any specific occasion.

"So he's at Tabora?" he asked.

"Palmerston? Yes. He's kept under house arrest there. I find it incredible that he still has supporters, but he does—my editor for one—so it's unlikely he'll go before the firing squad, as he deserves. You know he buggered up the constitution, too?"

"How so?"

"When he manipulated the Regency Act back in 1840 to ensure that Albert took the throne instead of Ernest Augustus of Hanover, he left no provision for what might happen afterward—no clear rules of succession for when Albert died. Ha! In 1900, I, like a great many others, was a staunch republican, so when the king finally kicked the bucket, I was happy to hear calls for the monarchy to be dismantled. Of course, equally vociferous voices were raised against the idea. Things got rather heated, and I, being a journalist, got rather too involved. There was public disorder, and I'm afraid I might have egged it on a little. When a man gets caught up in history, Richard, he loses sight of himself. Anyway, Palmerston was distracted, and that's when Bismarck pounced. I feel a fool now. In times of war, figureheads become necessary for morale. I should have realised that, but I was an idealist back then. I even believed the human race capable of building Utopia. Ha! Idiot!"

They slouched against the machines for a couple more minutes, the humidity weighing down on them, then resumed their trek, moving away from the tanks and up a gentle slope toward the ridge. The ground was dry, cracked, and dusty, with tufts of elephant grass standing in isolated clumps. There were also large stretches of blackened earth—"Where carnivorous plants have been burned away," Wells explained. "At least we're not due the calamity of rain for a few more weeks. The moment a single drop touches the soil, the bloody plants spring up again."

The Indian Ocean, a glittering turquoise line, lay far off to their right, while to their left, the peaks of the Usagara Highlands shimmered and rippled on the horizon.

"But let us not be diverted from our topic," Wells said. "I'm trying to recall your biographies. If I remember rightly, in 1859 you returned from your unsuccessful expedition to find the source of the Nile and more or less retreated from the public eye to work on various books, including your translation of *The Arabian Nights*, which, may I add, was a simply splendid achievement."

"*The Book of a Thousand Nights and a Night*," Burton corrected. "Thank you, but please say no more about it. I've not completed the damned thing yet. At least, I don't think I have."

He helped his companion past a fallen tree that was swarming with white ants and muttered, "It's odd you say that, though, about my search for the source of the Nile. The moment you mentioned it, I remembered it, but I feel sure I made a second attempt."

"I don't think so. It certainly isn't recorded. The fountains of the Nile were discovered by—"

Burton stopped him. "No! Don't tell me! I don't want to know. If I really am from 1863, and I return to it, perhaps I'll rewrite that particular item of history."

"You think you might get back to your own time? How?"

Burton shrugged.

"But isn't it obvious you won't?" Wells objected. "Otherwise we wouldn't be having this conversation, for you'd surely do something to prevent this war from ever happening."

"Ah, Bertie, there's the paradox," Burton answered. "If I go back and achieve what your history says I never achieved, you'll still be here, aware that I never did it. However, I will now exist in a time where I did. And in my future there'll be a Herbert George Wells who knows it."

"Wait! Wait! I'm struggling to wrap my brain around that!"

"I agree—it's a strain on the grey matter, especially if, like mine, it's as full of holes as a Swiss cheese. These days, I hear myself speak but have barely a notion of what I'm talking about."

Burton pulled a handkerchief from his pocket and wiped the sweat from the back of his neck. "But something tells me that if you go back into the past and make an alteration, then a whole new sequence of events will spring from it, establishing an ever-widening divergence from what had been the original course of history."

Wells whistled. "Yet that original has to still exist, for it's where you travelled back from."

"Precisely."

"So existence has been split into two by your act."

"Apparently."

"How godlike, the chronic argonaut," Wells mused.

"The what?"

"Hum. Just thinking out loud."

They joined a small group of officers who'd gathered at the top of the ridge. Wells indicated one of them and whispered, "That's General Aitken. He's in charge of this whole operation."

Burton tugged at his khaki uniform jacket, which he considered far too heavy for the climate. He felt smothered and uncomfortable. Perspiration was running into his eyes. He rubbed them. As they readjusted, the vista that sprawled beneath him swam into focus, and all his irritations were instantly forgotten.

Seen through the distorting lens of Africa's blistering heat, Dar es Salaam appeared to undulate and quiver like a mirage. It was a small white city, clinging to the shore of a natural harbour. Grand colonial buildings humped up from its centre and were clustered around the port—in which a German light cruiser was docked—while a tall metal structure towered above the western neighbourhoods. Otherwise, the settlement was very flat, with single-storey dwellings strung along tree-lined dirt roads and around the borders of small outlying farms.

A strip of tangled greenery surrounded the municipality—"They look small from here, but those are the artillery plants," Wells observed—and beyond them, the German trenches crisscrossed the terrain up to a second band of foliage: the red weed. The British trenches occupied the space between the weed and the ridge.

Like a punch to the head, Burton suddenly recalled the Crimea, for, as in that terrible conflict, the earth here had been torn, gouged, and overturned by shells. Flooded by heavy rains some weeks ago, the horrible landscape before him had since been baked into distorted shapes by the relentless sunshine. It was also saturated with blood and peppered with chunks of rotting human and animal flesh, and the stench assailed Burton's nostrils from even this distance. Bits of smashed machinery rose from the churned ground like disinterred bones. It was unnatural. It was hideous. It was sickening.

He unhooked his canteen from his belt, took a swig of water, and spat dust from his mouth.

"That's our target," said Wells, pointing at the metal tower. "If we can bring it down, we'll destroy their radio communications."

"Radio?" Burton asked.

Wells smiled. "Well I never! How queer to meet a man who isn't familiar with something that everyone else takes for granted! But, of course, it was after your time, wasn't it!"

Burton glanced uneasily at the nearby officers, who were peering at the sea through binoculars.

"Keep your voice down, please, Bertie," he said. "And what was after my time?"

"The discovery of radio waves. The technique by which we transmit spoken words and other sounds through the atmosphere to literally anywhere in the world."

"A mediumistic procedure?"

"Not at all. It's similar to the telegraph but without the wires. It involves the modulation of oscillating electromagnetic fields."

"That's all mumbo jumbo to me. What are they looking at?"

Wells turned to observe the officers, then raised his binoculars and followed the men's gaze.

"Ah ha!" he said. "The rotorships! Have a squint."

He passed the binoculars to Burton, who put them to his eyes and scanned the eastern sky, near the horizon, until two dark dots came into view. As they approached, he saw they were big rotorships, each with twelve flight pylons, wings spinning at the top of the tall shafts. The black flat-bottomed vessels were rather more domed in shape than those from his own time, and he could see guns poking out of portholes along their sides.

"*Astraea* and *Pegasus*," Wells said. "Cruiser class. The *Pegasus* is the one on the right."

"They're fast. What are those little things flying around them?"

"Hornets. One-man fighters. They'll swoop in to shoot at the ground defences."

"Actual insects?"

"Yes. The usual routine. Breed 'em big, kill 'em, scrape 'em out, shove steam engines into the carapaces. The method hasn't changed since your day. Look out! The *Königsberg* is bringing her cannon to bear!"

Burton directed the glasses to the city's harbour and saw that the decks of the seagoing vessel were swarming with men. A gun turret, positioned in front of its three funnels, was turning to face the oncoming rotorships. A few moments later, orange light blazed from the muzzle. Repetitive booms, lagging a few seconds behind the discharges, rippled out over the landscape, becoming thin and echoey as they faded away.

He looked back at the rotorships, both almost upon the city now. Puffs of black smoke were exploding around them.

Hornets dived down at the light cruiser and raked her decks with their machine guns.

"Come on, lads!" Wells cheered.

Burton watched men ripped into tatters and knocked overboard as bullets tore into them. A loud report sounded. He lowered the binoculars and saw that metal and smoke had erupted from the side of the *Pegasus*.

"She's hit!" Wells cried.

The rotorship listed to her left. As her shadow passed over the *Königsberg*, small objects spilled from beneath her. They were bombs. With an ear-splitting roar, the German vessel disappeared into a ball of fire and smoke. Fragments of hull plating went spinning skyward. Another huge detonation sounded as the ship's munitions went up.

The *Pegasus*, rocked by the shock wave, keeled completely over onto her side and arced toward the ground. She hit the southern neighbourhoods of Dar es Salaam and ploughed through them, disintegrating, until, when she finally came to rest, she was nothing but an unrecognisable knot of twisted and tattered metal slumped at the end of a long burning furrow. Hundreds of buildings had been destroyed, maybe thousands of lives lost.

Wells opened his mouth to say something but his words were drowned by thunder as the *Astraea* started to dump her payload onto the middle of the city. The noise slapped again and again at Burton's ears as the colonial district was pummelled and decimated. Soon, all he could see was a blanket of black smoke through which the red lights of Hades flickered, and gliding along above it, silhouetted against the glaring white sky, the menacing rotorship, drawing closer and closer to where the tip of the radio tower emerged from the expanding inferno.

Wells stood on tiptoe and put his mouth to Burton's ear, which was ringing with such intensity that the explorer could barely hear the correspondent's soprano voice: "We had no choice but to do it. I wonder, though—will the human race ever transcend the animalistic impulses that lead to such behaviour?"

Burton yelled back: "I suspect animals would be most offended to be associated with an atrocity like this! What of the people down there? What of the Africans?"

"Casualties of war. As I said, we had no choice!"

"But this isn't their bloody conflict! It isn't their bloody conflict, damn it!"

A quick succession of blasts marked the end of the radio tower. The *Astraea* slid over the belt of red weed and sailed northward with hornets buzzing around her.

The attack was already over.

Silence rolled back in from the surrounding countryside, broken only by occasional small explosions.

"She's probably on her way to give Tanga some of the same treatment," Wells said, watching the rotorship receding into the distance.

Burton stood silently, struggling to stay on his feet. His legs were trembling violently, and his heart hammered in his chest.

"Bismillah!" he muttered. "Bismillah!"

CHAPTER 3

THE EVE OF DEPARTURE

THE BAKER STREET DETECTIVE
Macallister Fogg's Own Paper!
Issue 908.
Every Thursday. Consolidated Press.
One Penny.
This Week:
Macallister Fogg and his lady assistant,
Mrs. Boswell, investigate
THE PERIL OF THE GRAVITY PIRATES!
by T. H. Strongfellow
Plus the latest instalments of:
DOCTOR TZU AND THE SINGING COBRA by Cecil Barry
FATTY CAKEHOLE'S DORMITORY EMPIRE
by Norman Pounder

"Take us up, Mr. Wenham, no higher than seven thousand feet, if you please." The order came from William Henson, the rotorship's first officer. He was a slender man, about fifty years old, with an extravagant moustache that curved around his cheeks to blend into bushy muttonchop whiskers. He wore tiny wire-framed spectacles that magnified his eyes while also accentuating his precise and somewhat stern manner.

He turned to Burton and Swinburne, who were standing next to Captain Lawless, having been invited up to the conning tower to witness the takeoff. "We have to keep her low, gentlemen, on account of our ventilation problems. Until we get the heating pipes fixed, flying at any greater altitude will have us all shivering in our socks."

A vibration ran through the deck as the engines roared. There was no sensation of movement, but through the windows curving around the front and sides of the tower, Burton saw the horizon slip downward.

"Here we go," declared Francis Wenham, the helmsman. He was at a control console at the front of the cabin, manipulating three big levers and a number of wheels; a beefily built man with pale blond, rather untidy hair, and a wispy goatee beard.

"One thousand five hundred feet," murmured the man at the station beside him. "Swing her forty degrees to starboard, please."

"Forty degrees to starboard, aye, Mr. Playfair."

The horizon revolved around the ship.

Playfair turned to Henson and said, "Course set, sir."

"Thank you. Ahead, Mr. Wenham. Get her up to forty knots."

"Aye, sir."

"Flight time to London, three and a half hours," Playfair noted.

Swinburne eyed the sharp-faced, dark-eyed navigator. "I didn't see him consult his instruments," he muttered to Lawless. "Did he just do that calculation in his head?"

"Yes," the captain answered quietly. "He's a wizard with mathematics, that one."

The meteorologist—short, very stout, very hairy, and wearing his bulging uniform jacket tightly buttoned—announced: "Clear going until we reach the capital, sir. Fog there."

"Thank you, Mr. Bingham."

The captain turned to a tall, heavily bearded man who'd just entered the cabin and said, "Ah, there you are. Sir Richard, Mr. Swinburne, this is Doctor Barnaby Quaint, our steward and surgeon. He'll give you a tour of the ship, see that you're settled into your quarters, and will make sure that you have whatever you require."

"Is there a bar on board?" Swinburne asked.

Quaint smiled. "Yes, sir, in the lounge, though it's closed at the moment. I dare say I could rustle you up a tipple, should you require it. Would you care to follow me, gentlemen?"

They took their leave of Lawless, left the command cabin, and descended a metal staircase. A short corridor led them past the captain's quarters on one side and the first officer's on the other, and through decorative double doors into the glass-encased observation deck.

They were greeted by Detective Inspectors Trounce and Honesty, Commander Krishnamurthy, Constable Bhatti, and Mrs. Iris Angell, who was beside herself with excitement.

"Who'd have thought!" exclaimed Burton's housekeeper. "Dirty old Yorkshire—see how pretty it appears from up here, Sir Richard!"

He stepped to her side and looked out at the little villages and patchwork fields passing below.

"The northern counties have some of the most beautiful countryside in all of England," he said. "Did you think it would be different?"

"Yes!" she exclaimed. "I expected horrible factories everywhere!"

"You'll find plenty of William Blake's 'dark Satanic mills' in and around the manufacturing cities, Mrs. Angell, but as you can see, the horror of the North felt by those in the South is generally quite unjustified."

Burton watched the scenery slide by for a couple more minutes then moved over to where Detective Inspector Honesty was standing alone.

"Hello, old fellow," he said. "I didn't see much of you at Fryston. Are you all set for Africa?"

Honesty turned to him. "I am. Wife unhappy but duty calls. Must finish this business. Stop interference from the future." The detective gazed back out of the window and his pale-grey eyes fixed on the horizon. "Africa. Exotic flora. Might collect specimens. Cultivate in greenhouse when we return."

"Are you an amateur horticulturalist? I didn't know."

Honesty looked back at Burton and the explorer noticed a strange light in the smaller man's eyes—an odd sort of remoteness about his manner.

"Should've been a landscape gardener. Always wanted to be. Joined the Force on account of my father. A Peeler. One of the originals. Very dedicated. Passionate about policing. Me—I'm just good at it. But gardening—well—" He paused and a small sigh escaped him. "There are different versions of history, Captain?"

"Yes."

"Maybe in one, I made another choice. *Thomas Manfred Honesty: Landscape Gardener.* Hope so."

He returned his attention to the vista outside.

Burton patted the detective's shoulder and left him. He felt troubled by his friend's detached air. Honesty hadn't been quite himself since last September's battle with the Rakes, when he'd had his fingers broken and been throttled almost to death by an animated corpse. It was, Burton thought, enough to unnerve any man.

Trounce approached him. "How long until we reach London? I'm eager to get back onto the trail of our murderer."

"A little over three hours." Burton lowered his voice. "I say, Trounce, what's your opinion of Honesty? Is he a hundred percent?"

Trounce glanced toward his colleague. "I'd say he's the most determined of us all, Captain. He's a man who likes everything to be just so. The idea that an individual can hop back through time and turn it all on its head doesn't sit well with him."

Burton gave a small nod of understanding. "The steward is taking us on a tour of the ship. Join us?"

"I will, thank you."

Leaving Honesty, Krishnamurthy, Bhatti, and Mrs. Angell—all of whom had been around the vessel earlier that morning—Burton, Swinburne, and Trounce followed Doctor Quaint back into the corridor. As they passed by the captain's rooms, a small, slightly pudgy boy emerged.

"All shipshape, Master Wilde?" the doctor asked.

"That it is, sir. Good morning to you, Captain Burton, Mr. Swinburne, Detective Inspector Trounce. Welcome aboard!" The boy grinned, habitually raising his hand to his nose in order to conceal his rather crooked and yellowing teeth.

"Hallo, Quips!" said Burton.

Quaint addressed the explorer: "I understand Master Wilde is with us at your recommendation, sir?"

"He is indeed."

"And I'm much obliged, so I am, Captain," Wilde said.

"By Jove, little 'un!" Trounce exclaimed. "If someone had told you a year ago that you'd be flying to Africa as a crewmember aboard the biggest rotorship ever built, would you have believed them?"

"I can believe anything provided it is incredible, Mr. Trounce."

"Ha! Quite so! Quite so! And I daresay it's a great deal better than going to school, hey?"

"I wouldn't know, never having suffered such an indignity. While education may be an admirable thing, it is well to remember that nothing worth knowing can be taught. Now then, I must get myself up to the captain to have these acquisition orders signed. There's much to be done, so there is, if we're to depart the country without leaving unpaid debts behind us. I'll see you later, gentlemen!"

"Good Lord!" Quaint said as Wilde disappeared up the stairs to the conning tower. "Where does he get those nimble wits from?"

"I have no idea," Burton answered. "Perhaps his diet of butterscotch and gobstoppers has affected his brain."

They moved on down the corridor, passing the crew's quarters, and entered the lounge, a large space stretching from one side of the ship to the other. There were tables and chairs, a small dance floor and stage, and, to Swinburne's evident satisfaction, a bar in one corner.

"How many passengers can the *Orpheus* accommodate, Doctor?" Burton asked.

"Two hundred, sir. The smoking room is ahead of us, and beyond that the dining room, then a small parlour, and the first-class cabins all the way to the stern, where the reading room is situated. From there we'll take the stairs down to the rear observation room, pass through the cargo hold to the galley and pantries, then the engine room, and on to the standard-class cabins in the prow end of the ship. As you can see, those rooms have access to this lounge via staircases on the port and starboard sides. Of course, the ship has a number of other rooms, but those are the main ones."

"Phew!" Trounce gasped. "Mr. Brunel certainly likes to work on a grand scale!"

They continued their tour, marvelling at the opulence that surrounded them—for every fixture and fitting, and every item of decor, had been hand-crafted from the finest materials—and eventually came to the galley, where they found Isabella Mayson unpacking foodstuffs and stocking the larders.

"By heavens, Miss Mason!" Quaint cried out. "You're making fast progress! The last time I looked in, this room was chock-a-block with unopened boxes!"

"A place for everything and everything in its place, Doctor Quaint," the young woman responded. "We took a great many supplies on board in York-shire and we'll be adding more when we get to London. If I don't have the kitchen in order by then, it'll mean more work and delayed meals. We wouldn't want that, would we?"

"Certainly not!" Quaint agreed.

Miss Mayson smiled at the steward and said, "I shall be serving an early lunch at half-past twelve, Doctor."

"Good!" Swinburne interjected. "I'm famished!"

Quaint led them out of the galley, past cabins given over to various ship-board functions, and into the first of the huge engine-room compartments. After Daniel Gooch had shown them around the massive twin turbines, they moved on to the standard-class cabins, where they encountered Sister Raghavendra, who was organising a small surgery. As Quaint explained, it was essential to have medical facilities aboard the ship, not only to cater for any passenger who might be taken ill, but also because some of the engi-neering duties were exceedingly hazardous. It was the job of the riggers, for example, to maintain the flight pylons, which sometimes meant crawling out onto them while the *Orpheus* was in mid-flight. They wore harnesses, of course, but a fall could still be damaging. Riggers had been known drop then swing into the side of their ship, suffering a crushing impact.

"Now that you have your bearings, gentlemen, I shall take my leave of you," the doctor said as they reached a staircase at the prow of the vessel. "There is much to be done before our principal voyage begins, as I'm sure you appreciate." He looked down at Swinburne. "I have to pass back through the lounge, sir. If you'd care to accompany me, I'll organise that breakfast tipple for you."

"Bravo!" Swinburne cheered. "That'll be just the ticket!"

"And you, sir?" Quaint asked Burton.

"Too early for me. I'll retire to my quarters to go over the expedition inventory."

"Then I shall see you at lunch, sir."

The top ends of four colossal copper rods poked out of the dense fog that blanketed London. Guided by Francis Wenham, HMA *Orpheus* slid into position between them and gently descended into the central courtyard of Battersea Power Station.

It was two o'clock in the afternoon.

"How times have changed," Swinburne commented as he and Sir Richard Francis Burton disembarked, wrapped tightly in their overcoats, top hats pressed onto their heads. "Who'd have thought, a couple of years ago, that we'd end up working with Isambard Kingdom Brunel?"

"How times *have* changed," Burton echoed. "That's the problem."

Herbert Spencer, the clockwork philosopher, emerged from the pall to greet them.

He was a figure of polished brass, a machine, standing about five-feet-five-inches tall. His head was canister-shaped, with a bizarre-looking domed attachment on top of it that was somewhat reminiscent of a tiny church organ. The "face" beneath it was nothing more than three raised circular areas set vertically. The topmost resembled a tiny ship's porthole, through which a great many minuscule cogwheels could be glimpsed. The middle circle held a mesh grille, and the bottom one was simply a hole out of which three very fine five-inch-long wires projected.

Spencer's neck consisted of thin shafts and cables, swivel joints and hinges. His trunk was a slim cylinder with panels cut from it, revealing gears and springs, delicate crankshafts, gyroscopes, flywheels, and a pendulum. The thin but robust arms ended in three-fingered hands. The legs were sturdy and tubular; the feet oval-shaped.

He was an astonishing sight; and few who saw him now would believe that not so many weeks ago he'd been a very human, grubby, and tangle-bearded vagrant.

"Hallo, Boss! Hallo, Mr. Swinburne!" he hooted.

His strange voice came from the helmet-shaped apparatus, recently created and added to the brass man by Brunel. Spencer spoke through it clearly but with a piping effect that sounded similar to the woodwind section of a band.

Burton returned the greeting: "Hallo. How are you, Herbert?"

"I reckons I've a touch of the old arthritis in me left knee," the philosopher said. "But can't complain."

"A screw loose, more like!" Swinburne suggested.

"P'raps. I tells you, though—it's a strange thing to be mechanical. I fear me springs may snap or cogs grind to a halt at any bloomin' moment. Speaking o' which, I have good news—I'll be comin' to Africa, after all."

"How so?" Burton asked as they crossed the courtyard. "Conditions will hardly be conducive to your functioning."

"Mr. Brunel's scientists have dreamt up a new material what they makes usin' a chemical process. They calls it polymethylene. It's brown, very flexible, but waxy in texture. It's also waterproof, an' can't be penetrated by dust. They've used it to tailor a number of one-piece suits for me, what'll entirely protect me from the climate."

"You're certain that you'll be shielded and that the material will endure? Remember, there are extremes of heat and cold, as well as mud and dust," Burton cautioned. "During my previous expedition the clothes literally rotted off my back."

They arrived at the tall doors of the main building. Spencer reached out and took hold of one of the handles. "The material will no doubt deteriorate over time, Boss," he said, "but they've supplied me with fifteen of the bloomin' outfits, so I daresay they'll last. Besides—" he gestured at the fog that surrounded them, "—if I can survive this funk, I can survive anythin'!"

"Then I'm delighted," Burton replied. "You were pivotal in our securing of the South American diamond, and your presence might be of crucial importance when—or, rather, if—we reach the African stone. Welcome to the team, Herbert!"

"Marvellous!" Swinburne added.

The clockwork man pulled the door far enough open for them to pass through.

"Enter, please, gents."

The two men stepped into the Technologists' headquarters and were almost blinded by the bright lights within.

Isambard Kingdom Brunel had built Battersea Power Station in 1837. At the time, he'd been full of strange ideas inspired by his acquaintance Henry Beresford, and had designed the station to generate something he referred to as "geothermal energy." The copper rods that stood in each corner of the edifice rose high above it like four tall chimneys, but they extended much farther in the opposite direction, plunging deep into the Earth's crust. Brunel, just thirty-one years old in '37 and still rather prone to exaggeration, had announced that these rods would produce enough energy to provide the whole of London with electricity, which could then be adapted to provide lighting and heat. Unfortunately, since its construction, the only thing Battersea Power Station had ever managed to illuminate was itself, although it was rumoured that this might soon change, for Brunel was thought to have discovered a means to significantly increase the output of the copper rods.

Shielding their eyes, Burton and Swinburne looked into the station and observed a vast workshop. A number of globes hung from the high ceiling. Lightning bolts had somehow been trapped inside them, and they bathed the floor beneath in an incandescent glare, which reflected off the surfaces of megalithic machines—contrivances whose functions were baffling in the extreme. Electricity fizzed, crackled, and buzzed across their surfaces, and shafts of it whipped and snapped across the open spaces, filling the place with the sharp tang of ozone.

Among all this, over to their right, there stood a bulky vehicle. Around twelve feet high and thirty-six in length, it was tubular in shape—the front half a cabin, the back half a powerful engine—and it was mounted on a large number of short jointed legs. Rows of legs also projected from its top and sides. At its rear, steam funnels stuck horizontally outward, while its front was dominated by a huge drill, which tapered from the outer edges of the vehicle to a point, the tip of which stood some eighteen feet in advance of the main body.

Spencer, noticing them looking at it, explained: "That's a Worm—one of the machines what they're usin' to dig the London Underground tunnels. They reckons Underground trains will make it easier for people to move around the city, now that the streets are so congested with traffic. But you won't find me gettin' into one o' them trains. I'd be afraid o' suffocatin'!"

"You can't suffocate, Herbert," Swinburne objected.

"Aye, so you says!"

Another contrivance caught their eye. Surrounded by a group of technicians and engineers, it was a large barrel-shaped affair on tripod legs with a myriad of mechanical arms, each ending in pliers or a blowtorch or a saw or some other tool. As Burton, Swinburne, and Spencer entered, it swung toward them, lurched away from the Technologists, and stamped over.

"Greetings, gentlemen," it said, and its voice was identical to Herbert Spencer's, except pitched at a low baritone.

"Hello, Isambard," Burton answered, for, indeed, this hulking mechanism was the famous engineer—or, more accurately, it was the life-maintaining apparatus that had encased him since 1859, earning him the nickname *the Steam Man*. The king's agent continued: "The crew of the *Orpheus* is standing ready to take delivery of the vehicles and further supplies. Is everything prepared?"

"Yes, Sir Richard. My people will tarry—harry—excuse me, *carry*—everything aboard."

"I say, Izzy!" Swinburne piped up, with a mischievous twinkle in his green eyes. "Has your new speech-rendering device broken?"

"No," Brunel answered. "But it is not currently interacting sufficiently—effusively—expectantly—I mean, *efficiently*—with the calculating elephants—um—*elements*—of my cerebral impasse—er, *impulse*—calculators. Unanticipated variegations—vegetations—my apologies—*variations* are occurring in the calibration of the device's sensory nodes."

"My hat!" Swinburne exclaimed. "The problem is obviously chronic! I didn't understand a single word you just said! It was absolute gibberish!"

"Algy," Burton muttered. "Behave yourself!"

"It's all right, Sir Pilchard—er, Sir Richard," Brunel interjected. "Mr. Spinbroom has not yet forgiven me for the way I treated him during the String Filled Sack affair. I mean the Spring Heeled Jack despair—um—*affair*. Kleep."

"Kleep?" Swinburne asked, trying to stifle a giggle.

"Random noise," Brunel replied. "A recurring poodle. I mean, problem."

The poet clutched his sides, bent over, and let loose a peal of shrill laughter.

Burton sighed and rolled his eyes.

"Mr. Brunel's speakin' apparatus is the same as me own," Herbert Spencer put in, raising a brass finger to touch the rounded arrangement of pipes on his head. "But, as you know, me intellect is knockin' around inside the structure o' black diamonds, whereas his ain't, and the instrument responds better to impulses from inorganic matter than from organic."

"Ah-ha!" Swinburne cried out, wiping tears from his eyes. "So you still have fleshly form inside that big tank of yours, do you, Izzy?"

"That's quite enough," Burton interrupted, pushing his diminutive assistant aside. He steered the conversation back to the business at hand: "Are we on schedule, Isambard?"

"Yes. We have to declare—compare—*repair* the ventilation and leaping—um, *heating*—system, but the League of Chimney Sweeps has guaranteed periphery—I mean, *delivery*—of a new section of pipe by six o'clock today, and the work itself will slake—*take*—but an hour or so."

Swinburne, who'd regained control of himself, asked, "Why can't you fabricate the pipe yourself?"

"Reg—parp—ulations," Brunel answered.

Burton explained: "The Beetle has recently secured the sole manufacturing and trading rights to any pipes through which his people must crawl to clean or service."

"That boy is a genius," Swinburne commented.

"Indeed," Burton agreed. "Very well, we'll leave you to it, Isambard. The ship's crew will help your people to load the supplies. The passengers will reconvene here tomorrow morning at nine."

"Would you like to suspect—*inspect*—the vehicles before you depart?"

"No time. We have a murder investigation under way. I have to go."

"Before you do, may I peek—*speak*—with you privately for a moment?"

"Certainly."

Burton followed Brunel and stood with him a short distance away. They conversed for a few minutes, then the Steam Man clanked off and rejoined the group of Technologists.

Burton returned.

"What was all that about?" Swinburne asked.

"He was telling me a few things about the babbage device that John Speke has fitted to his head. Let's go."

"Should I join you, Boss?" Spencer asked.

"No, Herbert. I'd like you to stay and check the inventory against the supplies loaded."

"Rightio."

Leaving the clockwork man, Burton and Swinburne walked out through the doors, crossed the courtyard, and joined Detective Inspectors Trounce and Honesty, Commander Krishnamurthy, Constable Bhatti, Isabella Mayson, Mrs. Angell and Fidget, and various other passengers at the foot of the rotorship's boarding ramp. Crewmembers D'Aubigny, Bingham, and Butler were also there, having been granted a few hours' shore leave.

The pea-souper swirled around them all, dusting their clothes and skin with pollutants, clogging their nostrils with soot.

"Are we all ready?" Burton asked his friends. "Then let us go and bid civilisation farewell, except for you, Mother Angell. I fully expect you to maintain its standards while we're gone."

The group walked out through the station gates and passed alongside the outer wall beside a patch of wasteland that stretched down to nearby railway lines—a location which held bad memories for the king's agent and his assistant, for two years ago they'd been pursued across it by wolf-men and had narrowly avoided being hit by a locomotive.

They followed a path down to Kirtling Street, which took them the short distance to Battersea Park Road. Here they waved down conveyances. Monckton Milnes's guests gradually disappeared, as they each caught cabs home. Mrs. Angell and Fidget climbed into a hansom, bound for 14 Montagu Place; Isabella Mayson took another, for Orange Street; and a growler stopped for Detective Inspector Honesty, Commander Krishnamurthy, and Constable Bhatti, ready to take them each in turn to their respective homes.

A fourth vehicle—a steam-horse-drawn growler—was hailed by Burton for himself, Swinburne, and Trounce.

"Scotland Yard, driver!" the latter ordered.

"Not to Otto Steinrück's house?" Burton asked, as he climbed into the carriage and settled himself on the seat.

"It's out in Ilford," came the reply. "Too far by cab, so I thought we'd each borrow one of the Yard's rotorchairs."

The growler swung out onto Nine Elms Lane and chugged along next to the Thames. Its passengers took out their handkerchiefs and held them over their noses, the stench from the river so intense it made their eyes water.

Burton looked out of the window. Somewhere along this road there was a courtyard in which a young girl named Sarah Lovitt had been assaulted by Spring Heeled Jack back in 1839—just one of many attacks Edward Oxford had committed while searching for his ancestor. That was twenty-four years ago, and in that short time Oxford's influence had totally transformed the British Empire. That one man could effect such a change so quickly seemed utterly incredible to Burton but it wasn't without precedent; after all, history was replete with individuals who'd done the same—the Caesars, Genghis Khans, and Napoleons. Oxford had caused the death of Queen Victoria. After that, his influence had been subtler; he'd simply made unguarded comments about the future to Henry Beresford. The marquess had passed that information on to Isambard Kingdom Brunel, whose remarkable creative talents had been set alight by the hints and suggestions, leading to the creation of the political and cultural juggernaut that was the Technologist caste.

While Brunel's Engineers and Eugenicists succumbed to their inventive zeal, Oxford's presence in the form of Spring Heeled Jack had also inspired an opposing force: the Libertines, who sought to change social policies and create a new species of liberated man.

All of these elements had given rise to a condition of rapidly growing chaos, as scientific developments and social experimentation accelerated without check. For Charles Darwin, the man they called "God's Executioner," who'd fallen under the sway of his cousin, the Eugenicist Francis Galton, the possibilities had been so overwhelming they'd pushed him beyond the bounds of sanity.

How many others? Burton thought. *How many have become something they should never have been?*

The growler turned left onto Vauxhall Bridge and joined the queue of vehicles waiting to pay the toll to cross.

"The devil take it!" Trounce grumbled. "For how long are we to sit here breathing in this funk?"

"I can barely see a thing," Swinburne said, leaning out and peering ahead. "There's no telling how far from the toll booths we are. Surely, Pouncer, you don't expect us to fly rotorchairs in this?"

"Oy!" the police officer objected. "Don't call me Pouncer! But you're right, of course. After all that fresh Yorkshire air, I forgot how damned impenetrable these London particulars can be."

Burton made a suggestion: "It's only a couple of miles to the Yard. Why don't we leg it there and borrow penny-farthings instead?"

Trounce agreed, and moments later they were crossing the bridge on foot, cursing the stink, cursing the traffic, and cursing the fog.

"I tell you, Captain, I'll be delighted to leave this bloody cesspool of a city behind for a few months," Trounce declared.

It was six o'clock by the time they reached Ilford, and, though the fog was thinner there, the daylight was fading and the ill-lit town was wreathed in gloom.

They steered their velocipedes along the Cranbrook Road, then turned left into Grenfell Place.

"We're looking for number sixteen," Trounce said.

A minute later, they found it: an isolated house set back from the road and concealed by a gnarled and unnaturally twisted oak tree.

"By Jove!" Trounce exclaimed. "Why would anyone want this monstrosity in their front garden?"

They opened the gate, passed through, ducked under the branches, and walked along the path to the front door. No lights were showing in the house.

Trounce exercised the door knocker with his usual vigour but was met with nothing but silence.

"This is a murder investigation," he said, taking two steps back, "so I have no qualms about breaking in. Stand aside, would you, while I put my shoulder to it."

Burton held up a hand. "No need for that, old chap." He produced a picklock from his coat pocket and went to work on the keyhole. Moments later, there was a click.

"Open sesame!" Swinburne commanded, with an effusive wave of his arms.

"Go back to the gate and stand guard, would you, Algy?" Burton asked. "We'll need to light lamps, and if our strangler returns while we're here and sees the windows blazing, he'll do a runner before we've a chance to nab him. Yell if you see anyone acting in a suspicious manner."

The poet nodded and moved away while Burton and Trounce entered the house. The Scotland Yard man took out a box of lucifers, struck one, and put it to a wall lamp in the hallway. It illuminated three doors and a flight of stairs.

The first door opened onto a small lounge. Trounce got another lamp going and the two men saw five chairs positioned around a coffee table on which ashtrays and empty glasses stood.

"It looks like there was a meeting of some sort," Burton observed. He checked a bureau and found it empty, then the cupboards of an armoire and found the same.

The second door led to a dining room in which they found nothing of interest, and the third door into a kitchen. Its pantry was empty.

"I fear our quarry is long gone," Trounce muttered.

The bedrooms upstairs added weight to his suspicion, for the wardrobes were bare and there were no personal possessions to be found anywhere.

"Let's take another look at the lounge," Burton suggested.

They returned to that room and began a thorough search of it. The king's agent picked through the ashtrays, lifting cigar butts to his nose.

"Revealing," he murmured. "Four different Germanic brands and one English."

"Look at this, Captain."

Burton moved over to where his friend was squatting by the fireplace.

Trounce pointed at a reddish-brown patch at the back of the hearth. "Is that dried blood?"

Burton crouched and examined the stain. "Yes, I think so. Well spotted. But how the blazes did blood get there?" He thought for a moment, then said: "Would you call Algy in, please?"

Trounce grunted, straightened, and left the room. While he was gone,

Burton pulled the ashes and half-burned coals out of the fireplace and pushed them to one side, careless of the mess he made on the hearthrug. He lifted out the grate and set that aside, too.

"There was a hansom outside," Swinburne said as he entered the room with Trounce behind him. "It trotted past in the normal manner. I don't think it was anything untoward. What's happening here?"

"You're the chimney expert," Burton said. "Have a look at this."

Swinburne cast his eyes over the fireplace. "It was recently cleaned," he noted.

"It was?"

"Yes. Look how thin the layer of soot is. Is that a bloodstain?"

"We think so."

"Give me your lantern, Richard."

Burton reached into his pocket and pulled out his clockwork lantern. He shook it open and wound it, then handed it over to his assistant.

Swinburne removed his topper and laid it on the coffee table, then ducked down, stepped into the fireplace, and raised the light into the chimney.

"I'm going up," he said, and, bracing his legs against either side of the opening, he began to climb.

"Be careful, lad!" Trounce cautioned.

"Don't worry," Burton said. "Vincent Sneed trained him well."

"Don't mention that cad!" came Swinburne's hollow voice. "I say! There's a sort of niche up here and a little stash of food. There are more bloodstains, too. I'm going to go all the way up to the roof."

Little showers of soot fell into the hearth, but less than Burton would have expected; evidently the poet was correct, and the chimney was fairly clean.

Five minutes passed, then scrapes and trickles of black dust and an occasional grunt indicated that Swinburne was on his way back down. His feet appeared, then the poet in his entirety, his clothes and skin blackened, his green eyes sparkling from his sooty face.

"My guess is that a chimney sweep was hired to clean the chimney then came back later to steal food from the house," he said. "It's not uncommon. Most of the boys are half-starved and those that lodge with master sweeps are often so brutalised that they occasionally seek refuge for a night in suitable chimneys."

"Suitable chimneys?" Trounce asked. "What constitutes a suitable chimney?"

Swinburne turned off the lantern and handed it back to Burton. "One like this, with a niche in it and a shelf wide enough for the nipper to sleep on."

"And the blood?" Burton asked.

"They shot him."

"What?"

"Halfway up there's a furrow in the brickwork with a bullet lodged at the end of it. That shot obviously missed. Another one didn't. There's blood smeared all the way to the top and a lot of it on the roof tiles. The lad got away by the looks of it, but I doubt he survived for long, the poor little blighter."

The three men were silent for a moment, then Swinburne said quietly: "And now I hate that Prussian swine even more."

They made a final search of the house in case they'd missed anything then turned off the lights, stepped out, and closed the front door behind them.

"I'll report to the Yard and will have a couple of constables sent over to keep watch on the place," Trounce said as they proceeded down the path.

"We have no choice but to leave the investigation in the hands of your colleagues now," Burton said, "which means even if they catch the wretch, we won't hear about it for some considerable time. There is, however, one last thing I can do."

"What?"

The king's agent pulled open the gate and they crossed to where their velocipedes were parked.

"I can visit the Beetle. He may know something about the injured sweep."

They started the penny-farthings' engines, mounted, and set off. As they turned back into Cranbrook Road and began to chug down the hill, Burton called, "We'll split up when we get to Mile End. I'll head off to Limehouse. Algy, you go home, get packed, and have a good night's sleep. Stay off the alcohol. Trounce, do what you have to do at the Yard then get yourself home to your wife. We'll reconvene at the *Orpheus* tomorrow morning."

This arrangement was followed, and just under an hour later, Burton was striding through the stifling fog along the banks of Limehouse Cut canal. The factories that lined it had finished production for the day, and the thousands of workers who toiled within them had dispersed, returning to their lodgings in the loathsome slum that was London's East End—or "the Cauldron" as it was more commonly known.

Burton had left his velocipede in the charge of a constable back on the High Road. It wouldn't do to bring such an expensive vehicle into this district. He'd left his top hat with the policeman, too. The men in this area were most often bare-headed or wore flat caps. Best not to stand out.

The king's agent did, however, carry his sword cane—with its silver panther-head handle—held in such a manner so as to be able to quickly unsheathe the blade should it become necessary.

He arrived at a towering factory that, unlike the others, stood derelict. Nearly every one of its windows was cracked or broken, and its doors were boarded up. He circled around it until he came to a narrow dock at the side of the canal. In a niche in the building's wall, he found iron rungs set into the brickwork. He climbed them.

The edifice was seven storeys high, and by the time Burton reached the roof, he was breathing heavily. Hauling himself over the parapet, he sat and rested a moment.

There were two skylights set into the flat roof with eight chimneys rising around them. The third one from the eastern edge had rungs set into its side, and, after the king's agent had got his breath back, he began to ascend it. Halfway up, he stopped to rest again, then pressed on until he came to the top of the structure. He swung himself onto the lip of the chimney and sat with one leg to either side of it. He'd picked up a number of stones on his way here, and now he retrieved three of them from his pocket and dropped them one by one into the flue. This signal would summon the Beetle.

Burton had never actually seen the strange leader of the League of Chimney Sweeps. All he knew about him was that he was a boy, he lived in this chimney, and he had a voracious appetite for books. The Beetle had been of significant help during the strange affair of Spring Heeled Jack, when he'd arranged for Swinburne to pose as a sweep—a move that led directly to the exposure of Darwin and his cronies—and since then Burton had visited regularly, always bringing with him a supply of literature and poetry. The Beetle was especially desirous of anything written by Swinburne, whose talent he practically worshipped.

Burton wrapped his scarf around the lower half of his face and waited.

From this height there was usually a stunning view across London but today the king's agent could barely see his own hand in front of his face. The fog was dense and cold, and the "blacks" were falling—coal dust that coalesced with ice at a higher altitude and drifted down like dark snow.

He frowned. The Beetle should have responded by now.

"Hi!" he called into the flue. "Are you there, lad? It's Burton!"

There was no answer. He dropped three more stones into the darkness and sat patiently. The minutes ticked by and there was still no sound of movement, no whispery voice from the shadows.

Burton called again, waited a little longer, then gave up.

Where was the Beetle?

Half an hour later, after retrieving his vehicle and headwear, Burton continued homeward. For a few minutes he thought a hansom was following him, but when he reached the main thoroughfares, he became so ensnarled in traffic that he lost sight of it.

Central London had ground to a complete halt, the streets jammed solid with a bizarre mishmash of technologies. There were horses pulling carts and carriages; prodigious drays harnessed to huge pantechnicons; steam-horse-drawn hansoms and growlers; velocipedes; and adapted arachnids and insects, such as harvestmen and Folks' Wagon Beetles, silverfish racers and omnipedes. Burton even saw a farmer trying to drive a herd of goats through the streets to Covent Garden Market.

It seemed to the king's agent that the past, present, and future had all been compressed into the capital's streets, as if the structure of time itself was deteriorating.

None of the vehicles or pedestrians was making any progress, being more engaged in battling one another than in moving forward. The horses were whinnying and shying away from the insects, the insects were getting tangled up in each other's legs and mounting the pavements in an attempt to pass one another, and among them all, cloaked in fog and steam, crowds of people were shouting and cursing and shaking their fists in fury.

Slowly, with many a diversion down dark and narrow side streets and alleyways, Burton made his way out of Cheapside, past the Bank of England, and along Holborn Road. Here, at the junction with Red Lion Street, he collided with another velocipede—whose driver had lost control after his vehicle's boiler burst and knocked the gyroscope out of kilter—and was almost forced into an enormously deep and wide hole in the road. Clutching at the barrier around the pit so as not to topple from his penny-farthing, Burton cursed vehemently, then reached down and turned off his engine. The other man, who'd fallen onto the cobbles, picked himself up and kicked his machine. "Stupid bloody thing!" he cried out, then looked up at the king's agent. "Bless me, sir, you almost came a cropper! Pray forgive me!"

"It wasn't your fault," Burton said, dismounting. "Are you hurt?"

"I've ripped my trouser knee and knocked my elbow but nothing more life-threatening than that. What's this whacking great crater all about?"

"They're building a station here for the new London Underground railway system. The Technologists say it'll make moving around the city a lot easier."

"Well, it couldn't be any more difficult," the man answered. "Strike a light! What was that?"

Something had whined past his ear and knocked off Burton's top hat.

"Get down!" the king's agent snapped, pushing the other man to the ground.

"Hey up! What's your game?"

"Someone's shooting!"

"I beg your pardon? Did you say shooting?"

The explorer scanned the milling crowd, then reached for his hat and snatched it up from the road. There was a hole in its front, near the top edge. At the back, an exit hole was set a bit lower.

"The shot was fired from slightly above ground level," he murmured.

"Shot? Shot?" the man at his side stammered. "Why are we being shot at? I've never done anything! I'm just a bank clerk!"

"Not we—*me*."

"But why? Who are you?"

"Nobody. Pick up your boneshaker and get out of here."

"But—I—um—should I call for a policeman?"

"Just go!"

The man scuttled sideways on his hands and knees, pushed his penny-farthing upright, and wheeled it away while crouching behind it, as if it might shelter him from further bullets. As he disappeared into the noisy throng, Burton also moved, sliding along the edge of the barrier with his eyes flicking left and right, trying to pierce the fog.

"Confound it!" he hissed. He had no idea where the shootist might be. In one of the nearby carriages, perhaps? On a velocipede? Not in a building, that much was certain, for the windows along this side of the street were nothing but faint rectangular smudges of light—no one could possibly have identified him through the intervening murk.

He decided to follow Falstaff's dictum that "discretion is the better part of valour," and, bending low, he retrieved his cane, abandoned his conveyance, and shouldered his way into the crowd. He ducked between the legs of a harvestman, squeezed past a brewery wagon, and hurried away as fast as the many obstructions would allow. It was a shame to leave the penny-farthing behind but he couldn't risk climbing up onto its saddle again—that would make him far too visible.

It was past eleven o'clock by the time he finally arrived at 14 Montagu Place. As he stepped in, Mrs. Angell greeted him.

"Hallo!" he said, slipping his cane into an elephant's-foot holder by the door. "Good show! You got home! What a state the streets are in!"

"It's pandemonium, Sir Richard," she agreed. "How are the delivery boys to do their job? We'll starve!"

"I'm halfway there already," he said, shrugging out of his coat and hanging it on the stand. "I haven't eaten since I don't know when!"

"Then you'll be pleased to hear that a bacon and egg pie has been waiting for you these three hours past. That should fill the hole in your stomach. I don't know what to do about the hole that appears to have found its way into your hat, though."

Burton took off his topper and eyed it ruefully. "Oh well, I don't suppose I'll need it where I'm going. Perhaps you'd consign it to the dustbin for me?"

"Most certainly not!" the old woman objected. "A fine headpiece like that should be repaired, not abandoned. What happened to it?"

"Someone took a pot-shot at me."

Mrs. Angell raised her hands to her face. "Oh my goodness! With a gun? Are you hurt?"

Burton placed the hat on the stand, then squatted to untie his bootlaces. "Not at all. The would-be assassin's aim was off."

He eased his boots off and stood in his stockinged feet.

"I missed a night's sleep and I'm weary to the bone," he said. "I'll change into something more comfortable and join you in the kitchen for supper, if you don't mind."

Mrs. Angell looked surprised. "Eat? In the kitchen? With me?"

Burton took his housekeeper by the shoulders and smiled fondly down at her. "My dear, dear woman," he said. "I shan't see you again for such a long time. How will I ever do without you? You've fed me and cleaned up after me; you've kept me on the straight and narrow when I would have strayed; you've put up with intruders and all manner of inconveniences; you didn't even complain when the Tichborne Claimant practically demolished the house. You are one of the world's wonders, and I'd be honoured to dine with you tonight."

With glistening eyes, Mrs. Angell said, "Then be my guest, Sir Richard. There is, however, a condition."

"A condition? What?"

"I shall boil plenty of water while we eat and, when we are finished, you'll carry it upstairs and take a bath. You reek of the Thames, sir."

Burton relaxed in a tin bathtub in front of the fireplace in his study. He'd shaved, clipped his drooping moustache, and scrubbed the soot and toxins from his skin.

He took a final puff at the stub of a pungent cheroot, cast it into the hearth, reached down to the floor and lifted a glass of brandy to his lips, drained it, then set it back down.

"Someone," he said to the room, "doesn't want me to go to Africa, that much is plain."

"Fuddle-witted ninny," murmured Pox, his messenger parakeet. The colourful bird was sleeping on a perch near a bookcase. Like all of her kind, she delivered insults even while unconscious.

Burton leaned back, rested his head on the lip of the tub, and turned it so that he might gaze into the flickering flames of the fire.

His eyelids felt heavy.

He closed them.

His breathing slowed and deepened.

His thoughts meandered.

In his mind's eye, faces formed and faded: Lieutenant William Stroyan, Sir Roderick Murchison, Ebenezer Smike, Thomas Honesty, Edwin Brundleweed. They shifted and blended. They congealed into a single countenance, gaunt and lined, with a blade-like nose, tight lips, and insane, pain-filled eyes.

Spring Heeled Jack.

Gradually, the features grew smoother. The eyes became calmer. A younger man emerged from the terrible face.

"Oxford," Burton muttered in his sleep. "His name is Edward Oxford."

His name is Edward Oxford.

He is twenty-five years old and he's a genius—a physician, an engineer, a historian, and a philosopher.

He sits at a desk constructed from glass but, rather than being clear, it is somehow filled with writing and diagrams and pictures that move and wink and come and go. The surface of the desk is flat and thin, yet the information dancing within it—and Burton instinctively knows that it *is* information— appears to be three-dimensional. It's disconcerting, as if something impossibly big has been stored in something very small—like a *djan* in a lamp— but this doesn't appear to bother Oxford. In fact, the young man has some sort of control over the material, for occasionally he touches a finger to the glass or he murmurs something and the writing and outlines and images respond by folding or flipping or metamorphosing.

A large black diamond has been placed on the desk.

Burton recognises it as the South American Eye of Nāga, which he'd discovered last year beneath the Tichborne family's estate. The dream disagrees with him. The stone was not found in 1862, it says. It was found in 2068.

Original history!

Oxford is fascinated by it. The structure of the stone is unique. He whispers, "Even more sensitive than a CellComp. More efficient than a Cluster-Comp. More capacity than GenMem."

What is he talking about? Burton wonders.

The dream twists away and repositions itself inside a day a few weeks later.

The diamond is filled with the remnant intelligences of a prehistoric race. They have inveigled their way into Oxford's mind.

He starts to think about time.

He becomes obsessed.

He becomes paranoid.

It happens that he shares his name with a distant ancestor who, in a fit of insanity, had attempted to assassinate Queen Victoria. A voice, from somewhere behind his conscious mind, insists: "That man besmirched your family's reputation. Change it. Correct it."

Why does this obscure fact suddenly matter? Why should he care about a forgotten incident that occurred near three hundred and fifty years ago?

It matters.

He cares.

He can think about little else.

The reptilian intelligence plants another seed.

Slowly, in Oxford's mind, a theory concerning the nature of time blossoms like a pervasively scented exotic flower. Its roots dig deeper. Its lianas entangle him. It consumes him.

He works tirelessly.

The dream convulses and fifteen years have passed.

Oxford has cut shards from the diamond and connected them to a chain of DNA-StringComps and BioProcs. They form the heart of what he calls a Nimtz Generator. It is a flat circular device. It will enable him to move through time.

To power it, he's invented the fish-scale battery, and has fashioned thousands of these tiny solar-energy collectors into a one-piece tight-fitting suit. He's also embedded an AugCom into a round black helmet. It will act as an interface between his brain and the generator. It will also protect him from the deep psychological shock that he somehow knows will afflict anyone who steps too far out of their native time period.

The boots of the costume are fitted with two-foot-high spring-loaded stilts. They appear wildly eccentric but they offer a simple solution to a complex problem, for when the bubble of energy generated by the Nimtz forms around the suit, it must touch nothing but air.

Oxford will literally jump through time.

It is the evening of 15th February, 2202. Nine o'clock. A Monday. His fortieth birthday.

Oxford dresses in attire suitable for the 1840s. He pulls his time suit on over the top of it and clips on his stilts. He attaches the Nimtz Generator to his chest and puts the helmet on his head. He picks up a top hat and strides out of his workshop and into the long garden beyond.

His wife comes out of the house, wiping her hands on a towel.

"You're going now?" she asks. "Supper is almost ready!"

"I am," he replies, "but don't worry—even if I'm gone for years, I'll be back in five minutes!"

"You won't return an old man, I hope!" she grumbles, and runs a hand over her distended belly. "This one will need an energetic young father."

He laughs. "Don't be silly. It won't take long."

Bending, he kisses her on the nose.

He instructs the suit to take him to five-thirty on the afternoon of 10th June, 1840. Location: the upper corner of Green Park, London.

He looks at the sky.

"Am I really going to do this?" he asks himself.

"Do it!" a voice whispers in his head, and before he can consciously make a decision, he takes three long strides, jumps, hits the ground with knees bent, and leaps high into the air. A bubble forms around him and he vanishes with a small detonation, like a little clap of thunder.

Pop!

Sir Richard Francis Burton jerked awake and tepid water slopped over the edge of his bath.

He shivered, sat up, and looked around his study, trying to identify the source of the noise. His attention was drawn to a thin wisp of steam rising from a tubular contraption on one of his three desks. He reached for a towel then stood, stepped out of the bath, and wrapped the thick cloth around himself. He crossed to the desk. The glass and brass apparatus was his direct connection to the prime minister and the king. Burton retrieved a canister from it, snapped it open, and pulled out a sheet of paper. He read the words: *Be prepared to receive the prime minister at 2 a.m.*

"Curse the man! That's all I need!"

Pox twitched a wing and chirped, "Stink fermenter!"

Burton looked at the clock on the mantelpiece. It was half-past one.

Rapidly drying himself, he went into his dressing room and put on loose white cotton trousers and a shirt, then wrapped his *jubbah*—the long and loose outer garment he'd worn while on his pilgrimage to Mecca, which he now used as a night robe—over the top of them. He slid his feet into pointed Arabian slippers and wound a turban around his damp hair.

By two o'clock, the bathtub had been removed, another Manila cheroot had been smoked, and Burton had sat and pondered his strange dream. There was much about it that he didn't understand—the curious glass desk, the sparsely furnished room in which it stood, some of the words that Edward Oxford had uttered—yet it seemed vividly real.

Did I just glimpse a distant future? The one that was meant to be before Oxford interfered?

Hearing the coughing of steam engines and rumble of wheels in the street outside, he stepped to the window and looked out in time to see Lord Palmerston's armoured six-wheeled mobile castle draw up.

He went downstairs and opened the front door.

Palmerston was standing on the step, with his odd-job men Gregory Hare and Damien Burke on either side of him.

"Do you consider that suitable attire, Captain Burton?" the prime minister asked.

"For two o'clock in the morning? Yes, sir," Burton replied, moving aside to let the men enter. "Do you consider it a suitable hour for visiting?"

"One cannot run an Empire and maintain respectable hours, sir."

"Up to the study, if you please."

Burton closed the door and followed them upstairs, noting that the prime minister's men were dressed, as ever, in outlandishly old-fashioned outfits.

"Last time I saw this room," Palmerston said as he entered the bookcase-lined chamber, "it was all but destroyed."

"You're referring to the occasion when we were attacked and you hid in my storeroom?" Burton responded.

"Now, now, Captain. Let us not get off on the wrong foot."

Palmerston placed his hat on one of the desks and took off his calfskin gloves. His fingernails were painted black. He didn't remove his tightly buttoned velvet frock coat but smoothed it down then sat in Burton's favourite saddlebag armchair and crossed his legs. He pulled a silver snuffbox from his pocket and said, "We must talk. I would have been here earlier but the streets were impassable."

Burke and Hare each sat at a desk. Burton took the armchair opposite Palmerston, who asked, "Your expedition is equipped and ready for departure?"

"It is."

"Good. Good. All running smoothly, then?"

"Yes. Unless you count two attempts on my life, one of which resulted in the death of my good friend Thomas Bendyshe."

Palmerston jerked forward. "What did you say?"

"A man named Peter Pimlico tried to poison me. He was hired by a Prussian named Otto Steinrück, who then killed him by strangulation to keep him quiet. And, earlier this evening, somebody sent a bullet my way."

Damien Burke, tall, hunchbacked, extremely bald, and sporting the variety of side whiskers known as "Piccadilly Weepers," cleared his throat and said, "This Germanic individual, Captain Burton—did you find out anything about him?"

"Only that he's portly, wears a large moustache, has pointed claw-like fingernails, and chews Kautabak tobacco."

Burke glanced at Gregory Hare, who was short and muscular, with white hair and a broad, pugnacious face. "Ah-ha," he said. "Do you agree, Mr. Hare?"

"I do, Mr. Burke," Hare answered. "Ah-ha."

"You know something of this individual?" Burton asked.

"Yes," Burke said. "I consider it highly likely that Otto Steinrück is not Otto Steinrück. It is almost certainly an alias. The man fits the description of a notorious Prussian spy named Count Ferdinand Graf von Zeppelin. You'll remember that last year he helped Richard Spruce and his Eugenicist colleagues to flee the country. A very dangerous man, Captain."

Burton nodded. "And one bent on preventing me from going to Africa, it would appear. I'm certain he's still working with Spruce, too."

"Why so?"

"The dead man had a foul-looking plant sprouting from the roof of his mouth."

"Hmm. That's interesting." Burke took a notebook from his pocket and scribbled something in it with a pencil.

Palmerston opened his snuffbox, took a pinch of brown powder, sprinkled it onto the back of his right hand, and raised it to his nose. He snorted it and his eyes momentarily widened.

It occurred to Burton that the prime minister's face had been stretched so taut by his Eugenicist treatments that those eyes appeared almost oriental.

"A complex situation," Palmerston muttered. "There are great moves being made, Captain, moves that will reshape the world, and you are in the thick of it."

"How so?"

"Tomorrow afternoon, I shall make an announcement to parliament. You'll be out of the country by then, so I came to give you the news personally. Excuse me—"

Palmerston turned his head to one side and let loose a prodigious sneeze. When he looked back, there were hundreds of deep wrinkles around his eyes and nose. Over the next few minutes, they slowly flattened out and disappeared.

"What news?" Burton asked.

"Lincoln has surrendered. America is ours."

Burton's jaw dropped. He fell back into his seat, speechless.

"Some time ago," Palmerston continued, "I told you that if this should occur I would demand of the Confederates the abolition of slavery as repayment for our role in their victory. I fully intend to do that. But not just yet."

Finally, Burton found his voice and asked, "Why not?"

"Because of *Blut und Eisen*."

"Blood and iron?"

"Three months ago, while you were clearing up the Tichborne business and our turncoat Eugenicists were defecting to Prussia, Chancellor Bismarck made a speech in which he declared his intentions to increase military spending and unify the Germanic territories. He said—and believe me, I can quote this from memory, for it is seared into my mind: 'The position of Prussia in Germany will not be determined by its liberalism but by its power. Prussia must concentrate its strength and hold it for the favourable moment, which has already come and gone several times. Since the treaties of Vienna, our frontiers have been ill-designed for a healthy body politic. Not through speeches and majority decisions will the great questions of the day be decided—that was the great mistake of 1848 and 1849—but by blood and iron.'"

Burton said, "I read accounts of the speech in the newspapers. Is he warmongering?"

Palmerston clenched his fists. "Indisputably. It is the first blatant move toward the world war Countess Sabina has predicted. There is no doubt that Bismarck is seeking to establish a Germanic empire to rival our own. Empires require resources, Captain Burton, and there is one vast untapped resource remaining in the world. I refer to Africa."

"So you suspect Bismarck will try to establish a foothold there?"

"I think he intends to carve it up and suck it dry."

"But what has this to do with America's slaves?"

"If a united Germany can count Africa among its territories, and if war breaks out, it will find itself with an almost limitless source of expendable manpower."

"Expendable?"

"I believe the term is 'cannon fodder.'"

The king's agent felt ice in his veins. "You surely aren't suggesting—" he began.

Palmerston interrupted him. "If we are faced with such a situation, we will require our own disposable units."

"You mean America's slave population?"

"Yes. A little over four million individuals, though I'm including women in that number."

Burton's jaw flexed spasmodically. "Hellfire, man! You're talking about human beings! Families! You're not only suggesting support for state-sanctioned slavery—you're talking about bloody genocide!"

"I mean to ensure the survival of the British Empire, whatever it takes."

"No!" Burton shouted. "No! No! No!" He slapped his hand down on the leather arm of his chair. "I won't stand for it! It's despicable!"

"You'll do whatever you're damned well ordered to do, Captain Burton," Palmerston said softly. "And what you are ordered to do is help me to ensure that no such circumstance ever arises."

"Wha—what?"

"Your primary mission hasn't changed—you are to retrieve the Eye of Nāga so that we might employ it to infiltrate and coerce the minds of our opponents. However, there is now a secondary purpose to your expedition. You are to employ your military and geographical experience to determine which are the most strategically advantageous African territories and how we might best secure them. I intend to claim that continent before Bismarck makes his move, and I'm relying on you to advise me how to do it."

Burton's heart hammered in his chest. His mind raced.

He looked into Lord Palmerston's impenetrable eyes.

"And if I do, sir, and if we make Africa a part of the British Empire, then what of the inhabitants? What of the Africans?"

The prime minister—returning Burton's gaze steadily and without blinking—replied: "They will be accorded the rights granted to all British subjects."

There was a moment of silence, broken only by Gregory Hare clearing his throat slightly, then Burton said, "You refer to the same rights enjoyed by those undernourished Britishers who toil in our factories and inhabit our slums? The same given to those who beg on our street corners and doorsteps? The same extended to servant girls abused and impregnated by their employers then thrown onto the streets where their only means of survival is prostitution? Is this the marvellous civilisation that you, the great imperialist, have to offer Africa?"

Palmerston shot to his feet and yelled, "Shut the hell up, Burton! Am I to endure your insolence every time we meet? I'll not tolerate it! You have your orders!" He stamped to the door, snapping his fingers at Burke and Hare. They rose and followed. He ushered them out first, then, with his hand on the doorknob, turned to face the explorer.

"Do your bloody job, Captain!" he snarled.

The prime minister stepped out of the room and slammed the door shut behind him.

"Illiterate baboon," Pox squawked.

"In the maelstrom of making history," Bertie Wells said, "very little of it is accurately recorded. When the time finally comes for an account of the events that have passed, human nature takes over."

He and Burton were in an ambulance sharing that rarity of rarities, a scrounged cigar. The oxen-drawn vehicle was part of a convoy, a seemingly never-ending line of soldiers and vehicles moving up from the south toward the port of Tanga, some hundred miles north of Dar es Salaam.

It was early morning but already ferociously hot. The troops were dripping sweat. They were exhausted, ill, and miserable. Occasional bursts of chanting broke out—the usual sad native dirges—but these quickly tailed off, overwhelmed by the rhythmic *tromp tromp tromp* of boots. At one point a company of Britishers broke into song, their mock cheerfulness shot through with resentful hatred. The tune was "What a Friend We Have in Jesus," but the lyrics were rather more colourful than those of the original hymn:

> When this lousy war is over, no more soldiering for me,
> When I get my civvy clothes on, oh how happy I shall be.
> No more church parades on Sunday, no more begging for a pass.
> You can tell the sergeant major to stick his passes up his arse.

The sergeant major in question harangued the men for a three-mile stretch after that.

Burton was sitting on the ambulance's tailgate, leaning against the side of the vehicle's open back. He couldn't stop scratching.

"Human nature?" he said. "What do you mean?"

Wells, perched on a bench just behind him, responded, "I'm of the opinion that we possess an inbuilt craving for narrative structure. We want everything to have a beginning, a middle, and an end. That way, we can make better sense of it." He looked down at Burton. "How many days did that uniform last before it got infested?"

"Four. The lice are eating me alive."

"Chin up, old man. It could be worse. Fever, trench foot, dysentery, having your bloody legs blown off—all the perils of wartime Africa."

"Bismillah! What are you people doing? You've created hell from an Eden!"

"Is my generation responsible, Richard, or is yours? I've heard people say over and over that we are all products of the past. They'd lay the blame for this war squarely at their fathers' feet. In other words, welcome to the world you created."

"Absolutely not! None of my contemporaries intended the creation of this *Jahannam*!"

"As you say. Besides, I disagree with the philosophy of what you might term *sequentialism*. The problem, as I see it, is that we don't truly understand the nature of the past. We mythologise it. We create fictions about actions performed to justify what we undertake in the present. We adjust the cause to better suit the effect. The truth is that the present is, and will always be, utter chaos. There is no story and no plan. We are victims of zeitgeist. I apologise for using a German word, but it's singularly appropriate. Are you familiar with it?"

"Yes. It translates as 'ghost tide,' or, perhaps, 'spirit of the age,' and refers to the ambience or sociopolitical climate of any given period."

"Exactly so, and in my view it's a phenomenon entirely independent of history. History doesn't create the zeitgeist, we create the history to try to explain the zeitgeist. We impose a sequential narrative to endow events with something that resembles meaning."

The ambulance jerked as its wheels bounced through a pothole. Burton's head banged against the vehicle's wooden side.

"Ouch!"

"How's your arm?" Wells asked.

"Aching. How's your leg?"

"Broken. How's your head?"

"Shut up."

"Have a cigar."

The war correspondent passed what remained of the "Hoffman" to the explorer, who glanced at its much-reduced length and muttered, "Your lungs are healthy, at least." He raised it to his lips and drew in the sweet smoke, savouring it while observing the column of men and vehicles that snaked back over the rolling landscape.

The supply wagons and ambulances were mostly towed by steam-horses or oxen. There were a few mangy-looking nonmechanical horses in evidence, too, including mega-drays pulling huge artillery pieces. Harvestmen stalked along beside the troops, and Scorpion Tanks thumped through the dust with their tails curled over their cabins, the guns at their ends slowly swinging back and forth.

"Hey! Private!" Burton called to a nearby Britisher. "Where are we?"

"In it up to our bloody eyeballs, chum!"

"Ha! And geographically?"

"I ain't got a bleedin' clue. Ask Kitchener!"

"We're almost there, sir," an African voice answered. "Tanga is a mile or so ahead."

"Much obliged!" Burton said. He turned Wells. "Did you hear that? We must be near your village. Shall we hop out here?"

"Hopping is my only option, unfortunately."

Burton slid from the tailgate into the ambulance, then moved to its front and banged his fist against the back of the driver's cabin. "Stop a moment, would you?"

He returned to Wells and, as the vehicle halted, helped him down to the ground and handed him his crutches. The two men put on their helmets, moved to the side of the column, and walked slowly along beside it.

"So what's your point, Bertie?"

"My point?"

"About history."

"Oh. Just that we give too much credence to the idea that we can learn from the past. It's the present that teaches the lesson. The problem is that we're so caught up in doing it that we can never see the wood for the trees. I say! Are you all right?"

Burton had suddenly doubled over and was clutching the sides of his head.

"No!" he gasped. "Yes. I think—" He straightened and took a deep, shuddering breath. "Yes. Yes. I'm fine. I'm sorry. I just had a powerful recollection of—of—of a man constructed from brass."

"A statue?"

"No. A machine. But it was—it was—Herbert."

"What? Me?"

"No, sorry, not you, Bertie. I mean, its—his—name is—was—is Herbert, too."

"A mechanical man named Herbert? Are you sure your malaria hasn't flared up again?"

Burton clicked his tongue. "My brain is so scrambled that the line between reality and fiction appears almost nonexistent. I'm not sure what that particular memory signifies, if anything. Perhaps it'll make more sense later. Where's the village?"

Wells pointed to a vaguely defined path that disappeared into a dense jungle of thorny acacias. The trees were growing up a shallow slope, and Burton could just glimpse rooftops through the topmost leaves. "Along there," Wells said. "Kaltenberg is right on the edge of Tanga—practically an outlying district. It was built by the Germans in the European style, on slightly higher ground. The occupants fled into the town a few days ago. We'll get a good view of the action from up there."

"I gather the role of war correspondents is to climb hills and gaze down upon destruction?"

"Yes, that's about it."

They left the convoy and followed the dirt track. The boles of the trees crowded around them, blocking the convoy from sight. The sky flickered and flashed through the foliage just above their heads. Mosquitoes whined past their ears.

"Who's Kitchener?" Burton asked.

"One of the military bigwigs. Or was. No one knows whether he's dead or alive. Damn this leg! And damn this heat. In fact, damn Africa and all that goes with it! I'm sorry, we'll have to slow down a little." Wells stopped, and, balancing himself on his crutches, struck a match and lit a cigarette. He took a pull at it then held it out to Burton.

"Thanks, Bertie, but I'll pass. My fondness for cheap cigars doesn't plummet to such depths. Besides, it would ruin the taste of my toffee."

"You have toffee?"

"I scrounged it from the ambulance driver. Four pieces. I'd offer you two but I fear they'd be wasted after that tobacco stick."

"You swine!"

Burton grinned.

"And don't do that with your ugly mug," Wells advised. "It makes you look monstrously Mephistophelian."

"You remind me of someone."

"Who?"

"I don't recall."

They set off again, the war correspondent swinging himself along on his crutches.

Burton said, "Remind me again why we're attacking Tanga."

"Firstly," Wells replied, "because we're trying to regain all the ports; secondly, because we want to raid German supplies; and thirdly, and most importantly, because it's believed the commander of the *Schutztruppe*, Generalmajor Paul Emil von Lettow-Vorbeck, is holed up there, and we would dearly love to deprive him of his existence. The man is a veritable demon. He has a military mind to rival that of Napoleon Bonaparte!"

By the time they reached the first of the Kaltenberg cottages, both men were sweating profusely. "Do you remember snow?" Wells muttered as they moved out from beneath the acacias and into the village. "What I wouldn't give for a toboggan ride down a hill with a tumble at the bottom." He stopped and said quietly, "Richard."

Burton followed his companion's gaze and saw, in a passageway between two cottages, the body of an Askari in British uniform. They approached and examined the corpse. A laceration curved diagonally across the African's face, the skin to either side of it swollen and puckered.

"That's a lurcher sting," Wells observed. "He's recently dead, I'd say."

"This was a bad idea, Bertie. We should have stayed with the column."

Wells shook his head. "It's the job of a war correspondent to watch and report, Richard. When we reach the other end of the village, you'll find that it offers an unparalleled view across Tanga. We'll see far more from here than we would if we were in the thick of it. Not to mention the fact that we'll stand a better chance of staying alive."

The silence was suddenly broken by a rasping susurration, similar to the sound of a locust, but shockingly loud and menacing.

"Hum. I might be wrong," Wells added, his eyes widening. "Where did that noise come from?"

"I don't know."

They stepped out of the passage and immediately saw a lurcher flopping out of one of the cottages they'd just passed. It was a hideous thing—a tangle of thorny tentacles and thrashing tendrils. From its middle, a red, fleshy, and pulsating bloom curled outward. Extending from within this, two very long spine-covered stalks rose into the air. They were rubbing together—a horribly frantic motion—producing the high-pitched ratcheting sound. The wriggling plant rolled forward on a knot of squirming white roots—and it moved fast.

"We've got to get out of here!" Burton cried out. "Drop your crutches, Bertie! I'm going to carry you!"

"But—"

Wells got no further. Burton kicked the crutches away, bent, and hoisted the shorter man up onto his shoulder. He started to run, heavy-footed.

"Bloody hell!" he gasped. "This is a lot easier with Algy!"

"Who?"

"Um. Algy. Bismillah! That's who you put me in mind of! How in blazes could I have forgotten him?"

"I don't know and right now I don't care. Run!"

Burton pumped his legs, felt his thigh muscles burning, and heard the lurcher rapidly drawing closer behind him.

"It's on us!" Wells yelled.

The famous explorer glimpsed a house door standing ajar. He veered toward it and bowled through, dropping Wells and banging the portal shut behind him. The lurcher slammed into it with terrific force, causing the frame to splinter around the lock. Burton quickly slid the bolts at the top and bottom into place. Thorns ripped at the wood outside.

"This door won't keep it out for long. Are you all right?"

"I landed on my leg," Wells groaned.

Burton helped the war correspondent to his feet. "Let's get upstairs. God, my head! I was just knocked sideways by memories!"

He gave support to his friend and they made their way up and through to the front bedroom. The other upper chamber was given over to storage.

The din of hammering tentacles continued below. Burton was breathing heavily. He lowered Wells onto a bed, then staggered back and leaned against a wall, pressing the palms of his hands into his eyes.

"Algernon," he whispered, and when he looked up, there were tears on his cheeks.

"What is it?" the shorter man asked.

Burton didn't answer. He was looking beyond his companion, at a dressing table mirror, and the face that stared back from it was that of a total stranger. It was all he could see. He fell into its black, despair-filled eyes and was overwhelmed by such a powerful sense of loss that his mind began to fracture.

"Richard!" Wells snapped. "Hey!"

The room sucked back into focus.

"Where am I?" Burton gasped. He felt hollow and disassociated.

Wordlessly, Wells pointed at the window.

After drawing a shuddering breath, Burton crossed to it, but he quickly stepped back when he saw thorny vines crawling over the glass.

"Manipulated and accelerated evolution," the war correspondent observed. "Another of the Eugenicists' ill-conceived monstrosities. That thing was once a man in a vehicle. Look at the damned thing now! So who's this Algy person?"

"Algernon Swinburne."

"The poet? Yes, of course, you knew him, didn't you?"

"He is—was—my assistant."

"Really? In what?"

"I have no idea. But I recall fleeing from a fire with him slung over my shoulder."

"Fire is what we need now. It's the only way we'll destroy the lurcher. Step a little farther back from the window, Richard. The stalks are strong enough to break through the glass."

Burton hastily retreated. He looked around the room at the furniture, the pictures, and the ornaments. Everything was crawling with ants and cockroaches. Even this fact stirred buried recollections. The name "Rigby" rose into his awareness then sank away again.

Wells said, "My leg is hurting like hell."

"Stay here while I have a poke about in the other room," Burton responded. He went out onto the landing and into the chamber beyond. Wells sat and massaged his right thigh.

A loud crack sounded from below as the front door split under the lurcher's continued assault.

Burton came back in.

"Any luck?" Wells asked.

"A whole bottle of it." Burton held up a wide-necked container. "Turpentine."

Wells pulled something from his jacket pocket. "And a box of four whole matches. Yours for the price of two pieces of toffee."

"Deal."

Burton crossed to the window and, after putting the bottle on the floor, used both hands to slide the sash up. It squealed loudly and jammed, with less than a foot of it open.

"Look out!" Wells shouted.

The explorer staggered back as two flailing stalks came smashing through the glass and wood, showering splinters over both men. The spiny appendages coiled and slashed around the room, gouging the furniture and ripping long gashes across the walls.

Wells, acting without thinking, threw himself back onto the bed, clutched the thin mattress, and rolled, wrapping it around himself. He lunged upright and dived at the window, letting out an agonised scream as pain knifed through his wounded leg. He landed across the stalks, pinning them to the floor. They bucked under him and curled back, slapping against the bedding, shredding it.

"Quick, man! I can't hold it!"

Burton sprang at the bottle, which was rolling over the floorboards, scooped it up, and untwisted the cap. Unable to get past Wells to stand directly in front of the window, he stuck his arm through it from the side and poured the turpentine, praying to Allah that it would land on the target.

"The lucifers, Bertie!"

"I dropped the bloody things!"

A ragged length of the mattress's cotton cover was ripped away exposing the horsehair stuffing beneath. The material flew into the air as one of the stalks whipped up and back down, thumping across the correspondent's body.

Burton, having spotted the matchbox lying on the floor, scrambled across the room. He crawled and rolled on broken glass.

"Have you got them?" Wells yelled.

"Yes!"

Snatching up the length of torn material, Burton reeled back to the front wall, thudded against it, and slid into a crouch beside the window.

Wells was suddenly sent spinning into the air as the long stalks jerked violently and slid from the room.

The battering noises ceased.

Burton, with a puzzled expression, stood and cautiously peered out of the window. The stalks were nowhere in sight. Carefully, he leaned out and looked down.

The lurcher was below, quivering and jerking as if in the grip of a seizure.

"What's happened to it?" he murmured.

He pulled a match from the box, struck it, put the flame to the torn cotton, and dropped the burning cloth onto the plant, which immediately exploded into flames.

As he watched, the fire turned from blue to yellow and started to belch thick black smoke.

He turned and started to speak but realised that Wells was unconscious.

"Bertie, are you all right?"

The war correspondent shifted and groaned.

Pulling away the tattered mattress, Burton helped his companion to sit upright. Wells's uniform was ripped and bloodstained.

"You're bleeding, Bertie."

"Nothing serious," his friend croaked. "So are you. Is it dead?"

"Yes. It was odd, though. The thing appeared to lose control of itself just before I set fire to it. Let's get out of here."

They limped from the bedroom and down the stairs, pulled open the wrecked front door, and tumbled out onto the street.

The lurcher had already been reduced to a twitching bonfire.

"Wait here," Burton said. "I'll get your crutches."

He retrieved them from outside the alley farther down the road and returned.

"You did exactly what he would have done," he said, handing over the sticks.

"Who?"

"Algernon Swinburne. He's the most fearless man I've ever known."

"That's where the comparison fails, then. I was scared out of my wits."

"You're a good chap, Bertie."

CHAPTER 4

DISASTER!

> 1 Six-inch sextant. 1 Four-inch sex-
> tant. 1 Mercurial horizon. 1 Pris-
> matic compass. 2 Pocket chronometers.
> 3 Thermometers to 212°. 3 Ditto
> smaller, in cylindrical brass cases.
> 2 Casella's apparatus for measuring
> heights by the boiling point: steam
> and 1 for water. 1 Book, having its
> pages divided into half-inch squares
> for mapping. Memorandum-books. 1 Nau-
> tical Almanac. 1 Thomson's *Lunar
> Tables*. 1 Galton's *Art of Travel*. 1
> Admiralty Manual. 1 Tables of Loga-
> rithms. *Hints to Travellers* by the
> Royal Geographical Society.
> —FROM BURTON'S INVENTORY NOTES,
> AFRICAN EXPEDITION, 1863

The *Orpheus* was over southern France by the time Sir Richard Francis Burton woke up. After two nights in a row with virtually no sleep, he'd been oblivious for the first hours of the voyage.

Now he stood on the observation deck, enjoying the view and feeling an immense sense of release. Departure always lifted his spirits, and as the shackles and restraints of civilisation fell away, he was giving himself up to that which he liked best: the lure and promise of the unknown.

Algernon Swinburne entered and joined him at the window.

"What ho! What ho! And what ho again! But you missed a top nosh-up at lunch, Richard!"

"I've been dead to the world, Algy. What have you been doing, apart from lining your stomach, that is?"

"I've been looking for that little imp Willy Cornish, but it seems our funnel scrubbers are already crawling about in the pipes."

"Sweltering work, I imagine. He'll emerge eventually. No doubt you'll catch up with him later."

"I suppose. I say, there's a bit of a flap on with Mr. Gooch and his people."

"Why so?"

"The four stern engines have gone wonky. I think it's something to do with the doo-dah forcing the thingamajig to bang against the wotsitsname. There's not much poetry in engineering, is there?"

"Not a lot. Are you quite all right?"

"I'm fine. No, I'm not. Oh, blast it, I don't know, Richard."

"Thinking about Tom?"

Swinburne heaved a sigh. "Yes. They'll be burying him this afternoon."

The poet reached into his jacket and pulled out Apollo's gold-tipped arrow. He examined its point. "We didn't catch his killer, and we're going to be away for such a long time that we probably never will."

"Don't be so sure. I found out last night that Otto Steinrück is actually Count von Zeppelin."

"What? What? The spy?"

"Yes. I'll be very surprised if his and our paths don't cross again in due course."

Swinburne's face took on a ferocious expression. "Good!" he snarled. "Good!" He held up the arrow and, in a melodramatic tone, declared: "This is the arrow of justice! I shall carry it with me until Tom Bendyshe is avenged!"

Burton patted his friend's shoulder.

They stood and watched the scenery slipping by far below. Ahead, France's south coast was visible.

Swinburne said, "I think I'll go and do some work."

"*Atalanta in Calydon?*"

"No. I've started a little something entitled 'A Lamentation.'"

"In memoriam?"

"I'm not entirely sure. It might concern another matter entirely. It's hard to tell. It's coming out of here—" he tapped the middle of his chest, "rather than here—" he put a finger to his head. "Maybe it'll make more sense to me when it's finished."

With that, he left the observation deck.

Burton's fathomless eyes fixed on the line of ocean at the horizon.

"Poems the poet cannot quite grasp. Dreams the dreamer cannot decipher. Mystery upon mystery. And still the Weaver plies his loom, whose warp and woof is wretched Man. Weaving the unpatterned dark design, so dark we doubt it owns a plan."

An hour passed, during which time he stood, motionless, lost in thought.

"Sir Richard," came a voice from behind him. He turned and saw Captain Lawless. "Do you feel a vibration beneath your feet?"

"I do," Burton answered. "Something to do with the stern engines?"

"Ah, you've heard. They're operating out of alignment with the forward engines and pushing us too hard. If we can't regulate our speed, we'll complete our voyage considerably ahead of schedule but in doing so the ship will have shaken herself half to pieces and won't be fit for the return journey. I don't much fancy being stuck in Zanzibar. I'm on my way down to engineering to see whether Mr. Gooch can cast some light on the matter. Would you care to accompany me?"

Burton nodded, and, minutes later, they found Daniel Gooch in an engineering compartment behind the furnace room. He'd removed a large metal panel from the floor and was on his knees, peering into the exposed machinery beneath. When he heard the two men approaching, he looked up and said, "There's a bearing cradle missing."

"A what?" Burton asked.

"A bearing cradle. It's a metal ring, twelve inches in diameter, housing a cog mechanism and greased ball bearings. It's an essential component in the system that synchronises the engines. There are four bearing cradles on the ship, each governing four of the flight shafts. The one for the stern engines has gone. Someone has removed it."

"Are you suggesting we've been sabotaged, Mr. Gooch?" Lawless asked.

"Yes, sir. I am."

"By someone on board?"

"That's very likely the case, sir."

Nathaniel Lawless's pale-grey eyes narrowed. He clenched his fists and addressed Burton. "I don't like the idea that one of my crew is a rogue, Sir Richard. Nor do I understand it. Why would anyone wish to interfere with your expedition?"

Burton clicked his teeth together. He glanced at Gooch, who got to his feet and stood with his metal arms poised over his shoulders, then turned back to Lawless. "How much do you know about my mission, Captain?"

"Only that you intend to discover the source of the River Nile. I've been instructed by Mr. Brunel to deliver you and your supplies to Zanzibar. I understand that the government has funded the entire undertaking. Is there something more?"

"There is."

"Then I ask you to tell me. You can count on my discretion. Mr. Gooch, would you leave us, please?"

"It's all right, Captain," Gooch said. "You have authority over me on this ship but, as a Technologist, I hold a more senior position and happen to know the details. I apologise for having kept them from you, but our superiors felt that certain aspects of this expedition should remain hush-hush."

Lawless looked from one man to the other. "That's all well and good, but if the *Orpheus* is in danger, I have the right to know why."

"Agreed," Burton said. "The truth, sir, is that while I hope to finally identify the source of the Nile, it is only a secondary consideration. The priority is to locate and retrieve a black diamond, known as the Eye of Nāga. In this endeavour, I am almost certainly opposed by a Prussian spy named Zeppelin."

Lawless's eyes widened. "Are you telling me that our saboteur is a Prussian agent?"

"In all probability, yes. I should say he was commissioned by Zeppelin to interfere with the ship."

Lawless raised a hand and ran it over his closely cropped white beard. His eyes flashed. "I'll keelhaul the bastard!"

"I'm not sure that's possible in a rotorship," Gooch muttered.

"I'll bloody well make it possible!"

"We have to catch him first," Burton observed.

"It's puzzling, though," said Gooch. "If the saboteur intends to delay your expedition, don't you think it rather peculiar that he's committed an act which causes the ship to fly faster—albeit destructively so; an act that'll cause you to arrive at Zanzibar considerably earlier than planned?"

Burton frowned. "That, Mr. Gooch, is a very good point. A very good point indeed!"

Burton spoke to Swinburne, Trounce, Honesty, Krishnamurthy, Bhatti, Spencer, Miss Mayson, and Sister Raghavendra, and arranged for them to patrol the ship, keeping a close watch on the crew and their eyes peeled for suspicious behaviour. He then returned to his quarters, intending to update his journal. Pulling a key from his pocket, he unlocked the door, pushed it open, and stopped in his tracks.

There was something on the desk.

He stepped into the room and looked around. The cabin was rectangular and of a medium size, carpeted, wallpapered, and well furnished. One of the thick ventilation pipes ran across the ceiling and four oil lamps were suspended two to each side of it. There were two other doors, one to the small bedchamber and the other to a tiny washroom.

The afternoon sun was sending a shaft of Mediterranean brilliance in through the porthole. Its white glare reflected brightly off the object, which hadn't been on the desk when Burton left the cabin a couple of hours earlier. He'd locked the door behind him. There were no other means of ingress.

He picked the thing up, went back out into the corridor, closed and locked the door, then knelt and squinted at the keyhole. He stood and paced away, heading toward the prow of the rotorship. Doctor Quaint was coming the other way.

"Doctor," Burton said. "May I have a minute of your time?"

"Certainly. I say! What have you there?"

Burton held up the object. "A mystery, Doctor. It was on the desk in my quarters. Tell me—who else has a key?"

"To your cabin? Just Sister Raghavendra and myself." Quaint reached into his pocket and pulled out a crowded key ring. "As stewards, we have access to all the passenger rooms." He picked through the keys one by one. "Here it is. This is yours."

"And have you used it today?"

"No, sir, I have not."

"Could you prove that, should it be necessary?"

Quaint bristled slightly. "Sister Raghavendra will attest that I've been working with her all morning, throughout lunch, and up until a few minutes ago, when I left her in order to report to the captain. I've just come from the bridge."

"Thank you, Doctor. I'm sorry to have troubled you. I'd better see the captain myself, I think."

"Very well." Quaint glanced again at the object.

Burton left the steward and proceeded along the corridor and up the metal stairs to the conning tower. He stepped onto the bridge, which was occupied by a number of crewmembers. Captain Lawless turned as he entered, saw what he was holding, and uttered an exclamation.

"Great Scott! Where did you find that?"

"On the desk in my cabin, Captain. Am I correct in assuming it's the missing bearing cradle?"

"You are. Let me see."

Burton handed the metal ring to Lawless, who examined it closely before pronouncing it undamaged. He addressed Oscar Wilde, who was cleaning a console at the back of the room.

"Master Wilde, would you run this down to the engine room, please? Ask Mr. Gooch to have it fitted as soon as we land at Cairo."

Wilde took the cradle and departed.

"In your cabin?" Lawless said. "How did it get there?"

"That's the question. I locked the door when I left and it was still locked when I returned. Doctor Quaint assures me that neither he nor Sister Raghavendra entered the room in my absence and I saw nothing to suggest the lock had been picked. That doesn't mean it wasn't, but in my experience there are usually tiny scratches left after that manner of break-in."

Lawless removed his captain's hat and rubbed his head. "Well, whatever method your intruder used, this is rather an inept way to implicate you."

"It would only implicate me if the stewards had found the bearing cradle while servicing my cabin. And you'd think it would at least be hidden under my bunk, rather than placed on top of my desk in broad daylight. Besides which, it makes no sense that I would sabotage my own expedition."

Lawless hissed softly, "Curse it! I won't rest until we find this bloody traitor!"

"Nor I," Burton whispered back. "I have my people patrolling the ship. Our villain will find it hard to cause any further damage without being caught in the act!"

The explorer remained on the bridge for the next three hours. He kept a close eye on the men at their stations, but saw nothing suspicious.

The Mediterranean slid beneath the big rotorship.

A hollow whistle sounded.

Lawless crossed to a brass panel in the wall and pulled a domed lid from it. As it came away, a segmented tube followed behind. Lawless flipped the lid open, blew into the tube, put it to his ear, and listened awhile. He then moved it to his mouth and said, "Hold him. I'll be right down."

He clicked the lid back into the panel and said to Burton, "Apparently your assistant is causing merry mayhem in the engine room."

"How so?"

Captain Lawless ignored the question and turned to his first officer. "Take command, please, Mr. Henson."

"Yes, sir."

"Mr. Playfair, how long to Cairo?"

"Two and a half hours, sir, unless we can slow her down. All four stern engines are already overheating, according to my instruments."

"Thank you. Mr. Bingham, report, please."

The fat little meteorologist replied, "Clear sailing all the way, sir. Not a cloud in the sky. Breeze is northwesterly, currently less than five knots but building."

"Mr. Wenham?"

"Steady going, sir."

"Good. Follow me, Sir Richard."

The aeronaut and explorer left the bridge, descended through the conning tower, and entered the corridor that ran the length of the rotorship.

"Mr. Swinburne claims to have caught our saboteur," Lawless said.

"Ah!" Burton replied.

They entered the lounge and descended the port-side staircase, then moved past the standard-class cabins and on into the first of the engine-room compartments. The rumble of the turbines sounded from the next chamber, muffled by thickly insulated walls.

Peering past pipes and four wide rotating pillars, Burton saw Trounce and Honesty gripping the arms of a very small person. Engineers were gathered around them, and Swinburne was dancing in front of the police officers and their captive, shrieking at the top of his voice.

"Tobias Threadneedle, my eye!" he screeched. "Liar! Brute! Traitor! Impostor!"

"What are you doing down here, Algy?" Burton asked as he and Lawless joined the group. "I thought you were working?"

"I found myself unable to write, Richard, so I came in search of inspiration, and what I found instead—" Swinburne raised his voice to a scream and pointed his finger, "—is the one and only Vincent Sneed—otherwise known as the Conk!"

Burton looked down at the short, wiry individual held in the grip of the two Scotland Yard men. He wasn't much bigger than a child, and owned a very unprepossessing stoat-like face, dominated by a perfectly huge nose. A ragged, nicotine-stained moustache concealed his lipless mouth. His thin black hair was long, greasy, and combed back over his narrow skull. He was pockmarked and sly-looking, and his beady little eyes—positioned almost on the sides of his gargantuan proboscis rather than to either side of it in the normal way—were flicking back and forth in a panicked manner.

"I bloody aren't!" he protested. "Me name's Threadneedle. Arsk 'im!" He nodded to a small boy standing nearby, a ragamuffin with sandy-blond hair.

Captain Lawless said, "And who are you, my lad?"

"Willy Cornish, sir," the boy answered nervously.

Daniel Gooch stepped forward, his mechanical arms slowly undulating to either side of him. "They are the ship's funnel scrubbers, Captain."

Willy Cornish nodded and pointed at the prisoner. "That's right, sir. And he's who he says he is—Tobias Threadneedle."

Swinburne let loose a tremendous howl and hopped up and down like a madman. "Willy! You know perfectly well this is Sneed!"

Cornish shifted uncomfortably and wrung his hands. "No, Carrots," he said, employing the nickname he'd given the poet during the time they'd spent together sweeping chimneys. "I know he looks like old Sneed, but he's Mr. Threadneedle, and he's all right, he is."

"All right? He's a rogue! A bully! A snake in the grass!"

"I ain't none o' them things!" the captive cried out, struggling to free himself.

"Here, less of that!" Trounce snapped.

"I'll have the cuffs on you!" Honesty threatened.

"I ain't done nuffink!" the prisoner protested.

"You sabotaged the ship!" Swinburne shouted.

"I bloody didn't!"

"You bloody did!"

"I bloody didn't!"

"SHUT UP!" Lawless roared. "You—" he jabbed a finger at Swinburne, "—calm down and explain."

"The explanation," Swinburne answered, "is that while this hound may be calling himself Tobias Threadneedle, he is actually, and without doubt, a scurrilous rogue by the name of Vincent Sneed. I worked side by side with him the year before last and he treated me abominably. I cannot be mistaken. Look at that nose of his! How many men do you think there are walking around with such a perfectly enormous beak?"

"Oy!" the prisoner objected.

"But you say Mr. Swinburne is mistaken?" Lawless demanded of Cornish.

"Y-yes, sir," the boy stuttered. "I kn-know Mr. Sneed, and this ain't him."

Swinburne groaned and slapped a hand to his forehead. "Why, Willy? Why are you supporting this blackguard?"

"Stop calling me them bleedin' names, you damned rat!" the accused man cried out.

"Algy," Burton said. "Even if this is Mr. Sneed—"

"It is!"

"—What makes you think it was he who sabotaged the ship?"

"Because he's a villain!"

"So your allegation is based on supposition rather than evidence?"

Swinburne sighed and muttered, "Yes, Richard. But isn't it enough that he's lying to us?"

Burton turned to Captain Lawless. "Is there a secure room available? I'd like to keep this man under guard while we get to the bottom of this."

"Use the first of the class-two passenger cabins," Lawless said, pointing toward the corridor they'd come through. "I have to get back to the bridge. I'll send the steward down with the key. Report to me when this is sorted out, please."

With that, the captain gave a last glance at the prisoner then marched away.

Burton addressed his assistant: "Algy, where is Herbert?"

"Holed up in his cabin, working on a philosophical treatise."

"Would you fetch him, please?"

The poet shifted his weight from one foot to the other, glowered at the big-nosed man, frowned at Willy Cornish, then nodded and followed after Lawless.

Burton positioned himself in front of the individual who called himself Tobias Threadneedle and said, "Did you take part in a riot at Speakers' Corner last summer?"

"No!" the man answered. He couldn't meet Burton's eyes, and kept raising his own to the ceiling, anxiously scanning the pipes and machinery above. The way he squirmed in Trounce and Honesty's grip suggested that he wasn't telling the truth.

"The two men holding you are police officers," Burton revealed.

Trounce added, "And we won't hesitate to arrest you and deliver you to a Cairo gaol if you're what Mr. Swinburne says you are!"

"Egyptian prison," Honesty murmured. "Very nasty. Foul places."

"Oh please, Mother! I ain't done nuffink!" their captive wailed. "I'm just a bleedin' funnel scrubber!"

"Sneed was at the riot," Burton stated. "As were these two fellows and myself. My assistant got into a scrap with him. None of us saw it, but our colleague, Mr. Spencer, did. He's on his way down now, and he'll either endorse Mr. Swinburne's assertion, or he won't. If you're Tobias Threadneedle, you have nothing to worry about. If you're Vincent Sneed, things are about to go very badly for you."

The prisoner let out a keening whine of despair.

Burton turned to Willy Cornish.

"I've heard good things about you, young man. I hope you're not telling fibs. I would be very disappointed indeed."

Willy burst into tears and buried his face in the crook of his arm.

Daniel Gooch approached Burton and said, in a low voice, "That bearing cradle, Sir Richard—I understand it appeared in your cabin under mysterious circumstances?"

"Yes."

"It's this fellow's duty—" one of Gooch's mechanical arms gestured toward Threadneedle, "—to keep the pipes clear on that side of the ship. He could have opened the ventilation panel in the pipe and entered your quarters through it."

"I see. Thank you, Mr. Gooch."

A few tense minutes passed while they waited for Herbert Spencer's arrival. When the clockwork philosopher entered the room—clanking along beside Swinburne, and with Pox squatting on his head—Threadneedle's little eyes widened and he stuttered, "Wha-wha-what's that thing?"

"Tosspot!" Pox squawked.

"Herbert," Burton said. "Have you seen this fellow before?"

The brass man stepped over to Threadneedle and nodded. "Yus, Boss. He were at the riot last summer. He got into a fight with Mr. Swinburne. He's Vincent Sneed."

The prisoner groaned and slumped.

Doctor Quaint walked in, glanced curiously at the scene, and handed a key to Burton. "Second-class cabin number one," he said.

"Thank you, Doctor." Burton addressed the Yard men: "Let us secure Mr. Sneed, gentlemen."

He led the way to the cabin, followed by the policemen and their prisoner.

Swinburne turned to Willy Cornish and placed a hand on the boy's shoulder. "Why were you protecting him, Willy? Has he threatened you?"

Willy looked up, his eyes swimming in tears. "I can't say, Carrots. I would, but I just can't!"

Swinburne shook his head and chewed his bottom lip. "There's something very wrong about all of this," he grumbled. "But how the blazes am I to get to the facts of the matter if you won't help?"

With a cry of anguish, Willy suddenly sped away, ducked under the arms of the engineers who tried to stop him, and leaped onto machinery lining one of the walls. He clambered up it like a little monkey until he reached a ventilation panel. Swinging it open, he disappeared into the pipe behind.

"My hat!" the poet muttered. "What on earth has got into him?"

The *Orpheus* landed at the Cairo Airfield at seven in the evening, and the crew got to work taking on a fresh load of Formby coal and refilling the water tanks.

Vincent Sneed had been left alone to stew in Standard Class Cabin 1. He was slumped on the bunk when a key turned in the lock and the door opened. Sir Richard Francis Burton entered followed by Detective Inspectors Trounce and Honesty and a tall dark-skinned man wearing a uniform with epaulettes and a sash. His face was eagle-like, adorned with a moustache and imperial, and his eyes were black. There was a fez on his head.

"Mr. Sneed," Burton said. "This is Al-Mustazi, the commissioner of the city police. He has men waiting outside. They will take you into custody until the British consul gets around to dealing with you. That could take a good few weeks, during which time you'll have to survive as best you can in Cairo's prison. I know you were born and raised in the Cauldron, and I know from personal experience what a hellhole that part of London is, but I can assure you that it will seem like Shangri-La in comparison to the conditions you are to experience shortly."

Sneed looked up, his little ferrety eyes filled with wretchedness. "I ain't done nuffink," he keened.

"Do you still maintain that your name is Tobias Threadneedle?"

The funnel scrubber swallowed, his Adam's apple bobbing on his scrawny neck.

"Yes," he whispered.

"Even though you've been identified by two people as Vincent Sneed?"

"Yes."

"Did you break into my quarters and deposit a bearing cradle in them?"

Burton noted that the little man's hands were trembling. He saw the eyes flick to the left and right, then up at the ceiling.

"I—I ain't done nuffink! Nuffink!"

Burton sighed. "Mr. Sneed, many a man has lied to me in the past and I have a practised eye. I can see by the way you hold yourself, by your every movement and expression, that you're not telling me the truth. I shall give you one final chance. Admit who you are, tell me why you placed the bearing cradle on my desk, then I shall see to it that you are shipped back to London with due dispatch. I'll even ask that no charges are brought against you. Obviously, you'll never work as a funnel scrubber again, but you can, at least, go back to being a master sweep."

A tear trickled down Sneed's cheek. "You don't understand," he said. "I knows I've been a bad 'un. P'raps a bit too strict, like, wiv the nippers. But I were only tryin' to get good work out o' them. I didn't mean no 'arm to that carrot-top. I were just trainin' 'im. An'—" he sucked in a shuddery breath and swallowed again, "—an' I don't mean no 'arm now, neither. I ain't done nuffink! I ain't done nuffink!"

"So you admit to the actions of Vincent Sneed yet still say you aren't him?"

The little man wrung his hands together then raised them to cover his face.

"Yes," he groaned.

"Does the name Zeppelin mean anything to you?"

Sneed parted his fingers and looked out from behind them. "Zephram?"

"Zeppelin."

"I don't know no Zeppelin."

Burton turned to Trounce and Honesty. "Would you hand the prisoner over to your Egyptian colleagues, please?"

The two detectives nodded, stepped forward, and hoisted Sneed up off the bed.

"No!" he screeched, writhing in their grip. "Get yer 'ands off me!"

"No nonsense, if you please!" Trounce snapped.

They bundled him out of the cabin, to where four Egyptian constables waited. Sneed howled.

Burton, speaking fluent Arabic in the local dialect, quietly addressed Al-Mustazi: "Despite my threats to the man, I'd prefer it if you kept him from the worst of it. I sent my parakeet to the consul as soon as we landed with a request that the prisoner be processed with due dispatch. He'll be handed over to British authorities and sent home in a few days but there's no need to tell him that. Let him think he's going to be in Cairo prison for the long haul, it may teach him a lesson."

Al-Mustazi murmured an acknowledgement, bowed, and departed.

Burton left the cabin and met Trounce and Honesty in the corridor. They headed up to the passenger lounge.

"Strange!" said Honesty. "Why so stubborn?"

"It's odd, I'll admit," Burton replied. "And there was something else rather peculiar, too. He kept glancing up at the ceiling."

"I noticed that," Trounce grunted. "I wonder why?"

The three men joined Swinburne, Krishnamurthy, Bhatti, and Herbert Spencer in the lounge. The clockwork philosopher was incapable of drinking or smoking but he enjoyed company and needed the mental relaxation, despite that his mind was an electrical field processed by a machine. With Pox on his head, he sat at the bar with the men, who sipped at their brandy and sodas and gazed at the scattered lights of the city's houses and minarets. Burton smoked one of his disreputable Manila cheroots, Trounce opted for a rather more expensive *Flor de Dindigul* Indian cigar, while Honesty and Krishnamurthy puffed at their pipes. Neither Swinburne nor Bhatti smoked. The poet compensated for it by consuming twice as much brandy.

"Steady on," Burton advised him.

"I need it," his assistant answered. "I'm frustrated. Willy Cornish is a splendid young man, and I can't for the life of me think why he would defend a scurrilous miscreant like Sneed. And now he's vanished into the pipes and probably won't emerge until he's starving!"

"Needs interrogating!" Honesty snapped. "Spill the beans. Tell us what Zeppelin is up to."

"Dribbly snot-rag!" Pox cawed.

"I don't understand it," Krishnamurthy said. "Why would the Prussian hire a villain Mr. Swinburne could recognise in an instant?"

"Perhaps he didn't know that we'd encountered Sneed before," Bhatti suggested.

Trounce snorted. "Pah! Too much of a coincidence! There's more to it, mark my words, lad!"

Burton nodded thoughtfully. "I agree," he murmured. "There's a deeper mystery here."

Doctor Quaint and Sister Raghavendra entered the chamber and began to light the oil lamps. Burton stood and wandered over to the young woman.

"Hello, Sadhvi. Have you settled into your duties?"

"Hello, Captain Burton. Yes. It's been a busy day. I'll go down to the kitchen in a minute to help Mr. Butler and Miss Mayson with the supper, then once that's cooked and eaten and tidied away, I'll retire to my cabin for a well-earned rest. Incidentally, I brought with me a volume of Mr. Swinburne's *Poems and Ballads* to read but I seem to have misplaced it. Might you ask him if he has a spare copy?"

"You can borrow mine. I'll have Quips deliver it to you. I should warn you, though—it's a mite vivid!"

"So I've heard, but I'm from India, Captain. I don't suffer the modesties, embarrassments, or fainting fits of your English ladies!"

Burton smiled. "Then you are most fortunate!"

On his way back to his friends, halfway across the small dance floor, the king's agent suddenly stopped and gazed up at the ceiling.

"By James!" he whispered. "Could it be? It would certainly explain a lot!"

When he sat down and picked up his drink, the others noticed that he wore a distracted expression.

"What's on your mind, Captain?" Bhatti asked.

"Hmm? Oh, I'm just—just thinking about—about—um—Christopher Rigby."

"Yikes!" Swinburne exclaimed. "He's going to be nothing but trouble!"

"Who's Rigby?" Herbert Spencer asked.

"Malodorous horse bucket!" Pox whistled.

"The parakeet has it!" Swinburne declared. "Lieutenant Christopher Palmer Rigby is the consul at Zanzibar and a fat-headed ninny of the first order. Richard repeatedly knocked him off the top spot in language examinations back when they were stationed in India, and Rigby, sore loser that he is, has never forgotten it. The rotter's made a career of besmirching our friend's reputation. I'd like to punch the hound right on the nose!"

"Thank you, Algy," Burton said. He explained further: "Rigby and I were in the East India Company's Eighteenth Bombay Native Infantry at Scinde, and he formed an immediate and irrational hatred of me from the outset. He'll cause problems for us when we land in Africa, of that I'm certain."

"King's agent!" Honesty barked. "Authority!"

"Possessing authority is one thing," Burton replied, "but expecting a man like Rigby to respect it is quite another."

Over the next hour, he barely said another word, and when they attended the captain's table for supper, the explorer appeared so preoccupied that his bearing came perilously close to impoliteness. Afterward, he muttered a few words about writing up his journals and retired to his cabin.

He lit one lamp and turned it down low, then got undressed, washed, put on his pyjamas, and wrapped himself in his *jubbah*. He lit a cheroot and relaxed in an armchair, his eyes focused inward, his mind working on a Sufi meditation exercise.

He finished the cigar.

A couple of hours passed.

He didn't move.

Then: *There!*

He'd heard a faint noise, a tiny rasping sound.

He waited.

Again, an almost imperceptible scrape.

He allowed a few minutes to tick by.

"You should have asked before borrowing Sister Raghavendra's copy of *Poems and Ballads*."

Silence.

He spoke again. "You made a scapegoat of Vincent Sneed. I have no fondness for the fellow, but why? What was the point?"

Thirty seconds or so passed.

A small, whispery voice said, "Distraction, Captain Burton."

"There you are! Hello, lad! I take it Sneed and Willy Cornish smuggled you onto the ship in the replacement section of pipe?"

"Yes. I had ordered the previous two funnel scrubbers to purposely damage a section in order to facilitate my presence here."

"So the Beetle, the chief of the League of Chimney Sweeps, finds himself en route to Africa. A bizarre circumstance indeed, and I imagine you must have a very good reason for leaving your chimney. Distraction, you say? Who are you trying to distract, and from what?"

Burton stood and moved to the middle of the room. He looked up at the grille in the thick ventilation pipe. Vaguely, he could discern something moving behind it.

"Don't turn the lamps up," came the whisper.

"I don't intend to. I know how you abhor light."

"One of my boys was killed."

"Who?"

"Bingo Stokes. He was ten years old, and one of the few not an orphan. But his father mistreated him terribly, and Bingo often sought refuge in a chimney."

"Ah. Now I understand. He cleaned the chimney of a house in Ilford, then went back there to steal food and spend a night in the flue."

"That is correct, Captain. And while he was there, he overheard four men plotting. Three were Prussians, but, fortunately, they spoke in English on account of the fourth man. That individual was instructed to bring down this ship, if he couldn't kill you first. Unfortunately, Bingo's presence was detected, and though he got away, he was shot. By the time he reached me, it was too late to save him. He bled to death, but not before repeating to me everything he'd heard."

"So there is still a saboteur at loose?"

"Yes, but I do not know who it is. I arranged to be smuggled aboard and I instructed Vincent Sneed to steal the bearing cradle."

"You're conversant with the engineering of the *Orpheus*?"

"I had already read a great deal of material pertaining to her construction."

Burton thought for a moment, then said, "So you alerted us to the fact that a saboteur was aboard by arranging a fairly harmless act of sabotage yourself?"

"Exactly, and in doing so, I made it difficult, if not impossible, for the Prussian agent to act, for your people were all on the lookout for suspicious behaviour. The first leg of your voyage was thus protected. I then placed the cradle in your room, knowing that Sneed would be recognised and accused."

"Why do that?"

"Because now Sneed's been dealt with, your enemy will think that you consider yourselves safe. He'll be of the opinion that he can act with impunity when, in truth, you'll be watching out for him."

Burton pondered this, then said, "You've done me a service, and I thank you, but I don't understand. Why such an extravagant scheme when you could've got a message to me before the *Orpheus* left Battersea?"

"If I had, what would you have done?"

"I'd have dismissed the entire crew, hired a new one, and had every inch of the ship thoroughly checked."

"And how long would that have taken?"

"Perhaps four days. Maybe five or six."

"Bingo Stokes learned something else. The man who owned the house, Steinrück, was taking care of some business in Yorkshire—"

"His real name is Zeppelin and he went there to arrange my poisoning."

"I see. I'm glad he failed. Upon completing this business, he was going to fly to Prussia to join an expedition to Central Africa led by Lieutenant John Speke. I realised, therefore, that warning you would result in a delay you can ill afford, for you are in a race."

"Bismillah!" Burton cursed. "I thought a rival expedition might be a possibility! So Speke and Zeppelin are already on their way?"

"They are, and that is why I chose the removal of the bearing cradle as my means of false sabotage, for I knew that it would result in a dangerous turn of speed. Maybe it will get you ahead in the game."

Burton smacked a fist into his palm and paced up and down. "Damnation!" he muttered.

"You have no time for this stopover in Cairo," the Beetle urged. "You must get this ship back into the air at once. The saboteur will make a move but he will undoubtedly lack the appropriate caution. Catch him, then catch up with your opponents."

Burton hurried across the room and snatched up his clothes. "What of you?" he asked as he started to dress.

"I will watch and listen and try to identify the agent. After you are delivered to Zanzibar, I'll remain with the ship while it returns to London. Willy Cornish—who, incidentally, has been following my orders—will facilitate my return to Limehouse."

"And Sneed?"

"He has a history of bullying my lads. This was his chance to redeem himself. He performed his part well and will be compensated for the inconvenience he is currently suffering."

Burton quickly buttoned up his clothes and tied his bootlaces. He stepped to the door and grasped its handle. "I have to tell my people what you've done, then get us moving," he said. "Thank you, lad. I'm in your debt."

First Officer William Henson had just dropped off to sleep when a hammering at his cabin door awoke him. Swearing under his breath, he pulled on a gown, yanked open the door, and was confronted by the captain.

"Sleep is cancelled, Mr. Henson. I need all hands on deck."

"Right away, sir. Is there a problem?"

"A change of schedule. No layover in Cairo. We're departing immediately. Mr. Gooch and the riggers will be recalibrating the four stern engines while we're in mid-flight. That means four external doors are going to be wide open in the sides of the engineering bay. We'll keep a low altitude, of course, but nevertheless I feel uneasy flying so exposed. I'd like you to oversee things down there until we're properly sealed up again."

"Certainly, sir, though I'm sure Mr. Gooch—"

"Will have everything under control. I don't doubt it, Henson, but since we have only three riggers and there are four engines that require attention, Mr. Gooch will be out on one of the flight pylons."

"Ah. I see. I'll get down there at once."

"You can shave and tidy yourself up first. There are some internal repairs and adjustments to be made before Gooch and his team go outside. Get down there within the hour, please."

"Yes, sir."

Henson's door was the first of a number to be knocked upon over the course of the next few minutes, and in very short measure the majority of the *Orpheus*'s aeronauts found themselves unexpectedly back on duty.

It was a few minutes past midnight.

The rotorship's flight crew gathered on the bridge. Sir Richard Francis Burton was there, watching each of them carefully. They looked bleary-eyed and dishevelled. Captain Lawless did not. His uniform was buttoned, his eyes were bright, and he was all efficiency.

"What's going on, sir?" Arthur Bingham, the meteorologist, asked.

"I'll have your report, Mr. Bingham, not your questions," Lawless snapped.

"Yes, sir. A wind has picked up. Rather strong. Easterly, currently at a steady twenty knots. No cloud."

"You heard that, Mr. Playfair?"

"Yes, sir," the navigator responded. "Taken into account. Course plotted to Aden."

"Good man. Mr. Pryce, call down to Mr. Gooch and have him start the engines."

"Aye, sir." Wordsworth Pryce, the second officer, moved to the speaking tubes. Moments later, a vibration ran through the rotorship.

"Engage the wings, Mr. Wenham."

"Engaging. Opening. Rotating . . . and . . . up to speed."

"Take us to two thousand feet."

On an expanding cone of steam, the *Orpheus* rose into the night sky and began to power into the southeast, leaving the ill-lit city of Cairo behind her. Above, the Milky Way arced across the heavens, but below, the narrow Red Sea and the lands to either side of it were wreathed in darkness, so it seemed that the ship was sailing through an empty void.

With her stern engines still operating abnormally, the huge vessel rattled and shook as she ate up the miles, speeding at almost 150 knots toward Aden, on the tip of the Arabian Peninsula.

In the engine room, the bearing cradle had been refitted, but it took Daniel Gooch and his fellow engineers almost four hours to reset the synchro-nisation system, which they achieved by shutting down the four rear engines one at a time while adjusting the various components to which the cradle was connected.

Now all that remained was to recalibrate each of those stern-most engines.

Gooch and the riggers Gordon Champion, Alexander Priestley, and Win-ford Doe, positioned themselves at the four hull doors and buckled them-selves into harnesses. They clipped safety straps to brackets above the portals.

First Officer Henson pulled a speaking tube from the wall.

On the bridge, his call was answered by Oscar Wilde, who said, "Captain Lawless, Mr. Henson is asking permission to open the external doors."

Lawless was standing by the window with Sir Richard Francis Burton. They were watching *al-fajr al-kaadhib*, the zodiacal light, which was rising column-like in the western sky. He said, "Tell him permission is granted, Master Wilde."

"Aye, sir," the boy replied. He relayed the message down to the engine room.

Lawless stepped over to the helmsman and stood beside him, quietly ordering, "Steady as she goes, please, Mr. Wenham."

"Aye-aye, sir, but—" Wenham hesitated.

"What is it?"

"I—um—I think—" The helmsman turned to Cedric Playfair, the navi-gator. "Shouldn't we still be over the Red Sea?"

"Yes," Playfair answered, glancing at his instruments.

"Then why is there desert below us?"

Lawless and Playfair both looked up and saw what Wenham had spotted—that the vaguest glimmers of light were skimming not over water, but sand dunes.

"Impossible!" Playfair gasped.

Burton joined them and watched as the navigator checked over his console.

"The compass says we're travelling south-southeast," Playfair muttered. "But if that were true, we'd be where we should be." He tapped the instrument, then bent, opened a panel in the console, reached in, and felt about, muttering: "Maybe something is interfering with—hello! What's this?" He pulled out a small block of metal, and as he did so, the compass needle swung from SSE to SE.

"A magnet!" Burton observed.

"How the devil—?" Playfair exclaimed.

Lawless clenched his teeth and bunched his fists.

"But it shouldn't make any difference!" Francis Wenham objected. "That compass is just for reference. It isn't used to set the course."

"He's right, sir," Playfair put in. "Mr. Wenham follows the instrumentation on his own console. It indicates the degrees to port or starboard he should steer the ship to maintain the course I set. Taking into account the compensation I calculated, if he's followed his indicators exactly, we should be slap bang over the Red Sea."

"And I have done," Wenham noted.

"Compensation?" Burton asked.

"For the wind, sir," Playfair replied.

Burton stepped back to the window. He turned and gestured for Oscar Wilde to join him.

"Yes, sir?" the boy asked.

"Can you find me some field glasses?"

"Right over here," said Wilde, crossing to a wall cabinet and returning with a large-lensed brass device. Burton took it and raised it to his face, clipping its bracket over his head. He turned back to the window, and with the fingers of both hands rotated the focusing wheels on either side of the apparatus.

The land below was wreathed in darkness, with just the tips of dunes visible in the faint light of *al-fajr al-kaadhib*. The field glasses threw them into sharp relief.

"Captain Lawless," Burton murmured, "I have a reasonably clear view of the sand dunes below us."

"What of it, Sir Richard?"

"They are entirely motionless. There is no sand rippling across their surface or spraying from their peaks. In other words, the strong wind Mr. Playfair just mentioned is nonexistent, at least at ground level, and since we're flying low—"

"If I've been taking into account a wind that isn't actually blowing, it would certainly explain our position," Playfair put in.

"Mr. Bingham!" Lawless roared, but when he turned to the meteorologist's position, he saw that it was unoccupied. "Where the devil is he?" he demanded.

"Mr. Bingham left the bridge some little time ago, so he did, sir," said Oscar Wilde.

"Playfair, Wenham, get us back on course! Sir Richard, come with me. We have to find my meteorologist. He has some explaining to do!"

Some minutes later, they located Arthur Bingham in the engine room, standing with Daniel Gooch, Shyamji Bhatti, and Winford Doe near one of the open hull doors. Doe was unbuckling his harness.

"Hallo, Captain Burton, Captain Lawless!" Bhatti called as they approached.

Gooch turned and said, "Almost done, Captain. Mr. Champion is just putting the finishing touches to the last of our wayward engines."

Lawless ignored the chief engineer and glared at the short, fat meteorologist. "You appear to have deserted your post without permission, Bingham."

"I—I just came down to watch Mr. Gooch at—at work, sir," Bingham responded.

"Worried he'd be blown off the pylon by the high winds, were you?"

Bingham took a couple of steps backward.

"Is there a problem?" Gooch asked.

Lawless's eyes flashed angrily. "There most certainly is!"

Bingham pulled a pistol from his pocket and brandished it at them. "Get back, all of you!"

"Bloody traitor!" Lawless snapped.

"Hey! Drop that!" Bhatti cried out.

Bingham swung the pistol toward the constable, then pointed it at Burton, then at Lawless. His lips thinned against his teeth and his eyes flashed threateningly.

Lawless said, "Why?"

"Because I have a wife and two children," the meteorologist snarled. "And I also happen to have a tumour in my gut and not many months to live. A certain party has agreed to pay my family a large amount of money in return for the sacrifice I'm about to make." He directed his gun back at the king's agent. "I wouldn't have to do it at all but for you, Burton. I followed you to Ilford and back and took a pot-shot at you."

"You ruined a perfectly good hat."

"It's a crying shame I didn't spoil the head it was adorning. If you'd have been decent enough to die then, this ship and its crew would have been spared."

"You're not the only man Zeppelin hired to kill me," Burton revealed. "The other was promised money and received instead the count's hands around his neck."

"Ah, so you know my employer, then! But what do you mean?"

"My other would-be assassin was strangled to death, Bingham. Had you managed to put a bullet in me, I have little doubt that Zeppelin's associates would have then put one in you. As for money being paid to your family, you can forget it. The Prussians will feel no obligation to you once you're dead."

"Shut your mouth!" Bingham yelled. His finger whitened on the trigger as he jerked his pistol back and forth between Burton, Lawless, and Bhatti.

"Give it up, man!" the latter advised. "Don't leave your family stained with the name of a traitor!"

The meteorologist backed away a step. "Not another word out of you!" he spat at Bhatti. "As for you, Burton, they want an end to your little jaunt to Africa, and this——" With his free hand, Bingham undid his tightly buttoned jacket and pulled it open. He wasn't the fat man they thought he was. He was a slim man made bulky by a vest fashioned from sticks of dynamite. "This will ensure they get what they want!"

"Hell's teeth!" Captain Lawless shouted. "Are you bloody insane, man?"

Bingham sneered nastily. "Blame your friend here, Lawless. He's left me with no choice but to eliminate you all."

"You do have a choice," Burton said. "Shoot me now and spare the ship."

"No. I've overheard you and your companions enough to know that, now they're on their way to Africa, they'd continue your mission without you. This is it for all of you."

He placed his left index finger over a button in the middle of his chest.

"Bingham! There are women and children on board!" Lawless bellowed.

"To protect my own woman, and my own children, I would do anything, even——"

Shyamji Bhatti suddenly threw himself at the meteorologist, thudded into him, and with his arms wrapped around the saboteur, allowed his momentum to send them both toppling out of the open hull door. There came a blinding flash from outside and a tremendous discharge. The floor swung upward and slapped into the side of Burton's head, stunning him and sending him sliding across its metal surface. Bells jangled in his ears. Through the clamour, as if from a far-off place, he heard someone yell: "We're going down!"

CHAPTER 5

THROUGH THE DESERT

"A Phenomenal Success."
FLOR DE DINDIGUL
A Medium-Mild Indian Cigar
"Will bear favourable comparison
with choice Havanas,
while the cost is about one-third."
Indian Tobacco, grown by Messrs. Slightly & Co.,
is eugenically enhanced for exquisitely choice
flavour and delicate aroma.
A DELIGHTFUL WHIFF
22/- per 100 from all good Tobacconists.

*S*ir Richard Francis Burton was leaning against a palm tree just beyond the final cottage of Kaltenberg. Beside him, Bertie Wells, sitting on a rock, was dabbing at a small wound on the back of his neck with a handkerchief. Burton had just used a penknife to dig a jigger flea out from beneath the war correspondent's skin.

From the trees around them, the shrieks and cackles of birds and monkeys blended into a cacophonous racket.

High overhead, eagles wheeled majestically through the dazzling sky.

The terrain in front of the two men angled down to the outlying houses and huts of Tanga.

Burton squinted, looking across the rooftops of the sprawling town to the ocean beyond. It was like peering through glass; the atmosphere was solid with heat. The humidity pressed against him, making his skin prickle. Respiration required a conscious effort, with each scalding breath having to be sucked in, the air resisting, as if too lethargic to move.

Wells pointed at a large building in the western part of the seaport.

"That's the railway terminal. Two major lines run from it—the Tanganyika, all the way west to the lake; and the Usambara, up to Kilimanjaro."

"Language is an astonishingly liquid affair," Burton muttered. "We pronounced it Kilima Njaro in my day. Like the natives."

"Perhaps some still do," Wells replied. "But it's the fluid quality that makes language an excellent tool for imperialists. Force people to speak like you and soon enough they'll be thinking like you. Rename their villages, towns, and mountains, and before they know it, they're inhabiting your territory. So Kilimanjaro it is. Anyway, as I was saying, that's the station and our forces need to capture or destroy it to slow down the movement of German troops and supplies." He indicated a twin-funnelled warship lying at anchor in the bay. "And that's HMS *Fox*. She's almost two decades obsolete but such is our desperation that we have to resort to whatever's available. She's been sweeping the harbour for mines. Look at her flags. Do you understand the signal?"

"No."

"It's a demand for surrender. The British Indian Expeditionary Force transports have already offloaded the troops onto the beaches. They're awaiting the order to attack. The *Fox*'s captain will lead the assault. He's probably waiting for Aitken to get our lot into position. It won't be long now."

Burton frowned. "The town looks uninhabited."

Wells glanced at his bloodstained handkerchief and pushed it into a pocket. "They're all hiding indoors," he said. "They've known the attack was coming for a couple of days."

Burton closed his eyes, removed his helmet, and massaged his scalp with his fingertips.

Wells looked at him and asked, "Is that tattoo of yours hurting?"

"No. It's just that—I don't know—I feel like I should be somewhere else."

"Ha! Don't we all!"

They lapsed into silence, broken a few minutes later when Wells said, "I have a theory about it. Your tattoo, I mean. It looks African in pattern. You still don't recall how you got it?"

"No."

"I think perhaps you were captured and tortured by some obscure tribe. There are still a few independent ones scattered about, especially up around the Blood Jungle where you were found. Certainly the state you were in suggests some sort of trauma in addition to the malaria and shell shock, and the tattoo possesses a ritualistic look."

"It's possible, I suppose, but your theory doesn't ring any bells. Why is it called the Blood Jungle?"

"Because it's red. It's the thickest and most impassable jungle on the whole continent. The Germans have been trying to burn it away for I don't know how long but it grows back faster than they can destroy it."

An hour passed before, in the distance, a bugle sounded. Others took up its call; then more, much closer.

Wells used a crutch to lever himself to his feet. He leaned on it, raised his binoculars, and said, "Here we go. Stay on your toes, we're closer to the action than I'd like."

A single shot echoed from afar and, instantly, the birds in the trees became silent. For a moment there was no sound at all, then came a staccato roar as thousands of firearms let loose their bullets. An explosion shook the port.

Below and to his left, Burton saw a long line of British Askaris emerging from the undergrowth, moving cautiously into the town. They had hardly set foot past the outermost shack before they were caught in a hail of gunfire from windows and doorways. As men fell and others scattered for cover, Wells let loose a cry: "Bloody hell!"

A stray bullet whistled past him and thudded into a tree.

"Get down!" Burton snapped. The two observers dived onto the ground and lay prone, watching in horror as the Askaris were shredded by the crossfire. It fast became apparent that armed men inhabited all the houses and huts. Tanga wasn't a town waiting to be conquered—it was a trap.

A squadron of Askaris ran forward, threw themselves flat, and lobbed grenades. Explosions tore apart wooden residences and sent smoke rolling through the air. Similar scenes unfolded all along the southern outskirts of the town as the allied forces pressed forward. Hundreds of men were falling, but by sheer weight of numbers, they slowly advanced.

A sequence of blasts assaulted Burton's eardrums as HMS *Fox* launched shells into the middle of the settlement. Colonial houses erupted into clouds of brickwork, masonry, and glass.

"There goes the Hun administration!" Wells shouted. "If we're lucky, Lettow-Vorbeck was in one of those buildings!"

A Scorpion Tank scuttled out of the smoke and into a street just below them. The cannon on its tail sent shell after shell into the houses, many of which were now burning. When a German soldier raced from a doorway, one of the Scorpion's claws whipped forward, closed around him, and snipped him in half.

Harvestmen were entering the town, too, firing their Gatling guns and wailing their uncanny "Ulla! Ulla!"

Forty minutes later, the last of the troops with whom Burton and Wells had travelled moved past the observation point and pushed on into the more central districts of Tanga. As the clamour attested, the battle was far from over, but it had passed beyond Burton and Wells's view now, so they were forced to judge its progress by the sounds and eruptions of smoke. A particularly unbridled sequence of detonations occurred in the eastern part of the town, and, shortly afterward, a Union Jack was spotted there by Wells as it was hoisted up a flagpole at the top of a large building.

"That's the Hotel Nietzsche!" Wells exclaimed.

Pain lanced through Burton's head.

"Nietzsche!" he gasped. "I know that name! Who is he?"

"Bismarck's advisor," Wells replied. "The second most powerful man in the Greater German Empire!"

"He—he's going to—he's going to betray Bismarck!" Burton said hoarsely. "He's going to take over the empire! This year!"

Wells regarded his companion, a confused expression on his face. "How can you possibly know that? You're from the past, not the future."

Burton was panting with the effort of remembering. "I—it—something—something to do with Rasputin."

"If Ras—"

"Wait!" Burton interrupted. "1914. It's 1914! Rasputin will die this year. I killed him!"

"You're not making any sense, man!"

Burton hung his head and ground his teeth in frustration. A tiny patch of soil just in front of his face suddenly bulged upward and a green shoot sprouted out of it. He watched in astonishment as a plant grew rapidly before his eyes. It budded and its flower opened, all at a phenomenal speed.

It was a red poppy.

Wells suddenly clutched at the explorer's arm. "What's that over there?"

Burton looked up and saw, writhing into the air from various places around the town, thick black smudges, twisting and spiralling as if alive. They expanded outward, flattened, then sank down into the streets. From amid the continuing gunfire, distant screams arose.

"What the hell?" Wells whispered.

Some minutes later, British troops came running out from between the burning buildings. They'd dropped their rifles and were waving their arms wildly, yelling in agony, many of them dropping to the ground, twitching, then lying still. One, an Askari, scrambled up the slope and fell in front of the two onlookers. He contorted and thrashed, then a rattle came from his throat, his eyes turned upward, and he died.

He was covered in bees.

"We've got to get out of here!" Wells shouted. "This is Eugenicist deviltry!"

Many more men were now climbing the incline toward them, all screaming.

Burton hauled Wells to his feet, handed him his crutches, then guided him from the observation point back into Kaltenberg. Behind them, gunfire was drawing closer.

"Counterattack!" Wells said. "Go on ahead, Richard. Get out of here. Don't let me slow you down."

"Don't be a blessed fool!" Burton growled. "What manner of ridiculous war is this that our forces can be routed by bees?"

Even as he spoke, one of the insects landed on the back of his hand and stung him. Then another, on his neck. And another, on his jaw. The pain was a hundred times worse than a normal sting and he yelled, slapping the insects away. Almost immediately his senses began to swim and his heart fluttered as the venom entered his system. He staggered but found himself supported on either side by a couple of British Tommies who began to drag him along.

"Come on, chum!" said one. "Move yer bleedin' arse!"

"Bertie!" Burton shouted, but it came out slurred.

"Never mind your pal," the other soldier snapped. "He's bein' taken care of. Keep movin'. Have you been stung?"

"Yes." Burton's legs had stopped functioning and he had tunnel vision; all he could see was the ground speeding by. There was a buzzing in his ears.

The soldiers' voices came from a long way away: "He's snuffed it. Drop him."

"No. He's just passed out."

"He's slowing us down. Aah! I've been stung!"

"I'll not leave a man. Not while he still lives. Help me, damn it!"

A shot. The whine of a bullet.

"They're on us!"

"Run! Run!"

Burton's senses came swimming back. Two men were dragging him along.

"I can walk," he mumbled, and, regaining his feet, he stood and opened his eyes.

Light blinded him. It glared down from the sky and it glared up from the sand.

He raised a hand for shade and felt a big bump over his right eyebrow. It was sticky with blood.

"Are you dizzy, Captain?" asked Wordsworth Pryce, the second officer of the *Orpheus*.

"You took quite a knock," observed another. Burton recognised the voice as that of Cyril Goodenough, one of the engineers.

His vision blurred and swirled then popped back into focus. He looked around, and croaked, "I'm fine. Somewhat dazed. We crashed?"

"The bomb destroyed our starboard engines," Pryce replied. "It's a good job we were flying low. Nevertheless, we turned right over and came down with one hell of a thump."

Burton saw the *Orpheus*.

The huge rotorship was upside down, slumped on desert dunes, its back broken, its flight pylons snapped and scattered. Steam was pouring from it and rising straight up into a clear blue morning sky. The sun was not long risen, but the heat was already intense. Long shadows extended from the wreckage, from the figures climbing out of it, and from the bodies they were lining up on the ground some way from the ship.

William Trounce was suddenly at his side. The detective's jacket and shirt were badly torn and bloodied but his wounds—lacerations, grazes, and bruises—were superficial; no broken bones.

"I think we've got everyone out now except the Beetle," he said. "The boy is still in there somewhere."

"What state are we in?" Burton asked, dreading the answer.

"Thirteen dead. First Officer Henson; Helmsman Wenham and his assistant D'Aubigny; Navigator Playfair; riggers Champion, Priestley, and Doe; the two firemen, Gerrard and Etheridge; Stoker Reece-Jones; and, of course, that cur Arthur Bingham. I'm afraid Daniel Gooch bought it, too."

Burton groaned.

"I'm told Constable Bhatti died a hero's death, heaven bless him," Trounce said.

"He did. There'd probably be no survivors at all but for his sacrifice. What of the wounded?"

"Tom Honesty is still unconscious. Captain Lawless was pierced through the left side. Engineer Henderson and the quartermaster, Butler, are both in critical condition with multiple broken bones and internal injuries. Miss Mayson has just had a dislocated arm snapped back into place. She'll be all right. Everyone else is battered, cut, and bruised in various degrees. Swinburne is fine. Mr. Spencer has a badly dented and twisted leg. Sister Raghavendra is unharmed, as are Masters Wilde and Cornish. Krishnamurthy was banged around pretty badly but has no serious injuries. He's devastated at the loss of his cousin, of course." Trounce paused, then said quietly, "What a confounded mess."

"And one that's fast heating up," added Pryce. "We're slap bang in the middle of a desert."

"I suppose the captain is out of action," Burton said to him, "which makes you the commanding officer. I suggest you order the wreck stripped of everything useful. As a matter of urgency, we should employ whatever suitable material we can find to build a shaded area beside it. Please tell me the ship's water tanks are intact."

"Half of them are. There'll be plenty enough water."

"Well, that's something, at least. Have some of it put into containers."

"I'll organise it at once."

Pryce strode off.

Trounce cleared his throat. "Um. Captain, this heat—it's not—that is to say, how should we treat our—um—what should we do with the dead?"

The muscles to either side of Burton's jaw flexed. His closed his eyes for a moment, then opened them and looked at his friend. "We can't bury them, William. These sands are permanently shifting. We can't leave them in the open—there are scavengers. Our only option is a pyre."

Trounce considered this for a moment, gave a brusque nod, said, "I'll get it done," and walked away.

Burton turned to Engineer Goodenough: "What of the cargo hold and the expedition's equipment?"

"It's intact, sir. The vehicles are relatively undamaged. Overturned, of course, but they just need to be righted. Your supplies look like they got caught up in a tornado but I daresay we can sort them out. I'll see to it."

"Thank you. I'll round up some help for you."

Burton walked over to where Doctor Quaint and Sister Raghavendra were treating the wounded. Thomas Honesty was sitting up now but obviously hadn't fully regained his wits; his eyes were glazed, his mouth hanging slackly open. There was blood all over his face.

The doctor looked up from Charles Henderson, who was semiconscious and moaning softly, and said, "Almost everyone on the bridge was killed. As for the rest, the extent of their injuries depended on where they were when the ship hit the ground." He stood, drew Burton aside, and continued in a low voice, "If we don't get the wounded to a hospital, they won't make it."

Burton examined the landscape. To the north, behind the fallen *Orpheus*, to the east, and to the south, pale sand undulated all the way to the horizon in a sequence of large dunes. To the west, a thin strip of green and brown terrain clung to the hilly horizon.

"If I can recover my instruments from the hold—and if they're undamaged—I will be able to establish our position, Doctor. Then we can work out how to get to the nearest settlement."

"But, as I say," Quaint replied, "these men need a hospital."

"I assure you, Doctor, the Arabians are masters at the medical arts. They invented surgery."

"Very well. I'll trust your judgement, sir."

Burton looked at the Sister. She gave a slight jerk of her head to indicate that she was all right. He moved away, feeling oddly detached. The front of his skull was throbbing, and the dry heat of the Arabian Peninsula was beginning to suck the moisture out of him. He knew that within a couple of hours it would become a furnace. Shelter was the priority now. The inside of the *Orpheus* wouldn't do—the sun would soon make a giant oven of it.

Swinburne approached with Oscar Wilde and Willy Cornish in tow. The two youngsters were wide-eyed and pale-faced. Wilde was cradling his right arm.

"Are you hurt, Quips?"

"Just a sprain, Captain Burton. I'm thinking it's my wits that are more shaken than my body. I'd only just left the bridge when the ship went down. Escaped by the skin of my teeth, so I did."

"And you, Master Cornish?"

"I bumped my head, Mr. Burton. Really hard."

"Me too. How is it now?"

"Not so bad, sir."

"Good boy. Algy, you appear to have escaped without a scratch."

"Don't ask me how," Swinburne replied, glancing across at the Sister's patients. "My hat! I was bounced around like a rubber ball. What infamy, Richard, that our enemies are prepared to kill innocent men, women, and children in order to stop our expedition."

"All the more reason why we must succeed," Burton growled. He regarded the stricken *Orpheus*. "Algy, when the engineers have made it safe, I want you and the boys to search the ship. Locate the Beetle."

"Is he alive, Mr. Burton?" Cornish asked anxiously.

"I don't know. But if he is, we need to get him out of there before he's cooked. Good Lord! What on earth is that?"

Burton gaped at an approaching figure. It looked something like an upright brown bear, but baggy and shiny and possessed of a strange, narrow head, upon which Pox squatted. The thing moved with an ungainly lurching motion, swaying unevenly from side to side as it drew closer. The parakeet held out first one wing, then the other, to stay balanced.

"Cripes! A monster!" Cornish exclaimed, diving behind Burton and clinging to his legs.

"Pestilent stench-monkey!" Pox whistled.

"Hallo, Boss," the creature beneath the bird hooted.

"Is that you, Herbert?"

"Aye. I've busted me arthritic leg. Got a whackin' great dent in it. Can't hardly walk straight! Otherwise I came through with just a scratch or two. I'm itchin' all over, though. It's these blinkin' polymethylene togs."

Swinburne snorted. "You can't possibly itch, Herbert. You're made of brass!"

"I know. But I tells you, I itch!"

Herbert was completely enveloped by the suit. Gloves encased his three-fingered hands, and his flat-iron-shaped feet were booted. The voluminous material billowed around his limbs and torso but was wrapped tightly against his head and held in place by two elasticated belts. There were three openings in the suit, through which the circular features of his "face" could be seen.

"I can't say your outfit is worthy of Savile Row," Burton noted, "but it looks functional and you're protected from wind-borne sand. Come on, let's give the crew a helping hand."

They moved to the back of the steaming hulk, from which supplies were being unloaded, and started to sort through them. Thirty minutes later, Swinburne, Cornish, and Wilde were given the all clear to enter the ship. They began their search for the Beetle.

Burton, meanwhile, found his surveying equipment, climbed to the top of a nearby dune, and took readings. He returned and approached Wordsworth Pryce, announcing: "We're about a hundred miles to the northeast of Mecca. Unfortunately, that city is forbidden to us. However, I'm familiar with this area. If the expedition travels south for a hundred and eighty miles, we'll come to the town of Al Basah, where we should be able to join a fast caravan that'll take us all the way to Aden."

Pryce looked surprised. "Surely you don't mean to continue with your expedition? What about your supplies? How will you transport them?"

"We have no choice but to keep going. Our mission is of crucial importance. The supplies will have to be abandoned, apart from whatever we can realistically carry. We'll purchase what we can when we get to Aden, then more at Zanzibar. There's also a large shipment awaiting us in the Dut'humi Hills in Africa."

Pryce shook his head. "But travelling nearly two hundred miles through this desert? The injured will never survive it."

"They won't have to. I want you and your men to use the vehicles to transport them westward until you encounter the ocean, then south along the coast to Jeddah, which has excellent medical facilities and a British Consulate. It's not far. If we work fast, you'll be ready to leave at sunset and you'll arrive there before dawn."

"But Captain Burton!" Pryce objected. "What about you and your people? You can't possibly walk to Al Basah!"

"If they don't receive proper attention soon, Lawless, Henderson, and Butler will die. Take the vehicles. I'm an experienced desert traveller and I happen to know that there's a chain of oases between here and the town. They're frequented by traders and there's a very high probability that we'll join a caravan within hours of setting forth."

The aeronaut gripped Burton by the arm. "Come with us, sir! You can get a ship and sail from Jeddah to Aden."

"We'll not all fit into the vehicles, Mr. Pryce. And strange as it might seem, caravans journey south far more frequently than ships do. Vessels sailing from Jeddah are normally bound for Cairo. We might wait for months for one that's going to Aden. But in Al Basah, camel trains leave on a daily basis and travel rapidly down through central Arabia. We might reach Aden in less than two months."

"Two months! But by golly, sir—that's a huge delay!"

Burton shook his head. "It might appear so, but it's nothing compared to the hold-ups I experienced during my first expedition. Believe me, Pryce, Speke will be encountering many similar hindrances. I remain confident that we can catch him up, despite this setback. Now, let's get those vehicles out of the cargo hold."

Frantic hours followed. Supplies were sorted and stacked beneath makeshift awnings, food and water were distributed, and two travois were constructed for Burton and his team to use to transport whatever they could manage.

The Beetle was finally located in a pipe in the heart of the wreck, which the desert heat had not yet reached. He was uninjured but hungry. Burton took him a bag of sausage rolls, some sliced meat, half a loaf of bread, and a canteen of water. He held the comestibles up to a panel in the pipe. It swung open, and a small pale-blue and mottled hand reached out and drew them into the darkness.

"Thank you, Captain," came a whisper. "And I'm very sorry."

"Sorry?"

"If I had warned you about the saboteur in London, you might have lost a week. Instead, my scheme has cost you the expedition."

"No, lad. As I just informed Mr. Pryce, this crash has put us maybe two months behind Speke."

"Then he has won!"

"Not a bit of it. Time in Africa is not the same as time in England. Where we can measure a journey in hours and days, in Africa, they must be measured in weeks and months and even years. And Speke is in incompetent traveller. He is certain to make mistakes, and they will cost him as much time as we have lost today."

"I hope so. And what of me, Captain? I appear to be somewhat disadvantaged."

"We've arranged transportation for you, lad."

"How so?"

"If you follow this pipe toward the stern and turn right at the second junction, you'll find that it ends at a grille. When you are there, signal by tapping. The engineers will then saw through the pipe behind you, leaving you in a six-foot-long section, the cut end of which they'll immediately seal."

"I do not want them to see me."

"They shan't. I'll be there to ensure your continued privacy."

"That is good of you. What will then happen?"

"The pipe will be loaded aboard one of our vehicles in the custody of William Cornish and Oscar Wilde. You'll travel to Jeddah by night—which will be cold, but that's better than being baked alive. It may take some time for Second Officer Pryce to arrange, but from the port you'll sail with the boys and the crew of the *Orpheus* to Cairo, and from there home to London. All those who'll accompany you have pledged to guard you en route. It will mean a long time in a cramped pipe, but you'll get home."

"That is most satisfactory, Captain. Thank you."

A little later, after Bloodmann and Bolling had cut and sealed the pipe, they and Burton carried it into the long tent-like structure that had been erected beside the ship. The six members of the explorer's expedition were resting there: Swinburne, Trounce, Honesty, Spencer, Krishnamurthy, and Sister Raghavendra; and so were the other nine surviving crew members: Pryce, Goodenough, Quaint, Beadle, Miss Mayson, the boys—Cornish and Wilde—and the injured men, Lawless, Henderson, and Butler.

Those who were conscious had a haunted look about their eyes—they'd all seen the tall column of smoke rising up from the other side of a nearby dune. They knew what it meant. They sat, silently bidding their friends goodbye.

Then they slept.

For the next few hours, the hottest of the day, the clockwork man kept lone vigil over the camp.

There wasn't a single sound from outside, but inside, the exhausted sur- vivors shifted restlessly and gave forth occasional moans, for even in their trauma-filled dreams, they could feel the arid air scorching their lungs.

Five hours later, when they awoke, they felt as desiccated as Egyptian mummies.

"By Jove!" Trounce croaked. "How can anyone live in this?"

"Are Arabs flameproof?" Krishnamurthy asked.

"It will cool rapidly over the next hour," Burton declared, pushing canvas aside and squinting out at the setting sun. "Then you'll be complaining about the cold."

"Can't imagine cold. Not now!" Honesty confessed.

"This is a land of extremes, old chap, and we have to take advantage of those few hours, twice a day, when the climate shows an iota of mercy."

One such period was soon upon them, and after a hasty meal, they stocked the two conveyances with fuel and food and water, and the aeronauts prepared to take their leave.

The vehicles were extraordinary. They were crabs—of the variety *Lio- carcinus vernalis*—grown to gigantic size, their shells cleaned out and fitted with steam machinery, controls, chairs, and storage cabinets. They walked forward rather than sideways, as they had done when alive, and their claws had been fitted with razor-sharp blades, designed to slice and rip through jungle.

Wordsworth Pryce reached up to the underbelly of one of them and opened a hatch, which hinged down, steps unfolding on its inside surface. One by one, Captain Lawless, Charles Henderson, and Frederick Butler were borne up on stretchers by Doctor Quaint and Cyril Goodenough.

"I'm not at all happy about this, Captain," Pryce said to Burton. "Could you not wait it out here? Myself and one of my men could drive back to you and ferry you south."

"That would mean us tarrying for two days," Burton replied, "and in that time, we could be well on our way. The Al Atif oasis is about five hours' walk from here. The chances are good that we'll be able to join a caravan to Al Basah from there. And you must bear in mind that, in travelling westward, you'll soon find yourself on firmer terrain, easy for the crabs to traverse. Southward lies only sand. It would quickly infiltrate the machinery and the vehicles would be rendered inoperable in short order. No, Mr. Pryce, this is the best way."

Pryce shook the explorer's hand. "Very well, Captain Burton. I wish you luck, and rest assured that the Beetle's privacy will be protected and he'll be escorted all the way back to his chimney in Limehouse."

With that, Pryce boarded the vehicle and pulled up the hatch.

Burton paced across to the second crab, into which Bolling and Blood-mann had just carried the Beetle's section of pipe. The stoker, Thomas Beadle, joined them.

Willy Cornish and Oscar Wilde lingered a moment to say goodbye.

"Quips, I'm sorry I dragged you into this," Burton said. "I thought I was doing you a favour."

Wilde smiled. "Don't you be worrying yourself, Captain. Experience is one thing you can't get for nothing, and if this is the price, I'm happy to pay it, for I'm having the experience of a lifetime, so I am!"

The boys entered the crab.

Burton turned to Isabella Mayson.

"Are you sure you want to remain behind and join our expedition, Miss Mayson? I warn you that we have many months of severe hardship ahead of us."

"There is barely room for another aboard the vehicles, Sir Richard," she replied. "And your group will need to be fed—a responsibility I'm happy to make my own. Besides, it will be better for Sadhvi to have another woman present. We must, at very least, tip our heads at propriety, do you not think?"

Burton pushed up the hatch and clicked it shut, then stood back as the two crabs shuddered into life with coughs and growls. Steam plumed from their funnels, and Wilde and Cornish and Doctor Barnaby Quaint waved from the windows as the two outlandish machines stalked away.

The sun sank.

Beside the *Orpheus*, eight people remained, standing in the gathering twilight watching their friends recede into the distance.

Pox the parakeet sang, "Crapulous knobble-thwacker!" and Burton muttered: "I couldn't have put it better myself."

One foot in front of the other.

Step. Step. Step. Step.

Eyes on the ground.

Ignore the cold.

"How far?" Krishnamurthy mumbled.

"Soon. By sunrise," Burton replied.

They were dragging a travois over the sand. It was loaded with food and water, cooking pots and lanterns, rifles and ammunition, tents, clothing, instruments, and other equipment. Krishnamurthy was certain it was getting heavier.

The Milky Way was splattered overhead, dazzling, deep, and endless. The full moon had risen and was riding low in the sky. The dunes swelled in the silvery light.

Step. Step. Step. Step.

A second travois was pulled by Trounce and Honesty.

The two women trudged along beside it.

Herbert Spencer, in his protective suit, limped a little way behind.

"Tired," Honesty said. "Four hours walking."

Trounce gave a guttural response.

Ahead, Algernon Swinburne reached the peak of the next dune and stood with his rifle resting over his shoulder. He looked back at his companions, waited for them to catch up a little, then disappeared over the sandy peak. Before the others had reached the base of the upward slope, the eastern sky suddenly brightened.

To Burton, the quickness of dawn in this part of the world came as no surprise; to the others, it was breathtaking. One minute they were enveloped by the frigid luminescence of the night, and the next the sky paled, the stars faded, and brilliant rays of sunshine transformed the landscape. The desert metamorphosed from cold naked bone to hot dry flesh.

They slogged across it.

Step. Step. Step. Step.

"Cover your eyes," Burton called.

On his recommendation, they were each wearing a *keffiyeh*—a square headscarf of brightly striped material, secured on the crown with a circlet, or *agal*—which they now pulled down across their faces. The light glared through the material but didn't blind them, and, as they came to the top of the dune, they could clearly see through the weave that the redheaded poet had reached its base and was starting up the next one.

"I can feel heat!" Krishnamurthy exclaimed. "Already!"

"It will become unbearable within the next two hours," Burton predicted. "But by that time we'll be encamped at Al Atif."

A few yards away, Honesty glanced toward the huge molten globe of the sun and whispered, "*Gladiolus gandavensis.*"

"What?" Trounce asked.

"A plant. Not a hardy one. Dislikes winter. Roots best kept in sand until mid-March. Then potted individually. You have to nurture them, William. Start them off in a greenhouse."

It was the first time, in all the years they'd worked together, that Thomas Honesty had used Detective Inspector Trounce's first name.

"I say, Honesty—are you all right, old fellow?"

The small, dapper man smiled. "Thinking about my garden. What I'll do when we get back. Do you like gardening?"

"My wife takes care of it. We only have a small patch, and it's given over to cabbages and potatoes."

"Ah. Practical."

Step. Step. Step. Step.

"William."

"Yes?"

"I was wrong."

"Wrong?"

"About Spring Heeled Jack. Didn't believe you."

"Nor did anybody else."

"But you were right. He was at Victoria's assassination."

"Yes, he was."

"Will you forgive me? Misjudged you."

"Already done, old fellow. Some considerable time ago."

"When we get back, there's something I'd like."

"What?"

"You and Mrs. Trounce. Come over. Have tea with Vera and me. In the garden."

"We'd be honoured."

"Maybe the gladioli will be out."

"That'll be nice."

"Ahoy there!" Swinburne shouted. "I see palms!"

"The oasis," Burton said.

"Praise be!" Krishnamurthy gasped.

"Arse!" Pox squawked.

They climbed up to the poet and stopped beside him. He pointed at a distant strip of blinding light. They squinted and saw through their lashes and *keffiyehs* that it was dotted with wavering palm trees.

"Please, Captain Burton, don't tell us that's a mirage!" Sister Raghavendra said.

"No," Burton responded. "That's real enough. It's just where it ought to be. Let's push on."

They each took a gulp of water from their flasks, then returned to the hard work of placing one foot in front of the other, on and on and on, not daring to look up in case the oasis was farther away than they hoped.

Step. Step. Step. Step.

Another hour passed and the temperature soared, sucking away what little strength remained in them.

Then, suddenly, they were in shade, green vegetation closed around them, and when they finally raised their eyes, they saw a long, narrow lake just a few yards ahead.

"Thank goodness!" Isabella Mayson exclaimed, sinking to the ground. "Let me catch my breath, then I'll prepare some food while you gentlemen put up an awning."

Forty minutes later, they were tucking into a meal of preserved sausages and bread and pickles, which they washed down with fresh water and a glass each of red wine—an indulgence Swinburne had insisted on bringing, despite Burton's directive that they keep their loads as light as possible.

They sighed and lay down.

"My feet have never ached so much," Trounce observed. "Not even when I was a bobby on the beat."

Herbert Spencer, sitting with his back against the bole of a palm tree, watched Pox flutter up into its leaves. The colourful bird hunkered down and went to sleep. The clockwork philosopher made a tooting sound that might have been a sigh. "For all your complaints, Mr. Trounce," he said, "at least you can enjoy the satisfaction of a good meal. All I ever get these days is a touch of oil applied to me cogs 'n' springs, an' that always gives me indigestion."

Trounce replied with a long, drawn-out snore, then rolled onto his side and fell silent.

Peace settled over the camp, and into it, Swinburne said softly:

"Here life has death for neighbour,
And far from eye or ear
Wan waves and wet winds labour,
Weak ships and spirits steer;
They drive adrift, and whither
They wot not who make thither;
But no such winds blow hither,
And no such things grow here."

"That's beautiful, Mr. Swinburne," Sister Raghavendra whispered.

The sun climbed and the heat intensified.

Three hours passed.

They were too tired to dream.

Herbert Spencer's polymethylene-wrapped canister-shaped head slowly turned until the three vertical circles of his face were directed at the king's agent. He watched the sleeping man for many minutes. Very quietly, the pipes on his head wheezed, "Time, Boss, is that which a man is always trying to kill, but which ends in killing him." Then he looked away and sibilated, "But for us, only equivalence can lead to destruction—or transcendence."

He sat, motionless.

"Wake up! Wake up! We're attacked!"

Herbert Spencer's trumpeting shocked them all out of their sleep.

"We're attacked! We're attacked!"

"What the devil—?" Trounce gasped, staggering to his feet.

"Grab your rifle," Burton snapped. "Be sharp and arm to defend the camp!"

He winced, realising that he'd uttered the very same words back in '55 at Berbera; the day a spear had transfixed his face; the day his friend William Stroyan had been killed; the day John Speke had begun to hate him.

There was a thud, and Trounce went down.

A wild-looking man stepped over him and jabbed the butt of a matchlock at Burton's head. The king's agent deflected it with his forearm, lunged in, and buried his fist in his assailant's stomach.

From behind, an arm closed around the explorer's neck and the point of a dagger touched his face just below the right eye.

"Remain very still," a voice snarled in his ear. Burton recognised the language as Balochi—a mix of Persian and Kurdish.

He froze, tense in the man's grip, and watched as brigands rounded up his companions. They were big men with intimidating beards and flowing robes, wide blue pantaloons, and colourful sashes around their waists. They were armed with matchlocks, daggers, swords, and shields.

Herbert Spencer—who they obviously regarded as some sort of exotic animal—was surrounded and roped. With his enormous strength, he yanked his captors this way and that, throwing them off their feet, until one of the bandits raised a gun and fired a shot at him, at which point Burton, afraid that his friend would be damaged, called, "Stop struggling, Herbert!"

The brass man became still, and his attackers wound him around and around with the ropes then bound him to a tree trunk.

"Goat ticklers!" Pox screeched from somewhere overhead.

Burton was dragged over to the others. The two women were pulled aside, and, with their arms held tightly behind their backs, were forced to watch as the men were lined up and pushed to their knees.

"I say!" Swinburne screeched. "What the dickens do you think you're playing at? Unhand me at once, you scoundrels!"

A heavily built warrior strode over. He sneered down at the diminutive poet and spat: "*Kafir!*"

"Bless you!" the poet replied. "Do you not have a handkerchief?"

The big man cast his eyes from Swinburne to Honesty, then to Trounce, Burton, and Krishnamurthy.

"Who leads?" he demanded.

"I do," said Burton, in Balochi.

The man moved to stand in front of him.

"Thou has knowledge of my language?"

"Aye, and I say to thee that there be no majesty and there be no might save in Allah, the Glorious, the Great, and in his name we ask for thy mercy and thy assistance, for we have suffered severe misfortune and have a long journey before us."

The Baloch threw his head back and loosed a roar of laughter. He squatted and looked into Burton's eyes.

"Thou speakest very prettily, Scar Face. I am Jemadar Darwaas. I lead the Disciples of Ramman. Who art thou?"

"Some call me Abdullah the Dervish."

"Is that so?" Darwaas pointed at Herbert Spencer. "And what is that?"

"It is a man of brass. A machine in which a human spirit is housed."

"So! A whole man in a whole mechanism this time! Like Aladdin's djan?"

"Like that, aye. He is concealed within material that protects him from the sand, for if grains of it got into him, he would die."

While he spoke, Burton took stock of the men into whose clutches his expedition had fallen. He judged there to be about sixty of them—all hardened desert warriors—marauders from Belochistan a thousand miles to the northeast.

"Thou art a storyteller, Abdullah."

"I speak the truth."

"Then I would cut through the material and look upon this miraculous brass man of thine."

"In doing so, thou shall kill him," Burton advised, "and what would he then be worth?"

Jemadar Darwaas grinned through his beard. "Ah," he said. "Now, O Abdullah, thou art truly speaking my language! He has value, eh?"

"The British government would pay a substantial ransom for him, and for these others, too," Burton said, indicating his companions with a jerk of his head. "Especially for the women, if they are unharmed."

Darwaas grunted. He drew his dagger and held it up, examining its sharp point. His eyes flicked from the blade to Burton's dark eyes. With a fluid motion, he stood, paced away, and began to speak in low tones with a group of his men.

William Trounce leaned close to Burton and whispered, "What was all that about?"

"I'm trying to talk him into holding us for ransom."

"Why do that?"

"Because it'll buy us some time," the king's agent replied.

Less than half an hour later, the brigands finished setting up their camp on the edge of the oasis, and the two women were taken to it and placed in a guarded tent.

Darwaas returned to the remaining captives, drew his scimitar, and levelled the point at Burton's face. "Thy people will be held until the British consul in Jeddah pays for their release," he said. "But thee, Abdullah the Dervish, thee I shall fight."

"Fight? For what purpose?"

"For no purpose other than I desire it."

The Jemadar ordered his men to clear a circular area. The prisoners were dragged to its boundary and the bandits gathered around. Burton was yanked up and pushed forward. A warrior threw down a scimitar. It landed at the explorer's feet, and he bent, picked it up, and noted that it was a well-balanced blade.

Sir Richard Francis Burton was a master swordsman, but he much preferred fighting with a point than with an edge. The point demanded skill and finesse; the edge required mainly strength, speed, and brutality, though there were also a few techniques associated with it, in which, fortunately, he was well schooled.

He held the blade, narrowed his eyes at his opponent, and sighed.

Before leaving the wreck of the *Orpheus*, he'd attached to his belt a leather holster, and in that holster there was a very odd-looking pistol. It was green and organic—actually a eugenically altered cactus—and it fired venomous spines that could knock a man unconscious in an instant. His captives had not removed it, and he wished he could draw it now, for he would far prefer to render the leader of the Disciples of Ramman senseless than to hack at him with a blade. Sword cuts, unless they were to the head, neck, or stomach, very rarely killed quickly. Instead, they condemned the victim to hours—even days—of excruciating agony, often followed by infection and a lingering death. He knew, however, that the moment he went for his gun, matchlocks would be jerked up and fired at him.

Jemadar Darwaas stepped closer and brandished his scimitar. "How didst thou come by that scar on thy face, Abdullah?" he asked.

"A spear," Burton responded. "Thrust by an Abyssinian."

"Didst thou kill him?"

"No."

"That was a mistake. My people say: 'When thy enemies attack—'"

"'—bathe in their blood,'" Burton finished.

"Ha! Thy knowledge is impressive. Hast thou lived among Allah's children?"

"I am *Hajji*."

"What? A pilgrim? A believer? I did not know. Now I shall honour thee doubly after I have spilled thy guts."

Darwaas suddenly lunged forward and swung his sword at Burton's head. The king's agent deflected it with ease and slashed back at his opponent, slicing through the front of Darwaas's robe. The Baloch jumped back and exclaimed, "Thou art practised with the sword, then?"

"Aye," said Burton, circling slowly. "And these are designed for fighting from horseback, not for face-to-face combat. Nevertheless, there are tactics that a man can employ with them when on foot. For example—" He paced forward, ducked, and, balancing on one heel, whipped around in a full circle, using his momentum to sweep his scimitar upward at a twenty-degree angle. Darwaas barely had time to react, only just managing to place his weapon between himself and Burton's blade, and when the two scimitars clanged together, his own was forced back hard against him, sending him staggering.

Burton immediately pressed his advantage, striking at his opponent's right side—a blow that was, again, turned aside with difficulty.

Darwaas teetered off balance, stumbled, and gasped, "By Allah! Thou art considerably more than I expected!"

"A man should not be precipitous in his choice of enemy," Burton advised. "And I am puzzled that thou hath chosen me. Wert thou paid to do so?"

"Aye, 'tis the case."

"When I told thee of the man of brass, thou didst exclaim, 'A whole man in a whole mechanism this time!' Perhaps, then, thou hast seen a man partially of metal? Mayhap it was his head that was half of brass, and this man was your paymaster?"

John Speke.

"I do not deny it. Enough talk. Let us fight."

Burton transferred his scimitar to his left hand. "Keep thy body loose, Jemadar, and control thy blade with the wrist, not with the entire arm. Now, strike at me."

"Art thou so confident?"

"Strike!"

The Jemadar gave a grimace. The duel wasn't going at all the way he'd have liked. He spat onto the sand and crouched a little, his sword arm held out. The two men moved around one another, their dark eyes locked.

With such speed that the movement was almost a blur, Darwaas launched himself at Burton and sliced sideways. His blade hit his adversary just below chest level, but Burton was braced against it, with his own weapon shielding him closely, held point downward, tight against his body from shoulder to mid-thigh. He immediately swept it out, up, and around, hooking it beneath the bandit's scimitar. He stepped in with knees bent and pushed upward. Darwaas's sword was instantly levered right out of his hand.

The gathered Baloch men cried out in amazement as their leader's weapon went spinning away, landing at the edge of the arena.

Darwaas stood stunned.

"The sword should be held against the body in defence," Burton stated, "else, as thou saw, in being knocked backward, it can do as much damage as the attacking blade. Also, this means that, for the defender, the muscles of the shoulders, arms, and wrists are relaxed—are not employed in resisting the offensive—and are thus free to fully power the counterattack."

Darwaas's face blackened. "Dost thou mean to humiliate me, dog?"

Burton shook his head. "I did not seek to fight thee, Jemadar. I desire only to—"

"Richard!" Swinburne shrieked.

Something impacted against the back of Burton's head. The world reeled around him and vanished.

A conflagration raged in his skull, needled his eyelids, clawed at his skin. He tried to move and found that he couldn't. Thirst consumed him.

He forced his eyes open and squinted up at the pitiless sun. Turning his head, he saw that he was on his back, with limbs spread out, his wrists and ankles bound with cord to wooden stakes driven deeply into the ground.

Dunes rose to either side.

He opened his mouth to shout for help but only a rattle emerged.

Grains of sand, riding a hot, slow breeze, blew against the side of his face.

He experienced a strange sense of déjà vu.

Is this a dream?

Jemadar Darwaas entered his field of vision.

"Art thou comfortable?" he asked. "Thy head aches, I fancy? My *moollah*—lieutenant—struck thee with a knob stick." The bandit chuckled. "By Allah, he knows how I hate to be bested! Thou art a fine swordsman,

Abdullah! Mayhap the tales told of thy race are true, for it is said that the British are undefeated in battle. Praise be to Allah that the lands of my people have no resources that thy people covet!" Darwaas held his arms out wide as if to embrace the entire desert. He grinned wickedly. "Let us see," he said, "how that land now judges thee, Britisher."

He turned away and climbed to the top of a dune, looked back once, spat, then descended the other side of the mound and passed out of sight.

Burton felt his flesh cracking.

It was mid-afternoon and the heat wouldn't abate for at least another three hours. If he survived it, he'd then have to endure the severe chill of night.

He moved his tongue in his mouth. It felt like a stone.

There was a spell of nothingness.

He sucked in a burning breath and realised that he'd been unconscious.

Think. Think, and hang on to the thoughts. John Speke and Count Zeppelin obviously stopped here and warned the bandits to look out for a crashed rotorship and to kill any survivors. How far ahead are they? Already at Aden, perhaps?

Think, and keep thinking!

Awareness slipped to one side and skidded into oblivion.

Awake.

Where?

He tried to form words, to call for help, but the slightest movement of his mouth increased the pain a thousandfold. The agony flared; an unbearable brilliance.

He sank into the centre of an inferno.

Flames.

Flames in a stone bowl hanging by chains from a ceiling so high that it is lost in shadows. Columns. A monolithic temple. It is on a hill in the centre of Kantapuranam, the capital city of Kumari Kandam, the land of the reptilian Nāga.

A man steps forward.

He is Brahmin Kaundinya, and he is wedded to the monarch's daughter, their union a symbolic pact to mark the end of conflict between the lizard race and humans. He has lived a year among them, and is now standing before K'k'thyima, the high priest.

Thin blue smoke from burning incense curls around the human's legs. Onlookers watch attentively. There are at least a thousand of them gathered in the temple, and many millions more in attendance mentally but not physically.

The man bows his respect to the priest.

"Not to me, soft skin," K'k'thyima hisses. "To the Joined." With a three-fingered clawed hand, he gestures to his right.

Kaundinya turns to a huge black diamond, which rests on a plinth of gold.

One of the three Eyes of Nāga.

Kaundinya bows again.

K'k'thyima says: "Thy wife may step to thy side."

The man turns around to look at his mate. "Come, and speak for me, that all may know my character," he says, following the ritual.

She moves to him. Like all of her race, she is about half his height; her skin segmented into a mosaic of leathery black, yellow, and green; her limbs short and thick; her head confusing to the human, for sometimes it seems to be one of seven heads, other times one of five, and occasionally the sole one. She is wearing extravagant jewellery and a chain-mail tunic.

"Husband," she says, "I am willing to speak."

The high priest, who also appears to have multiple heads, orders a human prisoner to be brought forward. As the man is escorted to the plinth, Kaundinya is addressed.

"Thou came as an emissary, O Kaundinya. Thou came to broker peace between the race of soft skins and the race of Nāga. Thou hast lived among us as one of us, and thou hast been husband to Kuma K'sss'amaya."

He turns to the female.

"Hast thou, my Kuma, been satisfied with the conduct of thy husband?"

"I have," she answers. "With intervention from our wise ones, that which divides our species was bridged, and the human gave to me a child. He is an attentive and dutiful father. He has respected our ways. He has learned much and has not judged. He brings peace."

The crowd emits an approving sibilance.

Kaundinya watches the high priest. A single head swims into focus. Its yellow eyes blink, their membranes sliding sideways: a sign of satisfaction. The head blurs. There are seven heads. There are five. There is one. There are seven.

"Pay honour to the Joined," K'k'thyima orders.

A blade slices through the prisoner's neck and his blood spurts over the irregular facets of the giant gemstone. He convulses and dies and his corpse is dragged out of the chamber.

"A sacrifice is always necessary, O Kaundinya, but the essence of he who gave his life will live on in the Eye."

The priest performs a number of ritualistic gestures, almost a dance, and intones: "The multitude are one. Individual thoughts are one thought. Separate intentions are one intention. The words of one are the words of all. The days that have been and the days that will come are eternally now."

He steps to the stone, leans over it, and, with one of his long forked tongues licks blood from its surface. He then dips the same tongue into a bowl containing black diamond dust.

With the organ extended, he returns to Kaundinya—who bows down— and runs it delicately over the human's shaven scalp, leaving a swirling, glittering hieroglyph.

K'k'thyima steps back. Kaundinya straightens.

The High Priest says: "Thou art invited into the Great Fusion, O Emissary. Dost thou accept the Joining?"

"I accept."

The crowd emits a throbbing susurration, a repetitive refrain. All the gathered priests extend and quiver their multiple neck crests, a dazzling display of vibrating colour.

From somewhere, a throbbing rhythm pulses and a melody of heart-wrenching beauty swells through the temple. Layer after layer is added to it. Its refrains are bafflingly complex, and they are constructed from tones that no human instrument has ever produced; tones that no human being can even properly comprehend.

Kaundinya tries to meet K'k'thyima's eyes but is unable to focus on any single head. He feels the music and the lizard's mesmeric power over-whelming all but one tiny and very well-concealed part of his consciousness, and he allows it.

He looks at the black diamond. His eyes fixate upon it. He feels himself pulled into its depths, the essence of his individuality breaking apart, distributing itself among the planes and lines and points and angles of the great stone.

Kaundinya remains passive as thousands upon thousands of other minds touch his. He loses his sense of independence and becomes enmeshed, soaking into a vast multiple consciousness.

He wills his identity farther and farther into the diamond. He fills it; exists in every part of it; becomes an ingredient in its very existence.

He is one with the Nāga.

He exists with them in the Eternal Now.

All but one tiny part of him.

Kaundinya is no ordinary man. Through rigorous education, meditation, and ritual, he has attained the absolute pinnacle of intellectual order and emotional discipline. Here, at the dawn of human history, his self-control is unmatched; and it will remain so until the end of that history.

The Nāga have been surreptitiously probing his mind from the moment he started to live among them. They have found only good intentions, only a desire for peace between the human race and their own.

Kaundinya's true purpose has never been exposed.

Now, the moment has arrived.

He flexes the one small knot of awareness that has not melted into the Joined and turns it inward, probing deep into the physical matter of his own brain.

He locates a major blood vessel and he wrenches at it.

A massive haemorrhage kills him in an instant, and at the moment his consciousness is destroyed, it sends an inexorable shockwave through the structure of the diamond.

The stone fractures and explodes into seven fragments.

The Joined are ripped apart.

Millions of Nāga drop dead.

The retorts of the shattering gem echo through the temple like rifle fire. The pieces fall from the plinth to the floor, their facets glinting like stars.

Rifle fire and stars.

Rifle fire. Stars.

Rifle fire. Stars.

Sir Richard Francis Burton opened his eyes.

It was night.

Stars filled the sky.

Rifle fire echoed across the desert.

A man screamed.

A camel brayed.

Voices argued in one of the languages of the Arabian Peninsula.

His eyelids scraped shut, time overbalanced and dropped away, and he opened them again and saw the dawn.

A figure climbed into view and stood looking down at him. A breeze tugged at her robes—for it was undoubtedly a woman, Burton could tell that from the curve of her hip, against which she rested the butt of her rifle.

"No," she said, in English. "It cannot possibly be you."

Her voice was deep and warm but filled with shock.

He tried to speak but his tongue wouldn't move. His skin was afire, yet the core of him, having suffered the night, was as cold as ice. He could feel nothing but pain.

The woman slipped and slithered down the sand then strode to his side and knelt, laying her weapon to one side. Her face was concealed by a *keffiyeh* and remained in shadow—silhouetted against the deep-orange sky. She unhooked a flask from her belt, unscrewed its top, and dribbled water onto his lips. It trickled into his mouth, through his teeth, over his tongue, and was so good that he passed out from the sheer relief of it.

When awareness returned, he was inside a tent and sunlight was beating against its roof. Sister Raghavendra smiled down at him.

"Lie still, Sir Richard," she said. "I have to apply more ointment to your skin."

"Give him warm water mixed with a spoonful of honey, please, Sadhvi."

The voice was the same melodious one he'd heard before. Impossibly familiar.

He tried to look but a stab of pain prevented him from turning his head.

Sister Raghavendra drizzled sweet liquid into his mouth.

"We were rescued," she said.

Consciousness escaped him yet again, only to be summoned back by the tinkle of camel bells and the flapping of the tent's canvas as it was battered by the *simoon*—the strong hot desert wind.

He'd been propped up into a semi-reclining position, with his back and head supported by soft pillows. Sadhvi Raghavendra was sitting to his left, Algernon Swinburne to his right. The owner of the deep female voice was standing at his feet, with her face still concealed by her Arabian headdress.

She was a tall woman, slender but curvaceous, and she radiated confidence and power. Her large clear eyes, above the scarf, were of a scintillating blue.

She reached up, pulled the material aside, smiled prettily, and said, "Are you *compos mentis*? You've been ranting about reptiles and temples and diamonds."

He tested his voice. "I think——" and found that it worked, albeit harshly. "I think my mind is in better order, though my body is burned to a crisp. Hello, Isabel."

"Hello, Dick."

Isabel Arundell, who'd once been his fiancée, was wearing a long white cotton shirt, white pantaloons, and an *abba*—a short-sleeved cloak of dark green woven from the finest of wools. A sword, a dagger, and a flintlock pistol were held in place by a multicoloured sash circling her slender waist. She manoeuvred them out of the way as she lowered herself onto a cushion and sat with her legs tucked to one side.

Burton rasped, "I thought you were running around with Jane Digby in Damascus."

Sadhvi handed him a canteen. He drank from it sparingly, knowing from experience that gulps would cause excruciating stomach cramps.

"We parted ways," Isabel replied. "I found her morals to be wanting."

"My hat, Richard!" Swinburne piped up. "We've experienced a miraculous intervention! Miss Arundell is leading a merry band of Amazonian warriors. They came galloping to our rescue on the most beautiful horses you've ever seen and gave the Disciples of Ramman a proper thrashing!"

Burton looked from his assistant back to Isabel, a question in his eyes.

She smiled again and said, "I seem to have acquired the habit of collecting about me women who've suffered at the hands of their husbands. When I opened a refuge in Damascus, there were objections from those same men. The continued existence of the place soon became untenable, so my companions and I left the city to live as Bedouins. We travelled south, through Syria, collecting more women on the way, until we arrived in Arabia, where we've survived by raiding the bandits who plunder the caravans."

"Extraordinary!" Burton wheezed. "How many of you are there?"

"A little over two hundred."

"Great heavens!"

"We saw a plume of steam, went to investigate, and discovered your downed ship. It was abandoned and a lot of supplies had been left behind. Don't worry—we have them with us. Then we followed your trail and happened upon the brigands."

"The women are armed to the teeth!" Swinburne enthused. "And they revere Miss Arundell as if she were the goddess herself! Guess what they call her!"

"Please, Algernon!" Isabel protested.

"What?" Burton asked.

"Al-Manat!"

THE PERILOUS SAFARI

Hardly we find the path of love, to sink the Self, forget the "I,"
When sad suspicion grips the heart, when Man, *the* Man begins to die:
[...]
How Thought is imp'otent to divine the secret which the gods defend,
The Why of birth and life and death, that Isis-veil no hand may rend.

Eternal Morrows make our Day; our *Is* is aye *to be* till when
Night closes in; 'tis all a dream, and yet we die, — and then and THEN?

And still the Weaver plies his loom, whose warp and woof is wretched Man
Weaving th' unpattern'd dark design, so dark we doubt it owns a plan.
[...]
Cease, Man, to mourn, to weep, to wail; enjoy thy shining hour of sun;
We dance along Death's icy brink, but is the dance less full of fun?
                    —SIR RICHARD FRANCIS BURTON,
                        THE KASÎDAH OF HÂJÎ ABDÛ EL-YEZDÎ

CHAPTER 6

THE EXPEDITION BEGINS

"It only requires a scientist to be told what variety of thing to look for, and where best to look, and it is inevitable that the thing will be found. So it was in the earliest days of Eugenics. The hints had been of the vaguest. They were passed from a madman to a drunkard, and from the drunkard to an engineer, and from the engineer to a naturalist, and from the naturalist to Mr. Francis Galton. Whether they seeded themselves in Mr. Galton's brain in anything resembling their original form seems doubtful—we all know how information is corrupted by travel—and yet, in that magnificent, terrifying mind of his, they blossomed, and he dazzled us all with his brilliance. Mr. Charles Darwin, in particular, was enthused to the point where, I regret to say, moral and ethical boundaries ceased to exist for him. To some extent, this happened to all of us in that little band of scientists. Unquestionably, I am now ashamed of certain of my actions whilst under the influence of that great wave of fervour and creativity that overtook us. And I feel somewhat responsible, too, for the dark turn Eugenics very quickly took after it was established as a unique scientific discipline, for it was I who, under Mr. Galton's direction, conjoined his and Mr. Darwin's brains, using techniques that I have since discovered are many, many decades ahead of their proper time. The thing that Darwin/Galton became, as a consequence of that operation, I now regard as a monstrosity, but while it existed I was in its thrall, and much against my better judgement, I was a principal in the horrible path that Eugenics trod. Oh that I could travel back and change everything! The death of Darwin/Galton liberated me and restored my proper senses, but with them I now suffer to witness the villainies of Eugenics; I see the terrifying speed at which its ghastly techniques develop; I see how it has moved so far beyond the original concept of guided evolution that it now perverts life dreadfully. Perhaps it is true that, as many claim, Mr. Darwin killed God. The existence of Eugenics rather suggests to me, I fear, that he did not, at the same time, succeed in destroying the devil."

—FROM *THE EUGENICISTS: THEIR HISTORY AND THEIR CRIMES* BY FLORENCE NIGHTINGALE, 1865

Edward Oxford thudded onto grass and bounced on his spring-heeled boots. Glancing around, he saw a rolling park surrounded by tall glass buildings whose sides flashed with advertising, and in the near distance, the ancient form of the Monarchy Museum, once known as Buckingham Palace, in which the relics of England's defunct royal families were displayed. A sonic boom echoed as a shuttle headed into orbit. People buzzed overhead in their personal fliers. His AugCom was functioning.

He checked that he was still holding the top hat he'd carried with him, then ran into the wooded corner of the park, not noticing that, in the long grass to his left, a white-haired man was lying unconscious with a sniper rifle, a jewel case, and a portmanteau bag at his side.

Oxford ducked into the trees and pushed through the undergrowth until he felt safe from prying eyes. He detached the Nimtz Generator from his chest and put it on the ground, pulled off his stilted boots and placed them beside it, then stripped off his fish-scale battery suit and draped it over a low branch. Reaching up to his helmet, he hesitated, then switched off the AugCom and removed the headgear. A foul stench assaulted his nostrils, a mix of raw sewage, rotting fish, and burning fossil fuels. He started to cough. The air was thick and gritty. It irritated his eyes and scraped his windpipe. He fell to his knees and clutched at his throat, gasping for oxygen. Then he remembered that he'd prepared for this and fumbled in his jacket pocket, pulling out a small instrument that he quickly applied to the side of his neck. He pressed the switch, it hissed, he felt a slight stinging sensation, and instantly he could breathe again. He put the instrument away and rested for a moment. The inability to catch his breath had been a perceptive disorder rather than a physical one. The helmet had protected him from the idea that the atmosphere was unbreathable; now a sedative was doing the job.

Unfamiliar sounds reached him from the nearby road: horses' hooves, the rumble of wheels, the shouts of hawkers.

He stood and straightened the reproduction mid-Victorian-era clothes that he'd worn beneath his time suit, placed the top hat on his head, and made his way to the edge of the thicket. As he emerged from the trees, a transformed world assailed his senses, and he was immediately shaken by a profound uneasiness.

There were no AugCom illusions now, and only the grass was familiar. Through dense, filthy air, he saw a massive expanse of empty sky. The tall glass towers of his own age were absent, and London clung to the ground. To his left, Buckingham Palace, now partially hidden by a high wall, looked brand new. Quaintly costumed people were walking in the park—no, he reminded himself, not costumed; they always dressed this way!—and their slow pace appeared entirely unnatural.

Despite the background murmur, London slumbered under a blanket of silence.

He started to walk down the slope toward the base of Constitution Hill, struggling to overcome his growing sense of dislocation.

Behind him, unseen, the unconscious man regained his wits, snatched up his things, staggered to his feet, and stumbled into the trees.

"Steady, Edward," Oxford muttered to himself. "Hang on, hang on. Don't let it overwhelm you. This is neither a dream nor an illusion, so stay focused, get the job done, then get back to your suit!"

He reached the wide path. The queen's carriage would pass this way soon. My God! He was going to see Queen Victoria! He looked around. Every single person was wearing a hat or bonnet. Most of the men were bearded or had moustaches. The women held parasols.

Slow motion. It was all in slow motion.

He examined faces. Which belonged to his ancestor? He'd never seen a photograph of the original Edward Oxford—there were none—but he hoped to recognise some sort of family resemblance.

He stepped over the low wrought-iron fence lining the path, crossed to the other side, turned around to face the hill, and loitered near a tree. People started to gather along the route. He heard a remarkable range of accents and they all sounded ridiculously exaggerated. Some, which he identified as working class, were incomprehensible, while the upper classes spoke with a precision and clarity that sounded wholly artificial. Details kept catching his eye, holding his attention with hypnotic force: the prevalence of litter and dog shit on the grass; the stains and worn patches on people's clothing; rotten teeth and rickets-twisted legs; accentuated mannerisms and lace-edged hand-kerchiefs; pockmarks and consumptive coughs.

"Focus!" he whispered.

He noticed a man across the way, standing in a relaxed but rather arrogant manner and looking straight at him with a knowing smile on his round face. He had a lean figure and a very large moustache.

Can he see that I don't belong here?

A cheer went up. The queen's carriage had just emerged from the palace gates, its four horses guided by a postilion. Two outriders trotted along ahead of the vehicle; two more behind.

Where was his ancestor? Where was the gunman?

Ahead of him, an individual wearing a top hat, blue frock coat, and white breeches reached under his coat and moved closer to the path. Slowly, the royal carriage approached.

Is that him?

Moments later, the forward outriders came alongside. The blue-coated man stepped over the fence and, as the queen and her husband passed, he took three strides to keep up with their vehicle, then whipped out a flintlock pistol and fired it at them. He threw down the smoking weapon and drew a second.

Oxford yelled, "No, Edward!" and ran forward.

They detected Zanzibar first with their nostrils, for, prior to the island darkening the horizon, the sultry breeze became laden with the scent of cloves. Then the long strip of land hove into view at the edge of the sapphire sea, its coral-sand beaches turned to burnished gold by the fierce sun.

"By Jove," William Trounce whispered. "What's the word for it? Sleepy?"

"Tranquil," Krishnamurthy suggested.

"Languidly basking in sensuous repose," Swinburne corrected.

"Whatever it is," said Trounce, "it's splendid. I feel as if I'm inside one of Captain Burton's tales of the Arabian Nights."

"More so than when you were actually in Arabia?" the poet enquired.

"Great heavens, yes! That was just sand, sand, and more sand. This is . . . romantic!"

"Seven weeks!" Krishnamurthy grunted. "Seven weeks on a blasted camel. My posterior will never recover."

Ahead, the land swelled seductively, coloured a reddish brown beneath its veils of green, which wavered and rippled behind the heavy curtain of air.

"What do you think, Algy?" Trounce asked. The members of Burton's expedition were all on first-name terms now—one of the more positive effects of their gruelling trek through central Arabia. They were also all burned a deep brown, with the exception of Swinburne, whose skin was almost as crimson as his hair had been before the sun bleached it the colour of straw.

The poet looked up at the detective, then followed his gaze to the prow of the ship—the Indian Navy sloop of war *Elphinstone*—where he saw Sir Richard Francis Burton standing with Isabel Arundell.

"If you're asking me whether the romance of Zanzibar is infectious, Pouncer, then I take it you haven't read Richard's account of his first expedition."

"There's little time for reading at Scotland Yard, lad. And, for the umpteenth time, don't call me Pouncer."

Swinburne grinned cheekily. "Apparently, the island's infections are nothing to celebrate. By the same token, I'd suggest that Richard and Isabel's relationship is probably not exactly as it appears from here."

He was correct. In fact, had he been able to eavesdrop upon their conversation, Swinburne would have reported to Trounce that Isabel was giving Burton "what for."

"You're a pig-headed, self-absorbed, stubborn fool," she said. "You have never failed to underestimate me or to overestimate yourself."

Burton fished a cigar from his pocket. "Do you mind if I smoke?" he asked.

"You'll not drive me away with tobacco fumes."

He put a flame to the Manila, inhaled the aromatic smoke, and gazed down at the water that gurgled and sparkled against the hull below. A few yards away, a shoal of flying fish shot out of the sea and glided some considerable distance before plunging back in.

Isabel pulled a small straw-coloured cylinder from a pouch at her waist and raised it to her lips. She struck a lucifer and lit its tip.

Burton smelled the tart fumes of Latakia and looked at her, raising his eyebrows.

"Good grief! Surely that's not a cigarette?"

"All the rage since the Crimea," came her murmured reply. "Do you object to a woman smoking?"

"I—well—that is to say—"

"Oh, stop stammering like an idiot, Dick. Let's set it out plainly, shall we? You disapprove of my lifestyle."

"Nonsense! I simply asked you why you have chosen to live as a Bedouin when you belong to the House of Wardour, one of the richest families in Britain."

"The implication being?"

"That you could have Society at your feet; that the comforts and advantages of an aristocratic life are yours to enjoy. You aren't Jane Digby, Isabel. She fled England after her scandalous behaviour made it impossible for her to remain there. Not so, you. So why endure the hardships and dangers of the nomadic life?"

"Hypocrite!"

"What?"

"How often have you railed against the constrictions and restraints of the Society you now endorse? How often have you purposely provoked outrage and challenged social proprieties at dinner tables with your shocking anecdotes? How often have you styled yourself the outsider, the man who doesn't fit in, the noble savage in civilised clothing? You glory in it, and yet you denounce Miss Digby! Really! They call you Ruffian Dick. I call you Poseur Dick!"

"Oh stop it, and tell me why you've settled upon this extraordinary lifestyle."

"Because I'm a woman."

"Indubitably. How is that an answer?"

"Just this: I accepted your proposal of marriage not just because I loved you, but because I saw in you the solution to my problem, and in me the solution to yours."

"Mine?"

"When we met, you had no security. You were adrift. I could have given you a sense of belonging."

A breath of wind pushed at them, driving away the scent of cloves and replacing it with the odour of putrefying fish. Burton wrinkled his nose, puffed at his cigar, and looked at the looming island.

"And in you," Isabel continued, "I might have found liberation from the suffocating corsets of the English gentlewoman. I mean that metaphorically, of course." She gave him a sideways glance. "Well, perhaps not entirely metaphorically."

Burton flashed a savage smile and turned his attention back to her.

"What I mean to say," Isabel continued, "is that I require something the Empire is not willing to give to a woman."

"You mean liberty?"

"And equality. I am not one to be laced-up and condemned to the parlour to while away my days crocheting antimacassars. Why should I allow my behaviour to be dictated by the protocols of a society in which I'm granted neither a voice nor representation?"

"I hardly think Bedouin women have a better time of it," Burton murmured.

"That's true. But at least they don't pretend otherwise. Besides, I'm not a Bedouin woman, am I? And the Arabs don't know what to make of me. To them, I'm a curiosity, whose foreign ways can be neither understood nor judged. I've found a niche where the only rules that apply are the ones I make myself."

"And you're happy?"

"Yes."

"In that case, Isabel—believe me—I don't disapprove. I detected both courage and resourcefulness in you very soon after our initial meeting, and I've always admired you for them. I salute your spirit of independence. And, incidentally, while it may be true that I was at one time uncertain of myself, I assure you that's not the case now. As the king's agent, I have a purpose. I no longer feel that I don't belong."

She sought his eyes. "But still there's no room for a wife."

He took another drag at his cigar, then looked at it with dissatisfaction and flicked it over the side of the ship. "When I called off our engagement, it was because I thought my new role would be dangerous for anyone too closely associated with me. Now I know for certain that I was right."

"Very well," she said. "And accepted. But if I can't support you as Isabel the wife, I shall most certainly do so as Al-Manat, the warrior."

"I don't want you in harm's way, Isabel. It was good of you to escort us through the desert to Aden, but there was no need for the Daughters of Al-Manat to sail with us."

"We will march with you to the Mountains of the Moon."

Burton shook his head. "No, you won't."

"Do you still imagine that, as my husband, you would have been in a position to command me? If so, I must disillusion you. Besides which, you are not my husband, and I take orders from no one. If I see fit to lead my women alongside your expedition, what can you do to stop me?"

"Nothing."

"Then our conversation is done."

With that, Isabel dropped her cigarette, crushed it beneath her heel, and paced away.

The *Elphinstone* manoeuvred through sharp coral reefs and steered toward a white Arabic town dominated by a plain square fort, which rose from among the clove shrubs, the coco-trees, and the tall luxuriant palms. Though the sun was high in the azure sky, the light it cast over the settlement was hazy and mellow, perhaps an effect of the high humidity, making the place appear beautiful in the extreme. However, twenty minutes later, when the steamer glided past the guard ship and into the mirror-smooth harbour waters where the rank stench of rotting molluscs and copra became overwhelming, the illusion broke. The idyllic landscape, seen up close, proved anything but. The shoreline was marked by a thick line of refuse, including three bloated human corpses upon which cur dogs were chewing, and the buildings were revealed to be in dire need of renovation.

Small fishing vessels now swarmed around the arriving sloop, and from them men shouted greetings and questions, and requested gifts, and demanded *bakhshish*, and offered fish and tobacco and alcohol at exorbitant prices. They were a mix of many races; those with the blackest skin wore wide-brimmed straw hats, while those of a browner cast wore the Arabic fez. Their clothing was otherwise the same: the colourful cotton robes common to so much of Africa.

Burton watched the familiar details unfold and thought, *I no longer feel that I don't belong.*

He'd been reflecting upon that statement ever since he'd made it. Now, while deck hands milled around making preparations to secure the vessel, it occurred to him that he hadn't adapted himself to British society at all— rather, British society was changing at such a pace, and with so little planning and forethought, that it had become extremely volatile, and, while this precarious state caused most of its people to feel unsettled, for some reason Burton couldn't comprehend, it was an environment he practically relished.

He stretched, turned, and walked over to Swinburne, Trounce, and Krishnamurthy.

Trounce grumbled, "It's not quite the paradise I expected, Richard."

Burton examined the flat-roofed residences, the Imam's palace, and the smart-looking consulates. Beyond them, and ill-concealed by them, the decrepit hovels of the inner town slumped in a mouldy heap.

"Zanzibar city, to become picturesque or pleasing," he said, "must be viewed, like Stanbul, from afar."

"And even then," Swinburne added, "with a peg firmly affixed to one's nose."

The ship's anchors dropped, and, with gulls and gannets wheeling and shrieking overhead, she came to a stop in the bay, nestling among the dhows and half a dozen square-rigged merchantmen. The British collier ship *Blackburn* was also there, waiting forlornly for the *Orpheus*.

As tradition demanded, the *Elphinstone* loosed a twenty-one-gun salute, and the detonations momentarily silenced the seabirds before rolling away into the distance. Strangely, no response came, either in the form of raised bunting or returned cannon fire.

"That's a curious omission. I wonder what's happening," Burton muttered. He turned to his friends and said, "The captain will order a boat lowered soon. Let's get ourselves ashore."

They had spent seven weeks in the Arabian Desert, two weeks in Aden, and ten days at sea. The expedition was considerably behind schedule. It was now the 19th of March.

Time to disembark.

Time to set foot on African soil.

Burton, Swinburne, Trounce, Honesty, and Krishnamurthy were met at the dock by a half-caste Arab who placed his hand over his heart, bowed, and introduced himself, in the Kiswahili tongue, as Saíd bin Sálim el Lamki, el Hináwi. He was of a short, thin, and delicate build, with scant mustachios and a weak beard. His skin was yellowish brown, his nose long, and his teeth dyed bright crimson by his habitual chewing of betel. His manner was extremely polite. He said, "Draw near, Englishmen. I am wazir to His Royal Highness Prince Sayyid Majid bin Said Al-Busaid, Imam of Muscat and Sultan of Zanzibar, may Allah bless him and speed his recovery."

Burton answered, in the same language: "We met when I was here last, some six years ago. Thou wert of great help to me then."

"I was honoured, Sir Richard, and am more so that thou doth remember me. I would assist thee again, and will begin by advising thee to accompany me to the palace before thou visit the consulate."

"Is there a problem?"

"Aye, there may be, but I should leave it for Prince Sayyid to explain. He is looking forward to seeing thee."

Eight men had accompanied Saíd. They were Askaris—a title created some years ago by the prince's grandfather, Sultan bin Hamid, to distinguish those Africans who took military service with him. Through means of immoderately wielded staffs, they now kept the hordes of onlookers, beggars, and merchants away from the group as it moved into the town.

"His Highness has been ill?" Burton enquired.

"With smallpox," Saíd answered. "But by Allah's grace, the worst of it has passed."

They entered a deep and winding alley, one of the hundreds of capricious and disorderly lanes that threaded through the town like a tangled skein. Some of the bigger streets were provided with gutters, but most were not, and the ground was liberally puddled with festering impurities, heaps of offal, and the rubble of collapsed walls. Naked children played in this filth, poultry and dogs roamed freely through it, and donkeys and cattle splashed it up the sides of the buildings to either side.

The fetor given off by the streets, mingled with the ubiquitous odour of rotting fish and copra, made the air almost unbreathable for the visitors. All of them walked with handkerchiefs pressed against their noses.

Their eyes, too, were assaulted.

Initially, it was the architecture that befuddled Burton's companions, for they had seen nothing like it before. Built from coral-rag cemented with lime, the masonry of the shuttered dwellings and public establishments to either side of the alleys showed not a single straight line, no two of their arches were the same, and the buildings were so irregular in their placement that the spaces between them were sometimes so wide as to not look like thoroughfares at all, and often so narrow that they could barely be navigated.

Slips of paper, upon which sentences from the Koran had been scribbled, were pinned over every doorway.

"What are they for?" Krishnamurthy asked.

"To ward off witchcraft," Burton revealed.

As for the inhabitants of Zanzibar, they appeared a confusing and noisy mélange of Africans and Arabs, Chinamen and Indians. The Britishers saw among them sailors and market traders and day labourers and hawkers and date-gleaners and fishermen and idlers. They saw rich men and poor men. They saw cripples and beggars and prostitutes and thieves.

And they saw slaves.

Swinburne was the first to witness the island's most notorious industry. As he and his friends were escorted through the crowded and chaotic Salt Bazaar—thick with musky, spicy scents, and where Saíd's men swung their staffs with even less restraint—the little poet let out a terrific yell of indignation. Burton, following his assistant's shocked stare, saw a chain gang of slaves being driven forward by the whip, approaching them through the crowd to the right.

Swinburne hollered, "This is atrocious, Richard! Why has our Navy not stopped it?"

"They can't be everywhere at once," the king's agent replied. "For all our successes on the west coast of Africa, here in the east the miserable trade continues."

The poet, gesticulating wildly in his frustration, made a move toward the slaves but was held back by his friend, who said, "Don't be a fool, Algy. More than forty thousand slaves pass through Zanzibar every year—you'll not change anything by causing trouble for us now."

Swinburne watched miserably as the captive men and women were herded past like animals, and he was uncharacteristically silent for a considerable time afterward.

Saíd led them into the main street leading up to the palace.

As they neared the blocky, high-windowed edifice, Thomas Honesty remarked on the tall purple clouds that had suddenly boiled up in the southeastern sky.

"It's the *Msika*," Burton told him. "The greater rain. This is the worst season to commence an expedition, but it lasts for two months and we can't delay."

"We're English," Honesty said, in his usual jerky manner. "Conditioned to rain."

"Not such as Africa has to offer, old thing. You'll see."

The palace, when they came to it, looked little better than a barracks. Roofed with mouldering red tiles, it was double-storied, square, and unencumbered by adornment.

They were ushered through the big entrance doors into a pleasant vestibule, then up a staircase and into a parlour. Saíd left them for a few moments before returning to announce that the prince was ready to receive them. The four men were then escorted into a long and narrow room, furnished with silk hangings, divans, tables, lamps, a plethora of cushions, and with colourful birds singing in its rafters.

Prince Sayyid Majid greeted them in the European manner, with a hearty handshake for each. He was a young man, thin, and possessed of a pleasant though terribly pockmarked countenance.

They sat with him on the floor, around a low table, and waited while two slaves served sweetmeats, biscuits, and glasses of sherbet.

"It pleases me to see thee again, Captain Burton," the prince intoned, in high-spoken Arabic.

Burton bowed his head, and employing the same language replied, "Much time has passed, O Prince. Thou wert little more than a child when I last visited the island. It pained me to hear of thy father's death."

"He taught me much and I think of him every day. May Allah grant that I never disgrace his name. I intend to continue his efforts to improve the island. Already I have cleared more land for *shambas*—plantations."

"And of thy father's intention to end the slave trade, O Prince—hast thou made progress in this?"

Sayyid Majid took a sip of his sherbet, then frowned. "There is one who opposes me—a man named el Murgebi, though most know him as Tippu Tip. His caravans penetrate far into the interior and he brings back many slaves. This man has become rich and powerful, and I can do little against him, for his supporters outnumber my own. Nevertheless—" The prince sighed and touched his nose with his right forefinger—a gesture Burton knew meant *It is my obligation.*

They talked a little more of the island's politics, until, after a few minutes, the prince revealed: "A very large force of Europeans has made its base on the mainland, Captain, in the village of Mzizima, directly south of here. Thy friend, Lieutenant Speke, was among them."

"He's no longer a friend of mine," Burton declared.

"Ah. Friendship is like a glass ornament; once it is broken, it can rarely be put back together the same way. I believe the men are of the Almaniya race."

"Germanic? Yes, I think that likely. Thou sayest Speke *was* with them? Is he no longer?"

"He and a number of men left Mzizima and are currently moving toward the central territories."

"Then I must follow them at the earliest opportunity."

The prince sighed. "The rains will make that difficult, and it pains me to tell thee, Captain, but also, thou hast been betrayed by Consul Rigby."

Burton's hands curled into fists.

The prince continued, "The British government shipped supplies here some weeks ago and instructed him to hire Wanyamwezi porters to transport them to the Dut'humi Hills, where they were to await thy arrival. The supplies consisted of trading goods—bales of cotton, rolls of brass wire, beads, the usual things—plus food, instruments, weapons and ammunition, and two of the spider machines—they are called harvestmen?"

"Yes."

"The men were never hired, and the goods never transported. A month ago, when the Almaniyas arrived, the consul handed the supplies over to them."

"Bismillah! The traitorous hound! Ever has Rigby sought to stand in my way, but I tell thee, Prince Sayyid, this time he hath defied those to whom he owes his position. This will ruin him."

"Aye, Captain, mayhap. But that is for the future. For now, we must put our energy into overcoming the obstacles this man hath set in thy path. To that end, I offer my resources. Tell me what I can do."

Over the next hour, Burton and the prince made plans, with the king's agent occasionally breaking off to translate for his companions.

By mid-afternoon, they all had tasks assigned to them. Honesty and Krishnamurthy headed back to the *Elphinstone* to join Herbert Spencer, Isabella Mayson, and Sadhvi Raghavendra in overseeing the transfer of the expedition's supplies and equipment to a corvette named *Artémis*. William Trounce, Isabel Arundell, and her followers were taken by Saíd bin Sálim to the prince's country ranch, there to select horses from his extensive stud, which, in the morning, they'd ship over to the mainland aboard a cargo carrier, the *Ann Lacey*.

Sir Richard Francis Burton and Algernon Swinburne, meanwhile, paid a visit to the British Consulate.

It was nine o'clock in the evening by the time they left the prince's palace. The rain had just ceased and the town was dripping. The filth, rather than being washed away, had merely been rearranged.

The king's agent and his assistant picked their way cautiously through foul alleyways until they arrived at their destination. Its gates, to their surprise, were open and unguarded. They passed through, crossed the small courtyard, and pushed open the entrance doors. The building was unlit and silent.

"This isn't right," Burton whispered.

"Does Rigby live here?" Swinburne asked.

"Yes, in the upstairs apartments, but let's check his office first."

The ground floor consisted of the entrance hall, a waiting room, a sparsely furnished parlour, a records office and a clerks' office, a library, and the main consulting room. All were empty and dark.

In the library, Burton, upon detecting a faint rustling, drew out his clockwork lantern, shook it open, wound it, and cast its light around.

The bookshelves were teeming with ants and termites.

"My hat!" Swinburne exclaimed. "What an infestation! What on earth has attracted them, Richard?"

"I don't know, but this is certainly excessive, even for Africa."

They moved back into the entrance hall and started up the stairs. Halfway up there was a small landing, where the steps made a turn to the right. The body of a man lay at an awkward angle upon it. Burton held his lantern over the face. He could see from the man's physiognomy that his skin would have been black in life; in death, it was a horrible ashen grey and had shrunk against the bones beneath. The lips had pulled back, exposing all the teeth, and the eyes had withdrawn to the back of the sockets.

The king's agent reached down and pressed a finger against the face.

"It feels like wood," he said. "Like all the blood and moisture have been sucked out of it."

"And that's how." Swinburne pointed to the dead man's left arm. Burton moved the light to better illuminate it. He saw that a leafy vine of a purplish hue was coiled around the wrist, and that the end of it, which was splayed flat and covered in three-inch-long thorns of wicked appearance, was pressed against the forearm and had pierced the skin many times over.

Talking a dagger from his belt, he carefully probed at the plant. Its leaves were dry and fell away at his touch. The vine itself was hard and desiccated. Raising the lantern, he followed its course and saw that it coiled away up the stairs and disappeared around a corner.

"Be careful, Algy," he said, and started toward the upper floor.

Swinburne followed, noting that the steps were swarming with beetles and cockroaches.

When they reached the hallway at the top, they saw that the vine twisted through an open doorway into a faintly illuminated chamber just ahead. Only a small part of the room was visible—the bulk of it obviously lay to the left of the portal—but the end they could see was so seething with insects that every surface seemed alive. Vines were clinging to the walls and floor and ceiling, too. Loops of vegetation hung down like jungle creepers, and through and around it, glowing softly, hundreds of fireflies were flitting.

Muttering an imprecation, Burton moved forward with Swinburne at his heels. They traversed the corridor then passed through the doorway, and, with insects crunching underfoot, turned and tried to interpret what they saw. It was difficult. No item of furniture could be properly discerned, for everything was crawling with life and half-concealed behind a tangle of thorny but dead-looking foliage. Furthermore, Burton's lantern caused the great many shadows to deepen, while the myriad fireflies made them wriggle and writhe, so that the entire space squirmed disconcertingly around the two men.

There was a shuttered window in the far wall. In front of it, what looked to be the squat and bulky main trunk of a plant humped up from the floor. Burton, ducking under a dangling creeper, stepped closer to it. He saw that it had corners and realised that what he was looking at was actually a desk, though it was hardly recognisable as such, distorted as it was by all the knotted limbs of the growth that covered it.

His lantern picked out a gnarl of woody protrusions that caught and held his attention. A few moments passed before he realised why.

It was because they resembled a hand.

The hairs at the nape of his neck stood on end.

He slowly raised the lantern and leaned closer. The protuberances grew from the end of a thick, vine-tangled branch which, a little way along its length, bent elbow-like upward before joining a hideously warped trunk— positioned just behind the desk—over which centipedes, spiders, ants, beetles, and termites scuttled in profusion. The insects were flooding in a downward direction. Burton followed their course upward, to where the trunk suddenly narrowed before then widening into a large nodule which angled backward slightly. There was a hole in it, and from this the creatures were vomiting.

Burton knew what he was going to see next, and with every fibre of his being he didn't want to set eyes on it, but the compulsion to lift the lantern higher couldn't be resisted, and its light crept upward from the hole, over the deformed nose and cheekbones, and illuminated Christopher Rigby's living eyes, which burned with hatred in his transfigured and paralysed face.

Burton's shock rendered him voiceless; he could only crouch and stare, his whole body trembling, his senses blasted by the appalling thing before him.

Rigby had been sitting at his desk when the metamorphosis came upon him. It had turned his flesh into plant tissue. Roots and creepers and vines and lianas had grown from him. Repulsive thorny leaves had sprouted. And, to judge from the corpse on the stairs, the thing he'd become was carnivorous, for it had sucked the blood from that unfortunate individual.

Now, though, with the exception of those demonic eyes, Rigby appeared to be dead, for he was withered and dried out, the majority of his leaves had fallen, and his body was riddled with termite holes.

Burton straightened. The eyes followed him. He noted that Rigby's neck had been crushed, then saw the same claw marks he'd noted on the corpse of Peter Pimlico, but they were deeper, more savage.

"The devil take him, Algy," he muttered. "This is Zeppelin's doing."

Swinburne didn't reply.

Burton turned, and for a second he thought his assistant had left the room. Then a flash of red drew his attention to the ceiling. To his horror, he saw the poet up there, flat against it, entwined by creepers.

"Algy!" he yelled, but his friend was limp, unconscious, and the explorer spotted a thorny extension pressed against the side of the small man's neck.

Spinning back to face Rigby, he yelled, "Let him go, damn you!"

A thick fountain of insects suddenly erupted from the consul's mouth, spraying into the air and landing on the desk, on the floor, and on Burton. The head creaked slowly into an upright position.

"You!" Rigby whispered. His voice sounded like dry leaves being disturbed by a breeze. "I have waited for so long."

"Release him!" Burton demanded. "Maybe I can help you, Rigby!"

"I don't want your help, Burton. I only want your blood!"

A liana dropped from above and encircled the explorer's neck. Burton, realising that he still held his dagger, brought it up, sliced through the creeper, and pulled it away from his skin.

"Zeppelin did this to you, didn't he?"

"Yes."

"A Prussian, Rigby! He's working against the Empire and I've been sent to stop him. You're British, man! Do your duty! Help me!"

"Were it anyone else, Burton, I would. But you, never! I'll die a traitor rather than aid you!"

Leafy tendrils wound around Burton's calves. He felt thorns cutting through his trouser legs, piercing his skin. He ducked as a spiny appendage whipped past his face.

There was no time for persuasion. No time for discussion. Swinburne was being bled to death and, at any moment, Burton himself would likely be overwhelmed.

He jabbed his dagger into his lantern, ripped the side of it open, then prodded the point of the weapon into the oil sack. Liquid spurted out and instantly ignited.

"Don't!" the consul rasped.

"I've suffered your jealousy and enmity for too many years, Rigby. It ends here."

Burton slammed the burning lantern onto the desk. Immediately, the burning oil splashed outward and the tinder-dry plant burst into flames, sending the king's agent reeling backward. The vines around his legs tripped him but then slithered away, thrashing back and forth.

Swinburne dropped and thudded onto the floor. Burton crawled on hands and knees over to him, feeling the spreading inferno scorching the hairs on the back of his head. With Rigby's screams ringing in his ears, he tore vines away from the poet, grasped him by the collar, and dragged him through the scuttling insects and out of the room.

The fire was expanding with frightening speed. It tore along the walls and over the ceiling, raged past the two men, and filled the corridor with roiling black smoke.

Holding his breath and staying low, Burton reached the top of the stairs and practically fell down them. He rolled onto the cadaver on the landing, then Swinburne rolled onto him, then all three tumbled down the remaining steps. The corpse's limbs broke like snapping twigs as it fell.

A blazing roof beam crashed onto the landing they'd just vacated, showering sparks and fragments of flaming wood onto them.

Burton stood, hoisted Swinburne onto his shoulder, and staggered across the reception hall, out into the courtyard, and through the consulate's gate.

He turned and looked back. There would be no saving the building, that much was plain, and Christopher Rigby, who'd hated him implacably for two decades, was being cremated inside it.

Burton felt no satisfaction at that.

He carried Swinburne back toward the Imam's palace.

Early the following day, on the East African coast below Zanzibar, two ships dropped anchor off a long, low, bush-covered sand spit some twenty miles south of the ivory- and copra-trading town of Bagamoyo.

The *Artémis* and *Ann Lacey* lowered their boats and began the long task of transporting men, mules, horses, and supplies to the mainland. In this, they were assisted by a hundred and twenty Wasawahili porters, who waited on the shore having been transported in a dhow from Bagamoyo by Saíd bin Sálim and his eight staff-wielding Askaris.

This part of the coast was known as the Mrima, or "hill land." Cut by deep bays, lagoons, and backwaters, its banks were thickly lined by forests of white and red mangroves, the tangled roots of which made passage through to the more open land beyond extremely difficult. There was, however, a humped shelf of black rock that cut through the trees and formed a path from the spit. Burton ordered that this be strewn with sand—and straw from the *Ann Lacey's* hold—so the horses might traverse it without slipping. One by one, eighty of the fine Arabian mounts were lowered by harness from the cargo vessel to the boat, then landed two at a time on the spit and led across the rock and through the mangroves to an encampment, an extensive patch of white sand bordered by a wall of verdure on three sides and by a low hill, held together by tough and bright-flowered creepers, to landward. Beyond this, more grass-covered hills swelled between mosquito-infested creeks, lagoons, and black fetid ooze.

The eighty horses were the first of four livestock shipments, and once they were ashore, the *Ann Lacey* steamed away to pick up the next consignment from Zanzibar.

Meanwhile, *Artémis* offloaded seventy bundles of trading specie, crates of food and books and equipment, Rowtie tents, weapons, ammunition, and all the other paraphernalia necessary for the safari.

Amid the perpetual whine and buzz of insects, Burton directed the construction of the camp. As soon as the first Rowtie was erected, Algernon Swinburne was carried by litter into it and made comfortable on a bunk.

"He's still unconscious," Sister Raghavendra told the king's agent. "He lost a lot of blood and also took a nasty knock to the head, but he'll get over it. I have no doubt he'll be bouncing around again in due course. His durability is astonishing. I remember remarking upon it that time he was assaulted by Laurence Oliphant. Nevertheless, I should allow him a week of undisturbed bed rest."

Burton shook his head. "I'm sorry, Sadhvi, but that won't be possible. We can't tarry here. We have to strike camp and start moving at the first glimmer of dawn tomorrow. But I'll assign porters to his stretcher. We'll carry Algy for as long as he needs."

"Very well. I'll stay close to him."

Saíd bin Sálim had been appointed *ras kafilah*—or guide—to the expedition. Thankfully, despite sharing the same name, he was not the man who'd acted in that capacity during Burton's first exploration back in '57. That particular Saíd had caused nothing but trouble, whereas the current *ras kafilah* immediately demonstrated his worth by assigning tasks to the Wasawahili and ensuring they earned their pay. In this, his eight "bully boys," as Trounce called them, were instrumental. With surprising rapidity, the camp was organised.

By the time the sun had set, two hundred and fifty horses and twenty mules were corralled at the southern end of the clearing; a semicircle of Rowtie tents had been erected at the northern end; the east side was crowded with *beit sha'ar*—Arabian goat-hair tents—occupied by the two hundred Daughters of Al-Manat; and the west side belonged to the porters, who sat or lay wrapped in blankets. Guards were posted, fires were lit, and chickens and vegetables and porridge were cooked and consumed.

The silence of the tropical night settled over the expedition, shattered now and then by the bellow of a bull-crocodile or the outré cry of a nocturnal heron. The atmosphere was stifling, the mosquitoes indefatigable.

Burton, his friends—with the exception of Swinburne—and Saíd had gathered in the main tent. The Englishmen wore light trousers and collarless shirts, unbuttoned at the neck and with sleeves rolled up. Isabella Mayson and Sister Raghavendra had donned summer dresses of a modest cut. Saíd and Isabel Arundell were in their Arabian robes. Herbert Spencer still wore his polymethylene suit but had wrapped around it the full robes of a Bedouin, his head completely concealed within a *keffiyeh*. He'd taken to walking with a staff, not only to compensate for his damaged leg, but also because it added to the impression that he was a leper—a disguise that caused the Wasawahili porters to give him a wide berth. Had they been aware of what really lay beneath those robes, superstitious dread would have caused them to desert in droves.

The group was sitting around a table upon which Burton had spread a large map. They examined it by the light of an oil lamp against which a repulsive moth was bumping.

"This was drawn up in 1844 by a French naval officer named Maizan," Burton told them. "As you can see, I have added extensive corrections and annotations. We are here—" he pointed to a spot on the map, then to another, farther inland, "—and this is the village of Kuingani. And beyond that, here we have the village of Bomani, and here, Mkwaju. If you march at two and a half miles per hour and don't stop at the first two villages, you'll reach the third in about four and a half to five hours."

Thomas Honesty shrugged. "Sounds too slow."

"Don't underestimate the terrain," Burton replied. "You'll find it hard going, and the pace I suggest won't be easy. And in addition to the difficulties of swamp and jungle, the hills that extend back from here, and which rise up along the length of the coast, belong to the Wamrima tribes. They are generally hostile and uncooperative."

"Who wouldn't be, with slavers preying on them?" Isabella Mayson murmured.

"Quite so. My point is this: strike camp at the crack of dawn, press on as hard as you can, stay alert, and keep your weapons to hand. Don't take any nonsense from the villagers. They will undoubtedly try to charge you an extortionate tax for passing through their territory. They refer to it as *hongo*— meaning 'tribute'—and they'll do everything possible to hamper your progress if they aren't satisfied with what they get. Pay only as Saíd advises— which will, anyway, be over the odds."

He said something to the guide in Arabic. Saíd looked at Krishnamurthy and addressed him in fluent Hindustani: "I speak thy tongue, sir."

"Ah, good, that's excellent!" Krishnamurthy responded.

Burton continued: "When you reach Mkwaju, rest and eat, but be ready to move on at a moment's notice. If everything goes to plan, by the time we catch up with you, it'll be the hottest part of the day. Despite that, we'll have to start moving again. I want to reach Nzasa, here—" He tapped another mark on the map. "That's another three-and-a-half-hour march. By the time we get there, I'm pretty sure we'll be too done in to go any farther, and the day's rains will be on their way, so this is where we'll camp for the night."

They talked for a little while longer, then Burton stood, stretched, and fished a cigar from his pocket. He addressed Isabel Arundell and William Trounce: "It's a new moon tonight, so we'll be operating by starlight alone. Isabel, when your women are done with their evening prayers, please begin your preparations. William, come have a smoke with me. The rest of you: bed—that's an order!"

"I'll work on me book, Boss," Herbert Spencer said. "Sleep is another pleasure I'm denied nowadays, but it ain't all bad—my *First Principles of Philosophy* is comin' on a treat!"

They bade each other goodnight.

Burton and Trounce stepped outside, lit up, and strolled slowly around the camp, sending plumes of blue tobacco smoke into the heavy air. It did nothing to drive away the mosquitoes. Trounce slapped at one that was attacking his forearm. "Bloody things!"

"They gather especially around swampy ground," Burton told him. "The places where miasmic gases cause malaria. The areas where the mosquitoes are thickest are the same areas where you're most likely to succumb."

"How long before I do?"

"The seasoning fever usually sets in fairly quickly. A fortnight at most, old chap, then you'll be sweating it out and gibbering like a loon for a month. I'm afraid it's inevitable."

Trounce grunted. "I hope Sadhvi is as good a nurse as you say she is!"

They watched Isabel's women saddling their horses, then discarded their cigar stubs, walked back to the main tent, and retrieved their shoulder bags and rifles.

"All right," said Burton. "Let's get on with it."

Ten minutes later, the two men were riding at Isabel's side and leading two hundred mounted Amazons up the hill. When they reached its brow, Trounce pulled his horse around—like Honesty and Krishnamurthy, he'd learned to ride during their trek through Arabia—and looked down at the camp. It seemed a tiny island, hemmed in on three sides by riotous vegetation, with the Indian Ocean glittering in the starlight beyond, and, behind him, the endless expanse of unexplored Africa.

"I feel that we're up against impossible odds," he said to Burton.

The king's agent replied, "We probably are."

Mzizima village was five miles south of the camp. Originally, it had been composed of thatch-roofed beehive huts and a *bandani*—a wall-less palaver house, just a thatched roof standing upon six vertical beams—which were all positioned in an orderless cluster around an open central space. Surrounding the village, amid cocoa, mango, and pawpaw trees, there had been fields of rice, holcus, sugarcane, and peas, separated by clumps of basil and sage. This cultivated land stretched to the edge of a mangrove forest in the south, to the hills in the west, and to a small natural bay on the coast.

In the distant past, the Wamrima inhabitants had been farmers of the land and fishers of the sea, but the slave trade had made lying, thieving, shirking, and evasiveness the tools of survival, reducing a once-prosperous village to a clump of hovels occupied by men and women who, in the knowledge that life could be literally or metaphorically taken from them at any moment, did not bother to apply themselves to the business of living.

And now the Prussians had come.

It was four o'clock in the morning. Sir Richard Francis Burton was lying on his stomach at the top of a bushy ridge to the north and was using the field glasses he'd retrieved from the *Orpheus* to spy upon the settlement. Only a few of its original structures remained—the palaver house being one of them—and in their place wood-built barracks of a distinctly European design had been erected. There were six of these, plus six more half-built, and beyond them a sea of tents that spread out into the once-cultivated fields. The canvas dwellings were especially numerous farther to the south, where mangroves had obviously been chopped and burned away. More half-erected wooden buildings were visible there, too.

"It looks like they're planning a permanent camp here," Trounce whispered. "Building a village a little to the south of the original one."

Burton grunted an agreement.

By the bright light of the stars, he could see that his stolen supplies were stacked up in the *bandani*. One of his harvestman vehicles squatted beside the structure. The other one was closer to his and Trounce's position, standing motionless at the outer edge of the tented area just in front of the ridge, obviously left there by its driver. A guard was standing beside it, with a rifle over his shoulder and a pipe in his mouth.

Mzizima was silent, with only a few men on patrol. Of the Wamrima, there was no sign, and Burton felt certain that the villagers had either been pressed into service as lackeys or killed.

"What the bloody hell is that?" Trounce hissed, pointing to the other side of the encampment.

Burton focused his glasses on the thing that flopped along there. Even before he caught a clear view of it, its shadowy shape caused him to shudder. Then it floundered into an area of silvery luminescence and he saw that it was a huge plant, propelling itself along on thick white roots. To Burton's astonishment, there was a man sitting in the thing, cocooned in a fleshy bloom and surrounded by flailing tendrils. He appeared to be steering the plant by thought alone, for there were coiling threadlike appendages embedded into the skin of his scalp, and when he moved his head, the grotesque vehicle turned in the direction he was looking.

"There are others," Trounce said. "They're patrolling the outer perimeter."

A few minutes later, it became apparent why.

One of the plants suddenly lunged forward and grabbed at something. A man, screaming wildly, was yanked out of the undergrowth and hoisted into the air. It was a Wamrima native, obviously trying to escape, and now he paid the price. Held aloft by creepers entangled around his wrists, he was mercilessly whipped by the plant's spine-encrusted limbs until his naked back was streaming blood, then he was cast back into the camp—sent spinning through the air to land in a heap between tents, where he lay insensible.

"This complicates matters," Burton said.

"Should we call it off?"

"No. We'll need those supplies if we're to catch up with Speke. He's got a tremendous lead on us, but if we have all our resources, we can cut straight through all the circumstances that will slow him down."

"What circumstances?"

"Mainly the obstructions the natives will throw in his path. I'm counting on his incompetence as an expedition leader, inability to communicate in any language other than English, and the fact that, believing us blown up on the *Orpheus*, he has no idea we're on his tail."

Fifteen minutes later, Pox swooped out of the sky and landed on Burton's shoulder.

"Message from Isabel Arundell!" the parakeet announced.

"Shhh!" Burton hissed, but it was an instruction the bird didn't understand.

"In position, you lumpish clotpole. Awaiting the word. Message ends."

"The guard by the harvestman is looking this way," Trounce said softly.

"Message to Isabel Arundell," Burton whispered. "Consider the word received. Beware. There are Eugenicist plants. Message ends."

Pox gave a squawk and flew away.

"It's all right," Trounce said. "He just saw Pox. Probably thinks it's nothing but a noisy jungle bird. He's giving his attention back to his pipe."

"I think it's time to take care of him, anyway," Burton said.

He pulled his spine-shooter from its holster.

Steadying the cactus gun on his left forearm, he took careful aim and gently squeezed the nodule that functioned as a trigger. With a soft *phut!*, the pistol fired.

Seven spines thudded into the guard's chest. He looked down at them, muttered, *"Was sind diese?"* then crumpled to the ground.

"Quietly now," Burton hissed. "To the outer tents. Stay low."

The two men slipped over the brow of the ridge and slithered silently down to the perimeter of the camp. They crouched in the dark shadow of a tent and waited.

When it happened, it did so with such suddenness that even Burton and Trounce, who were expecting it, were taken by surprise. One minute there was nothing but the sound of snoring men under canvas, the next the night was rent by rifle fire, the pounding of horses' hooves, and the ululation of women.

The Daughters of Al-Manat came thundering over the crest of the hill on the northwestern border of the camp, and even before a warning shout could be raised by the guards, they had stampeded over tents, set burning brands to three of the barracks, and wheeled their horses and raced back up the hill and out of sight.

The Prussian guards barely got a shot off, so panicked were they at this unexpected onslaught.

"Wir wurden angegriffen! Wir wurden angegriffen!" they bellowed. *"Vertei-digt das Lager!"*

Men blundered out of the burning buildings, came running out of the others, and emerged from the tents, rubbing their eyes and peering around in confusion. Gunfire banged and flashed from the summit of the hill. Many of the soldiers fell to the ground with bullets in them.

Snatching up their rifles, the Prussians raced to meet the attacking forces. Burton grabbed Trounce by the arm and pointed to the Eugenicist plant vehicles. They, too, were lumbering to the northwesternmost part of the settlement.

The gunfire from one particular area of the hills intensified. The Prussians returned it, shooting blind. While their attention was thus engaged, twenty riders burst out of the verdure a little farther to the south, dashed across an overgrown field, and put torches to two of the plant creatures. Burton could barely repress a cheer when the starlight revealed that Isabel Arundell was the leader of this cavalry charge. She held a pistol in one hand and a spear in the other, and, expertly controlling her mount with her knees, she sent her charge leaping across tents to another of the Eugenicist creations. Plunging her spear into the densest part of it, she reared her horse away from its lashing tendrils, brought her pistol to bear, and shot the plant's driver through the head. She barked a command, galloped away with her band following, and disappeared into the darkness.

The part of Mzizima closest to Burton and Trounce was almost entirely abandoned now.

"Let's move," Burton urged. "We have to get this done before the southern part of the camp joins the fray." He and Trounce crept forward until they reached the nearest of the two harvestmen. The explorer reached up to where he expected to find a small hatch in the machine's belly. In London, harvestmen were primarily employed to transport goods, which they carried in netting suspended from their bellies. It had been his intention to reclaim the two vehicles, load them up with the supplies, and walk them away while the Prussians were distracted. He now encountered a serious setback.

"Damn!" he said. "They've removed the confounded net! It's been replaced by a bracket. Looks like they intend to fix something else to the underside of the body."

"How will we transport our stuff?" Trounce asked.

"I don't know. Let's get to it first. Speed is of the essence!"

They ran forward, unnoticed amid the confusion.

One of the barracks, consumed by flames, collapsed, sending out a shower of sparks. Men yelled. Rifles cracked.

Pox fluttered onto Burton's shoulder.

"Message from Isabel churlish bladder-prodder Arundell. Hurry up, you foot-licker! Message ends."

The second harvester, standing beside the *bandani*, was intact. Burton pulled down its net and spread it out.

"Start loading it. As many crates as you can. Ignore the specie—it's the equipment we need."

"*Was machen Sie hier?*" a voice demanded.

Burton whirled, raised his spine-shooter, and shot the inquisitor down.

"Message to Isabel Arundell," he said. "We're loading the equipment now. There's only one harvestman. Maximum distraction, if you please. Message ends."

Pox departed.

Moments later, the Daughters of Al-Manat came pelting back down the hill with guns blazing. As they engaged at close quarters with the Prussians, Burton and Trounce lifted crate after crate from the *bandani* into the netting. At one point, the king's agent sensed movement at the periphery of his vision, looked up, and noted ten or twelve Africans running up the slope of the ridge and disappearing into the undergrowth.

"Good for you!" he grunted.

Two more soldiers noticed the Englishmen and both went down with venomous cactus spines in them.

"That's as much as she can take," Burton panted. They'd loaded about a third of the stolen supplies. "Get into her, stay low, and drive back the way we came. If I haven't caught up with you by the time you reach the sand spit, wait for me there."

William Trounce uttered an acknowledgement, climbed the rungs on one of the harvestman's legs, and settled into the driver's seat. He started the engine. Its roar was drowned out by the gunfire, but as the harvestman stalked away, with its loaded net swinging underneath and Burton running in its wake, its trail of steam was noticed and three of the Prussian plant vehicles started to converge on it.

"Keep going!" Burton yelled. "Get out of here!"

As they came abreast with the other harvestman, the king's agent quickly clambered up its leg, slipped into position, grabbed the control levers, and prayed to Allah that the machine was operational.

It was.

The engine clattered into life behind his seat, and he sent the conveyance striding into the path of the nearest plant. He raised his cactus gun and fired spines at the Prussian who was nestled in its bloom. They had no effect.

"Immune to the venom?" he muttered. "Maybe you're half-plant yourself!"

Burton sent his steam-powered spider crashing into the mutated flora. Tendrils wrapped themselves around his machine's legs and started heaving at it, attempting to turn it over. He repeatedly shot spines at its driver until the Prussian's face resembled a porcupine. The man remained conscious, snarled at the Britisher, and sent a vine whipping at the explorer's hand. It caught the cactus gun with such viciousness that the barrel was sliced completely in half. Burton cursed and dropped it.

The harvestman was jolted from side to side. Its carapace was battered and scored by swishing barbed limbs, and Burton felt it slewing sideways beneath him. Desperately hauling at its levers, he caused its front two legs to rise up and brought them sweeping down onto the soldier's chest. The man died instantly, his heart pierced through, and the plant bucked and threshed wildly, causing the harvestman to topple over. In the instant before it hit the ground, Burton dived out of it, rolled, and started running. He reached the bottom of the slope but it was too late; the two other plants were looming over him. Putting his head down, he pumped his legs as fast as he could and started up the hill. Creepers coiled at the periphery of his vision, reaching out to grab him. Suddenly, one hooked under his left arm and wrenched him into the air. Expecting to be flayed or ripped apart, Burton instead found himself flying over the ground and bumping against the side of a horse. He realised that it wasn't a creeper but a hand holding him. Unable to manoeuvre himself into a position where he could see his rescuer, he clutched at the rider's ankle in an attempt to steady himself—a female ankle!

The horse dashed up to the top of the ridge and skidded to a halt beside Trounce's harvestman. Burton was dropped unceremoniously onto the ground.

"William! Stop!" The commanding voice belonged to Isabel Arundell.

Trounce brought his machine to a halt.

"Get onto the net, Dick!" Isabel barked.

Burton looked up at her just as a bullet tore through a fold in her Bedouin robes, missing her flesh by less than an inch. She turned in her saddle, levelled her revolver, and fired six shots back into the camp.

"Move, damn it!" she yelled.

Burton snapped back into action. Three paces took him beneath the harvestman. He jumped up, gripped the net, and clambered onto it.

"Go, William!" Isabel shouted. "As fast as possible! Don't stop and don't look back! We'll keep the Prussians occupied for as long as we can."

"Isabel—" Burton began, but she cut him off: "We'll catch up with your expedition later. Get going!"

She reared her horse around, and, as she sent it plunging down the slope, she pulled a spear from over her shoulder and jabbed its point into one of the plant vehicles.

Trounce pulled back on a lever, his harvestman coughed and sent out a plume of steam, then went striding into the night with Burton swinging underneath.

"Bloody hell!" the explorer muttered to himself. "That woman has the strength of an ox and the courage of a lion!"

William Trounce didn't stop the harvestman until he'd travelled half the distance back to the expedition's campsite. There'd been no pursuit. Distant gunshots peppered the night.

He manoeuvred one of the spider's long legs inward until it was within Burton's reach. The king's agent climbed up it to the one-man cabin and sat on the edge of it with his legs inside and feet hooked under the seat.

"All right," he said, and Trounce got the vehicle moving again.

It was slow going. The harvestman was far heavier than a horse, and the pointed ends of its legs frequently sank deep into the sodden earth. By the time they reached the sand spit, the sun had risen, the vegetation was dripping with dew, and the land was steaming.

The sandy clearing where they'd camped was empty.

"Good," Burton said. "They're on their way. Maybe we can catch up with them before they reach Nzasa."

Pox glided down and landed on Trounce's head.

"Hey there! Get off!" the Scotland Yard man protested. The bird ignored him.

"Message from Isabel Arundell. We're going to withdraw and recoup. Eleven of my women killed, three injured. We shall wage an idle-headed guerrilla campaign over the next few days to prevent them following you. We'll catch up presently. Travel safely, wobble-paunch! Message ends."

"An idle-headed guerrilla campaign?" Trounce asked, in a puzzled tone.

"I think there's a parakeet insertion there," Burton said.

"Oh. Can you get the bloody parrot off my head, please?"

"Message for Isabel Arundell," Burton said. "My gratitude, but don't take risks. Disengage as soon as you can. Message ends."

The parakeet squawked its acknowledgement and launched itself into the air.

With Burton navigating, Trounce steered the harvestman up the hill on the western side of the clearing. They travelled over sandy soil, thick with thorn bushes, and, after a succession of rolling hills, descended into rich parkland dotted with mangoes and other tall trees. The sun was climbing behind them. The morning steam evaporated and the air began to heat up.

A little later, Pox rejoined them.

They came to a swamp and waded the harvestman through it, scattering hippopotami from their path.

"This would have sent Speke into a frenzy," Burton noted.

"What do you mean?"

"He's a huntsman through and through. He'll shoot at anything that moves and delights in killing. When we were out here in '57, he slaughtered more hippos than I could count."

The giant mechanised arachnid pitched and swayed as it struggled through the stinking sludge, then it finally emerged onto more solid ground and began to move with greater speed.

A few beehive huts came into view, and the inhabitants, upon seeing the gigantic spider approaching, bolted.

Burton and Trounce crossed cultivated land, passed the village of Kuingani, which emptied rapidly, and proceeded onto broad grasslands flecked with small forests and freestanding baobab trees possessed of bulbous trunks and wind-flattened branches. It was here that Trounce saw his first truly wide African vista and he was astonished at the apparent purity of the land. Giraffes were moving in the distance to his right; two herds of antelope were grazing far off to his left; eagles hung almost motionless high in the sky; and on the horizon, a long, low chain of mountains stretched from north to south. This Eden should, perhaps, have been caressed by the freshest of breezes, but the atmosphere was heavy and stagnant and filled with aggressive insects. The backs of Trounce's hands, his forearms, and his neck were covered with bumps from their bites.

After a further two hours of travel, Burton pointed and exclaimed: "Look! I see them!"

There was a village ahead, and around it many people were gathered. Burton could tell by the loads he saw on the ground that it was his expedition.

"That little collection of huts is Bomani," he told Trounce.

As the harvestman drew closer, the natives reacted as those before them had done and fled en masse.

"Well met!" Maneesh Krishnamurthy cried out as the harvestman came to a halt and squatted down with a blast of steam and a loud hiss. "They wanted all our tobacco in return for safe passage through their territory. You soon saw them off!"

"You've made good time," Burton noted, jumping to the ground.

"Saíd had us packed and moving well before sunup," Krishnamurthy revealed. "The man's a demon of efficiency."

Burton turned to the Arab: "Hail to thee, Saíd bin Sálim el Lamki, el Hináwi, and the blessings of Allah the Almighty upon thee. Thou hast fulfilled thy duties well."

"Peace be upon thee, Captain Burton. By Allah's grace, our first steps have been favoured with good fortune. May it continue! Thou hast caught up with us earlier than anticipated."

"Our mission did not take the time I expected. The Daughters of Al-Manat were ferocious and the Prussians barely looked in our direction. We were able to recover our supplies quickly. Are we fit to continue?"

"Aye."

"Very well. Have the porters take up their loads."

The *ras kafilah* bowed and moved away to prepare the safari for the next stage of the journey.

Burton spoke to Miss Mayson. "Swap places with William, Isabella. We'll take shifts in the harvester. It's more agreeable than a mule."

The young woman smiled and shook her head. "To be honest, I'd rather stay with my flea-bitten animal. I'm better with beasts than with machines."

"You're not uncomfortable?"

"Not at all. I feel positively liberated!"

It was Thomas Honesty who took over from Trounce in the end, for Sister Raghavendra also refused to give up her mount, preferring to ride alongside Swinburne's litter. The poet was awake but weak.

"My hat, Richard!" he said, faintly. "Was that really Christopher Rigby? What in blue blazes happened to him?"

"Count Zeppelin. I think he carries some sort of venom in his claws. Either he didn't pump much of it into Peter Pimlico or his talons were less well grown when he strangled him. Rigby, by contrast, received the full treatment."

"And it turned him into a prickly bush?"

"Yes. It was a close call, Algy. What devils the Eugenicists have become!"

"Not just them," Swinburne said, glancing at the harvestman. "If you ask me, all the sciences are out of control. I think my Libertine friends were right all along. We need to give more attention to the development of the human spirit before we tamper with the natural world."

Herbert Spencer limped over to them. "Mr. Saíd says we're all set for the off."

"Tell him to get us moving then, please, Herbert."

"Rightio. Pardon me, Boss, but would you mind windin' me up first? Me spring is a little slack."

"Certainly. Fetch me your key."

The clockwork man shuffled off.

"How are you feeling, Algy?" Burton asked his friend.

"Tip-top, Richard," Swinburne replied. "Do you think I might have a swig of gin, you know, to ward off malaria?"

"Ha! You're obviously on the mend! And no."

When Spencer returned, he stood with his back to Burton, and the king's agent, after first checking that the porters couldn't see what he was doing, felt around for the holes that had been cut in the back of the philosopher's many robes, and in the polymethylene suit beneath them. He pushed a large metal key through and into the opening in the brass man's back, then turned it until the clockwork philosopher was fully wound.

Spencer thanked him and went to help get the safari back under way.

It took half an hour for the crowd of men and animals to open out into a long line, like a gigantic serpent, which then slowly made its way westward.

What a site that column was! At its head, Burton and Trounce rode along on mules, the explorer noting everything in his journal, assessing the geography and geology as Palmerston had ordered, while the Scotland Yard man scanned the route before them with the field glasses. A few yards to the left, Honesty drove the harvestman, while behind, Isabella Mayson and Sister Raghavendra, with dainty parasols held over their heads, rode their mounts sidesaddle. Swinburne, in his stretcher, was carried by four of the Wasawahili, and behind him, the rest of the porters and pack mules followed, all heavily laden. Most of the men carried a single load balanced on their shoulder or head, while others shared heavier baggage tied to a pole and carried palanquin fashion. Each man also bore his private belongings upon his back—an earthen cooking pot, a water gourd, a sleeping mat, a three-legged stool, and other necessities.

The Wasawahili wore little, just rough cloth wound about their loins, and, when the rains came or the sun had set, a goatskin slung over their backs. Some had a strip of zebra's mane bound around their head; others preferred a stiffened oxtail, which rose above their forehead like a unicorn's horn; while many decorated their craniums with bunches of ostrich, crane, and jay feathers. Bulky ivory bracelets and bangles of brass and copper encircled their arms and ankles, and there were beads and circlets around their necks. At least half of them had small bells strapped just below their knees, and the incessant tinkling blended with the heavier clang of the bells attached to the mules' collars. This, along with ceaseless chanting and singing and hooting and shouting and squabbling and drumming, made the procession a very noisy affair, though not unpleasantly so.

At the rear of the long line, Krishnamurthy and Spencer rode their mules and kept their eyes peeled for deserters, but it was Saíd bin Sálim and his eight Askari bully boys who were, by far, the most industrious members of the party. With illimitable energy, they ranged up and down the column, keeping it under tight control and driving the men on with loud shouts of, "Hopa! Hopa! Go on! Go on!"

The expedition soon came upon one of Africa's many challenges: a forest, thick and dark and crawling with biting ants. They struggled through it, with low branches snagging at the loads the porters carried on their heads. Honesty had great difficulty in forcing the harvester through the unruly foliage.

They eventually broke free and descended a long gentle slope into a ragged and marshy valley. Here, the mules sank up to their knees and blundered and complained and had to be driven on by the energetic application of a *bakur*—the African cat-o'-nine-tails. After a long delay, with the fiery sun beating down on them, they reached firmer ground and struggled up through thick, luxuriant grass to higher terrain. From here, they could see the village of Mkwaju. Once again, the prospect of a gigantic spider approaching sent the villagers racing away.

"This is an advantage I hadn't anticipated," Burton told William Trounce. "They're too scared of the harvestman to hold us up with demands for *hongo*. Damnation! If only we had all our vehicles! Without the crabs to clear a route through the jungles, we'll soon reach a point where the harvester will be stymied and we'll be forced to abandon it."

Mkwaju was little more than a few hovels and a palaver house, but it was significant in that it was the last village under the jurisdiction of Bagamoyo. The expedition was now entering the Uzamaro district.

The sun was at its zenith, and the soporific heat drained the energy out of all of them, but they were determined to reach Nzasa before resting, so they plodded on, glassy-eyed, the sweat dripping off them.

The loss of the harvestman came much sooner than Burton expected. Less than two hours after he'd expressed his concern to Trounce, they encountered a thick band of jungle too dense to chop a wide enough path through and too high for the vehicle to pick its way across. Honesty ran the spider along the edge of the barrier for a mile southward, then back and for a mile to the north. He returned and shouted down from the cabin: "Stretches as far as the eye can see. No way through. Shall I go farther?"

"No," Burton called back. "It wouldn't do to get separated. I don't want to lose you! We'll have to leave it. We knew it was going to happen at some point. I suppose this is it. And at least the porters will be able to dump the coal supply."

Honesty turned off the machine's engine and climbed down a leg. "Should destroy it," he said. "Prussians might follow. Don't want them to have it."

Burton considered a moment then nodded. "You're right."

While the safari began to machete its way through the dense undergrowth, the king's agent and the detective tied a rope around the upper part of one of the harvestman's legs and used it to pull the vehicle over onto its side. Honesty drew his Adams police-issue revolver and emptied its chamber into the machine's water tank. They picked up rocks and used them to batter one of the spider's leg joints until it broke.

"That'll do," Burton said. "Let's press on to Nzasa. The sooner we get there, the better. We're all tired and hungry!"

The band of jungle sloped down to a narrow river. Mosquitoes swarmed over the water and crocodiles basked on its banks. The crossing was difficult, perilous, and uncomfortable, and by the time the expedition emerged from the tangle of vegetation on the other side, everyone was covered with mud, scratches, leeches, insect bites, and stings.

They moved out onto cultivated land and trudged past scattered abodes concealed by high grass and clumps of trees.

They were seeing kraals now—large round huts or long sheds built from sticks woven through with grass. Around these, in a wide circle, thorny barriers had been erected. Constructed by slaver caravans, their presence indicated that the inhabitants of this region were hostile and didn't welcome strangers at their villages.

The trail broadened and the going became easier. They slogged up a hill then descended into the valley of the Kinganí River—called *Wady el Maut* and *Dar el Jua*, the Valley of Death and Home of Hunger—which they followed until they spotted Nzasa, which Burton knew was one of the rare friendly settlements in the area.

He and Saíd rode ahead. They were met by three *p'hazi*, or headmen, each with a patterned cotton sheet wrapped around his loins and slung over his shoulder, each sheltering under an opened umbrella. The Africans announced themselves as Kizaya, Kuffakwema, and Kombe la Simba. The latter, in the Kiswahili language, greeted the two visitors with the words: "I am old and my beard is grey, yet never in all the days I have lived have I beheld a catastrophe like this—the *muzungo mbáyá* once again in the land of my people!"

Muzungo mbáyá translated as "the wicked white man."

"I understand thy dismay," Burton responded. "Thou remembers me not then, O Kombe?

The ancient chief frowned and asked, "I am known to thee?" He squinted at Burton, then his eyebrows shot up and he exclaimed: "Surely thou art not the *Murungwana Sana?*"

Burton bowed his head and murmured, "I am pleased that thou recollects me as such," for the words meant "real free man" and were the equivalent of being called a "gentleman."

Kombe suddenly gave a broad smile, his jet-black face folding into a thousand wrinkles, his mouth displaying teeth that had been filed to points. "Ah!" he cried. "Ah! Ah! Ah! I see all! Thou art hunting the *shetani?*"

"The devil?"

"Aye! The *muzungo mbáyá* of the long soft beard and gun that never ceases!"

"Thou art speaking of my former companion, John Speke? Thou hast seen him of late?"

"No, but a man from the village of Ngome, which is far north of here, came to us this many—" he extended the word to indicate the time that had passed: *maaaannny*, "—days ago and told of a bad man with bad men who came to his village intent on bad things. They were led by the *muzungo mbáyá*, and when he was described to me, I remembered the one thou callest Speke, though now they say his head is half of metal."

Burton said, "So his expedition is taking the northern trail eastward?"

"Aye, and killing and stealing as he goes. Dost thou mean to do the same?"

"Absolutely not! My people seek only to rest for a single night, and for this we shall pay with copper wire and cotton cloth and glass beads."

"And tobacco?"

"And tobacco."

"And drink that burns the throat in a pleasurable manner?"

"And drink that burns the throat in a pleasurable manner."

"I must consult with my brothers."

The three *p'hazi* stepped away and conversed out of Burton's earshot.

Saíd gave a snort of contempt and said, in a low voice, "They will come back and demand much *hongo* to allow us passage through their territory."

"Of course," Burton answered. "What else do they have to bargain with?"

Sure enough, Kombe returned with what amounted to an extravagant shopping list. Burton and Saíd, both experienced in such matters, bartered until an agreement was reached. The village would receive around two-thirds of the specie demanded—which, in fact, was a much better deal than the elders had expected.

Kombe, well satisfied, allowed the expedition to set up camp beside

Nzasa and announced that a feast would be held to honour the arrival of the *Murungwana Sana*.

Their first full day of African travel had exhausted them all. Isabella Mayson said to Burton, "I'm confused, Sir Richard. My body tells me we've travelled many miles, but my head says we've hardly progressed at all."

"Such is the nature of our task," he replied. "This was a good day. On a bad, a single step must be counted an achievement."

As the afternoon wore into evening, the tents were put up, the animals corralled, and the supplies secured.

The rains came.

There were no warning droplets or preliminary showers. One minute the sky was clear, the next it was a dark purple, then the *Msika* fell, a sheet of unbroken water. It hit the tents like an avalanche, and Burton, Saíd, Trounce, Honesty, Krishnamurthy, Spencer, Sister Raghavendra, and Miss Mayson— who'd all gathered in the biggest of the Rowties—had to raise their voices, first against the sound of the deluge pummelling the canvas, then against the cacophonous thunder, which grumbled without a pause.

"Excuse my language, ladies," Trounce shouted, "but bloody hell!"

"Can the tent stand it?" asked Krishnamurthy. "I think the ocean is being emptied on top of us!"

Honesty pulled the entrance flap aside and peered out. "Can't see a thing!" he called. "Solid water."

"There'll be two hours of this," Burton announced, "so if Sadhvi and Isabella don't mind, I propose a brandy and a smoke."

"I don't mind at all," Isabella said.

"Nor I," added Sadhvi. "In fact, I'll take a tipple myself."

A reedy sigh of frustration came from within Herbert Spencer's many robes and scarves.

Pox, perched as usual on the clockwork philosopher's head, gave a loud musical whistle, then squawked, "Flubberty jibbets!"

"Hurrah!" Krishnamurthy cheered. "That's a new one!"

"The nonsensical insults are definitely the most entertaining," Isabella agreed.

"By Jove!" Trounce blurted. "That reminds me. I say, Richard, those horrible plant things we saw at Mzizima—"

"What about them?" Burton asked.

"I was wondering, what with Eugenicist creations, such as Pox, here—"

"Pig-snuggler!" Pox sang.

"—always displaying a disadvantage in proportion to whatever talent the scientists have bred into them—"

"Yes?"

"Well, what might be the drawback to those vegetable vehicles, do you think?"

"That's a good question, William, and one I can't answer!"

Burton served brandies to them all, including the women, and the men lit their various cigars and pipes, with many a nervous glance at the tent roof, which was billowing violently under the onslaught of rain.

Sister Raghavendra distributed small vials of a clear liquid that she insisted they all add to their drinks. "It's a special recipe we use in the Sisterhood of Noble Benevolence to deal with fevers," she said. "Don't worry, it's quite tasteless."

"What's in it?" Honesty asked.

"A mix of quinine and various herbs," she answered. "It won't make you immune, but it will, at least, make the attacks shorter and less damaging."

The tent flap suddenly flew open and a drenched imp hopped in.

"Bounders!" it shrieked. "Cads! Fiends! Traitorous hounds! Taking a drink without me! Without *me*! Aaaiiii!"

The thing bounded to the table and, with wildly rolling eyes, snatched up the brandy bottle and took an extravagant swig from it. Banging the bottle back down, it wiped its mouth on its sleeve, uttered a satisfied sigh, belched, then keeled over like a toppled tree and landed flat on its back.

"Great heavens! Is that Algernon?" Herbert Spencer tooted.

Sister Raghavendra bent beside the sodden and bedraggled figure and put a hand to its forehead. "It is," she said. "And despite that display, he doesn't appear to be feverish at all."

Burton stepped over, lifted his assistant up, and carried him to a cot at the side of the tent. "Algy tends to operate, as a matter of course, at a level that most people would consider feverish," he said. "I think, on this occasion, he has simply overestimated his own strength."

"Indeed so," the nurse agreed. "Any man would require a week to recover from blood loss like Algernon experienced."

"In which case, Algy will probably need just a couple more days, for he is most certainly not *any* man!"

They dried their friend as best they could, made him comfortable, and let him sleep.

The rain eventually stopped as quickly as it had started, and the silence of another African night settled over them. They sat quietly, comfortable in each others' company, too exhausted for conversation.

A hyena cackled in the distance.

A shout came from the village.

One drumbeat sounded.

Then another.

All of a sudden, a deep, loud, rhythmic pulsation filled the air as many drums were pounded. A boy's voice hailed them from outside. Burton stepped out of the tent and a child, about ten years old, grinned up at him.

"O *Murungwana Sana*," he said, "the fire is lit and the meat is cooking and the women are restless and want to dance. The men desire news of the far off lands of the *Muzungu*—the white man. Wouldst thou attend us?"

Burton gave a bow. "We shall come with thee now."

So it was that the expedition's first day ended with a feast and a party, attended by all but the philosopher Herbert Spencer and the poet Algernon Swinburne.

In the tent, the brass man placed a stool beside the cot, sat on it, and leaned forward, bracing himself with his staff. Deep in the shadow of his *keffiyeh*, his metal face seemed to gaze unwaveringly at Burton's assistant.

And Swinburne dreamt of war.

CHAPTER 7

BATTLE AT DUT'HUMI

"To plunder, to slaughter, to steal, these things they misname
empire; and where they make a wilderness, they call it peace."
—TACITUS

Warm rain hammered against Burton's tin helmet and poured from its
brim down the back of his greatcoat. An explosion momentarily
deafened him, knocked him to his hands and knees, and showered him with
clods of mud and lumps of bloody flesh. The black water at the bottom of the
flooded trench immediately sucked at his limbs, as if the earth were greedy
for yet another corpse. A head floated to the surface. Half of its face was
missing. He recoiled in shock, splashing back to his feet, and ducked as
another pea burst just yards away. Men and women shrieked in agony, cried
out for their mothers, spat the same profanity over and over and over.

A seed thudded into a soldier's face. Blood sprayed. His helmet went
spinning. He slumped as if his bones had suddenly vanished, and slid into
the mire.

Burton stumbled on, sloshing forward, peering at the troops who were
lining the right side of the trench and firing their rifles over its lip. He eventually saw the man he was searching for—a big Askari with a patch covering
his right eye. He climbed up beside him and shouted into his ear: "Are you
Private Usaama?"

"What?"

"I'm looking for Private Usaama. I was told he knows Wells."

"I'm him. What wells?"

"Herbert Wells. The correspondent. I think he's with your company."

The man's answer was lost as a squadron of hornets swept overhead,
flying low, buzzing furiously, their oval bodies painted with the Union Jack,
their guns crackling.

"What did you say?" Burton hollered.

"I said if he hasn't bought it he'll be in the forward listening post. Keep on down the trench until you come to an opening on your right. It's there."

They both ducked as seeds howled past them and embedded themselves in the opposite wall of the trench. Rain-loosened dirt collapsed inward.

Burton jumped back down into the water and moved along, picking his way past the dead and the mutilated, whispering a Sufi meditation to keep himself sane.

A female Askari, who was propped against a pile of saturated sandbags, grabbed at his sleeve and said in a pleading tone: "I've lost my boot. I've lost my boot. I've lost my boot."

He looked down and saw that the woman's left leg was a ragged mess beneath the knee. The foot was missing.

"I've lost my boot. I've lost my boot."

He nodded helplessly and yanked his arm from her grasp.

Another explosion. More terrible screams.

The passage to the listening post, seen dimly through the downpour, was now just a few steps away. He waded toward it, the smell of cordite and rotting flesh and overflowing latrines thick in his nostrils.

Sirens wailed through the staccato gunfire and thumping detonations: "Ulla! Ulla! Ulla!"

He entered the narrow passage and pushed through the water to its end, which widened into a small square pit. Its sides were shored up with wood, its upper edges protected by sandbags. To his right, a mechanical contrivance rested on a table beneath a canvas hood. Nearby, a corpse lay half-submerged, its eyes gazing sightlessly at the sky. Straight ahead, a short and plump man was standing on a box and peering northward through a periscope. He had a bugle slung over his shoulder and his tin helmet was badly dented on one side.

"Bertie?"

The man turned. The left side of his face was badly disfigured by a burn scar. He was unshaven and smeared with dirt.

"Lieutenant Wells, if you don't mind," he shouted. "Who the devil are you?"

"It's me. Burton."

Wells squinted through the rain, then gave a sudden whoop of joy and jumped from the box. He splashed over to Burton and gripped him by the hand.

"It's true! It's true!" he yelled, his voice pitched even higher than usual. "By gum, Burton, it's been two years! I thought I'd imagined you! But look at you! Alive! In the flesh! The chronic argonaut himself!" Wells suddenly stepped back. "What happened to you? You look like a skeleton!"

"War has been happening to me, Bertie, and to you too, I see."

They both jerked down as something whistled overhead and exploded in the trenches behind them.

"This is the ugliest it's ever been," Wells shouted. "It's attrition warfare now. The Hun has abandoned all strategy but that of battering us into oblivion. Grab a periscope and join me. Ha! Just like when we first met! What happened to you after the Battle of the Bees?"

"The what?"

"Tanga, man!"

Burton took one of the viewing devices from the table and climbed onto the box beside Wells.

"I fell in with a group of guerrilla fighters. We spent eighteen months or so raiding Hun outposts around Kilimanjaro before I suffered a fever and severe leg ulcerations that had me laid up in a field hospital for seven weeks. While I was there, the guerrillas were killed by A-Spores. During my final week in the hospital, I heard from—" They both crouched as three explosions tore up the battlefield nearby. "—From another patient that you were heading to Dut'humi, for the attack on the Tanganyika Railway, so I hooked up with a company that was heading this way."

"I can't tell you how good it is to see you again!" Wells exclaimed. "By heaven, Richard, your inexplicable presence is the one spark of magic in this endlessly turgid conflict! Is your memory restored? Do you know why you're here?"

Burton peered through the periscope. He saw coils of barbed wire forming a barrier across the landscape ahead. Beyond it there were German trenches, and behind them, the terrain rose to a ridge, thick with green trees. The Tanganyika railway line, he'd learned, was on the other side of that low range.

"I remember a few more things—mainly that there's something I have to do. The trouble is, I don't know what!"

From over to their left, a machine gun started to chatter. Four more explosions sounded in quick succession and lumps of mud rained down on them. Someone screeched, coughed, and died.

"Forgive the mundanity," Wells said, "but I don't suppose you've got biscuits or anything? I haven't eaten since yesterday!"

"Nothing," Burton replied. "Bertie, the forest—"

"What? Speak up!"

"The trees on the ridge. There's something wrong with them."

"I've noticed. A verdant forest—and one that wasn't there two days ago!"

"What? You mean the trees grew to maturity in just forty-eight hours?"

"They did. Eugenicist mischief, obviously."

"They aren't even native to Africa. *Acer pseudoplatanus*. The sycamore maple. It's a European species."

"For a man whose memory is shot through you know far too much Latin. Down!"

They ducked and hugged the dirt wall as a pea thumped into the mud nearby and detonated.

Wells said something. Burton shook his head. He couldn't hear. His ears had filled with jangling bells. The war correspondent leaned closer and shouted: "The Hun have recently solved the problem with growing yellow pea artillery. The shrapnel from these projectiles is poisonous. If you're hit, pull the fragments out of your wound as fast as you can."

An enormously long, thin leg swung over the listening post as a harvestman stepped across it. Burton looked up at the underside of its small oval-shaped body and saw a trumpet-mouthed weapon swivelling back and forth. He straightened, wiped the rain from his eyes, and lifted the scope. A long line of the mechanised spiders was crossing the forward trenches and approaching the barbed-wire barrier. There were at least twenty vehicles. Their weapons began to blast out long jets of flame.

All of a sudden the downpour stopped, and in the absence of its pounding susurration, the loud clatter of the vehicles' steam engines and the roar of their flamethrowers sounded oddly isolated.

A strong warm breeze gusted across the battlefield.

Burton was shaken by a sense of uneasiness.

Wells obviously felt it too. "Now what?" he muttered.

A shell, fired from the German trenches, hit one of the harvestmen. "Ulla!" it screamed, and collapsed to the ground. Its driver spilled from the saddle, started to run, and was shredded by gunfire.

"Something's happening up on the ridge," Wells said.

Burton turned his attention back to the distant forest. He frowned and muttered, "Is there something wrong with my sense of perspective?"

"No," Wells answered. "Those trees are gigantic."

They were also thrashing about in the strengthening wind.

"This doesn't feel at all natural," Burton said.

"You're right. I think the Hun weathermen are at work. We'd better stand ready to report to HQ."

"HQ? Are you Army now, Bertie?"

"Aren't you? You're in uniform."

"My other clothes rotted off my back—"

Another pea burst nearby. A lump of it clanged off Burton's helmet.

"—and I was given these at the field hospital. No one has officially drummed me into service. I think they just assume I'm a soldier."

"Such is our state of disorganisation," Wells responded. "The fact is,

Richard, everyone is a soldier now. That's how desperate things have become. There's no such thing as a British civilian in the entire world. And right now, I'm assigning you as my Number Two. The previous, Private Michaels—" Wells gestured toward the half-submerged corpse Burton had barely registered earlier, "—poked his head over the sandbags, the silly sod, and got hit by a sniper. Be sure you don't do the same. Get over to the wireless."

Burton glanced back at the apparatus on the table. "Wireless? I—er—I don't know how to use it."

"Two years here and you still can't operate a bloody radio?"

"I've been—"

He was interrupted by whistles sounding all along the frontline trench.

"This is it!" Wells exclaimed. "The lads are going over!"

To the left and right of the listening post, Askari soldiers—with some white faces standing out among them—clambered from the waterlogged trenches and began to move across the narrow strip of no-man's-land in the wake of the advancing harvestmen. They were crouching low and holding bayoneted rifles. Seeds from the opposing trenches sizzled through the air. Men's heads were jerked backward; their limbs were torn away; their stomachs and chests were rent open; they went down, and when they went down, others, moving up from behind, replaced them. Peas arced out of the sky and slapped into the mud among them. They exploded, ripping men apart and sending the pieces flying into the air. Still the British troops pressed on.

"Bismillah!" Burton whispered as the carnage raged around him.

"Look!" Wells yelled. He pointed up at the ridge. "What the hell is that?"

Burton adjusted his viewer and observed through its lens a thick green mass boiling up from the trees. Borne on the wind, it came rolling down the slope and passed high above the German trenches. As it approached, he saw that it was comprised of spinning sycamore seeds, and when one of them hit the leg of a harvestman, he realised they were of an enormous size—at least twelve feet across. The seed didn't merely hit the spider's leg, either—its wings sliced right through it; they were as solid and sharp as scimitars. He watched horrified as thousands upon thousands of the whirling seeds impacted against the lofty battle machines, shearing through the long thin legs, chopping into the oval bodies, decapitating the drivers. As the harvestmen buckled under the onslaught, the seeds spun on toward the advancing troops.

"Take cover!" Wells bellowed.

Burton and the war correspondent dropped to their knees in filthy water and hugged the base of the observation pit's forward wall. Eight sycamore seeds whisked through the air above them and thudded into the back of the excavation. A ninth sliced Private Michaels' corpse clean in half. A green cloud hurtled overhead and mowed into the frontline trenches.

Its shadow passed. The wind stopped. Burton looked up at the sky. The rainclouds were now ragged tatters, fast disappearing, and the blistering sun shone between them down onto a scene of such slaughter that, when Burton stood, climbed back onto the box, and looked through his periscope, he thought he might lose his mind with the horror of what he saw. He squeezed his eyes shut. Ghastly moans and whimpers and shrieks of agony filled his ears. He clapped his palms over them. The stench of fresh blood invaded his nostrils.

He collapsed backward and fell full length into the trench water. It closed over him and he wanted to stay there, but hands clutched at his clothing and hauled him out.

"Run!" Wells cried out, his voice pitched even higher than usual. "The Germans are coming!"

Burton staggered to his feet. His soaked trousers clung to his legs; filthy liquid streamed from his jacket and shirt.

"Move! Move!" Wells shouted. He grabbed Burton and pushed him toward the connecting passage. As they splashed through it, the little war correspondent lifted his bugle to his lips and sounded the retreat. With the urgent trumpeting in his ears, Burton blundered along and passed into the forward trench. It looked as if hell itself had bubbled up out of the mud. The sycamore seeds were everywhere, their blades embedded in sandbags, in the earth, and in soldiers. The troops had been diced like meat on a butcher's slab; body parts were floating in rivers of blood; and in the midst of the carnage, limbless men and women lay twitching helplessly, their dying eyes wide with terror and shock.

As Burton and Wells raced from the foremost trench and made their way through the connecting ditches toward the rear, the smaller man blew the retreat with frantic desperation, while the taller, whenever he spotted a soldier still capable of moving, gathered wits enough to shout: "Withdraw! Withdraw!"

Eventually they came to the final trench, clambered out of it, their uniforms red with other men's gore, and began to run.

Burton glanced to either side and saw a straggling line of fleeing soldiers—so few!—then looked back and gasped: "What are they?"

Wells said something but it was lost as a barrage of explosive peas came whistling down, punched into the ground just behind them, and sent up huge spouts of mud.

The world slowed down, became utterly silent, and revolved majestically around Burton. The sky passed underneath. Men performed loose-limbed pirouettes through it. Some of the loose limbs weren't attached to the men.

I have to be somewhere.

The ground swung upward to meet him.

Time resumed.

The earth smacked into his face.

He coughed, groaned, spat soil from his mouth, and lifted himself onto all fours.

Wells was spreadeagled nearby.

Burton crawled over to him. His friend was alive and conscious and his mouth was moving but there was no sound. There was no sound anywhere.

Wells pointed at the trenches.

Looking back, Burton saw the *Schutztruppen* approaching. One of the Germans was very near. He was dressed in a slate-grey uniform and his helmet was spiked at its crown. He held in his hands, like a rifle, a long seedpod with a vicious thorn dripping venom at its end.

The *Schutztruppen* weren't human.

Burton pushed himself backward through the mud, kicking his feet, trying to get away. He couldn't take his eyes off the approaching soldier. Though a man in shape, the German's head was deformed—his jaws were pushed forward into a snout, and his slavering mouth was filled with long canines. He was a tawny-yellow colour, and black-spotted, and his golden eyes had vertical irises.

The name Laurence Oliphant jumped into Burton's mind, and in a flash he recalled a duel, a clashing of swords, with a man half human and half white panther. The memory was hallucinogenic in its power. He reached for his sword, looked into the thing's feline eyes, and whispered: "Good lord! What have you done to yourself?"

When his hand came whipping up there was not a sword in it, but a pistol, and without even thinking, he pumped four bullets into the German.

He watched as the trooper staggered, dropped the seedpod, and teetered to one side. The creature—a leopard given human shape—flopped to the ground. There were more approaching. Some of them were similarly formed from lithe jungle cats; others were bulky rhinoceros men, or vicious hyena things. Hardly any were fully human.

Fingers closed over Burton's arm. He jerked free of them and scrabbled away before realising they belonged to Bertie Wells. The war correspondent was on his feet. His mouth was working, and faintly, as if from a long way off, Burton heard: "Come on, man! We have to get out of here!"

A chunk of dirt was thrown up near his head. Something tugged violently at his wet sleeve and scored the skin beneath. It finally registered that he was being shot at.

He pushed himself to his feet and, with Wells, started to run as hard as he could.

They passed between two Scorpion Tanks whose tail cannon were spewing fire at the oncoming enemy troops. A pea smashed square into one and the war machine flew apart, sending shards of splintered carapace skittering past the two men.

Burton's hearing returned with a clap, and the dissonances of battle assaulted his already overwhelmed senses.

He and Wells veered to the right, ducked behind the swollen carcass of a long-dead mega-dray horse, and bolted through a field of broken wagons and wrecked wooden shacks.

They ran and ran and eventually reached the base of the Dut'humi Hills.

Seven British hornets, flying extremely low, came buzzing from behind the higher ground. They swept down, passed over the two men, and raked the battlefield with bullets. One of the giant insects was struck mid-thorax by an enemy cannon. It hit the earth and tumbled, enveloped in flames.

At the edge of the undergrowth, Burton noticed a bright poppy—a red beacon amid the foliage.

"This way!" he shouted, and pulled Wells toward it. They threw themselves past the little flower and into thick purplish vegetation. Careless of thorns, they heaved themselves through bushes, climbed over twisted roots, ducked under looped lianas, and forced their way uphill until the frightful noise of conflict began to fade behind them.

Vegetation snagged at and tore their uniforms. Wet leaves dripped on them, though they were already soaked to the skin. Still they kept going, passing over the brow of a jungly hill and down into a stinking swamp. They waded through it, thigh-deep, careless of crocodiles, and emerged onto firmer land where the terrain once again sloped upward. The vegetation was slightly less dense here, and they slowed to walking pace as they passed between tree boles, with a tightly packed canopy overhead.

Burton noticed another poppy off to his left. He steered his companion in that direction.

"There's a place I must go, Bertie."

"Where?"

"I wish I knew."

A prickly and malformed plant to Wells's right twitched spasmodically. Milky liquid spurted from it and hit the sleeve of the war correspondent's greatcoat. The material immediately started to smoulder.

Wells swore, ripped the garment open, and pulled it off, throwing it to the ground. He pushed Burton onward, leaving the plant and the coat behind.

"Bloody Eugenicist creations are starting to sprout up all over the place," he growled. "And they're all acid-spitting, bloodsucking, needle-shooting, poison-scent-emitting atrocities! Look at those, for instance—" He nodded toward the base of a nearby tree. Burton looked and saw a clump of bulbous white fungi.

"Those are Destroying Angel mushrooms—the species they get the A-Spores from. Not native to Africa until the Eugenicists meddled with them. Now they're everywhere!"

They steered carefully past a nest of pismire ants. They were natural, but nevertheless dangerous. Burton knew from painful experience that their bite was like the jab of a red-hot needle.

For the next hour, the two men forced their way onward. Twice more, Burton saw poppies and altered his direction in order to pass by them. He did not mention this to Wells.

Finally, with gasps of relief, they emerged into a small glade. It was carpeted with the bright-red blossoms, and in its very centre, upon a mound, a profusion of multicoloured flowers were thriving. A single beam of sunlight angled through tree branches and brightly illuminated the vivid reds, yellows, blues, and purples. The air was filled with pollen, which shone like gold dust in the shaft of light. Butterflies danced over the flowers. Everything was glowing with an almost supernatural radiance.

"A patch of beauty, at last!" Wells cried. "My eyes can hardly bear it! And look—your favourite poppy is everywhere!"

The two men threw themselves down beside the mound. For thirty minutes or so, they sat in silence, each dealing in his own way with the atrocities they'd witnessed.

Eventually, Burton spoke: "What is it about you, Bertie, that attracts death from the sky? When I first met you it was the spores. Then it was bees. This time, sycamore seeds. What next? Boulder-sized hailstones? Acidic rain? Explosive bloody bird shit?"

"Whatever else I might have to say about them," Wells responded, "I can't deny that the Germans are damned creative."

"Unquestionably. What the hell were those *Schutztruppen?*"

"The Eugenicists are turning animals into soldiers," Wells replied. "Because they're running out of Africans."

Burton groaned. "So the loathsome treatment of this continent now extends even to its flora and fauna? I swear to you, I wish a plague would wipe mankind from the face of this world! How despicable we are!"

The smaller man shrugged. "I don't think a plague is required—we're doing a pretty good job of it ourselves. You know, there was a time in my life when I fancied that we could all work together as equals for the good of the species, when I thought that our true nationality was *Mankind*. Now I recognise that I vastly overestimated the human race. We disguise imperialism as the spread of higher civilisation, but it's blatantly animalistic in its nature. We are no better than carnivores or carrion eaters. Having beast-men fighting this dreadful war is wholly appropriate."

He took a canteen from his belt and drank from it.

Burton said, "I remember you saying that Palmerston was responsible."

"Yes."

"And now you say the imperialistic drive is an animal impulse. Yet I can think of no one more divorced from nature than Palmerston!"

"Pah!" Wells snorted. He handed the canteen to Burton. "Did it never strike you that in his efforts to conquer the natural in himself, he was merely signposting the trait of his that he felt most vulnerable to? All those Eugenics treatments he paid for, Richard—they were the mark of the Beast!"

"Humph! I suppose."

"And where was nature better symbolised in your age than in Africa? No wonder this continent fell victim to his paranoia!"

Burton shook his head despairingly. "I don't know how you can endure it."

"Somehow, I still have hope," Wells answered, "or I could not live."

Burton took a gulp from the canteen. He coughed and spluttered as brandy burned its way down his throat.

"I was expecting water!" he croaked.

Wells watched two dragonflies flitting back and forth over the flowers. "It's ironic," he said softly.

"What is?"

"That I'm fighting the Germans."

"Really?"

"Yes, for in some respects, since he seized power, Nietzsche has expanded upon the beliefs I held as a younger man, and I feel strongly drawn to his philosophy." Wells looked at Burton. "You were right, by the way: Nietzsche did seize power in 1914 and Rasputin did die. According to our Intelligence agents, he suffered a brain haemorrhage. It happened in St. Petersburg, so your claim that you were responsible doesn't hold up—unless, that is, you possess extraordinary mediumistic powers, in which case I should deliver you to Colonel Crowley at the soonest possible moment."

Burton shook his head. "I have no such abilities, Bertie. So what is Nietzsche's philosophy?"

Wells sighed and was silent for a moment. Then he said: "He proposes an entirely new strain of human being. One that transcends the bestial urges."

A memory squirmed uncomfortably at the back of Burton's mind. He reached out, picked a flower from the mound, and held it in front of his face, examining its petals. They did nothing to aid his powers of recollection.

"The Greek *Hyperanthropos?*" he asked.

"Similar. The term he uses is *Übermensch*. A man free from the artificial limitations of moral codes." Wells snorted contemptuously. "Moral codes! Ha! As much as we invoke God with our exclamations and curses, we all know that he's dead. Your Darwin killed him outright, and the concept of supernaturally defined morals should have died with the deity!"

Burton held up an objecting hand and blew out a breath. "Please!" he exclaimed. "He was never my Darwin!"

"He was a man of your time. Anyway, without a God to impose ideas of right and wrong, mankind is left with a moral vacuum to fill. Nietzsche's *Übermensch* populates it according to an inner inclination that is entirely divorced from social, cultural, or religious influences. What blossoms within him is therefore utterly authentic. Such an individual will, according to Nietzsche, transcend his animal instincts. Furthermore, from amid all these singular standards of behaviour, certain common values will emerge, and they will be so completely in tune with the zeitgeist that human evolution will accelerate. God left a vacancy. We shall fill it."

Burton considered this for a moment, then said, "If I understand you correctly, the implication is that the zeitgeist, time itself, has some sort of beneficial purpose."

"Yes. Nietzsche posits that, through living as we do, we have impeded our proper relationship with time. We misunderstand it. We see only one aspect of it and we allow that to dominate us. It keeps us bound to the natural world. Only by becoming an *Übermensch* can an individual grow beyond it."

The sky suddenly grew darker. The sun was beginning to set.

Wells said, "You don't happen to be an *Übermensch*, I suppose? You have, after all, somehow managed to defy the normal limitations of time."

Burton gave a wry smile. "I very much doubt that I'm anything Nietzsche might aspire to."

He reached among the flowers and brushed idly at a flat moss-covered stone. "Beresford. That's who I've been trying to remember. Henry—um—Henry de La Poer Beresford. Yes! The Mad Marquess! Bismillah! Bertie! This *Übermensch* business is remarkably similar to something the creator of the Libertine and Rake movements came up with. He was obsessed with the idea of what he termed the *trans-natural man*, and he was inspired in that by—by—bloody hell!"

"What is it?" Wells asked, puzzled.

"By Spring Heeled Jack!"

"By folklore?"

"By Edward Oxford!"

"Are you referring to the man who assassinated Queen Victoria?"

"Yes—and no."

"You're not making any sense, Richard!"

"I'm—I'm trying to remember!"

Burton scrubbed furiously at the stone, as if cleaning it of moss might also clear his foggy memory.

"The Libertines," Wells said. "I believe they opposed the Technologists for a period but pretty much died out during the 1870s or 80s."

Burton didn't answer. He was leaning forward and frowning. Wells looked at him curiously then moved to his side. He reached out, pushed flowers out of the way, and, in the dwindling light, peered at the flat stone.

"Are those letters on it?" he asked.

"Yes," Burton murmured. "There's some sort of inscription."

Wells reached into his pocket and pulled out a dagger. "Here, use this."

Burton took it and used the blade to scrape the moss away. Words were revealed. They read:

Thomas Manfred Honesty
1816-1863
Lost His Life While
Liberating the Enslaved.
R.I.P.

On the morning the expedition departed Nzasa, having stayed there for a single night, Sir Richard Francis Burton sent Pox to Isabel to report his position. When the parakeet returned, it squawked: "Message from Isabel Arundell. We are still harassing the stinky-mouthed enemy. I have so far lost eighteen of my women to them. They are preparing a moronic party to follow you. We will try to hold them back. Grubby pants. Message ends."

With the threat of pursuit, Burton tried to establish a greater sense of urgency among his porters, but already his safari was assailed by problems. Upon packing to leave the village, it was discovered that two boxes of equipment were missing and three of the Wasawahili had deserted; one of the mules appeared to be dying; and water had found its way into three sacks of flour, rendering them unusable.

The explorer, who from previous experience had resigned himself to such misfortunes, put a bullet through the mule's head, discarded the flour, redistributed the loads, and got his people moving.

The second day saw them trek from Nzasa to Tumba Ihere. The route led over gently undulating grasslands and through miry valleys, past a bone-strewn burial ground where witches and other practitioners of *ucháwi*—black magic—had been burned at the stake, and across a fast-flowing stream where they lost another mule after it slipped and broke a leg.

They rested for an hour.

Swinburne abandoned his stretcher.

"I'm fine and dandy! In the pink! Fit as a fiddle!" he announced. "How far to the next village?"

"At least four hours' march," Burton replied. "You can't possibly be in full bloom. You had half your blood sucked out a couple of days ago."

"Pah! I'm perfectly all right. Confound it! I was hoping the village would be closer."

"Why?"

"Because I want to try that *pombe* African beer you once told me about!"

They started moving again, crossing a plain that seethed with wildlife, and for half an hour, Swinburne, who was now riding a mule while holding an umbrella over his head, amused himself by shouting the names of every species he spotted: "Zebra! Koodoo! Giraffe! Guinea-fowl! Lion! Quail! Four-legged thingummy!"

He then fell off his mount, having fainted.

They put him back onto the stretcher.

After wrestling their way through a long stretch of sticky red soil and onto firmer, hilly ground, they were met by men from the village of Kiranga-Ranga. These Wazamaro warriors each bore three long puckered scars extending across both cheeks from their earlobes to the corners of their mouths. Their hair was plastered down with ochre-coloured mud and twisted into a double row of knobs that circled their heads. They wore loincloths of unbleached cotton and had strings of beads looped around their necks, which were also fitted with tightly beaded bands, known as *mgoweko* collars. A solid ring of brass circled their wrists. They carried muskets, spears, bows with poisoned arrows, and long knives.

They were not friendly.

Tribute was demanded, haggled over, and finally paid in the form of two *doti* of cloth and some much-prized *sami-sami* beads.

The safari continued, meandering past fertile fields of rice, maize, and manioc before coming up against a snarled and riotous jungle, which they were still hacking through when the rains started. They eventually stumbled out of it, soaked to the skin and covered with ticks, and found themselves amid fetid vegetation from which misshapen dwarf mango trees grew, and in this unlikely spot—Tumba Ihere—they were forced to establish their camp.

That evening, in the main Rowtie, Isabella Mayson announced that she was feeling out of sorts. By the morning she was trembling with ague and hallucinating that ravenous birds were trying to peck out her eyes. Swinburne gave up his stretcher for her.

"I have developed a horror of the horizontal!" he declared.

"Sit on your mule," Burton instructed, "and don't overexert yourself."

The explorer ordered the commencement of the next march.

"Kwecha! Kwecha!" Saíd bin Sálim and his Askaris yelled. "Pakia! Hopa! Hopa!" Collect! Pack! Set out! Safari! A journey! A journey today!

So began the third day of their hike.

Pox made the daily flight eastward and back again. The report was not good. A ship had delivered two thousand Prussian reinforcements to Mzizima. The Daughters of Al-Manat had divided into two groups of ninety women, one continuing to wage a guerrilla campaign against the burgeoning town, the other harassing a contingent of men that had set off in pursuit of Burton's expedition.

"We have to move faster," the king's agent told Saíd.

"I will do all I can, Mr. Burton," the *ras kafilah* promised in his habitually polite manner, "and the rest is as Allah wills it."

They tramped through alternating bands of richly cultivated land and matted flora, with Saíd's Askaris forcing the porters to a brisk pace wherever possible, until they eventually found themselves in a large forest of copal trees that oozed resin and filled the air with a cloying perfume. Horseflies attacked them. Thomas Honesty was stung below the left eye by a bee and the side of his face swelled up like a balloon. Trounce started to feel a stiffness in his limbs. For an hour a strange whistling noise assaulted their ears. They never discovered its source.

They kept going.

About noon, Burton—who'd succumbed to the turgid heat and was gazing uncomprehendingly at the back of his mule's head—was roused by Swinburne, who, in his piping voice, suddenly announced:

> "The dense hard passage is blind and stifled
> That crawls by a track none turn to climb
> To the strait waste place that the years have rifled
> Of all but the thorns that are touched not of time.

The thorns he spares when the rose is taken;
The rocks are left when he wastes the plain.
The wind that wanders, the weeds wind-shaken,
These remain."

"What?" Burton mumbled.

"Police pottery," Swinburne replied. "Do you remember Matthew Keller in Leeds? Feels like a long time ago, durn't it?"

"I'm losing track," Burton replied. "Since we left the *Orpheus*, I've been forgetting to record the date in my journal. I don't know why. It's out of character."

He squinted against the glaring light and for the first time realised that the forest had been left behind; they were now traversing broad grain fields. He recognised the place—he'd passed through it during his previous expedition.

"We're approaching the village of Muhogwe. Its people have a reputation for violence but last time I was here they settled for mockery."

William Trounce cleared his throat and said, "My apologies, Richard." He slipped to the ground.

It was another case of seasoning fever.

"We're succumbing considerably sooner than I expected," Burton said to Sister Raghavendra as they lowered the police detective onto a litter.

"Don't worry," she replied. "There's usually a fairly long incubation period with this sort of affliction but the medicine I've been feeding you negates it. The stuff brings on the fever more rapidly, makes it burn more fiercely, and it's all over and done with in a matter of hours instead of weeks."

Burton raised his eyebrows. "I should have liked that during my previous expedition!"

They came to Muhogwe. It was abandoned.

"Either the slavers have taken the entire population, or the entire population has upped and moved to avoid the slavers," Burton observed.

"The latter, I hope," Swinburne responded.

Beyond the village it was all jungle and forest again, then a quagmire where they had to fire their rifles into the air to scare away a herd of hippopotami.

A slope led up to a plateau, and here they found a *boma*—a fenced kraal—and decided to set up camp. No sooner had they erected the last tent than the clouds gathered and the rain fell.

They ate and rested, except for Burton who braved the downpour to take stock of the supplies. He found that two more porters had run away and three bundles of specie were missing.

Night came. They tried to settle but the air smelled of putrefying vegetation, the mosquitoes were remorseless, and they all felt, to one degree or another, ill and out of sorts.

Hyenas cackled, screamed, and whined from dusk until dawn.

And so it went. The days passed and the safari crept along, seemingly at a snail's pace, and wound its way over the malarious plain of the Kinganí River toward the low peaks of the Usagara Highlands. Each in turn, they came down with fever then made an astonishingly rapid recovery. Burton was in no doubt that Sister Raghavendra was a miracle worker, for there could be no greater contrast than that between his first Nile expedition, during which he and John Speke had been permanently stricken with an uncountable number of ailments, and this, his second, where illness was the exception rather than the rule.

Isabel's reports came every morning. A force of four hundred men was now following in the expedition's tracks. The Daughters of Al-Manat were making daily attacks against them but nine more of her followers had been killed and the distance was closing between the two groups.

"If we can just make it to Kazeh before they catch up," Burton told his friends. "The Arabians there are well disposed toward me—they will loan us men and weapons."

They trudged on.

Plains. Hills. Forests. Swamps. Jungle. The land challenged their every step.

Sagesera. Tunda. Dege la Mhora. Madege Madogo. Kidunda. Mgeta. The villages passed one after the other, each demanding *hongo*, each whittling away at their supplies.

Desertions. Theft. Accidents. Fatigue. The safari became ever more frayed and difficult to control.

One night, they heard distant gunshots.

They were camped at Kiruru, a small and semi-derelict village located deep in a plantation of holcus, whose tall, stiff canes almost completely hid the ragged beehive huts and slumping *bandani*.

Herbert Spencer, freshly wound up, had been explaining to them some of his *First Principles of Philosophy* when the crackle and pops of rifle fire echoed faintly through the air.

They looked at each other.

"How far away?" Thomas Honesty asked.

"Not far enough," Maneesh Krishnamurthy grunted.

"It's from somewhere ahead of us, not behind," Burton noted.

"Lardy flab!" Pox added.

"Sleep with your weapons beside you," the explorer ordered. "Herbert, I want you to patrol the camp tonight."

"Actually, Boss, I patrol the camp every blinkin' night," the philosopher answered.

"Well, with extra vigilance tonight, please, and I think Tom, William, Maneesh, Algy, and I will stand shifts with you."

Burton turned to Saíd. "Wilt thou see to it that we are packed and on the move well before sunrise?"

Saíd bowed an acknowledgement.

The night passed without incident but the march the following morning was one of the worst they'd so far experienced.

They found themselves fighting through thick razor-edged grass, which towered over their heads and dripped dew onto them. The black earth was greasy and slippery and interlaced with roots that caught at their feet. The mules brayed in distress, refused to be ridden, and had to be forced along with swipes of the *bakur*, not moving until the cat had raised welts on their hindquarters.

Pox, who'd been sent to Isabel earlier, returned and shrieked: "Message from Isabel Big Nose Arundell. We have reduced their cretinous number by a quarter but they are less than a day behind you. Move faster, Dick. Message bleeding well ends."

"We're moving as fast as we bleeding well can!" Burton grumbled.

The grass gave way to a multitude of distorted palms, then to a savannah which promised easier going but immediately disappointed by blocking their progress with a sequence of steep *nullahs*—watercourses whose near-vertical banks dropped into stinking morasses that sucked them in right up to their thighs.

"I suspect this plain is always water-laden," Burton panted, as he and Krishnamurthy tried to haul one of the mules through the mire. "The water runs down from Usagara and this area is like a basin—there's no way for it to quickly drain. Were we not in such a confounded hurry, I would have gone around it. The ridge to the north is the best route, but it would've taken too long to get there. Bismillah! I hope they don't catch us here. This is a bad place for armed conflict!"

Krishnamurthy pointed ahead, westward, at plum-coloured hills. "Higher ground there," he said. "Hopefully it'll be easier going. The height would give us an advantage, too."

Burton nodded an agreement and said, "Those are the hills of Dut'humi."

They finally reached the slopes.

Burton guided his expedition along a well-trodden path, up through thick vegetation, over a summit, and down the other side. They waded through a swamp that sent up noxious bubbles of hydrogen sulphide with their every step. The rotting carcass of a rhinoceros lay at the far edge of the morass, and beyond it a long, sparsely forested incline led them to an area of tightly packed foliage. Monkeys and parrots squabbled and hooted in the branches around them.

They forced their way along the overgrown trail until they suddenly came to a clearing, where seven elderly warriors stood, each holding a bow with a trembling arrow levelled at them. The old men were plainly terrified and tears were streaming down their cheeks. They were no threat and they knew it.

Saíd called for the porters to halt, then stepped forward to speak to the old men, but one suddenly let loose a cry of surprise, dropped his weapon, pushed the Arab aside, and ran over to Burton.

"*Wewe! Wewe!* Thou art *Murungwana Sana* of Many Tongues!" he cried. "Thou wert here long long days ago, and helped our people to fight the *p'hazi* whose name is Manda, who had plundered our village!"

"I remember thee, *Mwene Goha*," Burton said, giving the man his title. "Thy name is Máví ya Gnombe. Manda was of a neighbouring district, and we punished him right and good, did we not? Surely he has not been raiding thy village again?"

"No, not him! The slavers have come!" The man loosed a wail of despair. "They have taken all but the old!"

"When did this happen?"

"In the night. It is Tippu Tip, and he is still here, camped beyond the trees, in our fields."

A murmur of consternation rose from the nearest of the porters and rippled away down the line. Burton turned to Saíd. "See to the men. Bring them into this clearing. Do not allow them to flee."

The *ras kafilah* signalled to his bully boys and they started to herd the porters into the glade.

The king's agent instructed Trounce, Honesty, Krishnamurthy, Spencer, Isabella Mayson, and Sister Raghavendra to help the Arab guard the men and supplies. He gestured for Swinburne to join him, then addressed Máví ya Gnombe: "*Mwene Goha*, I wouldst look upon the slavers' camp, but I do not wish the slavers to see me."

"Follow, I shall show thee," the elder said. He and his companions, who'd put away their arrows, led Burton and Swinburne to the far side of the clearing where the path continued.

Between the glade and the cultivated fields beyond there was a thick band of forest. The trail led halfway through this, then veered sharply to the left. The African stopped at the bend and pointed down the path.

"It is the way to the village," he said.

"I remember," Burton replied. "The houses and *bandani* are in another clearing some way along. I had arranged for a forward party of Wanyamwezi porters to meet us at thy village with supplies, but the plan went awry."

"Had they come, they would now be slaves, so it is good the plan did not work. *Murungwana Sana*, this is one of three paths from the village clearing. Another leads from it down to the plain and is better trodden than this."

"I was wondering why this one is so overgrown," said Burton. "The last time I was here, it was the main route."

"We changed it after Manda attacked us."

"And the third path?"

"Goes from the village, through the forest, to the fields. All these paths are now guarded by old men, as this one was. But let us not follow this way. Instead, we shall go through the trees here, and we will come to the fields at a place where the slavers would not expect to see a man, and will therefore not be looking. My brothers will meanwhile return to the village, for the grandmothers of those taken are sorely afraid."

"Very well."

Máví ya Gnombe nodded to his companions, who turned and continued down the trail, then he pushed through a sticky-leafed bush and disappeared into the undergrowth. Burton followed, and Swinburne stepped after him, muttering about leeches and ticks and fleas and "assorted creepy-crawlies."

They struggled on for five minutes, then the trees thinned, and the men ducked low and proceeded as quietly as possible. They came to a bush, pushed aside its leaves, and looked out over cultivated fields, upon which was camped a large slave caravan.

There were, Burton estimated, about four hundred slaves, men and women, mostly kneeling, huddled together and chained by the neck in groups of twelve. Arabian traders moved among and around them—about seventy, though there were undoubtedly more in the large tents that had been erected on the southern side of the camp.

A little to the north, a great many pack mules were corralled, along with a few ill-looking horses.

Swinburne started to twitch with fury. "This is diabolical, Richard!" he hissed. "There must be something we can do!"

"We're vastly outnumbered, Algy," Burton said. "And we have the Prussians breathing down our necks. But—"

"But what?"

"Perhaps there's a way we can kill two birds with one stone. Let's get back to the others."

They retraced their steps through the foliage until they emerged once again onto the path. Burton addressed the elderly African: "Máví ya Gnombe, go thou to thy village and bring all who remain there to the glade where we encountered thee. Do not allow a single one to remain behind."

The old man looked puzzled, but turned and paced away to do as commanded.

Burton and Swinburne returned to the clearing, where they found the porters restless and unhappy. The king's agent walked over to the bundle of robes that hid Herbert Spencer and reached up to the parakeet that squatted atop it. Pox jumped onto his outstretched hand, and Burton took the bird away from his companions and quietly gave it a message to deliver to Isabel. He included a description of their location, outlined a plan of action, and finished: "Report the enemy's numbers and position. Message ends."

Pox disappeared into the green canopy overhead.

As if turned on by a switch, the day's rainfall began. Everyone moved to the more sheltered edges of the glade.

Burton called his companions over and told them what he intended.

"You've got to be bloody joking!" Trounce exclaimed.

"Chancy!" Thomas Honesty snapped.

"Perilous!" Krishnamurthy grunted.

"Inspired!" Swinburne enthused.

"I see no other way," Burton said.

They ate a hurried meal while awaiting the parakeet's return.

The villagers arrived, pitifully few in number, and all elderly. Burton described to them what was soon to happen, and drilled into them that their silence would be essential. They huddled together, wet, miserable, and scared.

The expedition members took rifles and pistols from the supplies and began to clean and load them.

"You'll remain with the porters," Burton told the two women.

Isabella Mayson picked up a revolver, flicked open its chamber, and started to push bullets into it. "Absolutely not," she said.

Sister Raghavendra hefted a rifle. "Do you consider us too frail, Richard?"

"On the contrary, you have proven yourselves—"

"Equal to any man?" the Sister interrupted. "Good. Then we shall do what needs to be done and fight at your side, and don't you dare attempt to persuade us otherwise."

Burton gave a curt nod.

Forty minutes later, Pox returned.

"Message from Isabel Arundell. We are ready. Estimate a hundred and fifty thumb-sucking men fast approaching your position. You have an hour at most, chamber-pot lover. Be prepared."

"You all understand what you must do?" he asked his friends.

They gave their grim assent, pushed pistols into their belts, slung rifles over their shoulders, and divided into two teams of four: Trounce, Swinburne, Krishnamurthy, and Mayson; and Burton, Honesty, Spencer, and Raghavendra. Pox huddled on the explorer's shoulder.

Burton addressed Saíd: "To thee falls responsibility for the porters and villagers. It is vital that they neither flee nor make a sound."

"I understand."

The king's agent and his companions moved out of the glade and along the path. The rain hammered against the leaves around them, hissing loudly, soaking through their clothing, making the ground squelch beneath their feet.

They followed the trail as it veered to the right, and traipsed on until they eventually reached the abandoned village, which was some considerable distance from the original clearing. The second glade was much bigger. There were twenty or so beehive huts in it, and a well-built palaver house. A massive fig tree spread over the central space.

"The first shot is yours," Burton said to Trounce. "Judge it well. Don't be too eager."

"Understood."

Trounce led his team to the eastern edge of the village and they disappeared into the vegetation, following the path down the hill to the marshy ground where the rhinoceros carcass lay. Burton and the rest went in the opposite direction, cautiously proceeding along the trail toward the fields. Halfway along it, they left the path and pushed into the bushes and plants that crowded around the boles of the trees. Struggling through the roots and vines and thorns and branches, they made their way to the edge of the forest until, through the dripping verdure, they saw the cultivated land and the slave encampment.

The sun was low in the sky by now, and it turned the fringes of the passing clouds a radiant gold.

The rain stopped.

"It won't be long," Burton said softly. "Spread out. Don't shoot until I do. And remember—keep moving."

Honesty, Spencer, and Sadhvi Raghavendra slipped away.

Burton lay flat on his stomach and levelled his rifle, aiming at the slavers who were moving around their tents and captives.

He flicked a beetle from his cheek and crushed a leech that had attached to the back of his left hand.

Pox hopped from his shoulder to his head and mumbled, "Odious pig."

The shadows lengthened.

A seemingly endless line of ants marched over the mulch just in front of him. They were carrying leaf fragments, dead wasps, and caterpillars.

He heard Honesty sneeze close by.

A rifle cracked in the near distance.

All of a sudden, gunfire erupted and echoed through the trees, the sound rising up from the base of the hill on the other side of the village. Burton knew what it meant: the Prussians were very close, and Trounce and his team had opened fire on them.

Sheltered behind the roots of trees, the police detective's team could take pot-shots at the hundred and fifty Prussians with impunity. Not only were they concealed but they were also on higher ground, while the pursuing party had to struggle through the marsh before ascending a slope that, while forested, was considerably more open than the uppermost part of the hill.

Trounce, Swinburne, Krishnamurthy, and Isabella Mayson would be silently and invisibly moving backward as they picked off the enemy, drawing the Prussians toward the village and away from the other clearing.

The noise of battle had reached the Arabs. Burton watched as they grabbed rifles and gestured at the forest. A large group of them started running toward where he and the others were hidden.

He took aim at a particularly large and ferocious-looking slaver and shot him through the heart.

Immediately, rifles banged loudly as Honesty, Spencer, and Raghavendra opened fire.

Burton downed two more of the slavers, then, as the other Arabs started shooting blindly into the undergrowth, he crawled backward and repositioned himself behind a tangle of mangrove roots from where he could see the beginning of the path to the village.

Bullets tore through the foliage but none came close to him. He put his rifle aside and pulled two six-shooters from his belt. Four Arabs ran into view. He mowed them down with well-placed shots then crawled away to reposition himself once again.

Slowly, in this fashion, Burton and his friends retreated toward the village.

The slavers followed, and though they sent bullet after bullet crashing into the trees, they didn't once find a target.

On the other side of the empty settlement, Trounce and his companions were performing exactly the same manoeuvre. They had slightly less luck—a bullet had ploughed through Krishnamurthy's forearm and another had scored the skin of Isabella Mayson's right cheek and taken off her earlobe—but the effect was the same: the Prussians were advancing toward the village.

After some minutes, Burton came closer to the end of the path where it opened into the clearing. He fired off three shots and wormed his way under a tamarind tree whose branches slumped all the way to the ground forming an enclosed space around the trunk, and here he found Herbert Spencer collapsed and motionless in the dirt.

A rifle cracked, tamarind leaves parted, and Thomas Honesty crawled in. He saw the bundle of Arabian robes and whispered: "Herbert! Dead?"

"He can't die," Burton replied in a low voice. "He's clockwork. Fool that I am, I forgot to wind him up this morning—and the key is back with the supplies!"

"Manage without him. Almost there!"

"Let's get into position," Burton said. "Stay low—things are about to get a lot hotter around here!"

He dropped onto his belly and—followed by the Scotland Yard man—wriggled out from beneath the tamarind, through thorny scrub, and into the shelter of a matted clump of tall grass. Using his elbows, he propelled himself forward until he reached the edge of the village clearing. Honesty crawled to his side. They watched the action from behind a small acacia bush. The police detective glanced at it and murmured, "Needs pruning, hard against the stem."

Guns were discharging all around them, and they immediately saw that the thing they'd hoped for had come to pass. The slavers had entered the village from the west, while Trounce and his team had lured the Prussians into it from the east; and now the two groups, convinced that the other was the enemy, were blazing away at each other.

"Now we just lie low and wait it out," Burton said.

Four of the plant vehicles he'd seen at Mzizima were slithering into view, and cries of horror went up from the Arabs, who aimed their matchlocks at the creatures and showered them with bullets. Burton plainly saw the men sitting in the blooms hit over and over, but they appeared unaffected, apart from one who took a shot to the forehead. He went limp, and his plant thrashed wildly before flopping into a quivering heap.

Over the course of the next few minutes, the two forces battled ferociously while the king's agent and his friends looked on from their hiding places in the surrounding vegetation. Then a slight lull in the hostilities occurred and a voice shouted from among the slavers: "We shall not submit to bandits!"

A Prussian, in the Arabic language, yelled back: "We are not bandits!"

"Then why attack us?"

"It was *you* who attacked *us*!"

"You lie!"

"Wait! Hold your fire! I would parley!"

"Damn it!" Burton said under his breath. "We can't let this happen, but if any of us shoots now, they'll realise a third party is present."

"Is this trickery, son of Allah?" the Prussian shouted.

"Nay!"

"Then tell me, what do you want?"

"We want nothing but to be left alone. We are en route to Zanzibar."

"Why, then, did you set upon us?"

"I tell you, we did not."

Burton saw the Prussian turn to some of his men. They talked among themselves, holding their weapons at the ready and not taking their eyes from the Arabs, some of whom were crowded around the end of the western-most path, while others crouched behind the native huts.

Moments later, the Prussian called: "Prove to us that you are speaking the truth. Lay down your weapons!"

"And allow you to slaughter us?"

"I told you—we are not the aggressor!"

"Then you lay down your guns and withdraw those—those—plant abominations!"

Again, the Prussian consulted with his men.

He turned back to the slavers. "I will only concede to—"

Suddenly, one of the slavers—swathed in his robes and with his head wrapped in a *keffiyeh*—ran out from among his fellows, raised two pistols, and started blasting at the Prussians.

Immediately, they jerked up their rifles and sent a hail of bullets into the man. He was knocked off his feet, sent twisting through the air, and hit the ground, where he rolled then lay still.

The battle exploded back into life, and, on both sides, man after man went down.

A stray bullet ripped into the tall grass, narrowly missing Burton. He turned to make sure Honesty was unharmed but the Scotland Yard man had, at some point, silently moved away.

"Message to Isabel Arundell," Burton said to Pox. "Your company is requested. Message ends."

As the parakeet flew off, one of the plant vehicles writhed past Burton's position and laid into a group of slavers. Its spine-covered tendrils whipped out, yanked men off their feet, and ripped them apart. Some tried to flee but were shot down as the Prussians began to gain control of the clearing. One group of about twenty Arabs had secured itself behind a large stack of firewood in the *bandani*, and it wasn't long before they were the last remaining men of the slave caravan's force. The Prussians, by contrast, had about fifty soldiers left, plus the three moving plants. Individuals in both groups were drawing swords as ammunition ran out: wicked-looking scimitars on the Arabian side; straight rapiers on the Prussian.

Pox returned: "Message from Isabel Arundell. We had problems getting the buttock-wobbling horses through the bloody swamp but are now regrouping at the bottom of the hill. We'll be with you in a stench-filled moment. Message ends."

One of the mobile plants crashed into the barrier behind which the slavers were sheltering and lashed out at them, tearing their clothes and flaying their skin. Screaming with terror, they hacked at it with their scimitars, which, in fact, turned out to be a more efficient way to tackle the monster than shooting at it.

An Arab climbed onto the woodpile and jumped from it into the centre of the bloom, bringing his blade swinging down onto the head of the man sitting there. The plant shuddered and lay still.

The cavalry arrived.

The Daughters of Al-Manat, eighty strong and all mounted, came thundering into the village, emerging in single file from the eastern path. With matchlocks cracking, they attacked the remaining Prussians. Spears were thrust into the plant vehicles and burning brands thrown onto them.

Those few slavers who remained alive took the opportunity to flee and plunged away down the path, disappearing into dark shadow, for now the sky was a deep purple and the sun had almost set.

The last Prussian fell with a bullet in his throat.

The Daughters of Al-Manat had been savage—ruthless in their massacre of the enemy who, at Mzizima, had killed thirty or so of their number. Now they reined in their horses and waited while Sir Richard Francis Burton and the others emerged from the vegetation.

Krishnamurthy was holding his forearm tightly and blood was dribbling between his fingers. Isabella Mayson's right ear had bled profusely and her clothes were stained red. Swinburne, Trounce, and Sister Raghavendra were uninjured. They were all wet through and covered with dirt and insects.

"Well done," Burton told them.

"Where's Tom?" Trounce asked.

"Probably dragging Herbert out of the bushes—his spring wound down. Sadhvi, would you see to Isabella and Maneesh's wounds?"

While the nurse got to work, Burton indicated to Trounce the area where Spencer had been left, then paced over to Isabel Arundell, who was sitting on her horse quietly conversing with her Amazons.

"That was brutal," he observed.

She looked down at him. "I lost a lot of good women at Mzizima and on the way here. Revenge seemed . . . appropriate."

He regarded her, moistened his lips, and said, "You're not the Isabel I met twelve years ago."

"Time changes people, Dick."

"Hardens them?"

"Perhaps that is necessary in some cases. Are we to philosophise while slaves remain in shackles or shall we go and liberate them?"

"Wait here a moment."

He left her and approached Swinburne.

"Algy, I want you and Maneesh to leg it along to the other clearing. Bring the villagers, Saíd, and our porters back here. They can help move the bodies out to the fields. They'll need to start work digging a pit for a mass grave."

He returned to Isabel. She indicated a riderless horse, which he mounted. Holding burning brands to light the way, they led a party of ten of the Daughters out of the glade and along the path to the fields. Burton felt sickened by the slaughter he'd witnessed but he knew it was the only option. On the one hand, the Prussians would certainly have killed him and his party, but on the other, he couldn't allow the villagers to fall into the hands of Tippu Tip.

They rode out of the forest and approached the caravan. Five Arabs were guarding it.

"He who raises a weapon shall be shot instantly!" Burton called.

One of the guards bent and placed his matchlock on the ground. The others saw him do it and followed suit.

Burton and Isabel stopped, dismounted, and walked over to them.

"Where is el Murgebi, the man they call Tippu Tip?" Burton asked, in Arabic.

One of the men pointed to a nearby tent. Burton turned to Isabel's Amazons and said, "Take these men and make a chain gang of them. Then get to work liberating the slaves."

The women looked for confirmation from Isabel. She gave them a nod, then she and Burton strode over to the tent, pushed aside its flap, and stepped in.

By the light of three oil lamps, they saw colourful rugs on the ground, a low table holding platters of food, and piles of cushions upon which sat a small half-African, half-Arabian individual. His teeth were gold, and though he appeared less than thirty years old, his beard was white. He raised his turbaned head and they noted that a milky film covered his eyes. He was blind.

"Who enters?" he asked in a reedy voice.

"Thy enemy," Burton replied.

"Ah. Wilt thou take a sweet mint tea with me? I have been listening to the noise of battle. An exhausting business, is it not? Refreshment would be welcome, I expect."

"No, Tippu Tip, I will not drink with thee. Stand up, please."

"Am I to be executed?"

"No. There has been enough death this night."

"Then what?"

"Come."

Burton stepped forward, took the trader by the elbow, and marched him out of the tent and over to the chained-up slaves. Isabel followed and said nothing. Her women were busily releasing the four hundred captives, who, in a long line, were making their way toward the village.

As Burton had ordered, the five guards were now tethered together, with short chains running from iron collar to iron collar, and from ankle manacle to ankle manacle. Their hands were tied behind their backs. The king's agent positioned Tippu Tip at the front of the line and locked him in fetters, joining him to the chain gang but leaving his hands unbound. He then pulled the prisoners along, away from the crowd of slaves and out into the open field.

"What are you doing?" Isabel whispered.

"Administering justice," he replied, and brought them to a halt. "Aim your matchlock at Tippu Tip, please, Isabel."

"Am I to be a firing squad of one?"

"Only if he attempts to point this at us," the king's agent responded, holding up a revolver. He placed it in the Arabian's hand and stepped away. The slaver's face bore an expression of bafflement.

"Listen carefully," Burton said, addressing the prisoners. "You are facing east, toward Zanzibar. However, if you walk straight ahead, you will find yourselves among the villagers and slaves we have just liberated and they will surely tear you limb from limb. You should therefore turn to your left and walk some miles north before then turning again eastward. In the morning, the sun will guide you, but now it is night, a dangerous time to travel, for the lions hunt and the terrain is treacherous in the dark. I can do nothing to make the ground even, but I can at least give you some protection against predators. Thus, your leader holds a pistol loaded with six bullets. Unfortunately, he is blind, so you must advise him where to point it and when to pull the trigger to ward off anything that might threaten you, but be cautious, for those six bullets are the only ones you have. Perhaps if walking all the way to Zanzibar is too challenging a prospect for you—well, there are six bullets and there are six of you. Need I say more?"

"Surely thou cannot expect us to walk all the way to the coast in chains?" Tippu Tip protested.

"Didst thou not expect just that of thy captives?" Burton asked.

"But they are slaves!"

"They are men and women and children. Now, begin your journey, you have far to go."

"Allah have mercy!" one of the men cried.

"Perhaps he will," Burton said. "But I won't."

The man at the back of the line wailed, "What shall we do, el Murgebi?"

"Walk, fool!" the slave trader barked.

The chain gang stumbled into motion and slowly moved away.

"Tippu Tip!" Burton called after it. "Beware of Abdullah the Dervish, for if I set mine eyes on thee again, I shall surely kill thee!"

No one slept that night.

The liberated slaves carried the dead Arabs and Prussians along the path and into the fields, leaving them in a distant corner, intending to dig a mass grave when daylight returned. A number of Isabel's women stood guard over the corpses to prevent scavengers getting to them. The Africans were too afraid to do the job, believing that vengeful spirits would rise up and attack them.

Of the four hundred slaves, most had been taken from villages much farther to the west. This turned out to be a blessing, for Burton's porters had been so terrified by the sounds of battle and proximity of slavers that they'd overpowered Saíd and his men and had melted away into the night. No doubt they were fleeing back the way the expedition had come. Fortunately, their fear had outweighed their avariciousness and they'd departed without stealing supplies. The released slaves agreed to replace the porters on the understanding that each man, as he neared his native village, would abandon the safari in order to return home. Burton calculated that this would at least cover the marches from Dut'humi to distant Ugogi.

The Arab camp was stripped of its supplies, which were added to Burton's own and stored in the village's *bandani*. Tippu Tip's mules were also appropriated.

A large fire was built and the plant vehicles were chopped up and thrown into the flames.

The Daughters of Al-Manat corralled their hundred and eight horses.

"We're starting to lose them to tsetse bites," Isabel informed Burton. "Twelve, so far. These animals were bred in dry desert air. This climate is not good for them—it drains their resistance. Soon we'll be fighting on foot."

"Fighting whom?"

"The Prussians won't give up, Dick. And remember, John Speke almost certainly has a detachment of them travelling with him."

"Hmm. Led by Count Zeppelin, no doubt," Burton muttered.

"He may be taking a different trail from us," Isabel observed, "but at some point we're bound to clash."

Swinburne bounded over, still overexcited, and moving as if he'd come down with a chronic case of St. Vitus's dance.

"My hat, Richard! I can't stop marvelling at it! We were outnumbered on both sides yet came out of it without a scratch, unless you count the five thousand three hundred and twenty-six that were inflicted by thorns and hungry insects!"

"You've counted them?" Isabel asked.

"My dear Al-Manat, it's a well-educated guess. I say, Richard, where the devil has Tom Honesty got to?"

Burton frowned. "He's not been seen?"

"Not by me, at least."

"Algy, unpack some oil lamps, gather a few villagers, and search the vegetation over there—" He pointed to where he'd last seen the Scotland Yard man. "I hope I'm wrong, but he may have been hit."

Swinburne raced off to organise the search party. Burton left Isabel and joined Trounce at the *bandani*. The detective was rummaging in a crate and pulling from it items of food, such as beef jerky and corn biscuits.

"I'm trying to find something decent for us to chow on," he said. "I don't think the villagers will manage to feed everybody. I put Herbert over there. He still needs winding."

Burton looked to where Trounce indicated and saw the clockwork man lying stiffly in the shadow of the woodpile. The king's agent suddenly reached out and gripped his friend's arm. "William! Who found him?"

"I did. He was in a hollow under a tree."

"Like that?"

"Yes. What do you mean?"

"Look at him, man! He had Arabian robes covering his polymethylene suit. Where are they?"

"Perhaps they hindered his movement, so he took them off. Why is it important?"

Burton's jaw worked. For a moment, he found it impossible to speak. His legs felt as if they couldn't hold him, and he collapsed down onto a roll of cloth, sitting with one arm outstretched, still clutching Trounce.

"Bismillah! The bloody fool!" he whispered and looked up at his friend.

Trounce was shocked to see that the explorer's normally sullen eyes were filled with pain.

"What's happened?" he asked.

"Tom was next to me when the Prussians and Arabs started to powwow," Burton explained huskily. "We were near Herbert, just a little way past him. The parley threatened to ruin our entire plan. The Arab who lost patience with the conflab and ran out shooting saved the day for us. Except—"

"Oh no!" Trounce gasped as the truth dawned.

"I think Tom may have crawled back to Herbert, taken his robes, put them on, and—"

"No!" Trounce repeated.

They gazed at each other, frozen in a moment of anguish, then Burton stood and said, "I'm going to check the bodies."

"I'm coming with you."

They borrowed a couple of horses from Isabel and, by the light of brands, guided their mounts along the path to the fields then galloped across the cultivated ground to where the dead had been laid out. Dismounting, they walked up and down the rows, examining the corpses. The Prussians were ignored, but each time either man came to a slaver, he bent and pulled back the cloth that covered the corpse's face.

"William," Burton said quietly.

Trounce looked up from the man he'd just inspected and saw the explorer standing over a body. Burton's shoulders were hunched and his arms hung loosely.

Something like a sob escaped from the Scotland Yard man, and the world seemed to whirl dizzyingly around him as he staggered over to his friend's side and looked down at Thomas Manfred Honesty.

His fellow detective was wrapped in the robes—ragged and bloodstained—that he'd borrowed from Spencer. He'd been riddled with bullets and must have died instantly, but it was no consolation to Trounce, for the little man, who'd mocked him for nearly two decades over his belief in Spring Heeled Jack, had, in the past couple of years, become one of his best friends.

"He sacrificed himself to save us," Burton whispered.

Trounce couldn't reply.

They buried Thomas Honesty the next morning, in the little glade to the north of the village.

Burton spoke of his friend's bravery, determination, and heroism.

Trounce talked hoarsely of Honesty's many years of police service, his exemplary record, his wife, and his fondness for gardening.

Krishnamurthy told of the respect the detective inspector had earned from the lower ranks in the force.

Swinburne stepped forward, placed a wreath of jungle flowers on the grave, and said:

> "For thee, O now a silent soul, my brother,
> Take at my hands this garland, and farewell."

Sister Raghavendra softly sang "Abide with Me," then they filed back along the trail to the village, a subdued and saddened group.

For most of the rest of the day, Burton and his fellows caught up with lost sleep. Not so William Trounce. He'd found a large flat stone on the slope beneath the village, and, borrowing a chisel-like tool from one of the locals, he set about carving an inscription into it, sitting alone, far enough away from the huts that his chipping and scraping wouldn't disturb his slumbering companions. It took him the better part of the day to complete it, and when it was done, he took it to the glade, placed it on the grave, and sat on the grass.

"I'm not sure I really understand it, old chap," he murmured, "but apparently the whole Spring Heeled Jack business sent us all off in a different direction. None of us is doing what we were supposed to be doing, although I rather think I would have carried on as policemen no matter what."

He rested a hand on the stone.

"Captain Burton says this history we're in isn't the only one, and, in any of the others, meddlers like Edward Oxford might be at work, and whenever they tamper with events, they cause new histories. Can you imagine that? All those different variations of you and me? The thing of it is, my friend, I hope—I really hope—that, somewhere, a Tom Honesty will be tending his garden well into old age."

He sat for a few minutes more, then bent over and kissed the stone, stood, sighed, and walked away.

The tear he left behind trickled into the inscription, ran down the tail of the letter "y," and settled around a seed in Swinburne's wreath.

CHAPTER 8

TO KAZEH

Omne solum forti patria.
(Every region is a strong man's home.)
—SIR RICHARD FRANCIS BURTON'S MOTTO

T he clangour of the parade bell sounded and voices hollered: "*Aufwachen!*
Aufwachen!"

In Barrack 5, Compound B, of Stalag IV at Ugogi, Sir Richard Francis
Burton and his fellow prisoners of war dragged themselves wearily from their
bunks, quickly put on their grey uniforms, and tumbled out onto the dusty
parade ground, which was baking in the afternoon heat.

Obeying shouted orders, they arranged themselves into three rows,
facing forward, blinking and screwing up their faces as the glare of the white
sky burned the sleep out of their eyes.

"What now?" the man to Burton's right grumbled. "Surely they can't be
sending us back to the pass already?"

"They'll work us to death as long as they get the blasted road built,"
another man growled.

They were referring to the passage the prisoners had been carving
through the Usagara Mountains. Burton and his fellows had originally been
incarcerated at Stalag III, near Zungomero, on the other side of the range.
From there, they'd been escorted out daily, in a chain gang, to work on the
road. When the halfway point had been reached, three months ago, they'd
been marched to this new POW camp at Ugogi to commence the second half
of the route.

From his place midway along the second row, Burton looked up at the
guard towers. The man-things in them, standing with their mounted seed-
pods trained on the prisoners, appeared rather more alert than usual.

Over to the left, the gates in the high barbed-wire fence surrounding the compound were swinging shut, and inside, a large plant had just drawn to a halt, squatting down on its roots. A group of German officers stepped out of the vehicle.

"Bloody hell!" a man gasped. "That's Lettow-Vorbeck!"

"Which one?" Burton asked.

"The small bloke with the wide-brimmed hat. What the hell is he doing here?"

Burton watched as the officer, with a swagger stick under his right arm and a leather briefcase in his left hand, met with Oberstleutnant Maximilian Metzger, the camp commandant. They conversed for a few minutes then marched over to the lined-up prisoners and started walking from one end of the first row to the other. They gave each man a cursory glance, reached the end of the line, then proceeded down the second row.

When they reached Burton, they stopped and Metzger said: *"Hier, Generalmajor! Hier ist der gesuchte Mann!"*

Lettow-Vorbeck examined Burton's face. He pulled a photograph from his pocket, looked at it, and nodded.

"Sehr Gut gemacht! Bringen Sie ihn her!"

Metzger signalled to two rhino guards. They stamped over, took Burton by the elbows, and dragged him out of the line. He was taken across the parade ground, into the commandant's office, and pushed into a chair opposite a heavy desk. The guards stood to attention to either side of him.

Lettow-Vorbeck entered and barked: *"Lassen Sie uns allein!"*

The guards clicked their heels and thudded out.

There was a clockwork fan revolving on the ceiling. Burton leaned his head back, closed his eyes, and allowed the air to wash over his face. He was weary to the bone.

"Do you know who I am?" Lettow-Vorbeck said, in strongly accented English.

Without opening his eyes, Burton replied: "Generalmajor Paul Emil von Lettow-Vorbeck. You command the German forces in East Africa."

"That is correct. *Sehr gut.* So."

Burton heard a chair scrape on the floor and creak as the other man sat down. There was a soft thump—the briefcase being swung up onto the desk—and a click as it was opened.

"I have here a file in which you feature with some considerable prominence."

Burton didn't respond. He was hungry and thirsty, but most of all he needed to sleep.

"Private Frank Baker, captured on the western slopes of the Dut'humi Hills two years ago. You were alone—a refugee from the failed British assault on the Tanganyika Railway."

There was a long moment of silence. Burton had still not opened his eyes. He thought about Bertie Wells and the night they'd slept in the open, beside Thomas Honesty's grave. The temperature had plummeted after sunset, and during the hours of darkness both of them developed a fever. Burton's dreams had been filled with violence; with scenes of Prussians and Arabians slaughtering each other—and he'd woken up soaked with dew, filled with memories, and cursing himself. How could he have forgotten there was a village nearby? Just along the trail!

Wells was in the grip of hallucinations, which—to judge from his babbling monologues—involved insects crawling out of the moon, invisible madmen, and three-legged harvestmen. With what little strength remained to him, Burton had hauled the war correspondent to his feet and dragged him along an overgrown trail that eventually opened into another clearing where a decrepit village stood. Its menfolk were long gone—conscripted—and the remaining villagers were elderly and half-starved. Burton left Wells with them while he went to hunt game.

But he'd become the prey. Three lurchers had blundered out of the undergrowth and pursued him across boggy ground and into thick jungle. It was peculiar; he felt certain they could have caught him, but instead they appeared to be herding him along.

One of them sprouted poppies as it floundered after him.

By the time he'd eluded them, he was lost and in the grip of malaria.

The Germans found him unconscious at the side of a trail. Since then, he'd spent nearly two years in the Stalag III POW camp before his recent transfer to Ugogi.

Large parts of his memory had returned. He knew he was the king's agent. He was aware that Algernon Swinburne, William Trounce, Thomas Honesty, Maneesh Krishnamurthy, Herbert Spencer, Sister Raghavendra, Isabella Mayson, and Isabel Arundell had travelled to Africa with him. But he didn't know why, what had become of them, or how he'd been transported into the future.

He'd been here for four years. Four years!

Why? For what purpose?

"Why?" Lettow-Vorbeck said.

Burton opened his eyes and met those of the generalmajor. Behind the officer's head, pencil-thin shafts of light shone through the slats of the window shutter. Motes of dust entered them, blazed, then vanished into the shade. Against this illumination, Lettow-Vorbeck's features were very dark—almost silhouetted—but by some quirk, his eyes shone with an almost feral intensity.

"Why what?"

"Why are you British so destructive? Do you not believe in evolution?"

"Evolution? What do you mean?"

The officer drummed the fingers of his right hand on the desktop.

"The Greater German Empire seeks to advance the human species. We wish to liberate every man and every woman from slavery so that each can fulfil his or her greatest potential. So each can become an *Übermensch*. Perhaps this translates as 'Over Man,' *ja?*"

Burton gave a snort of disdain. "I don't think your Askaris feel particularly liberated."

"*Nein. Nein.* And it is the fault of your people. We are forced to employ the Africans to oppose British assaults on the infrastructure we are building here. Were it not for your people, Africa would have atmospheric railways and well-developed cities by now. And Europe would be a paradise, where trivial jobs and the necessities of survival are taken care of by plant life, leaving the human species free to explore its best potentials. Instead, we must assign our resources on both continents to resisting your vandalism."

Burton's breath whistled from between his teeth. "It's always the same," he said. "A madman creates a plan for the future of humanity, and, in unleashing it, causes untold suffering. Generalmajor, do I really need to point out that your vegetation is proliferating without check, or that while many individuals may be capable of advancing themselves, most are content to be well fed and sheltered and wish for little more?"

Lettow-Vorbeck nodded thoughtfully. "*Es trifft zu*, what you say of our plants. But that situation will be corrected once hostilities cease. As for your suggestion that the populace is not willing or able to evolve—I cannot agree. It is typical British thinking, for you built your Empire on the premise that an educated and privileged minority should benefit from the labours of a downtrodden majority."

Lettow-Vorbeck suddenly slapped his hand down on the thick dossier that lay before him. "So! *Lassen Sie uns auf den Punkt kommen!* No more—what is the expression?—beating around the bush?" He put his elbows on the desk and steepled his fingers in front of his face. "*Ich kenne die Wahrheit.* Your name is not Frank Baker. You are Sir Richard Francis Burton. You were born in the year 1821. You died in the year 1890. And you were sent to the year 1914 from the year 1863. *Es ist ein außerordentlicher Umstand! Unglaublich!*"

Burton sat bolt upright. His exhaustion fell away.

Lettow-Vorbeck gave a slight smile, his teeth white in the shadow of his face. "*Sehr gut. Sehr gut*, Herr Burton. I have your full attention now. You will listen to me, *ja*? I have a story to tell you. But first a question: do you possess *die telepathischen Fähigkeiten*?"

"Mediumistic abilities? No."

"Nor I. Hah! It is a misfortune! I should like them! You are aware, *ja*, that many people do? In increasing numbers, it appears. Your Colonel Crowley has his people—and they are strong—while we Germans have our weathermen, and, of course, the Kaiser himself, who is the greatest *Gedankenleser*—medium—of them all."

Burton's right eyebrow rose slightly. "Nietzsche styles himself emperor now, does he?"

"*Es ist angebracht, dass!*"

A large fly buzzed lazily around Lettow-Vorbeck's head and landed on the desk. The German picked up the dossier and whacked it down onto the insect. He flicked the flattened corpse onto the floor and resumed his former position.

"And in *Russland*, there was Grigori Rasputin, also a great *Gedankenleser*, who, as you may know, died of—how do you say *Hirnblutung*?"

"Brain haemorrhage," Burton answered.

"So. *Ja*. Thank you. He died of that two years ago. It is him my story concerns."

Burton remained silent.

Lettow-Vorbeck pointed a finger down at the report lying in front of him.

"This dossier was entrusted to me by Kaiser Nietzsche himself. It contains information that no other man is aware of—just he and I—and now I will tell you."

Still Burton said nothing.

"Thirteen years ago, after we were forced to destroy your nation's capital city, our troops discovered a number of black diamonds beneath the rubble of the Tower of London. They were the seven fragments of the Cambodian Eye of Nāga, and the seven of the African Eye. We know this because documents concerning them were also found, and, in these documents, another Eye—from South America, and also in seven pieces—was described. Of it, though, there was no sign. You know of what I speak, *ja*?"

"I'm aware of the Eyes of Nāga, Generalmajor," Burton said, "but I can't help you. I don't know where the South American stones are."

"That is not why you are here. We have already located them: our people have sensed their presence in Tabora—your last stronghold. We will recover them when we drive you from that place."

"So far, I believe, you've not been very successful in that endeavour."

"*Ich kann es nicht verleugnen!* The South American stones are being used to protect the city, Herr Burton, but the *Heereswaffenamt*—our Army Ordnance people—have a solution to that. A final solution! It will be put into operation soon and Tabora will be destroyed. But let us not stray from the subject—we must talk of the other Eyes, *ja*? For many decades, even before the Great War commenced, your people committed mediumistic acts of sabotage against German industry. When it was discovered that the diamonds were the tools your *Gedankenleser* had used to perpetrate their crimes, Bismarck passed them to Nietzsche, that he might employ them to—what is the word?—*accentuate* the talents of our own people. Nietzsche kept the Cambodian stones but sent the African ones to Rasputin, and the two men used the power of the Eyes to secure an alliance between Germany and Russland. Then, in 1914, Nietzsche overthrew Bismarck and Rasputin deposed the Tsar."

"Two traitors betraying their leaders," Burton said scornfully.

"Two visionaries," Lettow-Vorbeck countered, "committed to creating a better world."

Shouts penetrated the office from outside. The prisoners were being rounded up and marched out of the camp, on their way into the Usagara Mountains to continue work on the road.

Burton asked, "What has any of this to do with me?"

"We shall come to that. Nietzsche took control of the Greater German Empire, but before Rasputin could do similar in Russland, he died of the *Hirnblutung*. German agents retrieved the African stones and returned them to Nietzsche. Now we come to the interesting part of the story, for our emperor had spent considerable time probing the Cambodian fragments and he'd detected in them a remnant intelligence."

"Yes. The Nāga," Burton muttered.

"The mythical reptiles? *Nein, das ist falsch.*"

Burton looked surprised. "Then what?"

"A man. A philosopher named Herbert Spencer. It was little more than an echo, but some information could be gleaned from it; specifically that Spencer died in 1862 yet his intelligence somehow survived for a further year, before finally being extinguished in a temple filled with jewels."

"A temple? Where?"

"Somewhere here in Africa. Fascinating, *ja*? So now Nietzsche probed the African stones, also, and in them, too, he found the remains of a man—the residual memories—and in these, the temple was also present, but in greater detail, and Nietzsche saw that this mysterious place, encrusted with gems of unsurpassed value, was a vast device designed to channel enormous energy."

"To what purpose?"

"To transcend the boundaries of time, Herr Burton. And it was also recorded in the remnant memories that you, *mein Freund*, were sent through the device. It is how you came to 1914 from 1863."

"I was? Why?"

"You ask me that! *Es ist meine Frage!*"

Burton examined his blistered hands and frowned with frustration. "I don't remember. These past four years, I've been slowly piecing together what happened to me prior to my arrival in 1914, but there are still gaps."

"Ah. I am pleased. You admit who you are. And do you remember this temple?"

"No."

"That is unfortunate. The Kaiser knows only that it is located somewhere in the Ruwenzori Range, deep inside the *Blutdschungel*."

"The Blood Jungle? This Ruwenzori Range, was it—?"

"Once known as the Mountains of the Moon? *Ja.* That is the case. An area of Africa most important to you, I think!"

The German fell silent for a moment and considered Burton, who warily watched the other man's glittering eyes. Generalmajor Paul Emil von Lettow-Vorbeck, the explorer decided, was as dangerous as a venomous snake.

"Well," the generalmajor said, "we have attempted to burn away the *Blutdschungel* but it grows back so fast! It is impenetrable, it covers the mountains, and it is spreading. All these years we have made no progress into the region, but that, perhaps, is because we do not know where in it we should be going. So, we have a plan."

"And your plan involves me?"

"*Ja.* That is correct. As I have said, the Kaiser saw in the diamonds that the temple sent you to 1914. He therefore ordered me to find you. It has taken a long time. Africa is big! But, finally, here you are. A man from the past."

"So?"

"So you will locate the temple for us. You somehow found your way out of it and through the *Blutdschungel*, so obviously there is a route."

"But, I told you, I don't remember."

"I think this—" the German raised a hand and tapped his forefinger against the side of his head, "—will return to you."

Burton sighed. "So what now?"

"Now we shall escort you all the way to your Mountains of the Moon and you shall show us the way to this fabulous temple. With it, the Kaiser can send agents back in time to prevent the interference that has so delayed the expansion of the Greater German Empire! British interference, Herr Burton!"

Lettow-Vorbeck stood and slipped the dossier back into his briefcase.

He barked, "*Wache!*" and the two rhino guards returned. "*Ab mit ihm zum Transporter!*"

They hoisted Burton to his feet.

"Wait! Wait!" he urged.

Lettow-Vorbeck looked at him and asked, "*Haben Sie eine Frage?*"

"Yes," Burton replied. "Yes, I have a question. The memories imprinted in the African stones—whose are they?"

"Ah," Lettow-Vorbeck said. "*Ja. Ja.* This you should know! They belonged to a man named William Trounce."

"I'm dead!" Trounce announced. He waved a large earthenware jar in the air. "Not a drop left!"

"All is not lost!" Swinburne declared. He held up a second container, and the *pombe* in it sloshed invitingly. "I must say, though, Pouncer: while there may be life left in my jar, the invincible languor and oppression of this climate have sucked the very last drop of it from yours truly."

"But not the poetry," Trounce growled. "Invincible languor, my foot! Why can't you just say, the weather in Africa is as hot as hell, like any normal person would? Pass the beer."

After taking an immoderate swig from it, Swinburne handed the container to Trounce, who poured an extravagant amount of its contents into his mouth, swallowed, hiccupped, then said, "We've been on the blasted continent for so long that I'm even beginning to enjoy this foul brew."

He received a belched response.

The two men, dressed in light khaki suits, were relaxing beneath a calabash tree in the centre of Ugogi, a village that lay slightly more than halfway along their route to Kazeh. It had taken two weeks to reach here from Dut'humi, passing first through cultivated lands, then following the marshy bank of the Mgazi River, before chopping their way through thick dripping jungle of the most obstinately difficult kind, and crossing a quagmire, two miles wide, where a mule had sunk completely out of sight in the stinking, sulphurous mud.

Arriving at Zungomero, in the head of the Khutu Valley, they'd at last begun the climb onto higher terrain, escaping the dreadful and diseased swamps that had made the first stage of their safari so miserable. The foothills of the Usagara Mountains, which now rose all around, were densely forested and resplendent with jungle flowers and fruits; the air was laden with the scent of jasmine, sage, and mimosa blossoms; and fresh springs jumped and tinkled across the sloping land.

It had been the only pleasant stage of the trek. All too soon, the ascents and descents became so steep that the mules had to be relieved of their loads before attempting them, and the watercourses in the valleys grew deeper and stronger and more perilous to cross.

The climate changed, too. As they gained altitude, the temperature swung from one extreme to the other. The nights were raw, the days bright and hot. But it was the damp mornings that had the most impact, for thick mist bubbled out of the mountains and drowned the valleys around them in a milky sea, out of which peaks rose like islands. Visually, it was stunning, but it chilled them to the bone.

While passing through this region, Trounce developed severe ulcerations on his legs; so painful that he couldn't walk or sit on a mule without suffering. So they carried him on a litter and Sister Raghavendra collected wild herbs and experimented with them until she found a combination that, when applied as a poultice, eased the pain and hastened the healing process.

There were other troubles.

The people of the region, the Wasagara, were recalcitrant and, on one occasion, hostile. Fortunately, despite shouting loudly and shooting arrows, they lacked courage and were bad marksmen. Rifle fire, aimed over their heads, was enough to discourage them.

As always, the terrain did far more harm than its inhabitants. Four mules and five horses died, one porter broke his leg, and another fell to his death.

Equipment was damaged by mildew and rust. Food and clothes rotted.

And, of course, there were insects: biting, stinging, scratching, wriggling, tickling, burrowing, and bloodsucking insects. The travellers felt they were being eaten alive.

They struggled through it, crossed the mountains, and arrived at Ugogi on the other side.

The village, being the first port of call after the Usagara Range and the last before the dry lands, was a favourite stopping point for caravans, and had thus developed into a prosperous trading centre, which the slavers left untouched. Because it was 2,750 feet above sea level, it enjoyed a comfortable heat and refreshing breezes, and its surrounding hills were rich in cattle, and its plains in grain.

Ugogi's people welcomed the expedition. Partridge and guinea fowl were pushed into cooking pots and a feast was prepared. There was drumming and dancing and laughter. There was *pombe*.

Burton announced that they would rest in the village for three days before embarking on the four-day march across the western wilderness.

That first evening, with distended bellies and befuddled senses, everyone stumbled to their beds apart from Swinburne and Trounce, who decided to lie beneath the calabash, share a couple more jars of *pombe*, and gaze at the Milky Way—and Herbert Spencer, whose belly couldn't distend, much to his evident disappointment, and whose senses were powered by clockwork.

The brass man returned to his tent to work on the final chapters of his *First Principles of Philosophy*. His parting words were: "I'm feeling a little bilious, anyway, gents."

An oil lamp hung from a branch above Swinburne and Trounce. Mosquitoes danced around the light and big ugly moths regularly threw themselves violently into the glass.

"I bloody hate Africa!" Trounce proclaimed, with the trace of a slur. "Except for Ugogi. I bloody love Ugogi. What's your opinion, Algernon?"

"My opinion, my dear Detective Inspector William Ernest Pouncer Trounce, is that you are drinking far more than your fair share. Pass that jar back at once or I shall report to the witch doctor that you covet his wife!"

"Has he got a wife?"

"I don't know."

"Is there even a witch doctor?"

"Confound your deductive abilities! Give me the beer!"

Trounce handed over the jar.

Swinburne drank deeply, gave a satisfied sigh, and looked up at the branches.

"How did so many stars get tangled up in the tree, I wonder?"

"They're not stars, you ass. They're glowworms."

"I absolutely refuse to believe your perfectly logical explanation. Mine is far more poetical and therefore speaks of a greater truth."

Trounce grunted. "The greater truth being that you're three sheets to the wind, lad."

Swinburne blew a raspberry.

They lapsed into silence for a few minutes. A mongoose chirruped somewhere in the near distance. Farther away, something hooted mournfully. Swinburne hooted back at it.

"Seventeen," Trounce said.

"Seventeen what?"

"Mosquito bites on my right forearm."

"Ah, but look at this," Swinburne replied. He stuck his left leg into the air and pulled back the trouser leg. His ankle was swollen and the skin was dark and puckered around two small puncture marks. "Snake," he said. "Poisonous, too. That had Sadhvi going, I can tell you! She flapped about like a goose down a chimney before settling on the appropriate miracle cure!"

"Humph!" Trounce responded. He sat up, shifted until his back was to the poet, then yanked up his shirt. There was what appeared to be a bullet hole just above the small of his back.

"How about that, then? Hornet sting. Got infected. Worse than being stabbed with a stiletto."

Swinburne unbuttoned his own shirt and displayed his left armpit. Just below it, a cluster of nasty-looking swellings decorated his ribs.

"Boils," he revealed. "I shan't elaborate."

Trounce winced, then said, "You'll not beat this." He reached up, pressed his right nostril closed, and blew a hard breath out through the left. One of his ears emitted a startlingly loud whistle.

The unidentified animal hooted a reply from the darkness.

"My hat!" Swinburne exclaimed. "What's caused that?"

"I haven't a notion. It first did it when I blew my nose a few days ago, and it's been doing it ever since!"

The poet lifted the jar and gulped more beer. "Very well," he said, and wobbled to his feet. He stood swaying for a moment, then undid his belt, dropped his trousers, and showed the Scotland Yard man his pale white buttocks, which shone in the lamplight like the full moon. They appeared to be zebra-striped.

"Ye gods!" Trounce gasped.

"Three days ago," Swinburne slurred. "My mule was getting obstinate in one of the swamps. Saíd took a mighty swipe at it with that *bakur* of his, but, just as he lashed out, the blessed animal's hind legs suddenly sank about three feet down. I was sent sliding backward and received the cat myself!"

"Ouch! Did it hurt?"

"Deliciously!"

"You," said Trounce, reaching for the *pombe*, "are a very curious young man, Algernon."

"Thank you."

A few more minutes of quiet were suddenly broken by a loud gurgling rumble, which echoed across the village.

"Elephant," Trounce murmured.

"Thank goodness," Swinburne replied. "I thought it was you."

Trounce responded with a snore, which, as it happened, was a fair challenge to the nearby pachyderm.

Swinburne lay back down and considered the heavens. He reached into his jacket and pulled out Apollo's gold-tipped arrow of Eros, which he'd carried with him ever since the death of Thomas Bendyshe. He pointed it at the stars.

"I'm coming for you, Count Zeppelin," he whispered.

About half an hour later, he clambered to his feet and stretched. He looked down at his sleeping companion and decided to leave him there beneath the tree. Pouncer would be fine. Even a predator brave enough to enter the village would shy away from such volcanic rumblings and snorts. Besides, the Yard man would receive a rude awakening soon enough, when the nightly rain arrived.

The stars to the east were already being obscured by cloud. The downpours were coming later and later, and were far shorter in duration. Soon the rainy season would end.

"Herbert," Swinburne whispered. "I'll go and have a little chinwag with old tin-head."

He staggered away, stopped when his trousers slipped to his ankles, hauled them up, fastened his belt, and continued on until he came to the philosopher's tent.

He pushed through the flap.

"I say, Herbert, I'm not in the slightest bit sleepy. Shall we—"

He stumbled to a halt. The clockwork philosopher was sitting at a makeshift table and was completely motionless. Wrapped in robes, he looked somewhat akin to a bundle of laundry.

"Herbert?"

There was no response.

Swinburne stepped over to his friend, put a hand on his shoulder, and gave him a shove.

Herbert didn't budge.

He'd wound down.

The poet sighed and turned to leave, but as he did so, a book on the table caught his eye. It was a large notepad, on the cover of which was written the legend: *First Principles of Philosophy*.

Curious to see how far along Herbert had got with his project, Swinburne reached for the book, slid it toward himself, and opened the first page. He read:

> *Only equivalence can lead to destruction or a final transcendence.*
> *Only equivalence can lead to destruction or a final transcendence.*
> *Only equivalence can lead to destruction or a final transcendence.*
> *Only equivalence can lead to destruction or a final transcendence.*

The poet frowned and flipped the pages to the middle of the book.

Only equivalence can lead to destruction or a final transcendence.
Only equivalence can lead to destruction or a final transcendence.

He kept turning until he came to the last page upon which anything was written.

Only equivalence can lead to destruction or a final transcendence.
Only equivalence can lead to destruction or a final transcendence.
Only equivalence can lead to destruction or a final transcendence.

"My Aunt Agatha's blue feather hat!" he exclaimed.

The next day, William Trounce complained of a thumping headache, Maneesh Krishnamurthy collapsed with malarial fever, and a messenger arrived in Ugogi. The latter had run all the way from Mzizima with a dispatch for Isabel from those Daughters of Al-Manat who'd remained behind at the fast-expanding Prussian settlement. His first words to her, in Kiswahili, and translated by Burton, were: "You will pay me very well, I should think, for I have run far and far and far!"

Burton assured him that he'd be generously rewarded.

The man closed his eyes and recounted the message in a singsong voice. He spoke in Arabic, though he obviously didn't understand the language and was merely recounting what he'd been told, parrot fashion. He said: "O Al-Manat, peace and mercy and blessings of Allah upon thee, and upon those who follow thy lead, and upon those who travel with thee. May he grant safety, speed, and good fortune to this messenger, who, regrettably, must deliver to thee bad tidings, for a great many Prussians continue to arrive in Mzizima and they are now too strong for us to fight without thy wise counsel. A force of perhaps a thousand has departed the camp and is travelling westward. We follow and are striking them at intervals, in the manner thou taught us, though we are far fewer in number. May Allah protect us and you and give us all strength to endure."

Burton instructed Saíd to issue the man with a *doti* of richly patterned cloth, a box of *sami-sami* beads, and three coils of brass wire. The messenger, much pleased, joined the villagers to rest, drink beer, swap news, and boast of his newfound wealth.

"It sounds like an invasion force," Isabel said to Burton. "What is Bismarck up to, sending so many troops to Africa?"

"Palmerston thinks he's trying to establish a German empire, and that he intends to use Africa's vast natural—and human—resources to fuel it."

"So the Prussians are here to stake a claim?"

"It would appear so."

"Then we must stop them."

"I don't see how we can. Besides which, that's not what we're here for."

"But surely this is a challenge to the British Empire, Richard? Is it not our duty to do something about it?"

"What do you suggest?"

"We fight!"

Burton held his hands out wide in a gesture of disbelief. "Look at us, Isabel! We're nothing but a ragtag expedition! Our clothes are half-rotted off us! We look positively skeletal! We're exhausted and ill!"

"Will Palmerston send troops?"

"I consider that highly probable."

"Then once your mission is done, Richard, I shall lead my women against the Prussians until the British Army arrives."

The king's agent blew out a breath and shook his head. "I can't stop you, of course. You're the most obstinate woman I've ever met. You infuriate me—and it's why I fell in love with you. Just don't take unnecessary risks, please."

"We shall do what we do best: hit them and run. Then wait, and, when they least expect it, we'll hit them again, and then we'll run again."

The expedition spent the remainder of the day resting, writing journal entries, checking equipment, and socialising with their generous hosts.

Before sun-up the following morning, much recovered, the travellers set forth across the Marenga M'khali, a stretch of desert that would take four days to traverse. The ground was hard and cracked, the scrub thorny, and the horizon lumpy with low, quivering, and blurring hills.

Close up, the terrain was a rusty-brown shade, strewn over with rocks and rubble and tufts of brittle white grass. As it receded into the distance, it grew paler, bleaching to a soft yellow that eventually blended hazily into the washed-out-blue sky, which deepened in colour overhead.

The sun was like fire upon their necks in the mornings, and blinded them in the afternoons.

Burton, Swinburne, and Trounce were mounted on mules. Sister Raghavendra and Miss Mayson were riding with the Daughters of Al-Manat. Krishnamurthy was being borne along on a litter.

Saíd bin Sálim and his eight Askaris kept the liberated slaves moving despite their inclination to laze until sundown. Burton by now considered his *ras kafilah* a marvel of efficiency and industriousness. Between Saíd and Sister Raghavendra, the expedition had progressed with a minimum of annoyances and illnesses.

Herbert Spencer limped along at the back of the column of men.

Algernon Swinburne had said nothing to anyone about what he'd seen in the clockwork man's book. He didn't know why he kept it quiet—he simply felt no need to raise the subject. At one point, on the third day, when they were climbing onto higher ground and passing huge blocks of weathered granite, he had a sudden urge to speak to Herbert about the *First Principles of Philosophy*, but when he'd approached him, he heard Pox—on the philosopher's head—mutter, "Sweet cheeks," and changed his mind. Herbert was the only individual the parakeet ever complimented, and for some reason, hearing the messenger bird was enough to make the poet change his mind. Swinburne dropped the subject. He knew it was wrong to do so; he knew it made no sense; but he dropped it anyway.

The expedition did not cross the desert alone. Antelope and buffalo, giraffe and rhinoceros, elephants and zebra, in herds and alone, they all plodded along wearily, making their way toward the nearest watering holes. Burton watched and envied them their uncomplicated instincts. He wished his own possessed such clarity, and wondered whether he'd made the right choice in accepting the king's commission.

Marry the bitch, Burton. Settle down. Become consul in Fernando Po, Brazil, Damascus, and wherever the fuck else they send you. Write your damned books!

Those had been the words of Spring Heeled Jack, the man from the future. The "bitch" referred to was Isabel Arundell, and the speech had been a clue to the life he would have led had history not changed—perhaps the life he was *meant* to lead. In rejecting it, it now appeared that he'd inadvertently placed himself at the centre of a maelstrom that would shape the future of the world.

Why must it rest on my shoulders?

He watched the animals moving through the heat.

A horrible sense of inevitability settled over him.

The long slog continued.

Eventually, the desert became a featureless grassy plain, which disappeared into a tough, tightly packed jungle, and beyond it they reached the village of Ziwa, where they were received with war cries and a shower of poison-tipped arrows.

Five porters were killed and three mules went down before Saíd managed, through much shouting, to communicate the fact that the long line of men was not an invading army but a peaceful safari.

The headman argued that all *muzungo mbáyá* came to kill and steal. "Go!" he hollered. "Turn around and go all the way back to your own lands and remain in them! This place is our home and if you try to cross it we shall kill you with our arrows and then we shall take our spears and use them to kill you a second time!"

One of the lead porters laid down the bundle of cloth he'd been carrying on his head and stepped forward. "Goha!" he cried. "Do you not recognise me? It is Kidogo, who was stolen from this village by slavers some days and days and days ago!"

The *p'hazi* moved his head left and right as he examined the man. "H'nn! Yes, you are the son of Maguru-Mafupi, who was the son of Kibuya, who had pain in his joints and was the son of a man whose name I cannot remember but he had big ears. So now you, who were taken from us, are the slave of these white devils?"

"No! It was the one named Tippu Tip who put me in chains, but these men came and set me free. They set all these others free, too. And now I have come home, and I see my mother!"

Before the *p'hazi* could react, a caterwauling arose from behind the gathered warriors and a woman shoved her way through them and ran to the porter, throwing herself upon him.

"It is Kidogo, my son!" she wailed, and gave forth a loud ululation, which was quickly taken up by all the women of the village.

Goha threw down his bow and jumped up and down on it in a fit of temper. He yelled at Kidogo: "See what noise you have caused by coming home after being stolen from us? Now the women will expect a feast and drumming and dancing and we will have to dress in our finest cottons! Is there no end to the troubles and inconveniences caused by the *muzungo mbáyá?*"

Burton stepped forward and spoke in the man's language: "Perhaps, O *p'hazi*, if we provided the food?"

"And alcohol?"

"Yes. We have beer and gin and—"

Swinburne, who understood nothing except the words "beer" and "gin," whispered urgently: "Don't give him the brandy!"

"—and gifts."

"You will pay *hongo?*"

"We will pay."

Goha scratched his stomach and looked at Burton with interest. He shouted: "Kidogo! Tell your mother to be quiet! I can't think with all her clucking and twittering!"

The liberated slave nodded and guided his parent into the village. The ululations quietened. The headman huddled into a group with his warriors and they murmured and argued and complained, with many a glance at the white men. After a few minutes, Goha turned back to Burton. He bent and picked up his bow.

"See," he said. "You have been here but a little time and already you have broken my bow, which I have treasured my entire life, and which I made just yesterday. You people have skin like ghosts and cause destruction and misery and problems wherever you put your feet."

"We shall replace your weapon."

"Whatever you give me will not be as good. Is it true that you eat your dead and use their bones to make the roofs on your huts?"

"No, that is not true."

"Is it true that *Uzungu*—the White Land—is far across the water and in it bright beads grow underground and the men have more wives even than I?"

"How many wives do you have?"

"Eight."

"No, that, also, is not true, though my land is far across the water."

"I meant five."

"It is still not true."

"And the beads?"

"They do not grow underground."

"Is it true that the flowers and plants obey your will?"

"They will not obey my people but there are white men from a different land who possess some such control. They are my enemy. Have you seen them?"

"Yes. They came at night and took our cattle for meat and killed two of our women for no reason except that they like killing. They were angry because their porters kept running away and they tried to take the men of this village to replace them but we prevented that from happening, for we are fierce warriors."

"How did you prevent it?"

"By running fast and hiding in the jungle. Sit and eat and sing and dance with us and I will tell you more of them after you have given me some beer and a better bow than this excellent one, which you broke."

In this long-winded manner, Burton was invited to set up camp at the village, and while his friends and the porters enjoyed what turned out to be fine hospitality, Burton sat in conference with Goha and the other elders and learned that the whole region was aware that two expeditions were travelling toward the interior, and that one of them did not respect the customs of the people, while the other one did.

Of Speke's expedition, he was informed that it was perhaps three times the size of his own and comprised mainly of Prussians, with just a few African guides and maybe seventy porters. There were eight of the plant vehicles with it, and these, just as Burton's harvestman had done on the first day of the safari, caused great fear wherever they were seen.

Despite this, Speke's people were in complete disarray.

Confident that he could forge ahead by brute force alone, Burton's former travelling companion had opted not to carry specie and was refusing to pay *hongo*. As a result, his path through East Africa, which had thus far followed a route parallel to and some fifty miles north of Burton's own, had been made extremely hazardous by villagers, who'd run ahead to warn of his approach. Traps and obstructions had been set: the thorns of bushes to either side of the trail were smeared with poison; sharp spines were pushed point-upward into the mud of countless *nullahs*; and arrows and spears were launched from the undergrowth.

As it struggled through this, Speke's column of men had become ever more ragged. His porters were not paid, like Burton's, but were slaves, and they took every opportunity to slip away, often carrying equipment with them. As for the Prussian soldiers, not being accompanied by a Sister of Noble Benevolence, they had succumbed again and again to fevers and infections.

Just as Burton had suspected, Speke's long head start had been eaten away, and, frustrated, the traitor had recently attempted to solve his problems by leaving the northern trail to join the southern one, which the king's agent was following. The question was: how far in front was he?

As usual, establishing a realistic sense of time was a hopeless endeavour. When asked how long ago Speke had passed, Burton received the reply: "Days and days and days and days and days and days."

"How many?"

"This—" And Goha stretched out his arms to indicate a distance.

It was impossible to understand what he meant, and despite Burton's experience, and no matter how many different ways he asked the question, he didn't receive a comprehensible answer.

Later, he said to Swinburne, "Time is not the same in Africa as it is in Europe. The people here have an entirely different conception of it."

"Perhaps they are rather more poetical," Swinburne replied.

"What do you mean?"

"Maybe they measure time not by the beat of a second or minute or hour, but by the intensity of their reactions to a thing. If they feel very disgruntled by Speke's expedition, that means it was here not long ago. If they feel mildly irritated, but they remember that they were more annoyed before, then a greater amount of time must have passed. And if they feel fine, but recall once being upset, then obviously the reason for it occurred long ago."

"I never considered it that way," Burton confessed. "I think you might be on to something."

"Not that it helps much," his assistant noted. "We still can't establish when Speke was here. How much easier it would be if old Goha could tell us, 'Five o'clock last Sunday afternoon!'" He looked puzzled, and continued, "I say, Richard! What's the confounded day, anyway? I haven't a giddy clue!"

Burton shrugged. "Nor have I. I've haven't noted the date in my journal since—" He paused, then stretched out his arms. "This long ago."

They left Ziwa, trudged across broad, rolling savannahs, and climbed onto the tableland of the Ugogo region. From here, they could see in the distance to their rear, crowned with mist and cut through by streaks of purple, the pale azure mountains of Usagara. In front, in the west, the terrain sank into a wide tract of brown bushland, dotted with grotesquely twisted calabash trees through which herds of elephants roamed, then rose to a range of rough hills. South and northward, verdure-crowned rocks thrust up from an uneven plain.

The villages they encountered, as they traversed this country, were inhabited by the Wagogo people, who, not having suffered as much the decimating attentions of slavers, demonstrated less timidity and a greater degree of curiosity. They turned out of their settlements in droves to watch the *wakongo*—the travellers—passing by, and cried out: "Wow! Wow! These must be the good men who are chasing the bad ones! Catch them, *Murungwana Sana* of Many Tongues, for they killed our cattle and chased us from our homes!"

However, while the people in general appeared to regard Burton's safari as a force bent on vengeance for the crimes committed by Speke's, the village elders with whom the explorer spoke proved rather more suspicious. "What will happen to us," they asked, "when your people take the land?"

To this question, Burton had no reply, but it caused him more and more to think of Palmerston.

They will be accorded the rights given to all of our citizens.

The explorer felt increasingly uneasy.

They stopped for a day at a settlement called Kifukuru, the first where the Kinyamwezi language was spoken, rather than Kiswahili.

Swinburne entertained its inhabitants with a poetry reading. They didn't understand a word of it, of course, but they laughed uproariously at his odd twitches and hops, his jerky gestures and exaggerated facial expressions, and, for some obscure reason, they attached themselves to a stanza from "A Marching Song," and demanded that he repeat it over and over:

Whither we know, and whence,
And dare not care wherethrough.
Desires that urge the sense,
Fears changing old with new,
Perils and pains beset the ways we press into.

Something about the first line of this caused the audience great merriment—perhaps its rhythm, or the sound of the words—and throughout the rest of the day, the diminutive poet was followed everywhere by hordes of children, who chanted, "Widdawenow! Anwense! Andah! Notkah! Wedru!"

"My hat, Richard!" he exclaimed. "I feel like the blessed Pied Piper of Hamelin! Aren't these little scamps marvellous, though?"

"They're the future, Algy!" Burton replied, and was instantly stricken by an incomprehensible sadness.

The next morning, the expedition took up its baggage and moved on, and Burton carried with him a growing depression and irritability. It was obvious to the others that he was lost in thought. He sat on his mule with his dark eyes smouldering, and his jaw, hidden behind a long bushy beard, set hard.

The rainy season had ended now and the plain, clothed in long ossifying grass, was already a mosaic of deep cracks. It took them two days to cross it, during which time Burton spoke little, then they chopped their way through a jungle and emerged into a ten-mile-wide clearing. Here, a powerful Wagogo chief named Magomba, who'd caused problems for Burton in '57, did so again by demanding that *hongo* be paid not just for the explorer's expedition but also for Speke's, which had forced its way with violence through the area. Reparation was also demanded for seven men killed by the Prussian forces.

Magomba was jet black in colour and his skin was crisscrossed with thousands of fine wrinkles. From the back and sides of his half-bald head, a few straggly corkscrews of grey hair depended; the whites of his eyes were actually yellow; and his filed teeth were brown. Brass rings dragged his earlobes down to his shoulders.

He squatted, all bones and joints, on a stool in his village's *bandani*, chewed constantly at a quid of tobacco, and expectorated without mercy.

Burton and Saíd bin Salím sat cross-legged before him.

"There was *ucháwi*—black magic," Magomba said. "And I will not have *ucháwi* in my land."

"What happened, O Magomba?" Burton asked. "Explain to me."

"One of thy people—"

"Not mine!" Burton interrupted. "They are the enemy of my people!"

"One of thy people took a man by the neck and shook him until he dropped to the ground. The next morning, the man had turned into a tree. We had to cut off his head and burn him. Now, listen carefully whilst I tell thee of the tax thou must pay in order to pass through my domain."

Magomba's demands were extortionate. Burton and Saíd spent the entire afternoon haggling, and eventually paid ten patterned cloths, six coils of brass wire, seven blue cottons, a pocket watch, twenty-five brass buttons, four boxes of beads, a quarter of tobacco, and a bottle of port.

"Good," Magomba said. "Now I shall order a calf killed so that thy people may eat. It is good to see thee again, *Murungwana Sana*. Ever hast thou been my favourite of all the foul devils that plague this unhappy land."

The next morning, as the expedition prepared for departure, the old chief confronted Burton and said, "I have had the blue cottons counted. There are only seven rolls."

"It is what we agreed."

"No. Thou promised nine."

"You art mistaken. We said seven, and seven it is."

"I will accept eight, providing thou swears an oath."

"What oath?"

"Thou must give thy word not to strike my land with drought, nor with disease, nor with misfortune."

"Eight it is, then. And I swear."

Burton's porters hacked a route through the bordering jungle. The explorer led his people out of the clearing and, eventually, up into the hills and onto the glaring white plains of the Kanyenye region. Though the going was easier here, the heat was hellish and pertinacious gadflies assailed them all. The Daughters of Al-Manat had trouble controlling their horses, which constantly shied under the onslaught, and the pack mules bucked and kicked and shed their loads. As the ground gradually rose and became rockier, the expedition also suffered from a want of water, having used up their supply more rapidly than usual.

They started across rolling, very uneven ground, congested with gorse-like bushes and deeply pocked with holes and crevices.

Burton's calf muscles kept cramping, causing him such agony that he could barely keep from screaming.

Swinburne was thrown from his steed and landed among long, viciously sharp thorns. He emerged with his clothes in tatters and his body scratched and bleeding from head to toe. He announced, with much satisfaction, that it would sting for the rest of the day.

William Trounce slipped on stony ground and twisted his ankle.

Maneesh Krishnamurthy, who'd recovered from his malarial attack, was stung in his right ear. It became infected, and his sense of balance was so badly disturbed that he suffered severe dizziness and spent a whole day vomiting until he lapsed into unconsciousness. Once again, he had to be carried on a stretcher.

Isabella Mayson was prostrated by a gastric complaint that caused embarrassingly unladylike symptoms.

Isabel Arundell's horse collapsed and died beneath her, sending her crashing to the ground where she lay stunned until they revived her with smelling salts and a dash of brandy.

Herbert Spencer declared that he was experiencing shooting pains along his limbs, which was impossible, of course, but they'd all concluded that his hypochondriacal tendencies really did cause him discomfort.

Sister Raghavendra developed ophthalmia and could see nothing but blurred shapes and moving colours.

Two of Saíd bin Sálim's Askaris collapsed with fever, and the *ras kafilah* himself was stricken with an indefinable ague.

Nearly half of the Daughters of Al-Manat were beset by illness and infections.

Two more horses and three mules died.

Pox the parakeet flew away and didn't return.

As the sun was setting, they arrived in the district of K'hok'ho and wearily set up camp on open ground. No sooner had they lit a fire than angry warriors from the two nearby villages surrounded them and demanded that they move on. No amount of arguing would convince them that the expedition was anything other than an invading force, like the one before it. Tempers flared. A warrior stepped forward and thrust a spear into William Trounce's upper arm. Burton fought to control the Askaris, who stepped forward with scimitars drawn. "Stand down! We are going!" he shouted. "Kwecha! Kwecha! Pakia! Hopa! Hopa! Collect! Pack! Set out!"

Hurriedly, they struck camp and picked their way across the moonlit ground with the warriors escorting them on either side, mocking and jeering and threatening.

Sister Raghavendra, by touch alone, bandaged Trounce's arm.

"I'll need to stitch the wound, William, but we'll have to wait until we're safely away from these ruffians. Are you in pain?"

"By Jove, Sadhvi! Between this and the ankle, I'm having a fine day of it! I feel absolutely splendid! In fact, I thought I might top things off by repeatedly banging my head against a rock! What do you think?"

"I think you'd better chew on this." She handed him a knob of a tobacco-like substance. "These herbs have strong pain-relieving properties."

"What do they taste like?"

"Chocolate."

Trounce threw the herbs into his mouth and started chewing. He gave a snort of appreciation. His ear whistled.

The warriors yelled a few final insults and withdrew.

Burton, at the front of the column, crested the brow of a hill, looked down onto a small plain, and saw the stars reflected in a number of ponds and small lakes.

"We'll rest there," he said. "And let's hope that water is fresh."

The division between the days became ever more nebulous and confusing.

Consciousness and unconsciousness merged into a single blur, for when they slept, they dreamt of passing terrain, and when they were awake, they were so often somnambulistic that they might well have been dreaming.

From K'hok'ho into the land of Uyanzi, from village to village, through an ugly and desiccated jungle and over baked earth; then into the sandy desert of Mgunda Mk'hali, where lines of elephants marched in stately fashion, trunk to tail, past petrified trees filled with waiting vultures.

Mdaburu to Jiwe la Mkoa; Jiwe la Mkoa to Kirurumo; Kirurumo to Mgongo Thembo; Mgongo Thembo to Tura.

Days and days and days.

This long.

As they approached Tura, Burton said to Swinburne, "I keep seeing animal carcasses."

"Funny," the poet murmured. "I keep seeing a pint of frothy English ale. Do you recall The Tremors in Battersea? I liked that tavern. We should go back there someday."

The two men were walking. So many of the freed slaves had left them now—gratefully returning to their home villages—that all the animals were required to help carry the supplies, and there were no more spare horses.

Burton looked down at his assistant. The roots of Swinburne's hair were bright scarlet. The rest of it was bleached an orangey straw colour all the way to its white tips. It fell in a thick mass to below his narrow, sloping shoulders. His skin had long ago gone from lobster red to a deep dark brown, which made his pale-green eyes more vivid than ever. He had a thin and

245

straggly beard. His clothes were hanging off him in ribbons and he was painfully thin and marked all over by bites and scratches.

"I'm sorry, Algy. I should never have put you through all this."

"Are you joking? I'm having the time of my life! By golly, in a poetical sense, this is where my roots are! Africa is *real*. It's *authentic*! It's *primal*! Africa is the very *essence* of poetry! I could happily live here forever! Besides—" he looked up at Burton, "—there is a matter of vengeance to be addressed."

After a pause, Burton replied, "In that, you may not have to wait much longer. The dead animals I've been seeing—I think they were killed by a bloodthirsty hunter of our acquaintance."

"Speke!"

"Yes."

They came to Tura, the easternmost settlement of Unyamwezi, the Land of the Moon. Burton remembered the village as being nestled amid low rolling hills and cultivated lands; that it was attractive to the eye and a balm to wearied spirits after so many days of monotonous aridity. But when his expedition emerged from the mouth of a valley and looked upon it, they saw a scene of appalling destruction. Most of Tura's dwellings had been burned to the ground, and corpses and body parts were strewn everywhere. There were only fifty-four survivors—women and children—many wounded, all of them dehydrated and starving. Sister Raghavendra and Isabella Mayson—both recovering from their afflictions—treated them as best they could; but two died within an hour of the expedition's arrival, and during the course of the following night they lost eight more.

The camp was set up, and Burton gathered those women whose injuries were slightest. For a while they refused to speak and flinched away from him, but his generosity with food and drink, plus the presence of so many women in his party, especially Isabel Arundell, whom they took to almost straight away, eventually quelled their fears, and they explained that the village had been ravaged by "many white devils accompanied by demons who sat inside plants." This terror had descended upon them without warning or mercy, had killed the men, and had made away with grain and cattle and other supplies.

The sun, Burton was informed, had risen two times since the attack.

He gathered his friends in the village's half-collapsed *bandani*.

"Speke and the Prussians have not respected the customs of Africa at all," he observed, "but this degree of savagery is new."

"What prompted it?" Isabel Arundell asked. "John is a schemer but not a barbarian."

"Count Zeppelin is behind this carnage, I'm sure," Swinburne opined.

"Aye, lad," Trounce muttered. "I agree. They went through this place like a plague of locusts. Looks to me as if they badly needed supplies and hadn't the patience or wherewithal to trade."

"We're about a week away from Kazeh," Burton said. "It's an Arabic town, a trading centre, and it marks the end of our eastward march. It's where we'll restock with food, hire new porters, and buy new animals, before heading north to the Ukerewe Lake and the Mountains of the Moon. Speke will be following the same route and no doubt intended to obtain fresh provisions there too, but perhaps he couldn't make it. I'd lay money on him having squandered all his supplies between Mzizima and here."

"So Tura bore the brunt of his ineptitude," Krishnamurthy growled.

Some of the Daughters of Al-Manat were patrolling the outskirts of the village. One of them now reported that a body of men were approaching from the west. They were carrying guns, in addition to the usual spears and bows.

Burton hurried over to where the women of Tura were sitting together and addressed them in their own language: "Men are coming, perhaps Wanyamwezi. If they've heard what has happened here, they will assume my people are responsible and they will attack us."

One of the women stood and said, "I will go to meet them. I will tell them of the white devils who killed our men and I will say that you are not the same sort of devil and that even though you are white you have been good to us."

"Thank you," Burton replied, somewhat ruefully.

As he'd predicted, the new arrivals were Wanyamwezi. They stamped into Tura—two hundred or so in number—and levelled their weapons at the strangers. They were mostly very young men and boys, though there were a few oldsters, too. All were armed with matchlock rifles; all bore patterned scars on their faces and chests; all frowned at Burton and his associates; and all bared their teeth, showing that their bottom front two incisors had been removed.

From among them, a man stepped forward. He was tall, gaunt, and angular, but powerfully built, with long wiry pigtails hanging from his head. There were rings in his nose and ears and a profusion of copper bangles on his wrists and ankles.

"I am Mtyela Kasanda," he said. "They call me Mirambo."

It meant *corpses*.

"I am Burton," the king's agent responded. "They call me *Murungwana Sana* of Many Tongues."

"Dost thou see mine eyes?" Mirambo asked.

"I do."

"They have looked upon thee and they have judged."

"And what did they find?"

Mirambo sneered. He checked that there was priming powder in the pan of his matchlock. He tested the sharpness of his spear with a fingertip. He examined his arrow points. He cast an eye over his warriors. "Mine eyes see that thou art *muzungo mbáyá*, and therefore bad."

"My people are the enemy of those who destroyed this village. We found the women injured, and we helped them."

"Did doing so darken thy skin?"

"No, it did not."

"Then thou art still *muzungo mbáyá*."

"That is true, but, nevertheless, we remain the enemy of those who did this deed." Burton held his hands open, palms upward. "We have come to help thee."

"I will not be friends with any *muzungo mbáyá*."

Burton sighed. "I have learned a proverb from thy people. It is this: *By the time the fool has learned the game, the players have dispersed.*"

Mirambo turned his head a little, chewed his lip, and regarded Burton from the corners of his eyes. He coughed and spat, then said, "I understand thy meaning. If I do not choose, I will have no say in the outcome."

"That is probably correct."

There was a sudden commotion among the gathered warriors and a small man pushed his way to the front of them. He was wearing a long white robe and a white skullcap, with a matchlock rifle slung over his shoulder and a machete affixed to his belt. At the sight of him, Burton felt a thrill of recognition.

"Wow! I know this scar-faced man, O Mirambo," the newcomer announced. "I have travelled far and far with him. He is ugly and white, it is true, but he is not as those who passed before. He is fierce and loyal and good, though filled with crazy thoughts. I speak only the truth."

The Wanyamwezi chief pondered this for a few moments, then said to the man: "Give me *pombe*, Sidi Bombay."

The small man took a goatskin flask from one of his companions and handed it to the chief. Mirambo drank from it then passed it to Burton, who did the same.

"Now," Mirambo said. "Tell me of our foe."

The season of implacable heat arrived, and each morning they struck camp at 4 a.m., walked for seven hours, then stopped and did their best to shelter from it. It meant slow progress, but Burton knew Speke wouldn't be able to move any faster.

Their first three days from Tura saw them trekking over cultivated plains. The sky was so bright it hurt their eyes, despite that they wore *keffiyehs* wrapped around their faces.

The Daughters of Al-Manat, now supplemented by the vengeance-bent women of Tura and their children, rode and walked to the right of the porters.

Mirambo and his men marched on the other side of the column, keeping their distance, holding their matchlocks at the ready and their heads at an aloof angle. Sidi Bombay, though, walked along next to Burton's mule, for he knew the explorer of old, and they were firm friends.

A one-time slave who'd been taken to India then emancipated upon his owner's death, Bombay spoke English, Hindustani, and a great many African languages and dialects. He'd been Burton's guide during the explorer's first expedition to the Lake Regions in '57, and had then accompanied Speke on his subsequent trek in '60. Burton now learned that he'd also accompanied Henry Morton Stanley, last year.

As they pushed on across a seemingly unchanging landscape, Bombay cast light on some of the mysteries surrounding the latter two expeditions.

Burton already knew that, after discovering the location of the African Eye of Nāga in '57 but failing to recover the jewel, Speke had returned to Africa with a young Technologist named James Grant. They'd flown toward Kazeh in kites dragged behind giant swans, but, en route, had lost the birds to lions. He now learned that when they'd arrived at the town on foot, they'd hired Bombay to guide them north to the Ukerewe Lake, then west to the Mountains of the Moon.

"Mr. Speke, he led us into a narrow place of rocks. Wow! We were attacked by Chwezi warriors."

"Impossible, Bombay!" Burton exclaimed. "The Chwezi people are spoken of all over East Africa and all agree that they are long extinct. Their legendary empire died out in the sixteenth century."

"But perhaps no one has told them, for some have forgotten to die, and live in hidden places. They guard the Temple of the Eye."

"A temple? Did you see it?"

"No, Mr. Burton. It is under the ground, and I chose not to go there, for I met my fourth wife in an ill-lit hut and I have never since forgotten that bad things happen in darkness. So I remained with the porters and we held back the Chwezi with our guns while Mr. Speke and Mr. Grant went on alone. Only Mr. Speke came back, and when he did—wow!—he was like a man taken by a witch, for he was very crazy, even for a white man, and we fled with him out of the mountains and all the way back to Zanzibar. On the way, he became a little like he was before, but he was not the same. I think what he saw under the ground must have been very bad."

Stanley's expedition had also ended in disaster. The American newspaper reporter's team—five men from the Royal Geographical Society—had employed porters to carry rotorchairs from Zanzibar to Kazeh, then flew them north to locate the source of the Nile. They'd returned a few days later, on foot. Their flying machines had stopped working.

Bombay, who at that time was still living in Kazeh, was commissioned as a guide. He led Stanley to the Ukerewe, and the expedition started to circumnavigate it in a clockwise direction. But at the westernmost shore, Stanley became distracted by the sight of the far-off mountains and decided to explore them.

"I told him no, it is a bad place," Bombay said, "but—wow!—he was like a lion that has the musk of a gazelle in its nostrils and can think of nothing else. I was frightened to go there again, so I ran away, and he and his people went without me. They have not been seen again. This proves that I am a very good guide."

"How so?"

"Because I was right."

The safari trudged on.

The cultivated lands had fallen behind them. Now there was nothing but shallow, dry, rippling hills that went on and on and on.

"The same!" Swinburne wailed, throwing his arms out to embrace the wide vista. "The same! The same! Won't it ever change? Are we not moving at all?"

During the nights, swarms of pismire ants crawled out of the ground and set upon the camp. They chewed through tent ropes, infested the food supplies, shredded clothes, and inflicted bites that felt like branding irons.

On the fourth day, the safari left the region behind with heartfelt expressions of relief and entered the Kigwa Forest, a wide strip of gum trees and mimosas spread over uneven, sloping land. The boles were widely spaced but the sparse canopy nevertheless provided a little shade and for the first time in many weeks they weren't bothered by mosquitoes or flies.

They camped among the trees, dappled by shafts of pollen-thick light, with butterflies flitting around them and birds whistling and gabbling overhead. The scent of herbs filled their nostrils.

"We've travelled almost six hundred miles," Burton said. He was sitting on a stool in front of the main Rowtie, massaging his left calf, which felt bruised after his bout of cramps. Trounce was on a chair at a folding table.

The Scotland Yard man's beard reached halfway to his chest, and he'd had enough of it. He was attempting to crop it close to his chin with a pair of blunt scissors. "But how long has it taken us?" he asked.

"That's the question. It took me a hundred and thirty-four days to reach this spot during my previous expedition. I feel we've been considerably faster but I couldn't tell you by how much. It's very peculiar. All of us appear to have lost track of time. Do you want a hand with that, William? You appear to be struggling."

"If you wouldn't mind," the other man answered. "It's my bloody arm. The spear wound still hurts like blazes when I move it. So are you suggesting that something is having an adverse influence on us?"

Trounce stuck out his chin. Burton stood, took the scissors, and attacked his friend's facial hair.

"Perhaps. But the Mountains of the Moon are still at least two hundred miles away, so if the Eye of Nāga is responsible, then its emanations are reaching a damned long way."

"If it didn't affect your timekeeping back in fifty-seven," Trounce said, "then why would it be doing so now?"

"The only explanation I can think of is that there's an intelligence directing it."

"Which knows we're here? I don't like the sound of that."

"Nor I."

A few minutes later, Burton finished his hacking and held up a small round mirror so Trounce could examine the results.

"By Jove!" the detective exclaimed. "It's made no difference at all! I still look like a confounded Robinson Crusoe!"

Burton smiled, turned away, and watched as the Daughters of Al-Manat rolled out their prayer mats and began to praise Allah. He looked at Mirambo's warriors, sitting in a group on small portable stools, sharpening their weapons and cleaning their matchlocks. He observed Saíd redistributing the baggage among the remaining porters. He examined the horses and mules and saw that many were covered in tsetse bites. They wouldn't survive much longer.

A commotion over to his left attracted his attention. It was Swinburne, leaping around like a possessed forest sprite.

"Look! Look!" the poet cried, jabbing his finger in Herbert Spencer's direction.

Burton turned his eyes toward the robe-wrapped clockwork philosopher and saw that he was approaching with Isabella Mayson at his side. He had a colourful parakeet on each shoulder.

"Pox is back!" Swinburne cheered.

"Slippery sewer-sniffer!" Pox cawed.

"And he's been courting!"

"*She's* been courting," Isabella corrected.

Swinburne gave a screech. "What? What? You mean Pox is—is—?"

"Is a girl, yes. She always has been. I believe I pointed that out when I first introduced you to her."

Swinburne looked flummoxed. "I—I—I suppose the bad language caused me to assume the reverse."

"Danglies-clutcher!" Pox added.

The other bird let loose a piercing squawk.

"Parakeets usually mate for life," Isabella told Burton, "so perhaps you'd like to give a name to the new member of your family."

The king's agent groaned. "You don't mean to say I'll have to accommodate two of the beastly things when we return to London?"

Spencer piped, "At least only one of 'em will insult you, Boss."

"Sheep-squeezing degenerate!" Pox crowed.

"Monkey cuddler!" her mate added.

"Oh no!" Burton moaned.

"My mistake," Spencer admitted.

"Hah!" Swinburne cried out. "Malady is learning!"

They all looked at him.

"It's the perfect name," he said. "Don't you think Pox and Malady sound like they belong together?"

There was a pause, then William Trounce threw his head back and let loose a roar of laughter. "On the button, Algernon!" he guffawed. "On the blessed button! Oh my word! What more fitting remembrance of this endeavour could you have, Richard, than to leave Africa with a Pox and a Malady? Ha ha ha!"

Burton shook his head despairingly.

"Cheer up!" Swinburne grinned. "If I remember rightly, when you were a young soldier returning from India and its whorehouses, you brought back similar!"

Trounce doubled over and bellowed his mirth.

"Algy, there are ladies present," Burton said, glowering at his assistant.

Isabella made a dismissive gesture. "I rather think Africa has stripped me of all the social niceties, Richard. Try as any of you might, you'll not induce a fit of moral outrage in me!"

"I say! Could we make an attempt anyway?" Swinburne enthused.

"Certainly not."

Krishnamurthy came running over. "Shhh!" he urged. "Stop making such a confounded racket! Listen!"

They did so, and heard gunfire snapping and popping faintly in the far distance.

"Speke," Swinburne whispered.

"How far?" Trounce asked.

"It's difficult to say," Burton responded, "but we'd better stay on our toes."

The next morning, they proceeded with caution and with four Wanyamwezi scouting a little way ahead. Gunfire continued to crackle faintly from the west. It sounded like a battle was being fought. Burton unpacked all the spare rifles and distributed them among Mirambo's warriors, replacing the ancient matchlocks. He and the rest of his expedition kept their own guns cleaned, oiled, and loaded.

The forest was fairly easy going, its canopy high and the undergrowth light. Nevertheless, it required two more marches to traverse. When they finally emerged from it, they found themselves in a long valley through which sweet water bubbled in a wide stream. The hills to either side were swathed in bright-yellow grain, blazing so brightly that the travellers were forced to walk through it with eyes slitted, and the heat was so ferocious that Herbert Spencer compared this part of their trek to "walkin' on the surface of the bloomin' sun itself!"

The terrain gradually opened onto a flat plain, empty but for stunted trees. On the horizon ahead, low forested hills could be seen, though they folded and jumped in the distorting atmosphere. From the other side of them, the noise of battle raged on. The sound was carrying a long way.

They walked and walked and yet felt as if they made no progress.

"I can't judge the distance," Trounce muttered. "Those hills are like the mirages we saw back in Arabia. One minute they spring up right in front of us, the next they're not there at all."

"They're fairly close," Burton advised.

"And so is one heck of a scrap by the sound of it!"

"Wow! It is from Kazeh!" Sidi Bombay noted.

Burton walked back along the line of porters and mules to where Swinburne was striding along. The poet had a rifle slung across his shoulder and was holding an umbrella over his head.

"I'm going to gallop ahead to take a peek over those hills, Algy. Will you join me? Can you bear it during the hottest part of the day?"

"Rather! Anything to break the monotony of this flatland."

They stopped and waited for Isabel Arundell, who was riding near the middle of the column, to catch them up.

"I need two of your fittest horses," Burton said as she drew abreast of them. "Algy and I are going to reconnoitre."

"Very well, but I'm coming with you. If we're joining a battle, I want to see for myself how best to deploy my women."

"Very well."

Mounts were selected, supplies were packed into saddlebags, and the threesome rode back to the head of the safari.

Burton took the field glasses from Trounce and informed him of their intentions. "You're in charge while we're gone. Keep going until the heat gets too much. You'll not make Kazeh in a single march, or even the base of the hills, so stop when you must but don't erect the tents. Get what rest you can."

They kicked their heels into the sides of their mounts and raced away, leaving a cloud of dust rolling in their wake.

It took them an hour to catch up with one of Mirambo's scouts. They stopped to greet him and offer water but he ignored them, as if by doing so he could make the *muzungo mbáyá* cease to exist.

The entire afternoon was spent pushing the horses to their limits until, with the sun swelling and melting in front of their eyes, they arrived at the edge of the plain and threw themselves down beside a narrow stream. They drank deeply and washed the dust from their faces, splashed their steeds to cool them, then left them reined to trees but with enough slack to be able to reach the water.

Gunfire stammered and echoed around them.

"They've been fighting for three days, at least," Isabel noted.

"We'll take a look at the combatants presently," Burton said. "First, eat, rest, and attend to your weapons."

This was duly done, and slightly under an hour later they climbed the hill, passing through the trees, descended the other side, scrambled up the next slope, and crawled onto its summit. They looked out over the twilit plain on the other side. The sun had just set and the western horizon was blood-red, the sky above it deep purple and flecked with bright stars.

The land beneath was considerably more verdant than the ground they'd just crossed; large tracts had obviously been irrigated; there were grain fields and many trees, the latter casting very long shadows.

A little to the north, a monolithic verdure-topped outcrop of rock dominated the otherwise flat landscape, and just to the south of it, right in front of them, there was a small town, little more than a wide scattering of wooden houses and shacks, with a few larger residences at its centre.

Lights flashed all along its eastern and northern borders and the noise of gunfire punctured the African night.

Burton whispered, "The Prussians have Kazeh under siege!"

CHAPTER 9

THE PARTING OF WAYS

"We do not see things as they are. We see them as we are."
—THE TALMUD

The plant was roughly the shape of a boat. It moved on thick white roots that grew in tangled bunches beneath its squat, flattened, and elongated stem. From this, ten white flowers grew in pairs, aligned in a row. Their petals were curled around the men who sat in them, forming extremely comfortable seats. Sir Richard Francis Burton was in one of the middle blooms. Generalmajor Paul Emil von Lettow-Vorbeck was sitting beside him. *Schutztruppen* occupied the others. The driver's head was pierced just above the ears by thorny tendrils through which he controlled the conveyance. The soldier beside him was positioned behind a seedpod, which, to Burton, looked exactly like a mounted gun. From the rear of the vehicle, three long leaves curved upward and forward like a canopy, protecting the passengers from the sun.

It was a bizarre conveyance. It was also a very fast one.

They'd left Stalag IV at Ugogi yesterday and were travelling along a well-defined trail—almost a road—in a westerly direction.

As the landscape unfolded around them, another unfolded inside Burton. His lost memories were returning, and each one inserted itself into his conscious mind with a violent stab that made his eyes water and caused a curious sensation in his sinuses, as if he'd accidentally snorted gunpowder instead of snuff.

The vehicle scuttled over the Marenga M'khali desert, and he recognised it. A grassy plain, a jungle, and rolling savannahs—he'd seen them all before. He was familiar with every hill, every *nullah*. He'd walked this route.

He remembered his companions and felt the hollow grief of untimely deaths. He knew who Al-Manat had been.

Isabel. Whatever became of you?

As if reading his thoughts, Lettow-Vorbeck said, "This road, it is built on the old trail that you followed so many years ago, *ja?*"

"Yes, I think so."

"And the other trail, the one parallel to it, to the north, that is now our Tanganyika Railway Line, which the Greater German Empire employs to bring civilisation to Africa, and which your people attack and sabotage with such tedious frequency."

Burton shrugged. He was sick of this war. He'd had more than enough of the twentieth century.

The plant raced across dusty ground and climbed into the Ugogo region.

"Nearly two hundred miles westward," the generalmajor informed him, "then we shall steer north to avoid Tabora. An inconvenience, but one that we'll not have to put up with for much longer."

"The 'final solution' you spoke of before?"

"*Ja.* It is on its way, even now, Herr Burton. We have a great flying ship, the *L.59 Zeppelin*, following inland the river that so obsesses you. I speak of the Nile, of course."

Another missing shard of Burton's memory slammed into place, causing him to catch his breath and stifle a groan.

Lettow-Vorbeck continued, "The name *Zeppelin* is a very suitable one for *das Afrika Schiff*, I think, for it is widely held that a Zeppelin was present at the start of the war, and now a Zeppelin will be present at its end!"

The generalmajor suddenly frowned and peered inquisitively at his prisoner. "*Ja, ja,*" he said, thoughtfully. "You, also, were in Africa when all this began. Perhaps you met the Ferdinand Graf von Zeppelin of whom I speak? Maybe you can enlighten our historians and tell us how and where he died, for this is a great mystery."

Burton shook his head. "No, sir, I didn't and I cannot."

"Hmm, so you say, *aber ich denke, dass Sie mehr wissen. Richtig?*"

"No. I know nothing more."

The road bisected a rolling plain then ran through a chaotic jungle that had been burned back from the thoroughfare and was held at bay by tall wire fences.

Lettow-Vorbeck pointed. "You see there, the *unkontrollierbare Anlagen!*"

The "uncontrollable plants" were lurchers. There were many hundreds of them writhing against the barrier.

"We will see more as we approach the Lake Regions, for they are much more numerous near the *Blutdschungel*. What a nuisance they are!"

The hot air blew against Burton's face as the vehicle raced along, then the sun set and he fell asleep. When he awoke, it was early morning, and they were leaving the Uyanzi region and entering another blistering desert.

He stretched and yawned and said, "Generalmajor, where is all the wildlife? I haven't seen an elephant for years!"

"Elephants are extinct, *mein Freund*. As for the other creatures, our Eugenicists have adapted a great many for frontline warfare, and the rest have sought refuge in less battle-torn areas of the country; the South, primarily, where you British have no presence and where civilisation prospers in harmony with nature."

"No presence? South Africa was part of the British Empire in my day."

"That is so, and the Boers and the Zulus were not happy about it. My people offered them full independent rule, and, with our military assistance, they overthrew you. It took less than a year to drive the British out. After that, it was simply a case of establishing strong trade and industrial relations, and, before many years had passed, the South was very willingly incorporated into the Greater German Empire."

They soon left the desert and the road began to snake between small domed hills, finally emerging from a valley into a wide basin. The ground was torn up and dried into grotesque configurations; the trees were nothing but stumps; burned wreckage was strewn about; but there was something in this old battlefield that Burton recognised—its contours told him that this was where the village of Tura had stood. There was no sign of the settlement.

The driver shouted something.

"Ah," Lettow-Vorbeck said. "Now we leave the road and travel north. Later we shall go west again. You are hungry?"

"Yes."

The generalmajor snapped an order and the man sitting in front of Burton lifted a hamper onto his lap, opened it, and started to pass back packets of sliced meat, a loaf of bread, fruit, and other comestibles. With a shock, Burton noticed that the soldier's face was covered with short bristly fur and that his jaws extended forward into a blunt muzzle. His mouth was stretched into a permanent and nasty smile. A hyena.

They sped out of the hills onto a wide expanse of flatland broken only by a long ridge that ran along to the north of them.

The sun was high in the sky. The scenery around them jiggled in and out of focus as if struggling to maintain its reality.

"How will the *L.59 Zeppelin* destroy Tabora?" Burton asked.

Lettow-Vorbeck gave a peal of laughter and slapped his thigh. "Hah! I was wondering how long it would take before you asked me that!"

"I assumed you'd inform me that it's top secret."

"So *warum bitten Sie jetzt?*"

"Why do I ask now? Because this journey is interminable, Generalmajor, and I'm bored. Besides, it occurs to me that since I'm your prisoner, and I don't even know where Tabora is, and the attack is imminent, there can be little harm in you telling me."

"*Ja, das ist zutreffend.* Very well. In forty-eight hours, the *L.59 Zeppelin* will drop an A-Bomb on the city."

"And what is that?"

"You are aware of the A-Spores, *ja?*"

"An obscene weapon."

"Quite so. Quite so. But very effective. The bomb will deliver, from a very high altitude, a concentrated dose of the spores to the entire city. The Destroying Angel mushroom is among the most toxic species of fungus in the world, Herr Burton. Its spores kill instantly when they are breathed, but they are easily resisted with a gas mask. Not so the ones in the bomb, for they have been specially bred to such microscopic size that they will penetrate the pores of a person's skin. No one will escape."

"Barbaric!"

"Hardly so. It is a very sophisticated weapon."

"And still you claim the Greater German Empire is a superior civilisation?"

"It is you British who have driven us to such extremes."

"I hardly think that—"

The plant suddenly lurched to the left and the driver screamed: "*Gott im Himmel! Was ist das? Was ist das?*"

Burton looked to the right. The most incredible machine he'd ever seen was mounting the ridge. It was completely spherical, a gigantic metal ball about two hundred feet in diameter and painted a dark jungle green. A wide studded track was spinning at high speed vertically around it, providing the motive force. Burton guessed that the same gyroscopic technology that kept penny-farthings upright in his time was here employed to prevent the sphere from rolling to its left or right.

Four long multi-jointed arms extended from the sides of it. The upper pair ended in lobster-like claws, the lower in spinning circular saw blades. These were obviously used to tear through whatever vegetation couldn't be simply rolled over.

Three rows of portholes and cannon ports ran horizontally around the orb, and four curved chimneys pumped steam into the air from just below its apex.

A puff of smoke erupted from its hull. A loud bang followed, and another, even louder, as an explosion threw up the earth ahead of the German transport.

"Warning shot!" Burton shouted. "You have to stop! You'll never outrun it!"

"Halt! Halt!" Lettow-Vorbeck yelled.

The plant jerked to a standstill. The generalmajor stood, drew his pistol, pushed the barrel into the side of Burton's head, and waited as the sphere drew closer.

"I am sorry, Herr Burton, I will kill you rather than allow you back into British hands, but let us first see what they have to say."

There was a hard thud.

Lettow-Vorbeck looked down at the hole that had just appeared in the middle of his chest and muttered, "*Himmelherrgott!* Just that?"

He collapsed backward out of the plant.

Thud. Thud. Thud.

One after the other, in quick succession, the *Schutztruppen* slumped in their seats.

The rolling sphere drew to a stop, casting its shadow over the German vehicle. Burton watched as a thin wedge opened from it, angling down to form a sloping platform with a door at the top. There was a figure framed in the portal.

"Don't just sit there, you chump!" Bertie Wells called. "Come aboard!"

It was named the SS *Britannia*, and was captained by General Aitken himself—the director of all British military operations in East Africa—whom Burton remembered from the bombing of Dar es Salaam back in 1914.

"It's good to see you again, Bertie!" the famous explorer enthused as Wells and three British Tommies led him through the ship toward the bridge. "What happened to you? And how did you end up aboard this behemoth?"

"Adventures and perils too numerous to recount happened to me, Richard, but eventually I made my way to Tabora like everyone else. Practically every free Britisher in Africa—perhaps in the entire world—is there now."

"Bismillah!" Burton swore, grabbing at his friend's arm. "Praise to Allah that you rescued me now and not two minutes earlier!"

"What do you mean?"

"First, answer me this: how were my captors shot with that kind of precision at such a distance? I've never seen anything like it!"

"Marksmen with the new Lee-Enfield sniper rifles. A remarkable weapon—the most accurate long-range rifle ever manufactured."

"And these marksmen, would they have recognised the men they were shooting?"

"As Germans? Of course! The uniform is unmistakable."

They passed through a room lined with gun racks then rounded a corner into a corridor along which many men were moving.

"You should have examined the bodies, Bertie, instead of just leaving them there."

"Why so?"

"Because one of them was Generalmajor Paul Emil von Lettow-Vorbeck."

Wells stumbled to a halt, his mouth hanging open, eyes wide. His three companions stopped, too, but instinctively retreated a few paces, displaying a typically British sensitivity to Wells and Burton's need for a moment of privacy. Nevertheless, having heard the pronouncement, they gaped.

"Wha—what?" Wells stuttered, then his voice rose to a squeal: "We just killed Lettow-Vorbeck? We killed him? Are you sure?"

"He was holding a pistol to my head when he took a bullet through the heart."

Wells smacked a fist into his palm and let loose a whoop of triumph. "Bloody hell! This could change everything!"

"No, Bertie, it's too late."

"Too late? What do you mean, it's too late?"

Very quietly, Burton said: "In forty-eight hours, a German flying ship is going to drop a bomb on Tabora."

"That's nothing new. The plants fly over, we shoot 'em down."

"This one will be at a high altitude, and it's carrying an A-Bomb."

"A what?"

In a whisper, Burton explained, and as he did so, his friend's burn-scarred and sun-browned face turned white. Wells looked to the right and left, gestured to the three guards, indicating that they should wait, then pulled Burton back along the passage and into the gun room. He spoke quietly and urgently: "We have to tell Aitken, but don't give away too much about yourself. Keep your true identity under wraps, for starters. The situation is complicated, and there's no time to fill you in right now. Suffice to say, your impossible presence in Africa has been detected. Colonel Crowley himself sent us to rescue you—"

"Your so-called wizard of wizards?"

"Yes. Apparently he's been aware of an anomaly on the continent since

1914 and has been trying to identify it ever since. He finally traced it to the Ugogi Stalag, then homed in on you as you were being transported. He sent the *Britannia* to intercept the vehicle and retrieve you."

"But he doesn't know who I am?"

One of the Tommies appeared in the doorway, cleared his throat, and jerked his head to suggest that they should move on. Wells gave a slight nod. He guided Burton back into the corridor and they followed a few steps behind the three soldiers. They came to a staircase and started up it.

"All Crowley knows is that you don't belong in 1918," Wells whispered. "I think, through you, he's hoping to unlock the secrets of time travel."

"Lettow-Vorbeck had the same idea."

"Listen, this is important. My old editor, the man who used to run the *Tabora Times* before it folded, needs to see you. I don't know the full story, but there are moves being made, and we can't allow you to fall under the wizard's spell."

"What does that mean?"

"Crowley is a tremendously powerful mesmerist. Once pierced by those fiendish eyes of his, you'll have no willpower of your own."

"I'm no mean mesmerist myself," Burton pointed out.

Wells grunted. "I remember reading that. You're no match for our chief medium, though. But my editor has connections. He pulled a few strings and arranged that these men—" he gestured toward the three soldiers, "—and myself be aboard the *Britannia*. We're going to kidnap you."

"Kidnap?"

They reached the top of the stairs and started down a short passage.

"Just trust me, Richard."

The Tommies stopped at a door. One of them opened it, and Wells led Burton through onto the bridge.

The explorer found himself in a chamber filled with consoles and levers, wheels, pipes, and gauges. There were twelve crewmembers at various stations, but Burton's attention immediately centred on a tall man standing before a wide curved window.

"Private Frank Baker, sir," Wells announced.

The man turned. He was slim, with sad eyes, unevenly arranged features, and a clipped moustache, wearing a dark uniform with a double row of silver buttons and a peaked cap. He looked Burton up and down.

"You've attracted the attention of men in high places, Baker," he said. His voice was sharp and precise, with a nasal twang. "Why?"

Burton saluted. He staggered.

"It's all right," Aitken said. "Steady yourself. We're going over some hills."

"I didn't realise we were moving," Burton answered.

"The only time you'll feel it is on rough terrain, and even then not much. It's like being on an ocean liner. Answer the question."

"I honestly haven't the vaguest idea why there's any interest in me at all, sir. I've been in a POW camp for two years."

"And before that?"

"Civilian Observer Corps at Dar es Salaam and Tanga, then a guerrilla fighter until I was captured at Dut'humi."

"Where were they taking you?"

"To the Lake Regions, but they didn't tell me why."

"Sir," Wells interjected. "Apparently one of the men we just shot dead was Lettow-Vorbeck."

Burton watched as Aitken's Adam's apple bobbed reflexively. All the crew members turned and looked at the general. He cleared his throat, glared at them, and snapped, "Attend your stations!"

"There's something else, sir," Wells added. "I think you might prefer to hear it in private."

Aitken gazed at the little war correspondent for a moment, gave a brusque nod, then turned away and issued a sequence of orders to the bridge crew concerning the velocity and course of the ship. He returned his attention to Burton and Wells, jabbed a finger at them, and said, "You and you—follow me."

They did so, trailing after him back out into the corridor and through a door into the captain's office. Aitken positioned himself behind a desk but remained standing with his hands held behind his back.

"What do you have to tell me, Wells?"

"I think it best that Baker explains, sir."

"I don't give two bloody hoots who does the talking, just get on with it!"

Speaking slowly and clearly, Burton told him about Lettow-Vorbeck's A-Bomb.

Moments later, General Aitken collapsed into his chair.

Burton was confined to a cabin with Bertie Wells as his guard. He'd washed, thrown away his prison uniform, and dressed in clean, tick-free battle fatigues. A cup of tea and a plate of sandwiches had been provided.

"They've radioed ahead," Wells told him. "And so have I."

"And the city's being evacuated?"

"Evacuated? To where? There's no place to go. Tabora has been under siege for half a century, and all the rest of Africa is under German control. My guess is they'll try to get as many people as possible into underground bunkers. Whether that'll save them or not remains to be seen. If the spore cloud is dense enough, I don't suppose there'll be anywhere safe."

"Yet we're going back?"

"To rescue the top brass."

"And take them to—?"

"Your guess is as good as mine. I suppose it's possible there's another British enclave somewhere, a place only the bigwigs know about. Or maybe we'll head into one of Africa's wildernesses and lay low while Crowley experiments on you."

"I don't like the sound of that." Burton took a bite out of a sandwich and frowned thoughtfully while he chewed and swallowed. "Who did you radio?"

"I sent a coded message to my editor, told him about the A-Bomb."

"Will he be able to get to safety?"

"Probably not. As I say, the city is surrounded."

"Then how do we get in? How does the *Britannia* come and go?"

"We manage to keep a passage—we call it Hell's Run—open through the besieging German forces to the east of the city. The most ghastly fighting occurs along its borders, but Crowley and our mediums focus their efforts there and have so far prevented the Germans from closing the route."

A siren started to blare.

"That's the call to battle stations!"

The door opened and an Askari stepped in. "You're both ordered to the bridge," he said. "Tabora just radioed a message that's put the wind up Aitken. We're approaching the city now."

"What message?" Wells asked as they followed the African out of the room.

"I don't know the details, Lieutenant."

They passed along corridors and up stairs, with men rushing around them and the siren howling continuously. The moment they entered the bridge, Aitken rounded on Burton and snapped: "Baker, did Lettow-Vorbeck tell you anything about lurchers? Have the Germans regained control of them?"

"He pointed out a crowd of the plants," Burton replied, "and said they're most numerous up near the Blood Jungle, but control? No, quite the opposite."

"Well, that's damned strange. Tabora reports that thousands of them are approaching the city from the north."

Burton and Wells looked at each other. The explorer shook his head and shrugged, baffled.

"We're currently racing straight down the middle of Hell's Run, well away from German peashooters," Aitken said. "When was the last time you were here, Baker?"

"I've never been to Tabora, sir."

"You haven't? Well, take a peek out of the window. We're almost there."

Burton and Wells stepped over to the glass and looked out across the African landscape. The *Britannia* was travelling at a tremendous speed over flat ground. To the north and south of her, black clouds humped up into the blue sky. Lightning flickered inside them. Puffs of smoke rose from the ground beneath. There were flashes. Tiny dots could be seen flying through the air.

"Those are the edges of Hell's Run," Wells murmured. "As you can see, the Hun weathermen are at work. The storms are more or less constant, as is the fighting beneath them. Tabora is behind the hills you see ahead of us."

As he examined the terrain, Burton was overcome by a sense of déjà vu. He struggled for breath and clutched at Wells's arm.

The *Britannia* shot up a slope, over the crest of a hill, sank into the valley beyond, navigated up the next slope, and reached the second summit. Burton saw a wide plain stretched out below. Much of it was obscured by a blanket of dirty steam, which was particularly dark and opaque straight ahead, where, from out of the pall, there rose a tall rock topped with green vegetation.

"Kazeh!" Burton croaked. "Tabora is Kazeh!"

"Kazeh is under siege!"

Sir Richard Francis Burton, Algernon Swinburne, and Isabel Arundell had ridden back through the night to where Trounce and the expedition were bivouacked. All three of them were coated with dust and thoroughly exhausted, but there was no time to rest.

Burton fired his rifle into the air to rouse the camp and yelled: "Hopa! Hopa! Pakia!"

Trounce responded to the announcement with: "By the Prussians? Are there that many of them?"

"There's enough! We have to get moving! If they take the town, we won't be able to resupply for the next leg of the safari."

"But what the blazes are they up to?"

"It's the key to central East Africa, William. Whoever controls Kazeh controls the region all the way from Lake Tanganyika to Zanzibar, and up to the Mountains of the Moon. My guess is they mean to drive the Arabs out and make of it a Prussian base of operations."

Burton ordered Saíd bin Sálim to have the porters take up their loads. Mirambo silently appeared beside him and asked, "Will the coming day be that in which we fight?"

"Yes. I bid thee prepare thy warriors, O Mirambo."

"We are always prepared, *muzungo mbáyá*. It is wise to be so when devils such as thee walk the land."

The African stalked away.

Krishnamurthy, Spencer, Isabella Mayson, Sister Raghavendra, and Sidi Bombay gathered around the king's agent. He described to them the scene he'd witnessed.

Krishnamurthy asked, "Can we get into the town from the west?"

"Yes," Burton replied. "If we follow the hills south, remaining on this side of them, then cross when—"

"No. We can't enter the town at all," Isabel Arundell interrupted.

They all looked at her, surprised.

"It would be suicidal. I have a hundred and twenty fighters and another ninety or so on the way. Mirambo has two hundred boys. The Prussians already greatly outnumber us and there are a thousand more fast approaching. If we're in the town when they arrive, we'll be pinned down and we'll likely never get out again."

Burton nodded thoughtfully. "You're the expert in guerrilla tactics," he said, "and I'll bow to your expertise. What do you recommend?"

Isabel positioned herself directly in front of him and placed her hands on his shoulders. "The king made you his agent, Dick, and you have your orders. What is the distance from here to the Mountains of the Moon?"

"Something under two hundred miles."

"Then go. Forget about resupplying in the town. You and your people take two horses each and the bare essentials in supplies. No porters. Nothing but what you can carry. Travel as fast as you can. It's a race, remember? I have no doubt that John Speke is already on his way."

"And you?" Burton asked.

"Mirambo and I will lead our forces against the Prussians."

William Trounce interjected: "But why, Isabel? If we're going to bypass the town, why risk yourselves in battle at all?"

Isabel stepped back and pulled the *keffiyeh* from her head. The sickle moon had just risen over the horizon and its pale light illuminated her long blonde hair.

"Because despite these robes, I'm British, William. If what we saw at Mzizima, and what we are witnessing here at Kazeh, are the first skirmishes in a clash of empires, then it's my duty to defend that to which I belong—

besides which, if we don't keep the Prussians occupied here, they'll be able to rapidly establish outposts all the way to the Mountains of the Moon, making it almost impossible for you to get there."

For a long moment, no one spoke.

Isabella Mayson cleared her throat. "Richard," she said, "if you don't mind, I think I would like to stay and join the Daughters of Al-Manat."

"And I," added Sister Raghavendra. "Besides, you'll probably travel more quickly as a smaller group."

The explorer looked from one woman to the other, then his gaze went past Isabel and his eyes locked with Swinburne's, and even in the dim light, the poet could see in them a great depth of despair.

"I'm afraid Isabel is right," the poet said quietly. "We can't allow Speke to reach the Eye of Nāga before us. Equally, we can't let Kazeh fall to the Prussians. The only option is to split the expedition."

Burton leaned his head back and considered the stars. Then he closed his eyes and said, "And you, William?"

Trounce stepped forward and spoke in a low, gruff voice: "Am I supposed to run off and leave women to fight?"

Isabella Mayson whirled around to face him. "Sir! The fact that I wrote a book about cookery and household management doesn't mean I'm incapable of putting a bullet through a man's head! Have you forgotten this—" She pulled back her hair to reveal the notch in her right ear. "I fought by your side at Dut'humi. Was I any less effective than you? Did I scream? Did I faint? Did I start knitting a shawl?"

"No, of course not! You're as brave as they come. But—"

"No buts! No medieval nonsense about honour and chivalry! There isn't time for such indulgence! We have a job to do! Yours is to accompany Sir Richard and to retrieve that diamond!"

"Well said!" Isabel Arundell put in.

They all looked at Burton, who was standing stock-still.

Gunfire rattled from the town.

The cough of a lion sounded from afar.

Pox, on Herbert Spencer's head, muttered something unintelligible, and Malady responded with a click of his beak.

"All right! Enough!" Burton snapped, opening his eyes. "Sadhvi, will you prepare for us a pack of remedies and treatments?"

"Yes, certainly."

"Take Algy with you and instruct him in their use. Maneesh—"

Krishnamurthy moved closer. "Yes?"

"I'm sorry, but I have to give you a very difficult mission. Sidi Bombay says an aggressive tribe called the Chwezi live among the Mountains of the Moon, so there's every chance that we won't make it out. It's imperative that the government learns what is happening here. For that reason, I'm going to entrust you with my journals and reports. I want you and Saíd and his men to trek all the way back to Zanzibar. I'm going to pay our remaining porters to accompany you as far as Ugogi. There, you can hire more. Once you reach the island, catch the first ship home and report to Palmerston."

Krishnamurthy straightened his back and squared his shoulders. "You can rely on me, sir."

"I don't doubt it, my friend."

Burton next addressed Trounce and Bombay: "You two, Algy, Herbert, and I will depart at sun-up. Work with Isabella to get everything prepared. I'll join you presently. First though—" he took Isabel Arundell by the arm and steered her away, "—you and I need to talk."

They walked a short distance, then stopped and stood, listening to the battle and watching dark shapes moving across the plain near the horizon.

"Elephants," Isabel murmured.

"Yes."

"You don't have to say anything, Dick. I'm familiar with your hopelessness when it comes to goodbyes."

He took her hand. "Did you know that, had history never changed, this is the year we'd be celebrating our honeymoon?"

"How do you know that?"

"Countess Sabina. Palmerston's medium."

"I ought to slap your face for reminding me that you broke our engagement."

"I'm sorry."

"I know. Do you think we'd have been happily married?"

"Yes."

He was silent a moment, then: "Isabel, I—I—"

She waited patiently while he struggled to express himself.

"I'm filled with such regret I can barely stand it," he said, his voice breaking. "I've done everything wrong. Everything! I should never have accepted the king's commission. I panicked. Speke had ruined my career and reputation. Then he put a bullet into his head and people said it was my fault!"

"Which is when Palmerston threw you a lifeline."

"He did, but even with the situation as it was, I'm not certain I'd have accepted his offer had Spring Heeled Jack not assaulted me the night before."

"There you have it, Dick. You regret a decision you made, but how much can you blame yourself when you were under the influence of such extraordinary circumstances? We all like to fool ourselves that we are independent and that our minds are our own, but the truth is we're always swayed by events."

Burton smacked his right fist into his left palm. "Yes! That's exactly it! My decisions were made according to context. But have I ever properly understood it? Since the advent of Spring Heeled Jack, I feel like I've not had a firm grip on events at all. It's all slipped away from me. It feels to me as though things that should have occurred over a long stretch of history are all piling up at once—and it's too much! It's too confusing! Bismillah! I can sense time swirling through and around me like some sort of discordant noise. But—"

Burton paused and raised his hands to his head, pushing his fingertips into his scalp and massaging it through the hair, as if to somehow loosen blocked thoughts.

"What is it?"

"I have this feeling that time is—is—like a language! Damn it, Isabel! I have mastered more than thirty tongues. Why does this one elude me? Why can't I make any sense of it?"

Burton's eyes momentarily reflected the moonlight and Isabel saw in them the same torment Swinburne had spotted minutes ago.

He continued: "Tom Bendyshe, Shyamji Bhatti, Thomas Honesty—all dead; and we—we have pushed through pain and fever and discomfort to the point of utter exhaustion. That is the context in which I have to now judge my decisions, but I don't comprehend the significance of it! Surely there has to be one! Why can't I translate the language of these events?"

"I have never before known a man with your depth of intellect, Dick, but you're demanding too much of yourself. You haven't slept. You're overwrought. You're trying to do what no man—or woman—can do. The workings of time are obscure to us all. Your Countess Sabina, who has insight into so much more than the rest of us—does she understand it?"

"No. If anything, the more of it she observes, the more confused she gets."

"Perhaps, then, it cannot be deciphered by the living, which is why meaning is assigned retrospectively, by those who inhabit the future. By historians."

"Who weren't even a part of the events! Are future historians better placed to interpret the life of Al-Manat than you are? Of course not! But will their reading of your life make more sense than anything you can tell me now—or at any other point while you're alive? Yes, almost certainly."

"Are you afraid of how history will judge you?"

"No. I'm afraid of how I'm judging history!"

Isabel gave a throaty chuckle.

Burton looked at her in surprise and asked, "What's so funny about that?"

"Oh, nothing, Dick—except I imagined that perhaps you took me aside to tell me that you love me. How silly of me! Why on earth didn't I realise it was for nothing more than a philosophical discussion!"

Burton looked at her, then looked down and directed a derisive snort at himself.

"I'm an idiot! Of course I love you, Isabel. From the moment I first laid eyes on you. And it gives me a strange kind of comfort to know that there's another history, and in it we are together, and not parted by—" He gestured around them. "This."

"I always thought that if anything was going to come between us it would be Africa," she said.

"But it wasn't," Burton replied. "It was the Spring Heeled Jack business."

"Yes." Isabel sighed. "But I suspect that, somehow, those events, just like the River Nile, have their source here."

The freshly risen sun turned the plain the colour of blood. From the summit of a hill, Burton, Swinburne, Trounce, Spencer, and Sidi Bombay looked down upon it and watched as the expedition divided into three. One group, led by Maneesh Krishnamurthy, was heading back in the direction they'd all come; another—the Daughters of Al-Manat—was riding away, along the base of the hills, intending to set up camp among the trees to the southeast of Kazeh; while the third—Mirambo and his men—was moving into the forest directly east of the town.

Burton, with a savage scowl on his face, muttered, "Come on," pulled his horse around, and started along a trail that led northward. There were two horses, lightly loaded with baggage, roped behind his mount. Trounce had two more behind his. Swinburne's horse led the eighth animal, upon which Herbert Spencer was rather awkwardly propped, and the ninth horse was tethered behind that. The clockwork man wasn't heavy—his mount could easily carry him—but he'd only thus far ridden a mule sidesaddle, and wasn't used to the bigger beast.

Sidi Bombay's horse led no others, for the African frequently rode ahead to scout the route.

Traversing a long valley, they moved through the trees and, thanks to the scarcity of undergrowth and the canopy sheltering them from the sun, made rapid progress. They didn't stop to rest—nor did they speak—until they reached the edge of a savannah midway through the afternoon; and when they sat and shared unleavened bread and plantains, the conversation was desultory. Each man was preoccupied, listening to the distant gunfire, dwelling on those from whom they'd parted. Even the three screechers, Pox, Malady, and Swinburne, were subdued.

"We'll endure the heat and keep going," Burton muttered.

They resumed their journey, shading themselves beneath umbrellas, guiding their horses over hard, dusty ground, watching as herds of impala and zebra scattered at their approach.

The rest of the day passed sluggishly, with the interminable landscape hardly changing. The climate had all four men so stupefied that they frequently slipped into a light sleep, only to be awakened by Spencer shouting: "The bloomin' horses are stoppin' again, Boss!"

Shortly before sunset, they erected their one small tent beside a stony outcrop, ate, then crawled under the canvas to sleep. Sidi Bombay wrapped himself in a blanket and slumbered under the stars. Spencer, having had his key inserted and wound, kept guard.

In the few seconds before exhaustion took him, Swinburne remembered the clockwork philosopher's book, and the phrase: *Only equivalence can lead to destruction or a final transcendence.*

He wondered how he'd come to forget about it; why he hadn't mentioned it to anyone; then he forgot about it again and went to sleep.

Sir Richard Francis Burton dreamt that he was slumbering alone, in the open, with unfamiliar stars wheeling above him. There was a slight scuffing to his left. He opened his eyes and turned his head and saw a tiny man, less than twelve inches high, with delicate lace-like wings growing from his shoulder blades. His forehead was decorated with an Indian *bindi*.

"I don't believe in fairies," the explorer said, "and I've already looked upon your true form, K'k'thyima."

He sat up, and blinked, and suddenly the fairy was much larger, and reptilian, and it had one or five or seven heads.

"Thou art possessed of a remarkable mind, O human. It perceives truth. It is adaptable. That is why we chose thee."

Burton was suddenly shaken by a horribly familiar sensation: an awareness that his identity was divided, that there were two of him, ever at odds with each other. For the first time, though, he also sensed that some sort of physical truth lay between these opposing forces.

"Good!" the Nāga hissed. "Still we sing, but soon it will end, and already thou hears the echo of our song."

"What are you suggesting? That I'm sensing the future?"

The priest didn't answer. His head was singular. His head was multiple. Burton tried to focus on the strange presence, but couldn't.

"I dreamt of you before," he said. "You were in Kumari Kandam. This, though, is Africa, where the Nāga are known as the *Chitahuri* or the *Shay-turáy*."

"I am K'k'thyima. I am here, I am in other places. I am nowhere, soft skin, for my people were made extinct by thine."

"Yet the essence of you was imprinted on one of the Eyes; you lived on in that black diamond until it was shattered."

Again, the Nāga chose not to respond.

A flash drew Burton's eyes upward. He saw a shooting star, the brightest he'd ever witnessed. It blazed a trail across the sky, then suddenly divided into three streaks of light. They flew apart and faded. When he looked down, the Nāga priest was gone.

He lay back and woke up.

"It's dawn, Boss. I can still hear shots from Kazeh."

Herbert Spencer's head was poking through the entrance to the tent. It was wrapped in a *keffiyeh* but the scarf was pulled open at the front and the polymethylene suit beneath was visible, as were the three round openings that formed the philosopher's "face." Through the glass of the uppermost one, Burton could see tiny cogs revolving. Spencer was otherwise motionless.

A moment passed.

"Was there something else, Herbert?"

"No, Boss. I'll help Mr. Bombay to load the horses."

The philosopher withdrew.

Swinburne sat up. "I think I shall take lunch at the Athenaeum Club today, Richard, followed by a tipple at the Black Toad."

"Are you awake, Algy?"

The poet peered around at the inside of the tent.

"Oh bugger it," he said. "I am."

Burton shook Trounce into consciousness and the three of them crawled into the open, ate a hasty breakfast, packed, and mounted their horses.

Burton groaned. "I'm running a fever."

"I have some of Sadhvi's medicine," Swinburne said.

"I'll take it when we next stop. Let's see how far we can get today. Keep your weapons close to hand—we don't know when we might run into Speke."

They moved off.

Most of the day was spent crossing the savannah.

Vultures circled overhead.

The far-off sounds of battle faded behind them.

They entered a lush valley. Clusters of granite pushed through its slopes, and the grass grew so high that it brushed against the riders' legs.

"Wow! This is the place called Usagari," Bombay advised. "Soon we will see villages."

"Everyone move quietly," Burton ordered. "We have to slip past as many as we can, else the few boxes of beads and coils of wire we're carrying will be gone in an instant."

After fording a *nullah*, they rode up onto higher ground and saw plantations laid out on a gentle slope. Bombay led them along the edges of the cultivated fields, through forests and thick vegetation, and thus managed to pass four villages without being spotted. Then their luck ran out, and they were confronted by warriors who leaped about, brandishing their spears and striking grotesque poses that were designed to frighten but which sent Swinburne into fits of giggles.

After much whooping and shouting, Bombay finally established peaceful communication. The Britishers paid three boxes of beads and were given permission to stay at the village overnight. It was called Usenda, and its inhabitants proved much more friendly than their initial greeting had suggested. They shared their food and, to Swinburne's delight, a highly alcoholic beverage made from bananas, and gave over a dwelling for the explorers' use. It was a poor thing constructed of grass, infested with insects, and already claimed by a family of rats. Trounce was too exhausted to care, Swinburne was too drunk to notice, and Burton was so feverish by now that he passed out the moment he set foot in it. They all slept deeply, while Spencer stood sentry duty and Bombay stayed up late gossiping with the village elders.

When they departed the next day, the king's agent was slumped semi-aware in his saddle, so Trounce took the lead. He successfully steered them past seven villages and out of the farmed region onto uninhabited flatlands where gingerbread palms grew in abundance. It was easy going but took two days to traverse, during which time Burton swam in and out of consciousness. His companions, meanwhile, grew thoroughly sick of the unchanging scenery, which offered nothing to suggest that they might be making any progress.

At last, they came to the edge of a jungle and began to work their way through it, with Trounce and Spencer leading the way while Swinburne and Bombay guided the horses behind them. Burton remained mounted and insensible.

For what felt like hours, they fought with the undergrowth, until Spencer pushed a tangle of lianas out of their path and they suddenly found themselves face to face with a rhinoceros. It kicked the ground, snorted, and moved its head from side to side, squinting at them from its small, watery eyes.

They raised their rifles.

"Absolute silence, please, gentlemen," Trounce whispered. "The slightest noise or movement could cause it to charge us."

"Up your sooty funnel!" Pox screamed.

"Pig-jobber!" Malady squawked. "Cross-eyed slack-bellied stink trumpet!"

The rhino gave a prodigious belch, turned, and trotted away.

"My hat!" Swinburne exclaimed. "Malady has been learning fast!"

"Humph!" Trounce responded. "Next time we're confronted by a wild beast, I won't bother to unsling my rifle. I'll just throw parakeets."

It was close to nightfall by the time they broke free of the mess of vegetation and found a place to camp. Burton recovered his wits while the others slept, and he sat with Spencer, listening to the rasping utterances of lions and the chuckles and squeals of hyenas.

"How're you feelin'?" the philosopher asked.

"Weak. How about you?"

"Phew! I'll be glad when all this walkin' an' ridin' is over an' done with. It's playin' merry havoc with me gammy leg."

"Your leg is just dented, Herbert."

"Aye, but it aches somethin' terrible."

"That's not possible."

"Aye. Do you think, Boss, that I've lost some qualities that a man possesses only 'cos he's flesh?"

"What sort of qualities?"

"A conscience, for example; a self-generated moral standard by which a man judges his own actions. Old Darwin said it's the most important distinction between humankind an' other species."

"And you think it's a characteristic of corporeality?"

"Aye, an evolution of a creature's instinct to preserve its own species. Compare us to the lower animals. What happens when a sow has a runt in her litter? She eats it. What happens if a bird hatches deformed? It's bloomin' well pecked to death. What do gazelles do with a lame member of the herd? They leave it to die, don't they? Humans are the dominant species 'cos we're heterogeneous, but to support all our individual specialisations, we have to suppress the natural desire to allow the weak an' inferior to fall by the wayside, as it were, 'cos how can we evaluate each other when reality demands somethin' different from every individual? A manual labourer might consider a bank clerk too physically weak; does that mean he should kill the blighter? The clerk might think the labourer too unintelligent; is that reason enough to deny him the means to live? In the wild, such judgements apply, but not in human society, so we have conscience to intercede, to inhibit the baser aspects of natural evolution an' raise it to a more sophisticated level. As I suggested to you once before, Boss, where mankind is concerned, survival of the fittest refers not to physical strength, but to the ability to adapt oneself to circumstances. The process wouldn't function were it not for conscience."

Burton considered this, and there was silence between them for a good few minutes.

Spencer picked up a stone and threw it at a shadowy form—a hyena that had wandered too close.

"You're suggesting," Burton finally said, "that conscience has evolved to suppress in us the instinct that drives animals to kill or abandon the defective, because each of us is only weak or strong depending on who's judging us and the criteria they employ?"

"Precisely. Without conscience we'd end up killin' each other willy-nilly until the whole species was gone."

"So you associate it with the flesh because it ensures our species' physical survival?"

"Aye. It's an adaptation of an instinct what's inherent in the body."

"And you suspect that your transference into this brass mechanism might have robbed you of your conscience?"

"I don't know whether it has or hasn't, Boss. I just wonder. I need to test it."

They sat a little longer, then Burton was overcome by weariness and retired to the tent.

Travel the following morning proved the easiest since their arrival in Africa. The ground was firm, trees—baobabs—were widely spaced, and undergrowth was thinly distributed. Small flowers grew in abundance.

As they entered this district, Pox and Malady launched themselves from Spencer's shoulders and flew from tree to tree, rubbing their beaks together and insulting each other rapturously.

"It's love," Swinburne declared.

Almost before they realised it, they found cultivated land underfoot and a village just ahead. It was too close to avoid, so *hongo* was paid and, in return, a hut was assigned for their use.

They rested and took stock.

Sadhvi's medicine was driving the fever out of Burton. He ached all over but his temperature had stabilised and strength began to seep back into his limbs.

Trounce, though, was suffering. The spear wound in his arm had become slightly infected, and his legs were ulcerating again.

"I shall be crippled at this rate," he complained. He sat on a stool and allowed Swinburne to roll up his trouser legs.

"Yuck!" the poet exclaimed. "What hideous pins you have, Pouncer!"

"You're not seeing them at their best, lad."

"Nor would I want to! Now then, it just so happens that I'm the sole purveyor of Sister Raghavendra's Revitalising Remedies. Incredible Cures and Terrific Tonics, all yours for a coil of wire and three shiny beads! What do you say?"

"I say, stop clowning and apply the poultice or I'll apply the flat of my hand to the back of your head."

Swinburne got to work.

"Shame you can't do nothin' for mine," Spencer piped.

Burton, who, with Bombay, had been parleying with the village elders, walked over and plonked himself on the ground beside the Yard man.

"We need to navigate in a slightly more northeasterly direction," he said. "It will save us from having to pass through a densely populated region."

They departed before sun-up the next morning, descended into a deep and miry watercourse, struggled through bullrushes, then climbed to the peak of a hill just as the sun threw its rays over the horizon. The next few hours were spent crossing uneven ground cut through with marshy rivulets, each filled with tall, tough reeds. There were cairns dotted over the land for as far as the eye could see, as well as stubby malformed trees in which hundreds of black vultures sat in sinister contemplation.

"Yea, though I walk through the valley of Death," Swinburne announced.

"Spongy-brained measles rash!" Pox added.

A steep incline led them up onto firmer ground and into a forest. The two parakeets once again left Spencer's shoulders and travelled overhead, with Pox teaching Malady new insults.

Burton rode onto a fairly well-defined trail.

"This is the path I think Speke is following," he said.

"Wow!" Bombay answered. "It is the one he took before, when I was with him."

"Then we should proceed with caution."

They stopped to eat, then rode on at a brisk pace until they emerged from the trees at the head of a shadowed valley. Its sides were thickly wooded and a clear stream ran through its middle with reasonably open ground to either side. There were pandana palms in profusion, rich groves of plantains, and thistles of extraordinary size. In the distance, the land rolled in high undulations to grassy hills, which Burton identified as the districts of Karague and Kishakka.

Late in the afternoon, they approached a village and were surprised when the inhabitants, upon sighting them, ran away.

"By Jove! That hasn't happened since we had the harvestman," Trounce observed.

Riding among the huts, they noticed that the usual stocks of food were missing. There were also a couple of ominous-looking stains on the ground in the central clearing.

"It looks like they received some non-too-friendly visitors," the king's agent said. He unpacked two boxes of beads from one of the horses and placed them at the entrance to the chief's dwelling. "Let's leave them a gift, if for no other reason than to demonstrate that not all *muzungo mbáyá* are bad."

The remainder of the day was spent travelling through the rest of the valley before crossing fine, rising meadowlands to a stratified sandstone cliff, beneath which they rested for the night.

Another early start. Hilly country. Herds of cattle. Forests of acacias.

All around them, the trees were alive with a profusion of small birds, whistling and chirping with such vigour that, for the entire day, the men had to raise their voices to be heard above the din.

They left the boisterous tree-dwellers behind as the sun was riding low in the sky and drew to a halt on a summit, looking across a broad, jungle-thick basin. On the far side, they spotted movement on the brow of a hummock. Trounce lifted the field glasses, clipped them onto his head, and adjusted the focusing wheels.

"About twenty men," he reported. "On foot. And one of those plant-vehicle things."

"Let me see," Burton said.

His friend passed the magnifying device and Burton looked through it, watching the distant group as it disappeared from view.

"Speke," he said.

They decided to stop where they were, quickly set up the camp, and without bothering to eat first immediately fell into an exhausted sleep.

Herbert Spencer stood outside the tent, leaning on his staff. His shadow lengthened, turned a deep shade of purple, then dissipated into the gathering gloom. When they awoke in the morning, he was still there. Burton wound him up.

"I say, Herbert, is your mind still active when your spring is slack?" Swinburne asked as he prepared their breakfast.

"Yus, lad." The mechanical man tapped a gloved finger to his scarf-enshrouded head. "The babbage in here interprets the electrical field held in the diamonds an' translates its fluctuations as speech an' movement. In the other direction, it channels sensory information about the environment from this brass body to the gemstones, which the field interprets as sound an' sight. When the babbage has no bloomin' power, I have no idea what's happenin' around me, but I can still think."

"It must feel like you're trapped. I should probably go mad under such circumstances."

"You're already mad," Trounce put in.

One of the horses had died during the night. They redistributed its load, then, after eating, began the trek down the slope to the edge of the jungle. When they reached it, they found the verdure to be extravagantly abundant and chaotic, pressing in to either side of the narrow trail. Speke's party had passed this way recently, but there was very little evidence to suggest it, and guiding the horses past the thorny bushes and dangling ant-covered lianas proved extremely difficult.

"I'll set to with me machete, Boss," Spencer announced, limping to the front of the party.

He unsheathed his blade and began to swipe at the undergrowth. A man would have been exhausted by this very quickly but the clockwork philosopher's mechanical arm hacked without pause, widening the path, until four hours later they emerged onto a huge flat rock as big as a tennis court, surrounded on all sides by lush green vegetation.

Spencer moved onto it, stumbling slightly, then laid down his blade, pulled a 54-bore Beaumont-Adams revolver from his waistband, and said: "Shall we stop here awhile?"

Burton glanced at Trounce and replied, "Yes, I think William's ulcers are paining him. We'll lay up until the day's heat abates a little."

"I'm fine," the Scotland Yard man protested.

"Wow! It is a good place to rest, Mr. Trounce," said Sidi Bombay.

Pox and Malady, who'd been snuggled together on Spencer's head, suddenly squawked and flew into the trees.

"Yes, William," the brass man said in his hooting voice. "You should take the weight off your feet."

He lifted his gun, aimed carefully between Trounce's eyes, and pulled the trigger.

TIME

"Oh glory, that we wrestle
So valiantly with Time!"
—RICHARD MONCKTON MILNES

CHAPTER 10

TO THE MOUNTAINS
OF THE MOON

"Death must be so beautiful. To lie in the soft brown earth,
with the grasses waving above one's head, and listen to silence.
To have no yesterday, and no tomorrow. To forget time,
to forgive life, to be at peace."
—OSCAR WILDE

Eighteen-year-old PC53 William Trounce had failed to make his first arrest.

He always timed his beat so he'd reach Constitution Hill in time for Queen Victoria's spin around Green Park. He thought the young monarch—who was just three years into her reign—was taking a needless risk with these daily excursions. He understood her need to escape for a few precious moments from the stuffy formality of Buckingham Palace, but there were many who still thought her a puppet of the unpopular prime minister, Lord Melbourne, and they often took the opportunity to jeer and boo as she rode through the park in her open-topped carriage. Trounce considered it one of his essential duties to be there in time to move the naysayers along.

Today he was going to be late, and it was Dennis the Dip's fault. He'd spotted the notorious East End pickpocket on the Mall. The crook was, as usual, dressed as a gentleman and looked entirely at home among the well-heeled crowd that sauntered back and forth along the ceremonial avenue. He scrubbed up well, did Dennis, and easily passed muster as a gent so long as he kept his mouth shut. Were any of his fellow perambulators to hear him speak, though, they would have instantly recognised the harsh accent and mangled grammar of the Cauldron and would most certainly have given him a very wide berth indeed.

As it was, Dennis mingled with his potential victims with nary a glance of suspicion cast his way. No glances—but there was one unwavering gaze, and that belonged to PC53 Trounce.

It would have been a very satisfying first feather in his cap for the young constable if he'd ended the career of this particular villain today, but alas it was not to be. Dennis's eyes flicked from handbag to handbag, pocket to pocket, but his long, restless fingers remained in plain view the whole time, and Trounce had to settle for warning the man away.

"Oh bleedin' 'eck, I ain't up to nuffink, am I!" Dennis had whined. "Jest givin' me Sunday best an airing, that's all."

"It's Wednesday, Dennis," Trounce pointed out.

The thief objected and wriggled on the spot a little more before finally scurrying off, and Trounce resumed his beat, a mite disappointed that he'd still not "christened his badge" after two weeks on the beat.

At the end of the Mall he passed Buckingham Palace and turned right into the park. He preferred to walk along on the grass rather than on the Constitution Hill path itself; it was better to position himself behind the crowds that often gathered along Victoria's route, for the troublemakers nearly always hid at the back, where they could more easily take to their heels should anyone object to their catcalls.

He saw that Her Majesty's carriage, drawn by four horses—the front left ridden by a postilion—was already trundling along a little way ahead of him. He increased his pace to catch up, striding down a gentle slope with an excellent view of the scene. Despite the mild weather, the crowd was sparse today. There were no protests and few hurrahs.

He jumped at the sound of a gunshot.

What the hell?

Breaking into a run, he peered ahead and noticed a man wearing a top hat, blue frock coat, and white breeches walking beside the slow-moving carriage. He was throwing down a smoking flintlock and drawing, with his left hand, a second gun from his coat.

In an instant, horror sucked the heat from Trounce's body and time slowed to a crawl.

His legs pumped; his boots thudded into the grass; he heard himself shout: "No!"

He saw heads turning toward the man.

His breath thundered in his ears.

The man's left arm came up.

The queen stood, raising her hands to the white lace around her throat.

Her husband reached for her.

A second man leaped forward and grabbed the gunman. "No, Edward!" came a faint yell.

The scene seemed to freeze; the two men entwined; their faces, even from this distance, so similar, like brothers; each person in the crowd poised in mid-motion, some stepping forward, some stepping back; the queen upright in the carriage, wearing a cream-coloured dress and bonnet; her consort, in a top hat and red jacket, reaching for her; the four outriders turning their horses.

Christ! thought Trounce. *Christ, no! Please, no!*

A freakish creature suddenly flew past.

Tall, loose-limbed, bouncing on spring-loaded stilts, it skidded to a halt in front of him. Trounce stumbled and fell to his knees.

"Stop, Edward!" the weird apparition bellowed.

A bolt of lightning crackled from its side into the ground and the lean figure staggered, groaning and clutching at itself. Below, the two struggling men turned and looked up.

A second shot echoed across the park.

Mist-enshrouded Tabora was dirty and crowded and filled with oppressively monolithic buildings and bustling, noisy streets. Its many vehicles reminded Sir Richard Francis Burton of hansom cabs, except their steam-horses had been incorporated into the body of the cabin, so the things rumbled along on four wheels with no visible means of locomotion. Bertie Wells referred to them as "motor-carriages."

The two men were in one now, along with the three Tommies from the *Britannia*, one of whom was driving the contraption by means of a wheel and foot pedals. Burton watched him and thought the operation looked exceedingly complicated.

Upon the rolling sphere's arrival in the besieged city, the king's agent had been hustled out of the ship and marched straight to a rather more luxurious motor-carriage than the one in which he was currently sitting. He'd waited in it for a while before being joined by Wells, General Aitken, and a driver. The latter started the engine, steered the vehicle onto a broad street, and sent it rattling along until they reached the centre of the city. A second conveyance—the one Burton was now in—had followed behind.

He was escorted into a large square building that, from the outside, reminded him of London's Athenaeum Club but which, on the inside, proved far less opulent. Here, he was presented to twelve generals who, along with Aitken, acted in lieu of an elected government. They ordered him to explain how he'd come to be in the Ugogi POW camp and why he was being moved.

He answered the first part of the question truthfully. To the second part he said simply: "I don't know."

The men then requested a full description of Paul Emil von Lettow-Vorbeck and demanded that Burton recount everything the German had said to him. He told them as much as he could without revealing his identity.

Finally, they questioned him about the approaching *L.59 Zeppelin* and its payload, the A-bomb.

When he'd finished explaining, he was summarily dismissed.

Bertie Wells had taken him back outside and to the second car, in which the Tommies were waiting.

They were now on their way to a secret destination.

"We're supposed to be escorting you to Colonel Crowley," Wells said, "but we're disobeying orders. When he finds out, if we're lucky, we'll be court marshalled and executed by firing squad."

Burton looked at his companion and asked, "And if you're unlucky?"

"He'll use his mediumistic powers on us. I dread to think how that might turn out. One way or the other, though, this is a suicide mission."

"Bloody hell!" Burton exclaimed. "Why didn't you tell me that before? I'd rather face this Crowley character than have you sacrifice yourself!"

"Which is exactly the reason I kept it quiet. I'm only telling you now so you'll realise the importance of what we're doing. I trust my editor implicitly, despite his eccentricities, and if he says the future depends on him meeting you, then I'm willing to bet my life that it does. Here, strap on this pistol, you shouldn't be without a weapon."

Burton clipped the holster to his belt. He watched, amazed, as three smaller versions of the *Britannia* suddenly sped out of the billowing mist and swept past the motor-carriage. They were about eight feet in diameter and lacked the jungle-slicing arms of the bigger ship.

"What are those things?"

"Steam spheres. I suppose the nearest equivalent you had in your time was the velocipede."

Burton shook his head in wonder, then said, "Eccentricities?"

Wells smiled. "The old man has a rather unconventional sense of style and his, um, 'living arrangements' tend to raise eyebrows."

"Why so?"

"The gentleman he lodges with is, er, rather more than a friend, if you know what I mean."

Burton threw up his hands in exasperation. "Good grief! It's 1918 and that's still considered unconventional? Has the human race not evolved at all since my time?"

The driver swung the motor-carriage into a narrow side street and accelerated down to the end of it, drawing to a stop outside a plain metal door.

Bertie stepped out of the vehicle. Burton and the Tommies followed. The explorer wiped perspiration from his eyes and muttered an imprecation. Tabora possessed the atmosphere of a Turkish bath.

"Keep alert," the war correspondent said to the three soldiers. They nodded, drew pistols from their holsters, and stood guard at the door while Wells ushered Burton through it.

"Up the stairs, please, Richard."

The king's agent passed an opening on his left and ascended. There was an oil lamp hanging from the upper landing's ceiling, and by its light he saw that the walls were painted a pale lilac and decorated with colourful theatre posters, most of them dating from the 1880s. He reached the top and stopped outside a wooden door with a glowing fanlight above it. Wells reached past him and rapped his knuckles against the portal: *Knock. Knock-knock-knock. Knock-knock.*

"Code?" Burton asked.

"Open sesame," Wells replied.

Algernon Swinburne's face flashed before the explorer's mind's eye.

"Come," a voice called from the room beyond.

They pushed the door open and stepped through into a large chamber. It was lit by four wall lamps and reminded Burton of his study in Montagu Place, for it was lined with bookshelves, had two large desks, and was decorated with all manner of ornaments and pictures and nicknacks.

A crimson rug lay between four leather armchairs in the centre of the room. A heavyset man was standing on it, and, immediately, Burton felt that he'd seen him somewhere before. He was tall, rather fat, and appeared to be in his mid-sixties. His brown hair—which had obviously been dyed, for its roots were grey—was long and fell in waves to his shoulders. It framed a jowly face, with creases and wrinkles around the grey, indolent eyes, and full-lipped mouth. He was wearing a black velvet smoking jacket, inky-blue slacks, and leather button-up boots. There was a long cigarette holder between the pudgy ringed fingers of his left hand.

After a long pause, spent staring fixedly at the king's agent, the man drawled: "The tragedy of old age is not that one is old, but that one is young."

His voice was deep and mellow and lazy. It possessed an Irish lilt.

Burton almost collapsed.

"Quips!" he cried out. "Bismillah! It's Quips!"

Oscar Fingal O'Flahertie Wills Wilde grinned, displaying crooked teeth, threw his cigarette holder onto a table, rushed forward, and took Burton by both hands.

"Captain Burton!" he exclaimed. "You're alive and young again! By heavens! How have you done it? I demand to know the secret! To get back my youth I would do anything in the world, except take exercise, get up early, or be respectable!"

Burton gave a bark of laughter. "Still the rapier-sharp wit! The war hasn't blunted that, I see, and praise be to Allah for it! It's good to see you, lad! It's bloody good to see you!"

"Sure and begorra, he's calling me lad now! And here's me a quarter of a century his senior by the looks of it!" Wilde caught Burton as the explorer suddenly sagged. "Hey now, you're trembling all over! Come and sit down. Bertie, in the drinks cabinet—there's a decanter of brandy. Fetch it over, would you? Sit, Captain. Sit here. Are you feeling faint?"

"I'm all right," Burton croaked, but, to his horror, he suddenly found himself weeping.

"It's the shock, so it is," Wilde said. "A dash of brandy will put you right. Pour generously, Bertie, the captain probably hasn't tasted the good stuff for a long while."

"I haven't—I haven't tasted it at all since—since Dut'humi," Burton said, his voice weak and quavering.

Wells passed him a glass but Burton's hand was shaking so violently that Wilde had to put his own around it and guide the drink to the explorer's mouth. Burton gulped, coughed, took a deep shuddering breath, and sat back.

"Quips," he said. "It's really you."

"It is, too, Captain. Are you feeling a little more steady now?"

"Yes. My apologies. I think—I never—I never expected to find a little piece of home in this hellish world."

Wilde chuckled and looked down at himself. "Not so little any more, I fear." He addressed Herbert Wells: "Bertie, you'd best be getting off—we don't have much time. The devil himself will be snapping at our heels soon enough, so he will."

Wells nodded. "Richard," he said, "I'm going to prepare our escape. All being well, I'll see you within a couple of hours."

"Escape?"

Wilde said, "Are you fit to take a walk? I'll explain as we go."

"Yes." Burton drained his glass and stood up. "By 'the devil himself,' I assume you mean Crowley."

The three men moved to the door and started down the stairs.

"That I do, Captain."

They reached the lower hallway. Wells opened the street door and peered out. The three Tommies were waiting by the car. The little war correspondent nodded to Burton and Wilde and slipped out into the mist, closing the portal behind him.

Wilde gestured to the opening in the side wall. "Into the basement, if you please, Captain."

Burton stepped through and started down the wooden stairs he found beyond. "I don't understand Crowley and all this mediumistic business, Quips. The only evidence I've seen of it is the Germans occasionally manipulating the weather."

"When the Hun destroyed London, they killed most of our best mediums, which is horribly ironic, do you not think? Here we are. Wait a moment."

The stairs had ended in a large basement, which was filled with old furniture and tea chests. Wilde crossed to a heavy armoire standing against the far wall.

"Ironic?" Burton asked.

"Yes, because our clairvoyants didn't predict it! As a matter of fact, we now think their opposite numbers, on the German side, may have perfected some sort of mediumistic blanket that can render things undetectable."

"Such as the approaching A-Bomb, for instance?"

"Unfortunately, yes. Ah-ha! That's got it!"

Wilde had been fiddling with something behind the big wooden unit. Now the whole thing slid smoothly aside, revealing the entrance to a passage. He turned and grinned at Burton. "Do y'know, I became the captain of a rotorship thanks to you? Do you remember old Nathaniel Lawless? A fine gentleman!"

"I remember him very clearly, and I agree."

"After you wangled me the job on the poor old *Orpheus*, Lawless would never settle for another cabin boy. He sponsored my training, helped me rise through the ranks, and, before you know it, I was given captaincy of HMA *Audacious*. A lovely vessel, so she was, but the war had broken out by then and she was put to fiendish use. I soon found that I was losing myself in the mesmeric brutality of battle. As long as war is regarded as wicked, it will always have its fascination. When it's looked upon as vulgar, it will cease to be popular. It took me a few years, I must confess, to realise that vulgarity."

He indicated that Burton should follow and disappeared into the secret passage.

"So I had myself drummed out of the Air Force."

"How did you manage that?"

"Through what they call 'conduct unbecoming to an officer and a gentle-man.' I inspired the wrath of a certain Colonel Queensberry, and he rather gleefully put his proverbial boot to my backside. It caused a bit of a stir at the time, I can tell you."

"And afterward you became a newspaper man?"

"Aye, I did that—going back to my roots, as you might say—and I wound up in Tabora."

The passage made a sharp turn to the right. As they continued on, Burton looked at the small lights that, strung along a long wire, gave illumination. "How do these work?" he asked, pointing at one.

"Electricity."

"Ah! Like I saw on the *Britannia*! Was it Isambard who mastered the technique?"

"Good Lord!" Wilde cried out. "Brunel! I haven't thought of him in years! What a genius he was!"

"And for all his faults, loved by the public," Burton noted.

"To be sure! To be sure! Ah, what a delight it must be to be a Technologist! So much more romantic than being the editor of a newspaper! I can assure you that popularity is the one insult I have never suffered. But to answer your question: yes, he mastered electricity—in 1863, as it happens."

They hurried on, with Wilde panting and puffing as he propelled his bulk forward.

"Where are we going, Quips?"

"All in good time, Captain."

Burton began to wonder if the tunnel spanned the entire city.

"So the mediums," he said. "They were killed when London fell?"

"So they were. And we had no more of them until 1907, when Crowley came to the fore. In recent years he's focused his talents on defending this city, which is why the Germans have never managed to conquer it."

"Surely, then, he should be regarded as a hero? Why is it that no one seems to have a good word to say of him?"

Wilde shrugged. "That's a difficult one. There's just something about him. He's sinister. People suspect that he has some sort of hidden agenda. Here we are."

They'd reached a door. Wilde knocked on it, the same arrhythmic sequence Wells had used earlier. It was opened by a seven-foot-tall Askari—obviously of the Masai race—who whispered, "You'll have to be quick. There's some sort of flap on. They're going to move the prisoner."

Wilde muttered an acknowledgement. He and Burton stepped into what appeared to be a records room, followed the soldier out of it into a brightly lit corridor, and ran a short distance along it until they came to a cell door. However, when it was unlocked and opened, the room behind it proved to be not a cell at all but a very large and luxurious chamber, decorated in the English style, with Jacobean furniture and paintings on its papered walls.

In its middle, there was a metal frame with a wizened little man—naked but for a cloth wrapped around his loins—suspended upright inside it. He was held in place by thin metal cables that appeared to have been bolted straight through his parchment-like skin into the bones beneath. His flesh was a network of long surgical scars and he was horribly contorted, his arms and legs twisted out of shape, their joints swollen and gnarled, and his spine curved unnaturally to one side. His finger- and toenails were more than two feet long and had grown into irregular spirals. Bizarrely, they were varnished black.

Large glass bulbs also hung from the frame, and were connected to the figure by tubes through which pink liquid was pumping. Each one held an organ: a throbbing heart, pulsating lungs, things that quivered and twitched.

Burton saw all this in a single glance, then his eyes rested on the man's face and he couldn't look away.

It was Palmerston.

Henry John Temple, 3rd Viscount Palmerston, was bald, and the skin of his face was stretched so tightly that it rendered him almost featureless. But despite the eyes being mere slits, the nose a jagged hole, and the mouth a horribly wide frog-like gash; despite that the ears had been replaced by two brass forward-pointing hearing trumpets, riveted directly into the sides of his skull; despite all this, it was plainly Palmerston.

The old man's eyes glittered as he watched his visitors enter.

Wilde closed the door and stepped to one side of it. He gently pushed Burton forward. The king's agent approached and stopped in front of the man who'd once been prime minister. He tried to think of something to say, but all that came out was: "Hello."

Just above Palmerston's head, an accordion-like apparatus suddenly jerked then expanded with a wheeze. It gave a number of rapid clicks, expelled a puff of steam, then contracted and emitted a sound like a gurgling drain. Words bubbled out of it.

"You filthy traitorous bastard!"

Burton recoiled in shock. "What?"

"You backstabbing quisling!"

The explorer turned to Wilde. "Did you bring me here to be maligned?"

"Please allow him a moment to get it out of his system, Captain. It's been pent up for half a century."

"Prussian spy! Treasonous snake! You dirty collaborator!"

"I have no idea what he's talking about. Is he sane?"

"In a manner of speaking."

"How old is he?

"A hundred and thirty-four."

"You never bloody told me!" Palmerston gurgled.

"Have you finally run out of insults, Pam?" Burton asked.

"*Lord Palmerston*, you insolent cur! You never told me!"

"Told you what?"

The misshapen figure squirmed and stretched spasmodically.

Wilde said, "Calm yourself, please, Lord Palmerston. We don't have time for tantrums."

The ex-prime minister went limp. He glared at Burton with sulphurous hatred. The accordion-thing shook and rattled and groaned, expanded, blew out more steam, and squeezed shut.

"I sent you to Africa to find the Eye of Nāga. You succeeded in your mission but you neglected to report that, in the course of retrieving it, you'd visited the future!"

"Sir," Burton replied. "You must understand: you're berating me for something that, from my point of view, I haven't done yet."

"You saw this damned war. You saw that the Germans were running rampant over the entire globe. You saw that the British Empire had been reduced to this one small enclave. Yet you purposely kept it from me! You were working for the Prussians all along!"

"No, I was not."

"Then why?"

"How can I possibly account for decisions I haven't yet made?"

"Traitor!"

Burton looked at Oscar Wilde and gave a helpless shrug.

Wilde stepped forward. "Gentlemen, let us get straight to the point. Captain, if I might explain—Lord Palmerston is blamed by the majority of Britishers for the woeful position we find ourselves in."

"Yes, Bertie Wells expressed such a sentiment."

"Indeed. Fortunately, Bertie has acted counter to his views on the matter out of loyalty to me, for I, along with a few others, am of the opinion that Lord Palmerston only ever had the best interests of the Empire in mind when he made the decisions that led to this war."

Burton looked at the monstrosity hanging in the frame and murmured, "I don't disagree. But, Quips, those 'best interests' were envisioned according to the manner in which he comprehended the influences at play: the political landscape; the perceived shape of society and culture; the advice of his ministers; and so forth. In my opinion, his judgement of those things was erroneous in the extreme, and so too, inevitably, were his decisions."

Palmerston emitted a spiteful hiss.

Wilde nodded. "A fair statement, but is it not the case that the manner in which a man apprehends the present is shaped by his past?"

"Then where does the responsibility for his decisions lay? With Time itself? If so, then you're proposing that Palmerston is a victim of Fate."

"I am. Furthermore, I submit that you are, too. So perhaps you should stop striving to understand what is happening and, instead, simply allow it to play out however it will. You've just learned that you'll return to the past, which, I'm sure, is very welcome news indeed. Bertie is currently making arrangements to ensure that you get out of Tabora. When you do so, I suggest that you placidly follow whatever sequence of events leads you home."

Burton was suddenly filled with longing. How he missed Mrs. Angell, his comfortable old saddlebag armchair, his library, even Mr. Grub, the street vendor, whose pitch was on the corner of Montagu Place!

"Captain," Wilde continued, "just as Lord Palmerston made his decisions according to how the past taught him to gauge the state of affairs, so, too, will you. In 1863, you'll determine—you *did* determine—not to reveal that you had survived for a number of years in a war-torn future where you witnessed the death of the British Empire. Our history books, such as they are, don't reveal anything that casts light on why you took this course of action. Biographies written about you don't even mention that you were the king's agent, for that was a state secret. They say the second half of your life was lived quietly, indulging in scholarly pursuits. This is only partially true. What really happened is that you exiled yourself to Trieste, on the northeastern coast of Italy, from there to watch the seeds of war sprouting. You died in that city in 1890, ten years before the Greater German Empire invaded its neighbouring countries."

Sir Richard Francis Burton moistened his lips with his tongue. He raised his hand and put his fingertips to the deep and jagged scar on his left cheek, the one made by a Somali spear back in '55.

"Am I to take it that you're blaming me for the war?" he asked huskily.

"Yes!" Palmerston gurgled.

"No, not at all," Wilde corrected. "People are wrong to condemn Lord Palmerston, and Lord Palmerston is wrong to condemn you. You do not represent the evils of this world, Captain Burton—you represent hope."

"Because you think I can alter history?"

"Indeed so. Lord Palmerston and I were already aware that Crowley had, in 1914, detected an aberrant presence in Africa. When Bertie Wells told me—about eighteen months ago—that he'd met you, we realised what that aberration was and how it—you—could be employed to change everything."

"So whatever the circumstances I find when I return to 1863, you want me to somehow suppress the reactions that my own past has instilled in me, ignore what I consider to be my better judgement, and—" he turned to face Palmerston, "—and tell you everything I've seen here during the past five years?"

"Tell me *everything*, Burton!"

"Should I even describe your present—um—condition?"

"I insist upon it. I would like the opportunity to die naturally, with a little grace, at a much earlier time."

Burton sighed. "I'm sorry. It won't work."

"Why not?" Wilde asked.

"I will most assuredly do as you suggest, and I might succeed in creating a history in which this war never happens. If so, I'll have the good fortune to live in it. But you won't. Here, nothing will change. You won't wink out of existence and wake up in a new world. Instead, a new history will branch off from the moment I change my actions, and it will run parallel to this one."

"Is there then no hope for us?"

"If I understand the workings of time correctly, the only way to alter the circumstances in which you exist, as opposed to the future that lies ahead, would be to somehow change the past without leaving the present—like sitting on a tree branch and sawing it through behind you, at the trunk."

"Isn't that what we're doing by making this request?"

"Asking a person to perform an action is not the same as performing that action yourself."

"Captain, you're implying that time and history are entirely subjective."

"Yes, I rather think I am."

There came a knock at the door. It opened and the Masai guard poked his head into the room. "You have to get out of here," he said. "They're on their way. They're going to move Lord Palmerston onto the *Britannia*."

Wilde nodded and the guard withdrew.

"Don't allow them to move me!"

"The city is about to be destroyed, sir," Wilde said. "A select few will attempt to escape in the sphere. It appears you'll be among them."

Palmerston was silent for a moment, then: "Burton, do as we say. If it won't change this world, it will, at least, create another, better one, and Mr. Wilde and I can die knowing that somewhere, other versions of us lived better lives."

Burton looked at Wilde, who nodded and said, "We have to go."

"Wait!" Palmerston ordered. "Burton, I don't trust you. You have to demonstrate your loyalty."

"How?"

"Obey my final order. Without question!"

"What is it?"

"I have received so many Eugenicist treatments that I cannot die a natural death. That fiend Crowley has been feeding off my mental energy like a damned vampire to supplement his mediumistic powers. I cannot stand it any more. Take out your pistol right this minute and shoot me through the head."

Without hesitation, Burton drew his revolver, raised the weapon, looked Palmerston in the eyes, and pulled the trigger.

"They probably heard that!" Wilde exclaimed. "We'd better leg it!"

They left the cell and raced down the corridor. The Masai ushered them into the records room. Burton saw that the tunnel entrance was normally concealed behind a tall filing cabinet.

"Go through and I'll slide it back," the guard said. "Then I'll hold them at bay until I'm dead or out of ammo."

"You're a good fellow, so you are," Wilde said as he stepped through the opening.

"The word is out," the Masai replied. "It was announced on the wireless minutes ago. Everyone knows what's coming. It's the end. I might as well go out with a bang!" He vanished from view as he slid the filing cabinet into place.

"The fool!" Burton hissed. "Why doesn't he come with us?"

"Whenever a man does a thoroughly stupid thing, it's always from the noblest motives," Wilde replied. "Come on! Let's not make his death in vain!"

It took them fifteen minutes to reach the other end of the passage. They stepped out into Wilde's basement and the ex-editor panted: "I'm pooped!"

"You never abandoned your diet of gobstoppers and butterscotch, I take it?" Burton ventured.

"I never expected to be running along secret corridors at the age of sixty-four!" Wilde replied. "Up the stairs with you!"

They ascended, stopped at the front door, and Wilde opened it a crack and peeked out.

"Good!" he exclaimed. "Your motor-carriage is still there. The guards will take you to Bertie."

"You'll come too, of course!"

Wilde took Burton's hand and shook it. "No, old friend. This is where we must say goodbye. I'm too old to go hurrying out into the depths of Africa."

"But Quips! You'll be killed!"

"Yes. But thanks to the help you gave me when I was a boy, I have lived, Captain, and to live is the rarest thing in the world. Most people exist, that is all."

"But—"

"I want to spend my last hours with the man I love."

Burton put a hand to his friend's shoulder. "I'm glad you found happiness in this ugly world. What's his name?"

"Paul. He was a shopkeeper in his younger days—what people call a very ordinary man, but it happened that he brought to me extraordinary peace of mind and contentment."

Burton smiled, and his eyes filled with tears. "I fear I may weep in front of you again, Quips."

"The clock is ticking. Be off with you, man!"

Burton loosed an unsteady breath, opened the door, and stepped out into the hot mist of the Taboran night. He crossed to the motor-carriage where the three guards waited. One of them opened its door and gestured for him to enter.

"Captain!" Oscar Wilde called from the doorway.

The explorer turned.

"If the processes of time and history truly are subjective, do not be afraid of the past. If people tell you that it is irrevocable, do not believe them. The past, the present, and the future are but one moment. Time and space, succession and extension, are merely accidental conditions of thought. The imagination can transcend them."

Oscar Wilde smiled and closed the door.

Dawn wasn't far off. Tabora was enveloped in steam. A great crowd of people milled through it, moving alongside the motor-carriage in an easterly direction.

"Are they trying to leave the city?" Burton asked.

"I suppose so," one of the Tommies replied. "But to make it through Hell's Run, you either have to be in a very fast vehicle or crawling along on your own, keeping low and out of sight. A mob like this will never make it. They'll be slaughtered!"

"It's certain death if they stay," one of the other men noted, "so it's worth taking the risk. I'm going to chance it, for sure."

Burton watched in horror as shadowy forms occasionally emerged from the pall: people with fear in their eyes, carrying bags and bundles and children, looking hunted and desperate.

"Bismillah!" he muttered. "Nowhere to go, and very little chance of getting there. This is ghastly."

With delays and diversions, the vehicle made slow progress, and the three soldiers became increasingly nervous.

"I'm sorry, sir. We didn't count on this."

Screams and shouts came out of the cloud.

A line of steam spheres shot past.

Burton heard a gunshot.

The motor-carriage moved on.

Finally, they drew to a stop and the Tommies disembarked. The king's agent followed and was escorted to a door in the side of a warehouse. Stepping through, he entered a very expansive and well-lit space.

"Good! You made it!" Bertie Wells called.

The little war correspondent was standing beside one of two big harvestman machines. They were of the variety Burton had become familiar with here in the future—with a saddle on top of the carapace instead of a seat inside it—but they were slung rather lower to the ground than he'd seen in other models, with the middle joints of the legs rising high to either side of the body.

"Built for speed!" Wells announced.

"I assume we're to escape the city on these things?"

"Yes. We have to set off now while fortune favours us."

"In what manner is it doing that?"

Wells grinned. "The lurchers are attacking the Germans! Hell's Run is clear!"

"The lurchers? Why?"

"No one knows!"

Burton turned to his escort: "You men heard that?"

They nodded.

"So get going! Get out of the city. Africa's a big continent. Find a quiet valley, build a village, live off the land, stay out of trouble."

"And learn to speak German," one of the men said.

"Yes, that might be advisable."

They saluted and hastily departed.

Burton joined his friend by the giant arachnids. There were bulging pannier bags hanging against their sides. Wells reached up and patted one. "Food and supplies to keep us going for at least a couple of weeks." He touched a long leather sheath. "And Lee-Enfield sniper rifles. I'll start the engines. You go and open up." He indicated large double doors. Burton strode over and, with some difficulty, slid them apart. It was lighter outside: dawn was breaking. Mist rolled in around him as he returned to the now chugging harvestmen. Wells was already mounted on one. Burton reached up to the other's stirrup and hauled himself into its saddle. He took hold of the two control levers.

"Follow me!" Wells called.

The two spiders clanked out of the warehouse and onto a wide thoroughfare. For half a mile, the machines scuttled along the road, weaving in and out between other vehicles, with crowds surging along to either side of them. Then they passed the last outlying building and Wells led the way off the road and onto the dusty savannah, leaving the fleeing Taborans behind. He stopped his vehicle and Burton drew his own to a halt beside him. The mist was thinning and, through it, the huge orange globe of the sun was visible ahead of them.

"We'll go eastward across country," Wells said. "If we stay a little north of the exodus, we'll be closer to the German forces but free of the crowds."

"What's your destination, Bertie?"

"My only objective is to get past the end of Hell's Run. After that, I don't know. Where do we have to go to get you home to 1863?"

"To the Mountains of the Moon."

Wells shook his head. "We'll not get through the Blood Jungle. It's impassable."

"Nevertheless."

The war correspondent lifted his shoulders and let them drop. "Whatever you say. Onward!"

"Wait!" Burton snapped. He pointed to Wells's left, at the ground.

His friend looked down. "What the hell?" he uttered in astonishment.

A line of poppies was sprouting out of the hard earth.

Wells looked at Burton, a baffled expression on his face.

"It keeps happening," the king's agent said. "They bloom right in front of me, in an instant."

"It's impossible, Richard. How can they grow so fast? Have the Eugenicists made them?"

"*How* is one thing, Bertie, but I'm more interested in *why*!"

They watched as the flowers opened, a long line of them, snaking unevenly into the haze.

"North," Burton muttered. "Bertie, I want to follow them."

"It will take us straight into the German trenches. If the Hun doesn't do for us, the lurchers will."

"Maybe."

Wells reached down and unclipped the sheath containing his rifle. He took his pistol from its holster, checked that it was fully loaded, then slipped it back into place. He looked at Burton, smiled, and, in his high-pitched squeaky voice, said, "Well then: in for a penny, in for a pound!"

The two harvestmen scurried northward, following the line of red flowers, and disappeared into the mist.

"What the devil are you playing at?" William Trounce roared. "You nearly gave me a bloody heart attack!"

Herbert Spencer lowered the pistol, which, when he'd pulled the trigger, had done nothing.

"Herbert! Explain yourself!" Burton demanded.

"I'm sorry, William," Spencer said. "I didn't mean to scare you."

"How in blue blazes can shooting at a man's head not scare him, you tin-headed dolt?"

"But I didn't shoot, an' that's the point."

"Not for want of trying! I clearly saw you squeeze the trigger!"

"So did I," Swinburne added. He'd drawn his own weapon and was pointing it uncertainly at the philosopher.

"Yus, an'—as I expected—nothin' bloomin' well happened, did it!"

Burton paced forward and snatched the gun out of Spencer's hand. "As you expected? What are you talking about?"

"When we stepped onto this rock, Boss, I felt every spring in me body go slack. We've entered the Eye of Nāga's area of influence. None o' the guns will work now. Nor will any other mechanical device. Henry Morton Stanley couldn't fly his rotorchairs any farther than this. You'll remember they was found by Arabs, an' they weren't functionin' at all."

Swinburne directed his gun at the sky and squeezed the trigger. It felt loose under his finger. The weapon didn't fire.

Trounce scowled. "Firstly, Spencer, there was no need for a bloody demonstration, especially one that involved me! You've been fitted with voice apparatus—ruddy well use it! Secondly, why are you still standing?"

Burton answered before Spencer could. "We encountered this same emanation when we went after the South American Eye. The fact that Herbert's mind is embedded in the Cambodian stones gives him the ability to neutralise it."

"I say, Herbert!" Swinburne exclaimed. "If you radiate an opposing force, could you cast it wide enough to make our guns work? It would give us one up on the Prussians!"

"Perhaps a gun I was holdin' meself," Spencer replied.

"By thunder!" Trounce yelled furiously. "You see! What if your magic rays, or whatever they are, had worked on the pistol in your hand? You'd have blown my bloody head off!"

"All right, all right," Burton growled impatiently. "Let's leave it be. But if you ever pull a stunt like that again, Herbert, I'll throw your key into the middle of the Ukerewe Lake."

"I'm sorry, Boss."

Leading the horses, they moved to the edge of the rock, which the jungle overhung, and settled in the shade. The trees around them were crowded with blue monkeys that had fallen silent when the men appeared but which now took up their distinctive and piercing cries again—*Pee-oww! Pee-oww!*—and began to pelt the group with fruit and sticks. Sidi Bombay shouted and waved his arms but the tormentors took no notice.

"Confound the little monsters!" Trounce grumbled. "We'll not get any peace here!"

Swinburne removed the dressings from the detective's legs and applied fresh poultices. He checked the wound on his friend's arm. It was red and puckered but the infection had disappeared.

They abandoned the clearing and plunged back into the jungle, the men trailing behind Spencer as he swiped his machete back and forth, clearing the route. Pox and Malady had elected to sit on one of the horse's saddles rather than in their habitual position on the clockwork philosopher's head, causing Swinburne to wonder whether Spencer had fallen out of favour with the two parakeets as well.

The poet struggled with his thoughts. Hadn't he noticed something about the brass man's philosophical treatise back in Ugogi? Something unusual? What was it? Why couldn't he remember? Why was a part of him feeling ambivalent about Spencer? It didn't make sense—Herbert was a fine fellow!

Moving to Burton's side, he opened his mouth to ask if the explorer shared his misgivings. Instead, he found himself saying, "It's awfully humid, just like in the coast regions."

"Humph!" Burton replied, by way of agreement.

It was near sundown by the time they stumbled wearily out of the vegetation. They were at the base of a hill, with a wide, clear, and shallow stream crossing their path.

The horses drank greedily. One of them collapsed.

"It's done for, poor thing," Trounce said. "I'd put a bullet through its brain if I could. It's the proper thing to do."

"If our guns worked," Burton responded, "that would alert Speke to our presence."

"Allow me," said Spencer, limping over to the stricken animal. He bent, took its head in his hands, and twisted it with all his mechanical might. The horse's neck popped. It kicked and died.

They moved half a mile upstream, washed, ate, and set up camp.

Burton spoke to Pox: "Message for Isabel Arundell. Please report. Message ends. Go."

Pox blew a raspberry, took to the air, and disappeared over the jungle.

"Weasel thief!" Malady screeched, and flew after his mate.

The men sat quietly for a little while then entered the tent and almost immediately fell into a deep slumber.

Dawn came, and so did a warning from their clockwork sentry: "Rouse yourselves, gents! Twenty men approachin' an' they don't look very cheerful!"

Burton, Swinburne, and Trounce crawled into the open and rubbed the sleep from their eyes. They found Spencer and Bombay watching a gang of men, some way off, marching toward them. Their hair was fashioned into multiple spikes and held in place with red mud, their faces striped with ridged scars, their noses adorned with copper rings, and their shadows stretched across the golden hillside. They were armed with spears and held long oval shields.

"Wow! They are Wanyambo," Sidi Bombay advised. "A peaceful people."

"Not if their expressions are anything to go by," Burton observed. "Do you speak their language, Bombay?"

"Yes. I shall talk with them." The African set off to greet the newcomers, braving their scowls and brandished weapons. Burton and his friends watched as an argument commenced, gradually cooled to a heated debate, then settled into a passionate discussion, and, finally, became a long conversation.

Bombay returned. "Wow! These fine warriors are from the village of Kisaho. They say the *muzungo mbáyá* arrived at Kufro, which is nearby, and took all the food and weapons from the people. Wow! The jungle moved among them and killed nine men."

"The Prussian plant vehicle!" Burton murmured.

"And a mighty wizard took the chief by the neck and turned him into a tree which killed three more villagers by sucking out their blood. The men had to burn it to kill it." Bombay gestured back toward the Wanyambo. "These from Kisaho came to fight you but I told them that, although you are ugly and strange, you are an enemy of the wizard and you have come to punish the wicked white men. They will help."

"Tell them we will be honoured if they join us. Ask them to send a man running ahead to inform the villages that we are approaching, and that we are here to avenge the dead."

This was done, and the Britishers packed their tent and set off up the hill, following the warriors over its brow and down into the forested valley beyond.

They passed along a dirt path bordered by fruit-bearing trees and fragrant flowery shrubs, then stepped out into cultivated fields where peas grew in profusion. While they were crossing these, Pox and Malady returned.

"Message from Isabel Arundell. The Arabs are holding stinking cesspit Kazeh. My witless reinforcements from Mzizima have arrived but Prussian numbers are building steadily. We're keeping them occupied. Isabella and Sadhvi are safe. Mucous-bag Mirambo is injured but will recover. When you get home, tell Palmerston to send troops as a matter of urgency. May Allah guide and protect you. Bettawfeeq!"

"That means 'good luck,'" Burton explained in response to a puzzled look from Trounce.

"Are you going to send the bird to Maneesh?" the police detective asked.

"No. I fear it's too great a distance by now."

The whole day was spent crossing valleys and hills. On the next, they trekked over an alluvial plain until they reached the Kitangule Kagera, a river that, according to Speke's account of his earlier expeditions, flowed into the Ukerewe Lake. Crossing it proved so awkward that their supplies got soaked and another of the horses died.

The swelling terrain on the other side was alive with antelope, which scattered as the twenty Wanyambo led the Britishers up to the crest of a hill. From there they saw, stretching for miles and miles to their right, a rich, well-wooded, swampy plain containing large open patches of water.

A band of light blazed across the horizon.

Burton waved a fly away from his face and shaded his eyes.

"Bismillah!" he exclaimed. "Look at the size of it!"

"Is it a mirage?" Swinburne asked, squinting.

"No, Algy. That's it. That's the lake!"

"Ukerewe? Are you sure? It looks like the sea! Perhaps we've walked right across Africa—or we've wandered in an enormous circle!"

Burton cast his eyes around the landscape, taking in every topographical detail, making rapid mental calculations, adding it to his knowledge of the country to the southwest, around Lake Tanganyika.

"I think he was right all along," he murmured. "I think Speke got it. Ukerewe has to be the source!"

"But I don't want him to be right!" Swinburne objected. "He doesn't deserve it!"

They continued west.

The ground rose and fell, rose and fell, and rolled away to the hazy horizon. Through the moisture-heavy air, distant peaks faded into view, dark green at their base, blanching up to such a pale blue that they merged with the sky. Hovering above, as if floating, their jagged peaks were white.

"It's wonderful!" Swinburne enthused, jerking and waving his arms. "Snow in the middle of Africa! No one will believe it!"

"Our destination!" Burton announced. "The Mountains of the Moon!"

"Wow! I do not want to go there again," Sidi Bombay said softly. "But I shall because I am with you, and I am certain you will pay me very well indeed."

Yet another horse succumbed. The men were all on foot now, the baggage divided between the remaining animals. There wasn't much of it. Burton had no idea how they were going to make it back to Zanzibar.

As they progressed, villagers turned out to greet them and to press food and weapons into their hands. Word had spread like wildfire across the lands between the lake and the mountains, and now the air throbbed with drums— a deep, thunderous booming, ominous and threatening and incessant.

"I don't think we'll be taking Speke by surprise," Swinburne commented.

In one settlement, the *p'hazi* led them into a hut where four men lay groaning. Their skin was lacerated, in some places to the bone, and none were likely to live.

Bombay translated: "Warriors attacked Mr. Speke's people but the jungle thing killed many. Wow! Five died in this village, and the *p'hazi* says that in the next, Karagu, you will discover all the men gone, for there was a very big battle there."

"How far behind Speke are we?" Burton asked.

"He says the wicked *muzungo mbáyá* are four or five villages ahead."

"We're too done in to catch up with him today. Ask if we can stay here overnight."

Permission was granted, and the Britishers slept with drums pounding through their dreams.

In the morning, the women intoned a warlike chant as the expedition set off again. Burton, Swinburne, Trounce, Spencer, Bombay, and the twenty Wanyambo marched out of the village and onto marshy plains studded with rounded knolls, each topped by an umbrella cactus. They pushed through tall grasses where buffalo were numerous and mosquitoes were legion.

At noon, they arrived at Karagu, which was nestled against a strip of jungle, and found it half-wrecked and filled with keening women. The men, as the *p'hazi* had stated, were all dead.

On Burton's behalf, Bombay promised the women that vengeance would soon fall upon those responsible.

The expedition rested and ate a light meal, then prepared to move on.

"Kwecha!" Burton called. "Pakia! Hopa! Hopa!"

The Wanyambo gathered at the edge of the jungle. One of them shouldered through a screen of vegetation to the path beyond. He suddenly howled and came flying back out, cartwheeling over the heads of his fellows, spraying blood onto them. He thudded to the ground and lay still.

"What the—" Trounce began, then tottered back as the Prussian plant vehicle burst out of the undergrowth and plunged into the warriors. He cried out in horror as the thing's spine-covered tendrils lashed like whips, opening skin, sending blood splashing. The Wanyambo yelled in agony as their flesh was sliced and torn. Sidi Bombay was hoisted into the air and flung into the trees. The village women screamed and raced away. Trounce instinctively drew his pistol, aimed at the plant, and pulled the trigger. Nothing happened. He threw the weapon down in disgust and swore at himself.

"Stop it!" Swinburne shouted. He hefted a spear and charged forward, plunging the shaft into the centre of the repulsive bloom. Its point sank into the driver's stomach but had little effect. A thorny appendage slashed across the poet's forehead and sent him spinning away, with red droplets showering around him. He crashed into the side of a wrecked hut, which collapsed under the impact, burying the poet beneath sticks and dried mud.

The Wanyambo fought desperately, dodging and ducking, lunging in then backing away. They fell over one another and became wet with each other's blood. They went down and struggled up again. They threw and jabbed their spears until the huge weed-like thing was bristling with shafts. But despite their efforts, the plant continued to lurch back and forth, with the Prussian cradled in its bloom screeching furiously in incomprehensible German.

Burton looked this way and that, hoping to see fire somewhere in the village—sticks burning beneath a cooking pot, anything that he might fling at the plant to set it alight—but there was nothing. He snatched a spear from the ground and started to circle the monstrosity, looking for an opening that would allow him to leap in and drive the weapon through the Prussian's head. He got too close; a thick ropey limb smacked against his torso and ripped upward, shredding his shirt and flaying a long strip of skin from his chest. He stumbled and dropped to his knees.

"Stay back, Boss!" a voice piped.

A bundled mass of robes dived past Burton and launched itself into the writhing vegetation. Herbert Spencer landed on top of the driver and was immediately entwined by creepers. His robes and polymethylene suit were ripped apart as he fought with the frenzied, flailing appendages. A thick coil whipped around him, its thorns gouging deep scratches into his brass body.

The philosopher groped downward and forced his right hand into the fleshy petals. His three brass fingers slid over the driver's face. The man hollered and the plant shook and bucked as two of Spencer's digits found his eyes. The philosopher put his full weight on his arm and drove his fingers through the back of the Prussian's eye sockets and into the brain behind. The vehicle convulsed. Burton ran over and thrust his spear through the man's neck, severing the spine. The plant's tendrils flopped down, a tremor ran through it, then it was still.

Spencer fell backward and clanged onto the ground.

"Oof!" he piped.

The Wanyambo—those who weren't dead, unconscious, or in too much pain to notice—stared at him in astonishment. A metal man!

Burton tottered away from the Eugenicist creation, pulled what remained of his shirt off, and pressed the material against the deep laceration that angled up over his chest onto his left shoulder. He groaned with the pain of it, but, upon looking at the African warriors, saw that many had suffered much worse injuries.

He made his way over to Swinburne, who was crawling out from beneath the collapsed hut. Blood was streaming down the poet's face, dripping onto his clothing.

The king's agent called to Trounce, who was standing dazed. "William, are you hurt?"

"What? Huh, no."

"Come and bandage Algy, would you?"

The Scotland Yard man dragged a hand over his face as if to clear his mind, nodded, then ran over to the horses, which were being held on the far side of the village by a woman who'd had the foresight and courage to stop them from stampeding away. Pox and Malady were huddled on the saddle of one. The parakeets had slept through the entire drama.

Trounce retrieved the medical kit and returned to the poet.

Burton, meanwhile, spoke to Spencer: "Are you all right, Herbert?"

"Battered, Boss. Dented an' scratched all over—but tickin' an' serviceable."

Burton saw that the able-bodied among the Wanyambo had drawn together and were talking quietly, with many a gesture in Spencer's direction.

"I don't think our friends consider you a leper any more," he said.

Sidi Bombay crawled out of the undergrowth. "Wow! Mr. Spencer is like the thing called *pocket watch*, which you gave me long and long ago and which one of my six wives stole!"

"Yes, he is, Bombay," Burton agreed. "Can you explain that to the Wanyambo?"

"I shall try, though none of them has met my wives."

While Bombay joined the surviving warriors, Burton checked the injuries of the fallen. Three were dead and five too seriously hurt to continue on to the Mountains of the Moon. That left twelve—which meant his forces and Speke's were about even.

Bombay rejoined him and explained: "Wow! I told them that, just as the bad *muzungo mbáyá* has bad magic, so the good *muzungo mbáyá* has good magic. And Mr. Spencer is good magic."

"And they believed you?"

"Not at all. But they will continue with us to the mountains anyway."

"Good."

"They will not go into them, though, for the Wanyambo are afraid of the Chwezi, who you say don't exist."

"Very well. Help me with these injured, then we'll regroup and go after Speke. It's high time he and I brought our feud to an end—whatever it takes to do so."

Sidi Bombay stood motionless and gazed up at the mountains. He made clicking noises with his tongue.

Burton watched him, then stepped to his side and asked, "You are sure this is the route Speke took?"

Without moving, his eyes remaining glued to the scene ahead, Bombay answered: "Oh yes, this is it. Wow! It is an evil place. There is a bad feeling in the air, like when my wives stop speaking to me because I have come home drunk."

"It's certainly quiet," Burton replied. "An oppressive silence."

"There are no birds in the trees."

"There are two. We're having the devil of a time getting Pox and Malady down. Algy is climbing up to them."

"Your friend is like a little monkey."

"I'll be sure to tell him."

"I do not like these mountains, Mr. Burton. The Chwezi live here. The Chwezi who don't exist, and who serve the Batembuzi."

"And who are the Batembuzi?"

"They are the children of the gods who once ruled these lands. Long and long ago they disappeared into the underworld."

"We have no choice but to go on, Bombay," Burton said, "but you aren't obliged to accompany us. Do you want to remain here in the camp with the Wanyambo?"

"Wow! I want to, but I will not, because I have five wives and I expect you will pay me much more if I accompany you."

"I thought you had six wives?"

"I am trying to forget number four."

It was early in the morning. Two days had passed since the plant vehicle had attacked them. In that time they'd trekked across sodden and difficult terrain, and had at last reached the base of the Mountains of the Moon. They were now camped at the tree line.

A steep ravine lay ahead of them. Tall pointed rocks of a blueish hue stood like gateposts at the foot of the slope leading into it. According to Bombay, this was the path to the Temple of the Eye.

"I found them!" Swinburne announced as he shinned down the trunk of the Red Stinkwood tree into which the parakeets had vanished the night before. "They've nested in a hollow—and Pox has laid an egg!"

"By Jove!" Trounce exclaimed. "And what did the happy parents-to-be have to say on the matter?"

Swinburne jumped to the ground. "Pox called me a fumbling toad-gobbler, and Malady told me to sod off."

Burton moved away from Bombay and over to his friends. "It looks like this expedition has had a happy ending for one of our little family, anyway," he said. "Come on, let's leave them to it and get ourselves moving."

"I've divided what's left of the supplies into light packs," Trounce advised. "What equipment remains, we'll have to leave here."

Swinburne, looking up into the branches he'd just vacated, shook his head. "Why would they want to live in a place like this?" he asked. "There are no other birds."

"P'raps they likes their privacy," Herbert Spencer suggested.

"Maybe they need the space so they can begin a dynasty," Trounce offered.

The poet sighed. "I shall miss the foul-mouthed little blighters."

They hefted their bags, took up their spears, and started to scrabble up steep loose shale, sending rivulets of stone clattering down behind them.

Sir Richard Francis Burton, Algernon Swinburne, William Trounce, Herbert Spencer—with his discoloured, scratched, and dented body unencumbered by robes or polymethylene—and Sidi Bombay entered the Mountains of the Moon, and more than one of them had a question on his mind.

How many of us will come back?

CHAPTER 11

THE TEMPLE

"–the sombre range
Virginal, ne'er by foot of man profaned,
Where rise Nile's fountains, if such fountains be."
— José Basilio da Gama, *O Uruguay, Canto V*

Burton and Wells drew their harvestmen to a halt at the top of an incline and turned the vehicles to face the way they'd come. Beneath the mechanised spiders' feet, poppies grew in abundance. The red flowers weaved away in an irregular line, disappearing into the hazy distance, back toward the dirty grey smudge that marked the position of Tabora.

High overhead, looking enormous even though it was flying at a very high altitude, the *L.59 Zeppelin* drifted closer to the city.

It was a remarkable craft—a vegetable thing, like a gargantuan pointed cigar with ruffled seams on its sides. All along this join, oval bean-like growths swelled outward, and even from afar, it was apparent that they'd been hollowed out and fitted with portholes.

A giant purple flower grew from the rear of the vessel, similar in appearance to a tulip. Its petals were opening and closing, throbbing like a pulsing heart, driving the ship through the air.

"It's magnificent," Wells said. "And utterly horrible."

"Horrible because we know what it's carrying," Burton replied. "I wonder how big an area the A-Bomb will destroy? Surely the spores will drift?"

"Perhaps they're potent for only a few minutes," Wells mused. "But even if the effects are of short duration and confined to the city, thousands of people are going to die. There simply hasn't been time for everyone to get out. Look! Those dots rising up from Tabora—that's a squadron of hornets!"

"We need a rotorship."

"There are none. Our last was brought down more than a year ago."

The hornets—twelve of them—raced across the shrinking distance between the city and the German vessel. As they neared the bomb carrier, they exploded one after the other and fell to the earth trailing smoke behind them.

"No!" Wells shrilled. "What the hell happened?"

"There!" Burton pointed. "See the trails of vapour curving out from the *Zeppelin*? The Germans must have some sort of manoeuvrable shells."

"By heavens, Richard. Has it reached Tabora already? I can't tell."

"Any time now," Burton replied. "Be prepared to—"

Without warning, the sun erupted from the ground beneath the city. A blinding light blazed outward, and though Burton squeezed his eyes shut in an instant and clapped his hands over them, still he could see it. He heard Wells scream.

"Bertie, are you all right?" he yelled.

Wells groaned. "Yes. I think—I think it's passed."

Burton, realising that his friend was right, lowered his hands and opened his eyes. Wherever he looked, he saw a ball of fire.

"The damned after-image has blinded me," he said.

"Me too."

They sat with hands held to faces, waiting for their retinas to recover.

A strong wind hit them.

"Shockwave!" Wells exclaimed.

"No! It's going in the wrong direction," Burton noted, puzzled.

They looked up, blinking, vision returning.

A dense yellow mass of Destroying Angel spores was bubbling up from where the city stood—and as the two men watched, the billowing substance slowly revolved, as if around a central axis.

"The wind!" Wells said. "It's the blasted Hun weathermen! They're keeping that damned mushroom cloud in check, concentrating it in the city, preventing it from drifting!"

Burton moaned: "Quips! Poor Quips! Bismillah, Bertie! How many have just died?"

"Tens of thousands," Wells said, and his voice was suddenly deep and oily and unpleasant. "But I am not one of them."

Burton looked at the little war correspondent and was shocked to see that every visible part of his eyes had turned entirely black. There was a terrible menacing quality about them, and Burton couldn't tear his own away.

Wells gestured at the dying city.

"The generals are eager to locate a safe haven," he said, "so, regrettably, the SS *Britannia* is rolling in an easterly direction and will soon turn south, whereas you, I see, are heading north. Why is that, Private Frank Baker? Hah! No! That won't do! That won't do at all! Let us call you by another name. Let us call you Sir—Richard—Francis—Burton." He enunciated Burton's name slowly, emphasising each syllable, as if to drive home the point that he knew the explorer's true identity.

"Bertie?" Burton asked, uncertainly.

"Obviously not! Tell me, how did you do it?"

"How did I do what? Who are you?"

"Control the lurchers—make them open up a route through the besieging German forces?"

"Crowley?"

"Yes, yes! Now answer the question!"

"I didn't."

"What? You didn't control them? Then who—or what—did?"

"I have no idea. What do you want, Colonel?"

"I have seven black diamonds, Sir Richard, the fragments of the South American Eye of Nāga. There is much about them I do not understand." The black eyes glittered. The king's agent felt them penetrating his soul. "For example, you, sir, who should be three decades dead—your metaphorical fingerprints are all over them. Are they somehow responsible for transporting you from your time to mine?"

Burton didn't respond.

Wells—Crowley—regarded him silently.

The wind gusted past them.

"I shall tell you a secret, Sir Richard Francis Burton—something that, were it known by the generals aboard this ship, would prompt my immediate execution."

"What?"

"I am in contact with Kaiser Nietzsche."

"You're a collaborator?"

"Not in the sense you mean it. The German emperor and myself share a talent for clairvoyance. We've both detected through the diamonds that other realities exist, and that other versions of ourselves inhabit them. We want to know more. Your presence here appears to have some bearing on the matter." Wells gave an elaborate shrug and his oleaginous voice took on a carefree airiness. "But here we are: you fleeing in one direction and me fleeing in the other. Very inconvenient! I really should do away with this Wells fellow. He acted against me. But I shall allow him to live, for I sense that he's a vital ingredient in the shape of things to come."

"Crowley," Burton said. "Nietzsche dropped a bomb on you."

Wells emitted a thick chuckle. "Ah! So you doubt his commitment to me? Do not concern yourself. He gave me fair warning, and it was preordained that I would get away."

"You knew Tabora would be destroyed? You allowed all those people to die? Your countrymen?"

"Ordinary morality is only for ordinary people. The end of the British Empire was long overdue. I merely bowed to the inevitable."

"In the name of Allah, what kind of man are you?"

"Allah? Don't be ridiculous. And as for what I am, perhaps the embodiment of the Rakes, who, if I remember rightly, prospered in your age."

"You're an abomination!"

"I'm an individual who shares with Nietzsche the desire to create a superior species of man."

For the first time since he'd taken possession of Wells, Crowley took his eyes from Burton. He looked at the yellow cloud enveloping Tabora.

"Multiple futures," he said. "Different histories. Maybe some of them don't end like this. I should like to visit them." He returned his dreadful gaze to the explorer. "Perhaps we'll get it right in one of them, hey?"

He made Wells stretch and groan.

"Ho hum, Sir Richard! Ho hum! I've been here long enough. It's not comfortable. Has he told you how his leg is perpetually paining him? I don't know how he can bear it. Anyway, I'll say farewell. We shall meet again, sir; in this world or another version of it; maybe in your time, maybe in mine, maybe in another. But we shall meet again. And when we do—"

Wells smiled wickedly. The expression lingered, then the black faded from his eyes, they slipped up into his head, and he fell sideways from his saddle to the ground.

Burton hurriedly dismounted and threw himself down beside his friend. "Bertie! Bertie!"

The war correspondent rolled onto his side and vomited. He curled into a fetal position and moaned. "He was in my head. The filth, Richard! The filth of the man! He's the Beast personified!"

"Has he gone? Is he watching us?"

"He's gone. But he's going to come after you. Wherever—*when*ever—you are—he's coming after you!"

Burton helped Wells to sit up. The smaller man wiped his mouth and looked at the far-off mushroom cloud, and the flying machine shrinking to the south.

"It's finished," he said. "The Germans probably think they've won, but they're wrong. Everything is ending. This world is done for."

310

Burton could think of nothing to say, except: "I'm sorry, Bertie."

Wells stood, swayed slightly, and reached up to the stirrup of his harvestman.

"Let's get back on the trail. I want to find out where these poppies are leading us."

They clambered back into their saddles and turned their vehicles, sending them scuttling over the savannah.

For two days, they steered their harvestmen over what, to Burton, was eerily familiar territory.

He felt detached. All the connections to this world, formed over the past five years, were unfastening. Change was coming to him, of that he was certain, but he didn't know how.

Change, or, perhaps, restoration.

The Mountains of the Moon.

His destiny lay there.

Maybe it always had.

The trail of poppies led to those peaks, that was obvious even before the snow-capped summits rose over the horizon. He saw them, jagged and white, seeming to hover in the air above the blood-red base of the mountains.

"Red!" he exclaimed. "I remember this view—but the mountains were green!"

"That might have been true in the 1860s," Wells replied, "but the Blood Jungle has grown since then."

They raced over the empty landscape. Where there had once been villages, there were none. Were there had once been herds of antelope and zebra, there was nothing. Where fields had been cultivated, there was now rampant undergrowth.

Increasingly, they saw lurchers. The ungainly plants were shuffling over the hills and through the valleys with an unnerving air of sentience that prompted Wells to ask: "What are the damned things up to, Richard?"

"I know what you mean," the explorer replied. "They look purposeful, don't they? Do you remember the one that attacked us at Tanga? See how differently they move now! The mindless thrashing has been replaced by shudders and ticks, as if they're operating under some sort of restraint."

With so much of his memory restored, Burton recognised that the lurchers were the same species of plant as the vehicles the Prussians had used back in 1863—the same but horribly different, for there were no men enfolded in their fleshy petals—which meant, if there was something still controlling them, it wasn't necessarily human.

As they drew closer to the mountains, the vegetation grew thicker and wilder. Its flowers and fruits took on a reddish hue, deepening the farther they travelled, until blood-coloured blooms and berries and globular dew-dripping swellings of indiscriminate form surrounded them. The poppies guided the steam-driven spiders straight into the humid tangle, and, astonishingly, the chaotic verdure parted in front of them to allow their passage.

Shafts of light angled through the trees. Lianas drooped and looped and dangled. The air was heavy with scent, one minute perfumed, the next pungent with the stench of maggoty meat, then delightful again. Fat bees droned lazily through it. Dragonflies and butterflies flitted hither and thither. Seeds floated past on feathery wings. And in the canopy overhead, thousands upon thousands of parakeets squawked and screeched and cackled and whistled and cursed and insulted.

Burton started to laugh and couldn't stop.

Wells, who was at that point leading the way, looked back, raised his eyebrows, and asked: "What the heck has got into you?"

"Pox!" Burton cried out. "Pox and Malady! Ye gods! How many eggs did that confounded bird lay? Hah!" He raised his face to the sky and bellowed: "Pox! Pox! Pox!" then bent forward and was suddenly wracked by violent sobs, for too many memories were returning, and he knew for sure that he was going back, and he recalled what to.

Wells reined in his harvestman until it was beside the explorer's. "What is it, man? Are you all right?"

"I can't bear it," Burton whispered. "I can't bear it. It would be too much for any man. I have to find a way to change everything, Bertie. *Everything.*"

"Let's rest here," the war correspondent suggested. "There's some grub left in one of the packs. We'll eat and grab forty winks."

They turned off their vehicles' engines and dismounted. Beside them, a thick mass of crimson foliage suddenly rustled and parted like a pair of curtains, unveiling a short pathway to a beautiful poppy-filled glade.

"By golly! An invitation, if ever I saw one!" Wells exclaimed. "Whatever's behind your poppies obviously has power over this jungle, too!"

They walked into the open space and sat down. Wells had carried one of the panniers with him, and now opened it and pulled out a loaf of bread and a wedge of cheese. The two men ate.

Burton appeared lost in himself. His dark eyes were haunted, his cheeks sunken. Wells, feeling concerned, was watching him from the corner of his eye when something else caught his attention. At the edge of the clearing, a tree, heavy with large pear-shaped gourds, was moving. One of its branches, with creaks and snaps, was extending outward, into the open space. Burton, upon hearing it, turned his head and watched as the limb manoeuvred a gourd above them, then lowered it until it hung between the two men.

"A gift?" Wells asked.

Burton reached up to the red pumpkin-sized fruit. It snapped loose from the branch—which swung back out of the way—with ease, and as he lowered it, a small split opened in its top and an amber-coloured liquid sloshed out. He sniffed it, looked surprised, tasted it, and smacked his lips.

"You'll not believe this!" he said, took a swig, and passed the gourd to the war correspondent.

Wells tried it.

"It's—it's—it's brandy!"

They drank, they ate, they were insulted by parakeets.

Night came. They slept.

At dawn, the two men returned to their vehicles and continued along the trail of poppies.

"Either I'm riding a giant steam-powered spider through a benevolent living jungle with a man from the past," Wells pondered, "or I'm dreaming."

"Or stark staring mad," Burton added.

At noon, they came to a steep incline, bracketed on either side by tall pointed outcrops of blueish rock. Burton stopped his harvestman and peered through the branches at the mountains that towered ahead of them. He slid down from his saddle, bent, and examined the ground. The slope was comprised of shale bound together by a network of threadlike roots.

"This is it, Bertie."

"What?"

"This is the path that leads to the Temple of the Eye."

"Then onward and upward, I say!"

Burton remounted and steered his vehicle up the incline and into the mouth of a narrow crevasse. Thickly knotted vines grew against the rocky walls to either side and the ground was deep in mulch, from which poppies and other flowers grew in profusion.

As the walls rose and the shadows deepened, swarms of fireflies appeared, bathing the two travellers in a weird fluctuating glow.

They'd travelled for about a mile through this when the harvestmen passed a small mound of rocks—quite obviously a grave—and Burton, remembering who was buried there, was stricken with misery.

They went on, through thick foliage that parted as they approached, under hanging lianas that rose to allow them passage, over tangled roots that burrowed into the mulch so as not to trip the big machines.

And even in this place, so sheltered from the sunlight, parakeets ran riot through the vegetation, enthusiastically delivering their insults, which, as Wells noted, were invariably in English, despite that they were deep in the heart of German East Africa.

On, up, and the fissure opened onto a broad forested summit. Through the thick canopy, the men glimpsed distant snow-topped mountain peaks chopping at the sky.

"The Blood Jungle covers the whole range," Wells noted, "and has been gradually expanding beyond it for the past couple of decades."

The terrain angled downward, and the trail of poppies eventually led them into the mouth of a second crevasse, this one narrower and deeper than the previous. As they entered it, the verdure closed around them like a tunnel. Strange vermillion fruits hung from its branches, spherical and glowing with a ghostly radiance.

"I've never seen anything like it," Wells muttered. "I have the distinct impression that this is all one single plant. I feel as if we're inside a gigantic living thing."

Now the parakeets became less numerous, and a deep hush settled over them, broken only by the quiet chugging of the vehicles' steam engines and the buzzing of insects.

"We're being watched," Burton announced.

"What? By whom? Where?"

Burton pointed to a gap in the leaves up to his right. Wells squinted into the gloom and saw, vaguely illuminated by the red light, a naked man squatting on a branch. His skin was black and looked reptilian. There was a bow in his hands.

"Chwezi," Burton said. "The Children of the Eye. They won't harm us."

"How can you be sure?"

"I'm sure, Bertie."

They spotted more of the silent, motionless observers as they drove on, deeper and deeper into the gorge.

All of a sudden, there was daylight.

They'd emerged into a wide natural amphitheatre. Sunshine filtered through leaves and branches and slanted across such an unruly mass of vegetation that both men cried out in wonder. Branches and leaves and creepers and vines and lianas and stalks and stems and fruits and flowers were all jumbled together, all red, all climbing the surrounding cliffs, carpeting the ground, and drooping from overhead.

A colossal trunk rose from the centre of it all, dividing high above them into many limbs from which big fleshy leaves grew, and among which bizarre vermillion flowers blossomed. One of the branches was moving down toward them, with much groaning and screeching as its wood bent and stretched. It manoeuvred a giant flower, a thing with spiny teeth in its petals and odd bladder-like protuberances at its base, until it hung just in front of Burton.

The bladders inflated. The petals curled open to reveal a tightly closed bud-like knot. The bladders contracted. Air blew from between the lips of the bud making a high-pitched squeal, like a child's balloon being deflated. The lips moved and shaped the squeal into words.

The plant spoke.

"My hat, Richard! You took your giddy time! What the blazes have you been up to?"

From the deep indigo of the African sky, a thin line descended.

It wobbled and wavered through the hot compressed air, arcing down into the crevasse.

Sidi Bombay shouted, "Spear!" an instant before it emerged from the heat haze and thudded into his chest, knocking him backward. He sat on the rocky ground, looked at the vibrating shaft, looked at the sky, then looked at Burton.

"Wow!" he said. "Mr. Burton, please send a message to my fourth wife. Tell her—"

He fell backward and the shaft swung up into a vertical position.

Blood gurgled out of his mouth. His eyes reflected the azure heavens and glazed over.

"*Ambuscade!*" Burton bellowed. "Take cover!"

The Englishmen dropped their packs and dived into the shadow of an overhanging rock. Spears rained down, clacking against the rocky ground.

From behind a boulder, Burton peered up at the opposite lip of the gorge. Figures were silhouetted there. A spear thwacked against the stone inches from his face. He ducked back.

Spencer was beside him. "Are you all right, Herbert?" Burton asked.

"Yus, Boss."

"William!" the explorer shouted. "Are you fit?"

"As a fiddle! But I'd feel a lot better if our bloody rifles worked!" came the response from behind an outcrop some hundred and eighty feet away.

"Algy?" Burton called.

Swinburne—who'd thrown himself behind a rock off to Burton's right— leaped back into the open. He looked up and waved his arms like a lunatic.

"Hi!" he hollered at the shadowy figures overhead. "Hi there! You Prussians! Why don't you do us a favour and bloody well bugger off out of here?"

His voice bounced off the high walls. Spears descended and clattered around him.

"Algy!" Burton yelled. "Get under cover, you addle-brained dolt!"

Swinburne walked casually over to Burton and joined him behind the boulder.

"I'm trying to make them throw more of the bally things," he said. "They don't have an infinite supply."

"Actually, that's not too bad an idea," Burton muttered, "but poorly executed. Try to remember the difference between fearless and foolhardy."

He examined the rock-strewn fissure. The expedition's packs lay scattered, with multiple spear shafts rising out of them.

"There's not going to be much left that's usable in that lot—least of all the water bottles!" he grumbled.

Trounce's voice echoed: "How many bloody spears have they got up there?"

"Far fewer than before!" returned Burton. "Algy had it right—the more they waste, the better."

"Perhaps not such a waste," Swinburne said. "They're purposely trying to keep us pinned down, which suggests to me that some of them have gone on ahead."

Burton called: "William! Can you make it over here?"

"Watch me!" came the response.

Trounce leaped into view and sprinted across the intervening space, weaving from side to side as spears started to rain around him. He swept up three of the packs as he passed them, dragging them along, then, batting a falling shaft aside, hit the ground and slid into shelter in a cloud of dust.

"Phew! Am I in one piece?"

"Not a single perforation as far as I can see. How do you fancy a little bit more of that?"

The Scotland Yard man handed over the packs for Swinburne to check. "I don't much. My legs are still afire with damned sores. What's the plan?"

"We'll dart from cover to cover and keep moving. Don't so much as pause for breath in the open or you'll end up a pincushion!"

"Right you are."

The king's agent looked over at Sidi Bombay's body. Another death. Another friend lost. Another part of his world ripped out of him.

He wondered how much more of it he could take.

There was no option but to leave the African where he lay. Perhaps there'd be an opportunity to bury him later, if animals didn't get to the corpse first.

Trounce watched Swinburne reorganising the contents of the three bags, fitting it all into one pack. "What do we have?" he asked.

"Not a lot!" the poet replied. "One intact water bottle, a dented sextant, Herbert's key, an oil lamp, a box of lucifers, the field glasses from the *Orpheus*, and a small stock of food that looks as if it's been trampled by a herd of elephants."

"What took a hundred and twenty men to carry at the start of the expedition now takes one!" Burton muttered. "Throw away the sextant, and let's get on with it."

He took the bag, slung it over his shoulder, and pointed at fallen rocks farther up and to either side of the faint trail that wound through the middle of the crevasse. "William, you leg it to the base of the cliff, there. Algy, you dive beneath the overhang, there. And Herbert, you make for that boulder, there. I'm going to try for the rock at the bend in the trail—do you see it? From there, I'll survey the next stretch and call instructions to you. All ready? Good. Get set! Go!"

The three men—and one clockwork device—burst out of cover and dashed toward the locations the explorer had indicated. Spears started to fall, their points shattering as they landed.

Swinburne dived into cover first.

Burton was next, though his allotted position was farthest away.

Trounce stumbled when a rebounding shaft cracked painfully against the side of his face but made it without any more serious injury.

Herbert Spencer fared less well. Hampered by his damaged leg, his run was more of a fast shuffle, and three spears hit him. The first bounced from his shoulder with a loud chime.

"Ow! Bleedin' heck!" he piped

The second ploughed a furrow down his back.

"Aagh! They've got me!"

The third sliced through his left ankle, leaving his foot dragging behind him, attached by a single thin cable.

"Cripes! That's agony!" he hooted, falling into the shadow of the large boulder Burton had assigned to him.

"Ouch! Ouch! Ouch!" he said, and, reaching down, he tore the foot off completely and held it up so the others could see it. "Look at this!" he cried. "Me bloomin' foot's been chopped off!"

"Can you still walk, Herbert?" Burton called.

"Yus, after a fashion. But that ain't the point, is it?"

"What is the point?" Swinburne asked from his nearby position.

"That me bleedin' foot's come off, lad!"

"I'm sure Brunel will have you polished and repaired in no time at all after we get back to Blighty," Swinburne responded. "There's no need to worry."

"You're still missin' the point. Me foot's come off. It hurts!"

Burton, who'd identified points of cover among the rocks ahead, shouted instructions back to them.

They ran.

Herbert Spencer hobbled along, scraping his stump over the hard ground. A spear clunked into his hip and stuck there.

"Yow!" he cried. He yanked it out and threw it aside.

Another clanged off his head.

"Bloody hell! Bloody hell!"

He reached the sidewall, where it bulged outward, and collapsed into its shadow. He lay there, groaning.

"Herbert," Swinburne called. "For the umpteenth time: it's all in your mind! You can't feel pain!"

"Ready for more dodging?" Burton called.

"Wait a moment!" Trounce shouted. A spear tip had scooped a furrow across his thigh and blood was flowing freely. He tore off one of his shirt-sleeves and used it to bind the wound. "All set!"

Another mad dash, more spears—but far fewer this time—and they reached the space beneath a leaning slab without further injury.

"They must have stolen every spear from every village they pillaged," Swinburne noted. "Either that or they have a portable pointy-stick factory with them."

A wailing scream suddenly echoed and a body thumped into the gorge near to where they squatted. It was a white man, blond-haired and blue-eyed and dead. An arrow, striped red and black, was sticking out of his chest.

Shouts and screams sounded from above.

"They're being attacked!" Burton exclaimed.

"Who by?" Swinburne asked.

"Let's not dally to ponder that! Come on!"

They dashed out of their hiding place—the king's agent giving support to Trounce, and Swinburne to Spencer—and hurried along the cleft, leaving the embattled Prussians behind.

After they'd traversed perhaps two miles, the ground angled steeply upward. It was tough going.

Burton's stomach rumbled. Sweat dripped from the end of his nose.

He tried to remember what it felt like to sit in his old saddlebag arm-chair by the fire in his study.

"We're gettin' close, Boss," Spencer announced. "I can feel the Eye's presence."

The group struggled on through the fissure. By mid-afternoon, its walls had opened out and they emerged onto a low summit. The temperature plummeted, and suddenly they were shivering. The low mountains and hills they'd trekked through humped away to the rear; to either side, a long ridge zigzagged away to rising snow-covered peaks, which jaggedly heaped into the distance; and ahead, a long slope of crumpled strata plunged steeply downward and was split by a second shadowy crevasse.

Footing became precarious now; the ground was very uneven, with patches of loose slate-like rock that slipped from beneath their feet and rattled away down the incline.

They reached the fracture in the mountain's side and entered it. Darkness closed around them. Sheer rock faces soared up to the left and right, reaching such a height that the sky was reduced to nothing but a thin line of serrated blue.

They stopped for a moment while Burton rummaged in the pack for the oil lamp. Its glass was broken but it was functional. He struck a lucifer, put it to the wick, and moved on, illuminating the cracks and irregularities in their path.

"That's rummy!" Swinburne muttered. "No echoes!"

It was true: their footsteps and voices, the knocks and scrapes of displaced stones—every sound was sucked into an overwhelming silence.

The eerie atmosphere increased as the party moved ever deeper into the gloom.

"If Speke went on ahead while the Prussians tried to stick us with spears, then surely we must be hot on his heels by now," Trounce whispered.

Burton clenched his jaw and fists.

After a while, they found themselves catching swift movements from the corners of their eyes—indistinct things flitting through the shadows—but when they looked, there was nothing to see.

The thread of sky was so far away that the darkness was almost complete. Burton raised his lamp. It illuminated men, naked but for loincloths and necklaces of human finger bones, standing dark and motionless against the cliffs to either side. Their faces were scored by networks of scars, making their skin resemble the segmented hide of reptiles; they were holding bows fitted with red-and-black-striped arrows, and their eyes were fixed on Herbert Spencer.

"How many?" Swinburne hissed.

"Hard to tell. A lot," Burton replied. "Chwezi. It was obviously they who attacked the Prussians."

"Look at the way they're all a-gogglin' at me," Spencer said.

"I'm not surprised," Swinburne responded. "With all those dents and scratches, you're quite a sight!"

"Thank you, lad. But it ain't that. I reckons they can feel the diamonds what's in me head."

"They're closing in to the rear," Trounce warned.

The others looked back and saw a number of the Chwezi slowly moving toward them.

"But they've left the way ahead open," Swinburne observed. "Seems to me like they're here to escort us. Or do I mean herd us?"

"To the Eye?" Burton asked.

"It's in this direction, Boss," Spencer confirmed. "The emanations are very strong now."

"Then I suggest we allow ourselves to be guided."

The king's agent continued on along the narrow path, and Swinburne, Trounce, and Spencer trailed after him. The Chwezi stood in eerie silence, not moving until the Britishers had passed, then falling in behind.

Untouched by the sun, the mountain air grew increasingly frigid, and the men's breath clouded in front of their faces. Snow, piled at the sides of the crevasse, reflected the light of Burton's lamp, stark white in the black shadows, and ice glittered on the walls.

"This fault line," Swinburne said, "we climbed up through it on the other side of the mountain, and now we're descending through it on this. It's as if the whole peak has been split down its centre. What unimaginable energy must have caused that?"

"Not volcanic," Burton mumbled, distractedly. "This is metamorphic rock. You can see from the angle of the strata how subterranean pressures have pushed it upward." He frowned and looked up at the thin strip of blue sky high overhead. "You're right, though, Algy. There are very powerful geological forces at work here!"

Half a mile farther on, the chasm suddenly opened out to form a broad, bowl-shaped arena into which the sun shone, warming the air dramatically.

"Look!" Trounce said softly, and pointed ahead.

Across the space, the high wall was cut through as the great crack in the mountain's side continued, the mouth of it blocked by more of the silent Chwezi. Burton glanced about. He and his companions were surrounded.

"There's a cave," Spencer announced. He pointed to the right, at a gap in the ranks of encircling warriors, where a shadow in the rock concealed a blacker patch of darkness.

"Bombay said the temple was underground and accessible through a cave. I suppose that's it," Burton said. "And our escort obviously wants us to go down there."

He moved warily to the opening and extended his lamp into it, illuminating a deep hollow at the back of which he saw a narrow opening.

"Come on," he called, and ushered the others in with a wave of his hand. They filed past and he followed, stepping through the aperture in the rear wall while watching to see if the Chwezi were going to come in after them. They didn't.

He turned and saw a smooth rocky passage.

"Wait," he instructed. His friends stopped and he squeezed past them until he was in point position.

They moved on, following the irregular tunnel. It descended, bending to the right and to the left.

There were no sounds of pursuit.

After a while, the detective became aware of something peculiar. He ordered a halt and blew out his lamp's flame. By degrees, a faint bluish luminescence became apparent.

"What's that?" came Swinburne's whisper.

"Some sort of phosphorescent fungus or lichen, by the looks of it. Let's proceed without the lamp. Our eyes will adjust."

Gingerly, measuring every step as the passage inclined more steeply, they inched onward. As they did so, the glowing fungus became more prevalent until, a few yards farther on, it covered the walls entirely, lighting the way with a weird, otherworldly radiance.

The crooked corridor veered sharply to the left and plunged downward at a severe angle. They struggled to maintain their footing, slipping and stumbling until they were moving faster than they could help. Almost running, they plunged down and out onto the level floor of a fantastical chamber—a large domed grotto—so filled with ambient blue light that its every feature stood out in sharp focus.

They gasped, astonished at the spectacle.

Stalagmites, ranging from tiny to huge, rose from the floor, stretching toward stalactites of similar proportions, which hung from the high roof. Many of them had met and melded together to form massive asymmetrical pillars, giving the chamber the appearance of a gigantic organic cathedral.

Veins of glittering quartz were embedded in the walls, and serrated clumps of the crystal rose from the floor. On the far side of the chamber, a small fountain of clear water tinkled as it bubbled up from its underground source, spreading into a pool, roughly oval in shape and about twenty feet across at its widest point. Draining from it, a narrow stream had cut a channel through the stone floor to the centre of the cavern, where the kidney-shaped forty-foot-wide mouth of a sinkhole opened in the floor. The stream plunged into the darkness of this cavity, disappearing back into the depths of the Earth.

A number of tall wooden posts with roughly spherical masses stuck at their tops stood around the hole.

At the base of the walls, mushrooms—probably white but appearing pale blue in the light—stood clustered in groups; mushrooms of wildly exaggerated proportions, many of them more than twelve feet tall.

Trounce gasped: "Somebody pinch me!"

"Incredible!" Swinburne spluttered. "If an emissary of the fairy nation stepped forward and, on behalf of his monarch, welcomed us to his kingdom, I wouldn't be a bit surprised!"

They moved farther into the grotto and peered into the well. Trounce picked up a rock and dropped it in. They waited, expecting to hear a crack or splash echoing up from the darkness. Neither came.

"A bottomless pit," the Scotland Yard man muttered.

The men stepped over to the pool. Burton knelt and lifted a handful of water to his lips.

"Wonderfully pure," he said. "Thank heavens!"

They slaked their thirst.

"Boss," Spencer said.

Burton looked at the philosopher and saw that he was pointing at the nearest of the upright poles. The king's agent examined it and let out a gasp of horror.

The lump at its top was a desiccated human head. Though wrinkled and shrunken, it was unmistakably that of a European.

There were seven poles and seven heads. Burton examined them all. He recognised one. It was Henry Morton Stanley.

"These others must be the five men who travelled with him," he said. "Which leaves one extra."

A harsh voice rang out: "*Ja, mein Freund!* It is the head of poor James Grant!"

They whirled around.

Count Zeppelin stepped into view from behind a thick stalagmite. He was a tall and portly man with a completely bald head and a big white walrus moustache. His hands were gripped tightly around the neck of a second individual. It was John Hanning Speke. The vicious-looking claws at the end of Zeppelin's fingers were pressing against, but not yet piercing, the skin of the Britisher's throat.

"*Es ist sehr gut!*" said the count enthusiastically. "We have reached the end of our journey at last!"

"You bastard!" Swinburne hissed. "You've the blood of Tom Bendyshe and Shyamji Bhatti on your hands!"

"I do not know those people," Zeppelin answered. "And I do not care."

Burton whispered to Spencer: "Herbert, if you can make your revolver work, now is the time. On my command, draw it and shoot him."

"Rightio, Boss."

"And what is the death of one man," Zeppelin was saying, "or two, or even a hundred, when we—how do you say it, Herr Burton?—*wenn wir mit der Welt spielen?*"

"When we are gambling with the world. I would say the death of one man might make all the difference, Count Zeppelin. Hello, John. Your erstwhile ally seems to have you at a disadvantage."

Bedraggled and skinny to the point of emaciation, with his beard grown almost to his waist, Speke's pale-blue right eye was wide with fear. The left was a glass lens—part of the brass clockwork apparatus that had been grafted to his head, replacing the left hemisphere of his brain. It was a prototype constructed by Charles Babbage, designed to process the electrical fields stored in two fragments of the Cambodian Eye of Nāga. Those diamonds had been stolen before the scientist could properly experiment with them, so he'd passed the device over to a cabal of Technologists and Rakes, and they'd fitted it to Speke in order to gain control of him. Later, Babbage had constructed a much more sophisticated version of the device, and that now sat in Herbert Spencer's head, along with all seven of the Cambodian stones.

"Dick!" Speke gasped. "It wasn't me! It wasn't me! I didn't do any of it!"

"I know, John. You've been the greatest victim of them all."

"Please! We have to get out of here! They'll come for us!"

Zeppelin grinned. "He believes there are monsters in this place."

"I see only one," Swinburne snarled, stepping forward with his fists raised.

"Remain where you are, *kleiner Mann*," Zeppelin growled.

Burton said, "Let's not waste any more time. Now, Herbert."

The clockwork philosopher drew his revolver, aimed it at Zeppelin's head, and did nothing.

Burton sighed. He turned to William Trounce and asked, in an exasperated tone, "Have you noticed how he winds down at the most inconvenient of times?"

"I have!" the Yard man grumbled.

Count Zeppelin laughed nastily. "Your clockwork toy has become a statue. *Sehr gut!* Now, let us get to business. I want your little assistant to go around the rock behind me. He will find there a pack, and in it some lengths of rope. Have him fetch them, if you please."

"Up yours, you murdering git!" Swinburne spat.

"It would be more convenient for me to keep the lieutenant alive for a while longer, Herr Burton, but I am prepared to inject him with venom now, if necessary. It will cause him to transform in a most painful fashion. He is your enemy, *ja*? But he was once your friend. Are you prepared to watch him die?"

The count applied pressure to Speke's neck. The Englishman started to choke.

"Stop!" Burton barked. "Algy, fetch the ropes."

"But, Richard—"

"Just do it, please."

Swinburne hesitated, then stamped past Zeppelin and his captive, found the pack, retrieved the coils of rope, and returned to his former position.

"Don't—" Speke began, but was cut off and shaken hard.

"You will be quiet!" the count said. He looked at Trounce and demanded: "You there! Who are you?"

Trounce scowled. "I'm Detective Inspector William Trounce of Scotland Yard."

"Ha-ha! A policeman in Africa! Most amusing! You will kneel down and the little man will bind your wrists."

"I'll not kneel for you!"

"You are of no consequence to me, Detective Inspector. If you allow yourself to be tied, I give you my word that I will leave you here alive. Perhaps you will manage to free yourself and make your way out of this cavern, *ja*? But if you resist, I shall most certainly kill you like a dog." Zeppelin transferred his attention to Burton. "Do not doubt that I can defeat all three of you, Herr Burton!" He took his right hand from Speke's neck, held it up, and flexed his fingers. His claws gleamed in the phosphorescent light. "It takes but one scratch!"

"William," Burton said, quietly. "Do as he says, please."

Trounce looked shocked. "We can overpower him!" he hissed.

"The risk is too great. As he says: one scratch. I would prefer to keep you alive while this affair plays itself out."

"Kneel with your back to me, Herr Policeman. I wish to see that the rope is made tight."

Trounce slowly obeyed, his face livid with anger.

Burton said: "Go ahead, Algy."

The poet, whose eyes were also blazing with fury, squatted behind Trounce and began to tie his wrists.

"*Nein! Nein!*" Zeppelin shouted. "*Das ist ein* slipknot*! Ich bin kein Narr!* Do not try to deceive me! Do it properly!"

Swinburne cursed under his breath and started again.

When he'd finished, the count ordered the poet to rejoin Burton. He then dragged Speke forward, still holding him by the neck with just his left hand, and inspected the handiwork.

"*Das ist besser!*" he exclaimed.

He pulled a revolver from his belt and pointed it at the back of Trounce's neck.

"No!" Swinburne shrieked.

Burton looked on, his face mask-like.

Zeppelin noticed the explorer's expression and grinned at him. "You think perhaps that my pistol is useless, *ja?*"

He received no response.

"You are wrong, Herr Burton. Observe!"

The Prussian sliced the weapon upward into the bony side of Speke's head. The lieutenant slumped, and the count let him slip senselessly to the ground.

"Effective, do you not think?"

Zeppelin reversed the weapon and held it in his left hand like a club. He stepped closer to Trounce, pressed his knee between the detective's shoulder blades, and, with his right hand, reached down over the Yard man's face. He curled his fingers under the bearded chin and levered Trounce's head back until his spine was agonisingly arched and the Prussian's claws were pressed dangerously into the skin of his neck.

"Now, Herr Burton, you too will kneel and your assistant will tie you. If you do not do this, I will break this man's back."

"You gave your word!" Swinburne shrilled.

"I gave my word that I would leave him here alive. I did not say anything about the condition of his spine."

"Damn the man!" Burton muttered. He knelt, facing away from Zeppelin.

"As before, little assistant. None of your tricks!"

Swinburne bent over Burton and began to bind his wrists.

"What's the plan, then, Richard?" he whispered eagerly.

"I was hoping you'd tell me, Algy."

"Be quiet!" Zeppelin commanded.

Swinburne finished the job and stood back.

The count released Trounce. "*Das war einfach!*" he said. "It is more convenient to kill a man when he is on his knees, *nein?*"

He raised the revolver over Trounce, still holding it like a club, looked at Swinburne, and asked, "Do you wish to say goodbye to your friends?"

The poet's mouth fell open.

"Your word, Zeppelin!" Burton yelled.

The count laughed. "Who heard it except the men who will die here today? I will leave this place, by myself, with the Eye of Nāga in my hand and my honour intact! I will be a hero to the Germanic people!"

He swung the pistol up and back.

Swinburne let loose a scream of rage and flung himself forward. The Prussian turned and swiped at him, but the poet, with astonishing speed, ducked and rolled through Zeppelin's widespread legs. Snatching up a lump of quartz, he bounded to his feet and threw it with all his might into the side of his opponent's head.

Zeppelin staggered and groaned. He turned and hit out, blindly. Swinburne was already scampering clear and scooping up a fist-sized stone. He threw it and it cracked off the bigger man's kneecap, causing him to scream with pain.

"Bravo, lad!" Trounce cheered.

"Your aim is improving, Algy!" Burton called.

"I was trying to hit his nose!"

"Oh!"

"Come here!" Zeppelin roared, hopping on one leg.

"Not bloody likely!" Swinburne answered. Maintaining his distance, he picked up more crystals and rocks and started pelting the count with them.

"*Gott im Himmel!*" Zeppelin cried out. He backed away, coming perilously close to the lip of the sinkhole.

"Send him over the edge, lad!" Trounce urged.

In desperation, the Prussian hurled his revolver at Swinburne. It flew wide of the mark.

"Ha!" the poet squealed. He aimed at Zeppelin's uninjured knee, and, putting all his strength behind it, launched another stone. It caught the count in the middle of his forehead. The big man groaned and sat down hard, his eyes glazing over. Blood poured down his face.

Swinburne bent and lifted a large serrated lump of amethyst, heaved it over his head, and staggered toward the Prussian, intending to crack it down onto the man's skull.

"Algy!" Burton yelled. "Stay away from him!"

His assistant, oblivious to all but revenge, ignored the command and reached his opponent's side. He swung the amethyst higher.

Zeppelin's fist lashed out and caught him in the stomach. The crystal shattered on the rocky ground as Swinburne dropped it and doubled over. The count grabbed him by the neck and dug his claws in. He pushed himself to his feet and, standing behind the poet, yanked him around to face Burton and lifted him into the air.

Swinburne's eyes bulged. His face began to turn blue. He jerked and kicked in Zeppelin's grip. Black lines of venom crawled under his skin as the talons sank in.

"Don't!" Burton screamed.

"He is very irritating to me, Herr Burton!" Zeppelin explained, shaking his victim.

Swinburne's tongue protruded. His eyes started to roll up into his head.

"Let him go!" Trounce bellowed.

"I will be certain to do so, Herr Policeman—when he is dead! But see! He has a little life left in him still! How he kicks!"

With his last vestiges of strength, the poet reached into his jacket and pulled from it Apollo's gold-tipped arrow of Eros. He jerked it upward and backward over his shoulder. The point sank into Zeppelin's right eye.

With an agonised shriek, the Prussian reeled back, teetered on the edge of the sinkhole, and plunged into it, dragging Swinburne with him.

Suddenly: silence.

Burton and Trounce knelt, staring, unable to comprehend that their companion was gone. An incalculable interval passed; perhaps a moment, maybe an hour; to the two men, it felt as though time wasn't moving at all; then John Speke moaned and shifted and everything snapped back into focus.

"I say, chaps!" came Swinburne's voice. "Culver Cliff!"

Burton loosed a bark of laughter. On a previous occasion, when his assistant had been dangling over a precipice and holding on by his fingertips, he'd referred to that youthful escapade of his, when he'd climbed Culver Cliff on the Isle of Wight. It had become a symbol of his apparent indestructibility.

"Hold on!" Burton called. He struggled to his feet, his wrists still bound behind him, paced over to the lip of the well, and knelt beside it. Swinburne was just below, hanging on to a narrow shelf with both hands. His neck was bruised purple, and blood flowed from the puncture marks in it.

"William!" Burton snapped. "Get over here, put your back to me, and untie these confounded knots. Can you hang on there for a little longer, Algy?"

"Yes, Richard. But I feel jolly peculiar."

It was no wonder: the capillaries of the poet's face were black and appeared to be writhing beneath the skin. Small white buds were pushing through at the corners of his nose, and, even as Burton watched, leaves started to open amid his friend's long hair, like a laurel wreath.

"Hurry, William!" he hissed as he felt Trounce's fingers getting to work.

The whites of Swinburne's eyes suddenly turned green.

"I'm thirsty," he said.

"Almost there!" Trounce grunted.

"And my arms are aching," the poet added.

"Got it!" the Scotland Yard man announced, and Burton felt the ropes loosen. He yanked his wrists free, threw himself on his stomach, and reached down to his assistant.

"Grab hold!"

Hanging on to the ledge with just his left hand, Swinburne stretched the right up toward Burton.

"My hat!" he exclaimed and drew his hand back a little, for a bright-red flower had suddenly bloomed from the back of it. "It's—it's a poppy, Richard!"

His fingers slipped from their hold.

Swinburne dropped into darkness.

"Have you got him?" Trounce asked.

Burton didn't reply.

"Richard?"

The Yard man crawled around on his knees to face the explorer.

"Richard? Richard? Do you have him?"

The king's agent remained still, his tears dripping into the void beneath his face.

"Oh no," Trounce whispered huskily. "Oh no."

Burton untied Trounce.

John Speke stirred and sat up.

"Dick," he groaned. "I'm so sorry. I'm so sorry for everything." He touched the babbage embedded in his skull. "It was this damned thing. Every time I wound it up, it forced decisions upon me. I've been like an opium addict with it. Unable to stop!"

"But now?" Burton asked, dully. He felt remote. Disengaged. Broken.

"It was all about coming here," Speke responded. "The wretched thing was designed to make me fetch the black diamond for the Technologist and Rake alliance. When you killed the madmen behind that scheme, the compulsion to come here remained, but I had no sponsor, so it forced me to find one."

"The Prussian government."

"Yes. I guided Zeppelin here, and as soon as I set foot in the place, the device, having realised its purpose, stopped working."

An expression of sheer torment passed over his face.

"I still have the addiction, Dick. I'm on fire with the urge to wind it up again! But Babbage booby-trapped it. If I use it even once more, a timing mechanism will activate and it will explode!"

Herbert Spencer broke his pose and stepped forward. He spoke in an uncharacteristically precise voice: "The man you refer to was rather precious about his contraptions, wasn't he? I understand he booby-trapped them all to prevent others from discovering the secret of their construction." He aimed his pistol at the king's agent. "This revolver will operate perfectly well while it's in my grasp, Sir Richard. Don't you think it rather regrettable that destructive forces must so often be employed to achieve one's ends?"

Burton gasped and clutched at Trounce's arm for support.

Spencer made a piping noise that may have been a chuckle. "Pretending to have lost motive energy is by no means an original trick but it is an effective one. As you can see, I have power in my mainspring."

"What—what are you playing at, Herbert?" Burton stammered. "Why didn't you help us?"

"The song must be sung in the proper manner."

"Song? What are you talking about?"

"The Song of the Nāga. Let us not stand here discussing it. A demonstration will be far more effective. If you would all please step over to that outcrop of blue crystal—" The brass man gestured with his revolver toward the wall of the cavern where a tall formation of amethyst hunched up from the floor. They moved to it. There was a low opening in the wall behind, a space big enough for a man to crawl into.

Spencer said, "Go in first, please, Mr. Speke; then you, William; and you last, Sir Richard."

One by one, they entered what proved to be little more than a winding tube. Patches of phosphorescence illuminated its length.

Burton fought to quell his rising panic. He had an irrational fear of enclosed spaces. The passage into the grotto had been bad enough, but this was far worse.

As they inched along, flat on their stomachs, the clockwork man explained: "The fact of the matter is that I'm not Herbert Spencer and never have been. When he died in close proximity to the Cambodian diamonds, his mind was imprinted onto them, just as you thought, but it never had the power to motivate this mechanical body. It was I who did so, using his personality as a bridge—or a filter, if you will—through which to interact with you. Spencer is, I'm afraid to say, thoroughly suppressed. The poor man! I can feel his frustration, his eagerness to help you!"

"Then who are you?" the king's agent asked, fighting to keep his voice steady.

"I am K'k'thyima, high priest of the Nāga."

Burton, whose mind had barely functioned since the loss of Swinburne, struggled to make sense of this revelation.

"I dreamt of you. You sounded different."

"As I said, I employ the mind of Herbert Spencer in order to communicate. I could chin-wag more like what he bloomin' well does, if'n it'll make you feel more comfy, like."

"I'd prefer it if you didn't."

"A little farther, gentlemen. We're almost there."

Moments later, the three men wormed their way out of the tunnel and got to their feet. They stood paralysed, with hearts hammering and eyes popping.

What confronted them was virtually incomprehensible.

They were standing on a ledge, hundreds of feet above the floor of a vast cavern, which was ablaze with the strange azure radiance; and if the previous vault had seemed magical, then this one appeared miraculous!

A megalithic temple rose from the centre of the massive space. Its soaring walls, spires, and columns were decorated with complex geometrical designs and friezes. The men gazed in awe at its sweeping arches and curving arcades; at the many gargoyles and representations of lions and oxen and other, extinct, animals; and at the thick round central tower that rose to the distant ceiling and merged with it.

The entire temple complex—for there were many outbuildings squatting around the base of the edifice—was hewn from solid rock, and for many minutes, Burton, Trounce, and Speke stood silent and confounded, wondering what manner of tools had been employed to achieve this eighth—and foremost!—wonder of the world.

As the brass man scraped out of the tunnel behind them, Speke whispered, "I never knew! I never got this far! Both times, when I reached the grotto, the things came and dragged me out of it."

"Then when did you see the Eye?" Burton asked.

"I didn't. Not physically. But I had a clear vision of it."

"*What?* All this we've been through began with nothing but a *vision?*"

"I planted it in Mr. Speke's mind," K'k'thyima said.

"Things?" Trounce interrupted. "You said *things* dragged you out, Speke?"

"Yes. They were—they were—"

"They were the Batembuzi," the brass figure interjected. "Long ago, they served the Nāga and had an empire that covered all of the Lake Regions, but now this—" he swept out his arm to indicate the temple, "—is their home." He gestured to their right with his revolver. "The ledge goes down here and slopes around the wall to the floor. Follow it, please."

They walked slowly, as necessitated by the condition of the clockwork man's left leg.

The ledge narrowed for a stretch, and they had to press themselves against the cavern wall to navigate along it.

"Allow me to tell you a little of the Nāga," K'k'thyima said. "Long, long ago, we lived where the three Eyes had fallen: here, and in South America, and on the continent of Kumari Kandam—and though our colonies were separated, we bonded in a Great Fusion through means of the diamonds."

"Until Brahmin Kaundinya came along," Burton murmured.

"Ah, of course, you have studied the legend. Yes, your spy Kaundinya broke the Kumari Kandam Eye into seven fragments, causing the physical death of all the Nāga on that continent. Their essence lived on in the stones, of course, but now they were isolated, for the other two Eyes were whole, whereas theirs was shattered."

"Your Great Fusion requires the three Eyes to be in the same state?"

"It does."

The group was now about halfway down the path. Speke led the way, self-absorbed and tormented; Trounce followed, listening to what he considered a fairy tale; Burton was third in the line; and the clockwork man hauled himself along behind, holding his pistol aimed steadily at the back of the explorer's head.

K'k'thyima continued: "When a Nāga completes its lifespan, the Great Fusion offers the choice of true death—which many prefer—or a transcendence. Kaundinya's act of betrayal denied us all these options, and condemned us to eternity and eventual madness. Obviously, this is a situation that has to be corrected."

"Only equivalence can lead to destruction or a final transcendence," Burton said. "You can't put a broken diamond together again, so you have to shatter the other two stones to achieve equivalence."

"And restore the Great Fusion, yes. Incidentally, your friend Spencer is a very determined man. He is not happy that I borrowed his personality. He tried to leave a clue for the unfortunate Mr. Swinburne in his *First Principles of Philosophy*. It was all I could do to stop the poet from telling you about it."

"How did you do that?"

"I've been radiating a mesmeric influence to make you all consider me harmless and friendly."

They reached the cavern floor, and K'k'thyima directed them along a well-worn path toward the buildings at the foot of the temple.

"So we were at an impasse. We couldn't shatter the other two Eyes while our South American and African colonies still lived, for it would have physically killed them. Nor could we stand to exist in a state of disconnection. We thus lost the will to survive in the material realm, and allowed you soft skins to hunt us to extinction."

"But the essence of you continued to dwell in the Eyes?" Burton asked.

"Yes, and now we had to wait for your species to discover the diamonds."

"Why?"

"So that we might use you to bring equivalence. As high priest, I was the only one of my people whose essence spanned all of the stones, and I was able to channel the mesmeric abilities of my species through any of them. I was thus able to manipulate you soft skins. Ah, look! Here come the Batembuzi!"

Up ahead, figures were slouching out of doorways and sliding out of glassless windows. A large crowd of them gathered and loped forward to meet the approaching party. They were small and ape-like, with skin of a dull-white hue, and their eyes were strange and large and greyish-red. Shaggy flaxen hair descended to their shoulders and grew down their backs, and they moved with their arms held low, sometimes resorting to all fours. Thoroughly nightmarish in aspect, they proved too much for Speke. With a wail of terror, he threw himself backward.

"Hold him!" K'k'thyima ordered.

Burton and Trounce grabbed the lieutenant. He fought them, emitting animalistic whines of fear.

"They aren't going to harm you!" the priest said. "They'll just escort us into the temple,"

Speke finally quietened down when the hideous troglodytes, rather than attacking, simply fell into position beside the group.

As they entered among the squat buildings, the brass man instructed the Britishers to walk straight ahead to the central thoroughfare, then turn right and proceed along it. They followed his instructions and saw, some way ahead, the tall double doors of the temple entrance.

"Everything!" Burton suddenly exclaimed. "Bismillah! You orchestrated *everything*! You planted in Edward Oxford an irrational obsession about his ancestor so he'd travel back in time and cause all of the Eyes to be discovered! You manipulated Rasputin so you could occupy that clockwork body, commandeer Herbert Spencer's mind, and shatter the South American Eye! And you caused that damned babbage to be grafted onto Speke's brain so he'd lead me here!"

"That has been my song," K'k'thyima confessed. "And now we shall shatter the last of the Eyes and the Nāga will be free."

Passing blocky, unadorned buildings, they came to the foot of a broad set of steps leading up to the temple's imposing arched entrance. They ascended, and a group of Batembuzi put their shoulders to the doors and pushed. As the portals swung slowly inward, Burton asked, "But what of the fragments Oxford cut from the South American Eye for his time suit? Surely they unbalance the equivalence you seek?"

"Soon, Sir Richard, you will discover the beauty and elegance of paradox. Those shards were cut in a future where the stone was complete. I changed that future when, earlier in the same diamond's history, I broke it into seven. Thus the pieces could not be cut from it."

"I don't understand any of this," Trounce grumbled.

The clockwork man gave a soft hoot. "Do not be embarrassed, William. Non-linear time and multiplying histories are concepts that most soft skins struggle with. For your kind, it is virtually impossible to escape the imprisoning chains of narrative structure. We have come here to address that deficiency."

"Oh. How comforting."

They entered a prodigious and opulent chamber. Its floor was chequered with alternating gold and black hexagonal tiles. The walls were carved into bas reliefs, inset with thousands of precious gemstones, and the ceiling was a solid blanket of scintillating phosphorescence from which hung censers forged from precious metals and decorated with diamonds.

Oddly, though, the chamber reminded Burton and Trounce less of a temple and more of Battersea Power Station, for there were strange structures arrayed around the floor and walls; things that appeared to be half-mineral formation and half-machine, with, dominating the centre of the space, a thick floor-to-ceiling column made up of alternating layers of crystalline and metallic materials.

Despite the abundance of precious stones on display, there was an air of abandonment about the place. As they passed through the chamber and started up a winding stairwell, Burton noted that many of the gems had fallen from their housings in the patterned walls and were lying scattered around the floor. There were cracks and crumblings in evidence everywhere, and at one point they had to step over a wide hole where the stone steps had collapsed and fallen away.

"Straight ahead, please, gentlemen."

"My bloody legs!" Trounce groaned as they climbed higher and higher.

The stairs led up to a long, wide hall with gold-panelled double doors at its far end. Fourteen statues stood against the walls, seven to each side. They depicted Nāga, squatting on short plinths, some with one head, some with five, some with seven.

At K'k'thyima's command, the three men approached the doors. The brass man clanked past, holding his gun levelled at Burton's face, took hold of a handle with his free hand, and pulled one of the portals open far enough for the men to pass through it.

"Enter, please, gents."

They stepped into what turned out to be a medium-sized room. It was square and the walls were panelled with oblongs of phosphorescence. The tall ceiling was shaped like an upside-down pyramid, with an enormous black diamond the size of a goose egg fitted into an ornate bracket at its tip.

"The last unbroken Eye of Nāga!" K'k'thyima announced.

A stone altar was laid out beneath the gemstone. Metal manacles were fitted to it, and there were stains on its surface that Burton didn't want to examine too closely. Gold chalices, containing heaps of black-diamond dust, stood to either side. The explorer noted nasty-looking instruments, like something one might find in a surgery, arranged on a nearby block, and there were other items around the room that, again, looked somehow more machine than architecture or decoration.

"William, Mr. Speke, if you would move over there—" K'k'thyima gestured to one side of the chamber, "—and Sir Richard, I'd be much obliged if you'd climb onto the altar and lie down."

"Do you intend to sacrifice me, Nāga?"

The clockwork man gave his soft hooting chuckle. "Rest assured, you'll leave here alive. On you get, please, or—" he moved the pistol, aiming it at Trounce, "—or do I have to shoot William in the leg before you'll comply?"

Scowling ferociously, Burton sat on the altar, swung his legs up, and lay down. Immediately, he felt an energy, like static electricity, crawling over his skin.

With one hand, K'k'thyima closed the manacles around the explorer's wrists and ankles.

Speke, who'd been detached and withdrawn since they'd entered the temple, suddenly spoke up: "Wait! Whatever you're going to do, do it to me instead!"

"I'm afraid that wouldn't be at all satisfactory," K'k'thyima responded. "Only this man is suitable for the task."

Speke fell to his knees and held his hands out imploringly. "Please!"

"Quite impossible. Stand up, Mr. Speke, and be quiet. The song will not require you again until the final verse."

"Task?" Burton asked.

K'k'thyima picked up a wicked-looking knife from among the instruments on the nearby block.

Trounce stepped forward.

"Back, William! I intend no harm to your friend! See, I'm putting down the pistol now—" he placed his revolver next to Burton's head, "—but I'll slice his throat if you come any closer."

Trounce bit his lip and gave a curt nod. He returned to his former position.

The brass man took hold of Burton's hair and, working quickly, began to slice it off.

"You have a most remarkable mind, Sir Richard," he said. "When you wandered into this diamond's range of influence during your first expedition, we immediately recognised that you were the soft skin we'd been waiting for."

Burton winced as the blade scraped across his scalp.

The priest continued: "The one with an open and enquiring intellect; an observer, sufficiently separated from his own culture to be able to easily absorb the ways of others; one not disorientated by the unusual or unfamiliar."

"Why is that of any significance?"

K'k'thyima removed the last few strands of hair from the explorer's head and said, "William, Mr. Speke, I have to perform a delicate operation now. Do not interfere. If you try anything, he'll die, and so will you. Is that understood?"

Both men nodded.

The clockwork man put down the knife and took up a small bowl. It was partially filled with a sticky paste.

"Excellent!" he exclaimed. "The Batembuzi prepared everything well!"

He dipped the bowl into a chalice, scooping black diamond dust into it, then used a small instrument to work the dust into the paste. Limping to the head of the altar, he employed the same instrument to paint an intricate hieroglyph on Burton's naked scalp.

"It is of significance, Sir Richard, because it gives you the wherewithal to remain sane while experiencing history beyond the boundaries of your natural lifespan."

"Beyond the—" Burton began. He stopped and his eyes widened. "You surely don't intend to send me through time!"

"I intend exactly that."

The Nāga priest finished painting, put the bowl aside, and reversed the instrument he was holding. Its other end was needle-sharp.

"This will hurt," he said, and started to jab the point over and over into Burton's skin, working at such speed that his hand became a blur.

Burton groaned and writhed in pain.

"Time, Sir Richard. Time. Time. Time. You soft skins have such a limited sense of it. You think it's the beat of a heart, that its pulses are regular, that it marches from A to B to C. But there's much more to time than mere rhythm and sequence. There's a melody. There are refrains that arise and fade and arise again. Time can change pitch and timbre and texture. Time has harmonies. It has volume. It has accents and pauses. It has verses and choruses. Your understanding of it is tediously horizontal, but it has all these vertical aspects, too."

William Trounce snorted. "Even if all that gobbledegook is true," he growled, "so bloody well what?"

"Just this, Detective Inspector: when the ripples of consequence spread out from an action taken, they go in all directions, not just forward, as you soft skins would have it. All directions."

"Ruddy nonsense!"

K'k'thyima straightened up from his task and said, "Do you happen to have a handkerchief?"

Trounce shook his head, but Speke reached into his pocket, pulled out a square of cotton, and passed it to the clockwork priest. K'k'thyima used it to wipe the blood and excess paste from the explorer's freshly etched tattoo.

"All done," he announced. He picked up his revolver. "We shall now send our friend Sir Richard Francis Burton into the future, where he'll witness the music of time in all its glory. It is a gift from the Nāga to the race that destroyed us."

Burton said, "Why?"

"Because you have to learn! If you don't, this world is doomed! It is in your hands now, soft skin—teach the lesson you learn today."

"Hogwash!" Trounce spat.

"It's a terrible shame," K'k'thyima said, "and I'm truly sorry, but, as has ever been the case, the Eye requires a sacrifice to activate it. Your essence will, however, be imprinted on the stone, if that's any consolation, William."

He raised the pistol and shot Trounce through the head.

Burton screamed.

There was a blinding white flash.

CHAPTER 12

ESCAPE FROM AFRICA

"In despair are many hopes."
—ARABIC PROVERB

The prodigious plant quivered and the huge red flower swung upward into a sunbeam and unfurled its outer layer of spiny petals to soak in the light and heat. The air bladders at the top of its stalk expanded like balloons then contracted, and the resultant squeak possessed an oddly dreamy tone.

"One, who is not, we see; but one, whom we see not, is;
Surely this is not that; but that is assuredly this.

"What, and wherefore, and whence? for under is over and under;
If thunder could be without lightning, lightning could be without
        thunder."

The bloom shifted again with a woody creak and appeared to look back down at the two men, who sat on their harvestmen and gaped at it in utter astonishment.

Bertie Wells whispered the obvious: "It's a talking plant. A talking bloody plant!"

Two long narrow leaves, positioned a little way below the petals, stretched and curled in a gesture that resembled a man throwing out his hands. "So explain yourself, you rotter! Why did you ignore me for so long? Wasn't it obvious that I was calling you back? The poppies, Richard! The poppies!"

Burton turned off his harvestman's steam engine, toppled from his saddle, thumped onto the ground, and lay still.

337

Behind him, Wells hurriedly stopped his own machine, dismounted, and ran over to kneel at his friend's side.

"I say!" the flower exclaimed. "Who are you? What's wrong with Richard?"

"I'm Bertie Wells, and I think he's fainted. Probably out of sheer disbelief!"

"Ah," said the bloom, and added:

"Doubt is faith in the main; but faith, on the whole, is doubt;
We cannot believe by proof; but could we believe without?

"Why, and whither, and how? for barley and rye are not clover;
Neither are straight lines curves; yet over is under and over.

"Two and two may be four; but four and four are not eight;
Fate and God may be twain; but God is the same as fate."

"God is a proven fallacy," Wells muttered distractedly as he took a flask from his belt and splashed water onto Burton's face.

"Indeed he is," the plant agreed. "Darwin drove the sword home and left us with a void. What now, hey? What now? I say we should fill it with a higher sort of pantheism. What do you think, Mr. Wells?"

Without considering the fact that he'd somehow become engaged in a theological discussion with oversized vegetation—for he felt that to do so would lead to the inevitable conclusion that he'd gone completely barmy—Wells replied: "I feel man would be wise to work at correcting his own mistakes instead of waiting for intervention from on high, and should replace faith in an unknowable divine plan with a well-thought-out scheme of his own."

"I say! Bravo! Bravo!" the plant cheered.

"Ask a man what he thinks, and get from a man what he feels;
God, once caught in the fact, shows you a fair pair of heels."

Burton blinked, sneezed, lay still for a moment, then scrambled to his feet, swayed, and grabbed at one of his harvestman's legs for support.

He looked up at the flower.

It angled itself downward and squealed, "I didn't think you were the fainting type, Richard! A hangover, I suspect! Did you drink too much of my brandy? I exude it like sap, you know! A very ingenious process, even if I do say so myself!"

Very slowly, Burton replied, "You, Algernon, have *got* to be bloody joking."

"What? What? Why?"

"A *flower*?"

"Oh! Ha-ha! Not just a flower—a whole bally jungle! What a wheeze, hey?"

"But is it—is it really you?"

The blossom twisted slightly, a gesture like a man angling his head to one side in contemplation. It refilled its air bladders and squeaked:

"Body and spirit are twins; God only knows which is which;
The soul squats down in the flesh, like a tinker drunk in a ditch.

"More is the whole than a part; but half is more than the whole;
Clearly, the soul is the body; but is not the body the soul?"

With a sudden jerk, the flower dropped until it was just inches from Burton's face.

"Is there something wrong with your memory, old horse?"

"Yes. There's a lot wrong with it. I've spent the past five years trying to piece it together while being pursued, shot at, and bombed."

"And I suppose you've forgotten the poppy that sprouted from my hand?"

Burton flinched and put a hand to his head as an image flashed into his mind, bringing with it an overwhelming sense of loss. "Bismillah! I had! But I—wait! I think—I think—Culver Cliff!"

Swinburne shivered and rustled. "Unfortunately so."

With watering eyes, Burton squinted at the surrounding rock face.

"I know this place. There's—"

He looked to his right, to where one of the plant's thick limbs crossed the ground and dug into the surrounding cliff. There was a dark opening in the root-like growth, and he could see that it was hollow.

Disparate recollections slotted together.

"There's a cave," he said, hoarsely. "It's there! I remember now. A grotto! You killed Count Zeppelin!"

"Yes! The golden arrow of Eros straight into his eyeball! Good old Tom Bendyshe avenged! But the Prussian injected me with that horrible venom of his and the next thing I knew I was falling. It took me an age to grow back out of that pit and into daylight, I can tell you! Lucky for me that Zeppelin fell into it, too. He made very good fertilizer!"

A black pit.

Algernon Swinburne hanging by his fingertips.

A green shoot emerging from the back of the poet's hand. Petals unfurling. A red poppy.

"The poppies," Burton whispered. "Now I understand."

"Bloody typical!" the poet trumpeted. "I stretched myself to the absolute giddy limit to signpost the way back here, and you didn't even recognise what the confounded signs meant!"

"I'm sorry, Algy. Something happened to me in that cave—in Lettow-Vorbeck's temple! Yes, I remember now! It's in there, beyond the grotto!"

"Lettow-Vorbeck?" Swinburne asked.

Wells answered, "A German general, Mr. Swinburne. Apparently he's been trying to burn his way through your jungle to find this place."

"The swine! I felt it, too! Very unpleasant!"

Burton murmured, "I lost my memory in that temple. The shock of your death was part of it, Algy, but there was more. And it ended with me being projected through time."

Swinburne inflated his bladders, fluttered his petals, and said, "I know. You can imagine my surprise when, after having had nothing but Pox and Malady's foul-mouthed descendants for company for decade after decade, I suddenly saw you come stumbling into this clearing! You were ranting and raving like a Bedlam inmate! I tried to speak to you but you legged it through the gorge and out of the mountains like a man with the devil himself at his heels. By the way, what year is this?"

"I arrived in 1914. It's now 1918."

"My hat! Really?"

The flower angled upward as if regarding the sky.

"One and two are not one; but one and nothing is two;
Truth can hardly be false, if falsehood cannot be true."

It turned back to the two men.

"I find it rather difficult to measure time these days. I've had such a different sense of it since I—er—took root, so to speak. It's not at all the way I used to think of it. Can you conceive of time as a thing filled with paradoxes and echoes? What a magnificent poem it would make!

"Once the mastodon was; pterodactyls were common as cocks;
Then the mammoth was God; now is He a prize ox.

340

"Parallels all things are; yet many of these are askew;
You are certainly I; but certainly I am not you.

"Springs the rock from the plain, shoots the stream from the rock;
Cocks exist for the hen; but hens exist for the cock.

"God, whom we see not, is; and God, who is not, we see;
Fiddle, we know, is diddle, and diddle, we take it, is dee."

Swinburne arched his thick stalk and shook with a peal of high-pitched laughter. Leaves drifted down from his higher branches.

Wells leaned close to Burton and whispered, "I'm of the opinion that your friend, the giant plant, is rip-roaringly drunk!"

The explorer appeared not to hear the little war correspondent. "Vertical as well as horizontal qualities," he mumbled to himself. "Who else spoke to me about the nature of time?"

Swinburne loosed a sound that resembled a belch and directed his petals back at Burton.

"But for all my newfound perception," he said, "upon your appearance, I instantly recognised that you weren't where—or, rather, *when*—you belong; and I certainly didn't relish the thought of you being out there, beyond the mountains, among the savages."

"Actually, there aren't many left," Wells put in. "Most of those that remain are Askaris now."

Swinburne gave a scornful hiss. "I'm not referring to the Africans, Mr. Wells. I mean the Europeans!"

"Ah. Quite so."

"The barbarities that have been committed on this continent in the name of one ideology or another, this social policy or that—quite dreadful! And I mean to put an end to it. I shall soon have the strength to make the German vegetation—the red weed and the venomous plants—whither and die. Already I've gained influence over those horrible things the Prussians once employed as vehicles—"

Wells cried out: "Then it was you! You took control of the lurchers! You cleared the route out of Tabora for us!"

"Is that what you call them? Yes, of course it was me. Now I shall use them to rid this land of its armies. My influence is growing, Mr. Wells. My roots will one day reach from coast to coast. And when they do, I shall make a Utopia of Africa!"

"Utopia!" Wells's eyes glistened with hope.

"For as long as this version of history exists, Africa will be an Eden."

The flower bobbed low, until it was level with their faces.

"But," it squeaked, "this history should *not* exist. You have to go back, Richard, and you have to put an end to all such divergences."

Bertie Wells frowned and looked from the vermillion blossom to Burton and back again. "Mr. Swinburne," he said, "Richard has explained the phenomenon of alternate histories to me. Why can they not exist concurrently?"

"Time is a complex thing. It is like music. In addition to its rhythm, there is—"

"A melody," Burton interjected. "Refrains, pitch, timbre, and texture. Time has harmonies, volume, accents, and pauses. It has verses and—Bismillah! I've heard this before—from—from Herbert Spencer!" He looked confused. "But not Herbert Spencer."

"Good old tin-head!" Swinburne exclaimed. "I wonder what became of him?"

Burton pointed to where Swinburne's hollow root blocked the cave mouth. "He's in there!"

"I say! Is he? Was he then involved in your transportation here?"

The explorer struggled for an answer. Something felt very wrong. The clockwork philosopher had been a friend and ally, yet, for reasons he couldn't determine, when he thought of him now, he felt threatened and distrustful. "He was," he said, and immediately felt he'd uttered an untruth.

"Then you must go to him," Swinburne said. "And he must return you to 1863. For, to answer Mr. Wells's question, these alternate histories are proliferating and turning time into a cacophony. Imagine ten orchestras playing different tunes in the same theatre. The musicians would lose their way. Some would play the wrong melody by mistake. Musical expressions would be misplaced and mixed up. There'd be pandemonium. And that is what's happening. If this situation is allowed to continue unchecked, the borders between each version of reality will be breached. Diverse technologies will become horribly intermingled. People's personalities will be bent entirely out of shape. Events will develop in increasingly eccentric directions."

"But how can I reverse the damage?" Burton asked.

"I haven't a clue! I'm just a poet! But you'll find a way."

The king's agent looked at the opening in Swinburne's root. He didn't want to enter the cave; didn't want to see the grotto or the temple; and, especially, he didn't want to see Herbert Spencer.

He noticed a flower-strewn mound. It looked like a grave. The back of his mind seemed to flex, as if to divulge a secret, but the information didn't come—only deep sadness.

He addressed Wells: "Algy is right, Bertie. And that means I have to leave you now. I have to enter the temple."

"I'm coming with you."

"There's no need, and it might be dangerous."

"I've seen this thing through with you from the start. I need to be there at the finish."

Burton considered a moment, then nodded.

"Algy," he said, turning back to the vermillion blossom. "I'm sorry this happened to you."

"Sorry?" the poet responded. "Don't be sorry! This is everything I could have hoped for! My senses are *alive*, Richard! And *what* senses! I've never felt so engaged with life! So intoxicated by it! Finally, I feel the inexpressible poetry of sheer *being*! It's wondrous!"

Burton reached up and placed a hand on the side of the flower. "Then I'm happy for you, my friend."

Swinburne's petals squeezed into a pucker, and the flower slid forward and placed a dewy kiss on the explorer's forehead.

Drawing away, Swinburne said, "Off you go."

Burton reached up to his vehicle's saddle and lifted down his rifle. Seeing this, Wells stepped back to his harvestman and did the same. They walked together across the glade to the opening in the plant's root.

The king's agent looked back. The huge red flower had risen up into the sunbeam. Its petals were open. A trio of butterflies danced around it. He smiled and moved into the hollow limb.

Swinburne whispered:

"A wider soul than the world was wide,
Whose praise made love of him one with pride,
What part has death or has time in him,
Who rode life's lists as a god might ride?"

Sir Richard Francis Burton and Herbert George Wells walked through the hollow root and down into the grotto. They stepped out of an opening in the limb, crossed the chamber, and wriggled through the narrow tube in its wall to the shelf overlooking the vast cavern. After following the path down, they were met by the Batembuzi, who shepherded them to the Temple of the Eye.

The war correspondent gazed in disbelief at the monolithic edifice. "By gum," he said. "It dwarfs even the pyramids!" He glanced nervously at their escorts. "It's funny, though—I always imagined that it'd be the workers who ended up as troglodytes, rather than the priests."

"Historically, priests have probably lived underground more often than any other segment of the world's population," Burton commented.

Wells gave a dismissive grunt. "The power of faith over rationality."

"I used to think they were the opposite ends of a spectrum," Burton answered. "Now I'm not so certain."

"Surely you're not resurrecting God, Richard?"

"No. But perhaps I'm resurrecting myself."

"Ah. Faith in oneself. When confronting the unknown, perhaps that's the only thing one can truly hope for."

"I certainly have nothing else."

"You have my friendship."

Burton looked at Wells, reached out, and patted his shoulder.

"Yes. I do."

They trudged along the central thoroughfare, reached the steps to the temple entrance, climbed them, and passed through the tall double doors. The Batembuzi ushered them to the foot of the staircase then slunk away and were absorbed into the shadows.

"Are they even men?" Wells asked.

"I have no idea, but, according to legend, the Nāga managed to breach the natural divide between species to produce half-human offspring."

They ascended to the hall, walked between its statues, and stopped at the gold-panelled doors.

Burton gripped a handle and said, "The last of my lost memories are in here, Bertie. Do you really want to face them with me?"

"Most assuredly!"

The king's agent swung the door open and they entered the chamber beyond.

He recognised it instantly. Everything was as it had been fifty-five years ago, except: "The Eye has gone!" Burton pointed to the empty bracket at the tip of the upside-down pyramid.

"That's the guarantee that you'll return to 1863," Wells replied, "for obviously you removed the diamond and took it to London."

Burton added, "Where it was recovered by the Germans after the destruction of the city. I go back knowing that will happen, so why do I allow it?"

"You'll find out! I say! This must be your Mr. Spencer!" He pointed to the floor.

The clockwork man was lying beside the altar. His brass body was battered, scratched, and discoloured, its left leg bent out of shape and footless. What passed for his face was disfigured by a big indentation on the left side.

The speaking apparatus had been removed from his head and was sitting on the nearby block, among the various instruments.

Burton pointed out the exposed babbage to Wells.

"Do you see the seven apertures? They're where the Cambodian diamonds were fitted. They contained Spencer's mind and—and—"

"What is it, Richard?" Wells asked, noticing his friend's pained expression.

"K'k'thyima! I was wrong, Bertie—it wasn't ever Spencer! It was a Nāga priest named K'k'thyima. He used the power of the diamonds to send me into the future—but I don't understand; the diamonds are gone, so how can I return?"

Wells pointed to something on the altar.

"Perhaps that holds the answer."

Burton looked and recognised the key that wound the clockwork man. He picked it up.

"Help me turn this thing onto its stomach," he said, squatting beside the brass machine.

Wells did so, then watched as Burton inserted the key into a slot in the device's back and twisted it through a number of revolutions.

The two men stood back.

A ticking came from the figure on the floor. A click and a whir and a jerk of the footless leg, then it rolled over, sat up, and struggled upright. It looked at Sir Richard Francis Burton, saluted, and pointed at the altar.

A tremor ran through Burton's body. "Of course. I have black diamond dust tattooed into my scalp. It must be connected through time to the Eye in sixty-three."

He hesitated. "I'm torn, Bertie. My instincts object, but have I any other choice but to go through with this?"

"All the evidence tells us that you did, and therefore will. Hmm. I wonder. Does Fate eliminate paradox? Could Fate be a function of the human organism?"

Burton climbed onto the altar and lay down. He rested his sniper rifle between his body and left arm. "If it is, then perhaps these multiple histories are disrupting it, making us prone to paradox after paradox."

"Then you know what you have to do, Richard."

"What?"

"You have to seal your own fate."

Wells stood back as the clockwork man circled the altar, closing the manacles around Burton's wrists and ankles.

The explorer began: "Whatever the case, I—" then stopped with a strangled gasp as, without warning, the last missing fragment of memory returned to him.

"Oh no!" he hissed. "No no no!" He looked at Wells and bellowed: "Get the hell out of here, Bertie! Run! Run!"

"What—?"

"Run for your life! Get out!" Burton screamed, his voice near hysterical.

The clockwork man suddenly lunged at the war correspondent, grabbed his head with both hands, and twisted it violently. Bone cracked. Wells slumped to the floor.

"No!" Burton howled.

A bright flash.

The blinding light lingered in John Speke's one functional eye.

The gunshot left bells clanging in his ears.

The noise was gradually superseded by the sound of a man howling in pain and distress.

William Trounce fell against him and thudded onto the floor.

Speke blinked rapidly.

Vision returned.

Burton was on the altar. His head was thrown back and he was screaming hysterically. He'd undergone a shocking transformation. Where, seconds ago, his head had been shaved, tattooed, and smeared with blood, now it was covered by long snowy white hair. Where his face had been gaunt and savage and strong, now it was frail and lined and brutalised, as if the explorer had aged, and suffered intolerably.

His clothes were different. He was terribly emaciated. There was a rifle beside him.

K'k'thyima stepped back and placed the revolver on the block with the various instruments.

"Most satisfactory," he said. "A sacrifice was made and our intrepid traveller has returned. Mr. Speke, would you calm him down, please."

Speke breathed a shuddery exhalation and stepped to the altar. He took Burton by the shoulders and shook him slightly.

"Dick! Dick! It's all right, man! It's all right! Stop!"

Burton's eyes were wild. His lips were drawn back over his teeth. His screams gave way to words: "Bertie! Get out! Get out!"

"It's me, Dick! It's John! John Speke!"

"Get out. Get out. Get out."

Speke slapped him hard.

"Dick! Look at me! It's John!"

Burton's eyes fixed on him, focused, and sanity gradually bled back into them.

"Is it you, John?" he croaked. "John Speke?"

"Yes, it's me. We're in the Nāga temple. Do you remember?"

"I remember death. So much death."

Tears flowed freely and a sob shook the king's agent. "I have lost my mind. I can't take any more of it. Algy was—was—then William, and Bertie!" Burton looked over to K'k'thyima and suddenly screamed: "Get me out of these shackles, you damned murdering lizard!"

"Welcome back, Sir Richard," the Nāga priest said. He limped to the explorer's side and clicked open the manacles on Burton's left wrist and ankle, then moved around the altar, leaned past Speke, and liberated the other two limbs.

Burton sat, swung around, pushed himself to his feet, and sent a vicious right hook clanging into the side of the brass man's head. He stifled a groan as pain lanced through his hand, but was satisfied to see that he'd just created the big dent he'd noticed in the clockwork man's face in 1918.

"You bastard!" he hissed. "I'm going to tear you apart!"

"I wouldn't recommend it, soft skin. Don't forget where you are. This is 1863. You need me to remain here, in this room and in one piece, for fifty-five years, else how can I return you from 1918?"

"You damned well know it doesn't work like that! I'm here, now, and I won't disappear if I rip your bloody cogs out!"

"Perhaps not, but even if you had the strength to overpower me—which I assure you, you don't—do you really want to create yet another history—one that denies a path home to that alternate you, condemning him to exile in Africa of 1918?"

Burton swayed. Speke, looking bemused, steadied him. "What happened to you, Dick? You didn't go anywhere but your appearance is—is—"

Burton looked down at William Trounce's body. His face twisted into an expression of fury, then one of utter despair.

"I have spent four years in the future, John," he said, "and now I must prevent that future from occurring." He turned back to K'k'thyima. "How?"

The high priest shuffled back to the other side of the altar. He reached up and began to work the Eye out of its housing.

"That's the question, isn't it? How will you ever know whether what you're doing is, from the perspective of the time you just visited, any different from what you did?"

The black diamond came loose. K'k'thyima stepped back and held it up.

"You are on your own, Sir Richard. The Nāga are finally departing this world. We leave you to sing the final verse of our song."

The phosphorescence around the walls suddenly dimmed, its blue light concentrating around the diamond, and small crackles and snaps sounded, increasing in volume. Bolts of energy started to sizzle over the stone's many facets, then flared out, dancing across its surface and down K'k'thyima's arm. The Eye hummed, the sound rapidly deepening, causing Burton's and Speke's ears to pop before it passed below the range of human hearing.

Tiny fractures zigzagged across the Eye, and as each appeared, with a faint *tink!*, a small entity was expelled. To Speke's astonishment, they appeared to be tiny people with the wings of butterflies and dragonflies—fairies!—but Burton knew it was an illusion; that they appeared this way because the human mind wasn't able to process the things' true appearance, and so replaced it with a marvel from mythology. To him, the ejected forms were sparks of reptilian consciousness, sensed rather than seen. He'd witnessed the same dance around the South American stone when it had shattered.

The energy built to a storm-like frenzy, banging and clapping and sending out streaks of blue lightning that sputtered up the walls and across the floor and ceiling.

Speke cried out in fear: "What's happening, Dick?"

The king's agent yelled, "He's breaking the stone!"

Moments later, with a loud detonation, the enormous black diamond cracked and fell apart, dropping out of the brass man's hand and falling to the floor in seven equally sized pieces.

The room became still.

The bolts of energy vanished.

The smell of ozone hung in the air.

K'k'thyima bent and retrieved the stones.

"Equivalence! Though one or two or even all of the Eyes remain whole in some versions of history, in this one they are all divided into seven, thus, across all the realities, the Nāga can now transcend or die." He directed his misshapen face at Burton. "Our gratitude, Sir Richard. The Nāga thank you for the role you've played in our release."

"Oh just bugger off, why don't you?" the king's agent growled. He suddenly staggered, made a grab at Speke, missed, and fell to the floor, where he sat with his eyes open but glazed. Speke squatted beside him and felt his forehead.

"Feverish," he muttered. "And exhausted beyond endurance, by the looks of it."

"I don't know what to do," Burton mumbled. "How do I seal my own fate, Bertie?"

"Who's this Bertie he keeps mentioning?" Speke asked K'k'thyima.

"I don't know, Mr. Speke. Let's get him up." The brass man bent and hooked a metal hand through Burton's arm. Speke took the cue and supported the explorer on the other side. They pulled him upright and sat him on the altar.

"You had better be off, gentlemen," K'k'thyima said. "Our work here is done, at least for the next fifty-five years."

He opened Burton's shirt pocket and slipped the seven pieces of the African Eye into it. "You need to unscrew my speaking apparatus to expose the babbage. Remove the seven Cambodian stones and take them with you back to London. Leave my winding key on the altar, please. The babbage will have one function left to perform, which it'll fulfil in 1918, as you have seen."

"Damn you to hell," Burton whispered.

"On the contrary, I have chosen to transcend. Goodbye, Sir Richard Francis Burton."

K'k'thyima became silent.

For a few moments, the king's agent sat and did nothing, while Speke watched and fidgeted nervously; then the explorer stood and detached the clockwork man's speaking device. He pulled seven black diamonds out of the exposed babbage and put them into his pocket.

The brass device walked to the other side of the altar, saluted, and stopped moving.

Burton picked up his rifle and said to Speke: "Help me carry William outside. I want to bury him in the open."

It was night when they emerged into the cliff-ringed arena, both weary to the bone after manoeuvring Trounce's corpse through the narrow subterranean passages. To Burton, the bowl-shaped space felt strangely empty. He peered around it, remembered where he'd seen flowers growing on a mound, and, with Speke's help, laid Trounce to rest there, piling rocks onto him by the starlight.

Chwezi warriors stepped out of the shadows. Silently, they escorted the two men through the gorges on either side of the mountain, leading them each by the arm in utter darkness.

When they reached the spot where Sidi Bombay had fallen, Burton found his friend's corpse undisturbed, and a second burial mound was built before they continued on.

The king's agent, asleep on his feet, lost all awareness of the environment and his own actions until, suddenly, they emerged from the Mountains of the Moon and found the Wanyambo sitting around a small crackling fire. The warriors stared in superstitious dread at the Chwezi and backed away. The mountain tribe broke its silence. Words of reassurance were spoken. An oath was sworn. Obedience was demanded. Agreement was reached. The groups banded together—thirty men in all—and continued on eastward toward the Ukerewe Lake.

It was mid-morning by the time they reached the first village. Its inhabitants, fearing the Chwezi, immediately offered shelter and sustenance. Burton, not knowing what he was doing, crawled into a beehive hut and slept.

When he awoke, he was being borne along on a litter with Speke walking at his side. The lieutenant looked down and said, "You've been in a fever for three days. How are you feeling?"

"Weak. Thirsty. Hungry. Where's my rifle?"

"One of the Africans is carrying it."

"Get it. Don't take it from me again."

Another day. Another village. They stopped. They ate and drank.

Later, the king's agent sat with Speke in the settlement's *bandani* and watched the sun oozing into the horizon.

"Where are we, John?"

"I'm not certain. About a day's march from the northwestern shore of the lake, I hope. I didn't know what to do. Without this damned thing to help me—" he tapped the babbage embedded in the left side of his skull, "—I find it almost impossible to make decisions, so I'm following what it had originally intended me to do upon gaining the diamond, which is to circumnavigate the water to its northernmost point, then march northward. I think the Chwezi understood my intentions, though I've only been able to communicate through sign language."

Burton checked his pockets. The fourteen stones were still there.

"It seems as good a plan as any," he said. "As long as the Chwezi remain with us, the locals will supply what we need and we'll avoid demands for *hongo*."

Speke nodded and glanced at the other man. There was a disturbing lifelessness to Burton's voice, as if a large part of him had simply switched off.

The next afternoon, after mindlessly slogging over hill after hill, they caught sight of the great lake, stretching all the way to the horizon.

In a voice still devoid of emotion, Burton said, "I apologise, John. Had I seen this with my own eyes during our initial expedition, I would never have doubted your claims."

"It was my fault you didn't see it," Speke answered. "I became obsessed with the idea that my name alone should be forever associated with the solving of the Nile problem."

"The diamond influenced your judgement as soon as we were within range of it."

"Perhaps. Do you think we'll make it home?"

Burton looked down at himself. His tick-infested 1918 army fatigues were torn and rotting. His boots were cracked.

"I have reason to believe we will."

"And what then?"

Burton shook his head and shrugged.

Just before sunrise, they set out again. For a short time, Burton walked, then his legs gave way and he collapsed onto the litter. He drifted in and out of consciousness. Fever raged through him like a forest fire.

Sometimes he opened his eyes and there was blue sky; other times, the Milky Way. On one occasion, he rolled his head to the right and saw a mirror-smooth expanse of water covered by thousands of pelicans.

For a long time, he saw nothing.

A hand shook his shoulder.

"Isabel," he muttered.

"Dick! Wake up! Wake up!"

He opened his eyes and looked upon John Speke's lined, heavily bearded features, and his own reflected in the other's black, brass-ringed left-eye lens. He pushed himself up and found that a little strength had returned to him.

"What is it?"

"Listen!"

Burton looked around. They were on a slope. It concealed the landscape ahead and to the right, but on the left jungled hills rolled away before climbing to faraway mountains.

In front, from beyond the crest of the incline, mist was clouding into the sky.

A constant roar filled his ears.

"That sounds like—"

"Falling water!" Speke enthused. "Can you walk?"

"Yes."

The lieutenant took Burton's arm and helped him to his feet. With a gesture to the Chwezi and Wanyambo warriors, he indicated that they should stay put.

The two Britishers walked slowly toward the summit, Burton leaning heavily on his companion. The sun burned their faces. Mosquitoes darted around them. The air was heavy and humid.

They reached the top.

Below them, the earth was cut by a wide and deep rift into which, from the edge of the Ukerewe, a great mass of water hurtled. Thundering beneath billowing vapour, it crashed and splashed and frothed over rounded rocks, and cascaded through the arch of a permanent rainbow. Fish leaped from it, flashing in the sunlight, and birds darted in and out of the rolling cloud.

There could be no doubt.

It was the source of the River Nile.

Burton thought: *Here it begins. Here it ends. Not the source, but just another part of a circle.*

They stood silently for a long while, deafened by the sound of the falling water, then Speke roused himself, leaned close to Burton, put his mouth to the explorer's ear, and shouted: "We've done it, Dick! We've discovered it at last!" He clutched his companion's elbow. "And we did it together!"

Burton tore himself away and Speke took a step back, shocked by the ferocious expression on the other man's face.

"You can have it! I want nothing more to do with it! It's yours, Speke! The whole damned thing is yours!"

Over the next few days, they followed the river north, struggled across an extensive quagmire, pushed through thickets of water hyacinth, and found themselves on the shore of a second lake, smaller and much shallower than the Ukerewe. It was completely covered with water lilies and smelled of rotting vegetation.

"What shall we name it?" Speke asked.

"Why name it at all?" Burton growled. "It is what it is. A bloody lake."

The lieutenant shook his head despairingly and walked away. He couldn't understand the other's mood at all. Burton had hardly spoken since their discovery of the falls. He wasn't even bothering to acquire the Chwezi language, which was entirely out of character, for in Speke's experience Burton was driven by a mania to conquer every foreign tongue he encountered.

The Wanyambo warriors, now far from home and unwilling to go any farther, left them.

Over the next three days, the Chwezi guided the two Britishers around the southern shores of the lake to where, at its western tip, the river flowed out of it.

They followed the waterway. The land was boggy and swarming with snakes. Foul-smelling gasses bubbled out of the ground.

The sun rose and set and rose and set, and they lost count of the days. Mosquitoes bit every inch of their exposed skin. Their clothes fell to pieces and had to be replaced with cotton robes, donated by villagers. They wound rough cloth around their now bootless feet and walked with staffs, looking like a couple of heavily bearded skeletons, burned almost black, too exhausted to communicate, or even to think.

One of their guides, who'd been scouting ahead, returned and spoke quietly to his companions. He approached Burton and Speke and jabbed his finger first at one, then at the other, then toward a ridge that lay just to the south of the river, a couple of miles to the west.

He rejoined the other Chwezi and, as a man, they disappeared into the undergrowth.

Suddenly, the Britishers were alone.

"Well then," Speke said, shading his one functioning eye and peering at the nearby high land. "I suppose we're meant to go up there."

They set off through sucking mud and shouldered past stiff bullrushes until the terrain sloped upward, became firmer underfoot, and they climbed to the top of the ridge. On the other side of it, the Nile flowed into another vast lake, and on the near shore, just half a mile away, an air vessel was hovering about forty feet from the ground. It was a gargantuan cigar-shaped balloon with a long cabin affixed beneath it and pylons, with rotor wings at their ends, extending out horizontally from its sides. The ship, which must have been close to a thousand feet in length, was painted with a Union Jack and bore on its side the name HMA *Dauntless*.

A large camp of Rowtie tents lay in the shadow of the vessel.

Burton suddenly spoke: "John, I have to make a request of you."

"What is it?"

"Tell them nothing. Not now, and not when we return to London. Don't let on anything of what we've experienced here. The future may depend on it."

"Dick, I—"

"I need your word on it."

"Very well. You have it."

Burton took Speke's hand and shook it.

They stumbled down toward the camp and had crossed half the distance when they were spotted. A shout went up, men started running toward them, came close, and gathered around. One of them stepped forward.

"By James!" he exclaimed. "Is that you, Sir Richard?"

Burton's vision was swimming. The man in front of him blurred in and out of focus. Slowly, recognition dawned.

"Hello," the king's agent whispered. "I'm very happy to see that you've recovered from your injuries, Captain Lawless."

Everything toppled over and darkness rushed in.

CHAPTER 13

THE SOURCE

"We are each our own devil, and we make this world our hell."
—OSCAR WILDE

While Sir Richard Francis Burton was in Africa, electricity came to London. Now, in early 1864, thick cables were clinging to the walls of the city's buildings, looping and drooping over its streets, dripping in the fog, and quietly sizzling as they conveyed energy from Battersea Power Station across the nation's capital.

Street lamps blazed. House and office windows blazed. Shop fronts blazed. The permanent murk effortlessly swallowed the light and reduced it to smudged globes, which hung in the impenetrable atmosphere like exotic fruits.

In the gloomy gullies between, pedestrians struggled through an unyielding tangle of almost immobile vehicles. The legs of steam-driven insects were caught in the spokes of wheels, panicky horses were jammed against chugging machinery, crankshafts were hammering against wood and metal and flesh.

Animalistic howls and screams and curses sounded from amid the mess.

And to this, Burton had returned aboard His Majesty's Airship *Dauntless*.

The vessel was the first of her type, the result of Isambard Kingdom Brunel's solving of the gas-filled dirigible problem. Design faults had been corrected and unstable flammable gasses replaced. The *Dauntless* was a triumph.

A slow but long-range vessel, she was propelled by electric engines, which, lacking springs, should have been impervious to the deleterious influence that had so far prevented any machine from piercing Africa's heart.

Unfortunately, this had proved not to be the case.

Following the Nile upstream, the ship had reached the northern outskirts of the Lake Regions. Her engines had then failed. However, the wind was behind her, so Captain Lawless allowed the vessel to be borne along, powerless, until the air current changed direction, at which point he'd ordered her landing on the shore of a great lake.

The crew set up camp.

There were two passengers on board: John Petherick and Samuel Baker, both experienced explorers from the Royal Geographical Society. They prepared an expedition, intending to head south to search for Burton. The day prior to their planned departure, he and Speke had come stumbling into the camp.

Lawless and his engineers had taken it for granted that the engines were still dysfunctional. Burton, though, knew that the Nāga were no longer present in the black diamonds, so their influence should have vanished.

He was correct. The engines functioned perfectly. The *Dauntless* flew home and landed at an airfield some miles to the southeast of London. Damien Burke and Gregory Hare, Palmerston's odd-job men, were there to greet it. They took possession of the fourteen black diamonds—the seven fragments of the Cambodian Eye and the seven of the African.

"All the Nāga stones are in British hands now, Captain Burton," Burke said. "You've done excellent work for the Empire, isn't that so, Mr. Hare?"

"It most certainly is, Mr. Burke!" Hare agreed.

John Speke was taken into custody.

"He's a traitor," Burke observed. "The irony of it is that he'll no doubt be incarcerated in our chambers beneath the Tower of London, which is where the Eyes will go, too. One of the most disreputable men in the country held in the same place as what might well be our most precious resource. Such is the way of things."

Burton was taken to Penfold Private Sanatorium in London's St. John's Wood, where, for three weeks, the Sisterhood of Noble Benevolence fussed over him.

As his strength increased, so too did his anxiety. He had a terrible decision to make. By telling Palmerston about the future and revealing to him his fate, he might persuade him to abandon plans to use the Eyes of Nāga as a means for mediumistic espionage against Prussia; might convince him that sending troops to Africa would lead to disaster. But if he succeeded in this, it would mean no reinforcements for the Daughters of Al-Manat. Bertie Wells had told him that the female guerrilla fighters survived at least into the 1870s. In changing history, Burton would almost certainly condemn Isabel Arundell, Isabella Mayson, and Sadhvi Raghavendra to much earlier deaths.

Obviously, the future he'd visited had occurred because he'd favoured Al-Manat's survival over the 130-year-old Palmerston's direct order. As much as he loved Isabel, he had no idea why he might have done such a thing, for, in anyone's estimation, could three lives—even *those* three—be worth the savagery and destruction of the Great War?

He wrote much about this in his personal journal, examining the problem from every angle he could think of, but though he produced pages and pages of cramped handwriting, he could find no answer.

The solution finally came with a visit from Palmerston himself.

Two weeks into his treatment, Burton was sitting up in bed reading a newspaper when the door opened and the prime minister stepped in, announcing: "I'd have come earlier. You know how it is. Affairs of state. Complex times, Captain Burton. Complex times."

He took off his hat and overcoat—revealing a Mandarin-collared black suit and pale blue cravat—and placed them on a chair. He didn't remove his calfskin gloves.

Standing at the end of the patient's bed, he said, "You look bloody awful. Your hair is white!"

The king's agent didn't reply. He gazed dispassionately at his visitor's face.

Palmerston's most recent treatments had made his nose almost entirely flat. The nostrils were horizontal slits, as wide as the gash-like mouth beneath. A dimple had been added to the centre of his chin. His eyebrows were painted on, high above the oriental-looking eyes.

"You'll be pleased to hear, Captain, that not only do I fully endorse your recommendations, but I have acted upon them even in the face of virulent opposition led by no less than Disraeli himself," he announced.

Burton looked puzzled. "My recommendations, Prime Minister?"

"Yes. Your reports confirmed my every suspicion concerning Bismarck's intentions. Obviously, we cannot allow him to gain a foothold in East Africa, so British troops have already been conveyed there by rotorship, and I have more on the way. It's by no means a declaration of war on my part, but I do intend that they offer resistance to any efforts made by Prussia to claim territories."

Burton's fingers dug into the bedsheets beneath him. "My—my reports?" he whispered hoarsely.

"As delivered to us by Commander Krishnamurthy. A very courageous young man, Burton. He will be given due honours, of that you can be certain. And I look forward to receiving the remainder of your observations—those made between Kazeh and the Mountains of the Moon. Do you have them here?"

"N-no," Burton stammered. "I'll—I'll see that they're delivered to you." He thought: *Bismillah! Krishnamurthy!*

"Post-haste, please, Captain."

Burton struggled for words. "I—I wrote those reports before I had—before I had properly assessed the situation, Prime Minister. You have to—to withdraw our forces at once. Their presence in Africa will escalate hostilities between the British Empire and Prussia to an unprecedented degree."

"What? Surely you don't expect me to allow Bismarck free rein?"

"You have to, sir."

"Have to? Why?"

"Your actions will—will precipitate the Great War, the one that Countess Sabina has predicted."

Palmerston shook his head. "The countess is working with us to prevent exactly that. She and a team of mediums have already employed the Nāga diamonds to great effect." He pointed at Burton's newspaper. "No doubt you've read that a second Schleswig conflict has broken out between Prussia, Austria, and Denmark. We precipitated that, my dear fellow, by means of undetected mediumistic manipulations. I intend to tangle Bismarck up in so many minor difficulties that he'll never have the strength to challenge us in Africa, let alone establish his united Germany!"

Burton squeezed his eyes shut and raised his hands to his head in frustration. It was too late. The circumstances that would lead to all-out war had already been set into motion!

He thought rapidly. Now he understood the 130-year-old Palmerston's claim that he—Burton—had never revealed his visit to the future. The king's agent knew the way the prime minister's mind worked. Having already out-manoeuvred Benjamin Disraeli—a formidable political force—to get his way, Palmerston wouldn't under any circumstances backtrack, not even on his own advice! So what would he do instead? The answer was obvious: the prime minister would attempt to outguess his future self by ordering a pre-emptive strike; he'd throw every resource he could muster into defeating Bismarck before Prussia could properly mobilise its military might; and in doing that, in Burton's opinion, he was much more likely to incite the war at an earlier date than to prevent it.

Burton felt ensnared by inevitability.

"What's the matter?" Palmerston asked. "Should I call a nurse?"

The explorer took his hands from his head, feeling the ridges of his tattoo sliding beneath his fingertips.

"No, Prime Minister. I have a headache, that's all."

"Then I won't disturb you any further, Captain." Palmerston picked up his coat, shrugged it back on, took up his top hat, and said: "We've blown hot and cold, you and I, but I want you to know that I have renewed faith in you. You've done a splendid job. Absolutely splendid! Thanks to your actions, the Empire is secured."

He turned and departed.

Burton sat and stared into space.

A week later he was released from hospital and returned to his home at 14 Montagu Place.

Mrs. Angell, his housekeeper, was horrified at his appearance. He looked, she said, as if he'd just been dug out of an Egyptian tomb.

"You'll eat, Sir Richard!" she pronounced, and embarked on a culinary mission to restore his health. She also cleaned around him obsessively, as if the slightest speck of dust might cause his final ruination.

He put up with it stoically, too weak to resist, though there was one item he wouldn't allow her—or the maid, Elsie Carpenter—to touch, let alone dust: the rifle that leaned against the fireplace by his saddlebag armchair.

It was an anomaly, that weapon, and the image of it arose again and again in his Sufi meditations, though he couldn't fathom why.

A few days after his homecoming, a parakeet arrived at his study window. "Message from thick-witted Richard Monckton Milnes, otherwise known as Baron hairy-palmed Houghton. Message begins. I will call at three o'clock, bum-slapper. Message ends."

The new 1st Baron Houghton arrived on time and found Burton wrapped in his *jubbah* and slumped in his armchair beside the fireplace, with a cheroot in his mouth, a glass of port in his hand, and Fidget the basset hound stretched out at his feet. Whatever greeting Monckton Milnes had planned died on his lips at the sight of the explorer. He stood in the doorway of the study, his mouth hanging open.

Burton removed his Manila, set down his glass, and gave a half-grin. "What you see is the much-recovered model," he said, rising to his feet. He crossed to his friend and shook his hand. "You should have seen the state of me before! Hang up your coat, old man, and take a seat. Congratulations on your peerage. Would you prefer me to bow or pour you a drink?"

"Hell's bells, Richard! You look twenty years older!"

"I'm four years older. No, five, counting the year since you last saw me, the rest is down to the vicissitudes of Africa."

His visitor sat down and accepted a glass of port.

"By heavens, it's good to see you again. But five years? What are you talking about?"

"It will require a suspension of disbelief on your part."

"A little over a year ago you told me that Spring Heeled Jack was a man from the future and that history had been changed. Is what you have to tell me more incredible even that that?"

"As a matter of fact, yes, it is."

"Ouch! Very well, fire away. You talk and I'll drink."

Over the course of the next two hours, Burton told his friend everything that had happened in Africa, and he withheld nothing.

A long silence followed as Monckton Milnes digested the tale, along with the copious amount of port he'd gulped.

Burton showed him the rifle and pointed out the inscription on its stock: *Lee-Enfield Mk III. Manufactured in Tabora, Africa, 1918.*

"You have to change history," his guest said softly.

"That's the problem," Burton replied. "To do so I have to outmanoeuvre myself, as well as Palmerston."

"And if you succeed," Monckton Milnes interjected, "if you create yet another branch of history, you'll just be adding to the chaos poor Algernon warned of."

Burton sucked at his cigar. "Not so much *poor* Algernon. He seemed very content with his new form. But yes, you're correct. He told me to put an end to all the divergences, despite that doing so would wipe out the history in which he currently resides. How, though, am I to do that?"

He looked down at the rifle that lay across his legs. "How am I to do that?"

Quite without warning or obvious reason, the last words Burton had ever heard Detective Inspector Honesty speak leaped into his mind with such clarity they might have been muttered into his ear: *"Needs pruning, hard against the stem."*

Monckton Milnes, as Burton had requested, had spent the past year surreptitiously monitoring the prime minister. He reported that Palmerston had secretly quadrupled military spending, had reshuffled his cabinet so that it contained the most martial of his party's ministers, and was steadfastly refusing to make a decision regarding British America's slave population.

Burton thanked his friend, bade him goodbye, and spent the rest of the afternoon meditating.

That evening, he met Maneesh Krishnamurthy for dinner at the Athenaeum Club on Pall Mall. They grabbed each other by the elbows and shared a wordless greeting. Both grinned stupidly, both looked into the other's eyes, and both saw pain and loss.

They settled in the lounge and shared a bottle of wine.

"I've started on these foul-tasting things," the police commander said, opening a platinum cigarette case and pulling forth one of the little tubes of Latakia tobacco. "Much worse than my old pipe, but I had to trade the damned thing to get out of a jam at Madege Madogo and I haven't the heart to replace it. It was a gift from my cousin, bless him."

"I miss him," Burton murmured. "I miss them all."

He raised his glass in a silent toast. Krishnamurthy followed suit. They drained them in a single swallow and poured over-generous refills.

"Sir Richard, I know I look like I've been starved, beaten, and dragged backward through a thorn bush, but if you don't mind me saying so, you look considerably worse. What in blue blazes happened to you?"

"Time, Maneesh. Time happened to me."

For the second time that day—and only the second time since he'd got back—Burton gave an account of what had occurred after he and Krishnamurthy parted company outside Kazeh.

"By James, it's unbelievable, Sir Richard, but looking at what's happening in the world today, I can easily see how it might develop into the hellish conflict you describe."

"Unfortunately not *might*, but *will*."

They drank more. Too much. Krishnamurthy described his journey from Kazeh back to Zanzibar. Burton's head began to swim.

A concierge approached. "Excuse me, sir," he said. "A message for you. It arrived by runner."

Burton took the proffered note. He looked at Krishnamurthy. "This will be from Palmerston."

"How can you tell?"

"Because the only way a runner would know I'm here is if it was sent by someone who's having me watched."

He opened the note and read:

This morning, a military court found Lieutenant John Hanning Speke guilty of treason. He will be executed by firing squad at dawn on Friday. His final request is to see you. This has been permitted. Please attend with due dispatch. Burke and Hare will escort.

Henry John Temple, 3rd Viscount Palmerston

Burton cursed and passed the note to his friend.

Krishnamurthy read it and said, "Because he aided the Prussians?"

"Yes. But he was never acting under his own volition. From the very inception of this whole affair, Speke has been manipulated and taken advantage of."

"Will you go?"

"Yes."

The two men continued drinking until past midnight, then said farewell and made off—somewhat unsteadily—toward their respective homes.

On the city's main highways, electric lighting saturated the fog and made it glow a dirty orange. Black flakes drifted down and settled on Burton's shoulders and top hat. He wound a scarf around his face and, leaning heavily on his sword cane, walked a little way along Pall Mall then turned left onto Regent Street. Despite the late hour, the traffic hadn't cleared and the pavements were still crowded with bad-tempered pedestrians, so he turned right and took to the backstreets, which, though dark and filthy, at least afforded a quicker passage.

He cursed himself for drinking so much. He wasn't recovered enough to cope with drunkenness; it made him feel ill and weak.

From alley to alley, he walked past huddled shapes and broken windows, lost his bearings, and drifted too far northward.

He found himself in a network of narrow passages. A raggedly dressed man stepped out of the darkness and brandished a dagger. Burton drew his sword cane and smiled viciously. The man backed away, held up his hands, said, "No 'arm meant, guv'nor!" and ran away.

The explorer pushed on, turned left, stumbled over a discarded crate and kicked it angrily. Two rats emerged from beneath it and scurried away.

He leaned against a lamppost. He was shaking.

"Pull yourself together, you blockhead!" he growled. "Get home!"

He noticed a faded flier pasted to the post and read it:

> *Work disciplines your spirit*
> *Work develops your character*
> *Work strengthens your soul*
> *Do not allow machines to do your work!*

It was old Libertine propaganda. They'd been a force to be reckoned with a couple of years ago, but now the Technologists dominated and the Libertines were ridiculed in the newspapers. What, Burton wondered, would the world be like if the shoe had been on the other foot?

He resumed his journey.

What if Edward Oxford had never jumped back through time? The Libertines and Technologists owed their existence to him—would the world be so different if they'd never existed?

Edward Oxford.

It all went back to him. All the alternate histories had been made possible by his interference.

Burton turned another corner and stopped. He'd entered a long straight lane bordered by high brick walls, and despite the gloom and the fog, he recognised it—for he'd unconsciously drifted to the very spot where he'd had his first encounter with Oxford—with Spring Heeled Jack.

Richard Francis bloody Burton!
Your destiny lies elsewhere!
Do you understand?
Do what you're supposed to do!

The words echoed in his mind, and he said aloud now what he'd said then: "How can I possibly *know* what I'm supposed to do? How can I *know*?"

"What?" came a voice.

Burton turned. A vagrant had shuffled out of the fog.

"Was ye a-talkin' to me, mister?"

"No."

"I thought ye said sumfink."

"I did. I was—I was just thinking aloud."

"Ah, rightio. I do that. They say it's the first sign o' madness, don't they? Can ye spare a copper? I ain't 'ad nuffink to eat, not fer a couple o' days, least-ways."

Burton fished in his pocket, pulled out a coin, and flipped it to the man. He turned to go, but then paused and said to the beggar: "How can I possibly know what I'm supposed to do?"

"Heh! Ye just carry on carryin' on, don'tcha, mate! Fate'll do the rest!"

Burton sighed, nodded, and walked out of the alley.

Needs pruning, hard against the stem.
Do what you're supposed to do!
Lee-Enfield Mk III. Manufactured in Tabora, Africa, 1918.
The source of the Nile!
Edward Oxford.
The source!

Burton sat up, jolted out of his sleep.

Had that been Bertie Wells's voice or Algernon Swinburne's?

He looked at the four corners of his bedroom.

Nobody's voice. A dream.

He sat up, poured a glass of water from the jug on his bedside table, then opened a drawer and took out a small vial. Its label read *Saltzmann's Tincture.* He added three drops of its contents to the water, drank it, and stood up. After washing and wrapping his *jubbah* around himself, the king's agent went downstairs and was served a hearty breakfast by Mrs. Angell. He then went to his dressing room and outfitted himself in shabby workmen's clothing.

It was early on Thursday morning.

Burton caught a hansom to Limehouse. When it became ensnarled in traffic halfway there, he left it and walked the rest of the distance. He made his way along Limehouse Cut until he came to an abandoned factory, climbed one of its chimneys, and dropped three pebbles into its flue. The Beetle responded to the summons. The head of the League of Chimney Sweeps, who'd been safely transported from the Arabian Desert back to his home, reported that, on Captain Lawless's recommendation, Willy Cornish had received a government grant to put him through private schooling, while Vincent Sneed had been released from the Cairo prison and was now working as a funnel scrubber at an airfield in South London.

Satisfied, the king's agent left the mysterious boy with a satchel of books and made his way homeward.

It was almost midday by the time he turned the corner of Montagu Place. He saw Mr. Grub, his local street vendor, standing in the fog with a forlorn expression on his face.

"Hallo, Mr. Grub. Where's your barrow?"

"It got knocked over by a bleedin' omnipede, Cap'n," the man replied. "Smashed to smithereens, it was."

"I'm sorry to hear that," Burton replied. "But you have your Dutch oven, still?"

"Nope. It was crushed by one o' them lumbering great mega-dray horses."

"But Mr. Grub, if you can't sell shellfish or hot chestnuts, what the dickens are you standing here for?"

The vendor shrugged helplessly. "It's me patch, Cap'n. Me pa stood on it, an' his pa afore him! It's where I belong, ain't it!"

Burton couldn't think how to reply to that, so he settled for a grunted response and made to move away.

"'Scusin' me askin', Cap'n—"

The explorer stopped and turned back.

"Did you ever find it?"

"Find what, Mr. Grub?"

"The source, sir. The source of the Nile."

"Ah. Yes. As a matter of fact I did."

"Good on you! That's bloomin' marvellous, that is! An' was it worth it?"

Burton swallowed. His heart suddenly hammered in his chest. He blinked the corrosive fog from his eyes.

"No, Mr. Grub. It wasn't worth it at all. Not in the slightest bit."

The vendor nodded slowly, as if with deep understanding.

"Aye," he said. "I have it in mind that the source o' things ain't never what you expect 'em to be."

The king's agent touched the brim of his topper in farewell and walked the rest of the short distance home.

Burke and Hare were waiting for him.

"A moment, if you please, gentlemen. I'd like to change into more suitable clothing, if you don't mind."

He left them waiting in the hallway, went upstairs, removed his patched trousers and threadbare jacket, and put on a suit. He was on his way back down when Mrs. Angell came up from the kitchen, all pinafore and indignation.

"You'll not be going out again, Sir Richard!" she protested, with a scowl at Burke and Hare. "You'll leave him be, sirs! He's not a well man! He's infected with Africa!"

Damien Burke bowed and said, "I assure you, ma'am, I have nothing but the good captain's well-being in mind, isn't that so, Mr. Hare?"

"It is absolutely the case, Mr. Burke. Ma'am, were it not the last request of a condemned man, we wouldn't dream of imposing on Captain Burton."

"It's all right, Mrs. Angell," Burton interrupted. "The restorative quality of your incomparable cooking has put new life into me. I'm fit as can be."

"What condemned man?" the housekeeper asked.

"Lieutenant John Speke," Burke answered.

"Oh," the old dame replied. "Him."

She threw up her chin disapprovingly and stamped back to the kitchen.

"She blames Speke for all my ills," Burton remarked as he put on his overcoat. He lifted his topper from its hook and suddenly remembered that more than a year ago—or, from his point of view, more than five—a bullet had been fired through it. He examined it closely and saw no sign of the two holes. In his absence, Mrs. Angell had obviously paid for its repair.

He smiled, pushed the hat onto his head, and took his silver-handled sword cane from the elephant's-foot holder by the door.

"Let's go."

Nearly two hours later, they arrived at the Tower of London after a difficult journey in a horse-drawn growler.

"It would have been quicker to walk," the king's agent noted.

"Yes, Captain, my apologies," Burke replied. "The new underground railway system will solve many of the capital's ills, I hope, but I fear its opening is still some way off."

"Has Mr. Brunel encountered problems?"

"No, sir, he's still drilling the tunnels. It's a project of immense proportions. These things take time. Isn't that so, Mr. Hare?"

"It certainly is, Mr. Burke," Hare agreed.

They disembarked at the end of Tower Street and walked around the outer walls to the river-facing Bloody Tower Gate. The stench from the Thames was almost too much for Burton, and he snatched gratefully at the perfumed handkerchief proffered by Hare, pressing it to his nostrils. Palmerston's men appeared unaffected by the foul odour.

After a few whispered words with the Beefeater guards, the two odd-job men ushered the king's agent through the gate, across a courtyard, and into the Great Keep. They entered St. John's Chapel, and Hare opened a door in one of its more shadowy corners, indicating to Burton that he should descend the stairs beyond. The explorer did so.

Oil lamps lit the stone staircase, which went down much farther than he expected.

"You understand, Sir Richard, that the area we're about to enter is not generally known to exist and must remain a secret?" Damien Burke said.

"You can count on my discretion."

The stairs eventually ended at a heavy metal portal. Hare produced a key and unlocked it, and the three men stepped through into a wide hallway with doors along its sides. As they walked along, Burton observed small signs: *Conference Rooms 1 & 2*; *Offices A–F*; *Offices G–L*; *Administration Rooms*; *Laboratories 1–5*; *Clairvoyance Rooms 1–4*; *Vault*; *Weapon Shop*; *Monitoring Station*; *Canteen*; *Dormitories*.

At the end of the passage, they unlocked and passed through a door marked *Security*. The chamber beyond was rectangular and contained filing cabinets and a desk. There were six sturdy metal doors, each numbered.

A man at the desk rose and said, "Number four, gentlemen?"

Burke nodded. He turned to Burton. "You have thirty minutes, Captain. Mr. Hare and I will wait here."

"Very well."

Cell 4 was opened and Burton stepped into it. The door shut behind him. He heard a key turn in its lock.

The chamber looked more like a sitting room than a prison. There were shelves of books, a desk, a bureau, a settee and armchairs, ornaments on the mantelpiece, and pictures on the wall. A door stood open to Burton's right, and John Speke stepped out from what was evidently a bedchamber.

The lieutenant was barefoot, wearing trousers and a white cotton shirt, wrinkled and untucked.

"Dick!" he exclaimed. "I'm sorry, old fellow, I had no idea it was that time already!"

"Hallo, John. How are you feeling?"

"As healthy as a condemned man can expect." Speke waved toward the armchairs. "Come, sit down."

As they moved across the room, he leaned in close and quietly hissed: "They'll be listening."

Burton gave a slight nod of acknowledgement and sat down.

There was an occasional table beside Speke's chair. He took a decanter of brandy from it, poured two glasses, and handed one to his guest.

"Do you consider me guilty, Dick?"

"Absolutely not," Burton responded.

"Good. I don't care about anyone else. But I must ask your forgiveness. A weakness in my character caused me to take umbrage with you during our exploration of Berbera, and everything we've endured since stems from that act. I thought you considered me a coward. I was angry and resentful."

"And wrong, John. I never thought of you that way. But if it's forgiveness you need, then consider it granted."

"Thank you."

Hesitantly, Speke raised his glass. Burton leaned forward, clinked his own against it, and they drank.

"Do you remember all those dreadful days of illness in Ujiji?" Speke asked, referring to 1857, when they'd discovered Lake Tanganyika.

"How could I forget, John? I thought we were goners for sure."

"When I was at my lowest ebb, you used to sit beside my cot and read to me from Camoens. Would you do so again? I'd gain much comfort from it. They allowed me a volume of *The Lusiad*."

"Certainly."

Speke stood, crossed to a bookshelf, and returned with a book in his hand. He passed it to Burton and sat down.

"I've marked a page."

Burton nodded then opened the book where a loose leaf of paper poked out from the pages. He saw Speke's handwriting on the sheet and glanced up at his friend.

Speke met his eyes and held them a moment. His lens glinted.

Burton returned his attention to the book. He began to read aloud.

> "'Ah, strike the notes of woe!' the siren cries;
> 'A dreary vision swims before my eyes.
> To Tagus' shore triumphant as he bends,
> Low in the dust the hero's glory ends—'"

Such was his familiarity with the Portuguese poet that he continued automatically, reciting the verse, expressively and faultlessly, though his eyes and mind were on Speke's note. He read:

Dick,

    I have told no one of what occurred in the temple. Nor have we ever spoken to each other about it, for we were in no fit condition to converse in the days subsequent to those events, and, besides, I had little recollection of anything other than a bright flash and a deafening gunshot.

    But in recent days, the veil of light that blinded me seems to have lifted. What I witnessed has gained clarity in my mind, and I feel instinctively that it might be of importance to you.

    I shall try to describe what happened in its proper sequence, though, in truth, these are but facets of an instant.

    Dick, this thing that Darwin and his cronies attached to my head, this babbage device, contains antennae of such extreme sensitivity that they detect the electrical operations of a human brain. At the moment the brass man fired his pistol, those sensors were hit by a transmission of subtle electrical force. It was the—I'm sorry, but I know of no other way to describe it—the final mental exhalation of Mr. Trounce. This same burst of energy seemed to activate the downward-pointing pyramid above the altar. It suddenly blazed with light and lost its opacity. I was able, as if seeing through solid matter, to discern that its structure was comprised of alternating layers of material, one denser than the other.

    Simultaneously, a pale-blue lightning flashed from the diamond at the tip of the pyramid and jumped to the brass man's head, then from his to yours. In the slightest fraction of a second, your appearance altered—your hair became white, your clothes changed, and a rifle appeared beside you—and the energy then reversed direction, jumping from you back to the brass man, then to the diamond.

    As I say, this all occurred in a single moment, and I don't know what to make of it, except—this may be nonsense, but it seemed to me that the clockwork man somehow channelled and directed the force.

    I wish I could be of more help to you, but my time has run out.

    I cannot forget that we were once as brothers. I hope, when you remember me, you will think of that time, and not of the wicked things I have done.

    Your old friend,
    John Hanning Speke

Burton continued to recite Camoens, but his eyes flicked up and signalled gratitude to the other man. Surreptitiously, he slipped the letter into his pocket.

The half-hour ended and the door opened. Damien Burke leaned in and said: "Captain?"

Burton closed the book, put it down, stood, and shook Speke's hand.

"Goodbye, old fellow," he said.

Speke's mouth moved but he could find no words, and with his eye glistening, he turned away.

It was past three o'clock by the time the king's agent left the tower. He whistled for a hansom cab and ordered the driver to take him to Battersea.

"Bless me, sir! That's a relief!" the man said, climbing down from his seat. He took a couple of lumps of Formby coal from the scuttle at the back of the vehicle's steam-horse and put them into the furnace.

"Why so?" Burton asked.

"South of the river, ain't it! A lot less traffic south of the river! Can't move for love nor money on the main roads north o' the Thames, but south—we'll have you on your merry way, no trouble at all, sir. In you go. There's a blanket under the seat if you feel the chill."

The driver climbed back up to his seat, waited for Burton to settle, then—with an unnecessary "Gee up!"—squeezed the velocity lever and got the hansom moving.

As the cab rattled along Lower Thames Street and turned left onto London Bridge, the king's agent sat back, tied Gregory Hare's perfumed handkerchief around the lower half of his face, and focused on his breathing. Keeping it slow and steady, he imagined each breath entering first his left lung, then his right. He matched his respiration to the rhythm of a Sufi chant:

Allāhu Allāhu Allāhu Haqq.
Allāhu Allāhu Allāhu Haqq.
Allāhu Allāhu Allāhu Haqq.

He started to complicate the exercise, altering the tempo, establishing a cycle of four breaths, visualising oxygen saturating different parts of his body.

At the same time, he listened only to the chugging of the hansom's steam-horse, allowing it to block out all other noises.

By the time the vehicle reached the junction of Bankside and Blackfriars Road, Burton had slipped into a Sufi trance.

His mind drifted.

He saw formless light and colour; heard water and snatches of conversation:

"—*According to the evidence John Speke presented to the Society, the Nile runs uphill for ninety miles—*"

"—*The lake he discovered was, indeed, the source of the Nile—*"

The lights coalesced into a single bright ribbon, broad, snaking away through darkness, disappearing into the distance. He flew over it, following its course upstream.

"—Captain Burton! Did you pull the trigger?—"

"—Is there shooting to be done?—"

"—I rather suppose there is!—"

"—The source!—"

"—Don't step back! They'll think that we're retiring!—"

From far off to either side, he saw more ribbons of light. The farther upstream he flew, the closer they came.

"—Don't step back!—"

"—Step back!—"

"—Pull the trigger!—"

"—Step back!—"

"—The source!—"

Shining intensely, as if reflecting the sun, the ribbons began to converge around him.

"—Step back!—"

"—The source!—"

"—Needs pruning, hard against the stem—"

"—How can I reverse the damage?—"

"—You'll find a way—"

"—Is there shooting to be done?—"

"—I rather suppose there is!—"

"—Pull the trigger!—"

"—The source!—"

The bands of light joined into one blazing expanse. It shot upward in front of him. Burton gazed at it and became aware that it was falling water. He looked up and saw a rainbow.

The hansom cab jerked over a pothole, shaking his senses back into him.

He cried out: "Step back! The source needs pruning, hard against the stem! Pull the trigger!"

And, all of a sudden, he knew exactly what had to be done.

The hatch in the roof of the cab opened and the driver looked in.

"Did you say somethin', sir?"

"Yes. Make a detour to the nearest post office, would you?"

"Certainly, sir. We're just comin' up on Broad Street. There's one there."

A few minutes later, Burton paid for two parakeet messages. He sent the first bird to Commander Krishnamurthy: "Maneesh, hurry to my place and pick up the rifle next to the fireplace in my study. Bring it to Battersea Power Station. Utmost emergency. Great haste, please."

The second parakeet was sent to Mrs. Angell to alert her to the commander's mission. It went on: "Mrs. Angell, I have an unusual job for you.

You must do it at once, without hesitation or protest. Please remove from my study all my casebooks, journals, reports, and personal papers. Take them from the desks, from the drawers, and from the shelves nearest the window. Carry them into the backyard and make a bonfire of them. Do not leave a single one unburned. This is of crucial importance. Destroy them all, and do it at once."

The king's agent returned to the cab and, thirty minutes later, it delivered him to his destination.

The glaring lights of the Technologist headquarters were turning the thick fog around it into a swirling soup of glowing particles, here a sickening yellow, there a putrid orange, in many places a deep hellish red. Burton picked his way through the murk to the front entrance, hailed a guard, and was escorted to the main hall.

Isambard Kingdom Brunel appeared from amid buzzing machinery and clanked over to greet him.

"An unexpected pleasure, Sir Richard. It's been more than a year."

"You've corrected your speech defect, Isambard."

"Some considerable time ago. I'm afraid young Swinburne will be disappointed."

"Swinburne is dead," Burton said flatly.

"Dead?"

"Yes. Well, in a manner of speaking, anyway."

"I'm not sure what you mean, but I am truly sorry. What happened?"

Burton glanced at a nearby workbench around which a group of Technologists was gathered.

"May we speak in private?"

Brunel expelled a puff of vapour. The piston-like device on the shoulder of his barrel-shaped body paused in its pumping, then continued. The bellows on the other side creaked up and down insistently.

"Follow," he piped.

Burton trailed after the Steam Man, across the vast floor to where two of the huge Worm machines were parked. The explorer marvelled at the size of the burrowing vehicles—and, right there, the main area of difficulty in the scheme that had formed in the back of his mind found its solution.

Brunel reached out with a mechanical arm and opened a big hatch in the side of one of the Worms. He stepped in, gestured for Burton to follow, and pulled the doorway down behind the explorer. Lights came on automatically. The steam man hissed into a squat.

Burton pulled Speke's letter from his pocked and, wordlessly, handed it to the engineer. Brunel held it up with a metal pincer. It wasn't evident what part of his life-maintaining contraption functioned as eyes but something obviously did, and moments later he lowered the paper and said: "What does the alteration of your appearance signify? Does Algernon Swinburne's death relate to it?"

"I was sent through time to the year 1914, Isambard. What for John Speke was a split second lasted four years for me. Algy was killed in Africa last year, but was present, albeit in a different form, in the future I visited."

"A different form?"

Burton sat on a leather-upholstered chair and, for the final time, told the full story.

When he finished, the Steam Man raised the letter again.

"Hmm," he said. "This pyramid construction appears to have the elements of a battery. You say there were other structures of alternating layers in the temple?"

"Yes."

"And a great deal of quartz?"

"Along with other crystals and gemstones, yes—an almost inconceivable amount."

"Intriguing. My hypothesis, then, is that the entire temple was constructed to generate and store piezoelectricity."

"Piezoelectricity?"

"A very recent discovery, Sir Richard. Or so I thought. I now learn that it was, in fact, employed in ancient times!"

"But what is it?"

"Put simply, it is electrical power generated by certain substances, crystals especially, when they are distorted by pressure."

"Ah. And the temple—"

"Has the weight of a fractured mountain on top of it. That, Sir Richard, is a lot of power. Having it hit you in the head should have been enough to burn you to a cinder in an instant. Yet, instead, it projected you through time."

"It passed through Herbert Spencer—or rather through the priest K'k'thyima—first."

"It did. Or perhaps it would be more accurate to say that it passed through the seven stones of the Cambodian Eye. It seems to me that the intelligence in those stones was somehow able to control the force, and, I should think, set the coordinates for your destination in time."

"Good," Burton responded.

"Good, Sir Richard?"

"Yes."

"Why?"

"Because you've confirmed my own suspicions on the matter. If we are correct, my plan has, perhaps, some small chance of succeeding."

"You have a plan?"

"Of sorts."

"Then I think perhaps I had better hear it."

At four-thirty in the morning, a strong vibration shook the floor of the rooms beneath the Tower of London. It rapidly increased in intensity and a loud rumbling shocked the secret institution's staff out of their beds.

People, wrapped in dressing gowns, ran into the main hallway.

"Earthquake!" someone shouted.

Damien Burke, in a long nightshirt, nightcap, and slippers, yelled: "Up the stairs! Now! Everybody out!"

A guard unlocked the entrance door and the staff quickly filed out.

The floor cracked. A siren started to wail.

Gregory Hare, also in his sleeping clothes, pointed to a lone figure at the other end of the hallway—a woman, white-haired and fully dressed.

"Mr. Burke!" he called.

Burke followed his companion's pointing finger and saw the woman.

"Countess Sabina!" he shouted. "You must leave at once!"

The rumbling grew into a roar.

"I think not!" she mouthed, her voice lost in the din.

The floor in the middle of the hallway bulged and heaved. Dust erupted and filled the air as a spinning metal cone emerged from the ground and expanded upward. The deafening commotion caused Burke and Hare to press their hands to their ears. They blinked against the eddying dust and squinted through watering eyes at the massive drill as it thundered out of the floor and its tip bit into the ceiling. Shredded plaster and masonry exploded outward.

"Mr. Burke! Mr. Burke!" Hare bellowed, but the other man could hear nothing but the cacophonous machine.

The drill buried itself deeper and deeper into the roof, and, as it did so, the main body of the tunnelling machine rose into view. Steam belched out of holes in its sides until the atmosphere of the hallway was so thick that nothing could be seen, though electric wall lamps continued to glow.

Burke groped for Hare's arm, clutched it, put his mouth against the other man's ear, and yelled: "Find your way to the armoury. Bring weapons!"

He felt his colleague move away.

The noise suddenly died. There was a moment of absolute silence, then the rattle of debris as it continued to fall from the ceiling.

A clang and a creak.

Thumping footsteps.

A repetitive wheezing.

The hiss of escaping vapours.

Something moved in the murk—a shadow—then a man stepped out of the cloud. Though the bottom half of his face was concealed by a scarf and the eyes were behind leather-rimmed goggles, Burke recognised Sir Richard Francis Burton.

"Captain!" he exclaimed. "Thank goodness! What's happen—"

He was cut short as Burton's fist shot up and connected with his chin. Burke folded to the floor.

"My apologies, old thing," the king's agent murmured.

He moved back to the Worm. Two figures—Isambard Kingdom Brunel and Maneesh Krishnamurthy—were standing beside it.

"This way!" he snapped.

He led them toward the far end of the hall but stopped short when someone stepped into his path. He drew back his arm, his fingers bunched into a fist.

"No!" came a female voice. "It's me!"

"Countess! What are you doing here?"

"They've been using me in their campaign against the Prussians, Sir Richard. I can stand it no longer. Besides, I foresaw that you would come. There is a role for me to play. I must accompany you."

Burton hesitated, then said, "Get into the vehicle, Countess. We'll join you in a minute."

As she moved away, the explorer strode forward and kicked open the door to the security section. He entered, Krishnamurthy followed, and Brunel squeezed through after them.

"This one," Burton said, indicating the entrance to Cell 4.

He moved aside as the Steam Man's multiple arms raised cutting tools and applied them to the metal portal. Moments later, Brunel pulled the door from its frame and threw it aside.

"John!" Burton called.

"Dick, what's happening?"

"We're breaking you out of here! Explanations later! Come!"

Speke, still in his shirt and trousers, groped his way forward.

"This way, Mr. Speke," Krishnamurthy said, grabbing the prisoner's arm.

They hurried back out into the main hall.

A pistol was pressed into the side of Krishnamurthy's head.

"May I ask what you think you're doing?" Gregory Hare asked.

Burton wheeled to face Palmerston's man and cried out: "Hare, it's me! Burton!"

"What's happening here, Captain?"

"I have to take Speke! Hare, trust me, man! The future depends on this!"

"John Speke is a traitor. I can't allow you to remove him. Where is Mr. Burke?"

"Unconscious. I had to—" Burton suddenly shot forward and chopped at Hare's wrist with such force that the pistol went spinning away. He buried his fist in the man's stomach.

The breath whooshed out of Hare. He doubled over but clutched at Burton's clothing. As Krishnamurthy steered Speke out of the way, Palmerston's man yanked Burton backward, threw his ape-like arms around him, and squeezed.

"No!" Burton objected. "You have to—" But suddenly he couldn't say another word; his breath was cut off; he couldn't move. Hare's arms were unbelievably powerful. They tightened around the king's agent like a vice. He felt his ribs creak. Two of them snapped. Agony cut through him. He couldn't scream. Darkness closed in from the edges of his vision.

Then he was free and on his knees, gulping lungfuls of dust-filled air. He coughed and keeled over. Pain stabbed into his side. He saw Hare's face just inches away. The odd-job man was unconscious on the floor. Blood was oozing from his scalp.

Metal hooked beneath Burton's armpits and he was hauled upright, lifted off his feet, and borne to the door of the Worm.

"I rendered your attacker unconscious with a blow to the head," Isambard Kingdom Brunel explained.

"Wait! Stop!" Burton shouted. "Put me down."

The engineer complied. Burton clutched his left side and groaned. He pointed to a heavy door, barely visible through the steam and dust.

"The vault, Isambard! Get in there!"

The Steam Man clanged across the broken floor and started to work on the portal.

Burton stood, swaying, waiting. He turned his head to the side and spat. The taste of blood filled his mouth.

The siren was still wailing. He remembered the echoing "Ulla! Ulla!" of the wartime harvesters.

It happened, he reminded himself.

With a loud *thunk*, the vault door came loose. Brunel stepped aside, carrying it with him.

Burton limped forward and entered the chamber. He looked around and saw things he didn't understand: bizarre biological objects in bell jars; devices that looked like weapons; a necklace of shrunken non-human heads; a mirror that reflected a different room, and, when he looked into it, a different person.

"You were right, Algy," he muttered, for these things, he felt sure, had somehow slipped through from alternate versions of reality.

A flat jewel case caught his eye. He reached for it, opened it, and saw that it contained twenty-one black diamonds arranged in three rows of seven: the fragments of the Eyes of Nāga.

He snapped the case shut and was just about to leave with it when he noticed a particularly large leather portmanteau. He paced over to it, pulled it open, and saw white scaly material, a black helmet, a metal disk, and a pair of stilted boots inside. It was Edward Oxford's burned and battered time suit; the weird costume that had earned him the name "Spring Heeled Jack."

Burton picked up the bag and left the vault.

Krishnamurthy's voice came out of the dust cloud: "Hurry! This is taking too long! They'll be back any minute!"

The king's agent found the door of the Worm and clambered into the vehicle. He sat and let loose a sob as his ribs grated together. Brunel's great bulk entered. The Steam Man pulled the hatch shut.

"Are you all right, Countess?" Burton asked.

"Yes," the clairvoyant answered. "But you're hurt, Captain!"

"It's nothing."

"Dick—" Speke began.

Burton cut him off: "Let's get out of here first, John. Explanations later."

They manoeuvred themselves around the cabin until Brunel was comfortably at the controls. He set the engine roaring and reversed the Worm back into the tunnel it had drilled.

With the short legs around its circumference racing, the machine hurtled along underground, passing far beneath the River Thames, following the burrow westward until it angled upward and emerged from the wasteland at the front of Battersea Power station.

They all disembarked, striding and clanking and limping to the main doors, passing through them, crossing the courtyard, and entering the principal workshop.

Technologist personnel gathered around. Brunel ordered them to secure the building.

The group moved over to a workbench. Burton laid the diamond case and the portmanteau on it. Krishnamurthy walked away and returned with the Lee-Enfield rifle. "Here you are, Captain."

"Thank you, Maneesh. By the way, was Mrs. Angell organising a bonfire when you visited?"

"She was, sir, and she seemed rather distraught about it."

"If what I have in mind doesn't succeed," Burton said, addressing all of his friends, "then, at very least, I want the evidence of what has occurred destroyed. Thus I've instructed my housekeeper to burn all of my records."

"But why is that necessary?" Speke asked.

The Countess Sabina answered: "Different versions of history exist, Mr. Speke—I've seen them—and the boundaries between each are thin. If the wrong sort of person learned of this, they could make a Bedlam of all existence."

Burton thought of Aleister Crowley.

"We're almost ready," one of the technicians announced.

The king's agent turned to Speke. "Walk with me, John."

John Hanning Speke, lying flat on his back on a workbench, allowed Isambard Kingdom Brunel to remove the cover of the babbage in the left half of his skull.

The engineer used a pincer to indicate two hollows in the exposed mechanism.

"See, Sir Richard," he said. "These sockets were designed to receive two of the Cambodian stones."

Burton examined the cavities, then looked down at Speke. "You understand why we have to do this, John?" he asked.

"Yes," Speke replied. "Put them in."

The king's agent nodded to Brunel, and the engineer reached into the jewel case, retrieved a diamond, fitted it into one of the slots in Speke's babbage, and screwed down a delicate bracket to hold the stone in place. He repeated the process with a second gem, then replaced the cover of the device and stood back.

Speke sat up.

"Do you sense anything?" Burton asked.

"Nothing."

Countess Sabina stepped forward. "I do."

Burton looked at her. "What do you feel, Countess?"

"The Nāga intelligence has left the diamonds, Sir Richard, but the shape of it remains in them, like a mould, if you will. Mr. Speke has to allow his conscious mind to flow into it. That is the role I must play—I shall employ my mediumistic abilities to guide him."

The king's agent nodded, moved away with Isambard Kingdom Brunel, and asked him: "What of the rest of it, Isambard? Can you generate power enough?"

"Easily," Brunel replied. "My technicians are setting everything up now. But you realise that, if Mr. Speke cannot manage his part, you will be incinerated?"

"Believe me, I am very aware of that particular fact!"

They walked over to where Krishnamurthy stood by two workbenches. Technicians were positioning them beneath a hanging structure, a thing of multiple layers and looped cables. Brunel gestured toward it.

"This will feed power into Mr. Speke's device. If I have understood the process properly, he will then be able to channel it in the appropriate manner through the resonance that exists between the Cambodian stones and the diamond dust in your tattoo. The unique properties of the diamonds will then come into play and project you through time. Speke will guide you to the exact moment and location."

"But on previous occasions," Burton said, "a sacrifice—a death—has been required to activate the process."

Brunel pointed one of his clamp-ended arms at the workshop entrance. "We hope that will suffice."

Burton looked and saw a horse being led in.

Krishnamurthy addressed the king's agent: "Why are you aiming for 1840, Sir Richard? Didn't the first alternate history branch off three years earlier?"

"Edward Oxford's initial entry point into the past is the source of all the trouble," Burton replied. "If I kill him in 1837, he'll still arrive in 1840, and will still assassinate Queen Victoria, whereas, if I kill him in 1840, it will make it impossible for him to be thrown back to 1837."

"But that means you won't merely change 1840 onward—you'll change the past of the history you are actually in. As far as I understand this whole business, no one has done that before."

"Cause and effect in reverse, Maneesh."

Krishnamurthy scratched his head. "Yes. But what will happen to you? To us?"

"I can't be sure—it's all theoretical—but I suspect that all the alternate histories will metamorphose from the Actual to the Potential, if you see what I mean. Whatever act caused each of them to come into being will be nullified, and they'll detach from what was meant to be, like branches being pruned from a bush."

"Will we remember anything?"

"That, Maneesh, is a question I can't answer. Perhaps each individual's subjective apprehension of the world will readjust, returning to the original version of history."

"And you, Sir Richard? Won't you exist twice in the same time? How old were you in 1840?"

"Nineteen. I don't know what will happen to me. I'll deal with it when I get there."

Burton watched as Speke was escorted to one of the benches and lay down on it. Two Technologists affixed cables from the contraption above to the lieutenant's babbage.

"They are ready for you," Brunel said.

Burton took a deep breath. Holding his arm pressed to his injured side, he paced over to the bench beside Speke and gingerly positioned himself on it. He put the Lee-Enfield rifle down with its barrel resting on his shoulder.

Krishnamurthy crossed to another worktop and returned from it with the portmanteau and the jewel case. He placed them on Burton's chest and stomach. The explorer wrapped his arms around them.

"Good luck, sir," the police commander said. He moved to the end of the benches where the horse had been tethered, took hold of the animal's reins, and drew his police-issue Adams revolver.

Countess Sabina stepped closer to Speke.

The machine overhead began to hum.

"Is everyone in position and prepared?" Brunel piped loudly.

The gathered technicians answered in the affirmative.

Burton rolled his head to the side and said to Speke: "John. Thank you."

Speke looked back and gave a sad smile.

Brunel clanked over to a console and began to adjust levers and dials.

The apparatus hanging over the benches suddenly hummed—a deep, throbbing sound—and bolts of blue energy fizzed and spat across its surface.

"Now, please, Mr. Speke," Brunel said.

The lieutenant reached up to the key that poked out over his left ear and began to wind the babbage.

"I just felt the booby trap arm itself," he muttered. "Maybe thirty minutes, then it'll explode."

Countess Sabina said, "Try to remain calm, please, Mr. Speke. I'm establishing a mediumistic connection with you now."

She flinched, gasped, and whimpered: "Oh, you poor thing!"

"I can feel your presence," Speke groaned. "It's—it's—"

"Intrusive? I know, sir. I'm sorry."

"I'm awaiting your word, Countess," Brunel said.

"Not yet!" The woman put her fingertips to her temples and squeezed her eyes shut. "I can sense the diamonds. I have to feel my way into them. Follow me, if you can, Mr. Speke. I'm trying to connect with your mind, too, Sir Richard."

Burton felt his scalp crawling, as if insects were running over it.

"Power's building!" Brunel called. "Hurry!"

From head to toe, Burton's muscles suddenly locked tight. Pain shot through his side. He cried out.

"Now!" the countess screamed.

A jagged line of blue lightning shot out of the overhead machine, hit Speke's babbage, and jumped across to Burton's head. The king's agent screeched and jerked as his nerve endings seemed to catch fire.

"Krishnamurthy!" Brunel shouted.

The Flying Squad commander pushed his pistol against the horse's head and pulled the trigger. The animal collapsed.

Burton convulsed and began to lose consciousness.

"It hasn't worked!" Krishnamurthy shouted. "Turn off the power! You're killing them!"

"No!" the countess shrieked. She threw out her arms. Blood welled up in her eyes and ran down her cheeks. "It's me! I'm the sacrifice!"

"Countess!" Krishnamurthy yelled.

The cheiromantist flopped to the floor.

There was a flash of white light.

Sir Richard Francis Burton remembered his youth and his first independent visit to London. He'd been there before—he'd gone to school in Richmond when he was eight years old—but on this occasion he was nineteen, had come from Italy to enrol at Trinity College, Oxford, and was filled with grandiose ideas and a bottomless well of self-esteem.

As is so often the case with memories, they were conjured by his olfactory sense. His nostrils were filled with the gritty carbon smell of soot, the rotten stench of the Thames, the stale odours of unlaundered clothes and unwashed bodies, all lurking behind the powerful tang of grass.

Grass?

He opened his eyes. He was lying facedown in long grass at the edge of a thicket of trees. A man had just emerged from them and, not noticing Burton, was walking away, down a slope. The explorer heard him mutter: "Steady, Edward! Hang on, hang on. Don't let it overwhelm you. This is neither a dream nor an illusion, so stay focused, get the job done, then get back to your suit!"

Bismillah! That's Edward Oxford!

He was too late! He hadn't counted on losing consciousness. He'd intended to shoot the visitor from the future among the trees before making a fast getaway. What now?

Burton pushed himself to his knees and almost cried out as his ribs scraped against each other. He reached for his rifle, the jewel case, and portmanteau—all on the grass beside him—picked them up, and crawled into the thicket. He found a suitable spot, lay flat, and carefully—gritting his teeth against the pain—pulled himself forward until he was hidden beneath a bush. He looked out at Green Park.

Tick tick tick.

He could feel John Speke's babbage winding down. The black diamond dust in his scalp was somehow connected to it through the decades.

He leaned on his elbows, hefted the rifle in his hands, and glanced at the inscription on its stock.

1918!

He'd been fifty-five years into the future, now he was twenty-four years into the past.

He shook his head slightly, trying to dispel the odd sense of dislocation that lurked at the edges of his mind: the feeling that he possessed two separate identities. But, of course, it was the 10th of June, 1840, and he really was duplicated, for his much younger self was currently travelling through Europe.

If only that opinionated and arrogant youngster knew what life had in store for him!

Burton whispered: "Time changed me, thank goodness."

He peered through the rifle's telescopic sight.

"The question is, can I return the favour?"

The wooded area in which he was hidden covered the brow of a low hill overlooking the park. At its base, people had gathered along the sides of a path. It was a mild day. The men sported light coats, top hats, and carried canes. The women wore bonnets and dainty gloves and held parasols. They were all waiting to see Queen Victoria ride past in her carriage. Burton examined them, levelling the crosshairs at one person after another. Which of them was the man he'd seen moments ago? And where was that man's ancestor, the insane eighteen-year-old with two flintlock pistols under his frock coat?

"Damnation!" Burton groaned softly. His hands were shaking.

He considered his options. He knew the assassin was going to fire two shots at the queen. The first would miss. The second should, too, but Edward Oxford was going to tackle his ancestor, and, in doing so, he would inadvertently cause that second bullet to hit Victoria in the head.

If Burton killed Oxford too soon, the crowd would start hunting for the killer, providing a distraction that might allow the assassin to strike with greater accuracy. So he must wait until after the first shot. If he could then put a bullet in Oxford during the panic, the man from the future would die before he could change history, and his antecedent would almost certainly be blamed for the murder.

The king's agent shifted cautiously, trying not to disturb the bush that arched over him.

He noticed a man in the crowd. It was Henry de La Poer Beresford, the "Mad Marquess," the founder of the Libertines.

"I'll be dealing with you," he murmured, "twenty-one years from now."

A cheer went up. Queen Victoria's carriage, drawn by four horses, had emerged from the gate of Buckingham Palace, off to his left.

Two outriders—the Queen's Guards—trotted ahead of the royal conveyance, which was steered by a postilion. Two more followed behind. They drew closer to the base of the slope.

Tick tick tick.

"Come on," Burton whispered. "Where are you?"

A man wearing a top hat, blue frock coat, and white breeches stepped over the low fence onto the path. He paced along beside the slow-moving carriage, drew a flintlock from his coat, pointed it at the queen, and pulled the trigger.

The report echoed across the park.

Victoria, in a cream-coloured dress and bonnet, stood up in her carriage.

Prince Albert leaned forward and reached for her.

People started to scream and shout.

The man drew a second pistol.

Burton held his breath and became entirely motionless.

The assassin raised his arm and took aim.

The queen reached up to her white lace collar.

Burton made a tiny movement, shifting the crosshairs of his sight slightly to the left of the monarch's head, their centre-point hovering over the young gunman's face.

The man from the future, Edward Oxford, suddenly jumped from the crowd.

"No, Edward!" he bellowed.

The two men struggled.

Burton took aim. His finger tightened on the trigger.

In 1864, John Speke's babbage exploded.

The shockwave crossed time and hit Burton like a punch between the eyes. In a moment of total disorientation, he thought he saw a blue flash far off to his left, and a faint voice yelling: "Stop, Edward!"

The assassin fired.

Burton fired.

Queen Victoria's head sprayed blood. She fell backward out of the carriage.

Albert scrambled after her.

Edward Oxford, still alive, threw his ancestor to the ground, accidentally impaling the young man's head on the wrought-iron spikes atop the low fence.

"No!" Burton whispered.

A frantic police whistle sounded.

The crowd surged around the carriage. The outriders plunged into the mob, attempting to hold it back.

Oxford forced his way free and started to run up the slope.

"No!" Burton whispered again.

He snapped out of his shock and backed into the trees, pulling the jewel case and portmanteau with him, and found a place of concealment. He listened as Oxford reached the vegetation and pushed through it to where he'd left his suit, helmet, and boots.

Burton lunged forward, hooked an arm around the time traveller's throat, squeezed hard, and crushed his windpipe. He put his mouth against the man's ear and hissed: "You don't deserve this, but I have to do it again. I'm sorry."

With his right hand, he twisted Oxford's head until the neck snapped, then released his hold and allowed the corpse to crumple to the ground.

He stepped back into hiding.

Almost immediately, he heard a voice calling: "Step out into the open, sir! I saw what happened. There's nothing to worry about. Come on, let's be having you!"

It sounded familiar.

Burton remained silent.

"Sir! I saw you trying to protect the queen. I just need you to accompany me to the station to make a statement!"

There was a pause, then someone began to push their way into the thicket. A policeman emerged from the leaves and looked down at Oxford.

"By Jove!" he exclaimed. "What in the devil's name has happened here?"

Burton took up his rifle, raised it butt-forward over his shoulder, and stepped out of the undergrowth.

The policeman turned and looked him full in the face.

Burton hesitated. The young, square-jawed, and wide-eyed features were those of William Trounce.

"Who the heck——?" the constable began.

Burton cracked the rifle butt into the youth's forehead. Trounce's cockscomb helmet went spinning away. He moaned and collapsed. The king's agent leaned over him and checked that he was breathing. He was.

Screams and whistles filled the air.

Burton straightened and returned to the portmanteau and jewel case. He took them over to where Oxford had hung his time suit, and, taking down the clean, unmarked material, pushed it into the bag with the older, scorched version of itself. With difficulty, he managed to squeeze the helmet and boots in, too.

He took off his jacket and wrapped it around the rifle, then, picking everything up, made his way through the trees toward the high wall at the back of the thicket. Horses' hooves and voices sounded from the street beyond. He followed the barrier around the border of the park until he came to a tree stump hard up against the brickwork. Stepping onto it, he reached up and placed the rifle and jewel case on top of the wall. He looped his arm through the handles of the bulging portmanteau and hauled himself up and over, dropping to the ground on the other side. His ribs creaked, and for a moment he thought he might pass out. He leaned back against the bricks.

"Sangappa," came a voice.

The explorer looked up and saw a street sweeper standing on the pavement nearby.

"What?"

"Sangappa," the man repeated. "It's the best leather softener money can buy. They send it over from India. Hard to find and a mite expensive but worth every penny. There's nothing to top it. Sangappa. It'd do that overstuffed portmanteau of yours the world of good, take my word for it."

Burton used his sleeve to wipe beads of sweat from his forehead.

The street sweeper leaned on his broom and asked, "Are you quite all right?"

"Yes," Burton replied. "But I'm having a bad day."

"It looks like it. Don't you worry, you'll forget it by tomorrow!"

The man suddenly looked confused. He scratched his head.

"It's odd—I can't even remember this morning. I must be going loopy!"

He lifted his broom and stepped from the pavement into the street. With a look of bemusement on his face, he began to sweep horse manure from it and into the gutter.

Burton swallowed and licked his lips. He needed a drink. He was feeling strange and disorientated. He wasn't sure where he was, what he was doing, why he was doing it.

He retrieved the rifle and jewels and started to move away.

"Hey!" the man called after him. "Don't forget! Sangappa! You can buy it at Jambory's Hardware Store on the corner of Halfmoon Street." He pointed. "Thataway! Tell old Jambory that Carter the Street Sweeper sent you!"

Burton nodded and limped on. He tried to piece together what had just occurred, but his mind was a jumble.

He crossed the road, passed Jambory's Hardware Store, kept going, and entered Berkeley Street, where he saw an elderly man peering out of a ground-floor window. He stopped and examined the white-bearded and scarred face, the sharp cheekbones and deep, dark, tormented eyes.

The man gazed back.

The man moved when he moved.

What? No! It can't be! That's me! My reflection! But how? How can I be old? I'm—I'm nineteen! Just nineteen!

He looked down at his hands. They were brown and wrinkled and weathered. They were not the hands of a young man.

What has happened? How is this possible?

He stumbled away and passed through Berkeley Square into Davies Street, then onto Oxford Street, which was filled with horse-drawn traffic. Only horse-drawn. Nothing else. That surprised him. He had no idea why.

What am I expecting to see? Why does it all feel wrong?

Burton reached Portman Square, staggered into the patch of greenery at its centre, dropped his luggage, and collapsed onto a bench beneath a tree. He'd been walking toward Montagu Place, but it had just occurred to him that there was no reason to go there.

He laughed, and it hurt, and tears poured down his cheeks.

He cried, and thought he might die.

He was quiet, and suddenly hours had passed and a dense fog was rolling in with the night.

Muddled impressions untangled and emerged from behind a veil of shock. He tried to force them back but they kept coming. Around him, London vanished behind the murk. Inside him, the truth materialised with horrible clarity.

She had flinched to one side.

Just as he'd pulled the trigger, she'd moved.

The assassin's second bullet had clipped her ear.

Sir Richard Francis Burton's bullet had hit her in the head.

It was me. I did it.

He had killed Queen Victoria.

Here it begins.

Here it ends.

Not the source, but just another part of a circle.

He sat in Portman Square.

The thick fog embraced him.

It was silent.

It was mysterious.

It was timeless.

And, behind it, the world he had created was very, very real.

A LAMENTATION

by Algernon Charles Swinburne,
from *Poems and Ballads*, 1866.

I.

Who hath known the ways of time
Or trodden behind his feet?
There is no such man among men.
For chance overcomes him, or crime
Changes; for all things sweet
In time wax bitter again.
Who shall give sorrow enough,
Or who the abundance of tears?
Mine eyes are heavy with love
And a sword gone thorough mine ears,
A sound like a sword and fire,
For pity, for great desire;
Who shall ensure me thereof,
Lest I die, being full of my fears?

Who hath known the ways and the wrath,
The sleepless spirit, the root
And blossom of evil will,
The divine device of a god?
Who shall behold it or hath?
The twice-tongued prophets are mute,
The many speakers are still;
No foot has travelled or trod,

No hand has meted, his path.
Man's fate is a blood-red fruit,
And the mighty gods have their fill
And relax not the rein, or the rod.

Ye were mighty in heart from of old,
Ye slew with the spear, and are slain.
Keen after heat is the cold,
Sore after summer is rain,
And melteth man to the bone.
As water he weareth away,
As a flower, as an hour in a day,
Fallen from laughter to moan.
But my spirit is shaken with fear
Lest an evil thing begin,
New-born, a spear for a spear,
And one for another sin.
Or ever our tears began,
It was known from of old and said;
One law for a living man,
And another law for the dead.
For these are fearful and sad,
Vain, and things without breath;
While he lives let a man be glad,
For none hath joy of his death.

II.

Who hath known the pain, the old pain of earth,
Or all the travail of the sea,
The many ways and waves, the birth
Fruitless, the labour nothing worth?
Who hath known, who knoweth, O gods? not we.
There is none shall say he hath seen,
There is none he hath known.
Though he saith, Lo, a lord have I been,
I have reaped and sown;
I have seen the desire of mine eyes,

The beginning of love,
The season of kisses and sighs
And the end thereof.
I have known the ways of the sea,
All the perilous ways,
Strange winds have spoken with me,
And the tongues of strange days.
I have hewn the pine for ships;
Where steeds run arow,
I have seen from their bridled lips
Foam blown as the snow.
With snapping of chariot-poles
And with straining of oars
I have grazed in the race the goals,
In the storm the shores;
As a greave is cleft with an arrow
At the joint of the knee,
I have cleft through the sea-straits narrow
To the heart of the sea.
When air was smitten in sunder
I have watched on high
The ways of the stars and the thunder
In the night of the sky;
Where the dark brings forth light as a flower,
As from lips that dissever;
One abideth the space of an hour,
One endureth for ever.
Lo, what hath he seen or known,
Of the way and the wave
Unbeholden, unsailed-on, unsown,
From the breast to the grave?

Or ever the stars were made, or skies,
Grief was born, and the kinless night,
Mother of gods without form or name.
And light is born out of heaven and dies,
And one day knows not another's light,
But night is one, and her shape the same.

But dumb the goddesses underground
Wait, and we hear not on earth if their feet
Rise, and the night wax loud with their wings;
Dumb, without word or shadow of sound;
And sift in scales and winnow as wheat
Men's souls, and sorrow of manifold things.

III.

Nor less of grief than ours
The gods wrought long ago
To bruise men one by one;
But with the incessant hours
Fresh grief and greener woe
Spring, as the sudden sun
Year after year makes flowers;
And these die down and grow,
And the next year lacks none.

As these men sleep, have slept
The old heroes in time fled,
No dream-divided sleep;
And holier eyes have wept
Than ours, when on her dead
Gods have seen Thetis weep,
With heavenly hair far-swept
Back, heavenly hands outspread
Round what she could not keep,

Could not one day withhold,
One night; and like as these
White ashes of no weight,
Held not his urn the cold
Ashes of Heracles?
For all things born one gate
Opens, no gate of gold;
Opens; and no man sees
Beyond the gods and fate.

MEANWHILE, IN THE VICTORIAN AGE, AND BEYOND . . .

SIR RICHARD FRANCIS BURTON (1821–1890)

The year 1863 started well for Burton—he was at last able to enjoy a honeymoon with Isabel, a full year after they were married. Unfortunately, he then had to return to his consulate duties on the disease-ridden West African island of Fernando Po. He made various forays onto the mainland but was not much impressed by the slavery-ravaged tribal kingdoms he found there.

In August of 1864, he returned to England. Fourteen months earlier, John Hanning Speke and James Grant had come back in triumph from their expedition to find the source of the Nile. Now Burton and his former partner engaged in an unpleasant duel, and much was done to besmirch Burton's reputation. The conflict reached its climax in September, when, the day before they were scheduled to confront each another at a debate in the city of Bath, Speke died. He had shot himself in the left side of his body while out hunting. There is no clear evidence whether this was suicide or a tragic accident. Biographers generally agree that, preoccupied with the forthcoming debate, Speke was uncharacteristically careless with his weapon and probably discharged it by accident while climbing over a wall.

Burton appears to have gone off the rails for a time after this incident. Given the consulship of Brazil, he went to South America and, unlike all his other excursions, did not keep a journal or account of his travels. Witnesses, such as Wilfred Scawen Blunt, recalled that he was drinking heavily for much of the time. While in Buenos Aires, Burton fell in with a rather unscrupulous character—a fat man named Arthur Orton, who was passing himself off as Sir Roger Tichborne.

> "I ask myself 'Why?' and the only echo is 'damned fool! . . . the Devil drives.'"
> —From a letter to Richard Monckton Milnes, 31st May, 1863

"And still the Weaver plies his loom, whose warp and woof is wretched Man. Weaving th' unpattern'd dark design, so dark we doubt it owns a plan."

—From *The Kasîdah of Hâjî Abdû El-Yezdî*, 1870

"Zanzibar city, to become picturesque or pleasing, must be viewed, like Stanbul, from afar."

—From *Zanzibar, City, Island, and Coast*, 1872

ALGERNON CHARLES SWINBURNE (1837–1909)

Swinburne travelled widely in 1863, visiting Paris, Genoa, and Florence, and enjoyed perhaps his most productive period, writing many of his most celebrated poems.

"Here life has death for neighbour . . ."

—From "The Garden of Proserpine"

"The dense hard passage is blind and stifled . . ."

—From "A Forsaken Garden"

"One, who is not, we see; but one, whom we see not, is . . ."

—"The Higher Pantheism in a Nutshell" (complete poem quoted)

"A wider soul than the world was wide . . ."

—From "On the Death of Richard Burton"

HERBERT SPENCER (1820–1903)

In 1863, Spencer, having published the year before his *First Principles of a New System of Philosophy*, was rapidly emerging as one of the greatest ever English philosophers.

An extreme hypochondriac, he also had little patience for the excesses of Victorian attire, and preferred to wear a one-piece brown suit of his own design. Apparently, it made him look like a bear.

He said:

"Time is that which a man is always trying to kill, but which ends in killing him."

GEORGE HERBERT WELLS (1866-1946)

By 1914, H. G. Wells was an established and popular author, a pioneer of science fiction.

> "A time will come when a politician who has wilfully made war and promoted international dissension will be as sure of the dock and much surer of the noose than a private homicide. It is not reasonable that those who gamble with men's lives should not stake their own."

> "We were making the future, he said, and hardly any of us troubled to think what future we were making. And here it is!"

> "Our true nationality is mankind."

> "I hope, or I could not live."

RICHARD MONCKTON MILNES (1809-1885)

In 1863, Monckton Milnes was raised to the peerage, becoming the 1st Baron Houghton.

HENRY JOHN TEMPLE, 3RD VISCOUNT PALMERSTON (1784-1865)

1863, for Palmerston, marked the middle of his final term as British prime minister. Nicknamed "Lord Cupid" on account of his youthful appearance and rumoured affairs, he was a popular and capable leader.

WILLIAM SAMUEL HENSON (1812-1888)

A very industrious inventor, Henson is best known as an early pioneer in aviation. He created a lightweight steam engine that he hoped would power a passenger-carrying monoplane, the "Henson Aerial Steam Carriage," but was never able to perfect the design. He also invented the modern safety razor.

FRANCIS HERBERT WENHAM (1824–1908)

A British marine engineer, Wenham came to prominence in 1866 when he introduced the idea of superposed wings at the first meeting of the Royal Aeronautical Society in London. His concept became the basis for the design of the early biplanes, triplanes, and multiplanes that attempted flight, with varying degrees of success. Wenham is possibly the first man to have employed the term "aeroplane."

OSCAR WILDE (1854–1900)

In 1863, aged nine, Wilde started his formal education at Portora Royal School in Enniskillen, County Fermanagh.

"Education is an admirable thing, but it is well to remember from time to time that nothing that is worth knowing can be taught."

"I can believe anything provided it is incredible."

"Experience is one thing you can't get for nothing."

"The tragedy of old age is not that one is old, but that one is young."

"To get back my youth I would do anything in the world, except take exercise, get up early, or be respectable."

"As long as war is regarded as wicked, it will always have its fascination. When it is looked upon as vulgar, it will cease to be popular."

"Popularity is the one insult I have never suffered."

"Whenever a man does a thoroughly stupid thing, it is always from the noblest motives."

"To live is the rarest thing in the world. Most people exist, that is all."

"Do not be afraid of the past. If people tell you that it is irrevocable, do not believe them. The past, the present, and the future are but one moment in the sight of God, in whose sight we should try to live. Time and space, succession and extension, are merely accidental conditions of thought. The imagination can transcend them."

ISABELLA MAYSON (1836-1865)

Married to Samuel Beeton in 1856, Isabella was made famous by her *Book of Household Management*, which had been published in 1861. 1863 was the last healthy year of her life. In 1864, she contracted puerperal fever, which caused her death on 6th February 1865.

> "A place for everything and everything in its place."
>
> —From *The Book of Household Management*

FERDINAND GRAF VON ZEPPELIN (1838-1917)

Count Zeppelin was a German general who later became an aircraft manufacturer. In 1863, he acted as an observer for the Union during the American Civil War, during which time he made his first ascent in a balloon. After serving in the Austrian and Franco-Prussian wars, he became increasingly fascinated by the prospect of steerable balloons and devoted himself to their development. By the turn of the century, his name was synonymous with rigid-framed powered airships.

ALEISTER CROWLEY (1875-1947)

An influential occultist, Crowley challenged the moral and religious values of his time, promoting a libertine philosophy—"Do what thou wilt"—that earned him notoriety and the reputation for being "the wickedest man in the world."
He said:

> "Ordinary morality is only for ordinary people."

SIDI MUBARAK BOMBAY (1820-1885)

Captured by Arab slave traders when he was a young boy, Bombay was sold in exchange for some cloth, and was taken to India where he lived as a slave for many years. When his owner died, he was emancipated and returned to Africa, where he gained fame as a guide, working with Burton, Speke, Stanley, and Livingstone. In 1873 he traversed the continent from its east coast to its west.

MTYELA KASANDA (AKA MIRAMBO)

A Wanyamwezi warlord, he started out as a slave and ivory trader, travelling between Africa's great lakes and the coast, but later installed himself as king of the Urambo region. He was a sworn enemy of the Arabic traders at Kazeh. He died aged 44, after becoming too ill to rule.

GENERALMAJOR PAUL EMIL VON LETTOW-VORBECK (1870–1964)

The commander of the German East Africa campaign during the First World War.

MAJOR GENERAL ARTHUR EDWARD AITKEN (1861–1924)

Commander of the Indian Expeditionary Force "B" in Africa during the First World War.

JANE DIGBY (LADY ELLENBOROUGH) (1807–1881)

An English aristocrat, Digby was involved in numerous romantic scandals. She had four husbands and countless lovers before eventually settling in Damascus, where she married Sheikh Medjuel el Mezrab, who was twenty years her junior.

BLUT UND EISEN

Otto von Bismarck made his famous speech in support of increased military spending on 29th September 1862. "Blood and iron" was, in fact, *Eisen und Blut.* The words were reversed almost immediately by press reports and have remained that way in most accounts.

HMS *ORPHEUS*

The *Orpheus* was a Jason-Class Royal Navy corvette, constructed in Chatham Dockyard, England, in 1861. She was commanded by Captain Robert Burton and served as the flagship of the Australian squadron. On 7th February 1863, while navigating Manukau Harbour, New Zealand, the ship hit a sandbar and sank, with a loss of 189 men, including Captain Burton. Frederick Butler, a convicted deserter, served as quartermaster aboard the vessel.

THE BOMBING OF DAR ES SALAAM

Despite a number of prior skirmishes between British and German troops, the First World War didn't properly begin in East Africa until 8th August 1914, when the British launched an attack against Dar es Salaam. The naval vessels HMS *Astraea* and HMS *Pegasus* bombarded the city, the *Astraea* hitting and destroying the German radio station. The Germans responded by sabotaging the harbour so the British couldn't use it, which also had the effect of preventing their own ship, SMS *Königsberg*, from returning to port. Just over a month later, the *Pegasus* was docked at Zanzibar for repairs when the *Königsberg* launched a surprise attack and sank her. The *Königsberg* was herself eventually knocked out of action by British ships on 11th July 1915.

THE BATTLE OF THE BEES

Also known as the Battle of Tanga, this was an attempt by the British Indian Expeditionary Force to capture the German port, and became one of the worst defeats for the British in Africa during the First World War. The incident commenced when HMS *Fox* arrived at the port and gave the authorities an hour to surrender. The hour passed but no action was taken, which gave Generalmajor Paul Emil von Lettow-Vorbeck time to move German reinforcements into position. On 4th November 1914, street-to-street fighting began in the north and jungle skirmishes in the south. The British found themselves hard pressed, and when swarms of bees, disturbed by the conflict, attacked both sides, the British were routed and took to their heels. In retreating, they left behind all their equipment, which the Germans appropriated. In later propaganda, the British suggested that the bees had somehow been a fiendish trap set by the enemy.

L.59 ZEPPELIN

A German dirigible used during the First World War, *L.59 Zeppelin* was known as Das Afrika-Schiff ("The Africa Ship"). In 1917, it was commissioned to resupply Generalmajor Paul Emil von Lettow-Vorbeck's troops. Its journey to Africa was intended to be a one-way voyage—upon delivering its 50 tons of supplies, the ship would be cannibalised, its outer envelope used for tents, its frame used to build radio towers, etc. Following the course of the Nile, *L.59 Zeppelin* was halfway along the river when she received an "abort" order transmitted by Lettow-Vorbeck, who, in his battle with British forces, had been unable to secure a safe landing place for her. She returned to Germany. The following year, the dirigible mysteriously exploded over the Strait of Otranto in the Mediterranean, with a loss of all twenty-one crew.

THE SECOND SCHLESWIG WAR

Beginning on 1st February 1864, this was a renewal of hostilities between Prussia, Austria, and Denmark over control of the Duchies of Schleswig, Holstein, and Saxe-Lauenburg. The conflict continued until the end of October, when the Treaty of Vienna saw the territories ceded to Prussia and Austria. It confirmed Prussia's military might and thus advanced the cause of those who supported German unification.

THE BURNING OF SIR RICHARD FRANCIS BURTON'S JOURNALS AND PAPERS

Of all the controversies concerning Burton during his lifetime, none compared with what happened after his death in 1890. His widow, Isabel, made a bonfire of his personal journals, the vast majority of his papers, and the unpublished book he regarded as his magnum opus, his new translation of *The Perfumed Garden*, which he'd retitled *The Scented Garden*. Her act incited such anger and condemnation from those who'd known Burton, including Swinburne, that she lost many friends and badly stained her own reputation.

ABOUT THE AUTHOR

MARK HODDER was born in Southampton, England, but lived for many years in London. He is an ex-commercial copywriter, BBC web producer, journalist, and editor. After too many years running the rat race, he threw in the towel and moved to Valencia in Spain, seeking quality of life rather than quantity of income. After a few months teaching English as a foreign language, he wrote his first novel, *The Strange Affair of Spring Heeled Jack*, which won the Philip K. Dick Award in 2010. After that, there was no looking back, and Mark now works as a full-time novelist, thus fulfilling his wildest dreams, which he started having around the age of eleven after reading Michael Moorcock, Robert E. Howard, Edgar Rice Burroughs, Fritz Leiber, Jack Vance, Philip K. Dick, P. G. Wodehouse, and Sir Arthur Conan Doyle. In addition to speculative and detective fiction, he is interested in Buddhism, transcendentalism, all the ITC TV programmes of the 60s and 70s, and techie-gadgety things.